Qualitative Research in Higher Education: Experiencing Alternative Perspectives and Approaches

Edited by
Clifton Conrad, Anna Neumann,
Jennifer Grant Haworth, Patricia Scott

Daryl G. Smith, Series Editor

ASHE READER SERIES

GINN PRESS
160 Gould Street
Needham Heights, MA 02194

Cover photograph by Bill Stanton.
Copyright © Bill Stanton, International Stock.

ISBN 0–536–558417-6

BA 1464

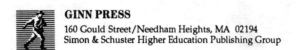

GINN PRESS
160 Gould Street/Needham Heights, MA 02194
Simon & Schuster Higher Education Publishing Group

Contents

PART VI   READING TEXT: EXAMPLES OF QUALITATIVE RESEARCH

PREFACE

Broadly defined, qualitative inquiry refers to research based on nonmathematical procedures and interpretations of qualitative data (such as words or pictures) or quantitative data (such as numbers). For the most part, qualitative researchers treat the "natural" or field setting as the primary location of data, emphasize the perspectives of individuals in the field as major sources of meaning and understanding, view themselves as the primary data-gathering instrument, emphasize open-ended approaches to data collection and analysis, place more emphasis on inductive than on deductive data analysis, and tend to report their findings from the "native's point of view."

From our perspective, a comprehensive reader on qualitative inquiry is needed in the field of higher education for four major reasons. First, while some people treat qualitative inquiry as if it were a unified approach, there is a growing appreciation among scholars across many fields of study that there is a variety of perspectives and approaches that need to be considered by qualitative researchers. Fueled by a growing disenchantment with positivist epistemology and quantitative modes of inquiry, researchers in many fields of study have articulated alternative world views, paradigms, and perspectives to guide qualitative inquiry—such as feminist, critical, and postmodernist perspectives. Alongside traditional approaches to qualitative inquiry such as ethnography, alternative approaches have emerged in recent years—such as grounded theory—as have new approaches to data analysis and reporting. Moreover, scholars are concerned with exploring various perspectives on reflexivity in qualitative inquiry, as demonstrated in the literature on ethical dimensions of qualitative research and on "trustworthiness," including the textual presence of the researcher, the researched, and the reader.

A second compelling reason for a reader on qualitative inquiry is that traditional quantitative approaches are limited in their ability to probe some of the central questions in higher education today. In short, due to the limitations (or the natural boundaries) of traditional methods, we have come to know certain topics within higher education—and dimensions of these topics—quite well while ignoring others. For example, we have considerable research on administrative behavior in diverse circumstances (e.g., crisis), a topic that is fairly amenable to traditional quantitative inquiry. Yet, we have little understanding of the belief systems, values, and attitudes that engender—and emanate from—various forms of administrative behavior, a topic that is more amenable to qualitative approaches.

In the last several years, many scholars in higher education have increasingly emphasized that qualitative research studies are needed to enhance our understanding of important issues in higher education. In the domain of student studies, for example, researchers have noted how our patterns of knowing within the field have been shaped—and constricted—by our reliance on traditional quantitative methods of inquiry. On completing an encyclopedic critical review of the research on how college affects students, conducted with Patrick Terenzini, Ernest Pascarella (1991, p. 463) admitted to "a very real feeling of personal discontent at how often and how severely we limit ourselves and what we can learn if we depend only on those approaches to understanding that have served us (however admirably) in the past." While asserting that traditional methods, rooted in logical positivism, "will continue to serve us usefully for a long time to come" (p. 463), Pascarella forcefully stated:

> . . . I have come to believe that we have mapped only part of the higher-education landscape with quantitative, logical positivist approaches—perhaps not even the most interesting part. It is my considered opinion that judicious and creative qualitative, naturalistic, or ethnographic approaches may simply be better and more sensitive ways of capturing many of the subtle and fine-grained complexities of college impact than more traditional quantitative approaches. . . . Pat [Terenzini] and I anticipate that in the next decade important, and probably landmark, contributions to our under-standing of college impact will be produced by ethnographic and naturalistic studies. As an extra treat, such studies may be more interesting and fun to read than studies based on more traditional social science methodologies (p. 464).

A third reason for the development of this reader relates directly to issues at the center of today's higher education agenda. In light of growing concerns about campus racism, gender bias, gender- and class-based conflict, and multiculturalism, there is a growing need for research methods that probe areas often deemed "unresearchable" because of their personal and highly subjective nature—for example, the dynamics of "silencing" in organizations or the perpetuation of culturally dominant views in a curriculum. Topics and concerns such as these lend themselves to qualitative research; they are, simultaneously, at the heart of campus life of the 1990s (see, for example, studies by Holland and Eisenhart 1990; Weis 1985). In this sense, qualitative research promises to contribute meaningfully to the "real life" efforts of higher education practitioners and other stakeholders in ways that traditional methods have been unable to do in recent times (Keller 1985).

Finally, traditional quantitatively-oriented approaches often seem to fit neatly within the bounds of traditional topic areas, e.g., student surveys contribute almost exclusively to our knowl-edge of students, financial analyses contribute primarily to our understanding of financial situa-tions. But qualitative methods typically do not fall neatly into such conventional categories. Rather, qualitative methods spread—often unpredictably—across multiple topical domains (e.g., a study of students may contribute to understanding of collegiate organization, faculty cultures, processes of curricular construction). As such, qualitative methods, in addition to pointing out new avenues for inquiry, also suggest an internal redefinition of the field of higher education as we currently know it, including a rearrangement of traditional topical domains. A recent example of the crosscutting features of qualitative work include Conrad, Haworth, and Millar's study of master's degree programs, work which cuts across several of the "traditional" topical domains of organiza-tion, curriculum, students, and faculty in a way that could not have been done through quantitative methods alone.

Our purpose in this volume is to help students and teachers prepare for, enter into, participate in, reflect on, and give voice to the experience of doing qualitative research. In doing so, we invite students of higher education to examine alternative perspectives and approaches to qualitative inquiry and their implications for designing, conducting, and reporting qualitative research. To this end, we have selected readings from a variety of fields, including writings that critically examine alternative perspectives and approaches as well as provide vivid examples of qualitative research.

We are aware that dividing this reader into separate sections runs the risk of maintaining a widespread impression—a false one, in our view—that qualitative research can be broken into discrete stages (e.g., that methods and techniques can be separated from the reporting of research). With the caveat that qualitative inquiry should be viewed instead as a holistic process, we have nonetheless chosen to divide the reader into sections on the grounds that the advantages of using such organizing categories outweigh this limitation.

Because this volume will be used primarily in courses that focus on qualitative inquiry, we have prepared an introductory chapter aimed at inviting faculty and students to reflect on the learning and teaching of qualitative research. In each of the six sections in the reader which follow, we provide a brief introduction to the general topic and describe the readings. At the end of the volume, we provide a bibliography of recommended readings that includes readings in each of the topics covered in the volume—including numerous examples of qualitative research studies.

References

Conrad, Clifton F. , Haworth, Jennifer Grant, and Millar, Susan Bolyard. *A Silent Success*. Baltimore, Maryland: The Johns Hopkins University Press, 1993.

Holland, Dorothy C. and Eisenhart, Margaret A. *Educated in Romance: Women, Achievement, and College Culture*. Chicago: University of Chicago, 1990.

Keller, George. "Trees Without Fruit." *Change* (January–February, 1985), pp. 7–10.

Pascarella, Ernest T. "The Impact of College on Students: The Nature of Evidence." *Review of Higher Education* 14 (Summer, 1991), pp. 453–466.

Pascarella, Ernest T. and Terenzini, Patrick T. *How College Affects Students*. San Francisco: Jossey-Bass, 1991.

Weis, Lois. *Between Two Worlds: Black Students in an Urban Community College*. Boston: Routledge and Kegan Paul, 1985.

Acknowledgments

This book represents a collaboration among Clifton Conrad, Anna Neumann, Jennifer Grant Haworth, and Patricia Scott. While Clif Conrad had lead responsibility, this volume is a result of our shared understandings and efforts.

The editors express their sincere appreciation to Daryl Smith (Series Editor), Brian Romer (Editor, Ginn Press), and members of the advisory board for their many valuable suggestions regarding the content of this book.

Advisory Board

Marilyn Amey, University of Kansas
Louis Attinasi, Jr., University of Houston
Estela Bensimon, Pennsylvania State University
John Creswell, University of Nebraska
Dorothy Finnegan, College of William and Mary
Zelda Gamson, University of Massachusetts at Boston
Mildred Garcia, Montclair State University
Patricia Gumport, Stanford University
Laura Rendon, Arizona State University
Gary Rhoades, University of Arizona
Frances Stage, Indiana University
John Thelin, College of William and Mary
Elizabeth Whitt, Iowa State University

INTRODUCTION

Notes on the Classroom as Field Setting: Learning and Teaching Qualitative Research in Higher Education

PATRICIA SCOTT, JENNIFER GRANT HAWORTH, CLIFTON CONRAD, AND ANNA NEUMANN[1]

Our discussions about this volume over the past year have reminded us of our personal experiences as qualitative researchers and have led us to consider how our own experiences in graduate courses might have better prepared us for doing qualitative research. Drawing on our collaboration, our personal experiences, and the literature—including selections in this volume—we wrote this chapter with two aims in mind: to explore some major challenges that we and others have faced in doing qualitative research and, in tandem, to suggest some learning and teaching opportunities—classroom activities, exercises, and assignments—that others might find useful in preparing for these challenges.

In this chapter, we invite readers to think of the qualitative methods research class as a re-created "field site" in which participants practice and reflect on qualitative research. Viewed in this way, the classroom becomes a place where participants experience first-hand the process of doing qualitative research, and do so in ways that support risk-taking and collaborative learning—ingredients we believe are at the heart of qualitative inquiry.

In keeping with this view, we have organized the chapter around five overlapping stages in qualitative research—each related to a particular section of this book. "Surveying the Terrain" explores the philosophical landscape of qualitative inquiry; "Learning From Others in the Field" discusses building rapport and enriching understanding through interviewing and observation; "Interacting with Self and Others" focuses on enhancing self-awareness and reflexivity; "Seeing the Forest Through the Trees" addresses data recording and analysis; and "Voicing our Adventure" emphasizes authorial role and textual strategy in writing-up qualitative research. In the remainder of this chapter, we explore various challenges and suggest classroom activities, exercises, and assignments that may help illuminate each of these five stages.

---

[1]Pat Scott and Jennifer Grant Haworth are doctoral students at the University of Wisconsin-Madison and are completing qualitative studies for their dissertations. A faculty member at the University of Wisconsin-Madison, Clif Conrad teaches a qualitative research course and has done qualitative studies of higher education curriculum. Anna Neumann is a professor at Michigan State University and has conducted qualitative studies on topics such as administrative team leadership and the college presidency.

Surveying the Terrain: Finding Our Bearings

Challenges

In our experience, one of the most difficult—but important—challenges qualitative researchers face is "finding our bearings." Deciding on the underlying assumptions to guide our inquiry is seldom done quickly or easily. As Pat explains, finding our bearings often requires that we explore new and difficult terrain:

> I think that perhaps the most important step in doing qualitative research is coming to grips with your own philosophical bearings. In reflecting on my own experiences, I recall encountering three challenges as part of this process.
>
> First, as I sat in my qualitative research and curriculum courses, I gradually (and uncomfortably) became aware that there was more than "one way" to view the world. Until this point, I had unwittingly embraced positivism and a functionalist perspective—a by-product of my social work training. Now I found myself reading qualitative studies that had been written from multicultural, feminist, and critical perspectives. My first reaction to these studies was that they were anecdotal and unscientific. As we discussed them in class, however, I remember how my instructors used these studies as springboards for examining the world from new vantage points which, in turn, got me thinking about the nature of reality and how people "come to know what they know."
>
> My interest heightened, I encountered a second challenge—conceptual understanding. When I began reading texts on qualitative methods and qualitative research studies, I was introduced to a potpourri of abstract concepts and confusing jargon. For starters, there were difficult concepts like epistemology, ontology, and axiology. Then there were the various perspectives—such as functionalism, interpretivism, critical theory, liberal and radical feminism, and postmodernism. Overwhelmed by the discourse, I found myself swimming in a sea of confusion. I wanted to initiate dialogue with others about my conceptual struggle, but I usually remained silent because I lacked the "appropriate" vocabulary and background to articulate intelligible—much less intelligent—questions.
>
> Throughout the process of developing a conceptual understanding of some of the competing assumptions and perspectives that inform qualitative research, I concurrently faced a third challenge: the realization that I needed to develop a paradigmatic foundation, a world-view, to inform my own inquiry. Before, I had firmly believed that an objective reality existed "out there" that I could discover through objective, detached investigation. Then the boon came down: I was introduced to a new philosophical perspective—post-positivism—that maintained that no single objective reality existed but that there were multiple constructed realities that were time and context-bound. Given these two sharply contrasting views of the world—positivism and post-positivism—I began to question which view best reflected my personal experience with and understanding of the world. This questioning prompted an introspective journey that has, over time, led me to carve out my own philosophical niche.

Pat's story conveys several of the challenges that await qualitative researchers as they reflect on and come to understand the dimensions (and limitations) of their "philosophical bearings." While this is intellectually (and often, emotionally) demanding, we believe that reflecting on our fundamental values and beliefs is crucial. Why? Because our personal philosophies inform and animate every aspect of qualitative inquiry: from the types of questions we ask to the way we collect "data," from the way we interact with informants to the way we craft and present our texts. Finding our philosophical bearings forces us to confront the assumptions that shape our own and others' views of reality and, in so doing, provides us with a roadmap for beginning to survey the qualitative landscape.

Classroom Opportunities

Pat's account suggests that finding our bearings is a complex, sometimes frustrating, process that may begin conceptually but soon evolves into a personal understanding of alternative ways of knowing. Below, we suggest several classroom activities that, based on our own and others' experiences, can be useful in facilitating and enriching this stage of research.

For starters, we suggest that class participants read selections in the first section of this volume ("Explicating Frames of Reference: The Multiple Faces of Qualitative Research") as a basis for exploring some of the major paradigms, world-views, and perspectives that inform qualitative inquiry. We have found Yvonna Lincoln and Egon Guba's (1985) chapter, for example, a useful introduction to the philosophical assumptions that inform and animate positivist and post-positivist (naturalistic or constructivist) paradigms. Readings by Evelyn Jacob (1988) and Joyce McCarl Nielson (1990) introduce a variety of world-views and perspectives—including symbolic interactionism, feminist theory, critical theory, and standpoint epistemology. And the case studies that John Milam (1990) presents have provided us with enriched understandings of functionalist, intepretivist, radical humanist, and radical structuralist perspectives.

In our experience, the abstractions discussed in these readings become much more real for class participants when they discuss and link what they have read to tangible situations in their own lives. This can be done in various ways. Clif, for example, asks students in his qualitative research course to read Lincoln and Guba's chapter and then to form two groups: the "positivists" and the "post-positivists." Each group is asked to outline the basic assumptions of their assigned paradigm, illustrate it using examples from their own educational experiences, reflect on their own assumptions, and indicate if they identify more with the positivists or the post-positivists. As an alternative to this dualism, Clif then asks students to read the chapter included in this volume entitled "A Positioned Subject Approach to Inquiry" (Conrad, Haworth, and Millar, 1993) and to compare the authors' "bearings" with positivism and post-positivism. Finally, as shown at the end of this chapter, Clif gradually introduces more layers of complexity by providing a class handout incorporating four "frameworks" (functionalist, interpretivist, critical theory, and postmodern) that he uses to raise "talking points" and invite discussion about the multiple faces of qualitative research.

In her educational foundations course, Jennifer requires teachers to form working groups to analyze a national, state, or district-wide policy document that affects their professional practice from a specific perspective (critical, functionalist, or interpretivist). After each group has completed their analysis, class members reassemble and share their analyses with one another. Like Clif, Jennifer has found that these kinds of activities not only help class participants to develop richer understandings of alternative world-views, paradigms, and perspectives, but also their awareness of the underlying assumptions that inform their own and others' inquiry and professional practice.

Along with reading and group discussion, we have found that "journaling" provides class members with another opportunity to explore their philosophical bearings. As an individual undertaking, journal-keeping prompts class members to think critically about, react to, and challenge classroom readings and discussions in ways that are personally meaningful to them. As a group activity, journal-keeping invites class members to share with one another (usually anonymously) their frustrations as well as their breakthroughs. In both instances, journaling provides class members with a safe forum to reflect on and respond to their own and others' ideas, wrestle with their emerging understandings, and contemplate their "philosophical niche."

Finally, role-playing can be useful in helping class participants—faculty and students alike—find their bearings. While a range of scenarios is possible, we suggest that class members role-play the implications of a post-positivist paradigm for teaching and learning and use their own qualitative research class as an illustration. The following questions could frame the role-play: How would teaching and learning be different in our classroom if we enacted a post-positivist perspective? How would traditional classroom roles and relationships change? How might this influence the classroom culture and how might the culture differ from the "typical" college classroom? How might class goals and grading change? Conversely, how would teaching and learning be different if we enacted a positivist paradigm? Based on our own and others' experiences, role-playing exercises often enhance the personal relevance of the philosophical views under discussion, facilitate participants' understanding of these views, and help class members appreciate that the philosophical choices they make have important implications for how they "come to know."

Learning From Others in the Field: Establishing Rapport and Learning Through Interviewing and Observation

Challenges

From our perspective, the most important challenge we face in the field is learning from others. This is not easy. Unlike in quantitative research, where interaction with "subjects" is more or less detached and accomplished through instruments which are developed and "perfected" *a priori*, in qualitative research we are the instrument and must spontaneously process and respond to complex situations and human beings.[2] As we see it, learning from others involves two challenges: establishing trusting relationships, and utilizing research strategies—such as observation and interviewing—in ways that help us genuinely learn from others.

In the field, developing relationships of trust is critical if people are to willingly confide in us and help us to understand. Establishing and maintaining this rapport, in our experience, is far more demanding than is usually recognized. As human beings, we may have beliefs and feelings that impede our rapport with others. For example, we may be acutely aware of our "outsider" status in the field, which may engender feelings of discomfort and isolation. We may feel watched or scrutinized and become self-conscious. We may experience embarrassment as we seem to commit one faux pas after another, or feel guilty about our personal biases and prejudices.[3] As Pat reminds us, maintaining trusting relationships is not easy:

> I had been a participant-observer in Professor Swanson's class for about two months and was gaining some valuable understandings. As usual, I was waiting out in the hallway until class began, when Kevin suddenly appeared and sat down next to me. He looked depressed and I remembered his run-in with Swanson on Tuesday. She had been handing back exams and, without warning, announced Kevin's "F" to the entire class. She then proceeded to lecture him on the merits of studying in front of his classmates. Mortified, Kevin sat quietly with his eyes downcast as he took this verbal beating. As we talked, I felt myself compelled to ask, "Are you alright about Tuesday?" Kevin seized the opportunity to vent his frustration and anger. He said he felt "humiliated" by the whole experience and felt like dropping the class. I wanted to say: "You should be angry. She had no right to embarrass you like that." But a voice inside me said "shut-up, don't say anything more." Somehow my internal voice worked out a compromise because I responded "some instructors don't realize their impact on students." This was obviously not the response Kevin wanted, but he grudgingly agreed and that ended the conversation—I thought. Swanson called me the next day, livid. Kevin, apparently bolstered by our conversation, confronted Swanson after class with a list of grievances and used my name in reference. After explaining and apologizing profusely, she allowed me to continue observing the class, but I knew our rapport would never be the same.

Along with building rapport, we have also come to appreciate the importance of using our research methods and techniques in ways that help us learn from others. While the two most basic field methods—participant-observation and interviewing—each pose special challenges, both require patience and skill if they are to enhance understanding. As an informant once advised William Whyte (1955, p. 303): "Go easy on that who, what, when, why, where stuff, Bill. You ask these questions and people will clam up on you. If people accept you, you can just hang around, and you'll learn the answers in the long run without even having to ask the questions."

To develop deeper understandings, whether through observation or interviewing, many texts on qualitative research tell us that we must patiently and skillfully listen with our "third ear" for the "meaning behind the message." In this vignette, Anna illustrates this point:

> One of the most important lessons I learned about interviewing was that I should not take my interviewees' words for granted. Interviewees often assumed that I knew what they meant, particularly when they talked about the intricacies of their institutional settings or, more difficult for me, about "abstractions" that were part of the vocabulary of the field—words like leadership, collaboration, mission, vision, goals, and so on. It's this latter piece—the abstractions—that I'm talking about here.
>
> This is what I encountered in the field: As an interviewer, I was trying to get into people's (administrators' and faculty members') minds about what leadership meant to them. I assumed that the word "leadership" would mean different things to different people and, therefore, that it would mean different things to the person I was interviewing and to me. My interviewees, of course, were not working from this assumption, and it took me a while to appreciate just what that meant in the fleeting seconds of an interview. The people I interviewed would use abstract words, like leadership, without checking that I was understanding what *they* were understanding. I learned to stop them—to make them back up. So if the word leadership came up in a person's response, I'd say, "You just used the word leadership. What do you mean by that?" But it didn't end there because that person's response might be something like, "It means having a vision." Since I wasn't sure just what "having a vision" meant to her, I'd have to ask her to back up again: "Tell me what the word vision means to you." And then the interviewee might come back with, "It means building a common image among the people in the college—the leader does that." But again, this was something that, analytically, I felt I had to pursue. So I might ask, "You just referred to the leader building a common image. *How* does a leader do that?" And if they looked puzzled I might add, "Getting people to have a similar image of a college can be a pretty difficult thing to do. Do you think it's possible to do that? What would be involved in getting that to happen?"
>
> What I learned from conversations such as these was how packed with stories any abstract word or phrase can be—people's individual stories of how they see things happening in settings that they share with others. I also learned how different the stories could be from person to person, even in a single place, and how little people really knew about each other's "stories of causality" in a shared social space. What I had to remember was to keep asking about those words and stories—not to take them for granted.

Classroom Opportunities

As our discussion—and Pat's and Anna's vignettes—suggest, we believe that developing rapport and learning to use field methods with patience and skill are critical to learning from others in the field. We now offer a few classroom activities that might prepare class participants to learn more effectively from others in the field.

As a point of departure, we suggest class discussions centered around the selections included in the second section of this volume ("Approaching Inquiry: Methods and Techniques"). Robert Crowson's (1987) article provides a useful overview of qualitative methods, including a discussion of building rapport. The other readings look at a range of methods and techniques for doing qualitative inquiry—including ethnography, grounded theory, and multiple case studies—all of which can provide a foundation for discussion of rapport-building and using field methods in ways that maximize learning from others in the field.

To help class members practice establishing rapport, we suggest an exercise by William Tierney and Yvonna Lincoln (1992, p. 10) that focuses on negotiating entry. In brief, they propose that students role-play the negotiation process in pairs, and that gatekeepers be instructed to "play hardball" and make entre difficult. According to Tierney and Lincoln, such tactics help prepare class members for the possibility of rejection, encourage them to practice persuasive communication, and allow them to experience the difficulty of building rapport while under fire.

Class members might also benefit from other experiences aimed at developing and maintaining rapport. For example, we sometimes ask students to discuss how they establish rapport in their everyday lives with new acquaintances, classmates/colleagues, and friends. We then build on this conversation by asking questions such as: "Which of these rapport-building skills could be transferred to the field?" and "Are there additional rapport-building skills unique to the field?" After the class has developed some basic rapport-building principles, we invite class members to practice (role-play) building rapport with different types of individuals (such as administrators, students, faculty) and to compare and contrast rapport-building techniques under different circumstances (such as in a classroom or at the student union). Throughout these activities, class members give one another feedback on their strengths and on potential areas for growth in their performance; in so doing, they develop their skills at listening to and learning from others "in the field." Class participants are also asked to identify the types of people with whom they might have difficulty establishing rapport and to consider how they might approach these kinds of people.

To enhance the observational skills of class participants, Annette Lareau (1987) describes an exercise where the entire class observes the same event and then shares their notes with one another (including the instructor). Lareau has class members observe a role-play situation, but a class could observe a public event (for example, a university senate meeting), a film, or even their own classroom. Lareau further suggests scheduling a number of these observation sessions but with variation. For example, she has students take notes on the same event but gives each a different question to guide their observation. These types of exercises invite class members to discuss criteria for good notetaking, to share and discuss any differences in one anothers' perceived "realities," and to examine issues of trustworthiness.

Finally, we believe that class members need to be provided with safe opportunities to practice their interviewing skills. Lou Attinasi, for example, told us that he has students interview one another in pairs (either alone or while the class observes) and then asks them to critique each other's performance. At some point during the term, students also submit an audiotaped interview and transcription for his feedback. In much the same vein, Clif invites class participants to role-play interviewing different types of respondents (such as nonverbal and verbose, students and faculty members), to conduct different types of interviews (informal and formal), and to explore different approaches to interviewing (structured, semi-structured, and unstructured). He then asks students to reflect upon what they learned from interviewees in these role-playing situations and encourages them to discuss how they could hone their interviewing skills to learn more from others in the field. We suggest that all of these exercises—from developing better rapport with informants to improving how we converse with them—can help class members become more effective at learning from others in the field.

Interacting with Self and Others in the Field: Developing Self-Awareness and Reflexivity

Challenges

Perhaps the most important challenge of qualitative research is developing self-awareness, the kind of self-awareness that enhances our reflexivity. As we define it, to be "reflexive" means that the researcher remains constantly aware that he or she is an integral part of the social world he or she is studying. It involves acknowledging and continuously reflecting on how our values, attitudes, feelings, and perspectives inform our research and field-related understandings.

We have found that reflexivity is seldom easy, or comfortable. Being reflexive can make us acutely aware of our feelings, idiosyncracies, insecurities, biases, values, and beliefs—and we sometimes learn things about ourselves that we would prefer not to learn. Yet, as many qualitative researchers have observed, reflexivity is vital. It reminds us to be more "ethical" in our interactions with others. It also reminds us to take account of our presence, thereby enhancing the "trustworthiness" of our research. Finally, it enriches our understandings. Jennifer suggests that reflexivity can lead to meaningful new insights into ourselves in concert with our research, as indicated in this journal entry she made while in the field:

> I walked into yet another faculty member's office, and step-by-step went through the interviewing rituals that had become a familiar part of my role as researcher/interviewer. After conversing for almost two hours with my latest "interviewee," I attempted to close the interview with my now familiar phrase, "Well, I've taken more of your time than I intended—I should really let you get back to your work." The middle-aged male faculty member replied, "Oh, that's OK. This has really been fun. I've learned a few things about myself today." I told him that he had been very informative, and that I, too, had enjoyed our conversation but that I had to run off to another interview. We exchanged business cards, shook hands, and wished each other well. As I rushed to my next appointment, I began to reflect on this person's words and silently said to myself, "I guess I learned a few things about myself today, too."

> Later that evening, upon revisiting the interview, I began to understand more fully that I was not a detached "researcher" out-on-the-road "interviewing" people about their experiences in master's programs. Rather, I began to see myself as an "interviewee" who was also being "researched" by the people with whom I spoke. Indeed, my middle-aged "subject" wanted to get to know me as much as I wanted to know him; he engaged me in an *inter-view*—or what I would term a relational dialogue— in which I learned about his attitudes and beliefs as well as my own. This reflexive moment helped me to appreciate that I not only sought to understand informants' experiences in master's education, but also that these same informants urged me to open up and *re-search* my views on the same topic.

Classroom Opportunities

Understanding reflexivity—and enhancing the self-awareness from which it springs—is not easy, but it has been our experience that this challenge gives us an unusual opportunity to be resourceful and creative in the classroom. Below, we offer several class exercises for helping class members prepare for this challenge.

To begin with, we suggest that class discussions be organized around the concept of reflexivity. We have found that the readings in the fourth section of this volume ("Interacting with Self and Others: Reflections In/On Qualitative Inquiry") can provide a useful point of departure for class discussion. Readings by Susan Krieger (1985) and Sara Lawrence Lightfoot (1983) introduce the concept of reflexivity, and those by Margaret LeCompte and Judith Preissle Goetz (1982) and Patti Lather (1986) explore the concept of reflexivity in relation to differing definitions of "trustworthiness" in qualitative research. And an essay by Annette Lareau (1989) in the third section of this volume is, in our view, a wonderful illustration of "reflexivity."

Journal writing often enhances self-awareness and reflexivity. Like Joanne Cooper (1993), we believe that journal writing can encourage "powerful, reflective practices which promote . . . learning and context-embedded critical thinking." By maintaining journals throughout an entire course, class members can explore their intuitive, creative, and affective selves; give "voice" to tacit thoughts that, when expressed, may give rise to valuable insights and understandings; and consider the rich details and meanings in their everyday experiences. One journal exercise that we have found particularly useful requires class members to sit in a comfortable place for a few minutes and keep a written account of their experience. Class members begin the exercise by asking themselves, "What am I aware of in this instant?" and they then note both internal (physical sensations, emotions, thoughts) and external (aspects of the surrounding environment) sources of awareness, where their awareness travels during this period, and any understandings they develop as a result of their experience (adapted from Kalven, Rosen, and Taylor, 1982, p. 83).

In addition, there are many exercises like the Johari Window and the Awareness Wheel that can help to foster self-awareness (adapted from Kalven, Rosen, and Taylor, 1982). In the Johari Window exercise, class members divide into groups of three and each group role-plays some aspect of entering or interacting in the field (such as negotiating entry and interviewing). After each role-play, group members give written or verbal feedback in four areas. The "Public Area" explores information that is known to both the self and others. Here group members review what the researcher said, how he or she approached the situation, and the respondent's observable reaction. The "Blind Spot" refers to feedback that is known to others but not the self. Group members share how they perceived and responded to the researcher during the role-play. The "Hidden Area" contains information that is known to the self and not others. Here, the researcher discloses his or her own thoughts, feelings, and internal reactions experienced during the role play. Finally, the "Unknown Area" contains feedback that is known neither to self or others. As Janet Kalven and her colleagues note, the information in this last area "is below the level of conscious awareness, but some elements of it may emerge in a free, open and supportive interchange" (p. 98). Dialogue about the "Unknown Area" can help to encourage the expression of tacit awarenesses that are rarely voiced and that are difficult to grasp and articulate.

Finally, the Awareness Wheel exercise trains participants to "distinguish between sensory impressions, thoughts, feelings, intentions, and actions" (Kalven, Rosen, and Taylor, 1982, p. 84). Once again, teams of students role-play some aspect of entering or interacting in the field and use the wheel to re-experience what they saw (sensory experience), felt (affective experience), wanted (intentions), and did (behavior) during the role play. This activity is useful both as a small group exercise and as an individual journal activity.

Seeing the Forest Through the Trees: Data Recording and Analysis

Challenges

In the field, data recording and analysis are central research activities. By data we mean the field notes, interview transcriptions, or documents generated through our observations, interviews, and field explorations. By analysis we mean the process through which we "make sense" of our data and come to understand our field experience.

Data recording poses challenges to every qualitative researcher, particularly in the construction of field notes—our written reminders of what we saw, heard, thought, experienced, and did in the field. We concur with Martyn Hammersley and Paul Atkinson (1983, p. 146) that a qualitative study without adequate field notes is "like using an expensive camera with poor quality film. . . . [T]he results will be poor. Only foggy pictures result." That said, writing field notes can be a formidable challenge, as Pat's account suggests:

> Field notes were a pain to write but the reasons for this changed over time. Initially, they were laborious. Being the quintessential perfectionist, I labored over them like I was writing my first novel—carefully separating my descriptive, methodological, and theoretical notes as suggested by Leonard Schatzman and Anselm Strauss (1973). Fortunately, my dissertation advisor suggested I discard this "anal-retentive" approach for a more relaxed one. I still remember the sensation of freedom I experienced when I finally "let 'er rip" and allowed everything to pour onto the page—the day's events, my hunches, confessions, impressions, problems, rantings, along with new understandings about myself and the field. They were cathartic and stimulated my creative juices and led to

some of my best thinking and analysis. I actually relished returning home after a day of observations and chronicling my encounters.

Soon enough, I encountered my next obstacle—writing. Prior to my field research, I prided myself on succinct prose that eliminated "superfluous" detail and cut straight to the point. But field notes required a different type of writing—writing that captured the richness of the field and recreated it on paper. Field notes were supposed to paint vivid portraits of people, activities, settings, conversations, and even my own thought processes with accuracy and style. Suddenly, I needed a rich vocabulary of adjectives and action verbs to portray and recreate colorfully these scenes on paper. Words never became so important.

As this challenge slowly receded, another challenge replaced it—discipline. After awhile field notes got very old. Each hour of observation required two to three hours of writing and intense reflection. Between the study and the field notes, I felt consumed by my research. Every aspect of my life seemed to revolve around the study. Needless to say, it took tremendous discipline to return home every day from the field site tired, only to spend another three to five hours writing. It was emotionally and physically draining. Occasionally, I gave into temptation and waited until the following day(s) to type my notes. But in those instances, I always paid a price. I could never recreate the field in quite the same way—conversations were fuzzier, observations less distinct, and my writing less spontaneous and flowing.

As Pat's description indicates, data recording generates a number of challenges. Still, these challenges often pale in comparison to data analysis. We know of no other aspect of the research process that generates more anxiety, procrastination, and diffidence on the part of researchers than data analysis. Put simply, we frequently become so immersed in the field and in recording our data that we "cannot see the forest through the trees." That said, this is also one of the most rewarding aspects of qualitative inquiry. Margaret Ely and her colleagues (1991, p. 86) communicate the intellectual and emotional challenges associated with data analysis in this way:

> The five of us have found that often the first analyses create a place where reality hits, where doubts, fears, and avoidances begin, where the theory and philosophy of qualitative research are put to a reality test. We have also found that this is a place of great value and rededication and personal joy. When the researcher gets right to it, it is an awesome, even frightening responsibility to bow to the fact that "self-as-instrument" inevitably means one must create ongoing meaning out of the evolving and evolved data, since raw data alone have little value. But it gives tremendous elation to know it can be done. Thus, the naturalistic researcher must come to rely on his/her own talents, insights, and trustworthiness and, in the end, go public with the reasoning that engendered the results, while accepting with equanimity that other people may make different meaning from the same data.

Throughout our research, analysis is a complex process that requires an intimate, ongoing, and reciprocal relationship between ourselves and our "data." As such, there is no step-by-step guide, no consensus in the literature on how best to approach it. Still, most authors of qualitative research texts suggest that we develop some way to code and categorize our data based on observed regularities, patterns, or other conceptual schemes. These categories are then refined, regrouped, and synthesized into larger conceptual or thematic units that we, in turn, construct into an overall theory or set of generalizations. Jennifer and Clif, who think of the process as "finding a story line," recall the data analysis experience they had working on a qualitative study of master's education:

> Some days we worked alone, reading program summary after program summary and recording recurring themes. Many more days we engaged in lively and spirited exchanges in which we worked together to understand and explain similarities and differences in stakeholders' master's experiences. We questioned one anothers' interpretations and assumptions, critically reviewed the evidentiary foundation for our emerging themes, and discussed alternative interpretations.

> Then one day, after mucking around with our data for several months, we serendipitously hit upon what came to be a unifying theme in "our" story about master's education: people make choices in

key program areas that have important consequences for how participants experience their master's programs. Armed with this new insight, we returned to our interview material and sought to understand the differing choices stakeholders made in their programs. We followed all the "rules" of comparative data analysis: we coded data into a range of categories—in our study, "decision-situations"—and proceeded to modify them in light of our evidence. After multiple iterations of this process (which literally took months in the case of one decision-situation), we finally made sense of our interview material in terms of five key decisions that stakeholders made in master's programs. We travelled many roads to get to this point, including scores of dead-end streets and cul de sac's.

While engaged in analyzing interview material for the master's study, our minds often wandered to that well-known classic, "The Wizard of Oz", which, unknown to us at the time, served as a metaphor for our experiences with this aspect of qualitative research. On many occasions, for example, we wanted to visit the Wizard and trade in our brains for new and improved models. On other occasions, we wanted to ask the Wizard for a shot of courage to keep us going through what at the time seemed like a neverending process. And, yes, there were occasions when our hearts beat faintly wondering if we would ever make sense of the mountain of paper and audio tape we had collected during our study. Yet in venturing to test our intellectual ability and stick-to-itiveness, we came to appreciate that we did not need a Wizard to get through the data analysis process after all.

As Jennifer and Clif's account suggests, data analysis is "mucky" business. Yet, when we finally make sense of our data in ways that help us emerge from the trees and see the forest, the personal and intellectual rewards associated with this stage of qualitative research can be enormous.

Classroom Opportunities

In our experience, the twin challenges of data recording and analysis are often short-shrifted in the classroom, leaving many students ill-prepared to deal with them successfully in the field. With this in mind, we offer some exercises to help bridge this gap.

We begin with some writing exercises. Since the writing process begins with field notes and extends through the writing of the final report, we and some of our colleagues have found it useful to involve students in writing exercises throughout the course. For instance, class members could bring in examples of colorful passages from well-regarded qualitative studies to explore how authors may use a variety of literary techniques to bring field scenes to life. It might also be helpful to invite a creative writing instructor to class. Students might also find it useful to practice their creative writing skills by observing some public event and, alone or in pairs, writing a short but vivid description of what they see.

Exercises such as these can be extended to field notes. After discussing the purpose, mechanics, types, styles, and criteria for "good" field notes, we encourage class participants to observe a short role-play (perhaps assigned to two or three students) and to write brief observational, theoretical, methodological, and reflexive notes to share in class. Further, class members could do a lengthier class observation (at least thirty minutes), jot notes as they observe, and later write complete field notes based on their jottings. Ideally, these exercises encourage class members to hone their writing skills, provide them with opportunities for feedback, and enhance their awareness of their individual writing styles.

We have learned that most class members also need practice with data analysis. We suggest two exercises in this regard. The first (adapted from Gunter, Estes, and Schwab, 1990, p. 190) is designed to help class members develop a "feel" for inductive thinking and data analysis and to demonstrate how groups may interpret and analyze the same data differently. In this exercise, class members break into teams of three or four persons and read a list of 20 to 40 terms.[4] Using inductive analysis, each team establishes a categorical system to group related terms and labels these groups accordingly. (Class members may find it helpful to write the nouns and labels on post-it notes and rearrange them on a board or other flat surface as groups of words are identified. This can help participants visually conceptualize relationships and groups.) Word groups can then be reanalyzed and combined into more meaningful complex categories—a process that requires each team to adopt a more wide-angled perspective. Finally, teams are asked to develop a "story line" that synthesizes and explains the relationship among their "data" groups in a one or two sentence summary and/or schematic drawing.

After this "warm up" exercise, we encourage class members to try a content analysis exercise developed by William Tierney and Yvonna Lincoln (1992). During the first hour of class, students are given copies of actual interview notes (names and identifying information omitted) and a supply of index cards. Students are instructed to extract data "units" from the notes and place them on 3 x 5 cards. In the second hour, students work in small groups to combine related data "units" into categories. Finally, each group presents and explains the rationale behind their data categories during the third hour of class.

A variation of this latter exercise involves using students' journal entries (adapted from Laureau, 1987). Class members first divide into groups of three or four. Using the question "How do students experience the qualitative research learning process?" as a guide, each group then extracts "data units" from their personal journal entries and forms a "storyline" that tells their collective "tale." Since they use their own "data" (journal entries), this exercise often makes the process more meaningful for students.

Voicing Our Adventure: Authorial Role and Textual Strategy

Challenges

In considering literally dozens of qualitative studies for inclusion in this volume, we realized that many qualitative researchers sidestep the challenge of voice. (By "voice," we refer to how authors present their research—and themselves—to their audience.) We came across few examples in which the author(s) discussed her or his role in "creating" the text, and even fewer where the author employed rhetorical and narrative conventions to communicate that role to the reader.

One of the most important challenges we face in doing qualitative inquiry is "finding our voice"—especially our authorial role and textual strategy. We believe, however, that "finding our voice" is a vital challenge. Writing, after all, is not a neutral activity. Rather, we—as authors—have a central role in constructing texts—including determining what story we will tell, how we will tell it, who we will tell it to, and our role in constructing it.

As Clif suggests, learning how to write-up qualitative research posed some difficult challenges for him[5]:

> In the last few years, as I have renewed my commitment to qualitative research, I have come to believe that communicating qualitative research is infinitely more challenging than writing-up quantitative studies that are anchored in logical positivism and an objectivist way-of-knowing. As I have come to appreciate from my reading and my interactions with others, writing-up qualitative research means "finding my voice" for every single text that I write. Put simply, it means addressing two major challenges: defining my role in the text, and developing a textual strategy consistent with that role.
>
> In defining my role in the text, my greatest challenge is to establish my role and voice in such a way that the text reflects my underlying philosophical and theoretical orientation, my research questions, my methods and techniques, my role in analysis, interpretation, and presentation of data, and how I choose to present myself—in short, my role in coming to know what I have learned. In addressing this challenge, I often find myself returning to qualitative research texts that address issues of "authorial role" and "voice." In each case, however, I address this challenge anew, for how I decide to

establish my role and voice in a particular text varies somewhat according to circumstances and my "position" in the inquiry.

My second major challenge is developing a textual strategy consistent with my role. In addressing this challenge, I usually begin by exploring alternative textual approaches—what John Van Maanan (1988) calls "tales"—and then seek to fashion a more specific strategy for writing that reflects my presence in *how* I came to know what I learned in concert with *what* I actually learned. In so doing, I gradually begin to craft my narrative in a way that I find to be in harmony with my role and the "story" I wish to tell. If I am persevering, and fortunate, I eventually find my voice—but never easily.

Classroom Opportunities

Because writing is so inextricably linked to the doing of qualitative research, we believe that writing needs to be targeted much more consciously in the classroom than—we suspect—is the case in many qualitative research courses. We agree with Paul Atkinson (1991, p. 172) that "apprenticeship in the craft skills of writing is an essential element in research training." In this vein, we offer the following exercises, activities, and assignments to help class members give written voice to their research.

To begin with, it is useful to introduce class members to various ways of writing-up qualitative research. Along with diverse authorial role and textual strategies, we have found it helpful for students to discuss: different organizational approaches (such as topical, thematic, natural history, and chronological), storylines, modes of presentation, narrative and rhetorical devices, and writing styles. The readings included in the fifth section of this volume ("Creating a Text: Writing Up Qualitative Research") may be useful in facilitating discussions. We also suggest that class members choose examples of qualitative research from section six ("Reading Text: Examples of Qualitative Research") and, in small groups, analyze them in terms of authorial role, textual strategy, organizational approach, narrative and rhetorical conventions, storyline, mode of presentation, and the like.

Along these same lines, it is beneficial to practice writing in new and different ways. We suggest that class members begin by practicing different ways of organizing texts (Hammersley and Atkinson, 1983, pp. 212–227). Class members could be asked to write about a previous class session—one which they all found memorable. Each participant could then select a different textual strategy and write a two-page narrative using their approach for the next class session. Participants could then critique each others' narratives in small groups by addressing questions such as: How well does the narrative illustrate the textual strategy? What are the related strengths and weaknesses? Does the author omit important details or information? Does the author include unnecessary information? What are the narrative's stylistic strengths and weaknesses? What is the authorial voice in the text? This exercise helps illustrate different textual approaches to the writing up of qualitative research. Moreover, because in this exercise everyone writes about the same class session, students can compare and contrast their narratives.

We likewise encourage class members to experiment with different authorial voices and textual strategies using John Van Maanen's (1988) six types of tales—realist, confessional, impressionist, critical, formal, and literary. For example, each participant could choose a memorable class event, describing it in six paragraphs, each reflecting a different authorial voice and textual strategy. Working in small groups, participants could then compare and critique each others' writing, stressing both strengths and weaknesses.

Finally, class members could critique their own texts. In his class, for example, Clif requires students to join a collaborative research team, conduct a pilot field study, present their findings to the entire class (both orally and in writing), and then participate in a class discussion about their final report. This exercise provides students with opportunities to write up qualitative research and to discover and define their own authorial role and voice.

A Concluding Note

Our purpose in this volume is to help participants in qualitative research courses prepare for, enter into, and give voice to the experience of qualitative inquiry. We have invited readers to view their research methods classroom as a *re-created* "field site" in which they confront challenges and participate in opportunities to experience qualitative inquiry in ways that encourage risk-taking and collaborative learning. We conclude by inviting readers to view our discussion in light of their own experiences, and to share other classroom activities with us and others who are invested in learning and teaching qualitative inquiry.

Endnotes

1. As Harry Wolcott (1988, p. 190) puts it: "The ethnographer is the research instrument, the villagers are the population. That instrument—the anthropologist in person—has been faulted time and time again for being biased, inattentive, ethnocentric, partial, forgetful, overly subject to infection and disease, incapable of attending to everything at once, easily distracted, simultaneously too involved and too detached—the list goes on and on. Be that as it may, what better instrument could we ever devise for observing and understanding human behavior?"

2. Rosalie Wax (1971, p. 370) has insightfully observed: "The person who cannot abide feeling awkward or out of place, who feels crushed whenever he makes a mistake—embarrassing or otherwise—who is psychologically unable to endure being, and being treated like, a fool . . . ought to think twice before he decides to become a participant observer."

3. Here is a list of terms we propose: dialogue, direction, energize, strategize, guide, unity, compromise, cooperate, motivate, convey, purposeful, participate, eye contact, groups, listen, rewards, collaborate, attitude, acknowledge, initaite, goals, plan, facilitiate, feedback, reflect, satisfy, vision, inspire, support, accept, and question.

4. In the course syllabus for his qualitative methods course, Clif forthrightly communicates his anxiety about writing, saying that this anxiety goes with the territory and hence the sooner we come to terms with it the better. In his words:

   I almost always experience anxiety about writing and, frankly, I am highly suspect of people who say that writing is easy for them. To be brutally honest, I think that writing is one of the hardest things to do—for me and many others. For in so doing, we have to demonstrate clear and compelling thinking to ourselves—and then communicate it to our audiences. Writing, for most of us, is bloody hard work—and I think that it's useful to admit that if we are to deal effectively with the writing process.

5. In addition, Clif has found that collaborative research teams are useful in many other ways as well—including as support groups. Indeed, his experiences mirror those of Margaret Ely and her colleagues (1991, pp. 100–101), who extol the virtues of support groups in the classroom: "The members of a suppport group can help each other in several key ways: offering emotioal support, suggesting new points a [sic] view, and establishing interim, reachable deadlines. While professors also offer emotional support . . . [they] cannot often achieve the level of intimacy that colleagues and fellow sufferers manage."

References

Atkinson, Paul. "Supervising the Text." *International Journal of Qualitative Studies in Education* 4 (April-June, 1991), pp. 161–174.

Burrell, Gibson, and Morgan, Gareth. *Sociological Paradigms and Organisational Analysis.* Portsmouth, New Hampshire: Heinemann, 1979.

Cooper, Joanne E. "Digging, Daring and Discovery: Sifting the Soil of Professional Life Through Journal Writing." In *Ethical and Social Issues in Professional Education*, edited by C. Brody and J. Wallace. New York: SUNY Press, 1993 (in press).

Crowson, Robert L. "Qualitative Research Methods in Higher Education." In *Higher Education: Handbook of Theory and Research* (Vol. 3), edited by John C. Smart. New York: Agathon Press, 1987, pp. 1–56.

Ely, Margot, Anzul, Margaret, Friedman, Teri, Garner, Diane, and Steinmetz, Ann McCormack. *Doing Qualitative Research: Circles Within Circles*. New York: Falmer, 1991.

Gunter, Mary Alice, Estes, Thomas H., and Schwab, Jan Hasbrouck. *Instruction: A Models Approach.* Boston: Allyn and Bacon, 1990.

Hamersley, Martyn and Atkinson, Paul. *Ethnography: Principles in Practice.* London: Tavistock Publications, 1983.

Jacob, Evelyn. "Clarifying Qualitative Research: A Focus on Traditions." *Educational Researcher* 17 (January-February, 1988), pp. 16–19, 22–24.

Kalven, Janet, Rosen, Larry, and Taylor, Bruce. *Value Development: A Practical Guide.* New York: Paulist Press, 1982.

Lareau, Annette. "Appendix: Common Problems in Field Work: A Personal Essay." In *Home Advantage: Social Class and Parental Intervention in Elementary Education*, by Annette Lareau. New York: Falmer Press, 1989, pp. 187–223.

Lareau, Annette. "Teaching Qualitative Methods: The Role of Classroom Activities." *Education and Urban Society* 20 (November, 1987), pp. 86–120.

Lather, Patti. *Getting Smart: Feminist Research and Pedagogy With/In the Postmodern.* New York: Routledge, 1991.

Lather, Patti. "Issues of Validity in Openly Ideological Research: Between a Rock and a Soft Place." *Interchange* 17 (Winter, 1986), pp. 63–84.

LeCompte, Margaret D. and Goetz, Judith Preissle. "Problems of Reliability and Validity in Ethnographic Research." *Review of Educational Research* 52 (Spring, 1982), pp. 31–60.

Lightfoot, Sara Lawrence. "Afterword: The Passion of Portraiture." In *The Good High School: Portraits of Character and Culture*, by Sara Lawrence Lightfoot. New York: Basic Books, 1983, pp. 369–378.

Lincoln, Yvonna S., and Guba, Egon G. "Postpositivism and the Naturalistic Paradigm." In *Naturalistic Inquiry*, by Yvonna S. Lincoln and Egon G. Guba. Beverly Hills, California: Sage, 1985, pp. 14–46.

Milam, John H., Jr. "Using Alternative Paradigms: Four Case Studies." In *Higher Education: Handbook of Theory and Research* (Vol. 8), edited by John C. Smart. New York: Agathon, 1992, pp. 305–344.

Nielsen, Joyce McCarl. "Introduction." In *Feminist Research Methods*, edited by Joyce McCarl Nielson. Boulder, Colorado: Westview Press, 1990, pp. 1–37.

Schatzman, Leonard and Strauss, Anselm L. *Field Research: Strategies for a Natural Sociology.* Englewood Cliffs, New Jersey: Prentice-Hall, 1973.

Tierney, William G., and Lincoln, Yvonna S. "Teaching Qualitative Methods in Higher Education." Paper presented at the annual meeting of the Association for the Study of Higher Education, Minneapolis, Minnesota, 1992.

Van Maanen, John. *Tales of the Field: On Writing Ethnography.* Chicago: University of Chicago Press, 1988.

Wax, Rosalie H. *Doing Fieldwork: Warning and Advice.* Chicago: University of Chicago Press, 1971.

Whyte, William F. *Street Corner Society: The Social Structure of an Italian Slum.* Chicago: University of Chicago Press, 1955.

Wolcott, Harry F. "Ethnographic Research in Education." In *Complementary Methods for Research in Education,* edited by Richard M. Jaeger. Washington, D.C.: American Educational Research Association, 1988, pp. 187–210.

Class Handout for Qualitative Research Methods: Functionalist, Interpretivist, Critical Theory, and Postmodern Frameworks

Professor Clif Conrad
University of Wisconsin-Madison

As we have discussed in class, there seem to be a bewildering number of paradigms, world-views, perspectives—philosophical frames-of-reference—that variously inform and animate the work of qualitative researchers. I make no pretense of advancing a bold new scheme for classifying these various frames-of-reference, but I would like to circulate this informal handout as a "tool"—a series of possible "talking points" for our collectively exploring some of the multiple faces of qualitative research.

Most qualitative researchers tend to work more or less out of one of four general "frameworks"—by which I mean simply a "frame" which broadly informs one's approach to inquiry. To complicate matters further, some researchers draw upon more than one of these frameworks and from diverse "perspectives" within them—including various feminisms. For example, there are individuals such as Patti Lather who work at the intersections of "post-positivism," critical theory, postmodernism, and feminism.

Below, under each of the four frameworks, I have attempted to identify the major focus of research, origins of the framework, major "perspectives" often associated with the framework, individuals sometimes linked with a framework or perspective and, in a highly informal manner, raised some possible implications for doing qualitative research.

Functionalist Framework

FOCUS: Predict and Control (Develop/Test Theory)

ORIGINS: This framework is anchored in nineteenth century positivism in which biological and mechanical analogies were adapted—mostly by sociologists—to the study of human behavior. Functionalists assume that, because they have endured, existing "systems" and "structures" are legitimate as well as desirable. In turn, they seek to understand how these systems and structures operate by using methods of research derived from the natural sciences. Moreover, most functionalists focus on how structures "cause" human behavior/action; they do not focus on how people create meaning. Well-known individuals associated with this tradition include: August Comte, Herbert Spencer, Emile Durkheim, Malinowski, A.R. Radcliffe-Brown, Ludwig Von Bertalanffy, Talcott Parsons, Robert Merton, David Easton, George Homans, Daniel Katz, Robert Kahn, and Richard Hall.

PERSPECTIVES:

"Structural Functionalism" (Organismic Analogy)
"Systems Theory"
"Conflict Functionalism"

SOME IMPLICATIONS FOR DOING RESEARCH:

1. Class Discussion: Sampling, open-endedness of design, generalizability, roles of researcher and "researched," data analysis and interpretation.

Interpretivist Framework

FOCUS: Understand/Explain

ORIGINS: This framework is historically anchored in nineteenth century German idealism and the concept of "verstehen" (understanding). Those using this framework posit that meaning is "socially constructed" by human beings. Hence, they focus not on "uncovering reality" but on generating understandings based on the interpretations of people (researchers and "researched"), that is, how people "experience," "interpret," and give "meaning" to their worlds. Major individuals: Wilhelm Dilthey, Max Weber, Edmund Husserl, Peter Berger, Thomas Luckman, and Clifford Geertz.

PERSPECTIVES:

"Interpretivist" (Clifford Geertz)
"Naturalistic" (Yvonna Lincoln and Egon Guba)
"Ethnomethodology" (Harold Garfinkel)
"Constructivist"
"Grounded Theory" (Barney Glaser and Anselm Strauss)
"Phemonenological" (Heidigger, Husserl)
"Symbolic Interaction" (George Herbert Mead)
"Hermeneutic" (Dilthey, Gadamer)
"Liberal Feminist"

SOME IMPLICATIONS FOR DOING RESEARCH:

1. Orientation of Research (De-Centering of Positivism/Objectivism): Positivists tend to view researchers as "subjects" and respondents as "objects", but most interpretivists take what conventionally have been viewed as "objects" (for example, faculty, students, administrators) and make them "subjects." In turn, researchers operating within this framework don't impose categories of observations (because "objects" are now "subjects") but, alternatively, focus on how subjects interpret/make sense of their worlds. Subjects are variously watched (observed) and interviewed in order to learn from them and to "understand."

Critical Theory Framework

FOCUS: Critique/Emancipate/Radical Change (Oppression Requires Explication and Social Change)

ORIGINS: As nicely explicated by Gibson Burrell and Garth Morgan (1979), there are two major intellectual traditions within Critical Theory: radical structuralist and radical humanism. As to the first and oldest tradition—radical structuralist—this tradition (while committed to radical change) has many similarities with the "functionalist" framework (emphasis on social structures) and "positivism" (realism, nomothetic, and determinist). Its origins lay in the "mature Marx" and Russian social theorists (such as Nikolai Bukharin), and this tradition has been continued by many Marxist and New Left social scientists such as Louis Althusser and Ralf Dahrendorf. This tradition is viewed as the more "conservative" of the two traditions and, over the last two decades, has been largely superseded by those working in the tradition of "radical humanism."

"Radical humanism" is linked to the work of the "early Marx" who took a much more "subjectivist" point of view (nominalism, ideographic, non-determinist), namely, that individuals create their world. (Note that this is similar to the interpretivist framework, but the foci of the two are different—for example, "critique and emancipation" versus "understanding.") In radical human- ism, the focus is on "human consciousness"—that human beings create meaning—rather than on "structures" (functionalist framework). Beginning in the 1920s, when Georg Lukacs and Antonio Gramsci revived interest in "subjectivist interpretations" of Marxist theory, this tradition was continued in the so-called Frankfurt School (cf. Max Horkheimer and Theodore Adorno) in Ger- many and later moved in part to the U.S. (In the United States during the 1940s, the term "critical theory"—rather than Marxism—gained widespread usage owing to widespread public concern with anything having to do with Marx.) Major individuals: Herbert Marcuse, Jurgen Habermas, Ivan Illich, Paulo Freire, and Henry Giroux.

Some underlying ideas informing Critical Theory include: 1) marginalization and emancipation (advanced capitalism has "marginalized" and "de-humanized" workers) [while critical theorists have traditionally focused on economic considerations (social class), many contempoary critical theorists focus on other forms of oppression especially as they relate to race, ethnicity, gender, and sexual orientation]; 2) culture is used by "dominant groups" to legitimate their interpretations of the world; 3) centrality and ubiquity of power; and 4) importance of "praxis" (linking theory with action).

PERSPECTIVES:

"Critical Theory"
"Neo-Marxist"
"Feminist"
"Praxis-Oriented"
"Freirian Participatory Action Research" (Paulo Freire)
"Hermeneutic"
"Critical Ethnography" (Neo-Marxist and Feminist)

SOME IMPLICATIONS FOR DOING RESEARCH:

1. Overall Orientation: Critical theorists orient their research (questions, analysis, reporting) to highlight "oppression" and to enable self-organization on the part of the "oppressed."

2. "Praxis" Orientation: Critical theorists engage in "action-oriented" research aimed at bringing together theory and practice in ways that are emancipatory and transformative for individuals.

3. Concepts/Variables: Critical theorists tend to use such categories as race, class, gender, and sexual orientation.

4. Reflexivity: As discussed by Patti Lather and Gary Anderson, among many others, critical theorists take "reflexivity" beyond where "interpretivists" take it. For critical theorists in higher education such as William Tierney, reflexivity refers to the ability of researcher to engage in a dialectical process among the constructs of the researcher, the informants, the data, the researcher's ideological suppositions, and the relevant socio-cultural forces. This "reflexivity" is conveyed in the written text.

5. Research Problem/Design/Procedure: Critical theorists ask questions such as: How might I actively involve the "researched" as partners in the study? How will the research "empower" those I am studying? What steps have I taken that will enable the "researched" to develop their own interpretations?

Postmodern Framework

FOCUS: Deconstruct

ORIGINS: The broad and elusive idea of "postmodernity" originally was applied to an architectural movement but today it is used widely as a descriptor of advanced societies as well as a lens for inquiry. At this juncture, "postmodern" is probably defined more by what it is not (modernism, that is, the emphasis on "rationalism" and traditional "scientific understanding") than what it "is." In broad strokes, however, most postmodernists question or reject "ethnocentric rationalism" (modernism) in favor of a way of looking at the world in which a plurality of voices cry out for their versions of reality (in other words, there is no single, or "essentialist," view of truth). Accordingly, the "grand theories and narratives" of modernism are replaced by subject-centered pluralist discourses which are marked by differences, opposites, paradoxes, and enigmas. While postmodernism can be traced to the "nihilism" of Friedrich Nietzsche, it has taken many forms and, in recent years, has been fueled in part by the work of many contemporary feminists such as Sandra Harding. At the risk of great oversimplification, a couple of central ideas seem to be important: 1) moral absolutes have been abandoned; 2) "grand narratives" have been abandoned; and 3) differences (race, gender, sexual orientation, and class) are highlighted. Individuals: Jacques Derrida, Michel Foucault.

PERSPECTIVES:

"Postmodern"
"Poststructural"
"Post-Paradigmatic Diaspora"
"Radical Feminist"

SOME IMPLICATIONS FOR DOING RESEARCH:

1. Emphasis on "Reflexivity" and "Language" and Related Implications: The researcher is aware of relationships between informants' beliefs ("positioned subjects"), data and data analysis, and the text. In turn, in the text the researcher should communicate how he/she is "positioned" and should make it clear to the reader how he/she may have influenced the study. Carried a step futher, traditional notions of the "omniscient author" and the passive voice are de-centered, and the researcher chooses how to give voice (her/his and Others) in the text. Thus, instead of the role of the "Great Interpreter" and the "authoritative" voice (third person), the postmodernist identifies her/his voice, seeks to highlights other voices (through quotations, narratives, stories, and the like) throughout the text, and informs the reader throughout of the position he/she assumes as author. Sometimes, the reader is invited to be a partner in creating the text.

2. REPORTING: Postmodernists are more likely to report their "findings" in a literary rather than a "scientific" way.

3. REPORTING: Poststructuralists seem to reject the "rationality" assumption of the other three "modernist" frameworks (functionalist, interpretivist, critical theory) that some "theories or explanations" are more robust/powerful than others. Instead, they suggest that all meaning is indefinite and that it depends on perspective ("radical relativist"). This has obvious implications for writing one's text. (A good many postmodernists don't believe that meaningful "action" can be taken because meaning shifts and is problemmatic. However, many feminist poststructuralists have sought to reintroduce "action" as central based on contingent understandings. [For an excellent example of a feminist poststructuralist doing research in education, see Patti Lather's *Getting Smart* (1991)].

Note: While I have drawn on many sources in preparing this handout, I am especially indebted to Gibson Burrell and Gareth Morgan (see *Sociological Paradigms and Organisational Analysis*). In addition, I have learned a great deal from conversations with Yvonna Lincoln and William Tierney as well as from their extensive writings.

PART I
Explicating Frames of Reference: The Multiple Faces of Qualitative Research

Postpositivism and the Naturalist Paradigm

YVONNA S. LINCOLN AND EGON G. GUBA

And as we think, so do we act.

(Schwartz and Ogilvy, 1979)

Paradigms and Paradigm Eras

The history of humankind is replete with instances of attempts to understand the world. Our curiosity has been directed at the same fundamental questions throughout time; our progress as inquirers can be charted by noting the various efforts made to deal with those questions. What is the world? How can we come to know it? How can we control it for our purposes? What is, after all, the *truth* about these matters?

The concept of truth is an elusive one. Julienne Ford, in her delightfully whimsical book, *Paradigms and Fairy Tales* (1975), asserts that the term *truth* may have four different meanings, which she symbolizes as $Truth_1$, $Truth_2$, $Truth_3$, and $Truth_4$. $Truth_4$ is the familiar *empirical* truth of the scientist; a claim in the form of hypothesis or predicate (an affirmation or denial of something) is T_4 if it is consistent with "nature" (or, in Ford's own language, "preserves the appearances."[1] $Truth_3$ is *logical* truth; a claim (hypothesis or predicate) is T_3 if it is logically or mathematically consistent with some other claim known to be true (in the T_3 sense) or ultimately with some basic belief taken to be T_1 (to which we shall return in a moment). $Truth_2$ is *ethical* truth; a claim is T_2 if the person who asserts it is acting in conformity with moral or professional standards of conduct.[2]

$Truth_1$, with which we are most concerned here, may be called *metaphysical* truth. Unlike the case of a claim's being T_2, T_3, or T_4, a claim that is said to be T_1 cannot be tested for truthfulness against some external norm such as correspondence with nature, logical deducibility, or professional standards of conduct. Metaphysical beliefs must be accepted at face value; as Aristotle knew (Reese, 1980, p. 70) and Ford affirms, basic beliefs can never be proven T_4—in conformity with nature—or $False_1$. They represent the ultimate benchmarks against which *everything else* is tested, for if there were something more fundamental against which a test might be made, then that more fundamental entity would become *the* basic belief whose truth (T_1) must be taken for granted.

Now certain *sets* of such basic or metaphysical beliefs are sometimes constituted into a *system of ideas* that "either give us some judgment about the nature of reality, or a reason why we must be content with knowing something less than the nature of reality, along with a method for taking hold of whatever can be known" (Reese, 1980, p. 352). We shall call such a systematic set of beliefs, together with their accompanying methods, a *paradigm*.[3]

25

Paradigms represent a distillation of what we *think* about the world (but cannot prove). Our actions in the world, including actions that we take as inquirers, cannot occur without reference to those paradigms: "As we think, so do we act." But, while paradigms are thus enabling, they are also constraining:

> A paradigm is a world view, a general perspective, a way of breaking down the complexity of the real world. As such, paradigms are deeply embedded in the socialization of adherents and practitioners: paradigms tell them what is important, legitimate, and reasonable. Paradigms are also normative, telling the practitioner what to do without the necessity of long existential or epistemological consideration. But it is this aspect of paradigms that constitutes both their strength and their weakness—their strength in that it makes action possible, their weakness in that the very reason for action is hidden in the unquestioned assumptions of the paradigm. (Patton, 1978, p. 203)

It is the authors' posture that inquiry, whether in the physical or social sciences, has passed through a number of "paradigm eras," periods in which certain sets of basic beliefs guided inquiry in quite different ways. We shall briefly describe these periods as prepositivist, positivist, and postpositivist, and show that each period had its own unique set of "basic beliefs" or metaphysical principles in which its adherents believed and upon which they acted. We shall take the position that the positivist posture, while discredited by vanguard thinkers in every known discipline, continues to this day to guide the efforts of practitioners of inquiry, particularly in the social or human sciences. Further, we shall argue that, since these methods are based on metaphysical principles that are dissonant with the principles guiding the vanguard development of substantive (discipline) thought, it is imperative that inquiry itself be shifted from a positivist to a postpositivist stance. *For, if a new paradigm of thought and belief is emerging, it is necessary to construct a parallel new paradigm of inquiry.*

Some Caveats

In discussing the eras through which paradigms have passed, it will be easy to assume that there exists somewhere *the* paradigm that past efforts at paradigm formation have approximated more and more closely. If science could successfully converge onto that paradigm, then it could quickly tease out its consequences, test them in the empirical world, and come, finally, to "true" understanding. A study of the history of science might be very important if we are to achieve an understanding of those successive approximations; it might be asserted, as Barnes suggests, that "the subject matter of the historian of science can only be demarcated by recognizing what it is in the past that exhibits causal continuity with present science" (cited in Hesse, 1980, p. 47). But, as Hesse (1980, pp. 4–5) points out:

> The present is in this crude sense the standard of truth and rationality for the past, and gives the inductivist historian grounds for the reconstruction of past arguments according to an acceptably inductive structure, and for judging past theories as simply false and often ridiculous. *Such inductive history is of course, among its other defects, self-defeating, because if all theories are dangerous and likely to be superseded, so are the present theories in terms of which the inductivist judges the past.* (emphasis added)

We may draw from these remarks the following caveat: Since all theories and other leading ideas of scientific history have, so far, been shown to be false and unacceptable, so surely will any theories that we expound today. This insight induces a certain degree of humility in claims for the "ultimate truth" (T_1) of anything that is asserted here. This book should therefore be regarded not as an attempt to make ultimately true (and modern) pronouncements, but as an effort to mark our place along the path of understanding—a path that unfortunately is never ending. We are not setting forth a new orthodoxy; instead, we aim to make it a little more difficult to hold onto the old.

A second caveat is that theories, whether scientific or otherwise, are remarkably immune to change; hence one cannot expect an easy time of it when proposing something as radical as a paradigm revision. Theories are, to borrow a term from modern organization theory, "loosely coupled" (Weick, 1976.) There is, as Hesse (1980) suggests, a "many-to-one" relation between theoretical and practical facts; it is possible to fit many different idealizations (theoretical facts) to a single practical fact:

> Many conflicting networks may more or less fit the same facts, and which one is adopted must depend on criteria other than the facts: criteria involving simplicity, coherence with other parts of science, and so on. Quine, as is well known, has drawn this conclusion explicitly in the strong sense of claiming that any statement can be maintained true in the face of any evidence: "Any statement can be held true come what may, if we make drastic enough adjustments elsewhere in the system." (Hesse, 1980, p. 86)

Thus the loosely coupled nature of theories makes it possible for scientists to squirm mightily before giving up a theory (or a paradigm). Any conflicting fact can be accommodated by making adjustments elsewhere in the system.

Along the same lines, Wimsatt (1981, p. 1340) has noted what he terms the "robustness" of prevailing theories, a robustness, he claims, that derives from the fact that portions of theory are "walled off from" (loosely coupled to) one another:

> The thing that is remarkable about scientific theories is that the inconsistencies are walled off and do not appear to affect the theory other than very locally. . . . When an inconsistency occurs, results which depend on one or more of the contradictory assumptions are infirmed. This infection is transitive; it passes to things that depend on these results, and to their logical descendants, like a string of dominos—until we reach something that has independent support. The independent support of an assumption sustains it, and the collapse propagates no further. If all deductive or inferential paths leading to a contradiction pass through robust results, the collapse is bounded within them, and the inconsistencies are walled off from the rest of the network. For each robust result, one of its modes of support is destroyed; but it has others, and therefore the collapse goes no further.

Thus the failure of a paradigm to be fully coherent, that is, entirely internally consistent,[4] can also be one of its chief defenses against challenge. As paradigms are assaulted by "facts" that do not fit, the facts can be walled off—a possibility only because the paradigm is loosely coupled. Further, even those elements of the paradigm that are most affected by the conflicting facts may be supported in independent ways—a fact that could not obtain if the paradigm were completely coherent. The result of this state of affairs is that it becomes possible for adherents of the paradigms to resist stoutly, even if at times irrationally, the efforts of others to replace it. Making it even a little more difficult to hold onto the old paradigm may itself turn out to be an enormously difficult task, not one to be taken on by the fainthearted!

The Prepositivist Era

Of the three "paradigm eras," the prepositivist is both the longest and the least interesting from a modern perspective; indeed, its lack of provocative acts and ideas is best illustrated by its very title—*pre*positivist. This era is simply a precursor to the more exciting period that followed. It ranges over a period of more than two millenia, roughly speaking, from the time of Aristotle (384–322 B.C.) to that of (but not including) David Hume (1711–1776). One might expect that "science" would have made enormous strides over such a long period, but it did not, largely because Aristotle (and many other prepositivists) took the stance of "passive observer" (Wolf, 1981). What there was in "physis," Aristotle argued, occurred "naturally." Attempts by humans to learn about nature were interventionist and unnatural, and so distorted what was learned. Wolf (1981, p. 22) comments:

Aristotle believed in natural motion. Humans' interference produced discontinuous and unnatural movements. And, to Aristotle, such movements were not God's way. For example, Aristotle envisioned the idea of "force." The heavy cart being drawn along the road by the horse is an unnatural movement. That is why the horse is struggling so. That is why the motion is so jerky and uneven. The horse must exert a "force" to get the car moving. The horse must continue to exert a "force" to keep the cart moving. As soon as the horse stops pulling, it stops exerting a "force" on the cart. Consequently, the cart comes to its natural place, which is at rest on the road.

Aristotle's mind was broad ranging enough to touch virtually every conceptual problem imaginable at his time. Not the least of these problem areas was that of logic. Aristotle contributed two principles, commonly known as the Law of Contradiction (which states that no proposition can be both true and false at the same time) and the Law of the Excluded Middle (which holds that every proposition must be either true or false), which when applied to noninterventionist or passive observations, seemed sufficient to generate the entire gamut of scientific understandings that were needed (Mitroff and Kilmann, 1978). Wolf further observes:

> Within the world of the mind, these thoughts occurred thousands of years ago. Scientists were passive then. It would take a while before they would attempt to reach out and touch, to try ideas and see if they worked. (p. 23)

When scientists did begin to reach out and touch, to try ideas and see if they worked, in short, when they became active observers, science passed into the positivist period. The movement was slow; Isaac Newton (1642–1727) is said to have commented that "if I have seen further, it is because I have stood on the shoulders of giants." But the number of giants was exceedingly small. Only a few workers had emerged who went beyond Aristotelian science, and it is useful to observe that they also came from essentially noninterventionist fields: three astronomers (Copernicus, 1473–1543; Galileo, 1564–1642; Kepler, 1571–1630) and a logician/mathematician (Descartes, 1596–1650). Further, their work did little to challenge the prevailing paradigm of inquiry, however much it may have exercised established religion. It did, however, pave the way for that challenge.

The Positivist Era

Positivism may be defined as "a family of philosophies characterized by an extremely positive evaluation of science and scientific method" (Reese, 1980, p. 450). Indeed, its early adherents saw in this movement the potential for the reform of such diverse areas as ethics, religion, and politics, in addition to philosophy, to which field it finally became confirmed. As a philosophy, the movement began early in the nineteenth century, primarily in France and Germany; its most powerful advocates in the twentieth century were formed into a group known as the Vienna Circle of Logical Positivists, which included philosophers and scientists such as Gustav Bergman, Rudolf Carnap, Philipp Frank, Hans Hahn, Otto Neurath, and Moritz Schlick, the last having founded the group. Schlick held an endowed chair at the University of Vienna that had been established in the memory of Ernest Mach, an extreme advocate of operationalism,[5] whose ideas the group proposed to promulgate.

But positivism had its major impact not in reforming ethics, religion, and politics, or even philosophy, but scientific method. The concepts of positivism provided a new rationale for the doing of science that amounted to a literal paradigm revolution, although that revolution took place so slowly and was so imperfectly perceived by even the major actors caught up in it that its revolutionary character was never appreciated. If it is difficult for a fish to understand water because it has spent all of its life in it, so is it difficult for scientists—and prepositivist scientists were no exception—to understand what their basic axioms or assumptions might be and what impact those axioms and assumptions have upon everyday thinking and lifestyle.

Given this slow and little-understood change, it is not surprising that different scientists and philosophers would have somewhat different views of just what positivism implied, and on what ground it stood. That confusion continues today, as can be seen from a reading of some representative authors on the topic. For example, David Hamilton, in a paper prepared for an informal workshop at the University of Illinois in 1976, suggests that positivism began with the publication of John Stuart Mill's *A System of Logic* in 1843. Hamilton (1976, p. 2) comments on this work:

> Historically, *A System of Logic* was a powerful interpretation, formalization, and defense of the secular ideologies which had emerged alongside the political, economic, and social revolutions of the late eighteenth and early nineteenth centuries. Its twentieth century importance, however, is rather different. Mill's *Logic* offered a coherent set of principles of procedure for use in the social and natural sciences. Although subjected to considerable criticism . . ., Mill's original formulations have survived till the present day as the dominant methodological paradigm.

Hamilton's summarizes Mill's assumptions as follows:

(1) The social and natural sciences have identical aims, namely, the discovery of general laws that serve for explanation and prediction.

(2) The social and natural sciences are methodologically identical.

(3) The social sciences are merely more complex than the natural sciences.

(4) Concepts can be defined by direct reference to empirical categories—"objects in the concrete."

(5) There is a uniformity of nature in time and space. Hamilton comments that this assumption, itself an induction, enabled Mill to overcome Hume's objections to logical inference and thereby invested induction with the same procedural certainty as syllogistic logic. We may note that such an argument has been found to be invalid by modern philosophers; see the discussion below about the problem of the underdetermination of theory.

(6) Laws of nature can be naturally (inductively) derived from data. Hamilton comments that Mill had little to say about theory because he held it to be isomorphic with "empirical uniformities."

(7) Large samples suppress idiosyncracies ("partial causes") and reveal "general causes" (the ultimate laws of nature).

A second example: Wolf (1981, p. 56) discusses positivism in the guise of Newtonian mechanics, which he says rested upon the following assumptions regarding the "physical and therefore mechanical world":

(1) Things move in a continuous manner. All motion, both in the large and in the small, exhibits continuity.

(2) Things move for reasons. These reasons were based upon earlier causes for motion. Therefore, all motion was determined and everything was predictable.

(3) All motion could be analyzed or broken down into its component parts. Each part played a role in the great machine called the universe, and the complexity of this machine could be understood as the simple movement of its various parts, even those parts beyond our perception.

(4) The observer observed, never disturbed. Even the errors of a clumsy observer could be accounted for by simply analyzing the observed movements of whatever he touched.

A third example: Schwartz and Ogilvy, whose work will occupy a considerable portion of our attention in Chapter 2, describe the Newtonian "world view" as holding that matter consists of very small particles that are assembled into larger and larger complexes. The essential ideas are captured by the metaphor of the billiard table.[6] The metaphor supports a deterministic physics—if we knew the masses, positions, and velocities of all the particles we could predict the future from the laws of physics. But Schwartz and Ogilvy (1979, p. 32) point out,

> Embedded within the mechanistic view of the world are three basic assumptions. The first is that there is a most fundamental level of reality (i.e., the basic building blocks) composed of the smallest particles and the complete set of forces that govern them. Once we find that fundamental level and the laws that govern it, the world laws that govern matter and energy on the very small scale must be very similar, and hopefully identical, to those that apply on the very large scale. The governing laws thus would be universal, so that we ought to be able to build a picture of planets moving about the sun out of an understanding of the particles of which matter is composed. Finally, there is the assumption that we, as observers, can be isolated from experiments and the world we are studying to produce an "objective" description.

A fourth example: Mary Hesse (1980, p. vii) a British epistemologist and historian of science, suggests that what she calls the "standard account" of scientific explanation within an "empirical philosophy" depends upon a series of assumptions:

> The most important of these are the assumptions of *naive realism*, of a *universal scientific language*, and of the *correspondence theory of truth*.

> These three assumptions between them constitute a picture of science and the world somewhat as follows: there is an external world which can in principle be exhaustively described in scientific language. The scientist, as both observer and language-user, can capture the external facts of the world in propositions that are true if they correspond to the facts and false if they do not. Science is ideally a linguistic system in which true propositions are in one-to-one relation to facts, including facts that are not directly observed because they involve hidden entities or properties, or past events or far distant events. These hidden events are described as theories, and theories can be inferred from observations, that is, the hidden explanatory mechanism of the world can be discovered from what is open to observation. Man as scientist is regarded as standing apart from the world and able to experiment and theorize about it objectively and dispassionately.

A fifth example: Hesse (1980, pp. 170–171) also presents a statement of what are taken to be the characteristics of empirical method described by Habermas, who was presumably himself drawing upon the work of Dilthey:

1. In natural science experience is taken to be objective, testable, and independent of theoretical explanation. . . .

2. In natural science theories are artificial constructions or models, yielding explanation in the sense of a logic of hypothetico-deduction: *if* external nature were of such a kind, *then* data and experience would be as we find them. . . .

3. In natural science the lawlike relations asserted of experience are external, both to the objects connected and to the investigator, since they are merely correlational. . . .

4. The language of natural science is exact, formalizable, and literal; therefore meanings are univocal, and a problem of meaning arises only in the application of universal categories to particulars. . . .

5. Meanings in natural science are separate from facts.

A sixth example: Harre (1981, p. 3) provides yet another formulation:

The positivist tradition in scientific methodology has been based upon the principle that the only reliable knowledge of any field of phenomena reduces to knowledge of particular instances of patterns of sensation. Laws are treated as probabilistic generalizations of descriptions of such patterns. The sole role of laws is to facilitate the prediction of future sensory experience. Theories are logically ordered sets of laws. In consequence theories are reduced to a logical apparatus necessary to the business of prediction. It follows that for a positivist, the task of understanding a theory is exhausted by two processes. Analysis of theoretical discourse is aimed at revealing its logical structure. The empirical content of the theory is supposed to be brought to light by identifying those logical consequences of the set of laws which purport to describe observations. There are, therefore, two sides of modern positivism; one logical and one empirical. Modern positivism is sometimes called "logical empiricism."

Harre goes on to raise the question of how it ever happens that positivism gains a foothold. He describes positivism as a kind of fallback position, a "positivist retreat" that occurs whenever there is a serious loss of confidence in current theory in some field. Scientists, he speculates, tend to take their theories and models very seriously, as representations of reality, as factual descriptions of what actually occurs. But, he goes on:

> If we are to take an imagined mechanism seriously as a possible representation of reality there ought to be some way of deciding between rival candidates for the role of best explanation. Sometimes the ingenuity of theorists produces a multitude of seemingly possible mechanisms, all capable of being imagined to produce close analogues of the empirically observed patterned regularities. But at the other extreme, it sometimes happens that the most talented and imaginative thinkers can make no headway at all in imagining any mechanism capable of simulating the behavior of the real world in the field they are investigating. The former situation brought on a positivist reaction among astronomers in the sixteenth century, the latter among subatomic physicists in the twentieth. At the heart of the positivist reaction is a denial that theory could represent hidden realities. According to positivism a science should be taken as no more than a well-attested body of rules for predicting the future course of observation. But these "internal" historical conditions are not sufficient to account for the retreat to positivism. Historical studies clearly reveal an odd twist to this retreat. As scientists abandon the search for a deep knowledge of nature they tend to adopt a militant, even an arrogant posture, sometimes persecuting those who hope to continue on the path of scientific tradition. A kind of glorying in ignorance is displayed, like the Paduan professors who refused to look through Galileo's telescope. Positivist retreats seldom last beyond a single generation of scientists, though the damaging effect of widespread abandonment of realism can sometimes be felt for a long time after the dominant figures have departed. (Harre, 1981, pp. 7–8)[7]

It is very clear from this sample of statements about positivism that there is no clear agreement about what either the philosophy or the method encompasses. Positivism can be reshaped, apparently, to suit the definer's purpose, and while there is certainly remarkable overlap in these statements there are also some inconsistencies and some idiosyncracies. One might venture to say that the particular form of definition offered by any commentator depends heavily upon the counterpoints he or she wishes too make. (The significance of that observation for the ways in which positivism will be interpreted later in this book should not be overlooked; we are "guilty" of the same "crime.") But it does seem to be the case that these authors do agree on one point: Positivism is passé. Harre's scathing comments noted a few paragraphs ago leave no doubt that he not only disagrees with the positivist position but believes it to be the product of small, confused minds who retreat to it because they lack any other viable alternatives. Such a harsh judgment is undoubtedly a strong overreaction, but hear some more temperate critics:

- Mary Hesse (1980, p. vii) having given it as her opinion that the three most important assumptions underlying positivism are naive realism, belief in a universal scientific language, and a correspondence theory of truth, goes on to comment, "Almost every assumption underlying this account has been subjected to damaging criticism."

- Schwartz and Ogilvy (1979, p.32), having described what they take to be the three basic assumptions of the Newtonian world view, add that "all of these basic assumptions are now being challenged by theoretical and experimental findings."

- Wolf (1981, pp. 51–56), after describing his view of the assumptions "concerning the physical ... world" of the Newtonian, comments, "But it would take nearly fifty years for the true [sic] story to be told"; with the "end of the mechanical age" coming into view because of certain unexplainable (in positivist terms) phenomena: the inability of physicists to find ether, that necessary component of wave theories of light, and their inability to deal with "the ultraviolet catastrophe," the failure of physicists to explain the colors of heated (glowing) objects.

Challenges to and Critiques of Positivism

What is the nature of the challenges to and critiques of positivism that have brought it to its metaphoric knees? Space precludes the level of treatment that such a question deserves, but one may point to the following issues:

(1) *Positivism leads to an inadequate conceptualization of what science is:*

- Hesse (1980, pp. 46–47) cites the work of Barry Barnes, who

asserts that all attempts to find demarcating criteria, that is, necessary and sufficient conditions for a belief system to be science, have failed. These failures include all verifiability and falsifiability criteria, and all specific appeals to experimentation and/or to particular kinds of inductive or theoretical inference. At best, he argues, the concept "science" must be regarded as a loose association of family resemblance characteristics involving, among other things, aversion to all forms of anthropomorphism and teleology, and consequent tendencies to secularism, impersonality, abstraction, and quantification.

While it would be inappropriate to argue that this failure is entirely produced by adherence to positivistic principles, it is clear that the paradigm has offered no way out of the dilemma.

- Positivism thoroughly confuses two aspects of inquiry that have often been called the "context of discovery" and the "context of justification." The former deals with the genesis or origin of scientific theories and the latter with testing them. Positivism excludes the former and focuses on the latter. The process of theory conceptualization is seen as noncognitive or nonrational and hence outside the pale. But any theory, no matter how bizarre its origins, is admissible so long as it is coherent (T_3) and testable (T_4). In terms of these constraints, much of Einstein's work, for example, would be considered nonscientific by positivists, who would hardly be persuaded by or interested in Einstein's thought (*gedanken*) experiments.

It may be the case, as Cronbach (1982) seems to suggest, that verification has taken precedence over discovery within positivism because proponents of that formulation could not devise a means for coming to grips with it systematically. He comments:

"Design of experiments" has been a standard element in training for social scientists. This training has concentrated on formal tests of hypotheses—confirmatory studies—despite the fact that R.A. Fisher, the prime theorist of experimental design, demonstrated over and over again in his agricultural investigations that effective inquiry works back and forth between the heuristic and the confirmatory. But since he could offer a formal theory only for the confirmatory studies, *that part came to be taken as the whole*. (pp. ix–x; emphasis added)

- Positivism severely constrains the possible uses or purposes of science to prediction and control. Indeed, what is often called the "pragmatic criterion" of success in science is that it should lead to increasingly successful prediction and control. Such a delimitation forces out of contention other legitimate purposes, as, for example, *verstehen* or understanding, description, problem responses, status determination, and so on. It focuses on what might be called *kennenschaft* to the virtual exclusion of *wissenschaft*.

Of course, none of these reasons are sufficient to lead to discarding positivism, but they are sufficient to lead to an extreme degree of discomfort among practicing scientists who would prefer to have a more solid conceptualization to use as a touchstone.

(2) *Positivism is unable to deal adequately with two crucial and interacting aspects of the theory-fact relationship:*

- *The underdetermination of theory, sometimes also called the problem of induction.* In deduction, given the validity of the premises, the conclusion must be true and it is the only conclusion possible. But in induction, there are always many conclusions that can reasonably be related to certain premises. Deductions are closed but inductions are open. Thus there is always a larger number of theories that can fit observations more or less adequately. Hence there cannot be convergence, no ultimate conclusions, no certain or "true" (T_1) theory. Nor is this situation helped by the fact that there is no agreement about what a theory is (a pattern, network, nomological net, hypothetico-deduction system) or what it is for (to systematize, uncover, predict, explain).

- *The theory-ladenness of facts, that is, the apparent impossibility of having "facts" that are not themselves theory-determined.* It is, many assert, impossible to have an observational language that is not also a theoretical language. The "truth" of propositions (facts on trial) cannot be determined except in relation to a true theory, but, as we have just seen, true theories cannot be derived because of the problem of underdetermination. Hence the reasoning is entirely circular.

(3) *Positivism is overly dependent on operationalism, which has itself been increasingly judged to be inadequate.*

- Operationalism is simply not meaningful or satisfying; recalling the quotation from Ford (see note 5), most people are more interested in fear than in the number of fecal boluses emitted every hour.

- Operationalism is too shallow, depending as it does almost entirely on sensations for its "facts" and refusing to deal with meanings or implications.

- Operationally defined facts are just as theory-laden as are any others.

- Despite the good intentions and the best efforts of the Vienna Circle of Logical Positivists, neither they nor any of their adherents have been able to rid science of its metaphysical underpinnings.

- The strict practice of operationalism results in a meaningful splintering of the world. Since nothing exists for the operationalist except through the instruments that measure it, even such conceptually close entities as two IQ scores measured by two different IQ tests must be asserted to be different *despite* a high correlation between them.

(4) *Positivism has at least two consequences that are both repugnant and unfounded:*

- *Determinism,* repugnant because of its implications for human free will and unfounded because of recent findings in many fields that argue strongly against it, for example, the Heisenberg Uncertainty Principle (Chapter 4).

- *Reductionism,* repugnant because it would make all phenomena including human phenomena ultimately subject to a single set of laws, and unfounded because of recent findings in many fields including mathematics and physics that rule out the possibility in those fields, for example, Gödel's Theorem (Chapter 5).

(5) *Positivism has produced research with human respondents that ignores their humanness, a fact that has not only ethical but also validity implications.*

- It has emphasized *exogenous* research—that is, research in which all aspects of the research, from problem definition through instrumentation, data collection and analysis, and use of findings, have been researcher-determined—to the virtual exclusion of *endogenous* research—that is, research in which the respondents have equal rights of determination.

- It has emphasized *etic* research—that is, research carried out with an outside (objective) perspective—to the virtual exclusion of *emic* research—that is, research carried out with an inside perspective (subjective).

(6) *Positivism falls short of being able to deal with emergent conceptual/empirical formulations from a variety of fields; three examples:*

- Gödel's Incompleteness Theorem, which states that no axiomatic system of mathematics is able to provide information about both the completeness and consistency of that axiomatic system; or, put another way, it asserts that no theory of mathematics asserted to be complete can also be internally consistent.

- Heisenberg's Uncertainty Principle, which asserts that the position and momentum of an electron cannot *both* be determined, because the action of the observer in making either measurement inevitably alters the other.

- Bell's Theorem, which asserts that no theory compatible with quantum theory can require spatially separated events to be independent.

The consequences of these three formulations, as well as others, for the basic premises of positivism, including ontology, objectivity, and causality, are devastating.

(7) *Positivism rests upon at least five assumptions that are increasingly difficult to maintain.* These five assumptions capture the most salient aspects included in the various definitions of positivism that have already been reviewed,[8] and will *form the basis for the counter-proposals that are the backbone of this book:*

- An ontological assumption of a single, tangible reality "out there" that can be broken apart into pieces capable of being studied independently; the whole is simply the sum of the parts.

- An epistemological assumption about the possibility of separation of the observer from the observed—the knower from the known.

- An assumption of the temporal and contextual independence of observations, so that what is true at one time and place may, under appropriate circumstances (such as sampling) also be true at another time and place.

- An assumption of linear causality; there are no effects without causes and no causes without effects.

- An axiological assumption of value freedom, that is, that the methodology guarantees that the results of an inquiry are essentially free from the influence of any value system (bias).

The consequences of these several critiques of positivism are sufficiently telling and widely appreciated that a significant number of vanguard scientists have abandoned that paradigm and moved into the postpositivist era. We shall describe next what are still clumsy and emergent efforts to carry out that move.

The Postpositivist Era⁹

Positivism has been remarkably pervasive. We have noted that its precursor era does not have a name of its own but is called, simply, the prepositivist era. Similarly, the new era has not yet gained sufficient credibility or self-assurance to have assumed a name of its own; it too is called by a simple name: postpositivism. The grip of *its* precursor is still on it; it is just as difficult for the modern-day scientist of whatever stripe to throw off the shackles imposed on thinking by the positivists as it was for Galileo's inquisitors to take his telescope, and what it revealed, seriously; or for Lavoisier's fellow chemists to be able to accept oxygen without simultaneously wondering where all the phlogiston had gone. The reader who has never contemplated postpositivist ideas may be in for a surprise; indeed, a rude shock. As the aphorism goes, "Expect the unexpected."

Perhaps the *most* unexpected aspect of postpositivism is that its basic tenets are virtually the reverse of those that characterized positivism—perhaps not so surprising, after all, when one contemplates that postpositivism is as much a reaction to the failings of positivism as it is a proactive set of new formations; reaction, too, is a form of "standing on the shoulders of giants."

An example: it will be recalled that Habermas, expanding on the ideas of Dilthey, outlined what he took to be the crucial axiomatic differences between hermeneutics and empiricism. In opposition to what he saw to be the five central aspects of positivism—objectivity, hypothetico-deductive theory, external lawlike relations, exact and formal language, and separation of facts from meaning—Habermas proposed five counterpoints, which Hesse (1980) declares have *now* come to characterize the natural sciences as well. Indeed, she asserts, the positions ascribed by Habermas to the empirical sciences, while valid at the time that he wrote, have been "almost universally discredited" (Hesse, 1980, p. 172). She goes on:

> Paralleling the five points of the [Habermas] dichotomy [of natural and human sciences], we can summarize this post-empiricist account of natural science as follows:
>
> 1. In natural science data is not detachable from theory, for what count as data are determined in the light of some theoretical interpretation, and the facts themselves have to be reconstructed in the light of interpretation.
>
> 2. In natural science theories are not models externally compared in nature to a hypothetico-deductive schema, they are the way the facts themselves are seen.
>
> 3. In natural science the law-like relations asserted of experience are internal, because what we count as facts are constituted by what the theory says about their interrelations with one another.
>
> 4. The language of natural science is irreducibly metaphorical and inexact, and formalizable only at the cost of distortion of the historical dynamics of scientific development and of the imaginative reconstructions in terms of which nature is interpreted by science.
>
> 5. Meanings in natural science are determined by theory; they are understood by theoretical coherence rather than by correspondence with facts. (pp. 172–173)

Objective reality has become very relative indeed!

Another instance: Rom Harre (1981), whose scathing dismissal of positivism was quoted above, also contrasts positivism with the "new paradigm." Where positivism is concerned with surface events or appearances, the new paradigm takes a deeper look. Where positivism is atomistic, the new paradigm is structural. Where positivism establishes meaning operationally, the new paradigm establishes meaning inferentially. Where positivism sees its central purpose to be prediction, the new paradigm is concerned with understanding. Finally, where positivism is deterministic and bent on certainty, the new paradigm is probabilistic and speculative.

Most of the distinguishing features of the postpositivist paradigm have emerged from fields such as physics and chemistry, customarily denoted as the "hard sciences." But the argument for the new paradigm can be made even more persuasively when the entities being studied are human beings.[10] For such research, Heron (1981) advances six arguments in favor of the postpositivist paradigm:

(1) *The argument from the nature of research behavior.* Heron argues that researchers cannot define one model of behavior for themselves and a different one for their respondents. If the basic model for research behavior is that of "intelligent self-direction," then, to be consistent, the same model must be applied to the respondents.

(2) *The argument from intentionality.* Heron (1982, p. 23) argues for the necessity of checking with the respondents to be sure that their intentionality and the researcher's interpretation of it coincide: "When I am interpreting such basic actions [as walking, talking, looking, pointing] in terms of their more complex intentions and purposes, than I need to check against the [respondent's] version of what he was about, for a person may walk, talk, or look or point to fulfill many different higher order intentions."

(3) *The argument from language.* Language formation is interpreted by Heron as an archetype of inquiry itself. When human beings communicate they must agree on the rules of language they will follow. Hence the use of language contains within itself the model of cooperative inquiry. Heron (1981, pp. 26–27) asserts:

> I *can* use the language to make statements about persons who have not contributed or assented to the formulation of those statements. . . . [But] to use language in this way is to cut it off from its validating base. . . . The result is a set of alienated statements hanging in an interpersonal void: statements about persons not authorized by those persons. . . . My considered view of your reality without consulting you is a very different matter from our considered view of our reality.

(4) *The argument from an extended epistemology.* Heron notes that while science as *product* takes the form of a set of propositional statements, the *process* of scientific inquiry involves not only propositional knowledge but also *practical* knowledge (the skills, proficiencies, or "knacks" of doing research) and *experimental* knowledge (knowing a person or thing through sustained encounters). He notes:

> What I am arguing . . . is that empirical research on persons involves a subtle, developing interdependence between propositional knowledge, practical knowledge, and experiential knowledge. The research conclusions . . . necessarily rest on the researcher's experiential knowledge of the [respondents]. This knowledge of persons is most adequate as an empirical base when . . . researcher and [respondent] are fully present to each other in a relationship of reciprocal and open inquiry, and when each is open to construe how the other manifests as a presence in space and time. (p. 31)

(5) *The argument from axiology.* Heron argues that the truth of a proposition depends on shared values. The data that researchers generate, he suggests, depend upon their procedural norms, which in turn depend upon their shared values. If the facts are about persons other than the researchers, "they have indeterminate validity, no secure status as truths, until we know whether those other persons assent to and regard as their own the norms and values of the researchers" (p. 33).

(6) *The moral and political argument.* Research in the conventional sense usually exploits people, Heron asserts, for knowledge is power that can be used against the people from whom the knowledge was generated. The "new paradigm" avoids some of these difficulties because

> (1) it honours the fulfillment of the respondents' need for autonomously acquired knowledge; (2) it protects them from becoming unwitting accessories to knowledge-claims that may be false and may be inappropriately or harmfully applied to others; (3) it protects them from being excluded from the formation of knowledge that purports to be about them and so from being managed and manipulated . . . in ways they do not understand and so cannot assent to or dissent from. (pp. 24–35)

But just what is this new postpositivist paradigm? If we accept that its axioms or assumptions are virtually the inverse of those of positivism, we are not *definitively* helped because, as we have seen, different writers have cast the positivist assumptions in different terms; hence postpositivism's definition depends upon whose positivistic description is followed.

Of course, some scholars insist that postpositivism is nothing more than an overreaction, and that it is time for a rapprochement that realigns positivism with the relativism that characterizes postpositivism. One such writer is Donald T. Campbell, who suggests that it is time to move into a post-postpositivist era, in which positivism and postpositivism are married off and live happily ever after. In his William James Lecture #5, delivered in 1977, for example, he describes science as a *social system*, with all the usual attributes of such a system: norms, jobs, communication channels, modes of recruiting and rewarding members and keeping them loyal, and so on. He says:

> But I want to assert that among all these belief-preserving mutual admiration societies, all of which share this common human tribalism, science is also different, with different specific values, myths, rituals, and commandments, and that these different norms are related to what I presume to be science's superiority in the improving validity of the model of the physical world which it carries. . . . In spite of the theory-ladenness and noisiness of unedited experimental evidence, it does provide a major source of discipline in science. . . . The experiment is meticulously designed to put questions to "Nature Itself" in such a way that neither the questioners, nor their colleagues, nor their superiors can affect the answer. . . . In our iterative oscillation of theoretical emphases, in our continual dialectic that never achieves a stable synthesis, we are now ready for a post-post-postitivist theory of science which will integrate the epistemological relativism recently achieved with a new and more complex understanding of the role of experimental evidence and predictive confirmation in science. (cited in Brewer & Collins, 1981, pp. 15–16)

Now this whole statement moves from hidden assumptions rooted in the positivist tradition. "Theory-ladenness" and the "noisiness of unedited experimental evidence" are treated as minor technical inconveniences. The place of values in inquiry is ignored and the delusion of objectivity is maintained in claims such as that experiments can be designed meticulously enough so that no one can influence the outcome, only "Nature Itself." But what this perspective misses completely is the fact that postpositivism is not merely a perturbation, a wrinkle, a new angle that simply needs to be accommodated to make everything all right. Postpositivism is an entirely new paradigm, not reconcilable with the old. Rapprochements, accommodations, compromises are no more possible here than between the old astronomy and Galileo's new astronomy, between phlogiston and oxygen, between Newtonian and quantum mechanics. We are dealing with an entirely new system of ideas based on fundamentally *different*—indeed, shaarply contrasting—assumptions, as the quotations from Mary Hesse, Rom Harre, and John Heron so vividly illustrate. What is needed is a transformation, not an add-on. That the world is round cannot be added to the idea that the world is flat. Nor is the notion of a paradigm transformation simply an intellectual fashion, as Pollie (1983) suggests. To make this point crystal clear, it is worth making a brief digression into the nature of axiomatic systems.

Features of Axiomatic Systems[11]

Axioms may be defined as the set of undemonstrated (and undemonstrable) "basic beliefs" accepted by convention or established by practice as the building blocks of some conceptual or theoretical structure or system. They are the statements that will be taken as Truth, in the sense proposed by Julienne Ford. Probably the best known and most widely experienced system of axioms is tht undergirding Euclidean geometry. Euclid set himself the task of formalizing what was known about geometry (literally, the measurement of earth or surveying) at his time; essentially, that meant systematizing the rules of thumb used by land surveyors, which had never been "proved" but which everyone knew had validity. It was Euclid's powerful insight that these rules could be "proved" by showing them to be logical derivatives from some simple set of "self-evident" truths; or, to use Ford's terminology, that they could be shown to be T_3 by demonstrating their consistency with the basic beliefs—the self-evident truths—taken to be T_1. Euclid began with four such basic beliefs, which have since come to be known as the axioms of Euclidean geometry (Hofstadter, 1979):

(1)   A straight line segment can be drawn joining any two points.

(2)   Any straight line segment can be extended indefinitely in a straight line.

(3)   Given any straight line segment, a circle can be drawn having the segment as radius and one end point as cnter.

(4)   All right angles are congruent.

With these four axioms, Euclid was able to derive ("prove") the first 28 of the eventually much larger set of theorems (statements show to be T_3), but the twenty-ninth proof he attempted turned out be tractable. In despair, and driven by the need to go on to other theorems, Euclid finally simply assumed it as a fifth axiom:

(5)   If two lines are drawn that intersect a third in such a way that the sum of the inner angles on one side is less than two right angles, then the two lines inevitably must intersect each other on that side if extended far enough.

The more modern way to state this axiom is as follows: Given a line and a point not on that line, it is possible to construct only one line through the point that is parallel to the given line.

As compared to the first four axioms, the fifth seems strained and inelegant; Euclid was sure that eventually he would be able to find a way of proving it in terms of the first four. But his hope was not to be realized in his lifetime or, indeed, ever; two millenia of effort by mathematicians have failed to provide a proof.

It is now known that a proof in Euclid's sense is impossible, but that fact was hidden from mathematicians' minds during many centuries when assiduous efforts were made to find it. Early attempts at proof were of the form that mathematicians would call *direct*, but, these having failed, *indirect* proof was sought, one variant of which is to assume the *direct opposite* of what one wishes to show and then to demonstrate that this opposite assumption leads to absurd conclusions (theorems). In that case, the original formulation rather than its opposite can be assumed to be correct. It was exactly this approach, however, that culminated in so-called non-Euclidean geometries, for not only were the consequences of non-Euclidean (opposite to Euclidean) axioms not absurd, they were in fact of great utility. One such geometry is called Lobachevskian; this form takes as its fifth axiom, "Given a line and a point not on that line, it is possible to draw a bundle of lines through the point *all of which* are parallel to the given line." Now this axiom flies in the face of all human experience; yet it yields results of great interest, for example, to astronomers.

One of the theorems "provable" (in the sense of T_3) from the Euclidean fifth axiom is that the sum of angles in a triangle is 180°. But the sum of angles of a Lobachevskian triangle is *not always 180°* but approaches 180° as the triangle becomes "small." An intuitive understanding of this point can be had from examining the (impossible in either geometry but useful for pedagogical purposes) triangle shown in Figure 1.1. Assuming we have a triangle with three angles of 40°, summing to 120°, it is clear that as the triangle is bisected from its 40° superior angle by a perpendicular bisector, each of the smaller triangles now has a sum of angles of 150°. Now of course all human experience argues that triangles *do* have a sum equal to 180°, but that is simply evidence for the fact that, within Lobachevskian geometry, *all earth-size triangles are small*. But astronomically sized triangles are very much larger, and astronomers find that Lobachevskian geometry provides a better "fit" to the phenomena that they investigate than does Euclidean.

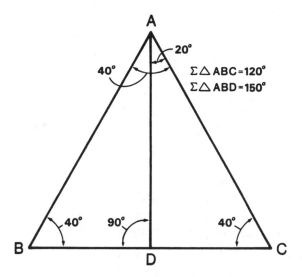

Figure 1.1: Smaller "Lobachevskian" triangles have large sum of angles (approaching 180°).

From this digression we may deduce several crucial points:

(1)   Axioms (basic beliefs) are arbitrary and may be assumed for any reason, even if only for the "sake of the game."

(2)   Axioms are *not* self-evidently true, nor need they appear to be so; indeed, some axioms appear to be very bizarre on first exposure.

(3)   Different axiom systems have different utilities depending on the phenomena to which they are applied. These utilities are *not* determined by the nature of the axiom system itself but by the *interaction* between the axioms and the characteristics of the area of application. Thus Euclidean geometry is fine for terrestrial spaces, but Lobachevskian geometry is preferred for interstellar spaces.

(4)   A decision about which of several alternative axiom systems to use in a given case is best made by testing the "fit" between each system and the case, a process analogous to testing data for fit to assumptions before deciding on which statistic to use in analyzing them.

We are ready now to deal with the axioms of the particular postpositivist paradigm we advocate in this book, which we will term the "naturalistic paradigm." The assumptions of that paradigm are briefly outlined in the next section and are contrasted with those of the positivist paradigm; the question of testing their "fit," particularly for use in human inquiry, is delayed for extended treatment in Chapters 3 through 7. The next section will also provide a preview of some of the methodological implications of the selected paradigm for actually doing research; these implications will be explored in detail in Chapter 8.

The Axioms of the Naturalistic Paradigm

We have made the point several times that the particular formulation of the positivistic paradigm that one adopts depends as much upon the countercase that one will propose as upon anything else; the selection of points is essentially arbitrary. This presentation is not different in that respect;

we hope, however, that the reader will agree that, first, we have selected to emphasize more salient rather than more bizarre aspects of positivism, and, second, that we have not misstated the position that a committed positivist would take on these points, whatever might be said about other points. The points of contrast that we have chosen are, we believe, crucial to an understanding of the naturalistic paradigm and the ways in which it differs, contrasts, and even conflicts with the positivistic.

Immediately following is a formal statement of the five axioms in both their naturalistic and positivistic versions; these are also summarized in Table 1.1 for convenience. The reader shoudl here acquaint him- or herself with the axioms and delay concerns about whether these axioms provide a better fit to the phenomena of socio behavioral inquiry until this matter comes under close scrutiny in later chapters.

Axiom 1: *The nature of reality (ontology)* (expanded in Chapter 3).

- *Positivist version:* There is a single tangible reality "out there" fragmentable into independent variables and processes, any of which can be studied independently of the others; inquiry can converge onto that reality until, finally, it can be predicted and controlled.

- *Naturalist version:* There are multiple constructed realities that can be studied only holistically; inquiry into these multiple realities will inevitably diverge (each inquiry raises more questions than it answers) so that prediction and control are unlikely outcomes although some level of understanding (*verstehen*) can be achieved.

Axiom 2: *The relaitionship of knower to known (epistemology)* (expanded in Chapter 4).

- *Positivist version:* The inquirer and the object of inquiry are independent; the knower and the known constitute a discrete dualism.

- *Naturalist version:* The inquirer and the "object" of inquiry interact to influence one another; knower and known are inseparable.

Axiom 3: *The possibility of generalization* (expanded in Chapter 5).

- *Positivist version:* The aim of inquiry is to develop a nomothetic body of knowledge in the form of generalizations that are truth statements free from both time and context (they will hold anywhere and at any time).

- *Naturalist version:* The aim of inquiry is to develop an idiographic body of knowledge in the form of "working hypotheses" that describe the individual case.

Table 1.1
Contrasting Positivist and Naturalist Axioms

Axioms About	Positivist Paradigm	Naturalist Paradigm
The Nature of reality	Reality is single, tangible, and fragmentable.	Realities are multiple, constructed, and holistic.
The relationship of knower to the known	Knower and known are independent, a dualism.	Knower and known are interaction, inseparable.
The possibility of generalization	Time- and context-free generalizations (nomothetic statements) are possible.	Only time- and context-bound working hypotheses (idiographic statements) are possible.
The possibility of causal linkages	There are real causes, temporally precedent to or simultaneous with their effects.	All entities are in a state of mutual simultaneous shaping, so that it is impossible to distinguish causes from effects.
The role of values	Inquiry is value-free.	Inquiry is value-bound.

Axiom 4: *The possibility of causal linkages* (expanded in Chapter 6).

- *Positivist version:* Every action can be explained as the result (effect) of a real cause that precedes the effect temporally (or is at least simultaneous with it).

- *Naturalist version:* All entities are in a state of mutual simultaneous shaping so that it is impossible to distinguish causes from effects.

Axiom 5: *The role of values in inquiry (axiology)* (expanded in Chapter 7).

- *Positivist version:* Inquiry is value-free and can be guaranteed to be so by virtue of the objective methodology employed.

- *Naturalist version:* Inquiry is value-bound in at least five ways, captured in the corollaries that follow:

  Corollary 1: Inquiries are influenced by *inquirer* values as expressed in the choice of a problem, evaluand, or policy option, and in the framing, bounding, and focusing of that problem, evaluand, or policy option.

  Corollary 2: Inquiry is influenced by the choice of the *paradigm* that guides the investigation into the problem.

  Corollary 3: Inquiry is influenced by the choice of the *substantive theory* utilized to guide the collection and analysis of data and in the interpretation of findings.

  Corollary 4: Inquiry is influenced by the values that inhere in the *context*.

  Corollary 5: With respect to corollaries 1 through 4 above, inquiry is either *value-resonant* (reinforcing or congruent) or *value-dissonant* (conflicting). Problem, evaluand, or policy option, paradigm, theory, *and* context must exhibit congruence (value-resonance) if the inquiry is to produce meaningful results.[12]

Following the naturalistic rather than the positivistic version of these key axioms has, as one might expect, enormous implications for the *doing* of research; these implications are very briefly sketched in the following section and will be pursued in more detail subsequently.

Implications for the Doing of Research

An inquirer doing research in the style or mode of the naturalist paradigm needs more than just the five axioms listed above as guides. In this section we shall describe very briefly some of the more important implications of the paradigm for actual research operations. The importance of these modes will be more fully appreciated as we return to them in more depth in Chapter 8.

We shall describe fourteen characteristics of operational naturalistic inquiry. These characteristics can be justified in two ways: (1) by their logical dependence on the axioms that undergrid the paradigm, and (2) by their coherence and interdependence. These fourteen characteristics display a synergism such that, once one is selected, the others more or less follow. Some attempt will be made in the paragraphs that follow to support these claims.

Logical Dependence Upon the Axioms

Characteristic 1: Natural setting. N (the naturalist) elects to carry out research in the natural setting or context of the entry for which study is proposed because naturalistic ontology suggests that realities are wholes that cannot be understood in isolation from their contexts, nor can they be fragmented for separate study of the parts (the whole is more than the sum of the parts); because of the belief that the very act of observation influences what is seen, and so the research interaction should take place with the entity-in-context for fullest understanding; because of the belief that context is crucial in deciding whether or not a finding may have meaning in some other context as well; because of the belief in complex mutual shaping rather than linear causation, which suggests that the phenomenon must be studied in its full-scale influence (force) field; and because contextual value structures are at least partly determinative of what will be found.

Characteristic 2: Human instrument. N elects to use him- or herself as well as other humans as the primary data-gathering instruments (as opposed to paper-and-pencil or brass instruments) because it would be virtually impossible to devise a priori a nonhuman instrument with sufficient adaptability to encompass and adjust to the variety of realities that will be encountered; because of the understanding that all instruments interact with respondents and objects but that only the human instrument is capable of grasping and evaluating the meaning of that differential interaction; because the intrusion of instruments intervenes in the mutual shaping of other elements and that shaping can be appreciated and evaluated only by a human; and because all instruments are value-based and interact with local values but only the human is in a position to identify and take into account (to some extent) those resulting biases.[13]

Characteristic 3: Utilization of tacit knowledge. N argues for the legitimation of tacit (intuitive, felt) knowledge in addition to propositional knowledge (knowledge expressible in language form) because often the nuances of the multiple realities can be appreciated only in this way; because much of the interaction between investigator and respondent or object occurs at this level; and because tacit knowledge mirrors more fairly and accurately the value patterns of the investigator.

Characteristic 4: Qualitative methods. N elects qualitative methods over quantitative (although not exclusively) because they are more adaptable to dealing with multiple (and less aggregatable) realities; because such methods expose more directly the nature of the transaction between investigator and respondent (or object) and hence make easier an assessment of the extent to which the phenomenon is described in terms of (is biased by) the investigator's own posture; and because qualitative methods are more sensitive to and adaptable to the many mutually shaping influences and value patterns that may be encountered.

Characteristic 5: Purposive sampling. N is likely to eschew random or representative sampling in favor of purposive or theoretical sampling because he or she thereby increases the scope or range of data exposed (random or representative sampling is likely to suppress more deviant cases) as well as the likelihood that the full array of multiple realities will be uncovered; and because purposive sampling can be pursued in ways that will maximize the investigator's ability to devise grounded theory that takes adequate account of local conditions, local mutual shapings, and local values (for possible transferability).

Characteristic 6: Inductive data analysis. N prefers inductive (to deductive) data analysis because that process is more likely to identify the multiple realities to be found in those data; because such analysis is more likely to make the investigator-respondent (or object) interaction explicit, recognizable, and accountable; because this process is more likely to describe fully the setting and to make decisions about transferability to other settings easier; because inductive data analysis is more likely to identify the mutually shaping influences that interact; and because values can be an explicit part of the analytic structure.

Characteristic 7: Grounded theory. N prefers to have the guiding substantive theory emerge from (be grounded in) the data because *no* a priori theory could possibly encompass the multiple realities that are likely to be encountered; because believing is seeing and N wishes to enter his transactions with respondents as neutrally as possible; because a priori theory is likely to be based on a priori generalizations, which, while they may make nomothetic sense, may nevertheless provide a poor idiographic fit to the situation encountered (the fact that a woman recounts a set of gynecological symptoms to her doctor that, in 80 percent of patients, indicates cervical cancer is not sufficient reason to schedule her for surgery without examination to determine whether she might not be one of the 20 percent); because the mutual shapings found in a particular context may be explicable only in terms of the contextual elements found there; and because grounded theory is more likely to be responsive to contextual values (and not merely to investigator values).

Characteristic 8: Emergence design. N elects to allow the research design to emerge (flow, cascade, unfold) rather than to construct it preordinately (a priori) because it is inconceivable that enough could be known ahead of time about the many multiple realities to devise the design adequately; because what emerges as a funciton of the interaction between inquirer and phenomenon is largely unpredictable in advance; because the inquirer cannot know sufficiently well the patterns of mutual shaping that are likely to exist; and because the various value systems involved (including the inquirer's own) interact in unpredictable ways to influence the outcome.

Characteristic 9: Negotiated outcomes. N prefers to negotiate meanings and interpretations with the human sources from which the data have chiefly been drawn because it is their constructions of reality that the inquirer seeks to reconstruct; because inquiry outcomes depend upon the nature and quality of the interaction between the knower and the known, epitomized in negotiations about the meaning of data; because the specific working hypotheses that might apply in a given context are best verified and confirmed by the people who inhabit that context; because respondents are in a better position to interpret the complex mutual interactions—shapings—that enter into what is observed; and because respondents can best understand and interpret the influence of local value patterns.

Characteristic 10: Case study reporting mode. N is likely to prefer the case study reporting mode (over the scientific or technical report) because it is more adapted to a description of the multiple realities encountered at any given site: because it is adaptabale to demonstrating the investigator's interaction with the site and consequent biases that may result (reflexive reporting); because it provides the basis for both individual "naturalistic generalizations" (Stake, 1980) and transferability to other sites (thick description); because it is suited to demonstrating the variety of mutually shaping influences present; and because it can picture the value positions of investigator, substantive theory, methodological paradigm, and local contextual values.

Characteristic 11: Idiographic interpretation. N is inclined to interpret data (including the drawing of conclusions) idiographically (in terms of the particulars of the case) rather than nomothetically (in terms of lawlike generalizations) because different interpretations are likely to be meaningful for different realities; and because interpretations depend so heavily for their validity on local particulars, including the particular investigator-respondent (or object) interaction, the contextual factors involved, the local mutually shaping factors influencing one another, and the local (as well as investigator) values.

Characteristic 12: Tentative application. N is likely to be tentative (hesitant) about making broad application of the findings because realities are multiple and different; because the findings are to some extent dependent upon the particular interaction between investigator and respondents (or object) that may not be duplicated elsewhere; because the extent to which the findings may be applicable elsewhere depends upon the *empirical* similarity of sending and receiving contexts; because the particular "mix" of mutually shaping influences may vary markedly from setting to setting; and because value systems, especially contextual values, may be sharply at variance from site to site.

Characteristic 13: Focus-determined boundaries. N is likely to set boundaries to the inquiry on the basis of the emergent focus (problems for researh, evaluands for evaluation, and policy options for policy analysis) because that permits the multiple realities to define the focus (rather than inquirer preconceptions); because focus-setting can be more closely mediated by the investigator-focus interaction; because boundaries cannot be satisfactorily set without intimate contextual knowledge, including knowledge about the mutually shaping factors involved; and because foci have no meaning in any event in abstraction from the local investigator value systems.

Characteristic 14: Special criteria for trustworthiness. N is likely to find the conventional trustworthiness criteria (internal and external validity, reliability, and objectivity) inconsistent with the axioms and procedures of naturalistic inquiry. Hence he or she is likely to define new (but analogous) criteria and devise operational procedures for applying them. Chapter 11 is devoted to this matter; here it is worth noting that the conventional criterion of internal validity fails because it implies an isomorphism between research outcomes and a single, tangible reality onto which inquiry can converge; that the criterion of external validity fails because it is inconsistent with the basic axiom concerning generalizability; that the criterion of reliability fails because it requires absolute stability and replicability, neither of which is possible for a paradigm based on emergent design; and that the criterion of objectivity fails because the paradigm openly admits investigator-respondent (or object) interaction and the role of values. The case will later be made that there exist substitute crieria (called credibility, transferability, dependability, and confirmability) together with corresponding empirical procedures that adequately (if not absolutely) affirm the trustworthiness of naturalistic approaches.

Coherence (Mutual Reinforcement) Among the Characteristics

A second justification for claiming that the above list of fourteen characteristics is justifiable for naturalistic inquiry is the fact that they display a remarkable coherence and interdependence. One simple illustration will suffice to make the point that each may be taken as a raison d'être for the others; and that the exclusion of any one of them would seriously damage all.

In doing research from a naturalistic perspective, N is forced into the natural setting because he or she cannot specify, without an a priori theory or hypothesis, what is important to control or even to study. Until N has spent some time in the setting he or she cannot specify the focus (problem, evaluand, or policy option) in more than rudimentary form, or place boundaries on it. N could not design a contrived study (an experiment, say) because he or she would not know what to contrive. If theory is to be grounded in data, those data must first be located and analyzed inductively. Since N cannot specify the precise form of the data to be sought, he or she must fall back on an open-ended adaptive instrument: the human being, who, like the "smart bomb," can identify and wend its way to (purposefully sample) the target without having been precisely preprogrammed to strike it. Humans find certain data collection means more congenial than others; they tend toward the use of qualitative methods that "extend" human senses: seeing, hearing, and tacit "sixth-sensing" that lead one to observation, interview, documentary analysis, and the like. These methods results in insights and information about the sending context so that the extent of transferability and applicability in some other receiving context may be judged. No aggregations, no generalizations, no cause-effect statements can emerge, but only idiographic interpretations negotiated with knowledgeable respondents; hence an air of tentativeness surrounds any proposed application. Finally, the case study mode lends itself well to the full description that will be required to encompass all of these facets and make possible understanding on the part of a reader (building on his or her own tacit knowledge and making "naturalistic generalization" possible). Judgments about the trustworthiness of such a process cannot be made with conventional criteria; criteria devised especially for and demonstrably appropriate to naturalistic inquiry are required.

An Overview

The remainder of this volume is devoted to a fuller explication of the ideas that have been introduced so sketchily in this chapter. Chapter 2 is an effort to provide further legitimation for the naturalistic paradigm by showing its resonance with a more encompassing new "paradigm of thought and belief" that draws upon *substantive* (rather then merely methodological) vanguard ideas from a wide variety of disciplines. Chapters 3 through 7 deal in more detail with each of the five axioms—reality, knower-known interaction, generalizability, causality, and values—and make the case that the naturalistic version of these axioms provides a better fit to sociobehavioral phenomena at least, if not to all phenomena. Chapter 8 deals in more detail with the first thirteen of the fourteen characteristics listed in this chapter, and closes out the first and more theoretical part of the book.

Beginning with Chapter 9, we attempt to provide more practical guidelines for the actual *doing* of naturalistic inquiry. That chapter discusses the design of a naturalistic study (although, as the reader can guess, the term "design" will be found to have a somewhat different meaning than is conventionally the case). Chapter 10 gives directions for actually carrying through a design. Chapter 11 returns to the theme of trustworthiness techniques. Chapter 12 outlines the procedures for inductive data processing, and Chapter 13 for writing the case study and closing out the inquiry with a general member check and audit.

Notes

1. The concept of "preservation of appearances" was common in medieval and early positivist periods.

2. The wisdom of taking T_2 on faith (as one often must) is called into question by the frequency with which it is discovered that one or another well-known scientist has "fudged" the data.

3. We are aware that this definition of *paradigm* is not that which scientists customarily use, that is, a model or pattern (as for example, a paradigm equation that illustrates the procedures for solving an entire class of equations). It is, however, consistent with the use of that term by Kuhn (1970) and others who have written in a similar vein about "paradigm revolutions."

4. A serious question can be raised whether any theory that aims at comprehensiveness can also be perfectly coherent. Gödel's Theorem in mathematics suggests that a comprehensiveness/coherence union is in principle impossible. See the excellent discussion in Hofstadter (1979).

5. We cannot resist citing a memorable paragraph from Julienne Ford (1975, p. 149), who, in describing operationism in terms of the concepts of Percy W. Bridgman, a staunch advocate, says:

    Bridgman's argument is quite simply that to be meaningful a variable must be defined in terms of the measurement operation that would be invovled in detecting it in reality. This view is usually termed *operationism* (though it is sometimes referred to as operation*alism*) and it amounts to the methodological assertion that any variable which cannot be directly represented by a measurement operation has no place in science. Thus a hypothesis like *"Those rabbits will be afraid"* is regarded as meaningless. However, the statement, *"Those rabbits will be seen to be emitting more faecal boluses per hour than is normal for rabbits"* is perfectly meaningful as far as Bridgman and his men are concerned. Fear, then, is meaningless to the operationist but an observably increasing defecation rate does have meaning. (Notice incidentally that Cockneys seem to think that Bridgman has a point: The Cockney rarely says "Huck is afraid", instead he says "Huck is shitting himself".)

6. This same metaphor also served David Hume in his critique of the concept of causality. See Chapter 6.

7. Harre's reference to the "Paduan professors who refused to look through Galileo's telescope" is a famous instance of what might be called the "reluctant mind," the mind that refuses to accept the need for a new paradigm and that capitalizes on what we earlier termed the "loose coupling" of theory. Galileo, it will be

recalled, had gotten himself into trouble with the Church (it was only in 1983 that the Church admitted having committed a major blunder in Galileo's case; *Time*, May 23, 1983, p. 58) because of his publications outlining a heliocentric universe, a formulation clearly at odds with the Church's position that the universe was geocentric. Ordered to an inquisition in 1633, he was censured and actually condemned to death, although the sentence was suspended in view of his abject recantation. But prior to the official "hearing." Galileo was visited in Padua by a group of inquisitors, composed (to the eternal shame of all academics) mainly of professors from the nearby university. According to the story, which may well be apocryphal, Galileo invited his visitors to look through his telescope at the moon and see for themselves the mountains and the craters that the marvelous instrument revealed for the first time. But his inquisitors refused to do so, arguing that whatever might be visible through the telescope would be a product not of nature but of the instrument. How consistent this position is with Aristotelian "naturalism"! Galileo's active intervention in building the telescope and viewing the moon through it were, to the inquisitors' prepositivist minds, an exact illustration of how the *active* observer could distort the "real" or "natural" order. Their posture was perhaps not so much a "glorying in ignorance," as Harre claims, but adherence to the best "scientific" principles of the time.

Another example of the fact that even the best thinkers of an era may have difficulty in throwing off the constraints imposed by the paradigm they follow can be found in the conversion of the field of chemistry from a phlogiston-based theory of combustion and calcination to an oxygen-based theory. The oxygen theory seemed to offer a better explanation of these two phenomena than did the phlogiston theory/and, indeed, offered an explanation of several other phenomena that had not been contemplated by the phlogiston theories: respiration and acidity. Chemists steeped in the phlogiston theory were accustomed to working with equations that included terms for either the absorption or emission of phlogiston. When Lavoisier provided a variety of evidence in support of the oxygen theory, many chemists were prepared to accept his formulation but stumbled over one crucial issue: What happened to the phlogiston in Lavoisier's equations? They could not understand that the very concept of phlogiston was foreign to the paradigm being offered by Lavoisier; that it did not require explanation in the new paradigm, that the construction of the new paradigm denied phlogiston's existence. For an instructive treatment of this important piece of chemical history, see McCann (1978).

8. The reader should recall at this point our earlier caveat about describing the positivist paradigm in terms that best accommodate the rebuttal or counterproposal that the critic intends to make.

9. The reader should be aware that we use term "postpositivist" to refer to paradigms that represent genuine breaks with the positivist tradition. A substantial number of writers who refer to their own work using this phrase are, in our terms, only *neo*positivists. They have attempted to respond to criticism of positivism by making adjustments or accommodations, not by radical revision. They represent modern-day counterparts of the "reluctant minds" that we have already encountered in our description of the "Paduan professors: or the phlogiston-oriented chemists. We shall return to this theme repeatedly throughout this book.

10. One notable difference between conventional and emergent paradigms can be detected in the terminology common to each to describe human entities being studied. Positivists tend to call them "subjects," or even "objects of inquiry," treating them as though they were equivalent to the inanimate objects encountered in physics and chemistry. We prefer to call them "respondents," a term that not only retains their humanness but reminds us of the interactive character of human inquiry.

11. The language of this and the following section follows closely Guba and Lincoln (1982).

12. This assertion is one of the most central in this book. If it were not the case that these various value aspects could be resonant or dissonant, one need not be too concerned about which paradigm was being used in any particular inquiry. But it is precisely because the foci of modern inquiry and the substantive theories used in their study may rest on assumptions that are inconsistent with those of the positivist paradigm that it is imperative to move to a paradigm that *is* resonant. The fact that the emergent substantive theories in virtually all disciplines are better supported by the naturalist paradigm will be argued in Chapter 2.

13. Hofstadter (1979) points out that adaptability and perfectability stand in a trade-off relationship to one another. The more perfect an instrument is for some specific purpose, the less adaptive it must be for other purposes. The human, while far from perfect as an instrument, is nevertheless infinitely adaptable.

Clarifying Qualitative Research:
A Focus on Traditions

EVELYN JACOB

There is considerable confusion in the educational literature about the nature of qualitative research. In this article I argue that a major source of the confusion arises from discussing qualitative research as if it is one approach. The discussion in the educational literature concerning qualitative research can be clarified by recognizing that qualitative research comes in many different varieties, which can be more clearly identified and understood by using the notion of research traditions. To apply this concept to the discussion of qualitative research, I describe briefly and compare six traditions from the disciplines of psychology, anthropology, and sociology. These traditions are human ethology, ecological psychology, holistic ethnography, cognitive anthropology, ethnography of communication, and symbolic interactionism. I conclude that we may increase our understanding of qualitative research by focusing our discussions at the level of traditions.

Until recently, educational research has drawn primarily from psychological traditions that operate within a positivistic approach. However, within the past 10 years educational researchers and psychologists such as Campbell (1978) and Cronbach (1975) have challenged scholars to transcend the limits of positivism. To address these challenges many scholars looked to literature in disciplines outside psychology and to literature in psychological traditions that previously have been disfavored by educational researchers.

Subsequent discussions addressed to the general education audience frequently examined the issues as if there were only one alternative to traditional positivism (e.g., Jacob, 1982; Lutz & Ramsey, 1974; Magoon, 1977; Rist, 1977; J.K. Smith, 1983; L. Smith, 1978; Wilson, 1977). Other authors acknowledged more than one alternative to positivism, but discussed the issues as if there were only a single alternative (e.g., Bogdan & Biklen, 1982; Erickson, 1977; Guba & Lincoln, 1981; Lincoln & Guba, 1985; Patton, 1980). Although authors have used many different labels for the alternative to positivism, I will use "qualitative" because it is the most widely used term.

Several themes have emerged from these discussions. Qualitative research has been characterized as emphasizing the importance of conducting research in a natural setting (Bogdan & Biklen, 1982; Lincoln & Guba, 1985; Patton, 1980; Wilson, 1977), as assuming the importance of understanding participants' perspectives (Bogdan & Biklen; Lincoln & Guba, Magoon, 1977; Patton; Rist, 1977; Wilson), and as assuming that it is important for researchers subjectively and empathetically to know the perspectives of the participants (Lincoln & Guba; Patton; Rist; J.K. Smith, 1983; Wilson). Qualitative research is also seen as free from predetermined theories and questions, with questions and theories emerging after data collection rather than being posed before the study begins (Bogdan & Biklen; Lincoln & Guba; Patton; Rist; Wilson). The central method of qualitative research is said to be participant observation (Bogdan & Biklen; Wilson).

Although these themes occur across several discussions, they are not uniformly agreed upon as the necessary characteristics of qualitative research. Moreover, when one looks more closely at individual discussions, the apparent unity of the qualitative approach vanishes, and one sees considerable diversity. What has been called "qualitative research" conveys different meanings to different people. Needless to say, this has caused considerable confusion among educational researchers (see J.K. Smith, 1983, p. 6).

In this article I argue that a major source of the confusion lies in discussing qualitative research as if it were *one* approach. The discussion in the educational literature concerning qualitative research can be clarified by recognizing that qualitative research in the noneducation disciplines comes in many different varieties. These varieties can be more clearly identified and understood by using the notion of research tradition.

Kuhn (1970) stated that within the sciences there are various groups of scholars who agree among themselves on the nature of the universe they are examining, on legitimate questions and problems to study, and on legitimate techniques to seek solutions. Such a group is said to have a "tradition." Kuhn further pointed out that a tradition can occur either as an entire discipline or as a school within a discipline. For the purposes of this article it is most useful to look at sub-disciplinary schools. This is the level at which most scholars in the social sciences operate, and it provides a good vehicle for resolving the confusion within education about qualitative research.

To apply the concept of traditions to the discussion of qualitative research, I shall describe and compare six representative traditions from the disciplines of psychology, anthropology, and sociology. These traditions are human ethology, ecological psychology, holistic ethnography, cognitive anthropology, ethnography of communication, and symbolic interactionism. I selected these traditions because they have been cited in the education literature as examples of qualitative research and because they provide an illustration of the range of approaches available from noneducation disciplines.

My purpose here is not to cover all of the qualitative traditions that could be included. Other qualitative traditions include ethnomethodology, structural-functionalism, psychological anthropology, and symbolic anthropology. Nor do I intend to attempt an in-depth study of any particular tradition. Instead, I intend to summarize briefly the main points of each tradition covered and, by contrasting the traditions, to illustrate the diversity of qualitative research.[1] References to further reading are provided in each section. Jacob (1987) presented a fuller discussion of the qualitative traditions examined here.

Traditions of Qualitative Research

In this section I briefly describe qualitative traditions by their historical roots, important assumptions, major foci, central questions, and common methods.

Human Ethology

Human ethology developed from the study of animal behavior within biology and is guided by the synthetic theory of evolution (Blurton Jones, 1972, p. 6; Charlesworth, 1978, p. 7). Ethologists emphasize the importance of understanding the range of naturally occurring behavior and its relationship to the environment in which an animal adapted. Most human ethologists conduct studies of naturally occurring behavior before conducting controlled experiments. They downplay the idea that humans are different from other animals (Blurton Jones, p. 7). For example, although many ethologists acknowledge that language is an important aspect of human behavior, they generally do not analyze human language, but code it merely as "talk" (e.g., Smith & Connolly, 1972, p. 78). Some recognize that there are subjective components to human behavior (e.g.,

Charlesworth, p. 9; Hinde, 1983), but most human ethologists are not interested in people's subjective perceptions of what they are doing (Blurton Jones & Woodson, 1979, p. 99).

Human ethologists focus on questions about immediate causation of behaviors, development of behaviors, biological functions of behaviors, and evolution of specific behaviors. Their primary units of analysis are individuals at the level of anatomically described motor patterns. Data comprise observations collected through videotapes or by nonparticipant observers. The observations are coded into anatomically defined behavior categories, and the data are analyzed quantitatively.

Blurton Jones (1972), Blurton Jones and Woodson (1979), Charlesworth (1978), Hinde (1982, 1983), and P.K. Smith (1974) presented some conceptual statements about human ethology. Blurton Jones, Hinde (1983), Hutt and Hutt (1970), and P.K. Smith (1974) provided discussions of its methodology.

Ecological Psychology

Ecological psychology was developed by Roger Barker, Herbert Wright, and their colleagues at the University of Kansas. They drew heavily on natural history field studies and the work of Kurt Lewin (Barker & Wright, 1955, p. 1). Ecological psychologists are interested in the relationships between human behavior and the environment; they see individuals and the environment as interdependent. They assume that there are subjective aspects to behavior which they examine in terms of the goals of human behavior. They also assume that there is a subjective aspect to the environment which they usually discuss in terms of a person's emotional reactions to the environment. For example, they might be concerned whether a boy does an activity unwillingly or unhappily (Barker & Wright, p. 202).

Ecological psychologists ask descriptive questions about either individuals' behavior and environment or about the features of behavior settings. One focus of their work is individuals' perceived environment and goal-directed behaviors, which they study using "specimen records." Under the specimen record methodology, nonparticipant observers write a narrative description of the behavior of one person over a substantial period of time (Schoggen, 1978, p. 43). This "stream of behavior" is then divided into segments based on goal-directed actions. Coders draw upon their ordinary knowledge and perceptions to infer the goals that actors intend to achieve, marking off sections of narrative descriptions into segments leading toward specific goals (Wright, 1967, pp. 25–27). These segments are coded and analyzed quantitatively (Wright).

The second focus in ecological psychology is the transindividual patterns of behavior associated with particular constellations of places, things, and times, which they study using "behavior setting surveys." In behavior setting surveys, researchers identify all possible behavior settings and then identify those which meet stringent tests for true behavior settings (Barker, 1968). These are then coded for their features and analyzed quantitatively to provide a comprehensive description of all the behavior settings in a particular community or institution during a stated period of time (Barker; Schoggen, 1978, p. 50).

Barker and his colleagues (Barker, Wright, Schoggen, & Barker, 1978; Barker & Wright, 1955) and Schoggen (1978) discussed the theory and methodology of both foci of ecological psychology. Wright (1967) presented the specimen record approach and Barker (1968) discussed the behavior setting approach in depth.

Holistic Ethnography

Holistic ethnography developed primarily from the work of Franz Boas in America and Bronislaw Malinowski in England. Culture, a central concept for holistic ethnographers, includes patterns *of* behavior and patterns *for* behavior. The concept of patterns of behavior is self-explanatory. Patterns for behavior are seen as systems of "standards for deciding what is, standards for deciding what can be, standards for deciding how one feels about it, standards for deciding what to do about it, and standards for deciding how to go about doing it" (Goodenough, 1971, pp. 21, 22). These standards are seen as shared group phenomena (Goodenough, pp. 36–42), leading to a certain predictability in social life, but without determining behavior (Barrett, 1984, p. 72).

Holistic ethnographers assume that certain aspects of human culture are central to understanding human life in all societies. These aspects include social organization, economics, family structure, religion, politics, rituals, enculturation patterns, and ceremonial behavior (Pelto, 1970, p. 18). Holistic ethnographers also assume that the various aspects of a culture form a unique, unified whole, with the parts being interdependent (Mead, 1970/1973, p. 246).

Holistic ethnographers focus on the study of the culture of bounded groups, with an interest in describing and analyzing the culture as a whole. Their goal is to describe a unique way of life, documenting the meanings attached to events and showing how the parts fit together into an integrated whole. They approach a particular culture with a minimum of preconceived ideas or theories beyond the general assumptions.

Although there is considerable diversity in how holistic ethnographers conduct their studies, most hold several basic tenets. First, holistic ethnographers gather empirical evidence directly themselves through "fieldwork," usually involving participant observation and informal interviews, in the culture they are studying (Malinowski, 1922/1961, pp. 7–8). Second, holistic ethnographers endeavor to document the participants' points of view, preferably through verbatim statements (Malinowski, p. 23). Third, holistic ethnographers collect a wide range of data using a wide range of methods (Malinowski). Analysis of the data is primarily qualitative.

Discussions of holistic ethnography are embedded in many discussions of anthropology as a whole. LeVine (1970/1973) and Sanday (1979) explicitly discussed the tradition. Edgerton and Langness (1974), Jongmans and Gutkind (1967), and Pelto (1970) treated holistic ethnographic methods in the context of other anthropological methods. Gutkind, Jongmans, Jonker, Kobben, Sankoff, and Serpenti (1967) presented an annotated bibliography of a wide range of anthropological field methods.

Cognitive Anthropology

Cognitive anthropology, which has been called ethnoscience or the "new ethnography," developed from pioneer work by Ward Goodenough and Charles Frake, who drew heavily on the methods of linguistics. Cognitive anthropologists have a mentalistic view of culture. They assume that each bounded group of individuals has a unique system for perceiving and organizing the world and that this culture is organized into categories which are systematically related to one another (Spradley, 1979, p. 93), with classes of phenomena being organized into larger groupings (Tyler, 1969, p. 7). Cognitive anthropologists also assume that a group's cultural knowledge is reflected in its language—specifically, in semantics (Tyler, p. 6).[2]

Cognitive anthropologists strive to identify phenomena that participants recognize and to understand how groups organize their cultural knowledge, primarily as it is expressed in a group's semantic system. Data, consisting of words and their meanings, are collected primarily through interviews and formal elicitation procedures. Informal interviews and observations provide preliminary data (Spradley, 1979). Data analysis is qualitative and involves the identification of "domains" of cultural knowledge, identification of how terms in each domain are organized, study of the attributes of terms in each domain, and discovery of relationships among cultural domains (Spradley, 1979, 1980).

Tyler (1969) presented a now classic introduction to cognitive anthropology. Spradley (1972, 1979) discussed the tradition and its associated methods, focusing on semantic data. In another volume (1980) Spradley applied the methods to observational data. Agar (1980, chap. 7) incorporated some techniques of cognitive anthropology into a broader discussion of anthropological methods.

Ethnography of Communication

Ethnography of communication, which has been called ethnography of speaking, micro-ethnography, or constitutive ethnography, developed from work in anthropology, sociology, sociolinguistics, and nonverbal communication (Erickson & Mohatt, 1982, p. 136; Erickson & Wilson, 1982, p. 42). Ethnographers of communication see culture as central to understanding human behavior. They assume that both verbal and nonverbal communication are culturally patterned even though the persons communicating may not be aware of this patterning (Erickson & Mohatt, p. 136; Philips, 1983, p. 4). They see context, which they define to include the participants in an interaction, as influencing the patterns of communication (Mehan, 1984, p. 175), and they assume that the social structure and "outcomes" of institutional processes are produced at least in part by the processes of face-to-face interaction (Erickson & Mohatt, p. 137; Mehan, 1984, p. 18),

Ethnographers of communication focus on the patterns of social interaction among members of a cultural group and among members of different cultural groups. They are interested in specifying the patterns and processes of face-to-face interaction and in understanding how these "micro" processes are related to larger "macro" issues of culture and social organization (Erickson & Mohatt, 1982, pp. 137–138; Erickson & Wilson, 1982, p. 43). Ethnographers of communication base their studies on participant observation data and on audio or video recordings of naturally occurring interactions (Erickson & Wilson, p. 43). The machine-recorded data are maximally continuous and comprehensive (Erickson & Wilson, p. 77). Researchers index the machine-recorded data from major social occasions, select segments for detailed analysis, repeatedly view the segments to develop and refine analytic categories, and code the data (Erickson & Mohatt; Mehan, 1979). Analysis of patterns may be either quantitative or qualitative.

Hymes (1972, 1974) and Gumperz (1968) presented conceptual discussions of ethnography of communication. Erickson (1977) also discussed the tradition. Erickson and Wilson (1982) reviewed methodological issues for the ethnography of communication tradition. Erickson (1986) discussed methods salient to his work, while Erickson and Shultz (1981) discussed their general approach to data analysis.

Symbolic Interactionism

Symbolic interactionism was developed by Herbert Blumer, drawing on the earlier work of G.H. Mead, Charles Cooley, John Dewey, and W.I. Thomas (Manis & Meltzer, 1978, p. xi). Symbolic interactionists see humans as qualitatively different from other animals. Whereas nonhuman animals act in response to other objects and events based on factors such as instinct or previous conditioning, humans act toward things on the basis of the meanings those objects have for them (Blumer, 1969, p. 2). Symbolic interactionists assume that meanings arise through social interaction (Blumer, p. 4), but that an individual's use of meanings is not automatic. "The actor selects, checks, suspends, regroups, and transforms the meanings in the light of the situation in which he is placed and the direction of his action" (Blumer, p. 5).

These assumptions affect how symbolic interactionists view the macro structures of society. They do not see macro structures as having a life of their own. "Human society is to be seen as consisting of acting people, and the life of the society is to be seen as consisting of their actions" (Blumer, 1969, p. 85).

Symbolic interactionists are interested in understanding the *processes* involved in symbolic interaction—i.e., they seek to know how individuals take one another's perspective and learn meanings and symbols in concrete instances of interaction (Denzin, 1978, p. 7; Ritzer, 1983, p. 308). To collect appropriate data, symbolic interactionists primarily use participant observation and open interviews. They also collect life histories, autobiographies, case studies, and letters (Meltzer, Petras, & Reynolds, 1975, p. 58). Analysis of these data is usually qualitative.

Blumer (1969), Manis and Meltzer (1978), and Rose (1962) discussed the basic assumptions and principles of symbolic interactionism. Becker (1970) and Blumer (1969) presented position papers on methodology in symbolic interactionism. Bogdan and Taylor (1975) and Schatzman and Strauss (1973) presented more concrete, "how-to" discussions.

Comparison of Traditions on Themes

As mentioned in the introduction, the educational literature on qualitative research contains several themes. In this section I compare the above six traditions on these themes and find considerable variability among the traditions.

Natural Setting

All the traditions examined here assume that the setting has an important influence on human behavior. All except cognitive anthropology collect most or all of their data in "natural" settings. Cognitive anthropologists use controlled elicitation techniques for much of their data; however, the question formats used in these techniques are derived from naturally occurring statements in the language.

Subjective Aspects of Human Behavior

Scholars in all of the traditions examined acknowledge that there is a subjective dimension to human behavior. However, they differ substantially in how they define the subjective dimension and the role they give it in their work. This dimension illustrates the diversity among the traditions.

Some human ethologists acknowledge that there are subjective components of human behavior (Charlesworth, 1978; Hinde, 1983). However, they generally are disinterested in this subjective aspect (Blurton Jones & Woodson, 1979, p. 99), and have paid little attention to it. Similarly, in their studies of behavior settings, ecological psychologists focus only on observable patterns of behavior.

In contrast, ecological psychologists make subjective aspects of human behavior a primary focus in their specimen record studies. First, they assume that individuals' behavior is directed by their goals (Barker & Wright, 1955, p. 179). Second, ecological psychologists also assume that individuals have subjective perceptions of their environment, which Barker and Wright define primarily in terms of the individual's emotional reactions to the environment.

Holistic ethnographers, cognitive anthropologists, and ethnographers of communication do not focus on the goals and emotions of individuals, but instead attempt to understand human society through the concept of culture, which is seen as involving a subjective component—shared patterns *for* behavior. While all three traditions share some basic assumptions about culture, they differ in further assumptions they make and how they use the concept of culture in their work. Some holistic ethnographers emphasize culture as a subjective phenomenon in their work, while others combine it with the study of observable behavior. Cognitive anthropologists assume that culture is reflected primarily in language, and specifically in semantics (Tyler, 1969, p. 6). They study a culture's categories and the organizing principles underlying them through the study of semantic systems in the language. Ethnographers of communication assume that verbal and nonverbal social interaction are culturally patterned (Erickson & Mohatt, 1982, p. 136; Philips, 1983, p. 4). They study cultural patterns of social interaction, and how these patterns are related to larger social "facts" (Erickson & Mohatt, pp. 137–138; Erickson & Wilson, 1982, p. 43).

Symbolic interactionists study the subjective aspects of human life by focusing on human life as a moving process in which participants are defining and interpreting each other's acts. They are concerned with understanding how these processes occur, how individuals are able to take one another's perspective and learn meanings in concrete instances of interaction (Denzin, 1978, p. 7; Ritzer, 1983, p. 308).

In sum, the six traditions examined take different approaches to the subjective. Ecological psychologists in their studies of behavior settings and human ethologists pay little attention to it. The five traditions that acknowledge the importance of the subjective in human life do this in diverse ways. In their specimen record studies ecological psychologists define the subjective in terms of individuals' goals and emotional reactions to their environments, while the three anthropological traditions define the subjective as culture. Symbolic interactionists define the subjective in terms of symbolic interaction processes and what individuals do with socially derived meanings.

Subjective Knowledge of Subjective Data

All of the traditions examined are interested in using objective means to study observable behavior. For example, human ethologists try to develop categories of behavior in terms of body parts and motor patterns without inferential or motivational labels (Blurton Jones, 1972, p. 12; Hutt & Hutt, 1970, p. 30; McGrew, 1972, p. 19). Ecological psychologists have produced extensive objective descriptions of the purposive, goal-directed behavior of individuals: "the description includes the manner in which the actions are carried out; the 'how' of everything done and said is of great importance" (Schoggen, 1978, p. 43). Many holistic ethnographers are interested in objectively documenting patterns of behavior in a culture, and ethnographers of communication, in their use of audio taped and videotaped data, are also concerned with collecting objective, retrievable records of social interaction (Mehan, 1979, pp. 18–20).

All of the traditions except human ethology are interested in subjective aspects of human behavior as well as observable behavior. The traditions have varying ideas about how best to know and study these subjective aspects. Ecological psychologists use detailed objective descriptions in specimen record studies as the base to infer the subjects' subjective states. "The inferences included are at a low level, the level of inference about feelings and motivations of others that is regularly employed by persons of normal social sensitivity in ordinary social intercourse in a culture with which they are familiar" (Schoggen, 1978, p. 43).

Holistic ethnographers, cognitive anthropologists, and ethnographers of communication want to report participants' culture objectively. One methodological tenet in holistic ethnography is that it is important to have verbatim statements of the participants in order to get their views of their world (Malinowski, 1922/1961, pp. 23, 25). Cognitive anthropologists place particular emphasis on removing the potential bias of the researcher's own cultural categories and use controlled elicitation techniques to minimize this influence. Ethnographers of communication often review taped data with participants to get their reports of the cultural meanings of the interactions recorded.

Some researchers in the holistic ethnographic tradition also discuss the role of the researcher's subjective experiences through participant observation as being an important way to know about the culture. The ethnographers are seen as data collection instruments themselves and their subjective "knowing" of the culture provides important information (Malinowski, 1922/1961).

Symbolic interactionists have made the strongest statements about subjective ways of knowing subjective aspects of human life. Blumer has stated that to truly document the processes of symbolic interaction researchers need to get "inside the experience of the actor" (Blumer, as quoted by Meltzer et al., 1975, pp. 57–58). This approach has been called "sympathetic introspection" (Meltzer et al., p. 51) and *verstehen* (Bogdan & Taylor, 1975, pp. 13–14).

To summarize, the traditions examined take different stances toward the kind of data needed to study the subjective aspects of human life. The continuum runs from traditions that want only objective evidence to those that regard subjective evidence as essential.

Theory and the Generation of Research Questions

All the traditions examined stress that descriptive studies should precede studies that test specific theories (Barker & Wright, 1955, pp. 13–14; Blumer, 1969, pp. 47–49; Blurton Jones, 1972, pp. 4, 14; Hymes, 1980; Tyler, 1969). The purpose of this descriptive phase is to discover what is happening in the natural setting, and in some cases to understand participants' meanings. All the traditions allow for the possibility of conducting studies focused on testing specific hypotheses after the necessary descriptive groundwork has been laid.

Although researchers in all of the traditions examined emphasize the importance of description and eschew preconceived ideas, they all hold some assumptions which guide the development of their descriptive questions. In each tradition these assumptions are related to what scholars in the tradition think should be the focus of study.

The traditions differ in the amount of discovery that is incorporated within the design of a single study. Human ethologists and ecological psychologists have predetermined questions and designs for individual studies which do not change during the course of the study. In contrast, holistic ethnographers, cognitive anthropologists, ethnographers of communication, and symbolic interactionists frequently develop specific questions and research goals after beginning a study (Blumer, 1969, p. 48; LeVine 1970/1973, p. 183; Spradley, 1979). The research design is seen as "an exploration into the unknown," in which the researcher needs to get background information on the specific group(s) being studied before formulating more specific questions (LeVine, p. 183).

In sum, the role of theory and the generation of research questions in the traditions examined here is complex. All of the traditions believe that descriptive studies should precede studies that test specific hypotheses. However, the traditions differ in the amount of discovery they incorporate within a single study. Two traditions have predetermined questions and designs for individual studies; four traditions, on the other hand, frequently allow specific research questions and related research designs to "emerge" during the course of a study.

Participant Observation

Participant observation plays various roles in the traditions examined. It is not used by human ethologists. Nor is it used by ecological psychologists for collecting specimen records or for describing behavior settings. However, it is sometimes used by ecological psychologists to identify behavior settings (Barker & Schoggen, 1973, pp. 49–50; Schoggen, 1978, p. 50).

Participant observation frequently is used by ethnographers of communication and cognitive anthropologists for preliminary data collection (Erickson & Wilson, 1982; Spradley, 1979). However, ethnographers of communication primarily use films or tapes to record sequences of social interaction (Erickson & Wilson, 1982, p. 43; Mehan, 1979, pp. 18–20), while cognitive anthropologists rely on open-ended interviews and controlled eliciting for their primary methods of data collection (Spradley, 1979).

Participant observation is a more central method for many holistic ethnographers and symbolic interactionists (Malinowski 1922/1961; Meltzer et al., 1975). However, most holistic ethnographers see participant observation as one component of the larger "fieldwork" (Clammer, 1984) and some holistic ethnographers emphasize open-ended interviews instead of observations (Agar, 1982). Symbolic interactionists see participant observation as the most important method of data collection but do use others, such as open interviews, life histories, autobiographies, and letters (Meltzer et al., p. 58).

In sum, none of the traditions examined use participant observation as the only method of data collection. One tradition does not use participant observation at all. One uses it for preliminary data collection to help identify units of analysis. Two traditions use it for preliminary data collection. And two traditions use it as a central method, along with other methods.

Discussion

Examination of the six traditions discussed above has shown that they present diverse approaches to qualitative research. The themes by which the educational literature has characterized qualitative research appear in varying ways among the different traditions.

Continuing to discuss qualitative research as if it were *one* approach can only increase the confusion in the education literature. The one-approach treatment has led to confusion and disagreement as authors have focused on identifying one set of "correct" features of qualitative research. The concept of traditions can help clear up this confusion by suggesting that different authors, drawing from different traditions or trying to present a transtradition approach, have focused on different features.

Viewing qualitative research as one approach may also lead to confusion when educational researchers study the noneducation literature in which qualitative traditions have developed. This literature confronts education scholars with diversity, not unity. Awareness of the various traditions will help educational researchers understand that the diversity is not a sign of misunderstanding or disagreement, but rather a reflection of various approaches.

Examining the differences among the traditions contributes to clarifying the discussion of qualitative research in education in another way. Not all the traditions cited in the education literature as examples of qualitative research seem to be appropriately treated as such. Specifically, human ethology, except for its emphasis on naturalistic description, follows a positivistic approach.

Awareness of traditions, I believe, is important not only to clarify qualitative research in education, but also to foster it. The one-approach view of qualitative research may inhibit this research by implying that researchers should incorporate all the features of qualitative research in any one research project. This may lead educational researchers who are uncomfortable with some of the features to reject qualitative research completely. In contrast, focus on the various traditions has shown that different themes represent different options for qualitative research, not invariable requirements. Moreover, these themes are implemented in varying ways by different traditions. Thus, researchers are presented with a range of research options, not just an all-or-nothing choice between qualitative research and positivistic research.

Educational discussions of qualitative research which treat it as one approach have focused on methods or assumptions, usually ignoring the issues of appropriate foci of study and levels of analysis. Both of these vary widely in the traditions examined above. Awareness of the different traditions can give educational researchers new viewpoints, open up new problems for study, and, in general, expand the range of ways available to address educational problems.

Work on this paper was supported in part by a summer stipend from George Mason University. I would like to thank Bruce Davis, David Fetterman, and Robert Stake for their helpful comments on drafts of the paper.

Notes

1. Although the six traditions discussed below are treated separately, they are not totally independent. For example, cognitive anthropology and ethnography of communication developed, in part, in response to what were seen as deficiencies in the holistic ethnography tradition. Symbolic interactionism is closely allied with cognitive anthropology in its emphasis on the cognitive aspects of culture. However, for our purposes here it is most useful to emphasize the differences rather than the similarities among the traditions.

2. Some recent work goes beyond the study of semantics to "multilexeme constructions interlinking items from disparate semantic domains" (Clement, 1976, p. 55). For some of this more recent work see Agar (1982), Clement, Dougherty (1985), and Holland (1985).

References

Agar, M. (1980). *The professional stranger: An informal introduction to ethnography*. New York: Academic Press.

Agar, M. (1982). Whatever happened to cognitive anthropology: A partial review. *Human Organization, 41,* 82–85.

Baker, R.G. (1968). *Ecological psychology: Concepts and methods for studying the environment of human behavior*. Stanford, CA: Stanford University Press.

Barker, R.G., Wright, H.F., Schoggen, M.F., & Barker, L.S. (1978). *Habitats, environments, and human behavior*. San Francisco: Jossey-Bass.

Barker, R.G., & Schoggen, P. (1973). *Qualities of community life: Methods of measuring environment and behavior applied to an American and an English town*. San Francisco: Jossey-Bass.

Barker, R.G., & Wright, H.F. (1955). *Midwest and its children*. New York: Harper & Row.

Barrett, R.A. (1984). *Culture and conduct: An excursion in anthropology*. Belmont, CA: Wadsworth.

Becker, H. (1970). *Sociological work: Methods and substance*. New Brunswick, NJ: Transaction Books.

Blumer, H. (1969). *Symbolic interactionism*. Englewood Cliffs, NJ: Prentice-Hall.

Blurton Jones, N. (1972). Characteristics of ethological studies of human behaviour. In N. Blurton Jones (Ed.), *Ethological studies of child behaviour* (pp. 33–30). Cambridge, England: Cambridge University Press.

Blurton Jones, N., & Woodson, R.H. (1979). Describing behavior: The ethologists' perspective. In M. Lamb, S.J. Suomi, & G.R. Stephenson (Eds.), *Social interaction analysis: Methodological issues* (pp. 97–118). Madison: University of Wisconsin Press.

Bogdan, R., & Biklen, S.K. (1982). *Qualitative research for education: An introduction to theory and methods*. Boston: Allyn and Bacon.

Bogdan, R., & Taylor, S. (1975). *Introduction to qualitative research methods*. New York: John Wiley & Sons.

Campbell, D.T. (1978). Qualitative knowing in action research. In M. Brenner, P. Marsh, & M. Brenner (Eds.), *The social contexts of method* (pp. 184–209). London: Croom Helm.

Charlesworth, W. (1978). Ethology: Its relevance for observational studies of human adaptation. In G. Sackett (Ed.), *Observing behavior: Vol. 1: Theory and applications in mental retardation* (pp. 7–32). Baltimore: University Park Press.

Clammer, J. (1984). Approaches to ethnographic research. In R.F. Ellen (Ed.), *Ethnographic research: A guide to general conduct* (pp. 63–85). London: Academic Press.

Clement, D. (1976). Cognitive anthropology and applied problems in education. In M.V. Angrosino (Ed.). *Do applied anthropologists apply anthropology?* (Southern Anthropological Society Proceedings, No. 10). Athens: University of Georgia Press.

Cronbach, L.J. (1975) Beyond the two disciplines of scientific psychology. *American Psychologist, 30,* 116–127.

Denzin, N.K. (1978). *The research act: A theoretical introduction to sociological methods.* New York: McGraw-Hill.

Dougherty. J.W.D. (Ed.). (1985). *Directions in cognitive anthropology.* Urbana: University of Illinois Press.

Edgerton, R.B., & Langness, L.L. (1974). *Methods and styles in the study of culture.* San Francisco: Chandler and Sharp.

Erickson, F. (1977). Some approaches to inquiry in school-community ethnography. *Anthropology and Education Quarterly. 8,* 58–69.

Erickson, F. (1986). Qualitative methods in research on teaching. In M.C. Wittrock (Ed.), *Handbook of research on teaching* (3rd ed., pp. 119–161). New York: Macmillan.

Erickson, F., & Mohatt, G. (1982). Cultural organization of participation structures in two classrooms of Indian students. In G. Spindler (Ed.), *Doing the ethnography of schooling: Educational anthropology in action* (pp. 132–174). New York: Holt, Rinehart, and Winston.

Erickson, F., & Schultz, J. (1981). When is a context? Some issues and methods in the analysis of social competence. In J. Green & C. Wallat (Eds.), *Ethnography and language in educational settings* (pp. 147–160). Norwood, NJ: Ablex.

Erickson, F., & Wilson, J. (1982). *Sights and sounds of life in schools: A resource guide to film and videotape for research and education* (Research Series No. 125). East Lansing: Michigan State University, College of Education, Institute for Research on Teaching.

Goodenough, W. (1971). *Culture, language, and society* (Addison-Wesley Module). Reading, MA: Addison-Wesley.

Guba, E., & Lincoln, Y. (1981). *Effective evaluation.* San Francisco: Jossey-Bass.

Gumperz, J. (1968). The speech community. In D.L. Sills (Ed.), *The international encyclopedia of the social sciences* (Vol. 9, pp. 381–386). New York: Macmillan & The Free Press.

Gutkind, P.C.W., Jongmans, D.G., Jonker, C., Kobben, A.J.F., Sankoff, G., & Serpenti, L.M. (1967). Annotated bibliography: Contents. In D.G. Jongmans & P.C.W. Gutkind (Eds.), *Anthropologists in the field* (pp. 217–271). Assen, The Netherlands: Van Gorcum.

Hinde, R.A. (1982). *Ethology: Its nature and relations with other sciences.* New York: Oxford University Press.

Hinde, R.A. (1983) Ethology and human development. In P. Mussen (Ed.), *Handbook of child psychology. Vol. II: Infancy and developmental psychology* (4th ed., pp. 27–93). New York: John Wiley & Sons.

Holland, D.C. (1985). From situation to impression: How Americans get to know themselves and one another. In J.W.D. Dougherty (Ed.), *Directions in cognitive anthropology* (pp. 389–411). Urbana: University of Illinois Press.

Hutt, S.J., & Hutt, C. (1970). *Direct observation and measurement of behavior.* Springfield, IL: Charles C. Thomas.

Hymes, D. (1972). Models of the interaction of language and social life. In J.J. Gumperz & D. Hymes (Eds.), *Directions in sociolinguistics: The ethnography of communication* (pp. 35–71). New York: Holt, Rinehart and Winston.

Hymes, D. (1974). *Foundations in sociolinguistics: An ethnographic approach.* Philadelphia: University of Pennsylvania Press.

Hymes, D. (1980). What is ethnography: In D. Hymes (Ed.), *Language in education: Ethnolinguistic essays* (pp. 88–103). Washington, DC: Center for Applied Linguistics.

Jacob, E. (1982). Combining ethnographic and quantitative approaches: Suggestions and examples from a study of Puerto Rico. In P. Gilmore & A. Glatthorn (Eds.), *Children in and out of school: Ethnography and education* (pp. 124–147). Washington, DC: Center for Applied Linguistics

Jacob, E. (1987). Traditions of qualitative research: A review. *Review of Educational Research, 57,* 1–50.

Jongmans, D.G., & Gutkind, P.C.W. (1967). *Anthropologists in the field.* Assen, The Netherlands: Van Gorcum.

Kuhn, T. (1970). *The structure of scientific revolutions* (2nd ed.). Chicago: University of Chicago Press.

LeVine, R.A. (1973). Research design in anthropological field work. In R. Naroll & R. Cohen (Eds.), *A handbook of method in cultural anthropology* (pp. 183–195). New York: Columbia University Press. (Original work published 1970).

Lincoln, Y., & Guba, E. (1985). *Naturalistic inquiry.* Beverly Hills, CA: Sage.

Lutz, F., & Ramsey, M. (1974). The use of anthropological field methods in education. *Educational Researcher, 3*(10), 5–9.

Magoon, A.J. (1977). Constructivist approaches in educational research. *Review of Educational Research, 47,* 651–693.

Malinowski, B. (1961). *Argonauts of the western Pacific.* New York: E.P. Dutton. (Original work published 1922).

Manis, J., & Meltzer, B. (Eds.). (1978). *Symbolic interaction: A reader in social psychology* (3rd ed.). Boston: Allyn and Bacon.

McGrew, W. (1972). *An ethological study of children's behavior.* New York: Academic Press.

Mead, M. (1973). The art and technology of fieldwork. In R. Narroll & R. Cohen (Eds.), *A handbook of method in cultural anthropology* (pp. 246–265). New York: Columbia University Press. (Original work published 1970).

Mehan, H. (1979). *Learning lessons: Social organization in the classroom.* Cambridge, MA: Harvard University Press.

Mehan, H. (1984). Language and schooling. *Sociology of Education, 57,* 174–183.

Meltzer, B.N., Petras, J.W., & Reynolds, L.T. (1975). *Symbolic interactionism: Genesis, varieties and criticism.* London: Routledge and Kegan Paul.

Patton, M.O. (1980). *Qualitative evaluation methods.* Beverly Hills, CA: Sage.

Pelto, P. (1970). *Anthropological research: The structure of inquiry.* New York: Harper and Row.

Philips, S.U. (1983). *The invisible culture: Communication in classroom and community on the Warm Springs Indian Reservation.* New York: Longman.

Rist, R. (1977). On the relations among educational research paradigms: From disdain to detente. *Anthropology & Education quarterly, 8,* 42–49.

Ritzer, G. (1983). *Sociological theory.* New York: Alfred Knopf.

Rose, A. (1962). A systematic summary of symbolic interaction theory. In A. Rose (Ed.), *Human behavior and social processes* (pp. 3–19). Boston: Houghton Mifflin.

Sanday, P.R. (1979). The ethnographic paradigm(s). *Administrative Science Quarterly, 24,* 527–538.

Schatzman, L. & A.L. Strauss. (1973). *Field research: Strategies for a natural sociology.* Englewood Cliffs, NJ: Prentice-Hall.

Schoggen, P. (1978). Ecological psychology and mental retardation. In G. Sackett (Ed.), *Observing behavior. Vol. I. Theory and applications in mental retardation* (pp. 33–62). Baltimore: University Park Press.

Smith, J.K. (1983). Quantitative versus qualitative research: An attempt to clarify the issue. *Education Researcher, 12*(3), 6–13.

Smith, L. (1978). An evolving logic of participant observation, educational ethnography, and other case studies. In L.S. Shulman (Ed.), *Review of research in education* (Vol. 6, pp. 316–377). Ithasca, IL: F.E. Peacock, for the American Educational Research Association.

Smith, P.K. (2974). Ethological methods. In B. Foss (Ed.), *New perspectives in child development* (pp. 85–137). Harmondsworth, England: Penguin.

Smith, P.K., & Connolly, K. (1972). Patterns of play and social interaction in pre-school children. In N. Blurton Jones (Ed.), *Ethological studies of child behaviour* (pp. 65–95). Cambridge, England: Cambridge University Press.

Spradley, J. (1972). Foundations of cultural knowledge. In J.P. Spradley (Ed.), *Culture and cognition: Rules, maps, and plans* (pp. 3–38). San Francisco: Chandler.

Spradley, J. (1979). *The ethnographic interview.* New York: Holt, Rinehart and Winston.

Spradley, J. (1980). *Participant observation.* New York: Holt, Rinehart and Winston.

Tyler, S. (1969). Introduction. In. S. Tyler (Ed.), *Cognitive anthropology* (pp. 1–23). New York: Holt, Rinehart and Winston.

Wilson, S. (1977). The use of ethnographic techniques in educational research. *Review of Educational Research, 47,* 245–265.

Wright, H.F. (1967). *Recording and analyzing child behavior.* New York: Harper and Row.

Using Alternative Paradigms: Four Case Studies

JOHN H. MILAM, JR.

Part I

Introduction

Most of the scholarship on paradigms in higher education is devoted to defining a specific language of assumptions, including the constructivist, critical theory, ethnocentric, ethnographic, Eurocentric, feminist, functionalist, interpretive, liberationist, Neo-Marxist, phenomenological, post-modernist, post-positivist, post-structuralist, radical humanist, and radical sociology paradigms. Although some scholars such as Attinasi (1990), Barrow (1991), Glazer (1990), Lincoln (1989), Tierney (1991), and Townsend (1991) acknowledge specific paradigm assumptions as being central to their work, little research has been done which explores the fundamental tensions between paradigms and how these relate to the conduct of research in higher education. Part of the problem may be that few scholars adopt the same language of assumptions which would allow them to make sense of and explore different paradigm points of view at the same time. There are numerous examples of scholars engaged in dialogue about the differences between paradigms. However, most battle maps for the "paradigm wars" are one-sided.

The purpose of this chapter is to contribute to this paradigm dialogue, not by offering yet another set of definitions, but by presenting case studies which use the critical lenses of different research perspectives. This design for case studies is based, in part, on an idea which Morgan (1983) had for a conference on organizational inquiry. He hoped that participants would critically examine methodologies of organizational research using the Burrell and Morgan (1979) paradigm schema. The complexities of researchers' perspectives did not fit easily into the paradigm definitions, however, and the participants abandoned Morgan's plan. Morgan asked:

> Was it possible to learn something from the assumptions underlying the different research perspectives? Although each perspective offered a logically coherent and internally consistent argument for conducting research in a particular way, this argument was ultimately derived from the ground assumptions on which it was based. Was it possible to raise and debate these assumptions? (Morgan, 1983, pp. 15–16).

The Burrell and Morgan (1979) paradigm schema has been shown to be useful in understanding the meta-theoretical assumptions of the core, higher education journal literature (Milam, 1991). With case studies of actual research within each paradigm, it may be possible to understand how scholars with an alternative paradigm might generate different research questions, assumptions, methods, and possibly findings. Perhaps interesting relationships, tensions, linkages, and dissonance between paradigms may be better understood by putting these questions in the context of actual research.

This chapter is divided into three sections. First, the theoretical framework of Burrell and Morgan (1979) for analyzing paradigms is presented. The literature about scholars' attitudes toward research perspectives is also discussed (Lincoln, 1989; Morgan, 1983; Schwandt, 1989; and Schwartz and Ogilvy, 1979). Next, four sets of case studies are presented which examine and critique examples of research from different paradigm perspectives. Finally, the results of the case studies are discussed. The dialogue about research which occurs in the case studies is analyzed according to the literature on attitudes about paradigms. The cognitive development theories of Perry (1970, 1981) and Belenky, Clinchy, Goldberger, and Tarule (1986) are suggested as metaphors to portray possible positions, stages, or levels of paradigm development.

Theoretical Background

Burrell and Morgan

In their work *Sociological Paradigms and Organizational Analysis*, Burrell and Morgan (1979) analyze organizational theory according to a two-dimensional paradigm schema. See Clark (1985), Conrad (1989), Griffiths (1983), and Milam (1989, 1991) for discussion of this schema for educational administration and higher education. Central to the Burrell and Morgan conception of paradigms is their belief that all social theories are based upon both a philosophy of science and a theory of the social world. These may be thought of in terms of different sets of implicit and explicit assumptions.

In the dimension of social science, the authors identify four types of assumptions:

(1)   ontological assumptions about the nature and essence of what is being studied: *realism* versus *nominalism*:

(2)   epistemological assumptions about the grounds for understanding knowledge: *positivism* versus *anti-positivism*;

(3)   assumptions concerning human nature, about the relationship between human beings and their environment: *determinism* versus *voluntarism*;

(4)   methodological assumptions about the ways to study and gather information about the social world: *nomothetic* versus *idiographic* methods.

These sets of opposite assumptions make up two sides of the social science dimension, which Burrell and Morgan label as the objective and the subjective. Methodological approaches which represent the objective approach include such techniques as causal modeling, survey questionnaires, and integrative literature reviews. Possible examples of subjective social science could include naturalistic inquiry, ethnography, and grounded theory building.

In the authors' work, sociological theory is considered under one of two mutually exclusive categories—the *sociology of regulation* versus the *sociology of radical change*. Regulation sociology is interested in understanding why society works the way it does and with integrating its mechanism and processes. Radical change sociology is based on the premise that conflict and contradiction are inherent in society and must form the basis for any social analysis The seven sets of assumptions are identified as follows:

(1)   Regulation sociology concerns the *status quo*, the way things currently are, and ways to maintain the patterns of the social system as a whole. Radical sociology is concerned with all elements of *radical change*, both at the structural level and at the level of subjective consciousness.

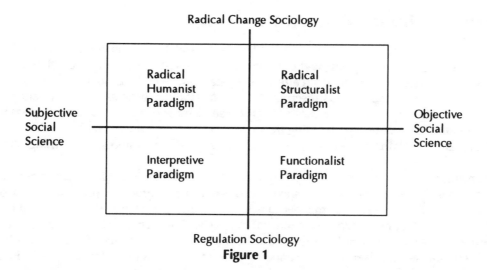

Figure 1

(2)   Understanding and maintaining the functions and processes of the *social order* is the concern of regulation sociology, where radical sociology identifies *conflicts* such as class, gender, and race which are imbedded in the fabric of society.

(3)   Regulation sociologists believe that values are developed autonomously. *Consensus* in terms of shared values regarded as a positive indication of integration. Radical sociologists believe that shared values are the result of modes of *domination*.

(4)   In regulation sociology, the *social integration and cohesion* of society are of primary concern. The radical sociology position recognizes that heterogeneity, imbalance, antagonistic and divergent forces are at work, ant that these contribute to social, economic, and other kinds of structural *contradictions*.

(5)   Maintaining the *solidarity* of how the patterns of society hold together is important to regulation sociology. *Emancipation* from the structures which limit potential is the concern of radical sociology.

(6)   Where regulation sociology is interested in the *need satisfaction* of society as an organism, radical sociology focuses on psychic and material forms of *deprivation* and how the system erodes human fulfillment.

(7)   Regulation sociology is rooted in understanding society as it already is, implicitly legitimizing the *actuality* of the status quo. Radical sociology offers visionary *potentiality* with alternatives to conflicts and contradictions.

Burrell and Morgan visualize their paradigm schema (Figure 1) as a grid with two dimensions and four cells. The four paradigms are defined by their position within the two dimensions of social science and sociology. The *functionalist* paradigm is based in objective social science and regulation sociology. The *radical structuralist* paradigm is also based in objective social science, but is rooted in radical change sociology. The *interpretive* and *radical humanist* paradigms both operate with subjective social science assumptions. While the interpretive paradigm is concerned with regulation sociology, the radical humanist holds a radical change sociological perspective.

Scholars' Attitudes Toward Paradigms

The extensive scholarship by Lincoln (1985, 1986, 1989) and Lincoln and Guba (1985, 1989) on naturalistic inquiry, constructivism, and paradigms is a frequent starting point in scholars' discussions of the methodological choices and alternative paradigms which guide their work. Analyzing paradigm evolution in the various disciplines, Lincoln (1989) identifies four different types of attitudes toward multiple paradigm discussions. These include: denying that the debate is important; recognizing the debate, but affirming the primacy of the scientific method; denying that there is a debate, and continuing as always; and intense curiosity and interest in learning about the debate.

According to Lincoln, scholars who critique paradigms fall into four categories: those who feel that traditional methods are impoverished and need more richness; those who focus on the exclusion of gender in research, as this pertains to values and the portrayal of women; those who make an exception for one or two new axioms of inquiry within their existing paradigm; and those who are able to see a whole paradigm, discarding former methods of inquiry for a new world view.

In discussing approaches to understanding multiple paradigms, Morgan (1983) identifies attitudes among scholars which he labels as supremacy, synthesis, dialectic, contingency, and anything goes. In supremacy, there is a search for the merits of one method or perspective over another. Scholars challenge assumptions to refine a research strategy. This approach "encounters the same kind of relativism as that with which it is trying to deal" (p. 378). In synthesis, scholars work to find an optimum way to do research within an all-embracing paradigm, combining the strengths of some approaches and minimizing the weaknesses of others. The dialectical attitude recognizes that a diversity of approaches is inevitable. Scholars need to work with multisided approaches, counterpoising insights in order for new debates to emerge, and seeking a kind of theoretical pluralism. Another attitude, labeled contingency, involves the recognition that there is no one best set of assumptions. Research tools are used in a practical way according to their usefulness. Competing insights are used in complex analysis, and there is no search for foundational truth. A final attitude, labeled "Anything Goes" is one of complete relativism, believing that synthesis is unnecessary. Theoretical and methodological anarchy is welcomed. Only the researcher is in the position to choose an approach.

Schwandt (1989) modifies the work of Morgan (1983) in an article entitled "Solutions to the Paradigm Conflict: Coping with Uncertainty." He suggests slightly different attitudes about multiple paradigms: Denial, refusing to admit the problem; Co-optation, acknowledging paradigm differences but claiming that they are resolvable; Supremacy, claiming that one paradigm is ultimately better than another; Replacement, creating a new paradigm that blends the tensions between others; Primacy of method, extracting methods away from philosophy and science into a vision of problem solving, with the choice of methods as the primary concern; and Anarchism, admitting no authority to any paradigm and resisting the search for an ideal.

Cognitive Development Theory

Cognitive development theory also provides a lens for viewing the attitudes of scholars toward multiple paradigm discussions. The work of Perry (1970, 1981) on stages and levels of cognitive and ethical student development offers a language for discussing dualism and relativism. Belenky, Clinchy, Goldberger, and Tarule (1986) act on the criticisms of Gilligan (1982) and suggest that the metaphor of "finding a voice" is useful in mapping women's development. Working with Moore, Thompson (1991) combines Perry with Belenky et al. in a revision of the Perry scheme used for student assessment at Evergreen State College. According to Thompson (1991, pp. 2–3), this does not fundamentally revise the cognitive epistemology used by Perry, but serves "to incorporate contemporary learning styles and styles of expression (along the lines of Belenky et al.)."

Perry's stages are labeled as dualism modified, relativism discovered, and commitment in relativism. The key terms are dualism, multiplicity, relativism, and commitment. Explained simply, dualism divides meanings as right or wrong. Multiplicity recognizes that diverse opinions are legitimate when right answers are unknown. Relativism sees the full diversity of opinions, values, and judgments, viewing knowledge as "qualitative, dependent on context" (Perry, 1981, p. 80). Commitment involves decisions or choices made with awareness of relativism. These stages are broken out into nine positions, with the positions considered as less important to development than the transitions. The nine positions are labeled as: (1) basic duality; (2) multiplicity prelegitimate; (3) multiplicity legitimate but subordinate; (4) multiplicity correlate or relativism subordinate; (5) relativism correlate, competing or diffuse; (6) commitment foreseen; (7) initial commitment; (8) orientation in implications of commitment; and (9) developing commitments.

Belenky, Clinchy, Goldberger, and Tarule (1986) find metaphors for voice within women's development. These include: silence, received knowledge, subjective knowledge, procedural knowledge, and constructed knowledge. The reader should refer to the case study for definitions of these five metaphors of voice. Thompson (1991) presents modifications of positions two through five of the Perry scheme in his monograph *Learning at Evergreen*. Position two is relabeled as dualism or received knowledge. Knowledge is "information from Authorities" and is basically dualistic. Position three is relabeled as early multiplicity, or separate, procedural knowing. It is recognized that some answers are unknown. There is no sense of relationships between methods. Position four is relabeled as late multiplicity, or subjective and connected knowing. Concerned with "how to think," students recognize diversity of opinions. Authorities "are observed to differ because of their methods and assumptions, and particularly their gender, class, and culture, afford competing points of view" (Thompson, 1991, p. 3). Two sub-positions are suggested—an oppositional stance and an adherent stance. Position five is relabeled contextual relativism or constructivism, and involves metathinking, or "thinking about thinking." The belief in absolute knowledge is suspended, though it is possible to construct "tentative theories and models, some of which are demonstrably more appropriate than others to the context at hand" (p. 4).

Case Studies

Four case studies were developed as part of this author's dissertation research (Milam, 1989) and were revised for the purposes of this chapter. Each case study represents an example of research from one of the four Burrell and Morgan paradigms and consists of four parts.

These examples were located as part of a larger content analysis of the core, higher education journal literature (Milam, 1991). To determine the paradigmatic content of a piece of higher education research, 64 content analysis questions were used to look for implicit meta-theoretical assumptions. The language for each question comes directly from key phrases in the Burrell and Morgan definitions. Decision rules and dichotomous, a priori coding categories are used to catalog examples within the four paradigms, two dimensions, and eleven sets of assumptions. The content analysis techniques are chosen to ensure validity and replicability through extensive documentation and coding notes, peer debriefing, use of a methodological log, and memo-writing. The trustworthiness of the human author as a coding instrument is assessed and refined through pilot testing of the questions, memo-writing techniques, and decision rules.

Examples for case studies of the functionalist and radical structuralist paradigms were located in the content analysis of the journal literature. Other sources were required to locate a useful piece of research from the radical humanist and interpretive paradigm perspectives. All four research examples are coded as having a majority of the assumptions in their paradigm definitions for the social science and sociology dimensions.

Pascarella, Ethington, and Smart's (1988) article entitled "The Influence of College on Humanitarian/Civic Involvement Values" was chosen to represent the functionalist paradigm. For the radical structuralist paradigm, Loo and Rolison's (1986) article entitled "Alienation of Ethnic Minority Students at a Predominantly White University" was selected. Logan's (1988) article entitled "A Study of Four Undergraduate Computer-Writers" is an example of the interpretive paradigm. The monograph *Women's Ways of Knowing: The Development of Self, Voice, and Mind* by Belenky, Clinchy, Goldberger, and Tarule (1986) serves as an example of the radical humanist paradigm.

The first part of each case study consists of a synopsis of the research problem, methodology, and findings, using the language of assumptions of its particular paradigm. The research is then critiqued according to the critical lenses and language of the three alternative paradigms. The product of each case study consists of four different treatments of the same topic.

Part II

Functionalist Case Study: College's Influence on Values

Pascarella, Ethington, and Smart's (1988) article entitled "The Influence of College on Humanitarian/Civic Involvement Values" represents an example of research in the functionalist paradigm. The authors present a longitudinal, causal model based on the work of Tinto, Astin and Kent, Lacy, and Chickering. This model posits that the type of institution attended by a student is a function of precollege characteristics, and that precollege characteristics and institution attended together influence many aspects of the college experience. Different college outcome characteristics are viewed as a function of these variables.

In order to observe the impact of institutional characteristics, the authors restricted the sample of students to those who had attended only one institution. The 4,843 students were enrolled in 379 four-year colleges and universities. Longitudinal data were collected from responses to the 1971 Cooperative Institutional Research Program (CIRP) Freshmen Survey and to the 1980 CIRP Postcollege Survey. HEGIS files were used to gather matching institutional data.

The student precollege variables include: (1) scores on the 1971 humanitarian/civic involvement values measure, a factorially derived scale; (2) family socio-economic status (SES); (3) age; (4) secondary school achievement; and (5) secondary school social accomplishment. The institutional characteristics include: (6) selectivity; (7) size; and (8) whether the college or university is predominantly black. The college experience variables include: (9) whether the student is a social science major; (10) college grade point average; (11) social leadership experiences; and (12) familiarity with faculty/staff. Student post-college variables include: (13) highest degree attained; and (14) whether the student is employed in a social service occupation.

The dependent measure consists of scores on the 1980 humanitarian/civic involvement values measure, which uses the same 1971 scale. One post-college variable, employment in a social service occupation, is added to the 1980 survey. In the causal model, the measure of social leadership experiences is defined as the sum of four items assessing involvement. These include self-reports of being president of a student organization, serving on an university or department committee, editing a publication, or having a major part in a play. The 1971 and 1980 values involvement scales are based on the personal importance of six activities associated with civic and humanitarian involvement. These include activities such as cleaning up the environment, helping others who are in difficulty, participating in a community action program, becoming a community leader, influencing social values, and influencing the political structure.

The GEMINI statistical computer program is used by the authors to calculate indirect effects and estimate their significance. Structural equations are used to regress endogenous variables on exogenous variables and other antecedent endogenous variables in the causal model. These equations produce standardized and metric regression weights which are interpreted as direct effects. Preliminary analyses are performed to test whether or not direct effects vary by race and/or sex.

The results of the equations show that the causal model explains between 12.6 and 18.8 percent of the variance in scores on the 1980 humanitarian/civic involvement scale, depending on the subgroup population. Of the precollege variables, scores on the 1971 values measure are the only predictor which has a significant direct effect on all four sub-groups' 1980 scores. Most of the influence of these variables is indirect. None of the institutional characteristics has a significant direct effect on scores. Of the college experience variables, only social leadership experience shows a significant direct effect for all groups but black women. Some "pronounced racial differences" are found in the direct effects of the educational attainment and occupational outcome variables. For example, the effect on values development of being in a social service occupation is greater for whites than blacks. For whites, post-college employment has an impact on values development "above and beyond the influence of student precollege characteristics and the college experience"; whereas, for blacks, occupation has "little incremental impact on black student values"(p. 432). Highest academic degree awarded also has a significant indirect effect only for white males and females.

Based on the results, the authors conclude that "neither institutional selectivity nor predominant race had other than a trivial influence on the development of humanitarian/civic values" (p. 429). This means that:

> Irrespective of individual student race or gender, the humanizing of individual values is no more likely to occur at a selective college than at a nonselective college; nor does it appear to be much influenced by the institution's racial composition (p. 429).

Secondly, the findings suggest that;

> . . . the undergraduate college experience had a significant unique impact on the humanizing of values that is independent of the individual characteristics the student brings to college, the selectivity, size and predominant race of the institution attended, and subsequent educational attainment and postcollegiate occupation (p. 429).

Finally, Pascarella et al. conclude that: (1) social involvement has a positive impact on the development of humanitarian and civic values; (2) the type of involvement which most contributes to values development differs by race and sex; and (3) the indirect effects of outcome variables should be considered, since there are few direct effects.

Criticism of the Pascarella Study Employing the Interpretive Paradigm

From an interpretive standpoint, Pascarella et al.'s attempt to define variables and data elements of civic and humanitarian involvement values is futile and the use of sophisticated data analytic techniques inappropriate. To begin, the four sets of "variables" used in the causal model are simply labels for making sense of the world. Such data variables as "secondary school achievement" and "civic involvement values" are not "real." They are the result of the researchers' perceptions of the social world. In other words, Pascarella et al. fail to recognize that student experiences in college are the product of individual cognition and that reality is a social construction. Psychological processes of student and adult development are much more complicated than this research study allows for, or than most models and theories of student, adult, or human development allow for.

To an interpretive researcher, theory should be used differently than is done in this study. The interpretive researcher sees the need for grounded theory and theory as it relates to particularized situations, but the generalizability of theory is viewed as problematic. Functionalist researchers like Pascarella et al. believe that knowledge is expanded by the accumulation of new theories. This is why the research of Astin and Kent, Chickering, and Tinto is cited as a foundation of the study. However, the development of knowledge is not always a cumulative process.

Another criticism concerns the way in which civic and humanitarian values are separated out from other types of attitudes and values. How do the definitions used for humanitarian and civic values differ from other values? Why were these definitions chosen? The study places singular importance on one measure: graduates having been employed in a social service occupation. Is this to say that people employed in other occupations do not hold similar values? The scale used to measure values involvement consists of student responses to how important they rate "activities" associated with civic and humanitarian involvement. Hundreds of other college activities which are important to student development could have been included. The inherent value judgments of the CIRP survey must be questioned.

In their deterministic search for cause and effect relationships, the researchers are interested in environmental and situational behavioralism. The authors find a correlation between participation in an elite handful of social activities and scores on the values scale. An interpretive researcher would ask: Why are these "social leadership activities" particularly meaningful in terms of long-range values development. These activities seem to have been taken from an outdated image of college life. Also, there is no sense of the cultural diversity of human lives in a large university setting.

Where the results are interpreted in terms of direct and indirect effects, the researchers should have been looking from an interpretivist perspective into possible patterns and regularities. There is no need to "prove" anything about development, to establish one correct causal model. Pascarella et al. should have turned to qualitative techniques found in ethnography and naturalistic inquiry to examine research questions related to values and attitudes. Individual human nature and values development can only be understood from the point of view of students.

The findings of the study are suspect. For example, the interpretation is made that, for black alumni, post-college occupation has "little incremental impact on black student values" (p 429). It is shown that the type of job obtained by blacks makes little difference to the values they hold about civic life and humanitarian concerns. This generalization is not credible. Of course employment has an effect on values, as does income level. What is important is not statistically measuring the degree of indirect effect for subgroups, but investigating and understanding the nature of racial differences in occupational outcome and educational attainment. The pre-existing constructs of the survey items may have prevented the researchers from exploring the pertinent, subjective data about students.

Another questionable finding is that there is no difference between traditionally black institutions and predominantly white institutions in how individual values are humanized. Certainly it is likely that the culture and experiences of the two institutional types differ greatly, just as the lives of black and white students differ. If the authors want to draw conclusions about black and white students in these institutions, then they should study real people, not just match HEGIS data to 15-year-old CIRP data. It seems as if the CIRP database guided the inquiry more than did any a priori research question and design.

In addition, from an interpretivist perspective, institutions are more relativistic than the authors are willing to admit. This apparent lack of appreciation for institutional complexity is evident in the interpretation that institutional selectivity has no influence on values. Selectivity does make a difference in how students develop values because this factor is related to many other things—institutional resources, diversity of the student body, quality of the faculty, and the role of teaching in the mission of the institution, to name a few. All of these aspects of the complex college world need to be taken into account. To isolate one aspect of college in a causal model is like looking at a painting without being able to see the picture as a whole, because the viewer is engrossed in trying to identify and label the brushes and pigments the artist used.

Criticism of the Pascarella Study Employing the Radical Structuralist Paradigm

In the Pascarella study, values development is portrayed as an autonomous, voluntary, and spontaneous process; it is not. Radical structuralists assume that values are ordinarily imposed on some members of society by others. From this perspective, the question needs to be asked: Whose values are these that the authors are promoting? A radical structuralist analysis may show that the ideal humanitarian and civic involvement values promoted by Pascarella et al. are those of white, Anglo-Saxon, Protestant, middle class males between the ages of 18 and 22 attending quality, four-year institutions. It is important to note that, although the sample may have been random and diverse in sub-population representation, the causal model of values development is not that complex.

The article assumes that all students should hold the values of wanting to become involved in certain civic and humanitarian involvement activities. If students come to share these values, then the college environment is assumed to have been successful in its mission of student development. For the radical structuralist, these shared values are a sign of the success of the forces of domination. Individual values are subordinated for dominant values.

From a radical structuralist perspective, Pascarella et al. do not adequately recognize that many subtle forms of coercion are involved in the manipulation and control of students in order for them to develop the "correct" values. A number of economic, political, religious, and social forces work to socialize and indoctrinate students. What Pascarella and Astin label as "social leadership experiences," radical structuralists might term "conditioning." Student involvement in these traditional leadership activities reinforces norms and dominant codes of behavior by which students are taught to lead their lives.

The theoretical frameworks used for analyzing student involvement and student development are inadequate because these theories are fixed, stagnant, and overly rigid in their view of the human condition. This kind of research does not generate any new alternatives, nor is it truly concerned with student potential. Growth and development are considered by functionalists as everyday processes. Change is thought to be an ordinary, empirical reality. That Pascarella failed to introduce any form of radical change as a process in students' lives is understandable—due to the total lack of attention paid to the conflicts and contradictions embedded in college society. In fact, values of blacks, whites, men and women are discussed without any reference to the contradictions among and between these different groups. The authors introduce variables of sex and race in the way all functionalists do. They do not understand or take into account the manner in which their limited view of gender and race issues affects the results. The college experiences of men and women will vary significantly because women are oppressed by a patriarchal society and because minorities are discriminated against. It is also necessary to account for the impact on students' lives of oppression from other sources, such as political systems, economic status, sexual orientation, family structures, and religious beliefs.

The authors find "pronounced racial differences" in educational attainment and occupational outcome. Of course whites go on to graduate and professional school at a greater rate. They do not face the same patterns of discrimination. Minorities do not have the same opportunities to hold elite, social service jobs. Instead, they are forced by the system to take lower-status, service employment. The study implies that all things are equal for those with a four-year college degree. What about "pronounced economic class differences" between low-income and high-income students and the effect of these on educational attainment and occupational outcomes?

Another example of differences in the viewpoints held by the radical structuralist and the functionalist is found in the way in which the authors interpret their finding that "predominant race" had only a trivial influence on values development. Is this to mean that there is no difference between predominantly white and traditionally black institutions when it comes to student development of values? Certainly, the environment faced by blacks in white universities is much less conducive to positive growth and development of self-esteem than that of black institutions, which support and nurture a community based in black culture. This finding is probably not accurate. Race does have a significant effect on values development.

The finding that none of the institutional characteristics has an effect on values development is only accurate from the point of view of the authors' narrow, functionalist definition of values. If the researchers had paid attention to institutional characteristics as these affect values through forces of domination, deprivation, and oppression, then significant direct and indirect effects would probably have been found. Once it is clear whose values are being reinforced, then findings may point out that predominantly white institutions cause greater problems for black students in terms of alienation of values than do traditionally black institutions. A different kind of institutional selectivity may, indeed, have a significant effect on values. Institutions may select those students who will fit into their value systems, and reject those who would challenge the value structure. Institutional selectivity probably does have a significant effect on values development.

A radical structuralist would not question the finding that participation in social leadership activities has a significant influence on values. The finding would be turned around, though, to question whether the influence is actually negative, not positive. Perhaps participation in such activities works in the other direction. Participation in these activities represents training in and acceptance of a particular political philosophy with inherent oppressive features which are ignored here.

The researchers could not change the data elements used in the original 1971 CIRP surveys. It may have been possible for them to have had input into the post-college 1980 survey. If they had the opportunity, they might have included items to determine whether black and women students had a "choice" in their having joined a service profession, or whether it is the only job they could get. Which of the "social service" jobs are high status and which are dead-end? Too many questions about social tensions are not addressed in the Pascarella study.

Criticism of the Pascarella Study
Employing the Radical Humanist Paradigm

The Pascarella study fails to recognize the major theme of radical humanism: the alienation of human consciousness through domination by ideological superstructures. A radical humanist critique of the research addresses radical change issues of alienation, domination, deprivation, and oppression at the level of subjective consciousness. Each of these must be considered as part of any study of civic and humanitarian involvement values in college students.

In their functionalist perspective, the authors use data elements in the causal model to understand what happens to college students in their development of values. However, no such data elements as "socio-economic status" and "secondary school achievement" actually exist. These variables are a creation of the researcher, labels without meanings except for what the researchers assign to them. The only discernible data element to be studied is "human consciousness." The realist ontology needs to be exchanged in favor of a more nominalist perspective if the study is to deal with human beings.

From a radical change standpoint, consciousness is dominated by ideological superstructures which drive a wedge between the self and true consciousness. Radical humanists hope to change the social world by releasing consciousness from these forms of domination. Embedded in the functionalist sociology of regulation, this study offers little in understanding this dialectic of consciousness.

Idiographic methods would have been much more appropriate where nomothetic, quantitative methods are used. To the radical humanist, quantitative tests, measurements, and instruments do not fit the subjective nature of how civic and humanitarian values are developed in the consciousness of college students. Pascarella et al.'s positivist search for laws, causal relationships, and empirical hypotheses is without utility. The social world can only be understood by getting close to students' lives, by entering their frame of reference through such qualitative approaches as naturalistic inquiry and ethnography. The quantitative data gathering and analytic techniques chosen for this study are mismatched to the true purpose of such research, which is to understand the place of values in consciousness.

From a radical humanist point of view, the civic and humanitarian values discussed in the Pascarella article are part of the ideological constructions set up to control people by telling them how they should be and act in society. If students hold the "right" values about civic life, then they will want to influence other people's values and the political structure. The authors legitimize this form of domination. A radical humanist researcher would ask: Where do these ideals come from? Where does the language of values originate in the first place? What is the significance of this essentialist philosophy of cultural transmission within the mission of higher education? What purposes do values as an ideological construction serve in colleges and universities and in the larger society? To the radical humanist, all such ideological norms serve to alienate consciousness.

Radical humanist researchers would challenge the whole concept of what is being explored with the four sets of variables. From their perspective, the pre-college characteristics would fail to account for how human beings become alienated from their own selves. The variables on institutional characteristics would fail to recognize the ideological superstructures which stunt and limit potential. College experiences are discussed without any mention of contradictions and conflicts among different college constituencies Finally, the post-college occupation variables consist of two elitist measures, degree attainment and employment in a social service occupation, neither of which acknowledges the inherent inequality and inequity of occupational class.

Pascarella et al. appear to have only a minimal understanding of how higher education has become a sort of "psychic prison" when they analyze the negative "psychosocial" effects of institutional size. Such psychosocial effects are part of the profound sense of alienation experienced by students.

None of the empirical findings of the study hold up to the scrutiny of the radical humanist's expectations for subjective social science and radical sociology. Too much is going on in the college world to expect that scores on the 1971 CIRP survey are any indication of values development. The college world is too complex for this kind of neat, sequential prediction. Similarly, the statement that institutional characteristics, especially selectivity and predominant race, have no significant effect on values development is not credible. Of course, all of these factors and many more will influence any individual's attitudes and values about civic life and humanitarian concerns. The oppressive nature of these factors, such as the world of discrimination at a southern, predominantly white university, will certainly affect values formation. Human actions are just too complex to be explained in a linear, causal model of values development.

The authors' findings about racial differences in educational attainment and occupational outcomes are probably useful on a surface level. Racial differences, as discussed in these findings, fail to include larger issues such as Afrocentricity. A radical humanist critique of this study might agree with the findings as somewhat true; but would have to ask: So what? The findings do not tell the reader about the sociological problems faced by minority students. That social leadership activities have an effect on values development seems correct on the surface. Generalization of these findings to other contexts is not appropriate.

Radical Structuralist Case Study: Alienation of Ethnic Minorities

The article by Loo and Rolison (1986) entitled "Alienation of Ethnic Minority Students at a Predominantly White University" was chosen to represent the radical structuralist paradigm. This article begins with an analysis of the social processes and structures which influence the university environment for ethnic minority students. The authors recognize that goals for civil rights and equal access have not been realized for ethnic minorities. They suggest that some of the forces which preclude equal opportunity and academic success are ethnic isolation, sociocultural alienation, malintegration, racism, discrimination, cultural domination, and socioeconomic class disadvantages. Tinto's concept of academic and social integration is applied to the study of ethnic minorities in predominantly white institutions. What Tinto terms malintegration, Loo and Rolison define as alienation. The authors depart from Tinto in their focus on academic alienation, examining "perceptions of academic difficulty and satisfaction" instead of grade performance. Willie's theory of race relations also guides the research.

A small, public university in the University of California system was chosen as the site for the study. This institution has unique features which make it appropriate for the research problem, including "segregated" cluster colleges, a disproportionately small number of minorities, and nontraditional use of narrative evaluations in place of grades.

Semi-structured interviews are considered to be an appropriate data gathering method, because "for a sensitive topic like alienation, interviews that used ethnically relevant, open and closed questions were deemed preferable to alienation scales" (p. 62). Random sampling and stratification are used to choose students for interviews. Intentional oversampling of the minority population is done in order to detect differences between minority groups. The final sample consists of 163 undergraduate students, of whom 67 percent are members of minority groups and 33 percent are white. Examination of between group differences in the data is done with Chi-Square analyses.

For the most part, the interviewing is done by students of the same race. This is an important consideration, the authors argue, because with white interviewers there may be a "tendency" for "responses to be affected by a 'white socially desirable bias'" (p. 63). A structured schedule of both closed and open-ended questions is used. These questions are broken out into six theoretically derived categories, including sociocultural alienation, academic difficulties, thoughts of dropping out, academic satisfaction, university supportiveness and unsupportiveness, and ethnic representation.

Demographic characteristics are described first. The authors show that white and minority students differ significantly in terms of class backgrounds, parental occupation and education, ethnicity of home community, and whether the university's location is their hometown. They conclude that minority students feel significantly greater sociocultural alienation than do white students. Approximately 40 percent of the minorities interviewed state that their values are reflected just "a little" or "not at all" by the university. Greater social isolation is also experienced by these students.

A majority of the black and Chicano students interviewed believe that minorities experience greater academic difficulties than whites. White students' perceptions of these difficulties for minorities are evenly divided, with 53 percent believing that whites face the same difficulties as minorities. Academic difficulties are traced by some Chicano and black students to poor high school preparation. Others point to the socioeconomic and cultural differences between minorities and whites as variables affecting academic problems. Some ethnic minorities say that they have to deal with a kind of "culture shock" which requires them to expend energies that could go to other things.

There are no significant differences between the percentages of white and minority students who consider dropping out, but there are differences in the reasons for leaving. White students usually think about dropping out because of academic factors. For ethnic minorities, sociocultural alienation is as much a reason for dropping out as any academic factor.

The university environment is perceived from "vastly different perspectives" by whites and minorities. Sixty-three percent of white students feel that the university is supportive of minorities, as opposed to only 28 percent of Chicanos and blacks. The greatest sources of support, according to minorities, come through student services. Whites and minorities also have "vastly different views about how the university lacked support for minority students." One student feels that there is more "lip service" than "actual service." Another feels that "The university is doing the minimum." Two related problems are brought out by the interviews: the small number of minorities on campus; and the fact that there are "few social activities geared towards minority students" (p. 68).

The authors conclude that minority students experience significantly greater feelings of alienation than do white students, and that these feelings are the result of ethnic isolation and cultural domination. This form of sociocultural alienation is different than alienation which is caused by academic dissatisfaction. Even when minorities are doing well academically, they may experience feelings of alienation when the proportion of minorities on campus is small. When minority students feel alienated academically, this may be related to poor high school preparation, lower socioeconomic status, parental education attainment, and the "culture shock" of "encountering a class and culture distinctly different from their background" (p. 72). In their analysis of white and minority students' perceptions about academic and sociocultural alienation, Loo and Rolison find that whites are basically unaware of the greater academic difficulties faced by minorities.

Criticism of the Loo and Rolison Study
Employing the Functionalist Paradigm

From a functionalist perspective, the topic explored in this study is important to fulfilling higher education's mission of equal opportunity and access. It is unfortunate that, in their efforts to understand the problems felt by ethnic minority students at predominantly white universities, Loo and Rolison employ a radical sociological perspective. This makes the study less useful to scholars who may wish to build on their research.

The authors cite Tinto's early work on attrition as relevant to their study. Because the adaptation of Tinto focuses on a different definition of academic satisfaction, one must question the theoretical framework. It is difficult to believe that Tinto's concept of malintegration is the same problem which the authors discuss. Sociocultural domination of values is not really part of Tinto's work. Willie's theory of how white values suppress minority values is what the authors are really interested in investigating. Use of this second theoretical framework, however interesting it may be to the authors, involves a major departure from Tinto's empirical model.

A functionalist believes that the conflict between white and minority students is only one of many processes and functions in college; that students' values are developed autonomously and spontaneously, not as a result of values domination, and that there are no contradictions between campus groups which cannot be worked out. The radical structuralist perspective on cultural domination is simply too radical. To a functionalist, it seems almost paranoid and conspiratorial in tone.

The choice of university for the case study is a problem. The university represents all of the anomalies of the minority experience in higher education, such as the formation of ethnic enclaves. The use of a narrative evaluation system by the university instead of grades makes the study of academic satisfaction questionable, since the Tinto model uses grades, not evaluations, as the measure of academic integration.

The results suggest that some minorities in this setting feel alienated and/or isolated by the university community. Issues of ethnic isolation are confused by the discussion of "segregated" enclaves within the university's eight colleges. These residential communities present fascinating portraits of integration and socialization at work in a complex, multiracial setting. What is the relationship between membership in an ethnic enclave and academic satisfaction? There are many different factors which could affect the academic satisfaction and integration of students, including experiences of discrimination and racism in the social world outside the university walls.

These peculiar features in the university setting make its use for data gathering inappropriate. From a functionalist standpoint, the case study has minimum generalizability. If external validity is important to the researchers, then the contextual features of the case work are far too idiosyncratic. Perhaps the oversampling of minorities should have been left for another study focusing on between-minority group differences.

The use of same-race interviewers was intended to alleviate what the authors called a "white socially desirable bias" in responses. There are many other types of problems which occur with this kind of interview. Deviation from a structured interview protocol may be a problem, due to the authors' (and perhaps the interviewers') ideological predisposition. This makes all of the data suspect.

The major finding of the research, that some minority students experience social and academic alienation that may be related to isolation and culture shock, is probably true, but certainly not new. This has been a concern of affirmative action, access, remediation, and retention programs for some time. The authors' radical position makes it sound as if nothing has ever been done to alleviate these problems.

All of the findings are supported with Chi-Square analyses, though more robust statistical tests would be welcome. The study's results are incomplete, though. For instance, the finding that white and minority students think about dropping out for different reasons is quite striking. There is a major difference, however, between thinking about dropping out and actually doing so. The authors do not interview students who dropped out, so it is impossible to tell if their reasons are not as much academic as cultural. Tinto's conception of attrition has much to say about drop-out behavior, but this use of Tinto's model is so convoluted by the radical sociology position that it is difficult to know where it should be applied.

Some of the other findings may be more easily assimilated within a functionalist view. It is highly probable that ethnic clustering is perceived differently by whites and minorities. This is because whites are not part of these enclave experiences, and therefore do not have adequate mechanisms for understanding what is happening in them, The finding that minorities experienced greater social isolation needs to be examined more fully. Perhaps there are other types of social interactions which take place which need to be included in the data gathering. Since the definition of isolation is not clear, the finding about social isolation is unclear. It seems obvious that whites would favor enrollment if more minorities on campus, especially since this sample is from California.

The finding that some minorities do not feel that the university is supportive of them is too general. The same is true of the finding that 40 percent of the minorities interviewed feel that their values are not reflected or are reflected just "a little" by the university. This interpretation is weak. It tells the reader nothing except that the university environment is culturally diverse and perceived in different ways.

Criticism of the Loo and Rolison Study Employing the Interpretive Paradigm

Since the interpretive paradigm represents the exact opposite of the assumptions of the radical structuralist paradigm, both sociology and social science criticisms of the Loo and Rolison study would be raised by an interpretivist. To begin, the research is too bound by theory, too grounded in a particular social analysis. A priori definitions of social determinants limit the exploration of possible social forces and shape the researchers' perceptions of them. This discussion of minority alienation is therefore one-sided. The authors fail to look for larger patterns and processes which are part of the coordinating, integrating, and cohesive mechanisms of society.

To an interpretive researcher, the discussion of conflict, domination, and contradiction must be moved from the structural to the subjective. Research problems and questions should be concerned with understanding subjective experiences, examining the university in all of its multidimensional complexity. Psychological processes such as feelings of alienation and isolation may be part of the college experience. However, these processes are much more complicated than these theories suggest. The environmental, situational, and behavioral variables which are discussed offer, at best, an incomplete portrait of human activities. Such determinants may play a role in patterns of integration, but to attribute any person's actions of feelings to one or more of these variables is to deny the depth and complexity of human affairs.

Shared values are seen by the interpretive researcher as a sign of integration, whereas the radical structuralist views them as a sign of the success of the forces of domination. Although heterogeneity and imbalance may be pointed out as incongruities within the university, these problems are actually part of the integrating and cohesive processes being worked out in society as a whole. Radical structuralists believe that racial conflicts are evidence of deep, societal contradictions. They do not understand that, over time, different constituencies can co-exist peacefully and compatibly. What radical structuralists label as conflict and contradiction are simply pieces of the puzzle of integration which keep the social world moving forward, albeit somewhat slowly at times.

The emphasis on sociocultural domination is far too mechanistic, deterministic, and radical for an investigation of how values may or may not be influenced by culture. Cultural domination does not occur simply because social efforts exist to preserve and protect values and norms. It is clear that the researchers operate with value judgments about what constitutes minority alienation and that their efforts to be "objective" are unsuccessful since it is impossible for them to be detached.

The definitions and labels used by Loo and Rolison to describe alienation, academic difficulties, university supportiveness, and attitudes toward minority admissions are not "real," because empirical definitions are themselves the product of subjective value judgments. The interpretivist views these labels as the result of researchers' perceptions of the social world and of their theoretical frameworks. The search for significant differences between whites and minority groups through Chi-Square analyses is futile. Researchers must recognize that experiences in higher education are the creation of individual cognition and consciousness and part of the social construction of reality. It is only at the subjective level that the problem of alienation may be understood in a meaningful way.

Research on minority experiences should be based upon first-hand evidence from subjective accounts. Principles of ethnography and naturalistic inquiry should guide the inquiry. With the interviews, Loo and Rolison should have tried to get inside the university's frame of reference, to learn the language of today's minority and white college students, and to tell their stories.

It is unfortunate that the authors spend so much time trying to generalize from data that do not lend themselves to this kind of nomothetic analysis. Interpretation should have been left to the reader, based on her or his feelings about the study's trustworthiness. No attempts to form conclusions should have been made, as these are inappropriate.

Criticism of the Loo and Rolison Study Employing the Radical Humanist Paradigm

To a radical humanist, the determinist reliance on examining the social world from environmental, situational, and behavioral perspectives is a major weakness of the Loo and Rolison study. Human actions are much more complex than the Tinto and Willie theories imply. The social world of domination and deprivation in the university must be analyzed from a more contextual and relativistic perspective. It is of utmost importance that researchers be able to understand the sources of alienation which are inherent in the totality of universal consciousness and which converge in the context of the social construction called "higher education."

Radical humanists believe that only by entering the minority student frame of reference and getting to know students who are oppressed can researchers investigate issues of alienation. Quantitative measures, tests, and data analytic techniques do not fit this kind of subjective inquiry. Social science knowledge is not be expanded by the accretion and accumulation of hypotheses and the acknowledgment of Chi Square differences. The creation of a radical humanist perspective on alienation is an holistic process.

Alienation is not a variable to be measured. If scholars are to participate in alleviating oppression, then research must focus on subjective consciousness, in all its dark and human frailty. Essentially, the world of the university acts as a sort of cognitive wedge, driven between the consciousness of minorities and their true selves. In the psychic prison of higher education, all people are alienated from their true selves and from each other.

The findings of the Loo and Rolison study are not surprising to a radical humanist. Minorities do feel culturally alienated and socially isolated. Their values are certainly not reflected by the university. It is no wonder that they have more academic difficulties, or that they drop out for different reasons than white students do. The university does not support them, just as it denies their cultural values. Ethnic clustering seems to have been the only way in which they have been able to survive amidst domination and oppression.

The results of the study actually tell the radical humanist reader very little about the nature of the alienation and isolation which minorities experience. The radical structuralist approach is useful only up to a certain point because of its positivist orientation. To really understand oppression at the level of consciousness, it is necessary that subjective assumptions about social science replace the traditional, positivist assumptions.

Interpretive Case Study:
Four Undergraduate Computer-Writers

In the article entitled "A Study of Four Undergraduate Computer-Writers," Logan (1988) uses ethnographic techniques and case studies to present a portrait of four undergraduate students who learn to use computers in their writing. The author's approach to educational research is based on assumptions underpinning what she describes as "interpretive inquiry."

The study focuses on one semester's writing class in a computer lab. Document analysis, observation, and interviews are used as ethnographic techniques. First, a computerized form of questionnaire is designed to elicit comments and reflections from students about their computer-writing skills. This procedure is abandoned because it does not gather the kind of information in which the researcher is interested. As part of her participation as instructor, the author then uses observation techniques to look for clues to the computer-writing processes at work for different students. Field notes of these observations are recorded. However, the author believes that this technique also does not offer the kinds of information she hopes to gather. Therefore, a series of informal "casual conversations" are initiated with students during the lab time. Out of these conversations comes the author's decision to do interviews.

Students' selection for interviews is based on three criteria, including: (1) their "ability to articulate" their experiences using computers in writing; (2) their not having a computer at home to use; and (3) their having time to work in the lab and be interviewed. Two students who met these criteria are interviewed twice; once three weeks into the semester, and again two weeks before the end of the semester. Two additional students are chosen for one-time interviews to serve as "sources of 'disconfirming or confirming evidence'" (p. 136). It is hoped that these different data gathering methods will serve as forms of "triangulation."

The design of the open-ended interviews is "guided by the same general topic, but the sequence and nature of questions are determined by the subject's responses." The first question Logan uses is: "I was wondering if you would tell me something about your experiences with writing at a computer." During the progress of the interview, efforts are made to incorporate Spradley's three types of ethnographic questions. The interviews are recorded and transcribed. In addition, the author has access to students' written work for document analysis.

The data analytic approach involves "descriptive analysis of the meanings which these four writers assign to the activity of writing at a computer" (p. 138). In the article, case studies are presented for the two main students, Karen and Ellen. The case description is broken up into the two topics of attitudes about computers and writing strategies.

An example of how attitudes about computers are described is found in the following passage: "She [Ellen] expresses some ambivalence about the impact of computers on society in general, implying that somehow they are less authentic, not the real thing." Ellen explains:

> I think it would be a good idea to go back and see how it is to do it on a typewriter. . . . To open their minds up and say "Wow, look what it is that this thing can do." They take it for granted. And I think it's really important as computers become the pencil of the future that they learn the process of what they're really doing (p. 138)

The data on writing strategies are illustrated in this interview with Karen:

> Slow, just when you think you're halfway across, it sucks you back in. And it's never ending process. For me it is. I have to keep going back through the manual the manual that you gave us and re-read everything. . . . I always have to go back through to move text or to make any of the changes. For me it's just, ugh! I still don't like them [computers] (p. 142).

In her analysis, Logan writes that Karen "seems to want to blame the computer for some of her writing problems" (p. 143). During the second interview, Karen "seemed a lot more antagonistic toward computers" (p. 142). Logan explains that:

> For Karen, the computer seems to represent the enemy out there to be conquered because it's so "up and coming." Perhaps because she sees it this way, it presents more difficulty for her. She seems more willing to accept her inability to "learn the computer," just as she is willing to accept her writing deficiencies as a "fact of life." One of her final remarks to me as she turned in her typed final paper was, "Well, I guess the computer won!" This comment along with the one in her last interview ("I still don't like them") suggests that she took the endeavor to be a personal confrontation, likened to "trudging through a swamp" (p. 144).

Summarizing the results of different ethnographic techniques, Logan explains that:

> Some dominant patterns of meaning surface in the description of these four computer-writers. As we consider these patterns, it is important to remember that they are offered not as findings, results, or conclusions . . . (p. 144).

Three important patterns of meaning emerge from this study. The first is that Ellen sees the computer as a technical "tool, something which she can use to write more efficiently." Second, Karen is interested in learning about the computer because it is "up and coming." For her, the computer also "seems to represent the enemy out there to be conquered . . ." Learning the computer is "a personal confrontation." In the cases of Bob and Angie, "the computer is not at issue; it is a given" (p. 144). Both have prior computer experience and, unlike Ellen and Karen, are primarily interested in getting the system to work for them.

Logan concludes by analyzing the patterns of meanings in terms of their implications for practice. No attempt is made to generalize from these case studies. The author warns that:

> Knowing how four writers perceived a semester's experience of writing with a computer does not tell us how four other students during a different semester of even during the same semester perceived

it. Nor does it tell us how these same four students might perceive it in another setting.... One value, it seems, of such an irreplicable [sic] study is that knowing how meaning was made in this classroom community might provide us with new lenses for looking at others (p. 145).

Criticism of the Logan Study Employing the Functionalist Paradigm

To a functionalist, the Logan study of computer-writers is poor research; the research problem is framed in such a subjective manner that the study does not accomplish anything. Methodologically, there are problems in the data gathering and data analytic techniques.

A functionalist would question whether case studies of this sort can generate information that is useful in any cumulative sense. There are a number of disciplines which can be brought to bear on the problem of understanding how learning labs may be used in teaching computers and writing. Sociology, psychology, education, along with the sub-fields of educational technology and cognitive development, have much to offer this topic of study, which better fits a behavioral treatment.

It is important to question whether the methodological design could have sustained the author's conclusions. First, the author tries a computerized questionnaire. The data on this procedure are not even reported. The reader is simply told that the data are not reported because the author didn't get the kind of data she was looking for. Then, the author tries to observe students in the lab. Again, the reader is told that this procedure does not obtain the type of information desired. Logan settles on interviews for data gathering. This might be an appropriate choice, using interviews to gather exploratory, qualitative data. The choice to interview only two students may limit the amount of insight to be gained into patterns in the data, since there is little room for redundancy.

Numerous problems may be expected in the data analysis when interviews are completely open-ended and non-sequential. It is impossible to know how problems in the content analysis are worked out by the author.. The methods of document analysis of students' writings are not discussed. The cases are filled with the instructor's personal, subjective interpretation, despite statements to the contrary about not wanting to generalize. Logan's use of "descriptive analysis" is inadequate. All that the reader is left with is a sequence of simplistic anecdotal quotes about students' perceptions of their attitudes about computers and their writing strategies. Overall, the structure of the case studies is not useful.

One might predict that the results of such data gathering and analysis would be poor, and this is the case in the concluding sections of the article. There are no correlations, laws, or relationships to be found in the data, only what Logan calls "patterns of meanings." These three "meanings" are basically "meaningless." So what if Ellen sees computers as a tool and Karen used computers because they are trendy? The reader is told that Bob and Angie already know about computers. How does this affect their use of the lab? What about the four students' learning processes? Do they do anything in the lab? Does the curriculum meet their needs? Do they develop any skills? Do computers make a difference in their writing? These subjective accounts fail to illustrate any of these basic questions, or, for that matter, to be of interest to the reader.

Since the study's findings consist only of patterns of meanings, a functionalist researcher would question whether the data from two students represent a pattern. It is possible that these meanings are entirely idiosyncratic. For example, Karen's attitudes about computers being "trendy" may represent nothing at all but an off-hand remark. For this reason, all of the findings about patterns of meanings which Logan discusses are suspect. How does the reader know if students accept computers as writing tools? The fact that Angie has a computer at home may not be linked to her success in using computers or her acceptance that they are "a given." The relationship between Bob's having a background of computer science courses and his success in the lab is not substantiated by the "pattern" of his interview comments.

Even though Logan says she isn't going to generalize, the implications of the study sound like concluding recommendations. Any possible links between the implications, the "patterns of meaning," and the data are missing from the article. To make these kinds of recommendations a researcher is expected to have analyzed data with some degree of precision.

Criticism of the Logan Study
Employing the Radical Structuralist Paradigm

For the radical structuralist, any form of critical analysis must recognize the inherent contradictions and conflicts which plague the college environment. Logan neglects to mention the role of technology in reinforcing class structures or the influence of computer technology in maintaining and preserving racial, gender, class, economic, and geopolitical superstructures in society. There is no understanding in this research of the ways in which technology is used to control and manipulate people's lives by dehumanizing work and reifying technical knowledge. Human worth is devalued in favor of technological competency. Also, there is no appreciation of the dominating power relationship which is the basis for pedagogy—that of professor over student.

To the radical structuralist, Logan's study simply reinforces the status quo, accepting that this is the way things are in society and that nothing can or should be done to change it. The learning laboratory, which is supposed to help teach students to use computers in their writing, does something entirely different, though. Students are conditioned into believing that technology will help them, that it will make them better students, that if they learn to use computers they will get better jobs because of their new skills. Through computer-writing, students come to accept a dominant belief system about the role of technology which subtly and unconsciously degrades the human condition. These mechanisms of oppression are legitimized by Logan, who accepts technology without questioning its impact. This is not to say that there is no place for computers or computer-writing software, but that their use should not facilitate oppressive class structures.

Both of the students in the case studies are women. It is obvious that neither of them is successful from the instructor's point of view in learning to use computers in their writing. One woman, Karen, even says that she does not like computers. Why should she? The expectation of the author, who seems unable to "objectively" separate herself from her role as instructor, is that Karen should like computers because they are good for her. The truth is that her experience with the computer has led to her self-image being belittled. Computers are described by Karen as the "enemy." For her, trying to learn word processing becomes a big "confrontation." These are not just words. They are cries for help, statements about the profound feelings of oppression and domination experienced by this student. The computer lab confronts her with sexist stereotypes and self-fulfilling prophecies of women's science abilities. The computer program tries to make her writing into what the programmer thinks it should be, grammatically and anatomically correct. No wonder she does not feel particularly creative. The learning laboratory is an artificial and dehumanizing setting. There are probably no windows in the lab. Certainly, there are no feelings of liberation or empowerment being developed as part of this new technology.

Two additional students are interviewed for confirmation of the data. It is interesting to note that both of these students seem to have met Logan's unspoken criteria of success in computer-writing. One of these students, Bob, faces none of the fears of success with technology that the two women feel, in part because he has already had computer courses. Angie does well, according to Logan, because she owns her own computer and regularly uses Wordperfect for word processing.

A radical structuralist reading of these limited, subjective data would suggest that Ellen and Karen are oppressed by computer technology. The computer-writing lab reinforces a particular form of domination. Bob is privileged because he fits into the norms of the technological elite. He also has an easier time of it because he is part of male-dominated society. Angie definitely fits into the researcher's bias for a middle class image of students, since she has the luxury to buy her own home computer and software. Through these four examples, one glimpses the processes by which training in technology legitimizes oppressive power. Ellen and Karen are deprived of their potential as producers and consumers of technology because they do not fit into the mold of computer "user." Since they are women, can not afford to buy their own computers, and are de-selected out of other computer science prerequisites, they lose this opportunity to become "computer literate." As an interpretive researcher, Logan fails to address these problems of class and gender.

There are certain expectations about the conduct of social science which Logan obviously does not meet. To the radical structuralist, Logan's subjective approach to social science does not constitute good research. The only data offered in the case studies are anecdotal. The scientific approach requires that data elements and variables be empirically grounded and defined with precise, technical language. Logan's observation procedures did not solicit the type of data she desired. This may be because the techniques are not very rigorous or objective. Open-ended interviews may be useful for data exploration, but these are inappropriate for prediction and explanation. Logan has no hypotheses, no empirical data, no conclusions, and no generalizations.

The "pattern of meaning" that Ellen sees computers as an effective writing tool also shows something the interpretive researcher is not looking for—students' resigned indifference to giving up their freedom in exchange for technological bondage. Bob and Angie, who both see computers as "a given," readily accept Logan's values about computers. It is possible that these are not patterns at all, but entirely idiosyncratic, since each pattern comes from only one subject.

Criticism of the Logan Study
Employing the Radical Humanist Paradigm

Logan describes computers and technology as if they are value-free. From a radical humanist perspective, this is simply not the case. Where computer technology is discussed as a liberating element in society, it needs to be recognized as a negative and dominating force as well. In Logan's mind, only good could come from technology. The author seems to be blind to the reality that the two women interviewed for the case studies are alienated by their experiences with computers. She does not see that there are many forms of deprivation, oppression, and domination at work in the computer lab.

There is something to be learned from the data, though. Karen's comment that she did not like computers is a clue. The computer is the "enemy." She admits that "the computer won," and that learning to write on a computer is a "personal confrontation," like "trudging through a swamp" (p. 144).

Here, technology is reified and Karen's human worth devalued. She is alienated by her experience with computers. The dialogue between the student and professor, as depicted in the article, is an example of the communicative distortion which takes place in power relationships. The author's attitudes about computers do not allow her to observe what is taking place in the form of technological domination and oppression. Logan legitimizes the status quo of technological domination by criticizing Karen for her lack of acceptance of technology.

The author does not express much concern for creativity. In the context of a single classroom experience, Karen's potential as a computer user, her feelings of ability and talent as a writer, and her self-esteem as a person, are eroded. What if she has a learning disability? Like many others, she will be quickly passed over for selection into the technological elite because she does not meet the expectations of the professor, who acts as expert and judge. The lab staff serve as the gatekeepers of potential, passing out grades and possibilities for development and fulfillment.

Most researchers, like Logan, fail to understand what technology does to people. Karen sees computers as the enemy. The learning lab is not educating her to the possibilities of writing poetry, novels, or non-fiction. She is being trained to take her place as a second-class citizen. This higher education experience is inculcating her with values of passivity, submissiveness, how self-esteem, and low self-worth.

Moreover, from a radical humanist perspective, this kind of research perpetuates ideological hegemony by stultifying human creativity. To the radical humanist, the computer lab represents a kind of "psychic prison." The computer-writing curriculum drives a cognitive wedge between the self and true consciousness. There is no appreciation of cognitive development or of the psychology of critical thinking and writing skills. Through using these computer programs, students are taught to write correctly. Ideas are not important; grammar, spelling, and correct text analysis are. Engagement with any of the fundamental questions of human life is devalued. What is important to Logan is that Ellen and Karen learn to subordinate their originality and creativity by using a word processor, spelling checker, and text analyzer.

These case studies of how four undergraduates learn to do computer-writing represent larger societal tensions between science and the humanities, a false duality which is being played out in the totality of higher education. Science and computer technology triumph over the arts and humanities in general education and in the major. This new technology curriculum has become anti-human.

To an interpretive researcher like Logan, change is a superficial, ephemeral, everyday part of life. To a radical humanist, change means much more. True change takes place through the development of new modes of cognition and consciousness. Scholars have a responsibility to encourage alternatives to the status quo by envisioning radical changes in the ideological super-structures of technology. Subjective data gathering and analytic techniques such as used by Logan have a unique place in mapping the alienation of human consciousness. In this study, however, the technological bias of the researcher seems to reinforce and compound the profound sense of alienation felt by the two women.

Radical Humanist Case Study: Women's Ways of Knowing

In their book *Women's Ways of Knowing: The Development of Self, Voice, and Mind*, Belenky, Clinchy, Goldberger, and Tarule (1986) present the results of a five-year research study on women's epistemology. From their perspective, most theories of development fail to identify "aspects of intelligence and modes of thought that might be more common and highly developed in women" (p. 7). This lack of significant research on women's development is a result of the male-dominated world of scholarship in developmental psychology and in all of the academic disciplines.

An emergent, naturalistic design using interviews and case studies was chosen in order to "explore with the women their experience and problems as learners and knowers as well as to review their past histories for changing concepts of the self and relationships with others" (p. 11). The authors describe their developmental assessment approach as being similar to that used by Perry (1970), which involves "an open and leisurely interview that establishes rapport and allows presuppositions and frames of reference of the interviewee to emerge. We share Perry's commitment to this phenomenological approach" (p. 10).

Gilligan's conception of women's development, portrayed as a process of "finding a voice," is crucial to the authors' understanding of gender differences and to their articulation of women's development, as distinct from men's. Rather than be guided in their data gathering and analysis by existing theoretical constructs and developmental research, the researchers "wanted to hear what the women had to say in their own terms rather than test our own preconceived hypotheses" (p. 11).

A total of 135 women were selected for interviews, including 90 women who attended or were recent alumni from one of six colleges, and 45 women who were being served by one of three family agency programs. The academic institutions encompass a wide variety of educational philosophies. The family agencies are considered as "invisible colleges." All of the agency programs are organized and run by women. This gives the authors a chance to find out "what kinds of institutions for promoting growth and development women would create for themselves if they were not so dominated by masculine images, theories, founders, or administrators" (p. 13). Also, by paying attention to mothering, which is the focus of various program services, it might be possible to "hear themes that were especially distinctive in the woman's voice" (p. 13). This diversity of respondents allows the researchers to "see the common ground that women share, regardless of background" (p. 13).

All 135 women are interviewed in-depth at least once, sometimes twice. The sets of interviews offered comparison data that could be used in case studies of development over time for approximately one-third of the women. A series of qualitative content analysis procedures are used to code and classify the interview data. First, the interview sections for assessing scores on the Perry, Kohlberg, and Gilligan development schemes are separated out and blind coding of these sections is done. Where Perry focuses on stages and positions of development which followed a clear sequence, Belenky et al. are interested in "epistemological *perspectives* from which women know and view the world" (p. 15). Applying the Perry scheme to Gilligan's concept of "finding a voice," the authors identify five distinct epistemological perspectives which they call "women's ways of knowing."

The interview transcripts are coded into a number of emergent and a priori categories. Contextual analysis follows the use of ethnographic techniques to preserve the data intact and place them into epistemological categories. Two other kinds of analyses are done. One of the a priori coding categories distinguishes women's epistemologies in terms of what the authors call "educational dialectics." These eleven educational dialectics consist of "bimodal dimensions." Each side of the dimensions represents a preferred mode of learning. Statements from each woman are grouped under each dialectical mode. Throughout the interviews, the authors also pay attention to the influence of two social institutions on women's development—the family and formal education.

One result of the data analyses surprises the authors. They recognize the notion of "finding a different voice" which Gilligan heard "as women talked about personal moral crises and decisions." But, as they note, "What we had not anticipated was that 'voice' was more than an academic shorthand for a person's point of view . . ." but a "metaphor that can apply to many aspects of women's experience and development" (p. 18).

In their description of five "epistemological perspectives from which women know and view the world" (p. 15), the researchers caution that these are not to be interpreted as stages, positions, or sequences of development. The categories are not intended by the authors to be fixed or exhaustive. The authors state that their "intention is to share not prove our observations" (p. 16).

These five epistemological perspectives are (1) silence; (2) received knowledge, or listening to the voices of others; (3) subjective knowledge, including the inner voice, and the quest for self; (4) procedural knowledge, including the voice of reason, separate knowing, and connected knowing; and (5) constructed knowledge, or integrating the voices.

Approximately one-third of the book *Women's Ways of Knowing* is devoted to understanding the effects of family life and formal education on women's development. Stories of family life are told as case studies of each epistemological perspective.

For the silent women, there is violence instead of dialogue at home. "Everyone in this small group experienced some form of gross neglect and/or sexual abuse, by one or both of their parents" (p. 159). These women need, somehow, to gain a voice if they are to break out of the cycle of being a victim or perpetrator of family violence. For received knowers who listen to the voices of others, there is one-way talk, inequality, and male domination, without any hope of rebellion against oppressive and sexually abusive authority. Those subjective knowers who listen to their inner voice are, on the contrary, able to "revolt and rebel against their parents" (p. 168), questioning authority. In this position, there comes the first "criticism of conventional female goodness," (p. 174) as the ideal of selflessness is questioned. In the family life of procedural knowers who are working to integrate the voices of reason and feeling, there is more of a dialogue and connectedness between mothers and daughters. Integrating the voices of reason and feeling, constructed knowers have themes of connectedness between mothers and daughters, using mothers in developing the voice of reason and fathers in developing the voice of emotion.

The authors observe that "women often feel alienated in academic settings and experience 'formal' education as either peripheral or irrelevant to their central interests and development" (p. 4). Most of the women who are interviewed feel that they have "often been treated as if they were stupid" (p. 194). In college, the focus on knowing does not involve development of the self and of voice, but acceptance of a new form of authority, that of faculty over student. Rarely are school experiences considered as "powerful learning experiences" (p. 200). A "tyranny of expectations" is at work, the authors find, in which connected knowing is devalued as a dialectic and separate knowing is praised. The masculine preference in each dimension is promoted as the mode for both sexes, and the modes preferred by women are down-played and/or criticized.

The differences between male and female students are contrasted in the chapter entitled "Toward an Education for Women." For women, confirmation of the self as a knower and acceptance into the college community of relationships are "prerequisites rather than consequences of development" (p. 194). In the concluding chapter entitled "Connected Teaching," the authors envision a philosophy of education for women's development that replaces "traditional separate education" with "connected teaching," and which pays attention to women's educational dialectics of connected knowing.

Criticism of the Belenky Study Employing the Interpretive Paradigm

To an interpretivist, this analysis is unmistakably based on a combination of feminist critique, radical sociology, Gilligan's and Perry's theories of development, and psychoanalytic theory. The researchers make a number of radical sociological assumptions about the existence of domination, contradiction, deprivation, emancipation, and potentiality—criticisms that do not have a place within the interpretive paradigm. They simply represent the views of one particular ideological perspective on the problems of the social world.

The primary goal of developmental research on women should be to understand the subjectively created social world, as it is, in terms of ongoing patterns and processes of human growth and development. The power relationships of male domination discussed by the radical humanist position are a theoretical interpretation. To an interpretivist, values about home, family and education are acquired more autonomously than is suggested.

As for the overall findings of the study, these are frightening in their depiction of possible barriers to development which some women face. The metaphor of "voice" is useful in understanding part of what women feel is going on in their lives. It is interesting to look at the metaphor of voice from five different epistemological perspectives. Although this epistemology is grounded in a nominalist, constructivist approach to subjective knowing, it seems that the authors could not resist implying sequential stages and hierarchical levels of development.

The description of modes of how some women learn is interesting, but still somewhat Manichean. Although these polarities may be useful as a starting point, gender issues in learning are much more complex. It is probably true that some women learn in modes which are different from how some men learn, although it is questionable whether the two are at opposite poles. Here the radical sociological position intrudes in the interpretation of the data. Perhaps institutions of higher education do favor certain modes, as the authors suggest. It is implausible, though, to attribute complex processes to male domination and hierarchical power relationships. To the interpretivist, research with women about their development is only useful up to a point. The very nature of developmental psychology is hierarchical. The authors' methodological ideals for subjective inquiry are compromised because they are so engaged with their ideological approach.

Criticism of the Belenky Study
Employing the Functionalist Paradigm

From a functionalist perspective, the sociological assumptions which undergird the Belenky study are simply unfounded. Instead of taking the traditional approach to the topic, they are interested in male domination and oppression. Values are acquired much more autonomously than the research suggests. The preferred learning modes which the authors describe are probably not the result of domination, deprivation, and oppression. It is absurd to assume that any of these learning dialectics exist as polar opposites between the sexes.

Significant gender-related behavioral problems do occur within the psychosocial process of integration, but these are not a sign of inherent contradictions or conflicts. These are natural imbalances and problems of heterogeneity which are caused by tensions between the sexes and by the panoply of human activities. Natural gender differences, which have both a physiological and psychological basis, should not be construed as representing any kind of authoritarian power relationship of men over women. Research needs to be done on differences between the sexes that can be attributed to the processes of growth and development, and to gender-specific developmental behavior. Research must pay attention to the environmental, situational, and behavioral determinants which are part of the integrating, coordinating, and cohesive mechanisms built into society.

Through the institutions of the family unit and higher education, the status quo of the social world is maintained. Men and women complement one another in their social lives, and their psychological development is basically compatible. This is not to make light of the tragic data about incest, sexual abuse, and family violence which the interviews bring out. One must recognize, though, that these deviations are not the norm. For many women, family life and education are developmentally stimulating and fulfilling parts of normal human existence. Belenky et al. criticize the institutions of family life and education for legitimizing and reinforcing oppression. A functionalist views the family unit and colleges and universities as important societal mechanisms which help balance divergent social processes.

To the functionalist, the entire approach to research used in the Belenky study is too subjective. Empirical data should be gathered which describe the relationship between the sexes in quantitative terms. Self-reports of how women learn and know about the world can be a useful source of data which might, conceivably, serve as a starting point in developmental research; but these are just subjective accounts. How can the reliability of these anecdotal reports be adequately measured? Other data sources with more integrity, such as instruments and tests, should be used to assess the validity of the interview data. If the interview protocol is valuable, then the data may be used to determine whether they support the epistemological schema.

The authors' "observations" are not objective. As researchers, their perceptions about women's development and their feminist belief structures influence their ability to gather and analyze the data dispassionately and rationally. Empirical precision should be of the utmost importance if any form of interpretation is to be done. All of the data coding is suspect. It is unclear which coding categories emerged and which were guided by theory.

The authors state that they do not want to make hypotheses, but that they want the data to speak for themselves. Still, subtle, hidden causal models are being defined in the description of the five epistemological positions. While attempting to be naturalistic and subjective on the surface, the feminist ideology implies that domination is a cause and that oppression is an effect. The authors are not successful in maintaining both a subjective and a radical change perspective. Perhaps they do not intend to. From a functionalist point of view, however, the mix of methods and ideology is problematic and makes the results much less useful.

Based on the data presented, it is difficult for the functionalist reader to accept the conclusion that women learn best through dialectical modes which support "connected knowing," or that "connected teaching" is useful in facilitating women's development. Overall, this study fails to substantiate any interpretations or conclusions that might be useful in future research. Researchers wishing to build on this developmental schema will have to remove the data from the many radical sociology interpretations which surround them. Any reporting of results should be done in a straight forward and scholarly manner that is not embedded in social commentary.

Criticism of the Belenky Study
Employing the Radical Structuralist Paradigm

From a radical structuralist point of view, this study of *Women's Ways of Knowing* is an excellent example of feminist discourse. It offers an original and compelling argument about family life and higher education as barriers to the development of women. Several general criticisms need to be raised, though, about the social science assumptions.

The devastating effects of male domination are discussed at a microcosmic level which is too subjective. Research on women's development should not fall victim to the "tyranny of data." In this study, the subjective data overshadow the a priori theoretical framework of radical sociology. The primacy of theory should be maintained. The authors incorporate a theoretical perspective, but fail to fully admit it that it guides their methodological choices. The subjectivity which is at the heart of this study must be avoided. If the male academic establishment is to be confronted, it should be done with empirically sound documentation of oppression.

Some of the findings of the study are more credible than others. It is important for scholars to document the fact that women learn differently than men, that men's ways of learning and knowing about the world have been valued, while women's ways have been criticized and scorned. The eleven educational dialectics and dimensions represent modes by which men oppress and devaluate women's ways of knowing.

To a radical structuralist, the concept that human beings subjectively create their own reality is fundamentally unsound. The world is not a social construction. Here, the subjective nature of the data lead to misinterpretations about the nature of oppression in the social world. Barriers to development are real and tangible. They may be empirically tested and measured with nomothetic precision. Reality is the same, whether or not people develop different epistemological perspectives with which to see it.

The force and power of the critique is greatly diminished by the authors' nominalist assumptions about the social world. If this kind of research is to be taken seriously by the scholarly community, it is imperative that researchers remain objective social scientists who dispassionately employ methodological rigor to find new ways of tearing down barriers to women's development.

An alternative feminist model of women's development could be envisioned which suggests women's potential once they are emancipated from the structures of patriarchal society. Once an alternative feminist vision is put forward, it is possible to facilitate education for development by fostering activities which have a positive effect on women's development.

Discussion

Using the Burrell and Morgan definitions to develop alternative research strategies, the case study approach produces interesting illustrations of relationships, tensions, linkages, and dissonance between paradigms. The two dimensional schema seems to be useful for critiquing and defending the problem, questions, methods and findings of higher education research.

There are a number of limitations in the Burrell and Morgan schema and in the content analysis methodology. It is not possible to translate all of the different paradigm languages (constructivist, neo-Marxist, feminist, etc.) into the two dimensions and eleven sets of assumptions. Rather, the schema is offered as a starting point to help scholars share a common language to explore what it is to have a different paradigm perspective. The context of the case studies in actual research is designed to breathe life into the language of assumptions.

Sometimes, the cases read like caricatures of a perspective. While this in not intended, it is recognized that each paradigm critique could be made more complex. Except for Pascarella et al.'s example of functionalism, the content analysis results show that none of the authors are "pure" in their reflection of only one paradigm. In the case studies, each piece of research is treated as if it were. This undoubtedly holds authors to an idealistic standard with which they might not choose to be identified.

Another limitation of the case study process is its fundamentally dualistic nature. From one paradigm perspective, the other three are always inadequate in one or both dimensions of assumptions. All four cases are written as dualistic, black/white, right/wrong treatments. Morgan (1983) and Schwandt (1989) label this attitude among scholars as one of supremacy. The cases are seen as "some sort of decisive test to determine which is superior" (Schwandt, 1989, p. 384). One purpose behind writing the four cases is to foster what Morgan (1983) defines as a dialectical attitude, trying to facilitate a multisided diversity of approaches in a sort of "theoretical pluralism." The case study method does not, though, allow the reader to weigh the merit of two opposing paradigm perspectives at the same time.

Morgan describes the problem of "reframing our view of knowledge." Scholars need to:

> find a way of dealing with the possibilities that relativism signifies. In order to find such an approach, it is necessary to reframe our view of knowledge in a way that gets beyond the idea that knowledge is in some sense foundational and can be evaluated in an absolute way, for it is this idea that ultimately leads us to try and banish the uncertainty associated with relativism, rather than simply to deal with it as an inevitable feature of the process through which knowledge is generated (Morgan, 1983, pp. 372–373).

Do arguments for reframing the discussion of multiple paradigms reflect only the interpretive point of view? Functionalists may not believe that the dominance of one paradigm in research is a limitation. Rather, this may be seen as a sign of the field of higher education's maturation and coherence. If scholars decide that something important is to be learned from challenging the dominant paradigm and exploring alternative paradigms, then the dynamic for change may mean moving from dualism to relativism.

There are interesting similarities between the cognitive development literature and the discussions of Morgan (1983), Schwandt (1989), and Lincoln (1989) about scholars' attitudes toward paradigms. Translating Belenky et al. (1986), Perry (1970, 1981), and Thompson (1991) to attitudes about multiple paradigms, an interesting developmental map may be created which explains possible movement between dualism, multiplicity, relativism, and commitment in regard to a particular research paradigm.

While it is inappropriate here to suggest any empirical basis to this developmental approach to paradigms, it may be useful to explore the similar language of paradigmatic and developmental assumptions. If scholars are to be able to reframe their view of knowledge, then it is necessary to move away from dualism to multiplicity to simple relativism to more advanced stages of paradigm development.

Perry's idea of fostering development by presenting concepts which are one stage above students' current developmental level may be useful for thinking of the debate as an educational process. Rather than confronting other scholars over their lack of sensitivity to oppression or their not having recognized the utility of new axioms of inquiry, it may be more useful to take up the debate with language which is one stage above many listeners' or readers' current level of paradigm development. Dualists would be exposed to multiplistic perspectives, multiplistic scholars would encounter relativists, and relativists would be exposed to scholars who have made a commitment to conducting research in an alternative paradigm.

Such a strategy might use the case studies of this chapter in the following manner: To those dualists who believe that functionalism is the essence of good research, the case studies suggest that there are multiple perspectives on paradigms which are worth paying attention to. It is interesting to note that entirely different findings might result if an alternative problem statement and methodology were used. Multiplistic scholars who are already beginning to explore the language of different paradigms might be struck with the limitations of the case studies as being dependent on the contest of theory and methodology. To relativistic scholars who recognize and appreciate the diversity of paradigms, the cases might allow them to explore approaches and make tentative commitments to a paradigm. Scholars who have made a commitment to a research paradigm may find it too limiting, and move back into relativism.

Perry's definitions of ways in which students deflect cognitive development might help scholars in understanding their own and others' problems in adjusting to different attitudes toward paradigms. A possible rephrasing of Perry might be: (1) Temporizing—in which scholars postpone movement away from their traditional paradigm. (2) Escape—where scholars abandon their responsibility to be aware of and debate paradigm issues. On a higher level, the multiplicity and relativism of the debate are exploited in order to avoid commitment. (3) Retreat—in which scholars avoid the complexity and ambiguity of the paradigm debate by retreating to dualism, showing little tolerance for other paradigms.

It is important to recognize and move beyond these possible barriers to paradigm development. The primary purpose of this chapter has been to use case studies to help the reader explore multiple paradigm perspectives. Reviewing this chapter, it is obvious that it meets the definitions of a functionalist approach to paradigms. The chapter is limited by its reach for a rational, positivist explanation of what paradigms have to offer scholars in their research.

The use of a hierarchical developmental scheme is inherently functionalist. While Belenky et al. state specifically that their model of women's development is not intended to be hierarchical, it is easy to fall into using the language of sequences stages, levels, and positions. Most researchers who offer modifications of Perry retain the same sequence, though others may add or modify some positions. It may be most useful to think of this model of paradigm development as a metaphor. While it brings images to mind, human nature is much too complex to be discussed in this manner.

It is important that continued dialogue about paradigms be moved to a higher level. Too often, the mode of discussion has been one of confrontation. Feminists such as Glazer (1990) and Townsend (1991) confront scholars with the exclusion of gender in research and the patriarchal nature of the research enterprise. Lincoln (1985, 1989) confronts positivists with the axioms of naturalistic inquiry. This type of scholarship is critical to the evolution of paradigms. As the modified Perry/Belenky developmental scheme suggests, though, a confrontational posture will not necessarily foster development. Instead, the debate must be taken to a variety of levels and involve learning different paradigm development languages.

Perry's positions seven through nine for commitment in relativism suggest a language for a higher level of discussion about multiple paradigms. How might this level of discussion take place among higher education scholars? In Pascarella and Terenzini's (1991) synthesis of research, *How*

College Affects Students, they discuss research on Perry's theory of intellectual and ethical student development. Some striking parallels to attitudes about paradigms may be seen in the authors' description of position nine, commitment. Translating their language to the attitudes about paradigms, the following image of higher education researcher/scholars may be drawn:

Having affirmed their lives and responsibilities as researchers in a pluralistic society, scholars make commitments to specific ideas, ideologies, perspectives, methods, and assumptions. These commitments are seen as "dynamic and changeable." Scholars must believe in their own assumptions, yet be open and willing to learn about alternative approaches, Commitments to the social science or sociological perspective of a specific paradigm point of view are "modifiable, subject to new evidence and understanding about who one is and how the world is. Commitments may be made, but they are not immutable . . ." "This process of construction and reconstruction does not end with college. Indeed, it is a lifelong process" (Pascarella and Terenzini, 1991, p. 30). Scholars should recognize that they will retrace the paradigm journey over and over, but hopefully "more wisely."

As Perry explains, the path of development is "neither the straight line nor the circle, but a helix, perhaps with an ever expanding radius to show that when we face the 'same' old issues we do so from a different and broader perspective" (Perry, 1981, p. 97).

The author wishes to thank David L. Clark, his dissertation advisor, and Clifton L. Conrad, a more recent advisor, for their assistance and encouragement in the preparation of this chapter.

References

Attinasi, L.C., Jr. (1990). Phenomenological inquiry and higher education research. Paper presented at the Annual Meeting of the Association for the Study of Higher Education, Portland, Oregon, November 2, 1990.

Barrow, C.W. (1991). *Universities and the Capitalist State: Corporate Liberalism and the Reconstruction of American Higher Education, 1892–1928*. Madison: University of Wisconsin Press.

Bateson, G. (1972). *Steps Toward an Ecology of Mind*. New York: Ballantine.

Belenky, M.F., Clinchy, B.M. , Goldberger, N.R., and Tarule, J.M. (1986). *Women's Ways of Knowing: The Development of Self, Voice, and Mind*. New York: Basic Books.

Burrell, G., and Morgan, G. (1979). *Sociological Paradigms and Organisational Analysis*. London: Heinemann Educational Books.

Clark, D.L. (1985). Emerging paradigms in organizational theory and research. In Y. S. Lincoln (ed.), *Organizational Theory and Inquiry: The Paradigm Revolution*. Beverly Hills: Sage Publications.

Conrad, C. F. (1989). Meditations on the ideology of inquiry in higher education: exposition, critique, and conjecture. *Review of Higher Education* 12(3): 199–220.

Gilligan, C. (1982). *In A Different Voice: Psychological Theory and Women's Development*. Cambridge: Harvard University Press.

Glazer, J.S. (1990). Feminism and professionalism: the case of education and business. Paper presented at the Annual Meeting of the Association for the Study of Higher Education, Portland, Oregon, November 1, 1990.

Griffiths, D.E. (1983). Evolution in research and theory: a study of prominent researchers. *Educational Administration Quarterly* 19(3): 201–221.

Kuhn, T.S. (1970) *The Structure of Scientific Revolutions*. Second Edition. Chicago: University of Chicago Press.

Lincoln, Y.S. (1986). A future-oriented comment on the state of the profession. *Review of Higher Education* 10(2): 135–142.

Lincoln, Y.S. (ed.). (1985). *Organizational Theory and Inquiry: The Paradigm Revolution*. Beverly Hills: Sage Publications.

Lincoln, Y.S. (1989). Trouble in the land: the paradigm revolution in the academic disciplines. In J. C. Smart (ed.), *Higher Education: Handbook of Theory and Research in Higher Education*, Vol. V. New York: Agathon Press.

Lincoln, Y. S., and Guba, E.G. (1989). Ethics: the failure of positivist science. *Review of Higher Education* 12(3): 221–240.

Lincoln, Y.S., and Guba, E.G. (1985). *Naturalistic Inquiry*, Beverly Hills: Sage Publications.

Logan, S.W. (1988). A study of four undergraduate computer-writers. *Collegiate Micro-computer* 6(2): 135–145, 176.

Loo, C.M., and Rolison, G. (1986). Alienation of ethnic minority students at a predominantly white university. *Journal of Higher Education* 57 (1): 58–77.

Milam, J.H., Jr. (1989). *Paradigms of Theory in Higher Education*. Doctoral Dissertation, University of Virginia. Ann Arbor: University Microfilms International. #9023474.

Milam, J.H., Jr. (1990). Paradigms of theory in higher education. Paper presented at the Annual Meeting of the Association for the Study of Higher Education, Portland, Oregon, November 2, 1990.

Milam, J.H., Jr. (1991). The presence of paradigms in the core higher education journal literature. *Research in Higher Education* 32(6): 651–668.

Morgan, G. (1983). *Beyond Method: Strategies for Social Research*. Beverly Hills: Sage Publications.

Overman, E.S. (1987) Policy physics: exploring the convergence of quantum physics and policy science. *Management Science and Policy Analysis Journal* 4(2): 30–39.

Pascarella, E.T., Ethington, C.A., and Smart, J.C. (1988). The influence of college on humanitarian/civic involvement values. *Journal of Higher Education* 59(4): 412–437.

Pascarella, E.T., and Terenzini, P.T. (1991). *How College Affects Students*. San Francisco: Jossey-Bass Publishers.

Perry, W.G. (1970). *Forms of Intellectual and Ethical Development in the College Years: A Scheme*. New York: Holt, Rinehart, and Winston.

Perry, W.G. (1981). Cognitive and ethical growth. In A. Chickering (ed.), *The Modern American College: Responding to the New Realities of Diverse Students and a Changing Society*. San Francisco: Jossey-Bass Publishers.

Schwandt, T.A. (1989). Solutions to the paradigm conflict: coping with uncertainty. *Journal of Contemporary Ethnography* 17(4): 379–407.

Schwartz, P., and Ogilvy, J. (1979). *The Emergent Paradigm: Changing Patterns of Thought and Belief.* Menlo Park, CA: SRI International.

Terenzini, P.T., and Pascarella, E.T. (1991) Twenty years of research on college students: lessons for future research. *Research in Higher Education* 32(1): 83–92.

Thompson, K. (1991). *Learning at Evergreen: An Assessment of Cognitive Development.* Olympia, Washington: Washington Center for Improving the Quality of Undergraduate Education.

Tierney, W.G. (1991). *Official Encouragement, Institutional Discouragement: Minorities in Academe—The Native American Experience,* Norwood, NJ: Ablex. Working Draft.

Townsend, B.K. (1991). The impact of feminist scholarship upon the study of higher education: an analysis of two higher education journals. Paper presented at the Annual Meeting of the Association for the Study of Higher Education, Boston, MA, November 2, 1991.

Introduction: Feminist Research Methods

Joyce McCarl Nielsen

Feminist research methods is an exciting, emergent, and potentially revolutionary academic sub-discipline, but by its very nature it is also controversial. Some writers and researchers have questioned whether it is possible to identify certain methods as distinctly feminist; some have suggested that the expression itself may be a contradiction in terms. As Parlee (1986:5) observed, "The notion of 'feminist methodology' strikes some of us as absolute nonsense while others take it for granted as a useful concept."

To understand this controversy, we must first understand what traditional social scientists mean by *methods*. In the first part of this Introduction, I describe scientific method as it is usually formally presented and show that, at first glance, it does seem contradictory to feminist-based inquiry. In the second section I demonstrate that there is an identifiable feminist approach to research that is grounded in both an older positivist-empirical tradition and in a newer postempirical one.[1] I argue, too, that feminist methods (in the broadest sense of that term) is part—perhaps the best part—of a larger intellectual movement that represents a fundamental shift away from traditional social science methodology. Thus feminist research is contributing to a transformation of what traditionally has been called methods in the same way that feminist scholarship has transformed substantive academic disciplines and subdisciplines from literary criticism to history, anthropology, and psychology.[2]

Scientific Method as a Way of Knowing

Most people understand the term methods to mean the scientific method; the scientific method, in turn, is best seen as one of the ways people (especially scholars) have tried to answer the question, "How do we know what we know?" When we say, for example, that the earth is round, that aggression is a common response to frustration, that women has a distinctive moral developmental history, that men excel at math, or that human infants need love and care in order to thrive, on what grounds do we base these assertions? What would we consider evidence or proof for such statements if they were challenged, as these particular statements have been at one time or another?[3] Do we most trust self-reflective knowledge, practical reasoning, or traditional authority as the final arbiter of what is right and what is real?

The history of Western philosophy shows that some fairly well-defined schools of thought—what philosophers call epistemologies, or theories of knowledge—have characterized different historical times and places. Examples are Greek rationalism, which posited logic as the final test of truth; seventeenth- and eighteenth-century empiricism, which held sense perception to be the sole source of valid human knowledge; Hegelian dialectics, where thought proceeds by contradiction and the reconciliation of contradiction; dialectical materialism, the method of Karl Marx, who regarded knowledge and ideas as reflections of material conditions; and mysticism, which holds that knowledge is communicable only in poetic imagery and through metaphor, if at all. Certainly the unquestioned authority of the scientific method as the best way to study both natural and social-cultural phenomena has characterized our own time.

Two distinguishable and dominant tendencies within the scientific tradition of method are, of course, rationalism and empiricism. The dominance of pure reason or logic (to the point of virtual absence of interest in observation) is the earlier mode. In discussions about the nature of the physical world, for example, early Greek philosophers made such statements as "What is, is," and "What is not, is not," or "Thou canst not know nor utter what is not—that is impossible" (Parmenides, cited in Jones, 1970:21). An example of seventeenth-century (versus classical) rationalism is Descartes's famous statement, "I think; therefore, I am." This statement is considered true because it would be a contradiction in terms to both think and not be. The first part of the statement makes the negation of the second part illogical. The fact that Descartes's ontological reality (his sense of existence or being) was grounded in thinking rather than, say, feeling or loving—he did not say "I feel (or love); therefore, I am"—illustrates an extraordinary trust in rational thought.

Empiricism, the second dominant theme, is probably more familiar to modern readers. This is the process of directly observing, recording, or monitoring the social and natural world. Contemporary physical scientists, for example, use sophisticated and elaborate measuring instruments to examine and manipulate aspects of the natural world. Although there are other ways to justify what we think we know (for example, divine revelation), the combination of rationalist (which now often takes the form of logic) and empiricism in modern science captures the dominant trends in Western thinking.

In spite of changing dominant epistemologies, one issue—which we will call "objectivism versus relativism" for now—has characterized the Western discourse on knowledge. Because of its importance to understanding feminist methods, I will outline this issue. Its relevance to the definition of feminist methods, how feminist inquiry is both similar to and different from other ways of knowing, and how feminist research fits into the particular historical context of contemporary epistemology will become clear.

At least since Plato's time there has been a tendency to take an either/or position about whether it is possible to obtain absolute or indubitable knowledge about the world. At one extreme are the many well-known philosophers (for example, Descartes, Kant, Spinoza, Hegel, Schopenhauer) who spent much of their lives searching for a foundation or basis for arriving at absolute knowledge. This search has mainly taken the form of assuming that there is some objective (that is, independent of the knower) world that is knowable. At the other extreme are those (like the Greek sophists or contemporary philosopher of science Paul Feyerabend) who answer the question "How can we be sure of what we know" with a despairing "We can't, not really." Their argument is that there is no final, ultimate measure of truth that all can agree on. The modern version of this kind of skepticism is relativism, which asserts that all knowledge is culture-bound, theory-bound, and/or historically specific—that is, understandable and valid only within a specific time, place, theory, or perspective.[4] Some distinguish between cognitive and moral relativism, arguing that we *can* be certain about scientifically based knowledge of the natural world but that moral or ethical judgments are relative—that is, dependent on one's values, which are culture-bound. Others say that everything we know (including knowledge about the physical world) is contextual. Some relativists argue further that because there are no sure grounds for choosing between competing explanations or theories, such different and sometimes contradictory ideas, thoughts, or claims are equally good or valid. This idea is sometimes called pluralism.

The dilemma of how we can be sure of our knowledge has been with us a long time. Yet it takes on new urgency and seriousness in contemporary society because of the recent loss of faith in science by social scientists and the redefinition of scientific method as we have understood it. This point will be elaborated on later.

Scientific Method in Textbooks

Even though most people have some sense of what is meant by doing something "scientifically," it is surprisingly difficult to say exactly what makes science scientific. This is partly because what is now called science developed over a period of several hundred years. During this time it evolved from a small reform movement (against authority based on tradition) characterized by little specialization and minimal division of labor into a large-scale, government- and military-sponsored, bureaucratic and specialized complex.

A second reason it is difficult to define what science essentially is arises from the claim that science is a method, or a way of knowing, that different disciplines have in common rather than a subject matter. Although people often think of science as comprising those disciplines that deal with the physical/natural world (astronomy, physics, geology, chemistry), philosophers of science and scientists themselves define science more abstractly as comprising disciplines that use scientific methods to gain or develop knowledge. We can tentatively and briefly define scientific method as including an appeal to empirical evidence, experimentation (defined as the purposeful manipulation of physical matter or events in order to gauge their effects), and the use of inductive and deductive logic. (Deduction is inference that follows necessarily from premise to conclusion; induction is inference from the particular—usually an observation—to a more general statement.)

But as Bernstein (1976), Harding (1986), and others pointed out, it is difficult to find a procedure or combination of procedures common to all of the disciplines we now call scientific. Astronomy, geology, and math, for example, are not primarily experimental, whereas physics is. And, of course, people who do not call themselves scientists routinely use empirical evidence as well as deductive and inductive reasoning.

Even more interesting is that physics is considered the model of science—"The most real of sciences" to use Haraway's (1981:475) phrase. Yet it is unlike the different disciplines we call scientific, at least in terms of (1) its considerable use of experimentation and formal logic, (2) the comparative simplicity of its subject matter, which is neither self-reflective nor intentional (as is human behavior, which is, of course, the subject matter of the social sciences), and (3) its minimal use of interpretation (Harding, 1986). This is significant because the social sciences, in their quest for academic respectability during their formative years, adapted physics and its methods as a model. Thus they not only made the assumption that the social world could be explored and studied in the same way as the physical world, but they also chose to emulate a form of science that is not very representative.

The argument I make in this chapter (shared by many others) is that on close analysis of what scientists actually do as opposed to what they and others say they do, the scientific method is inherently less distinguishable from other ways of knowing than previously thought. I will demonstrate this by first considering the scientific method that is endorsed by social scientists in their methods textbooks.

Most texts list a set of interrelated assumptions that are shared by social scientists who adopt a naturalistic approach to social phenomena but that are usually unstated and/or nonconscious in their particular works. The first assumption is that the social world is knowable (in the certain, nonrelativistic way discussed earlier) and in the same way that the natural world is knowable—that is, through observation and recording of what appears as "objective" reality by a subjective (independent) researcher. This is the "objectivity" assumption—that there is an objective (independent of the subjective knower) reality to be known. This assumption presumed, in turn, a distinction or separation between the subjective knower and the objective to be known world. This second assumption is referred to as the subject-object separation assumption. An extension of this is the idea that the subjective should not infect objective truth—that evaluative concerns of the subjective knower should be excluded.

A third assumption, called the empirical assumption, is that verification of one's claims about the social world should be based on the use of the senses, which, it is assumed, will give accurate and reliable information about human behavior. We observe through touch, sight, smell, hearing, and seeing, though sometimes indirectly with the use of measurement; information gained through the senses is considered the way to be "objective." The key word here is observe. It is also assumed that different observers exposed to the same data will come to more or less the same conclusions; thus intersubjective verification is not only possible but desirable.

The fourth assumption is that there is order in the social world, that social life is patterned, and that this pattern takes a predominantly cause-and-effect form. In other words, things don't just happen. This is called the cause-and-effect assumption, and it is reflected in the overall goal of the social scientist (in the naturalistic tradition, at any rate): to develop universal laws about the social world or social behavior—that is, generalizations that hold true across time and place and in many different conditions or situations. Notice that this purpose assumes that in spite of historical and cultural variation there is something permanent and regular about social life that can be captured in generalizations and abstract laws. This is a rationalist assumption—that social life is orderly, rational.

The fifth and final assumption is that there is a unity of the sciences (including the social sciences) insofar as they all share the same method of going about learning about the world, and that it is the best, if not the only, legitimate way to ground knowledge. Methods texts also assert that scientific conclusions—that is, the body of scientific knowledge at any given time—are always tentative (open to subsequent modification) and that the rules and procedures of science minimize subjectivity and personal bias.

These assumptions, then, are associates with a knowledge-generating approach that emphasizes rationality ("no contradictions"), impersonality ("the more objective, the better"), and prediction and control of events or phenomena studied. That is, it is a short step from discovering regularities to predicting them and then to controlling them. Indeed, this seems to be the end product of much science. In the natural sciences prediction and control are used presumably for human benefit. The social sciences have been less successful in this regard, yet the goal of much research is to explain and thereby solve what are defined as social problems. (An indeterminate world view, in contrast to a deterministic [cause and effect] one, means some degree of unpredictability or lack of pattern, thus making control and intervention difficult, if not impossible.

The Feminist Challenge: A First Look

Oakley's (1981) study of the transition to motherhood for fifty-five women is a good starting point for understanding feminist research. She discovered quickly that textbook advice about interviewing (for example, to maintain a certain distance between yourself and the interviewee, to "parry," or avoid, answering questions so as not to influence the answers of the interviewee, and so on) not only would not work but would also limit her ability to communicate with respondents in a way that would generate worthwhile and meaningful information. She asks how one can parry questions like "Have you got any children?" "Did you breast feed?" "Do you think my baby's got too many clothes on?" and "Why do some women need caesareans?" (p. 42). It would be obviously rude to evade or dodge such questions and then turn around and ask the respondents to answer similarly personal and matter-of-fact questions. Her successful research strategy turned out to be quite the opposite of what textbooks advocated. She not only answered questions, thereby becoming an important source of information and reassurance about the unknowns and anxieties related to childbirth, but established and continued to maintain a friendship with over a third of the women participants even after the study was over. In short, she got involved. The obviously successful consequences of her involvement directly challenges the subject-object separation referred to earlier.

A second example of feminist research—Freeman's (1975) study of the women's movement of the 1960s—also illustrates the lack of relevance of traditional scientific methodology to high-quality research.[5] I cannot capture all the complexity and richness of this study in a short space, but the gist of her argument is that two branches of the women's movement (the younger and the older) were involved in creating the conditions that led the movement to emerge at the time that it did. These conditions included a cooptable communication network (established in part by the New Left movement), a crisis (the circumstances surrounding passage of Title VII of the 1964 Civil Rights Act), and a sense of relative deprivation (when rewards are perceived to be incommensurate with effort or contribution). More important for our discussion is how she arrived at this assessment: Her research depended heavily on her participation in the movement. She traveled to and attended both informal and formal meetings and conventions; she interviewed key persons in different factions of the movement and recorded their talks; she monitored the movement through newspaper accounts and did library research to check relevant historical and legal documents. In brief, the work was multimethodological and required the researcher's personal involvement—hardly the recipe for "objective," scientifically sound work in the ideal sense described earlier.

These are not unique examples. Others have described feminist research as contextual, inclusive, experiential, involved, socially relevant, multimethodological, complete but not necessarily replicable, open to the environment, and inclusive to emotions and events as experienced (Reinharz, 1983). Feminist inquiry is much more than this list of characteristics, but for now the point is that given the obvious contrast between it and textbook definitions of scientific research, the expression "feminist research methods" does seem to be a contradiction in terms. It would seem that feminist research cannot be methodological in the sense of scientific method as presented thus far. My argument, however, is that the sketch (given earlier) of the scientific method as presented in textbooks is a false or at least incomplete picture of the scientific research process as we now know it. To elaborate, I will first outline what is referred to as the crisis in contemporary philosophy of science and then trace some of the events that led up to this crisis. In this context, then, we will take a second and closer look at the nature of feminist inquiry and expand on its part of this contemporary drama.

The Postempirical Crisis in Knowledge

Considered the only way to sure and respectable knowledge, science as a way of knowing has dominated modern life. In the past 25 years, however, we have seen the development of what philosophers of science call the postempirical period, which is characterized by the realization that the scientific method is not the ultimate test of knowledge or basis for claims to truth that we once thought it was. This realization is critical because there seems to be nothing to replace science— what can we depend on, if not science? Without some agreed-upon foundation for knowing we are extremely uncomfortable. I should add, however, that the sense of crisis is expressed more by philosophers, historians of science, epistemologists, sociologists of knowledge, and those in related disciplines than by practicing social scientists, and even less by practicing natural scientists. Though many factors have contributed to this new skepticism and ensuing crisis in knowledge, several are particularly important here. These include two traditions of thought in the social sciences: the interpretive and the critical.

The Hermeneutic Tradition

The interpretive, of hermeneutic, tradition can be defined briefly as a theory and method of interpreting meaningful human action. Those working in this tradition represent an exception to the dominant trend in the social sciences because they question the wholesale applications of natural science methods to the study of social life, even though they share some of the textbook assumptions listed earlier. Specifically, they are concerned with the importance of meaning in social interaction and argue that limiting research to observable human action misses the most important part of the story. To explain and understand any human social behavior, they argue, we need to know the meaning attached to it by the participants themselves.

Nevertheless, it is important to note that they endorse the subjective-objective distinction. Max Weber, for example, whose work initially inspired development in this tradition, argued that studying social phenomena involves studying conscious human agents who attach sense or meaning to their actions. Thus the social sciences are inherently different from the natural sciences, and a full understanding of social action must involve *verstehen* (empathetic understanding). At the same time, he believed that although true objectivity is impossible, the social scientists should attempt to remain value-free. Notice here the implicit acceptance of the subjective-objective distinction, which distinguishes these earlier critics of the scientific method (as applied to social phenomena) from later critics who not only reject the subjective-objective distinction but question whether traditional scientific method is the appropriate description of what both natural and social scientists do.

Schutz (1967), who has probably done the most to develop and legitimize an interpretive method in the social sciences (especially for sociologists), made a strong case for the importance of meaning and its inseparability from human action. As Bernstein (1976:145) said, for Schutz, "[Human] action is intrinsically meaningful; it is endowed with meaning by human intentionality, i.e., by consciousness. . . . We are continuously ordering, classifying, and interpreting our ongoing experiences according to various interpretive schemes." But how can we, as subjective, meaning-producing persons ourselves, be objective about the subjective meanings of others?

Schutz argued that social scientists must "bracket"—that is, hold in abeyance or set aside temporarily—the pragmatic and private concerns that dominate their own everyday lives and thus assume the attitude of a disinterested observer. In other words, by suspending their own subjectivity, researchers can be "objective" about the subjectivity of others. This way of acknowledging and studying subjective meaning objectively, then, illustrates endorsement of the subjective-objective dichotomy. Whether researchers are actually able to bracket their own subjectivity in the way Schutz described, however, is a question we will consider later.

The value of work in this tradition is that it has provided alternative research models—especially during a period of otherwise naturalistic hegemony. Participant observation, for example, which is a research strategy of direct participation in and observation of the community, social group, or event being studied, characterizes research in this tradition. Indeed, the two examples of feminist research I presented earlier could have been labeled interpretive as well as feminist. If it sounds contradictory to say both that these research projects benefited from the investigators having gotten involved and that they fit a research style modeled on the basis of a disinterested researcher-observer, it is partly because there is some question about whether a researcher can ever be really disinterested. In any case it is difficult to determine what it is to be "disinterested."

As you will see, feminist work has an interpretive dimension that attempts to transcend or move beyond concerns about personal prejudgments. Furthermore, there is a gap between the way research is presented and the way it is executed on a daily basis. A number of published case histories or "inside" stories of research projects illustrate this point rather well (for example, Becker, 1971; Horowitz, 1976; Bell and Newby, 1977; Roberts, 1981). This point is important because it buttresses the argument made earlier that traditional conceptions of science, especially as depicted in textbooks, are somewhat inaccurate.

In any case, in the context of the positivist (scientific) tradition, research strategies (for example, interviewing, participant observation) used by phenomenologists generate data that are considered less "objective" than that produced by physical scientists,[6] yet they are considered "scientific" to the extent that they share with positivism the underlying assumption that there is indeed an objective reality that is separate and separable from the (subjective) researcher. Thus phenomenologists differ more from positivistic social scientists with respect to their belief in how one can best know and understand that reality than with the assumption that it is objectively knowable.

The overall effect of the interpretive tradition is that it has kept alive the critique of (but not replaced) the natural science model that stresses objectivism, which is still the majority view. It has provided a legitimate alternative for those who want to stay within the scientific tradition, but incorporate the subjective into their research.

Critical Theory

Critical theorists (also referred to as the Frankfurt School) have also argued against the wholesale use of a science model for social inquiry and at the same time have been critical (in a debunking sense) of the practice of natural science itself. Criticism in this tradition means more than a negative judgment; it refers to the more positive act of detecting and unmasking, or exposing, existing forms of beliefs that restrict or limit human freedom. Thus it differs from the hermeneutic tradition in its purpose. To adopt Habermas's (1970) trichotomous identification of the cognitive interests that generate the different research/knowledge traditions considered here, we can say that the positivists' goal is to predict and control, the hermeneutics' is to understand, and the critical theorists' approach is to emancipate—that is, to uncover aspects of society, especially ideologies, that maintain the status quo by restricting or limiting different groups' access to the means of gaining knowledge.

Thus, theory is "critical" because it departs from and questions the dominant ideology, creating at least the possibility of being "outside" of that ideology. The dominant ideology in this context is usually that of capitalistic political and economic organization. Take, for example, the beliefs that individuals are naturally competitive and that people get pretty much what they deserve; ideas like these help to justify the status quo, so that social patterns such as extreme individualism, competitiveness, and poverty appear to be inevitable or natural.

What does critical theory have to do with our discussion of methods and feminist inquiry? In direct contrast to the positivism that goes with the endorsement of the scientific method, the critical tradition rejects the idea that there can be "objective" knowledge. Proponents of the tradition argue that there is no such thing as an objectively neutral or disinterested perspective, that everyone or every group (including themselves) is located socially and historically, and that this context inevitably influences the knowledge they produce. Knowledge, in short, is socially constructed.[7]

This assertion bring us back to the perennial issue of methods, introduced earlier as the issue of foundationalism (the belief in a basis for absolute knowledge) versus relativism. The question is, if every group's knowledge is grounded in history and social structure, then whose view should prevail? And what criteria should we use to decide? Writers in the critical tradition have provided several answers to this question, but I will elaborate on only one because it is relevant to feminist inquiry—this is the notion of standpoint epistemology.

Standpoint Epistemology

Briefly described, standpoint epistemology begins with the idea that less powerful members of society have the potential for a more complete view of social reality than others, precisely because of their disadvantaged position. That is, in order to survive (socially and sometimes even physically), subordinate persons are attuned to or attentive to the perspective of the dominant class (for example, white, male, wealthy) as well as their own. This awareness gives them the potential for what Annas (1978) called "double vision," or double consciousness—a knowledge, awareness of, and sensitivity to both the dominant world view of the society and their own minority (for example, female, black, poor) perspective. For example, given that blacks in our culture are exposed to dominant white culture in school and through mass media as well as in interaction with whites, we can see how it is possible that blacks could know both white and black culture while whites know only their own. The same might be said about women vis-à-vis men.

To the extent that women as a group are socially subordinate to men as a group, it is to women's advantage to know how men view the world and to be able to read, predict, and understand the interests, motivations, expectations, and attitudes of men. At the same time, however, because of the division of labor by sex found in all societies and sex-specific socialization practices, sex segregation, and other social processes that guarantee sex differences in life experience, women will know the world differently from men. It is almost as though there is a separate women's culture, which is certainly not the dominant one. Feminists use terms like "underground," "invisible" or "less visible," or "the underside" to describe women's culture, history, and lives. This does not mean that all women are acutely aware of what they share with other women. But members of the subordinate group in any dominant-subordinate relational system will have the potential for this awareness.

The standpoint notion is based on several premises outlined by Hartsock (1983). The first is that one's material life (what one does for a living and related facts such as the quality of one's material surroundings) structures and limits one's understanding of life. Being a coal miner, for example, would lead to quite a different understanding (standpoint) than being chief executive officer of a corporation. A second premise is that members of more powerful and less powerful groups will potentially have inverted, or opposed, understandings of the world. Third, the dominant group's view will be "partial and perverse" in contrast to the subordinate group's view, which has the potential to be more complete. The dominant group's view is partial and perverse because, according to Hartsock, so long as the group is dominant, it is in the members' interest to maintain, reinforce, and legitimate their own dominance and particular understanding of the world, regardless of how incomplete it may be.

Hartsock gave the example of the worker's versus the owner's view of the process of production. The owner sees it as a matter of exchange: the purchase and sale of labor power. The worker has the potential to see—is in the position to see—the real point of production, which is, in the final analysis, the continuation of the species. Jagger (1983) even more dramatically contrasted evaluations of the social order from the viewpoints of owner and worker in Western capitalistic society, using the terms "Eden" and "hell" to represent their respective viewpoints. These examples illustrate that the standpoint of the more politically powerful group is considered by these analysts as being more superficial than false. It does not get to a deeper or underlying meaning of social life, which is accessible to the subordinate. A final but important point made by Hartsock is that the less powerful group's standpoint has to be developed or acquired through education (including, presumably, consciousness-raising); its conscious distinctiveness from the usually more widely shared dominant group's view cannot be taken for granted. Without conscious effort to reinterpret reality from one's own lived experience—that is, without political consciousness—the disadvantaged are likely to accept their society's dominant worldview. Indeed, because the less advantaged are often denied access to formal education, they are likely to be less knowledgeable than the dominant group. The point, however, is that according to standpoint epistemology—which has the main premise that one's everyday life has epistemological consequences and implications—the disadvantaged have the potential to be more knowledgeable, in a way, than the dominant group.

We will say more about standpoint epistemology in relation to "feminist" standpoints later. For now, the point is that the methodology of the critical tradition has provided an alternative to the otherwise dominant view of the scientific method and its assumptions.[8] And, as you will see, both Marxist and socialist feminists have built on this tradition in ways that are directly relevant to our question about the definition of feminist research methods.

Conclusion. These two alternative traditions, the interpretive-hermeneutic and the critical, are easily distinguishable from each other in terms of subject matter focus, purpose, specific methodologies, level of analysis, and so on. Yet they have both contributed to postempirical epistemology by providing the impetus and inspiration for developing a satisfactory alternative to empirical-analytical social science. More recent developments along these lines by Bernstein (1983), Gadamer (1975, 1980), Habermas (1984), and Hekman (1986), as well as by feminists, are delineated in a later section of this chapter.

To be discussed next are two events, one from within the practice of science itself and one from the history of science, which have also contributed to an erosion of the philosophers' and social scientists' endorsement of scientific methods. This erosion challenges the assumption of objectivity within the study of the natural world itself.

Science as Paradigm Shifting

In 1962 Thomas Kuhn published *The Structure of Scientific Revolutions*. Based on a historical analysis of the progress and success of Western science, his book redefined science in a way that had the effect of demythologizing it as pure truth in an ultimate sense. Until recently, most people thought of science as a cumulative process of the discovery of increasingly correct descriptions of the physical world. That is, there seemed to be an increasingly better fit between the theories of science and what we thought of as an independent, physical reality. The phenomenal success of scientific inquiry seemed to be a function of continuously testing increasingly accurate theories about nature against what was considered a given empirical reality. Kuhn's analysis challenged this conception of science, describing it instead as a social-historical process of paradigm transitions.

Paradigms are defined in two basic ways. First, as "the entire constellation of beliefs, values, techniques and so on shared by members of a given [scientific] community" (Kuhn, 1970:175). An example of such a constellation is the mechanical worldview of Newtonian physics. Second, paradigms are defined as concrete puzzle solutions that are like schema and are used as models to complete the full development of a particular theory. The mathematical expression, $f = ma$, for example, has various transformations that are similar in form but slightly different in content. That is, its specifics change as it is used to describe the movement of a simple pendulum, a gyroscope, or a vibrating string. Thus the use of this equation is an example of a puzzle-solution in physics. A paradigm shift, then, is a process whereby new ways of perceiving the world come to be accepted. According to Kuhn, paradigms function as maps or guides; they dictate the kinds of problems or issues that are important to address, the kinds of theories (explanations) that are acceptable, and the kinds of procedures that will solve the problems defined. At least they function this way until a new paradigm succeeds the old.

For example, it took several hundreds of years for scientists to exhaust all the possibilities presented by Isaac Newton's laws of motion, the paradigm that replaced Aristotelian laws of motion. Thus the work done in the aftermath of Newton's laws was carried out in the context of a single, widely accepted paradigm until Albert Einstein's work led to a rather different worldview and a new paradigm.

How do these transitions come about? Two conditions prompt them, according to Kuhn. The first is the presence and awareness of anomalies—that is, phenomena that either do not fit, contradict, or cannot be explained by the existing dominant paradigm. What is important is not only that they exist (because at any given time there are always anomalies) but that scientists take note of them and define them as counterinstances that challenge the truth or accuracy of the dominant paradigm, rather than defining them as irrelevant, bothersome, and unimportant minor deviations.

The second condition necessary for a paradigm transition (or what amounts to a scientific revolution) is sthe presence of an alternative paradigm, one that can account for both the phenomena that the earlier paradigm explained *and* the anomalies that it did not. During periods of what Kuhn called normal science, there is widespread agreement about the veracity of a paradigm, and the scientific work consists mainly of "mopping up" operations because it is primarily elaborating on and developing the implications of the paradigm. The work that occurs during transition or crisis periods, when two or more paradigms compete (for example, Galileo's heliocentric worldview versus the earth-centered model it replaced; Einsteinian versus Newtonian models of time/space) is called extraordinary science.

Kuhn's argument can be summarized by saying that data or observations are theory-laden (that is, the scientist only sees data in terms of their relevance to theory); that theories are paradigm-laden (explanations are grounded in worldviews); and that paradigms are culture-laden (worldviews, including ideas about human nature, vary historically and across cultures).

Kuhn's work and the discussion it generated contributed to the development of the postempiricist crisis of knowledge in several ways. First, it challenged the idea that the scientific process itself should not be examined in the same way that other phenomena are—that is, scientific statements themselves are now seen as more relative or specific to a given historical period and/or paradigm rather than as universals, as they are presented in science texts. As Bloor (1977) discussed, even mathematical principles are socially and historically grounded. Though the truth or correctness of "one plus one equals two" seems immutable, the meaning and interpretation of the number "one," for example, was different for the Greeks than it is for us. As Harding (1986) notes, they regarded one as the first (in the sense of a generator) of a lineage but not as an odd (as opposed to even) integer as we do.

Second, though Kuhn may not have intended it, his work challenged the idea of a fixed, absolute reality against which we test our notions about the natural world. Given Kuhn's description of science, it seems that objective reality changes with changing paradigms. After a scientific revolution, said Kuhn (1970:135), "The data themselves had changed. . . . Scientists work in a different world" because what they take to be the empirical world is shaped by the paradigms they use to understand it.

Third, Kuhn's work has prompted a closer look (if not just at the physical world) at what criteria are actually used to decide which of several competing paradigms about the natural world is more correct. Of course, scientists continue to use traditional criteria such as a paradigm's or theory's predictive accuracy, reliability, scope, consistency, fruitfulness, simplicity, or elegance. But Kuhn's analysis showed, in addition, the importance of agreement, or consensus, on the part of the scientific community, especially during a period of extraordinary science. Rather than clear-cut criteria and critical empirical tests, the criteria used were based on shared values, reasoned judgment, and the convincingness of an argument.

For example, the notion of the crucial experiment—one that produces results such that one of two or more competing theories can be ruled out—was seriously challenged. Again, because theories are incommensurable—they are grounded in distinct or separate frames of reference—there are no fixed criteria for determining one as more correct than the other. Theories and paradigms are comparable, of course, but the criteria are "open," and that openness includes discourse with other scientists. This idea poses a problem for some people because of its potential to lead to an inescapably relativistic view of our knowledge about the world. The question is whether subsequent paradigms are really progressive improvements compared to their predecessors or just different. Are all theories equally valuable and the dominance or acceptance of any one dependent on the outcome of scientists' talk and persuasion? There is a hermeneutic or interpretive dimension to science, which is increasingly being recognized by philosophers and historians of science (Giddens, 1982:14; Hekman, 1986; Heelan, 1983; Lyotard, 1984; Toulmin, 1982).

• • •

From Paradigm Shift to Feminist Standpoints and Dialectical Processes

If feminist inquiry represents a paradigm shift, it is a shift toward what Hartsock (1983), Harding (1986), Jaggar (1983) and others called feminists standpoints.[9] Standpoint is defined by Jaggar as "a position in society from which certain features of reality come into prominence and from which others are obscured" (p. 382). Feminist standpoints begin with but do not end with women's experiences, and as in the case of other standpoint epistemologies, they are more than perspectives. They involve a level of awareness and consciousness about one's social location and this location's relation to one's lived experience. In this section I develop more in depth the nature of feminist standpoints.

Following Hartsock (1983), we first note that much of women's work in modern industrial societies (childrearing and housework, but also some market work) (1) involves an emphasis on change (versus statis); (2) is characterized by interaction with natural substances (versus work that separates one from nature); (3) emphasizes quality versus quantity; and (4) involves in most activities a mind/body unity that is not found in administrative, intellectual, and managerial work. In short, traditional women's work involves everyday contact with material necessities (clothes, meals, bodies) and attention to natural changes in natural substances. I should add that these aspects of women's work are also often characteristic of the work of working-class and blue-collar men.

Further differences between women's work and most men's work include the fact that women simply work more (that is, more hours per day); that a greater proportion of their work is unpaid; that it is structured more by repetition; and that it is sensuous. Finally, women's reproductive work (childbearing and childrearing) involves more body involvement and is more relational and interpersonal. Smith (1979) made a similar distinction between women's work as being in the "bodily mode" and men's work in the "abstract, conceptual mode."

Given these differences in everyday work activities as well as in socialization experiences by sex,[10] women's and men's perspectives are not only (potentially) very different, but inverted, or at odds with each other. The premise here is: You are what you do. Further, Hartsock and feminist standpoint advocates argue that women are more able to see the viewpoints of both men and women, and thus a woman's understanding is potentially more complete, deeper, and more complicated. The implication for developing a specifically feminist epistemology is that a woman's perspective (if transformed through consciousness-raising) will lead to more accurate, more complex knowledge.

This last aspect of the standpoint concept is what makes it both promising and problematic. On the one hand, the potential for transcendence is there—that is, the perspective of a more complex understanding of social relations could promote change for the betterment of all or have a liberating effect. On the other hand, the standpoint concept implies that one group's perspective is more real (better or more accurate) than anothers. And "more accurate" implies that there are some criteria for accuracy. So again we are confronted with the problematic idea of an objective reality.

A second problem with standpoint epistemologies in general and feminist standpoints in particular is that they imply that the more oppressed or more disadvantaged group has the greatest potential for knowledge construction. If the group's view is less superficial and more encompassing than others', its knowledge should prevail. When carried to its logical conclusion, however, the implication of this notion is that the greater the oppression, the broader or more inclusive one's potential knowledge is, a conclusion that few scholars can agree with. This conclusion leads one into a discussion that is not very productive about who is more oppressed (and how to prove it) and therefore potentially more knowledgeable.

Dialectical processes. More relevant for our purposes is Westkott's (1979) description and analysis (which appear in this book) of the dialectical tension that characterizes both women's experience and feminist research. As developed by Westkott, *dielectical* refers to discontinuities, oppositions, contradictions, tensions, and dilemmas that form part of women's concrete experience in patriarchal worlds—dilemmas that are realized only with a feminist consciousness.

Consider, for example, that according to tests that measure popular, ideal sex stereotypes such as the Bem Sex Role Inventory (Bem, 1976), a woman in our society who is gullible and yielding is conforming to a feminine ideal. Yet these same attributes would limit one's ability to be effective in the world at large. Or consider the normative expectation that women (and, earlier, U.S. Blacks) present themselves as smiling and cheerful. Compliance means conforming to a stereotyped role and some degree of social invisibility. Noncompliance means risking being labeled bitchy, difficult, or angry (Frye, 1988). Similarly, a young woman's decision about being sexually active puts her in a no-win situation: If she chooses to be active, she risks social censure as well as pregnancy and/or the side effects of dangerous contraceptives. If she chooses not to be sexually active, she risks being defined as prudish or frigid. Also consider a woman's conformity to body-damaging and body-limiting fashions such as high heels, girdles, panty hose, tight skirts, and so on. Nonconformity is better for her body but it means she appears different and even weird. As Westkott put it, women "oppose the very conditions to which they conform."

Westkott's examples of dialectical tension focus on the contradictions of women scholars and researchers—for example, that women feminist scholars are both "inside," or part of, their disciplines and "outside" of them due to their feminist perspectives, and that women's creativity often expresses a discontinuity between consciousness and action. The notion of dialectical tension and the creativity it generates is well developed in the Westkott chapter in this book. The point is that dialectical processes characterize feminist inquiry in many different ways and at different levels. This is evident in many of the contributions to this book. Sometimes it is explicit, as in Anderson et al., who illustrate the importance in obtaining oral history of gently probing and listening for a woman's subjective meanings of her behavior, which are often at variance with the meanings internalized from the larger society. A dialectical theme is also evident in Tsing's account of Induan Hiling, a female shaman in the Meratus Mountains of Indonesian Borneo, who endorsed and used the spiritual tradition of her culture yet simultaneously challenged and revised it. The dialectical theme is even more dramatically or forcefully expressed in Ferree's report of working-class women in Germany who are neither completely in the public nor the domestic sphere, but stand precariously between the two. Finally, Kushner's reinterpretation of the meaning of suicide for women (and men) suggests that when a woman takes her own life it may be a behavioral way of rebelling against the situation she is in, though this theory contradicts the assumed nonaggressive nature of women.

From Feminist Standpoints to Fusion of Horizons

I said earlier that feminist inquiry is contributing to a transformation of methodology and resolution of the epistemological crisis by producing exemplary research in a reconstructive postempirical context. The postempirical period has been characterized by many efforts to identify and delineate research strategies that are alternatives to positivism—for example, Gergen (1982) and Reason and Rowan (1981). Most of these efforts are bets described as "contextual" in that they are variations of the relativistic theme we outlined earlier. They are satisfying and sophisticated because they build on the recognition that social knowledge itself is socially constructed in context and in interaction with others. But they do not directly answer the lingering question, How do we know what we know? In other words, they do not explicitly lead the researcher out of the "either" (objectivism) /or (relativism)" dilemma with which we began this Introduction. Without agreed-upon, demonstrable criteria, how does one argue for a given feminist interpretation?

Yet out of the postempirical context, such criteria are being developed. As a tentative guideline, we can adapt Bernstein's (1976:xiv) formula: "An adequate, comprehensive . . . social theory must be at once empirical, interpretive, and critical." Empirical, interpretive, and critical: These are our criteria for now. Several other writers (Bowles, 1984; Farganis, 1986; Kasper, 1986; Wolff, 1975) have explicitly proposed the integration of epistemological aspects of feminism with the hermeneutic and critical theory traditions. And though they did not consider feminist inquiry, both Hekman's (1986) and Bernstein's (1983) syntheses of major contemporary writers in these traditions can be appropriated for our purposes.

Bernstein argued first that we (postempiricist researchers) can move "beyond relativism and objectivism" to endorse a new approach to knowledge and research. By this he meant that we are now abandoning (and rightly so) the either/or stance about irrefutable knowledge that I described at the beginning of this Introduction. In other words, there is something in between a foundation for irrefutable knowledge and relativism with all its problems: a synthesis of several major ideas from the traditions we outlined earlier.

To begin this synthesis, consider the problem of anthropologists studying another culture. To understand a culture other than their own, researchers can relate to the object of understanding (the other culture) in several possible ways. The first is to study the other culture using the standards or norms of the researchers' own cultures as criteria against which the other society is evaluated. This, of course, is ethnocentrism at its worst and is considered unacceptable, although Western research-ers are often nonconsciously ethnocentric. A second possibility is for the researchers to do as Schutz advocated and "bracket" (that is, hold in abeyance) their own judgments, beliefs, norms, and standards while studying the other culture. But this is what more recent hermeneutic thinkers have said is impossible. Gadamer, in particular, argued the opposite of earlier writers, asserting that one cannot escape from one's own assumptions or worldview. He said that there is no such thing as knowledge outside of a frame of reference.

A third possibility is to adopt the view of the alien culture—to "go native" as anthropologists say. Though not always practical, going native can be considered a form of relativism—that is, acknowledging the coexistence and legitimacy of different perspectives. It tends, however, to lead to the skeptical position described earlier: that there is no way to decide which interpretation of a culture is "better," and thus all are equally correct.

Bernstein likened the dilemma of trying to study another culture without being ethnocentric or going native to that of choosing among alternative paradigms or theories in the natural sciences and to considering alternative interpretations of works of art or literature. These are both different manifestations of the same problem because the processes involved (choosing, judging, weighing evidence for or against a given argument, and so on) and the outcome are partly determined on the basis of dialogue with other members of the scientific or academic community.

One could argue that there is no need to determine one view as more correct, that a plurality of views could prevail. But at some point—such as when important decisions have to be made—some view of reality must be endorsed. To develop a policy about abortion, for example, one would have to take a stance in an area where there are conflicting, seemingly irreconcilable views. Or consider the practice of introducing or imposing Western technology and normative standards—exploitive factory-based manufacturing and other forms of commercialization—into non-Western cultures. The British government's outlawing and eventual eradication of suttee (the practice of burning or burying women alive with their deceased husbands) in Hindu India is another case in point.[11] Whose standards of rationality, meaning, or ethics should prevail? During an official state visit, former First Lady Rosalyn Carter walked behind the then President Carter in order to conform to the host country's norms. Yet that behavior contradicted another normative standard: that women and men be treated equally. Though this is a single instance, it is a public, visible example of the issue at hand. So the question is not just whose standards should prevail but what criteria we use when different groups' standards conflict, compete, or differ. In these cases, decisions have to be made and they inevitably reflect assumptions, or theories, about human nature and social relations between children and adults and men and women.

The dilemma, then, is that once one rejects objectivism, the alternative seems to be a kind of relativism that is not very satisfying. This problem involving the various possible relations between the researcher and the researched captures the crisis in modern epistemology. Further, these examples illustrate the extent to which ethical and practical policy issues are part of the larger process of knowledge formation.

Let us go back to the argument that one cannot separate oneself from one's own historical, cultural context. Gadamer (1976), building on (but differentiating himself from) the hermeneutic tradition, argued that it is precisely through the interplay between one's existing cognitions or values (what he called prejudgments) and the elements of other cultures or new theories that one develops knowledge. In other words, one's prejudgments, or prejudices, makes one more open-minded than closed-minded when one puts these prejudgments at risk, testing them through exposure to and encounter with others' prejudgments. Prejudgments, in Gadamer's (1976:9) words, "constitute the initial directedness of our whole ability to experience. Prejudices are biases of our openness to the world. They are simply conditions whereby we experience something—whereby what we encounter says something to us. . . ."

Prejudgments, then, are the means by which one reaches the truth. Gadamer argued further that prejudice is the ontological condition of humans in the world. Rather than bracketing them, we should use prejudgments as essential building blocks or components for acquiring new knowledge. To know, one needs to be aware of one's own prejudice but one cannot, indeed, should not, try to transcend them. It is necessary to go back and forth between the old and new theories, paradigms, cultures, or worldviews to create a new synthesis. (In fact, one of the weaknesses of earlier [Schutzian] phenomenology is that the emphasis on individual intent in order to find the meaning of behavior makes it difficult to develop and acknowledge the fact that meaning is intersubjective, negotiated, and therefore collective rather than individual [Hekman, 1986].)

This back and forth process is captured in Westkott's characterization of feminist inquiry as dialectical and in Gadamer's notion of "fusion of horizons," which we can now use to more completely describe feminist inquiry. *Horizon* in this context refers to the full range of one's standpoint and includes the particulars of one's situation (for example, historical time, place, culture, class; any number of contextual variables are appropriate here). The *fusion* results from seeking knowledge while grounded in a perspective (in this case, feminism) that cannot be bracketed or held aside during the inquiry process. So one's horizon is described as necessarily limited and finite. At the same time, however, it is open to relating or connecting with horizons other than one's own (for example, feminist work does not ignore men the way androcentric work ignores women). The resulting fusion represents an enlargement, broadening, or enrichment of one's own horizon (as when feminist work is more inclusive than previous work).

The fusion of horizons concept carries the double, or dual, vision and dialectical notions a step further than do standpoint epistemologies because it indicates a transcendent third and new view, or synthesis. This next step in knowledge generation is captured in expressions like beyond- or post-feminism. Too often, such expressions are used by people who show no indication of ever having had a feminist perspective. Even so, some contemporary feminist writers hint at a "next step." Support for a beyond-feminist notion, for example, can be found in results from some women studies integration projects (described earlier as organized, formal programs designed to integrate the new scholarship on women into the curriculum, usually via faculty development). Faculty are expected to become familiar with the new scholarship and revise a targeted course accordingly. Evaluation of these projects supports the notion that faculty often move through a series of stages, from male-centered to increasingly female-centered ways of thinking, with the final stage variously described in post-feminist terms (Nielsen and Abromeit, 1989; Tetreault, 1985). This pattern is similar to what is described by the fusion idea, where one's view is enlarged and broadened by the clashing of two cultures; in this case, however, it is male-dominated versus feminist paradigms that clash.

To further clarify this fusion notion and at the same time incorporate more fully the critical and emancipatory element of feminist inquiry, I will use a metaphor: Consider an ordinary everyday conversation between two people. If the context or setting is free enough—if the two people respect and trust each other and are roughly equal in materialistic terms—then both are free to engage in unlimited dialogue, and the resulting conversation is potentially very constructive, creative, and somewhat indeterminant (that is, not very predictable). Even if one of the parties has an agenda (or prejudgments, to use Gadamer's term), the course of the conversation and its outcome are not predictable. Because verbal interaction is so dynamic, the discussants' ideas, thoughts, beliefs, and statements get developed, modified, and expanded in the course of being juxtaposed with other ideas, thoughts, theories, and so on.

This is what happens (or can happen if the process of knowledge development is completely free) in our pursuit of knowledge. To the extent that knowledge formation is a dialogic process, as we have seen, it is an open process that requires a context of equality. Knowledge construction requires the material and social conditions that promote freedom and equality and that have no obstacles to open dialogue. It is in this way that we incorporate a critical dimension into our blueprint for knowledge. Feminist work is emancipatory in that it identifies obstacles to the kind of equality necessary for dialogue. Our agenda for knowledge construction, then, includes removing the structural features and barriers that distort or limit open, free dialogue.

Addressing the emancipatory element of feminist work more directly, Smith (1977, 1979), Westkott (1983), and others have argued that feminist research is *for* rather than *about* women. We should not forget that the original impetus for feminist inquiry was to find an educational strategy for eradicating sexism. Our goal after all is women's liberation, and we assume that creative and scholarly work can contribute to reaching it. As Westkott (1983) said, we cannot leave out the emancipatory element—that is, the opposition to as well as understanding of sexism, the judging of as well as seeing sexism. Both theory and "praxis" (the inseparable action component of critical theory)[12] are vital to feminist inquiry. Westkott talked about the importance of holding criticism (of sexism in society) in tension with vision (a new feminist worldview) as well as the importance of the interaction between social knowledge and self-knowledge, which produces both anger about the distance from knowledge of women's subordination. In a phrase, "The personal becomes intellectual, and the intellectual, personal" (Westkott, 1983:211).

The feminist scholarship included in this text is implicitly or explicitly critical. Two chapters describe women's active involvement in both organized and individually motivated efforts for social change (the chapters by Gluck and Tsing). Two chapters describe and criticize male-only perspectives in documentation and the research process itself: Kushner criticizes the stereotypes that inform statistics on suicide, and Hyde criticizes how statistically derived but miniscule sex differences in cognitive ability are misused. Fishman's analysis of how women do the work of everyday conversation between intimates is more implicitly critical, as is Kathlene's elaboration and implied celebration of a contextualist approach to public policy formation.

So far we have talked about some of the interpretive and emancipatory aspects of feminist research. We can now broaden our characterization of feminist work to include its empirical aspect by justifying empirical as a criterion. Throughout this Introduction, I have been somewhat inconsistent in my presentation of empiricism. On the one hand, I presented it as part of the classical, objective tradition that many are saying has run its course. On the other hand, I said that one criterion I used for choosing the articles for this book was empirical content—that they include at least some data or observations relevant to the writer's argument. As Haraway (1981) pointed out, it is contradictory to expose bad science (that is, biased work that is presented as objective truth)—thereby implicitly showing the constructed character of all science—and then to produce feminist science with its own facts. If *all* facts are theory-laden and thus laden with value and history, how can we say feminist facts are any truer than androcentric or nonfeminist ones? To the extent that it is more complete, more inclusive, more comprehensive, and more complex, feminist work comes closer to realizing, or at least better exemplifying, the fusion of horizons process we have described here. Further, there are several reasons for preferring some form of empiricism to presentations that are empty of empirical reference.

First, it would be archaic to endorse a return to nonempirical inquiry. In this respect, I would argue that we should retain the element of empiricism in any definition of what good inquiry is for the same reason that it was originally advocated: to help protect and guard against the use of superstition or personal bias (rather than evidence) as a basis for knowledge, though we have to acknowledge that the empiricist element does not guarantee much. But more substantively, we can justify the use of facts and observations with the use of a modified, distinctive definition of the term *objective*, one that distinguishes it from *objectivism*. Ricoeur (1977) made this distinction when he described both social action and written text as objective in the sense that, once performed (or written), both are "outside" of the actor, creator, or initiator. This attribute makes them available to the rest of the world, to the public. This sense of objectivity is consistent with our interpretation of knowledge production as a communal, intersubjective, dialogic examination or observation of facts and can be distinguished from objectivism, the assumption of a reality that is separate and distant from a subjective knower. In this way, "objectively" shared empirical evidence is part of the fusion of horizons that seems to be the beginning or basis of a viable postempirical epistemology. A final reason for preferring empirical to nonempirical work is that the rest of the world is still grounded in empiricist science. To convince others, to even talk to others, we need facts, observations, and data to support our arguments. As Weisstein (1979:187) said, "Evidence became a friend of mine."

Conclusion

We started this Introduction with a question of what constitutes knowledge. It seems appropriately feminist to end it with a request that knowledge address itself to the "big" but practical questions. Bowles (1983:42) said it well. "For me, that means, what do we need to know in order to survive? (This takes us to such 'problems' as nuclear power and ecology.) And, if we do survive, what do we have to know in order to live relatively peacefully and happily together? (This takes us to such 'problems' as the relationship between people of different sexes and races and classes.)"[13]
But enough talk *about* feminist methods. Let us consider some exemplary feminist inquiry. This book contains works by authors from various social science disciplines (sociology, history, anthropology, and political science). In Part I, the authors elaborate and develop some of the themes I have introduced. Included are contributions by Keller, who provides a well-developed and fascinating explanation for the masculine character of science itself; Westkott, whose work has already been discussed to some extent; Cook and Fonow, who very specifically and concretely described feminist methodologies; and Anderson et al., whose presentation of oral history sets the stage for Part 2.

In Part 2, Gluck exemplifies feminist inquiry through oral history; Tsing presents a combination of anthropological fieldwork and feminist literary analysis; Ferree reviews some unusual survey and interview work with women workers; Kushner reanalyzes and reinterprets data on sex differences in suicide rates; Hyde challenges arguments for sex differences in cognitive abilities with a reanalysis of quantitative data; and Fishman and Kathlene present two kinds of linguistic analysis.

Notes

1. "Postempirical" refers rather generally to a turning point in contemporary philosophy of science, epistemology, sociology of knowledge, and related fields. This turning point is characterized by work toward the development of an alternative to information about events leading up to this transition and the nature of the developing alternatives follow.

2. For accounts of the substantive impact feminist scholarship has had on various disciplines, see Du Bois et al. (1985), Farnham (1987), Langland and Gove (1983), Spender (1981), and Stacey and Thorne (1985).

3. See the chapter by Hyde in this volume for a challenge to the popular notion that men excel at math.

4. In contrasting foundationalism, defined by Hekman (1986:8) as belief in "an indubitable element of human existence that can 'ground' human knowledge" with relativism, I am following Bernstein (1983). He showed that the objectivism-relativism contrast is more relevant to contemporary epistemological issues than is the older objective-subjective dichotomy.

5. Freeman's work received the American Political Science Association's prize for the best work on women and politics in 1975.

6. Sometimes less and more objective data are called *soft* and *hard*, respectively. The hard-soft distinction, with its implicit evaluation that hard is better, is just one of many examples of genderisms in science (see Keller, 1985).

7. Some, but not all, writers in this tradition exempt knowledge about the physical world from this claim.

8. As an important part of what is called received, or generally accepted, knowledge, scientific methods and products can be seen as supporting the status quo, or serving the interests of the majority or dominant group. This does not mean that they always have done so. There are many historical and contemporary cases of scientists and scientific knowledge representing minority views, and opposing a nonscientific dominant view (for example, religious views that conflict with scientific views). However, science (along with its accompanying technology) has become a dominant worldview and to that extent serves someone's interests.

9. Though the cited authors mostly use the term feminist standpoint in the singular, they recognized, of course, that there are many different feminist standpoints. I use the plural to underscore that often overlooked fact.

10. Here Hartsock accepted the theories of Chodorow (1978) and Dinnerstein (1976) that a woman's sense of self is more relational and a man's is more separated, autonomous, and abstract. For more on this theme, see these authors' works and the chapters by Kathlene and Keller in this volume.

11. I do not endorse the practice of suttee; but I would like to point out that in order to endorse a relativistic stance about others' values and social practices and be consistent, one would have to apply this stance to all those practices, whether one agrees with them or not. In other words, it would seem somewhat inconsistent to tolerate women walking behind men but then draw the line at suttee. This is simply imposing one's own values on another culture. Of course, I realize that women walking behind men is not as serious or harmful a practice as is suttee, but they are both practices that reflect women's lower social and political status. Wearing high heels does not have the same consequences as clitoridectomy, but both practices are body-deforming and related to gender.

12. Marx used the term *praxis* to distinguish between what one does and what one thinks and to distinguish revolutionary practice from other types of activity.

13. Bowles's statement might be considered a contemporary version of Tolstoy's statement, "The only question important for us [is] 'What shall we do and how shall we live?'" (cited in Bernstein, 1976:47).

References

Aiken, Susan Hardy, Karen Anderson, Myra Dinnerstein, Judy Lensick, and Patricia Maccorquodale. "Trying Transformations: Curriculum Integration and the Problem of Resistance," *Signs: Journal of Women in Culture and Society*, Vol. 12, No. 2, 1987:255–275.

Annas, Pamela J. "New Worlds, New Words: Androgyny in Feminist Science Fiction," *Science-Fiction Studies*, Vol. 5, 1978:143–156.

Becker, Howard. *Sociological Work.* London: Allen Lane, 1971.

Bell, Colin, and Howard Newby. *Doing Sociological Research.* New York: Free Press, 1977.

Bem, Sandra L. "Probing the Promise of Androgyny," pp. 48–62 in A.G. Kaplan and J.P. Bean (eds.). *Beyond Sex-Role Stereotypes: Readings Toward a Psychology of Androgyny.* Boston: Little, Brown, 1976.

Bernstein, Richard J. *The Restructuring of Social and Political Theory.* New York: Harcourt Brace Jovanovich, 1976.

————. *Beyond Objectivism and Relativism: Science, Hermeneutics, and Praxis.* Philadelphia: University of Pennsylvania Press, 1983.

Bloor, David. *Knowledge and Social Imagery.* London: Routledge & Kegan Paul, 1977.

Bowles, Gloria. "Is Women's Studies an Academic Discipline?" pp. 32–45 in Gloria Bowles and Renate Duelli Klein (eds.) *Theories of Women's Studies.* London: Routledge & Kegan Paul, 1983.

————. "The Uses of Hermeneutics for Feminist Scholarship," *Women's Studies International Forum*, Vol. 7, No. 3, 1984:185–188.

Chodorow, Nancy. *The Reproduction of Mothering: Psychoanalysis and the Sociology of Gender.* Berkeley: University of California Press, 1978.

Dinnerstein, Dorothy. *Teh Mermaid and the Minotaur: Sexual Arrangements and Human Malaise.* New York: Colophon Books/Harper and Row, 1976.

Du Bois, Ellen Carol, et al. *Feminist Scholarship: Kindling in the Groves of Academe.* Urbana and Chicago: University of Illinois Press, 1985.

Farganis, Sondra. "Social Theory and Feminist Theory: The Need for Dialogue," *Sociological Inquiry*, Vol. 56, No. 1, 1986:50–68.

Freeman, Jo. *The Politics of Women's Liberation.* New York: David McKay, 1975.

Frye, Marilyn. "Oppression," pp. 37–40 in Paula S. Rothenberg (ed.) *Racism and Sexism: An Integrated Study.* New York: St. Martin's Press, 1988.

Gadamer, Hans-Georg. *Truth and Method.* Translated and edited by Garrett Barden and John Cumming. New York: Seabury Press, 1975.

————. *Philosophical Hermeneutics.* Translated by David E. Linge. Berkeley: University of California Press, 1976.

————. *Dialogue and Dialectic.* Translated by P. Christopher Smith. New Haven: Yale University Press, 1980.

Gergen, Kenneth J. *Toward Transformation in Social Knowledge.* New York: Springer-Verlag, 1982.

Giddens, Anthony. *Profiles and Critiques in Social Theory.* Berkeley: University of California Press, 1982.

Habermas, Jurgen. *Knowledge and Human Interest.* Translated by J. Shapiro. London: Heinemann, 1970.

————. *The Theory of Communicative Action.* Boston: Beacon Press, 1984.

Haraway, Donna J. "Animal Sociology and a Natural Economy of the Body Politic, Part II: The Past Is the Contested Zone. Human Nature and Theories of Production and Reproduction in Primate Behavior Studies," *Signs: Journal of Women in Culture and Society,* Vol. 4, No. 1, 1978:37–60.

————. "In the Beginning Was the Word: The Genesis of Biological Theory," *Signs: Journal of Women in Culture and Society,* Vol. 6, No. 3, 1981:469–481.

Harding, Sandra. *The Science Question in Feminism.* Ithaca, N.Y.: Cornell University Press, 1986.

————. *Feminism and Methodology.* Bloomington: Indiana University Press, 1987.

Hartsock, Nancy C.M. "The Feminist Standpoint: Developing the Ground for a Specifically Feminist Historical Materialism," pp. 283–310 in Sandra Harding and Merrill B. Hintikka (eds.) *Discovering Reality.* Dordrecht, Holland: D. Reidel Publishing Co., 1983.

Heelan, Patrick. "Natural Science as a Hermeneutic of Instrumentation," *Philosophy of Science.* Vol. 50, 1983:181–204.

Hekman, Susan. *Hermeneutics and the Sociology of Knowledge.* Note Dame, Ind.: University of Notre Dame Press, 1986.

Horowitz, Irving L. *The Rise and Fall of Project Camelot: Studies in the Relationship Between Science and Practical Politics.* Cambridge: MIT Press, 1976.

Jaggar, Alison M. *Feminist Politics and Human Nature.* Totowa, N.J.: Rowman and Allanheld; Sussex: The Harvester Press, 1983.

Jones. W.T. *The Classical Mind,* 2nd ed. San Diego, Calif.: Harcourt Brace Jovanovich, 1970.

Kasper, Anne S. "Consciousness Re-Evaluated: Interpretive Theory and Feminist Scholarship," *Sociological Inquiry,* Vol. 56, No. 1, 1986:30–49.

Keller, Evelyn Fox. *Reflections on Gender and Science.* New Haven, Conn.: Yale University Press, 1985.

Kuhn, Thomas S. *The Structure of Scientific Revolutions.* 2nd ed. Chicago: University of Chicago Press, 1970.

Langland, Elizabeth, and Walter Gove (eds.). *A Feminist Perspective in the Academy: The Difference It Makes.* Chicago: University of Chicago Press, 1983.

Lyotard, Jean Francois. *The Post-Modern Condition: A Report on Knowledge.* Translated by Geoff Gennington and Brian Massumi. Minneapolis: University of Minnesota Press, 1984.

Nielsen, Joyce McCarl, and Jeana Abromeit. "Paradigm Shifts and Feminist Phase Theory in Women Studies Curriculum Transformation Projects," paper presented at the annual meeting of the American Sociological Association, San Francisco, Calif., August 1989.

Oakley, Ann. "Interviewing Women: A Contradiction in Terms," pp. 30–61 in Helen Roberts (ed.) *Doing Feminist Research.* London: Routledge & Kegan Paul, 1981.

Parlee, Mary Brown. "Feminism and the 'New Psychology,'" paper presented at the Center for the Study of Women and Society, CUNY Graduate Center, New York, May 1, 1986.

Reason, Peter, and John Rowan (eds.). *Human Inquiry: A Sourcebook of New Paradigm Research.* Chichester: John Wiley & Sons, 1981.

Reinharz, Shulamit. "Experiential Analysis: A Contribution to Feminist Research," pp. 162–191 in Gloria Bowles and R.D. Klein (eds.) *Theories of Women's Studies.* London: Routledge & Kegan Paul, 1983.

Ricoeur, Paul. "The Model of the Text: Meaningful Action Considered as a Text," pp. 316–334 in Fred Dallmayr and Thomas McCarthy (eds.) *Understanding and Social Inquiry*. Notre Dame, Inc.: University of Notre Dame Press, 1977.

Roberts, Helen. *Doing Feminist Research*. London: Routledge & Kegan Paul, 1981.

Rubin, Gayle, "The Traffic in Women: Notes on the 'Political Economy' of Sex," pp. 157–210 in Rayna R. Reiter (ed.) *Toward an Anthropology of Women*. New York: Monthly Review Press, 1975.

Schutz, Alfred. *Collected Papers*, Vol. 1. Edited and with introduction by Maurice Natanson. The Hague: Martinus Nijhoff, 1962.

—————. *The Phenomenology of the Social World*. Translated by George Walsh and Frederick Lehnert. Evanston, Ill.: Northwestern University Press, 1967.

Smith, Dorothy E. "Some Implications of a Sociology for Women," pp. 15–29 in Nona Glazer and Helen Youngelson Wachere (eds.) *Woman in a Man-Made World*, 2nd ed. Chicago: Rand McNally, 1977.

—————. "A Sociology for Women," pp. 135–188 in Julia A. Sherman and Evelyn Tonton Beck (eds.) *The Prism of Sex: Essays in the Sociology of Knowledge*. Madison: University of Wisconsin Press, 1979.

Spender, Dale (ed.). *Men's Studies Modified: The Impact of Feminism and the Academic Disciplines*. New York: Pergamon Press Ltd., 1981.

Stacey, Judith, and Barrie Thorne. "The Missing Feminist Revolution in Sociology," *Social Problems*, Vol. 32, No. 4, 1985:301–316.

Tetreault, Mary Kay Thompson. "Feminism Phase Theory: An Experience-Derived Evaluation Model," *Journal of Higher Education*, Vol. 56, No. 4, 1985:363–384.

Toulmin, Stephan. "The Construal of Inquiry: Criticism in Modern and Post-Modern Science," *Critical Inquiry*, Vol. 9, 1982:93–111.

Weisstein, Naomi. "Adventures of a Woman in Science," pp. 187–204 in Ruth Hubbard, Mary Sue Henifin and Barbara Fried (eds.) *Women Look at Biology Looking at Women: A Collection of Feminist Critiques*. Cambridge: Schenkman Publishing Co., 1979.

Westkott, Marcia. "Women's Studies as a Strategy for Change: Between Criticism and Vision," pp. 210–218 in Gloria Bowles and Renate Duelli Klein (eds.) *Theories of Women's Studies*. London: Routledge & Kegan Paul, 1979.

Wolff, Janet. "Hermeneutics and the Critique of Ideology," *Sociological Review*, Vol. 23, No. 4 (new series), 1975:811–828.

Learning from the Outsider Within: The Sociological Significance of Black Feminist Thought*

PATRICIA HILL COLLINS

Black women have long occupied marginal positions in academic settings. I argue that many Black female intellectuals have made creative use of their marginality—their "outsider within" status—to produce Black feminist thought that reflects a special standpoint on self, family, and society. I describe and explore the sociological significance of three characteristic themes in such thought: (1) Black women's self-definition and self-valuation; (2) the interlocking nature of oppression; and (3) the importance of Afro-American women's culture. After considering how Black women might draw upon these key themes as outsiders within to generate a distinctive standpoint on existing sociological paradigms, I conclude by suggesting that other sociologists would also benefit by placing greater trust in the creative potential of their own personal and cultural biographies.

Afro-American women have long been privy to some of the most intimate secrets of white society. Countless numbers of Black women have ridden buses to their white "families," where they not only cooked, cleaned, and executed other domestic duties, but where they also nurtured their "other" children, shrewdly offered guidance to their employers, and frequently, became honorary members of their white "families." These women have seen white elites, both actual and aspiring, from perspectives largely obscured from their Black spouses and from these groups themselves.[1]

On one level, this "insider" relationship has been satisfying to all involved. The memoirs of affluent whites often mention their love for their Black "mothers," while accounts of Black domestic workers stress the sense of self-affirmation they experienced at seeing white power demystified—of knowing that it was not the intellect, talent, or humanity of their employers that supported their superior status, but largely just the advantages of racism.[2] But on another level, these same Black women knew they could never belong to their white "families." In spite of their involvement, they remained "outsiders."[3]

This "outsider within" status has provided a special standpoint on self, family, and society for Afro-American women.[4] A careful review of the emerging Black feminist literature reveals that many Black intellectuals, especially those in touch with their marginality in academic settings, tap this standpoint in producing distinctive analyses of race, class, and gender. For example, Zora Neal Hurston's 1937 novel, *Their Eyes Were Watching God*, most certainly reflects her skill at using the strengths and transcending the limitations both of her academic training and of her background in traditional Afro-American community life.[5] Black feminist historian E. Frances White (1984) suggests that Black women's ideas have been honed at the juncture between movements for racial and sexual equality, and contends that Afro-American women have been pushed by "their marginalization in both arenas" to create Black feminism. Finally, Black feminist critic Bell Hooks captures the unique standpoint that the outsider within status can generate. In describing her small-town, Kentucky childhood, she notes, "living as we did—on the edge—we developed a particular way of seeing reality. We looked both from the outside in and from the inside out . . . we understood both" (1984:vii).

In spite of the obstacles that can confront outsiders within, such individuals can benefit from this status. Simmel's (1921) essay on the sociological significance of what he called the "stranger" offers a helpful starting point for understanding the largely unexplored area of Black female outsider within status and the usefulness of the standpoint it might produce. Some of the potential benefits of outsider within status include: (1) Simmel's definition of "objectivity" as "a peculiar composition of nearness and remoteness, concern and indifference"; (2) the tendency for people to confide in a "stranger" in ways they never would with each other; and (3) the ability of the "stranger" to see patterns that may be more difficult for those immersed in the situation to see. Mannheim (1936) labels the "strangers" in academia "marginal intellectuals" and argues that the critical posture such individuals bring to academic endeavors may be essential to the creative development of academic disciplines themselves. Finally, in assessing the potentially positive qualities of social difference, specifically marginality, Lee notes, "for a time this marginality can be a most stimulating, albeit often a painful, experience. For some, it is debilitating . . . for others, it is an excitement to creativity" (1973:64).[6]

Sociologists might benefit greatly from serious consideration of the emerging, cross-disciplinary literature that I label Black feminist thought, precisely because, for many Afro-American female intellectuals, "marginality" has been an excitement to creativity. As outsiders within, Black feminist scholars may be one of many distinct groups of marginal intellectuals whose standpoints promise to enrich contemporary sociological discourse. Bringing this group—as well as others who share an outsider within status vis-a-vis sociology—into the center of analysis may reveal aspects of reality obscured by more orthodox approaches.

In the remainder of this essay, I examine the sociological significance of the Black feminist thought stimulated by Black women's outsider within status. First, I outline three key themes that characterize the emerging cross-disciplinary literature that I label Black feminist thought.[7] For each theme, I summarize its content, supply examples from Black feminist and other works that illustrate its nature, and discuss its importance. Second, I explain the significance these key themes in Black feminist thought may have for sociologists by describing why Black women's outsider within status might generate a distinctive standpoint vis-a-vis existing sociological paradigms. Finally, I discuss one general implication of this essay for social scientists: namely, the potential usefulness of identifying and using one's own standpoint in conducting research.

Three Key Themes in Black Feminist Thought

Black feminist thought consists of ideas produced by Black women that clarify a standpoint of and for Black women. Several assumptions underlie this working definition. First, the definition suggests that it is impossible to separate the structure and thematic content of thought from the historical and material conditions shaping the lives of its producers (Berger and Luckmann 1966; Mannheim 1936). Therefore, while Black feminist thought may be recorded by others, it is produced by Black women. Second, the definition assumes that Black women possess a unique standpoint on, or perspective of, their experiences and that there will be certain commonalties of perception shared by Black women as a group. Third, while living life as Black women may produce certain commonalties of outlook, the diversity of class, region, age, and sexual orientation shaping individual Black women's lives has resulted in different expressions of these common themes. Thus, universal themes included in the Black women's standpoint may be experienced and expressed differently by distinct groups of Afro-American women. Finally, the definition assumes that, while a Black women's standpoint exists, its contours may not be clear to Black women themselves. Therefore, one role for Black female intellectuals is to produce facts and theories about the Black female experience that will clarify a Black woman's standpoint for Black women. In other words, Black feminist thought contains observations and interpretations about Afro-American womanhood that describe and explain different expressions of common themes.

No one Black feminist platform exists from which one can measure the "correctness" of a particular thinker; nor should there be one. Rather, as I defined it above, there is a long and rich tradition of Black feminist thought. Much of it has been oral and has been produced by ordinary Black women in their roles as mothers, teachers, musicians, and preachers.[8] Since the civil rights and women's movements, Black women's ideas have been increasingly documented and are reaching wider audiences. The following discussion of three key themes in Black feminist thought is itself part of this emerging process of documentation and interpretation. The three themes I have chosen are not exhaustive but, in my assessment, they do represent the thrust of much of the existing dialogue.

The Meaning of Self-Definition and Self-Valuation

An affirmation of the importance of Black women's self-definition and self-valuation is the first key theme that pervades historical and contemporary statements of Black feminist thought. Self-definition involves challenging the political knowledge-validation process that has resulted in externally-defined, stereotypical images of Afro-American womanhood. In contrast, self-valuation stresses the content of Black women's self-definitions—namely, replacing externally-derived images with authentic Black female images.

Both Mae King's (1973) and Cheryl Gilkes' (1981) analyses of the importance of stereotypes offer useful insights for grasping the importance of Black women's self-definition. King suggests that stereotypes represent externally-defined, controlling images of Afro-American womanhood that have been central to the dehumanization of Black women and the exploitation of Black women's labor. Gilkes points out that Black women's assertiveness in resisting the multifaceted oppression they experience has been a consistent threat to the status quo. As punishment, Black women have been assaulted with a variety of externally-defined negative images designed to control assertive Black female behavior.

The value of King's and Gilkes' analyses lies in their emphasis on the function of stereotypes in controlling dominated groups. Both point out that replacing negative stereotypes with ostensibly positive ones can be equally problematic if the function of stereotypes as controlling images remains unrecognized. John Gwaltney's (1980) interview with Nancy White, a 73-year-old Black woman, suggests that ordinary Black women may also be aware of the power of these controlling images in their everyday experiences. In the following passage, Ms. White assesses the difference between the controlling images applied to Afro-American and white women as being those of degree, and not of kind:

> My mother used to say that the black woman is the white man's mule and the white woman is his dog. Now, she said that to say this: we do the heavy work and get beat whether we do it well or not. But the white woman is closer to the master and he pats them on the head and lets them sleep in the house, but he ain't gon' treat neither one like he was dealing with a person (1980:148).

This passage suggests that while both groups are stereotyped, albeit in different ways, the function of the images is to dehumanize and control both groups. Seen in this light, it makes little sense, in the long run, for Black women to exchange one set of controlling images for another even if, in the short run, positive stereotypes bring better treatment.

The insistence on Black female self-definition reframes the entire dialogue from one of determining the technical accuracy of an image, to one stressing the power dynamics underlying the very process of definition itself. Black feminists have questioned not only what has been said about Black women, but the credibility and the intentions of those possessing the power to define. When Black women define themselves, they clearly reject the taken-for-granted assumption that those in positions granting them the authority to describe and analyze reality are entitled to do so. Regardless of the actual content of Black women's self-definitions, the act of insisting on Black female self-definition validates Black women's power as human subjects.

The related theme of Black female self-valuation pushes this entire process one step further. While Black female self-definition speaks to the power dynamics involved in the act of defining images of self and community, the theme of Black female self-valuation addresses the actual content of these self-definitions. Many of the attributes extant in Black female stereotypes are actually distorted renderings of those aspects of Black female behavior seen as most threatening to white patriarchy (Gilkes, 1981; White, 1985). For example, aggressive Afro-American women are threatening because they challenge white patriarchal definitions of femininity. To ridicule assertive women by labeling them Sapphires reflects an effort to put all women in their place. In their roles as central figures in socializing the next generation of Black adults, strong mothers are similarly threatening, because they contradict patriarchal views of family power relations. To ridicule strong Black mothers by labelling them matriarchs (Higginbotham, 1982) reflects a similar effort to control another aspect of Black female behavior that is especially threatening to the status quo.

When Black females choose to value those aspects of Afro-American womanhood that are stereotyped, ridiculed, and maligned in academic scholarship and the popular media, they are actually questioning some of the basic ideas used to control dominated groups in general. It is one thing to counsel Afro-American women to resist the Sapphire stereotype by altering their behavior to become meek, docile, and stereotypically "feminine." It is quite another to advise Black women to embrace their assertiveness, to value their sassiness, and to continue to use these qualities to survive in and transcend the harsh environments that circumscribe so many Black women's lives. By defining and valuing assertiveness and other "unfeminine" qualities as necessary and functional attributes for Afro-American womanhood, Black women's self-valuation challenges the content of externally-defined controlling images.

This Black feminist concern—that Black women create their own standards for evaluating Afro-American womanhood and value their creations—pervades a wide range of literary and social science works. For example, Alice Walker's 1982 novel, *The Color Purple*, and Ntozake Shange's 1978 choreopoem, *For Colored Girls Who Have Considered Suicide*, are both bold statements of the necessity for Black female self-definition and self-valuation. Lena Wright Myers' (1980) work shows that Black women judge their behavior by comparing themselves to Black women facing similar situations and thus demonstrates the presence of Black female definitions of Afro-American womanhood. The recent spate of Black female historiography suggest that self-defined, self-valuating Black women have long populated the ranks of Afro-American female leaders (Giddings, 1984; Loewenberg and Bogin, 1976).

Black women's insistence on self-definition, self-valuation, and the necessity for a Black female-centered analysis is significant for two reasons. First, defining and valuing one's consciousness of one's own self-defined standpoint in the face of images that foster a self-definition as the objectified "other" is an important way of resisting the dehumanization essential to systems of domination. The status of being the "other" implies being "other than" or different from the assumed norm of white male behavior. In this model, powerful white males define themselves as subjects, the true actors, and classify people of color and women in terms of their position vis-a-vis this white male hub. Since Black women have been denied the authority to challenge these definitions, this model consists of images that define Black women as a negative other, the virtual antithesis of positive white male images. Moreover, as Brittan and Maynard (1984:199) point out, "domination always involves the objectification of the dominated; all forms of oppression imply the devaluation of the subjectivity of the oppressed."

One of the best examples of this process is described by Judith Rollins (1985). As part of her fieldwork on Black domestics, Rollins worked as a domestic for six months. She describes several incidents where her employers treated her as if she were not really present. On one occasion while she sat in the kitchen having lunch, her employers had a conversation as if she were not there. Her sense of invisibility became so great that she took out a pad of paper and began writing field notes. Even though Rollins wrote for 10 minutes, finished lunch, and returned to work, her employers showed no evidence of having seen her at all. Rollins notes,

> It was this aspect of servitude I found to be one of the strongest affronts to my dignity as a human being. . . . These gestures of ignoring my presence were not, I think, intended as insults; they were expressions of the employers' ability to annihilate the humanness and even, at times, the very existence of me, a servant and a black woman (1985:209).

Racist and sexist ideologies both share the common feature of treating dominated groups—the "others"—as objects lacking full human subjectivity. For example, seeing Black women as obstinate mules and viewing white women as obedient dogs objectifies both groups, but in different ways. Neither is seen as fully human, and therefore both become eligible for race/gender specific modes of domination. But if Black women refuse to accept their assigned status as the quintessential "other," then the entire rationale for such domination is challenged. In brief, abusing a mule or a dog may be easier than abusing a person who is a reflection of one's own humanness.

A second reason that Black female self-definition and self-valuation are significant concerns their value in allowing Afro-American women to reject internalized, psychological oppression (Baldwin, 1980). The potential damage of internalized control to Afro-American women's self-esteem can be great, even to the prepared. Enduring the frequent assaults of controlling images requires considerable inner strength. Nancy White, cited earlier, also points out how debilitating being treated as less than human can be if Black women are not self-defined. She notes, "Now, you know that no woman is a dog or a mule, but if folks keep making you feel that way, if you don't have a mind of your own, you can start letting them tell you what you are" (Gualtney, 1980:152). Seen in this light, self-definition and self-valuation are not luxuries—they are necessary for Black female survival.

The Interlocking Nature of Oppression

Attention to the interlocking nature of race, gender, and class oppression is a second recurring theme in the works of Black feminists (Beale, 1970; Davis, 1981; Dill, 1983; Hooks, 1981; Lewis, 1977; Murray, 1970; Steady, 1981).[9] While different socio-historical periods may have increased the saliency of one or another type of oppression, the thesis of the linked nature of oppression has long pervaded Black feminist thought. For example, Ida Wells Barnett and Frances Ellen Watkins Harper, two prominent Black feminists of the late 1800s, both spoke out against the growing violence directed against Black men. They realized that civil rights held little meaning for Black men and women if the right to life itself went unprotected (Loewenberg and Bogin, 1976:26). Black women's absence from organized feminist movements has mistakenly been attributed to a lack of feminist consciousness. In actuality, Black feminists have possessed an ideological commitment to addressing interlocking oppression yet have been excluded from arenas that would have allowed them to do so (Davis, 1981).

As Barbara Smith points out, "the concept of the simultaneity of oppression is still the crux of a Black feminist understanding of political reality and . . . is one of the most significant ideological contributions of Black feminist thought" (1983:xxxii). This should come as no surprise since Black women should be among the first to realize that minimizing one form of oppression, while essential, may still leave them oppressed in other equally dehumanizing ways. Sojourner Truth knew this when she stated, "there is a great stir about colored men getting their rights, and not colored women theirs, you see the colored men will be masters over the women, and it will be just as bad as before" (Loewenberg and Bogin, 1976:238). To use Nancy White's metaphors, the Black woman as "mule" knows that she is perceived to be an animal. In contrast, the white woman as "dog" may be similarly dehumanized, and may think that she is an equal part of the family when, in actuality, she is a well-cared-for pet. The significant factor shaping Truth's and White's clearer view of their own subordination than that of Black men or white women is their experience at the intersection of multiple structures of domination.[10] Both Truth and White are Black, female, and poor. They therefore have a clearer view of oppression than other groups who occupy more contradictory positions vis-a-vis white male power—unlike white women, they have no illusions that their whiteness will negate female subordination, and unlike Black men, they cannot use a questionable appeal to manhood to neutralize the stigma of being Black.

The Black feminist attention to the interlocking nature of oppression is significant for two reasons. First, this viewpoint shifts the entire focus of investigation from one aimed at explicating elements of race or gender or class oppression to one whose goal is to determine what the links are among these systems. The first approach typically prioritizes one form of oppression as being primary, then handles remaining types of oppression as variables within what is seen as the most important system. For example, the efforts to insert race and gender into Marxist theory exemplify this effort. In contrast, the more holistic approach implied in Black feminist thought treats the interaction among multiple systems as the object of study. Rather than adding to existing theories by inserting previously excluded variables, Black feminists aim to develop new theoretical interpretations of the interaction itself.

Black male scholars, white female scholars, and more recently, Black feminists like Bell Hooks, may have identified one critical link among interlocking systems of oppression. These groups have pointed out that certain basic ideas crosscut multiple systems of domination. One such idea is either/or dualistic thinking, claimed by Hooks to be "the central ideological component of all systems of domination in Western society" (1984:29).

While Hooks' claim may be somewhat premature, there is growing scholarly support for her viewpoint.[11] Either/or dualistic thinking, or what I will refer to as the construct of dichotomous oppositional difference, may be a philosophical lynchpin in systems of race, class, and gender oppression. One fundamental characteristic of this construct is the categorization of people, things, and ideas in terms of their difference from one another. For example, the terms in dichotomies such as black/white, male/female, reason/emotion, fact/opinion, and subject/object gain their meaning only in *relation* to their difference from their oppositional counterparts. Another fundamental characteristic of this construct is that difference is not complementary in that the halves of the dichotomy do not enhance each other. Rather, the dichotomous halves are different and inherently opposed to one another. A third and more important characteristic is that these oppositional relationships are intrinsically unstable. Since such dualities rarely represent different but equal relationships, the inherently unstable relationship is resolved by subordinating one half of each pair to the other. Thus, whites rule Blacks, males dominate females, reason is touted as superior to emotion in ascertaining truth, facts supersede opinion in evaluating knowledge, and subjects rule objects. Dichotomous oppositional differences invariably imply relationships of superiority and inferiority, hierarchical relationships that mesh with political economies of domination and subordination.

The oppression experienced by most Black women is shaped by their subordinate status in an array of either/or dualities. Afro-American women have been assigned the inferior half of several dualities, and this placement has been central to their continued domination. For example, the allegedly emotional, passionate nature of Afro-American women has long been used as a rationale for their sexual exploitation. Similarly, denying Black women literacy—then claiming that they lack the facts for sound judgment—illustrates another case of assigning a group inferior status, then using that inferior status as proof of the group's inferiority. Finally, denying Black women agency as subjects and treating them as objectified "others" represents yet another dimension of the power that dichotomous oppositional constructs have in maintaining systems of domination.

While Afro-American women may have a vested interest in recognizing the connections among these dualities that together comprise the construct of dichotomous oppositional difference, that more women have not done so is not surprising. Either/or dualistic thinking is so pervasive that it suppresses other alternatives. As Dill points out, "the choice between identifying as black or female is a product of the patriarchal strategy of divide-and-conquer and the continued importance of class, patriarchal, and racial divisions, perpetuate such choices both within our consciousness and within the concrete realities of our daily lives" (1983:136). In spite of this difficulty, Black women experience oppression in a personal, holistic fashion and emerging Black feminist perspectives appear to be embracing an equally holistic analysis of oppression.

Second, Black feminist attention to the interlocking nature of oppression is significant in that, implicit in this view, is an alternative humanist vision of societal organization. This alternative world view is cogently expressed in the following passage from an 1893 speech delivered by the Black feminist educator, Anna Julia Cooper:

> We take our stand on the solidarity of humanity, the oneness of life, and the unnaturalness and injustice of all special favoritisms, whether of sex, race, country, or condition. . . . The colored woman feels that woman's cause is one and universal; and that . . . not till race, color, sex, and condition are seen as accidents, and not the substance of life; not till the universal title of humanity to life, liberty, and the pursuit of happiness is conceded to be inalienable to all; not till then is woman's lesson taught and woman's cause won—not the white woman's nor the black woman's, nor the red woman's, but the cause of every man and of every woman who has writhed silently under a mighty wrong (Loewenberg and Bogin, 1976:330–31).

I cite the above passage at length because it represents one of the clearest statements of the humanist vision extant in Black feminist thought.[12] Black feminists who see the simultaneity of oppression affecting Black women appear to be more sensitive to how these same oppressive systems affect Afro-American men, people of color, women, and the dominant group itself. Thus, while Black feminist activists may work on behalf of Black women, they rarely project separatist solutions to Black female oppression. Rather, the vision is one that, like Cooper's, takes its "stand on the solidarity of humanity."

The Importance of Afro-American Women's Culture

A third key theme characterizing Black feminist thought involves efforts to redefine and explain the importance of Black women's culture. In doing so, Black feminists have not only uncovered previously unexplored areas of the Black female experience, but they have also identified concrete areas of social relations where Afro-American women create and pass on self-definitions and self-valuations essential to coping with the simultaneity of oppression they experience.

In contrast to views of culture stressing the unique, ahistorical values of a particular group, Black feminist approaches have placed greater emphasis on the role of historically-specific political economies in explaining the endurance of certain cultural themes. The following definition of culture typifies the approach taken by many Black feminists. According to Mullings, culture is composed of

> the symbols and values that create the ideological frame of reference through which people attempt to deal with the circumstances in which they find themselves. Culture . . . is not composed of static, discrete traits moved from one locale to another. It is constantly changing and transformed, as new forms are created out of old ones. Thus culture . . . does not arise out of nothing: it is created and modified by material conditions (1986a:13).

Seen in this light, Black women's culture may help provide the ideological frame of reference—namely, the symbols and values of self-definition and self-valuation—that assist Black women in seeing the circumstances shaping race, class, and gender oppression. Moreover, Mullings' definition of culture suggests that the values which accompany self-definition and self-valuation will have concrete, material expression: they will be present in social institutions like church and family, in creative expression of art, music, and dance, and, if unsuppressed, in patterns of economic and political activity. Finally, this approach to culture stresses its historically concrete nature. While common themes may link Black women's lives, these themes will be experienced differently by Black women of different classes, ages, regions, and sexual preferences as well as by Black women in different historical settings. Thus, there is no monolithic Black women's culture—rather, there are socially-constructed Black women's cultures that collectively form Black women's culture.

The interest in redefining Black women's culture has directed attention to several unexplored areas of the Black female experience. One such area concerns the interpersonal relationships that Black women share with each other. It appears that the notion of sisterhood—generally understood to mean a supportive feeling of loyalty and attachment to other women stemming from a shared feeling of oppression—has been an important part of Black women's culture (Dill, 1983:132). Two representative works in the emerging tradition of Black feminist research illustrate how this concept of sisterhood, while expressed differently in response to different material conditions, has been a significant feature of Black women's culture. For example, Debra Gray White (1985) documents the ways Black slave women assisted each other in childbirth, cared for each other's children, worked together in sex-segregated work units when pregnant or nursing children, and depended on one another when married to males living on distant farms. White paints a convincing portrait of Black female slave communities where sisterhood was necessary and assumed. Similarly, Gilkes' (1985) work on Black women's traditions in the Sanctified Church suggests that the sisterhood Black women found had tangible psychological and political benefits.[13]

The attention to Black women's culture has stimulated interest in a second type of interpersonal relationship: that shared by Black women with their biological children, the children in their extended families, and with the Black community's children. In reassessing Afro-American motherhood, Black feminist researchers have emphasized the connections between (1) choices available to Black mothers resulting from their placement in historically specific political economies, (2) Black mothers' perceptions of their children's choices as compared to what mothers thought those choices should be, and (3) actual strategies employed by Black mothers both in raising their children and in dealing with institutions that affected their children's lives. For example, Janice Hale (1980) suggests that effective Black mothers are sophisticated mediators between the competing offerings of an oppressive dominant culture and a nurturing Black value-structure. Dill's (1980) study of the childrearing goals of Black domestics stresses the goals the women in her sample had for their children and the strategies these women pursued to help their children go further than they themselves had gone. Gilkes (1980) offers yet another perspective on the power of Black motherhood by observing that many of the Black female political activists in her study became involved in community work through their role as mothers. What typically began as work on behalf of their own children evolved into work on behalf of the community's children.

Another dimension of Black women's culture that has generated considerable interest among Black feminists is the role of creative expression in shaping and sustaining Black women's self-definitions and self-valuations. In addition to documenting Black women's achievements as writers, dancers, musicians, artists, and actresses, the emerging literature also investigates why creative expression has been such an important element of Black women's culture.[14] Alice Walker's (1974) classic essay, "In Search of Our Mothers' Gardens," explains the necessity of Black women's creativity, even if in very limited spheres, in resisting objectification and asserting Black women's subjectivity as fully human beings. Illustrating Walker's thesis, Willie Mae Ford Smith, a prominent gospel singer featured in the 1984 documentary, "Say Amen Somebody," describes what singing means to her. She notes, "it's just a feeling within. You can't help yourself. . . . I feel like I can fly away. I forget I'm in the world sometimes. I just want to take off." For Mother Smith, her creativity is a sphere of freedom, one that helps her cope with and transcend daily life.

This third key theme in Black feminist thought—the focus on Black women's culture—is significant for three reasons. First, the data from Black women's culture suggest that the relationship between oppressed people's consciousness of oppression and the actions they take in dealing with oppressive structures may be far more complex than that suggested by existing social theory. Conventional social science continues to assume a fit between consciousness and activity; hence, accurate measures of human behavior are thought to produce accurate portraits of human consciousness of self and social structure (Westkott, 1979). In contrast, Black women's experiences suggest that Black women may overtly conform to the societal roles laid out for them, yet covertly oppose these roles in numerous spheres, an opposition shaped by the consciousness of being on the bottom. Black women's activities in families, churches, community institutions, and creative expression may represent more than an effort to mitigate pressures stemming from oppression. Rather, the Black female ideological frame of reference that Black women acquire through sisterhood, motherhood, and creative expression may serve the added purpose of shaping a Black female consciousness about the workings of oppression. Moreover, this consciousness is shaped not only through abstract, rational reflection, but also is developed through concrete rational action. For example, while Black mothers may develop consciousness through talking with and listening to their children, they may also shape consciousness by how they live their lives, the actions they take on behalf of their children. That these activities have been obscured from traditional social scientists should come as no surprise. Oppressed peoples may maintain hidden consciousness and may not reveal their true selves for reasons of self-protection.[15]

A second reason that the focus on Black women's culture is significant is that it points to the problematic nature of existing conceptualizations of the term "activism." While Black women's reality cannot be understood without attention to the interlocking structures of oppression that limit Black women's lives, Afro-American women's experiences suggest that possibilities for activism exist even within such multiple structures of domination. Such activism can take several forms. For Black women under extremely harsh conditions, the private decision to reject external definitions of Afro-American womanhood may itself be a form of activism. If Black women find themselves in settings where total conformity is expected, and where traditional forms of activism such as voting, participating in collective movements, and officeholding are impossible, then the individual women who in their consciousness choose to be self-defined and self-evaluating are, in fact, activists. They are retaining a grip over their definition as subjects, as full humans, and rejecting definitions of themselves as the objectified "other." For example, while Black slave women were forced to conform to the specific oppression facing them, they may have had very different assessments of themselves and slavery than did the slaveowners. In this sense, consciousness can be viewed as one potential sphere of freedom, one that may exist simultaneously with unfree, allegedly conforming behavior (Westkott, 1979). Moreover, if Black women simultaneously use all resources available to them—their roles as mothers, their participation in churches, their support of one another in Black female networks, their creative expression—to be self-defined and self-valuating and to encourage others to reject objectification, then Black women's everyday behavior itself is a form of activism. People who view themselves as fully human, as subjects, become activists, no matter how limited the sphere of their activism may be. By returning subjectivity to Black women, Black feminists return activism as well.

A third reason that the focus on Black women's culture is significant is that an analytical model exploring the relationship between oppression, consciousness, and activism is implicit in the way Black feminists have studied Black women's culture. With the exception of Dill (1983), few scholars have deliberately set out to develop such a model. However, the type of work done suggests that an implicit model paralleling that proposed by Mullings (1986a) has influenced Black feminist research.

Several features pervade emerging Black feminist approaches. First, researchers stress the interdependent relationship between the interlocking oppression that has shaped Black women's choices and Black women's actions in the context of those choices. Black feminist researchers rarely describe Black women's behavior without attention to the opportunity structures shaping their subjects' lives (Higginbotham, 1985; Ladner, 1971; Myers, 1980). Second, the question of whether oppressive structures and limited choices stimulate Black women's behavior characterized by apathy and alienation, or behavior demonstrating subjectivity and activism is seen as ultimately dependent on Black women's perceptions of their choices. In other words, Black women's consciousness—their analytical, emotional, and ethical perspective of themselves and their place in society—becomes a critical part of the relationship between the working of oppression and Black women's actions. Finally, this relationship between oppression, consciousness, and action can be seen as a dialectical one. In this model, oppressive structures create patterns of choices which are perceived in varying ways by Black women. Depending on their consciousness of themselves and their relationship to these choices, Black women may or may not develop Black-female spheres of influence where they develop and validate what will be appropriate, Black-female sanctioned responses to oppression. Black women's activism in constructing Black-female spheres of influence may, in turn, affect their perceptions of the political and economic choices offered to them by oppressive structures, influence actions actually taken, and ultimately, alter the nature of oppression they experience.

The Sociological Significance of Black Feminist Thought

Taken together, the three key themes in Black feminist thought—the meaning of self-definition and self-valuation, the interlocking nature of oppression, and the importance of redefining culture—have made significant contributions to the task of clarifying a Black women's standpoint of and for Black women. While this accomplishment is important in and of itself, Black feminist thought has potential contributions to make to the diverse disciplines housing its practitioners.

The sociological significance of Black feminist thought lies in two areas. First, the content of Black women's ideas has been influenced by and contributes to on-going dialogues in a variety of sociological specialties. While this area merits attention, it is not my primary concern in this section. Instead, I investigate a second area of sociological significance: the process by which these specific ideas were produced by this specific group of individuals. In other words, I examine the influence of Black women's outsider within status in academia on the actual thought produced. Thus far, I have proceeded on the assumption that it is impossible to separate the structure and thematic content of thought. In this section, I spell out exactly what form the relationship between the three key themes in Black feminist thought and Black women's outsider within status might take for women scholars generally, with special attention to Black female sociologists.

First, I briefly summarize the role sociological paradigms play in shaping the facts and theories used by sociologists. Second, I explain how Black women's outsider within status might encourage Black women to have a distinctive standpoint vis-a-vis sociology's paradigmatic facts and theories. I argue that the thematic content of Black feminist thought described above represents elements of just such a standpoint and give examples of how the combination of sociology's paradigms and Black women's outsider within status as sociologists directed their attention to specific areas of sociological inquiry.

Two Elements of Sociological Paradigms

Kuhn defines a paradigm as the "entire constellation of beliefs, values, techniques, and so on shared by the members of a given community"(1962:175). As such, a paradigm consists of two fundamental elements: the thought itself and its producers and practitioners.[16] In this sense, the discipline of sociology is itself a paradigm—it consists of a system of knowledge shared by sociologists—and simultaneously consists of a plurality of paradigms (e.g., functionalism, Marxist sociology, feminist sociology, existential sociology), each produced by its own practitioners.

Two dimensions of thought itself are of special interest to this discussion. First, systems of knowledge are never complete. Rather, they represent guidelines for "thinking as usual." Kuhn (1962) refers to these guidelines as "maps," while Schutz (1944) describes them as "recipes." As Schutz points out, while "thinking as usual" is actually only partially organized and partially clear, and may contain contradictions, to its practitioners it provides sufficient coherence, clarity, and consistency. Second, while thought itself contains diverse elements, I will focus mainly on the important fact/theory relationship. As Kuhn (1962) suggests, facts or observations become meaningful in the context of theories or interpretations of those observations. Conversely, theories "fit the facts" by transforming previously accessible observations into facts. According to Mulkay, "observation is not separate from interpretation; rather these are two facets of a single process"(1979:49).

Several dimensions of the second element of sociological paradigms—the community formed by a paradigm's practitioners—are of special interest to this discussion. First, group insiders have similar worldviews, acquired through similar educational and professional training, that separate them from everyone else. Insider worldviews may be especially alike if group members have similar social class, gender, and racial backgrounds. Schutz describes the insider worldview as the "cultural pattern of group life"—namely, all the values and behaviors which characterize the social group at a given moment in its history. In brief, insiders have undergone similar experiences, possess a common history, and share taken-for-granted knowledge that characterizes "thinking as usual."

A second dimension of the community of practitioners involves the process of becoming an insider. How does one know when an individual is really an insider and not an outsider in disguise? Merton suggests that socialization into the life of a group is a lengthy process of being immersed in group life, because only then can "one understand the fine-grained meanings of behavior, feeling, and values . . . and decipher the unwritten grammar of conduct and nuances of cultural idiom" (1972:15). The process is analogous to immersion in a foreign culture in order to learn its ways and its language (Merton, 1972; Schutz, 1944). One becomes an insider by translating a theory or worldview into one's own language until, one day, the individual converts to thinking and acting according to that worldview.

A final dimension of the community of practitioners concerns the process of remaining an insider. A sociologist typically does this by furthering the discipline in ways described as appropriate by sociology generally, and by areas of specialization particularly. Normal foci for scientific sociological investigation include: (1) determining significant facts; (2) matching facts with existing theoretical interpretations to "test" the paradigm's ability to predict facts; and (3) resolving ambiguities in the paradigm itself by articulating and clarifying theory (Kuhn, 1962).

Black Women and the Outsider Within Status

Black women may encounter much less of a fit between their personal and cultural experiences and both elements of sociological paradigms than that facing other sociologists. On the one hand, Black women who undergo sociology's lengthy socialization process, who immerse themselves in the cultural pattern of sociology's group life, certainly wish to acquire the insider skills of thinking in and acting according to a sociological worldview. But on the other hand, Black women's experienced realities, both prior to contact and after initiation, may provides them with "special perspectives and insights . . . available to that category of outsiders who have been systematically frustrated by the social system" (Merton, 1972:29). In brief, their outsider allegiances may militate against their choosing full insider status, and they may be more apt to remain outsiders within.[17]

In essence, to become sociological insiders, Black women must assimilate a standpoint that is quite different than their own. White males have long been the dominant group in sociology, and the sociological worldview understandably reflects the concerns of this group of practitioners. As Merton observes, "white male insiderism in American sociology during the past generations has largely been of the tacit or de facto . . . variety. It has simply taken the form of patterned expectations about the appropriate . . . problems for investigation" (1972:12). In contrast, a good deal of the Black female experience has been spent coping with, avoiding, subverting, and challenging the workings of this same white male insiderism. It should come as no surprise that Black women's efforts in dealing with the effects of interlocking systems of oppression might produce a standpoint quite distinct from, and in many ways opposed to, that of white male insiders.

Seen from this perspective, Black women's socialization into sociology represents a more intense case of the normal challenges facing sociology graduate students and junior professionals in the discipline. Black women become, to use Simmel's (1921) and Schutz's terminology, penultimate "strangers."

> The stranger . . . does not share the basic assumptions of the group. He becomes essentially the man who has to place in question nearly everything that seems to be unquestionable to the members of the approached group. . . . To him the cultural patterns of the approached group do not have the authority of a tested system of recipes . . . because he does not partake in the vivid historical tradition by which it has been formed (Schutz, 1944:502).

Like everyone else, Black women may see sociological "thinking as usual" as partially organized, partially clear, and contradictory, and may question these existing recipes. However, for them, this questioning process may be more acute, for the material that they encounter—white male insider-influenced observations and interpretations about human society—places white male subjectivity at the center of analysis and assigns Afro-American womanhood a position on the margins.

In spite of a lengthy socialization process, it may also be more difficult for Afro-American women to experience conversion and begin totally to think in and act according to a sociological worldview. Indeed, since past generations of white male insiderism has shaped a sociological worldview reflecting this group's concerns, it may be self-destructive for Black women to embrace that worldview. For example, Black women would have to accept certain fundamental and self-devaluing assumptions: (1) white males are more worthy of study because they are more fully human than everyone else; and (2) dichotomous oppositional thinking is natural and normal. More importantly, Black women would have to act in accordance with their place in a white male worldview. This involves accepting one's own subordination or regretting the accident of not being born white and male. In short, it may be extremely difficult for Black women to accept a worldview predicated upon Black female inferiority.

Remaining in sociology by doing normal scientific investigation may also be less complicated for traditional sociologists than for Afro-American women. Unlike Black women, learners from backgrounds where the insider information and experiences of sociology are more familiar may be less likely to see the taken-for-granted assumptions of sociology and may be more prone to apply their creativity to "normal science." In other words, the transition from student status to that of a practitioner engaged in finding significant facts that sociological paradigms deem important, matching facts with existing theories, and furthering paradigmatic development itself may proceed more smoothly for white middle class males than for working-class Black females. The latter group is much more inclined to be struck by the mismatch of its own experiences and the paradigms of sociology itself. Moreover, those Black women with a strong foundation in Black women's culture (e.g., those that recognize the value of self-definition and self-valuation, and that have a concrete understanding of sisterhood and motherhood) may be more apt to take a critical posture toward the entire sociological enterprise. In brief, where traditional sociologists may see sociologists may see sociology as "normal" and define their role as furthering knowledge about a normal world with taken-for-granted assumptions, outsiders within are liable to see anomalies.

The types of anomalies typically seen by Black female academicians grow directly from Black women's outsider within status and appear central in shaping the direction Black feminist thought has taken thus far. Two types of anomalies are characteristically noted by Black female scholars. First, Black female sociologists typically report the omission of facts or observations about Afro-American women in the sociological paradigms they encounter. As Scott points out, "from reading the literature, one might easily develop the impression that Black women have never played any role in this society" (1982:85). Where white males may take it as perfectly normal to generalize findings from studies of white males to other groups, Black women are more likely to see such a practice as problematic, as an anomaly. Similarly, when white feminists produce generalizations about "women," Black feminists routinely ask "which women do you mean?" In the same way that Rollins (1985) felt invisible in her employer's kitchen, Afro-American female scholars are repeatedly struck by their own invisibility, both as full human subjects included in sociological facts and observations, and as practitioners in the discipline itself. It should come as no surprise that much of Black feminist thought aims to counter this invisibility by presenting sociological analyses of Black women as fully human subjects. For example, the growing research describing Black women's historical and contemporary behavior as mothers, community workers, church leaders, teachers, and employed workers, and Black women's ideas about themselves and their opportunities, reflects an effort to respond to the omission of facts about Afro-American women.

A second type of anomaly typically noted by Black female scholars concerns distortions of facts and observations about Black women. Afro-American women in academia are frequently struck by the difference between their own experiences and sociological descriptions of the same phenomena. For example, while Black women have and are themselves mothers, they encounter distorted versions of themselves and their mothers under the mantle of the Black matriarchy thesis. Similarly, for those Black women who confront racial and sexual discrimination and know that their mothers and grandmothers certainly did, explanations of Black women's poverty that stress low achievement motivation and the lack of Black female "human capital" are less likely to ring true. The response to these perceived distortions has been one of redefining distorted images—for example, debunking the Sapphire and Mammy myths.

Since facts or observations become meaningful in the context of a theory, this emphasis on producing accurate descriptions of Black women's lives has also refocused attention on major omissions and distortions in sociological theories themselves. By drawing on the strengths of sociology's plurality of subdisciplines, yet taking a critical posture toward them, the work of Black feminist scholars taps some fundamental questions facing all sociologists. One such question concerns the fundamental elements of society that should be studied. Black feminist researchers' response has been to move Black women's voices to the center of the analysis, to study people, and by doing so, to reaffirm human subjectivity and intentionality. They point to the dangers of omission and distortion that can occur if sociological concepts are studied at the expense of human subjectivity. For example, there is a distinct difference between conducting a statistical analysis of Black women's work, where Afro-American women are studied as a reconstituted amalgam of researcher-defined variables (e.g., race, sex, years of education, and father's occupation), and examining Black women's self-definitions and self-valuations of themselves as workers in oppressive jobs. While both approaches can further sociological knowledge about the concept of work, the former runs the risk of objectifying Black women, of reproducing constructs of dichotomous oppositional difference, and of producing distorted findings about the nature of work itself.

A second question facing sociologists concerns the adequacy of current interpretations of key sociological concepts. For example, few sociologists would question that work and family are two fundamental concepts for sociology. However, bringing Black feminist thought into the center of conceptual analysis raises issues of how comprehensive current sociological interpretations of these two concepts really are. For example, labor theories that relegate Afro-American women's work experiences to the fringe of analysis miss the critical theme of the interlocking nature of Black women as female workers (e.g., Black women's unpaid domestic labor) and Black women as racially-oppressed workers (e.g., Black women's unpaid slave labor and exploited wage labor). Examining the extreme case offered by Afro-American women's unpaid and paid work experiences raises questions about the adequacy of generalizations about work itself. For example, Black feminists' emphasis on the simultaneity of oppression redefines the economic system itself as problematic. From this perspective, all generalizations about the normal workings of labor markets, organizational structure, occupational mobility, and income differences that do not explicitly see oppression as a problematic become suspect. In short, Black feminists suggest that all generalizations about groups of employed and unemployed workers (e.g., managers, welfare mothers, union members, secretaries, Black teenagers) that do not account for interlocking structures of group placement and oppression in an economy as simply less complete than those that do.

Similarly, sociological generalizations about families that do not account for Black women's experience will fail to see how the public/private split shaping household composition varies across social and class groupings, how racial/ethnic family members are differentially integrated into wage labor, and how families alter their household structure in response to changing political economies (e.g., adding more people and becoming extended, fragmenting and becoming female-headed, and migrating to locate better opportunities). Black women's family experiences represent a clear case of the workings of race, gender, and class oppression in shaping family life. Bringing undistorted observations of Afro-American women's family experiences into the center of analysis again raises the question of how other families are affected by these same forces.

While Black women who stand outside academia may be familiar with omissions and distortions of the Black female experience, as outsiders to sociology, they lack legitimated professional authority to challenge the sociological anomalies. Similarly, traditional sociological insiders, whether white males or their nonwhite and/or female disciples, are certainly in no position to notice the specific anomalies apparent to Afro-American women, because these same sociological insiders produced them. In contrast, those Black women who remain rooted in their own experiences as Black women—and who master sociological paradigms yet retain a critical posture toward them—are in a better position to bring a special perspective not only to the study of Black women, but to some of the fundamental issues facing sociology itself.

Toward Synthesis: Outsiders Within Sociology

Black women are not the only outsiders within sociology. As an extreme case of outsiders moving into a community that historically excluded them, Black women's experiences highlight the tension experienced by any group of less powerful outsiders encountering the paradigmatic thought of a more powerful insider community. In this sense, a variety of individuals can learn from Black women's experiences as outsiders within: Black men, working-class individuals, white women, other people of color, religious and sexual minorities, and all individuals who, while from social strata that provided them with the benefits of white male insiderism, have never felt comfortable with its taken-for-granted assumptions.

Outsider within status is bound to generate tension, for people who become outsiders within are forever changed by their new status. Learning the subject matter of sociology stimulates a reexamination of one's own personal and cultural experiences; and, yet, these same experiences paradoxically help to illuminate sociology's anomalies. Outsiders within occupy a special place—

they become different people, and their difference sensitizes them to patterns that may be more difficult for established sociological insiders to see. Some outsiders within try to resolve the tension generated by their new status by leaving sociology and remaining sociological outsiders. Others choose to suppress their difference by striving to become bonafide, "thinking as usual" sociological insiders. Both choices rob sociology of diversity and ultimately weaken the discipline.

A third alternative is to conserve the creative tension of outsider within status by encouraging and institutionalizing outsider within ways of seeing. This alternative has merit not only for actual outsiders within, but also for other sociologists as well. The approach suggested by the experiences of outsiders within is one where intellectuals learn to trust their own personal and cultural biographies as significant sources of knowledge. In contrast to approaches that require submerging these dimensions of self in the process of becoming an allegedly unbiased, objective social scientist, outsiders within bring these ways of knowing back into the research process. At its best, outsider within status seems to offer its occupants a powerful balance between the strengths of their sociological training and the offerings of their personal and cultural experiences. Neither is subordinated to the other. Rather, experienced reality is used as a valid source of knowledge for critiquing sociological facts and theories, while sociological thought offers new ways of seeing that experienced reality.

What many Black feminists appear to be doing is embracing the creative potential of their outsider within status and using it wisely. In doing so, they move themselves and their disciplines closer to the humanist vision implicit in their work—namely, the freedom both to be different and part of the solidarity of humanity.

Notes

*I wish to thank Lynn Weber Cannon, Bonnie Thornton Dill, Alison M. Jaggar, Joan Hartman, Ellen Messer-Davidow, and several anonymous reviewers for their helpful comments about earlier drafts of this paper. Correspondence to: Department of Afro-American Studies, University of Cincinnati, ML 370, Cincinnati, OH 45221.

1. In 1940, almost 60 percent of employed Afro-American women were domestics. The 1970 census was the first time this category of work did not contain the largest segment of the Black female labor force. See Rollins (1985) for a discussion of Black domestic work.

2. For example, in *Of Women Born: Motherhood as Experience and Institution*, Adrienne Rich has found memories of her Black "mother," a young, unstereotypically slim Black woman she loved. Similarly, Dill's (1980) study of Black domestic workers reveals Black women's sense of affirmation at knowing that they were better mothers than their employers, and that they frequently had to teach their employers the basics about children and interaction in general. Even though the Black domestic workers were officially subordinates, they gained a sense of self-worth at knowing they were good at things that they felt mattered.

3. For example, in spite of Rich's warm memories of her Black "mother," she had all but forgotten her until beginning research for her book. Similarly, the Black domestic workers in both Dill's (1980) and Rollins' (1985) studies discussed the limitations that their subordinate roles placed on them.

4. For a discussion of the notion of a special standpoint or point of view of oppressed groups, see Hartsock (1983). See Merton's (1972) analysis of the potential contributions of insider and outsider perspectives to sociology. For a related discussion of outsider within status, see his section "Insiders as 'Outsiders'" (1972:29–30).

5. Hurston has been widely discussed in Black feminist literary criticism. For example, see selected essays in Walker's (1979) edited volume on Hurston.

6. By stressing the potentially positive features of outsider within status, I in no way want to deny the very real problem this social status has for large numbers of Black women. American sociology has long identified marginal status as problematic. However, my sense of the "problems" diverge from those

espoused by traditional sociologists. For example, Robert Park states, "the marginal man . . . is one whom fate has condemned to live in two societies and in two, not merely different but antagonistic cultures (1950:373)." From Park's perspective, marginality and difference themselves were problems. This perspective quite rationally led to the social policy solution of assimilation, one aimed at eliminating difference, or if that didn't work, pretending it was not important. In contrast, I argue that it is the meaning attached to difference that is the problem. See Lorde (1984:114–23 and passim) for a Black feminist perspective on difference.

7. In addition to familiarizing readers with the contours of Black feminist thought, I place Black women's ideas in the center of my analysis for another reason. Black women's ideas have long been viewed as peripheral to serious intellectual endeavors. By treating Black feminist thought as central, I hope to avoid the tendency of starting with the body of thought needing the critique—in this case sociology—fitting in the dissenting ideas, and thus, in the process, reifying the very systems of thought one hopes to transform.

8. On this point, I diverge somewhat from Berger and Luckmann's (1966) definition of specialized thought. They suggest that only a limited group of individuals engages in theorizing and that "pure theory" emerges with the development of specialized legitimating theories and their administration by full-time legitimators. Using this approach, groups denied the material resources to support pure theorists cannot be capable of developing specialized theoretical knowledge. In contrast, I argue that "traditional wisdom" is a system of thought and that it reflects the material positions of its practitioners.

9. Emerging Black feminist research is demonstrating a growing awareness of the importance of including the simultaneity of oppression in studies of Black women. For example, Paula Giddings' (1984) history of Afro-American women emphasizes the role of class in shaping relations between Afro-American and white women, and among Black women themselves. Elizabeth Higginbotham's (1985) study of Black college women examines race and class barriers to Black women's college attendance. Especially noteworthy is the growing attention to Black women's labor market experiences. Studies such as those by Dill (1980), Rollins (1985), Higginbotham (1983), and Mullings (1986b) indicate a new sensitivity to the interactive nature of race, gender, and class. By studying Black women, such studies capture the interaction of race and gender. Moreover, by examining Black women's roles in capitalist development, such work taps the key variable of class.

10. The thesis that those affected by multiple systems of domination will develop a sharper view of the interlocking nature of oppression is illustrated by the prominence of Black lesbian feminists among Black feminist thinkers. For more on this, see Smith (1983), Lorde (1984), and White (1984:22–24).

11. For example, African and Afro-American scholars point to the role dualistic thinking has played in domestic racism (Asante, 1980; Baldwin, 1980; Richards, 1980). Feminist scholars note the linkage of duality with conceptualizations of gender in Western cultures (Chodorow, 1978; Keller, 1983; Rosaldo, 1983). Recently, Brittan and Maynard, two British scholars, have suggested that dualistic thinking plays a major role in linking systems of racial oppression with those of sexual oppression. They note that

> there is an implicit belief in the duality of culture and nature. Men are the creators and mediators of culture—women are the manifestations of nature. The implication is that men develop culture in order to understand and control the natural world, while women being the embodiment of forces of nature, must be brought under the civilizing control of men . . . This duality of culture and nature . . . is also used to distinguish between so-called higher nations or civilizations, and those deemed to be culturally backward. . . . Non-European peoples are conceived of as being nearer to nature than Europeans. Hence, the justification . . . for slavery and colonialism . . . (1984:193–94).

12. This humanist vision takes both religious and secular forms. For religious statements, see Andrews' (1986) collection of the autobiographies of three nineteenth-century, Black female evangelical preachers. For a discussion of the humanist tradition in Afro-American religion that has contributed to this dimension of Black feminist thought, see Paris (1985). Much of contemporary Black feminist writing draws on this religious tradition, but reframes the basic vision in secular terms.

13. During a period when Black women were widely devalued by the dominant culture, Sanctified Church members addressed each other as "Saints." During the early 1900s, when basic literacy was an illusive goal for many Blacks, Black women in the Church not only stressed education as a key component of a sanctified life, but supported each other's efforts at educational excellence. In addition to these psychological supports, the Church provided Afro-American women with genuine opportunities for influence, leader-

ship, and political clout. The important thing to remember here is that the Church was not an abstract, bureaucratic structure that ministered to Black women. Rather, the Church was a predominantly female community of individuals in which women had prominent spheres of influence.

14. Since much Black feminist thought is contained in the works of Black women writers, literary criticism by Black feminist critics provides an especially fertile source of Black women's ideas. See Tate (1983) and Christian (1985).

15. Audre Lorde (1984:114) describes this conscious hiding of one's self as follows: "in order to survive, those of us for whom oppression is as American as apple pie have always had to be watchers, to become familiar with the language and manners of the oppressor, even sometimes adopting them for some illusion of protection."

16. In this sense, sociology is a special case of the more generalized process discussed by Mannheim (1936). Also, see Berman (1981) for a discussion of Western thought as a paradigm, Mulkay (1979) for a sociology of knowledge analysis of the natural sciences, and Berger and Luckmann (1966) for a generalized discussion of how everyday knowledge is socially constructed.

17. Jackson (1974) reports that 21 of the 145 Black sociologists receiving doctoral degrees between 1945 and 1972 were women. Kulis et al. (1986) report that Blacks comprised 5.7 percent of all sociology faculties in 1984. These data suggest that historically, Black females have not been sociological insiders, and currently, Black women as a group comprise a small portion of sociologists in the United States.

References

Andrews, William L. (ed.)
    1986 Sisters of the Spirit. Bloomington, IN: Indiana University Press.
Asante, Molefi Kete
    1980 "International/intercultural relations." Pp. 43–58 in Molefi Kete Asante and Abdulai S. Vandi (eds.), Contemporary Black Thought. Beverly Hills, CA: Sage.
Baldwin, Joseph A.
    1980 "The psychology of oppression." Pp. 95–110 in Molefi Kete Asante and Abdulai S. Vandi (eds.), Contemporary Black Thought. Beverly Hills, CA: Sage.
Beale, Frances
    1970 "Double jeopardy: to be Black and female." Pp. 90–110 in Toni Cade (ed.), The Black Woman. New York: Signet.
Berger, Peter L. and Thomas Luckmann
    1966 The Social Construction of Reality. New York: Doubleday.
Berman, Morris
    1981 The Reenchantment of the World. New York: Bantam.
Brittan, Arthur and Mary Maynard
    1984 Sexism, Racism and Oppression. New York: Basil Blackwell.
Chodorow, Nancy
    1978 The Reproduction of Mothering. Berkeley, CA: University of California Press.
Christian, Barbara
    1985 Black Feminist Criticism: Perspectives on Black Women Writers. New York: Pergamon.
Davis, Angela
    1981 Women, Race and Class. New York: Random House.
Dill, Bonnie Thornton
    1980 "'The means to put my children through': child-rearing goals and strategies among Black female domestic servants." Pp. 107–23 in LaFrances Rodgers-Rose (ed.), The Black Woman. Beverly Hills, CA: Sage.
    1983 "Race, class, and gender: prospects for an all-inclusive sisterhood." Feminist Studies 9: 131–50.

Giddings, Paula
    1984 When and Where I Enter . . . The Impact of Black Women on Race and Sex in America. New York: William Morrow.
Gilkes, Cheryl Townsend
    1980 "'Holding back the ocean with a broom': Black women and community work." Pp. 217–31 in LaFrances Rodgers-Rose (ed.), The Black Woman. Beverly Hills, CA: Sage.
    1981 "From slavery to social welfare: racism and the control of Black women." Pp. 288–300 in Amy Smerdlow and Helen Lessinger (ed.), Class, Race, and Sex: The Dynamics of Control. Boston: G.K. Hall.
    1985 "'Together and in harness': women's traditions in the sanctified church." Signs 10:678–99.
Gwaltney, John Langston
    1980 Drylongso, a Self-portrait of Black America. New York: Vintage.
Hale, Janice
    1980 "The Black woman and child rearing." Pp. 79–88 in LaFrances Rodgers-Rose (ed.), The Black Woman. Beverly Hills, CA: Sage.
Hartsock, Nancy M.
    1983 "The feminist standpoint: developing the ground for a specifically feminist historical materialism." Pp. 283–310 in Sandra Harding and Merrill Hintikka (eds.), Discovering Reality. Boston: D. Reidel.
Higginbotham, Elizabeth
    1982 "Two representative issues in contemporary sociological work on Black women." Pp. 93–98 in Gloria T. Hull, Patricia Bell Scott, and Barbara Smith (eds.), But Some of Us Are Brave. Old Westbury, NY: Feminist Press.
    1983 "Laid bare by the system: work and survival for Black and Hispanic women." Pp. 200–15 in Amy Smerdlow and Helen Lessinger (eds.), Class, Race, and Sex: The Dynamics of Control. Boston: G.K. Hall.
    1985 "Race and class barriers to Black women's college attendance." Journal of Ethnic Studies 13:89–107.
Hooks, Bell
    1981 Ain't I a Woman: Black Women and Feminism. Boston: South End Press.
    1984 From Margin to Center. Boston: South End Press.
Jackson, Jacquelyn
    1974 "Black female sociologists." Pp. 267–98 in James E. Blackwell and Morris Janowitz (eds.), Black Sociologists. Chicago: University of Chicago Press.
Keller, Evelyn Fox
    1983 "Gender and science." Pp. 187–206 in Sandra Harding and Merrill Hintikka (eds.), Discovering Reality. Boston: D. Reidel.
King, Mae
    1973 "The politics of sexual stereotypes." Black Scholar 4:12–23.
Kuhn, Thomas S.
    1970 The Structure of Scientific Revolutions. 2d Edition. Chicago: [1962] University of Chicago Press.
Kulis, Stephen, Karen A. Miller, Morris Axelrod, and Leonard Gordon
    1986 "Minority representation of U.S. departments." ASA Footnotes 14:3.
Ladner, Joyce
    1971 Tomorrow's Tomorrow: The Black Woman. Garden City, NY: Anchor.
Lee, Alfred McClung
    1973 Toward Humanist Sociology. Englewood Cliffs, NJ: Prentice-Hall.
Lewis, Diane
    1977 "A response to inequality: Black women, racism and sexism." Signs 3:339–61.

Loewenberg, Bert James and Ruth Bogin (eds.)
  1976 Black Women in Nineteenth-century Life. University Park, PA: Pennsylvania State University.
Lorde, Audre
  1984 Sister Outsider. Trumansburg, NY: The Crossing Press.
Mannheim, Karl
  1954 Ideology and Utopia: An Introduction to the Sociology of [1936] Knowledge. New York: Harcourt, Brace & Co.
Merton, Robert K.
  1972 "Insiders and outsiders: a chapter in the sociology of knowledge." American Journal of Sociology 78:9–47.
Mulkay, Michael
  1979 Science and the Sociology of Knowledge. Boston: George Allen & Unwin.
Mullings, Leith
  1986a "Anthropological perspectives on the Afro-American family." American Journal of Social Psychiatry 6:11–16.
  1986b "Uneven development: class, race and gender in the United States before 1900." Pp. 41–57 in Eleanor Leacock and Helen Safa (eds.), Women's Work, Development and the Division of Labor by Gender. South Hadley, MA: Bergin & Garvey.
Murray, Pauli
  1970 "The liberation of Black women." Pp. 87–102 in Mary Lou Thompson (ed.), Voices of the New Feminism. Boston: Beacon Press.
Myers, Lena Wright
  1980 Black Women: Do They Cope Better? Englewood Cliffs, NJ: Prentice-Hall.
Paris, Peter J.
  1985 The Social Teaching of the Black Churches. Philadelphia: Fortress Press.
Park, Robert E.
  1950 Race and Culture. Glencoe, IL: Free Press.
Rich, Adrienne
  1976 Of Woman Born: Motherhood as Experience and Institution. New York: Norton.
Richards, Dona
  1980 "European mythology; the ideology of 'progress'." Pp. 59–79 in Molefi Kete Asante and Abdulai S. Vandi (eds.), Contemporary Black Thought. Beverly Hills, CA: Sage.
Rollins, Judith
  1985 Between Women, Domestics and Their Employers. Philadelphia: Temple University Press.
Rosaldo, Michelle Z.
  1983 "Moral/analytic dilemmas posed by the intersection of feminism and social science." Pp. 76–96 in Norma Hann, Robert N. Bellah, Paul Rabinow, and William Sullivan (eds.), Social Science as Moral Inquiry. New York: Columbia University Press.
Schutz, Alfred
  1944 "The stranger: an essay in social psychology." American Journal of Sociology 49:499–507.
Scott, Patricia Bell
  1982 "Debunking sapphire: toward a non-racist and non-sexist social science." Pp. 85–92 in Gloria T. Hull, Patricia Bell Scott, and Barbara Smith (eds.), But Some of Us Are Brave. Old Westbury, NY: Feminist Press.
Simmel, Georg
  1921 "The sociological significance of the 'stranger'." Pp. 322–27 in Robert E. Park and Ernest W. Burgess (eds.), Introduction to the Science of Sociology. Chicago: University of Chicago Press.
Smith, Barbara (ed.)
  1983 Home Girls: A Black Feminist Anthology. New York: Kitchen Table, Women of Color Press.

Steady, Filomina Chioma
    1981 "The Black woman cross-culturally: an overview." Pp. 7–42 in Filomina Chioma Steady
    (ed.), The Black Woman Cross-culturally. Cambridge, MA: Schenkman.
Tate, Claudia
    1983 Black Women Writers at Work. New York: Continuum.
Walker, Alice
    1974 "In search of our mothers' gardens." Pp. 231–43 in, In Search of Our Mothers' Gardens. New
    York: Harcourt Brace Jovanovich.
Walker, Alice (ed.)
    1979 I Love Myself When I Am Laughing . . . A Zora Neal Hurston Reader. Westbury, NY:
    Feminist Press.
Westkott, Marcia
    1979 "Feminist criticism of the social sciences." Harvard Educational Review 49:422–30.
White, Deborah Gray
    1985 Art'n't I a Woman? Female Slaves in the Plantation South. New York: W.W. Norton.
White, E. Frances
    1984 "Listening to the voices of Black feminism." Radical America 18:7–25.

Research as Praxis

Patti Lather

The author, who is concerned with the methodological implications of critical theory, explores issues in the developing area of emancipatory research. She defines the concept of "research as praxis," examines it in the context of social science research, and discusses examples of empirical research designed to advance emancipatory knowledge. The primary objective of this essay is to help researchers involve the researched in a democratized process of inquiry characterized by negotiation, reciprocitiy, empowerment—research as praxis.

The attempt to produce value-neutral social science is increasingly being abandoned as at best unrealizable, and at worst self-deceptive, and is being replaced by social sciences based on explicit ideologies. (Hesse, 1980, p. 247)

Since interest-free knowledge is logically impossible, we should feel free to substitute explicit interests for implicit ones. (Reinharz, 1985, p. 17)

Scientists firmly believe that as long as they are not conscious of any bias or political agenda, they are neutral and objective, when in fact they are only unconscious. (Namenwirth, 1986, p. 29)

Fifty years ago the Italian neo-Marxist, Gramsci, urged intellectuals to adhere to a "praxis of the present" by aiding "developing progressive groups" to become increasingly conscious of their own actions and situations in the world (quoted in Salamini, 1981, p. 73). This essay explores what it means to do empirical research in an unjust world. In it I discuss the implications of searching for an emancipatory approach to research in the human sciences.[1] It is written from the perspective of one who believes that, just as there is no neutral education (Freire, 1973), there is no neutral research (Hall, 1975; Reason & Rowan, 1981; Westkott, 1979). Bearing in mind the words of Gramsci, my objective is to delineate the parameters of a "praxis of the present" within the context of empirical research in the human sciences.[2]

I base my argument for a research approach openly committed to a more just social order on two assumptions. First, we are in a postpositivist period in the human sciences, a period marked by much methodological and epistemological ferment. There has been, however, little exploration of the methodological implications of the search for an emancipatory social science. Such a social science would allow us not only to understand the maldistribution of power and resources underlying our society but also to change that maldistribution to help create a more equal world. Second, research that is explicitly committed to critiquing the status quo and building a more just society—that is, research as praxis[3]—adds an important voice to that ferment.

My exploration of postpositivist, praxis-oriented research draws on three research programs— feminist research,[4] neo-Marxist critical ethnography (Masemann, 1982; Ogbu, 1981), and Freirian "empowering" or participatory research (Hall, 1975, 1981). Each of these research programs opposes prevailing scientific norms as inherently supportive of the status quo; each is premised on a "transformative agenda" with respect to both social structure and methodological norms; each is, in other words, concerned with research as praxis (Rose, 1979, p. 279). All three of these postpositivist research programs are examples of what Hesse (1980), borrowing from Althusser,[5] terms the "epistemological break" of developing a critical social science with an openly emancipatory intent (p. 196). After brief overviews of praxis-oriented, new paradigm research and of recent efforts in radical educational theorizing aimed at creating an empirically informed Marxism, the essay focuses on the development of empowering approaches to generating knowledge.

The Postpositivist Era

Research paradigms inherently reflect our beliefs about the world we live in and want to live in (Bernstein, 1976; Fay, 1975; Habermas, 1971; Hesse, 1980). Currently we are in a period of dramatic shift in our understanding of scientific inquiry. Lecourt (1975) has termed this present era "the decline of the absolutes" (p. 49; see also Bernstein, 1983; Smith & Heshusius, 1986). No longer does following the correct method guarantee true results, rather, "method does not give truth; it corrects guesses" (Polkinghorne, 1983, p. 249). It is increasingly recognized that the fact/value dichotomy simply drives values underground. Facts are never theory-independent (Hesse, 1980, p. 172); they are as much social constructions as are theories and values. Whereas positivism insists that only one truth exists, Rich (1979) argues: "There is no 'the truth,' [nor] 'a truth'—truth is not one thing, or even a system. It is an increasing complexity" (p. 187). Postpositivism has cleared methodology of prescribed rules and boundaries. The result is a constructive turmoil that allows a search for different possibilities of making sense of human life, for other ways of knowing which do justice to the complexity, tenuity, and indeterminacy of most of human experience (Mishler, 1979).

Broadly speaking, postpositivism is characterized by the methodological and epistemological refutation of positivism (Bernstein, 1976, 1983; Mitroff & Kilmann, 1978); much talk of paradigm shifts (Eisner, 1983; Phillips, 1983; Smith, 1983); and by the increased visibility of research designs that are interactive, contextualized, and humanly compelling because they invite joint participation in the exploration of research issues (Reason & Rowan, 1981; Reinharz, 1979, 1983; Sabia & Wallulis, 1983). Postpositivism is marked by approaches to inquiry which recognize that knowledge is "socially constituted, historically embedded, and valuationally based. Theory serves an agentic function, and research illustrates (vivifies) rather than provides a truth test" (Hendrick, 1983, p. 506). What this means is that "scholarship that makes its biases part of its argument" has arisen as a new contender for legitimacy.[6]

Research programs that disclose their value-base typically have been discounted, however, as overly subjective and, hence, "nonscientific." Such views do not recognize the fact that scientific neutrality is always problematic; they arise from a hyperobjectivity premised on the belief that scientific knowledge is free from social construction (Fox-Keller, 1985; Harding, 1986). Rather than the illusory "value–free" knowledge of the positivists, praxis-oriented inquirers seek emancipatory knowledge. Emancipatory knowledge increases awareness of the contradictions hidden or distorted by everyday understandings, and in doing so it directs attention to the possibilities for social transformation inherent in the present configuration of social processes. Admittedly, this approach faces the danger of a rampant subjectivity where one finds only what one is predisposed to look for, an outcome that parallels the "pointless precision"of hyperobjectivity (Kaplan, 1964). Thus a central task for praxis-oriented researchers becomes the confrontation of issues of empirical accountability—the need to offer grounds for accepting a researcher's description and analysis—and the search for workable ways of establishing the trustworthiness of data in new paradigm inquiry.

Research as Praxis

The foundation of postpositivism is the cumulative, trenchant, and increasingly definitive critique of the inadequacies of positivist assumptions[7] in light of the complexities of human experience (Bernstein, 1976; Cronbach, 1975; Feinberg, 1983; Giroux, 1981; Guba & Lincoln, 1981; Kaplan, 1964; Mishler, 1979). Postpositivism argues that the present orthodoxy in the human sciences is obsolete and that new visions for generating social knowledge are required (Hesse, 1980; Reason & Rowan, 1981; Rose, 1979; Schwartz & Ogilvy, 1979). Those committed to the development of a change-enhancing, interactive, contextualized approach to knowledge-building have amassed a body of empirical work that is provocative in its implications for both theory and, increasingly, method.

Several examples of this work are available. Consider Bullough and Gitlin's (1985) case study of one middle school teacher, a study designed to encourage rethinking the meaning of resistance and its place in theories of cultural and economic reproduction within the context of teachers' work lives. Their research design included the teacher's written response to a preliminary interpretation of the data, which is an example of the most common form of an emancipatory approach to research—the submission of a preliminary description of the data to the scrutiny of the researched. In an earlier study, Willis (1977) focused on the school-to-work transition in the lives of twelve working-class British "lads." The most oft-cited example of neo-Marxist critical ethnography, Willis's work both identifies the area of resistance to authority as a corrective to the overly deterministic correspondence theories then popular in neo-Marxist circles (see Apple, 1980–81; Bowles & Gintis, 1976) and builds into his research design an attempt to take the research findings back to the lads for further dialogue. McRobbie (1978) conducted a similar study inquiring into the effects of socialization into femininity on the lives of working-class British females. Finally, a more praxis–oriented example is Mies's (1984) action-research project in Germany, designed to respond to violence against women in the family. A high visibility street action attracted people who were then interviewed regarding their experience with and views on wife-beating. The resulting publicity led to the creation of a Women's House to aid victims of domestic abuse. A desire for transformative action and egalitarian participation guided consciousness-raising in considering the sociological and historical roots of male violence in the home through the development of life histories of the women who had been battered. The purpose was to empower the oppressed to come to understand and change their own oppressive realities (see also Anyon, 1980, 1981, 1983; Berlak & Berlak, 1981; Everhart, 1983; Hall, 1981; McNeil, 1984; Miller, 1986; Roberts, 1981; Tripp, 1984).

Such examples are part of a rich ferment in contemporary discourse about empirical research in the human sciences, a discourse that spans epistemological, theoretical, and, to a lesser degree, methodological areas. Within radical educational circles, for example, there have been several calls for eliminating the dichotomy between empirical work and the construction of emancipatory theory (Anyon, 1982; Ramsay, 1983; Wexler, 1982). There are, however, few clear strategies for linking critical theory and empirical research.

This failure to probe the methodological implications of critical theory has led to a number of difficulties for praxis-oriented research. The abundance of theoretically guided empirical work affiliated with the "new sociology of education" attests both to the conceptual vitality offered by postpositivist research programs and to the danger of conceptual overdeterminism. This nondialectical use of theory leads to a circle where theory is reinforced by experience conditioned by theory. Marxism's history of sectarianism and "theoretical imperialism" (Thompson, 1978; see also Bottomore, 1978) gives evidence of the need for open, flexible theory-building grounded in a body of empirical work that is ceaselessly confronted with, and respectful of, the experiences of people in their daily lives. Far too often, however, one is left with the impression that neo-Marxist empirical work is conducted to provide empirical specificities for a priori theory (Hargreaves, 1982; Lather, in press). Such work demonstrates the continued relevance of Thompson's (1978, p. 13) assertion that too much of Marxist social theory is an "immaculate conception which requires no gross empirical impregnation"[8] (see also Comstock, 1982, p. 371; Kellner, 1975, p. 149; Krueger, 1981, p. 59; Wright, 1978, p. 10).

Additionally, neo-Marxist empirical studies are too often characterized by an attitude toward the people researched that is captured in the words of one research team: "We would not expect the teachers interviewed to either agree with or necessarily understand the inferences which were made from their responses" (Bullough, Goldstein, & Holt, 1982, p. 133). Given the all-male research team and the largely female teacher subjects, one could make much of the gender politics involved in such a statement. But the issue here is the implications of such a stance for the purposes of emancipatory knowledge-building and the empowerment of the researched. One of the central tasks of my argument is to encourage those of us who do critical inquiry to demonstrate how our attitude differs from what Reinharz (1979) has termed the "rape model of research" (p. 95) so characteristic of mainstream social science: career advancement of researchers built on their use of alienating and exploitative inquiry methods.

The difficulties which continue to characterize critical inquiry raise two central questions about the effort to develop a style of empirical research that advances emancipatory knowledge. First, what is the relationship between data and theory in emancipatory research? In grounded theory-building the relationship between data and theory, according to Glasser and Strauss (1967), is that theory follows from data rather than preceding it. Moreover, the result is a minimizing of researcher-imposed definitions of the situation, which is an essential element in generating grounded theory. Given the centrality of a priori theory in praxis-oriented research, it is evident that emancipatory theory-building is different from grounded theory-building. Understanding those differences requires a probing of the tensions involved in the use of a priori theory among researchers who are committed to open-ended, dialectical theory-building that aspires to focus on and resonate with lived experience and, at the same time, are convinced that lived experience in an unequal society too often lacks an awareness of the need to struggle against privilege. Second, growing out of the first question, how does one avoid reducing explanation to the intentions of social actors, by taking into account the deep structures—both psychological and social, conscious and unconscious—that shape human experience and perceptions, without committing the sin of theoretical imposition? This question is tied to both the issue of false consciousness (defined later in this essay) and the crucial role of the researcher vis-à-vis the researched in emancipatory inquiry. An exploration of both of these central questions comprises the remainder of this essay.

For praxis to be possible, not only must theory illuminate the lived experience of progressive social groups; it must also be illuminated by their struggles. Theory adequate to the task of changing the world must be open-ended, nondogmatic, informing, and grounded in the circumstances of everyday life; and, moreover, it must be premised on a deep respect for the intellectual and political capacities of the dispossessed. This position has profound substantive and methodological implications for postpositivist, change-enhancing inquiry in the human sciences.

Empowering Approaches to the Generation of Knowledge

For persons, as autonomous beings, have a moral right to participate in decisions that claim to generate knowledge about them. Such a right . . . protects them . . . from being managed and manipulated . . . the moral principle of respect for persons is most fully honored when power is shared not only in the application . . . but also in the generation of knowledge . . . doing research on persons involves an important educational commitment: to provide conditions under which subjects can enhance their capacity for self-determination in acquiring knowledge about the human condition. (Heron, 1981, pp. 34–35)

Krueger (1981) notes that "there are hardly any attempts at the development of an alternative methodology in the sense of an 'emancipatory' social research to be explored and tested in substantive studies" (p. 59). Along these lines, Giddens (1979) suggests that the task of a critical social science is to explore the nature of the intersection between choice and constraint and to center on questions of power. Is this not equally true of the research situation itself? Insofar as we have come to see that evolving an empowering pedagogy is an essential step in social transformation, does not the same hold true for our research approaches?

I am arguing for an approach that goes well beyond the action-research concept proposed over thirty years ago by Levin, which has given rise to "a very active and lively field" in Britain and Australia over the past decade (Tripp, 1984, p. 20). While Tripp (1984) and Grundy (1982) note the existence of some critical and emancipatory teacher-based action research, the vast majority of this work operates from an ahistorical, apolitical value system which lends itself to subversion by those "who are tempted to use merely the technical form as a means of engineering professional teacher development" (Tripp, 1984, p. 20).

An emancipatory social research calls for empowering approaches to research whereby both researcher and researched become, in the words of feminist singer-poet Chris Williamson, "the changer and the changed." For researchers with emancipatory aspirations, doing empirical research offers a powerful opportunity for praxis to the extent that the research process enables people to change by encouraging self-reflection and a deeper understanding of their particular situations. In an attempt to reveal the implications that the quest for empowerment holds for research design, I will focus on three interwoven issues: the need for reciprocity, the stance of dialectical theory-building versus theoretical imposition, and the question of validity in praxis-oriented research.

The Need for Reciprocity

No intimacy without reciprocity. (Oakley, 1981, p. 49)

Reciprocity implies give-and-take, a mutual negotiation of meaning and power. It operates at two primary points in emancipatory empirical research: the junctures between researcher and researched and between data and theory. The latter will be dealt with in the next section of this essay; I here address reciprocity between researcher and researched.

Reciprocity in research design is a matter of both intent and degree. Regarding intent, reciprocity has long been recognized as a valuable condition of research fieldwork, for it has been found to create conditions which generate rich data (Wax, 1952). Everhart (1977), for example, presents reciprocity as "an excellent data gathering technique" (p. 10) because the researcher moves from the status of stranger to friend and thus is able to gather personal knowledge from subjects more easily. He traces his evolution from detachment to involvement in a study of student life in a junior high school where he comes to recognize "the place of reciprocity in productive fieldwork" (p. 8). I argue that we must go beyond the concern for more and better data to a concern for research as praxis. What I suggest is that we consciously use our research to help participants understand and change their situations. I turn now to those who build varying degrees of reciprocity into their research designs for the purpose of empowering the researched.

Laslett and Rapoport (1975), who studied school dropouts in Britain, build a minimal degree of reciprocity into their research designs. They term their approach "collaborative interviewing and interactive research." A central component of their strategy is to repeat interviews at least three times. The repetition is "essential to deal with the feelings roused, often covertly, in order to 'unlock' deeper levels of data content" (p. 973). Furthermore, they urge "giving back" to respondents a picture of how the data are viewed, both to return something to the participants and to check descriptive and interpretive/analytic validity.

A Marxist survey researcher, Carr-Hill (1984), expands the use of reciprocity to identify, through initial interviews, a group of twelve to fifteen people with whom the researcher engaged in a series of open discussions about the mismatch between formal education and the way people live their lives. This resulted in a collectively generated survey given to one hundred people, a survey couched in the language of respondents and "in terms of the social categories through which they perceive the world" (p. 281). Additionally, interested participants attended evaluation seminars where survey results stimulated respondents "to critically analyze their own educational history and its relation to their present life-styles" (p. 281).

A maximal approach to reciprocity in research design can be found in the work of two evaluators involved in a four-year project to assess the curricular reform movements of the 1960s (Kushner & Norris, 1980–81). The goal of their research was to move people from articulating what they know to theorizing about what they know, a process the researchers term "collaborative theorizing" (p. 27). This methodology is characterized by negotiation; negotiation of description, interpretation, and the principles used to organize the first-draft report. While they admit that final drafts are usually the preserve of the researcher, Kushner and Norris suggest that the attractiveness of this approach is that all participants, within time constraints, are allowed a role in negotiation of the final meanings of the research. Such collaboration, they contend, offers "an opportunity to extend the range of theories and meanings . . . to give participants the dignity of contributing to theorizing about their worlds . . . [and] through sharing meaning-production . . . [to] develop significant understandings of schooling and education" (p. 35).

A final example is provided by Tripp (1983). He explores what it means for interviews to be coauthored and negotiated in a conscious effort to democratize the research situation. In his case studies of alienation and the school-to-work transition, Tripp held one-to-one and group discussions "as a means of developing participants' views" (p. 32). The resulting coauthored statements constituted an agreed-upon account of the views of the participants. Tripp cautions, however, that "the negotiation process must be clearly bounded" (p. 38) because participants often wish to "unsay" their words. In Tripp's view, "the right to negotiate [on the part of research participants] was replaced by the right to comment" (p. 39). Researchers are not so much owners of data as they are "majority shareholders" who must justify decisions and give participants a public forum for critique.

Tripp's research design, however, is not fully interactive. Reciprocity in the negotiation of meaning is limited to the early stages of investigation. No attempt is made to involve research participants in either the interpretation of the descriptive data or the construction of empirically grounded theory. The lack of involvement of research participants in these later stages of the research process makes possible a situation where the entire issue of false consciousness is skirted. False consciousness is the denial of how our commonsense ways of looking at the world are permeated with meanings that sustain our disempowerment (Bowers, 1984; Gramsci, 1971; Salamini, 1981); it is a central issue in any maximal approach to reciprocity.

In order to address this issue, Fay (1977) argues that we must develop criteria/theories to distinguish between people's reasoned rejections of interpretations and theoretical arguments and false consciousness. Fay pinpoints this as a glaring omission, a black hole,[9] if you will, in critical theory: a lack of knowledge about "the conditions that must be met if people are going to be in a position to actually consider it [critical theory] as a possible account of their lives" (p. 218). Fay is pointing out that the creation of emancipatory theory is a dialogic enterprise. Both the substance of emancipatory theory and the process by which that theory comes to "click" with people's sense of the contradictions in their lives are the products of dialectical rather than top-down impositional practices.

Dialectical practices require an interactive approach to research that invites reciprocal reflexivity and critique, both of which guard against the central dangers to praxis-oriented empirical work: imposition and reification on the part of the researcher. As Comstock (1982) argues, "dialogic education is integral to every research program which treats subjects as active agents instead of objectifying them and reifying their social conditions" (p. 386). Yet, notably more often than in either feminist or Freirian praxis-oriented research, the neo-Marxist researcher's self-perceived role is as "interpreter of the world" (Reynolds, 1980–81, p. 87), exposer of false consciousness. This nondialectical, nonreciprocal perception of the role of the researcher confounds neo-Marxist researchers' intent to demystify the world for the dispossessed. Respondents become objects—targets of research—rather than active subjects empowered to understand and change their situations. As a result, neo-Marxist praxis-oriented work too often falls prey to what Fay (1977) notes as the irony of domination and repression inherent in most of our efforts to free one another (p. 209). In the name of emancipation, researchers impose meanings on situations rather than constructing meaning through negotiation with research participants.

There are at present few research designs which encourage negotiation of meaning beyond the descriptive level. The involvement of research participants in data interpretation as well as (to take one further step toward maximal reciprocity) theory-building remains largely an "attractive aspiration" (Kushner & Norris, 1980–81, p. 35). But as Fay notes, feminist consciousness-raising groups provide a model for how to begin to flesh-out the nature of maximal reciprocity: the involvement of research participants in the construction and validation of knowledge.

Throughout the late 1960s and 1970s, thousands of small grassroots groups formed to provide a way for women to exchange thoughts, experiences, and feelings. From this movement emerged the feminist maxim: the personal is political. What were once thought to be individual problems were redefined as social problems that require political solutions. For Fay (1977), the lesson from these groups is that

> coming to a radical new self-conception is hardly ever a process that occurs simply by reading some theoretical work; rather, it requires an environment of trust, openness, and support in which one's own perceptions and feelings can be made properly conscious to oneself, in which one can think through one's experiences in terms of a radically new vocabulary which expresses a fundamentally different conceptualization of the world, in which one can see the particular and concrete ways that one unwittingly collaborates in producing one's own misery, and in which one can gain the emotional strength to accept and act on one's new insights.
>
> The experience of the Women's Movement confirms that radical social change: through rational enlightenment require some mechanism for ensuring that those conditions necessary for such enlightenment will be established and maintained. (p. 232)

Following Fay (1977), I propose that the goal of emancipatory research is to encourage self-reflection and deeper understanding on the part of the persons being researched at least as much as it is to generate empirically grounded theoretical knowledge. To do this, research designs must have more than minimal reciprocity. The following is a summary of some of the procedures and theory necessary to attain full reciprocity in research:

— Interviews conducted in an interactive, dialogic manner, that require self-disclosure on the part of the researcher. An example of self-disclosure can be found in Oakley's (1981) research with women and their experience of motherhood. Arguing the need for interactive self-disclosure, Oakley emphasizes a collaborative, dialogic seeking for greater mutual understanding. This is opposed to mainstream interview norms where interview respondent's questions about the interviewer's own life are deflected (see also Acker, Barry, & Esseveld, 1983; Hanmer & Saunders, 1984).

— Sequential interviews or both individuals and small groups to facilitate collaboration and a deeper probing of research issues.

— Negotiation of meaning. At a minimum, this entails recycling description, emerging analysis, and conclusions to at least a subsample of respondents. A more maximal approach to reciprocity would involve research participants in a collaborative effort to build empirically rooted theory.

— Discussions or false consciousness which go beyond simply dismissing resistance to Marxist interpretations as such. We need to discover the necessary conditions that free people to engage in ideology critique, given the psychological hold of illusion—"the things people cling to because they provide direction and meaning in their lives" (Fay, 1977, p. 214). There is a dialectic between people's self-understandings and researcher efforts to create a context which enables a questioning of both taken-for-granted beliefs and the authority that culture has over us (Bowers, 1984). There, in the nexus of that dialectic, lies the opportunity to create reciprocal, dialogic research designs which not only lead to self-reflection but also provide a forum in which to test the usefulness, the resonance of conceptual and theoretical formulations.

Dialectical Theory-Building versus Theoretical Imposition

I do not believe that imposing Marxist rather than bourgeois categories is socialist practice. (Carr-Hill, 1984, p. 290)

The goal of theoretically guided empirical work is to create theory that possesses "evocative power" (Morgan, 1983, p. 298). By resonating with people's lived concerns, fears, and aspirations, emancipatory theory serves an energizing, catalytic role. It does this by increasing specificity at the contextual level in order to see how larger issues are embedded in the particulars of everyday life. The result is that theory becomes an expression and elaboration of politically progressive popular feelings, rather than an abstract framework imposed by intellectuals on the complexity of lived experience.

Building empirically grounded theory requires a reciprocal relationship between data and theory. Data must be allowed to generate propositions in a dialectical manner that permits use of a priori theoretical frameworks, but which keeps a particular framework from becoming the container into which the data must be poured. The search is for theory which grows out of context-embedded data, not in a way that automatically rejects a priori theory, but in a way that keeps preconceptions from distorting the logic of evidence. For example, Ramsay (1983) aptly criticizes Anyon's critical ethnographies (which focus on the effects of class and gender on the structure of U.S. public school classrooms) for telling us more about her predispositions than about the phenomena studied. Anyon's (1980, 1981) *certainty* and *clear-cutness* are particularly problematic, for, as Ramsey notes, "while we would agree that there is no such thing as 'value-free' or objective research, we would argue that there is a need to keep as open a frame of reference as is possible to allow the data to generate the propositions" (p. 316).

Theory is too often used to protect us from the awesome complexity of the world. Yet, "the road to complexity" is what we are on in our empirical efforts (Clark, 1985, p. 65). Moving beyond predisposition requires a set of procedures that illuminates the ways that investigators' values enter into research (Bredo & Feinberg, 1982, p. 439; Feinberg, 1983, pp. 159–160). Anchoring theoretical formulations in data requires a critical stance that will reveal the inadequacies of our pet theory and be open to counter-interpretations. Apple (1980–81), in cautioning that conceptual validity precedes empirical accuracy, neglects the largely undialectical role that theory plays in most critical ethnography. Empirical evidence must be viewed as a mediator in a constant mutual interrogation between self and theory. Otherwise, neo-Marxist theory will fail to transcend "the hubris of the social sciences" still present in the two emergent alternatives to positivist orthodoxy—

the interpretive and critical paradigms (Moon, 1983, p. 28). As Acker, Barry, and Esseveld (1983) note, "An emancipatory intent is no guarantee of an emancipatory outcome" (p. 431). The struggle, of course, is to develop a "passionate scholarship" (Du Bois, 1983) which can lead us toward a self-reflexive research paradigm that no longer reduces issues of bias to canonized methodology for establishing scientific knowledge (Cronbach, 1980; Goddard, 1973, p. 18).

The search for ways to operationalize reflexivity in critical inquiry is a journey into uncharted territory. Sabia and Wallulis (1983) make clear the danger: too often critical self-awareness comes to mean "a negative attitude towards competing approaches instead of its own self-critical perspective" (p. 26). Guidelines for developing critical self-awareness, hence, are rare. Nevertheless, while the methodological implications of critical theory remain relatively unexplored (Bredo & Feinberg, 1982, p. 281), the need for research approaches which advance a more equal world is receiving some attention (Acker, Barry, & Esseveld, 1983; Apple, 1982; Comstock, 1982; Fay, 1975, 1977). Various suggestions for operationalizing reflexivity in critical inquiry can be drawn from that small body of work.

First, critical inquiry is a response to the experiences, desires, and needs of oppressed people (Fay, 1975). Its initial step is to develop an understanding of the world view of research participants. Central to establishing such understandings is a dialogic research design where respondents are actively involved in the construction and validation of meaning. The purpose of this phase of inquiry is to provide accounts that are a basis for further analysis and "a corrective to the investigator's preconceptions regarding the subjects' life-world and experiences" (Comstock, 1982, p. 381).

Second, critical inquiry inspires and guides the dispossessed in the process of cultural transformation; this is a process Mao characterized as "teach[ing] the masses clearly what we have learned from them confusedly" (quoted in Freire, 1973, p. 82). At the core of the transformation is "a reciprocal relationship in which every teacher is always a student and every pupil a teacher" (Gramsci quoted in Femia, 1975, p. 41). Thus, critical inquiry is a fundamentally dialogic and mutually educative enterprise. The present is cast against a historical backdrop while at the same time the "naturalness" of social arrangements is challenged so that social actors can see both the constraints and the potential for change in their situations.

Third, critical inquiry focuses on fundamental contradictions which help dispossessed people see how poorly their "ideologically frozen understandings" serve their interests (Comstock, 1982, p. 384). This search for contradictions must proceed from progressive elements of participants' current understandings, or what Willis (1977) refers to as "partial penetrations"; the ability of people to pierce through cultural contradictions in incomplete ways that, nevertheless, provide entry points for the process of ideology critique.

Fourth, the validity of a critical account can be found, in part, in the participants' responses. Fay (1977) writes: "One test of the truth of critical theory is the considered reaction by those for whom it is supposed to be emancipatory.... Not only must a particular theory be offered as the reason why people should change their self-understandings, but *this must be done in an environment in which these people can reject this reason*" (pp. 218–219, italics in original). The point is to provide an environment that invites participants' critical reaction to researcher accounts of their worlds. As such, dialogic research designs allow praxis-oriented inquirers both to begin to grasp the necessary conditions for people to engage in ideology critique and transformative social action, and to distinguish between what Bernstein (1983) calls "enabling" versus "blinding" biases on the part of the researcher (p. 128).

Fifth, critical inquiry stimulates "a self-sustaining process of critical analysis and enlightened action" (Comstock, 1982, p. 387). The researcher joins the participants in a theoretically guided program of action extended over a period of time.

Earlier in this essay, I argued for reciprocity as a means to empower the researched. Here reciprocity is employed to build more useful theory. Research designs can be more or less participatory, but dialogic encounter is required to some extent if we are to invoke the reflexivity needed to protect research from the researcher's own enthusiasms. Debriefing sessions with participants provide an opportunity to look for exceptions to emerging generalizations. Submitting concepts and explanations to the scrutiny of all those involved sets up the possibility of theoretical exchange—the collaborative theorizing at the heart of research which both advances emancipatory theory and empowers the researched.

A strictly interpretive, phenomenological paradigm is inadequate insofar as it is based on an assumption of fully rational action.[10] Sole reliance on the participants' perceptions of their situation is misguided because, as neo-Marxists point out, false consciousness and ideological mystification may be present. A central challenge to the interpretive paradigm is to recognize that reality is more than negotiated accounts—that we are both shaped by and shapers of our world. For those interested in the development of a praxis-oriented research paradigm, a key issue revolves around this central challenge: how to maximize the researcher's mediation between people's self-understandings (in light of the need for ideology critique) and transformative social action *without becoming impositional.*

Comstock (1982) says that the critical researcher's task is to stimulate research participants into "a self-sustaining process of critical analysis and enlightened action" (p. 387). Doing such work in a nonelitist and nonmanipulative manner means that one wants to be not a "one-way propagandist," but rather like the Cobbett written about by Thompson (1963): Cobbett acknowledged "the aid which he is constantly deriving from those new thoughts which his thoughts produce in their minds." Thompson notes: "How moving is this insight into the dialectical nature of the very process by which his own ideas were formed! For Cobbett, thought was not a system but a relationship" (p. 758).

For theory to explain the structural contradictions at the heart of discontent, it must speak to the felt needs of a particular group in ordinary language (Fay, 1975, p. 98). If it is to spur toward action, theory must be grounded in the self-understandings of the dispossessed even as it seeks to enable them to reevaluate themselves and their situations. This is the central paradox of critical theory and provides its greatest challenge. The potential for creating reciprocal, dialogic research designs is rooted in the intersection between people's self-understandings and the researcher's efforts to provide a change-enhancing context. Such designs would both lead to self-reflection and provide the forum called for by Fay (1977) whereby the people for whom the theory is supposed to be emancipatory can participate in its construction and validation.

In sum, the development of emancipatory social theory requires an empirical stance which is open-ended, dialogically reciprocal, grounded in respect for human capacity, and yet profoundly skeptical of appearances and "common sense." Such an empirical stance is, furthermore, rooted in a commitment to the long-term, broad-based ideological struggle to transform structural inequalities.

Issues of Validity

> The job of validation is not to support an interpretation, but to find out what might be wrong with it. . . . To call for value-free standards of validity is a contradiction in terms, a nostalgic longing for a world that never was. (Cronbach, 1980, pp. 103–105)

What does empirical rigor mean in a postpositivist context?[11] If validity criteria are the products of the paradigms which spawn them (Morgan, 1983), what validity criteria best serve praxis-oriented research programs? The need to systematize as much as possible the ambiguity of our enterprise does not mean that we must deny the essential indeterminacy of human experience—"the crucial disparity between the being of the world and the knowledge we might have of it" (White, 1973, p. 32). My point is, rather, that if illuminating and resonant theory grounded in trustworthy data is desired, we must formulate self-corrective techniques that check the credibility of data and minimize the distorting effect of personal bias upon the logic of evidence (Kamarovsky, 1981).

Currently, paradigmatic uncertainty in the human sciences is leading to the reconceptualization of validity. Past efforts to leave subjective, tacit knowledge out of the "context of verification" are seen by many postpositivists as "naive empiricism." Inquiry is increasingly recognized as a process whereby tacit (subjective) knowledge and propositional (objective) knowledge are interwoven and mutually informing (Heron, 1981, p. 32; Polanyi, 1967). The absence of formulas to guarantee valid social knowledge forces us to "operate simultaneously at epistemological, theoretical and empirical levels with self-awareness" (Sharp & Green, 1975, p. 234). Our best tactic at present is to construct research designs that demand a vigorous self-reflexivity.

For praxis-oriented researchers, going beyond predisposition in our empirical efforts requires new techniques and concepts for obtaining and defining trustworthy data which avoid the pitfalls of orthodox notions of validity. The works of Reason and Rowan (1981) and Guba and Lincoln (1981) offer important suggestions in this regard. Reason and Rowan advise borrowing concepts of validity from traditional research but caution us to revise and expand those concepts in ways appropriate to "an interactive, dialogic logic" (p. 240). Their notion of validity is captured in the phrase "objectively subjective" inquiry (p. xiii). Guba and Lincoln argue for analogues to the major principles of orthodox rigor. They state that in order to fulfill the minimum requirement for assessing validity in new paradigm research the techniques of triangulation, reflexivity, and member checks should be enlisted. Building on these, I offer a reconceptualization of validity appropriate for research that is openly committed to a more just social order.

First, triangulation is critical in establishing data-trustworthiness, a triangulation expanded beyond the psychometric definition of multiple measures to include multiple data sources, methods, and theoretical schemes. The researcher must consciously utilize designs that allow counterpatterns as well as convergence if data are to be credible.

Second, *construct validity* must be dealt with in ways that recognize its roots in theory construction (Cronbach & Meehl, 1955). Our empirical work must operate within a conscious context of theory-building. Where are the weak points of the theoretical tradition we are operating within? Are we extending theory? Revising it? Testing it? Corroborating it? Determining that constructs are actually occurring, rather than they are merely inventions of the researcher's perspective, requires a self-critical attitude toward how one's own preconceptions affect the research. Building emancipatory social theory requires a ceaseless confrontation with and respect for the experiences of people in their daily lives to guard against theoretical imposition. A *systematized reflexivity* which reveals how a priori theory has been changed by the logic of the data becomes essential in establishing construct validity in ways that contribute to the growth of illuminating and change-enhancing social theory.

As an example, Acker, Barry, and Esseveld (1983), in a noteworthy effort to reconstruct "the social relations that produce the research itself"(p. 431), write that "our commitment to bringing our subjects into the research as active participants [has] influenced our rethinking of our original categories . . ."(p. 434). As part of their self-reflexive essay on their research into the relation between changes in the structural situation of women and changes in consciousness, they explore the tension "between letting the data speak for itself and using abstracted categories." They ask, "How do we explain the lives of others without violating their reality?" (p. 429). Contrast this with Willis's (1977) classic ethnography where there is no clear indication how the researcher's perspectives were altered by the logic of the data. Without this account, one is left viewing the role of theory in this research (which is so strongly shaped by a priori conceptions) as being nondialectical, unidirectional, an imposition that disallows counter-patterns and alternative explanations (see also Lather, in press; Walker, 1985).

Third, *face validity* needs to be reconsidered. Kidder (1982) contends that although it has been treated lightly and dismissed, face validity is relatively complex and inextricably tied to construct validity. "Research with face validity provides a 'click of recognition' and a 'yes, of course' instead of 'yes, but' experience" (p. 56). Face validity is operationalized by recycling description, emerging analysis, and conclusions back through at least a subsample of respondents: "Good research at the nonalienating end of the spectrum . . . goes back to the subjects with the tentative results, and refines them in light of the subjects' reactions" (Reason & Rowan, 1981, p. 248). The possibility of encountering false consciousness, however, creates a limit on the usefulness of "member checks" (Cuba & Lincoln, 1981) in establishing the trustworthiness of data. False consciousness, an admittedly problematic phenomenon (Acker, Barry, & Esseveld, 1983), however, does exist. For reasons illuminated by Gramsci's (1971) theories of hegemony, most people to some extent identify with and/or accept ideologies which do not serve their best interests. Thus, an analysis which only takes account of actors' perceptions of their situations could result in research being incorrectly declared invalid. The link between face and construct validity and the possible false consciousness of research participants is an area that very much needs empirical exploration. Perhaps the best that can be suggested at this point is that, just as reliability is necessary but not sufficient to establish validity within positivism, building face validity into new paradigm research should become a necessary but not sufficient approach to establishing data credibility.

Fourth, given the emancipatory intent of praxis-oriented research, I propose the less well-known notion of *catalytic validity* (Brown & Tandom, 1978; Reason & Rowan, 1981, p. 240). Catalytic validity represents the degree to which the research process reorients, focuses, and energizes participants toward knowing reality in order to transform it, a process Freire (1973) terms conscientization. Of the guidelines proposed here, this is by far the most unorthodox; it flies directly in the face of the positivist demand for researcher-neutrality. The argument for catalytic validity is premised not only within a recognition of the reality-altering impact of the research process, but also in the desire to consciously channel this impact so that respondents gain self-understanding and, ultimately, self-determination through research participation.

Efforts to produce social knowledge that will advance the struggle for a more equitable world must pursue rigor as well as relevance. By arguing for a more systematic approach to triangulation and reflexivity, a new emphasis for face validity, and inclusion of catalytic validity, I stand opposed to those who claim that empirical accountability either is impossible to achieve or is able to be side-stepped in praxis-oriented, advocacy research. Lack of concern for data credibility within praxis-oriented research programs will only decrease the legitimacy of the knowledge generated therein. Praxis-oriented research can only benefit from agreed-upon procedures which make empirical decision-making public and hence subject to criticism. Most important, if we do not develop such procedures, our theory-building will suffer from a failure to protect our work from our passions and limitations. I join Lecourt (1975) in his call for an "ardent text" (p. 49) grounded in "the real motion of knowledge" (p. 79) which is as tied to passion as to "objectivity." The tension between advocacy and scholarship, however, can be fruitful only to the extent that it pushes us toward becoming vigorously self-aware in our efforts to develop a praxis-oriented research paradigm.

Summary

This essay has one essential argument: a more collaborative approach to critical inquiry is needed to empower the researched, to build emancipatory theory, and to move toward the establishment of data credibility within praxis-oriented, advocacy research. The present turmoil in the human sciences frees us to construct new designs based on alternative tenets and epistemological commitments. My goal is to move research in many different and, indeed, contradictory directions in the hope that more interesting and useful ways of knowing will emerge. Rather than establishing a new orthodoxy, we need to experiment, document, and share our efforts toward emancipatory research. To quote Polkinghorne (1983): "What is needed most is for practitioners to experiment

with the new designs and to submit their attempts and results to examination by other participants in the debate. The new historians of science have made it clear that methodological questions are decided in the practice of research by those committed to developing the best possible answers to their questions, not by armchair philosophers of research" (p. xi).
Let us get on with the task.[12]

Notes

This essay is a revision of papers originally presented at the Sixth Annual Curriculum Theorizing Conference, Dayton, October 1984, sponsored by the *Journal of Curriculum Theorizing* and the University of Dayton, and the annual meeting of the American Educational Research Association, Chicago, March 1985.

1. Polkinghorne (1983) traces the history of the term "human science." He argues that "behavioral science" retains the specter of behaviorism and its prohibition against including consciousness as a part of scientific study. "Social science" carries connotations of seeking a knowledge characteristic of the natural sciences in its law-seeking mode of inquiry. "Human science," he argues, is more inclusive, using multiple systems of inquiry, "a science which approaches questions about the human realm with an openness to its special characteristics and a willingness to let the questions inform which methods are appropriate" (Appendix, p. 289).

2. In another article (Lather, 1984), I explore what Gramsci's concept of "developing progressive groups" means in a contemporary context by arguing that women presently constitute a "developing progressive group" ripe with potential for assuming a position at the center of a broad-based struggle for a more equal world.

3. Morgan (1983) distinguishes between positivist, phenomenological, and critical/praxis-oriented research paradigms. While my earlier work used the term "openly ideological," I find "praxis-oriented" better describes the emergent paradigm I have been tracking over the last few years (Lather, in press). "Openly ideological" invites comparisons with fundamentalist and conservative movements, whereas "praxis-oriented" clarifies the critical and empowering roots of a research paradigm openly committed to critiquing the status quo and building a more just society.

   Praxis-oriented means "activities that combat dominance and move toward self-organization and that push toward thoroughgoing change in the practices of . . . the social formation" (Benson, 1983, p. 338). Praxis is, of course, a word with a history. In this essay, I use the term to mean the dialectical tension, the interactive, reciprocal shaping of theory and practice which I see at the center of an emancipatory social science. The essence of my argument, then, is that we who do empirical research in the name of emancipatory politics must discover ways to connect our research methodology to our theoretical concerns and commitments. At its simplest, this is a call for critical inquirers to practice in their empirical endeavors what they preach in their theoretical formulations.

4. Feminist research is not monolithic: some researchers operate out af a conventional positivist paradigm, others out of an interpretive/phenomenological one, while others still—an increasing number—use a critical, praxis-oriented paradigm concerned both with producing emancipatory knowledge and with empowering the researched. (see Acker, Harry, & Esseveld, 1983; Bowles & Duelli-Klein, 1983; Roberts, 1981; Westkott, 1979).

5. It was actually French philosopher Bachelard who originated the concept or epistemological break, which Althusser then applied to the work of Marx (see Lecourt, 1975). Epistemological break means a rupture in the established way of conceptualizing an issue, a rupture which essentially *inverts* meaning. Hesse (1980), for example, uses the term to characterize those who argue not only *against* the possibility of an "objective" social science but *for* the possibilities inherent in an explicitly value-based social science with emancipatory goals.

6. Phrase used by Anyon in a session of the annual meeting of the American Educational Research Association, Montreal, April 1984.

7. The basic assumptions of positivism are four: (1) the aims, concepts, and methods of the natural sciences are applicable to the social sciences; (2) the correspondence theory of truth which holds that reality is knowable through correct measurement methods; (3) the goal of social research is to discover universal laws of human behavior which transcend culture and history; and (4) the fact-value dichotomy, the denial of both the theory-laden dimensions of observation and the value-laden dimensions of theory. For an overview and critique of each of the three paradigms, the positivist, the interpretive, and the critical/praxis-oriented, see, respectively, Bredo and Feinberg (1982), Carr and Kemmis (1983), and Bernstein (1976).

8. Two examples of the dangers of conceptual overdeterminism leading to theoretical imposition (the lack of a reciprocal relationship between data and theory) in the new sociology of education are correspondence theory, which posited an overly deterministic mirror-image relationship between schools and the needs of corporate capitalism (Apple, 1979; Bowles & Gintis, 1976), and the wishful thinking which saw resistance in every inattentive student and recalcitrant teacher (for critiques, see Bullough & Gitlin, 1985; Giroux, 1983).

9. Sears (1983) first used this term in a conference paper.

10. The inadequacies of an overreliance on rationality in human behavior are eloquently captured in Ascher's letter to de Beauvoir, a letter written to "clear the air" after Ascher had written a biography of de Beauvoir: "I don't think you ever grasped sufficiently the way the unconscious can hold one back from grasping a freedom consciously chosen. Too often I see your sense of freedom being based on a rationalism that denies that murky inner world over which we have as little, or much, control as the world outside us. And, in fact, control would be your word, not mine. For I believe we have to love this deep inner self and try to be in harmony with it" (Ascher, DeSalvio, & Ruddick, 1984, p. 93; see also Harding, 1982).

11. Issues of validity in openly ideological research are dealt with much more fully in Lather (in press).

12. To avoid becoming "an armchair philosopher of research" myself, I am presently engaged in what I see as a long term effort to explore student resistance to liberatory curriculum in an introductory women's studies course (Lather, 1986). My theoretical concern is with the processes of "ideological consent" (Kellner, 1978, p. 46), especially the enabling conditions which open people up to ideology critique and those which limit these processes (A. Berlak, 1986).

References

Acker, J., Barry, K., & Esseveld, J. (1983). Objectivity and truth; Problems in doing feminist research. *Women's Studies International Forum, 6*(4), 423–435.

Anyon, J. (1980). Social class and the hidden curriculum of work. *Journal of Education, 62,* 67–92.

Anyon, J. (1981). Social class and school knowledge. *Curriculum Inquiry, 11,* 3–42.

Anyon, J. (1982). Adequate social science, curriculum investigations, and theory. *Theory into Practice, 21,* 34–37.

Anyon, J. (1983). Accommodation, resistance, and female gender. In S. Walker & L. Burton (Eds.), *Gender and education* (pp. 19–38). Sussex, Eng.: Falmer Press.

Apple, M. (1979). *Ideology and curriculum.* Boston: Routledge & Kegan Paul.

Apple, M. (1980–1981). The other side of the hidden curriculum; Correspondence theories and the labor process. *Interchange, 11* (3), 5–22.

Apple, M. (1982). *Education and power.* Boston: Routledge & Kegan Paul.

Ascher, C., De Salvio, L., & Ruddick, S. (Eds.). (1984). *Between women.* Boston: Beacon Press.

Benson, J. K. (1983). A dialectical method for the study of organizations. In G. Morgan (Ed.), *Beyond method: Strategies for social research* (pp. 331–346). Beverly Hills, CA; Sage.

Berlak, A. (1986). *Teaching for liberation and empowerment in the liberal arts: Toward the development of pedagogy that overcomes resistance.* Unpublished paper.

Berlak, A., & Berlak, H. (1981). *Dilemmas of schooling: Teaching and social change.* New York: Methuen.

Bernstein, R. (1976). *The Restructuring of social and political theory.* New York: Harcourt Brace Jovanovich.

Bernstein, R. (1983). *Beyond objectivism and relativism: Science, hermeneutics, and praxis.* Philadelphia: University of Pennsylvania Press.

Bottomore. T. (1978). Marxism and sociology. In T. Bottomore & R. Nisbet (Eds.), *A history of sociological analysis* (pp. 118–148). London: Hunemann.

Bowers, C. A. (1984). *The promise of theory: Education and the politics of cultural change.* New York: Longman.

Bowles, G., & Duelli-Klein, R. (Eds.). (1983). *Theories of women's studies.* Boston: Routledge & Kegan Paul.

Bowles, S., & Gintis, H. (1976). *Schooling in capitalist America: Educational reform and the contradictions of economic life.* New York: Basic Books.

Bredo, E., & Feinberg, W. (Eds.). (1982). *Knowledge and values in social and educational research.* Philadelphia: Temple University Press.

Brown, D., & Tandom. R. (1978). Interviews as catalysts. *Journal of Applied Psychology, 63,* 197–205.

Bullough, R., & Gitlin, A. (1985). Beyond control: Rethinking teacher resistance. *Education and Society, 3,* 65–73.

Bullough, R., Goldstein, S., & Holt, L. (1982). Rational curriculum: Teachers and alienation. *Journal of Curriculum Theorizing, 4,* 132–143.

Carr, W., & Kemmis, S. (1983). *Becoming critical: Knowing through action research.* Deakin, Australia: Deakin University Press.

Carr-Hill, R. (1984). Radicalizing survey methodology. *Quality and Quantity, 18,* 275–292.

Clark, D. (1985). Emerging paradigms in organizational theory and research. In Y. Lincoln (Ed.), *Organizational theory and inquiry: The paradigm revolution* (pp. 43–78). Beverly Hills, CA: Sage.

Comstock, D. (1982). A method for critical research. In E. Bredo and W. Feinberg (Eds.), *Knowledge and values in social and educational research* (pp. 370–390). Philadelphia: Temple University Press.

Cronbach, L. (1975). Beyond the two disciplines of scientific psychology. *American Psychologist, 30,* 116–127.

Cronbach, L. (1980). Validity on parole: Can we go straight? *New Directions for Testing and Measurement, 5,* 99–108.

Cronbach, L., & Meehl, P. (1955). Construct validity in psychological tests. *Psychological Bulletin, 52,* 281–302.

Du Bois, B. (1983). Passionate scholarship; Notes on values, knowing and method in feminist social science. In G. Bowles and R. Duelli-Klein (Eds.), *Theories of Women's Studies* (pp. 105–116). Boston: Routledge & Kegan Paul.

Eisner, E. (1983). Anastasia might still be alive, but the monarchy is dead. *Educational Researcher, 12*(5), 13–14, 23–24.

Everhart, R. (1977). Between stranger and friend; Some consequences of "long term" fieldwork in schools. *American Educational Research Journal, 14,* 1–15.

Everhart, R. (1983). *Reading, writing and resistance: Adolescence and labor in a junior high school.* Boston: Routledge & Kegan Paul.

Fay, B. (1975). *Social theory and political practice.* London: Allen & Unwin.

Fay, B. (1977). How people change themselves: The relationship between critical theory and its audience. In T. Ball (Ed.), *Political theory and praxis* (pp. 200–233). Minneapolis: University of Minnesota Press.

Feinberg, W. (1983). *Understanding education: Toward a reconstruction of educational inquiry.* New York: Cambridge University Press.

Femia, J. (1975). Hegemony and consciousness in the thought of Antonio Gramsci. *Political Studies, 23,* 29–48.

Fox-Keller. E. (1985). *Reflections on gender and science.* New Haven, CT: Yale University Press.

Freire, P. (1973). *Pedagogy of the oppressed.* New York: Seabury.

Giddens, A. (1979). *Central problems in social theory.* Berkeley: University of California Press.

Giroux, H. A. (1981). *Ideology, culture, and the process of schooling.* Philadelphia: Temple University Press.

Giroux, H. A. (1983). Theories of reproduction and resistance in the new sociology of education: A critical analysis. *Harvard Educational Review, 53,* 257–293.

Glaser, B., & Strauss, A. (1967). *The discovery of grounded theory: Strategies for qualitative research.* Chicago: Aldine.

Goddard, D. (1973). Max Weber and the objectivity of social science. *History and Theory, 12,* 1–22,

Gramsci, A. (1971). Selections from the prison notebooks of Antonio Gramsci [1929–1935] (Q. Hoare & G. Smith, Eds. & Trans.). New York: International Publishers.

Grundy, S. (1982). Three modes of action research. *Curriculum Perspectives,* 3(2), 22—34.

Guba, E., & Lincoln, Y. (1981). *Effective evaluation.* San Francisco: Jossey-Bass.

Habermas, J. (1971). *Theory and practice.* Boston: Beacon Press.

Hall, B. (1975). Participatory research: An approach for change. *Prospects,* 8(2), 24–31.

Hall, B. (1981). The democratization of research in adult and non-formal education. In P. Reason and J. Rowan (Eds.), *Human inquiry* (pp. 447–456). New York: Wiley.

Hanmer, J., & Saunders, S. (1984). *Well-founded fear: A community study of violence to women.* London: Hutchinson.

Harding, S. (1982). Is gender a variable in conceptions of rationality? *Dialectica, 36,* 225–242.

Harding, S. (1986). *The science question in feminism.* Ithaca, NY: Cornell University Press.

Hargreaves, A. (1982). Resistance and relative autonomy theories: Problems of distortion and incoherence in recent Marxist analyses of education. *British Journal of Sociology of Education, 3,* 107–126.

Hendrick, C. (1983). A middle-way methatheory. [Review of *Toward transformation in social knowledge.*] *Contemporary Psychology, 28,* 504–507.

Heron, J. (1981). Experimental research methods. In P. Reason and J. Rowan (Eds.), *Human inquiry* (pp. 153–166). New York: Wiley.

Hesse, M. (1980). *Revolution and reconstruction in the philosophy of science.* Bloomington: Indiana University Press.

Kamarovsky, M. (1981). Women then and now: A journey of detachment and engagement. *Women's Studies Quarterly, 10*(2), 5–9.

Kaplan, A. (1964). *The conduct of inquiry: Methodology for behavioral science.* San Francisco: Chandler.

Kellner, D. (1975). The Frankfurt School revisited. *New German Critique, 4,* 131–152.

Kellner, D. (1978). Ideology, Marxism, and advanced capitalism. *Socialist Review, 42,* 37–65.

Kidder, L. (1982, June). Face validity from multiple perspectives. In D. Brinberg and L. Kidder (Eds.), *New directions for methodology of social and behavioral science: Forms of validity in research* (No. 12, pp. 41–57). San Francisco: Jossey-Bass.

Krueger, M. (1981). In search of the "subjects" in social theory and research. *Psychology and Social Theory, 1*(2), 54–61.

Kushner, S., & Norris, N. (1980–1981). Interpretation, negotiation and validity in naturalistic research. *Interchange, 11*(4), 26–36.

Laslett, B., & Rapoport, R. (1975). Collaborative interviewing and interactive research. *Journal of Marriage and the Family, 37,* 968–977.

Lather, P. (1984). Critical theory, curricular transformation, and feminist mainstreaming. *Journal of Education, 166,* 49–62.

Lather, P. (1986, June). *Empowering research methodologies: Feminist perspectives.* Paper presented at the annual meeting of the National Women's Studies Association, Champaign, IL.

Lather, P. (in press). Issues of validity in openly ideological research: Between a rock and a soft place. *Interchange.*

Lecourt, D. (1975). *Marxism and epistemology.* London: National Labor Board.

Masemann, V. (1982). Critical ethnography in the study of comparative education. *Comparative Education Review, 26,* 1–15.

McNeil, L. (1984, April). *Critical theory and ethnography in curriculum analysis.* Paper presented at annual meeting of American Educational Research Association, New Orleans, LA.

McRobbie, A. (1978). Working class girls and the culture of femininity. In Women's Study Group (Ed.), *Women take issue: Aspects of women's subordination* (pp. 96–108). London: Hutchinson.

Mies, M. (1984). Towards a methodology for feminist research. In E. Altbach, J. Clausen, D. Schultz, & N. Stephan (Eds.), *German feminism: Readings in politics and literature* (pp. 357–366). Albany: State University of New York Press.

Miller, J. (1986). Women as teachers: Enlarging conversations on issues of gender and self-control. *Journal of Curriculum and Supervision, 1*(2), 111–121.

Mishler, E. (1979). Meaning in context: Is there any other kind? *Harvard Educational Review, 49,* 1–19.

Mitroff, I., & Kilmann, R. (1978). *Methodological approaches to social science*. San Francisco: Jossey-Bass.

Moon, J.D. (1983). Political ethics and critical theory. In D. Sabia & J. Wallulis (Eds.), *Changing social science: Critical theory and other critical perspectives* (pp. 171–188). Albany: State University of New York Press.

Morgan, G. (Ed.). (1983). *Beyond method: Strategies for social research*. Beverly Hills, CA: Sage.

Namenwirth, M. (1986). Science through a feminist prism. In R. Bleir (Ed.), *Feminist approaches to science* (pp. 18–41). New York: Pergamon Press.

Oakley, A (1981). Interviewing women: A contradiction in terms. In H. Roberts (Ed.), *Doing feminist research* (pp. 30–61). Boston: Routledge & Kegan Paul.

Ogbu, J. (1981). School ethnography: A multilevel approach. *Anthropology and Education Quarterly, 12*, 3–29.

Phillips, D.C. (1983). After the wake: Postpositivistic educational thought. *Educational Researcher, 12*(5), 4–12.

Polanyi, M. (1967). *The tacit dimension*. Garden City, NY: Anchor Books, Doubleday.

Polkinghorne, D. (1983). *Methodology for the human sciences: Systems of inquiry*. Albany: State University of New York Press.

Ramsay, P. (1983). A response to Anyon from the Antipodes. *Curriculum Inquiry, 13*, 295–320.

Reason, P., & Rowan, J. (1981). Issues of validity in new paradigm research. In P. Reason & J. Rowan (Eds.), *Human inquiry* (pp. 239–252). New York: Wiley.

Reinharz, S. (1979). *On becoming a social scientist*. San Francisco: Jossey-Bass.

Reinharz, S. (1983). Experiential analysis: A contribution to feminist research. In G. Bowles & R. Duelli-Klein (Eds.), *Theories of women's studies* (pp. 162–191). Boston: Routledge & Kegan Paul.

Reinharz, S. (1985). *Feminist distrust: A response to misogyny and gynopia in sociological work*. Unpublished manuscript. [Expanded version of Reinharz, S. (1985). Feminist distrust: Problems of context and content in sociological work. In D. Berg & K. Smith (Eds.), *Clinical demands of social research* (pp. 153–172). Beverly Hills, CA: Sage.]

Reynolds, D. (1980–1981). The naturalistic method and educational and social research: A Marxist critique. *Interchange, 11*(4), 77–89.

Rich, A. (1979). *On lies, secrets, and silence: Selected prose, 1966–1978*. New York: Norton.

Roberts, H. (1981). *Doing feminist research*. Boston: Routledge & Kegan Paul.

Rose, H. (1979). Hyper-reflexivity: A new danger for the counter–movements. In H. Nowotny & H. Rose (Eds.), *Counter-movements in the sciences: The sociology of the alternatives to big science* (pp. 277–289). Boston: Reidel.

Sabia, D., & Wallulis, J. (Eds.). (1983). *Changing social science: Critical theory and other critical perspectives*. Albany: State University of New York Press.

Salamini, L. (1981). *The sociology of political praxis: An introduction to Gramsci's theory*. Boston: Routledge & Kegan Paul.

Schwartz, P., & Ogilvy, J. (1979, April). *The emergent paradigm: Changing patterns of thought and belief.* (Values and Lifestyles Program Report No. 7). Menlo Park, CA: Stanford Research Institute (S.R.I.) International.

Sears, J.T. (1983, October). Black holes of critical theory: Problems and prospects of ethnographic research. Paper presented at Fifth Annual Curriculum Theorizing Conference, Dayton.

Sharp, R., & Green, A. (1975). *Education and social control: A study of progressive primary education.* Boston: Routledge & Kegan Paul.

Smith, J.K. (1983). Quantitative vs. qualitative research: An attempt to clarify the issue. *Educational Researcher, 12*(3), 6–13.

Smith, J., & Heshusius, L. (1986). Closing down the conversation: The end of the quantitative-qualitative debate among educational inquirers. *Educational Researcher, 15*(1), 4–12.

Thompson, E.P. (1963). *The making of the English working class.* New York: Pantheon Books.

Thompson, E.P. (1978). *The poverty of theory and other essays.* New York: Monthly Review Press.

Tripp, D.H. (1983). Co-authorship and negotiation: The interview as act of creation. *Interchange, 14*(3), 32–45.

Tripp, D.H. (1984, August). *Action research and professional development.* Discussion paper for the Australian College of Education Project, 1984–1985. Murdock, Australia: Murdock University.

Walker, J.C. (1985). Rebels with our applause: A critique of resistance theory in Paul Willis's ethnography of schooling. *Journal of Education, 167*(2), 63–83.

Wax, R. (1952). Reciprocity as a field technique. *Human Organization, 11,* 34–41.

Westkott, M. (1979). Feminist criticism of the social sciences. *Harvard Educational Review, 49,* 422–430.

Wexler, P. (1982). Ideology and education: From critique to class action. *Interchange, 13*(1), 53–78.

White, H. (1973). Foucault decoded: Notes from underground. *History and Theory, 12,* 23–54.

Willis, P. (1977). *Learning to labor: How working class kids get working class jobs.* New York: Columbia University Press.

Wright, E.O. (1978). *Class, crisis and the state.* London: National Labor Board.

Mediations on the Ideology of Inquiry in Higher Education: Exposition, Critique, and Conjecture

CLIFTON F. CONRAD

Throughout the 1980s, there have been lively and unfettered debates in many disciplines and fields regarding the purposes of inquiry, alternative paradigms, and perspectives, and the processes and products of inquiry. Meanwhile, aside from the writings of a handful of individuals (G. Keller 1986; Peterson 1986)—most notably Yvonna Lincoln (Lincoln and Guba 1985)—the higher education literature has been curiously silent. Not surprisingly, our scholarship continues to reflect conventional approaches to inquiry. I am deeply concerned about our reluctance—as individuals and as a profession—to reconsider the meaning and conduct of inquiry in the field of higher education.

The purpose on my essay is to reflect on some distinguishing features of our dominant ideology of inquiry—an ideology that is not a "bloodless abstraction" (Palmer 1987, 22) but the prime determinant of what we know about higher education and how we know it. Toward that end, I will examine four conventional beliefs that guide research in our field. These sometimes overlapping beliefs concern stakeholders, aims of inquiry, paradigm and modes of inquiry, and inquiry perspectives. For each, I will briefly describe the belief, offer a critique, and conjecture about future inquiry. I conclude the essay by suggesting some basic tenets for a renewed culture of inquiry to guide our community of scholars.

I have consulted with many friends and colleagues throughout the preparation of this paper; some of the ideas and perspectives considered here reflect that counsel. At the same time, preparing this essay has been a personal journey. My reflections are not those of a distant observer, but of one who has been passionately involved in higher education research for nearly two decades. In no small measure, then, this essay is part autobiographical, reflecting my continuing struggle to make sense out of my own research as well as the work of others. My criticisms and conjectures are aimed at my own scholarship as well as the research of others in our community of scholars.

Stakeholders: Inquiry for Whom?

Prevailing Belief:

> *Inquiry in higher education should be primarily oriented to scholarly peers rather than to other major stakeholding audiences (administrators/faculty, public policy-makers, and the educated public).*

Most research by faculty in higher education is oriented to scholarly peers rather than other stakeholders—such as higher education decision-makers and pratictioners as well as the public-at-large. Our research agendas, our emphasis on specialized knowledge, our frameworks and modes of inquiry, our rhetoric and the products of our inquiry—all reflect this conventional belief. The telltale signs are everywhere: specialized books and journal articles that report the results of technical studies; research topics that mirror the interests of scholars more than practitioners; the emphasis on quantitative rather than qualitative ways of knowing; and a rhetoric of inquiry that enshrines academic language and a "stripped-down, cool style" (Firestone 1987, 17) at the expense of a more public prose.

Like other core beliefs in our ideology of inquiry, this one is rooted in the widespread practice of viewing higher education as an academic discipline rather than as a field of study. For many of us, our individual and collective legitimacy and stature within the academy are seen as closely allied with the disciplinary modes and its basic premise that scholarly peers constitute the major audience for research. Tellingly, this view is reflected in our affirmation that the most significant research in higher education has been done by individuals—such as Burton Clark—who have been trained in an academic discipline and whose research, in general, is oriented more to like-minded scholars than to other stakeholding audiences.

Critique and Conjecture

Perhaps not least because the reward structure in higher education supports it, this prevailing belief has seldom been challenged within our field. Without relinquishing my commitment to the central role of academic scholarship and peer review, I find this belief self-serving and limiting in several major respects. First, our seemingly uncritical acceptance of higher education as a discipline seems to have undermined our sense of ethical responsibility to audiences outside of our peers. Administrators and faculty throughout higher education, public policy-makers, and the educated public—all have legitimate claims to and a stake in research about higher education. As citizens of colleges and universities, do we not bear a primary—rather than a secondary—responsibility to generate and disseminate knowledge that will benefit others as well as ourselves and our scholarly community?

Second, I strongly suspect that our disciplinary orientation and primary allegiance to our scholarly peers has isolated us from the agendas, perspectives, and insights of other stakeholders—especially from their self-reflections on their experience, which might provide a wellspring for generating some genuinely new ideas about higher education. With few exceptions, our research follows narrow disciplinary research agendas and restricted lines of inquiry, and echoes the extant literature. Our resulting isolation from higher education decision-makers and practitioners is not, I fear, unrelated to what many of us consider the harsh truth about too much of recent higher education literature: it is lifeless and pedestrian, inward-looking and parochial, the product of assembly-line research that has generated few new findings or challenging ideas.

In the context of these meditations, I think it is long past time that we view higher education not narrowly as an academic discipline but more broadly as a field of study. By that I mean that higher education should be viewed as a field like public administration, one that is multi-disciplinary and organized around subject matter rather than a particular method of inquiry. and as a field of study, I propose that we conceptualize our inquiry in terms of a stakeholder-centered model is which the needs of all major stakeholders—not just our scholarly peers—provide the lodestar for inquiry.

Besides our scholarly community, who are those stakeholding audiences that have a legitimate stake in higher education research? From my perspective, there are three major audiences: (1) administrators and faculty throughout higher education, who need knowledge about everything from assessment and student learning to leadership and resource allocation; (2) public policy-makers, from the institutional to the state and federal levels, who need a better knowledge base to inform their decisions about higher education governance, finance, planning, and quality; and (3) the educated public, individuals who need and wish to be more informed about our colleges and universities.

In what ways can we make our inquiry more responsive to these—and perhaps other—stakeholder groups? Drawing on recent discussions with individuals from these groups, as well as conversations with my scholarly peers, I think that we need to give special attention to at least five aspects of our inquiry: our scholarly aims, our inquiry paradigm and modes of inquiry, our inquiry perspectives, our research agendas, and our approaches to disseminating our findings. Let me briefly consider only the last two here, since I later discuss the others.

To begin with, I think we need to encourage research agendas that are more responsive to the concerns and needs of our stakeholders—with at least one eye fixed on the foreseeable future. Marketing, program review, technology transfer, economic development and competitiveness, minority recruitment and retention, evaluating the effectiveness of campus services—all are topical areas of substantial contemporary importance that have received relatively little scholarly attention but which seem likely to engage administrators until well into the next century. Besides teaching and learning, college and university faculty will continue to be interested in research that addresses post-tenure evaluation, graduate and professional education, leadership and program quality, faculty governance, equity, and reward structures. Public policy-makers—from governors and state-wide higher education agencies to legislative bodies at the state and federal level—are likely to need research that addresses a variety of topical areas: accountability, assessment, higher education and economic development, institutional purpose and mission, governance of state higher education systems, federal and state funding of low-income students, and the creative use of limited resources. Finally, the educated public—that corpus of individuals who are concerned about higher education for a variety of reasons—increasingly needs greater knowledge and understanding about such topics as institutional quality, the costs of higher education, and the purposes and integrity of our colleges and universities.

If we are serious about a stakeholder-centered model of inquiry, we also need to reexamine our approaches to dissemination of information. At the present time, most of us rely on traditional means of scholarly communication—books, monographs, journal articles, conference papers—aimed mostly at our scholarly peers. Aside from the ASHE/ERIC Research Report Series, which has been successfully targeted at administrators and faculty, this association has not much concerned itself with disseminating findings to audiences outside of ourselves (Newell 1986). Furthermore, very few scholars within our field have been concerned about dissemination. A recent exception is the report (Stark and Lowther 1988) and materials circulated by the Professional Preparation Network at the University of Michigan that includes self-study guides for faculty concerned about integrating liberal arts goals with professional students' educational experiences.

Owing in part to the diversity of subgroups within each of the stakeholding audiences I have identified, this is a complex issue that is unlikely to yield easy solutions. As a point of departure, however, let me suggest several considerations that might inform our discussion of dissemination. First, rather than establish costly new vehicles to disseminate our scholarship, we should encourage our colleagues to share their work through existing and emerging modes of dissemination that are utilized by various subgroups within each of our stakeholder audiences. For example, our administrative stakeholders are served by many diverse associations—such as the Council for the Advancement and Support of Higher Education (CASE), the College and University Personnel Association (CUPA), and the American Council on Education (ACE). In addition to practitioner journals, many of these associations have a monograph series and a newsletter, and more than a few are experimenting with innovative modes of communication such as electronic networking. A general and educated audience may be reached through such periodicals as *The New York Review of Books*, *Commentary*, *Harper's* and *The New Republic*, as long as scholars are willing and able to communicate in a "public idiom" (Jacoby 1987, 7).

Second, to enhance our exchange with our various audiences, we should encourage our colleagues to reexamine their rhetoric of communication. Instead of the objectivist language of traditional scientific inquiry and obfuscatory verbiage, we need to adapt our language to our respective audiences. For example, most administrators and policy-makers place a premium on a language that is clear and forthright; the educated public is likely to favor rhetoric that is stimulating as well as informative. And all of our stakeholding audiences—save a few of our scholarly peers—are likely to be most receptive to writers that use an active voice, convey "neighborliness" (Savage 1988), and are openly invitational.

Third, in recognition of the complexity as well as the importance of this issue, I propose that ASHE establish a special task force on the feasibility of dissemination. This association might serve as a broker or clearinghouse between higher education researchers and our various audiences propose ways to involve the policy and practitioner communities in adapting our research to specific audiences and contexts, and draw on the considerable body of literature on dissemination—including the journal *Knowledge: Creation, Diffusion, and Utilization*—to examine relations in our field between knowledge creation and knowledge use (DeMartini and Whitbeck 1986).

Aims of Inquiry

Prevailing Belief:

> *Inquiry in higher education should be aimed at developing a specialized knowledge rather than more broadly aimed at developing generalized knowledge.*

Not only do we produce knowledge for a narrow audience, but most of the knowledge we develop is highly specialized. Grounded in our overarching faith in higher education as a discipline, our philosophy of inquiry, and our commitment to research that addresses the intellectual concerns and sensibilities of a scholarly audience, most higher education researchers strongly believe in the sanctity of highly specialized knowledge. This belief is reflected in the disproportionate number of narrow, univariate, and technical studies that dominate our conference proceedings, our journals (Silverman 1982, 1987), and our professional discourse. With few exceptions, the greatest prestige in our field is accorded those who produce highly specialized studies on such topics as student attrition and faculty scholarly productivity.

Critique and Conjecture

Although there is a compelling need for specialized knowledge and technical studies, I find this core belief limiting. First, and most troubling, it has encouraged higher education researchers to focus their energies on gathering facts—on the acquisition of information. Preoccupied with data-gathering for narrow descriptive purposes, we have not emphasized understanding and interpretation that goes much beyond empirical generalization, narrow speculation, and low-level theory. We have too infrequently asked large and significant questions, and our knowledge base can be justifiably criticized as narrow, fragmented, and "esoteric" (Velben 1924, 237).

Second, while some of our studies have yielded information that has been useful to higher education practitioners, our specialized knowledge—on balance—has not been viewed as valuable by administrators and faculty throughout higher education, by policy-makers, or by the general public. A few observers have publicly and caustically criticized us for conducting "small studies of small questions" (Weiner 1986, 160), and producing "junk" and "piffle" (in G. Keller 1985, 8); perhaps more painfully—and telling—most of us are acutely aware that our major constituencies remain indifferent to our research. Based on my discussions with various stakeholders, it seems to me that our major audiences are less in need of highly specialized knowledge *per se* or "hands-on" knowledge than in generalized knowledge that addresses large and significant issues and offers illuminating perspectives and insights on those issues.

For these reasons, as well as my conviction that the legitimacy and long-term future of our field depend on the support of our stakeholders, I suggest that our research be aimed not exclusively at developing specialized knowledge but more broadly at developing generalized knowledge as well. This generalized body of knowledge would include observations, concepts, generalizations, and theories; and it would reflect a depth and breadth of understanding and interpretation that reaches beyond mere factual knowledge and seeks to address the needs of our major stakeholders. It would, of course, be built on "disciplined inquiry" (Cronbach and Suppes 1969, 17–18), that is, according to rigorous and widely accepted rules of scholarly inquiry that transcend specific methods.

If we are to enlarge our aims beyond narrow technical studies and broaden our conception of knowledge, our inquiry—in my judgment—should not be driven exclusively by narrow disciplinary research questions, by our paradigm, or by our modes of inquiry. For heuristic purposes, let me suggest four approaches to inquiry that seem especially well suited to developing generalized knowledge: problem-centered, interpretive, interpretive, and future-centered.

Problem-centered inquiry, as I define it, refers to interdisciplinary research that addresses large and significant issues and problems confronting higher education. As in many natural science disciplines and some professional fields, problem-centered inquiry is organized around major problems and issues that concern stakeholders—such as the political economy of universities. In addition to identifying issues, problem-centered research can involve stakeholders in the design, execution, and dissemination of research. If our research is to become more problem-centered in the future, we should especially encourage institutional and public policy studies (Fincher 1987) and evaluation studies (Rogers and Gamson 1982)—provided, of course, that they go beyond description and either contribute to theory-based knowledge or significantly enhance our general understanding of, for example, a proposed student aid policy or an innovation in liberal education. At present, policy studies have gained some legitimacy in our field, but our literature includes relatively few such studies; evaluation studies are rarely accepted for publication, perhaps on the ground that they are often atheoretical even though they may contribute substantially to our general understanding. Beyond these two types of studies, most of our research could be more problem-centered and interdisciplinary, while continuing to draw on such traditional quantitative techniques as survey research and content analysis as well as the full repertoire of qualitative techniques.

By integrative inquiry I mean research and scholarship that seeks to "knit together what has already been learned" (Heclo 1974, x), including findings from the relevant academic disciplines (Clark 1974). Reviews of the literature that integrate studies narratively can be especially useful in developing syntheses of what is known about specific topics; *Higher Education: Handbook of Theory and Research* has been an excellent vehicle for integrative reviews of the literature. At the same time, it seems to me that two additional kinds of studies are needed if integrative inquiry is to become more central to our scholarship: studies based on secondary analysis (Cook 1974), and meta-analytic studies (Glass, McGaw, and Smith 1981). Large amounts of both qualitative and quantitative data in our field could be analyzed and reanalyzed to provide syntheses of what is known. Significantly, some of the most highly regarded scholarship on higher education—such as Jencks and Riesman's *The Academic Revolution* (1968)—have relied heavily on secondary analysis. Meta-analysis—the statistical analysis of the overall findings of numerous empirical studies—can be a powerful tool for developing quantitative summaries of individual studies as shown, for example, in a recent study of the economic value of higher education (Leslie and Brinkman 1988).

Interpretive inquiry refers to primary research that aims at making meaning of a particular or general behavior(s), events(s), or context(s) as a foundation for holistic understanding that reaches beyond mere facts. In doing so, it may not lead to generalization beyond the particular and the development of theory; even if it does not, however, it can nevertheless constitute generalized knowledge if it contributes to the depth—if not the breadth—of our understanding. While some quantitative techniques such as content analysis can be used in interpretive inquiry, qualitative techniques are probably most appropriate for this kind of in-depth inquiry. Within the last decade, a growing number of field studies and case studies have been introduced into our literature, seeming to presage a greater emphasis on interpretive inquiry. From my perspective, however, many of these studies fall far short of markedly enhancing our understanding: straightforward narrative and description receive more attention than analysis, explanation, and interpretation. In short, there remains a gulf between qualitative research as a springboard to first-rate interpretive inquiry and the bulk of qualitative studies that have been conducted in higher education.

Finally, I have a strong sense that we need to encourage inquiry that is future-centered if we are to enlarge our scholarly aims. By future-centered I mean normative scholarship that imagines, idealizes, and speculates about the future of higher education. What, for example, should be the future of the comprehensive university, multi-campus systems, graduate education, the two-year college? At the present time, both scholars of higher education and our stakeholders give such topics little attention. To be sure, a few scholars have accentuated the value of "futures-research," and such studies may be a useful vehicle for thinking about the future, But it seems to me that we should begin to think broadly about initiating various kinds of normative inquiry regarding the future of higher education. There are traditions of philosophical inquiry, for example, that may be especially helpful for thinking about the future.

In summary, I believe strongly that we need to go beyond highly specialized knowledge to embrace inquiry that contributes to generalized knowledge. As conveyed far more eloquently in a quotation attributed to Oliver Wendell Holmes, Jr.:

> There are one-story intellects,
> Two-story intellects,
> And three-story intellects with skylights.
> All fact collectors who have
> No aims beyond their facts
> Are one-story men.
> Two-story men compare, reason,
> Generalize, using the labor of
> Fact Collectors as their own.
> Three-story men idealise,
> Imagine, predict—
> Their best illumination comes
> From above the skylight.

Inquiry Paradigm and Modes of Inquiry

Prevailing Belief:

> *Inquiry in higher education should be guided by the positivist ideal of the natural and physical sciences and quantitative modes of inquiry.*

Our emphasis on specialized knowledge is, of course, closely connected to our philosophy of inquiry. Fundamental to this philosophy is the fact that we live in an age that worships science and within a social institution that celebrates a particular view of science—positivism—that has long been associated with inquiry in the natural and physical sciences. While a growing number of social scientists (Bellah et al. 1985) have questioned the appropriateness of both positivism and quantitative modes of inquiry in social science research, scholars in our field have continued to work out of a positivist paradigm as reflected—among other ways—in the emphasis we place on verification rather than discovery, on "objective, value-free" inquiry, and on quantitative studies and "analytic science" (Silverman 1982, 1987). (Although quantitative modes of inquiry are associated with positivism, I do not suggest that the two are coextensive. There are countless examples of qualitative studies that are positivistic in orientation.)

Critique and Conjecture

Having nested most of our inquiry within a traditional positivist paradigm, we can be justifiably proud of the many valuable empirical studies conducted by higher educationists. At the same time, however, it seems to me that inquiry in higher education has been unduly stifled by our commitment to the traditional positivist epistemology and quantitative modes of inquiry. The problem is that in our quest to be "scientific," to make a science of higher education, we have uncritically embraced the ontological and epistemological foundations of the positivist ideal and tended to emphasize quantitative techniques at the expense of qualitative modes in inquiry.

On the basis of my reading of and reflection on the pertinent literature in philosophy and the sciences, I have been persuaded that the traditional positivist paradigm is too narrow and inherently limiting. A major thread in twentieth-century science and philosophy has been the systematic undermining of this ideal (Phillips 1987; Rabinow and Sullivan 1979). In our field, only Yvonna Lincoln has critically examined positivism in a series of publications (Lincoln 1988, 1989; Lincoln and Guba 1985, 1986, 1987, 1988) that have stimulated and sharpened my own thinking.

In particular, logical positivism and, to a lesser extent, Comtean positivism, have suffered a barrage of legitimate criticism, including the discrediting of the verifiability principle of meaning and the view that scientific knowledge is produced only from an objective observational base. To be sure, some closet Hempelians and unrepentant Comteans remain, and the critics of positivism have not approached agreement on what a "new philosophy of science" should entail. Nonetheless, the literature in the philosophy of science argues persuasively that the traditional positivist paradigm is inadequate (Bernstein 1983, 1985; Feyerabend 1978; Habermas 1971, 1984; Lakatos 1970; Phillips 1987).

It is long past time for scholars in our field to transcend the limits of a narrow positivism. For some, this means abandoning the positivist paradigm and substituting an alternative—a "post-positivist" (Schwartz and Ogilvy 1979) or "naturalistic" paradigm (Lincoln and Guba 1985). While sympathetic to these critics, I have some serious reservations. First, they are excessive in their "tenderness" and "charity"—their extreme relativism about what constitutes knowledge—and, in some cases, their rejection of scientific methods (Phillips 1987, 83–84). Second, there is a stridency and naiveté about their defense of an alternative paradigm that can be irritating. They tend to ignore the rich past of anthropology and sociology, such as the work of the Chicago School of Sociology, that stressed participant observation and fieldwork. Third, I am simply not persuaded that the Manichean, or "either-or" ("positivist" versus "naturalistic"), choice that has been introduced is as clear-cut as some critics suggest. For example, while Lincoln and Guba's (1985, 36–43) naturalistic paradigm is based on some meta-theoretical assumptions that contrast sharply with traditional positivism, many of the implications they draw for doing research are not at odds with positivist inquiry but rather reflect different emphases in knowledge creation—such as the need for research to be conducted in a natural setting.

What do I suggest? In objecting to a narrow-minded scientism, I do not think we should abandon the positivist paradigm. Rather, in the tradition of Campbell (1978) and Cronbach (1975)—and informed in part by Lincoln and Guba (1985)—we should abandon our paradigm for inquiry. In a very preliminary way, let me suggest several principles that might guide a more broadly conceived paradigm:

1.   Instead of assuming that there is a single "objective reality," we should explore the probability that there are "multiple constructed realities" (Berger and Luckmann 1973), though of course it does not necessarily follow that all constructions of reality are equally valid or powerful.

2.   Instead of assuming that inquiry is "objective and value-free" because we have used objective methods, we should assume that inquiry is value-bound and that the researcher cannot be completely separated from "what is known" (Lincoln and Guba 1985, 37–38).

3. While we should seek to develop nomothetic knowledge in the form of generalizations free from both time and context, we must recognize that in many instances only time-and context-bound ideographic knowledge is possible, acknowledging the legitimacy and importance of this kind of knowledge.

4. Following Popper (1959), we should view inquiry as following a meandering course in which tentative "knowledge claims" are subject to ongoing criticism, refutation, and revision. All claims must be subject to "organized skepticism" (Merton 1973, 277). In light of these points of view, it follows that our inquiry should place major emphasis on research in natural settings, and on discovery as well as verification, inductive as well as deductive data analysis, purposive sampling as well as random sampling, qualitative as well as quantitative modes of inquiry, and emergent designs as well as fixed designs.

Turning specifically to modes of inquiry, I am clearly not suggesting that we jettison quantitative techniques of research. Rather, in light of the limitations of traditional positivism as well as specific limitations of quantification—including "reductionism" and "distortion of truth" (Hamilton 1976; Pascarella 1982; Popper 1968; Rist 1980)—we should recognize the legitimacy of qualitative ways of knowing within the context of a broadened inquiry paradigm.

There are at least four qualitative "traditions" (Jacob 1987, 1988) in the social sciences and the humanities that are especially appropriate for research in higher education. Although these are widely known, I mention them to draw attention to their possible applicability to research in higher education. One such tradition, grounded theory, was developed by two sociologists (Glaser and Strauss 1967; Glaser 1978). It is a multi-faceted research strategy, which usually draws heavily on case study research that is designed to maximize flexibility in the generation of theory (Conrad 1982). Another qualitative method from sociology, symbolic interactionism (Denzin 1978; Ritzer 1983), has rarely been used in higher research. Yet the processes involved in symbolic interaction—that is, how people take another's perspective and derive meaning in specific situations—may provide valuable tools for a holistic understanding of, for example, leadership behavior in higher education.

Still another qualitative method—ethnography—was developed initially by anthropologists. Ethnography (Sandy 1979) focuses on the study of culture within particular settings, and it is organized around extensive field observation and a range of qualitative data. Although it has been used by a small number of researchers in our field (London, 1978), its possibilities for widespread use in higher education have scarcely been realized. Finally, from the humanities, I suggest a hermeneutic approach. Hermeneutics, an interpretative mode of inquiry, has been applied in curriculum studies at the secondary level. In higher education, it could be used to address problems in such areas as student development, curriculum, and evaluation.

Inquiry Perspectives

Prevailing Belief:

Inquiry in higher education should be guided by a functionalist perspective rather than by non-traditional inquiry perspectives, for example, neo-Marxist or feminist.

Just as we have sought to emulate the natural sciences through our commitment to a narrow positivism, so we have adopted a functionalist perspective from the natural sciences. Rooted originally in a model derived from the biological sciences and shaped by many sociologists and anthropologists over the last century, a functionalist perspective is one that has incorporated some diverse intellectual traditions: the structural-functionalism of Malinowski and Radcliffe-Brown, the systems theory advanced by Parsons and Buckley, and the conflict functionalism of Merton and

Coser. Yet in spite of this diversity, this perspective maintains an underlying unity (Burrell and Morgan 1979), namely, that there is patterned order in social life and that the purpose of inquiry is thus to explain how and why various social phenomena affect social stability. More specifically, a functionalist perspective focuses on integration, strain, and crisis as well as systemic differentiation; and it views conflict as problematic, unnatural, or something to be resolved, rather than being inherent and structured. Although few in our field explicitly acknowledge it, most of the research in higher education has been shaped (wittingly or unwittingly) on the anvil of a functionalist framework—from the questions we pose, to our research designs, to the lens through which we interpret our findings.

Critique and Conjecture

As a young graduate student in political science and sociology, I spent countless hours in abstract discussion of the virtues and limitations of a functionalist perspective. Despite some misgivings, I, like nearly all of my peers in the field of higher education, found myself conducting most of my research out of such a perspective. Today, however, I am concerned that our entrenched ideological commitment to a functionalist perspective excludes other frameworks at a high cost.

To begin with, we have become prisoners of a narrow, inherently conservative framework that has led us to focus on justifying the status quo in higher education. In turn, we have neglected to address critical and tough-minded questions about our colleges and universities. For example, most higher education researchers assume that there is pluralism and decentralization of power in American higher education and thus do not examine the question of whether there is a concentration of power in academe and, if so, the consequences of such a concentration for institutional governance and leadership, personnel, and academic programs. In my own area of curriculum research, higher education researchers assume that academic programs are shaped largely by factors internal to colleges and universities and therefore do not consider the extent to which the political economy in general and individual benefactors in particular—foundations, corporations, federal and state government—affect curriculum.

The functionalist perspective not only has limited the kinds of research questions asked, it has also blinded us to the viewpoints of many of our stakeholders. As Robert Merton has noted, "the concept of function involves the standpoint of the observer, not necessarily that of the participant" (1968, 7). In other words, most researchers in our field take the viewpoint of the observer and observe what they think is important, not what the observed may think is salient. By separating the "researcher" from the "researched," we have isolated ourselves from the voices of many of the participants and stakeholders in higher education that we are studying—including women, students in general, persons of color, and people from a full range of ethnic and socioeconomic backgrounds. Like other perspectives, a functionalist perspective is not neutral, and this orientation has almost always insulated our research designs and our data analysis and interpretation from the "reality constructions" of many of our stakeholders.

Without rejecting a functionalist perspective and with a full realization that "pluralism itself is a form of ideology" (Lincoln 1988, 14), I urge my colleagues to consider using alternative perspectives in the conduct of their inquiry. We all know that a variety of intellectual currents cut across such fields as philosophy, literature, political sociology, and history, providing the impetus and underpinnings for a growing number of alternative inquiry perspectives. These perspectives include critical, radical humanist, deconstructionist, feminist, neo-Marxist, realist, and radical structuralist (Bernstein 1983; Habermas 1971; Burrell and Morgan 1979). Each of these perspectives merits consideration; though as with any perspective, each should be considered with a full awareness of the limitations of narrowly partisan views.

At least partly because they respond to my stated reservations about a functionalist perspective, I would especially like to draw attention to two of these perspectives—one rooted in the nineteenth century, the other in the twentieth. The first, a neo-Marxist perspective, has been widely used by a growing number of scholars in the social sciences, the humanities, and the professions (Ollman and Vernoff 1982). The possibilities of such a framework to illuminate the study of higher education are splendidly illustrated in a new book on university-industry partnerships and the development of higher education policy. In a richly textured case study of the Business Higher Education Forum, Sheila Slaughter (1989) uses a neo-Marxist framework to analyze relations between changes in the political economy—as filtered through class, the state, and knowledge (ideology)—and the shaping of business/university alliances, science policy, and higher learning.

The second perspective—a feminist perspective—has been propelled by the contemporary women's movement. It informs an outpouring of feminist scholarship and reflects so many themes and voices—sometimes conflicting and contradictory—that it defines easy definition. While the academy has been reluctant to accept feminist scholarship, surely only the most curmudgeonly and sexist among us would question the assertion that a growing body of first-class scholarship in recent years has been guided by feminist persuasions (BuBois et al. 1985; Ferguson 1984; E. Keller 1985). Though examples in our field of research based largely on a feminist perspective are few, there are encouraging signs. Patricia Gumport's (1987) study of the emergence of feminist scholarship nicely illuminates the interacting processes by which this new field has gained legitimacy and become institutionalized in American higher education.

This discussion of inquiry perspectives can be aptly summarized with a quotation attributed to Jose Ortega y Gasset: "Reality happens to be, like a landscape possessed of an infinite number of perspectives, all equally veracious and authentic. The sole false perspective is that which claims to be the only one there is."

Beyond Ideological Hegemony: A Vision of Community

As students of higher education, many of us have been guided by a dominant ideology regarding the generation and dissemination of knowledge in our field. I have grown uneasy about our seemingly uncritical acceptance of that ideology while at the same time, I am skeptical of those who would substitute one orthodoxy for another. Yet because inquiry is at the heart of our community, I would like to conclude by suggesting some basic tenets to guide inquiry in our community of scholars:

- We should view higher education not as a narrow academic discipline but as a field of study in which the needs of our major stakeholders—scholarly peers, administrators and faculty, public policy-makers, and the educated public—provide the touchstone for inquiry. Within the context of a stakeholder-centered model of inquiry, we especially need to develop research agendas that are more responsive to our stakeholders, introduce new approaches to disseminating our research findings, produce generalized as well as specialized knowledge, broaden our inquiry paradigm and ways of knowing, and utilize nontraditional inquiry perspectives.

- Instead of reifying highly specialized knowledge at the expense of generalized knowledge— much less pitting one against the other—we should elevate the importance of generalized knowledge and encourage four general approaches to inquiry consonant with that end: problem-centered, integrative, interpretive, and future-centered.

- Without diminishing the contribution of our traditional research paradigm and quantitative modes of inquiry, we should more forthrightly acknowledge the limitations of the positivist paradigm and associated ways of knowing. In turn, we need to broaden our inquiry paradigm and draw on qualitative approaches from the humanities and social sciences—such as grounded theory, ethnography, symbolic interactionism, and hermeneutics.

- We should acknowledge the limitations of a functionalist perspective and, in turn, draw more heavily upon other inquiry perspectives used in the social sciences and humanities such as neo-Marxist and feminist perspectives.

In closing, I look forward to participation in a community that is more responsive to and valued by its stakeholders—indeed, a community held together by a shared commitment to its various stakeholders—more invitational and catholic about its research aims and agendas, more introspective about the strengths and limitations of its positivistic heritage, more open to the possibilities of alternative perspectives and ways of knowing as well as the diverse voices of scholars in other disciplines and fields. Perhaps most important, I look forward to a community more willing to engage in ongoing critique and conjecture about inquiry in higher education. For many of us, relaxing our grip on our ideological heritage will not come easy. But I have a strong conviction that our growth and maturity as a field—and as individuals—demand it.

Bibliography

Bellah, Robert N., Richard Madsen, William M. Sullivan, Ann Swidler, and Steven M. Tipton. *Habits of the Heart*. Berkeley: University of California Press, 1985.

Berger, Peter L., and Thomas Luckmann. *The Social Construction of Reality*. London: Penguin, 1973.

Bernstein, Richard J. *Beyond Objectivism and Relativism: Science, Hermeneutics, and Praxis*. Philadelphia: University of Pennsylvania Press, 1983.

Bernstein, Richard J., ed. *Habermas and Modernity*. Cambridge, Mass.: MIT Press, 1985.

Burrell, Gibson, and Gareth Morgan. *Sociological Paradigms and Organizational Analysis*. Portsmouth, N. N.: Hienemann Education Books, 1979.

Campbell, Donald T. "Qualitative Knowing in Action Research." In *The Social Contexts of Method*, edited by Michael Brenner, Peter Marsh, and Marylin Brenner, 184-209. London: Croom Helm, 1978.

Clark, Burton R. "The Professor-Disciplinarian." In *Higher Education: A Developing Field of Study*, edited by Fred F. Harcleroad, 282–302. Iowa City, Ia.: American College Testing Program, 1974.

Conrad, Clifton F. "Grounded Theory: An Alternative Approach to Research in Higher Education." *Review of Higher Education 5* (Summer 1982): 239–49.

Cook, Thomas D. "The Potential and Limitations of Secondary Evaluations." In *Educational Evaluation: Analysis and Responsibility*, edited by Michael W. Apple, Michael J. Subkoviak, and Henry S. Lufler, 155–222. Berkeley, Calif.: McCutchan, 1974.

Cronbach, Lee J. "Beyond the Two Disciplines of Scientific Psychology." *American Psychologist 30* (February 1975): 116–27.

Cronbach, Lee J., and Patrick Suppes. *Research for Tomorrow's Schools: Disciplined Inquiry in Education*. New York: Macmillan, 1969.

De Martini, Joseph R., and Les B. Whitbeck. "Knowledge Use as Knowledge Creation." *Knowledge: Creation, Diffusion, Utilization. 7* (June 1986): 383–96.

Denzin, Norman, K. *The Research Act: A Theoretical Introduction to Sociological Methods*. New York: McGraw-Hill, 1978.

DuBois, Ellen C., Gail P. Kelly, Elizabeth L. Kennedy, Carolyn W. Korsmeyer, and Lillian S. Robinson. *Feminist Scholarship: Kindling in the Groves of Academe*. Chicago: University of Illinois Press, 1985.

Ferguson, Kathy E. *The Feminist Case Against Bureaucracy*. Philadelphia: Temple University Press, 1984.

Feyerabend, Paul. *Against Method: Outline of an Anarchistic Theory of Knowledge*. London: Verso, 1978.

Fincher, Cameron. "Policy Analysis and Institutional Research." In *Key Resources on Higher Education Governance, Management, and Leadership*, edited by Marvin W. Peterson and Lisa A. Mets. San Francisco, Calif.: Jossey-Bass, 1987.

Firestone, William A. "Meaning in Method: The Rhetoric of Quantitative and Qualitative Research." *Educational Researcher* 16 (October 1987): 16–21.

Glaser, Barney G. *Theoretical Sensitivity*. Mill Valley, Calif.: Sociology Press, 1878.

Glaser, Barney G., and Anselm L. Strauss. *The Discovery of Grounded Theory*. Chicago: Aldine, 1967.

Glass, Gene U., Barry McGaw, and Mary Lee Smith. *Meta-Analysis in Social Research*. Beverly Hills, Calif.: Sage Publications, 1981.

Gumport, Patricia J. *The Social Construction of Knowledge: Individual and Institutional Commitments to Feminist Scholarship*. Ph.D. diss., Stanford University, 1987.

Habermas, Jürgen. *Knowledge and Human Interests*. Boston: Beacon Press, 1971.

_____. *The Theory of Communicative Action: Reason and Rationalization of Society*. Boston: Beacon Press, 1984.

Hamilton, David. *Curriculum Evaluation*. London: Open Books, 1976.

Heclo, Hugh. *Modern Social Politics in Britain and Sweden*. New Haven, Conn.: Yale University Press, 1974.

Jacob, Evelyn. "Traditions of Qualitative Research: A Review." *Review of Educational Research* 57 (Spring 1987): 1–50.

_____. "Clarifying Qualitative Research: A Focus on Traditions." *Educational Researcher* 17 (January-February 1988): 16-19, 22–24.

Jacoby, Russell. *The Last Intellectuals*. New York: Basic Books, 1987.

Jencks, Christopher, and David Riesman. *The Academic Revolution*. Garden City, N.Y.: Doubleday & Company, 1968.

Keller, Evelyn Fox. *Reflections of Gender and Science*. New Haven, Conn.: Yale University Press, 1985.

Keller, George. "Trees Without Fruit: The Problem with Research about Higher Education." *Change* 17 (January-February 1985): 7–10.

_____. "Free at Last? Breaking the Chains that Bind Education Research." *Review of Higher Education* 10 (Winter 1986): 129–34.

Lakatos, Imre. "Falsification and the Methodology of Scientific Research Programmes." In *Criticism and the Growth of Knowledge*, edited by Imre Lakatos and Alan Musgrave, 91–195. Cambridge, England: Cambridge University Press, 1970.

Leslie, Larry L., and Paul T. Brinkman. *The Economic Value of Higher Education*. New York: American Council of Education and Macmillan, 1988.

Lincoln, Yvonna S. "The Role of Ideology in Naturalistic Research." Paper presented at the annual meeting of the American Educational Research Association, New Orleans, La., April 1988.

_____. "Trouble in the Land: The Paradigm Revolution in the Academic Disciplines." In *Higher Education: Handbook of Research in Higher Education,* edited by John C. Smart, vol. 5. New York: Agathon Press, [1989, inpress].

Lincoln, Yvonna S., and Egon G. Guba. *Naturalistic Inquiry.* Beverly Hills, Calif.: Sage Publications, 1985.

_____. "Research, Evaluation, and Policy Analysis: Heuristics for Disciplined Inquiry." *Policy Studies Review* 5 (February 1986): 545–65.

_____. "Ethics: The Failure of Positivist Science." Paper presented at the annual meeting of the American Educational Research Association, Washington, D.C., April 1987.

_____. "Criteria for Assessing Naturalistic Inquiries as Reports." Paper presented at the annual meeting of the American Educational Research Association, New Orleans, La., April 1988.

London, Howard B. *The Culture of a Community College.* New York: Praeger, 1978.

Merton, Robert K. *Social Theory and Social Structure.* New York: Free Press, 1968.

_____. "The Normative Structure of Science." In *The Sociology of Science: Theoretical and Empirical Investigations,* edited by Robert Merton, 267–78. Chicago: University of Chicago Press, 1973.

Newell, L. Jackson. "The Discourse of a Learned Society." *Review of Higher Education* 10 (Fall 1986): iii–v.

Ollman, Bertell, and Edward Vernoff. *The Left Academy: Marxist Scholarship on American Campuses.* New York: McGraw-Hill, 1982.

Palmer, Parker J. "Community, Conflict, and Ways of Knowing." *Change* 19 (September-October 1987): 20–25.

Pascarella, Earnest T. "Perspectives on Quantitative Analysis for Research in Postsecondary Education." *Review of Higher Education* 5 (Summer 1982): 197–211.

Peterson, Marvin W. "Critical Choices: From Adolescence to Maturity in Higher-Education Research." *Review of Higher Education* 10 (Winter 1986): 142–50.

Phillips, D. C. *Philosophy, Science, and Social Inquiry: Contemporary Methodological Controversies in Social Science and Related Applied Fields of Research.* New York: Pergamon Press, 1987.

Popper, Karl R. *The Logic of Scientific Discovery.* New York: Basic Books, 1959.

_____. Conjectures *and Refutations: The Growth of Scientific Knowledge.* New York: Harper, 1968.

Rabinow, Paul, and William M. Sullivan, eds. *Interpretive Social Science.* Berkeley: University of California Press, 1979.

Rist, Ray C. "Blitzkrieg Ethnography: On the Transformation of a Method into Movement." *Educational Researcher* 9 (February 1980): 8–10.

Ritzer, George. *Sociological Theory.* New York: Alfred Knopf, 1983.

Rogers, Terry Heitz, and Zelda F. Gamson. "Evaluation as a Developmental Process: The Case of Liberal Education." *Review of Higher Education* 5 (Summer 1982); 225–38.

Sanday, Peggy R. "The Ethnographic Paradigm(s)." *Administrative Science Quarterly* 24 (December 1979): 527–38.

Savage, Mary C. "Can Ethnographic Narrative Be a Neighborly Act?" *Anthropology and Education Quarterly* 19 (March 1988): 3–19.

Schwartz, Peter, and James Ogilvy. *The Emergent Paradigm: Changing Patterns of Thought and Belief.* Analytical Report #7, Values and Lifestyles Program. Menlo Park, Calif.: SRI International, 1979.

Silverman, Robert J. "Journal of Manuscripts in Higher Education: A Framework." *Review of Higher Education* 5 (Summer 1982): 181–96.

_____. "How We Know What We Know: A Study of Higher Education Journal Articles." *Review of Higher Education* 11 (Autumn 1987): 3–59.

Slaughter, Sheila S. *The Higher Learning and High Technology: Higher Education Policy and University-Industry Partnerships.* Albany: State University of New York Press [1989, in-press].

Stark, Joan S., and Malcolm A. Lowther. *Strengthening the Ties that Bind: Integrating Undergraduate Liberal and Professional Study.* Report of the Professional Preparation Network. Ann Arbor: University of Michigan, 1988.

Veblen, Thorstein, *The Theory of the Leisure Class: An Economic Study of Institutions.* New York: B. W. Huebsch, 1924.

Weiner, Stephen S. "Shipyards in the Desert." *Review of Higher Education* 10 (Winter 1986): 159–64.

PART II
APPROACHING INQUIRY: METHODS AND TECHNIQUES

Qualitative Research Methods in Higher Education

ROBERT L. CROWSON

Some of you may have wondered what became of our College Ghost. Because we had a ghost, and there are people in this room who saw him.

"The Ghost Who Vanished by Degrees," in *High Spirits*, by Robertson Davies (1982).

Ghost tracking is certainly a bit beyond the pale of current, state-of-the-art research methods. Nevertheless, Robertson Davies's amusing account of the ghost haunting a graduate college, seeking, 'lo those many years, a chance to complete his examination for the Ph.D. ("I shall never be at peace without it"), captures well the spirit of a qualitative approach to understanding in higher education. Institutions of higher learning are filled with ghosts (even a few demons now and then). Traditions left inviolate from the Middle Ages, a system of governance that defies rational explanation, an edifice haunted by departmental rivalry and conflict, a professoriate that slips ethereally into and out of strange institutional roles and relationships, and organizational "sagas" (Clark, 1970) that live on and on in collective memory through a changing society—all of these, ghostlike, are essential elements of college and university environments.

It is only recently that scholars have recognized the productive and the definitional importance of some hard-to-measure (almost ghostly) characteristics of organizations (Peterson, 1985). Among these are the phenomena of loose coupling (Weick, 1976, 1984); organized anarchy (Cohen and March, 1974; March and Olsen, 1976); the organizational culture (Deal and Kennedy, 1982; Jelinek, Smircich, and Hirsh, 1983); organizational socialization (Van Maanen, 1976; Van Maanen and Schein, 1979); institutional myths (Martin et al., 1983; Sproull, 1981); and organizational learning (Hedberg, 1981). In the study of organizations, increased attention is being directed toward the use of research methods that probe into the above subtleties of institutional life, that seek an understanding of an environmental now know to be much more complex than first imagined, and that strive for theory formation rather than theory testing and generalization. In this search for greater understanding, the use of qualitative research methodology is receiving new interest and paradigmatic development.

There are, to be sure, a number of works of a qualitative research genre that can be regarded as "classics" in the literature on higher education. Among these are such outstanding case studies as *Boys in White* (Becker et al., 1961); *The Open Door College* (Clark, 1960); *Personality and Social Change* (Newcomb, 1943); and *The Distinctive College* (Clark, 1970). Additionally, higher education is deep in essays, commentaries, and reminiscences by some of its (and the nation's) outstanding figures. While not research in a traditional sense, such contributions as Kerr's *The Uses of the University* (1964), Barzun's *The American University* (1968), and Bell's *The Reforming of General Education* (1966) all provide the from-experience-toward-theory backdrop that is a central element of the qualitative approach. Finally, some notable institutional histories and biographies have enriched the field, including Morison's *The Founding of Harvard College* (1935), Storr's *Harper's University* (1966), and James's biography of *Charles W. Eliot* (1930).

Nevertheless, the qualitative research tradition is not strong in the study of higher education. While case studies, commentaries, and histories are in evidence, investigations employing participant observation, nonfocused interviewing, disguised observation, and other techniques that are usually associated with a more ethnographic approach to data are in rather short supply (Tierney, 1985). There has been some effort to understand college student cultures through ethnographic-type methods (Bushnell, 1962; Becker, Geer, and Hughes, 1968; Cottle, 1977; Lamont, 1979). There has also been some study of the internal working of higher education institutions in terms of their organizational cultures (Riesman and Jencks, 1962; London, 1978; Clark, 1972); their administrative dynamics (Baldridge, 1971; Miller, 1978; Hendricks, 1975; Tierney, 1983); and their efforts at curriculum reform (Grant and Riesman, 1978). The literature is not deep, however, and neither a widely shared methodology of qualitative research in higher education nor a clear delineation of the key topics and questions calling for study has yet surfaced—despite the urgency of such observations as Marvin Peterson's (1985) plea that we must "try to understand what holds together these fascinating institutions as organizations.'

Purpose of the Review

It is the purpose of this review to examine the literature appropriate to an improved appreciation of the role of qualitative research methods in the study of higher education. Our focus will primarily be upon the methodological traditions offered by anthropology and qualitative sociology, leaving for another reviewer the growing methodological interest in the application of historical inquiry to organizational analysis (Mattingly, 1983). The central task of our review is to highlight the key elements of and issues in qualitative research methodologies, as these methods may apply to the special institutional circumstances and conditions of work in postsecondary education in the United States. Thus, the review treats three major topics: (1) guiding principles of qualitative research methodology; (2) methodological issues in the application of qualitative research to higher education; and (3) considerations in the implementation of qualitative research in higher education.

A first key question, of course, is the definitional: Just what is qualitative research methodology? As interest in the topics has spread, it has received many labels and generated some infighting as to the most appropriate definition (Van Maanen, Dobbs, and Faulkner, 1982). To some researchers, the preferred descriptive term is *ethnography*, or with a more restrained meaning, *ethnomethodology*. Ethnography has been historically associated with anthropological method[1]; and although it has strict constructionists (e.g., Wolcott, 1984) and those who interpret loosely (e.g., Le Compte and Goetz, 1982), an emphasis upon the study of culture (usually through a lengthy period of participant observation) is the methodological focus (Spradley, 1980; Sanday, 1979). *Ethnomethodology* is a term coined by Garfinkel (1967) to represent a more sociology-based approach to understanding (e.g., using symbolic interaction theory) (Mehan and Wood, 1975; Psathas, 1979). Ethnomethodologists are less holistic than traditional ethnographers,[2] focusing intently on the meanings (and language) that individuals use to make sense of (to impute reality to) their own worlds (Geertz, 1973; Schwartz and Jacobs, 1979).

A descriptor of recent vintage is *naturalistic inquiry* (Guba, 1978; Lincoln and Guba, 1985). It is important to note that naturalistic inquiry starts its argument at the epistemological (presenting itself as an alternative philosophic paradigm), in contrast with the conventional approach to scientific inquiry (logical positivism). The basic assumptions of naturalistic inquiry are fundamentally at odds with positivism and are *not* reconcilable (Lincoln and Guba, 1985, p. 33) with the positivistic tradition. For example, while positivism assumes a discoverable reality in nature which (once known) can be predicted and controlled, the naturalist posits only "multiple constructed realities," which may not be controlled and, at best, can be understood. While positivism separates the researcher and the object of inquiry, naturalism argues that knower and known are inseparable. Positivism assumes that, through science, inquiry can proceed toward generalizable truth statements and toward a knowledge of cause-effect linkages. Alternatively, naturalism argues that working hypotheses (rather than lawlike generalizations) and "mutual simultaneous shaping" (rather than causation) are at the heart of the methodology. Using these differing philosophic assumptions as guides, the scholar would do research in the style of the naturalist paradigm—including inductive data analysis, purpose sampling, the development of grounded theory, and the use of an emergent research design (Lincoln and Guba, 1985, pp. 36–43).

Thus, within the rubric of something we'll call the *qualitative research method,* there is room for wide interpretation. Van Maanen et al. (1982) warn that a clear and concise definition of qualitative research at this time is most difficult. From a specific press toward cultural understanding (ethnography) to the larger suggestion of an alternative philosophic paradigm (e.g., naturalistic), the field encompasses a cornucopia of foci, assumptions, and techniques. Variously labeled *field research, case study research, descriptive research,* and, of course, *ethnography* and *qualitative research,* neither the method nor its descriptors are clear. At best, it can be said that to work "in the style " of the qualitative research is to consistently employ such practices of data collection as participant observation, the discovery and use of unobtrusive measures, informal interviewing, life history construction, content analysis, and videotaping—and to seek from one's data an *understanding* of the phenomena observed rather than some generalizable knowledge or explanation, prediction, and control.

One definitional point that must be heavily emphasized, however, is that it would be wrong to conceive of research methodology as a single continuum—with conventional quantitative inquiry at one end and the qualitative approach to research (naturalism) at the other end. Smith and Heshusius (1986) have observed that despite their fundamentally different epistemological traditions, quantitative and qualitative approaches have tended of late to be treated as potentially compatible systems of investigation. Basic philosophic differences are ignored in the interest of concentrating upon *procedures* from both traditions that can be cooperatively employed to serve a line of research. The differences are "deepistemologized," and the principal concern then becomes how to perform qualitative inquiry (Smith and Heshusius, 1986, p. 7).

Although this review is also focused upon the procedural, with little attention given to the underlying philosophical controversies, it is not our claim that a thorough understanding of qualitative inquiry can be left at the how-to-do-it stage. There *are* fundamental differences between the quantitative (positivist) and qualitative (phenomenological) research traditions. Qualitative research is not just another approach to "scientific" understanding in the conventional sense (Smith and Heshusius, 1986; Lincoln and Guba, 1985). Some of these fundamental differences become immediately apparent, below, as the review opens with a discussion of the guiding principles that surround qualitative research methodology.

Principles of Qualitative Research

It is above all a central goal of *understanding* that forms one of the method's important procedural principles. Its other key points of departure are a norm of researcher proximity, an emphasis upon analytic induction, and an appreciation of the value-bound context of most inquiry. We will discuss each of these principles in some detail, proceeding from this discussion to the consideration of key research issues in the special context of higher education.

The Search for Understanding

Mehan and Wood (1975) use an example from a study of the Azande of Africa (Evans-Pritchard, 1937) to illustrate the central problem of understanding. When faced with important decisions in their lives, the Azande consult and oracle. This consultation consists of gathering the bark from a certain type of tree, preparing the bark in a special ceremony, and feeding it to a chicken. The decision to be made is posed in simple yes-or-no terms, and the death of the chicken signals an affirmative or negative action. For extremely important decisions, however, the Azande take the second step of feeding the substance to another chicken and reversing the meaning of the chicken's death. If the first chicken's survival indicated that the oracle had said yes, then the second chicken's death would provide the same message.

Mehan and Wood remark that our Western scientific understanding tells us that the tree bark contains a poisonous quality that kills some chickens. Our understanding stops there, however. What do the Azande do when the oracle contradicts itself? What happens to their faith in the process when the answer given by the oracle is contradicted by later events? Our Western rationalism forces us to questions such as these in the face of many mysteries and contradictions left blatantly unanswered. To the Azande, however, there are no contradictions. The Azande are not even aware of the poisonous properties of the tree. Faith in the power of the oracle is explanation enough (pp. 8-9).

To *understand* the Azande is a tall order for us. We must somehow learn to see the world in their terms, from their perspective. The contradictions that perplex us aren't theirs. To know something in their culture is a far cry from "knowing something" in ours. Of course, if one were to turn the direction of the research around, the Azande might be equally perplexed by the tendencies of our decision makers to acquire, but then ignore, stacks of number-filled computer printouts; to meet endlessly with colleagues without ever reaching "yes" or "no" conclusions; and to make a decision, only to change it immediately when "politics" intervene.

The development of understanding as a central research objective has been attributed most prominently to Max Weber (using the German term *Verstehen*).[3] The researcher who is concerned with understanding seeks to observe and interpret human behavior from the observed actor's own frame of reference—developing an appreciation of the world as others experience it, and becoming acquainted with the subjective states of mind of other people (Schwartz and Jacobs, 1979, pp. 17–20). The search for understanding is often considered to be in direct contrast with the central goal of conventional or positivist inquiry, which purportedly seeks an objectively determined fact or causation in the study of social phenomena. The philosophic cornerstone of qualitative methodology is its effort to describe and render understandable the world of subjective experience rather than to discover its "truths" or generalizable cause-effect relationships.

An interesting illustration of this perspective is Seymour Sarason's (1982) suggestion that we indulge in a bit of fantasy—examining our educational institutions as if we were beings from outer space poised on invisible platforms above these institutions and trying to figure out "what's going on" (pp. 96–98). As observers, we might possibly start out with questions about obvious regularities—the perplexing patterns of human behavior that are noticeable down below. While Sarason's own outer-spacers were intrigued by elementary schools, the discernible regularities of colleges and universities are no less a puzzle. Posed above an urban university such as the one served by this author, our nonearthly being may ask why so many young-looking adults are in evidence during daylight hours while persons in their apparent middle years predominate in the evenings. Why do large groups of people congregate periodically in rooms with rows of seating facing one individual who talks a great deal while all others remain silent and write? Why do some of these groups appear to meet as often as five times in seven days, while others meet for longer periods as few as three times or even only once in seven days? Why does the person speaking to the large group spend so much of the rest of his time sitting silently alone in a small room with a desk, except when sitting around a table at irregular intervals with other speakers, all often talking at once? Why do extremely large groups of persons congregate once or twice a week in the evening without a speaker and show such enthusiasm watching the movement of a ball on a floor below them?

In short, without great sophistication or methodological elaboration, the one guiding theme of qualitative research is to assume a mantle of almost childlike curiosity, trying to understand—or even in the simple words of Baldridge (1971), trying to "find out how a situation ticks" (p. 31). This sense of curiosity (playing the role of the cultural ingenue) in the search for understanding is even conveyed clearly in the language that researchers have used to describe the purpose(s) of their work. From existing research of the qualitative genre in higher education, for example, some common descriptors have been (1) "acquiring a 'feeling' for the dynamics of the situation" (Baldridge, 1971, p. 31); (2) "discovering phenomena whose existence we were unaware of at the beginning of the research" (Becker et al., 1961, p. 18); plus (3) "discovering and investigating the unexpected" (London, 1978, p. 151). It would appear, again, that ghost tracking is not just an amusing bit of Robertson Davies; it is also a fundamental principle of the qualitative research method.

The Norm of Researcher Proximity

If understanding (in Weber's sense of *Verstehen*) is the prime goal, a norm of researcher proximity is the central procedural principle in most qualitative research. The person who is trying to understand should be there, at hand, as events occur and as behavior is exhibited. It is the researcher who is the main instrument of investigation (Burgess, 1984). Furthermore, it is the researcher as not only observer but additionally as *participant* in the events and behaviors under study that provides the foundation for *Verstehen*.

Becker and Geer (1960) explain the importance of participant observation, rather than mere observation, as follows:

> In general, the participant observer gathers data by participating in the daily life of the group or organization that he studies. He watches the people he is studying to see what situations they ordinarily meet and how they behave in them. He talks with the other participant and discovers their interpretations of the events he has observed. (p. 269)

To Becker and others (e.g., Wilson, 1977; Cusick, 1983; Dorr-Bremme, 1985), the essential value in the dual role of both observer and participant comes from an actual sharing in the events under study. By participating, and not just observing, the researcher does not simply witness and describe but, by participating, comes to the fuller understanding that belongs uniquely to the members of that culture. The result, ideally, will be description and interpretation of phenomena that move from an outsider account toward an assessment of events that approaches *Verstehen*—for a "true understanding of the reality can be had only if one will join in the creation." (Cusick, 1983, p. 132).

There are methodological problems aplenty in this researcher role, of course, and we will discuss some of these later in this chapter. Additionally, qualitative methods do not demand that participant observation be employed as the only means of gathering data. Formal and informal interviewing, nonparticipant observation, documentary analysis, even questionnaires and paper-pencil examinations can be employed by qualitative researchers to enhance understanding. Indeed, a cornerstone of the method is the notion that wherever possible, the researcher should strive for a "thick description" of phenomena (Geertz, 1973). A thick description is a many-sided glimpse of events (using a variety of data sources), enabling the reader of a research report to form his or her own understanding of the findings (Lincoln and Guba, 1985).

Nevertheless, participant observation is a mainstay of the method. Researcher proximity is considered a necessary if not sufficient condition of meaningful inquiry. Two correlate notions that normally accompany the proximity norm, furthermore, are immersion and the study of "natural settings." Beyond proximity, the qualitative researcher must seek to examine behavior as it occurs naturally (Wilson, 1977). Individuals are influenced by their settings and are furthermore wrapped in these settings within intricate "webs of significance" (Geertz, 1973, p. 5). A strand or two removed from the web, or examined closely without a simultaneous appreciation of the structure of the entire web, could give a false impression of the observed culture. Additionally, beyond proximity, the scholar must be sufficiently immersed in the research setting to appreciate wide varieties of meaningful behavior (Naroll and Cohen, 1970; Pelto and Pelto, 1978). Face-to-face contact and verbal behavior are to be observed, to be sure, but gestures, positions, facial expressions, visual signals, and the like are also vital routes toward understanding for the fieldwork investigator, all contributing to the total message of the research setting (Dorr-Bremme, 1985).

Indeed, immersion and naturalism have been such important constructs in qualitative inquiry that for many years a "school of hard knocks approach" was considered the proper pedagogical methods in the training of ethnographers (Cohen and Naroll, 1970). It was felt that a researcher would learn best if simply thrown into a culture, for technique rests ultimately on the idiosyncratic person and personality of the ethnographer. Cohen and Naroll (1970) write:

> The field worker was simply told to bring back as much material as possible documenting the way of life of the people he had lived among. To plan more rigorously would probably bias observation, it was thought; or even worse, it would prevent the collection of valuable—and often disappearing—data. (pp. 7–8)

The Emphasis upon Analytic Induction

Not only is the qualitative researcher expected to "be there," observing and bringing back whatever data seem appropriate to understanding; the method asks additionally that the inquiry seek to build understanding inductively, from the ground up (Lincoln and Guba, 1985). The point is captured best by Glaser and Strauss (1967) in the title of their influential book *The Discovery of Grounded Theory*. In place of the standard deductive activities of the scientific method, involving the formulation of hypotheses and the specification of data categories *a priori* before entering the field (Wilson, 1977), the qualitative researcher seeks to build, from the observed data, a bit of inductive knowledge. This knowledge is often in the form of tentative, working hypotheses (Lincoln & Guba, 1985, p. 38). The working hypotheses are "grounded" in the individual case and are both time- and context-bound and thus are not to be confused with data-based generalizations.

The argument in support of such an inductive emphasis is that the investigator of natural phenomena is more than likely to be abysmally ignorant of the field setting. The more precise the prior hypothesis and the more carefully structured the research design, the better the likelihood of missing meaningful behaviors and important occurrences as they fortuitously appear (Levine, 1970). The exigencies and characteristics of the research setting itself (Cohen and Naroll, 1970), and even the "feel" of the research setting (Baldridge, 1971), should direct the researcher, rather than a prior set of ideas or hypotheses. The researcher must actually enter the field and develop a sense (a feel) for what is meaningful, trusting to intuition as thoroughly as to reason. Even, strangely, in those settings that the scholar would be presumed to know well (e.g., university departments, families, and grocery stores), ignorance is abundant. To live in a setting is a far cry from being asked to study it (Psathas, 1973).

Methodological controversy has arisen as to what role any prior theorizing at all should play in qualitative research. From a purist's perspective, Psathas (1973) writes, "No presuppositions, whether they come from scientific theories or commonsense knowledge of social structures, are to influence the observer or cloud his vision" (p. 7). Researchers should set aside prior assumptions and what they think they already know about the setting, adopting the stance of completely disinterested observers (Psathas, 1973). Campbell (1975) labels such expectations naive. No culture can be observed in its entirety, and what one does "see" will surely be colored by investigator subjectivity. In recent years, fieldworkers have become more comfortable with a bit of prior focusing and sharpening in qualitative inquiry, recognizing that decisions on what to include as data and how to describe what has been observed are inevitable (Pelto and Pelto, 1978). While maintaining their flexibility and eclecticism, these fieldworkers of a more realist persuasion are willing to shape the specific themes, issue, and questions of their inquiry (Dorr-Bremme, 1985). The recognition, of course, is that the investigator's theoretical point of view does color a study and will shape the inductive vision of reality that appears in the researcher's findings. This brings us to the fourth major principle of qualitative research.

An Appreciation of the Value-Bound Context of Inquiry

"The ethos of social science," writes Gunnar Myrdal (1969), "is the search for 'objective' truth" (p. 3). In practice, continues Myrdal, students of society are highly unlikely to be able to liberate themselves very far from the powerful hold of (1) the normative and theoretical heritage (the reigning paradigms) of their field of inquiry; (2) the influence of their own cultural milieu; and (3) the influences stemming from their own personalities. To these, Lincoln and Guba (1985) would add the problematic influence of values that reside within the research setting itself (p. 38). In short, all research, whether qualitative or quantitative, is heavily value-bound.

Persons engaged in qualitative research, particularly ethnographers, have long been aware of the coloration that ideas and beliefs place upon any interpretation of the world as it "really is." Influenced heavily by phenomenological theory (e.g., Husserl, 1952; Schutz, 1967), those who work within the ethnographic tradition have been careful not only to recognize but to try to compensate for the role that subjectivity plays in the interpretation of observed behavior (Jehenson, 1973p; Rist, 1979). Ethnographic methods emphasize skills in suspending observer preconceptions (the term *bracketing* is used to describe this effort), and ethnographers seek instead to become sufficiently immersed in the culture under study to be able to take on and understand events from an insider's perspective (Wilson, 1977; Rist, 1979).

Recognizing that their efforts to suspend their own values may be far less than complete, phenomenology-minded researchers stress that one further necessary check is for observers to state their own biases clearly, hopefully to mitigate thereby some unintendedly subjective effects (Fetterman, 1984b; Dorr-Bremme, 1985). Myrdal (1969) cautions that such statements of value premises in social science research should be (1) explicit, and not concealed in implied assumptions (2) purposefully and volitionally selected; and (3) part of a consistent and thus not mutually incompatible system of values (pp. 63–64).[4]

Interestingly, one of the principal methodological debates within the qualitative research tradition, one tied closely to the problems raised by value-boundedness, is the contrast between emic and etic approaches to ethnography. The emicist seeks to discover and describe the pattern of a culture in terms of the meanings and idea systems that natives employ *in that culture*. The eticist looks for systems, patterns, and meanings in observed behavior from the standpoint of constructs defined *by the researcher*. From the emic perspective, only statements about the single culture under study can be reported; from the etic viewpoint, cross-cultural comparisons, using the same re-searcher-derived concepts, are possible (Pelto and Pelto, 1978, pp. 54–66). The emic-etic debate illustrates the continuing struggle between the recognition of subjectivity (both observer and observed) and the scientific aspiration nevertheless toward objective knowledge, or at least a bit of theory building that permits some proportions about human behavior. Campbell (1970) argues that this struggle between a recognition of subjectivity and a search for objectivity can at best produce a compromise, a middle ground of "hypothetical realism"—where constructs built from observation can be only "fallibly known, through a process of hypothetical models only indirectly confirmed" (p. 69).

In brief summary, the qualitative approach to inquiry in higher education rests upon four key procedural principles. *First*, the central research objective is to understand rather than to explain, predict, or control. Procedurally, a search for understanding asks the researcher to seek to appreciate each setting through the perspectives of its natives, and to satisfy an anthropologistlike curiosity about the behaviors that have been observed ("What's going on here?"). The *second* procedural principal suggests that understanding *(Verstehen)* emerges most readily if the researcher is himself or herself the prime instrument of data collection. A norm of researcher proximity surrounds the method. Being there, on hand, as behavior occurs and/or is reported (e.g., through interviewing) assists critically in meeting the *third* procedural principle: an emphasis upon analytic induction. The method asks its adherents to build interpretive understanding from the ground up rather than, in a hypothesis-testing sense, from the top down. Whether inductive or deductive, the qualitative approach recognizes *fourth* that the search for understanding is heavily value-laden. The setting, the researcher, the larger culture, and even the intellectual assumptions one brings to the process of *Verstehen*—all color the inquiry.

Methodological Issues in Qualitative Research in Education

All four of the guiding procedural principles of qualitative research raise methodological questions of special importance for inquiry in higher education. Among these are issues of (1) familiarity; (2) selection; and (3) trustworthiness. Implicit in the emic-etic debate is the question of whether a person closely familiar with a culture under study (an insider) or a person less familiar but perhaps more curious (an outsider) would be the better observer of natural phenomena. Furthermore, in a method emphasizing thick description and holistic understanding, centrally important methodological decisions surround questions of what to observe, where to observe, and what to focus upon in observation (sampling and selection issues). And in a method seeking neither objective and generalizable truth nor merely subjective storytelling (but some middle ground of theory development), problems of reliability and validity (trustworthiness) must be treated carefully. We will develop each of these issues in terms of their special saliency for the qualitative study of colleges and universities.

The Issue of Familiarity

In this review of ethnographic research in higher education, Tierney (1985) finds it exceedingly strange that higher education has not been thoroughly subjected to qualitative-style inquiry. The paradox is that colleges and universities display many of the characteristics considered particularly appropriate for anthropological fieldwork. Studies of well-defined subcultures (e.g., towns, tribal villages, and communities) have been favored by ethnographers because they tend to have delimitable boundaries and populations, are relatively complete social systems, and are small enough to be covered (in transportation terms) economically by a single researcher (Pelto and Pelto, 1978, pp. 177–178). Residential colleges and universities similarly are self-contained, with definable boundaries and with their activities carried out in close member proximity. Furthermore, the researcher in higher education would have the benefit of prior intimate knowledge of the language and the technology of the institution under study. Thus, he or she would also be able to enjoy the luxury of minimal acclimatization or socialization time, plus the possible benefit of full immersion "at home," where one earns a living as well as conducts inquiry (Messerschmidt, 1981; Tierney, 1985).

One of the strongest arguments for "insider research" (Aguilar, 1981) in higher education is the benefit that cultural familiarity accords any researcher who is faced with trying to understand a not-easily-illuminated and frequently arcane slice of daily life. In his ethnographic study of a

Himalayan village, Berreman (1962) observed, "Every ethnographer, when he reaches the field, is faced immediately with accounting for himself before the people he proposes to learn to know. Only when this has been accomplished can he proceed to his avowed task of seeking to understand and interpret the way of life of those people" (p. 269). It was only with time, patience, and careful "impression management" that Berreman was able to unearth the purposefully concealed dark secrets of his Himalayan subjects sufficiently to provide a meaningful ethnography.

Institutions of higher education are replete with their own innumerable dark secrets (even ghosts). Marsland (1985) cautions that the most informative windows upon organizational culture in higher education are often its special sagas (Clark, 1972); heroes; symbols, including metaphors (Cohen and March, 1974); and organizational rituals (providing a continuity with the past). These (usually hidden or at least masked) insights into daily life are not immediately apparent to the casual observer, nor are they likely to be shared freely with an unsocialized outsider. The university as a culture is complex, awash in contradictions (e.g., trade-offs between community and scholarship), and even flawed in places (Weick, 1984). Furthermore, Masland (1985) claims that in institutions where the culture is relatively "weak," the cultural themes will not stand out clearly and may be replete with hard-to-interpret anomalies.

An informed and culturally acceptable insider may also be better placed than an outsider to interpret observed behaviors within their appropriate institutional context. Cultures are multilayered and nested one within another (Dorr-Bremme, 1985). They involve for every person a variety of cultural attributions and a varied, lifelong chain of prior cultural experiences (Becker and Geer, 1960; Van Maanen, 1984). Indeed, in his study of differences between the graduate business schools of Harvard and MIT, Van Maanen (1984) concludes the prior socialization, the cultural impact of the business school, and the job placement and success of business school graduates all combine into a larger "culture of orientation" for individuals that cannot be easily or cleanly separated into one formative institutionalized influence versus another. Even to an insider, just what is the relevant social context of the institution under study is not readily ascertainable.

A strong argument for insider research, or at least a long period of immersion for the outsider, is fashioned additionally by Rosalie Wax (1971). Wax argues that understanding, while a desired outcome of research, is in more ways a necessary *precondition* of useful fieldwork. She writes, "A researcher cannot simply learn a few basic 'rules of fieldwork,' drop himself among an alien people like a man from Mars, and then proceed to acquire understanding. As any researcher or explorer he will fare better if he anticipates what he will confront and prepares himself accordingly" (p. 15). Furthermore, she continues:

> Perhaps the most egregious error that a fieldworker can commit is to assume that he can win the immediate regard of his hosts by telling them that he wants to "become one of them" or by implying, by word or act, that the fact that they tolerate his presence means that he *is* one of them. Indeed, this is the mistake that all experienced fieldworkers warn against. (p. 47)

While never really "one of them," the successful fieldworker must nevertheless acquire sufficient member knowledge to be able to understand shared frames of reference and to appreciate what is often covert and implicit in the social world under study. Furthermore, it helps significantly if the fieldworker is able easily to blend into the local context, thereby being less likely to alter social situations by his or her presence (Aguilar, 1981). In *Making the Grade* (1968), Howard Becker and his colleagues asked the question, "What is it like to be a college student?" They wanted to answer this question in the *students'* terms, learning about life in college through the students' eyes, and discovering in the process that this is a tough methodological job (Becker et al., 1968, p. 2).

Critics of insider research argue, however, that it is exactly the perspective of a man from Mars that *should* be emphasized in qualitative research (Stephenson and Greer, 1981). Researchers who are too much at home within a culture are apt to find little to arouse their curiosity—failing to recognize interesting, strange, or unusual patterns simply because they are too thoroughly acculturated, too familiar with the setting. Furthermore, insiders may experience member-type pressures with the setting. Furthermore, insiders may experience member-type pressures and expectations. They may be expected by those whom they are interviewing and observing to take a stand on current issues (e.g., organizational turf battles and leader personality conflicts). They may also experience pressure to produce an advocacy-oriented report, and they may feel reluctant to ask "certain questions" known to be politically charged or personally threatening. Insiders may also not receive the openness and relaxed honesty that respondents may accord an "ignorant" outsider; and finally, they may not enjoy the allowances for mistakes (e.g., dropping in uninvited on sensitive meetings that members often permit strangers (Aguilar, 1981; Stephenson and Greer, 1981). Stephenson and Greer (1981) conclude that fieldworkers studying the familiar must work exceptionally hard to place "stranger value" upon all that is familiar, recording as much detail as possible regardless of their sense of its relevance and adopting an "artificial naiveté" throughout the study (p. 24).

Becoming a stranger is of course exceptionally difficult for those persons (usually institutionally affiliated academics themselves) who would undertake fieldwork in higher education. The setting is familiar; moreover, the researcher is already aware of respective roles within the institution (e.g., administrator, teacher, student, and staff member) and is aware of the many norms and taboos that accompany role relationships. In a methodological appendix to his ethnographic study of a community college, for example, London (1978) discussed his difficulties in observing college classes. The instructors, used to autonomy, tended to feel evaluated and sought frequently to draw the fieldworker into class discussions as a colleague and coteacher. Fears of evaluation were also evident in postclass efforts by teachers to elicit some feedback: "What have you found out?" or "How's the study going?" (p. 162). On their part, the community college students frequently tried to turn the researcher into an informant or an adviser, sensing that the observer had developed an "in" into that mysterious world of college administration and faculty affairs that is effectively denied them within traditionally fashioned institutional relationships (London, 1978, pp. 156–164).

Realistically, the researcher, no matter how hard he or she tries, can probably never assume the mantle of a complete stranger nor be fully naive. Indeed, in his study of college reward structures, Thomas Cottle (1977) openly recognized the formative forces of his own college days in the 1950s and the guidance received from his own parents as influences upon his contemporary observation of college life. Thus, in the practice of inquiry, some advanced warning, a bit of introspection, a knowledgeable sensitivity about the higher education setting is probably called for in understanding the responses likely among one's research subjects (e.g., faculty, students, and staff). As Wilson (1977, p. 248) points out, the subjects' cautiousness regarding the intent of the investigation, their desire to exhibit appropriate behavior, their interest in being evaluated positively, and their hope for a special personal relationship with the researcher—all these are forces that shape behavior under many research designs. Nevertheless these forces would bear special consideration in higher education—with its strange combinations of cultivation alongside suspicion of intellect, egalitarianism and elitism, avant-gardism in juxtaposition with conservatism, and freedom amidst conformity (Kerr, 1964).

The Issue of Selection

Marsland (1985) suggests that to understand organizational culture in higher education, the researcher should attend most particularly to the details of daily life. But just what are these details? In answer, Masland offers four key "windows" upon an organizational culture. These are institutional sagas or stories, organizational heroes and the examples they set, organizational symbols and/or metaphors, and organizational rituals (Masland, 1985, pp. 160–163). To other scholars, however, the details of daily life might be better observed, and more instructive, if close attention is paid to (1) the routine interactions (both verbal and nonverbal) of organizational participants

(Dorr-Bremme, 1985); (2) the uses that people make of their time in organizations (Mintzberg, 1973); (3) the physical traces, episodic records, and other unobtrusive measures that pervade organizations (Webb et al., 1966); and even (4) the occasional pathologies of organizational existence (e.g., lying, stealing, or cheating) (Smircich, 1983, p. 353). In an interesting and unusual insight, for example, Abraham Maslow (1965) suggests that the level of "grumbling" in an organization is a key indicator of its state of being.

Although the fundamental goal of the qualitative-minded researcher is traditionally a holistic portrayal of culture, recognizing that cultures are in fact integrated wholes, it is obvious that inquiry into *all* of the many details of daily life is well past the grasp of the observer. Limits must be placed upon the scope of research, a sampling of organizational behavior must occur, and a selecting and focusing of attention must take place. In a pure sense, the qualitative researcher would wish to avoid the biases that accompany a predetermined structuring of his or her observations; nevertheless, reality demands some sharpening and focusing (Cohen and Naroll, 1970). All of the people and all of the events in a social situation cannot be studied; sampling and selection are essential.

Becker et al. illustrate the problem in their now classic study, *Boys in White* (1961). Their central research interest was to discover what medical school did to medical students. While recognizing that a medical school is a social system (with relationships between participants), the researchers decided not to focus equally upon all participants, electing instead to make the student their central concern and to study other aspects of the organization (e.g., the faculty) only as these aspects affected students. Even here, not all of the students could possibly be studied. Should one group of students be observed through the four years of medical school? Should different groups be studied for shorter periods of time? Should all types of students be studied, or should high and low deviants be left alone? The decision was to observe groups of students in a variety of situations (i.e., in differing departments and stages of training), as well as at leisure, including their casual conversations, mealtimes, and get-togethers at fraternity houses. The researchers furthermore discovered that an encyclopedic recording of every event or every remark they observed was not a research possibility. They conceded:

> We did leave things out. What was included or left out of our field notes depended very much on the problems we were pursuing at the time. We carried on a running analysis of the materials we gathered and, as we became aware of certain problems, made a greater effort to include materials which bore on those problems and tended to prove or disprove provisional hypotheses we were entertaining. (Becker et al., 1961, p. 27)

Not only, then, did Becker and his colleagues have to make some critical decisions "up front" about whom to study and under what conditions, but throughout the investigation, they found themselves (while on the run as observers) refocusing, revising, selecting this, and neglecting that.

Burgess (1984) notes that its focus upon natural settings poses special problems of sampling and selection for the qualitative method. Events are complex and multidimensional; much of importance can easily escape the observant eye and ear. People seldom hold still for the ethnographer; conversations are not always recordable; and human behavior is irrepressibly immune to the logic and consistency that scholars would much prefer to impute to it.

Three key selection decisions must be made by the qualitative researcher. These are where to conduct field research (what site), whom to observe (or interview, etc.) at the field site, and what behaviors to observe. For the first of these (the research site), Spradley (1980) suggests four guidelines.

1. *Simplicity.* If at all possible, the observed situations should be simple rather than complex, for example, few people rather than many, all at once; a setting with some observable boundaries rather than one in constant flux; situations with a beginning and end, or at least some semblance of time parameters, rather than intermittent and discontinuous.

2. *Accessibility.* Qualitative research is intrusive and intensely personal. Private lives are under a microscope, organizational secrets are laid bare. While representativeness (facilitating generalizability) is a key sampling criterion in traditional research, ease of access (seldom easy) is a legitimate criterion for the ethnographer. The site to be studied is one that lets you in.

3. *Unobtrusiveness.* To study a situation "naturally," the researcher should try to blend in. In general, settings in which the observer dresses wrong, is too old or too young, speaks differently, or otherwise appears to be out of place will yield inadequate results. As Philip Cusick (1983) puts it, "The major consideration is what to do with one's own self. One has a physical presence. How will he (or she) fit it into the setting he (or she) wants to study? Often the possibility of participation in some form in the activities of the research site (with its danger of biasing the data) is to be preferred to the role of being there with nothing to do and in the process standing out like a sore thumb (p. 136).

4. *Permissibleness.* Although access is a first step, a fruitful setting should also allow the researcher free or least-restricted entry into all of its activities. Permissibleness often depends upon the real or perceived threat that the observer presents to participants—no small problem for the student of organizations, with their tradition of managers, workers, clients, overseers (e.g., trustees), suppliers, and political supporters or detractors, who are often at odds with one another.

The second key selection decision is whom to observe, and three approaches to a sampling of research subjects or informants are suggested by Burgess (1984).

1. *Theoretically directed sampling.* Originally offered by Glaser and Strauss (1967), the selection of subjects for observation can grow directly out of a developing conceptual framework. In sampling, a theoretically relevant set of events or subjects is located; and as the study proceeds, further sampling branches off or evolves into the development of a more completely grounded theory. In other words, the selection of subjects, like the evolution of the theory, proceeds from an initially vague to an increasingly well-honed state of understanding.

2. *Judgment and opportunistic sampling.* In judgment and opportunistic sampling, the focus is less upon the fit between a developing theory and a set of informants and more upon an adaptation of data collection to the special circumstances and vagaries of each research site. One makes use of informants wherever one can find them, taking advantage of opportunities that arise; and one establishes a "feel" for the research site over time, using judgment to find occasions and settings where valuable data are at hand. In his study of student culture in a community college, for example, London (1978) learned through experience which settings to avoid (e.g., being seen with certain teachers) and where rich data on student behavior were most likely to be found (e.g., the game room, the lounges, and the hallways).

3. *Snowball sampling.* Typically, in ethnographic-style research, the investigator finds that some individuals are immediately approachable, open, and accepting, while others display an obvious reluctance to be the subjects of inquiry. By finding some people (often just a few initially) with whom to associate regularly, the researcher establishes an entree, learns the ropes, and gains an opportunity to be put in touch with friends and acquaintances. Eventually, a chain of informants has been selected.

Finally, third, a key selection decision involves the determination of what behaviors or events to observe. As discussed earlier, it makes little sense to try to study "the details of daily life" without giving considerable thought to what is worth investigator attention and what is not. Qualitative inquiry can produce a rich array of data from interviews, observations, unobtrusive measures, written records, nonverbal cues, even questionnaires and other paper-and-pencil instruments. Deciding what to observe can be approached in much the same manner as the selection of a field site and the selection of subjects—in that sampling can be guided by an emerging theory—but it is also likely to build, change, and adapt as the study proceeds. Each element sampled is influenced by preceding elements, with perhaps a bit of targeting of what is most salient as the study proceeds (Lincoln and Guba, 1985).

As with the issue of familiarity, however, decisions regarding the selection of where, whom, and what to study are replete with special problems in the qualitative study of higher education. As Crane shows, in *Invisible Colleges* (1972), even the boundaries of institutions of higher learning are poorly defined in spatial terms. Many persons in the professorial ranks consider their closest colleagues—and, in fact, their institutional brethren—to be other scholars within their own disciplines across the nation, and indeed the world, rather than persons in other disciplines inhabiting next-door offices at Riveredge U., with whom they seldom interact and do not share a common vocabulary.

The extremely loosely coupled nature of higher learning, furthermore, poses inordinate problems to those who would study the daily life of an institution. Faculty and staff members come and go; much of their work is conducted in isolation and is hidden from one another. Students are of all types and proclivities and, with their wide diversity, are poorly described by such terms as the *student body*. Disciplinary distinctions, role differentiation, independence of activity and time use, disorder, and a diffusion of power and responsibility abound (Perkins, 1973). One common methodological suggestion, to illustrate the problem, is to focus upon "critical incidents" in the life of an organization (Miles and Huberman, 1984). Yet the qualitative-minded researcher in higher education would be poorly advised to focus upon the occasional student demonstration or heated debate in the faculty senate as an example of a critical incident, rather than decisions made in quiet secrecy within faculty meetings and administrative offices deep within the bowels of the institution.

The Issue of Trustworthiness

An ongoing criticism of research produced through qualitative methods is that it seldom has any truth value. With its tendency to report upon isolated, one-at-a-time case studies; to provide long, drawn out, but usually a theoretical, stories of observed phenomena; and to ignore many of the canons of representative sampling, plus reliability and validity—the method offers little opportunity for the development of confidence in its reportage and a sense of truth or generalizability in its conclusions (Filstead, 1970; Cook and Reichardt, 1979; LeCompte and Goetz, 1982). Even such widely acclaimed, enormously influential, and popularly read anthropologists as Margaret Mead and Oscar Lewis have been criticized for a tendency to reflect their subjective assumptions and value judgments in their writing rather than the culture under study "as it really was" (Pelto and Pelto, 1978; Freeman, 1983).

In an early treatment of the problem, Howard Becker (1970b) outlined some reasons that observational methods conform poorly to traditional standards of scientific inquiry. *First,* qualitative researchers are usually more interested in a thorough understanding of an organization than in narrow relationships between specific, often abstract, variables. The essence of understanding is more enticing to the researcher than *post hoc* explanations or conclusions. *Second,* the design of qualitative research typically takes place while the research is already underway. The research site may be insufficiently understood at the beginning of the study to identify relevant data, let alone test *a priori* hypotheses. As the study continues, the analysis of data and the selection and definition of problems or foci for investigation proceed interactively, each providing direction for the other.

Finally, *third,* the qualitative researcher is typically faced at the end of his study with the task of trying to make some sense out of an almost overwhelming complexity of information, to fashion a bit of grounded theory, and to search for a sensible model rather than to test it. In this most difficult effort, notes Becker, "observers usually view currently available statistical techniques as inadequate to express their conceptions and find it necessary to use words" (p. 196).

In this discussion, Becker used a term that has since been selected by Lincoln and Guba (1985) as a key concept in establishing the trustworthiness of qualitative inquiry (replacing the traditional notions of realizability and validity). This term is *credibility. Reliability* refers, of course, to the capacity of study to be replicated—to yield the same results to a researcher who uses the same methods as a prior investigator. Because qualitative research occurs in natural settings, changes in design as the setting indicates, depends heavily upon the idiosyncrasies of each researcher, and often involves vague and intuitive insights into the setting and its data, the replicability of a piece of qualitative research is often quite problematic (LeCompte and Goetz, 1982). Qualitative research has a better claim to validity, particularly internal validity, where the researcher claims that his or her explanations match closely the actual conditions of life within the observed setting. External validity (which refers to the generalizability of a set of findings, a study's comparability and translatability) is much more difficult, however. Without acceptable reliability as a precondition, external validity is not likely (LeCompte and Goetz, 1982; Lincoln and Guba, 1985).

Lincoln and Guba (1985) argue that neither of these terms *(reliability* or *validity)* is really appropriate to the naturalistic research paradigm. They stake out a strong position, claiming that naturalistic inquiry is not just an added wrinkle upon conventional scientific methodology (positivism). Naturalistic inquiry is a new research paradigm, fundamentally different from positivism, and *"not* reconcilable with the old" (pp. 32–33). To score naturalistic inquiry as either unreliable or invalid because its methodological controls are not strong, therefore providing little chance of supporting or rejecting rival hypotheses, fails to recognize a difference between the two paradigms in their basic assumptions about the nature of reality. While positivism assumes the existence of a tangible, objectively identifiable body of facts just waiting to be discovered, the naturalistic paradigm sees no single reality or generalizable truth. There are, instead, "multiple construed realities" that cannot be pried apart into fragments of understanding without damaging the whole. There is no ultimate benchmark of truth (or even of replicability), but numerous mental constructions that together seek not truth but a bit of *Verstehen* (Lincoln and Guba, 1985, pp. 294–296).

Furthermore, to fault naturalistic inquiry for its lack of external validity (while recognizing that it often does provide more internal validity) fails to note a basic difference between paradigms on the question of transferability. To the conventional method, the representatives of the original sample is essential, because generalizability is the aim. The naturalist desires no generalizability (the goal rather is *Verstehen*), and the naturalist cannot know the settings for which generalizability might be sought. The burden of proof in the naturalist case rests with the person who would make a direct application of findings elsewhere rather than with the original investigator, as in the conventional method (Lincoln and Guba, 1985, pp. 296–298).

Lincoln and Guba do not, however, reject standards of careful, well-designed research. They suggest that the focus should be upon the "trustworthiness" and "confirmability" of data produced qualitatively rather than upon its adherence to conventional notions of reliability, validity, objectivity, or generalizability (p. 300). The qualitative researcher can meet a trustworthiness norm by emphasizing the following:

1. *Credibility.* The data and findings that are produced through naturalistic inquiry will more likely to be credible if they are acquired through (a) prolonged engagement (e.g., with sufficient time spent to learn the culture and to build trust); (b) persistent observation (thereby uncovering that which is most relevant to a developing understanding), and (c) the use of triangulation (using multiple data sources and collection methods).

2. *Transferability.* While external validity is not the goal, the naturalist does assist the person interested in making a transfer by engaging in a thick description of the setting studied. As Lincoln and Guba (1985) summarize, it is *"not* the naturalist's task to provide an *index* of transferability; it *is* his or her responsibility to provide the *data base* that makes transferability judgments possible on the part of potential appliers" (p. 316).

3. *Dependability and confirmability.* While conventional reliability (in terms of replicability) is not applicable, the reader of a naturalistic inquiry should be confident that the process of inquiry is consistent, internally coherent, and ethically aboveboard. Furthermore, the reader should be confident that the findings are grounded in the data, logical in terms of the data, and acceptable (e.g., negative cases accounted for and an "audit" of the study carried out) (Lincoln and Guba, 1985, and 301–327).

Suggestions for methodological sophistication in qualitative research (e.g., using triangulation, thick description, and confirmability audits) will be discussed in further detail later in this chapter. As an *issue* in the study of higher education, however, trustworthiness is an especially salient concern. LeCompte and Goetz (1982) sum it up quite succinctly in noting that the researcher's central concern should be directed toward an accurate portrayal of the client's "lifeways."

But as Robertson Davies's "ghost" reminds us, an accurate rendition of the folkways, subtle nuances, shadings, and inconsistencies of college and university environments is not a simple task. The ways in which even its participants may believe budgetary resources to be distributed may be out of touch with the reality of the allocatory process (Salancik and Pfeffer, 1974). The modern image of the university as an institution rendering teaching and public service may be vital to its own self-concept and to the picture it presents to the world, but deep inside (and the cause of strain between image and reality), the demand for scholarly productivity (publish or perish) remains well intact (Caplow and McGee, 1958). Beneath a facade of gentlemanly discourse, intellectual fervor, and collegial cooperation, the internal political dynamics of the university are often rough-and-tumble—with faculty rivalries, jealousies, and "dirty deeds" flavoring mightily the institutional atmosphere (Morris, 1981).

Furthermore, beyond such contradictions between image and reality, a faithful and accurate rendition of life in higher education encounters many of the threats to internal validity first suggested by Campbell and Stanley (1963). *History*, for example, affects the nature of the data collected. Institutions of higher education present complex and mysterious histories. They are both adaptively modern and unchangeably medieval at the same time (Perkins, 1973; Clark, 1983). They are highly variable, with formative sagas from their past that create unique adaptations to changing contemporary events (Clark, 1970, 1972). They are deeply rooted in a stable and predictable time frame of student registration, class scheduling, activities calendars, and degree conferring—while being simultaneously filled institutionally with unusual freedom in the allocation that participants make of their own available time. Participants (particularly the professoriate) can sometimes even serve the institution well by being away from it for months (occasionally years) at a stretch.

Mortality, a second threat to validity, refers to the changes in groups over time as a result of losses and gains in membership. Although coming and going is a normal part of all institutional settings, institutions of higher education (even residential colleges) are lade with growth and attrition. Differences, for example, in the attitudes, motivations, and aspirations of students abound (Pascarella, 1985); thus, a set of interviews with, and observations of, one group of students at one point may yield a far different picture from the one collected six months later at the same institution but with a now-reconstituted group.

Similarly, the *selection* of study participants (whom to observe and interview) is a threat and has already been discussed as a separate issue on its own. Complex institutional environments are filled with subgroups, factions, and a multihued events. An adequate inventory of subgroups is recommended (LeCompte and Gaetz, 1982) if a study's findings are not to be misleadingly underrepresentative of the variety and complexity of behaviors in the setting. However, even to an informed "insider" in a small residential college, thoroughly socialized and long at home, an adequate inventory of subgroups and factions could be a Herculean job. The range of possible events and groupings in any institution of higher education is a distinct challenge to the validity-minded researcher.

In sum, the use of qualitative methods in the study of higher education must pay special attention to three key issues. The first of these is the issue of *familiarity*. More than likely, those who study institutions of higher education will be persons with a deep insider's knowledge of the college and university culture. Such familiarity can be a benefit; it can also be handicap. Is an insider or an outsider more likely to be the better judge of what's "really going on" in academic setting? Additionally, the *selection* of what, whom, and where to study can be an important methodological problem. With their structural looseness, their complexity and variability, their independence of individual behavior, and their diffusion of power and responsibility, institutions of higher education do not yield easily to a search for understanding. Furthermore, vital to qualitative inquiry, whatever the research setting, is the pursuit of *trustworthiness*. While traditional, scientific standards of reliability and validity should not be applied, the qualitative research is no less interested than the positivist-oriented scholar in as accurate and credible a rendition of institutional lifeways as possible.

Use of Qualitative Research Methods in Higher Education

All three of the key methodological issues (familiarity, selection, and trustworthiness) impact heavily upon what John Van Maanen (1979b) labels the relationship between "first-order" and "second-order" conceptions of what is going on in a fieldwork setting. First-order conceptions are informants' notions about what is happening, and second-order conceptions are the researcher's interpretations. Or in simpler terms, first-order concepts can be considered the "facts" of fieldwork, while the second order applies theory and explanation to these facts. The second-order concepts are dependent upon the fieldworker's faith in the quality and accuracy of the facts (Van Maanen, 1979b, p. 542).

This most difficult translation from qualitatively research "fact" into grounded "theory" is the central theme of the third major section of this chapter. The practical use of qualitative research methods in higher education is explored, with special concern for analytical accuracy. With its press toward constructed reality (a search for understanding), its norm of researcher proximity, its emphasis upon analytic induction, and its appreciation of the value-bound context of most inquiry, the qualitative method faces interesting and unusual problems in the development of a *disciplined* form of inquiry, leading to confidence in the findings unearthed. In this section of the chapter, four components of the qualitative method in use are examined vis-a-vis research settings in higher education. The practical concern is with analytical accuracy. The components are (1) researcher entrance and rapport; (2) ethical problems in field studies in higher education; (3) data collection and design strategies; and (4) data analysis.

Entrance and Rapport

Gaining entrance to a research site and establishing rapport are often difficult and time-consuming tasks. In an ethnographic-style inquiry involving this author as part of a team observing the workaday lives of school principals within one large city school system, as many years were spent in gaining access to the schools (three years) as were spent in the observation (an additional three years) (Morris et al., 1984). Without care taken in securing entree and in the establishment of a role (rapport) that facilitates the collection of data, the accuracy of trust-worthiness of the findings becomes problematic.

John Van Maanen (1979a) has noted the "fact" that organizational settings are full of fiction. People are prone, especially when under observation, to put forth appearances. For one thing, the researcher "can be misled because informants want it that way. People lie, evade, and otherwise deceive the fieldworker in numerous and inventive ways"—often covering up the things that matter most to them (e.g., hidden failings, taboo-violating activities, and flagrant mistakes) (p. 544). Additionally, the researcher can be misled because the informants are themselves wrong about aspects of their own work site. Not all informants are good informants, equally knowledgeable about their own organization—as any university student knows who tries to learn "the facts" about course and graduation requirements from his or her faculty adviser. Finally, the researcher can be misled because informants are unaware of reasons for their own activities. People take a lot of things for granted in organizations (e.g., a categorizing or labeling of clients, or endemic rules violations), and the researcher can similarly be blinded if unquestioningly accepting the informants' own perceptual screen (Van Maanen, 1979a, pp. 544–548).

People are probably as likely to lie (either intentionally or unintentionally) in educational organizations as in any other institutional setting. Despite its apparent openness, the educational organization is typically a closed-in place. Persons sitting in college classrooms are expected to be either students (with ascribed roles of listening, responding to questions, producing effort, and discussing) or instructors (with the jobs of lecturing, asking questions, assigning work, and leading discussions). Departmental faculty meetings are typically intimate while at the same time often discursive and sometimes acrimonious affairs. Significant differences in individual ideology and perspective become apparent in crucial decisions about tenure, teaching assignments, new faculty searches, and program development or revision. Stephen Wilson (1977) observes that in every ethnographic study in education in which he has been involved, concerns have been expressed about the researcher's identity: Who is this person? What role is he or she about to play? Whose side is this person on? Perhaps most important, can I be myself while this person is around? Without care in entry and close attention to rapport on the part of the researcher, the discovery of only "appearances" is the likely research outcome.

Both Greer (1970) and Rist (1975) have talked about "the research bargain" or "the issue of reciprocity" in securing both access to and trust from the persons inhabiting a research site. In many ways, fieldworkers are at the mercy of those whom they are studying if their research is to be successful. Patterns of reciprocity are essential if interactions are to develop profitably and to achieve the stability required for deeper understanding. In his study of an urban elementary school, Rist (1975) was careful to assist teachers wherever possible (e.g, threading the film projector, moving tables, carrying heavy packages, and tacking pictures on a wall), to converse with teachers informally over coffee or at lunch and at school functions, and to listen to but maintain confidentiality in the constant flow of gossip around the school. Similarly, with school administrators, a bit of help writing a grant proposal and locating some hard-to-obtain learning materials cemented a relationship. With students, Rist was careful to avoid becoming part of the authority structure of the school and additionally attempted to be interested and supportive when children showed him their work.

With similar observations more pointedly directed toward research in higher education, Blanche Geer (1970, p. 82) warns that in studying a college, the fieldworker should start with "a cynical view of the enmities possible" in the three-level hierarchy of the organization (administrators, faculty, and students). Echoing Wax (1971) and also Richardson (1970), Geer argues that successful access requires substantial knowledge about an organization *before* the beginning of fieldwork, particularly foreknowledge of organizational structures and the distribution of power. Understanding is, at least in part, a precondition of qualitative research, as well as its outcome.

While Rist suggests reciprocity, Geer calls (in higher education) for a "period of bargaining" in the development of entry and rapport. The bargaining effort can be tricky and time-consuming. Often, the college administrator or staff member must be led to understand that the researcher is not just on a fishing expedition (despite the looseness of the design) and is not simply engaged in a bit of muckraking, looking for blemishes and bad spots that could well prove to be embarrassing to the organization. Researchers are often asked to share reports and findings with administrators before publication, cleaning up anything perceived to be harmful to the college. Furthermore, researchers are often pushed by administrators to direct their attention toward problems *they* want solved.

Similarly, bargains must be struck with faculty members, and even with students (particularly student leaders). Geer (1970) suggests paying courtesy calls on social scientists on the faculty, sharing ideas and publications, and generally engaging faculty members in repeated conversations to assure them of anonymity and confidentiality. Student leaders often tend to be a particularly suspicious lot, requiring cultivation, and proving to be not unlikely to "check with the administration and faculty to discover what sort of bargain was made with them" (p. 86).

Writing in 1970, Blanche Geer may have been overly attuned to, and full of caution following, the years of campus turmoil and dissent of the 1960s. Nevertheless, it is well recognized by qualitative methodologists that access most often requires careful researcher negotiation and is intensely personal. Researchers must often have wide latitude to choose freely where to observe and to whom to talk, but they face in the process the creation of an unusual institutional role—a role that, on the one hand, legitimizes an array of unhindered information-gathering behaviors but, on the other hand, avoids as much as possible established patterns of social expectation within the research setting (Pelto and Pelto, 1978). It is not easy; and the researcher often finds himself or herself creating and filling a new role within the organization—one with a good deal of helping behavior with simultaneously a chance to step back and watch objectively all that is going on. There is an urge to carve out a bit of usefulness, a sense that one's services are needed (Cusick, 1983). But Pelto and Pelto (1978) warn, "The local people do not forget that the anthropologists will ultimately leave them, carrying their notebooks, films, and other information-storing apparatus back to that other world from whence they came" (1978).

Thus, access and trust (and therefore analytical accuracy) often require a bit of bargaining and the negotiation of some form of jointly insider-while-at-the-same-time-outsider role for the qualitative researcher. In the process, however, the fieldworker encounters another major methodological dilemma: the Heisenberg problem. This problem was first brought to scientific attention by Werner Heisenberg, a German microphysicist, who in the 1920s enunciated his now famous principle of indeterminacy. According to this principle, there is a certain uncorrectable randomness in the behavior of subatomic particles, because there is no way for a physicist to observe and catalog their movements without simultaneously disturbing those movements. The very energy developed by electron microscopes to illuminate the target area alters the energy configuration of the particles under study. In short, the observer of phenomena disturbs and shapes the phenomena under study just by being there.[5]

While some enthnographic purists have argued that the researcher should in no way interfere with the culture under study, realism shows that, like the impact of the electron microscope, that of the fieldworker upon the setting is inevitable. Pelto and Pelto (1978) conclude, "The dilemma of the fieldworker, then, is not *whether* to interfere in the local cultural scene but *how much* to interfere" (p. 186). At what point does observer involvement intrude inordinately upon the naturalness of the setting? What point does fieldworker involvement destroy the objectivity of the researcher, the ability to step back and analyze the events observed under a somewhat dispassionate eye? How can the fieldworker maintain balance and fairness while at the same time first establishing and then maintaining close, reciprocal interaction with his or her informants?

This dilemma is probably as acute in research into higher education as in the study of any other organizational setting. Burgess (1984), drawing heavily upon Gold (1958), describes four fieldworker roles: the complete participant, the participant as observer, the observer as participant, and the complete observer. Each role, discussed briefly below, presents a trade-off between involvement and objectivity.

First, the *complete participant* conceals the observer portion of the role from other individuals in the setting. Data are collected covertly, without the knowledge or consent of other participants. Beyond some possible ethical considerations, the difficulties are that the researcher will "go native" and lose the ability (and also the time) to reflect and analyze the data at hand. Complete participation in any organizational setting, furthermore, involves committee chairmanships, taking sides on policy issues, making organizational enemies as well as friends, becoming involved in difficult questions of administration (e.g., alternative usages of available resources), and engaging in some personal corporate striving or ladder-climbing. As mentioned early in the chapter, the literature in higher education is insightfully rich in a backward glance at itself by some of its major figures (e.g., Kerr, 1964; Barzun, 1968; Bell, 1966; Riesman, 1958; Perkins, 1966). Nevertheless, the complete participant will often find it difficult to be fully objective and openly critical in a look backward at an institutional setting that he or she has probably played a role in building and/or altering.

The *participant as observer*, as a second alternative, is a more common fieldworker role. The researcher does not conceal his or her research interest; indeed, it is made known that the primary reason for the fieldworker's being there is to observe, not to participate. The researcher conveys the understanding that he or she wishes considerable freedom of movement and open access to all social situations and potential informants. However, the fieldworker also contributes, as participant, to the work of the organization and establishes legitimacy with informants by assisting the institution, just as they do, with its daily work load. The dangers in this role are that the fieldworker (1) can be easily seduced into more and more participation and less observation; (2) may meet closed doors and rebuffs as observer because of his or her alliances as participant; and (3) may interfere as participant with events that as pure observer he or she would have been advised to simply record (Pelto and Pelto, 1978; Spradley, 1980; Burgess, 1984). In the study of higher education, furthermore, the role of participant in any form can place obstacles in the path of observation. Whether one chooses to participate in the guise of faculty member, student, nonacademic staff member, or administrator, some doors and interactions are likely to open to one role more than to another.

The third fieldwork role is *observer as participant*. As the reversal of the two key terms indicates, the emphasis is placed upon observation with lessened participation. The observer role is made known, and the participation that occurs is more incidental and opportunistic (e.g., building trust through reciprocity) than long-term and structured. Because the fieldworker is likely to participate over less time and only on the periphery of the organizational culture, the danger is that the research will never penetrate deeply into insider understandings (Burgess, 1984, p. 82). While there is less chance that the fieldworker will go native, he or she may be hard pressed to penetrate below the appearances and the entree offered the casual tourist. The fieldworker may be particularly susceptible to publicity release interpretations of the work of the institution rather than its operable work life.

Finally, fourth, the *complete observer* role avoids all participation and its attendant biases in favor of pure observation. Eavesdropping and data collection or event recording can occur without the knowledge of participants and without the obligations that are placed on those who become involved in institutional affairs. The central dangers are that the complete observer will learn little of the insider's world and will be barred from much activity that requires negotiated entree. Pure observation may be easily pursued in higher education at its many large-group encounters (e.g., student centers, campus coming and goings, sports contests, student registration periods, and large-group lectures). However, in its many intimate and hard-to-penetrate gatherings (e.g., a tenure review board, a college executive committee, a student dormitory bull-session, small-group instructional seminars, a Ph.D. examination, and the chancellor's advisory committee), an observer role without a participation overlay is unlikely.[6]

Thus, one key barrier to analytical accuracy and trustworthiness in qualitative research within higher education is the problem of gaining access and establishing rapport. Organizations, and the individuals serving within them, are not averse to a portrayal of appearances to those who are not yet fully accepted within the institutional culture. Acceptance often involves a bit of bargaining, reciprocity, and even active participation, the attendant danger, as the fieldworker moves back and forth between participation and observation, is that the data will be affected by researcher interference. Later, in a discussion of data analysis issues, some techniques offered by Lincoln and Guba (1985) to assist trustworthiness (e.g., member checks, peer debriefings, and independent audits) will be explained and considered.

Ethical Problems

Pelto and Pelto (1978, p. 186) write about the moral conflict that fieldworkers face whenever their values conflict with events in the community under study. Especially poignant for ethnographers is the setting filled with human misery that could be prevented—with changes in sanitation, child rearing, crop producing, medical and dietary practices, and so on, or with changes in local power relations, governmental programs, and the like. The traditional research axiom is that the fieldworker must learn to endure the psychological tension of a hands-off approach, to observe and record but not try to change. The opposite viewpoint is expressed by Charles Valentine (1968), who argues that the fieldworker *should* become an activist on behalf of his or her subjects—"to act from the ethical position that he has major obligations to the people he is studying" (pp. 188–189).

Higher education institutions are unlikely (in most settings at least) to tax the fieldworker's conscience about unrelieved misery. However, moral conflicts of a similar type do develop. Fetterman (1984c, p. 215) reminds us that the researcher must respect informants' rights (e.g., to confidentiality and anonymity). The fieldworker must, realistically, work as well to stay on the good side of his or her subjects, maintaining, as mentioned earlier, the system of obligations and sharing and reciprocity that may have, only with difficulty and over time, provided the key to researcher access. But Fetterman observes additionally that the researcher must also be considerate of the taxpayer (ibid.). Whether the research is supported by government funds, or the agency under study is (or both), a commitment to a morality beyond the miniculture under investigation may be required.

Barnes (1970) provides additional perspective upon the dilemma. He notes that the foci of ethnographic-style studies are no longer just illiterate tribes in remote areas, but communities and institutions whose members can read, write letters, and even sue the researcher. Furthermore, the ethnographer more and more often finds himself or herself in situations where the code of values undergirding the setting is not strange or foreign, or so unusual as to warrant a fully detached (even amused at times) luxury of pure observation. Barnes concludes:

> More and more the ethnographer finds himself in situations in which he cannot avoid evaluating the actions of his informants in terms of his own code. If he refrains from acting on these evaluations, it is because of the way he has defined his role as a scientific investigator and not because of the cultural gulf between him and his informants. (pp. 240–241)

If reprehensible, morally wrong, even illegal activities are observed, should they be fully reported, ignored, glossed over, masked, or covered up? If reported, is damage done to the trust that was offered the fieldworker in permitting access and in opening private, institutional lives to close inspection? If not reported, can the study be considered a trustworthy portrayal of life as it really is in an institution?

Colleges and universities are not widely recognized, of course, as work settings where ethical transgressions and extralegal actions are likely to be in widespread evidence. Qualitative research has been more common in law enforcement occupations, the health professions, and social service bureaucracies, where consideration of the ethical has much day-in and day-out saliency (see, for example, Lipsky, 1980). Nevertheless, the fieldworker who penetrates student subcultures in higher education should not be surprised to find behaviors running the gamut from rule breaking to illegality. Furthermore, beneath a facade of professorial respectability, institutional life in higher education is no less immune than other types of organizations to examples of racism, sexism, favoritism, falsification, and immorality. Indeed, some would argue that modern institutional life in higher education brings inescapable ethical dilemmas to those who would administer its affairs. For example, Morris (1984) argues that college deans are imbued with a sense of service to their faculty members. Yet, as administrators, they must also work on behalf of the organization as a whole. In this larger effort, they often find themselves *using* people—their motivations, drives, and skills—to serve the corporate good. The interests of the entire organization come first, and on behalf of these interests,

> It is sometimes necessary to withhold certain kinds of information and deal it out, piece by piece, to the people who must use it, deliberately keeping it from others, especially those who may use the information in a disruptive and destructive way. The messages that flow across an administrator's desk are of a special sort. Although not literally personal, they are nevertheless privileged, an adjective which could never be applied to any sort of information in the academic marketplace. (p. 131)

Thus, using people, withholding information, bending the rules, playing favorites, and shading the facts are not at all uncommon behaviors in any organizational setting that is filled with just plain old human beings. The organization against the individual, one special interest opposing another, inequitably distributed power, purely personal motivations and needs, friends helping one another out—these are among the "stuff" of organizational life. They exist below the easily visible organizational surface or are hidden as skeletons (even ghosts) in organizational closets, but when unearthed, they be embarrassing and even destructive.

The crunch for the qualitative research comes at the point of the report. Fetterman (1984c) writes:

> Fieldwork conducted in highly political settings can be more dangerous than fieldwork in the streets of the inner city. An ethnographic report rich in detail is potentially as dangerous as it may be helpful—depending on how the material is presented and who uses the information. (p. 225)

In consideration of these time-bomb qualities, a number of guidelines for reporting are typically offered.

First, it is commonly suggested that the researcher should, above all, maintain agreements concerning confidentiality or anonymity (Lincoln and Guba, 1985). By carefully masking respondent identities, one can take the edge off much disclosure that may be potentially damaging to participants. Nevertheless, a *second* guideline that is also commonly suggested goes a step further (Fetterman, 1984c; Barnes, 1970; Fichter and Kolb, 1970). The suggestion is that research findings prior to dissemination should be shared with and cleared by those most closely concerned. Informants may be asked to check the accuracy of statements and may be asked if they will agree to statements about themselves (even if identities are masked) that may appear in print (Barnes, 1970, p. 245).

Third, it is suggested that the writing of a report should not be interpretive or evaluative, except in sections explicitly intended for such purposes (e.g., a set of conclusions attempting to establish a bit of grounded theory) (Lincoln and Guba, 1985). A report that is liberally dosed with the researcher's own moral outrage, that delightedly highlights organizational or individual aberrations, and that points a finger in abhorrence at ethical transgressions can add little to the central research objective of *Verstehen*.

On the other hand, and an added part of the researcher's dilemma, those who offer guidelines on reporting suggests that (1) the inquiry has obligations to whomever supplied funds for the investigation to the present the data honestly and with thoroughness, and (2) the researcher's colleagues and social scientists in general have a claim upon a serious, honest, and professionally competent report. Although assurances of anonymity, clearance, and cautious efforts to avoid moralizing are certainly in order, the fieldworker also owes a debt to his or her discipline (and even to society itself) to report thoroughly upon what was observed (warts and all) if the result is a bit of knowledge, some understanding, that has heretofore been unavailable (Fichter and Kolb, 1970). Whichever way one turns, concludes Fetterman (1984c), "guilty knowledge and dirty hands are at the heart of the fieldworker experience" (p. 231).

Data Collection and Design Strategies

Becker and Geer (1960) urge the qualitative researcher to take account of as much of an organization's complexity as time and effort will allow. Quite simply, the collection of data and the design of research strategies should be broad based and comprehensive enough to capture maximum understanding from the natural environment. Yet, the design must simultaneously be open-ended and flexible—with an emerging structure, as the uncovered data and their analyses indicate. The trick, as Lincoln and Guba (1985) put it, is to provide an opportunity for some "hard thinking" in an open-ended way that does not come across as "sloppy inquiry (p. 225).

Lincoln and Guba contrast the conventional perspective upon research design with that of naturalistic inquiry. A bit of a paradox is encountered, in that conventional design standards require precisely what is impossible for the qualitative researcher to specify in advance. While the conventional asks for the clear statement of a research problem and the statement of an *a priori* theoretical perspective (usually with hypotheses to be tested), the naturalist merely begins with a bit of focus in inquiry (which often changes) and a theory that emerges from the study. Convention also asks for representative sampling (in aid of generalization), operational definitions of the variables to be studied, and carefully specified data collection and analysis procedures (capable of testing the hypotheses offered). However, sampling for the naturalist is contingent and serial, data collection is opportunistic, and data analysis is open-ended and inductive. The design of a naturalistic inquiry cannot be tightly structured in advance; "it must emerge, develop, unfold" (Lincoln and Guba, 1985, p. 225).

It does not, however, unfold sloppily. Certainly, qualitative research is personalistic, with no investigator working quite as another does (LeCompte and Goetz, 1982). Nevertheless, the search for understanding (and, hopefully, some theory building) demands that careful attention be given to credibility. Two characteristics of qualitative research with important credibility overtones are (1) its provision for multiple strategies of data collection and (2) its concern for continuous checking, probing, verifying, and confirming as data collection and analysis proceed (Owens, 1982; Burgess, 1984; Lincoln and Guba, 1985).

Multiple Data Collection Strategies

Terms heard often in the discussion of field research methods are "thick description" (Geertz, 1973) and "triangulation" (Denzin, 1970, 1978). The concept of thick description suggests that it is the responsibility of the researcher to provide sufficient scope and depth in reporting to enable the reader to understand and separately interpret the study's findings. While transferability is not the central goal of qualitative research, thick description can make it possible for the reader to make his or her own applications to similar settings. In like fashion, the concept of triangulation calls for the use of multiple method of data collection (e.g., participant observation plus interviewing, document examination, and even questionnaires). Multiple sources of (cross-referenceable) data and multiple investigators (e.g., as part of a research team) can also be modes of triangulation, as can the use of the same methods on different occasions.

As Jick (1979) points out, one fundamental assumption behind the triangulation argument is that somehow the weaknesses embedded within each single method will be compensated for by the strengths of the other(s). The direct, to-the-problem, but possibly "rehearsed" product of the interview can be balanced by the spontaneity of on-site observation (e.g., of the overheard conversation, the chance remark, the here-and-now, and the knee-jerk reaction to events). The sometimes unfathomable parade of observed events, helter-skelter, one atop another, can be clarified and rooted in time and setting through the more leisurely examination of documents and records. Nevertheless, the strengths of a counterbalancing of methods are by no means automatically ensured, and, warns Jick (1979), "Multimethods are of no use with the 'wrong' question (p. 609).[7]

In parallel with the emergent and adaptive approach to research design that is urged for qualitative inquiry, Douglas (1976) offers three principles for the use of mixed data collection strategies. *First*, the mixture should not be too tightly controlled at the outset of research. *Second*, adaptability and flexibility in the selection of method should be maintained throughout the study. A *third*, the mix should attempt to progress from natural (e.g., pure observation) to more controlled methods (e.g., focused interviews), as findings in the study accumulate. Douglas's three principles are consistent with the Becker and Geer (1960) observation that fieldwork often proceeds through a number of distinct (but overlapping and interwoven) analytical stages: (1) an initial period of focusing and selection and definition of problems; then (2) a descriptive inquiry into the existence and distribution of phenomena; and finally (3) the incorporation of observations into a bit of initial theorizing.

Amidst all of this adaptation and reshuffling, it is the researcher who is the central instrument of data collection (Lincoln and Guba, 1985). Some manner of direct observation is the mainstay of the qualitative research tradition, but the approach is rich in its variety of data collection strategies. A few of the major strategies will be discussed, briefly, as they apply to research in higher education.

Observation. The generally favored form is participant observation, despite its demand that the fieldworker play two (somewhat incompatible) roles simultaneously; observer *and* group member. The phenomenon of participation provides an intimacy with, and a sharing of, the world of the observed that is often considered essential to the central goal of understanding (Denzin, 1970). While there is a range of styles of participation (from immersion to occasional), the decided strength of the method is its opportunity to perceive reality from an insider perspective, and therefore to give the study internal validity. Observational data (and particularly participant observation data) are, of course, subject to the vagaries of time and place. The fieldworker sees what happens while he or she is there. Furthermore, as a participant, the fieldworker helps to fashion somewhat what is to be seen; and, as a participant, the fieldworker helps to fashion somewhat what is to be seen; and, as a participant, the fieldworker may even find it necessary to serve in a role that limits what is to be seen (e.g, a student cut off from faculty councils or a member of a humanities department having minimal communication with the hard sciences departments). London (1978) illustrates the problem clearly in his study of the culture of a community college:

> A minor difficulty of this method was the awkwardness of being seen in the company of one group by students with whom I had spent the previous day(s); moving from clique to clique, I feared being seen as having switched allegiances, although I never heard any such accusations. There were occasions, for example, when a student would see me with a student or group of students he had vilified earlier, or with a teacher for whom he had expressed a particular distaste. (pp. 164–165)

Thus, while participant observation is the much-preferred style (because of its internal validity), the study of higher education does to adapt to it easily. To be sure, persons engaged in studies of colleges and universities are likely to be uncommonly well situated (as insiders and participants) to conduct inquiry into their own professional environments. Indeed, as mentioned earlier, the literature is rich in insider essays, retrospectives, and critiques. Nevertheless, the professorial role is a strange species of organizational participation, one not unduly well placed to provide a holistic understanding. Much of one's work life is spent in isolation and, even when teaching, cut off from widespread collegial interaction. Loneliness is considered a virtue, necessary to the completion of work—and much sought after, even reveled in by many, if not most, scholars. The slice of institutional life (despite the rich variety of life forms) that is open to each role incumbent in higher education is usually quite circumscribed.

Nonparticipant observation, despite its drawbacks of access and outsider status ("what in the world is that person doing here"?) can probably be used productively to study much in higher education. Ethics aside, covert (or undercover) observation is possible in many institutional subsettings (e.g., large-group gatherings, libraries, and movements of individuals spatially around a campus). The discrete observation of nonverbal behaviors and the gathering of unobtrusive measures (e.g., of groupings of individuals, body movements, spatial relationships between people, touching, physical arrangements of buildings on the campus, and traffic patterns) in college and university settings offers a richly varied menu of data gathering opportunities. And with careful attention given to access (properly explaining the intent of the study), the nonparticipating outsider is probably as welcome an observer in the inner councils of higher education administration as in any other organizational setting. The institutional culture understands and appreciates research, while in other organizations, the natives may wonder "why this person doesn't go out and get a real job."

Again, the central power of observation as a data collection tool is its inquiry into a natural, dynamic environment on its own terms (Guba and Lincoln, 1981). Lincoln and Guba (1985) suggest that this power can be maximized if considerate attention is given to the process of accurately recording observed phenomena. For example, observational notes can often be organized into theory-generating categories at the time of event occurrence. Time logs of events can assist data reconstruction and interpretation, as can maps of spatial arrangements and sociometric-style diagrams of the interaction patterns of individuals. "Debriefing sessions" (e.g., with other researchers), after a researcher leaves the setting, can produce observational insights that do not immediately occur to the fieldworker himself or herself (Lincoln and Guba, 1985, p. 275). There is, however, no standard operating procedure, no right or wrong methodology, in the use of observation. Settings differ in their demands and opportunities, and fieldworkers differ in their skill and creativity. Again, London (1978) provides an interesting and illustrative methodological vignette in his study of a community college:

> To remember important points from student's classes I would often take very brief notes while doodling. For example, to record the seating arrangement I would make a series of "Xs" and "Os" to designate males and females; to help reconstruct a dialogue I would write key words or letters on a slip of paper or a book jacket while appearing to be nonchalantly perusing the room. Similarly, during conversations with students I would sometimes doodle and let them have a view of the doodle, yet hidden in it were symbols to help me recall as faithfully as possible what was said. (p. 165)

Interviewing. In the interest of triangulation, the interview (either structured or unstructured) provides an opportunity to gather data in the respondents' own words, to focus inquiry more pointedly toward a study's central questions, to draw data efficiently from a setting, and to seek information directly from the persons who are most in the know in a setting. A vital tool in its own right, the interview can also be a valuable complement to observation. In studies that are primarily observational, interviewing is often likely to be unfocused (or at least open-ended) and opportunistic (occurring as time and place permit). To be sure, however, qualitative research and the idea of triangulation can also be well served through the use of carefully focused interviews (and/or surveys) at prearranged times with representatively sampled informants.

The major strength of interviewing (e.g., its opportunity to focus, its collection of the respondents' own words, and its efficiency) are also its central weakness. The interviewee is much more in control of the data than is the case in pure observation and knows (although some interviewing is covert) that he or she is providing data. Furthermore, the fluid (although time-consuming) nature of participant observation is stopped short in the interview. Other natural events of possible theoretical import may be flying by, unnoticed, while an interview is in progress. Nevertheless, the utility of the interview as a tool of triangulation is well recognized. An illustration of that importance, as well as of the tool's difficulties, is provided in another excerpt from the work of London (1978):

> The interviews consisted of a series of open-ended questions, some of which were modified slightly to suit the chemistry and idiosyncrasies of each interview. The chief problem in the interviews was the sensitive nature of the questions concerning the career transition and how successfully or unsuccessfully it had been made.
>
> As I began asking about the discrepancy between expectations and reality, I often sensed that teachers knew what I was getting at—that we were discussing or about to discuss the extent to which their careers had soured. Having seen me in their classes and having talked with me during the year, they knew I was familiar with their work problems, and many of them did reveal intimate thoughts. In three interviews I had the unverifiable feeling that teachers were not being honest and that there was nothing I could do to uncover the truth. (p. 168)

The varieties and forms of interviewing are many. Lincoln and Guba (1985) suggest that interviews can be categorized by "their degree of *structure*, their *degree of overtness*, and the *quality of the relationship* between the interviewer and respondent" (p. 268). Structures range from focused to unfocused, with focused (more highly structured) interviewing more likely to be employed when time is limited, when the data to be elicited (and therefore the appropriate questions to be asked) are clear, and/or when the interview is being used to corroborate understandings that have already been established. Overtness/covertness carries some ethical overtones—with moral judgment generally weighted toward informing respondents fully of the fact of the interview, as well as of its purpose, and of how respondents' contributions will be used. Similarly, relationships between interviewer and respondent can range from hostile to emphatic (Massarik, 1981), with the suggestion that effort in most qualitative research should be directed toward establishing the trust and rapport with respondents necessary to natural data collection.

One decided advantage of the interview in the study of organizations is the opportunity it provides for a glance backward as well as forward (speculatively) in time. Subjects can be asked to reconstruct past events as well as to project (from their own experience) the course of future occurrences ("What do you think is likely to happen next?"). A technique favored by sociologists some decades ago, and receiving renewed attention with the current interest in qualitative inquiry, is the development of the "life history." The life history is often a participant's glance backward at a lifetime of experience, captured in the participant's own words, with the participant's as well as the researcher's interpretations of those experiences (Denzin, 1970). Although interviewing will loom large in the life history, the compilation of documents (e.g., letters, autobiographies, diaries, and archival records) and the administration of questionnaires (e.g., attitude measures and interest inventories) can be appropriately added to the database.

The life history is a bit of contemporary organizational historiography that can be particularly useful in the study of higher education. With its structural looseness, the academic organization may be especially susceptible to the influence of an idiosyncratic personality upon its development and day-by-day work life. Certainly a Hutchins, an Eliot, or a Channing will receive marked attention, but throughout each college or university, there tend to be individuals (often little known outside the institution) whose careers leave a decided mark upon the course of intrainstitutional affairs. Furthermore, in a setting marked less by bureaucratic and hierarchic control than by the order induced through tradition and collegialism, the amalgam of beliefs, ideologies, and values embedded within the personalized life histories of its membership may be the best guide of all to the vitally important "culture" of an institution (Sproull, 1981).[8]

The importance of interviewing in the study of higher education (but bolstered by observation) is also underscored in an interesting argument by Howard Becker (1970a). Drawing upon his study of medical students, Becker argues that the values of any social group are likely to combine evidence of two polar opposites. His subjects were idealistic about their chosen profession (e.g., wanting to "help humanity" and eschewing great financial reward) and at the same time determinedly cynical about medical science and its program of professional training. In his observational data, typically gathered in group settings (e.g., at lunch and during teaching rounds), Becker found that "cynicism was the dominant language and idealism would have been laughed down" (p. 105). Consequently, he found himself systematically underestimating the idealism of his subjects—until, in interview situations, with questions asked in a sympathetic fashion, the depth of the medical ideal surfaced again and again. Conversely, notes Becker, had he relied solely upon the interview for his data, platitudes and official ideologies (mouthing the "right" slogans) might have been his sole harvest. It was only because of the acceptance emerging from his close observation of the students that informal and casual interviewing showed both cynicism *and* the admission of a deeply held (and real rather than merely voiced) idealism.

Documentation. Organizations are, of course, full of documents, in fact full of so many of varying categories (e.g., official and unofficial, draft version and final version, in-house and public, and formal and informal) that easily usable research taxonomies have not been forthcoming (Lincoln and Guba, 1985). Despite an increasing openness (under the Freedom of Information Acts) and despite the burgeoning quantity of paper produced by the photocopying machine (along with the voluminous records housed in computers), gaining access to documents and records can be a difficult and frustrating job.

Certainly an individual's right to privacy is an important ethical matter, but of even greater concern to the researcher is the presumably quite simple act of just finding appropriate and relevant documentation. Some records are readily available, of course, but many more that are filled with insights into the inner workings of an organization are deeply hidden in a committee chairperson's right-hand desk drawer, a former department head's personal papers, a secretary's unfathomable filing system, or a long-forgotten manila folder deep in the recesses of a four-drawer file. Documents, like money, tend to be "washed" as they rise from the bottom to the top of an organization, or as they proceed from inside to outside (public) view. Suitably and creatively unearthed, an organization's day-by-day flow of documentation can have important corroborative value for the qualitative researcher.

The essential research skill is a capacity for good-sleuthing. Lincoln and Guba (1985) capture the essence of the document hunt well in suggesting three principles of document or record retrieval. *First,* the researcher should begin with

> the assumption that if an event happened, some record of its exists (especially in today's heavily documented society). To put it another way, every human action "leaves tracks." (p. 278)

The tracks may not always be very readable, may often disappear only to reappear in unlikely locations, and may often lead to dark caves or dead ends. Nevertheless, successful tracking can be helped by the *second* relevant principle, that is, knowing generally (perhaps through prior observation) how the institution works: "One can imagine the tracks that *must* have been left by the action." Then, *third,* by knowing one's way around, "One knows where to look for the tracks" (Lincoln and Guba, 1985, p. 278).

Thus, document hunting and ghost tracking are two not at all dissimilar endeavors. On the other hand, the search for and access to relevant documents should be somewhat easier in higher education than in other types of organizations. Colleges and universities are fond of storing much of their documentary history in their own libraries. The loose structure of governance in institutions of higher education produces large numbers of carbon (or Xerox) copies and layers of committee approval for many, many intrainstitutional decisions. The primary tasks of teaching and research (particularly funded research) are well surrounded by legalisms requiring a full documentation of steps in the degree-conferring process (from admissions records to examination decisions), the research endeavor (from human subjects' protection to expenditure audits), and the professorial role (from affirmative action in hiring to tenure protection). Furthermore, most institutions of higher learning are unusually open (as organizations) in providing for a public scrutiny of their short- and long-term plans, budgets, and staff faculty work loads, as well as salaries, debates over institutional governance (e.g, minutes of faculty senate meetings), and even many of their institutional foibles (often gleefully highlighted in a student-run campus newspaper).

On the other hand, much of the important documentation that is produced in higher education may be accessed only with difficulty. Ethics and legality protect the records of individual students and faculty members. A Byzantine structure of committees and countervailing and overlapping approval functions typically buries many key decision-related documents in strange places. The looseness of the organization and its tradition of autonomy can lead to a wide gap between official and unofficial documentation (e.g., as a course syllabus for History 302 beers little resemblance to the catalog description of the course). And the extreme diversity of the organization (from an Office of Slavic and East European Studies, to an Integrated Systems Laboratory, to a Program in Speech Pathology) produces annually an overwhelming blizzard of paperwork—easily snowing under the researcher who, lightly clothed, sets naively out to track relevant documents.

As with the other data collection strategies, documents and records must be scrutinized carefully for their biases, inaccuracies, representativeness, and overall credibility. Interestingly, the continued ghostliness of it all is attested to in the language that Barzun and Graff (1977) use to describe the process of verification, in their book on historical method. The authors talk of "worming secrets out of manuscripts," "undoing the knots in facts," and "destroying myths" (pp. 94–97). In this subtle job of good sleuthing, the power of triangulation is again apparent. Just as ethnographers suggest the confirming assistance of the document, historians warn that good history demands the larger appreciation of a relevant culture. Barzun and Graff (1977) write:

> the investigator's original fund of knowledge must embrace even more than a well-populated chronology; it must include an understanding of how people in other eras lived and behaved, what they believed, and how they managed their institutions. This kind of mastery fills the mind with images and also with questions, which, when answered and discussed, make for what we term depth. (pp. 98–99)

Checking, Probing, Verifying, and Analyzing

Thus, quite clearly, the demands of qualitative research requires a flexible and opportunistic mixture of data collection strategies. Caveats, however, are offered by Lincoln and Guba and by Yin, Lincoln and Guba (1985) warn that naturalistic inquiry tends to be particularly vulnerable to attacks that it is "loosely-goosey." It is important, therefore, despite the emergent design characteristic, for researchers to plan carefully the measures to be taken to increase the credibility of their studies. Yin (1984) similarly argues the need for the development of a "chain of evidence" as the researcher moves through the investigation and from one state of inquiry to another.

With detailed attention to what they label "building trustworthiness," Lincoln and Guba (1985) offer the following methodological suggestions. The *first* is to give careful attention to the maintenance of at least four different types of field journals. In addition to the mandatory log of interview or observational data, the fieldworker should (1) keep careful track of his or her day-to-day activities, as a kind of calendar of appointments; (2) maintain a personal log, like a fieldwork diary, in which one reflects upon what seems to be happening in the field (e.g., initial hypotheses, introspections, and frustrations); and (3) keep a methodological log, detailing decisions made in the ongoing, emergent design of the study. Additional systematizing is offered by Miles and Huberman (1984), who suggest the use of "contact summary sheets," initial or first-level coding, and "memoing" as questions, reflections, and themes occur to the researcher.

The *second* methodological suggestion offered by Lincoln and Guba is to institute safeguards against the various forms of distortion that plague qualitative inquiry. Some of the key areas of distortion have been discussed earlier in this chapter (e.g., building rapport without going native and guarding against the Heisenberg problem). While they may not be totally eliminated, distortions can lose much of their harmful effect if they are recognized as problems (e.g., an awareness of possible fieldworker or respondent bias, and if countermeasures or checking are attempted).

Third, trustworthiness is assisted by team interaction and the use of debriefing. If a research team is engaged in the inquiry, all members of the team should meet often to share observations and to agree on the emergent design (not always easy with the heavy consumption of time in most qualitative research). Furthermore, a "debriefer" (a professional peer who is not involved in the inquiry) should have a "no holds barred conversation" with the members of the research team at periodic intervals (Lincoln and Guba, 1985, p. 283).

Fourth, trustworthiness can be helped through the accumulation of referential adequacy materials. *Referential adequacy* is a concept attributed by Lincoln and Guba to Eisner (1975). It calls for a laying aside (an "archiving") of a portion of the data that are collected in a study—not including them in the data analysis—until after tentative findings and interpretations have been reached. Then, the archived data can be retrieved (as still raw data) and tested against the conclusions already drawn. Lincoln and Guba recognize that this technique asks a lot of the fieldworker who has struggled mightily to obtain a few data, but the opportunities for comparison and corroboration are well worth the effort (Lincoln and Guba, 1985, p. 314).

Finally, *fifth,* a key suggestion and "the single most important trustworthiness technique," according to Lincoln and Guba (1985, p. 283), is the development of an "audit trail." Drawing upon the dissertation work of Halpern (1983), Lincoln and Guba urge the qualitative research team to engage an outside auditor, who will examine the records emanating from an inquiry with an eye to their confirmability, dependability, and credibility. Among the classes of records to be placed in audit would be (1) raw data (e.g., documents, field notes, and interview or survey results); (2) all data analysis efforts; (3) "process notes" (e.g., research design and trustworthiness considerations); (4) "materials relating to intentions and dispositions" (e.g., the research proposal, personal notes); and (5) "instrument development information" (e.g., interview schedules, questionnaires, and observation schemata). The auditor should be called in at the beginning of the study; should be given an opportunity to become thoroughly familiar with the inquiry and its records (making a determination of the study's auditability); and should be formally "locked in" to the audit (e.g., through a contract), with conditions of timing, format, and product clearly specified. In determining the trustworthiness of an inquiry, the auditor may undertake such actions as checking the adequacy of the overall design; making sure that findings can be traced back to the raw data; looking for inquirer bias, the extent to which negative evidence was taken into account, and whether all data have reasonably been accounted for; and exploring the extent to which the study might have been unduly influenced by "practical matters" (e.g., accommodations, subject interests, and sponsor deadlines) (Lincoln and Guba, 1985, pp. 319–327).

Data Analysis

However, despite the emphasis placed upon preparing for and planning systematically toward a defense of trustworthiness, the charge of looseness still surrounds the all-important task of *analyzing* qualitative data. In 1960, Becker and Geer observed that "the data of participant observation do not easily lend themselves to ready summary" (p. 279). In 1982, LeCompte and Goetz were still noting that "The analytic processes from which ethnographies are constructed often are vague, intuitive, and personalistic" (p. 40). The central difficulty lies in the need to maintain the flexibility, opportunism, idiosyncracy, and holism required to maximize the inductive potential of an inquiry, providing the many checks that lead the skeptical reader toward a sense of confidence in the study's report.

As mentioned earlier, Miles and Huberman (1984) have helped recently in offering a variety of displays for the presentation of qualitative data. The authors note that the typical and traditional mode of display has been the narrative—usually a descriptive report, a case study, telling the "story" of the setting under examination. The narrative, claim Miles and Huberman (1984, p. 79), is by itself a weak form of display—only vaguely ordered, often monotonous and overloading, and difficult to abstract from. As a complement to the narrative, and as an aid in data analysis, Miles and Huberman (1984) provide illustrations of numerous display formats. For example, a "context chart" can be used to show graphically the interrelationships between the participants in a setting; a "time-ordered matrix" provides a ready chronology of observed events; an "effects matrix" organizes the data in terms of one or more perceived outcomes; and a "critical incidents chart" lists the events seen to be influential or decisive during the course of some identifiable process (e.g., a period of change or an implementation phase).

As an organizing framework for understanding the treatment of qualitative (in their case, ethnographic) data, Goetz and LeCompte (1981, 1984) describe five analytic strategies that can be arrayed along a continuum of inductive constructive-subjective to deductive-enumerative-objective dimensions of research. To the left, at the most open or inductive end of the continuum, is the technique of analytic induction—a simple scanning of the data for relationships and categories, developing out of this effort some working hypotheses and typologies. A second strategy, and a small step to the right on the continuum, is the technique of "constant comparison," offered by Glaser and Strauss (1967) and summarized carefully by Lincoln and Guba (1985). With an eye toward the development of grounded theory, the art of constant comparison calls for a coding of the incidents applicable to each category of data that emerges, an integration of categories and their properties (making category properties explicit), and then a formation of the theory. At each stage of analysis, which occurs in tandem with the period of fieldwork, there is a constant comparison of newly observed events with old, of initial categorization with maturing, of an early feel for the data with later assignments of incidents to categories, and of early sense making with emergent theorizing. Data collection and processing, research implementation and research design, description and explanation—all occur simultaneously in a back-and-forth process of progressive understanding.

The three remaining data-analysis strategies discussed by Goetz and LeCompte are considered by Lincoln and Guba to be less typical of naturalistic inquiry. Each moves father to the right along the subjective-objective continuum. The first strategy, "typological analysis," uses externally derived theoretical categories, which are applied to the new data. Similarly, the fourth and fifth strategies move, respectively, toward deductive and verificatory approaches—through the use of "enumerative systems" and "standardized protocols." From these perspectives, write Lincoln and Guba (1985, p. 336), data analysis tends to be predetermined, with observations coded into categories that were decided upon well before initial entry into the field.

Perhaps a more interesting and certainly clearer exemplar of data analysis in qualitative research can be provided by drawing once again upon one of the few classic observational studies in higher education: Howard Becker et al.'s *Boys in White* (1961). Becker and his research team recognized that mere anecdote and illustration, while not uncommon forms of analysis in qualitative research, do not provide sufficient power of conclusion for the skeptical reader (Becker and Geere, 1960, p. 279). Since it is impossible for a report to include all of the data that have been collected, letting the reader form his or her own sense of understanding, some form of data reduction beyond the anecdotal must be undertaken.

And here's the rub. Where does one start? What "handle" does one place upon the data? What categories does one select (e.g., ongoing relationships, patterns of interaction, time usage, or particular events)? Becker et al., chose to analyze their medical school data from the viewpoint of "perspectives"—or the ideas and actions that the students themselves gave expression to in solving their own collective problems. The perspectives, in turn, were organized by area of application (e.g., student faculty relationships). Each perspective had to be gleaned tentatively from the data, initially from just a few incidents or a few statements, then firmed up or confirmed as it became clear that the perspective was a common conceptual framework for students in *their own* definitions of the situations they faced (Becker and Geer, 1960, p. 280).

The actual coding of their data was by observed "incidents" (often cross-coded in more than one perspective and area). In description, Becker and Geer (1960) wrote:

> If, for example, we decided that we will consider as part of our tentative formulation of the perspective that students cheat on examinations or that they believe cheating is a good way to solve their problems, then we would code separately each observation of cheating and each complete statement by a student expressing the attitude that cheating is all right. (p. 281)

As the incidents began to accumulate, it became possible to refine and describe more specifically the content of each perspective—leading toward the eventual formation of concluding statements about the attitudes and actions that, in common gave expression to the basic perspective(s) (Becker and Geer, 1960, p. 282).

In concert with the evolving definition of each perspective, the investigators fleshed out their understanding by checking each perspective's frequency, range, and collective character. For example, a frequency check might include a tabulation of the number of positive items of a perspective in use, compared with negative instances (e.g., an alternative perspective is used in dealing with the same problem). A check of range would seek to establish how widely instances of a perspective might be distributed through the observational situations. And a check of collective character would ask how widely shared a perspective seemed to be and how legitimate (e.g., a proper way to act) students deemed the perspective.

But in concluding their methodological note, Becker and Geer (1960, p. 288) recognize, with others who peruse the qualitative genre of inquiry, that there are few formal tests of researcher judgment and few clear guides to data analysis. Miles (1979) puts it in strong terms: "We found that the actual process of analysis during case-writing was essentially intuitive, primitive, and unmanageable in any rational sense" (p. 597). At best, one can ask for a reasoned calculation of the plausibility of a study's findings in the light of possible alternatives. Personality, subjectivity, "judgment calls" (McGrath, Martin, and Kulk, 1982), chance, opportunism, timing, motivation, intuition, structural conditions, and rapport: these enter into a complex process of observation and sense making, questioning and answering, collecting and categorizing, designing and theorizing, initiating and concluding, forging ahead and revising—all occurring at the same time. Solid technician, logician, and skeptic to be sure, but the qualitative researcher must also perform as a creative intellectual craftsman (Burgess, 1984)—flexible, aware, innovative, and responsive—ready to adapt creatively to a decidedly ghostly world. As in the creation of settings (Sarason, 1972), their analysis must be a work of art.

In sum, a review of qualitative research methods *in use* in the study of higher education has focused upon four components. These are (1) entrance and rapport; (2) the ethics of field study; (3) data collection and design strategies; and (4) data analysis. Entrance and rapport must frequently be carefully negotiated by the researcher. Furthermore, the fieldworker role often involves a bit of a trade-off between active involvement (even interference) in the setting under study and the opportunity to remain uninvolved, to step back for a more detached (perhaps more objective) appraisal of what is happening. As understanding deepens, so does the fieldworker's moral involvement. What are the ethical obligations of the researcher to her or his subjects, to the scholarly community, to the larger public? Understanding through qualitative inquiry can be deeply revealing, and therefore also ethically frustrating. Methodologically, its revelations are best achieved through an emergent research design, a strategy of data collection that remains open-ended and flexible and at the same time intensive, comprehensive, and thoughtful. Multiple data collection techniques (each with its own gains and losses) help to provide a thick description and a triangulated view of the research setting. And while not as tightly designed nor as much aimed at transferability as conventional inquiry, qualitative methods and their analyses are nevertheless thoroughly concerned with establishing the trustworthiness while preserving the creativity of their naturalism-based insights and interpretations.

Conclusion: The Future of Qualitative Research in Higher Education

In the end, Robertson Davies's (1982) ghost completed his Ph.D.:

> "Consider it yours," said I.
> "You meant that I may present myself at the next Convocation?"
> "Yes...."
> "I shall; Oh, I shall," he cried, ecstatically, and as he faded before my eyes I heard his voice from above the skylight in the Round Room, saying, "I go to a better place than this, confident that as a Ph.D. I shall have it in my power to make it better still." (p. 21)

There is no doubt that with the current, widespread interest in the improvement of qualitative research methods, there is an opportunity to make inquiry into the complex world of higher education "better still." In a discussion of emerging developments in postsecondary organization theory and research, Peterson (1985) urges the greater use of intensive qualitative studies but also notes that inquiry into higher education is becoming a "methodological maze"—increasingly complex and sophisticated but also confused and fragmented. A danger is that increasingly complicated research methods "may tend to make post-secondary organizational research either less useful or more difficult for administrators to comprehend" (Peterson, 1985, p. 10). It is on this note of need for usefulness and help in comprehension that this chapter ends—by examining three, final methodological issues surrounding qualitative research in higher education. These are issues in (1) the use of qualitative research in policy analysis and administration; (2) the conduct of research in a setting where one is employed; and (3) the use of multisite and multimethod research strategies.

Research and Policy

There is a developing interest in the use of qualitative inquiry to inform administrative and policy questions (Eddy and Partridge, 1978; Herriott and Friestone, 1983; Marshall, 1984; Tierney, 1985). However, it is not entirely clear just how this facilitative and practical use of fieldwork can most effectively be carried out. As Marshall (1984) puts it, two key questions are, *first*, how can qualitative researchers convince policymakers that their studies are as valuable as quantitative reports, and *second*, how can qualitative inquiry be most useful in the policymaker's search for policy-relevant information?

With its tendencies toward particularism rather than generalizability, description rather than prescription, broad rather than problem-specific study, and lengthy rather than quick-answer inquiry, qualitative research is by no means easily fit into the administrative art (Mulhauser, 1975).

Nevertheless, it has been suggested that many difficult-to-measure elements in institutional life and management not only call for enhanced understanding but are potentially significant tools of organizational improvement. For example, policy- and administration-oriented qualitative research can instructively provide (1) a richer managerial appreciation of that amorphous but powerful entity we call the *organizational culture* (Clark, 1980; Dill, 1982; Smircich, 1983; Masland, 1985; Deal and Kennedy, 1982); (2) a more thoroughgoing grasp of the subtle nuances, unintended effects, and changes and resistances that are elicited in efforts at program evaluation (Fetterman, 1984a; Guba, 1978; Tierney, 1985); and (3) an improved sense of the available mechanisms for managerial control (Cohen and March, 1974; March and Olsen, 1976) plus leadership (Yukl, 1981; Pfeffer, 1977)—amidst an institutional environment known for its weak, formal controls and its ambiguous attitudes toward administrative leadership.

As a special branch of qualitative inquiry, policy-oriented research is, however, filled with hazards. Tierney (1985, p. 102) suggests that the researcher should avoid pressures toward such problem-specific questions as: How can the institution "raise a half million dollars from recently graduated alumni"? Unless such questions can be broadened (e.g., a look at the quality of life at the school with institutional giving as a component), the fieldworker should stay well out of the practical problems arena. Similarly, Everhart (1984) warns that in policy research, the fieldworker may be constrained by funding agencies of governing bodies toward results in narrowly prespecified areas or toward investigations that use only certain data sets—giving up in the process the qualitative researcher's freedom to make the most of whatever the research setting provides.

Finally, Marshall (1984) suggests that policy-oriented research may require an array of special fieldworker approaches and abilities that would not be expected in less political environments. For example, researchers may need to persuade reluctant administrators that noncooperation in the provision of information could embarrass the institution. Or they may find that overcoming barriers to access and cooperation requires that "they appear as valuable, politically knowledgeable people with important connections in high places" (p. 239). However, Marshall (1984, p. 239) also refers to the Becker and Meyers (1974) finding that by often blithely walking unannounced into a "top official's inner sanctum as if one belonged there," one can successfully produce a flow of data. And a valuable fieldworker role in a charged organizational environment may often be a conscious mask of wide-eyed, naive innocence—appearing harmless as a listener but fascinated, and amply offering such encouraging expressions as "Really?" and "No kidding!" (Marshall, 1984, p. 241).

Researching at Home

It makes good sense to assume that many qualitative researchers who wish to study institutions of higher learning will focus, at least initially, upon settings in which they are employed. The convenience that accrues, plus ease of access and the head start of institutional foreknowledge (even to the point of knowing where many "ghosts" are hiding), augurs well for a search for understanding that begins at home. The gains and losses associated with insider versus outsider research have, of course, been summarized earlier in this chapter. Assuming stranger value within a setting to gain the distance and detachment that is often associated with creative and insightful data analysis must be offset against the benefits of cultural familiarity and the understanding in depth that can accompany the insider role.

Wade (1984) and Rossman (1984) have both described their experiences as researchers in higher education settings where they are also employed. The experience of "switching hats" was particularly problematic for Wade, for she was employed as a student affairs administrator and was simultaneously engaged in the study of the world of black undergraduate students at a major university. Understandably, many of her subjects had questions about her real place (organizational spy?) in the university community, distrusting her ability to change roles from administrator to researcher without an ongoing residue of superior-subordinate attitudes and perspectives. She found herself having to pay dues for the intrusion into her subjects' lives by providing them with special counseling, insider information, and representation (e.g., defending their interests within the university environment).

Wade (1984, p. 219) observed that persons engaged in inquiry within their place of employment can put aside any thoughts of operating as totally unaligned researchers. Indeed, both she and Rossman (who studied Ph.D. candidates) found that, to be observers, it was necessary to carve out for themselves a new *employment* role: nonjudgmental observer to be sure, a sympathetic ear for gripes and frustrations, an information provider, a finder of bureaucratic loopholes, and even occasionally a spokesperson. As mentioned earlier, Pelto and Pelto (1978) warned that the local people do not forget that the anthropologist will ultimately leave them. However, the researcher "at home" should be warned that the local people know the researcher will *not* be leaving them.

Multisite and Multimethod Research

Herriott and Firestone (1983) observe that the last decade has "seen the emergence of a new form of qualitative research, one intended to strengthen its ability to generalize while preserving in-depth description" (p. 14). This new form is the multisite qualitative study. The multisite study is aimed at cross-site comparison without a loss of within-site understanding.

This combination of depth and breadth, of generalization along with thoroughgoing description, is not at all an easy methodological task (Cook and Reichardt, 1979; McGrath, 1982). Among the key issues are the following: *First,* to what extent do instrumentation and the focus of observation need to be standardized? Although a single researcher can conceivably study more than one setting (but not many more), the likelihood is that a team of researchers will be used. When the researcher is the central instrument of data collection, does one need to structure away idiosyncratic researcher bias and perspective, as well as the impact of within-site variability, by demanding common observer foci and an agreed sense of "just what it is we're looking for"? Similarly, *second,* does multisite qualitative research require (or at least lead to) a stress upon data reduction toward standardization and ease of comparison at the possible expense of potentially meaningful, specific detail? And, *third,* do the gains of a broader understanding using (presumably) less time in data collection per site offset the benefits of long-term immersion at a single site (Firestone and Herriott, 1984; Miles, 1979)?

One gain in multisite research is a strengthened opportunity (even a near necessity) to mix qualitative and quantitative methods (Cook and Reichardt, 1979; Jick, 1979; Yin, 1984). Jick (1979, pp. 608–609) suggests that efforts to do so can help produce greater confidence in results, elicit creativity in problem definition, discover unusual or deviant dimensions of phenomena, and lead to more inclusive theorizing. Such approaches as the case survey (Yin and Heald, 1975) and the case cluster method (McClintock, Brannan, and Maynard-Moody, 1979) are suggested as ways to create common units of analysis among separate case studies.

A Final Word

Nevertheless, as a concluding thought to this chapter, and as a concluding thought to our interest in improving the methodology (and hence the credibility) of qualitative research, it should be noted, as anthropologist Harry F. Wolcott (1985) warns us, that a careful and complete articulation of its *method* is *not* the central concern of the qualitative (specifically, the ethnographic) research tradition. Wolcott (1985) writes:

> to the ethnographer *method itself is not all that important.* It never was and never will be. What ethnographers strive for is to "get it right," and in the long run the elusive "it" of determining just

what constitutes the cultural dimensions of behavior in any particular social setting creates more difficulty than the also-elusive rightness of the account. (p. 201)

Neither field technique, nor access to and rapport with subjects, nor the length and depth of site-level immersion are of the importance that is achieved in a sense of cultural understanding (*Verstehen*) that is gained from a broad observation of human behavior in its social context. Concludes Wolcott (1985): "Let educational researchers of other persuasions do the counting and measuring they do so well. Ethnographers have their commitment . . . to cultural interpretation" (p. 202). As in Robertson Davies's (1982) story of the college ghost, it is perhaps the qualitative researcher more than any other scientist who quite simply appreciates the need to take the time (sometimes very large blocks of it) necessary to perform the "act of mercy" of a bit of insight into (and an understanding of) what our strange institutions of higher learning are all about:

> "You have come at last," said the Ghost. "I have waited for you long—but of course you are busy. Every professor in this university is busy. He is talking, or he is pursuing, or he is in a journey, or preadventure he sleepeth. But none has time for an act of mercy." (p. 15).

Acknowledgements. A sincere thank you is due Yvonna S. Lincoln, Ernest T. Pascarella, and Van Cleve Morris for their forthrightly critical and extremely helpful comments on an earlier draft of this manuscript.

Notes

1. Rist (1979) notes that Malinowski (1922) is one of the first anthropologists to employ the term *ethnography* as a descriptor of his observation of and participation in the tribal cultures of Trobriand Islanders.

2. The oldest tradition in ethnography is the study of culture as an integrated whole (holism). Sanday (1979) shows, however, that the modern ethnographic paradigm is internally differentiated, with less emphasis upon holism in many quarters and more emphasis upon the provision of "observational data on preselected functionally relevant categories" (p. 536).

3. Weber's use of *Verstehen* is actually interpreted fully and given its modern research meaning by Talcott Parsons, in his edited volume of Weber's *Theory of Social and Economic Organization* (1947, pp. 87–88).

4. A recent approach to the problem of value-laden inquiry, which has received the philosophical label *critical theory*, asserts that research is inevitably value-determined and that all inquiry therefore serves some value agenda. Critical theorists have been active in exploring the metaphors, ideologies, and social structures (particularly socioeconomic class) that pervade our ways of thinking about the world (Lincoln and Guba, 1985; Morgan, 1980; Ortony, 1979; Schubert, 1986).

5. This is, of course, an occurrence that is by no means limited to qualitative research methods and observational studies. As Lincoln and Guba (1985, p. 95) point out, famous instances of measurement effect upon the phenomena under study are widely known (e.g., the Hawthorne effect and the Pygmalion effect).

6. Burgess (1984, pp. 83–84) makes clear that for most researchers, the adoption of *one* fieldworker role, from among these four, is less likely than the choice of different phases and places in the course of the research. Roles are seldom consistent throughout a study and may vary with differing informants and subsettings.

7. One attractive point flowing naturally out of the concept of triangulation is the argument for a mixing of both qualitative and quantitative methods (Jick, 1979; Ianni and Orr, 1979). The central difficulty, however, is that graduate training programs seldom prepare individuals adequately in more than one method, and researchers fall easily into the habit of using that one method, as it is most comfortable for them, in study after study, whatever the research problem or field setting (McGrath, Martin, and Kulka, 1982).

8. Donovan (1964) used the technique of life history informatively in an ambitious study (combining questionnaire and interview strategies) of nearly 300 faculty members at Catholic colleges and universities—assembling his data into a "social profile of the Catholic academic man" (p. 11).

References

Adams, R.N., and Preiss, J.J. (1960). *Human Organization Research: Field Relations and Techniques.* Homewood, IL: Dorsey.

Aguilar, J.L. (1981). Insider research: an ethnography of a debate. In D.A. Messerschmidt (ed.), *Anthropologists at Home in North America: Methods and Issues in the Study of One's Own Society,* pp. 15–26. Cambridge: Cambridge University Press.

Baldridge, J.J. (1971). *Power and Conflict in the University: Research in the Sociology of Complex Organizations.* New York: Wiley.

Barnes, J.A. (1970). Some ethical problems in modern fieldwork. In W.J. Filstead, *Qualitative Methodology: Firsthand Involvement with the Social World,* pp. 235–260. Chicago: Markham.

Barzun, J. (1968). *The American University: How It Runs, Where It Is Going.* New York: Harper & Row.

Barzun, J., and Graff, H.F. (1977). *The Modern Researcher* (3rd ed.). New York: Harcourt Brace Jovanovich.

Becker, H.S. (1970a). Interviewing medical students. In Filstead, *Qualitative Methodology: Firsthand Involvement with the Social World,* pp. 103–106.

Becker, H.S. (1970b). Problems of inference and proof in participant observation. In Filstead, *Qualitative Methodology: Firsthand Involvement with the Social World.* pp. 189–201. Markham.

Becker, H.S., and Geer, B. (1960). Latent culture. *Administrative Science Quarterly* 5; 303–313.

Becker, H.S., Geer, B., Hughes, E.C., and Strauss, A.L. (1961). *Boys in White: Student Cultures in Medical School.* Chicago: University of Chicago Press.

Becker, H.S., Geer, B., and Hughes, E.C. (1968). *Making the Grade: The Academic Side of College Life.* New York: Wiley.

Becker, T.M., and Meyers, P.R. (1974). Empathy and bravado: Interviewing reluctant bureaucrats. *Public Opinion Quarterly* 38; 605–613.

Bell, D. (1966). *The Reforming of General Education: The Columbia College Experience in Its Natural Setting.* New York: Columbia University Press.

Berger, P.L., and Luckman, T. (1973). *The Social Construction of Reality.* London: Penguin.

Berreman, G.D. (1962). *Behind Many Masks: Ethnography and Impression Management in a Himalayan Village.* Ithaca, NY: Society for Applied Anthropology.

Bess, J.L. ed. (1984). *College and University Organization: Insights from the Behavioral Sciences.* New York: New York University Press.

Best, J.H. (Ed.). (1983). *Historical Inquiry in Education: A Research Agenda.* Washington, DC: American Educational Research Association.

Blau, P.M. (1973). *The Organization of Academic Work.* New York: Wiley.

Bogdan, R. (1972). *Participant Observation in Organizational Settings.* Syracuse, NY: Syracuse University Press.

Bogdan, R., and Biklen, S.K. (1982). *Qualitative Research for Education.* Boston: Allyn & Bacon.

Bolman, L.G., and Deal, T.E. (1984). *Modern Approaches to Understanding and Managing Organizations.* San Francisco: Jossey-Bass.

Burgess, R.G. (1984). *In the Field: An Introduction to Field Research.* London: George Allen & Unwin.

Bushnell, J.H. (1962). Student culture at Vassar. In N. Sanford (ed.), *The American College.* New York: Wiley.

Campbell, D.T. (1975). Degrees of freedom and the case study. *Comparative Political Studies* 8; 178–193.

Campbell, D.T. (1970). Natural selection as an epistemological model. In R. Naroll and R. Cohen (eds.), *A Handbook of Cultural Anthropology.* Garden City, NY: Natural History Press.

Campbell, D.T., and Stanely, J.C. (1963). *Experimental and Quasi–Experimental Designs for Research.* Chicago: Rand McNally.

Caplow, T., and McGee, R.J. (1958). *The Academic Marketplace.* New York: Basic Books.

Clark, B.R. (1983). *The Higher Education System: Academic Organization in Cross-National Perspective.* Berkeley: University of California Press.

Clark, B.R. (1980). *Academic Culture* (Working paper, IHERG-42). New haven, CT: Yale University, Higher Education Research Group.

Clark, B.R. (1972). The organizational saga in higher education. *Administrative Science Quarterly* 17:179–194.

Clark, B.R. (1970). *The Distinctive College: Antioch, Reed and Swarthmore.* Chicago: Aldine.

Clark, B.R. (1960). *The Open Door College: A Case Study.* New York: McGraw-Hill.

Cohen, M.D., and March, J.G. (1974). *Leadership and Ambiguity: The American College President.* New York: McGraw-Hill.

Cohen, R., and Naroll, R. (1970). Method in cultural anthropology. In R. Naroll and R. Cohen (eds.), *A Handbook of Cultural Anthropology.* Garden City, NY: Natural History Press.

Cook, T.D. and Reichardt, C.S., eds. (1979). *Qualitative and Quantitative Methods in Evaluation.* Beverly Hills, CA: Sage.

Cottle, T.J. (1977). *College—Reward and Betrayal.* Chicago: University of Chicago Press.

Crane, D. (1972). *Invisible Colleges: Diffusion of Knowledge in Scientific Communities.* Chicago: University of Chicago Press.

Cronbach, L.J. and Suppes, P. (1969). *Research for Tomorrow's Schools: Disciplined Inquiry in Education.* New York: Macmillan.

Cusick, P.A. (1983). *The Egalitarial Ideal and the American High School.* New York: Longman.

Daalder, H., and Shils, E. (1982). *Universities, Politicians, and Bureaucrats: Europe and the United States.* Cambridge: Cambridge University Press.

Davies, R. (1982). The ghost who vanished by degrees. *High Spirits.* Markham, Ontario: Penguin.

Deal, T.E., and Kennedy, A.A. (1982). *Corporate Cultures: The Rites and Rituals of Corporate Life.* Reading, MA: Addison-Wesley.

Dentler, R.A., Baltzell, C., and Sullivan, D.J. (1983). *University on Trial: The Case of the University of North Carolina,* Cambridge, MA: Abt Books.

Denzin, N.K. (1970). *The Research Act: Theoretical Introduction to Sociological Methods.* Chicago: Aldine.

Denzin, N.K. (1978). *Sociological Methods.* New York: McGraw-Hill.

Dill, D.D. (1982). The management of academic culture: Notes on the management of meaning and social integration. *Higher Education* 11:303–320.

Donovan, J.D. (1964). *The Academic Man in the Catholic College*. New York: Sheed & Ward.

Dorr-Bremme, D.W. (1985). Ethnographic evaluation: A theory and method. *Educational Evaluation and Policy Analysis* 7:65–83.

Douglas, J.D. (1976). *Investigative Social Research*. Beverly Hills, CA: Sage.

Eddy, E.M., and Partridge, W.L. (eds.). (1978). *Applied Anthropology in America*. New York: Columbia University Press.

Eisner, E.W. (1975). *The Perceptive Eye: Toward the Reformulation of Educational Evaluation*. Occasional papers of the Stanford Evaluation Consortium. Stanford, CA: Stanford University.

Ellen, R.F. (1984). *Ethnographic Research: A Guide to General Conduct*. London: Academic Press.

Evans-Pritchard, E.E. (1937). *Witchcraft, Oracles and Magic Among the Azande*. London: Oxford University Press.

Everhart, R.B. (1984). Dilemmas of fieldwork in policy research: A critique. *Anthropology and Education Quarterly* 15:252–258.

Fetterman, D.M.,ed. (1984a). *Ethnography in Educational Evaluation*. Beverly Hills, CA: Sage.

Fetterman, D.M. (1984b). Ethnography in educational research: The dynamics of diffusion. In Fetterman *Ethnography in Educational Evaluation*, pp. 21–35.

Fetterman, D.M. (1984c). Guilty knowledge, dirty hands, and other ethical dilemmas: The hazards of contract research. In Fetterman, ed., *Ethnography in Educational Evaluation*, pp. 211–236.

Fichter, J.H., and Kolb, W.L. (1970). Ethical limitations on sociological reporting. In Fielstead, *Qualitative Methodology: Firsthand Involvement with the Social World*, pp. 261–274. Chicago: Markham.

Filstead, W.J., ed. (1970). *Qualitative Methodology: Firsthand Involvement with the Social World*. Chicago: Markham.

Firestone, W.A., and Herriott, R.E. (1984). Multisite qualitative policy research: Some design and implementation issues. In Fetterman, *Ethnography in Educational Evaluation*, pp. 63–88.

Freeman, D. (1983). *Margaret Mead and Samoa: The Making and Unmaking of an Anthropological Myth*. Cambridge: Harvard University Press.

Garfinkel, H. (1967). *Studies in Ethnomethodology*. Englewood Cliffs, NJ: Prentice-Hall.

Geer, B. (1970). Studying a college. In R.W. Habenstein (ed.), *Pathways to Data: Field Methods for Studying Ongoing Social Organizations*. Chicago: Aldine.

Geertz, C. (ed.). (1973). *The Interpretation of Cultures*. New York: Basic Books.

Glaser, B.G., and Strauss, A.L. (1967). *The Discovery of Grounded Theory*. Chicago: Aldine.

Goetz, J.P., and LeCompte, M.D. (1984). *Ethnography and Qualitative Design in Educational Research*. Orlando, FL: Academic Press.

Goetz, J.P. and LeCompte, M.D. (1981). Ethnographic research and the problem of data reduction. *Anthropology and Education Quarterly* 12:51–70.

Gold, R.L. (1958). Roles in sociological field observations. *Social Forces* 36:217–223.

Grant, G., and Riesman, D. (1978). *The Perpetual Dream: Reform and Experiment in the American College.* Chicago: University of Chicago Press.

Guba, E.G. (1978). *Toward a Methodology of Naturalistic Inquiry in Educational Evaluation.* Los Angeles: University of California Center for the Study of Evaluation.

Guba, E.G., and Lincoln, Y.S. (1981). *Effective Evaluation.* San Francisco: Jossey-Bass.

Habenstein, R.W., ed. (1970). *Pathways to Data: Field Methods for Studying Ongoing Social Organizations.* Chicago: Aldine.

Halpern, E.S. (1983). *Auditing Naturalistic Inquiries: The Development and Application of a Model.* Unpublished doctoral dissertation, Indiana University.

Hanson, M. (1984). Exploration of mixed metaphors in educational administration research. *Issues in Education* 11:167–185.

Hedberg, B. (1981). How organizations learn and unlearn. In P.C. Nystrom and W.H. Starbuck (eds.), *Handbook of Organizational Design,* Vol. 1. Oxford: Oxford University Press.

Heisenberg, W. (1958). *Physics and Philosophy.* New York: Harper & Row.

Hendricks, G. (1975). University registration systems: A study of social process. *Human Organization* 34:173–181.

Herriott, R.E., and Firestone, W.A. (1983). Multisite qualitative policy research: Optimizing description and generalizability. *Educational Researcher* 12(February): 14–19.

Husserl, E. (1952). *Ideals: General Introduction to Pure Phenomenology.* New York: Macmillan.

Ianni, F.A.J., and Orr, M.T. (1979). Toward a rapprochement of quantitative and qualitative methodologies. In T.D. Cook and C.S. Reichardt (eds.), *Qualitative and Quantitative Methods in Evaluation Research.* Beverly Hills, CA: Sage.

James, H. (1930). *Charles W. Eliot, President of Harvard University, 1869–1909.* Boston: Houghton Mifflin.

Jehenson, R. (1973). A phenomenological approach to the study of the formal organization. In G. Psathas (ed.), *Phenomenological Sociology: Issues and Applications.* New York: Wiley.

Jelinek, M., Smircich, L., and Hirsch, P., eds. (1983). Organizational culture. *Administrative Science Quarterly* 28:331–338.

Jick, T.D. (1979). Mixing qualitative and quantitative methods: triangulation in action. *Administrative Science Quarterly* 24:602–611.

Kerr, C. (1964). *The Uses of the University.* Cambridge: Harvard University Press.

Krathwohl, D.R. (1980). The myth of value-free evaluation. *Educational Evaluation and Policy Analysis* 2:37–45.

Lamont, L. (1979). *Campus Shock: A Firsthand Report on College Life Today.* New York: E.P. Dutton.

LeCompte, M.D., and Goetz, J.P. (1982). Problems of reliability and validity in ethnographic research. *Review of Educational Research* 52:31–60.

Levine, R.A. (1970). Research design in anthropological field work. In R. Naroll and R. Cohen (eds.), *A Handbook of Method in Cultural Anthropology.* Garden City, NY: Natural History Press.

Lincoln, Y.S. and Guba, E.G. (1985). *Naturalistic Inquiry.* Beverly Hills, CA: Sage.

Lipsky, M. (1980). *Street-Level Bureaucracy: Dilemmas of the Individual in Public Services.* New York: Russell Sage.

London, II.B. (1978). *The Culture of a Community College.* New York: Praeger.

Malinowski, B. (1922). *The Argonauts of the Western Pacific.* London: Routledge & Kegan Paul.

March, J.G., and Olsen, J.P. (1976). *Ambiguity and Choice in Organizations.* Bergen, Norway: Universitetsforlaget.

Marshall, C. (1984). Elites, bureaucrats, ostriches, and pussycats: Managing research in policy settings. *Anthropology and Education Quarterly* 15:235–251.

Marshall, C. (1984). Research dilemmas in administration and policy settings: An introduction to the special issue. *Anthropology and Education Quarterly* 15:194–201.

Martin, J., Feldman, M.S., Hatch, M.J., and Sitkin, S.B. (1983). The uniqueness paradox in organizational stories. *Administrative Science Quarterly* 28:438–453.

Masland, A.T. (1985). Organizational culture in the study of higher education. *The Review of Higher Education* 8:157–168.

Maslow, A. (1965). *Eupsychian Management.* Homewood, IL: Richard Irwin.

Massarik, F. (1981). The interviewing process re-examined. In P. Reason and J. Rowan (eds.), *Human Inquiry: A Sourcebook of New Paradigm Research.* New York: Wiley.

Mattingly, P.H. (1983). Structures over time: Institutional history. In J.H. Best (ed.), *Historical Inquiry in Education: A Research Agenda.* Washington, DC: American Educational Research Association.

McCall, G.J., and Simmons, J.L., eds. (1969). *Issues in Participant Observation: A Text and Reader.* Reading, MA: Addison-Wesley.

McClintock, C.C., Brannon, D., and Maynard-Moody, S. (1979). Applying the logic of sample surveys to qualitative case studies: The case cluster method. *Administrative Science Quarterly* 24:612–629.

McDonald, S., Redlinger, L., and Edwards, W. (1980). *The Heisenberg Problem: Comments on Observer Effects in the Field Work Situation.* Paper presented at the Annual Meeting of the American Educational Research Association, Boston, April.

McGrath, J.E. (1982). Dilematics: The study of research choices and dilemmas. In J.E. McGrath, J. Martin, and R.A. Kulka (eds.), *Judgment Calls in Research.* Beverly Hills, CA: Sage.

McGrath, J.E., Martin, J., and Kulka, R.A. (1982). *Judgment Calls in Research.* Beverly Hills, CA: Sage.

McHenry, D.E., and Associates (eds.). (1977). *Academic Departments.* San Francisco: Jossey-Bass.

Mehan, H., and Wood, H. (1975). *The Reality of Ethnomethodology.* New York: Wiley.

Messerschmidt, D.A. (ed.). (1981). *Anthropologists at Home in North America: Methods and Issues in the Study of One's Own Society.* Cambridge: Cambridge University Press.

Miles, M. (1979). Qualitative data as attractive nuisance: The problem of analysis. *Administrative Science Quarterly* 24:590–601.

Miles, M., and Huberman, A.M. (1984). *Qualitative Data Analysis: A Sourcebook of New Methods.* Beverly Hills, CA: Sage.

Miller, P. (1978). Administrative orientations from anthropology. In E. Eddy and W. Partridge (eds.), *Applied Anthropology in America*. New York: Columbia University Press.

Mintzberg, H. (1973). *The Nature of Managerial Work*. New York: Harper & Row.

Morgan, G. (1980). Paradigms, metaphors, and puzzle solving in organization theory. *Administrative Science Quarterly* 25:605–621.

Morison, S.E. (1935). *The Founding of Harvard College*. Cambridge: Harvard University Press.

Morris, V.C. (1981). *Deaning: Middle Management in Academe*. Urbana, IL: University of Illinois Press.

Morris, V.C. (1984). Plato's "philosopher-king": Position impossible. In P.A. Sala (ed.), *Ethics, Education and Administrative Decisions: A Book of Readings*, pp. 129–133. New York: Peter Lang.

Morris, V.C., Crowson, R., Porter-Gehrie, C., and Hurwitz, Jr., E. (1984). *Principals in Action: The Reality of Managing Schools*. Columbus, OH: Charles E. Merrill.

Mulhauser, F. (1975). Ethnography and educational policy. *Human Organization* 34:311–319.

Myrdal, G. (1969). *Objectivity in Social Research*. New York: Pantheon Books.

Naroll, R., and Cohen, R. (eds.). (1970). *A Handbook of Method in Cultural Anthropology*. Garden City, NY: Natural History Press.

Newcomb, T. (1943). *Personality and Social Change: Attitude Formation in a Student Community*. New York: Dryden Press.

Ortony, A., ed. (1979). *Metaphor and Thought*. Cambridge: Cambridge University Press.

Owens, R.G. (1982). Methodological rigor in naturalistic inquiry: Some issues and answers. *Educational Administration Quarterly* 18:1–21.

Pace, C.R. (1968). Methods of describing college cultures. In K. Yamamoto (ed.). *The College Student and His Culture*, pp. 193–205. Boston: Houghton Mifflin.

Pascarella, E.T. (1985). College environmental influences on learning and cognitive development: A critical review and synthesis. In J.C. Smart (ed.), *Higher Education: Handbook of Theory and Research*, Vol. I, pp. 1–61. New York: Agathon Press.

Patterson, F. and Longworth, C.R. (1966). *The Making of a College*. Cambridge, MA: MIT Press.

Pelto, P.J., and Pelto, G.H. (1978). *Anthropological Research: The Structure of Inquiry* (2nd ed.). Cambridge: Cambridge University Press.

Perkins, J.A., ed. (1973). *The University as an Organization*. New York: McGraw-Hill.

Perkins, J.A. (1966). *The University in Transition*. Princeton, NJ: Princeton University Press.

Peterson, M.W. (1985). Emerging developments in postsecondary organization theory and research: Fragmentation or integration. *Educational Researcher* 14:5–12.

Pfeffer, J. (1977). The ambiguity of leadership. *Academy of Management Review* 2:104–112.

Psathas, G. (ed.). (1979). *Everyday Language: Studies in Ethnomethodology*. New York: Irvington.

Psathas, G. (ed.). (1973). *Phenomenological Sociology: Issues and Applications*. New York: Wiley.

Reisman, D. (1958). *Constraint and Variety in American Education*. Garden City, NY: Doubleday.

Reisman, D. (1980). *On Higher Education: The Academic Enterprise in an Era of Rising Student Consumerism*. San Francisco: Jossey-Bass.

Reisman, D., and Jencks, C. (1962). The viability of the American college. In N. Sanford (ed.), *The American College*. New York: Wiley.

Richardson, S.A. (1970). Training in field relations skills. In W.J. Filstead, *Qualitative Methodology: Firsthand Involvement with the Social World*, pp. 155–163.

Rist, R.C. (1975). Ethnographic techniques and the study of an urban school. *Urban Education* 10:86–108.

Rist, R.C. (1979). On the means of knowing: Qualitative research in education. *New York Education Quarterly* (Summer), 17–21.

Rossman, G.B. (1984). "I owe you one": Considerations of role and reciprocity in a study of graduate education for school administrators. *Anthropology and Education Quarterly* 15:225–233.

Salancik, G.R., and Pfeffer, J. (1974). The bases and use of power in organizational decision making: The case of the university. *Administrative Science Quarterly* 19:453–473.

Sanday, P.R. (1979). The ethnographic paradigm(s). *Administrative Science Quarterly* 24:527–538.

Sarason, S.B. (1972). *The Creation of Settings and the Future of Societies*. San Francisco: Jossey-Bass.

Sarason, S.B. (1982). *The Culture of the School and the Problem of Change* (2nd ed.). Boston: Allyn & Bacon.

Schubert, W.H. (1986). *Curriculum: Perspective, Paradigm, and Possibility*. New York: Macmillan.

Schutz, A. (1962, 1964). *Collected Papers, Vols. 1 and 2*. The Hague: Martinus Nijhoff.

Schutz, A. (1967). *The Phenomenology of the Social World*. Evanston, IL: Northwestern University Press.

Schwartz, H., and Jacobs, J. (1979). *Qualitative Sociology: A Method to the Madness*. New York: Free Press.

Seeley, J.R. (1967). *The University in America*. Santa Barbara, CA: Center for the Study of Democratic Institutions.

Smircich, L. (1983). Concepts of culture and organizational analysis. *Administrative Science Quarterly* 28:339–358.

Smith, J.K., and Heshusius, L. 91986). Closing down the conversation: The end of the quantitative— qualitative debate among educational inquirers. *Educational Researcher* 15:4–12.

Spradley, J.P. (1980). *Participant Observation*. New York: Holt, Rinehart, & Winston.

Sproull, L.S. (1981). Beliefs in organizations. In P.C. Nystrom and W.H. Starbuck (eds.), *Handbook of Organizational Design*, Vol. 2. Oxford: University Press.

Stephenson, J.B., and Greer, L.S. (1981). Ethnographers in their own cultures: Two Appalachian cases. *Human Organization* 40:123–130.

Storr, R. (1966). *Harper's University: The Beginnings. A History of the University of Chicago*. Chicago: University of Chicago Press.

Tierney, W.G. (1985). Ethnography: An alternative evaluation methodology. *The Review of Higher Education* 8:93–105.

Tierney, W.G. (1983). Governance by conversation: An essay on the structure, function, and communicative codes of a faculty senate. *Human Organization* 43:172–177.

Valentine, C.A. (1968). *Culture and Poverty: Critique and Counterproposals*. Chicago: University of Chicago Press.

Van Maanen, J. (1976). Breaking-in: Socialization to work. In R. Dubin (ed.), *Handbook of Work, Organization, and Society*. Chicago: Rand McNally.

Van Maanen, J. (1984). Doing new things in old ways: The chains of socialization. In J.L. Bess (ed.), *College and University Organization: Insights from the Behavioral Sciences*, pp. 211–247. New York: New York University Press.

Van Maanen, J. (1979a). The fact of fiction in organizational ethnography. *Administrative Science Quarterly* 24:539–550.

Van Maanen, J., ed. (1979b). Qualitative methodology. *Administrative Science Quarterly* 24:520–526.

Van Maanen, J., and Schein, E.H. (1979). Toward a theory of organizational socialization. In B. Staw (ed.), *Research in Organizational Behavior*, Vol. 1. Greenwich, CT: JAI Press.

Van Maanen, J., Dobbs, Jr., J.M., and Faulkner, R.R. (1982). *Varieties of Qualitative Research*. Beverly Hills, CA: Sage.

Wade, J.E. (1984). Role boundaries and paying back: "Switching hats" in participant observation. *Anthropology and Education Quarterly* 15:211–224.

Wax, R.H. (1971). *Doing Fieldwork: Warnings and Advice*. Chicago: University of Chicago Press.

Webb, E.J., Campbell, D.T., Schwartz, R.D., and Sechrest, L. (1966). *Unobtrusive Measures: Nonreactive Research in the Social Sciences*. Chicago: Rand McNally.

Weber, M. (1947). *The Theory of Social and Economic Organization*, ed by T. Parsons. New York: Free Press.

Weick, K.E. (1984). Contradictions in a community of scholars: The cohesion accuracy tradeoff. In J.L. Bess (ed.), *College and University Organization: Insights from the Behavioral Sciences*, pp. 15–29. New York: New York University Press.

Weick, K.E. (1976). Educational organizations as loosely coupled systems. *Administrative Science Quarterly* 21:1–19.

William, G. (1958). *Some of My Best Friends Are Professors*. New York: Abelard–Schuman.

Wilson, S. (1977). The use of ethnographic techniques in educational research. *Review of Educational Research* 47:245–265.

Wolcott, H.F. (1984). Ethnographers sans ethnography. In Fetterman, *Ethnography in Educational Evaluation*, pp. 177–210.

Wolcott, H.F. (1985). On ethnographic intent. *Educational Administration Quarterly* 21:187–203.

Yin, R.K. (1984). *Case Study Research: Design and Methods*. Beverly Hills, CA: Sage.

Yin, R.K., and Heald, K.A. (1975). Using the case survey method to analyze policy studies. *Administrative Science Quarterly* 20:371–381.

Yukl, G.A. (1981). *Leadership In Organizations*. Englewood Cliffs, NJ: Prentice Hall.

Critical Ethnography in Education: Origins, Current Status, and New Directions

GARY L. ANDERSON

Interpretivist movements in anthropology and sociology have recently merged with neo-Marxist and feminist theory to produce a unique genre of research in the field of eduction known as "critical ethnography." Critical ethnographers seek research accounts sensitive to the dialectical relationship between the social structural constraints on human actors and the relative autonomy of human agency. Unlike other interpretivist research, the overriding goal of critical ethnography is to free individuals from sources of domination and repression. This review traces the development of critical ethnography in education, including a brief discussion of its view of validity; discusses its current status as a research genre; and describes criticisms and suggests new directions.

Critical ethnography in the field of eduction is the result of the following dialectic: On one hand, critical ethnography has grown out of dissatisfaction with social accounts of "structures" like class, patriarchy, and racism in which real human actors never appear. On the other hand, it has grown out of dissatisfaction with cultural accounts of human actors in which broad structural constraints like class, patriarchy, and racism never appear. Critical theorists in education have tended to view ethnographers as too atheoretical and neutral in their approach to research. Ethnographers have tended to view critical theorists as too theory driven and biased in their research. And so it goes.

This methodological and theoretical debate in the field of education parallels a reassessment of dominant ideas and methodologies under way in the social sciences and humanities. Geertz's (1983) phrase "blurred genres" characterizes the fluid borrowing that has occurred across disciplines, bringing with it new perspectives and new debates in educational research. In this review I trace the development of critical ethnography in the field of education, including a brief discussion of its view of validity; discuss its current status as a research genre; and describe criticisms and suggest new directions.

In the social sciences, the political and intellectual ferment of the 1960s challenged the grand theories and methodological orthodoxy of a previous generation. In sociology the Parsonian notions of function and system equilibrium have been viewed by many as too ahistorical and apolitical to do justice to the richness and diversity of social life. In anthropology, analysis shifted away from taxonomic descriptions of behavior and social structure toward thick descriptions and interpretations of symbol and meaning. And, everywhere, research methods tied to the assumptions of a positivism borrowed from the natural sciences are increasingly viewed as incapable of providing conceptually sophisticated accounts of social reality.

In most accounts by historians of science, a new paradigm challenges the dominant paradigm in the field. What characterizes the present postpositivist world of the social sciences is a continued attack on positivism with no single clearly conceived alternative. Within disciplines and fields generally, broad paradigms and grand theories are increasingly found lacking in their ability to provide guidance in asking and answering persistent and seemingly intractable social questions. In periods when grand theories are in disarray, attention turns to epistemological issues and modes of representation. According to Marcus and Fischer (1986),

> The most interesting theoretical debates in a number of fields have shifted from the level of substantive theoretical issues to the level of method, to problems of epistemology, interpretation, and discursive forms of representation themselves. (p. 9)

Thus, the current situation, although chaotic, is also full of opportunity. Current theoretical and methodological dissatisfaction has led to a resurgence of interest in intellectual traditions such as phenomenology, hermeneutics, feminism, and Marxism. Critical ethnography as a form of representation and interpretation of social reality is one of the many methodological experiments that have grown out of the ferment.

Critical Ethnography and Education

In the field of education, critical ethnography is the result of the convergence of two largely independent trends in epistemology and social theory. The epistemological movement was the result of a shift in research paradigms within the field of education that reflected an attempt to "break out of the conceptual cul-de-sac of quantitative methods" (Rist, 1980, p. 8). Of all the qualitative research traditions available, ethnography most captured the imagination of researchers in the field of education (Atkinson, Delamont, & Hammersley, 1988; Jacob, 1987). Although ethnographies of schooling have been done by a small group of anthropologists for some time, the ethnography "movement" began in the field of education during the late 1960s and early 1970s. The works of Cusick (1973), Henry (1963), Jackson (1968), Ogbu (1974), Rist (1973), Smith and Geoffrey (1968), Smith and Keith (1971), Wolcott (1973), and others provided examples of the genre that later educational ethnographers would emulate.

Critical ethnography also owes a great debt to interpretive movements in the fields of anthropology and sociology. Influenced by phenomenology, structuralism, semiotics, hermeneutics, and linguistics, interpretive ethnographers in anthropology raised fundamental questions about both the practice of ethnography and the nature of culture. Tracing their lineage to Malinowski's (1922) concern with "the native's point of view," they engaged in discussions of the nature of "local knowledge" and viewed social life as consisting of negotiated meanings (Geertz, 1973, 1983). While interpretivists in anthropology were shifting their attention from the functionalist notions of systems maintenance and equilibrium to what Geertz (1983) called "the analysis of symbol systems" (p. 34), qualitative sociologists were intensifying their epistemological attack on the pervasiveness of positivist assumptions in their field. In sociology the traditions of symbolic interactionism and ethnomethodology provided legitimation for ethnographic methods. Both interactionists and ethnomethodologists were concerned with social interaction as a means of negotiating meanings in context. The result of the interpretivist movements in both disciplines was to highlight the importance of symbolic action and "to place human actors and their interpretive and negotiating capacities at the centre of analysis" (Angus, 1986a, p. 61).

At the same time the ethnography "movement" was beginning in education, "neo-Marxist" and feminist social theorists in other disciplines were producing works that soon would make their way into American educational discourse (Althusser, 1971; Bernstein, 1971; Bourdieu & Passeron, 1977; Braverman, 1974; Chodorow, 1978; de Beauvoir, 1953; Foucault, 1972; Freire, 1971; Genovese, 1974; Giddens, 1979; Gramsci, 1971; Habermas, 1975; Horkheimer, 1972; Jameson, 1971;

Lacan, 1977; Lukacs, 1971; Marcuse, 1964; Millet, 1970; Oakley, 1972; Poulantzas, 1975; Williams, 1961). This "critical" thrust would raise serious questions about the role of schools in the social and cultural reproduction of social classes, gender roles, and racial and ethnic prejudice.

The interpretivists' focus on human agency and local knowledge appealed greatly to many neo-Marxists and feminists who were trapped in the theoretical cul-de-sac of overdeterminism. Analyses of economic and patriarchal determinism were increasingly viewed as inadequate social explanations for persistent social class, race, and gender inequities. Bowles and Gintis's (1976) impressive structuralist account of the role of American schooling in social reproduction and the theoretical and epistemological critiques that followed it (Cohen & Rosenberg, 1977; Cole, 1983) were a watershed. They accelerated the search for representations of social reality capable of providing social explanations sensitive to the complex relationship between human agency and social structure.

The British "new sociology" had already produced several prototypes for a dialectical representation of social structure and human agency (McRobbie & Garber, 1976; Sharp & Green, 1975; Willis, 1977). Also, Orthodox Marxist conceptions of false consciousness and economic determinism had long been under attack by the Frankfort School critical theorists, but the methodological implications of their critique were generally left unclear. Willis (1977) described how ethnography provides a methodological vehicle for theoretical advances in Marxism.

> The ethnographic account, without always knowing how, can allow a degree of the activity, creativity and human agency within the object of study to come through into the analysis and the reader's experience. This is vital to my purposes where I view the cultural, not simply as a set of transferred internal structures (as in the usual notions of socialization) nor as the passive result of the action of dominant ideology downwards (as in certain kinds of Marxism), but at least in part as the product of collective human praxis. (pp. 3–4)

Thus, ethnography allowed Willis to view the working-class adolescents who were his cultural informants as more than victims of "false consciousness": He viewed them as rational social actors who understood or "penetrated" the structural constraints on their social class but who nevertheless, through their very resistance to the dominant school culture, adopted the attitudes that condemned them to a life of factory labor. The resulting theory of resistance or cultural production and the emphasis on human "agency" or "praxis" is echoed by critical feminists:

> Insofar as a deterministic emphasis served to underscore the larger structural facility of women's oppression by demonstrating how women's personalities, ambitions, attitudes, behaviors and role acquisitions are products of patriarchal culture and patriarchal institutions, it was extremely significant. Nonetheless, it is now time to move beyond such models to explore more critically the relationship between macrostructural conditions and the immediate, concrete realities which women and men create and share, albeit differentially. . . . A critical feminism will attempt to overcome the aforementioned inadequacies of gender-role research in two primary ways. Metatheoretically, it will seek to eliminate assumptions of a micro-macro dualism in its analysis of social arrangements and social life by focusing analysis upon the interpenetration of structure and consciousness in the situations and relationships of everyday life. Epistemologically and methodologically, it will replace the positivistic methods of conventional sociology with those of a critical ethnography which attempts . . . to probe the lived-realities of human actors and the conditions informing both the construction and possible transformation of these realities. (DiIorio, 1982, pp. 22–23)

As the 1980s began, ethnographic methods, as well as critical theory and critical feminism,[1] were well entrenched among a small segment of American educational researchers. This uneasy alliance raised serious questions about the compatibility of theory-driven social agendas on one hand and the phenomenological research methods on the other. To many, their marriage seemed, at once, both an epistemological contradiction and an inevitability.

Critical Ethnography and the Issue of Validity

Throughout the development of critical ethnography as a research genre, perhaps its most serious methodological challenge has been the "validity issue." Educational researchers using qualitative methods have, over the years, had to work hard to legitimate their methods to the educational research establishment. The longstanding practice of ethnography in anthropology has provided many educational researchers with a legitimate methodological tradition. Ironically, however, while anthropologists have been moving in the direction of experimentation with more "literary" approaches to ethnography (Clifford & Marcus, 1986; Van Maanen, 1988), educational researchers have been moving to systematize ethnographic research in an attempt to make it more scientific, often even invoking the language of positivism to do so (Goetz & LeCompte, 1981; Kirk & Miller, 1985). The elaborate data analysis procedure of ethnographic semantics (Spradley, 1979, 1980) and microethnography (Green & Wallet, 1981) have been particularly popular in education because they lend legitimacy to ethnographic accounts and protect educational ethnographers from accusations of mere "story telling." To the extent that these procedures provide the reader with a record of the decision-making process that produced the final analysis, they are valuable. To the extent that they suggest that the final analysis is more the result of methodological rigor than the creative act of researcher interpretation, they are attempts to fit ethnography into a positivistic framework.

Critical ethnographers are in a double bind. They are often viewed with skepticism not only by the educational research establishment, but also by fellow ethnographers who have taken care to build procedures for "objectivity" into their work (see the critique of Willis by Hammersley & Atkinson, 1983; the critique of Everhart by Cusick, 1985a, 1985b; and the critique of Anyon by Ramsey, 1983). Critical ethnography is, after all, what Lather (1986a) called "openly ideological research." The apparent contradiction of such value-based research with traditional definitions of validity has left critical ethnography open to criticism from both within and outside of the ethnographic tradition.

Of course, critical ethnographers engage in standard practices associated with what Lincoln and Guba (1985) called the "trustworthiness" of ethnographic research, such as member checking and triangulation of data sources and methods. Nevertheless, their agenda of social critique, their attempt to locate their respondents' meanings in larger impersonal systems of political economy, and the resulting conceptual "front-endedness" of much of their research raises validity issues beyond those of mainstream naturalistic research. (For a more complete discussion of these issues than will be found in this review, see Angus, 1986a; Comstock, 1982; Lather, 1986a, 1986b; Masemann, 1982; Reynolds, 1980–1981; Simon & Dippo, 1986; Thomas, 1983; and West, 1984.)

Like other ethnographers—particularly those who define themselves as interpretivists—critical ethnographers aim to generate insights, to explain events, and to seek understanding. They also share with interpretivist ethnographers the view that the cultural informant's perceptions of social reality are themselves theoretical constructs. That is, although the informant's constructs are, to use Geertz's (1973) expression, more "experience-near" than the researcher's, they are, themselves, reconstructions of social reality.

Where critical ethnographers differ is in their claim that informant reconstructions are often permeated with meanings that sustain powerlessness and that people's conscious models exist to perpetuate, as much as to explain, social phenomena. Critical ethnographers, therefore, attempt to ensure that participants in research "are not naively enthroned, but systematically and critically unveiled" (Thompson, 1981, p. 143). This view is not limited to cultural informants but is also applied to the social science constructs employed by ethnographers. Analytic categories commonly used to build theory in sociology and anthropology, categories such as "family," "property," "stratification," "political," "economic," and so forth, "can be seen not as concepts designed for the analytic description of what surrounds us, but as concepts which are themselves part of that process which is the reproduction of our own social form" (Barnett & Silverman, 1979, p. 13).

Thus, according to critical ethnographers, analytical categories that are not viewed wholistically become ideological in what they lead to the reproduction of a particular set of social relationships.

> In order to deal critically with our categories of analysis, we must have an analysis of them: an analysis which , if it does not relate them to a world larger than those categories, can be accused of merely participating in the reproduction of this social form. (Barnett & Silverman, 1979, p. 13)

Thus, critical ethnographers in education do not view such categories as "giftedness," "dropouts," "management," "public relations," "effective" schools, or even "education" as nonproblematic. Rather, by placing them in a more wholistic social context, they are able to highlight their ideological aspects and the interests that benefit from the maintenance of current definitions.

For critical ethnographers wholism involves more than simply documenting those outside forces and macrostructural elements that impinge on the local cultural unit under analysis. A critical wholism recognizes that "the 'outside forces' are an integral part of the construction and constitution of the 'inside,' the cultural unit itself, and must be so registered, even at the most intimate levels of cultural process . . ." (Marcus & Fischer, 1986, p. 77). For the critical ethnographer, the cultural construction of meaning is inherently a matter of political and economic interests. According to critical ethnographers, the ideological nature of knowledge resides in the embeddedness of commonsense knowledge (and social science knowledge as well) in political and economic interests.

The critical ethnographer's concern with unmasking dominant social constructions and the interests they represent, studying society with the goal of transforming it, and freeing individuals from sources of domination and repression continues to make any discussion of validity, as defined by both positivist and interpretivist researchers, difficult. The most thorough attempt to address this problem has been Lather's (1986a) reformulations of construct and face validity and the addition of what she refers to as catalytic validity or "the degree to which the research process reorients, focuses, and energizes participants in what Freire (1973) terms 'conscientization'" (p. 67). Catalytic validity has been achieved, according to Lather, if respondents further self-understanding and, ideally, self-determination through their participation in the research. Erickson (1989) has also recently attempted to define what he called "critical validity": "I have come to see that relativist ethnography is itself evaluative when it reports absences, for example, 'neutrally' as absence rather than critically as the result of silencing" (p. 6).

Lather (1986b) summed up the tension that an "openly ideological" critical ethnography must resolve.

> Building empirically grounded theory requires a reciprocal relationship between data and theory. Data must be allowed to generate propositions in a dialectical manner than permits use of a priori theoretical frameworks, but which keeps a particular framework from becoming the container into which the data must be poured. (p. 267)

Critical Reflexivity

Perhaps the most pressing issue facing critical ethnographers today with respect to the validity or trustworthiness of their accounts is the exploration of reflexivity, that is, self-reflective processes that keep their critical framework from becoming the container into which the data are poured. Of course, the notion of reflexivity in ethnographic research is not new. In fact, unless ethnography is viewed as mere naturalistic description, the issue of reflexivity is at the center of any discussion of ethnographic method. Most discussions of reflexivity include reflection on the relationship between theory and data (Glaser & Strauss, 1967) and the effects of the researcher's presence on the data collected (Hammersley & Atkinson, 1983; Lincoln & Guba, 1985). The critical ethnographer also attempts to integrate and systematize two other forms of reflection—self-reflection (i.e., reflection on the researcher's biases) and reflection on the dialectrical relationship between structural/historical forces and human agency. Reflexivity in critical ethnography, then, involves a dialectical process among (a) the researcher's constructs, (b) the informants' commonsense constructs, (c) the research data, (d) the researcher's ideological biases, and (e) the structural and historical forces that informed the social construction under study.

Noblit (1989) suggested yet another kind of reflexivity that takes into account the reader of ethnographic accounts. According to Noblit, readers create their own text from the ethnography, and this text represents a new signification. The reader's text is the result of cumulative reflexivity: "All prior reading gives a context to all future reading. Moreover, one's perspective is not simply one's own. It derives from social interaction" (p. 14). In this way readers draw on perspectives available to them in their interpretive communities. (For an example of an interpretation standoff based on differing interpretive communities, see the exchange of critiques by Everhart, 1985a, 1985b, and Cusick, 1985a, 1985b.)

Little progress has been made in exploring methods that promote the kind of reflexivity required of the critical ethnographer. Collaborative and action research methods (Brown & Tandon, 1983; Carr & Kemmis, 1983) and the negotiation of research outcomes between the researcher and the researched (Anderson & Kelley, 1987; Kushner & Norris, 1980–1981) provide the beginnings of a better understanding of reflexivity among researchers, data, and informants. However, with few exceptions (see Reinharz, 1983; Westheimer, Steward, & Reich, 1989), the potential of systematic self-reflexivity in critical research has yet to be explored in depth.

Current Status of Critical Ethnography

Although still in their infancy, critical ethnographies have been written in a number of educational subfields and, although the following discussion will be limited to those written in English, in a number of languages. The following review represents the outline of a research program that explores schools as sites of social and cultural reproduction mediated through human agency by various forms of resistance and accommodation.

The emergence of critical ethnography in education occurred in England, following on the heels of the emergence of the British "new sociology" (Young, 1971). The 1970s in both Britain and the United States saw the cross-fertilization of sociological phenomenology (particularly the works of Berger & Luckmann, 1967; Garfinkel, 1967; and Shutz, 1962) and Marxian social analysis. The tension between the phenomenological and the structural is evident in the introduction to one of the earliest critical ethnographies.

> In the same way that Marx was against starting his analyses of society and history at the level of consciousness but rather sought for the basic societal structures which regulate interindividual action, so we need to develop some conceptualization of the situations that individuals find themselves in, in terms of the structure of opportunities the situations make available to them and the kinds of constraints they impose. (Sharp & Green, 1975, p. 22)

Alarmed by what they saw in Britain as a rush to phenomenology, Sharp and Green (1975) wished to warn researchers of the dangers of losing sight entirely of the structural.

Others, like Willis, came to critical ethnography with the opposite concern. Viewing ethnography as an antidote to structuralism, they were reacting to the absence of human agency in so many Marxist social accounts. Early British critical ethnographers, then, attempted to achieve a balance between the phenomenological concern with human agency and the Marxian conception of social structure.

American critical ethnographers, influenced greatly by Willis (1977) and Bowles and Gintis (1976), also viewed ethnographic methods as a way out of what many saw as structural overdeterminism. Following Marx, Bowles and Gintis's (1976) "correspondence principle" argued that there was a correspondence between schooling and the social relations of production in the work place.

> The structure of social relations in education not only inures the student to the discipline of the work place, but develops the types of personal demeanor, modes of self-presentation, self-image, and social-class identifications which are the crucial ingredients of job adequacy. (Bowles & Gintis, 1976, p. 131)

If the correspondence principle were true, then schools—whether wittingly or unwittingly—were serving a social reproductive function. That is, they served to reproduce a stratified work force whose members were taught to accept their class position. Early American critical ethnographers set out to empirically document, through field study, the nature of this correspondence. Perhaps the most impressive attempt was Anyon's (1980, 1981) case study of classrooms in five different schools, each serving students from different social class backgrounds. Anyon documented the differences in curriculum knowledge and educational experience that students from different social class backgrounds received.

Although serving to lend credence to the correspondence principle, this use of ethnography did little to peer inside the black box of how people let themselves get reproduced, or as Willis (1977) put it:

> The difficult thing to explain about how middle class kids get middle class jobs is why other kids let them. The difficult thing to explain about how working class kids get working class jobs is why they let themselves. (p. 1)

American critical ethnographers, drawing on theoretical and methodological critiques of a correspondence approach to social reproduction (Apple, 1982; Giroux, 1983), turned to theories of social production that view the process of social and cultural reproduction as one filled with complex forms of resistance and accommodation (see Weiler, 1988, for a cogent discussion of the social production/reproduction distinction).

Willis's (1977) work introduced a grounded version of resistance theory and became the standard for critical ethnographies written during the 1980s. In Willis's analysis of the behavior and attitudes of the "lads" who participated in the school's counterculture, he showed that the "lads" did partially penetrate the system that oppressed them and that their "inappropriate" behavior was a form of resistance. Although Willis and Anyon emphasized social class in their accounts, they were acutely aware of the need to understand the ways in which race and gender intersect with social class to reproduce structures of domination in society. In fact, Anyon's later work focuses on forms of resistance and accommodation and the relationship between gender and class.

Weis (1985) extended these categories to black students in an urban community college. Weis portrayed the ways urban black students are caught between the world of the dominant culture of the institution and the subordinate culture of the black urban underclass. This subordinate culture was not portrayed as inferior—on the contrary, it has many superior characteristics. For example, the cooperative nature of the urban black community was illustrated through the tolerance shown for women who bring their children to class.

> While children are often disruptive in the classroom, students do not complain. . . . They understand only too well that tomorrow *they* might have to bring their children to class for similar reasons. Male students, while not the primary caretakers of children, know that their nieces, nephews, sons, daughters or children of friends may also be there. (Weis, 1985, p. 113)

Weis described this subculture as in dialectical opposition to the dominant culture and showed how, in Genovese's (1974) words,

> [Blacks] have developed their own values as a force for cohesion and survival, but in so doing, they widened the cultural gap and exposed themselves to even harder blows from a white nation that

could neither understand their behavior not respect its moral foundations. (cited in Weis, 1985, p. 156)

In another attempt to understand the implications of resistance theory in a multiracial American context, McLeod (1987) studied two groups—one white and one black—of male adolescent "hall hangers" in a Boston housing project. McLeod found that it was the white group rather than the black group that was most alienated from school and that engaged in resistance. McLeod used this finding to explore resistance theory and the complex interactions of race and social class. Other studies that have explored the dynamics of race, gender, and class in student subcultures include those of Angus, 1986b; Aggleton, 1987; Aggleton and Whitty, 1985; Brah and Minhas, 1985; Corrigan, 1979; Humphries, 1981; Jenkins, 1983; and Macpherson, 1983.

A persistent criticism of educational critical theory is its tendency toward social critique without developing a theory of action that educational practitioners can draw upon to develop a "counter-hegemonic" practice in which dominant structures of classroom and organizational meaning are challenged. As Yates (1986) has pointed out,

> Because such theories have been confined to what not to do, or to forms of action outside the situation of teachers, teachers have developed their own forms of action, ranging from trying to tell students what is wrong with society, to trying to avoid controlling students, to emphasizing participation and nice relationships. (p. 128)

Although many critical ethnographies have attempted to address implications for practitioners (for example, see Willis, 1977, Chap. 9, "Monday Morning and the Millennium"), few have taken critical practitioners as objects of study. One of the advantages of ethnographic case study research has been its ability to study outliers. In some research programs the outliers are of more interest to the researcher than those cases that fall within a normal distribution. Some critical ethnographers are beginning to seek examples of practitioners who are attempting to put critical theory into practice (Comstock, 1982).

An example of this trend is Weiler's (1988) study of feminist teachers and administrators. Through the use of female practitioners' life histories and classroom observation, Weiler explored the beliefs and practices of teachers and administrators as they attempted to create what she called "feminist counter-hegemony" in schools. She attempted to unravel the complex interrelationships of administrators, teachers, and students as they negotiated and mediated meaning in schools and classrooms. Through her study of what she referred to as the "gendered discourse of the class-room" (p. 136), Weiler showed how teachers' meaning is both affirmed and contested by different students and how, therefore, the possibilities of and obstacles to counter-hegemonic teaching are revealed.

More generally, an impressive critical ethnographic research program of gender and schooling has been developing (Amos & Parmar, 1981; Eder & Parker, 1987; Fuller, 1980; Gaskell, 1985; Kelly & Nihlen, 1982; Kessler, Ashenden, Connell, & Dowsett, 1985; McRobbie & Garber, 1976; McRobbie, 1978; Nihlen & Bailey, 1988; Okazawa-Rey, 1987; Smith, 1987; Thomas, 1980; Wilson, 1978).

In the field of teacher education several critical ethnographers have explored the social reproduction of teachers' roles and have found evidence of teacher resistance. Goodman (1985) and Ginsburg and Newman (1985) studied preservice teacher education and explored the processes through which teachers take on their professional roles. Their studies emphasized the contested nature of occupational socialization and implications for teacher education programs. Aber (1986); Bullough, Gitlin, and Goldstein (1984); Ginsburg and Chaturvedi (1988); Kanpol (1988); Sears (1984); and Smyth (in press) described various forms of teacher resistance within a school context. All of these studies illustrate the extent to which commonsense conceptions of teacher roles inhibit teacher resistance.

As role becomes less taken-for-granted, less ideologically embedded, and as teachers begin to evaluate how they might create more humane and educative life spaces within schools, resistance becomes those acts that press up against role boundaries. (Bullough, et al., 1984, p. 342)

Although critical ethnographies have focused on students and teachers both in and out of classrooms, administrators have received less attention. Critical perspectives on administration are largely theoretical (see Anderson, 1989; Bates, 1984; Foster, 1986; Sirotnik & Oakes, 1986; Smyth, 1989). The few critical studies that have been conducted have explored the cognitive politics of the management of meaning (Anderson, 1988, in press; Gronn, 1984; Rosenbrock, 1987). These studies have portrayed administrators as the managers of organizational meaning, the custodians of organizational legitimacy, and the definers of organizational and social reality.

Besides administration, other areas in which critical ethnographies remain sparse, but in which some groundwork has been laid, are curriculum (Anyon, 1980, 1981; Bennett & Sola, 1985; Everhart, 1983; Mikel, 1987), early childhood (Miller, 1986), vocational education (Simon, 1983; Valli, 1986), parent and community role in schooling (Anderson Brantlinger, 1985; Connell, Ashenden, Kessler, & Dowsett, 1982; Ogbu, 1974), comparative education (Arias-Godinez, 1984; Wexler, 1979), higher education (Gumport, 1987; Pazmino-Farias, 1986), counseling (Roberts-Oppold, 1984), private schools (Angus, 1988; McLaren, 1986), tracking and dropouts (Fine, 1986; Oakes, 1985), and policy (Everhart, 1985c, 1988).

Criticisms and New Directions

The purpose of the following section is not to merely reveal the shortcomings of critical ethnography but to draw together and disseminate models from other disciplines and criticisms from within education to lay a groundwork for further theoretical and methodological advancement. A new generation of critical ethnographers will have to move beyond theories of social production/reproduction within schools to other methodological approaches and levels of analysis. As critical ethnographers turn their attention to subfields such as administration, special education, and teacher education, the theoretical framework that grew out of the study of student subcultures will be inadequate for the study of other areas of education.

The following discussion of criticisms and new directions will be divided into the following areas: (a) expanding and shifting the locus of analysis, (b) empowering informants, and (c) critiquing ideology.

Expanding and Shifting the Locus of Analysis

According to Wexler (1987), there have been major changes in U.S. social institutions that critical ethnography, as it is currently practiced, is unable to capture. He argued that critical ethnographic accounts fail to focus on broad social transformations (e.g., postindustrialism and poststructuralism) and social movements, as well as "historically specific 'local' institutional reorganizations" (p. 12). This is, in Wexler's view, due in part to a division of labor that has developed among academics who are increasingly specialized and compartmentalized across, as well as within, fields and disciplines. It is also due in part to a result of the lack of a sense of historicity capable of analyzing broad shifts in social institutions. Critical ethnography, Wexler argued, is ahistorical in that its preoccupation with education's role in social and cultural reproduction keeps it from analyzing much greater and broader changes in social and cultural forms.

Similarly, Wexler (1987) argued that the locus of analysis of critical ethnography is too site specific. In spite of its claim to wholism and its reliance on abstract social theories and categories such as "class" and "state," critical ethnography "languishes within the school institution, outside of social history," leading to the "omission of politically interested social analyses of the infrastructure of education and of its social institutional dynamics" (Wexler, 1987, p. 55). Thus, critical ethnographers are accused of ignoring "questions of finance, political regulation, governance, organizational dynamics, and specific historical, inter-institutional relations" (Wexler, 1987, p. 55).

Wexler perceived this lack of wholism as more than simply a "levels of analysis" issue. Schools, he believes, are no longer the primary educational institutions and, therefore, no longer the primary locus of analysis. Rather, at this historical juncture

> the relation between mass discourse and individual formation and motivation is the emergent educational relation. Where the forces of production become informational/communicational, semiotic, and the formation of the subject occurs significantly through mass discourse, then it is that relation which is the educational one. The mass communications/individual relation now already better exemplifies the educational relation than does the school, which as we know it, with all its structural imitations of industrial and, later, corporate productive organization, is being surpassed, as new modes of education develop. (Wexler, 1987, p. 174).

No examples of the type of critical analysis Wexler called for exist in education, although studies of the effects of mass communication on culture were reported in Hall (1980) and ethnographies of political economy were reviewed by Marcus and Fisher (1986). Also, Feinberg's (1983) broader definition of social reproduction may help a new generation of critical ethnographers to rethink current narrower views of the process.

The term *empowerment* has entered the mainstream of educational discourse and, consequently, its radical currency has been devalued. In a radical sense, however, empowerment occurs through "conscientizacao," which makes humans subjects rather than objects of history (Freire, 1971). "Subjects" are those who know and act; "objects" are those who are known and acted upon. According to Freire (1971),

> Doubt regarding the possible effects of *conscientizacao* implies a premise which the doubter does not always make explicit: It is better for the victims of injustice not to recognize themselves as such. In fact, however, conscientizacao does not lead men [sic] to "destructive fanaticism." On the contrary, by making it possible for men [sic] to enter the historical process as responsible subjects, conscientizacao enrolls them in the search for self-affirmation and thus avoids fanaticism. (p. 20)

Several research strategies are available to the critical ethnographer concerned about informant empowerment. Those discussed below are oral history methods, use of informant narratives, and collaborative research.

Oral history methods. Wexler (1987) made a connection between empowering research methods and the restoration of historicity to research accounts.

> The practice of oral history counters the elite assumption of the unreflected silence of ordinary people and makes their self-representing expressions authoritative. Where traditional history plays a role in social legitimation, the life history movement works to disperse authority. . . . Life history research offers as a model of social relations in education not system reproduction and resistance, but hermeneutic conversation. As research, it refuses to separate research and practice. It aims to amplify the capacity for intentional and historical memory. (p. 95)

Not only is oral history offering a challenge "to the accepted myths of history, to the authoritative judgment inherent in its tradition" (Thompson, 1978), but it also represents a longstanding methodological tradition in the field of anthropology. With few exceptions (see Weiler, 1988), life history methods have been ignored by critical ethnographers.

Use of informant narratives. Other attempts to empower informant understandings can be found in the use of informant "accounts" (Gilbert & Abell, 1983) and "narratives" (Mischler, 1986). According to Mischler, most current research methods do not give voice to the concerns of social actors and the ways they construct meaning. He argued that research interviewers have tended to code the responses of informants as if they existed independent of the contexts that produced them.

He also argued that researchers, instead of viewing the stories that respondents tell about their experiences as digressions from the topic at hand, should, in fact, elicit such stories. These stories can then be submitted to close narrative analysis in much the same way that a literary critic might approach a text.

> The effort to empower respondents and the study of their responses as narratives are closely linked. They are connected through the assumption . . . that one of the significant ways through which individuals make sense of and give meaning to their experiences is to organize them in a narrative form. As we shall see, various attempts to restructure the interviewee-interviewer relationship so as to empower respondents are designed to encourage them to find and speak in their own "voices." (Mischler, 1986, p. 118)

Mischler went on to cite several examples of studies in which respondents such as battered women and flood victims were encouraged to become more active participants in discourse with researchers. He also suggested a link to social action.

> There is, however, an additional implication of empowerment. Through their narratives people may be moved beyond the text to the possibilities of action. That is, to be empowered is not only to speak in one's own voice and to tell one's own story, but to apply the understanding arrived at to action in accord with one's own interests. (p. 119)

Another related attempt to empower the voice of informants and to restore its historicity can be found in the work of Soviet literacy critic Mikhail Bakhtin. Quantz and O'Connor (1988) argued cogently that through the concepts of "dialogue" and "multivoicedness," Bakhtin provides a framework for examining cultural continuity and change. According to Quantz and O'Connor,

> His (Bakhtin's) ideas show us that culture should be seen as a collection of historical events laden with a range of possibilities and shaped by the power resources of the individuals present. . . . In trying to understand human behavior, we must be cognizant that some voices are legitimated by the community and, therefore, vocalized, while others are nonlegitimated and therefore, unspoken. . . . Thus, the multiple voices within the individual and within the community struggle to control the direction of the acceptable dialogue, ideological expressions may be reinforced, reinterpreted, or rejected. . . . By recognizing and recording the multiple voices occurring within communities, we should be able to analyze the specific factors which affect the formation in historical situations of legitimated collusions and subsequent social actions. (1988, pp. 98–99)

What makes the concepts of multivoicedness and legitimated and nonlegitimated voice so powerful is Bakhtin's view that inward speech that becomes outwardly vocalized is probably that which is most compatible with the socially organized ideology. Multiple voices within the individual and within the community are in a constant struggle for legitimacy. Thus, neither a unified individual nor a consensual society is possible because both inward and outward speech are dialogical and social. Wexler's appeal to life history method and Mischler's advocacy of informant narratives may, in fact, represent means of access to the informant's inner dialogue.

Collaborative research. Concerns with informant empowerment are also evident in the increasing use of collaborative action research, which owes much to Friere's (1971) work, in which the empowerment of the powerless and the eradication of their "culture of silence" becomes the goal. It also owes much to feminist researchers who have critiqued the aloofness and distancing methods of traditional male-oriented research, whether quantitative or qualitative. An example of critical feminist work is the much-cited action study done by Mies (1983). Because she is both a researcher and a member of an action group establishing a house for battered women, her research and action agendas merge into a study of women's life histories aimed at "mobilizing the public at large about the problem" (p. 133).

This more activist research, with its emphasis on the application of critical theory to practice and its effort at researcher/practitioner collaboration, also responds to recent criticisms from within critical research. For example, Aronowitz and Giroux (1985) decried the nagativism of critical researchers who hold out little practical advice or hope for change to practitioners. They called for a "language of possibility" and an emphasis on "counter-hegemony" through which the dominant social assumptions that permeate everyday life are challenged. Wexler (1987) has criticized critical ethnographers for acting like voyeurs, viewing their research subjects' lives with the detachment characteristic of television viewing. There is an increasing awareness among critical ethnographers that if educational critical ethnography shares with applied educational research the goal of social and educational change, then it must address its impact on educational practitioners. According to Wilis, there is an immobilizing tautology implicit in most critical research—"nothing can be done until the basic structures of society are changed, but the structures prevent us making any changes" (p. 186).

Erickson (1986) has criticized radical research that views teachers and students as victims of structural inequality for just this reason. Following Edmonds (1979), he pointed out that differences in student achievement between classrooms with similar socioeconomic backgrounds indicate that teachers and principals can make a difference in student achievement. Cazden (1983) made a similar point:

> Social change of all kinds—from nuclear disarmament and removal of toxic wastes from the environment to more effective education in individual schools—requires some combination of the technical and the political. Asserting the importance of one does not negate the necessity of the other. (p. 39)

Unless critical ethnographers can provide an approach to educational and social change that includes both the technical and the political, that is, both sound techniques within the school and an effective political program outside the school, even critical practitioners may succumb to either hopelessness or lowered expectations.

Although top-down, outside-in approaches to critical ethnography are still the rule, the tendency toward collaborative action research and the negotiation of research outcomes with informants indicate a growing willingness among researchers to truly ground their critical analyses in the "trenches" of educational practice.

Critiquing Ideology

Although techniques of ethnomethodology and discourse analysis as a critique of ideology have been used extensively by critical feminists (Harding, 1987; Smith, 1987), critical sociolinguists (Fowler & Kress, 1979; Kress & Hodge, 1979), and other social theorists (Habermas, 1970), there has been little evidence in practice of a recognition by critical ethnographers in education that language is a social phenomenon that is enmeshed in relations of power and processes of social change. This may be in part because critical ethnographers have tended to favor macroanalysis, insisting that the lack of a wholistic approach to ethnography by microethnographers renders them incapable of revealing the broader social forces that inform the lives of social actors in specific social settings. They have further criticized microethnography for its tendency "to direct the attention of policymakers toward personal change without structural change" (Ogbu, 1981, p. 13).

Although the attribution of the methodological "narrowness" to microethnography and discourse analysis may have been justified at one time, this no longer seems to be the case. Theoretical advances in multilevel analysis (Knorr-Cetina & Cicourel, 1981) and discourse analysis (Thompson, 1984) make a critical approach to the ethnography of communication, both at the level of microsocial interaction and mass communication, not only plausible but imperative. As Thompson (1984) pointed out, a longstanding interest among discourse analysts is that of

> the relations between linguistic and *non-linguistic activity*. Traditionally such an interest was expressed in terms of the links between language and perception, language and thought, language and culture; but in recent years, discourse analysts have paid increasing attention to the ways in which

language is used in specific social contexts and thereby serves as a medium of power and control. It is this increasingly sociological turn which has rendered discourse analysis relevant to, though by no means neatly integrated with, some of the principal tasks in the study of ideology. For if the language of everyday life is regarded as the very *locus* of ideology, then it is of the very utmost importance to examine the` methods which have been elaborated for the analysis of ordinary discourse. (p. 99)

Critical educational theorists have appropriated many of the theoretical aspects of the work of such linguists as Pierre Bourdieu and Basil Bernstein. Categories like "cultural capital" and "symbolic violence" (Bourdieu & Passeron, 1977) or "elaborated" and "restricted" codes (Bernstein, 1971) turn up frequently in critical educational discourse. However, critical ethnographers in education, with few exceptions (see Collins, 1987), seem to underestimate in their own work the potential of sociolinguistic analysis to systematically explore how relations of domination are sustained through the mobilization of meaning.

Conclusion

Lather (1986a) divided critical research into three overlapping traditions: feminist research, neo-Marxist critical ethnography, and Freirian empowering research.[2] I have combined these under the critical ethnography rubric to emphasize the commonalities in their research programs and to highlight those areas where they can learn from each other. The largely phallocentric, distancing tendencies of much neo-Marxist ethnography are increasingly challenged by the merging, collaborative tendencies of feminist research. Likewise, critical feminists, drawing on neo-Marxist theory, are struggling with the ways patriarchy intersects with social class and race in women's oppression. Issues of gender equity and social equality become inseparable in critical feminist research. Freire's work has inspired critical pedagogists, if not critical ethnographers, to explore the relevance of emancipatory approaches to educational settings in the U.S. (Finlay & Faith,1980; Fiore & Elsasser, 1982).

Although there is a growing body of epistemological and methodological analysis in the writing on critical ethnography, there is as yet little practical advice. Critical ethnographers need to begin sharing insights from their research on such concepts as how to write a reflective journal, how to negotiate outcomes with informants, how to gain and maintain site access when doing controversial research, and how to systematize reflexivity. I have tried to capture some of the tensions in this marriage of critical social theory and ethnographic methods. The future of the marriage will depend on an ongoing dialogue between social theory and the day-to-day experience of the critical ethnographer in the field.

Notes

The author wishes to thank Ann Nihlen, Paul Pohland, and the reviewers for their suggestions.

1. The theoretical debates within feminism are complex. Glazer (1987) provided some flavor of the current theoretical positions.

    Liberal feminists believe that oppression results from socialization processes and the legal system, while radical feminists believe it results from women's biology and history and men's need and power to dominate. Marxist feminists, on the other hand, believe oppression results from capitalists' subordination of women in the interests of capital accumulation and profit and maintaining control over the means of production. (p. 298)

    Without entering into the radical versus Marxists feminist debate, what critical feminists ethnographies in education have in common is a concern with understanding the ways social class, race, and patriarchy intersect to reproduce current social relations. Although there may be some advantage to retaining a separate category for critical feminists ethnography, ideally all critical ethnography is interested in the intersection of class, race, and gender.

2. In the "origins" section of this article, I have included Freire's work under a broad neo-Marxist umbrella.

References

Aber, J. (1986). *Toward reconceptualizing teacher training in composition: An ethnographic account and theoretical appraisal.* Unpublished doctoral dissertation, The Ohio State University.

Aggleton, P. (1987). *Rebels without a cause.* London: Falmer.

Aggleton, P.J., & Whitty, G. (1985). Rebels without a cause? Socialization and subcultural style among the children of the new middle classes. *Sociology of Education, 58,* 60–72.

Althusser, L. (1971). *Lenin and philosophy, and other essays* (Ben Brewster, Trans.). New York: Monthly Review Press.

Amos, V., & Palmar, P. (1981). Resistances and responses: The experiences of black girls in Britain. In A. McRobbie & T. McCabe (Eds.), *Feminism for girls.* London: Routledge & Kegan Paul.

Anderson Brantlinger, E. (1985). Low-income parents' opinions about the social class composition of schools. *American Journal of Education, 93,* 389–408.

Anderson, G.L. (1988). *A legitimation role for the school administrator: A critical ethnography of elementary school principals.* Unpublished doctoral dissertation, The Ohio State University.

Anderson, G.L. (1989, March). *The management of meaning and organizational legitimacy.* Paper presented at the annual meeting of the American Educational Research Association, San Francisco.

Anderson, G.L. (in press). Toward a critical constructivist approach to school administration: Invisibility, legitimation, and the study of non-events. *Educational Administration Quarterly.*

Anderson, G.L., & Kelley, D. (1987, April). *Negotiating organizational reality: The mutual validation of research outcomes.* Paper presented at the annual meeting of the American Educational Research Association, Washington, DC.

Angus, L. (1986a). Developments in ethnographic research in education: From interpretive to critical ethnography. *Journal of Research and Development in Education, 20,* 59–67.

Angus. L. (1986b). Pupils, power and the organization of the schools. *The Journal of Educational Administration, 24,* 5–17.

Angus. L. (1988). *Continuity and change in Catholic schooling: An ethnography of a Christian Brothers college in Australian Society.* London: Falmer Press.

Anyon, J. (1980). Social class and the hidden curriculum of work. *Journal of Education, 161,* 67–72.

Anyon, J. (1981). Social class and school knowledge. *Curriculum Inquiry, 11,* 3–41.

Apple, M. (Ed.). (1982). *Cultural and economic reproduction in education.* Boston: Routledge & Kegan Paul.

Arias-Godinez, B. (1984). *Nonformal education through radio and the social reproduction/transformation of a rural community in Veracruz, Mexico.* Unpublished doctoral dissertation, University of Houston.

Aronowitz, S., & Giroux, H. (1985). *Education under siege: The conservative, liberal and radical debate over schooling.* South Hadley, MA: Bergin & Garvey.

Atkinson, P., Delamont, S., & Hammersley, M. (1988). Qualitative research traditions: A British response to Jacob. *Review of Educational Research, 58,* 231–250.

Barnett, S., & Silverman, M.G. (1979). *Ideology and everyday life: Anthropology, neo-Marxist thought, and the problem of ideology and the social whole.* Ann Arbor: University of Michigan Press.

Bates, R. (1984). Toward a critical practice of educational administration. In T. Sergiovanni & J. Corbally (Eds.), *Leadership and organizational culture* (pp. 260–273). Urbana: University of Illinois Press.

Bennett, A., & Sola, M. (1985). The struggle for voice: Narrative, literacy, and consciousness in an East Harlem school. *Journal of Education, 167,* 88–110.

Berger, P., & Luckmann, T. (1967). *The social construction of reality.* Garden City, NY: Doubleday Anchor.

Bernstein, B. (1971). *Class, codes and control.* London: Routledge & Kegan Paul.

Bourdieu, P., & Passeron, J. (1977). *Reproduction in education, society, and culture.* London: Sage.

Bowles, S., & Gintis, H. (1976). *Schooling in capitalist America.* New York: Basic Books.

Brah, A., & Minhas, R. (1985). Structural racism or cultural difference: Schooling for Asian girls. In G. Weiner (Ed.), *Just a bunch of girls.* Milton Keynes, England: Open University Press.

Braverman, H. (1974). *Labor and monopoly capital.* New York: Monthly Review Press.

Brown, L.D., & Tandon, R. (1983). Ideology and political economy in inquiry: Action research and participatory research. *The Journal of Applied Behavioral Science, 19,* 277–294.

Bullough, R.V., Gitlin, A.D., & Goldstein, S.L. (1984). Ideology, teacher role, and resistance. *Teachers College Record, 86,* 339–358.

Carr, W., & Kemmis, S. (1983). *Becoming critical: Knowing through action research.* Victoria: Deakin University Press.

Cazden, C.B. (1983). Can ethnographic research go beyond the status quo? *Anthropology & Education Quarterly, 14,* 33–41.

Chodorow, N. (1978). *The reproduction of mothering: Psychoanalysis and the sociology of gender.* Berkeley: University of California Press.

Clifford, J., & Marcus, G. (1986). *Writing culture: The poetics and politics of ethnography.* Berkeley: University of California Press.

Cohen, D., & Rosenberg, B. (1977). Functions and fantasies: Understanding schools in capitalist America. *History of Education Quarterly, 17,* 113–137.

Cole, M. (1983). Contradictions in the educational theory of Gintis and Bowles. *Sociological Review, 31,* 471–488.

Collins, J. (1987). Language and class in minority education. *Anthropology and Education Quarterly, 16,* 299–307.

Comstock, D. (1982). A method for critical research. In E. Bredo & W. Feinber (Eds.), *Knowledge and values in social and educational research* (pp. 370–390). Philadelphia: Temple University Press.

Connell, R.W., Ashenden, D., Kessler, S., & Dowsett, G. (1982). *Making the difference: Schools, families, and social division.* North Sydney: George Allen and Unwin.

Corrigan, P. (1979). *Schooling the Smash Street kids.* London: Macmillan.

Cusick, P. (1973). *Inside high school: The student's world.* New York: Holt, Reinhart & Winston.

Cusick, P. (1985a), Review of *Reading, writing and resistance. Anthropology and Education Quarterly, 16,* 269–272.

Cusick, P. (1985b), Comment on the Everhart/Cusick reviews. *Anthropology and Education Quarterly, 16,* 246–247.

deBeauvoir, S. (1953). *The second sex.* New York: Knopf.

Dilorio, J. A. (1982). Nomad vans and lady vanners: A critical feminist analysis of a van club. Unpublished doctoral dissertation, The Ohio State University.

Eder, D., & Parker, S. (1987). The cultural production and reproduction of gender: The effect of extracurricular activities on peer-group culture. *Sociology of Education, 60,* 200–213.

Edmonds, R. (1979). Effective schools for the urban poor. *Educational Leadership, 37,*15–24

Erickson, F. (1986) Qualitative methods in research on teaching. In M. C. Wittrock (Ed.), *Handbook of research on teaching* (pp. 119–161). New York: Macmillan.

Erickson, F. (1989, March). *The meaning of validity in qualitative research.* Paper presented at the annual meeting of the American Educational Research Association, San Francisco.

Everhart, R. B. (1983). *Reading, writing, and resistance.* London: Routledge & Kegan Paul.

Everhart, R. B. (1985a). Review of *The Egalitarian ideal and the American high school. Anthropology and Education Quarterly, 16,* 73–77.

Everhart, R. B. (1985b). Comment on the Cusick/Everhart reviews. *Anthropology and Education Quarterly, 16,* 247–248.

Everhart, R. B. (1985c). On feeling good about oneself: Practical ideology in schools of choice. *Sociology of Education, 58,* 251–260.

Everhart, R. B. (1988). *Practical ideology and symbolic community: An ethnography of schools of choice.* New York: Falmer Press.

Feinberg, W. (1983). *Understanding education: Toward a reconstruction of educational inquiry.* Cambridge: Cambridge University Press.

Fine, M. (1986). Why urban adolescents drop into and out of public high school. *Teachers College Record, 87,* 395–409.

Finlay, L., & Faith, V. (1980). Illiteracy and alienation in American colleges. Is Paulo Freire's pedagogy relevant? *Radical Teacher, 8,* 28–37.

Fiore, K., & Elasser, N. (1982). Strangers no more: A liberatory literacy curriculum. *College English, 44,* 169–181.

Foster, W. (1986). *Paradigms and promises: New approaches to educational administration.* Buffalo: Prometheus Books.

Foucault, M. (1972). *The archeology of knowledge and the discourse of language.* New York: Harper & Row.

Fowler, R., & Kress, G.R. (1979). Critical linguistics. In R. Fowler, B. Hodge, G. Kress, & T. Trew (Eds.), *Language and control* (pp. 186–199). London: Routledge & Kegan Paul.

Freire, P. (1971). *Pedagogy of the oppressed.* New York: Herder & Herder.

Fuller, M. (1980). Black girls in a London comprehensive school. In R. Deem (Ed.), *Schooling for women's work* (pp. 52–65). London & Boston: Routledge & Kegan Paul.

Garfinkel, H. (1967). *Studies in ethnomethodology.* Englewood Cliffs, NJ: Prentice-Hall.

Gaskell, J. (1985). Course enrollment in the high school: The perspective of working class females. *Sociology of Education, 58,* 48–59.

Geertz, C. (1973). *The interpretation of cultures.* New York: Basic Books.

Geertz, C. (1983). *Local knowledge.* New York: Basic Books.

Genovese, E. (1974). *Roll, Jordan, roll: The world the slaves made.* New York: Vintage Books.

Giddens, A. (1979). *Central problems in social theory: Action, structure, and contradiction in social analysis.* London: Macmillan.

Gilbert, G.N., & Abell, P. (1983). *Accounts and action: Surrey conferences on sociological theory and method.* London: Gower.

Ginsburg, M., & Chaturvedi, V. (1988). Teachers and the ideology of professionalism in India and England: A comparison of cases in colonial/peripheral and metropolitan/central societies. *Comparative Education Review, 32,* 465–477.

Ginsburg, M.B., & Newman, K.K. (1985). Social inequalities, schooling, and teacher education. *Journal of Teacher Education, 36,* 49–54.

Giroux, H. (1983). *Theory and resistance in education.* South Hadley, MA: Bergin & Garvey.

Glaser, B., & Strauss, A. (1967). *The discovery of grounded theory.* Chicago: Aldine.

Glazer, N. (1987). Questioning eclectic practice in curriculum change: A Marxist perspective. *Signs: Journal of Women in Culture and Society, 12,* 293–304.

Goetz, J.P., & LeCompte, M.D. (1981). Ethnographic research and the problem of data reduction. *Anthropology and Education Quarterly, 12,* 51–70.

Goodman, J. (1985). Field-based experience: A study of social control and the student teachers' response to institutional constraints. *Journal of Education for Teaching, 11,* 26–49.

Gramsci, A. (1971). *Prison notebooks.* New York: International Publishers.

Green, J., & Wallet, C. (Eds.). (1981). *Ethnography and language in educational settings.* Norwood, NJ: Ablex.

Gronn, P. (1984). "I have a solution. . .": Administrative power in a school meeting. *Educational Administration Quarterly, 20,* 65–92.

Gumport, P. (1987). *The social construction of knowledge: Individual and institutional commitments to feminist scholarship.* Unpublished doctoral dissertation, Stanford University.

Habermas, J. (1970). Toward a theory of communicative competence. In H.P. Dreitzel (Ed.), *Recent sociology* (pp. 114–148). New York: Macmillan.

Habermas, J. (1975). *Legitimation crises.* Boston: Beacon Press.

Hall, S. (Ed.). (1980). *Culture, media, language: Working papers in cultural studies.* 1972–79. London: Hutchinson.

Hammersley, M., & Atkinson, P. (1983). *Ethnography: Principles in practice.* London: Tavistock.

Harding, S. (Ed.). (1987). *Feminism and methodology*. Bloomington: Indiana University Press.

Henry, J. (1963). *Culture against man*. New York: Random House.

Horkheimer, M. (1972). *Culture theory: Selected essays*. New York: Herder and Herder.

Humphries, S. (1981). *Hooligans or rebels?* Oxford: Martin Robertson.

Jackson, P. (1968). *Life in classrooms*. New York: Holt, Rinehart & Winston.

Jacob, E. (1987). Qualitative research traditions: A review. *Review of Educational Research, 57*(1), 1–50.

Jameson, F. (1971). *Marxism and form*. Princeton, NJ: Princeton University Press.

Jenkins, R.P. (1983). *Lads, citizens and ordinary kids: Working-class youth life-styles in Belfast*. London: Routledge & Kegan Paul.

Kanpol, B. (1988). Teacher work tasks as forms of resistance and accommodation to structural factors of schooling. *Urban Education, 23*, 173–187.

Kelly, G., & Nihlen, A. (1982). Schooling and the reproduction of patriarchy: Unequal workloads, unequal rewards. In M. Apple (Ed.), *Culture and economic reproduction in education* (pp. 162–180). London and Boston: Routledge & Kegan Paul.

Kessler, S., Ashenden, R., Connell, R., & Dowsett, G. (1985). Gender relations in secondary schooling. *Sociology of Education, 58*, 34–48.

Kirk, J., & Miller, M. (1985). *Reliability and validity in qualitative research*. Beverly Hills, CA: Sage.

Knorr-Cetina, K., & Cicourel, A.V. (1981). *Advances in social theory and methodology: Toward an integration of micro- and macro-sociologies*. London: Routledge & Kegan Paul.

Kress, G.R., & Hodge, R. (1979). *Language as ideology*. London: Routledge & Kegan Paul.

Kushner, S., & Norris, N. (1980–1981). Interpretation, negotiation, and validity in naturalistic research. *Interchange, 11*, 26–36.

Lacan, J. (1977). *Ecrits: A section*. London: Tavistock.

Lather, P. (1986a). Issues of validity in openly ideological research: Between a rock and a soft place. *Interchange, 17*, 63–84.

Lather, P. (1986b). Research as praxis. *Harvard Educational Review, 56*, 257–277.

Lincoln, Y.S., & Guba, E.G. (1985). *Naturalistic inquiry*. Beverly Hills, CA: Sage.

Lukacs, G. (1971). *History and class consciousness*. Cambridge, MA: MIT Press.

Macpherson, J. (1983). *The feral classroom*. London: Routledge & Kegan Paul.

Malinowski, B. (1922). *Argonauts of the western Pacific*. London: Routledge.

Marcus, G.E., & Fischer, M.J. (1986). *Anthropology as cultural critique: An experimental moment in the human sciences*. Chicago: University of Chicago Press.

Marcuse, H. (1964). *One dimensional man*. London: Routledge & Kegan Paul.

Masemann, V.L. (1982). Critical ethnography in the study of comparative education. *Comparative Education Review, 26*, 1–15.

McLaren, P. (1986) *Schooling as a ritual performance*. Boston: Routledge & Kegan Paul.

McLeod, J. (1987). *Ain't no makin it: Leveled aspirations in a low income neighborhood.* San Diego: Westview.

McRobbie, A. (1978). Working class girls and the culture of femininity. In Women's Study Group. *Women take issue: Aspects of women's subordination* (pp. 96–108). London: Hutchinson.

McRobbie, A., & Garber, J. (1976). Girls and subcultures. In S. Hall & T. Jefferson (Eds.), *Resistance through rituals* (pp. 209–222). London: Routledge & Kegan Paul.

Mies, M. (1983). Towards a methodology of feminist research. In G. Bowles & R. Duelli Klein (Eds.), *Theories of women's studies* (pp. 117–139). Boston: Routledge & Kegan Paul.

Mikel, E. (1987). *Dilemmas of knowledge and issues of democratic schooling in the pedagogy of three experienced high school social studies teachers.* Unpublished doctoral dissertation, Washington University.

Miller, D. (1986). *Infant/toddler day care in high, middle, and low socio-economic settings: An ethnography of dialectical enculturation and linguistic code.* Unpublished doctoral dissertation, University of Houston.

Millet, K. (1970). *Sexual politics.* New York: Avon Books.

Mischler, E. (1986). *Research interviewing: Context and narrative.* Cambridge, MA: Harvard University Press.

Nihlen, A., & Bailey, B. (1988). Children's display of gender-schemas through interaction with nontraditional workers. *Anthropology and Education Quarterly, 19,* 155–162.

Noblit, G. (1989, March). *Armchair educational ethnography.* Paper presented at the annual meeting of the American Educational Research Association, San Francisco.

Oakes, J. (1985). *Keeping track: How schools structure inequality.* New Haven, CT: Yale University Press.

Oakley, A. (1972). *Sec, gender, and society.* New York: Harper and Row.

Ogbu, J. (1981). School ethnography: A multilevel approach. *Anthropology and Education Quarterly, 12,* 3–29.

Okazawa-Rey, M. (1987). *Teaching for liberation and for social change: An ethnographic study.* Unpublished doctoral dissertation, Harvard University.

Pazmino-Farias, C. (1986). *University reform, stratification and social reproduction in Venezuela.* Unpublished doctoral dissertation, Stanford University.

Poulantzas, N. (1975). *Classes in contemporary capitalism.* London: New Left Books.

Quantz, R.A., & O'Connor, T.W. (1988). Writing critical ethnography: Dialogue, multi-voicedness, and carnival in cultural texts. *Educational Theory, 38,* 95–109.

Ramsey, P.D. (1983). Fresh perspectives on the school transformation-reproduction debate: A response to Anyon from the antipodes. *Curriculum Inquiry, 13,* 295–320.

Reinharz, S. (1983). Experiential analysis: A contribution to feminist research. In G. Bowles & R. Duelli Klein (Eds.), *Theories of women's studies* (pp. 162–191). Boston: Routledge & Kegan Paul.

Reynolds, D. (1980–1981). The naturalistic method and education and social research: A Marxist critique. *Interchange, 11,* 77–89.

Rist, R.C. (1973). *The urban school: A factory for failure.* Cambridge: MIT Press.

Rist, R.C. (1980). Blitzkrieg ethnography: On the transformation of a method into a movement. *Educational Researcher, 9*(2), 8–10.

Roberts-Oppold, N. (1984). *The religious context of misogynous relational violence: An ethnographic study.* Unpublished doctoral dissertation, University of South Dakota.

Rosenbrock, P. (1987). *Persistence and accommodation in a decade of struggle and change: The case of women administrators in division 1A intercollegiate athletics programs.* Unpublished doctoral dissertation, University of Iowa.

Schutz, A. (1962). *Collected papers, vol. 1.* The Hague: Martinus Nijhoff.

Sears, J. (1984). *A critical ethnography of teacher education programs at Indiana University: An inquiry into the perceptions of students and faculty regarding quality and effectiveness.* Unpublished doctoral dissertation, Indiana University.

Sharp. R., & Green, A. (1975). *Education and social control: A study in progressive primary education.* London: Routledge & Kegan Paul.

Simon, R.I. (1983). But who will let you do it? Counter-hegemonic possibilities for work education. *Journal of Education, 165,* 235–256.

Simon, R.I., & Dippo, D. (1986). On critical ethnographic work. *Anthropology & Education Quarterly, 17,* 195–202.

Sirotnik, K., & Oakes, J. (1986). *Critical perspectives on the organization and improvement of schooling.* Boston: Kluwer Nijhoff.

Smith, D.E. (1987). *The everyday world as problematic: A feminist sociology.* Boston: Northeastern University Press.

Smith, L.M., & Geoffrey, W. (1968). *The complexities of an urban classroom.* New York: Holt, Rinehart & Winston.

Smith, L.M., & Keith, P.M. (1971). *Anatomy of educational innovation.* New York: John Wiley.

Smyth, J. (Ed.). (1989). *Critical perspectives on educational leadership.* London: The Falmer Press.

Smyth, J. (in press). A critical pedagogy of classroom practice. *Journal of Curriculum Studies.*

Spradley, J.P. (1979). *The ethnographic interview.* New York: Holt, Rinehart & Winston.

Spradley, J.P. (1980). *Participant observation.* New York: Holt, Rinehart & Winston.

Thomas, C. (1980). Girls and counter-school culture. In *Melbourne working papers.* Melbourne: Melbourne University.

Thomas, J. (1983). Toward a critical ethnography: A reexamination of the Chicago legacy. *Urban Life, 11,* 477–490.

Thompson, J.B. (1981). *Critical hermeneutics.* Cambridge: Cambridge University Press.

Thompson, J.B. (1984). *Studies in the theory of ideology.* Berkeley: University of California Press.

Thompson, P. (1978). *The voice of the past: Oral history.* Oxford: Oxford University Press.

Valli, L. (1986). *Becoming clerical workers.* Boston and London: Routledge & Kegan Paul.

Van Maanen, J. (1988). *Tales of the field: On writing ethnography.* Chicago: University of Chicago Press.

Weiler, K. (1988). *Women teaching for change: Gender, class & power.* South Hadley, MA: Bergin & Garvey.

Weis, L. (1985). *Between two worlds: Black students in an urban community college.* Boston: Routledge & Kegan Paul.

West, W.G. (1984). Phenomenon and form in interactionist and neo-Marxist qualitative educational research. In L. Barton & S. Walker (Eds.), *Social crisis and educational research* (pp. 256–285). London: Croom Helm Ltd.

Westheimer, M., Stewart, D., & Reich, M. (1989, Feb.). *Insights: The power and necessity of critical reflection.* Paper presented at the 10th annual University of Pennsylvania Ethnography in Education Research Forum, Philadelphia.

Wexler, P. (1979). Educational change and social contradiction: An example. *Comparative Education Review, 23,* 240–255.

Wexler, P. (1987). *Social analysis of education: After the new sociology.* London: Routledge & Kegan Paul.

Williams, R. (1961). *The long revolution.* London: Chatto & Windus.

Willis, P. (1977). *Learning to labor.* New York: Columbia University Press.

Wilson, D. (1978). Sexual codes and conduct: A study of teen-age girls. In C. Smart & B. Smart (Eds.), *Women, sexuality, & social control* (pp. 65–73). London: Routledge & Kegan Paul.

Wolcott, H. (1973). *The man in the principal's office: An ethnography.* New York: Holt, Rinehart & Winston.

Yates, L. (1986). Theorizing inequality today. *British Journal of Social of Education, 7,* 119–134.

Young, M. (Ed.). (1971). *Knowledge and control.* London: Collier-Macmillan.

Ethnographic Research in Education

Harry F. Wolcott

Cultural anthropologists conducting ethnographic research describe their activities with a modest phrase: they say they are "doing fieldwork." Several years ago anthropologist Rosalie Wax (1971) took that very phase, *Doing Fieldwork*, for the title of a fine account of her research experiences and some lessons she wanted to draw for future fieldworkers. It has not always been fashionable among anthropologists to concern themselves with methodological issues per se, but in the past two decades they have become both more self-conscious and more explicit about their research.

In recent years, ethnographic research has also been acknowledged, and to some extent even welcomed, as an alternative research strategy for inquiring into education. It is hard to imagine that ethnography will ever wring educational research from the iron grip of the statistical methodologists, but it is comforting to note the current receptivity among educators to other ways of asking and other ways of looking. Today one often hears educators discussing "ethnography" or the "ethnographic approach." The fact that educators use terms like ethnography and ethnographic approach does not, of course, assure that they have a clear sense of how ethnographers conduct their research or what ethnographic research shares in common with related approaches like participant observation studies, field studies, or case studies.

Let me illustrate how educators use the term without necessarily understanding it. One large-scale, federally funded educational project completed in the 1970s made it possible to employ a number of full-time "on-site" researchers to live in rural communities in order to document change processes in the schools and to study school-community interaction. Not all the researchers involved in the project were anthropologists, but the anthropologists among them—trained observers schooled in ethnographic techniques—were inclined to refer to their research as fieldwork and to describe their efforts as ethnography.

After living somewhat apprehensively under the watchful gaze of his resident 24-hours-a-day, 365-days-a-year ethnographer, the superintendent of schools in one of those rural communities received a preliminary copy of a report that had been prepared by the researcher. The superintendent's subsequent reaction, I'm told, was to note with a sigh of relief, "The stuff's okay. It's just pure anthropology."

In fact, the report he read was essentially history—an overview of the community's founding and early days. But I think it instructive to realize that the superintendent had been in association with a full-time anthropologist/ethnographer for months and months, knew that the project would include a major effort in descriptive research, and still had but the faintest idea of what to expect in the completed account. Something of a mystique does surround fieldwork—for insiders as well as outsiders to the process—and I intend here to explore the basis for that mystique. I will not entirely dispel it, but I want to suggest that the *real* mystique surrounding ethnography, as any experienced ethnographer will attest, is not in doing fieldwork but in subsequently organizing and analyzing the information one gathers and in preparing the account that brings the ethnographic process to a close.

Ethnography as Both Process and Product

Ethnography refers both to the research *process* and to the customary *product* of that effort—the written ethnographic account. Essentially I will limit this discussion to describing the research techniques anthropologists use in doing fieldwork. That is a sufficient task for me as author of a chapter, but it is not sufficient to make an ethnographer out of an interested reader. The necessary next stop is to embark on a program of extended reading in cultural anthropology, giving particular attention to ethnographic accounts and examining how different ethnographers have conceptualized and written about different cultural systems. The references and annotated materials accompanying this chapter include a number of such studies. If possible, one should also enroll in anthropology classes in order not only to learn about the field but to appreciate the range of interest and perspectives extant among anthropologists themselves.

Ethnography means, literally, a picture of the "way of life" of some identifiable group of people. Conceivably, those people could be any culture-bearing group, in any time and place. In times past, the group was usually a small, intact, essentially self-sufficient social unit, and it was always a group notably "strange" to the observer. The anthropologist's purpose as ethnographer was to learn about, record, and ultimately portray the culture of this other group. Anthropologists always study human behavior in terms of cultural context. Particular individuals, customs, institutions, or events are of anthropological interest as they relate to a generalized description of the lifeway of a socially interacting group. Yet culture itself is always an abstraction, regardless of whether one is referring to Culture in general or to the culture of a specific social group.

Here, I recognize, would be the proper place to provide a crisp definition of culture, yet I am hesitant to do so. The arguments concerning the definition of culture, what one anthropologist refers to as "this undifferentiated and diffuse variable," continue to comprise a critical part of the ongoing dialog among anthropologists. To what extent, for example, does culture consist of what people *actually* do, what they *say* they do, what they say they *should* do, or to *meanings* they assign to such behavior? Does culture make prisoners of us or free us from a mind-boggling number of daily decisions? Does culture emanate from our minds, our hearts, or our stomachs; from our ancestors, our totems, or our deities? And if someone really devised a culture-free test, could we ever find a culture-free individual to take or to interpret it?

In terms of understanding the ethnographer's task, I draw attention to one relatively recent definition of culture that I have found instructive, a definition proposed by anthropologist Ward Goodenough (1976):

> The culture of any society is made up of the concepts, beliefs, and principles of action and organization that an ethnographer has found could be attributed successfully to the members of the society in the context of his dealings with them. (p. 5).

The appeal of this definition for me lies in Goodenough's notion that the ethnographer "attributes" culture to a society. That idea serves as a reminder of a number of critical points. First, the ultimate test of ethnography resides in the adequacy of its explanation rather than in the power of its method. Second, culture cannot be observed; it can only be inferred. Third, the preoccupation with culture per se, discerning its components and their interrelationships in any particular society in order to make explicit statements about them, is the professional task ethnographers have chosen for themselves.

Without ordinarily having to go so far as to try to make it all explicit or to try to obtain as comprehensive and "holistic" a view as the ethnographer might seek, all human beings are similarly occupied with trying to discern and to act appropriately within the framework of the macro- and micro-cultural systems in which they operate as members of particular societies. We all have to figure out and become competent in numerous microcultural systems and in at least one macro-cultural system (cf. Goodenough, 1976). Everyone, anthropologists included, does it out of necessity; ethnographers also do it as part of their professional commitment. Ordinarily an outsider to the group being studied, the ethnographer tries harder to know more about the cultural system he or she is studying than any individual who is a natural participant in it, at once advantaged by the outsider's broad and analytical perspective but, by reason of that same detachment, unlikely ever totally to comprehend the insider's point of view. The ethnographer walks a fine line. With too much distance and perspective, one is labeled aloof, remote, insensitive, superficial; with too much familiarity, empathy, and identification, one is suspected of having "gone native." Successful ethnographers resolve that tension between involvement and detachment (see Powdermaker, 1966); others go home early.

In my opportunities for ethnographic research—inquiries into the social behavior of particular culture-bearing groups of people—I have most often been in modern, industrial settings and never, anywhere in the world, have I met anyone "primitive." Yet in confess that whenever I conjure up an image of an ideal ethnographer, I always envision him or her pulling a canoe up on a beach and stepping into the center of a small group of huts among lightly clad villagers in an exotic tropical setting. The imagery is not entirely a figment of my imagination, for it was in conducting research among exotic, or at least unfamiliar, peoples that anthropology got its start and anthropologists built their discipline. Anthropologists have only recently begun to examine how their earlier traditions and experiences in exotic and numerically manageable settings both limit and expand the range of work they might do now and in the future (see, for example, Messerschmidt, 1981).

My old-fashioned image of the ethnographer-at-work evidences still more elements that contribute to a fieldwork mystique and that continue to exert an influence in contemporary settings. The exotic continues to have its appeal, not only for the romantic notions involved but for the fact that one's capabilities for observing, recording, and analyzing what Malinowski (1922/1961) referred to as the "imponderabilia of actual life" are presumed to be enhanced in unfamiliar settings.

I should not pass over that point too quickly. When we talk about ethnographic research in schools, we face the problem of trying to conduct observations *as though* we were in a strange new setting, one with which we actually have been in more or less continuous contact since about the age of six. Anthropologists continue to debate whether cross-cultural experience should be a prerequisite for conducting ethnographically oriented research in schools.

Note that I pictured my ideal ethnographer traveling alone. I might have included a spouse or field assistant, but I definitely do not picture a team of researchers or technical assistants. My image also assumes that the anthropologist is there to stay—to become, for a while, part of the village scenery rather than to remain only long enough to have each villager fill in a questionnaire, submit to a brief interview, or complete a few test items. Tradition even informs the expectation of how long my ideal ethnographer should remain in the field: at least one year. That is not to say that all ethnographic studies are of 12 months' duration; rather, in the absence of other determinants, one is advised to remain at least long enough to see a full cycle of activity, a set of events usually played out in the course of a calendar year.

Note also that my image of ethnographic research is an image of people. The ethnographer is the research instrument, the villagers are the population. That instrument—the anthropologist in person—has been faulted time and time again for being biased, inattentive, ethnocentric, partial, forgetful, overly subject to infection and disease, incapable of attending to everything at once, easily distracted, simultaneously too involved and too detached—the list goes on and on. Be that as it may, what better instrument could we ever devise for observing and understanding human behavior?

If we could actually step into my dream and inquire of my image ethnographer how she or he planned to carry out fieldwork in a newly-arrived-at-setting, it might be disconcerting to hear a somewhat ambiguous response posing a number of possible ideas but suggesting a certain hesitancy about pursuing any one of them to the exclusion of the others. I doubt that an old-fashioned ethnographer would be the least bit embarrassed to confess that after doing some mapping and a village census, she or he wasn't sure just what would be attended to next. Such tentativeness not only allows the ethnographer to move into settings where one cannot frame hypotheses in advance but also reflects the open style that most (not all) ethnographers prefer for initiating fieldwork. That tentativeness is not intended to create a mystique, but to those comfortable only with hypothesis testing, an encounter with someone equally intrigued by discovering instead what the hypotheses *are* can be an unsettling experience. The hardest question for the ethnographer is not so difficult for researchers of other bents: What is it that you look at when you conduct your research? The answer is, of course, "It depends."

What one looks at and writes about depends on the nature of the problem that sends one into the field in the first place; on the personality of the ethnographer; on the course of events during fieldwork; on the process of sorting, analyzing, and writing that transforms the fieldwork experience into the completed account; and on expectations for the final account, including how and where it is to be circulated and what its intended audiences and purposes are. The mystique surrounding ethnography is associated with being in the field because we all harbor romantic ideas of "going off to spend a year with the natives." It is easy to lose sight of the ethnographer's ultimate responsibility to return home and to prepare an account intended to enhance our common human understanding.

Nonetheless, what anthropologists ordinarily do in the course of their fieldwork, regardless of whether their field site is an island in the Pacific Ocean or a classroom in the intermediate wing of the local elementary school, provides us with a way of looking at ethnographic research in action. So let me turn to a point-by-point examination of the customary research techniques of the anthropologist doing fieldwork.

Ethnographic Research Techniques

The most noteworthy thing about ethnographic research techniques is their lack of noteworthiness. No particular research technique is associated exclusively with anthropology. Furthermore, there is no guarantee that one will produce ethnography by using a variety of these techniques. I can make that statement even more emphatically: There is no way one could ever hope to produce an ethnography simply by employing many, or even all, of the research techniques that ethnographers use. Ethnography, as Frederick Erickson (1977) has reminded us, is *not* a reporting process guided by a specific set of techniques. It is an inquiry process carried out by human beings and guided by a point of view that derives from experience in the research setting and from the knowledge of prior anthropological research.

Unlike prevailing tradition in educational research, a preoccupation with method is not sufficient to validate ethnographic research. Ethnographic significance is derived socially, not statistically, from discerning how ordinary people in particular settings make sense of the experience of their everyday lives. As anthropologist Clifford Geertz (1968) has observed, "Anthropological interpretations must be tested against the material they are designed to interpret; it is not their origins that recommend them" (p. vii).

None of the field research techniques that I am about to describe, including ethnography's mainstay, "participant observation," is all that powerful or special. The anthropologist's trade secret, freely disclosed, is that he or she would never for a minute rely solely on a single observation, a single instrument, a single approach. The strength of fieldwork lies in its "triangulation," obtaining information in many ways rather than relying solely on one. Anthropologist Pertti Pelto has described this as the "multi-instrument approach." The anthropologist himself is the research instrument, but in his information gathering he utilizes observations made through an extended period of time, from multiple sources of data, and employing multiple techniques for finding out, for cross-checking, or for ferreting out varying perspectives on complex issues and events. By being on the scene, the anthropologist not only is afforded continual opportunity to ask questions but also has the opportunity to learn which questions to ask.

There is no standard approach even for enumerating the most commonly employed fieldwork practices. The list that I present is adapted from a discussion by authors Pertti and Gretel Pelto in their text *Anthropological Research: The Structure of Inquiry* (1978). My adaptation of the Peltos' list is designed to emphasize two major strategies in fieldwork: participant-observation and interviewing. Many anthropologists summarize fieldwork practice by referring only to those two terms, and some insist that "participant-observation" says it all.

In that sense, participant-observation causes some confusion. Like the term ethnography, it has come to have two meanings. Sometimes it refers to the particular technique of being a participant-observer, one of the important ways anthropologists obtain information. Collectively it can also refer to *all* the techniques that comprise fieldwork, and thus it serves as a synonym for fieldwork itself. Here I use it in the former, more restricted sense—participant-observation as a particular technique.

The review of research techniques that follows is organized into four sections representing four basic research strategies. Each strategy is illustrated by a familiar set of techniques and could be expanded to include still others. The four strategies include the two critical ones already noted—*participant-observation* and *interviewing*—augmented by two others, *use of written sources* and *analysis or collection of nonwritten sources*. Taken together, these four categories are sufficiently inclusive to encompass virtually everything ethnographers do to acquire information.

I should warn that approaching the topic of field techniques this way is better adapted to writing about fieldwork than to doing it. When one is in the field, matters of sequence and sensitivity in using different techniques can be far more important than the choice of them. Problems of "gaining entrée and maintaining rapport," coupled with the absolutely endless task of note writing, account for a good portion of the fieldworker's attention and energy. In the "bush," such everyday concerns as potable water, food purchase and preparation, sanitation, or even a reliable way to receive and send mail, may take precedence over all else. Whatever the contemporary equivalents of those seemingly romantic problems, I call attention here to the techniques themselves, not to how and when one uses them or how information learned through these techniques is subsequently processed. Those facets require one to *think* like an anthropologist, not just to act like one. I have limited this discussion to what fieldworkers do, rather than to how they think about and interpret the information they get. Some important contrasts with more conventional educational research approaches will be apparent in this discussion and will provide the opportunity for summary remarks following the outline of techniques.

Participant-Observation

Participant-observation is such an integral part of fieldwork that some anthropologists might not think to include it in compiling a list of explicit techniques. I know that other anthropologists are appalled when they find colleagues appearing to reify the obvious fact that, as circumstances permit, their research strategy includes their presence among members of a group they are studying. We should be circumspect in describing participant-observation as a formal research technique and recognize ambiguity and contradictions in this seemingly simple solution to pursuing ethnographic research (cf. Martin, 1966/1968). Obviously, we are all participant-observers in virtually everything we do, yet we do all claim to be ethnographers. We are ethnographic observers when we are attending to the cultural context of the behavior we are engaging in or observing, and when we are looking for those mutually understood sets of expectations and explanations that enable us to interpret what is occurring and what meanings are probably being attributed by others present.

I think it is fair to ask anyone who claims title as a participant-observer to provide a fuller description about how each facet—participant, observer, and the precarious nexus between them—is to be played out in an actual research setting. As it turns out, each facet is intertwined with a host of conditions, many of which are quite beyond the control of the ethnographer. Even if we could assume that every ethnographer was equally capable of getting as involved as he or she wanted, and of always having an exquisite sense of just how involved that should be, there are other constraints on the extent to which one can engage in or observe human social behavior. And schools, like other formal institutions, impose rather strict constraints on how anyone—insider or outsider alike—may participate in them. When outsiders come to school as interested observers, it is pretty hard to distinguish among a social scientist, a professor of education, a parent, or a teacher visiting from another school. Schools offer few role options, but one role that is well structured is observer-visitor. Most studies conducted in schools as "participant-observer" research are really "observer" studies augmented by an occasional chance to talk briefly with students or teachers (Khleif, 1974).

If taking a more active role than "observer" seems warranted in conducting ethnographic research in schools, I should point out that there are costs as well as benefits. In my own initiation to fieldwork (Wolcott, 1967), occupying the role of teacher in a cross-cultural classroom may have made a genuine participant-observer study possible, but it also diverted from my research effort the energy that full-time teaching demands. Richard King (1967, 1974) and Gerry Rosenfeld (1971) are two other researchers whose ethnographic studies are from the teacher's perspective. More recently, Sylvia Hart (1982) found that by volunteering as a classroom aide she achieved an optimum balance between opportunities to participate and to observe in studying the social organization of one school's reading program. A few anthropologists have attempted to take the role of the student in the classroom (e.g., Burnett, 1969; Spindler & Spindler, 1982). It always amuses me to think of that huge George Spindler, a major contributor to anthropology and education, sitting at his third-grade desk in a German village. But is worth nothing that of the relatively few accounts obtained from the perspective of either the teacher or the student as participant-observer, the researchers who have conducted them represent several disciplinary interests—sociology (e.g., Everhart, 1983; McPherson, 1972), social psychology (e.g., Smith & Geoffrey, 1968), education (e.g., Cusick, 1973)—rather than only anthropology.

For my own purposes I have found it useful to make distinctions among different participant-observer styles to take into account whether the researcher has (and is able to use) the opportunity to be an *active participant*, is (or eventually becomes) a *privileged observer*, or is at best a *limited observer*. Regardless of ethnographic pedigree or prior experience, most fieldworkers in schools are privileged observers, not active participants. In some settings, the ethnographer must be satisfied with the role of limited observer; in such cases, other field techniques assume great importance. (I might note here that I think the role of active participant has been underutilized in educational research. I encourage those pursuing ethnographic approaches to give careful consideration to opportunities for being active participants rather than passive observers. In traditional fieldwork, one really had no choice.)

Interviewing

Interviewing comprises the second major category of fieldwork techniques. Again I point out that the same techniques I mentioned here in association with ethnography are also used by sociologists, social psychologists, collection agencies, psychiatrists, and the CIA. The only distinction the ethnographer would be sure to draw is between his cherished and respected (and sometimes paid) informant and someone else's subjects or (sometimes paid) informers.

I will briefly introduce seven specific types of interview used by anthropologists: key-informant interview, life history interview, structured or formal interview, informal interview, questionnaire, projective techniques, and—primarily because we are considering school-related research—standardized tests and related measurement techniques.

One should recognize, of course, that I use the category "Interviewing" in a very broad sense. How else can I consider the collection of life history data, conducting a structured interview, and administering an IQ test to be a common set of activities? I include as an interview activity anything that the fieldworker does that intrudes upon the natural setting and is done with the conscious intent of obtaining particular information directly from one's subjects.

In the participant-observer role, ethnographers let the field setting parade before them. In the interviewer role, ethnographers take a critical step in research that can never reversed—they ask. And regardless of whether they ask you the sum of nine plus eight, what you "see" in a set of printed cards or drawings, or to tell your life story, they have imposed some structure upon the setting. In that sense, ethnographers are like other field researchers. But they are also different, in at least two ways. First, they are less likely to put too much faith in any one instrument, set of answers, or techniques. And second, they are more likely to be concerned with the suitability of the technique in a *particular* setting than with the standardization of the technique across different populations. Ethnographers are more likely to prepare a questionnaire after coming to know a setting well rather than beginning a study by using a questionnaire already constructed (or mailing it in lieu of ever visiting at all). Or, given some highly standardized instrument like an intelligence test, they might even try "destandardizing" it, as Richard King (1967) did with Indian pupils in the Yukon Territory when he set out to see whether his pupils couldn't literally get smarter every week through practice and instruction in how to take standardized tests.

The idea of *key-informant interviewing*, the most purely "anthropological" of any of the techniques under discussion here, flies quite in the face of a prevailing notion in education research that truth resides only in large numbers. Anthropologists are so fond of their special term "informant" that they are inclined to refer to all their subjects that way. But informant has a special meaning—it refers to an individual in whom one invests a disproportionate amount of time because that individual appears to be particularly well informed, articulate, approachable, or available. For the anthropological linguist, one key informant is as large a sample as one needs to work out the basic grammar of an unknown language. Ethnographers do not usually rely that heavily on a single informant, but unwittingly or not, I suspect that most fieldworkers rely on a few individuals to a far greater extent than their accounts imply. Inscriptions in completed ethnographies attest to the contribution informants have made to the doing of ethnography (see also Casagrande, 1960).

Researchers using ethnographic techniques in schools have not made extended use of key informants in studies of contemporary education. My hunch is that most of us feel so well versed about what goes on in schools that we become our own key informant in school research. I refer to this approach as "ethnography-minus-one" (Wolcott, 1984). The phrase ethnography-minus-one serves notice that in school-related studies it is often the researcher who is telling us what everything means (and perhaps even how things *should be*) rather than allowing those in the setting to give *their* vision of *their* world (cf. Malinowski, 1961). This is another of the problems we face in doing descriptive research in settings already familiar, where our subjects are *us* rather than *them*.

The *life history* or biographical approach, while not uniquely anthropological, is uniquely suited to anthropology because it helps to convey how the social context that is of such importance to the ethnographer gets played out in the lives of specific individuals. Life history also helps anthropologists get a feeling for how things were before they arrived on the scene and for how people view or choose to portray their own lives (see, for example, Langness & Frank, 1981). Given pervasive anthropological interests in how things change and how they stay the same, attention to life history adds a critical historical dimension to the ethnographic account at the same time that it provides focus on somebody rather than on everybody.

As I have come to understand the extent to which personal ambitions of educators exert a driving force in American education, I have been thinking about the possibility of adapting a life history approach to help us learn more about the impact of personal careers on the dynamics of public education. Alternatively, looking at the "life history" of educational innovations, projects, fads, or movements provides an opportunity for discerning pervasive "patterns" in educator behavior (see, for example, Wolcott, 1977).

I contrast *structured formal interviews* with *informal interviews*, the next two techniques I wish to introduce, in order to emphasize that being in the field provides the ethnographer with almost unlimited opportunity to talk informally with subjects. Informal interviewing—that is, interviewing that does not make use of a fixed sequence of predetermined questions—is possible because the ethnographer is the research instrument. Ranging as it does from casual conversation to direct questioning, informal interviewing usually proves more important than structured interviewing in an extended study (see also Agar, 1980). It is my impression that being on the scene also facilitates getting information from people reluctant to provide a structured interview but willing to talk casually to a neutral but interested listener. I have found that people often will grant a lengthy face-to-face interview although they may insist they are too busy to fill out a questionnaire.

I include *questionnaires* to point out that "relatively systematic" procedures popular among some researchers may also be used by ethnographers, particularly when they are working in settings with sophisticated, literate, and busy people from whom some base-line census data might be helpful, warranted, and perhaps all one can hope to get. But I have seen anthropologists register surprise when colleagues claim that mass survey techniques comprise part of their customary field procedures. I think that most anthropologists would feel obliged to explain why they employed such techniques in a particular setting, just as researchers of other orientations might feel an obligation to explain why they did not use them on a particular occasion. In connecting census data or genealogical data, or in following the formal eliciting techniques of the so-called "new" ethnography or "ethnoscience" approaches, ethnographers follow procedures that are entirely systematic—but they utilize them because they deem them appropriate for understanding the case at hand rather than to sprinkle their findings with ritual doses of scientific legitimacy.

It is important to remember that, unlike most research reported by educators or psychologists, the ethnographer never intends to base a study on the findings of only one technique, one instrument, or one brief encounter. Take a look at the appendices anthropologists include with their studies. They do not ordinarily provide copies of questionnaires or interview schedules; instead, they provide additional information about their subjects: maps; household composition; glossaries; descriptions of ceremonies, songs, chants, magic; maybe a report about the fieldwork experience; but not a copy of a mailed questionnaire form and the accompanying cover letter.

I have included *projective techniques* in this listing more to record an era in fieldwork than to describe customary practice, particularly if the topic brings to mind such standbys as the use of Rorschach Ink Blot cards or pictures from the Thematic Apperception Test. Ever in search of a unifying theory of humankind, anthropologists were intrigued by the psychoanalytic interpretations of the Freudians; in the 1930s and 1940s it was common for anthropologists not only to use projective tests and to cast their observations in psychoanalytic terminology but also to undergo psychoanalysis before venturing into the field. Those interests permeate much of the ethnography recorded in that period. Not many ethnographers today could produce a set of Rorschach cards, although anthropologists continue to share interests with psychologists and psychiatrists. However, given the diversity that the fieldworker confronts, there is obvious appeal in using any technique that can be administered to everyone alike. George and Louise Spindler continue to report success with their Instrumental Activities Inventory, a set of culture-specific drawings used to elicit comments from young respondents about the kind of activities in which they expect to engage, ranging in choice from traditional/rural to modern/urban (Spindler & Spindler, 1965, 1982).

The final type of interview activity I include here, *standardized tests and other measurement techniques*, serves as a reminder that any fieldworker may use virtually any kind of test as a way of eliciting information. For all the obvious attractions of obtaining quantifiable data so well known to educational researchers, however, I should point out that fieldworkers are often reluctant to use such materials themselves and may object vigorously to being required to administer tests or questionnaires selected or devised by others in connection with a large-scale research project. As educators, we are inclined to forget how intrusive test-taking can be and how different it is to test *in* school, where evaluation is a way of life, and to test in populations *out* of school. Anyone who has listened to an adult describe the trauma associated with having to take a driving test (or even the written examination required to obtain a driver's license) after years of not taking tests is reminded how tests can frighten and alienate.

I have not forgotten the experience of a colleague who wished to obtain some test-like data early in the course of his first fieldwork. He began by making a house-to-house census in the village where he was conducting research. While collecting that information, he also decided to explore the sociometrics of villager interaction and their perceptions of personal power and influence. Because he was residing in the village, was accepted by the villagers, and had requested their cooperation through both formal and informal channels, they dutifully answered his questions about private and personal judgments. But, once having complied, for the next three months no one volunteered further information on *any* topic. Only slowly did he regain the rapport he once had and then lost. Questioning can be rude work. Ethnography is not intended to be rude business. Persistent, maybe, but not rude.

Use of Written Resources

In order to emphasize the importance of historical documents and public records in ethnographic research, I use the term *archives* to refer specifically to one type of written sources and use a broad catch-all term, *other written documents*, to include everything else. The importance of archival materials in ethnographic research may reflect the close link between colonial administrations and the early development of both British and American anthropology. In any case, it is important to note that anthropologists use all kinds of written records; they do not limit themselves to what is available in libraries.

Like historians, ethnographers find primary documents of all sorts—letters and diaries, for example—of great value. In working with populations that include school-age children, ethnographers have sometimes sponsored essay contests to encourage young people to write of their experiences (e.g., Kileff & Kileff, 1970). I have already mentioned fieldwork of my own in which I found that assuming the duties of village teacher seemed to hamper my opportunity for interaction. I was so busy keeping school that I often had a little idea of what was going on in the village. Eventually, I discovered that the problem had compensating side. My customary classroom practice of having students write in class every day was providing not only a daily account of village events but the extra bonus of the students' own views of those events as given in the seclusion of written rather than spoken comments. Furthermore, the youngsters chronicling the events were at an age when they moved easily throughout the village, more easily than I could and far more easily than did their circumspect elders. My only hesitancy in relating this episode is that it took me so long to realize how valuable my students' written accounts were in my efforts to learn about village life.

Analysis or Collection of Nonwritten Sources

Far too many "data-gathering" procedures are designed with an overriding concern for getting data that are manageable, codable, punchable. To date, ethnographers seem impressed by what computers can do but they are not so intimidated that they have begun to think like them. They still collect their information in a variety of forms, rather than with an eye to the degrees of freedom afforded by a punchcard or computer program. Perhaps that is why some anthropologists have an expressed preference for the term "fieldwork" rather than for the phrase "data gathering."

It is hard to envision a scene in which colleagues eagerly assemble to see what a quantitatively oriented researcher has brought back to the office after an intense interlude of data gathering. It is hard to imagine an ethnographer who would not have collected pictures, maps, or examples of local handiwork, even if the field site was a nearby classroom. The wall adornments of anthropologists' offices and homes display the results of compulsive collecting. But the use of nonwritten sources is primarily for examination and illustration, not ornamentation, and the linguist with his tapes, or the ethnographer with his photographs, films, or artifacts, find such primary materials invaluable in analysis and write-up, as well as in later testing the adequacy of his developing descriptions and explanations.

I trust I have provided sufficient examples of this fourth and last major category, nonwritten sources, to make the case for the importance of *maps, photographs and film, artifacts,* and *video and audio tapes,* in pursuing ethnographic research. These are virtually indispensable aids in all field-work. The use of photography, particularly in ethnographic filmmaking, has received special attention (J. Collier & M. Collier, 1986; Heider, 1976) and has been applied effectively in classroom research, particularly for examining nonverbal communication (J. Collier, 1973; M. Collier, 1979; Erickson & Wilson, 1982).

The subject of mapping brings me full circle to participant-observation, for one of the first things the ethnographer is advised to do in a new field setting is to make a map. Just think how interesting it would be to teachers, and how natural an activity for an ethnographer, to prepare a map of a school and school-ground, to plot how different categories of people at the school move through its space, and to probe reasons they might offer to explain how things happen to be used or placed as they are. Is that the principal's car or a handicapped employee's car in the specially marked parking space? Why is the nurse's office so near the front office? Do nurses usually have offices? If the principal is the instructional leader of the school, why is the Instructional Materials Center so far from his or her office? How do new students learn about "territory" in the school? Under what circumstances can certain territory be invaded? You see how quickly one thing can lead to another—and how a knowledge of the setting and the people in it helps one get a sense of which questions to ask, of whom, when, and in what manner.

Preparing the Written Account

As I have noted, for me the real mystique of ethnography is in the process of transforming the field experience into a completed account. Rosalie Wax (1971) wisely counsels would-be ethnographers to allow at least as much time for analyzing and writing as one plans to spend in the field. I can only underscore that time for analyzing and writing should be reckoned in equivalents of "uninterrupted days." Fair warning is hereby given that the time commitment is great in terms of customary expectations for research in education. My own fieldwork-based doctoral dissertation added two years to my graduate program in education and anthropology—one full year in research, a second full year to write it up.

It is in the write-up, rather than in the fieldwork, that the materials become ethnographic. What human beings do and say is not psychological, sociological, anthropological, or what have you.

Those disciplinary dimensions come from the structures we impose on what we see and under-stand. It is in the ethnographer's pulling together of the whole fieldwork experience, an activity informed by the observations and writings of other anthropologists, that the material takes ethno-graphic shape as both description of what is going on among a particular social group and a cultural interpretation of how that behavior "makes sense" to those involved (see Wolcott, 1985). As the term ethnography has caught on in educational research, I think astute observers who have produced excellent descriptive accounts have frequently been tempted to tack on the label ethnog-raphy as though it were synonymous with observation itself (see Wolcott, 1980). Let me emphasize again that one might utilize all the field research techniques I have described and not come up with ethnography, while an anthropologist might possibly employ none of the customary field research techniques and still produce an ethnographic account (or at least a satisfactory ethnographic reconstruction).

I should also note that not every cultural anthropologist cares that much about producing ethnography. Some are more theoretically or philosophically inclined. These days some have become interested in method, the analysis of other people's data, or computer solutions to classic anthropological problems. The more action-oriented look for ways to make better use of the huge corpus of data already available. One journal in the field of cultural anthropology (*American Ethnologist*) went so far as specifically to exclude descriptive ethnographic studies from its purview during its first 5 years of publication. Nevertheless, descriptive ethnographic accounts are the building blocks of the discipline of cultural anthropology, just as fieldwork itself is the *sine qua non* of the cultural anthropologist.

Only recently—since about the mid 1960s—have anthropologists given much explicit attention to their research approach. Even less attention has been directed to the difficult business of organizing and writing, other than to repeat well-worn maxims that fieldwork amounts to naught if the notes are not transformed into an ethnographic account, to advise neophyte fieldworkers to begin writing early (preferably to complete a first draft while still in the field), and to acknowledge, more with awe than with instruction, when an occasional ethnographer seems to have made a literary as well as a scholarly contribution. Critical attention to ethnographics as texts has only begun (Marcus & Cushman, 1982; Marcus & Fischer, 1986).

For the beginning writer of a descriptive account, I can offer a few suggestions that have proven useful in my own work and in guiding the work of others. First, I suggest that every effort be made to couple the writing task to ongoing fieldwork. It is splendid indeed if one is able to follow the advice to prepare a first draft while fieldwork is still in progress. In attempting to set down in writing what you understand, you become most acutely aware of what you do *not* understand and can recognize "gaps" in the data while time remains to make further inquiry. But lacking the time, practice, or perspective required for drafting a full account, one can nonetheless begin to "think" in chapters, sections, or expanded outlines, and thus keep tuned to the difficult task sometimes dismissed as simply "writing up one's notes."

Wherever and whenever the task of writing begins, a second bit of advice is to begin at a relatively "easy" place where you are well informed and know (or should know!) what you are talking about. One good starting point is to describe your fieldwork: where you went and what you did. That material may subsequently become part of your first chapter, or an appendix, or a separate, publishable paper. Another good starting point is to begin with the descriptive portion of the account, resisting any temptation to begin making inferences or interpretation but simply telling the story of what happened. Not only will this help to satisfy the anthropological preference for providing a high ratio of information to explanation (Smith, 1964), but it also invites your reader into the interpretive act because he or she shares access to your primary sources. Description and interpretation need not be so dramatically separated in the final account (i.e., treated as separate chapters), but I think it a valuable exercise for someone new to descriptive writing to begin by preparing an "objects" account as free as possible from one's own inferences and preferences.

My next bit of advice might seem to have come from a short course on writing, but I came upon it in the instructions for assembling a wheelbarrow: Make sure all parts are correctly in place before tightening. There is a certain fluidity in developing an ethnographic account. Problem and interpretation remain in flux and in turn influence decisions about what must be included or may be deleted from the descriptive narrative. In that sense, ethnographic accounts can *finished* but they are never really *completed.*

Finally, let me offer the advice here that I frequently give to my students and colleagues: I would not be inclined to use the term "ethnography" in my title or to lay claim to be providing ethnography in my written account unless I was quite certain that I wanted and needed to make that claim. That point goes beyond merely finding an appropriate title, and I will turn to it in concluding this discussion.

"Doing Ethnography" Versus "Borrowing Ethnographic Techniques"

Armed with a list of fieldwork techniques such as those reviewed above, and duly cautioned about the critical complementary tasks involved in the subsequent write-up, is a neophyte researcher ready to start "doing" ethnography? I think not. Let me repeat reservations noted earlier and then attempt to provide a perspective on ethnographic research.

First, none of these fieldwork techniques is exclusive to anthropology, so no single one, including participant-observation, guarantees that the results will be ethnographic.

Second, although one can be reasonably certain that the anthropologist will use several techniques, there is no magic formula. Anthropologists conduct their studies of human social behavior by watching and by asking. When you stop to think about it, most of us have been doing those two things, and for basically the same reasons—to acquire cultural knowledge—since we first were able to watch and, subsequently, to ask. Our continued practice in that regard is scant basis for thinking that we will suddenly start producing ethnography instead of merely continuing to act appropriately. At the same time, here is a gentle reminder to all researchers. In learning to become functioning human beings, we ourselves have relied on numerous sources, numerous techniques, and ample time for attending to multiple significant facets in our lives, not just to a few that were easy to understand or that satisfied rigorous statistical tests.

I thing a certain reserve is warranted in educational research when we claim to be "doing ethnography" yet restrict our research arena solely to schools. The anthropologists conducting research in educational settings would expect to attend to a broad cultural context, but educational researchers do not ordinarily attempt to produce ethnographies or even "micro-ethnographies" per se. Rather than make the claim that they are doing ethnography, when that is neither what they are doing nor what they intend to do, I think educational researchers are well advised to display some modesty in noting in their research how they may at times avail themselves of several techniques for getting their information, how their approach may have been influenced by the characteristic long-term thoroughness of the fieldworker, or how their perspective or analysis may have been informed at least in part by relevant prior work in anthropology. I think it useful to distinguish between anthropologically informed researchers who *do ethnography* and educational researchers who frequently *draw upon ethnographic approaches* in doing descriptive studies.

It is not the techniques employed that make a study ethnographic, but neither is it necessarily what one looks at; the critical element is in interpreting what one has seen. In research among pupils in classrooms and in other learning environments—work generated out of ethnographic interests—a few ethnographically oriented researchers have been looking at smaller units of behavior, such as classroom teaching and learning styles, or at the classroom "participant structures" through which teachers arrange opportunities for verbal interaction (Philips, 1972). They are developing an ever-increasing capacity for examining fine detail—for example, in repeated viewings of filmed or videotaped segments of classroom behavior. But they are also embedding their analysis in cultural context. (See Wolcott, 1982, for a discussion of "styles" of descriptive research.)

We know we do not need to describe everything. We seek to identify those dimensions critical to our understanding of human social behavior and then to describe them exceedingly well. With his pithy phrase, "It is not necessary to know everything in order to understand something," anthropologist Geertz (1973, p. 20) reminds us that we may make headway through modest increments.

I am distressed when I hear educators lament that we have made no progress toward providing *an* ethnography of schooling, but I am also concerned when I hear others imply that we will someday complete *the* ethnography of schooling. The task of description, and thus the potential for ethnography, is endless. We need to look for those purposes in education to which ethnographic research seems best suited, an issue that continues to excite much discussion in the field of anthropology and education.

I think ethnography is well suited to answering the question, "What is going on here?" That is, anthropologically, a question of behaviors and, especially, a question of meanings. Such inquiry proceeds best under conditions where there will be time to find out, and where there is reason to believe that knowing "what-things-mean-to-those-involved" could conceivably make a difference. It also requires some understanding of how one particular instance, or event, or case, or individual, described in careful detail, is not only unique but also shares characteristics in common with other instances or events or cases or individuals. The ethnographer looks for the generic in the specific, following a "natural history" approach that seeks to understand classes of events through the careful examination of specific ones. Geertz (1973) reminds us that there is no ascent to truth without a descent to cases.

The ethnographer, like other social scientists, is concerned with the issue of "representativeness" but approaches that problem differently, by seeking to locate the particular case under study among other cases. The question, as Margaret Mead once noted, is not "Is this case representative?" but rather, "What is this case representative of?" You conduct your research where you can, with whatever available key informant or classroom or family or village best satisfies your research criteria, and then you undertake to learn how that one is similar to, and different from, others of its type.

The ethnographer's concern is always for context. One's focus moves constantly between figure and ground—like a zoom lens on a camera—to catch the fine detail of what individuals are doing and to keep a perspective on the context of that behavior. To illustrate: An ethnographer assisting in educational program evaluation ought to be looking not only at the program under review but at the underlying ethos of evaluation as well. What meaning does evaluation have for different groups or individuals? How do certain people become evaluators of others? Who, in turn, evaluates them? Or, in studying cases of conscious efforts to introduce educational change, ethnographers ought to be looking at the "donors" of change as well as at the recipients or targets of it. Frederick Erickson has posed a question that guides much current ethnographic research in classrooms: What do teachers and children have to know in order to do what they are doing?

The Role of Ethnographic Research in Education

Will ethnographic research become a potent force in shaping the course of formal education? I would like to tell you that it will, since it is the kind of research that most interests me. But I am pessimistic. I don't believe that educational research of any type has yet had great impact on educational practice, and descriptive research portraying how things really are does not seem to capture the imagination of those impatient to make them different.

In and of themselves, ethnographic accounts do not point the way to policy decisions; they do not give clues as to what should be done differently, nor do they suggest how best to proceed. Ethnographic attention tends to focus on how things are and how they got that way, while educators are preoccupied with what education can become. Educators tend to be action-oriented, but ethnography does not point out the lessons to be gained or the action that should be taken. Worse still, anyone who takes the time to read a descriptive account will probably realize that the complexity of the setting or problem at hand has been increased rather than decreased.

We have not yet found or created a strong constituency of informed consumers who have realistic expectations about ethnographic research in education. Perhaps that is where you can help. Let me conclude with three recommendations for how you might simultaneously benefit from and participate in furthering the use of ethnographic approaches in educational research.

First, expand your reading in professional education to include descriptive studies. Like the linguist who can amaze you by explicating rules of your own language that you never knew you knew, ethnographers' accounts of education should have a ring of authenticity to you as a native member of the group being described. And they ought to help you better understand the central process in which you are engaged both professionally and personally: human learning. If they do not, speak out regarding how, in your perception, observers are missing the point about what is going on or what teachers are trying to accomplish. It is not too unlikely that even in trying to explicate the difference between what observers see and what teachers try to do, you will begin to understand the important and useful distinction between what we do and what we say we do, between culture "on the ground" and culture as a system of mutual expectations about what ought to be.

Second, become familiar with the variety of field techniques described here and watch for instances where a multi-instrument approach would be preferable to relying on only one source of information. You might even watch yourself in action as teacher or administrator and ask whether, in your own professional circumstances, you tend to place too much reliance on too few ways of finding out. It is a ready trap for practitioner and researcher alike.

Third, take a cue from the ethnographer and develop a keener appreciation for context in educational research. Whether reading the research reports of others or trying to understand a setting in which you yourself are a participant, keep probing for more, rather than fewer, factors that may be involved. Researchers have a tendency (and, realistically, an obligation) to oversimplify, to make things manageable, to reduce the complexity of the events they seek to explain. Ethnographers are not entirely free from this tendency; if they were, they would not set out to reduce accounts of human social behavior to a certain number of printed pages or a reel of film. But they remain constantly aware of complexity and context. There are no such things as unwanted findings or irrelevant circumstances in ethnographic research. I wonder if it is the characteristic researcher inattention to broader contexts that makes educational research appear so irrelevant to its practitioners. If so, the ethnographic concern for context may be the most important contribution this approach can make.

References

Agar, M.H. (1980). *The professional stranger: An informal introduction to ethnography.* New York: Academic Press.

Burnett, J.H. (1969). Ceremony, rites, and economy in the student system of an American high school. *Human Organization, 28*(1), 1–9.

Casagrande, J.B. (1960). *In the company of man.* New York: Harper and Brothers.

Collier, J., Jr. (1973). *Alaskan Eskimo education: A film analysis of cultural confrontation in the schools.* New York: Holt, Rinehart and Winston.

Collier, J., Jr., & Collier, M. (1986). *Visual anthropology: Photography as a research method.* Albuquerque: University of New Mexico Press.

Collier, M. (1979). *A film study of classrooms in western Alaska.* Fairbanks, AK: Center for Cross-Cultural Studies.

Cusick, P.A. (1973). *Inside high school: The student's world.* New York: Holt, Rinehart and Winston.

Erickson, F. (1977). Some approaches to inquiry in school-community ethnography. *Anthropology and Education Quarterly, 8*(2), 58–69.

Erickson, F., & Wilson, J. (1982). *Sights and sounds of life in schools: A resource guide to film and videotape for research and education.* (Research Series No. 125). East Lansing: Michigan State University Institute for Research on Teaching.

Everhart, R.B. (1983). *Reading, writing and resistance: Adolescence and labor in a junior high school.* Boston: Routeledge and Kegan Paul.

Geertz, C. (1968). *Islam observed.* Chicago: University of Chicago Press.

Geertz, C. (1973). Thick description. In C. Geertz, *The interpretation of cultures.* New York: Basic Books.

Goodenough, W.H. (1976). Multiculturalism as the normal human experience. *Anthropology and Education Quarterly, 7*(4), 4-7.

Hart, S. (1982). Analyzing the social organization for reading in one elementary school. In G. Spindler (Ed.), *Doing the ethnography of schooling: Educational anthropology in action.* New York: Holt, Rinehart and Winston.

Heider, K.G. (1976). *Ethnographic film.* Austin, Texas: University of Texas Press.

Khleif, B.B. (1974). Issues in anthropological fieldwork in schools. In G.D. Spindler (Ed.), *Education and cultural process.* New York: Holt, Rinehart and Winston.

Kileff, C., & Kileff, P. (Eds.). (1970). *Shona customs: Essays by African writers.* Gwelo, Rhodesia (Zimbabwe): Mambo Press.

King, A.R. (1967). *The school at Mopass: A problem of identity.* New York: Holt, Rinehart and Winston.

King, A.R. (1974). The teacher as a participant-observer: A case study. In G.D. Spindler (Ed.), *Education and cultural process: Toward an anthropology of education.* New York: Holt, Rinehart and Winston.

Langness, L.L. & Frank, G. (1981). *Lives: An anthropological approach to biography.* Novato, CA: Chandler and Sharp Publishers.

Malinowski, B. (1961). *Argonauts of the western Pacific.* New York: E.P. Dutton and Co. (Original work published 1922.)

Marcus, G.E., & Cushman, D. (1982). Ethnographies as texts. *Annual Review of Anthropology, 11,* 25–69.

Marcus, G.E. & Fischer, M. (1986). *Anthropology as cultural critique.* Chicago: University of Chicago Press.

Martin, M. (1966/1968). Understanding and participant observation in cultural and social anthropology. *Boston studies in the philosophy of science, IV,* 303–330.

McPherson, G.H. (1972). *Small town teacher.* Cambridge, MA: Harvard University Press.

Messerschmidt, D.A. (Ed.). (1981). *Anthropologists at home in North America: Methods and issues in the study of one's own society.* New York: Cambridge University Press.

Pelto, P.J. & Pelto, G.H. (1978). *Anthropological research: The structure of inquiry* (2d ed.). New York: Cambridge University Press.

Philips, S.U. (1972). Participant structures and communicative competence: Warm Springs children in community and classroom. In C. Cazden, V.P. John, & D. Hymes (Eds.), *Functions of language in the classroom.* New York: Teachers College Press. (Reprinted 1985 by Waveland Press.)

Powdermaker, H. (1966). *Stranger and friend: The way of an anthropologist.* New York: W.W. Norton.

Rosenfeld, G. (1971). *"Shut those thick lips!": A study of slum school failure.* New York: Holt, Rinehart and Winston.

Smith, A.G. (1964). The Dionysian innovation. *American Anthropologist, 66,* 251-265.

Smith, L.M., & Geoffrey, W. (1968). *The complexities of an urban classroom.* New York: Holt, Rinehart and Winston.

Spindler, G.D., & Spindler, L. (1965). The Instrumental Activities Inventory: A technique for the study of the psychology of acculturation. *Southwestern Journal of Anthropology, 21,* 1-23.

Spindler, G.D., & Spindler, L. (1982). Roger Harker and Schonhausen: From the familiar to the strange and back again. In G. Spindler (Ed.), *Doing the ethnography of schooling: Educational anthropology in action.* New York: Holt, Rinehart and Winston.

Wax, R.H. (1971). *Doing fieldwork: Warnings and advice.* Chicago: University of Chicago Press.

Wolcott, H.F. (1967). *A Kwakuitl village and school.* New York: Holt, Rinehart and Winston. (Reprinted 1984 by Waveland Press.)

Wolcott, H.F. (1977). *Teachers versus technocrats: An educational innovation in anthropological perspective.* Eugene, OR: Center for Educational Policy and Management, University of Oregon.

Wolcott, H.F. (1980). How to look like an anthropologist without being one. *Practicing Anthropology, 3*(1), 6-7, 56-59.

Wolcott, H.F. (1982). Differing styles of on-site research, or, "If it isn't ethnography, what is it?" *Review Journal of Philosophy and Social Science, 7*(1,2), 154-169.

Wolcott, H.F. (1984). Ethnographers sans ethnography: The evaluation compromise. In D.M. Fetterman (Ed.), *Ethnography in educational evaluation.* Beverly Hills, CA: Sage Publications.

Wolcott, H.F. (1985). On ethnographic intent. *Educational Administration Quarterly, 21*(3), 187-203. (Republished in G. & L. Spindler, Eds., *Interpretive ethnography of education: At home and abroad.* Hillsdale, NJ: Lawrence Erlbaum Associates, 1987, pp. 37-57.)

Suggestions for Further Reading

Just as the ethnographer attends both to what people do and to what people say they do, a student can learn about ethnographic research both by reading the accounts produced by ethnographers and by reading what ethnographers say they do or how they advise others to go about their research. The references suggested here for further study distinguish between ethnography dealing specifically with education and ethnography in more traditional settings.

Ethnographic Studies of Formal Educational Settings: Bibliographies, Edited Collections, and Series

Burnett, J.H. (1974). *Anthropology and education: An annotated bibliographic guide*. New Haven, CT: Human Relations Area Files Press.

Roberts, J.I., & Akinsanya, S.K. (Eds.). (1976). *Schooling in the cultural context: Anthropological studies of education*. New York: David McKay Company.

Rosenstiel, A. (1977). *Education and anthropology: An annotated bibliography*. New York: Garland Publishing Company.

Spindler, G.D., & Spindler, L. (Eds.). *Case studies in education and culture*. New York: Holt, Rinehart and Winston. This series contains 16 titles, each published as a separate monograph. Although no longer in print, the studies are widely available in libraries, and several have been reissued by Waveland Press, P.O. Box 400, Prospect Heights, IL 60070. The following titles may be of particular interest:

Collier, J., Jr. (1973). *Alaska Eskimo education*.

Hostetler, J., & Huntington, G. (1971). *Children in Amish society*.

Jocano, F.L. (1969). *Growing up in a Philippine barrio*.

King, A.R. (1967). *The school at Mopass*.

Rosenfeld, G. (1971). *"Shut those thick lips!": A study of slum school failure*. (Reissued by Waveland Press, 1983.)

Singleton, J. (1967). *Nichu: A Japanese school*. (Reissued 1982 by Irvington Publishers, 551 5th Avenue, New York, NY 10176.)

Warren, R.L. (1967). *Education in Rebhausen*.

Wolcott, H.F. (1967). *A Kwakiutl village and school*. (Reissued by Waveland Press, 1984.)

Wolcott, H.F. (1973). *The man in the principal's office: An ethnography*. (Reissued by Waveland Press, 1984, with update)

Spindler, G.D. (Ed.). (1982). *Doing the ethnography of schooling: Educational anthropology in action*. New York: Holt, Rinehart and Winston.

Spindler, G.D. (Ed.). (1987). *Education and cultural process: Anthropological approaches*. Prospect Heights, IL: Waveland Press.

Spindler, G., & Spindler, L. (1987). *Interpretive ethnography of education: At home and abroad*. Hillsdale, NJ: Lawrence Erlbaum Associates.

Statements About Using an Ethnographic Approach in Educational Research

Bogdan, R.C., & Biklen, S.K. (1982). *Qualitative research for education: An introduction to theory and methods*. Boston: Allyn and Bacon.

Cassell, J. (1978). *A fieldwork manual for studying desegregated schools*. Washington, D.C., National Institute of Education. This manual, with its valuable bibliography compiled by Murray Wax, is useful to anyone interested in ethnography in education, not just to those inquiring into desegregated schools.

Erickson, F. (1977). Some approaches to inquiry in school-community ethnography. *Anthropology and Education Quarterly, 8*(2), 58–69.

Erickson, F. (1984). What makes school ethnography "ethnographic?" *Anthropology and Education Quarterly, 15*(1), 51–66.

Erickson, F., & Wilson, J. (1982). *Sights and sounds of life in schools: A resource guide to film and videotape for research and education.* (Research Series No. 125). East Lansing: Michigan State University Institute for Research on Teaching.

Smith, L.M. (1957). The micro-ethnography of the classroom. *Psychology in the Schools, 4,* 216–221.

Smith, L.M. (1982). Ethnography. In *Encyclopedia of educational research* (5th ed.). New York: Macmillan Free Press.

Wolcott, H.F. (1975). Criteria for an ethnographic approach to research in schools. *Human Organization, 34*(2), 111–127.

Wolcott, H.F. (1981). Confession of a "trained" observer. In T.S. Popkewitz & B. Robert Tabachnick (Eds.), *The study of schooling: Field based methodologies in educational research and evaluation.* New York: Praeger.

Wolcott, H.F. (1985). On ethnographic intent. *Educational Administration Quarterly, 21*(3), 187–203.

Anthropological Accounts About Ethnographic Research in General

Agar, M.H. (1980). *The professional stranger: An informal introduction to ethnography.* New York: Academic Press. The style, the emphasis on interview data, and the attention to early stages in fieldwork make this a valuable introductory book.

Bowen, E.S. (1954). *Return to laughter.* New York: Harper and Brothers. This is one of the earliest personal accounts of fieldwork experience.

Cesara, M. (1982). *Reflections of a woman anthropologist: No hiding place.* New York: Academic Press.

Geertz, C. (1973). Thick description: Toward an interpretative theory of culture. In C. Geertz, *The interpretation of cultures.* New York: Basic Books.

Heider, K.G. (1976). *Ethnographic film.* Austin: University of Texas Press.

Kimball, S.T., & Partridge, W.L. (1979). *The craft of community study: Fieldwork dialogues.* Gainesville: University Presses of Florida.

Langness, L.L., & Frank, G. (1981). *Lives: An anthropological approach to biography.* Novato, CA: Chandler and Sharp.

Marcus, G.E., & Clifford, J. (1985). The making of anthropological texts: A preliminary report. *Current Anthropology, 26*(2), 267–271.

Marcus, G.E., & Fischer, M. (1986). *Anthropology as cultural critique.* Chicago: University of Chicago Press.

Naroll, R., & Cohen, R. (1970). *A handbook of method in cultural anthropology.* New York: Natural History Press. (Also in paperback edition, Columbia University Press, 1973.)

Pelto, P.J., & Pelto, G.H. (1978). *Anthropological research: The structure of inquiry* (2d ed.). New York: Cambridge University Press. These authors present a point-by-point discussion of each of the techniques described in the chapter.

Powdermaker, H. (1966). *Stranger and friend: The way of an anthropologist*. New York: W.W. Norton.

Spindler, G.D., & Spindler, L. (Eds.). (1965 ff.). *Studies in anthropological method*. New York: Holt, Rinehart and Winston. This series contains 15 monographs describing particular facets of fieldwork or relating the ethnographer's experiences during a particular study. The series is long out of print, but copies can usually be found in social science libraries.

Spindler G.D. (Ed.). (1970). *Being an anthropologist: Fieldwork in eleven cultures*. New York: Holt, Rinehart and Winston.

Spradley, J.P., & McCurdy, D.W. (1972). *The cultural experience: Ethnography in complex society*. Chicago: Science Research Associates. This little classic presents a short introduction to the "New Ethnography" followed by 12 beginning ethnographies conducted by Spradley and McCurdy's undergraduate students using that approach.

Wax, R.H. (1971). *Doing fieldwork: Warnings and advice*. Chicago: University of Chicago Press.

An Ethnographic Sampler

(Original date of publication is given but most of these classics are available in paperback editions. Mead and Turnbull are good authors to read first.)

Firth, Raymond: *We, the Tikopia* (1936).

Malinowski, Bronislaw: *Argonauts of the western Pacific* (1922).

Mead, Margaret: *Coming of age in Samoa* (1927); *Growing up in New Guinea* (1930).

Simmons, Leo (Ed.): *Sun chief: The autobiography of a Hopi Indian* (1942).

Thomas, Elizabeth M.: *The harmless people* (1958).

Turnbull, Colin: *The forest people: A study of the pygmies of the Congo* (1961); *Wayward servants: The two worlds of the African pygmies* (1965). (See also *The Mbuti pygmies: Change and adaptation*. New York: Holt, Rinehart and Winston, 1983.)

Contemporary Ethnography

Edgerton, R.B. (1967). *The cloak of competence: Stigma in the lives of the mentally retarded*. Berkeley: University of California Press.

Estroff, S.E. (1981). *Making it crazy: An ethnography of psychiatric patients in an American community*. Berkeley: University of California Press.

Messerschmidt, D.A. (Ed.). (1981). *Anthropologists at home in North America: Methods and issues in the study of one's own society*. New York: Cambridge University Press.

Ogbu, J. (1974). *The next generation: An ethnography of education in an urban neighborhood*. New York: Academic Press.

Taylor, C. (1970). *In horizontal orbit: Hospitals and the cult of efficiency*. New York: Holt, Rinehart and Winston.

Suggested General Reading for Learning About the Field of Cultural Anthropology

Benedict, R. (1934). *Patterns of culture.* Always available in paperback editions, this best-seller gives an excellent portrayal of cultural diversity although its anthropology is dated.

Geertz, C. (1973). *The interpretation of cultures.* New York: Basic Books. To a collection of his previously published articles Clifford Geertz added a brilliant introductory essay that makes this book a "must."

Keesing, R.M. (1981). *Cultural anthropology: A contemporary perspective* (2d ed.). New York: Holt, Rinehart and Winston. Virtually any introductory text or collection of readings in cultural anthropology provides a good introduction to the field. Keesing's book is cited here as an especially good example of a single-author text that has undergone several revisions.

Kluckhohn, C. (1949). *Mirror for man.* Like Benedict's *Patterns of culture,* this book's timelessness has been proven through repeated printings.

The Forum

The study materials noted above offer the interested student an opportunity to become more familiar with ethnography by reading widely among readily available materials. In addition, there are several national organizations whose members include individuals with particular interests in ethnographic research and whose annual meetings and journals provide a forum for scholarly exchange. Attendance at their meetings or inspection of their journals is an excellent way to learn about current issues, find others who share interest in a specific problem, or begin an active organizational involvement. Details about subscriptions and memberships may be obtained by writing to the addresses listed.

Council on Anthropology and Education, 1703 New Hampshire Avenue, NW, Washington, DC, 20009. (Publication: *Anthropology and Education Quarterly.*)

American Educational Research Association, 1230 17th Street, NW, Washington, DC, 20036. (Association publications: *American Educational Research Journal; Educational Researcher; Review of Educational Research.*)

Society for Applied Anthropology, P.O. Box 24083, Oklahoma City, OK 73124–0083. (Publications: *Human Organization, Practicing Anthropology.*)

Study Questions

1. What are the differences, if any, between the role of hypotheses in ethnographic research and in more quantitative research methods, such as experimental research or correlational research?

2. Is it correct to say that in ethnographic research, in contrast to other research methods in education, decisions on the collection of specific data evolve, rather than being prespecified?

3. Discuss the role of "triangulation" or the "multi-instrument approach" in ethnographic research. Given an example of the way you might employ triangulation in an educational research study.

4. If you were to attempt to develop an ethnographic account of a third-grade class over the period of an entire school year, what roles might allow you to be a participant-observer? What are some possible advantages and limitations for each role?

5. What types of interviewing techniques might be employed in ethnographic research in education? Give an example of how life history interviews might be used in an ethnographic study of a school system.

6. Survey research is usually considered a separate research method. Is it therefore appropriate for an ethnographic researcher to use survey techniques? In using survey research methods, is an ethnographer stepping outside of his/her role and abandoning ethnography?

7. Could an ethnographer use standardized tests in gathering information about third-grade students? If so, would the ethnographer be likely to use the tests in the same way they are used by a school system's director of testing? How would these two uses of standardized tests likely differ?

8. Are "key informants" critical in doing ethnographic research on a school system in the United States? Discuss the relative usefulness of key informants in studying U.S. school systems and Japanese school systems, assuming *you* were attempting to do the research.

9. We usually think of ethnographic research as an attempt to portray a culture in its present-day totality. If this is correct, can historical records, whether formal or informal, play a role in developing an ethnography? Can you give an example of the way historical documents might be used in ethnography? Can you give an example of the way historical documents might be used in ethnographic research in education?

Qualitative Methods in a Team Approach to Multiple-Institution Studies

Elizabeth J. Whitt and George D. Kuh

Qualitative research methods produce data in the form of words which are then analyzed by "human instruments" (the investigators) (Lincoln and Guba 1985). These methods are particularly useful for exploring such "hard-to-measure" features of institutions of higher education as cultures, values, norms, and beliefs (Crowson 1987, 1; Peterson, 1985). Although qualitative methods have occasionally been used in studies of college and university life (e.g., Clark 1970; Heath 1968; Leemon 1972), investigations involving multiple sites and multiple investigators are rare (Crowson 1987; Tierney 1985). Yet qualitative studies of multiple institutions, such as Gerald Grant and David Riesman's (1978) portrayal of students and faculty at successful experimental colleges and Eugene Rice and Ann Austin's (1988) analysis of faculty morale in "exemplary" liberal arts colleges, permit in-depth understanding and broad comparisons of different college and university contexts (Crowson 1987; Herriot and Firestone 1983).

The purposes of this article are: (1) to describe the team approach used in the College Experiences Study, a qualitative investigation of fourteen institutions with reputations for providing unusually rich out-of-class learning opportunities for their undergraduate students (Kuh, Schuh, Whitt, Andreas, Lyons, Strange, Krehbiel, and MacKay 1991), and 92) to explain the usefulness of such an approach in higher education research. We discuss, first, the conceptual framework used to guide the inquiry and, second, research methods, including data sources, data collection, and data analysis. Finally, we offer several conclusions about the efficacy of the team approach to multi-site research in higher education.

Theoretical Framework

Colleges and universities are complex organizations characterized by loose coupling and cultures that are difficult to measure or quantify (Dill 1982; Kuh and Whitt 1988; Morgan 1984; Schein 1985; Weick 1976). Given these characteristics, qualitative methods, with their superiority to other research methods in identifying values, assumptions, expectations, and behavior (Goetz and LeCompte 1984; Van Maanen 1979a), can be particularly useful in higher education research. The superiority of qualitative methods for studying complex organizations and processes stems from five principles inherent to qualitative research: (1) a search for understanding, (2) investigator proximity, (3) inductive analysis, (4) familiarity with the setting and phenomena under investigation, and (5) an appreciation of the value-laden nature of inquiry (Crowson 1987).

The "central goal" (Crowson 1987, 4) of qualitative research is understanding, rather than the identification of causes or generalizability. Hence, investigators attempt to see and appreciate the setting studied from the perspectives of the persons within it and strive to interpret what is seen in light of participants' frames of reference. In addition, the investigators' findings and interpretations must be presented in such a way that both participants (insiders) and outsiders achieve greater understanding of the setting and its cultures (Schein 1985).

In order to attain understanding, investigators must study behaviors as they occur and hear the thoughts and words of participants first-hand (Crowson 1987; Van Maanen 1979a). Immersion in the setting enables investigators to gather multiple perspectives and observe many and varied behaviors and events (Chaffee and Tierney 1988; Crowson 1987). In this way they can provide the thick description needed for outsiders to understand the setting and for insiders to judge the accuracy of the investigators' portrayal.

Qualitative data are analyzed inductively (i.e., understanding is developed from observed data) rather than deductively (i.e., formulating hypotheses and identifying data categories or variables *a priori*) (Crowson 1987; Lincoln and Guba 1985). At the outset of the study, investigators are not aware of all that they do not know (Lincoln and Guba 1985); hence, the development of preconceived hypotheses or explanations of what is going on is likely to inhibit consideration of all possible meaningful behavior and events. An inductive approach allows the setting and the investigators' growing knowledge of the setting to shape the research process.

Effective field research using qualitative methods requires that the investigators be familiar not only with appropriate inquiry techniques but also with the phenomena under study. Familiarity with the setting (or type of setting), people, and processes to be examined prepares investigators for at least some of what they should look for or might see. Also, knowledgeable investigators are likely to be more credible and less visible to the "natives" in the setting (Crowson 1987). At the same time, too much familiarity can be inhibiting; unusual events or patterns may be ignored, and/or alternative explanations or questions may be dismissed.

Qualitative research acknowledges that inquiry is value laden, not value free. Investigators are bound by the values of their inquiry paradigm (e.g., positivist or naturalist) and cultural context, as well as by the values extant in the research setting; these values influence what the investigators see and the meanings they make (Crowson 1987; Lincoln and Guba 1985; Van Maanen 1979b). Investigators bias and the influence of contextual values can be offset somewhat by rigorous and prolonged focus on the perspectives of insiders (Crowson 1987) as well as by continuous feedback from insiders about the emerging findings and interpretations. Steps taken in this study to cope with these and other methodological problems are described next.

Research Methods

The Research Team

The ambitious scope of the College Experiences Study required multiple investigators. One or two individuals could not have conducted the number of interviews and observations required to provide a rich description of fourteen colleges and universities. Also, as mentioned above, each investigator had to be familiar with qualitative research methods, different types of institutions of higher education, and the phenomenon to be studied—student learning outside the classroom.

The research team consisted of nine members: four faculty, including a former college president and university provost, a former academic dean and department chair, the head of a preparation program in college student affairs administration, and a former dean of students; three student life administrators, including one chief student affairs officer with twenty-five years of experience at private institutions of higher education, one associate vice president for student affairs at an urban university who also had extensive experience with residence life, and one dean of students who had served at both commuter and residential universities; and two graduate students, one of whom had experience in student affairs administration at a women's college and at large public universities.

Data Sources

In May and June 1988, the team used a two-stage nomination process to identify a small number of four-year colleges and universities reputed to provide high-quality out-of-class experiences for undergraduates. Fifty-eight experts representing a variety of experiences, viewpoints, and constituencies in higher education (scholars, association leaders, accreditation agency representatives, presidents) participated in one or both rounds of the nomination process. They were asked to identify up to five institutions in each of the following categories: (1) residential colleges with fewer than five thousand students; (2) residential colleges/universities with five thousand or more students; (3) urban-commuter institutions (i.e., those with a high proportion of commuting and part-time students); (4) single-sex colleges; and (5) historically black colleges.

The research team met for three days in August 1988 to review research methods and to select, from among the nominated institutions, the colleges and universities to be included in the study. Focusing primarily on the results of the second round of nominations, the team—after a series of discussions—identified the fourteen institutions. Several factors influenced the selection process: (1) previous studies of the institution, if any, (2) the geographic region of the country in which the institution was located, and (3) the form of institutional control. We assumed that regional context and form of control influence both the characteristics of students and an institution's environment and, hence, the student experience (Kuh and Whitt 1988); therefore, we wanted all regions of the country represented and a balance between public and private institutions.

We claim no scientific sampling process. However, we polled and interviewed experts, then carefully developed and reviewed the final list of nominations together; the process satisfied us that this set of colleges and universities could offer useful information about fostering learning outside the classroom.

Prior to the campus visits, members of the site team obtained and reviewed written information about the institution, including institutional histories, catalogs, admissions materials, and institutional reports describing student characteristics. We provided a list of desired interviewees (i.e., president, chief academic officer, chief student affairs officer, faculty, students) to a contact person at the institution so that those interviews could be scheduled in advance.

Various members of the research team served as site-visit coordinator; this person was responsible for working with the campus contact person to arrange interviews, lodging, and airport transportation. The site-visit coordinator also worked with site team members to decide who would do which interviews and deal with any scheduling problems that arose. Because delayed flights and campus emergencies occasionally disrupted the interview schedule, we learned early to be flexible. For example, bad weather and flight delays kept one college president out of town during our visit, and we interviewed him by telephone.

The first round of site visits was conducted by teams of two to four (depending on the size of the institution) investigators from mid-September through early December 1988; the teams typically spent three or four days at each institution, again, depending on the size of the institution and scheduling constraints. After the first round of visits, the entire research team met to decide if second visits were necessary. Teams of two to four investigators made second visits to twelve institutions between January and May 1989.

Data Collection

Data collection (interviews, observations, document analysis) and analysis were conducted concurrently so that existing data could inform the collection and interpretation of additional data (Lincoln and Guba 1985; Miles and Huberman 1984). As we analyzed the data we also identified additional questions that needed to be asked or gaps in our understanding of a particular institution. For example, analysis of our first visit to one university revealed contradictory information about the quality of student life: some faculty described students' activities as too social and frivolous, while other faculty and students described widespread involvement in a variety of educationally purposeful projects, including extensive community service. During our second visit, we pursued this issue with more faculty, students, and administrators, and were able to portray student experiences in a way that was deemed accurate by all groups.

Participants

Because all of the events and people in a setting cannot be studied, some sort of sampling process was needed, although this necessarily limited the scope of the research and restricted the investigators' attention to some extent (Crowson 1987; Miles and Huberman 1984). Our theoretical framework and knowledge of college and university life, particularly the undergraduate student experience, guided our initial selections of what to observe and whom to interview.

The institutional contact person, usually the chief student affairs officer or her designate, was asked to schedule the initial round of interviews. We initially selected participants using status sampling (Dobbert 1984). In this instance, status sampling required interviews with the president, chief academic and student affairs officers, their principal assistants, faculty members, profession staff who worked directly with students, student leaders, and other students. The principle of inclusion was stressed to the contact person; we needed as many and diverse perspectives as possible (Miles and Huberman 1984; Schein 1985). For example, we wanted to be certain that we talked with students who held formal leadership roles as well as some who were not well-integrated into the dominant student culture(s) and social system. We also wanted to talk with faculty who did not have much contact with students outside of class, as well as those who did, for example, advisors to student organizations.

Once at the site, we employed a variant of snowball sampling to expand the participant pool (Crowson 1987; Dobbert 1984). At the conclusion of each interview, we asked participants to identify others whose opinions and/or out-of-class activities and experiences differed from their own, such as students who seemed less (or more) involved in campus life and faculty who had been at the institution for a longer (or shorter) period of time. We also did impromptu interviews in cafeterias, library foyers, student centers, residence halls, fraternity and sorority houses, and other living units.

All participants signed a consent form giving permission to use information obtained from them in the study. They were assured that their participation was voluntary and that they could withdraw from the study at any time (Dobbert 1984), although no one did.

Interviews

Our primary methods of data collection were interviews with individuals and focus groups (Merton, Fisk, and Kendall 1956; McMillin 1989). We interviewed approximately thirteen hundred persons during the course of the study. Focus groups are semi-structured discussion groups that meet only once and concentrate on a specific topic, such as factors related to students' out-of-class experiences. Focus groups are particularly useful for obtaining in-depth information about attitudes, values, and beliefs which may not be apparent in observations of behavior or individual interviews, and for generating ideas and insights at the outset of a study (McMillin 1989). The interaction and discussion among focus group members in response to open-ended questions from investigators can elicit rich information about participants' experiences and interpretations (McMillin 1989). Our focus group interviews turned out to be lively group discussions; the investigators' main functions were keeping the group on task and making sure that everyone had an opportunity to speak.

The degree of structure imposed on our interviews varied from less to more as the investigation proceeded (Crowson 1987; Lincoln and Guba 1985). To provide a general sense of direction for the interview process, we developed initial questions for each category of participant (e.g., president, student) based on the purposes and research questions of the study (Kuh, et al. 1991). All investigators at all of the sites used these interview protocols. The team added questions as interviewing progressed and additional clarification became necessary or as we needed to add new types of information, such as about differences across institutional types. For example, one of the team members found the question, "What is special about your college?", very useful in evoking a wide range of institutional images and perceptions. All of the investigators decided to begin each interview in that way.

Interviews were audiotaped with the participants' permission so that all of the information could be accurately retrieved. Transcripts were made of interviews that were deemed to be especially useful (e.g., student leaders, minority students, faculty). The investigators compiled interview data on interview summary forms (Miles and Huberman 1984) to identify themes, questions, and reactions generated by each interview. This information was used to develop additional questions and during data analysis.

Observations

A secondary source of data was observing programs, events, and activities that took place during the campus visits. Information from observations typically was used to generate topics for interviews (Barley 1983) and fell into three categories: (2) regularly scheduled events (e.g., convocations, concerts), (2) spontaneous events (e.g., frisbee matches), and (3) events conducted for the purpose of our visit (e.g., residence hall tours). We did not actively participate in the events observed; rather, we recorded notes and impressions on observation summary forms to facilitate the process of identifying additional questions and emergent themes (Dobbert 1984).

Documents

Documents were another secondary source of information and, like observations, provided topics and questions for interviews while helping team members understand the institutional context (Dobbert 1984). The following documents, obtained before campus visits, were particularly useful: handbooks (e.g., policy, procedure, faculty, student, and staff), promotional pamphlets (e.g., admissions viewbooks, student organization recruitment brochures), institutional mission and goal statements, institutional histories, and other documents that referred to the integration of students' out-of-class experiences with the academic mission of the institution.

In addition to printed documents, we reviewed video tapes and slide presentations used for institutional advancement and recruitment purposes. Other relevant documents also surfaced during campus visits, among them student newspapers, planning documents, and "table tents" advertising events and activities. Data gathered from document analyses were recorded on document summary forms. The forms on which we summarized interviews, observations, and document analyses were based on Miles and Huberman's (1984). Each type of form was a different color so that it could be easily identified. (We generated a lot of paper!)

Data Analysis

The process of analyzing the data collected in this study was complicated, not only because of the large amount of data obtained by nine investigators at fourteen institutions, but also because we needed to focus simultaneously on analyzing data within the individual institutional sites and across sites. Our decision at the outset of the study to use common summary forms and data coding facilitated both within-site and cross-site data analysis.

Within-site Analysis

We drew again on Miles and Huberman to develop a coding scheme that enabled us to identify categories for the purpose of organizing and retrieving data. Categories encompassed a single theme, containing those units of data that related to the same content (Lincoln and Guba 1985). The research team formulated a preliminary list of category codes from the conceptual framework, objectives, and questions of the study. These categories were: (1) the role of faculty, staff, students, and others regarding out-of-class experiences, (2) descriptions and roles of student subcultures, (3) descriptions and roles of institutional history and traditions, (4) descriptions and roles of institutional policies and practices, (5) descriptions and roles of institutional mission, (6) characteristics of student involvement in out-of-class life, (7) tentative explanations and speculations, and (8) other (creating additional categories as necessary).

At the end of each day of a campus visit, the members of the site team met to talk about their experiences. These meetings were intended to: (1) generate questions for subsequent interviews, (2) identify events to observe, documents to review, or people to interview, (3) begin (or, in the case of later first-round or second-round visits, continue) to identify themes and patterns in the data collected, and (4) "recharge" tired researchers by recounting the highlights and unusual experiences of their day. Team meetings were recorded, either on tape or by written notes, for use in writing the case report and planning for the second round of visits.

After each site visit, each investigator completed a case analysis form in which data from interviews, observations, and documents were placed in the categories developed by the group. These forms, as well as interview tapes and notes, were forwarded to the investigator designated as the site coordinator. The first task of the site coordinator was to compile all of the site data, including notes from team meetings on-site. The coordinator then assigned the data to categories; case analysis forms from the other investigators were used to assess the completeness of these categories. Placing data in categories at this point served two purposes. First, having the site data in categories enabled the development of a case report that summarized findings and conclusions for the first visit. Second, categorization of the site data provided a basis for analysis of data across sites, a process which is described below.

The case report of the first visit served as an "interim site summary," synthesizing what was known about; the site and identifying remaining questions to be explored (Miles and Huberman 1984, 75). The case report was then circulated among all members of the research team to inform data collection at other sites. The report was also sent to participants at the institution so that they could confirm or deny the investigators' constructions of their words and feelings (Lincoln and Guba 1985; Miles 1979). During the second round of site visits, debriefing meetings were held with groups of participants, many of whom had been interviewed in the first round. They were asked about their reactions to the interim case report: Did it fit their view of the "reality" of their institution? Were there important themes, people, or events that had been overlooked in the first visit? Had the investigators misinterpreted or misunderstood something that had been communicated? What else did we need to know to understand and accurately describe their institution and student learning outside the classroom? Information and insights from these debriefing sessions enabled us to deepen our understanding of the institutions from the perspectives of insiders and to alter the case reports as necessary to conform more closely to those perspectives. For example, many Stanford participants thought that our interim site summary of Stanford University overemphasized what was positive and underemphasized problems, no doubt because our purpose was to discover what each institution was doing well. Nevertheless, we incorporated additional information that enabled us to provide what was, in the eyes of participants, a more balanced and more accurate portrayal of Stanford. We return to the issue of participant debriefings in the section on trustworthiness.

After the second round of visits, we repeated the process used to record and analyze site data, incorporated new data into the revised case reports, and once again sent them to participants at each institution for their reactions and suggestions. Long after the conclusion of the campus visits, we continued to receive occasional BITNET comments and suggestions from participants which we incorporated into our "final" case reports for each institution.

Cross-site Analysis

Data from all of the first-round campus visits were compiled and analyzed at a meeting of the research team in December 1988. For the purposes of cross-site analysis, we "standardized" data from the individual sites by means of common categories and common reporting formats (i.e., interview, observation, and document summary forms; case analysis forms; interim site reports) (Miles and Huberman 1984, 152). We then used a four-stage process to analyze the standardized data: (1) development of a meta-matrix, (2) clustering of data, (3) identification of patterns, and (4) development of propositions (Miles and Huberman 1984).

In developing meta-matrices, "the basic principle is the basic inclusion of all relevant data" (Miles and Huberman 1984, 152). The project director developed a meta-matrix from summaries of within-site analyses. Data from each institution were described by categories: (1) the role of faculty, staff, students, and others regarding out-of-class experiences, (2) descriptions and roles of student subcultures, (3) descriptions and roles of institutional history and traditions, (4) descriptions and roles of institutional policies and practices, (5) descriptions and roles of institutional mission, (6) characteristics of student involvement of out-of-class life, and (7) tentative explanations and speculations.

Once the meta-matrix was prepared, the team members clustered data to identify commonalities and differences in categories across sites (Miles and Huberman 1984). In addition, we described commonalities and differences according to the five types of institutions: small residential, large residential, urban-commuter, single-sex, historically black. Except in the case of urban-commuter institutions, the various institutional types had many more elements in common than differences (Kuh et al. 1991).

The cluster of "things in common" was then examined to identify patterns or themes emerging in each category. From those themes, we developed a set of propositions to describe and explain, however tentatively, factors and conditions associated with high-quality out-of-class experiences for undergraduates. An example of a tentative proposition was that a distinctive and clearly communicated institutional mission was associated with student involvement in educationally purposeful activities. The propositions were discussed in debriefings with participants and evaluated during the second round of institutional visits.

In mid-March 1989, after half of the second-round visits were completed, the team met to analyze data from those visits and reconsider the propositions identified in December. As a result of new information (both from second-round interviews and debriefings with participants), we expanded and altered the original set of factors and conditions. For example, in December we had identified egalitarianism as a condition of environments which encouraged students to take advantage of learning opportunities. In March, it was clear that, at some of the institutions, such as Miami University and Xavier University, distinctions were made among roles and statuses; however, these distinctions were consistent with the institutional mission and also appeared to foster student involvement in out-of-class learning (Kuh et al. 1991). Hence, we revised our original proposition to focus on interpersonal distinctions in a *variety* of forms, all of which were consistent with the mission of the institution in which they were found.

At our final team meeting in June 1989, we looked at the data from the rest of the second-round visits and incorporated additional information and insights into our propositions; at that point, our task was mostly one of filling in and refining, rather than adding to or deleting from, the factors and conditions. The bulk of our time at that meeting was spent in trying to identify the policy and practice implications of our findings.

Because space limitations preclude a description of all of the findings and conclusions of the College Experiences, two examples must suffice. First, we concluded that a distinctive and clearly communicated institutional mission encourages student involvement in learning. At Involving Colleges (our shorthand term for the fourteen institutions), students, faculty, and administrators had a shared understanding of the institution's mission and could talk about its meaning for their lives. We also concluded that institutions that see the college experience in holistic terms encourage student involvement. Involving Colleges blurred the boundaries between the academic and the nonacademic and saw educational opportunities in all aspects of students' lives. (For a thorough discussion of the findings of the study, see Kuh et al. 1991.)

Team Functioning

The foregoing description may seem to portray a systematic, methodical, even dry, process of group analysis. Not so. Our team discussions were intense, lively, and challenging, characterized as much by arguments as by agreement, as much by talking side roads as following a planned route. Four "rules" did, however, emerge from our discussions: (1) everyone was expected to contribute to the process of analysis, (2) we made decisions about conclusions to be drawn from the data and propositions by consensus, although divergent views on some matters persist, (3) thinking aloud was encouraged, and (4) every attempt was made to avoid taking things personally, as in cases where, despite the rules, someone's idea was attacked as "bad." On occasion, feathers were ruffled, but we confronted problems openly and dealt with them. Periodic breaks to get away from one another (to jog, take naps, etc.) were helpful.

Team members took turns playing the roles as gatekeeper, encourager, moderator, and recorder. (All team meetings were taped as well.) Some people talked more than others; some preferred to take notes and summarize; some had a high need to stay on task while others needed to ramble (although even the most task-oriented among us came to recognize that taking tours down side roads often led us to fruitful new territories). The project director took responsibility for making sure that we accomplished what we needed to, although we always needed more time together than we had. Follow-up "meetings" took place by phone or BITNET after we returned to our home institutions.

Establishing Trustworthiness

The principles of qualitative research described earlier—seeking understanding, allowing the research design to emerge, using a human instrument to study natural settings, familiarity with the setting and phenomena being studied, primary reliance on interviews with respondents—can create discomfort for researchers socialized to standards of conventional scientific inquiry (Crowson 1987). For example, replicability (necessary to establish reliability) is probably impossible and even, by the standards of some inquiry paradigms, undesirable (Lincoln and Guba 1985). Also, oral data can be particularly misleading as respondents knowingly or unknowingly try to place their experiences, ideas, and institution in the best possible light (Van Maanen 1979b). The complexities and contradictions of institutions of higher education further muffle attempts to accurately portray "reality" to the satisfaction of both natives and outsiders (Crowson 1987). "The central difficulty," observed Robert Crowson, "lies in the need to maintain the flexibility, opportunism, idiosyncrasy, and holism required to maximize the inductive potential of an inquiry, while providing the many checks that lead the skeptical reader toward a sense of confidence in the study's report" (1987, 40).

With these difficulties in mind, we adopted the standard of trustworthiness to answer the question, "How can an inquirer persuade his or her audiences (including self) that the findings of an inquiry are worth paying attention to, worth taking account of?" (Lincoln and Guba 1985, 290; see also Crowson 1987). Criteria for trustworthiness include credibility (the investigators' constructions of the setting are credible to the participants), transferability (the study may be useful in another context), dependability (the reporting of results considers possible changes over time), the confirmability (the data can be confirmed by someone other than the inquirer) (Lincoln and Guba 1985).

Credibility

Triangulation, peer debriefing, and member checks were used to establish credibility (Lincoln and Guba 1985). Triangulation is a technique for judging the accuracy of data and requires multiple data sources and/or multiple methods of data collection. Multiple sources of data may include various "copies" of one kind of source, such as multiple participants, and different sources of the same information. In this study, data were obtained from five different types of institutions of higher education. In addition, at every institution, participants in nine general categories (i.e., students, presidents, chief academic officers, chief student affairs officers, faculty, student affairs staff, institutional historians, alumni/ae, and trustees) were interviewed. All nine types of participants at all five types of institutions were asked to provide information about the out-of-class experiences of undergraduates, the role of institutional agents and policies in those experiences, and the connection, if any, between out-of-class experiences and the academic mission of the institution.

Peer debriefing by the inquirer is used: (1) to ensure that the inquirer is aware of her or his personal perspectives and perceptions—the researcher's "perceptual screen" (Van Maanen 1979b, 548)—and the impact they have on the study, (2) to develop and test next steps to be taken, and (3) to test hypotheses emerging from the data. Debriefing sessions were particularly critical for this study as nine "human instruments" were involved. For example, two teams of investigators conducted first-round visits to Wichita State and Grinnell in mid-September. All nine members of the research team then held a conference call to debrief the first visits, make adjustments to interview protocols (e.g., asking "what is special about your institution?" of all participants), and to identify unforeseen sources of information that were found to be beneficial (e.g., admissions and development videos).

Recall also that team members met at the end of each day of interviews to discuss findings, plan for additional questions and interviews, and to discuss tentative conclusions. In addition to follow-up phone and BITNET conferences, we also conducted debriefings at four research team meetings held during the course of the study. At these debriefings we tested ideas, obtained feedback on methods, and discussed next steps.

Member checks are, in effect, debriefing sessions with participants for the purpose of testing the data, analytical categories, interpretations, and conclusions—in short, for judging the credibility of the findings of the study (Lincoln and Guba 1985). Participant debriefings occurred throughout the study and were informal as well as formal. At the end of most interviews, the investigators reviewed what they had heard with the participants, seeking immediate feedback and clarification. Also, after the first round of site visits, we began to "recycle" data among participants at each institution. Participants from each category received the site team's interim case report about their institution. We held conversations with participants, either by phone or in person during the second site visit, to obtain reactions to the questions, comments, concerns, and experiences participants described in the first round. This process focused later interviews and reinforced the constructions that were emerging through data analysis. Case reports developed from the second round of visits were also circulated among participants for their reactions, which were then incorporated in the final case reports.

Finally, copies of our propositions regarding institutional factors and conditions associated with high quality out-of-class experiences of undergraduates were sent to participants at the fourteen colleges and universities. We used their reactions to the propositions to inform the second round of site visits and during the process of developing conclusions for the study.

Transferability

To address the issue of transferability (i.e., can the finds of the study be used in another context?), investigators must demonstrate the degree of similarity between the sending (the setting of the study) and receiving (the setting to which the study may be applied) contexts (Lincoln and Guba 1985). Therefore, investigators must provide a thick description of the sending context so that someone in the potential reviewing context may assess the similarity between them and, hence, the transferability of the findings. Thick description entails the broadest and most thorough information possible (Lincoln and Guba 1985). In reporting the findings and conclusions of the study, we strove to describe institutional factors, conditions, and themes across sites as accurately and as extensively as possible, including the participant statements from which they were derived.

Dependability and Confirmability

To meet criteria for dependability (the reporting of results considers possible changes over time), the inquirer must provide evidence of the appropriateness of the inquiry decisions made throughout the study (Lincoln and Guba 1985). Confirmability (the data can be confirmed by someone other than the inquirer) is demonstrated by showing that the findings are based on the data and that the inferences drawn from the data are logical (Lincoln and Guba 1985). Dependability and confirmability can be established by an audit, in which an external auditor examines both the processes and the products of the study. During the course of the study, we developed an audit trail (Lincoln and Guba 1985) comprising: (1) raw data, including tapes, interview notes, and documents; (2) products of data reduction and analysis, including field notes, interview and document summary forms, and case analysis forms; (3) products of data reconstruction and synthesis, including category descriptions, case reports, and ongoing reports of findings and conclusions; (4) process notes, including notes on methodological decisions and trustworthiness criteria; and (5) materials relating to the intention and disposition of the research team, including notes of debriefings, team meeting minutes and tapes, and staff correspondence.

Conclusions

Now that the study has been completed, we can draw four conclusions about the research approach and methods used. First, multi-site qualitative research using multiple investigators is time consuming. The collection of data for a rich description of one college or university and information needed for institutional comparisons requires extended time on site by several investigators, doing interviews and observing the life of the campus. Some would say, perhaps, that two rounds of three- and four-day visits cannot be considered "extended" time on site. We would certainly agree that we could have learned more with more time and money (a topic we will discuss below), but we are satisfied that our results are credible to participants in the setting and add to knowledge about student learning outside of the classroom.

Obtaining feedback from participants also demanded a great deal of time. Sending reports to participants, waiting for them to read the reports, and waiting for their written comments took weeks (even, in some cases, months). Therefore, patience and commitment to the necessity of this input are essential. In addition, the analysis of data across institutions to identify the factors and conditions that encourage learning outside of class required four two- and three-day team meetings in which we thoroughly discussed institutional reports and individual constructions. The process of achieving some shared vision—that is, shared among ourselves as well as shared between investigators and "natives"—of the places we visited and their commonalities and differences was protracted and intense.

Our visits also involved significant time and effort on the part of the institutions we visited. Our contact persons developed interview schedules, mailed sets of documents to site team members, arranged for meeting rooms and (in many cases) lodging, made sure that we had transportation from and to airports, and helped us cope with such inevitable problems as cancelled interviews and dead tape recorder batteries. The hospitality and assistance of the people at the institutions were a tremendous help and a highlight of our experience.

Second, multi-site research involving a team of investigators can be (and was) expensive, in terms of money as well as time. The study was funded by grants from the Lilly Endowment, Inc., the National Association of Student Personnel Administrators, and the Education Services Division for the Marriott Corporation. Without external funding we could not have done such a large-scale and in-depth study. What we could have done with less money, what we could have done without, or even what we could have done with more funds, are debatable questions. More funds might have enabled additional site visits, which would probably have provided more insights about the institutions. More money also might have enabled us to add a category of institutions, such as two-year colleges, or community colleges. Less funding might have limited us to fewer institutions or, perhaps, to concentrate on campuses in one region of the United States.

Third, the composition of the research team was absolutely critical to the success of the study. We knew at the outset that we faced a complex and lengthy task, although just how complex and how lengthy emerged only as the study proceeded. Thus, another important qualification for investigators embarking on this type of research (besides those mentioned earlier) is willingness to commit time, not only to site visits, but to all of the process of data reduction, analysis, writing, thinking, sharing, and debating that follow. These tasks tested our stamina, time schedules, and, occasionally, egos. Working with a focus group, conducting an effective interview, and trying to understand a new setting require a lot of energy. However trite it may seem, anyone undertaking such a study should be conscientious about getting enough sleep and exercise and eating well.

Some of the team members had more time to give to the project than others and so took on more site visits and more writing tasks. Some of the team members were more conscientious than others about completing summary forms and responding to requests for information. This will happen in any group project and decisions should be made in advance about how, or whether, the group (or the project director) will respond.

We also recommend that team members talk in advance about the authorship of products of the study and about participation in opportunities like paper presentations or consultations that might arise from the study. Some flexibility in these matters is important, as group members may be more or less involved in writing tasks than they anticipated or have more or less time and interest for other work related to the study. Nevertheless, an early and honest discussion of expectations about the distribution of work and credit, the ways in which decisions about authorship and other opportunities will be made and by whom, and means for handling disagreements can help team members avoid misunderstandings and resentments. Do not assume, however, that one conversation at the outset will be enough; these matters will have to be revisited at points throughout the study and, in some cases, after it is completed. Although these issues—authorship, contributions, participation—are awkward to address (and most of us would prefer to pretend that they do not exist or will take care of themselves), they can affect group morale and even the effectiveness of the research process. Therefore, a commitment to professionalism and openness in relationships among team members as well as in the conduct of research is essential.

In addition to committing their time and energy, team members also, knowingly or unknowingly, committed themselves to learn (about qualitative research methods, about the institutions and their faculty, staff and students, about their own assumptions, values, and attitudes, about other team members), to suspend judgment (about the institutions in the study, about the ideas and assumptions of other team members), and to share openly their ideas, questions, and feelings. For ten months, we worked together almost constantly, a situation that occasionally tested our patience and sense of humor but that also provided each team member with a tremendously powerful and satisfying learning experience, as well as lifelong friends and colleagues.

Finally, despite the demands of this type of research, we believe that it works—that it enabled us to obtain rich and accurate descriptions of the individual institutions and to identify factors and conditions across institutions that seem to foster high quality out-of-class learning experiences for undergraduate students. Evidence of our success, and the effectiveness of our approach, can be found in: (1) feedback from students, faculty, and administrators at the participating institutions that our case reports are "very accurate" portrayals of the institutions, and (2) positive and affirming responses from various audiences about what we discovered (e.g., at annual meetings of the American Council on Education, American Educational Research Association, National Association of Student Personnel Administrators; and in requests to conduct "campus audits" of student life elsewhere).

An additional benefit of our research has been the press of self-examination and self-discovery that our visits and reports have precipitated at the institutions we visited. We often heard the comment, "I hadn't really thought about this before." Some institutions used our reports to stimulate change, such as deferring sorority rush at Miami and developing a new student affairs philosophy statement at Grinnell. Others, like Iowa State, have used their participation in the study as a mark of distinction in publicity releases and as a selling point for prospective students. Thus, our process of discovery and understanding has affected both the knower and the known.

Summary

In this article, we have described how nine investigators used qualitative research methods in a study of out-of-class experiences for undergraduates at fourteen colleges and universities. Despite the high levels of time, energy, and resources required to conduct the study, the team approach proved to be effective in discovering, understanding, and appreciating the myriad institutional elements that work together to encourage students to take advantage of learning and personal development opportunities outside the classroom.

Although our description of what we did and how we did it is (we think) accurate, this study, like most human experiences, was infinitely more complicated than we can describe here. That point is not made to discourage researchers from multi-site, multi-investigator projects (indeed, we look forward to participating again in similar studies); rather, we hope that those who undertake such efforts do so with a clear understanding of their myriad pitfalls *and* pleasures.

Bibliography

Barley, Stephen R. "Semiotics and the Study of Occupational and Organizational Cultures." *Administrative Science Quarterly* 28 (1983): 393–`413.

Chaffee, Ellen E., and William G. Tierney. *Collegiate Cultures.* New York: American Council on Education—Macmillan, 1988.

Clark, Burton R. *The Distinctive College: Antioch, Reed, and Swarthmore.* Chicago: Aldine, 1970.

Crowson, Robert L. "Qualitative Research Methods in Higher Education." In *Higher Education: Handbook of Theory and Research, Vol. 3,* edited by John C. Smart, 1–55. New York: Agathon, 1987.

Dill, David D. "The Management of Academic Culture: Notes on the Management of Meaning and Social Integration." *Higher Education* 11 (1982): 303–30.

Dobbert, Marion L. *Ethnographic Research: Theory and Application for Modern Schools and Societies.* New York: Praeger, 1984.

Grant, Gerald, and David Riesman. *The Perpetual Dream: Reform and Experiment in the American College.* Chicago: University of Chicago Press, 1978.

Goetz, Judith P., and Marilyn D. LeCompte. *Ethnography and Qualitative Design in Educational Research.* Orlando, Fla.: Academic Press, 1984.

Heath, Douglas H. *Growing Up in College: Liberal Education and Authority.* San Francisco: Jossey-Bass, 1968.

Herriott, Robert E., and William A. Firestone. "Multisite Qualitative Policy Research: Optimizing Description and Generalizability." *Educational Researcher* 12 (1983): 14–19.

Kuh, George D., John H. Schuh, Elizabeth J. Whitt, Rosalind E. Andreas, James W. Lyons, C. Carney Strange, Lee E. Krehbiel, and Kathleen A. MacKay. *Involving Colleges: Successful Approaches to Fostering Student Learning and Development Outside the Classroom.* San Francisco: Jossey-Bass, 1991.

Kuh, George D., and Elizabeth J. Whitt. *The Invisible Tapestry: Culture in American Colleges and Universities.* ASHE-ERIC Report Series. No. 1. Washington, D.C.: Association for the Study of Higher Education, 1988.

Leemon, Thomas A. *The Rites of Passage in a Student Culture.* New York: Teachers College Press, 1972.

Lincoln, Yvonna S., and Egon G. Guba. *Naturalistic Inquiry.* Beverly Hills, Calif.: Sage, 1985.

McMillin, James H. *Focus Group Interviews: Implications for Educational Research.* Paper presented at the annual meeting of the American Educational Research Association, San Francisco. 1989.

Merton, Robert K., M. Fisk, and P.L. Kendall. *The Focused Interview.* New York: Free Press, 1956.

Miles, Matthew B., and A. Michael Huberman. *Qualitative Data Analysis: A Sourcebook of New Methods.* Beverly Hills, Calif.: Sage, 1984.

Morgan, G. *Images of Organization.* Beverly Hills, Calif.: Sage, 1984.

Peterson, M.W. "Emerging Developments in Postsecondary Organization Theory and Research." *Educational Researcher* 14 (1985): 5–12.

Schein, Edward H. *Organizational Culture and Leadership.* San Francisco: Jossey-Bass, 1985.

Tierney, William G. "Ethnography: An Alternative Evaluation Methodology." *Review of Higher Education* 8 (1985): 93–105.

Van Maanen, J. "Reclaiming Qualitative Methods for Organizational Research: A Preface." *Administrative Science Quarterly* 24 (1979a): 520–26.

_____. "The Fact of Fiction in Organizational Ethnography." *Administrative Science Quarterly* 24 (1979b): 539–50.

Weick, K.E. "Educational Organizations as Loosely Coupled Systems." *Administrative Science Quarterly* 21 (1976): 1–19.

A Positioned Subject Approach to Inquiry

Clifton Conrad, Jennifer Grant Haworth, and
Susan Bolyard Millar

We learned from our review of the literature that few studies have examined master's education on its own terms and that the range of voices represented in the published conversation has been limited. On the basis of these understandings, we decided to conduct a broad-based study of master's education in the United States. In brief, we used an open-ended, multicase study design in which the perspectives of diverse stakeholders—people who have a vital stake in master's education, whom we variously refer to as "positioned subjects," stakeholders, and interviewees—animated our inquiry throughout. Altogether we interviewed nearly eight hundred people associated with forty-seven master's programs in thirty-one colleges and universities, including institutional and program administrators, faculty, students, alumni, and employers of program graduates.

Since the study was informed throughout by our understanding of interviewees, ourselves, and our readers as positioned subjects, we begin the chapter by briefly describing our positioned subject approach. We then describe our multicase study design (including our selection of cases and interviewees) and, in turn, discuss our fieldwork procedures, analytic processes, and the textual approach we used in writing this book.[1]

Positioned Subjects as an Approach to Research

From the beginning of the study, we wanted our research to focus on how diverse stakeholders interpreted their master's experiences within their own particular settings. At the same time, we wanted our research to allow us to generalize about master's education on a national level. By studying master's education at the individual program level and then generalizing across programs, we would be in a position to interpret stakeholders experiences in master's education.

To these ends, we chose a positioned subject approach to inquiry, one that assumes that people, as positioned subjects (where *subjects* refers to people with particular needs, perceptions, and capabilities for action, and *position* refers to the environment in which they are located), actively interpret and make sense of their everyday worlds.[2] In brief, this approach provided us with a strategy for research and analysis: we would focus on how people understood and interpreted master's experiences within programs—including how they made sense of them and what they valued in them—always from their own standpoints, or perspectives. In so doing, we viewed each program in terms of this positioned subject approach, namely, that each program was located, or positioned, within a particular setting and that, by understanding various patterns across these programs, we could develop a broad-based understanding of master's education in the United States. Moreover, like the stakeholders we interviewed, we also viewed ourselves, and our readers, as positioned subjects who interpret and make meaning based on our experiences and perspectives.

Multicase Study Design

Consonant with our positioned subject approach, we used a multicase study design that placed the perspectives of the individuals we interviewed at the center of our research.[3] We first developed a representative sample of 47 case studies and then selected a representative sample of 781 interviewees. To flesh out our design, we discuss our overall sampling strategy then turn to our selection of cases and interviewees.

Sampling Strategy

Our sampling strategy, including our selection of case studies as well as interviewees within cases, was based on a major premise in multicase study design: if a credible claim is to be made that our findings can be generalized from individual interviewees to each case study as a whole, and from a group of cases to master's education in this country, then the sample must be *substantively* representative of the population it claims to represent. To provide for substantitive representativeness, contextual characteristics of the population which may be theoretically relevant must be represented in the sample. There is no need, however, as Greene and David emphasized, to "require adequate representation on every conceivable variable, parameter, or factor that one might think of. In particular, there is no reason to prefer—let alone require—a sample that includes all the principle selection factors in every combination with each other (i.e., a 'fully-crossed' design). If there is a substantive reason for a particular combination of factors to be included in the sample, that is sufficient; otherwise, no particular combination of factors is more essential than any other" (1981, 30).[4]

Following this reasoning, we used a sampling strategy in which we intentionally selected cases across the nation, and interviewees within each case (program), which represented those program and interviewee characteristics we believed might be theoretically relevant. Hence, at the national level, we selected cases that varied in terms of characteristics such as field of study, institutional type, and type of control, along with other characteristics such as geographic location, instructional delivery system, and program prestige.[5] At the program level, we selected individuals representing six different stakeholder groups, including institutional administrators, program administrators, faculty, students, alumni, and employers of alumni. Below we discuss how we chose our sample of forty-seven cases and our within-case interviewees.

Selection of Case Studies To provide for heterogeneity (substantive representativeness) in terms of discipline, we selected eleven fields of study which represented diverse professional and liberal arts and sciences fields and which, among other considerations, varied in terms of their annual production of master's degrees. We selected five programs in each of nine fields along with one program in two fields (sociology and computer science), for a total sample of forty-seven programs.[6]

Our forty-seven-case sample was distributed across eleven fields of study as follows: five established professional fields, four emerging professional fields in the liberal arts and sciences (including one interdisciplinary field), and two traditional fields in liberal arts and sciences. From established professional fields, we selected business, education, engineering, nursing, and theater. We chose business, education and engineering because, in recent years, over one-half of all master's degrees awarded annually were in these three fields. Given the range of specializations offered by most of the programs in these three disciplines, we chose subfields that recently granted the largest number of master's degrees within their respective fields: in business, business administration; in engineering, electrical engineering; and in education, teacher education. We selected nursing because it grants the largest percentage of master's degrees in the health sciences and chose theater as a representative field in the performing arts.

In terms of emerging professional fields, we chose applied anthropology, computer science, environmental studies, and microbiology as representative fields in the traditional liberal arts and sciences in which, in recent years, a nonuniversity job market has developed for master's-educated people. (Environmental studies also was chosen because it is an interdisciplinary field in which a growing share of master's degrees have been awarded in recent years.) In the traditional liberal arts and sciences, we selected English and sociology as core disciplines representing the humanities and social sciences, respectively. (Applied anthropology and microbiology also are representative fields in the social and biological sciences.)

Further, to represent the range of institutions offering master's programs in the United States, we selected cases on the basis of differences in terms of institutional type and type of control (i.e., public or private). In terms of institutional type, we chose our forty-seven cases from among four types of institutions which we identified for purposes of this study: national universities, regional colleges and universities, liberal arts colleges, and specialty institutions.[7] The forty-seven case studies, chosen to reflect national data on master's degrees awarded, were distributed as follows: national universities, eighteen programs; regional colleges and universities, twenty-one programs; liberal arts colleges, five programs; and specialty institutions, three programs.[8] The thirty-one institutions represented in the sample include seven national universities, sixteen regional colleges and universities, five liberal arts colleges, and three specialty institutions.[9] With respect to type of control, nearly two-thirds of the forty-seven programs in our sample (that is, thirty-one programs) were located in public institutions, with the remainder (sixteen programs) being located in private (independent) institutions.[10] (Table 2.1 shows the distribution of cases by field of study and institutional type. Table 2.2 shows the distribution of case studies by institutional type and by type of control.)

Since master's programs in this country vary in other ways that might be theoretically relevant, we also chose programs that differed in terms of the following characteristics: geographic location (East, West, South, or Midwest), levels of degree offerings in departments (master's-only, bachelor's and master's, bachelor's, master's, and doctorate), student attendance patterns (full-time, part-time, mix), type of delivery system (traditional day/evening, nontraditional weekend/summer, nontraditional satellite), percentage of students who are minorities (high or low), and program prestige ("prestigious" or "nonprestigiuos"). In addition, we included four programs located in four predominately black institutions and one program at a predominately women's institution. Table 2.3 shows the distribution of the forty-seven cases across these six characteristics as well as by field of study, institution type, and type of control.[11]

Selection of Interviewees Consonant with our positioned subject approach, we chose to interview individuals who represented various stakeholder positions within the forty-seven master's programs in our sample, including institutional administrators, program administrators, faculty, students, alumni, and employers. We selected these specific stakeholder groups on the grounds that each had a major stake in master's education.[12] In addition, we strove to diversify our sample by interviewing people who differed in terms of personal characteristics such as minority status and gender, among others. Table 2.4 shows the distribution of people interviewed by stakeholder group, minority group status, sex, field of study, and institutional type.

To identify people to interview we relied on a program liaison from each of the forty-seven cases included in the study.[13] These individuals chose interviewees[14] on the basis of written criteria we had outlined in our formal request for their assistance.[15] For the most part, program liaisons were able to select interviewees according to these criteria, though sometimes practical considerations limited their ability to comply fully with our request.

We acknowledge that our interview selection method has a positive, or at least a systematic non-negative, bias that is linked to our procedure of asking program liaisons to select interviewees.[16] Although we ran the risk that program liaisons might select individuals who would describe their probrams in a highly favorable light, we used this procedure for two reasons. The first is that selecting interviewees ourselves would have been impossible given our time constraints; we were unable to spend more than three days visiting each program, and we did not wish to spend out time selecting interviewees then scheduling interviews. The second reason is that we suspected, on the grounds that this would have been intrusive, many programs would have declined to participate if we had insisted that we choose interviewees.

Table 2.1
Distribution of Case Studies, by Field of Study and Institutional Type

Field of Study	Institutional Type			
	National	Regional	Lib. Arts	Specialty
Established professional				
Business	2	2	1	
Education	1	3	1	
Engineering	2	2		1
Nursing	2	2		1
Theater	2	2		1
Emerging professional (Arts and sciences)				
Applied anthropology	2	3		
Computer science	1			
Environmental studies	2	1	2	
Microbiology	1	4		
Traditional arts and sciences				
English	2	2	1	
Sociology	1			
Total	18	21	5	3

Note: Four prominently black institutions and one predominantly women's college were represented in the sample. A total of thirty-one institutions were included in the sample.

Table 2.2
Distribution of Case Studies, by Institution Type and Type of Control

Institutional Type	Type of Control		Total
	Public	Private	
National universities	14	4	18
Regional colleges and universities	15	6	21
Liberal arts colleges	1	4	5
Specialty institutions	1	2	3
Total	31	16	47

Table 2.3
Characteristics of Case Study Sample

Pseudonym institution	Field of study	Type 1 = National 2 = Regional 3 = Liberal Arts 4 = Specialty	Control 1 = Public 2 = Private	Location 1 = East 2 = West 3 = South 4 = Midwst	Degree Levels[a] 1 = M only 2 = B+M 3 = B+M+D	Student Attendance 1 = Full-time 2 = Part-time 3 = Mix	Delivery System 1=Traditional (Day/Eve) 2=Nontrad. (Wknd/Sum) 3=Nontrad. (Satellite)	Percentage of Minority Students 1 = High 2 = Low	Program Prestige 1 = Prestigious 2 = Non-prestigious
Pierpont University	Business	1	2	1	1	1	1	2	1
Major State University		1	1	4	3	1	1	2	2
Parks-Beecher University[b]		2	2	3	2	1	1	1	2
Peterson University		2	2	1	2	2	2	2	2
St. Joan's College		3	2	2	2	2	2	2	2
Major State University	Education	1	1	4	3	3	1	2	1
Laramie University		2	2	2	1	2	2	2	2
Chester College		2	2	1	3	2	1	2	2
Southwest State University		2	1	2	3	2	2	2	2
Lake College		3	2	4	2	2	2	2	2
Major State University	Engineering	1	1	4	3	3	1	2	2
Prestige State University		1	1	2	3	1	1	2	1
Middle State University		2	1	3	3	3	1 and 3	2	2
Moore A&T University[b]		2	1	3	2	1	1	1	2
United Technological University		4	2	2	1	2	3	2	2
Major State University	Nursing	1	1	4	3	2	1	2	2
Barrett State Medical Center		1	1	2	3	2	1	2	1
Peterson University		2	2	1	2	2	1	2	2
Southern State University		2	1	3	3	2	1	2	2
Western State Medical Center		4	1	2	3	2	1	2	2
Major State University	Theater	1	1	4	3	1	1	2	2
Phelps University		1	2	1	1	1	1	2	1
Helena State University[c]		2	1	3	2	1	1	2	2
Trafalgar College		2	2	1	2	3	1	2	2
National Conservatory College		4	2	2	1	1	1	2	1

Table 2.3 (Continued)

Institution	Field							
Land-Grant University		1	2	2	2	1	2	2
Atlantic State University		1	1	2	1	1	2	2
City-State University	Applied anthropology	1	3	2	2	1	2	2
Southwest State University		1	2	2	1	2	2	2
Southeast State University		1	3	3	2	1	2	1
Major State University		1	4	3	1	1	2	2
Phelps University		2	1	3	1	1	2	1
Urban State University[b]	English	1	4	2	2	1	1	2
Southwest State University		1	2	2	1	1	2	2
Longmont College		2	1	1	2	2	2	2
Phelps University		2	1	1	1	1	2	1
Major State University		1	4	1	1	1	2	2
Carver A&M University[b]	Environmental studies	1	1	1	1	1	2	2
Vernon College		1	3	2	2	1	2	2
Walton State College		1	2	1	3	1	2	2
Major State University		1	4	3	1	1	2	1
Southwest State University		2	2	3	1	1	2	2
Mountain State University	Microbiology	1	2	3	1	1	2	2
Middle State University		2	3	2	1	1	2	2
Appleby State University		2	4	2	1	1	2	2
Major State University	Sociology	1	4	3	1	1	2	1
Major State University	Computer Science	1	4	3	1	1	2	1

aM = master's degree
B = bachelor's degree
D = doctoral degree
bPredominantly black institution
cPredominantly women's institution

Table 2.4
Distribution of Interviewees

By stakeholder group		By field of study	
Institutional administrators	85	Established professional	
Program administrators	95	Business	78
Faculty	167	Education	76
Students	184	Engineering	90
Alumni	147	Nursing	90
Employers	103	Theater	76
Total	781	Total	410
By minority status		Emerging Professional	
African-American	60	Applied anthropology	100
Asian-American	12	Computer science	15
International	19	Environmental studies	71
Hispanic	11	Microbiology	89
Native American	3	Total	275
White nonminority	676		
Total	781	Traditional arts and sciences	
		English	82
By sex		Sociology	14
Men	430	Total	96
Women	351		
Total	781	Grand total	781
By institutional type			
National universities	303		
Regional colleges and universities	333		
Liberal arts colleges	84		
Specialized institutions	61		
Total	781		

Interview Process: Dialogue between Positioned Subjects

In keeping with our positioned subject approach, we viewed our interviews as "dialogues between positioned subjects."[18] As such, we presented ourselves not as "invisible" observers but as participants in a conversation.[19] Our conversations were not balanced exchanges, however, as we encouraged interviewees to do most of the talking. Except when interviewing current students, we met one-on-one with each interviewee to allow both parties to concentrate on a single, sustained dialogue.[20] We arranged group interviews with students, one of us meeting with three or four students, because we thought students were most comfortable with this arrangement. We taped almost all of our interviews (with the permission of each interviewee) and took notes.[21]

In terms of our interview protocol, we developed a broad set of topics that we sought to address in each interview. In general, these topics were concerned with how interviewees experienced their master's program, including its "character," its "quality" and value, and those attributes they felt contributed most to student and faculty learning. Rather than using these topics as a formal interview protocol, however, we choose to give each interviewee as much responsibility as possible for establishing the overall direction of the dialogue. To prepare interviewees for our openended interviews, we provided each, in advance, with three-page description of the research project and our interview process.

In our interviews, we explained that we wanted to learn what they thought was important for us to know about their master's program. Some interviewees, to be sure, needed to be verbally prompted: Could you tell us what you expected from this program? What do you think are the most important characteristics of the program? What have you and others gotten out of the program? Generally speaking, however, people needed relatively little prompting. They not only described, interpreted, and evaluated their experiences but also often provided information and perspective on program history as well as external and internal factors influencing the program. Once they felt that we genuinely wanted to understand their views on the program and grew accustomed to the open-endedness of our interview approach, most interviewees seemed to enjoy establishing the general direction of the dialogue.

We tried to limit the amount of prompting with specific questions—because this would have tended to turn the dialogue into a testing ground for our emerging "themes," which may or may not have been interviewees' themes—but we inevitably provided interviewees with various inter-active cues. Our notetaking, in particular, sometimes provided a stimulus to interaction. By pausing to take notes, we often communicated to interviewees that we believed what they had said was particularly important. They frequently responded to such cues by commenting on our notes, either explaining that what we had written was not that important or, as was more often the case, elaborating on the point. We also noticed during the course of the study that we became better at interacting with interviewees, such as noticing when they needed to pause and reflect and allowing these moments of silence. We found, too, that, as we became more skilled at listening, the people we interviewed often told us that they had learned a great deal about themselves and their program during the interview.

Upon reflecting on what the 781 interviewees told us, we want to emphasize that most people seemed remarkably candid with us. We attribute their candidness to several factors. For one thing, interviewees appreciated our promise to keep their responses confidential. For another, most interviewees seemed to accept our explanation that our aim was to listen carefully to their perspectives as the basis for understanding stakeholder's experiences—not to evaluate their particular programs per se. For still another, we often noticed how most interviewees, as positioned subjects, seemed to enjoy the opportunity to express their views about their master's program.

From our perspective, the validity of our interview approach was enhanced through what researchers in the social sciences refer to as "triangulation." To begin with, triangulation—collecting and analyzing data across multiple data sources—was built into our sample inasmuch as each of the stakeholder groups "stood" in different positions with respect to their programs. In broad terms, faculty and program administrators held the most permanent and interior positions, since they were formally responsible for the program and often had long-term "insider" perspectives. Current students and alumni held partly interior and partly exterior standpoints: they were intimately involved in their program yet were also "visitors" who passed through it. Employers and institutional administrators, meanwhile, tended to speak from exterior standpoints and, while generally less informed than other stakeholders, provided a valuable check on insiders' perspectives as well as an alternative source of understanding.

Analysis as Positioned Subjects

Program-level Analysis

Just as triangulation was built into our case study design in the way we selected interviewees, it was also built into the analysis process in which we engaged as researchers. Since at least two of us conducted interviews in the same program at the same time, we continually engaged and "worked off" one another while we were in the field, frequently meeting over meals and during the evening hours to discuss our interviews.[22] These meetings helped us identify the occasional interviewee whose perspective seemed "out of kilter" with those of other interviewees.[23] They also helped each of us to listen and react more independently of personal biases.[24] Moreover, our frequent interactions in the field helped us to develop a better sense of our interview data, thereby enabling us to be more perceptive in our subsequent interviews. In addition, whenever possible we also read beforehand all the written materials that we asked each program liaison to send us and thus were able to include these materials in our ongoing efforts to "triangulate."[25]

Upon completing interviews in each case study, we summarized each and, using our tapes, transcribed long sections of many. One member of the research team then developed a case study summary (from 80 to 170 pages in length) based on all interview summaries as well as written documents provided by the program. While completing this work, we continued to triangulate and learn from each other's perspectives. In this fashion, we were able to use all the interviewees' perspectives to formulate a program portrait that incorporated what each had said and yet was more complete that what any one of them had presented.

The format we used for program summaries changed over time, as we discerned emerging themes in our interview data. By the midpoint of the study, we had established a format that helped us more quickly tune into various themes that we identified across interviews, while allowing us to retain the individuality of different stakeholders' voices. Our underlying purpose in producing these summaries was to understand, identify, and describe those themes that were shared by interviewees both within and across stakeholder groups in a given program. In effect, we attempted to renarrate, in their terms, the "stories" they told us about their particular program.

Cross-Program-Level Analysis

Our cross-program analysis, which mirrored the process we used in analyzing individual programs, began early in the study as we became attuned to themes, or patterns, in our fieldwork. Periodically, after several new program summaries had been completed, we paused to read and discuss them as a group. These discussions helped us discern patterns across programs, but we avoided drawing conclusions so that we would remain open to emerging themes throughout the duration of the study. As a result, we had a vast amount of relatively unanalyzed information by the time all the program summaries were completed and we were ready to begin our cross-program analyses.

We began the process of developing themes across the forty-seven programs in our sample by reading and discussing the individual summaries on a case-by-case basis. At first we were overwhelmed by the diversity of stakeholder perspectives. Despite this diversity, both across individuals and programs, we began to develop various themes that helped us to understand both similarities and differences across programs. Stakeholders in some programs, for example, spoke repeatedly about the sense of community in their programs, while interviewees in other programs described their experiences as more competitive and individualistic. Over the course of almost six months of intensive analysis, we developed patterns and themes that we tested and retested against our interview material. In so doing, we observed that many of the themes that stakeholders raised were ones we had not foreseen. It is noteworthy that many of the themes showed little association with the attributes built into our sample, such as field of study, type of control, and a full-or part-time student population. Moreover, we realized that, depending on the characteristics and themes to which we were attuned, we learned different kinds of things about master's programs. We could clearly see that the meaning of our "data" changed depending on which themes we were using to make sense of them.

Throughout this period of analysis, our central problem was to decide which set of characteristics across programs would allow us to develop an analysis that helped us most to understand stakeholder's master's experiences and one that accurately reflected the voices of the nearly eight hundred people we interviewed. To that end, we chose to view our interview material primarily in terms of five key types of decisions that stakeholders told us, directly and indirectly, they made about their master's programs. These five decision-situations were instrumental in the process we used to articulate four different types of master's programs which, from our perspective, embody the major differences among the master's programs in our sample. This analytical process is further explicated in parts 2 and 3 of the book.

Writing and Reading as Positioned Subjects

Conventional academic writing uses the present tense and the third-person passive voice, a textual style that presents the author as anonymous. From our perspective, this writing style makes invisible the very strength of our approach to inquiry, which assumes that we, like the people we interviewed as well as our readers, are positioned subjects who actively interpret and make meaning out of our interview material as we select certain themes, and not others, from individuals located in specific times and places. As Dorinne Kondo put it, "style and theory are inseparable in the process of writing" (1990, 48), and "the real challenge is *to enact our theoretical messages*" (43). Throughout this book, we try to use a writing style that "enacts" our positioned subject approach to the study.

During transitional passages in the book, when we want to involve the reader directly in the research and analysis process, we use the present tense and write in the first-person voice, self-consciously, or "reflexively" (as at this moment). Throughout most of the rest of the book—except when we quote directly from interviewees, when we present whatever tense they used—we use the past tense. When in past tense, we use the first-person voice when we want to remind the readers of our presence as interviewers and analysts and the third-person voice when we seek to engage the reader more imaginatively, as if "from the native's point of view" (Geertz 1983). We understand that some readers may, at first, find this unconventional use of tense and voice somewhat awkward, but readers of earlier drafts of this book have told us that they easily adjusted to it.

As part of our textural strategy, we also seek to pay attention to our readers as positioned subjects and, in turn, invite them to view us as positioned subjects. We strongly believe that readers will be better able to respond to our work if, as in face-to-face conversation, they have enough information to position us in terms of our backgrounds and experiences. As Renato Rosaldo has noted: "Because researchers are necessarily both somewhat impartial and somewhat partisan, somewhat innocent and somewhat complicit, their readers should be as informed as possible about what the observer was in a position to know and not know" (1989, 69). We invite our readers to view us as positioned subjects (along with themselves and our interviewees); in so doing, we conclude the chapter by presenting personal sketches of those of us involved in the study.[26]

Clifton Conrad was born in North Dakota and grew up in an upper middle-class family. He was educated at major public universities in mainstream social science (history, political science, and sociology) and earned his Ph.D. in higher education from the University of Michigan. In addition to serving as a professor at four colleges and universities, he has been a department chair and associate dean. He is currently a professor at the University of Wisconsin-Madison. His scholarly work includes studies of quantitive correlates of graduate program quality. Throughout the master's study, it was Clif who repeatedly urged us to remember that, as positioned subjects, our primary concern as analysts was to maintain fidelity to representing the full range of stakeholder voices and perspectives both in our analysis and in our writing.

Jennifer Grant Haworth was born in Wisconsin and raised in a working-class family. She joined the master's project after completing her master's degree at Columbia University and gaining experience teaching high school teachers and working as an institutional planning analyst and grants writer at an independent liberal arts college. She is nearing completion of her Ph.D. in higher education at the University of Wisconsin-Madison. Although most of her formal education has been mainstream sociology, she recently has revived her interest in interpretivist approaches to inquiry. Throughout the study, Jennifer constantly reminded us that our primary challenge as positioned subjects was to listen closely to our interviewees and to constantly reexamine how our assumptions may have influenced our interpretations of interviewee accounts.

Susan Bolyard Millar was born in New York and raised in a middle-class Euro-American family. She received her Ph.D. in anthropology from Cornell University, where she was trained in the interpretive tradition, a tradition in which she continues to work. She has done extensive fieldwork in Indonesia, taught women's studies courses at the University of Wisconsin-Madison, and worked as a policy analyst for a state higher education agency. As a positioned subject, Susan was especially critical of what has become known in recent social science and literary criticism as "objectivist" approaches to inquiry and analysis—as well as of radical "subjectivist" approaches. It was Susan who suggested a positioned subject approach to inquiry and analysis and who helped us to approach our fieldwork and to write in ways consistent with this approach.

We also benefited greatly from the perspectives of a fourth person, Karen Prager, who worked as a research associate during eighteen months of case study research. Prior to joining the project, Karen had earned an M.F.A. in theater from Columbia University, acted in many theatrical productions, taught elementary and junior high school students in an urban school system, and worked as a journalist. As a positioned subject, Karen especially made us aware of the historical and social context of the disciplines included in the study, and she often brought a fresh "outsider" perspective.

Grounded Theory: An Alternative Approach to Research in Higher Education

CLIFTON F. CONRAD

For well over a century, most social science research has emphasized controlled, experimental, quantitative procedures. The crucial underpinning of this epistemology is the theory of absolute objectivity (Douglas, 1976). In brief, this theory draws a sharp line between subjective and objective so that the internal, subjective experience of human beings is clearly distinguished from objective reality, which is viewed as external to the consciousness of individuals. The subjective is seen as being, like Plato's shadows of the cave, uncertain and untrue, while the objective is viewed as certain, absolute truth. According to the theory of absolute objectivity, subjectivity is controlled or eliminated and objectivity is ensured through the traditional scientific method.

In addition to embracing this epistemology of "logical positivism," social science has also emphasized the testing or verification, rather than the generation, of theory. In part because many social scientists believe that there are outstanding theories aplenty but few confirmations of them, and in part because quantitative methods have become more sophisticated in recent years, the discovery of new theories has received scant attention. Scholars who want to generate theory, rather than test theory through quantitative techniques, have often had to face sharp criticism from their colleagues.

Despite the dominance of logical positivism and verification in modern social science over the last decade, there nevertheless has been vigorous debate over theory and method. The most heated discussions have concerned method, and a growing number of social scientists have attacked the absolutist conception of objectivity and its concomitant emphasis on quantification (Douglas, 1976; Johnson, 1975). Others argue that many of the existing theories do not fit the data and are simply untenable. They propose that social science research should place more emphasis on theoretical advancement (Glaser and Strauss, 1967).

Out of these debates over theory and method have emerged numerous attempts to formulate alternatives to logical positivism, alternatives that reject the absolutist view of objectivity and the exclusive emphasis that is placed on quantification and verification. These alternatives include phenomenology, ethnomethodology (or "neopraxiology"), participant observation, naturalistic approaches, illuminative evaluation, ethnography, and grounded theory. While there are some important differences among these approaches, they have two common characteristics that distinguish them from mainstream social science research. First, with some qualification, all assert that too much attention has been focused on verification of extant theory at the expense of generating new theory. Second, all reject the subjective-objective dualism, asserting instead that there is an interdependency between the "knowing subject" or observer and the objects of knowledge. As a consequence, these alternative approaches emphasize the validity and relevance of "qualitative" data, for purposes of both generation and verification of theory.

Within higher education, discussion of theory and method has mirrored the larger social science debate, although markedly less attention has been given to alternative methodologies. The current of mainstream social science—with its exclusive emphasis on verification and quantification—has swept along higher education scholars. Still, a growing number of researchers in the field have begun to explore the possibilities of employing alternative methodologies.

This article considers but one of the alternative approaches to traditional social science theory and research. Grounded theory has been selected for three reasons. First, I am persuaded that of all the alternative approaches it responds most directly and effectively to the theoretical and methodological issues now being raised, without falling prey to the excesses (such as solipsism) of some of the other approaches. Second, grounded theory, which employs the constant comparative method, does not perpetuate the mindless dualisms (such as quantitative versus qualitative research) that have militated against the careful examination of theory and method in higher education. It offers instead an approach to research that can serve as a bridge for reconciling mainstream research with many of the legitimate questions being raised by proponents of alternative approaches. Third, while there is little published research in higher education using any of the alternative methodologies, there is at least some research using grounded theory. Several journal articles using grounded theory have recently been published, and at least three dissertations and a handful of unpublished studies have employed this approach.

The remainder of this article is divided into four sections. The first section explicates grounded theory as an approach to research and presents key features of the strategy. In the second section, the approach is amplified through a discussion of how grounded theory was applied to higher education in a study of academic change. The third section discusses the potential uses of grounded theory as a research strategy in higher education. The last section identifies the major strengths of the approach and concludes that careful examination of grounded theory can help to reanimate and illuminate debate over the purposes and techniques of research in higher education.

Grounded Theory as a Research Strategy

Overview of the Constant Comparative Method

Grounded theory may be defined as theory generated form data systematically obtained through the constant comparative method. An inductive method of discovering theory, constant comparison has been elaborated most systematically by Glaser and Strauss (1967) and was further developed by Glaser (1978). Since the original Glaser and Strauss publication on grounded theory remains the classic statement, this discussion is based largely upon its delineation of the constant comparative method. Before reviewing the method it is important to point out that a substantial number of social scientists have not unjustly criticized Glaser and Strauss for failing to explicate their method adequately so as to guide research. Accordingly, this discussion aims to simplify and clarify the constant comparative method and to illustrate its application to higher education research.

The constant comparative method is a multi-faceted approach to research designed to maximize flexibility and aid the creative generation of theory. The method combines systematic data collection, coding, and analysis with theoretical sampling in order to generate theory that is integrated, close to the data, and expressed in a form clear enough for further testing.

Glaser and Strauss identify four overlapping stages in the comparative method (1967, pp. 101-113). First, the researcher collects and then codes his data into as many categories of analysis as possible. These categories or concepts (or variables) are abstracted by the researcher on the basis of constant comparisons of data incidents with other data incidents. As concepts are developed which are supported by the data, the researcher begins thinking in terms of the theoretical properties of each concept: its dimensions, its relationship to other concepts, and the conditions under which it is pronounced or minimized.

The first stage blends into the second as the analysis moves increasingly from comparing data incident with data incident to comparing the data with properties of the concepts that have been abstracted during the comparison of incidents. In the third stage, continuing analysis and further refinement of concepts and their relationships gradually leads to the development of theory. The theory continues to be delimited as a smaller set of higher level concepts emerges. Finally, when the research is satisfied that the theory has been integrated and the requirements of theoretical saturation have been met, the theory is presented in a discussion format or as a set of propositions. In order to help facilitate understanding of the constant comparative method, it is instructive to examine its central features.

Collection and Treatment of Data

Data collection is guided initially by the major research question(s) and later by the requirements of theoretical sampling, the process of collecting data for comparative analysis in order to facilitate the generation of theory. The researcher begins by collecting and recording a wide range of data that are pertinent to the research question. The type and range of data collected are limited only by the imagination and energy of the investigator. For example, a researcher might choose to make field observations, conduct interviews, identify pertinent library materials and caches of miscellaneous documents (such as speeches, letters, or committee minutes), and search for unobtrusive sources of data. While most researchers using this method tend to rely exclusively on qualitative data, the possibilities of quantitative data should not be minimized (Glaser & Strauss, 1967, pp. 185–220). Surveys, for example, can provide a rich source of data for generating theory. Through the data collection process, data are continually and systematically sorted, analyzed, and coded as the researcher seeks to abstract from the data concepts, their properties, and their relationships (Schatzman & Strauss, 1973, pp. 108–127). The coding process is central to the analysis, for it provides the bridge between data and theory (Glaser, 1978, p. 55). Coding forces the researcher to move from the empirical to the conceptual and theoretical level by identifying the underlying patterns in the data. Subsequently, the concepts and relationships that are developed through the coding process guide data collection and analysis in their turn through a process referred to as "theoretical sampling."

Theoretical Sampling

Collecting data by theoretical sampling means that as a set of concepts is delineated and a primitive theory emerges, this theory controls further data collection. That is, the researcher collects, analyzes, and codes his data and then decides what data to collect next and where to find them solely on the basis of the emerging theory. Put another way, the universe of data to be collected is delimited through the use of theoretical criteria. The search for data relevant to the generation and verification of the theory continues until all of the major concepts and their interrelationships have been theoretically saturated. The criterion for saturation is that no additional data can be found that further embellish the theory.

Verification of Grounded Theory

As noted above, the constant comparative method, coupled with theoretical sampling, stimulates the gradual development and refinement of concepts, their properties, and their relationship to one another. These concepts and relationships are subject to verification throughout the investigation. As the research progresses, some concepts and hypotheses are eliminated because they are refuted or insufficiently supported by the data, while others are supported or modified by the data. As work nears completion, most of the investigator's time is spent searching for additional evidence to support or reject key concepts and theoretical propositions. This continues until the requirements of theoretical saturation are satisfied. What remains is a grounded theory based on and validated by empirical evidence. It should be noted, however, that the traditional rules of verification are relaxed somewhat in order to promote the discovery of theory, hence, for example, the use of theoretical instead of random sampling.

Summary

The comparative method is not built upon a predetermined design of data collection and analysis but is a method of continually redesigning research in light of emerging concepts and interrelationships among variables. Through the technique of constant comparative analysis, data are collected from a variety of sources to ensure a rich comparative data base. Controlled throughout by theoretical sampling, the comparative method of continuous coding and analysis lends itself to different methods of data collection which yield a diversity of data, but data that are collected and analyzed only as they relate to the generation and verification of the emerging theory (Conrad, 1978, p. 103).

An Application of Grounded Theory to Higher Education Research

An introduction to the constant comparative method would be woefully lacking if it failed to provide the reader with some sense of the richness, complexity, and movement that characterize this research strategy in action. Accordingly, I have chosen a piece of higher education research that will both suggest the dynamic of discovery that pervades this approach and illustrate how the method can be applied to a research problem in higher education. The research selected is a study of academic change that I completed in the mid-seventies (Conrad, 1975, 1978).

This study of academic change was organized around two central research questions: What are the major sources of academic change? What are the major processes through which academic change occurs? Through the application of the constant comparative method, I attempted to generate a theory of academic change that responded to these questions.

Consonant with the guidelines of theoretical sampling, I began the research by selecting institutions on the basis of their relevance to the research problem. Thus, only institutions that had recently changed their undergraduate curriculum were considered. Eventually, four diverse institutions were selected which met the sample criterion: University of Rochester, Aquinas College, Western Michigan University, and Ohio State University.

The first visit to each of the four schools yielded a wide range of data. Interviews were a major source, but a large amount of primary and secondary materials was also gathered: 1) minutes from committees, ad hoc groups, and faculty senates; 2) personal files of committee members; 3) miscellaneous published and unpublished reports; 4) campus newspaper articles; 5) speeches; 6) letters; and 7) tapes of faculty meetings. Although I actively searched for relevant quantitative data in each of the four research settings, the research problem did not easily lend itself to quantitative techniques, and no quantitative data were used in the study.

Confronted by a large body of data during the initial round of field visits, I immediately began to analyze as well as record the data. Using the coding process as a tool for linking the data to the emerging theory, I gradually began to abstract core concepts, their central properties, the conditions under which they were maximized or minimized and, in a preliminary way, their relationship to other concepts. The constant comparison of the data required that I move back and forth between the empirical and the conceptual levels. In the process, many concepts were abandoned for lack of sufficient support or because they were disconfirmed by new data. However, theoretical properties gradually emerged as concepts and relationships were explored, developed, refined, and further tested against new data collected through the process of theoretical sampling.

My search for a grounded theory of academic change began with a visit to the University of Rochester, where a broad organizational and sociological perspective initially guided data collection and analysis. Data analysis suggested that while underlying conflict seemed to be a precondition of academic change, conflicts became visible only when external or internal pressures threatened the status quo. Several major pressures, or sources of change, were derived from the data: curriculum practices at other institutions, faculty subcultures, and organizational turnover. In addition, the evidence at Rochester suggested a political cast to the overall change process, and I began to explore relationships between interest group pressures, conflict, and change. Significantly, one aspect of the change process emerged as central: the role of an administrative change agent who provides the major impetus for the reexamination of the curriculum by selecting a controlling mechanism for change (Conrad, 1978, p. 105).

A crude theoretical scaffold or framework, composed of a tentative set of concepts and relationships, was developed early at the University of Rochester and further expanded, modified, and tested in subsequent visits to Aquinas College, Western Michigan University, and Ohio State University. This framework was gradually and judiciously erected in order to ensure that additional or alternative explanations of curriculum change were not overlooked, and that framework guided the ongoing process of data collection and analysis. Its dynamic character cannot be overemphasized. Not infrequently, concepts that seemed important in one setting were unsupported or refuted in another. In other instances, I added and tested new concepts, which resulted in the modification of the framework throughout the study.

To illustrate the ongoing dynamic between discovery and verification, it is instructive to review selected findings from Aquinas College, the second institution visited. At Aquinas the political metaphor of academic change assumed a more prominent place and was given sharper focus in the emerging framework. Data from a large number of interviews supported the interpretation that prior to the initiation of efforts to bring about curriculum change, conflicts concerning the academic program had been emasculated. Gradually, however, the Aquinas community had become overtly divided over the issue of curriculum change. Eventually, a new president was selected who agreed to take the position only on the condition that the college would undertake a major self-study of the curriculum. Through careful analysis of the particular circumstances leading to the selection of this new president, I was able to illuminate and refine the relationship between a fragmented and politicized social structure and administrative intervention in the process of academic change.

While the political image of change and the critical role of the administrative change agent were supported and more clearly defined at Aquinas, I also developed and tested other concepts and relationships there. To cite one example, the concept of "power exertion," as contrasted with more static notions such as "power holding" and the ambiguous term "power," emerged as a core concept in explaining academic change.

The emphasis on discovery, as well as an ongoing concern with verification, continued to guide data collection as visits were made to Western Michigan and Ohio State. I explored alternative explanations of the change process and resisted the tendency toward premature closure, and this resulted in several new concepts, for example, "structural reorganization" as a major source of change. While many of the concepts and relationships derived from the data at the first two institutions were confirmed at Western Michigan and Ohio State, the evidence from the latter two schools led to a considerable refinement of several of these concepts, their properties, and their relationship to academic change. Following the first round of field visits, the theoretical framework was translated into a tentative theory of academic change.

I returned to all of the sample institutions except for the University of Rochester. During this second phase, I placed major emphasis on verification of the theory and gradually delimited the universe of data. Interviews, in particular, were oriented toward testing, elaborating, and refining the theory. After the second round of field visits and additional analysis, I decided that no additional data that would embellish the theory further could be found. The theory of academic change was then codified into a set of formal propositions (Conrad, 1975, pp. 65–261; 1978, pp. 108–110).

The Uses of Grounded Theory

To conclude this presentation of grounded theory, it may be instructive to suggest some of the potential uses of grounded theory as a research strategy in higher education. First, and most obvious, grounded theory is appropriately used when the major purpose of research is theory development. The methodology of the approach, featuring constant comparison and theoretical sampling, is designed to foster the creative generation of theory.

As of this writing, most (if not all) of the published studies in the higher education literature which have used grounded theory have been in the area of academic change. In addition to the research on academic change discussed earlier (Conrad, 1978), Newcombe and Conrad (1981) recently completed a study using the constant comparative method to generate a theory of mandated academic change. Given the paucity of theory in higher education, the application of grounded theory research to other substantive areas might yield rich dividends. For example, this approach seems particularly suited to such areas as curriculum, college environment, impact studies, and even organizational and administrative behavior.

Second, grounded theory can readily be used in tandem with other research strategies, whether the generation or the verification of theory is the primary focus of the research. For example, a recent study used ethnography, constant comparison, and quantitative techniques to generate a grounded theory of literacy development in community colleges (Richardson, Martens, Fisk, Okun, and Thomas, 1981). The combining of different research strategies, often referred to as "triangulation," can lead to greater confidence in research findings in the field. There are few areas of research in higher education that would not benefit by combining quantitative techniques with the qualitative techniques of grounded theory.

Finally, while grounded theory can consider both qualitative and quantitative data, it is an approach particularly suited to qualitative data, since it provides a systematic set of procedures for collecting and analyzing such data. Yet, to repeat an earlier theme, higher education has made little use of grounded theory, even in qualitative research. Since many of the research problems in higher education are not always well-served by relying exclusively on quantitative data, qualitative techniques such as those used to develop grounded theory merit serious consideration in contemporary research.

It is important to note that research whose major purpose is verification is not best conducted using grounded theory as the sole methodology. While verification does play a central role in grounded theory, verification procedures are systematically relaxed in order to facilitate the discovery of theory. Hence traditional strategies are more appropriate if verification is the primary concern. At present, most higher education research remains oriented toward the testing of theory and as long as that bias continues, researchers may dismiss grounded theory as inappropriate to all research agendas in the field. The concluding section addresses both the bias toward theory-testing and the bias against qualitative research, and suggests that a reexamination of theory and method in higher education is long overdue.

Reexamining Theory and Method in Higher Education: The Possibilities of Grounded Theory

As an approach to research, grounded theory has so far been embraced by relatively few researchers in higher education. Since higher education as a field of study has long reflected the twin emphases of mainstream social science on quantification and verification, it is hardly surprising that grounded theory is often dismissed as yet another "soft" approach to research that rejects these traditional emphases and stresses instead theory development and qualitative techniques. To be sure, advocates of grounded theory have failed to defend their approach adequately on at least two counts. First, supporters of grounded theory, in both higher education and the social sciences, have failed to elucidate the methodology in such a manner that it can be applied easily and consistently to a range of research questions. Second, some researchers have presented grounded theory as a competing, rather than complementary, approach to the traditional research paradigm by implying that the constant comparative method rejects traditional emphases on verification and quantification. As a result, it has been easy for higher education researchers to dismiss grounded theory for the wrong reason, namely, that it seems to contravene the scientific method.

While proponents of grounded theory may have contributed to its lack of acceptance, whether by poorly presenting the approach or by failing to communicate the methodology effectively, the suggestion that grounded theory opposes, rather than complements, traditional emphases on verification and quantification is based on a fundamental misunderstanding. As I wish to make abundantly clear, verification is an important part of the constant comparative method, and grounded theory is theory that has been tested through verification procedures. What some interpret as an antagonism between grounded theory and traditional methods concerning the importance of verification is, on the contrary, only a difference in the relative emphases placed on verification and generation of theory. Similarly, I have shown in this article that the grounded theory approach does not reject quantitative methods; rather, it simply places greater emphasis on qualitative data while, at the same time, using quantitative data when they are obtainable and pertinent to the particular research problem under investigation. In short, grounded theory complements traditional emphases and offers a strategy for reconciling generation with verification of theory and qualitative techniques with quantitative techniques—all in a manner consistent with modern science.

Two major strengths of grounded theory can be identified. The first major strength of grounded theory lies in its possibilities for redirecting higher education research away from an exclusive emphasis on verification and toward the development of theory. Since many of our paradigms and theoretical frameworks (almost all of them borrowed from the social sciences) do not appear to fit the data, it seems a propitious time to redirect our energies. As an inductive and systematic method aimed at discovering theory, constant comparison is especially suited to this task.

The second major strength of grounded theory lies in the important role in research that it assigns to qualitative data. In recent years the objective-subjective dualism, which has provided the justification for the dominance of "quantitative" over "qualitative" techniques, has come under sustained criticism. An increasing number of philosophers of science have attacked the validity of the objective-subjective distinction, yet mainstream social science and higher education research continue to embrace the "objectivity" of quantitative research as against the "subjectivity" of qualitative research. Notwithstanding the politics of social science, there are no longer any compelling reasons for rejecting qualitative research. In the field of higher education, qualitative data can be a rich source of data both for generating and testing theory, and such data are often more easily obtainable than quantitative data. Through the constant comparative method, grounded theory provides a strategy both for doing qualitative research alone and for combining qualitative and quantitative research.

In conclusion, this examination of grounded theory has explored its potential uses, its strengths and limitations, and its potential for reconciling quantitative with qualitative research and theory generation with theory verification—in short, its possibilities as a research strategy. The discussion of grounded theory has been placed within the context of the need to reanimate and sharpen the debate over theory and method in the field of higher education.

References

Conrad, C. F Toward a theory of academic change (Doctoral dissertation. University of Michigan, 1975).

_____. A grounded theory of academic change. *Sociology of Educahon*, 1978, *51*, 101–112.

Douglas, J. *D. Investigative social research*. Beverly Hills. Califomia: Sage, 1976.

_____. *The relevance of sociology*. New York: Appleton Century-Crofts, 1970.

Glaser, B. G *Theoretical sensitivity*. Mill Valley, Califomia: The Sociology Press, 1978.

Glaser, B. G. and Strauss, A. L. *The discovery of grounded theory*. Chicago: Aldine, 1967.

Johnson, J. M. *Doing field research*. New York: The Free Press, 1975.

Newcombe, J. P. & Conrad, C. F. A theory of mandated academic change. *Journal of Higher Education*, 1981, *52*, 555–577.

Richardson, R C. Jr., Martens, K. J., Fisk, E. C., Okun, M. A., Thomas, K. J. Draft report for the study of literacy development in the community college. Report to the National Institute of Education, contract number 400–78–0071, September, 1981.

Schatzman, L. and Strauss, A. L. *Field research*. Englewood Cliffs, New Jersey: Prentice-Hall, 1973.

Stories of Experience and Narrative Inquiry

F. MICHAEL CONNELLY AND D. JEAN CLANDININ

Although narrative inquiry has a long intellectual history both in and out of education, it is increasingly used in studies of educational experience. One theory in educational research holds that humans are storytelling organisms who, individually and socially, lead storied lives. Thus, the study of narrative is the study of the ways humans experience the world. This general concept is refined into the view that education and educational research is the construction and reconstruction of personal and social stories; learners, teachers, and researchers are storytellers and characters in their own and other's stories. In this paper we briefly survey forms of narrative inquiry in educational studies and outline certain criteria, methods, and writing forms, which we describe in terms of beginning the story, living the story, and selecting stories to construct and reconstruct narrative plots. Certain risks, dangers, and abuses possible in narrative studies are discussed. We conclude by describing a two-part research agenda for curriculum and teacher studies flowing from stories of experience and narrative inquiry.

Educational Researcher, Vol. 19, No. 5, pp. 2–14

What matters is that lives do not serve as models; only stories do that. And it is a hard thing to make up stories to live by. We can only retell and live by the stories we have read or hear;. We live our lives through texts. They may be read, or chanted, or experienced electronically, or come to us, like the murmurings of out mothers, telling what conventions demand. Whatever their form or medium, these stories have formed us all; they are what we must use to make new fictions, new narratives.

(Heilbrun 1988, p. 37, *Writing a Woman's Life.*)

Narrative inquiry is increasingly used in studies of educational experience. It has a long intellectual history both in and out of education. The main claim for the use of narrative in educational research is that humans are storytelling organisms who, individually and socially, lead storied lives. The study of narrative, therefore, is the study of the ways humans experience the world. This general notion translates into the view that education is the construction and reconstruction of personal and social stories; teachers and learners are storytellers and characters in their own and other's stories.

It is equally correct to say "inquiry into narrative" as it is "narrative inquiry." By this we mean that narrative is both phenomenon and method. Narrative names the structured quality of experience to be studied, and it names the patterns of inquiry for its study. To preserve this distinction we use the reasonably well-established device of calling the phenomenon "story" and the inquiry "narrative." Thus, we say that people by nature lead storied lives and tell stories of those lives, whereas narrative researchers describe such lives, collect and tell stories of them, and write narratives of experience.

Perhaps because it focuses on human experience, perhaps because it is a fundamental structure of human experience, and perhaps because it has a holistic quality, narrative has an important place in other disciplines. Narrative is a way of characterizing the phenomena of human experience and its study which is appropriate to many social science fields. The entire field of study is commonly referred to as *narratology*, a term which cuts across such areas as literary theory, history, anthropology, drama, art, film, theology, philosophy, psychology, linguistics, education, and even aspects of evolutionary biological science. One of the best introductions to the scope of this literature is Mitchell's book *On Narrative*.[1]

Most educational studies of narrative have counterparts in the social sciences. Polkinghorne's history of "individual psychology" (1988, pp. 101–105) from the mid-1800's described narrative-related studies that have educational counterparts. His categories of case history, biography, life history, life span development, Freudian psychoanalysis, and organizational consultation are represented in the educational literature. These categories of inquiry tend, as Polkinghorne noted, to focus on *an individual's* psychology considered over a span of time. Consider, for example, the long standing regular use of anecdotal records in inquiry into child development, early childhood education, and school counselling. This focus sets the stage for one of the most frequent criticisms of narrative, namely, that narrative unduly stresses the individual over the social context.

Narrative inquiry may also be sociologically concerned with groups and the formation of community (see Carr's narrative treatment of community, 1986). Goodson's (1988) historical discussion of teachers' life histories and studies of curriculum in schooling gave a sociologically oriented account of life history in sociology, anthropology, and educational studies. Goodson saw autobiography as a version of life history. However, given recent educational developments in works such as *Teacher Careers* (Sikes, Measor, & Woods, 1985), *Teachers' Lives and Careers* (Ball & Goodson, 1985), and *Teacher Careers and Social Improvement* (Huberman, 1988) in which the focus is on professionalism, it would appear reasonable to maintain a distinction between biography/ autobiography and life history. Goodson assigned to the Chicago school the main influence on life history work through sociologists such as Park and Becker. Polkinghorne emphasized Mead's (also Chicago school) philosophical theories of symbolic interaction.

Berk (1980), in a discussion of the history of the uses of autobiography/biography in education, stated that autobiography was one of the first methodologies of the study of education. Shifting inquiry from the question What does it mean for a person to be educated? to How are people, in general, educated? appears to have led to the demise of autobiography/biography in educational studies. This decline paralleled the decline of the study of the individual in psychology as described by Polkinghorne. Recently, however, Pinar (1988), Grumet (1988), and Pinar and Grumet (1976) developed with their students and others a strong autobiographical tradition in educational studies.

Three closely related lines of inquiry focus specifically on story: oral history and folklore, children's story telling, and the uses of story in preschool and school language experiences. Dorson (1976) distinguished between oral history and oral literature, a distinction with promise in sorting out the character and origins of professional folk knowledge of teaching. Dorson named a wide range of phenomena for narrative inquiry that suggest educational inquiry possibilities such as material culture, custom, arts, epics, ballads, proverbs, romances, riddles, poems, recollections, and myths. Myths, Dorson noted, are the storied structures which stand behind folklore and oral history, an observation which links narrative to the theory of myth (e.g., Frye, 1988). The best known educational use of oral history in North America is the Foxfire project (Wigginton, 1985, 1989).

Applebee's (1978) work is a resource on children's story telling and children's expectations of story from teachers, texts, and others. Sutton-Smith's (1986) review of this literature distinguished between structuralists approaches, which rely on *schema* and other cognition theory terms (e.g., Mandler, 1984, Schank & Abelson, 1977), and meaning in a hermeneutic tradition (e.g., Erwin-Tripp & Mitchell-Kernan, 1977; Gadamer, 1982; McDowell, 1979). A curricular version of this literature is found in the suggestion (Egan, 1986; Jackson, 1987) that school subject matter be organized in story form. Jackson wrote that "even when the subject matter is not itself a story, the lesson usually contains a number of narrative segments all the same" (p. 307) and Egan suggested a model that "encourages us to see lessons or units as good stories to be told rather than sets of objectives to be obtained" (p. 2).

Applebee's work is an outgrowth of the uses of story in language instruction, a line of enquiry sometimes referred to as the work of "the Cambridge group." Much of this work has a curriculum development/teaching method focus (e.g., Britton, 1970) but there are also theoretical (e.g., Britton, 1971; Rosen, 1986) and research traditions (e.g., Applebee, 1978; Bissex & Bullock, 1987; Wells, 1986). Lightfoot and Martin's (1988) book in honor of Britton gives an introduction to this literature. Recently this work has begun to establish a counterpart in studies of adult language and second language learning (Allen, 1989; Bell, in press; Conle, 1989; Cumming, 1988; Enns-Connolly, 1985, in press; Vechter, 1987). In our work on curriculum, we see teachers' narratives as metaphors for teaching-learning relationships. In understanding ourselves and our students educationally, we need an understanding of people with a narrative of life experiences. Life's narratives are the context for making meaning of school situations. This narrative view of curriculum is echoed in the work of language researchers (Calkins, 1983) and general studies of curriculum (B. Rosen, 1988; Lightfoot & Martin, 1988; Paley, 1979).

Because of its focus on experience and the qualities of life and education, narrative is situated in a matrix of qualitative research. Eisner's (1988) review of the educational study of experience implicitly aligns narrative with qualitatively oriented educational researchers working with experiential philosophy, psychology, critical theory, curriculum studies, and anthropology. Elbaz's (1988) review of teacher-thinking studies created a profile of the most closely related narrative family members. One way she constructed the family was to review studies of "the personal" to show how these studies had an affinity with narrative. Another entry point for Elbaz was "voice" which, for her, and for us (Clandinin, 1988), aligns narrative with feminist studies (e.g., Personal Narratives Group, 1989). Elbaz's principal concern is with story. Using a distinction between story as "primarily a methodological device" and as "methodology itself," she aligned narrative with many educational studies which, although specific researchers may not be conscious of using narrative, report data either in story form or use participant stories as raw data.[2] There is also a collection of educational literature that is narrative in quality but which is not found in review documents where it might reasonably appear (e.g., Wittrock, 1986). We call this literature "Teacher's Stories and Stories of Teachers." This name refers to first- and second-hand accounts of individual teachers, students, classrooms, and schools written by teachers and others.[3]

In this paper we see ourselves as outlining possibilities for narrative inquiry within educational studies. The educational importance of this line of work is that it brings theoretical ideas about the nature of human life as lived to bear on educational experience as lived. We have not set out to contribute to the long tradition of narrative in the humanities, nor to bridge the gap between the humanities and the social sciences in educational studies, desirable as that clearly is. In the remainder of the paper we explore various methodological issues of narrative inquiry.

Beginning the Story: The Process of Narrative Inquiry

Many accounts of qualitative inquiry give a description of the negotiation of entry into the field situation. Negotiating entry is commonly seen as an ethical matter framed in terms of principles that establish responsibilities for both researchers and practitioners. However, another way of understanding the process as an ethical matter is to see it as a negotiation of a shared narrative unity. We wrote about it (Clandinin & Connelly, 1988) in the following way:

> We have shown how successful negotiation and the application of principles do not guarantee a fruitful study. The reason, of course, is that collaborative research constitutes a relationship. In everyday life, the idea of friendship implies a sharing, an interpenetration of two or more persons' spheres of experience. Mere contact is acquaintanceship, not friendship. The same may be said for collaborative research which requires a close relationship akin to friendship. Relationships are joined, as MacIntyre (1981) implies, by the narrative unities of our lives. (p. 281)

This understanding of the negotiation of entry highlights the way narrative inquiry occurs within relationships among researchers and practitioners, constructed as a caring community. When both researchers and practitioners tell stories of the research relationship, they have the possibility of being stories of empowerment. Noddings (1986) remarked that in research on teaching "too little attention is presently given to matters of community and collegiality and that such research should be construed as research *for* teaching" (p. 510). She emphasized the collaborative nature of the research process as one in which all participants see themselves as participants in the community, which has value for both researcher and practitioner, theory and practice.

Hogan (1988) wrote about the research relationship in a similar way. "Empowering relationships develop over time and it takes time for participants to recognize the value that the relationship holds. Empowering relationships involve feelings of 'connectedness' that are developed in situations of equality, caring and mutual purpose and intention" (p. 12). Hogan highlighted several important issues in the research relationship: the equality between participants, the caring situation, and the feelings of connectedness. A sense of equality between participants is particularly important in narrative inquiry. However, in researcher-practitioner relationships where practitioners have long been silenced through being used as objects for study, we are faced with a dilemma. Practitioners have experienced themselves as without voice in the research process and may find it difficult to feel empowered to tell their stories. They have been made to feel less than equal. Noddings (1986) is helpful in thinking through this dilemma for narrative inquiry. She wrote that "we approach our goal by living with those whom we teach in a caring community, through modeling, dialogue, practice and confirmation. Again, we see how unfamiliar this language has become" (p. 502).

In this quotation, Noddings was speaking of the teaching-learning relationship, but what she said has significance for thinking about researcher-practitioner relationships as well. She drew attention to the ways we situate ourselves in relation to the persons with whom we work, to the ways in which we practice in a collaborative way, and to the ways all participants model, in their practices, a valuing and confirmation of each other. What Hogan and Noddings highlighted is the necessity of time, relationship, space, and voice in establishing the collaborative relationship, a relationship in which both researchers and practitioners have voice in Britzman's (in press) sense. Britzman wrote:

> Voice is meaning that resides in the individual and enables that individual to participate in a community. . . . The struggle for voice begins when a person attempts to communicate meaning to someone else. Finding the words, speaking for oneself, and feeling heard by others are all a part of this process. . . . Voice suggests relationships: the individual's relationship to the meaning of her/his experience and hence, to language, and the individual's relationship to the other, since understanding is a social process.

In beginning the process of narrative inquiry, it is particularly important that all participants have voice within the relationship. It implies, as Elbow (1986) noted, that we play the "believing game," a way of working within a relationship that calls upon connected knowing in which the knower is personally attached to the known. Distance or separation does not characterize connected knowing. The believing game is a way of knowing that involves a process of self-insertion in the other's story as a way of coming to know the other's story and as giving the other voice. Elbow emphasized the collaborative nature of the believing game when he wrote "the believing game . . . is essentially cooperative or collaborative. The central event is the act of affirming or entering into someone's thinking or perceiving" (p. 289).

> In narrative inquiry, it is important that the researcher listen first to the practitioner's story, and that it is the practitioner who first tells his or her story. This does not mean that the researcher is silenced in the process of narrative inquiry. It does mean that the practitioner, who has long been silenced in the research relationship, is given the time and space to tell her or his story so that it too gains the authority and validity that the research story has long had. Coles (1989) made a similar point when he wrote "but on that fast-darkening winter afternoon, I was urged to let each patient be a teacher: hearing themselves teach you, through their narration, the patients will learn the lessons a good instructor learns only when he becomes a willing student, eager to be taught" (p. 22). Narrative inquiry is, however, a process of collaboration involving mutual storytelling and restorying as the research proceeds. In the process of beginning to live the shared story of narrative inquiry, the researcher needs to be aware of constructing a relationship in which both voices are heard. The above description emphasizes the importance of the mutual construction of the research relationship, a relationship in which both practitioners and researchers feel cared for and have a voice with which to tell their stories.

Living the Story: Continuing the Process of Narrative Inquiry

What should be clear from the previous description is an understanding of the process as one in which we feel continually trying to give an account of the multiple levels (which are temporally continuous and socially interactive) at which the inquiry proceeds. The central task is evident when it is grasped that people are both living their stories in an ongoing experiential text and telling their stories in words as they reflect upon life and explain themselves to others. For the researcher, this is a portion of the complexity of narrative, because a life is also a matter of growth toward an imagined future and, therefore, involves retelling stories and attempts at reliving stories. A person is, at once, engaged in living, telling, retelling, and reliving stories.

Seeing and describing story in the everyday actions of teachers, students, administrators, and others requires a subtle twist of mind on behalf of the enquirer. It is in the tellings and retellings that entanglements become acute, for it is here that temporal and social, cultural horizons are set and reset. How far of a probe into the participants's past and future is far enough? Which community spheres should be probed and to what social depth should the inquiry proceed? When one engages in narrative inquiry the process becomes even more complex, for, as researchers, we become part of the process. The two narratives of participant and researcher become, in part, a shared narrative construction and reconstruction through the inquiry.

Narrative inquiry in the social sciences is a form of empirical narrative in which empirical data is central to the work. The inevitable interpretation that occurs, something which is embedded even in the data collection process, does not make narrative into fiction even though the language of narrative inquiry is heavily laced with terms derived from literary criticism of fiction. A number of different methods of data collection are possible as the researcher and practitioner work together in a collaborative relationship. Data can be in the form of field notes of the shared experience, journal records, interview transcripts, others' observations, story telling, letter writing, autobiographical writing, documents such as class plans and newsletters, and writing such as rules, principles, pictures, metaphors, and personal philosophies. In our later discussion of plot of scene, the importance of the narrative whole is made clear. The sense of the whole is built from a rich data source with a focus on the concrete particularities of life that create powerful narrative tellings. In the following we draw small excerpts from several narrative studies. These excerpts are illustrative of the variety of narrative data sources and ways of collecting narrative data.

Field Notes of Shared Experience

Field records collected through participant observation in a shared practical setting is one of the primary tools of narrative inquiry work. There are numerous narrative studies (Clandinin, 1986, 1989; Hoffman, 1988; Kroma, 1983) that make use of field notes. An example of field notes taken from a narrative study with an intern teacher (Clandinin & Connelly, 1987) is given below.

> Marie sent them off to get started in the haunted house. She gave the other children their choice of centers and then they walked over and watched the students at the haunted house. They had built a haunted house with the large blocks. They had made a number of masks that they moved up and down. The walls moved which they said was the Poltergeist. They showed this for two or three minutes and the other students clapped. Then they went off to their centers and the children at the block center continued to work on their haunted house. (notes to file, October 22, 1985)

These notes are a small fragment of the notes used in a narrative study, which explored the ways in which the intern teacher (Marie) constructed and reconstructed her ideas of what it meant to teach using themes in primary classroom setting. The researcher participated in the situation with the children, the intern teacher, and in recording the field notes. The researcher's notes are an active recording of her construction of classroom events. We term this *active recording* to suggest the ways in which we see the researcher expressing her personal practical knowing in her work with the children and the intern teacher, and to highlight that the notes are an active reconstruction of the events rather than a passive recording, which would suggest that the events could be recorded without the researcher's interpretation. Journals made by participants in the practical setting are another source of data in narrative inquiry. Journal records can be made by both participants, researcher or practitioner. The following journal excerpt is taken from Davies (1988). Davies, a teacher, has kept a journal of her ongoing classroom practice for a number of years as a participant in a teacher researcher group. In the following journal excerpt she wrote about her experiences with one of her student's journals in which Lisa, the student, figures out her writing.

> This episode with Lisa makes me realize that we're still moving forward in the "gains" of this experience. I've been wondering about when the natural "peak" will occur, the moment I feel we've gone as far as we can without the downslide effect—the loss of momentum. I just have to watch for the natural ending. I see time as so critical. Kids need and get the time with each other—kid to kid time responding is so important—they make their connections just as we make ours in the research group. (p. 20)

In this journal entry, Davies is trying to make sense of her work with the children in her classroom as they work in their journals. Yet she is also trying to understand the parallels between her experiences of learning through participating in the teacher researcher group with the work that is going on with the children in her classroom.

Interviews

Another data collection tool in narrative inquiry is the unstructured interview. Interviews are conducted between researcher and participant, transcripts are made, the meetings are made available for further discussion, and they become part of the ongoing narrative record. There are many examples of interviews in narrative inquiry. Mishler (1986) has completed the most comprehensive study of interview in narrative inquiry. We have chosen to highlight a sample of an interview from the work of Enns-Connolly (1985). The following excerpt is taken from her case study with a language student in her exploration of the process of translation.

Brian, Student: The situation about which he was talking I've thought about a lot.

Esther, Researcher: Mhmmm.

B: Mainly because, um, I've often been concerned that my own political beliefs might lead me in certain situations into a similar kind of thing.

E: Yeah, that's interesting because um you're thinking of it politically—as a political—as a consequence of politics which um, well this background—do you recall the background of this particular author? Like I'm sure that's probably a real factor in, in his writing. He's writing immediately after the Second World War after coming back from Russia and his war experiences and everything, and uh—For me, though, I don"t know—I guess that just for me it's not political—I'm not focusing on the fact that it's the consequences of a political situation, but I'm focusing on the whole idea of a human being being along and probing into himself and coming to terms with himself, and I see it more as somebody in the face of death. Like, for me death was really—like the presence of impending death was a really big thing that I was concerned about and I saw him as a person in the face of death and trying to—as reacting to impending death.

B: I saw him as a person who was just desperately trying to survive. Not survive in the face of death, but survive in the face of his own, his own capacity to break down mentally, I guess. (pp. 38–39)

What Enns-Connolly explores in her work with the German student are the ways in which a translator's personal practical knowledge is shaped by and shapes the translation. The above interview segment is one in which both participants narratively come to understand the ways in which their narrative experiences shape their translation of a particular text.

Story Telling

There are many powerful examples of the uses of individual's lived stories as data sources in narrative inquiry. These are as diverse as Paley's (1981, 1986) work with children's stories to Smith, Prunty, Dwyer, and Kleine's (1987) Kensington Revisited project. The following is an example of a story drawn from Connelly and Clandinin's (1988) work with a school principal, Phil. Phil told the following story of his experiences as a child as a way of explaining one of his actions as principal at Bay Street School.

He had been sent to school in short pants. He and another boy in short pants were caught by older students who put them in a blanket. Phil had escaped while the other boy was trapped. He went home saying he was never going to go back to that school again. He said he understood about being a member of a minority group but he said he didn't look like a minority. He said you understood if you've had the experience. (notes to file, April 15, 1981)

This story is part of Phil's storying and restorying of the ways in which he administers an inner-city school. Many stories are told by participants in a narrative inquiry as they describe their work and explain their actions. The tendency to explain through stories can easily be misinterpreted as establishing causal links in narrative inquiry. We later discuss this matter under the heading of the illusion of causality in narrative studies.

Letter Writing

Letter writing, a way of engaging in written dialogue between researcher and participants, is another data source in narrative inquiry. For many narrativists, letter writing is a way of offering and responding to tentative narrative interpretations (Clandinin, 1986). The following, another way of thinking about letter writing, occurs within the narrative study of a group of practitioners. The practitioners are exploring the ways in which they work with children in language arts. The following example is taken from Davies (1988), one of the teacher researchers.

I really realized just how important written response is to all of us in the research group. That made me think of the same thing for kids, which is what I'm doing now with their logs/journals of thinking. I have a reason to do these journals and that acts to focus my teaching and their learning. I really see the value, it's a lifelong one, for them as well as me. (p. 10)

Another participant in the group responds to Davies's comment in the following way in a written response similar to a response to a letter.

The notion of trusted friends has been built in your classroom since the beginning of the year. These journals are part of your evolving curriculum and as such they come into the curriculum at exactly the right time for the children to make the best possible use of them. They are working so well because they are a natural outgrowth of everything that has gone before. These kids are so open, so trusting, so sensitive, so caring, so everything! The usual kid school journals are an activity that the teacher comes up with to address some part of the mandated curriculum. Kids treat the activity like any of the regular sorts of assignment—for the teacher. The latest "chapter," the journal writing, really highlights the similarities between our group and what goes on in our classroom—the empowerment, validation, voice, sense of community, caring, connectedness are all there. (p. 10)

The exchange is drawn from a two-year study that narratively looks at teachers' experiences with writing and the ways in which their ways of knowing are expressed in their classroom practices.

Autobiographical and Biographical Writing

Another data source in narrative inquiry is autobiographical and biographical writing. Autobiographical writing sometimes appears in stories that teachers tell or in more focused autobiographal writing. We see an example of such writing in Conle's (1989) work.

To mind comes the image of a young teenager standing by a row of windows in a classroom which has become more spacious by open folding doors which usually separate it from the adjoining room. It is gym period in a small Ontario high school in the mid 50's and two grade 10 classes are enjoying a break in routine, a snowball dance. It started with one couple who then each asked a partner and so on. The girl by the window has been waiting. No one asked her yet. The crowd around her is getting smaller and smaller. Finally she is the only one left. She stays until the bell rings and everyone files out. "Perhaps no one noticed," she thinks, but a friend remarks, "Oh, you didn't dance!"

I have never forgotten the incident. Many years later a colleague and I talked about it in a discussion about my early years in Canada as an immigrant teenager. We wondered how those early experiences might have shaped my interest in teaching English as a second language? What did I remember of this episode and why did I remember it at all? (p. 8)

What Conle draws attention to is the ways in which her experience shapes her interest in, and ways of constructing, particular research and teaching interests. Other research references to autobiographical/biographical writing as a data source for narrative inquiry are, for example, Rose (1983) on the parallel lives in the marriages of well-known Victorian writers, Grumet (1988) on womens's experiences, and Pinar (1988), Olney (1980), and Gunn (1982) on method.

Other Narrative Data Sources

There are other data sources that narrative inquirers use. Documents such as class plans and newsletters (Clandinin, 1986), writing such as rules and principles (Elbaz, 1983), picturing (Cole, 1986), metaphors (Lakoff & Johnson, 1980), and personal philosophies (Kroma, 1983) are all possible data sources for narrative inquiry. See Connelly and Clandinin (1988) for a more extended discussion of these various resources.

Writing the Narrative

At the completion of a narrative study, it is often not clear when the writing of the study began. There is frequently a sense that writing began during the opening negotiations with participants or even earlier as ideas for the study were first formulated. Material written throughout the course of the inquiry often appears as major pieces of the final document. It is common, for instance, for collaborative documents such as letters to be included as part of the text. Material written for different purposes such as conference presentations may become part of the final document. There may be a moment when one says "I have completed my data collection and will now write the narrative," but even then narrative methodologies often require further discussion with participants, such that data is collected until the final document is completed. Enns-Connolly's (1985) letters to her student in the German language is an example where data collection and writing were shared through final drafts, thesis hearing, and subsequent publication. It is not at all clear when the writing begins.

It is important, therefore, for narrative researchers to be conscious of the end as the inquiry begins. The various matters we describe below are, of course, most evident in one's writing. But if these matters have not been attended to from the outset, the writing will be much more difficult.

What Makes a Good Narrative?
Beyond Reliability, Validity and Generalizability

Van Maanen (1988) wrote that for anthropology, *reliability* and *validity* are overrated criteria whereas *apparency* and *verisimilitude* are underrated criteria. The sense that the mainstay criteria of social science research are overrated is shared by Guba and Lincoln (1989), who reject the utility of the idea of generalization and argue that it "be given up as a goal of inquiry" and replaced by "transferability." Van Maanen, in discussing the origin of his book, writes that "the manuscript I imagined would reflect the quirky and unpredictable moments of my own history in the field and likely spoof some of the maxims of the trade. The intent was to be less instructive than amusing. Along the way, however, things grew more serious" (pp. xi–xii). This is a telling remark coming as it does as a story in a researcher's own narrative of inquiry. It is a helpful reminder to those who pursue narrative studies that they need to be prepared to follow their nose and, after the fact, reconstruct their narrative of inquiry. For this reason books such as Elbaz's (1983) *Teacher Thinking* and Clandinin's (1986) *Classroom Practice* end with reflective chapters that function as another kind of methods chapter. What are some of these more serious matters that guide the narrative writer in the creation of documents with a measure of verisimilitude?

Like other qualitative methods, narrative relies on criteria other than validity, reliability, and generalizability. It is important not to squeeze the language of narrative criteria into a language created for other forms of research. The language and criteria for the conduct of narrative inquiry are under development in the research community. We think a variety of criteria, some appropriate to some circumstances and some to others, will eventually be the agreed-upon norm. It is currently the case that each inquirer must search for, and defend, the criteria that best apply to his or her work. We have already identified apparency, verisimilitude, and transferability as possible criteria. In the following paragraphs we identify additional criterion terms being proposed and sued.

An excellent place to begin is with Crites' (1986) cautionary phrase "the illusion of causality" (p. 168). He refers to the "topsy-turvy hermeneutic principle" in which a sequence of events looked at backward has the appearance of causal necessity and, looked at forward, has the sense of a teleological, intentional pull of the future. Thus, examined temporally, backward or forward, events tend to appear deterministically related. Because every narrativist has either recorded classroom and other events in temporal sequence (e.g., field notes) or has solicited memory records, which are clearly dated (e.g., stories and autobiographical writing), and intentional expectations (e.g., goals, lesson plans, purposes, and time lines), which often tend to be associated with temporal targets, the "illusion" can become a powerful interpretive force for the writer. Adopting what might be called "the principle of time defeasibility," time may be modified to suit the story told. We make use of this notion in graduate classes, for example, in which students are often encouraged to write their own narrative by beginning with present values, beliefs, and actions and then to move to their childhood or early schooling experiences. Narrative writers frequently move back and forward several times in a single document as various threads are narrated. Chatman (1981) makes use of temporal defeasibility in his distinction between "storied-time" and "discourse-time." His is a distinction between events-as-lived and events-as-told, a distinction central to the writing of good narratives and for avoiding the illusion of causality.

If not causality, what then? Narrative explanation derives from the whole. We noted above that narrative inquiry was driven by a sense of the whole and it is this sense which needs to drive the writing (and reading) of narrative. Narratives are not adequately written according to a model of cause and effect but according to the explanations gleaned from the overall narrative or, as Polkinghorne (1988) said, on "change from 'beginning' to 'end'" (p. 116). When done properly, one does not feel lost in minutia but always has a sense of the whole. Unfortunately, this presents a dilemma in the writing because one needs to get down to concrete experiential detail. How to adjudicate between the whole and the detail at each moment of the writing is a difficult task for the writer of narrative.

One may fulfill these criterial conditions and still wonder if the narrative is a good one. Crites wrote that a good narrative constitutes an "invitation" to participate, a notion similar to Guba and Lincoln's (1989) and our own (Connelly, 1978) idea that case studies may be read, and lived, vicariously by others. Peshkin (1985) noted something similar when he wrote, "When I disclose what I have seen, my results invite other researchers to look where I did and see what I saw. My ideas are candidates for others to entertain, not necessarily as truth, let alone Truth, but as positions about the nature and meaning of a phenomenon that may fit their sensibility and shape their thinking about their own inquiries" (p. 280). On the grounds suggested by these authors, the narrative writer has an available test, that is, to have another participant read the account and to respond to such questions as "What do you make of it for your teaching (or other) situation?" This allows a researcher to assess the invitational quality of a manuscript already established as logically sound.

What are some of the marks of an explanatory, invitational narrative? Tannen (1988) suggested that a reader of a story connects with it by recognizing particulars, by imagining the scenes in which the particulars could occur, and by reconstructing them from remembered associations with similar particulars. It is the particular and not the general that triggers emotion and moves people and gives rise to what H. Rosen (1988) called "authenticity" (p. 81). This theme is picked up as integral to plot and scene in the next section.

Robinson and Hawpe (1986), in asking the question What constitutes narrative thinking? identify three useful writing criteria: *economy, selectivity,* and *familiarity* (p. 111–125). With these criteria they argue that stories stand between the general and the particular, mediating the generic demands of science with the personal, practical, concrete demands of living. Stories function as arguments in which we learn something essentially human by understanding an actual life or community as lived. The narrative inquirer undertakes this mediation from beginning to end and embodies these dimensions as best as he or she can in the written narrative.

Spence (1982) writes that "narrative truth" consists of "continuity," "closure," "aesthetic finality," and a sense of "conviction" (p. 31). These are qualities associated both with fictional literature and with something well done. They are life criteria. In our studies we use the notions of *adequacy* (borrowed from Schwab, 1964) and *plausibility.* A plausible account is one that tends to ring true. It is an account of which one might say "I can see that happening." Thus, although fantasy may be an invitational element in fictional narrative, plausibility exerts firmer tugs in empirical narratives.

We can understand the narrative writer's task if we examine significant events in our lives in terms of the criteria here describes. Life, like the narrative writer's task, is a dialectical balancing act in which one strives for various perfections, always falling short, yet sometimes achieving a liveable harmony of competing narrative threads and criteria.

Structuring the Narrative: Scene and Plot

Welty (1979) remarks that time and place are the two points of reference by which the novel grasps experience. This is no less true for the writing of empirical narratives. Time and place become written constructions in the form of plot and scene respectively. Time and place, plot and scene, work together to create the experiential quality of narrative. They are not, in themselves, the interpretive nor the conceptual side. Nor are they on the side of narrative criticism. They are the thing itself.

Scene: Place is where the action occurs, where characters are formed and live out their stories and where cultural and social context play constraining and enabling roles. Welty writes the following on the construction of scene:

> Place has surface, which will take the imprint of man—his hand, his foot, his mind; it can be tamed, domesticated. It has shape, size, boundaries; man can measure himself against them. It has atmosphere and temperature, change of light and show of season, qualities to which man spontaneously responds. Place has always nursed, nourished and instructed man; he in turn can rule it and ruin it, take it and lose it, suffer if he is exiled from it, and after living on it he goes to it in his grave. It is the stuff of fiction, as close to our living lives as the earth we can pick up and rub between our fingers, something we can feel and smell (p. 163).

It may be that place and scene (rather than time and plot) is the more difficult construction for narrativist researchers. Documents frequently contain brief character sketches and brief descriptions of classrooms, principal's offices, and the like. Setting these scenes in interesting relief is a puzzling writing task because these matters are "as close to our living lives as the earth we can pick and rub between our fingers" and depend, therefore, on writing talents for making the plain and prosaic, interesting and invitational.

It is less customary to set the scene in physical terms than in character terms. To describe seating arrangements, pictures, and layouts on classroom walls in a way that helps tell the narrative and enhance its explanatory capability is no easy task. The necessary field records for the construction of scene are often missing at the time of writing as one tends, during data collection, to focus on people rather than things.

Character and physical environment need, in the writing of narrative, to work in harmony with a third feature of scene, namely, context. Context may consist of characters and physical environments other than the classroom. For instance, department heads, principals, school, and community all bear on a classroom scene and need, depending on the inquiry, to be described. Setting the context of scene may be more troublesome to the writer than the other two features because context is "out of sight" and requires active searches during data collection. Nevertheless, difficult as it may be to write scenes composed of character, physical environment, and context, they are essential to narrative and are "as informing as an old gossip" (Welty, p. 163).

Plot: Time is essential to plot. If time were not insubstantial, one might say that time is the substance of plot. Welty develops this point in a metaphorical way. She says that "many of our proverbs are little nut shells to pack the meat of time in" (p. 164) and proceeds to give incipient plot examples such as "pride goeth before destruction" and "he that diggeth a pit shall fall into it." These temporal constructions which she calls "ingots of time" are also "ingots of plot" (p. 164).

They are both story containers and conveyors of stories, expressions that "speak of life-in-the-movement" with a beginning and an end. They mark what Kermode (1967) calls the tick-tock structure of story. With the addition of the middle, a basic explanatory plot structure of beginning, middle, and end is in place.

From the point of view of plot, the central structure of time is past-present-future. This common-sense way of thinking about time is informative of the temporal orientation taken in various lines of narrative and narratively oriented work. For example, narrative data sources may be classified according to their relative emphasis on the past, present, and future. Story telling and autobiography, for instance, tend to be located in the past; picturing and interviewing tend to be located in the present; and letter writing, journals, and participant observation tend to be located in the future. From the point of view of the narrative writer, then different kinds of data tend to strengthen these different temporal locales.

In addition to these methodological consequences of the three-part structure of time, Carr (1986) related the structure to three critical dimensions of human experience—significance, value, intention—and, therefore, of narrative writing. In general terms the past conveys significance, the present conveys value, and the future conveys intention. Narrative explanation and, therefore, narrative meaning, consists of significance, value, and intention. By virtue of being related to the structure of time, these three dimensions of meaning help a writer structure plots in which explanation and meaning themselves may be said to have a temporal structure. Furthermore, this structure helps convey a sense of purpose on the writing as one deals with various temporal data and fits them into past, present, or future oriented parts of the narrative.

We use an adaptation of this temporal plot structure as a device to initiate data collection. The device is based on White's (1981) distinction between annals, chronicles, and narratives in the narrative study of history. Annals are a dated report of events in which there is no apparent connection between the events. A person might, for example, simply search their memory for important life events with no particular interpretive agenda in mind. As events emerge, their date of occurrence is recorded and the event described. The same may happen in the ongoing record of participant observation where one may have no clear idea of the meaning of the events described but in which one makes dated records nonetheless.

Chronicles somewhat resemble Welty's ingots of time and plot in which events are clearly linked as, for example, a series of events from one's elementary school years or, perhaps, a series of events from one's years as a sports fan, or from a marriage, or during the time of a particular government with a particular educational policy, and so forth. Although it is clear that the events in a chronology are linked, the meaning of the events, and the plot which gives the explanatory structure for linking the events, is unstated. It is these matters which, when added to the chronology, make it a narrative. There is, of course, no clear separation of each of these ways of linking events. Nevertheless, the distinction is a useful one both in data collection and in the writing of the narrative.

In our own work, especially in teaching but also in research, instead of asking people at the outset to write a narrative we encourage them to write a chronology. We avoid asking people to begin by writing biographies and autobiographies for the same reason. People beginning to explore the writing of their own narrative, or that of another, often find the chronology to be a manageable task whereas the writing of a full-fledged autobiography or narrative, where one stresses plot, meaning, interpretation, and explanation, can be baffling and discouraging. Looked at from another point of view, many amateur biographies are often more akin to chronologies than narratives. The linking themes that transform the annals into a chronology are often mistaken for an account of plot and meaning. In the end, of course, it is of no real theoretical significance what the writing is called because all chronicles are incipient narratives and all narratives reduce to chronicles as one pursues the narrative, remembers and reconstructs new events, and creates further meaning. For inquiry, the point is that a heartfelt record of events in one's life, or research account of a life, does not guarantee significance, meaning, and purpose.

The creation of further meaning, which might be called "the restorying quality of narrative," is one of the most difficult of all to capture in writing. A written document appears to stand still; then narrative appears finished. It has been written, characters' lives constructed, social histories recorded, meaning expressed for all to see. Yet, anyone who has written a narrative knows that it, like life, is a continual unfolding where the narrative insights of today are the chronological events of tomorrow. Such writers know in advance that the task of conveying a sense that the narrative is unfinished and that stories will be retold and lives relived in new ways is likely to be completed in less than satisfactory ways. Furthermore, even when the writer is personally satisfied with the result, he or she needs always to remember that readers may freeze the narrative with the result that the restorying life quality intended by the writer may become fixed as a print portrait by the reader.

Multiple "I's" in Narrative Inquiry

In an earlier section, we wrote about the multiple levels at which narrative inquiry proceeds. We described each participant, researcher and teacher, as engaged in living, telling, retelling, and reliving their stories as the narrative inquiry proceeds.

Part of the difficulty in writing narrative is in finding ways to understand and portray the complexity of the ongoing stories being told and retold in the inquiry. We are, as researchers and teachers, still telling in our practices our ongoing life stories as they are lived, told, relived and retold. We restory earlier experiences as we reflect on later experiences so the stories and their meaning shift and change over time. As we engage in a reflective research process, our stories are often restoried and changed as we, as teachers and/or researchers, "give back" to each other ways of seeing our stories. I tell you a researcher's story. You tell me what you heard and what it meant to you. I hadn't thought of it this way, am transformed in some important way, and tell the story differently the next time I encounter an interested listener or talk again with my participant.

As researchers writing narratively, we have come to understand part of this complexity as a problem in multiple "I's." We become "plurivocal" (Barnieh, 1989) in writing narratively. The "I" can speak as researcher, teacher, man or woman, commentator, research participant, narrative critic, and as theory builder. Yet in living the narrative inquiry process, we are one person. We are also one in the writing. However, in the writing of narrative, it becomes important to sort out whose voice is the dominant one when we write "I."

Peshkin (1985) addressed an aspect of this problem in writing about the researcher's personal qualities elicited in the research process. Although Peshkin's reference was to the data collection process, his comments are also helpful in thinking about the writing of narrative:

> Thus fieldworkers each bring to their sites at least two selves—the human self that we generally are in everyday situations, and the research self that we fashion for our particular research situations . . . participant observation, especially within one's own culture, is emphatically first person singular. The human I is there, the I that is present under many of the same political, economic, and social circumstances as when one is being routinely human and not a researcher. . . . Behind this I are one's multiple personal dispositions . . . that may be engaged by the realities of the field situation. Because of the unknown and the unexpected aspects of the research field, we do not know which of our dispositions will be engaged. (p. 270)

Although in this quotation Peshkin addressed a dual "I," researcher and person, he suggested that the issue of multiple "I's" in writing narrative is more complex. There are more "I's" than person and researcher within each research participant. Peshkin acknowledged what he calls the personal dispositions as drawn out by the situation. In narrative inquiry we see that the practices drawn out in the research situation are lodged in our personal knowledge of the world. One of our tasks in writing narrative accounts is to convey a sense of the complexity of all of the "I's" all of the ways each of us have of knowing.

We are, in narrative inquiry, constructing narratives at several levels. At one level it is the personal narratives and the jointly shared and constructed narratives that are told in the research writing, but narrative researchers are compelled to move beyond the telling of the lived story to tell the research story. We see in Clandinin's (1986) work her story with Stephanie and Aileen as an expression of teacher images as well as a research story of a way of understanding classroom practice. In Enns-Connolly's (1985) work there is her story with Brian as well as a story of understanding the translation process as an expression of the personal practical knowledge of the translator as it is drawn forth in the experience of reading the text. This telling of the research story requires another voice of researcher, another "I."

In this latter endeavor we make our place and our voice as researcher central. We understand this as a moving out of the collaborative relationship to a relationship where we speak more clearly with the researcher "I." In the process of living the narrative inquiry, the place and voice of researcher and teacher become less defined by role. Our concern is to have a place for the voice of each participant. The question of who is researcher and who is teacher becomes less important as we concern ourselves with questions of collaboration, trust, and relationship as we live, story, and restory our collaborative research life. Yet in the process of writing the research story, the thread of the research inquiry becomes part of the researcher's purpose. In some ways the researcher moves out of the lived story to tell, with another "I," another kind of story.

Risks, Dangers and Abuses of Narrative

The central value of narrative inquiry is its quality as subject matter. Narrative and life go together and so the principal attraction of narrative as method is its capacity to render life experiences, both personal and social, in relevant and meaningful ways. However, this same capacity is a two-edged inquiry sword. Falsehood may be substituted for meaning and narrative truth by using the same criteria that give rise to significance, value, and intention. Not only may one "fake the data" and write a fiction but one may also use the data to tell a deception as easily as a truth.

In this section we do not give a complete listing of possible deceptions nor a list of devices for revealing unintentional and intentional deceptions. Rather, we simply remind potential narrative inquirers to listen closely to their critics. Our view is that every criticism is valid to some degree and contains the seed of an important point.

Take, for example, one of the central tenets of narrative, that is, the intersubjective quality of the inquiry. To dismiss criticism of the personal and interpersonal in inquiry is to risk the dangers of narcissism and solipsism. Narrative inquirers need to respond to critics either at the level of principle or with respect to a particular writing. It is too easy to become committed to the whole, the narrative plot, and to one's own role in the inquiry and to lose sight of the various fine lines that one treads in the writing of a narrative.

One of the "multiple I's" is that of the narrative critic. Empirical narrativists cannot, as Welty claims fictional writers can, avoid the task of criticism. She writes that "story writing and critical analysis are indeed separate gifts, life spelling and playing the flute, and the same writer proficient in both is doubly endowed. But even he can't rise and do both at the same time" (p. 107). Empirical narrativists cannot follow this dictum but must find ways of becoming "I, the critic." To accomplish this, Dalley (1989) experimented with different tenses, uses of pronoun, and text structure in an autobiographical study of bilingualism.

A particular danger in narrative is what we have called "the Hollywood plot," the plot where everything works out well in the end. "Wellness" may be a thorough and unbending censure, such as is sometimes found in critical ethnographies, or a distillation of drops of honey, such as is sometimes found in program evaluations and implementations. Spence (1986) called this process "narrative smoothing." It is process that goes on all the time in narrative both during data collection and writing. The problem, therefore, is a judicial one in which the smoothing contained in the plot is properly balanced with what is obscured in the smoothing for narrative purposes. To acknowledge narrative smoothing is to open another door for the reader. It is a question of being as alert to the stories not told as to those that are. Kermode (1981) called the untold stories "narrative secrets" to which a careful reader will attend. Unlike the case in fiction, which is Kermode's topic, the empirical narrativist helps his or her reader by self-consciously discussing the selections made, the possible alternative stories, and other limitations seen from the vantage point of "I the critic."

Selecting Stories to Construct and Reconstruct Narrative Plots

Because collaboration occurs from beginning to end in narrative inquiry, plot outlines are continually revised as consultation takes place over written materials and as further data are collected to develop points of importance in the revised story. In long-term studies, the written stories, and the books and papers in which they appear, may be constructed and reconstructed with different participants depending on the particular inquiry at hand. Our work in Bay Street School is illustrative. There are many computer disks of field records and interview transcripts. There are also file cabinets full of memoranda; school, board of education, and government documents; and newspaper clippings. It is obvious that only a small portion of it may be used in a paper, report, or even a book. We cannot summarize in formats that condense the volume in a way that data tables condense survey results. Because we know that a sense of the entire inquiry is useful context for readers, a descriptive overview is required. A "narrative sketch," something like a character sketch except that it applies to the overall inquiry is useful. It is primarily a chronicle of the inquiry. Like the notes playgoers receive as they are escorted to their seats, it has broad descriptions of scene and plot and a number of subsketches of key characters, spaces, and major events that figure in the narrative. A narrative sketch might be called an ingot of time and space.

In selecting how to use the data, there are choices of form and substance. Choices of substance relate to the purposes of the inquiry which, at the time of writing, may have evolved from the purposes originally conceived for the project and in terms of which much of the data was collected. Once again our work at Bay Street School is illustrative. the original purpose defined in our National Institute of Education grant proposal was to better understand policy utilization from the participant's points of view. The current purpose is to understand, through narrative, something of a school's cultural folk models (see Johnson, 1987) and to link these to a participant's personal knowledge and to the policy and community context. Thus, data collected and, therefore, shaped by one purpose is to be used for another. Our first task is to satisfy ourselves that the data is suitable to our new purpose.

The broad outlines of plot are contained in statements of narrative purpose. Which records are most telling? No matter how familiar they are with their data, narrative writers need to search their memories, both human and computer, for significant events preparatory to writing in much the same way that individuals search their memories and files for important life events in preparation for writing a biography. If one has worked as a team the process is richer as events can be brought to mind, discussed, and refreshed in detail with reference to field records.

Practical considerations of space and imagined audience eventually determine the quantity of data contained in the written narrative. Some narrative researchers deal with detailed accounts of experience whereas others prefer theory and abstraction. As noted earlier, both are important and a balance needs to be struck.

Another influence on the selection of data used in the final document is the form of the narrative. Eisner (1982) has stressed the need to experiment with "forms of representation." Narratives may be written in a demonstration mode or in an inductive mode, the former adopting more standard social scientific forms and the latter opening up possibilities imagined by Eisner. In the demonstrative mode, data tend not to speak for themselves but instead are used in exemplary ways to illustrate the thoughts of the narrative writer. In an inductive mode, data more clearly tell their own story. It is in this latter mode that researchers such as Beattie (in press) and Mullen (in press) are experimenting with different literary forms.

Our final section refers again to the restorying quality of narrative. Once a writer selects events it is possible to do at least three very different things with them. The first, which we have termed *broadening*, occurs when we generalize. An event recalled will be used in a chronicle or incipient narrative to make a general comment about a person's character, values, way of life or, perhaps, about the social and intellectual climate of the times. These generalizations appear as character and social descriptions, long-hand answers to the questions What sort of person are you? or What kind of society is it? Although these are interesting questions, they are not, as stated, narrative ones. A useful rule of thumb is to avoid making such generalizations and to concentrate on the event, in a process we have termed *burrowing*. We focus on the event's emotional, moral, and aesthetic qualities; we then ask why the event is associated with these feelings and what their origins might be. We imagine this to be somewhat like Schafer's (1981) narrative therapy. This way of approaching the event is aimed at reconstructing a story of the event from the point of view of the person at the time the event occurred. The third thing to do with the story follows from this. The person returns to present and future considerations and asks what the meaning of the event is and how he or she might create a new story of self which changes the meaning of the event, its description, and its significance for the larger life story the person may be trying to live. These questions often emerge at the point of writing, after the data are collected. Thus, whether one feels that the appropriate task is broadening, burrowing, restorying, or all three, additional data collection is a likely possibility during the latter stages of writing. In long-term studies, where the inquiry purpose has evolved (as it has in our Bay Street work), and where some participants may have retired or moved to other positions, maintaining collaboration on the construction and reconstruction of plots may become a task requiring special ingenuity.

This observation brings us to our final point on narrative inquiry, which is that it is common in collaborative ventures to either work with participants throughout the writing, in which case records of the work itself constitute data, or to bring written documents back to participants for final discussions. Thus, the process of writing the inquiry and the process of living the inquiry are coincident activities tending, perhaps, to shift one way or the other and always to work in tandem.

Concluding Observations

Recently we have tried to make sense of narrative inquiry for school curricula and for possible altered and new relations among curriculum researchers and teacher participants (Clandinin & Connelly, in press). Jackson (1987) wrote a telling paper on the first topic, the uses of narrative for school curricula. We plan to use our few remaining paragraphs to comment on the researcher-participant topic. These comments may be of interest to some who are not in curriculum studies or who work with participants other than teachers. Basically, we see that what is at stake is less a matter of working theories and ideologies and more a question of the place of research in the improvement of practice and of how researchers and practitioners may productively relate to one another. Narrative and story as we imagine them functioning in educational inquiry generate a somewhat new agenda of theory-practice relations. One part of the agenda is to let experience and time work their way in inquiry. Story, being inherently temporal, requires this. By listening to participant stories of their experience of teaching and learning, we hope to write narratives of what it means to educate and be educated. These inquires need to be soft, or perhaps *gentle* is a better term. What is at stake is the creation of situations of trust in which the storytelling urge, so much a part of the best parts of our social life, finds expression. Eisner (1988) wrote that this spirit of inquiry is already taking root. Researchers, he said, are "beginning to go back to the schools, not to conduct commando raids, but to work with teachers" (p. 19).

The second part of a possible agenda crept up on our awareness as we worked at stilling our theoretical voices in an attempt to foster storytelling approaches in our teaching and school-based studies. We found that merely listening, recording, and fostering participant story telling was both impossible (we are, all of us, continually telling stories of our experience, whether or not we speak and write them) and unsatisfying. We learned that we, too, needed to tell our stories. Scribes we were not; story tellers and story livers we were. And in our story telling, the stories of our participants merged with our own to create new stories, ones that we have labelled *collaborative stories*. The thing finally written on paper (or, perhaps on film, tape, or canvas), the research paper or book, is a collaborative document; a mutually constructed story created out of the lives of both researcher and participant.

We therefore think in terms of a two-part inquiry agenda. We need to listen closely to teachers and other learners and to the stories of their lives in and out of classrooms. We also need to tell our own stories as we live our own collaborative researcher/teacher lives. Our own work then becomes one of learning to tell and live a new mutually constructed account of inquiry in teaching and learning. What emerges from this mutual relationship are new stories of teachers and learners as curriculum makers, stories that hold new possibilities for both researchers and teachers and for those who read their stories. For curriculum, and perhaps for other branches of educational inquiry, it is a research agenda which gives "curriculum professors something to do" (Schwab, 1983).

Notes

1. Narrative inquiry may be traced to Aristotle's *Poetics* and Augustine's *Confessions* (See Ricoeur's, 1984, use of these two sources to link time and narrative) and may be seen to have various adaptations and applications in a diversity of areas including education. Dewey's (1916, 1934, 1938a, 1938b) work on time, space, experience, and sociality is also central. Narrative has a long history in literature where literary theory is the principal intellectual resource (e.g., Booth, 1961, 1979; Frye, 1957; Hardy, 1968; Kermode, 1967; Scholes & Kellogg, 1966). The fact that a story is inherently temporal means that history (White, 1973, 1981) and the philosophy of history (Carr, 1986; Ricoeur, 1984, 1985, 1988) which are essentially the study of time, have a special role to play in shaping narrative studies in the social sciences. Therapeutic fields are making significant contributions (Schafer, 1976, 1981; Spence, 1982). Narrative has only recently been discovered in psychology although Polkinghorne (1988) claims that closely related inquiries were part of the field at the turn of the century but disappeared after the second world war when they were suffocated by physical science paradigms. Bruner (1986) and Sarbin (1986) are frequently cited psychology sources. Among the most fundamental and educationally suggestive works on the nature of narrative knowledge is Johnson's philosophical study of bodily knowledge and language (1981, 1987, 1989, and Lakoff & Johnson, 1980). Because education is ultimately a moral and spiritual pursuit, MacIntire's narrative ethical theory (1966, 1981) and Crites's theological writing on narrative (1971, 1975, 1986) are especially useful for educational purposes.

   The first broadly conceived methodologically oriented book on the use of narrative in the social sciences came out of the therapeutic fields, such as Polkinghorne's *Narrative Knowing and the Human Sciences* (1988). This book was preceded by Mishler's more narrowly focused *Research Interviewing: Context and Narrative* (1986). Van Maanen's 1988 publication, written from the point of view of anthropology, gives a critical introduction to the ethnography of story telling both as subject matter and as ethnographers's written form. Reason and Hawkins (1988) wrote a chapter titled *Storytelling as Inquiry*. Undoubtedly others will follow.

2. On this basis, for Elbaz, works such as Shulman's (1987) research on expert teachers, Schon's (1987, in press) reflective practice, Reid's (1988) policy analysis, Munby's (1986) study of teacher's metaphors, and Lincoln and Guba's (1985) naturalistic approach to evaluation qualify as narratively related work.

3. Some illustrations of teachers' stories are those by Coles (1989), Barzun (1944), Reiff (1972), Booth (1988), Natkins (1986), Paley (1982, 1986), Calkin (1983), Steedman (1982), Armstrong (1980), Dennison (1969, Rowland (1984), and Meek, Armstrong, Austerfield, Graham, and Placetter (1983). Examples of "stories of teachers" are those by Yonemura (1986), Bullough (1989), Enns-Connolly (in press), selected chapters in Lightfoot and Martin (1988), several chapters in Graff and Warner (1989), Smith et al's *trilogy* (1986, 1987, 1988), Kilbourn (in press), Ryan (1970), and Shulman and Colbert (1988). Jackson's (1968) *Life in Classrooms* plays an especially generative role with respect to the literature of teachers' stories and stories of teachers.

References

Allen, J.P.B. (1989). The development of instructional models in second language education. *Annual Review of Applied Linguistics, 9,* 179–192.

Applebee, A.N. (1978). *The Child's concept of story: Ages two to seventeen.* Chicago: University of Chicago Press.

Armstrong, M. (1980). *Closely observed children: Diary of a primary classroom.* London: Writers and Readers in association with Chameleon.

Ball, S.J., & Goodson, I.F. (1985). *Teachers' lives and careers.* London: Falmer Press.

Barnieh, Z. (1989). *Understanding playwriting for children.* University of Calgary.

Barzun, J. (1944). *Teacher in America.* New York: University Press of America.

Beattie, M. (in press). *Teacher planning and inquiry as curriculum development.* Unpublished doctoral dissertation, University of Toronto, Toronto.

Bell, J. (in press). *Narrative self-study: The acquisition of literacy in a second language.* Unpublished doctoral dissertation, University of Toronto, Toronto.

Berk, L. (1980). Education in lives: Biographic narrative in the study of educational outcomes. *The Journal of Curriculum Theorizing, 2* (2), 88–153.

Bissex, G., & Bullock, R., (Eds.), (1987). *Seeing ourselves: Case-Study research by teachers of writing.* London: Heinemann.

Bleich, D. (1988). *The double perspective: Language, literacy, and social relations.* New York: Oxford University Press.

Booth, W.C. (1961). *The rhetoric of fiction* (2nd ed.). Chicago: University of Chicago Press.

Booth, W.C. (1979). *Critical understanding.* Chicago: University of Chicago Press.

Booth, W.C. (1988). *The vocation of a teacher: Rhetorical occasions 1967–1988.* Chicago: University of Chicago Press.

Britton, J. (1970). *Language and learning.* London: Allen Lane.

Britton, J. (1971). *Introduction to A.R. Luria, speech and the development of mental processes in the child.* London: Penguin.

Britzman, D. (in press). *Practice makes practice: A critical study of learning to teach.* New York: SUNY Press.

Bruner, J. (1986). *Actual minds, possible worlds.* Massachusetts: Harvard University Press.

Bullough, R.V. (1989). *First-Year teacher: A case study.* New York: Teachers College Press.

Calkins, L.M. (1983). *Lessons from a child: On the teaching and learning of writing.* Melbourne: Heinemann.

Carr, D. (1986). *Time, narrative, and history.* Bloomington: Indiana University Press.

Chatman, S. (1981). What novels can do that films can't (and vice versa). In W.J.T. Mitchell (Ed.), *On narrative* (pp. 117–136). Chicago: University of Chicago Press.

Clandinin, D.J. (1986). *Classroom practices: Teacher images in action.* London: Falmer Press.

Clandinin, D.J. (1988). *Understanding research on teaching as feminist research.* Paper presented at the meeting of the Canadian Society for the Study of Education, Windsor, Ontario.

Clandinin, D.J. (1989). Developing rhythm in teaching: The narrative study of a beginning teacher's personal practical knowledge of classrooms. *Curriculum Inquiry, 19* (2), 121–141.

Clandinin, D.J., & Connelly, F.M. (1987). *Narrative experience and the study of curriculum.* Washington, DC: The American Association of Colleges for Teacher Education. (ERIC Document Reproduction Service No. ED 306 208.)

Clandinin, D.J., & Connelly, F.M. (1988). Studying teachers' knowledge of classrooms: Collaborative research, ethics and the negotiation of narrative. *The Journal of Educational Thought, 22* (2A), 269–282.

Clandinin, D.J., & Connelly, F.M. (in press). Narrative and story in practice and research. In D. Schon (Ed.), *The Reflective turn: Case studies of reflective practice.* New York: Teachers College Press.

Cole, A.L. (1986). *Teachers' spontaneous adaptations: A mutual interpretation.* Unpublished doctoral dissertation, University of Toronto, Toronto.

Coles, R. (1989). *The call of stories: Teaching and the moral imagination.* Boston: Houghton Mifflin.

Conle, C. (1989). *Stories toward an interpretive thesis.* Ontario Institute for Studies in Education, Toronto.

Connelly, F.M. (1978). How shall we publish case studies of curriculum development? *Curriculum Inquiry, 8* (1), 78–82.

Connelly, F.M., & Clandinin, D.J. (1988). *Teachers as curriculum planners: Narratives of experience.* New York: Teachers College Press.

Crites, S. (1971). The narrative quality of experience. *Journal of the American Academy of Religion, 39* (3), 391–411.

Crites, S. (1975). Angels we have heard. In J.B. Wiggins (Ed.), *Religion as story* (pp. 23–63). Lanham: University Press of America.

Crites, S. (1986). Storytime: Recollecting the past and projecting the future. In T.R. Sarbin (Ed.), *The storied nature of human conduct,* (pp. 152–173). New York: Praeger.

Cumming, A. (1988). *The orchestration of ESL performance.* Working paper, University of British Columbia.

Dalley, P. (1989). *Mes langues, mes couleurs: A question of identity.* Unpublished master's thesis, University of Toronto, Toronto.

Davies, A. (1988). Two caring communities: A story of connected empowerment and voice. Unpublished manuscript, University of Calgary.

Dennison, G. (1969). *The lives of children*. New York: Vintage Books.

Dewey, J. (1916). *Democracy and education*. New York: Macmillan.

Dewey, J. (1934). *Art as experience*. New York: Capricorn Books.

Dewey, J. (1938a). *Experience and education*. New York: Collier Books.

Dewey, J. (1938b). *Logic: The theory of inquiry*. New York: Henry Holt.

Dorson, R.M. (1976). *Folklore and fakelore: Essays toward a discipline of folkstudies*. Cambridge, MA: Harvard University Press.

Egan, K. (1986). *Teaching as story telling: an alternative approach to teaching and curriculum in the elementary school*. London: Althouse Press, Faculty of Education, University of Western Ontario.

Eisner, E.W. (1982). *Cognition and curriculum: A basis for deciding what to teach*. New York: Longman.

Eisner, E.W. (1988). The primacy of experience and the politics of method. *Educational Researcher, 20*, 15–20.

Eisner, E.W. (in press). *The enlightened eye: On doing qualitative inquiry*. New York: Macmillan.

Elbaz, F. (1983). *Teaching thinking: A study of practical knowledge*. London: Croom Helm.

Elbaz, F. (1988, September). *Knowledge and discourse: The evolution of research on teacher thinking*. Paper presented at the Conference of the International Study Association on Teacher Thinking meeting of the University of Nottingham, England.

Elbow, P. (1986). *Embracing contraries: Explorations in teaching and learning*. Oxford: Oxford University Press.

Enns-Connoly, E. (1985). *Translation as interpretive act: A narrative study of translation in university-level foreign language teaching*. Unpublished doctoral dissertation, University of Toronto, Toronto.

Enns-Connolly, E. (in press). Translation and the translator: A narrative study of personal practical knowledge in the construction of meaning. *Curriculum Inquiry*.

Erwin-Tripp, S., & Mitchell-Kernan, C. (1977). *Child discourse*. New York: Academic Press.

Frye, N. (1957). *Anatomy of criticism*. Princeton, NJ: Princeton University Press.

Frye, N. (1988). *On education*. Markham, Ontario: Fitzhenry & Whiteside.

Gadamer, H.G. (1982). *Truth & method*. New York: Crossroad.

Goodson, I. (1988). Teachers' life histories and studies of curriculum and schooling. In I.F. Goodson (Ed.), *The making of curriculum: Collected essays*, (pp. 71–92). Philadelphia, Falmer Press.

Graff, G., & Warner, M. (Eds.). (1989). *The origins of literacy studies in America: A documentary anthology*. New York: Rurledge, Chapman and Hall.

Grumet, M.R. (1988). *Bitter milk: Woman and teaching*. Amherst, MA: University of Massachusetts Press.

Guba, E.G., & Lincoln, Y.S. (1989). *Personal communication*. Beverly Hills, CA: Sage.

Gunn, J.V. (1982). *Autobiography: Toward a poetics of experience*. Philadelphia: University of Pennsylvania Press.

Hardy, B. (1968). Towards a poetics of fiction: An approach through narrative. *Novel, 2,* 5–14.

Hoffman, L. (1988). Teacher personal practical knowledge. Unpublished master's thesis, University of Calgary.

Hogan, P. (1988). A community of teacher researchers: A story of empowerment and voice. Unpublished manuscript, University of Calgary.

Huberman, M. (1988). Teacher careers and social improvement. *Journal of Curriculum Studies, 20* (2), 119–132.

Jackson, P.W. (1968). *Life in classrooms.* Chicago: Holt, Rinehart & Winston.

Jackson, P.W. (1987). On the place of narration in teaching. In D. Berliner and B. Rosenshine (Eds.), *Talks to teachers* (pp. 307–328). New York: Random House.

Johnson, M. (Ed.). (1981). *Philosophical perspectives on metaphor.* Minneapolis: University of Minneapolis Press.

Johnson, M. (1987). *The body in the mind: The bodily basis of meaning, imagination, and reason.* Chicago: University of Chicago Press.

Johnson, M. (1989). Embodied knowledge. *Curriculum Inquiry, 19* (4), 361–377.

Kermode, F. (1967). *The sense of an ending: Studies in the theory of fiction.* London: Oxford University Press.

Kermode, F. (1981). Secrets and narrative sequence. In W.J.T. Mitchell (Ed.), *On narrative* (pp. 79–97). Chicago: University of Chicago Press.

Kilbourn, B. (in press). *Constructive feedback: Learning the art.* Toronto: OISE Press.

Kroma, S. (1983). Personal practical knowledge of language in teaching. Unpublished doctoral dissertation, University of Toronto, Toronto.

Lakoff, G., & Johnson, M. (1980). *Metaphors we live by.* Chicago: University of Chicago Press.

Lightfoot, M., & Martin, N. (Eds.). *The word for teaching is learning: Essays for James Britton.* London: Heinemann.

Lincoln, Y.S., & Guba, E.G. (1985). *Naturalistic inquiry.* Beverly Hills, CA: Sage.

MacIntyre, A. (1966). *A short history of ethics.* New York: Macmillan.

MacIntyre, A. (1981). *After virtue: A study in moral theory.* Notre Dame, IN: University of Notre Dame Press.

Mandler, J.M. (1984). *Stories, scripts and scenes: Aspects of schema theory.* Hillsdale, NJ: Lawrence Erlbaum.

McDowell, J. (1979). *Children's riddling.* Bloomington, IN: University of Indiana Press.

Meek, M., Armstrong, S., Austerfield, V., Graham, J., & Placetter, E. (1983). *Achieving literacy: Longitudinal studies of adolescents learning to read.* London: Routledge and Kegan Paul.

Mishler, E.G. (1986). *Research interviewing: Context and narrative.* Cambridge, MA: Harvard University Press.

Mitchell, W.J.T. (Ed.). (1981). *On narrative.* Chicago: University of Chicago Press.

Mullen, C. (in press). *The self I dream: A narrative reconstruction of a personal mythology.* Unpublished master's thesis, University of Toronto, Toronto.

Munby, H. (1986). Metaphor in the thinking of teachers: An exploratory study. *Journal of Curriculum Studies, 18,* 197–209.

Natkins, L.G. (1986). *Our last term: A teacher's diary.* Lanham, MD: University Press of America.

Noddings, N. (1986). Fidelity in teaching, teacher education, and research for teaching. *Harvard Educational Review, 56* (4), 496–510.

Olney, J. (Ed.). (1980). *Autobiography: Essays theoretical and critical.* Princeton, NJ: Princeton University Press.

Paley, V.G. (1979). *White teacher.* Cambridge, MA: Harvard University Press.

Paley, V.G. (1981). *Wally's stories: Conversations in the kindergarten.* Cambridge, MA: Harvard University Press.

Paley, V.G. (1986). *Molly is three: Growing up in school.* Chicago: University of Chicago Press.

Personal Narratives Group. (1989). *Interpreting women's lives.* Bloomington: Indiana University Press.

Peshkin, A. (1985). Virtuous subjectivity: in the participant-observer's eyes. In D. Berg & K. Smith (Eds.), *Exploring clinical methods for social research* (pp. 267–281). Beverly Hills: Sage.

Pinar, W.F., & Grumet, M.R. (1976). *Toward a poor curriculum.* Dubuque, IA: Kendall/Hunt.

Pinar, W.F. (1988). Whole, bright, deep with understanding: Issues in qualitative research and autobiographical method. In W.F. Pinar (Ed.), *Contemporary curriculum discourses* (pp. 135–153). Scottsdale, AZ: Gorsuch Scarisbrick.

Polkinghorne, D.E. (1988). *Narrative knowing and the human sciences.* New York: State University of New York Press.

Reason, P., & Hawkins, P. (1988). Storytelling as inquiry. In P. Reason (Ed.), *Human inquiry in action: Developments in new paradigm research,* (pp. 79–101). Beverly Hills, CA: Sage.

Reid, W.A. (1988). Institutions and practices: Professional education reports and the language of reform. *Educational Researcher, 17,* 10–15.

Ricoeur, P. (1984). *Time and narrative: Vol. I.* Chicago: University of Chicago Press.

Ricoeur, P. (1985). *Time and narrative: Vol. II.* Chicago: University of Chicago Press.

Ricoeur, P. (1988). *Time and narrative: Vol. III.* Chicago: University of Chicago Press.

Reiff, P. (1972). *Fellow teachers: Of culture and its second death.* Chicago: University of Chicago Press.

Robinson, J.A., & Hawpe, L. (1986). Narrative thinking as a heuristic process. In T.R. Sarbin (Ed.), *Narrative psychology* (pp. 111–125). New York: Praeger.

Rose, P. (1983). *Parallel lives.* New York: Vintage Books.

Rosen, H. (1986). The importance of story. *Language Arts, 63* (3), 226–237.

Rosen, B. (1988). *And none of it was nonsense.* Portsmouth, NH: Heinemann.

Rosen, H. (1988). The autobiographical impulse. In D. Tannen (Ed.), *Linguistics in context: Connecting observation and understanding* (pp. 69–88). Norwood, NJ.: Ablex Publishing Corp.

Rowland, S. (1984). *The enquiring classroom.* London: Falmer Press.

Ryan, K. (1970). *Don't smile until Christmas: Accounts of the first year of teaching.* Chicago: University of Chicago Press.

Sarbin, T.R. (Ed.). (1986). *Narrative psychology: The storied nature of human conduct*. New York: Praeger.

Schafer, R. (1976). *A new language for psychoanalysis*. New Haven, CT: Yale University Press.

Schafer, R. (1981). Narration in the psychoanalytic dialogue. In W.J.T. Mitchell (Ed.), *On narrative* (pp. 25–50). Chicago: University of Chicago Press.

Schank, R.C., & Abelson, R.P. (1977). *Scripts, plans, goals and understanding: An inquiry into human knowledge structures*. Hillsdale, NJ: Lawrence Erlbaum.

Scholes, R., & Kellogg, R. (1966). *The nature of narrative*. Oxford: Oxford University Press.

Schon, D. (1987). *Educating the reflective practitioner*. San Francisco: Jossey-Bass.

Schon, D. (Ed.). (in press). *Case studies in reflective practice*. New York: Teachers College Press.

Schwab, J.J. (1964). The structure of the disciplines: Meanings and significances. In G.W. Ford & L. Pugno (Eds.), *The structure of knowledge and the curriculum*, (pp. 1–30). Chicago: Rand McNally.

Schwab, J.J. (1983). The practical 4: Something for curriculum professors to do. *Curriculum Inquiry*, *13* (3), 239–265.

Shulman, L.S. (1987). Knowledge and teaching: Foundations of the new reform. *Harvard Educational Review*, *57* (1), 1–22.

Shulman, J.H., & Colbert, J.A. (Eds.). (1988). *The intern teacher casebook*. San Francisco: Far West Laboratory for Educational Research and Development.

Sikes, P.J., Measor, L., & Woods, P. (1985). *Teacher careers: Crises and continuities*. London: Falmer Press.

Smith, L.M., Kleine, P.F., Prunty, J.P., & Dwyer, D.C. (1986). *Anatomy of educational innovation: A mid to long term re-study and reconstrual. Book 1: Educational innovators: Then and Now*. Philadelphia: Falmer Press.

Smith, L.M., Kleine, P.F., ,Prunty, J.P., & Dwyer, D.C. (1987). *Anatomy of educational innovation: A mid to long term re-study and reconstrual. Book 2: The fate of an innovative school: The history and present status of the Kensington School*. Philadelphia: Falmer Press.

Smith, L.M., Kleine, P.F., ,Prunty, J.P., & Dwyer, D.C. (1986). *Anatomy of educational innovation: A mid to long term re-study and reconstrual. Book 3: Innovation and change in schooling: History, politics, and agency*. Philadelphia: Falmer Press.

Spence, D.P. (1982). *Narrative truth and historical method*. New York: Norton & Company.

Spence, D.P. (1986). Narrative smoothing and clinical wisdom. In T.R. Sarbin (Ed.), *Narrative psychology: The storied nature of human conduct*, (pp. 211–232). New York: Praeger Special Studies.

Steedman, C. (1982). *The tidy house*. London: Virago Press.

Sutton-Smith, B. (1986). Children's fiction making. In T.R. Sarbin (Ed.), *Narrative psychology: The storied nature of human conduct*, (pp. 67–90). New York: Praeger.

Tannen, D. (1988). Hearing voices in conversation, fiction, and mixed genres. In D. Tannen (Ed.), *Linguistics in context: Connecting observation and understanding*. Norwood, NJ: Ablex Publishing Corp.

Van Maanen, J. (1988). *Tales of the field: On writing ethnography*. Chicago: University of Chicago Press.

Vechter, A.R. (1987). *Je Suis la langue: An alternative approach to second language curriculum*. Unpublished doctoral dissertation, University of Toronto, Toronto.

Wells, G. (1986). *The meaning makers*. Portsmouth, NH: Heinemann.

Welty, E. (1979). *The eye of the story: Selected essays and reviews*. New York: Vintage Books.

White, H. (1973). *Metahistory: The historical imagination in nineteenth-century Europe*. Baltimore: John Hopkins University Press.

White, H. (1981). The value of narrativity in the representation of reality. In W.J.T. Mitchell (Ed.), *On narrative*. Chicago: University of Chicago Press.

Wigginton, E. (1985). *Sometimes a shining moment: The foxfire experience*. New York: Doubleday.

Wigginton, E. (1989, February). Foxfire Grows Up. *Harvard Educational Review, 59* (1), 24–49.

Wittrock, M.C. (Ed.). (1986). *Handbook of research on teaching* (3rd ed.). New York: Macmillan.

Yonemura, M.V. (1986). *A teacher at work: Professional development and the early childhood educator*. New York: Teachers College Press.

PART III
DOING FIELDWORK: DATA COLLECTION AND ANALYSIS

Appendix
Common Problems in Field Work:
A Personal Essay

Annette Lareau

In his appendix to *Streetcorner Society*, William Foote Whyte describes why twelve years after his book was originally published he decided to write a detailed portrait of how he did his famous study. He reports that he was teaching a methods course and had trouble finding 'realistic descriptions' of the fieldwork process:

> It seemed as if the academic world had imposed a conspiracy of silence regarding the personal experiences of field workers. In most cases, the authors who had given any attention to their research methods had provided fragmentary information or had written what appeared to be a statement of the methods the field worker would have used if he had known what he was going to come out with when he entered the field. It was impossible to find realistic accounts that revealed the errors and confusions and the personal involvement that a field worker must experience (Whyte 1981, p. 359).

Three decades later the problem remains: realistic descriptions of how research data are collected are unusual. Most studies by sociologists who use qualitative methods devote a short section to the research methodology: they describe the number of respondents, the selection of the sample, and general procedures for data collection. But, as Whyte complained, these studies—some of which are exemplary works—rarely portray the process by which the research was actually done, nor do they give insight into the traps, delays, and frustrations which inevitably accompany field work (but see Walford 1987).

This lack of realistic portraits is a problem, for they are not simply to assuage readers' desires for more personal information about the author, or to get—for those of us with more malicious inclinations—'the dirt' on a project. Rather, they give qualitative researchers a formal avenue for reporting how they proceeded with data collection and analysis. Without these details, it is hard to tell when researchers did an exemplary job in the data collection and analysis and when they did a 'quick and dirty' job. It is agreed, of course, that one should establish a rapport with one's respondents, be sensitive to the field setting, take comprehensive field notes, analyze your your data carefully, and write it up in a lively and accurate fashion. What that actually means, and what researchers actually do, is often anybody's guess. Most studies do not reveal their inner-workings, and good writing can cover up awkwardly collected and poorly documented field work.

In his appendix Whyte chose to do his 'bit to fill the gap' (1981, p. 359), and in this appendix I have decided to do my bit as well. One of the biggest problems is that this entails writing up my mistakes as well as my successes. In most lines of work, including teaching, almost everyone is

313

forced to admit to having made mistakes from time to time. But admitting mistakes in field work seems more difficult. Partly, this is because we often have an overly romantic notion of field work, which emphasizes the glory of 'going native' and glosses over the difficulties and problems of the endeavor. The implicit message is that mistakes are rare. Partly, this reluctance is an artifact of a scholarly tradition in which a public discussion of 'inner-workings' is considered unseemly and unnecessary. Finally, admitting to mistakes in fieldwork raises questions about the quality of the body of the research and the conclusions drawn from it. Given these considerations, it is hardly surprising that so little has been written about actual experiences in the field. Likewise, it is clear that all of us who are engaged in qualitative research could greatly benefit from a more frank sharing of our experiences.

My project has strengths as well as weaknesses. There are parts of the data set in which I am fully confident and parts which I think are considerably weaker. This assessment is implied in the way in which the work is written up, but in my view it is worth making this more explicit. So, in a fit of immodesty as well as honesty, I provide my own assessment of the strengths of the project, and I identify my successes as well as failings as a researcher.

This appendix consists of two parts. In Part I, I review the background for the study, access and entrance to Colton and Prescott, my role in the classroom, the selection of families, the interviews, and my assessment of the major mistakes I made in the research. I also briefly summarize the logistics of data analysis. In Part II, I turn to the development of the conceptual model and my struggle to formulate the research question.

It is my hope that readers will find this 'exposé' of a research project useful, not only for gaining insight into this particular study but for detailed examples of how to cope with common problems in field research. As I bumped about in the field not knowing what I was doing I often felt—incorrectly, as it turned out—that I was making a terrible mess of things, that my project was doomed, and that I should give up the entire enterprise immediately. This negativism came from my persistent feeling that, despite my having had a research question when I started, I didn't truly know what I was doing there. In part, my gloom signaled the continuing struggle to clarify the intellectual goals of the project.

As I have discovered, using qualitative methods means learning to live with uncertainty, ambiguity, and confusion, sometimes for weeks at a time. It also means carving a path by making many decisions, with only the vaguest guide-posts and no one to give you gold stars and good grades along the way. It has its rewards. Yet, there were times in the field that I would have killed for an inviolable rule to follow—an SPSSX command to punch into the computer and let the results spill out. I found it exhausting, as well as exhilarating, to be constantly trying to figure out what to do next. It is unlikely that qualitative work will ever have specific research rules to punch into a computer, but it can—and in my opinion should—offer novice researchers more concrete guidance on matters of data collection, data analysis, and writing up of qualitative work. This appendix is one, small contribution toward that process.

Part I: The Method of Home Advantage

Personal Background

I grew up in a white, upper-middle-class family; my father and mother worked as school teachers.[1] When I was in college, I spent three months in a small, predominantly black community in rural California, working in the schools as a teacher's aide and helping children with their homework in the evenings in their homes. After I graduated from college I thought about becoming a school teacher, and had there been jobs available I might have done so.

Instead, I got a job interviewing prisoners in City Prison for the San Francisco Pre-Trial Release Program. The program was commonly called the OR Project because it released defendants without bail on their own recognizance (OR).[2] Every day at 6.30 a.m. or at 5.00 p.m. I went inside City Prison. There, with one or two other co-workers, I made a record of who had been arrested, called them out to be interviewed, and spoke with them in the waiting room, through double-paned plastic windows and over telephones. Typically, I interviewed three to eight persons per day in the prison itself, then, in the office, I usually interviewed (by telephone) another ten or fifteen persons throughout the day. Each case needed three references—people who knew the defendant well and could verify the information collected, particularly the defendant's address, contact with relatives, and employment history. Over the course of two years, I did a lot of interviews.

The conditions for interviewing in this job were not exactly ideal. The telephones in City Prison did not work well; one or two were regularly out of order, and the ones that did work sometimes had static, so conversations were often conducted in a shout. Another OR worker was often sitting right next to me (about one foot away) also shouting interview questions. For each interview I would talk over the telephone (through the window) to a defendant, using my right hand to plug my ear so that I could hear his/her response. Once I heard the answer, I would balance the telephone on my left shoulder, use my left hand to secure the paper, and write down the answer. Throughout the interview other defendants stared down at the scene, and bailsmen, lawyers, families, and the guard with the door keys were all within ear shot. The defendants were often in crisis: many were dazed, angry, and adjusting to City Prison.

When I finished that job, I thought (modesty aside) that I had become an outstanding interviewer. I knew, particularly in telephone interviews with the families of respondents, that I often could get people to cooperate when other interviewers failed. I also knew that my interviews were very detailed, accurate, and, despite my truly terrible handwriting (a tremendous liability in field work), were considered to be among the best in the office. From that job I developed a love of interviewing as well as a desire to avoid ever being arrested and put in prison.

After I quit this job, I entered graduate school at the University of California, Berkeley, where I also worked intermittently as an interviewer. The twin experiences of working for two years as a full-time interviewer and working part-time on several research projects meant that I approached the field work for this study with uneven skills. In retrospect, I believe that this background had an important influence on the quality of the data I collected. I discovered I was more comfortable as an interviewer than as a participant-observer. While the months in the classroom provided crucial information for this study, my field notes, for a complicated set of reasons which I explain below, were not as comprehensive, focused, or useful as they should have been. The interviews were much better. I felt I had a good rapport with the mothers and fathers I interviewed and I have confidence in the validity of the results.

The fact that the interviews were tape-recorded was also a major advantage. As my research lurched from studying everything in front of me in the field setting to a specific topic, my interests in a particular interview also shifted. Had I taken notes instead of tape-recording, I am certain that the comprehensiveness of my interview notes would have varied according to which question in the field setting seized my interest at that moment.[3] Although tape recorders do introduce an effect, particularly during the initial stages of an interview, I would not plan a new research project without them. In my opinion, they provide a form of insurance on the accuracy and comprehensiveness of data collected in the face of shifting intellectual concerns.

The Beginning of the Project

The research proposal, in its original formulation, was to study social class differences in family life and the influence of these family patterns on the process of schooling and on educational performance. I had grand plans. I was going to link class differences in family-school relationships to achievement patterns. I had hoped to study three rather than two schools; interview six families in each school; and I wanted to supplement the qualitative study with a quantitative analysis of a national data set of family-school relations. Almost immediately reality began to set in. Although I still think it would have been a good idea to have had a third school that was heterogeneous in students' social class, I also still think it would have been too much work. Without any real idea of where to begin, even comparing two schools seemed like two schools too many.

I did have a rough idea of what types of schools I wanted. I decided to study two specific social classes—white working-class and upper-middle-class parents. In this regard, as I note in the text, I followed in the footsteps of others in defining social class, notably Rubin (1976) and Kohn and Schooler (1983). I also wanted schools with a large number of white children to prevent the confounding of race. I ultimately sought two homogeneous schools with a concentration of children in each of the two social classes. Since most schools in the greater Bay Area are, in fact, segregated by social class, and to a lesser extent by race, this initial focus provided hundreds of schools as possible sites. I was timid about approaching schools. I worried about why a school would ever admit me. At times simply getting in seemed insurmountable, a problem discussed extensively in the literature.[4] In the end I used a different strategy for each school.

Access and Entrance at Colton

About two years before I began, I visited Colton school (and four other schools in the district) and interviewed the principal and vice-principal as a graduate research assistant on another project. The principal investigator of that project had asked for schools with a range of students by social class and Colton was the low socio-economic school. It was considered to be one of the best run schools in the district and I liked the principal and the vice-principal. In addition the school had a large number of white working-class students, a relatively unusual pattern. After a lot of stalling, I wrote the principal a letter (which unfortunately I have lost) asking for permission to visit one first grade classroom to learn about family-school relationships. I then called him and set up a time to talk about the project with him and the vice-principal.

To my astonishment, both of these administrators were very positive. We met for about fifteen minutes in the teachers' room (they had my letter in front of them) and most of the discussion centered on choosing a teacher. They had five teachers to choose from; I left the choice to them. They recommended one of their best first grade teachers, Mrs. Thompson, and I accepted their choice. I knew it would be difficult to get one of their worst teachers and there were not, at least in my mind, any compelling analytic reasons for asking for one. (In fact, I preferred to have two good teachers in schools with good leadership. If I did, indeed, find class differences in family-school relationships, I don't want those findings commingled with and confounded by questions about the quality of the teachers or administrators.) After our brief chat, the principal and the vice-principal said they would talk to the teacher for me and suggested that I return the following week. I left the school completely elated. I felt as if I might, after all, get this project off the ground.

The next week I returned, fifteen minutes late (I forgot my map and got lost), and the vice-principal took me to the classroom, where class was in progress. After the children went out to lunch, Mrs. Thompson joined me at the table in the back of the classroom where I had been sitting. My notes from this encounter are sketchy at best:

> I summarize [the] project as an effort to learn about non-school factors [influence on achievement]. She says what do you want to do next; I say just observe, and then select five children and start to interview the parents. In the meantime, though, just observe and if I can help out in any way in the classroom then I am happy to do so. I also say that I realize that it is a busy time of the year (tell her my mother was a teacher for 18 years) and that if I become a burden she should feel free to tell me. We then talk about when I will come next; she doesn't know exactly when class starts (she says, 'I just listen to the bells') and so checks chart on the wall. . . . We determine I will come Monday at 9.04.

From out first encounter on, Mrs. Thompson was extremely nice, very friendly, and always tried to be helpful. Although I would like to think it is something I did to put her at ease, I think that basically she is a very nice person who goes through life being considerate and helpful.

In what became a play within a play, Mrs. Thompson and other Colton staff were very helpful with the project and, without consulting parents, provided extraordinary materials. The teachers and staff simply gave me the test scores for all of the children in the class without any concern about consent forms or parents' permission. The principal, in considering the project, did not express any concern about the burden on parents and never suggested that I clear the project with the district office. And I never asked him if this was necessary. This was a mistake because for the rest of the project I was unnecessarily worried about what would happen if the district research officer found out about it. I also needed some district statistics and finally had to call the office and ask for them, without mentioning why I needed them. In addition, the principalship changed between the first and second year of the study; both the principal and vice-principal left. I wrote a letter to the new principal and he agreed to cooperate and to be interviewed, but he might not have. This would have been extremely costly since I was almost one-half of the way through the study. As a result, I now believe in getting the highest official's formal approval for a project early on. I think it is very wise to contact respondents through informal channels but, once having secured access, it is important to gain official approval as well. This is usually not very hard to do (after you are already in the door).

Sometimes I puzzled about why Colton teachers and administrators cooperated so easily. The principal and vice-principal were interested in the research question; all of them thought family involvement in education was important but, although it was never articulated, they mainly seemed to think that being studied was part of their job. They had other researchers before me and expected others after me so they did not seem to treat it as a 'big deal' and were unruffled, helpful, and a bit *blasé* about the entire matter.

Access and Entrance at Prescott

At Prescott it was another story. There I was not given any real difficulty but the goals of the project were closely scrutinized. The district and school administrators expressed concern about the perspective of parents and the burden on parents, but the fact that both a district official and the principal were also graduate students appeared to be helpful in ultimately securing permission. Whereas I was never even asked about consent forms at Colton, the principal at Prescott asked that I get a separate slip from the six parents giving her their permission to release test scores to me. She felt that the human subjects permission form, although important, was not specific enough to cover the release of those materials. Knowing I had consent forms for only six families, the principal would never have released the test scores for the rest of the class to me.[5]

Part of this greater formality and rigidity at Prescott may have been related to my point of contact with the school. At Prescott I went through the district office which increased the emphasis on the procedures for approval of research projects (such as consent forms). I ended up at Prescott, rather than another school, through informal networks or the 'strength of weak ties' (Granovetter 1973). When I was looking for an upper-middle-class community Charles Benson, a very helpful member of my dissertation committee, suggested I think of Prescott. One of his graduates students (whom I knew slightly) worked as a district official, and at his suggestion I called her and then wrote her a letter.

That letter is reprinted in an end note.[6] It has many problems and it is much too long. Access letters should state the problem very briefly and then summarize accurately what the officials are being asked to do. In my letter the most important part (what I was asking them to do) is buried. The content of the letter I wrote to the district official was different than what I planned to tell the teacher and principal. Given that the district official was another graduate student I felt that I somehow owed her a longer, more academic explanation, but I had planned to adopt a much more vague approach with the teacher and parents. This strategy backfired because the district official forwarded the letter I wrote to her to the principal, who in turn gave it to the classroom teacher. I was quite upset at myself for this at the time as I should have known that might be a routine procedure. The lesson from this for me is that it is foolish to think, even if you are fellow graduate students, that one person should get one version of your project (when you are requesting access) and another person should get another. It is better to draft one version suitable for everyone.

Moreover in this age of bureaucracy, unless you are lucky, you will have to write a letter formally requesting access to a site. Another end note presents an introductory letter which, given what I know today, I wish I had written.[7] It is much shorter, more direct, and it focuses primarily on what I need from the site. Respondents do not need to be told, nor are they generally interested in, the details of the intellectual goals of the project (but see Walford 1987a). They seem mainly interested in knowing how much work you are asking them to do.

I now think that before I go into the field, I need a very short and very simple explanation for what I am doing there. When I began I had a one sentence description I was comfortable with: 'I want to learn more about how families help children in school.' If the listener wanted more information, however, I floundered. My answer, inevitably long and rambling, made both the person who asked the question and me squirm. Since that time I have been bored and perplexed when a simple question to a graduate student ('What are you studying?') produced a long, ambiguous, and defensive treatise.

As a matter of politeness, many people ask researchers what they are planning to do while in the field. It is essential to have a fleshed-out response prepared well in advance. In fact, in my bossy moments, I think that no researcher should begin a field study without memorizing a jargon-free summary of her/his intentions. This will save many awkward moments, increase rapport with people in the field, and help prevent the problem of respondents feeling particularly 'on stage' when they begin to engage in the activities in which they know that you are interested. A brief, accurate, and general statement will not of itself produce good rapport, but it is a better beginning point than a long and confused one.[8]

After receiving a copy of my letter (which was a mini-paper) the principal called me. She explained that the school was concerned about overburdening parents but that she was a graduate student as well and was sensitive to problems of research. Her biggest concern seemed to be the choice of the teacher. I wanted a self-contained first grade classroom; that year Prescott had only one first grade and one split classroom. There was only one choice and that was Mrs. Walters.

I don't know what the principal, Mrs. Harpst, told Mrs. Walters. I do know that Mrs. Walters was originally reluctant to have me in her classroom. As she told me later, she was afraid I would be a 'critical presence.' She agreed to participate, however, and the principal, in another telephone exchange, told me what day to begin the field work. Consequently I entered the school without ever meeting the principal face-to-face, and although I was at school regularly I did not meet her for several weeks. The first day I appeared at school, Mrs. Walters' welcome was cool. She showed me where to hang up my coat and put my purse but said very little in answer to my questions. Her aide, Mrs. O'Donnell, was much warmer and bubbly. Mrs. Walters told the children who I was while they were waiting in line outside the classroom. Her comments were:

> Today we have a visitor named Miss Lareau. She hasn't been in a classroom for a long time and so she wanted to visit our class and see how you work and talk and play.[9]

Mrs. Walters' classroom was much smaller than Mrs. Thompson's, and there was no free table at the back of the room. I felt painfully and obviously out of place that first day, as I listened to Mrs. Walters talking to the children outside the classroom and watched Mrs. O'Donnell work in the corner on some papers. They had not suggested where to sit or stand and I felt continually in the way. Finally, I found a chair in an empty space at the back of the classroom. When the children walked in they all stared at me intently and then walked to their seats, still staring. I was uncomfortable, Mrs. Walters seemed uncomfortable, and the children seemed uncomfortable as well, although, as I explain below, they quickly adjusted to my presence.

My entrance to Prescott therefore was less smooth than at Colton for many reasons, including Mrs. Walters' general discomfort at having me in the classroom, her lack of control over being selected as a research subject and, on top of that, her having been shown my overly complicated letter. I was worried that the focus on social class described in the letter might have had an important influence on Mrs. Walters' behavior. She never seemed to remember what I was studying; she consistently treated me as if I were an educator studying the curriculum (which I was not) rather than someone interested in family involvement in schooling. As I noted in my field notes:

> Mrs. Walters seems very interested in explaining the logic of learning activities to me. She carefully explains the bucket program and the 'hands on training' they are receiving. . . . This pattern, of Mrs. Walters repeatedly telling me about the curriculum, makes me think that she sees me as an educator with the tools to evaluate a good or bad learning program. And/or, [it makes me think] she is worried about being evaluated.

Over time my relationship with Mrs. Walters gradually warmed up. I considered the day she told me that she originally hadn't wanted me in the classroom to be a watershed. I felt that I had reached some level of acceptance but it took more time and more work than my relationship with Mrs. Thompson. As I complained in my field notes, 'I often feel at a loss for words [with her].' Being somewhat shy myself, I felt ill at ease with her when we were alone together and I often seemed to fumble in my efforts to chat with her. But the aide was so friendly and got along so well with both Mrs. Walters and me that, when she was there, the social interaction was quite comfortable and pleasant. During recess the three of us would go get a cup of coffee and visit together. When the aide was not there (in the afternoon or when she was sick) relations between Mrs. Walters and me were much more formal. Like some older married couples, Mrs. Walters and I both seemed to be more comfortable in the classroom with the children between us than trying to negotiate socializing together in a quiet classroom. At first I almost dreaded recess and lunch time with Mrs. Walters, and I felt that I truly did not know what to do with myself. If Mrs. Walters was doing an errand my choices were to sit in the classroom (which I felt self-conscious about since I never saw any aides or teachers do this), sit in the teachers' room (where I didn't know any of the teachers and conversation seemed to grind to a halt with my presence), or go to the bathroom and then return to the classroom looking busy (I did that a lot).

From this I learned that I had difficulty 'hanging out' and that I was happier in more structured situations, such as when class was in session or when I was interviewing someone. I also concluded that life would have been easier if, during the very first days in the field, I had come to school more frequently than twice a week for a few hours. If I had stayed all day and come three or four days in a row during the first week I would have been introduced to all of the staff and become more integrated. As it was I was introduced to a few staff members, but after that I saw a lot of familiar faces but was never introduced to them. Today I am much better at being able to say, 'I don't think we have met, although I have seen you around. My name is. . . .' But at that time I felt tongue-tied and often moved in and out of the teachers' lounges in both schools without talking or getting to know the other teachers.

Although I came to feel accepted in the classroom in both Prescott and Colton I never felt very comfortable outside the classroom. This meant that my study was essentially restricted to single classrooms, and I lost the possibility of learning about the organizational dynamics at each school. Even today I feel that if I had been a more skilled field worker, had become more comfortable on the site, had been better at easing my way into informal settings and simply 'hanging out,' that I would have learned more than I did. In particular I might have learned more about routine conflicts between parents and teachers in other classrooms, disagreements among teachers about how to manage parents, and principal-teacher relationships. I also might have gotten onto a more human footing with Mrs. Walters and, for example, learned more about sensitive issues, including how she felt about parents breathing down her neck and who she really was. As it stands the manuscript treats these issues only superficially.

My Role in the Classroom

Someone told me once that in field work: *You need to know who you are and what you are doing there.* This is good advice, but such certainty is often hard to come by at the beginning since, even if you have one idea, the context may lead you to different ones. My role in the classroom differed between the two schools and this turned out to be another source of information about family-school relationships.

At Colton it was rare for adults to be in the classroom unless they were teachers or teachers' aides. In addition, children were almost always sitting at desks doing their work; they were not working on projects that needed individual supervision. As a result there was not much that Mrs. Thompson needed me to do. Sometimes I would help out with art projects; for example, helping children open glue bottles and wiping up spilled glue. Mostly, however, I watched the lessons from the back of the classroom. This was facilitated by the fact that the classroom was quite large, there was a table in the back of the room at which I could comfortably sit, and the table was five or six feet from the nearest desk, giving me a little distance. I was not grossly disrupting the class by sitting there. I was not completely passive: I helped children line up, I went with them out to recess, I mediated disputes on the playground at children's requests, I went with them to the library, and frequently chatted with children in the class about things that were important to them (e.g., their toys, the pictures they drew). I knew the names of the children in the class and many of the children would wave and say hello to me when I walked across the playground as I came and went at school.

At Prescott, however, the classroom organization, spatial arrangements, and increased presence of parents on the school site led me to interact with children more and in different ways than at Colton. Mrs. Walters wanted me to come to school to volunteer during 'independent time.' In these one hour periods three times per week, the class was divided into four 'stations' and different projects were available in each station. Mrs. Walters scheduled a parent volunteer to be in the classroom during these times. This left four adults (including myself) to supervise the children as they worked independently. Children frequently had questions and particularly in the beginning of an hour in which the children were working on a new project all the adults were busy answering questions. Once the project got underway there was less to do as children went to work at their own pace.[10]

The problem was, as many parents so bitterly complained, that not all the children worked. Most did work consistently, but many would—for brief periods of time— break classroom rules by poking, hitting, or fussing at each other. Some children, including four or five boys, hardly did any work at all. The children seemed to operate under an implicit classroom rule that if an adult was watching you then you behaved and worked. I was ambivalent about what my role was to be; I didn't want to be a teacher or a disciplinarian. Like a favorite aunt or family friend, I was hoping to avoid discipline issues altogether. I wrote about this ambivalence in my notes:

> I am unsure as to what my role should be when children are not working productively or are 'acting out' with squabbles and minor fights. It is noteworthy that most of the children ignore me and continue their disputes in my presence (while with Mrs. Walters and usually with Mrs. O'Donnell the dispute is changed or is dropped).

The children quickly realized that I would not scold them and force them to work, as a result they would continue to misbehave in front of me. This made me uncomfortable. On the one hand I didn't want to be scolding children on the other hand I didn't want Mrs. Walters to feel that I was not helping out and doing what adults normally did in the classroom. Consequently I sometimes looked foolish and ineffective in the classroom, as this example makes clear:

> [Today] two boys were pushing each other in their chairs while they were supposed to be playing the numbers game. I came up behind them and said something weak/mild such as, 'Are you boys playing the numbers game?' They obviously were not as they continued to shove and push each other. Mrs. Harris then saw them and came over and said harshly, 'Jonathan, Roger. Stop that this instant! Now sit up and sit in your chairs and behave!' (She physically pushed them apart and pushed their chairs closer to their desks).

Clearly, Mrs. Harris was not ambivalent about controlling children. As my notes reflect, I began to think that I might have to get off the fence and take a more assertive role:

> When I started volunteering I wanted to disrupt the [classroom] activities as little as possible and so I made a concerted effort to stay away from the teacher/disciplinarian role. I am discovering, however, that in the world of children the adult/child split means I am often forced into the teacher/ disciplinarian role. Otherwise I am seen as powerless, not threatening, and the object of a great deal of acting out behavior when the children are not under the teacher's rule.

I didn't write down the actual date that I finally decided to abandon my passive role, but by about one third of the way through the field work I was controlling the children more and following the roles of the parents and teachers. This seemed to help; I felt more comfortable in the classroom and the children, Mrs. Walters, and Mrs. O'Donnell began to treat me like another parent or teachers' aide. I helped children with their stories, their art work, and various projects. I gave tests, I dictated problems which they wrote on the board, and supervised children, enforcing classroom rules when we went to the auditorium for a special event. When Mrs. Walters left school to have an operation six weeks before the end of the semester, I continued to visit the classroom. By then I was integrated into the classroom, and Mrs. Chaplin, Mrs. Walters' replacement, seemed to accept my presence. I helped organize the report cards and the games on the last day of school.

As I discuss in the text, my relationship to parents mirrored the pattern of family-school relationships in the two schools: I had much more contact with parents at Prescott than at Colton and the parents at Prescott scrutinized my activities much more closely than they did at Colton. There were advantages and disadvantages to this. The advantage of my more active role in the classroom at Prescott was that I worked with some of the parents and was, in many ways, a valuable assistant to Mrs. Walters, which she appreciated. The drawback was that I couldn't take notes in the classroom. I only tried that once in Mrs. Walters' class. The room was too small to accommodate a desk for me so I had to write on my lap; and I was only two or three feet away from the children's desks so my note-taking distracted them. Also, I was often there for independent time and Mrs. Walters needed adults to walk around and help children as they worked independently. As a result I had to try to recreate notes after I left the site. This increased the amount of time that field work demanded and produced notes with fewer quotes than at Colton.[11]

When I entered the field I had planned to select the parents of children at the end of the school year, after I had observed in the classroom. Seeking a balance by gender and achievement levels, I decided to select a boy and a girl from the high, medium, and low reading groups for interviews. In each school, I wanted five children from intact families (although their parents could be remarried) and one child from a single-parent family. At Colton, since almost one half of the class was non-white, and around a quarter were from single-parent homes, only about one third of the children were potential candidates. One day after school, Mrs. Thompson and I sat down with the reading groups. We chose a boy and a girl from each reading group. Whenever possible Mrs. Thompson recommended children whose parents she knew from having interacted with them at the school. As a result, the Colton families I interviewed were somewhat more active in their children's schooling than the average parent. After we had made the choices, she gave me a booklet with the names, addresses, and telephone numbers of the families and I copied them out. She also gave me test scores for the entire class.

Mrs. Walters was gone from Prescott by the end of the year. One afternoon after school, as we were cleaning up the classroom, the teacher's aide, the replacement teacher (Miss Chaplan), and I talked about whom to select for the study. The decisions were as follows, I selected Donald since he was clearly the highest achiever in the class and I had met his parents at Open House. Mrs. O'Donnell also told me that Donald's parents were enthusiastic about the study and were hoping to be selected. Such flattery is hard to resist. I selected Carol and Emily because I had met their mothers and observed them in the classroom. I selected Jonathan, although I had not met his mother, because he was the lowest achieving boy. I added Allen in part because both Jonathan and Donald were well behaved and I wanted someone who was more of a troublemaker. Allen fitted that bill. The children represented almost one quarter of the class but, since five of the six mothers volunteered in the classroom, a slightly higher percentage of mothers active in school. After we selected the children I copied down the names and addresses of the families.

With these two sessions the sample was set. At Colton, however, two of the families moved during the summer after first grade before I had interviewed them. In the second year of the study I needed to add two more families, a boy and a girl, one of whom was from a single-parent family. Because I had not anticipated this, I did not have other names and addresses from which to choose. During the next year I visited Colton occasionally, and I discovered that Mrs. Sampson's second grade class had a white girl, Suzy, who was a high achiever and whose parents visited the school frequently. Her father was a sheriff and her mother was a student. The teacher gave me their telephone number and I contacted them. Because of scheduling difficulties I had only one interview with them, but it was a long one and both the mother and father participated in it (with their eight-month-old girl sitting on my lap for much of the time).

The other child I added to the study, Ann-Marie, was in Mrs. Sampson's class, and Mrs. Sampson frequently mentioned her in informal conversations. I checked my field notes and I had a lot of notes about her from first grade. I decided to add her in the second year because I had been following her; she was from a single-parent family, and she seemed to exemplify important tensions that can occur between parents and schools. This choice was costly, however, as it upset the gender balance and left me with four girls and two boys in the Colton sample. Ann-Marie's mother did not have a telephone but Mrs. Sampson told me when their parent-teacher conference would be held. So, with a show of confidence I didn't actually feel, I simply went to the conference and spoke to Ann-Marie's mother there. She agreed, with no resistance, to be in the study. This scrambling around to add respondents to the study could have been avoided if I had started the year by following a pool of ten or fifteen families, expecting that some would have moved (or dropped out of the other reasons) by the second year.

In reflecting on the choice of families, I continue to feel that the children at both Colton and Prescott schools were a reasonably good sample of the classroom. There were no glaring omissions in terms of discipline problems, achievement levels, temperament, popularity, and parent involvement in schooling. At both schools I had a range of parents, from the most heavily involved to the least involved in school site activities and, according to teachers, in educational activities at home. Still, the sample was small and non-random so I cannot confirm this impression.

In addition to the twelve families in my sample I interviewed both principals, the first and second grade teachers at both schools, and the special education teacher at Colton. I interviewed the first grade teachers in the summer after first grade; the interviews with the second grade teachers and the principals were about a year later. The interviews ranged over a number of issues, including teachers' ideas of the proper role of parents in schooling, and their assessment of the level of educational support which the families were providing for their children. These discussions of the individual children were very helpful; they provided a useful contrast to parents' assessment of their behavior. At times teachers provided me with information which I would have liked to have asked parents about, as when Mr. Thompson told me she sent Jill to the nurse because of body odor. Unfortunately the demands of confidentiality precluded me from probing these issues as much as I would have liked. I did ask parents general questions; if they did not discuss the issue I was look for, then I simply dropped it. To have done otherwise would have violated the teachers' confidentiality.

Requesting Interviews

In requesting interviews with parents I followed a different strategy for each school. In a qualitative methods class I took, Lillian Rubin cautioned against writing letters to working-class families asking them to participate in a study. She said that it was usually better to telephone, since working-class families did not read as much nor did they routinely receive letters on university stationary. This advice made sense to me and I followed it. I telephoned the Colton mothers, verbally explained the study and asked permission to visit them in their homes. At Prescott, I sent parents a letter describing the study and requesting their participation. I then telephoned a few days later and set up a time for the interview. These written requests for participation did not go out at the same time. They were sent out about a week before I was able to schedule the interview. At both schools the requests and the interviews were staggered over a period of several months.

All of the mothers at Colton and Prescott agreed to participate with little hesitation. The fact that I had been in Mrs. Walters'' and Mrs. Thompson's classes seemed to help in gaining access to the children's homes. After In interviewed the mothers at the end of first grade, I told them I would like to return a year later. All of the mothers were agreeable to this. At the end of the second interview with each mother, I asked if I could interview the father as well. I interviewed all five Prescott fathers (Gail lived in a single-parent family). At Colton, I succeeded in interviewing only three of the five fathers. Mrs. Morris and Mrs. Brown were doubtful and reluctant to arrange for me to interview their husbands, and I did not press my request. I regret that now—I think with a bit of pressure I could have interviewed Mr. Morris, since I met his at school once and at home once. I never even saw Mr. Brown. He never went to school and his wife said that he was very shy. I doubt that, even if I had pursued it, I would have gained his cooperation. In addition, because of scheduling difficulties, I only interviewed Jonathan's mother (Prescott) once rather than twice.

In my telephone conversations and my letters to mothers asking for permission to interview them, I said the interviews would last about an hour and fifteen minutes ('depending on how much you have to tell me'). It turned out that the interviews took much longer; they always took at least ninety minutes and in most cases two hours. I discovered this very quickly and should have changed what I told parents but, again fearing rejection, I didn't. Now I would. It is a risk but, if it were happening to me, I would be irritated if I had set aside an hour and the interview took two. Furthermore, for reasons I don't completely understand, when I was in their offices or homes respondents rarely told me that it was time to go. Instead, adopting etiquette norms regarding guests, they seemed to wait me out. It was easy to delude myself and think that the respondents were enjoying the conversation so much that they didn't mind it going overtime, and in some cases that was true. But it was rude of me knowingly to conceal the true length of the interview (even by fifteen minutes to a half-hour) when I made my initial requests. It violated both the spirit and the letter of the notion that a researcher must respect her/his subjects.

My Perceived Role with Parents

The Prescott parents did not have any trouble figuring out who I was and what I was doing. They knew what graduate school was, they knew what a dissertation was, and they understood the concept of someone doing research on education without being an educator. Many had friends and relatives in doctoral programs. My general introduction was followed by questions from Prescott parents about my specific academic and career goals (e.g., 'Is this for your dissertation?').

The Colton parents did have difficulty figuring out who I was and what I was doing there. All of the mothers asked me if I was planning to become a teacher. When I said no, that I was working on a research project for the university, I generally drew nods accompanied by looks of confusion. In the beginning I often said I was a 'graduate student.' I dropped that description after a mother asked me if that meant I was going to graduate soon. From then on, I said that the university did a lot of studies and I was working on a research project to find out how families helped children in school. If mothers continued to ask questions about my plans I often took them through a brief explanation of the higher education system: 'After graduating from high school some people go to college. After four years of college people graduate and get a Bachelor's degree. After than, some people go on to more school, do research and get another degree. That is what I am trying to do now.' Overall, I would say that the Colton parents seemed to think that I was friendly, but that I was from a foreign land 'over there,' a world they had little contact with and did not understand. Even without that understanding, however, they were willing to participate in the project.

One consequence of this confusion was that Colton mothers mistakenly thought I worked at the school. My efforts to establish myself as being independent of the school took on new vigor after my first visit to Jill's home, which was early in the interviews. I had finished the interview, had packed everything up, and was standing in the kitchen, chatting. Suddenly I saw that on the wall of the kitchen was a calendar, and on that day's date was written 'visit from school,' with the time of our interview. I considered that to be very bad news; it could, and probably did, shape what the mother was willing to tell me. But the interview was over; it was too late to do anything more.

Thereafter, with parents, especially Colton parents, I stepped up my efforts to convince them that I was not from the school by stressing at the beginning of the interview, and repeating it in different ways at different times during the interview, that I did not work there ('Now, I am not from the school and there is something I don't understand very well . . .'). Although I can't be certain, I think these strategies worked; with some probing, all of the Colton parents did express criticisms of the school, although, as I show in the text, they were of a different character than at Prescott.

The Interviews

The interviews took place in the homes, in the living room or dining room. The interviews with mothers who worked in the home were often in the middle of the day, the ones with the fathers and the mothers who worked outside the home took place in the evening or at the weekend. In some cases the houses were quiet; in others children, dogs, house-cleaners, and the telephone frequently intervened. The interviews were open-ended and were set up to be more like a conversation than an interview. I had an interview guide but I sometimes varied the order of the questions, depending on how the interview was evolving. I had a tape recorder and I did not take notes during the interview. Instead, I tried to maintain eye contact, nod frequently, and make people feel comfortable. In the course of these and other interviews, I have discovered that each interview guide has its own rhythm. I have found that there is a particular time (often one eighth of the way through the interview) when the respondent should be 'with you.' If the respondent is not 'with you', it usually means that the interview is in trouble.[12]

In my interviews in people's homes, I found that within fifteen minutes of my arrival we should be set up and ready to begin the interview. Fifteen minutes into the interview things should be more relaxed; the respondent should look less tense and be sitting more comfortably in the chair; the original tension in the room and interpersonal awkwardness should be easing up; and there should be a sense of movement and revelation. Usually that happened, occasionally it did not. Some respondents (like some students in an examination) never seemed to settle into the rhythm. The situation remained awkward all the way through. In those instances I often discontinued the interview and started chatting. I asked the respondents questions about their house, their dog, their clothes, their pictures, their car. (Or I talked about myself, my clothes, local shopping malls I have been in, my family, my childhood fights with my brothers and sisters). My goal was to try to put these people at ease, make myself seem less intimidating, find something that we had in common, and—I suppose—to portray myself as a 'regular person,' one that they could talk to easily. In addition, I was interested in hearing them talk about something they cared about and could discuss with ease. That was helpful, for it gave me a sense of the tone and demeanor which I was striving for when I went back to the interview questions.[13]

Sometimes these conversational diversions, while hardly subtle, did seem to help. Respondents seemed to relax and began to forget the tape recorder. (Noticing that I didn't turn off the tape recorder or apparently mind wasting tape on a discussion of the family dog seemed to help some respondents to relax.) A few interviews—my first interview with Laura's mother at Colton and my interviews with Gail's mother at Prescott—never seemed to 'click' fully. There were good moments followed by awkward ones. For example, when I arrived at Laura's house the television was on and the mother didn't turn if off; in fact, she continued to stare at it from time to time, and comment about it during the interview. It was one of my first interviews in a home and I didn't have the nerve to ask her to turn it off. Now I always make sure that the television is off or, if others are watching it, I move the interview to another room. One of the first things I say after I get set up with the tape recorder is, 'Do you mind if we turn off the television for a while? I'm afraid this tape recorder is quirky and the television really causes problems. It shouldn't be too long.' I also thank them when they do turn off the television and again, when I am leaving, apologize if they missed any of their favorite programs because of the interview.

Considering the number of interviews, having two or three awkward ones was not very many, but I found such occasions to be extremely depressing. I tried to take comfort in Lillian Rubin's comment that it 'happens to everyone.' She confided that, after trying everything she could think of to enliven a failing interview with no success, she would simply finish the interview as quickly as possible and 'get out of there.' I still consider that to be good advice.

Data Analysis

I did two data analyses on this project. The first was half-hearted; the second time I was more systematic as I followed many of the ideas in Matthew Miles and A. Michael Huberman's (1984) very good book on data analysis, *Qualitative Data Analysis: A Sourcebook of New Methods*. Fortunately, the results did not change when I analyzed the data more carefully, although the second attempt did highlight themes I had not seen before. Readers interested in data analysis generally are referred to Miles and Huberman. In this section, I simply summarize the steps I took in the two analyses.

In my first effort, I finished collecting the data and then, based on what I had learned, I wrote it up. I felt that I had to portray the data accurately and I carefully reviewed my interviews and field notes. I also drew heavily on the notes I wrote after each interview: a short statement (usually three pages, single-spaced) which summarized the key issues in the interview.[14] During this period I transcribed sections of tapes where I felt there were important quotes, making carbon copies of these transcriptions. One copy of these quotes was put into a file, with the folders organized by child; the carbon copy was cut up and glued onto index cards. I also made numerous charts, sketching out the responses of parents to different issues, a precursor to 'data displays.' But the entire process was informal.

The second time I analyzed the data, the analysis was much more comprehensive and systematic. First, I spent hours listening to tapes: I purchased a portable tape recorder (a 'Walkman') and listened to tapes in the house, as I rode my bike, made dinner, and went about my life. In addition, all of the interviews were transcribed verbatim. It took an average of ten to fifteen hours for me or the secretaries in my department to transcribe a two hour interview, depending on sound quality. The shortest interview was ten pages, single-spaced: the longest was twenty-five pages, single-spaced. For a few interviews, only critical sections (anywhere from seven to fifteen pages of single-spaced quotes per interview) were transcribed. In all, had thirty-seven interviews with typed quotes, each interview quite lengthy.

I cut these single-spaced transcriptions up into the individual quotes (with a code name on each quote) and glued them on five by eight inch index cards. Colton was yellow, Prescott was white, and the teachers in both schools were blue. I ended up with over one thousand index cards. At first the cards were simply in groups by school and by child. Then they were sorted by basic categories: parents' view of their proper role, their educational activities in the home, and their complaints about Mrs. Walters. I also had categories for family life, including children's lessons outside of school and the social networks among parents in the community. Teachers' cards were grouped according to what educational activities they sought from parents.[15]

As the analysis continued, I tried to clarify my research question in the light of the literature. In particular I tried to see how my data could modify, challenge, or elaborate known findings. The cards continued to be in piles by major analytic categories (all over the living room floor), but the composition of these groups shifted as I reviewed the quotes, thought about the research question, looked for negative examples, and tried to clarify the differences within the schools as well as between them. For example, during the first analysis I focused on parents' educational activities at home and their attendance at school events. Gradually I realized that Colton and Prescott parents' actions went beyond helping at home. Parents in the two schools differed in how much they criticized the school and supplemented the school program. I also found omissions in the literature on this issue. This shifted the focus from looking at social class differences in parents' support (i.e., how much parents complied with teachers' requests) to the more inclusive notion of linkages.

As I pursued this idea the analytic categories became more numerous: teachers' wishes for parent involvement; parents' beliefs regarding their proper role, information about schooling, scrutiny of teachers, interventions in school site events, criticisms of teachers, educational aspirations for their children; and possible explanations of why parents were—or were not—involved in schooling. Differences between mothers and fathers and the disadvantages of parents' involvement were two other categories.

During this time I maintained index cards about each child in the study. These quickly became inefficient and cumbersome because the case studies of children were incomplete and I was 'borrowing' cards from the analytic piles to supplement information on each child. Finally I developed a dual system. For each child I had a collection of transcribed interviews on paper for the mother (both interviews) and the father. I also had the comments that the teacher had made about the child. These typed interviews were all paper-clipped together and put in three piles (Colton, Prescott, and educators). In addition, copies of all of the interviews were cut and pasted onto hundreds of index cards which were kept in analytic categories within open cardboard boxes (with rubber bands grouping cards in subcategories), and rearranged slightly as the analysis developed. Ultimately the chapters of this book mirrored the boxes of cards.

Following Miles and Huberman, I also made numerous 'data displays.' For example, I created matrices with the children listed in rows and various types of parent involvement in columns (i.e., reviewing papers after school, reading, attending Open House, attending conferences). I also produced matrices on select issues: in one chart I compared the criticisms Colton and Prescott parents had of school, in another I displayed what parents said was their proper role in schooling. The information on the cards duplicated the data displays (on large pieces of poster board) which provided a quick, visual overview of the evidence. Put differently, the cards showed me what I had, as the groups of cards provided stacks of evidence in support of ideas; the data displays showed me what I didn't have—as the cells revealed missing cases or showed exceptions to the pattern. Producing these matrices was time-consuming, but they were very helpful in displaying the strengths and weaknesses of the argument. Together the coding categories, sorting system, and dual system of case studies and analytic categories gave me a chance to look for other patterns, and increased my confidence in the accuracy of my interpretation of the data.

Mistakes: Lessons from the Field

I made one very serious mistake in the field; I fell behind in writing up my field notes. Writing up field notes immediately is one of the sacred obligations of field work. Yet workers I have known well all confessed that they fell behind in their field notes at one time or another. Researchers are human:—we get sick; we have an extra glass of wine; we get into fights with our spouses; we have papers to grade, due the next day; or we simply don't feel like writing up field notes immediately after an interview or a participant-observation session. On top of that, at least for me, writing field notes is both boring and painful: boring, because it repeats a lot of what you just did and it takes a long time to write a detailed description of a fifteen-minute encounter/observation; painful, because it forces you to confront unpleasant things, including lack of acceptance, foolish mistakes in the field, ambiguity about the intellectual question, missed opportunities in the field, and gaping holes in the data. To be sure, there is a tremendous sense of satisfaction in having placed on paper the experiences of the day and then adding these to the top of a neat and growing pile. But the time! Initially, one hour in the field would take me three hours to write up. Missing sessions of writing field notes can, like skipping piano practice, get quickly out of hand . . . exponentially, in fact.

If I wrote up my interviews two or three days later, I put 'retrospective notes' (or retro for short) at the top of the first page. In many cases I believe that I could have recreated, even several weeks later, a good account of what happened in the classroom, but I imposed on myself a certain 'code of honor.' If I missed my deadline and didn't write the event up within a few days of its occurrence, I wouldn't allow myself to write it up a week or two later and use my recollections as field notes I was sure that the information would be distorted. So there were notes that, I never wrote up despite my best intentions. My delinquencies multiplied because I didn't stop going into the field; gaining acceptance in the field is dependent on being there and being part of things. The more I went the more interesting things I saw, and the more people told me about up-coming events that they encouraged me to attend (i.e., the Easter Hat parade, a play coming to school). Like a greedy child on Christmas Day who keeps opening package after package without stopping to play with them and then asks for more, I dept going to the field, didn't write it up, but went back to the field anyway for fear of missing something really important. I usually went to the field three times per week (alternating schools), or about a dozen times per month. I don't know exactly how many transgressions I committed. My best estimate is that I completed about 100 hours of observation, with more hours at Prescott than at Colton, and I failed to write notes on about one eighth of my field work. Today I faithfully record in my calendar when I go into the field, where I go, and how long I stay. In my current and figure work I want to be able, to state, as Lubeck (1984; 1985) did, how many hours of field work the study is based on. This record of visits to the field also helps me keep track of sets of field notes land interviews.

In spite of these omissions I had, of course, quite a large amount of data. I was in the classrooms for several months and had stacks of carefully written notes of routine activities. Many studies (Lightfoot 1983) have been based on far less, but it was a serious breach of field methods and, although I cannot prove it, one that I am convinced is more common than is noted in the literature. In hindsight, the writing up of field notes was linked to the renowned problem of 'going native.' I liked being in the classrooms; I liked the teachers, the children, and the activities—making pictures of clovers for St. Patrick's Day, eggs for Easter, and flower baskets for May. I liked being there the most when I felt accepted by the teachers and children. Thinking about taking notes reminded *me* that I was a stranger, forced me to observe the situation as an outsider, and prevented me from feeling accepted and integrated into the classroom. Writing up my field notes was a constant reminder of my outside status. It was also a reminder of the ambiguous status of my intellectual goals; I knew only vaguely where I was going with the project. I also worried I might be making the wrong decisions, such as when I began to take a more active role in the class at Prescott or spent most of the time at Prescott during independent time (when Mrs. Walters needed help) rather than visiting the classroom regularly at other points in the day. There was a lurking anxiety about the field work: Was it going right? What was I doing? How did people feel about me? Was I stepping on people's toes? What should I do next?—and this anxiety was tiring.

The few times when I forgot about note-taking and observing and just enjoyed being there, I felt a tremendous sense of relief. I liked the feeling of giving up being a researcher and simply being a teacher's aid. The seduction of participation sometimes overshadowed the goal of participation; and the cost was a lack of carefully collected information. If I could do it over, I would arrange things so that I had a different set of choices. I would change my schedule and slow down the project. Although it was advantageous to be in both schools at once, in the interest of completeness I would now probably do one school at a time. I was also in a hurry to get through graduate school, a goal that now seems short-sighted. As a result I have developed what I call the Lareau Iron Law of Scheduling:

> Never (and I mean never) go into the field unless you have time that night, or in the next twenty-four hours, to write up the notes.

Such rigidity may seem hard to enforce because presence in the field is critical to sustaining access and rapport. There is also the 'somewhere else' problem (Walford 1987) that something critically important will take place and you will miss it. But whatever happens will often happen again, particularly if it is part of the routine social interaction that qualitative workers are usually trying to study.

This iron law of scheduling can be carried out, it just takes self-restraint. And it is crucial: field work without notes is useless and destructive. It is useless without documentation the observations cannot and should not be incorporated into the study; it is destructive because worrying about missing notes takes away valuable time and energy from the project, creates new problems, undermines competence, and turns a potentially rewarding process into a burdensome one. In my experience at least, it is not worth it.

A Hybrid Pattern

In most of the classic studies, the researchers were sustained by grants and field work was all that they did. Today such full-time devotion to field work is uncommon because difficulty securing full-time funding means that researchers are balancing other economic commitments while in the field. For graduate students, making ends meet often means working as a research assistant on someone else's project. For faculty, it means continuing to meet teaching obligations while doing field work. Although researchers would love to face only a computer when they leave the field, many in fact must go to committee meetings, write lectures, go to work, pick up children, fix dinner, etc. For many researchers, a hybrid pattern of commitments has replaced the single commitment model of fieldwork that characterized the community studies of the past.

This new hybrid patterns affects the character of field work in many ways. In my case other obligations severely curtailed the amount of time I could spend in the field. I was working twenty hours per week, I had many school obligations, I had to run my own household, and I was living in an area with family and friends in the immediate vicinity. It was often hard to find six to ten hours a week to go to the schools. In addition I felt the strain of straddling two different worlds. I would leave Prescott school and, with my head swimming with thoughts about how I should have handled Allen poking Jonathan, drive to the university, try to find a parking place in the middle of the day, and go to work as a sociology teaching assistant. It was disorienting. Because being in the field required more formal attire than was the norm among students at the university, I found myself constantly explaining to people I met in the hallway why I was so dressed up. I felt on stage and out of place when I was visiting the classroom, but I also felt myself a misfit at the university. I had trouble getting used to this; it seemed as if I could never establish a routine.

I think that researchers need to take seriously this hybrid pattern of research and analyze the differences it makes in access, entrance, rapport, data collection, and data analysis. It seems to me, for example, that access must be negotiated over longer periods of time, and more often, when the worker is moving in and out of the field than when she/he is living there (see Bosk 1979). Data collection is slower when the researcher is in the field less often, and moving in and out of the field is a strain, though possibly less of a strain than living in an unfamiliar environment for months at a time (Powdermaker 1966). Although data collection takes longer, data analysis and the clarification of the research question may move along more quickly under this hybrid pattern. Being in a university environment as well as in a field setting provides more people with whom to discuss the research question. This ready availability of sounding boards may help the researcher move ahead more rapidly with the data analysis.

Whether a commitment pattern is hybrid or single, all qualitative researchers inevitably experience errors and confusion in their research. In the course of defining the problem, negotiating access, beginning observations, and conducting interviews, many decisions must be made, some of which—in retrospect—are regrettable. This is true in all research, but in qualitative methods the mistakes are usually carried out and observed by the researcher first hand (rather than being committed by others and reported—or note reported—to the principal investigator by subordinates). Qualitative researchers also work in naturalistic settings and they lack opportunities to 'rerun' the data. Moreover, overwhelmed by the immediacy of the field setting, the sheer amount of data collected, and the many possibilities which the project offers, some researchers—temporarily or permanently—lost sight of their intellectual question(s). I turn now to a discussion of this problem.

Part II: Problems with the Research Question

Blinded by Data

Two months into my field work, a graduate seminar on participant-observation was offered by Michael Burawoy. Thinking that it might be useful to have others to talk to about the project I enrolled in the course.[1] As I soon discovered, Burawoy (1979) viewed qualitative data as data that tried to help answer a question. He allowed that the mode of inquiry might be very different than the mode of presentation in the final report, but he was interested in having us—all of us—answer sociological questions. 'So what?' was the question of the quarter.

As Burawoy soon discovered, I resisted this approach. More precisely, I was ambivalent and confused about how to write up the data I was collecting, which grew, literally, by the hour. Data collection is an absorbing process and it pleased me to add more and more field notes to the pile and make arrangements to complete interviews. Still, the sheer amount of data sometimes seemed overwhelming and I did not feel prepared to analyze it. I had unconsciously accepted the methodology of survey research which consists of four steps: a) formulate a problem; b) collect data; c) analyze it; and d) write it up. I was overextended simply trying to get to both schools, take notes, write up the notes, work as a teaching assistant, and keep up with Burawoy's class. As far as I was concerned, the analysis could wait.

My ambivalence, however, centered less on the problem of not having time to do it and more on the proper strategy for analyzing and writing up qualitative research—a problem which ultimately haunts almost all qualitative researchers. I wanted to describe social reality, to supply the details and the vivid descriptions that would draw my readers in and carry them along; I hoped to produce the holistic and seamless feeling of many of the ethnographies that I had read. Some of the many works in this genre are analytical. *Tally's Corner* (Liebow 1968), *Worlds of Pain* (Rubin 1976), and *Everything in Its Path* (Erikson 1976) all have arguments—but the analysis seems subordinate to the data. They certainly aren't written in the now-I-am-going-to-discuss-three-ideas' style which characterized everything I had written during graduate school. Captivated by some of the ethnomethodology and anthropology I had read, I was eager to abandon explicitly intellectual questions and 'simply' describe social reality. More to the point, I believed that was what good ethnographers did. Describing reality provided intrinsically interesting information. The intellectual ideas, tucked away in a concluding chapter or footnotes, did not spoil or constrain the novelistic portrayal of reality. I had hoped to use my own data to draw compelling pictures which would not—to use a favorite expression of mine at the time—violate the complexity of social reality. But I was also interested in ideas. I had waded through Bourdieu and found his approach useful. I was genuinely interested in the way in which social stratification was reproduced, and in the contribution made to children's life chances, by the interactions between parents and teachers.

As my field work progressed, I struggled to determine the 'proper' relationship between theory and qualitative data. I had framed a question before I began my field work, but once I got caught up in the drama of actually being in the field my original question became hazy. I had trouble linking the data back to the original question or modifying the original question. Instead, I was preoccupied by the characters—Mrs. Walters, Mrs. Thompson, the children, and even my own role in the research process.

This intellectual confusion is reflected clearly in my field notes. My notes—and I know that I am not alone in this—had some sensitive concepts (Glaser and Strauss 1967) but then were all over the map. They were a hodge podge of observations made on the basis of shifting priorities. One day I recorded the curriculum and how children interacted with the materials, their skills and how they displayed them. Another day I looked at how the teacher controlled the classroom and her methods of authority. Another day I looked at my role in interacting with the children, how I responded when children started breaking classroom rules in front of me, and my relationships to the teacher and the aide. Observations on the relationships between the aide and the children, the aide and the teacher, the parents and the children, all flow indiscriminately through my field notes. I wrote detailed descriptions of special events (e.g., a school play, a description of an easter egg dyeing project). I also watched for and noted hallmarks of social class: labels on clothing, vacation plans, parents' appearances in the classroom, and different relationships between parents and teachers. Anything and everything that went on in the classroom I tried to record. In my efforts to capture social reality as comprehensively as possibly, I forgot about the need for a focus.

Burawoy had no such memory lapse. He read a sample of my field notes and promptly advised me to narrow my interests. He also asked me (as well as the other members of the class) to spend a paragraph or two at the end of each set of field notes analyzing what was going on in the notes. After each session of observation, we were to write out our notes and then evaluate them in light of our question. We were expected to assess what we had learned, what new questions had been raised by our observations, and how we planned to proceed. Burawoy's advice was excellent.

Today I make my graduate students do the same thing, but, as with much, if not most, good advice (i.e., to lose weight or stop smoking) it was easier to give than to follow. I found the required analyses extremely difficult to do. I hated them. Worse yet, I did them only when I had to—the ten times I was required to give them to Burawoy.

Part of the reason that I avoided these analyses was that they highlighted the murkiness of my intellectual purpose. Methodologically I was clearer; I wanted to provide a rich description of social reality. The problem was that my romance with ethnomethodology didn't help me frame my research question in a way that would allow an answer that made a theoretical contribution. I was asking, 'How does social class influence children's schooling?' The answer was supposed to be a description of social reality. What I lacked was another, more conceptual, question: 'Do these data support one interpretation and suggest that another interpretation is not as useful?' or to be more specific, 'Can we understand parents' involvement in schooling as being linked to their values? Does cultural capital provide a better explanation for why parents are involved in school?' These questions have 'yes' or 'no' answers which can be defended using data from the study. By framing a 'how' question I could not provide a similarly defensible answer. I could not show that one explanation was superior; I could not demonstrate that these data helped to address an important issue. In short, I could not answer the 'So what?' question.

At the time I did not really understand the implications of posing the 'wrong' question. I analyzed my notes as rarely as possible and I didn't really notice that my goals changed hourly. I was more focused on building rapport with the teachers, taking comprehensive notes, trying to get the notes typed up, and getting permission to interview parents and teachers so I could complete the next stage of the project.

Burawoy, however, *was* concerned about the way I framed my study. He expressed this in all of our meetings. From our first discussion (following his review of my field notes), he repeatedly cautioned me to think the study through 'in greater analytical detail'. This advice sailed right by me or more accurately I ignored it. In the sixth week of the quarter I wrote a paper on what I had learned from my observations. It was long and my first effort to assess what I had learned from almost five months of research. It was all description: how teachers at Prescott and Colton looked, how they interacted with the children, how much math the children knew, where the children took their vacations, and a little about children's feelings about their academic ranking in the class. I discussed parents, noting that Colton parents were rarely there, seemed more deferential, and didn't seem to know as much as Prescott parents. The paper was vivid in parts and dull in others but it didn't define a question. It was an unfocused description of classroom life in two schools.

Burawoy's reaction to the paper, strongly worded and highly critical, proved to be the turning point in the conceptual development of the project. His comments made it clear that I could not continue to conduct a study that posed no problem and articulated no argument. He noted:

> . . . One's reaction to what you have written has to be, so what? What is so surprising? At no point do you attempt to present plausible alternatives to your findings . . . I would like to see you produce a theoretical beginning to this paper. I want you to use the literature to highlight the significance of the data you have collected . . . I really think you have to develop an argument, particularly as I presume this will be part of your thesis.

The chair of my dissertation, Troy Duster, gave me the same feedback although in a different way. Slowly I began to realize that quotes and field notes (which I found fascinating of course) would have to be applied to an intellectual problem. An unfocused thick description' would not do.

Using my original formulation of the problem and my conversations with others in my department, I began to try to link up the data with the intellectual problem. I wrote another, much shorter, paper noting the significant correlation between social class and educational achievement and arguing that this correlation was linked to parent involvement in schooling. This attempt was, as Burawoy commented, 'a major advance' over my earlier paper, but I still had a long way to go.

In retrospect, part of my problem was that the question I was framing was too heavily embedded in quantitative models. I was trying to unravel the way in which class difference in family life influenced schooling *and shaped achievement*. I seriously thought I could provide some kind of causal model using qualitative data. Today, that goal strikes me as outlandish. The strength of qualitative data is that it can illuminate the *meaning* of events. It cannot demonstrate that parent behavior 'a' has a stronger effect on achievement than parent behavior 'b' in a sample of two classrooms.

This preoccupation with achievement as a dependent variable and steady immersion in the quantitative literature made me overlook qualitative sociological studies that could provide a suitable framework for my project. I had not read many of the socio-linguistic studies that had been done in the United States, nor was I familiar with the work of cultural anthropologists. I unwittingly ignored the work of potential role models—people who had used similar methods successfully and whose studies could provide valuable examples.

I also failed to realize that just as an individual develops a personal identity most researchers develop an intellectual identity, one that often includes a theoretical as well as a methodological orientation. This identity does not usually change significantly over a single research project, although it might be modified in some ways. I began my project admiring radically different types of qualitative research; my own intellectual identity was in flux. I failed to realize that my multiple admirations were prompting me to strive for mutually incompatible goals. This was not, I have come to realize, an idiosyncratic pattern for I have observed many novice researchers do the same.

For example I admired many ethnomethodological and phenomenological studies in which the flesh and blood of real life is portrayed in vivid detail. Yet most of these studies emphasize that it is critical that the researcher's description remains true to the actor's subjective experience. I do not embrace this view. I believe my respondents should be able to agree that I have portrayed their lives accurately, but I do not want to restrict myself to 'folk explanations'. It does not trouble me if my interpretation of the factors influencing their behavior is different from their interpretation of their lives. Parents at Prescott and Colton schools cannot be expected to be aware of the class structure of which they are a part, nor of the influence of class on behavior. I want to be able to make my own assessment, based on the evidence I have gathered and my understanding of social structural factors. It is difficult, if not impossible, to provide a detailed, comprehensive portrayal of social reality (particularly using the actor's subjective experience) which also selects out elements of that experience to build a focused, coherent argument. A comprehensive portrait and a focused argument are different goals. As with many things in life, you cannot do everything. You have to choose.

This is why it is very helpful for a researcher to know her/his intellectual identity at the beginning of a research project. If you know what you believe in, what type of work you are trying to do, what you would consider acceptable and what you would consider unacceptable, you have a framework and general parameters for your research. You are also better prepared to make compromises: what kinds of weaknesses in your research are you willing to live with and what are completely unacceptable? Being clear about matters such as these can improve both the quality and the quantity of data collection. Well-defined, mutually compatible goals make it easier to focus in the field and also contributes to better organized data.

The Lone Ranger Problem

Even with a clear intellectual identity and a general theoretical question, almost all research questions undergo modification in the light of the data. A favorite description for this in qualitative methods courses is that the research 'evolves.' Many researchers adopt the myth of individualism here. The lone researcher collects the data and, aided by her/his powers of sensitive observation and skill in writing up field notes, the researcher's initial question 'evolves' and becomes more focused. After having collected the data, the researcher retreats into her/his study to write it up and then emerges with a coherent work.

This is a mistaken view of the research process. Research, like everything else, is social. Ironically, this is more obvious in the physical sciences, where researchers must share expensive laboratory equipment, than it is in the social sciences. In the physical sciences, faculty, post-doctoral fellows, graduate students, technicians, and (occasionally) undergraduate assistants all share the same work space—and equipment. Lab interactions and lab politics are a routine part of the work process. Social scientists, even those collaborating on large research projects, rarely work together in such a way. Usually the research team meets periodically for a couple of hours and co-workers may share a computer or an office, but they spend much more of their work time alone than do their colleagues in the physical sciences. Still, the research process in sociology is social. Researchers do not get ideas from vacuums; they arise from a social context. The impact of historical factors on academic agendas is testimony to that fact (Karabel and Halsey 1977). And the ideology of individualism notwithstanding, advances in conceptual models also depend crucially upon an exchange of ideas.

In my own case, my argument (and the relationship between the conceptual model and the data) went through four or five stages, becoming narrower and less sweeping at each point. As the question became clearer my data collection became more focused as well. I began to collect information about parents and I looked closely at the differences between the two schools. I ultimately dropped my effort to explain achievement, and developed an interest in the debates on cultural capital and, to a lesser extent, parent involvement in schooling. To say that my research question 'evolved' is true, but this is far too passive a description. Just as reproduction of the social structure does not happen automatically, so the narrowing and refining of a research project is not an automatic process. Qualitative researchers take steps to *produce* a more focused research question. Participant-observation, writing up field notes, and reflecting on field notes are the steps which are normally emphasized in the literature but there are others. Talking to colleagues is critical to the development of a question. Writing up the results and having the work critically reviewed is another important step. Comparing your findings to the literature and seeing how your conclusions modify the literature is also useful.

Today my rule of thumb is that every third visit to the field should be followed by some kind of effort to push the question forward. This can be a one hour conversation with a colleague (by telephone if necessary), a comparison with other studies, or a long memo which is then reviewed and criticized by others. Such efforts must include reflections on the overall goals of the project, the theoretical question, the data, and the remaining gaps. The analysis at the end of field notes and this 'state of the question push' are similar but not identical. The former is focused around a particular event or dynamic in the field setting; the latter is broader, more reflective, and—most importantly—more social. It is an effort to reach out and place the study in a social context to get others' feedback, to evaluate the study in terms of its contributions to the field. It is not usually very difficult to arrange this social interaction, but it must be solicited by the researcher; it will not happen automatically.

Thus, all of the conceptual advances in this project were linked to the production and criticism of written work. Writing was helpful because it required that I organize, systematize, and condense volumes of information. It helped me struggle to build the argument and it allowed me to assess the evidence in a new way. The criticism of others, particularly the comments of colleagues around the country, challenged me to rethink some of my ideas. Although I had many enjoyable sessions talking about the project and bouncing ideas around, I learned less from talking and listening than I did from writing. One consequence of this is that every few months or so (depending on the pace of data collection) I write a paper about my current project. (A deadline, such as giving a talk about the research, is helpful here.) These working papers are not polished and in most cases are not publishable.

Overall it was the social interaction (especially the criticism from others) that helped advance my work. While the lone scholar image has its appeal, it does not accurately portray the actual process in qualitative—or quantitative—research.

Writing It Up

After I signed a book contract and was committed to finishing this project, I began to ask colleagues who did qualitative research what books they considered exemplary models of writing up a qualitative project. I was shocked at how much trouble people had thinking of exemplary books. Moreover, when they did recommend books they were not usually within the field of the sociology of education. Several people recommended *Tally's Corner* (Liebow 1967). One colleague recommended Charles Bosk's book *Forgive and Remember* (Bosk 1979), a study of the socialization of medical residents into surgery. It is a compelling book and, I believe, a useful model. Another suggested *Everything in Its Path* (Erikson 1976), an award winning book which portrays the destruction of a community by the failure of traditional support systems following a dam burst.

When I began to reflect on the books that didn't make the list (only 99 per cent of the available literature), it became clear that there were many ways that qualitative researchers could end up producing mediocre books—even those beginning with interesting ideas and good evidence. Many studies represent good solid work but they have a plodding tone and analysis; they lack lively writing. Others seem as though the author(s) had not accurately represented the community under investigation and/or had missed important things in field research. Some books had good ideas and an interesting argument but seemed to be unsystematic in the analysis and portrayal of evidence. Others were long on ideas and short on data, while some lacked an argument all together.

The downfall of many of these books lies in their failure to integrate theory and data. In my own case, as I began to try to write up the results of this study, I would career rather abruptly from discussions of theory and the research problem to presentation of the data. I also presented very few quotes. Detailed—and negative—comments from reviewers helped me see the error of my ways. Mary Metz, a guest editor for *Sociology of Education*, summarized the complaints of reviewers, complaints that I have echoed in my own reviews of other manuscripts using qualitative methods:

> You need to work with your data and decide what can be learned from it and then present your theory tersely as it will help us understand those findings and put them in context.

The reviewers also complained that I made sweeping generalizations without enough evidence to back them up, another common problem in manuscripts based on qualitative research.

I used the reviewers' and the guest editor's criticisms to improve my dissertation. I cited and used more qualitative research and I worked to change the focus from a heavily theoretical piece to a more empirically grounded one, but problems remained. I over-shortened the literature review and the quoted material was not integrated with the text. Following Aaron Cicourel's advice, I labored to integrate the data with the analysis, supply more data and be more 'aggressive' in showing 'what is missing empirically and conceptually' from other studies.

Cicourel's advice was useful again as I prepared to write this book; it reminded me to use the data to build an argument. Nevertheless, while I knew that adding more data would strengthen my argument, I wasn't clear how much additional data to include. I had an urge to add almost everything. Finally, in a move of some desperation, I turned to books and articles that I admired and counted the number of quotes per chapter or page; most averaged one quote per printed page. The quotes were not evenly spread throughout the chapters; there would be pages without any quotes and then three or four quotes per page. Most of these studies also provided examples in the text. Of course the right number of quotes depends on many factors, but the count gave me a ball park figure for my own writing which I have found useful. The problem of linking theory and data is an ongoing struggle. I made a rule that every chapter had to have an argument. I also remembered, although I did not always follow, the advice that someone passed on to me that every paragraph should be linked to the argument. I tried to show that my interpretation was a more compelling way of looking at the data than other interpretations. In other words I tried to answer the question, 'So what?'

It will be for others to judge how well I have done in connecting the theoretical argument and the research data. I know that I have done a better job of integration with this book than I did with the written work that preceded it, notably drafts of papers and the dissertation. I used almost none of my dissertation in preparing this book. Instead I began again, adding probably three to four times as many quotes and streamlining and increasing the aggressiveness of the thesis. This pattern of modest improvement in linking theory and data gives me hope: maybe experience will help. In fact a comparison of first and second books does suggest that some people get much better at this as they go along; others however do not, and a few seem to get worse.

Reflections on the Making of Home Advantage

This project had its share of mistakes but it also had its successes. The design, which included interviews with both parents and teachers, is unusual as most studies do one or the other. This yielded insights that would not have been possible if I had studied families or schools. It was also helpful to follow children over time and clarify that parents adopted similar modes of interaction regardless of the teacher. It was very important to supplement the interviews with classroom observation which improved the interviews and enabled me to 'triangulate' in a way that would have been impossible with interviews alone.

In the end I did have a good rapport with the staff, particularly the classroom teachers I worked with most closely. On her last day of school Mrs. Walters gave me a hug goodbye; Mrs. Thompson thanked me warmly for being in her classroom. In both schools children ran up and gave me a goodbye hug on the last day of school. By the end of the interviews I felt I had genuinely come to know and enjoy many of the mothers and fathers, and I was also certain that in several cases the feelings were mutual. This was a reward. There are plenty of awkward moments in field work, even among the best researchers, but there are also rewards and signs, little and big, of acceptance. These are important to notice and remember. This is harder to do than one would think. Moments of foolishness and the damage they have wrought are easy to worry about. I spent a lot of time fretting about the mistakes I made in this study. They scared me so I wanted to try to hide them; I worried about each and every one of them, and they overshadowed my assessment of the project. This kind of self-criticism, in which the impact of each criticism is five times that of each compliment, is not productive.

It was productive, however, to spend time thinking about the strengths and weaknesses of the study and the confidence which I have in the results. As this appendix and the format of the book make clear, I have confidence in the validity of the interviews. I feel that I was helped by my previous experience as an interviewer. Although it is difficult to prove, I am confident in the quality of the data—that I did not lead, badger, or trap respondents in interviews, that I listened to them carefully and was able to get them to talk in an honest and revealing way. The field notes were also carefully recorded. When I went into the field I thought I would find evidence of institutional discrimination. I thought, as Bowles and Gintis, Cicourel and Kitsuse, and others had suggested, that the teachers were going to differ significantly in their interactions with parents of different social class. I did not find evidence to support this position. When I did not find it I looked for other explanations rather than trying to force the evidence into that intellectual frame. The project did not have as many field notes focused directly on the intellectual problem as I would have liked, but the ones that were there were carefully done.

Can we learn anything from a study of two first grade classes, twelve families, four teachers, and two principals? Yes, I think we can use a small, nonrandom sample to improve conceptual models. This study shows that a very high proportion of parents would agree that they want to be 'supportive' of their children's schooling but that they would mean very different things by this. It suggests that family-school models are inadequate. Researchers do not spend enough time addressing the differences in objective skills which social class gives to parents. Independent of parents' desires for their children, class gives parents an edge in helping their children in schooling. My confidence in the validity of the findings is bolstered by the fact that they elaborate a pattern that has been noted by many researchers, although often only in passing. They also mesh with the conclusions of other recent works (Baker and Stevenson 1986; Stevenson and Baker 1987; Epstein 1987).

Although not a form of systematic evidence, I must add, that just as after you learn a new word you see it everywhere, after I finished this study I began to notice that social class differences in family-school relationships are as evident in the Midwestern city where I now live and work as it was in the West Coast communities I studies. I see working-class neighbors and friends take a 'hands-off' attitude toward their children's schooling, emphasizing their own inadequacies and turning over responsibility to the school. I see upper-middle-class families, particularly academic couples, trying to monitor and control their children's schooling. I think that while there may be aspects of the argument that need modification, the overall pattern, that class gives people resources which help them comply with the demands of institutions, is really there. Other research, using multiple methodologies, is necessary to establish that and to illuminate the interactive effects of class and parent involvement; for example, working-class parents are much less likely to make requests of the school staff, and when they do make such requests are more likely to have them honored than upper-middle-class parents.

What this study cannot do is provide an assessment of how important individuals' competencies are relative to other factors influencing parent involvement (i.e., values, teachers' roles), nor can it evaluate how common parents' actions are, including parents' supervising teachers and compensating for weaknesses in the classroom. A small sample imposes restrictions that cannot be surmounted with felicitous phrases such as 'one half of the sample believed. . .' Large-scale, representative studies are much better for describing the proportion of people who share certain beliefs, and internal variations, while addressed here, can be better elaborated with a larger group. What qualitative methods can do is illuminate the meanings people attach to their words and actions in a way not possible with other methodologies. Although I admire many quantitative studies, they are in some ways 'unnaturally' straightforward. Data analysis and computer analysis have a much smaller range of options and there is less of a domino effect than occurs in qualitative work. Quantitative research does not have the ambiguity and uncertainty of field work.

In my view qualitative work is more cumbersome and more difficult than survey research at almost every stage: formulation of the problem, access, data collection, data analysis, and writing up the results. It is more time consuming; it is harder to spin off several publications; and, to add insult to injury, it is considered lower status by many members of the profession. But it adds to our knowledge in a critical and important way. It is that pay-off that draws me back, despite all I have learned about the enormous commitment of time and energy that qualitative research demands. If it were not one of the only ways of gaining insights into the routine events of daily life and the meaning that makes social reality, qualitative methods would not have a lot going for it. It is too much work. But it is one of the only ways, and possibly the only way, to achieve such insights. The usefulness of these insights rests, however, on the character of our research. Exchanging notes on our disappointments and successes in field research is an important step in increasing the quality of our work.

Notes

1. I am indebted to William F. Whyte's work not only for the idea of writing an appendix but also for providing a model of how to write one. I have shamelessly adopted elements of his organizational structure, including this one, in my appendix. Readers will note, however, a difference in the content and goals of the two appendices. Whyte's appendix elaborates issues of access, entry, and the formulation of the intellectual problem. He also provides a very good discussion of ethics and holding the line between researcher and native. My goals are somewhat different. Although I briefly review the issues of access and entry, my focus is on the practical considerations of data collection, data analysis, and the writing up of the results. I do, however, also discuss the task of formulating an intellectual problem in qualitative research.

2. My job was to help determine if recently arrested defendants were qualified to be released on their own recognizance. To help indigent defendants save bail money, the Own Recognizance Project (OR Project) would prepare cases by providing a summary of the social ties a defendant had to the area, including her/his correct address, contact with relatives, and employment history. Unlike bail, which was simply a matter of producing the money and the collateral, OR cases required judges' signatures. Primarily because of negative publicity, many judges were very reluctant to exercise the OR option. Although the San Francisco City Prison was not as bad as some prisons, most people found prison so uncomfortable that they wanted to get out as soon as possible. For them OR was too slow and too chancy so they bailed out instead.

3. Unfortunately for those of us not trained in shorthand, it is not possible to write down every single word and idea in an interview, particularly if you are trying to maintain eye contact and build a rapport with the subject. Without a tape recorder researchers must do some editing while taking notes. For most of us this means that some particularly interesting passages are written in more detail than others. Yet what is considered interesting changes as the project and the research question develop, thus note-taking is inevitably altered by these intellectual questions.

4. Whyte (1981) has a good discussion of the problems of access, but almost all books on qualitative research methods discuss the problems. The writing on qualitative methods has increased radically in recent years and there are many good pieces around. Bogdan and Biklen (1982), while directed at research in education is a useful overview. Other works include Silverman (1985), Agar (1986), and from a somewhat different perspective Glaser and Strauss (1967). Although older, Schatzman and Strauss (1973) provide a succinct discussion of key issues. In more specialized discussions, Gorden (1987) focuses on interviewing, Kirk and Miller (1986) the problems of reliability and validity in qualitative work, Macrorie (1985) the task of writing up one's results, and Punch (1986) on the politics of fieldwork. Erickson (1986) also has a useful overview of the steps in a qualitative research project using studies of teaching as an example. Finally, for reflections on the research process, see Rabinow (1977), Georges and Jones (1980), Van Mannen (1988), Simon and Dippo (1986), and Schon (1987).

5. As part of the human subjects approval process at the university, I wrote consent forms for all of the parents, children, teachers, and others I interviewed. [Since I was not disrupting the classroom activities, I was not required to gain consent forms from all of the children in the classes.] These forms briefly described the goals of the project and the methodology, including that parents and teachers would be interviewed. Before I gave parents and teachers the forms I stressed that these forms were routine and added that they were developed after serious abuses by researchers, such as prisoners being given drugs without being told. Although I agonized over the content of the form almost no one read it. Only two parents—a lawyer and his wife—read the form carefully before signing; the remaining parents and educators signed it with only a glance.

6. My letter to Prescott was as follows:

Dear Mrs. Finnegan:

This letter is in regard to our recent telephone conversation regarding my request to conduct a small research project in your district. As I mentioned, I am a graduate student in a doctoral program at University of California, Berkeley, in the sociology department. As part of my dissertation research, I am conducting a study on social class variations in the family-school relationship for young children. As you probably know, the social standing of a child's family is a key predictor of educational outcome. The purpose of the research is to examine the process through which social position affects the educational process. In particular, the research will focus on the impact which the social position of professional-middle-class and working-class families has on day to day experience of school life.

I would like to conduct a very small pilot study on these issues in Prescott School District. The research would involve one first grade classroom in your district. The study would include interviews with the teacher, principal, school secretary, and five families of the children in the classroom. In addition, I would like to observe the children in the classroom for a short time, perhaps amounting to six or eight visits. All of the interviews would be 'semi-structured' interviews with open-ended questions. The interviews would last a little more than one hour and would be tape recorded. All of the persons in the study would be assured of confidentiality.

The interviews will cover a number of issues in family life and school life. The study will ask both parents and the child questions about the family's approach towards schooling. The parents' view of schooling, the way in which the parents convey this view to the child and the behavior of the parents will be explored. In addition, the conflicts between parents regarding education and the proper type of educational experience will be studied. The purpose of this study is to *compare* differences between working-class and professional-middle-class families in their view of the ideal family-school relationship. The interviews in your district will provide a basic description of the family-school relationship for a small number of families of relatively high socio-economic status.

A slightly different set of issues will be taken up with the teacher, principal, and school secretary (the secretary is included as the front office often is the first point of contact between families and schools). First, it is important to note that I would like to request that the school send a letter to the families indicating that the researcher has the permission of the district to conduct the interviews. I would be happy to contribute in any way possible to the writing and mailing of such a letter.

Secondly, the interviews with the teacher, principal, and school secretary will focus on the amount of information which school personnel have about family life. Questions will focus on the types of information which school staff learn about families, and the informal ways in which this information is gathered. In addition, the research will solicit the perceptions of school staff regarding the way in which family life shapes the day to day educational experience for young children. It is important to emphasize that the purpose of the study is *not* to evaluate teachers, schools, or parents. Indeed, the specific teaching style of a teacher is really of very limited interest as the study seeks to understand social class patterns of family-school interaction.

These brief comments are intended to provide you and your colleagues with better insight into the concerns of the research project. If you or anyone else in the district has further questions, I would be happy to provide additional information. I appreciate your consideration of this request and look forward to hearing from you in the future.

Sincerely,

Annette Lareau

7. With hindsight, this is the letter I would write today:

Dear Mrs. Finnegan:

Thank your for taking the time to speak with me the other day. As we agreed, I am writing to request permission to conduct a study in your school district.

In this project, I am interested in learning more about how families help children in school. I would like to visit one first grade classroom in the district on a regular basis this school year (e.g., two times a week). My visits would be scheduled to be at a convenient time. Having worked in classrooms, I know how important it is to take an unobtrusive role in the classroom. I would be happy to work as a classroom volunteer if the teacher would like.

In addition, at a convenient time, I hope to interview the parents of five children in this classroom, as well as the teacher, principal, and school secretary. The interviews will last an hour or so. All information collected would be kept confidential; neither the identity of Prescott school district, nor that of any parents or teachers, would ever be revealed.

I am requesting permission to observe in the classroom and for you, or the school staff, to supply names and addresses of parents, with the understanding that parents may refuse to cooperate in the study. For your information, I have attached a sample copy of the letter which I would mail to parents.

I know that you, and the teachers, lead busy lives. Teachers have reported that the experience of working on this research project was interesting and pleasant. If it would be helpful, I would be happy to make a brief presentation about the project to school staff. If you would like any other information, please feel free to contact me at (618) 453-2494.

Again, I appreciate your consideration of my request. I look forward to hearing from you in the future.

Sincerely,

Annette Lareau

8. I always told people. that there was another school involved and that the school was of a different level of affluence. In the beginning I used the term 'socio-economic status'; that really raised eyebrows. I now realize that it is much too long a term and much too academic to be useful.

9. Having come from Berkeley I found this 'Miss Lareau' title to be astounding in the 1980s, but it happened in all of my interactions in the school. No one called me Ms. Lareau, and many people asked me: 'Is it Miss or Mrs.?' Unmarried teachers, including Miss Chaplan, used the term Miss in all of their interactions. It didn't really bother me, however, and I never asked to be called Ms. I didn't really care what they called me. I was just glad to be in a school doing field work.

10. I met several mothers, including Allen's and Emily's, during these periods. As children's work got underway the mothers would often chat with me and ask me questions about my study. They also observed me in the classroom and my interactions with the children. Mrs. Walters often complained about mothers visiting during volunteering saying, 'You get more work out of one parent than two.' In my own case it meant that mothers were watching me just as they watched Mrs. Walters. There were also indications that mothers discussed me and my study in their conversations with one another. Thus my role with parents paralleled that of the teachers; Prescott mothers knew more about me, scrutinized, and questioned me much more closely than Colton parents.

11. If there was a statement which I thought was important I would repeat it to myself over and over again while in the classroom and write it down immediately after I left—usually in my car before I drove away. Most of the field notes from Prescott do not have direct quotes; if there are quotes, however, I am quite confident of their accuracy.

12. While interviewing defendants in City Prison for the OR Project I found that by two or three minutes into the interview I needed to have the defendant calmed down, no longer trying to tell me the story of his or her arrest, and concentrating on the names of three persons (with telephone numbers) who could act as references, otherwise I felt the interview was in trouble. This 'transition point,' therefore, varies from study to study, depending on both the length and the substance of the interviews.

13. Although I believe I was almost always genuine in my admiration for aspects of the respondents' lives, the content of my compliments and 'fishing expeditions' varied according to social class. In Colton I found myself discussing television programs, admiring respondents' house plants and, to a lesser extent, their clothes. In Prescott I talked about classical music preferences, houses, and house decorations.

14. In these summaries I wrote a description of the respondents, the house, and key parts of the interview. I also listed critical quotes and their location on the tape (i.e., 'good quote about criticisms of school, end of side one').

15. These categories had been the analytic structure of my dissertation which had seven chapters: 1) a literature review and statement of the problem, 2) a description of the research methods, 3) a description of the two schools and the amount of parent involvement in each school, 4) parents' attitudes towards their role in schooling and the degree to which they complied with teachers' requests, 5) family life (i.e., lessons, gender roles, kinship ties) and the influence on family-school relationships, 6) teachers' wishes for parent involvement, and 7) the importance of cultural capital in shaping family-school relationships.

16. The class had a distinct (and very effective) structure. We were divided into groups of four, in roughly similar intellectual areas. We were to meet twice a week outside class to compare and discuss each other's field notes and problems in the field. Twice during the quarter we made presentations in class and shared our field notes with the entire class. Burawoy also read our field notes and commented on them. Course requirements included a critical literature review to help formulate a problem, a paper based on the field work, and ten sets of field notes.

Recording and Organizing Data

Martyn Hammersley and Paul Atkinson

There is a sense in which it is impossible ever to record all the data acquired in the course of fieldwork. As Radcliffe-Brown notes:

'However exact and detailed the description of a primitive people may be, there remains much that cannot be put into such a description. Living, as he must, in daily contact with the people he is studying, the field ethnologist comes gradually to "understand" them, if we may use the term. He acquires a series of multitudinous impressions, each slight and often vague, that guide him in his dealings with them. The better the observer the more accurate will be his general impression of the mental peculiarities of the race. This general impression it is impossible to analyze, and so to record and convey to others. Yet it may be of the greatest service when it comes to interpreting the beliefs and practices of a primitive society. If it does not give any positive aid towards a correct interpretation, it at least prevents errors into which it is only too easy for those to fall who have not the same immediate knowledge of the people and their ways.'

(Radcliffe-Brown 1948b:230)

In fact, such tacit knowledge is a ubiquitous phenomenon, extending even to physical science, as Michael Polanyi(1958) has shown. The existence of an inevitable residue of 'multitudinous impressions' or 'tacit knowledge' cannot be ignored. However, it does not negate the responsibility of the social scientist to be as explicit as possible about the data by means of which his or her theories have been generated, developed, and tested.

While it is possible to rely on memory to preserve this data over the course of the research, and some reliance on memory is unavoidable, there are limits to the amount of data that can be retained in this way. There is also a serious danger of distortion. We all know how memory can play tricks. A particular danger is that the data will be subconsciously transformed in line with emerging theory. In order to prevent this, it is essential to employ some system of recording data as, or soon after, they are collected.

There are several methods ethnographers use for recording their data, most notably fieldnotes, audio-taping, video-taping, and filming. Which of these is the most appropriate depends very much on one's purposes, the nature of the setting, and the financial resources available, though these techniques are not mutually exclusive. Their usefulness also varies according to the type of data to be recorded.

Observational Data

Fieldnotes are the traditional means in ethnography for recording observational data. In accordance with ethnography's commitment to discovery, fieldnotes consist of relatively concrete descriptions of social processes and their contexts. The aim is to capture these in their integrity, noting their various features and properties, though clearly what is recorded will depend on some general sense of what is relevant to the foreshadowed problems of the research. As we noted in Chapter 1, while it is impossible to provide any description without some principle of selecting what is and is not important, there are advantages (as well as disadvantages) in adopting a wide focus. At least prior to the closing stages of data collection, then, there is no attempt to code systematically what is observed in terms of existing theoretical categories. Indeed, the main purpose is to identify and develop what seem to be the most appropriate theoretical categories.

The construction and collection of fieldnotes is not something that is (or should be) shrouded in mystery: it is not an especially esoteric activity. On the other hand, it does constitute a central research activity, and it should be carried out with as much care and self-conscious awareness as possible. A research project can be as well organized and theoretically well informed as you like, but with inadequate note taking, the exercise will be like using an expensive camera with poor quality film. In both cases, the resolution will prove unsatisfactory, and the results will be poor. Only foggy pictures result.

The compilation of fieldnotes may appear to be a straightforward matter. However, like most aspects of intellectual craftsmanship, some care and attention to detail are prerequisites, and satisfactory note taking needs to be worked at. It is a skill demanding continual reassessment of purposes and priorities and of the costs and benefits of different strategies. Thus, the standard injunction, 'write down what you see and hear', glosses over a number of important issues. Among other things, the fieldworker will have to ask *what* to write down, *how* to write it down, and *when* to write it down.

Let us deal with this last point first: when to write notes? In principle, one should aim to make notes as soon as possible after the observed action that is to be noted. Most fieldworkers report that while they can train themselves to improve recall, the quality of their notes diminishes rapidly with the passage of time: the detail is quickly lost, and whole episodes can be forgotten or irreparably muddled.

The ideal would be to make notes during actual participant observation. But this is not always possible, and even when it is possible, the opportunities may be very limited. There may be restrictions arising from the social characteristics of the research setting, as well as from the nature of the ethnographer's social position(s) *vis-à-vis* the hosts.

If the research is covert, then note taking in the course of participation will often be practically impossible. In most settings, participants are not visibly engaged in a continual process of jotting down notes, seizing notebooks during conversations, and similar activities. In many circumstances, such activity would prove totally disruptive to any 'natural' participation. It is hard to think of Laud Humphreys (1970), for example, taking copious notes while acting as 'watchqueen' in public lavatories and observing casual homosexual encounters. In a few contexts, of course, writing may be such an unremarkable activity that covert note taking is feasible. In a covert study of students' timewasting strategies in a university library, spasmodic writing on the part of the ethnographer would be possible, though care would have to be taken not to appear too diligent!

However, overt research does not solve the problem of note taking. To some extent our comments concerning covert participation apply here as well. The conduct of note taking must be broadly congruent with the context of the setting under scrutiny. In some contexts, however well 'socialized' the hosts, open and continuous note taking will be perceived as threatening or inappropriate, and will prove disruptive to the action. In other contexts, fairly extensive notes can be recorded without undue disruption. Thus, for example, Whyte (1981) reports how he took on the role of secretary to the Italian Community Club because it enabled him to take notes unobtrusively in their meetings.

The possibility of on-the-spot note taking may vary across situations even within a single setting, as the case of studying a medical school illustrates:

'The quantity and type of on-the-spot recording varied across recurrent types of situation. During "tutorials", when one of the doctors taught the group in a more or less formal manner, or when there was some group discussion, and conducted in one of the teaching rooms, then it seemed entirely natural and appropriate that I should sit among the students with my notebook on my knee and take notes almost continuously. At the other extreme I did not sit with my notebook and pen whilst I was engaged in casual conversations with students over a cup of coffee. Whereas taking notes during a University class is a normal thing to do, taking notes during a coffee-break chat is not a normal practice. To have done so openly in the latter context would have been to strain the day-to-day relationships that I had negotiated with the students. Whilst I never pretended that everything I saw and heard was not "data", it would not have been feasible to make continuous notes. . . . Less clear-cut was my approach to the observation and recording of bedside teaching. On the whole I tried to position myself at the back of the student group and make occasional jottings: main items of information on the patients, key technical terms, and brief notes indicating the 'shape' of the session (e.g. the sequence of topics covered, the students who were called on to perform and so on). As I did this over a period I discovered that a substantial amount of the interaction could be recalled and summarized from such brief and scrappy jottings.'

(Atkinson 1976:24-5)

Even in situations where note taking is 'normal', however, such as in tutorials, care must be taken if disruption is to be avoided:

'I feel it much easier to write when the students write, and listen when they do; I have noticed that when I attempt to write when the students are not, I attract (the tutor's) attention and on a few such occasions she seems to falter in what she is saying. . . . Similarly when all the students are writing and I am not, but rather looking at her, I again seem to "put her off". And so it is that I've become a student, sometimes slightly at the loss of my self-esteem when I find myself lazily inserting a pencil in my mouth. (Fieldnotes: February, third year.)'

(Olesen and Whittaker 1968:28)

Many of the initial fieldnotes that ethnographers take, then, are jottings, snatched in the course of the observed interaction. A common joke about ethnographers relates to their frequent trips to the lavatory where such hasty notes can be scribbled in private soon after the action. Even the briefest of notes can be valuable aids in the construction of an account. As Schatzman and Strauss suggest:

'A single word, even one merely descriptive of the dress of a person, or a particular word uttered by someone usually is enough to "trip off" a string of images that afford substantial reconstruction of the observed scene.'

(Schatzman and Strauss 1973:95)

Moreover, it is important to record even things that one does not immediately understand because these might turn out to be important later. Even if it proves possible to make fairly extended notes in the field, they, like brief jottings, will need to be worked up, expanded upon, and developed.

Many social activities have a timetable of their own, and it may prove possible to match phases of observation with periods of writing up fieldnotes in accordance with such timetables. For instance, in the medical-school study referred to earlier, most of the clinical teaching that formed the main focus of the observation took place during the morning; the afternoon was devoted to laboratory work in the various medical sciences. Thus, it proved possible to undertake three or four hours of sustained observation before lunch, and to spend the afternoon and/or evening in writing up full notes. (The afternoon was also available for other forms of data collection such as interviewing and analysis.)

In other settings, the phasing of observation and writing will be much less straightforward to organize, but there are usually times when participants are engaged in activities that are not relevant to the research. At the very least, they sleep at regular times and at the risk of fatigue notes can be written up then. Carey (1972) reports a rare exception, that of 'speed freaks' (those addicted to amphetamines), who, under heavy doses, stay awake for several days in a hyperactive state:

'The peculiar round of life wherein people stay up for three, four, or five days at a time and then sleep for several days posed enormous practical difficulties for the research. Our conventional commitments (family, friends, teaching responsibilities) had to be put aside for a time so that we could adapt ourselves more realistically to this youthful scene. As we became more familiar with this particular universe, we developed a crude sampling plan that called for observations at a number of different gathering spots, and this relieved us somewhat from a very exacting round of life. If we were interested, however, in what happened during the course of a run when a small group of people started shooting speed intravenously, it meant that one or two fieldworkers had to be present at the beginning and be relieved periodically by other members of the team until the run was over. Fatigue was a constant problem and suggests that more than one fieldworker is required in this type of research.'

(Carey 1972:82)

Clearly, in such cases, finding time to write up fieldnotes poses particularly severe problems. The problem remains serious, however, even with less exhausting schedules. But some time for writing up fieldnotes must always be set aside. There is no advantage in observing social action over extended periods if inadequate time is allowed for the preparation of notes. The information will quickly trickle away, and the effort will be wasted. There is always the temptation to try to observe everything, and the consequent fear that in withdrawing from the field, one will miss some vital incident. Understandable though such feelings are, they must, in most circumstances, be suppressed in the interests of producing good-quality notes. Nevertheless, the trade-off between data collection and data recording must be recognized and resolved continually in the manner that seems most appropriate given the purposes of the research. Thus, for example, the organization of periods of observation, with alternating periods of writing and other work, must be done with a view to the systematic sampling of action and actors (Chapter 2).

It is difficult to overemphasize the importance of meticulous note taking. The memory should never be relied on, and a good maxim is 'If in doubt, *write it down*'. It is absolutely essential that one keep up to date in processing notes. Without the discipline of daily writing, the observations will fade from memory, and the ethnography will all too easily become incoherent and muddled. The overall picture will become fuzzy.

What of the *form* and *content* of fieldnotes? One can never record everything; social scenes are truly inexhaustible in this sense. Some selection has to be made. However, the nature of this is likely to change over time. During the early days of a research project, the scope of the notes is likely to be fairly general, and one will probably be reluctant to emphasize any particular aspects; indeed, one will probably not be in a position to make such a selection of topics. As the research progresses, and emergent issues are identified, then the notes will become more restricted in subject matter. Moreover, features that previously seemed insignificant may come to take on new meaning, a point that Johnson illustrates from his research on social workers:

'Gradually I began to "hear different things said" in the setting. This happened through a shift in attention from what was said or done to how it was said or done. The following excerpts from the fieldnotes illustrate several instances of my changing awareness. From the notes near the end of the sixth month of the observations:

"Another thing that happened today. I was standing by Bill's desk when Art passed by and asked Bill to cover the phone for a couple of minutes while he walked through a request for County Supp over to Bess Lanston, an EW supervisor. Now I don't know how many times I've heard a comment like that; so many times that it's not even problematic any more. In fact, it's so routine that I'm surprised that I even made any note to remember it. The striking feature about this is that in my first days at Metro [the social work agency] I would have wanted to know all about what kind of form he was taking over there, what County Supp was, why and how one used it, got it, didn't get it, or whatever, who and where Bess Lanston was, what she did and so on. But all the time I've missed what was crucial about such a comment, the fact that he was *walking* it through. Before I would have only heard what he was doing or why, but today, instead, I began to hear the how. "'

(Johnson 1975:197)

As theoretical ideas develop and change, what is 'significant' and what must be included in the fieldnotes also changes. Over time, notes may also change in *character*, in particular becoming more concrete and detailed. Indeed the preservation of concreteness is an important consideration in fieldnote writing. For most analytic purposes, compressed summary accounts will prove inadequate for the detailed and systematic comparison or aggregation of information across context or across occasions. As far as possible, therefore, speech should be rendered in a manner that approximates to a verbatim report and non-verbal behaviour in relatively concrete terms; this minimizes the level of inference and thus facilitates the construction and reconstruction of theory.

Below we reproduce two extracts from notes that purport to recapture the same interaction. They are recognizably 'about' the same people and the same events. By the same token, neither lays any claim to completeness. The first obviously compresses things to an extreme extent, and the second summarizes some things, and explicitly acknowledges that some parts of the conversation are missing altogether:

'1. The teacher told his colleagues in the staffroom about the wonders of a progressive school he had been to visit the day before. He was attacked from all sides. As I walked up with him to his classroom he continued talking of how the behaviour of the pupils at X had been marvellous. We reached his room. I waited outside, having decided to watch what happened in the hall in the build up to the morning assembly. He went into his classroom and immediately began shouting at his class. He was taking it out on them for not being like the pupils at X.

2. (Walker gives an enthusiastic account of X to his colleagues in the staffroom. There is an aggressive reaction.)

GREAVES: Projects are not education, just cutting out things.

WALKER: Oh no, they don't allow that, there's a strict check on progress.

HOLTON: The more I hear of this the more wishy washy it sounds.

(. . .)

WALKER: There's a craft resources area and pupils go and do some dress-making or woodwork when they want to, when it fits into their project.

HOLTON: You need six week's basic teaching in woodwork or metalwork.

(. . .)

HOLTON: How can an immature child of that age do a project?

WALKER: Those children were self-controlled and well-behaved.

HOLTON: Sounds like utopia.

DIXON: Gimmicky.

(. . .)

WALKER: There's no vandalism. They've had the books four years and they've been used a lot and I could see the pupils were using them, but they looked new, the teacher had told them that if they damaged the books she would have to replace them herself.

(. . .)

HOLTON: Sounds like those kids don't need teaching.

((Walker and I go up to his room: he continues his praise for X. When we reach his room I wait outside to watch the hall as the build up for the morning assembly begins. He enters his room and immediately begins shouting. The thought crosses my mind that the contrast between the pupils at X he has been describing and defending to his colleagues and the "behaviour" of his own pupils may be a reason for his shouting at the class, but, of course, I don't know what was going on the classroom.))

((   )) = observer descriptions.

(. . .) = omission of parts of conversation in record.'

(Hammersley 1980)

The second version is much more concrete in its treatment of the events; indeed, much of the time the speech of the actors themselves is preserved. We can inspect the notes with a fair assurance that we are gaining information on how the participants themselves described things, who said what to whom, and so on. When we compress and summarize we do not simply lose 'interesting' detail and 'local colour', we lose vital information.

The actual words people use can be of considerable analytic importance. The 'situated vocabularies' employed provide us with valuable information about the way in which members of a particular culture organize their perceptions of the world, and so engage in the 'social construction of reality'. Situated vocabularies and folk taxonomies incorporate the typifications and recipes for action that constitute the stock-of-knowledge and practical reasoning of the members of any given culture. Arensberg and Kimball provide an example from their study of interpersonal relations among family members in rural Ireland:

'The relations of the members of the farm family are best described in terms of the patterns which uniformity of habit and association build up. They are built up within the life of the farm household and its daily and yearly work. The relations of the fathers to sons and mothers to sons fall repeatedly into regular and expectable patterns of this kind that differ very little from farm to farm.

If we are to understand them, then, we must trace them out of this setting and see in what manner they offer us explanation of Irish rural behaviour. In terms of a formal sociology, such as Simmel might give us, the position of the parents is one of extreme superordination, that of the children of extreme subordination. The retention of the names "boy" and "girl" reflects the latter position. Sociological adulthood has little to do with physiological adulthood. Age brings little change of modes of address and ways of treating and regarding one another in the relationships within the farm family.'

(Arensberg and Kimball 1968:59)

Recently, there has been increased attention to the significance of the terminologies used by participants. A number of classic ethnographic studies have included lexicons of local terms. Examples include the studies of prison inmates by Sykes (1958) and Giallombardo (1966), and Davis's (1959) account of cab-drivers' evaluations of their clients (their 'fares').

The potential richness and detail of the connotations of such members' terms can perhaps be illustrated by reference to just one term from one such collection. American hospital speech includes the term 'gomer', which is part of the rich and colourful situated vocabulary characteristic of most medical settings. George and Dundes summarize its use:

'What precisely is a "gomer"? He is typically an older man who is both dirty and debilitated. He has extremely poor personal hygiene and he is often a chronic alcoholic. A derelict or down-and-outer, the gomer is normally on welfare. He has an extensive listing of multiple admissions to the hospital.

From the gomer's standpoint, life inside the hospital is so much better than the miserable existence he endures outside that he exerts every effort to gain admission, or rather readmission to the hospital. Moreover, once admitted, the gomer attempts to remain there as long as possible. Because of the gomer's desire to stay in the hospital he frequently pretends to be ill or he lacks interest in getting well on those occasions when he is really sick.'

(George and Dundes 1978:570)

Of course, this brief account glosses over a wide range of uses and connotations associated with this one folk term. In practice, the research worker will not be content simply to generate such a composite or summary definition, important though that may be in summing up one's understanding and cultural competence. The important task is to be able to document and retrieve the actual contexts of use for such folk terms.

In a study of tramps, Spradley (1970) identified a number of categories of actors who seemed to have their own languages: tramps themselves, social workers, police officers, counsellors, judges, court clerks, lawyers, guards, not to mention the ethnographer. Such languages are not, of course, totally selfcontained and mutually unintelligible. However, they are major markers of cultural difference constitutive of differing, and differentially distributed, definitions of the situation. They include the specialized languages of occupational groups, underworld argot, local sayings, and regionally and class-based dialects.

Making fieldnotes as concrete and descriptive as possible is not without its cost, however. Generally the more closely this ideal is approximated, the more restricted the scope of the notes. Unless the focus of the research is extremely narrow, some concreteness and detail will have to be sacrificed for increased scope. Even in the relatively detailed fieldnotes on an incident in a school staffroom quoted earlier, the level of concreteness and detail varied somewhat within the account. Such variations will follow, among other things, current assessments of the relative importance for subsequent analysis of the various features of the scene. There is no neutral observation language in which any scene can be described completely and definitively. Even in the case of recording language 'word for word', interpretation plays its part. Not only is it usually impossible to record everything that is said, and indeed we generally 'tidy up' speech when we write it down, omitting repetitions, hesitations, false starts, and so on, but accompanying non-verbal behaviour cannot usually be recorded unless its significance is of obvious importance. To one degree or another, then, selection, summary, and interpretation are always involved. That this involves dangers is clear, but so is the neglect of the wider context in which the events occurred. Some trade-off between detail and scope in note taking is inevitable and must be determined according to the priorities of the research.

Whatever the level of concreteness of fieldnotes, it is essential that direct quotations are clearly distinguished from summaries provided by the researcher, and that gaps or uncertainties in the quotations are clearly indicated. When we refer back to notes, there must be no ambiguity on that score. One should not have to puzzle 'Is that what they themselves said?' Even when only isolated or fragmented sequences can be recalled and noted, they should be kept typographically distinct from the observer's own descriptive glosses.'

Equally important is that records of speech and action should be located in relation to *who* was present, *where*, at what *time*, and under what *circumstances*. When we come to the stage of analysis, when one will be gathering together, categorizing, comparing, and contrasting instances, then it may become crucial that one can distinguish the circumstances surrounding an activity, such as the audience, and the main participants (see Chapter 8).

Spradley suggests one elementary checklist that can be used to guide the making of field records, and adherence to which would normally allow one to approximate to the provision of context we have referred to:

1. Space: the physical place or places.

2. Actor: the people involved.

3. Activity: a set of related acts people do.

4. Object: the physical things that are present.

5. Act: single actions that people do.

6. Event: a set of related activities that people carry out.

7. Time: the sequencing that takes place over time.

8. Goal: the things people are trying to accomplish.

9. Feeling: the emotions felt and expressed. '

(Spradley 1980:78ff)

Such lists are very crude and rest on arbitrary classifications such as that between acts, activities, and events. Nevertheless, they indicate a range of relevant features of context that might need to be noted.

We have seen, then, how the process of fieldnote writing is shot through with decisions about when and what to record. Indeed, very often these decisions take on the form of dilemmas: higher quality notes can often only be bought at the risk of missing important data; concreteness may sometimes have to be sacrificed to gain the necessary descriptive scope. However, there is one way in which it may seem that some of these dilemmas can be avoided: by the use of a tape recorder. The tension between note writing and observation can be eased, for example, by taping fieldnotes rather than writing them up. As Schatzman and Strauss (1973:97) note, this saves time. However, they also point to some problems, not the least of which is the temptation to generate a huge backlog of under-analysed tapes.

Even more tempting as a solution to the dilemmas involved in fieldnote writing is to resort to electronic recording techniques, audio or audio/visual, in the actual course of observation. While neither provides a complete record—selection is still involved in the placing of the cameras and/or microphones—clearly they provide a much more accurate and detailed account of events than can be provided in notes. And, indeed, these techniques are a very important resource especially where the research focuses on the details of social interaction. The work of McDermott (1976) provides an example. McDermott video-taped two reading groups in a first-grade classroom, looking at the detail of interpersonal interaction, verbal and non-verbal. He was able to show that while interaction in one group looked orderly and in the other disorderly, and was viewed as such by the teacher, what occurred was simply a different kind of order, in part sustained by the teacher's attitude, and that this had dire consequences for the achievement levels of the pupils. There has been similar detailed work on interactional processes by conversational analysts using audio-taping.

Where research is concerned with this level of detail, electronic recording is probably essential. Where the focus is wider, where every word spoken and gesture made is not relevant, such techniques are still useful because of the accuracy and concreteness they provide. However, their advantages must be weighed against some important disadvantages.

Of course, permission will not always be given for their use and this may restrict the range of settings from which an appropriate site for the research can be chosen, or restrict the parts of a setting that can be studied. For example, while teachers will often permit their lessons, and even their staff meetings (Hargreaves 1981) to be tape-recorded or even video-taped, these techniques are unlikely to be allowed in staffrooms. Moreover, even where permission is given, awareness that proceedings are being recorded may significantly affect what occurs. This is particularly true where recorders are carried around and switched on and off to capture particular events, as Altheide illustrates from his research in a TV newsroom:

'I used a tape recorder mainly for debriefing, although I also used it for recording in the setting. In this way, data collection and data recording were combined. However, I found that, with some exceptions, the recorder disrupted the naturalness of the conversation. This occurred during a talk I was having with an anchorman who was making a documentary about alcoholism. His fascinating comments about using actors to play alcoholics because "real alcoholics talk too much", prompted me to ask him if he would mind if I got my recorder. When I turned it on, he cleared his throat and began lecturing me on the magnitude of alcoholism in Western City, never returning to the original topic.

In other situations the recorder did not disrupt the event. One reporter's explanation about how he 'reduced' an interview was recorded without distortion. I know this to be true since I had watched him reduce other interviews in the same way. A few cameramen and reporters permitted me to routinely record their work and assessments of the news scene, while others, like the cameraman who threatened to throw me out of the car, did not approve. However, the recorder did have a situated significance for all workers. '

(Altheide 1976:213)

The effects of audio- and audio-visual recording vary considerably across people and settings. We would expect TV workers to be particularly sensitive, for example, and recording may be easier and less obtrusive where interaction is confined to a single, small setting, as in the case of school lessons or college tutorials. Moreover, the effects of the presence of recording equipment often dissipate over time.

The development of the cheap portable cassette recorder has made audio-recording relatively easy. Moreover, the small size of these machines makes them relatively unobtrusive. There are, of course, technical limitations on what can be recorded in this manner. It is an obvious point, but one of some significance, that only the soundtrack of a setting is recorded in this way, nonverbal behaviour and the physical environment of activities must still be recorded by fieldnotes. Indeed, sometimes this may have to be recorded in considerable detail if the audio-tape is to be comprehensible, as Walker and Adelman indicate in reporting their research on 'open' classrooms:

'Initially we experimented with sound tape recordings-keeping records over several weeks. These proved interesting in this context because, to a surprising extent they were incomprehensible. We do not mean this in the strictly technical sense of noise and distortion; we could hear the words but for much of the time we simply could not make complete sense of what was being said. We had previously made similar recordings in more orthodox classrooms and found them quite self-explanatory, even when reduced to transcript, but in this situation we were unable to apply any of the usual techniques of analysis. . . . For the most part transcripts prepared from tape recordings made of the teacher in this class revealed talk that was, for much of the time, fragmented, truncated, interrupted, unclear and cluttered with curious hesitations and pauses. Yet we knew from extensive observation that this class was one where a complex division of labour and considerable differentiation of tasks were in operation. From observation our impression was that talk in these classrooms was articulate and fluent, moreover, in all the time we had observed we could not recall any complaint that a child had been unable to understand the teacher, or misunderstood what she was saying. The transcripts came to us as something of a surprise. '

(Walker and Adelman 1972:8–9)

It was in response to this experience that Walker and Adelman synchronized film records with sound recordings. They often discovered then that identifying who was being addressed allowed them to make sense of what was being talked about: 'The talk we found strangely frustrating in transcript because it seemed fragmented, awkward and illogical, often came alive when seen in context, seeming economical, vivid and apt' (1972:10).

There are also, of course, technical limits to the scope of the interactions that can be recorded. Walker and Adelman's example of school classrooms provides a striking example of this too. Where lessons are very formal and predominantly oral, the whole lesson can be captured on tape with high fidelity. As we move towards the progressive end of the spectrum, however, not only does the quality and so the intelligibility of the recording decline, because of higher background noise produced by increased movement of pupils about the room, but the scope of the recording becomes more restricted. It is no longer possible to capture the whole lesson; one can only record fragments of it since the teacher and the pupils move about the room and the very organization of the lesson is decentralized. And there are many more social occasions that are like informal than formal teaching. Moreover, even in the case of recordings of traditional teaching, it is a mistake to assume that the whole event has been captured on tape. Not only is non-verbal behaviour- such as reading and written work—missing, but some talk may escape the recording, such as that between the teacher and individual pupils, or among pupils themselves. Similarly, in audio recordings of court proceedings, the public talk will be preserved, but not usually the private talk, between judge and counsel at the bench, among lawyers, and between them and their clients. How significant this is depends on the purpose of the research, of course, but the selectivity involved must not be forgotten since it may have implications for what conclusions can be legitimately drawn from the data.

While video-recording and filming avoid some of these problems, they are, of course, more expensive and likely to be more intrusive. Moreover, they share another somewhat ironic feature with audio-recording: they produce too much data. Schatzman and Strauss's remarks about taping fieldnotes—that transcription still remains to be done and that keeping in touch with the data so that theoretical sampling can proceed becomes more difficult—are even more true where events in settings are recorded themselves. While transcription is not always essential—one can simply treat the tape as a document, indexing, summarizing, and/or copying sections of it (see p. 163)—even then a considerable amount of time is required, probably more than is involved in writing up extended fieldnotes. When using audio- and video-recording techniques, it is very easy to record more data than one can ever actually use. One may also find that one's purpose and findings are constrained by the very techniques used. The use of audio- and video-recording devices does not avoid the dilemma of detail versus scope, though it may obscure it. While they provide data of great concreteness and detail, precisely because of this they may obscure longer term patterns; detailed pictures of individual trees are provided but no sense gained of the shape of the forest.

We noted in Chapter 1 that in ethnography the ethnographer is the research instrument. What we have said about audio- and video-recording techniques should make clear that they are no replacement for the participant observer and his or her fieldnotes. They may, however, be a useful supplement, depending on the nature of the setting and the purposes of the research. Used selectively, to provide detailed data on particularly important events or a sample of events, or used as a check on fieldnotes, they can be very helpful.

Interview Data

In the case of the highly structured interviews typical of survey research, the problem of recording responses is minimized because they are usually brief and generally fall into one or other pre-coded category. The interviewer simply rings one or other code, or at most writes in a few words in the space provided. With ethnographic interviews, on the other hand, generating lengthy responses not structured to fit a pregiven set of categories, the problem of recording looms large. It is, of course, possible to take notes and here much the same considerations—what is to be noted, when, and how—arise as in the case of observational fieldnotes. Once again reliance will most likely have to be placed on jotted notes, and the dilemma of summarizing versus verbatim reporting is just as acute. Similarly, note taking can prove disruptive, much as in the 'tutorial cited by Olefin and Whittaker (1968), with the interviewee becoming self-conscious about what is being written down; though the effects are probably lessened because note taking is a standard feature of interviews. However, the need to take notes makes the kind of reflexive interviewing we advocated in Chapter 5 very difficult, if not impossible, since much of the interviewer's attention is taken up with recording what has been said; especially since not just the informant's responses, but also the interviewer's questions should be recorded.

Given these problems, the advantages of audio-recording are considerable. While interviewees will sometimes not give permission (because, for example, 'you can't argue with a tape'), agreement is generally forthcoming once it is explained that the purpose is simply to aid note taking and that confidentiality will be maintained. Moreover, taperecording, particularly using a portable cassette recorder, may actually reduce reactivity rather than increase it. When the recorder is not in the informant's immediate line of sight, he or she is more likely to forget that the recording is being made than when the interviewer is hastily scribbling throughout the conversations. The tape recorder provides a more complete, concrete, and detailed record than fieldnotes, though once again non-verbal aspects and features of the physical surroundings are omitted. For this reason it is usually advisable to supplement the tape recording with jotted notes covering these matters.

Problems of processing the tapes arise, of course. Once again transcription may be necessary, though sometimes taking notes from the tape will prove adequate. Either way, rather more time is involved than simply filling out jotted notes, though the product is far more effective as a record of the interview.

Documents

Some documents are freely available and can be retained for later use. This is often true, for example, of such items as promotional material, guides of one kind or another, and circulars. Other documents can be bought relatively cheaply. Even where documentary sources are not produced in large numbers, the researcher may be able to produce copies for retention. Photocopiers are available in some settings, of course, and the ethnographer may be allowed access to them. Alternatively, it may sometimes be possible to borrow documents for short periods in order to copy them. Of course, there are constraints of time and finance here. Even if the copying can be done at no cost, time spent photocopying is time that otherwise might have been spent reading the documents, or in participant observation, or interviewing. For this reason, copying documents *in toto is* not necessarily the most effective recording strategy. While it avoids the dangers of omitting something important or losing the context of what is recorded, this has to be balanced against costs in time and money.

Frequently, because multiple copies are not available and photocopying is not possible, or is too costly, there is no alternative to note taking. Here too, though, there are different strategies available. One can index a document so that the relevant sections of it can be consulted as appropriate at later stages of the research. This can be done relatively quickly, but it requires easy and repeated access to the documentary sources. Alternatively, one may summarize relevant sections of material or copy them out by hand. The choice between summarizing and copying revolves around a dilemma that we have already met in recording observational and interview data. By summarizing one can cover much more material in the same time, thus releasing scarce time for work of other kinds. On the other hand, summarizing involves some loss of information and introduces interpretation. In producing a summary one must not only decide on the important points that require mentioning, but also translate these into general categories.

These three modes of note taking—indexing, copying, and summarizing—are not mutually exclusive, of course, and each should be used according to the accessibility of the documents and the anticipated nature of the use to which the notes will be put. Both these considerations may vary across different documents or even sections of documents. Where access to the documents is difficult and the precise wording used is likely to be important, there is little alternative to making painstaking copies. Where the need is for background information, summaries might be sufficient. Incidentally, it should be noted that notes need not necessarily be written on the spot; where access to documents is restricted it may be more efficient to read the indexes, summaries, or relevant sections into a portable taperecorder. In general, these will need to be written or typed out later and similar considerations arise as in the case of taperecording fieldnotes.

Analytic Notes and Memos

While reading documents, making fieldnotes, or transcribing audio or video tapes, promising theoretical ideas often arise. It is important to make note of these because they may prove useful when analysing the data. At that stage any contributions should be gratefully accepted! It is important though, to distinguish analytic notes from accounts provided by participants and from observer descriptions. This can be done typographically by encasing them in square or double brackets, for example, or by labelling them in some way.

Equally important is regular review and development of analytic ideas in the form of analytic memos. These are not fully developed working papers, but periodic written notes whereby progress is assessed, emergent ideas are identified, research strategy is sketched out, and so on. It is all too easy to let one's fieldnotes, and other types of data, pile up day by day and week by week. The very accumulation of material usually imparts a very satisfactory sense of progress, which can be measured in physical terms, as notebooks are filled, interviews completed, periods of observation ticked off, or different research settings investigated. But it is a grave error to let this work pile up without regular reflection and review: under such circumstances that sense of progress may prove illusory, and a good deal of the data collection could be unnecessarily aimless.

As we have emphasized, the formulation of precise problems, hypotheses, and an appropriate research strategy, is an emergent feature of the research programme itself. This process of progressive focusing means that the collection of data must be guided by the unfolding but explicit identification of topics for inquiry. The regular production of research memoranda will force the ethnographer to go through such a process of explication, and prevent any aimless drifting through the collection of data. Ideally, every period of observation should result in both processed notes, and reflexive monitoring of the research process. As such memoranda accumulate, they will constitute preliminary analyses, providing the researcher with guidelines through the corpus of data. If this is done there is no danger of being confronted at the end of the day with a more or less undifferentiated collection of material, with only one's memory to guide analysis.

The construction of such notes therefore constitutes precisely that sort of internal dialogue, or thinking aloud, that is the essence of reflexive ethnography. Such activity should help one avoid lapsing into the 'natural attitude', and 'thinking as usual' in the field. Rather than coming to take one's understanding on trust, one is forced to question *what* one knows, *how* such knowledge has been acquired, the *degree of certainty* of such knowledge, and what further lines of inquiry are implied.

These analytic notes may be appended to the daily fieldnotes, or they may be incorporated into yet a fourth variety of written account, the fieldwork journal. Such a journal or diary provides a running account of the conduct of the research. This includes not only a record of the fieldwork, but also of the ethnographer's own personal feelings and involvement. The latter is not simply a matter of gratuitous introspection or narcissistic self-absorption. As we point out elsewhere in this book, feelings of personal comfort, anxiety, surprise, shock, or revulsion are of analytic significance. In the first place, our feelings enter into and colour the social relationships we engage in during fieldwork. Second, such personal and subjective responses will inevitably influence one's choice of what may be noteworthy, what is regarded as problematic and strange, and what appears to be mundane or obvious. One often relies implicitly on such feelings, and their existence and possible influence must be acknowledged and, if possible, explicated in written form. Similarly, feelings of anxiety can pose limitations on data collection, leading to a highly restricted sort of tunnel vision. Although some commentators have drawn attention to the importance of recording one's feelings (e.g. Johnson 1975), the following remark from Olesen and Whittaker remains broadly true: 'The reading of most fieldwork studies leaves the impression that fieldworkers glide silkily and gracefully through the process without a twinge of anxiety or a single *faux pas*' (1968:44). Yet it seems unlikely that the intense personal involvement and commitment called for by ethnography commonly proceeds in such a smooth and 'silky' manner.

One of us (Atkinson) found some explicit reference to personal feelings of some value, for instance, in studying the Edinburgh medical school. One's own personal reactions to clinical encounters—fascination, revulsion, and embarrassment for example—cannot simply be used to extrapolate to the feelings of others such as doctors and medical students. However, they can be used to alert one to possible issues, such as the process of socialization that has been referred to as 'training for detached concern', or the 'cloak of competence', whereby medical practitioners' most extreme feelings may be masked or neutralized. Participation can be used to simulate the experience of other participants, and thus the researcher's own feelings can be an important form of data in their own right:

> '(O.C. I *feel* quite bored and depressed on the ward tonight. I wonder if this has anything to do with the fact that there are only two attendants working now. With only two attendants on, there are fewer diversions and less bantering. Perhaps this is why the attendants always complain about there not being enough of them. After all, there is never more work here than enough to occupy two attendants' time so it's not the fact that they can't get their work done that bothers them.)
>
> (O.C. Although I don't show it, I tense up when the residents approach me when they are covered with food or excrement. Maybe this is what the attendants feel and why they often treat the residents as lepers.)'
>
> (Bogdan and Taylor 1975:67)

There is, then, a constant interplay between the personal and emotional on the one hand, and the intellectual on the other. Private response is thus transformed, by reflexive analysis, into potential public knowledge. The fieldwork journal is the vehicle for such transformation. At a more mundane level, perhaps, the carefully made fieldwork journal will enable the conscientious ethnographer painstakingly to retrace and explicate the development of the research design, the emergence of analytic themes, and the systematic collection of data. The provision of such a 'natural history' of the research is a crucial component of the final report.

Storing and Retrieving Data Records

It is usual to organize written data records chronologically as a running record in which the data is stored by time of collection. Once analysis begins, however, reorganization of the data in terms of topics and themes generally becomes necessary. The first step here is to segment the data. Often there are 'natural' breaks in the material that can be used to break it up into chunks that can then be allocated to particular categories. This is usually the case with participant observation fieldnotes that often consist of notes on a sequence of incidents, each of which can be treated as a separate segment. Sometimes, particularly in the case of transcripts, 'natural' breaks are so few and far between that, simply for practical purposes, the data must be broken up in a more artificial way. Little seems to be lost by this.

The first categories in terms of which the data is normally reorganized are usually relatively descriptive, relating to particular people or types of people, places, activities, and topics of concern. The reorganization of the data in this way provides an important infrastructure for later data retrieval. However, it can also play an active role in the process of discovery, as the Webbs note:

> 'It enables the scientific worker to break up his subject-matter, so as to isolate and examine at his leisure its various component parts, and to recombine the facts when they have been thus released from all accustomed categories, in new and experimental groupings. . . .'

> (Webb and Webb 1932:83)

Moreover the selection of categories is of some significance:

> 'As I gathered my early research data, I had to decide how I was to organize the written notes. In the very early stage of exploration, I simply put all the notes, in chronological order, in a single folder. As I was to go on to study a number of different groups and problems, it was obvious that this was no solution at all.

> I had to subdivide the notes. There seemed to be two main possibilities. I could organize the notes topically, with folders for politics, rackets, the church, the family, and so on. Or I could organize the notes in terms of the groups on which they were based, which would mean having folders on the Nortons, the Italian Community Club, and so on. Without really thinking the problem through, I began filing material on the group basis, reasoning that I could later redivide it on a topical basis when I had a better knowledge of what the relevant topics should be.

> As the material in the folders piled up, I came to realize that the organization of notes by social groups fitted in with the way in which my study was developing. For example, we have a college-boy member of the Italian Community Club saying: "These racketeers give our district a bad name. They should really be cleaned out of here". And we have a member of the Nortons saying: "These racketeers are really all right. When you need help, they'll give it to you. The legitimate business-man—he won't even give you the time of day." Should these quotes be filed under "Racketeers, attitudes toward?" If so, they would only show that there are conflicting attitudes toward racketeers in Cornerville. Only a questionnaire (which is hardly feasible for such a topic) would show the distribution of attitudes in the district. Furthermore, how important would it be to know how many people felt one way or another on this topic? It seemed to me of much greater scientific interest to be able to relate the attitude to the group in which the individual participated. This shows why two individuals could be expected to have quite different attitudes on a given topic. '

> (Whyte 1981:308)

The allocation of data to categories in ethnography differs from the kind of coding typical in quantitative research and even some other qualitative research (Goode and Hatt 1952). Here there is no requirement that items be assigned to one and only one category, or that there be explicit rules for assigning them:

> 'We code (the fieldnotes) inclusively; that is to say if we have any reason to think that anything might go under the heading, we will put it in. We do not lose anything. We also code them in multiple categories, under anything that might be felt to be cogent. As a general rule, we want to get back anything that could conceivably bear on a given interest. . . . It is a search procedure for getting all of the material that is pertinent. '

> (Becker 1968:245)

Indeed, Lofland (1971) argues that in the case of analytic categories it pays to be 'wild', to include anything, however long a shot.

The identification of categories is a central element of the process of analysis. As a result, the list of categories in terms of which the data is organized generally undergoes considerable change over the course of the research. In particular, there is typically a shift towards more analytic categories as theory develops. In some research on staffroom talk in an inner-city secondary school (Hammersley 1980), the exchanges recorded in the fieldnotes were initially categorized according to whether they related to the teachers' views of pupils on the one hand, or to other aspects of teaching and the life of teachers on the other. As the analysis progressed, however, more refined and theoretically relevant categories were developed, concerning, for example, the 'crisis' that the teachers saw facing them, the way in which teachers traded 'news' about pupils, and how they sought to explain why pupil performances were so 'bad' despite their best efforts.

Organizing and reorganizing the data in terms of categories can be done in a number of different ways. The simplest is 'coding the record'. Here data is coded, that is assigned to a category, on the running record itself, or a copy of it. Comments relating the data to descriptive or analytic categories are written in the margin or on the back of each page. (Clearly, provision has to be made for this in the format employed for writing up notes and transcribing tapes.) The advantage of this procedure is that it can be done relatively quickly and it allows analysis of an item in the immediate context in which it is recorded. On the other hand, the amount of time subsequently taken up with reading through the running record finding items relevant to a particular category may be prohibitive with anything but the smallest data sets.

In more sophisticated versions of 'coding the record', an analytic index is produced. Here each data segment is assigned an identifying mark: a number, or letter, or combination of the two. (It is often useful, where different types of data have been collected—for example, observational and interview fieldnotes—to distinguish between them so that the status of any data segment can be identified at a glance.) A list of categories is prepared, and constantly up-dated as new categories emerge, with the codes for the segments of data relevant to each category listed under it, these too being updated as new data comes in. This requires a little more time and effort than simply coding the record. However, it greatly facilitates the speed and rigour of data retrieval. Indeed, analytic memos can be combined with an index, a file card being prepared for each category, providing a definition, relevant further information, and discussion of the relationship of the concept to others, etc. At the same time, the items of data relevant to that category can be listed by number on the card. The cards would need to be kept in some kind of order, perhaps alphabetical, to facilitate ready access.

An alternative method of data organization, used by Whyte, the Webbs, and many other ethnographers, is physical sorting. Here, multiple copies need to be made of each segment of data and a copy is filed under all of the categories to which it is relevant. With this system, when it is time for detailed analysis of a particular category all the relevant data is readily available, there is no need to sift through the running record to find the relevant data segments. An additional advantage is that all the items relevant to the same category can be put side by side and compared. On the other hand, considerable time and expense may be involved in producing the number of copies of the data necessary (this number depends on the number of categories any particular segment is relevant to). Furthermore, a large number of file folders and perhaps several filing cabinets may be required to store the data.

More recently, more sophisticated systems of data filing and retrieval have been developed. For example, punched cards have been used (Becker 1968:245-46). This is a development of physical sorting, but here only one copy of the data additional to the running record is required. Each segment of data is written on, or affixed to, a punched card. The holes around the edge of the card are used to represent the categories and an index noting which numbered hole relates to which category is maintained. Where a data segment is relevant to a particular category, the hole is clipped; the holes representing categories to which the item is not relevant are left intact, or vice versa.

With this system all the data can be kept together in the form of cards, in no particular order. When the materials relevant to a particular category are required a long needle pushed through the appropriate hole and lifted brings out or leaves the relevant cards (depending on whether the holes representing relevant categories have been clipped or left intact). Moreover, as with physical sorting, all the relevant data can be scanned simultaneously, but without the need for multiple copies and at a considerable saving in storage space. Furthermore, with this system sub-sorts identifying data relevant to two or more categories can be carried out. On the other hand, however, punched cards, needle, and clippers are fairly expensive and some time is taken in putting the data on the cards and punching them, though once this is done retrieval is easier than with any other system with the exception of physical sorting.

As one might expect, computers have also started to be used in data filing. Some ethnographers have used main frame computers to prepare analytic indexes. The advantage over manually prepared indexes is that the computer is able to carry out sub-sorts, listing items of data relevant to two or more categories. Of course, this requires computer time and an appropriate program. Alternatively, the data can be typed directly into the computer. Each segment is given an identifying number and an index is prepared on the computer listing the categories and the items relevant to each. With an appropriate program the computer is able to present all the material relevant to a particular category, sequentially on a video screen or to print it out. In principle this system is the one that gives most ready access to the data, especially given the declining cost of microcomputers. It combines the advantages of all the other systems. The disadvantages lie in the problems of expense and possible system breakdown, and in the fact that this strategy for handling data is still largely unproven. At the moment programs for filing, sorting, and retrieving ethnographic data are not easily available, but it is likely that they soon will be. An example of such a program is discussed in Drass (1980).

As with most other aspects of ethnographic technique, there is no ideal storage and retrieval system; the advantages and disadvantages of each strategy will take on varying importance according to the purposes of the research, the nature of the data, and the resources available to the researcher. Indeed, different methods may be appropriate for different data sets within the same research project. As a general guide, where the amount of data is relatively small, coding the record and analytic indexing are strong options. Where there is a large amount of data but each item is relevant to only one or two categories, physical sorting is probably the best technique. Where the amount of data is large and many items are likely to be relevant to a large number of categories (this depends on the categories as much as the data, punched cards have great advantages. With cheap and ready access to a microcomputer, and available back-up maintenance, computer filing is probably the best method all round, though as yet this possibility remains largely unexplored.

Conclusion

While it is probably impossible to render explicit all the data acquired in fieldwork, every effort must be made to record it. Memory is an inadequate basis for analysis. Of course, data recording is necessarily selective and always involves some interpretation, however minimal. There is no set of basic, indubitable data available from which all else can be deduced. What is recorded, and how, will depend in large part on the purposes and priorities of the research, and the conditions in which it is carried out. Moreover, in using various recording techniques we must remain aware of the effects their use may be having on participants and be prepared to modify the strategy accordingly. Similarly, there is no single correct way of retrieving the data for analysis. The various systems differ in appropriateness according to one's purposes, the nature of the data collected, the facilities and finance available, as well as personal convenience. And here, too, their use must be monitored in terms of changing purposes and conditions.

As with other aspects of ethnographic research, then, recording, storing, and retrieving the data must be reflexive processes in which decisions are made, monitored, and, if necessary, re-made in light of methodological and ethical considerations. At the same time, however, these techniques play an important role in facilitating reflexivity. They provide a crucial resource in assessing typicality of examples, checking construct-indicator linkages, searching for negative cases, triangulating across different data sources and stages of the fieldwork, and assessing the role of the researcher in shaping the nature of the data and findings. In short, they facilitate the process of analysis, a topic to which we turn in the next chapter.

Finding Your Way Through the Forest: Analysis

David M. Fetterman

I went to the woods because I wished to live deliberately, to front only the essential facts of life, and see if I could not learn what it had to teach.

—Henry David Thoreau

Analysis is one of the most engaging features of ethnography. It begins from the moment a fieldworker selects a problem to study and ends with the last word in the report or ethnography. Ethnography involves many levels of analysis. Some are simple and informal, others require some statistical sophistication. Ethnographic analysis is iterative, building on ideas throughout the study. Analyzing data in the field enables the ethnographer to know precisely which methods to use next, as well as when and how to use them. Analysis tests hypotheses and perceptions to construct an accurate conceptual framework about what is happening in the social group under study. Analysis in ethnography is as much a test of the ethnographer as it is a test of the data.

The fieldworker must find a way through a wilderness of data, theory, observation, and distortion. Throughout the analytical trek, the fieldworker must make choices—between logical and enticing paths, between valid and invalid but fascinating data, and between genuine patterns of behavior and series of apparently similar but distinct reactions. Choosing the right path requires discrimination, experience, attention to both detail and the larger context, and intuition. The best guide through the thickets of analysis is at once the most obvious and most complex of strategies: clear thinking.

Thinking

First and foremost, analysis is a test of the ethnographer's ability to think—to process information in a meaningful and useful manner. The ethnographer confronts a vast array of complex information and needs to make some sense of it all—piece by piece.

The initial stage in analysis involves simple perception. However, even perception is selective. The ethnographer selects and isolates pieces of information from all the data in the field. The ethnographer's personal or idiosyncratic approach, together with an assortment of academic theories and models, focuses and limits the scope of inquiry. However, the field presents a vast amount of material, and in understanding day-to-day human interaction, elementary thinking skills are as important as ethnographic concepts and methods.

A focus on relevant, manageable topics is essential and is possible through the refinement of the unit of analysis. But then the fieldworker must probe those topics by comparing and contrasting data, trying to fit pieces of data into the bigger puzzle—all the while hypothesizing about the best fit and the best picture.

Many useful techniques help the ethnographer to make sense of the forests of data, from triangulation to use of statistical software packages requiring a mainframe computer. All these techniques, however, require critical thinking skills—notably, the ability to synthesize and evaluate information—and a large dose of common sense.

Triangulation

Triangulation is basic in ethnographic research. It is at the heart of ethnographic validity, testing one source of information against another to strip away alternative explanations and prove a hypothesis. Typically, the ethnographer compares information sources to test the quality of the information (and the person sharing it), to understand more completely the part an actor plays in the social drama, and ultimately to put the whole situation into perspective.

During my study of dropouts, students often came to show me their grades. One young friend told me he earned straight A's that semester. I compared his verbal information with a written transcript, the teacher's verbal confirmation, and unsolicited information from his peers. His grades were excellent, but information from his teacher and his peers suggested an "attitude problem." According to them, "success went to his head." Thus one program goal—better grades— had a problematic side effect—an overbearing attitude. This outcome was in conflict with another program goal: cooperation and harmonious relationships with others in the program. This piece of information was extremely useful to me in understanding the strengths and weaknesses of the program. In this case, triangulation not only verified the student's claims about his grades, but also provided useful data about his role in the program. This information became more important in later conversations, in which he provided data that were more difficult to verify using conventional inquiry methods. A natural by-product of triangulation in this example was additional documentation about the student's overall growth or progress in the program, as well as about the health of the program overall.

Triangulation works with any topic, in any setting, and on any level: It is as effective in studying the high school classroom as it is in studying higher education administration. The trick is to compare comparable items and levels during analysis. In studying postsecondary institutions, I usually break down my unit of analysis into manageable pieces, such as school, department, or laboratory. Then I select the most significant concerns that emerged during the initial review period. I focus on those concerns throughout the study, refining my understanding of them by working with people in the field. I confirm some hypotheses, learn about new dimensions of the problems, and crystallize my overall conception of how the place operates by constantly triangulating information. Later, I use triangulated information about an individual faculty member and generalize some of these data to universitywide concerns.

One faculty member complained about the lack of funding for his laboratory during a funding hiatus, while he was between grants. A review of past records and interviews with other principal investigators to learn what they thought of the situation and with other faculty members to discover what they had done during past crises revealed that his concern was widespread. Funding crises had a direct impact on the principal investigator's ability to maintain academic continuity in the department. A principal investigator's research program can come to a grinding halt without funds to pay the researchers. A comparison of this faculty member's complaint with other faculty complaints and internal memoranda established that funding was a real problem for the research laboratories and merited further investigation. Additional interviews with various government agency officials and university deans revealed that from a bureaucratic perspective the problem was merely a paperwork issue. Whether or not to fund a certain project was not in question. The bureaucratic structure simply created normal delays in processing renewal papers for additional funding. Therefore, the issue was really how to handle a paperwork delay, not how to survive between different grants. The difference between these two situations is enormous. In most cases money for these laboratories was promised and would be coming to the principal investigator—eventually. One dean indicated that he was already aware of working on this problem. Unfortunately, he had never discussed it with other deans, directors, or principal investigators. Thus the principal investigators and their researchers were left to worry about what was essentially a paper problem. The larger issue that emerged from this triangulation effort was the lack of communication within the school and between the school and a variety of government agencies. The right hand didn't know what the left hand was doing. Here, the by-products of triangulation were as useful as its primary use in validating information.

Triangulation always improves the quality of data and the accuracy of ethnographic findings. During the emergency room study, triangulation was invaluable in clearing up an elementary misunderstanding. The department's assistant director complained about one of the residents during an interview: "If you want to find fraud, you should look at Henry. Henry works half the time he is supposed to for twice the pay." This information came from a presumably credible source. However, I thought it odd that he hadn't acted on this information, given his role in the organization. Fortunately, a bookkeeper overheard the assistant director's comment and pulled me aside the next day to say, "I thought you should know Henry is one of our best doctors. The only reason the [assistant director] bad-mouths him is because Henry is dating his ex-wife." Observations of the assistant director's ex-wife picking up Henry at the end of his shift, a review of the time records, and interviews with the nurses and the director all confirmed the bookkeeper's information. In this case, both serendipitous and systematic triangulation were invaluable in providing a reality test and a baseline of understanding.

Triangulation can occur naturally in conversation as easily as in intensive investigatory work. However, the ethnographer must identify it in subtle contexts. A recent discussion during a meeting with school superintendents in Washington, D.C., illustrates this point. A prominent superintendent, managing one of the largest districts in the nation, had just finished explaining why school size made no difference in education. He said that he had one 1,500-pupil school and one 5,000-pupil school in his district that he was particularly proud of, and that the school size had no effect on school spirit, the educative process, or his ability to manage. He also explained that he had to build two or three new schools next year, either three small schools or one small school and one large one. A colleague interrupted to ask which he preferred. The superintendent replied, "small ones, of course; they are much easier to handle." He had betrayed himself in this one phrase. Although the administrative party line was that size made no difference—management is management no matter how big or small the unit—this superintendent revealed a very different personal opinion in response to a casual question. Such self-contained triangulation, in which an individual's own statements support or undermine his or her stated position, is a useful measure of internal consistency. Later comments by this administrator continued to undermine his official position. He said that students in the small school blamed their athletic losses on school size. According to one student, "The big schools have the resources." This brief anecdote provided an additional insight into the district cosmology. Although people held different views about ideal school size, the issue of size was a critical focal point shared by all—from student to superintendent. This type of information provides a handle that aids the ethnographer in grasping a community's fundamental ideas and values. (See Webb et al., 1966, for a detailed discussion about triangulation.)

Patterns

Ethnographers look for patterns of thought and behavior. Patterns are a form of ethnographic reliability. Ethnographers see patterns of thought and action repeat in various situations and with various players. Looking for patterns is a from of analysis. The ethnographer begins with a mass of undifferentiated ideas and behavior, and then collects pieces of information, comparing, contrasting, and sorting gross categories and minutiae until a discernible thought or behavior becomes identifiable. Next the ethnographer must listen and observe, and then compare his or her observations with this poorly defined model. Exceptions to the rule emerge, variations on a theme are detectable. These variants help to circumscribe the activity and clarify its meaning. The process requires further sifting and sorting to make a match between categories. The theme or ritualistic activity finally emerges, consisting of a collection of such matches between the model (abstracted from reality) and the ongoing observed reality.

Any cultural group's patterns of thought and behavior are interwoven strands. As soon as the ethnographer finishes analyzing and identifying one pattern, another pattern emerges for analysis and identification. The fieldworker can then compare the two patterns. In practice, the ethnographer works simultaneously on many patterns. The level of understanding increases geometrically as the ethnographer moves up the conceptual ladder—mixing and matching patterns and building theory from the ground up. (See Glaser & Strauss, 1967, for a discussion about grounded theory.)

Observation of the daily activity of a middle-class family might reveal several patterns. The couple goes to work every day, dropping off their child in the day-care facility. They receive their paychecks every other week. Rituals such as grocery shopping and doing laundry recur every weekend. Combining these preliminary patterns into a meaningful whole makes other patterns apparent. The stresses and strains of a family in which both husband and wife must hold down full-time jobs and bring up a family, the emphasis on organization and planning, even of usually spontaneous activities, and a variety of other behaviors and practices become more meaningful and understandable in this context. The observer can make preliminary inferences about the entire economic system by analyzing the behavior that is subsumed within the pattern, as well as the patterns themselves. Ethnographers acquire a deeper understanding of and appreciation for a culture as they weave each part of the ornate human tapestry together, by observing and analyzing the patterns of everyday life.

Key Events

Key or focal events that the fieldworker can use to analyze an entire culture occur in every social group. Geertz (1973) eloquently used the cockfight to understand and portray Balinese life. Key events come in all shapes and sizes. Some tell more about a culture than others, but all provide a focus for analysis (see also Geertz, 1957).

Key events, like snapshots or videotapes, concretely convey a wealth of information. Some images are clear representations of social activity, others provide a tremendous amount of embedded meaning. Once the event is recorded, the ethnographer can enlarge or reduce any portion of the picture. A rudimentary knowledge of the social situation will enable the ethnographer to infer a great deal from key events. In many cases, the event is a metaphor for a way of life or a specific social value. Key events provide a lens through which to view a culture. They range from the ritual observance of the sabbath to the emergency response to a burning building in a small kibbutz. The sabbath is a ritualized key event that occurs every week. Ceremonial garb (or lack thereof), the orchestration of prayers, and the social activity that follows the service provide a highly condensed version of the culture's religious life. A fire is a key event that compels the ethnographer to observe, analyze, and act simultaneously. A participant observer has contradictory obligations. The ideal stance is simply to observe and record what happens in such a situation, but as a participant the researcher has an ethical obligation to help put out the fire. These obligations need not be mutually exclusive, however. Typically, the ethnographer simply joins in at the appropriate level depending on the danger, the amount of experience in the field with a certain group, and the behavioral norms in that situation. A fire in a small kibbutz settlement brings everyone running out of their houses to form a bucket brigade until the heavy fire-fighting equipment arrives. Involvement in this situation allows simultaneous observation and analysis. Informal leadership roles become apparent in such a crisis. The event is also a test of the cooperation the community professes to depend on. The technological sophistication of the people who fight the fire is a good indicator of their knowledge base, values, economic resources, and/or degree of social interaction or isolation from the mainstream. Other rare events—like funerals, weddings, and rites of passage—also offer excellent opportunities for in-depth analysis.

A classic key event in modern offices is the introduction of computers. Individuals act out most of the hidden dimensions of social life in these situations. Formal and informal hierarchies become apparent through action and memoranda. Who decides who will have a computer? Who will use a computer as a status symbol first and a functional piece of equipment last? Subterranean tensions—that have nothing to do with computers and that remain buried in daily interaction—come to the surface during such key events. Observing the schism between people who fear this innovation and those who embrace it, how staff members accept or reject the computer, and how its use changes the group's social dynamics can be an all-consuming but revealing task.

A fistfight erupted during a basketball game at one of the CIP sites. On the surface, this key event indicated the volatility of the social group and the occasion. On a deeper level, the fight was more revealing about the program's social dynamics. One fighter had been in the program for some time, the other was new. The new member threatened to have his group take over the program and "trash it." The old member was protective of the program, viewing it, as his peers did, as a "a big family." Thus he protected the program in a way both parties would understand. The fight was actually a minidrama in the bigger struggle between the two groups. It was also a rite of passage into the program: The display of loyalty said more about the program to the new participants than the fight itself.

Key events are extraordinarily useful for analysis. Not only do they help the fieldworker understand a social group, but the fieldworker in turn can use them to explain the culture to others. The key event thus becomes a metaphor for the culture. Key events also illustrate how participation, observation, and analysis are inextricably bound together during fieldwork.

Maps

Visual representations are useful tools in ethnographic research. Having to draw a map of the community tests an ethnographer's understanding of the area's physical layout. It can also help the ethnographer chart a course through the community. Like writing, mapmaking forces the ethnographer to abstract and reduce reality to a manageable size—a piece of paper. The process of drawing also crystallizes images, networks, and understandings and suggests new paths to explore. Maps, flowcharts, and matrices all help to crystallize and display consolidated information.

Flowcharts

Flowcharts are useful in studies of production line operations. Mapping out what happens to a book in a research library—from the time it is received on the shipping dock to the time it is cataloged and available on the shelf—can provide a baseline of understanding about the system. Flowcharting a social welfare program is also common in evaluation. The analytic process of mapping the flow of activity and information can also serve as a vehicle to initiate additional discussions.

Organizational Charts

Drawing organizational charts—of a program, department, library, or kibbutz—is a useful analytic tool, as Chapter 2 discusses in the section on structure and function. It tests the ethnographer's knowledge of the system much as drawing a map or a flowchart does. Both formal and informal organizational hierarchies can be charted for comparison. In addition, organizational charts can measure changes over time, as people move in and out or up and down the hierarchy. Organizational charts clarify the structure and function of any institutional form of human organization.

Matrices

Matrices provide a simple, systematic, graphic way to compare and contrast data. The researcher can compare and cross-reference categories of information to establish a picture of a range of behaviors or thought categories. Matrices also help the researcher to identify emerging patterns in the data.

The construction of a matrix was valuable during the first stage of my study of state-funded art programs. Art programs fell into various categories, such as music, dance, theater, painting, and sculpture; these categories became column titles on a spread sheet. The rows consisted of other categories: geographical location, size, funds, consortia, and other relevant variables. I located the specific programs in the appropriate boxes or cells. This exercise provided an immediate picture of the range of variation across programs, the types of programs in each category, geographic clusters, and many other valuable pieces of information. In addition, these data helped me to select a smaller, stratified sample within the population for in-depth fieldwork.

Similarly, a matrix helped to identify themes across sites during the dropout study. Rites of passage were noted in the appropriate cell. By designing the matrix according to academic calendar years, I could record changes over time. The researcher can develop a matrix by hand on paper, on a spread sheet (paper or software), or with the assistance of a database software program. (See Miles & Huberman, 1984, for a detailed presentation of the use of matrices in qualitative research.)

Content Analysis

Ethnographers analyze written and electronic data in much the same way that they analyze observed behavior. They triangulate information within documents to test for internal consistency. They attempt to discover patterns within the text and seek key events recorded and memorialized in print.

The dropout program study produced volumes of written records to review: teaching and counseling manuals, administrative guides, research reports, newspaper articles, magazine articles, and hundreds of memoranda. Internal documents received special scrutiny to determine whether they were internally consistent with program philosophy. The review revealed significant patterns. For example, the role of religion in these programs was evident. The literature contained testimonial statements that the program owed its success to the "direct involvement of religious leaders." Lease agreements often specified a church in which to house the program. Letters from the organization's leader—himself a minister—were written in pastoral tones.

Similarly, the program philosophy was easy to detect after a study of the program's public documents, in conjunction with daily observation. The program espoused a self-help, middle-class approach to life with a flavor of the Puritan ethic. Program pamphlets contained routine references to "the work ethic," "individual responsibility for success," "marketable skills," and enabling the disenfranchised to "claim their fair share of the [economic] pie." In numerous instances, I recorded certain words and phrases to determine their frequency in the text. I often inferred the significance of a concept from its frequency and context in the text. The program's magazine articles, editorials, and memoranda documented key events such as celebrations of civil rights legislation and reverse discrimination court cases, racial incidents, and local ethnic events. The organization's official position on these events told much about its politics and fundamental values.

The ethnographer can analyze data culled from electronic media in precisely the same fashion as written documentation. Because this material is often in a database or in a format that can easily transfer into a database, extensive manipulation—sorting, comparing, contrasting, aggregating, and synthesizing—is even simpler. In my higher education studies, most content analysis takes place on-line or through downloading to a database. Management philosophy is easily detectable from on-line meeting minutes, budgets, arguments, and policy statements (and drafts). A brief review of a department's budget provides vital information about its values: People put their money in areas they care about. A comparison of content analysis data with interview and observational data can significantly enhance the quality of findings.

Statistics

Ethnographers use nonparametric statistics more often than parametric statistics because they typically work with small samples. Parametric statistics require large samples for statistical significance. The use of nonparametric statistics is also more consistent with the needs and concerns of most anthropologists. Anthropologists typically work with nominal and ordinal scales. Nominal scales consist of discrete categories, such as sex and religion. Ordinal scales also provide discrete categories as well as a range of variation within each category—for example, reform, conservative, orthodox variants within the category of Judaism. Ordinal scales do not determine the degree of difference between subcategories.

The Guttman (1944) scale is one example of a useful ordinal scale in ethnographic research. In studying folk medicators, I used a Guttman scale to illustrate pictorially the range of attitudes toward the use of modern Western medicine from most receptive to most resistant to change in the community. A correlation of the Guttman scale scores with such variables as age, education, immigration status, and related value system variables identified population segments that would be most interested in educational material about alternative medicating practices. This information provided a target group and suggested an efficient use of limited educational resources, while respecting the wishes of those who were not interested in learning more about modern medicating practices. (See Pelto, 1970, for additional discussion of the Guttman scale.)

A chi-square test provided an insight into enrollment trends in the study of gifted and talented education programs. The test indicated that Hispanics had the most statistically significant increase in that program (Fetterman, 1988). Another popular nonparametric statistical tool in anthropology is the Fisher Exact Probability Test. However, all statistical formulas require that certain assumptions are met before application to any situation. A disregard for these variables in the statistical equation is as dangerous as neglect of comparable assumptions in the human equation in conducting ethnographic fieldwork. Both errors result in distorted and misleading efforts at worst and waste valuable time at best.

Ethnographers use parametric statistics when they have large samples and limited time and resources to conduct all the interviews. Survey and questionnaire work often requires sophisticated statistical tests of significance. Ethnographers also use the results of parametric statistics to test certain hypotheses, cross-check their won observations, and generally provide additional insight.

Student test scores were essential to one portion of the CIP study. The sponsors wanted to know if the students' reading and math capabilities improved as a result of their participation in the program. Gains in reading scores were statistically significant. From the sponsor and the ethnographer's perspective, this was a useful finding. The gains in math scores were statistically significant, but less spectacular than the gains in reading scores. This particular finding provided the ethnographer a unique opportunity to interact with the psychometrician in a significant—

interpretive—fashion. The statistical calculation delivered an outcome, but not the process behind it. Ethnographic description was useful in explaining why the math gains were not as spectacular as those in reading. The answer was simple: The math teaching positions were vacant during most of the study. The program had difficulty recruiting and maintaining math teachers given the competitive market for these individuals.

The test outcomes were a product of traditional psychometric approaches, including control and comparison group data using analysis of covariance and standardized gain procedures. This information was both useful to sponsors and the ethnographer and valuable in providing a focal point for further inquiry and data comparison.

Problems with Statistics

The use of statistics in ethnography has many problems. Meeting the assumptions that a specific test requires is a particularly sticky problem. One of the most common assumptions of inferential statistics is that the sample is random. Typically, ethnography uses stratified judgmental sampling rather than a truly randomized selection. The use of parametric statistics requires large samples. However, most ethnographers work with small groups. The issues of expertise and appropriateness raise further difficulties.

In many instances, sophisticated statistical approaches are inappropriate in ethnography in particular, and in social science in general. The first criterion is always the appropriateness of the tool for the problem. The second criterion—a subset of the first—is the methodological soundness of the application. A third criterion involves ethics. Is use of a certain tool at a given time with a certain population ethical? The ethical question comes under discussion in Chapter 7.

No design or technique is good or bad per se. The application, however, can be useful or useless, appropriate or inappropriate. The use of an experimental design and related statistical formulas to study the impact of an educational program or treatment on a population of former dropouts, near dropouts, and "push outs" (those the schools are no longer obligated to serve because they are too old or too disruptive) is conceptually sound. In the abstract, this approach could shed light on possible gains in math and reading scores by students in the program (compared with scores by students in the program (compared with scores of students in the control group). However, the application of this design to generate sophisticated statistical inferences about most educational programs is inappropriate on strict methodological grounds. The assumptions of the design are rarely met. A classical experimental design involves a double-blind approach. The individual delivering the treatment, the individual receiving it, and the individual in the control group do not know who is really receiving treatment. In most educational treatments, teachers know whether they are delivering an educational treatment or not, and the students know whether they have been accepted into the educational program or not. Instead of a double-blind experiment, the treatment group receives a positive treatment; rejected students receive a negative treatment. Thus students receiving treatment may display a Hawthorne effect, while rejected students may display a John Henry effect—overcompensating to demonstrate that they can do well in spite of the rejection. These forms of reactivity and contamination severely undermine the credibility of any outcome. (See Fetterman, 1982b, for a detailed discussion of this problem. See also Cook & Campbell, 1979.)

Another problem with statistical tests is perceptual. Statistics demonstrate correlations, not causality. Yet people frequently fall into the trap of inferring causality from statistical correlation. Also, as Mark Twain said, "There are three kinds of lies—lies, dammed lies, and statistics." A competent individual can manipulate figures to say almost anything. Statistical findings can be mesmerizing for some individuals. Computer-generated findings are ten times as credible for no better reason than technological sophistication. Computer-generated statistical errors can be particularly troublesome (if not materially significant) because they are reproduced incorrectly throughout related databases for long periods of time before detection. Countervailing forces or tests cannot easily compensate for such systemic problems.

This brief review of problems should not dampen the spirits of an enterprising ethnographer. Ethnography has ample use for experimental designs, quasi-experimental designs, and associated statistical analyses, including multiple regression analysis and factor analysis (see Britan, 1978; Maxwell, Bashook, & Sandlow, 1986). This brief review merely highlights some of the complexity statistical analyses can create—in ethnography or any other social science. (For a useful presentation of statistics for the social sciences, see Blalock, 1979; Hopkins & Glass, 1978.)

Crystallization

Ethnographers crystallize their thoughts at various stages throughout an ethnographic endeavor. The crystallization may bring a mundane conclusion, a novel insight, or an earth-shattering epiphany. The crystallization is typically the result of a convergence of similarities that spontaneously strike the ethnographer as relevant or important to the study. Crystallization may be an exciting process or the result of painstaking, boring, methodical work. This research gestalt requires attention to all pertinent variables in an equation. Gross errors can be misleading and lethal to any investigation. For example, a long line of cars with their lights on, all proceeding down the same street in the same direction, might suggest a funeral procession. However logical this conclusion might appear, it may also be dead wrong. Additional data from informal interviews or more disciplined and detailed observations are necessary. For example, identification of a hearse in the procession or a confirming word from one of the individuals involved would immeasurably improve the credibility of this conclusion. Another significant piece of information involves time. If the observer leaves out one vital piece of information—say, that the researcher saw this long chain of cars with their lights on at night—the credibility and probability of this conclusion are severely eroded. Participation at the funeral itself lends a great deal of face validity to the conclusion or crystallized conception.

Every study has classic moments when everything falls into place. After months of thought and immersion in the culture, a special configuration gels. All the subtopics, miniexperiments, layers of triangulated effort, key events, and patterns of behavior form a coherent and often cogent picture of what is happening. One of the most exciting moments in ethnographic research is when an ethnographer discovers a counterintuitive conception of reality—a conception that defies common sense. Such moments make the long days and nights worthwhile. During a recent study of research administration in higher education, I found after months of work that the situation had a counterintuitive solution. The administration consisted of two separate divisions serving separate departments in the university. The director of the two divisions was contemplating merging them into one unit. Logically, the merger would achieve greater efficiency by eliminating redundant staff positions and sharing resources. I was asked to comment on this plan. During the course of the study, I found that not only two separate divisions, but also two separate cultures existed in conflict in research administration, as well as many subcultures. One group had a client-representative (or client-centered) approach to serving faculty. When a faculty member asked his or her client representative about a problem, the representative would find the answer. The representative would find the information from a colleague in administration if unable to answer the question, instead of sending the faculty member round-robin to seek the answer from other administrators. Thus the faculty member typically dealt with only one person. This group was a cohesive team, substituting for one another as necessary. The faculty was very pleased with this division's performance.

The second team was organized according to function, ranging from accounting to a sponsored projects office. In general, most staff members in this division were isolated or buffered from faculty. Their interactions were primarily with faculty secretaries and administrative assistants.

This division was rife with territories and factions. The division's most notable subcultures were the old guard and the new guard. The old guard believed that the existing system had worked for many years and wanted to maintain the status quo. The new guard expressed a desire to experiment with new systems, including computerizing many functions. The faculty was not satisfied with this division's performance. Faculty members with questions would have to know the right person to call or make several calls to find the right person for the function. Moreover, the warring factions often prevented any work from taking place because people on various sides wouldn't talk to each other.

Both divisions were aware of the merger potential. Because of a historical animosity between the two divisions, neither wanted the merger. The client-representative service group feared losing its tightly knit social organization. This division's faculty members feared losing the group's excellent service. Staff in the second division did not want a client-representative approach. They were accustomed to working within a specific function, without any knowledge of their peers' activities. From their perspective, the functional approach was as effective as the client-representative approach.

When the director and the dean asked me to comment on the proposed plan to consolidate research administration, I explained that research administration stood at an organizational crossroads. Many organizational configurations were possible to improve overall performance. However, merging the two divisions was not a solution. Although the merger seemed logical, it would not be productive. Combining the divisions would escalate existing culture conflict and significantly reduce overall efficiency. Mixing the client-representative group with the functionally oriented division would rip the social fabric of the groups apart and diminish their capacity to serve faculty. Similarly, the imposition of the client-representative approach on the functionally oriented group would catalyze conflict. The functionally oriented group would interpret collaboration as territorial invasion, prying, or even spying.

My recommendation was not to merge the two units, regardless of the short-term financial benefits. Instead, I suggested that the client-representative division remain untouched. The functionally oriented group needed to know that its social organization was respected, but it also needed assistance in reducing internal strife and developing smoother contact with clients. Both groups agreed with my descriptions and recommendations. The overall ethnographic description of research administration convinced the dean to make the counterintuitive decision not to merge the divisions.

This counterintuitive conclusion or crystallization derived from a detailed study of each culture and its various subcultures. The emic perspective helped to put the entire picture together in my formal etic or social scientific role. (Also see Fetterman, 1981b, for other case examples.)

Analysis has no single form or stage in ethnography. Multiple analyses and forms of analyses are essential. Analysis takes place throughout any ethnographic endeavor, from the selection of the problem to the final stages of writing. Analysis is iterative and often cyclical in ethnography (see Goetz & LeCompte, 1984; Hammersley & Atkinson, 1983; Taylor & Bogdan, 1984). The researcher builds a firm knowledge base in bits and pieces, asking questions, listening, probing, comparing and contrasting, synthesizing, and evaluating information. The ethnographer must run sophisticated tests on data long before leaving the field. However, a formal, identifiable stage of analysis does take place when the ethnographer physically leaves the field. Half the analysis at this stage involves additional triangulation, sifting for patterns, developing new matrices, and applying statistical tests to the data. The other half takes place during the final stages of writing an ethnography of an ethnographically informed report.

Computer Storage and Manipulation of Field Notes and Verbal Protocols: Three Cautions

CHRISTOPHER M. CLARK

It has become fashionable to propose, as a solution to some of the technical and mechanical challenges of working with a large volume of qualitative information (for example, field notes from a year of observation and interaction, or transcripts of teachers thinking aloud while planning or during clinical interviews), that a large mainframe computer and special software be used to assist with data analysis. I would like to raise three cautions about this proposed approach, for it seems to me that computer storage and manipulation of such information could cause as many serious problems as it might solve. the three cautions concern labor and expense, access and control, and reductionism.

Caution #1: Labor and Expense. To store qualitative-descriptive information in a mainframe computer, one must type the entire corpus at least one more time than is the case in more conventional approaches. This is time-consuming, expensive, and a possible source of error. Obtaining appropriate software, training personnel in proper use of software, and user and storage charges levied by the computer center can also amount to significant expenses.

Caution #2: Access and Control. It has been my experience in working on more quantitatively oriented projects that one member of a research team tends to become the "computer expert," that is, the person who masters the intricacies of actually interacting with the computer and the information stored therein. I have no reason to believe that this phenomenon would not also happen when qualitative information is stored in a computer. Functionally, what this means is that one or two persons control access to the information, and typically these are not the same persons who did the fieldwork. The potentially thought-provoking data are removed, by one or two steps, from contact with the people who would be in the best position to make sense of those data. "Browsing" through the corpus would be much less likely to be done by the people who could make the most of this process.

A second kind of access problem can also develop when field notes are stored in mainframe computer files. This is the problem of unauthorized access to the information by persons who are clever with computers but who have no legal or moral right to see this information, some of which might be threatening to the privacy, reputation, or employment of the people described. As researchers, we typically promise confidentiality and anonymity to the teachers and students whom we study. But can we be confident that we can keep such promises when we know that even elaborately protected computer files have been accessed by unauthorized persons?

A third kind of access problem is related to the idea of "secondary analysis," the practice, sometimes followed by quantitative researchers, of obtaining a data set compiled by someone else and analyzing these data a second time for (usually)new purposes. Storing field notes or interview protocols in computer files would make secondary analysis in qualitative research more likely, and this would be a dangerous development. Dangerous, because the packaging of raw qualitative information in voluminous computer files could easily give the impression that these files constitute the complete data set—the corpus within which meaning resides. But field notes are not, *ipso facto*, data. Rather they constitute an incomplete and selective record of events and impressions recorded by the fieldworker. The interpretive meaning of these events does not reside in the notes, but must be recreated by the fieldworker who was present at the time, in the context, attending to and remembering much more than what is literally recorded in field notes. To ship off a computer tape containing hundreds of pages of text for "analysis" by persons who were not present when the notes were made constitutes electronic decontextualization and virtually guarantees misinterpretation.

Caution #3: Reductionism. Computers and the characteristics of their software exert powerful influences on how one might read, interrogate, manipulate, and make use of a large corpus of text. The nature of these systems encourages (and requires) coding and counting as the two major ways of working with computer files. Coding of a large volume of text entails thousands of analytic and categorical decisions about where sensible units of analysis begin and end, and what category (or categories) each unit represents. The labor is enormous, and a considerable amount of the meaning, feeling, and realistic ambiguity of human speech and social interaction is lost when it is diced into T-unit-sized bits. Functionally, the computer is capable of manipulating codes, not meaning, and whatever computer analyses may be done are severely bounded by the constraints imposed in data reduction via coding. And the damage done by coding is difficult to work around, for one's primary index for interrogating the text electronically becomes the coded categories.

A concern related to the reductionistic lock of coding systems follows from the wonderful ability of computers to count. Because this is one of the genuine strengths of computer technology, there would certainly be a temptation to make use of it in computer-assisted analyses of qualitative information. Frequency counts of key words or (more likely) of coded categories of thought and action units would be easy to generate, and the resulting precise numbers would give the illusion of standing for objective and valid "hard data." Some might be tempted to run a correlational analysis or even an analysis of variance to test for significant differences between classrooms or teachers of methods of instruction. But to do so would be to throw away what interpretive approaches to inquiry are truly good for and to try to spin gold from flax. Frequency of occurrence of a word or code may have nothing to do with its importance or functions or meaning. Absence of word, thought, or behavior is often more significant than presence. Lack of variability at the frequency count level may obscure phenomenologically important variance in how the nuances of teaching-learning situations are experienced and perceived by the participants. But the computer is insensitive to nuance.

In conclusion, I urge you to weigh the possible costs of using computers as devices for storing, manipulating, and analyzing qualitative information. I leave it to the proponents of such approaches to describe and promote the promised benefits and potential gains.

PART IV

INTERACTING WITH SELF AND OTHERS: REFLECTIONS IN/ON QUALITATIVE INQUIRY

New Methods for the Study of a Reform Movement

Gerald Grant

The Research Project on Competence-Based Education out of which this book has grown was itself an experiment in social research and an effort at reform of research methods. This final chapter therefore treats the project itself as a "case" and gives a concrete account of its conception and evolution in the hope of indicating not only what we did but how and why we did it, so that students of other movements can consider adopting our methods in whole or in part. It explains how we arrived at our conclusions and points to the limits of our generations, in order to ask whether our approach justifies its costs in comparison with more common ways of organizing a research enterprise. It illustrates the problems that researchers are likely to encounter in evaluating reform programs, including those of confidentiality, reciprocity, and trust, and it examines the politics of evaluation at the institutional and federal levels. Finally, it analyzes the project and this book in light of larger philosophical and epistemological questions that are inherent in all social research but that are all too often ignored in reports of research.

Our research project was an experiment in the sense that it posed a test of the question: What is the best way to study an emergent large-scale social movement or educational reform in order to produce the greatest yield of useful knowledge to policy makers and potential participants in such a movement or reform—not merely descriptive information about particular programs but knowledge about what it would mean to foster more widespread adoption of the reform? The need for such an approach to the evaluation of broad-aim social programs and their potential consequences have been stated by Weiss and Rein, among others. In criticizing the misapplication of "controlled" experimental designs to evaluation research during the past decade, they have called for a more qualitative, process-oriented approach that would be "concerned with what form [an] action program actually [takes], and with the details of its interaction with its surroundings, from which may be formed an inductive assessment of its consequences" (1971, p. 296). Similarly, Parlett and Hamilton (1972) have urged adoption of "illuminative" methods of evaluation that are more concerned with description and interpretation that with measurement and prediction. Such evaluations would study how an innovative program operates, how it both influences and is influenced by its environment, how those directly involved in the program perceive it, and what its most significant features, critical processes, and unintended consequences appear to be. This chapter attempts to show how our project constitutes a response to these proposals for new forms of evaluation and, at the same time, to illustrate how our inferences and generalizations about the competence-based education movement are grounded in field research rather than being the product of "armchair assessment" or typical social criticism.

Our project was also innovative both in the interdisciplinary character of our team and in the field research techniques we adopted. The more than a dozen original members of the team brought to its training in history, law, medicine, philosophy, psychoanalysis, English literature, education, and sociology. These multi-disciplinary foundations enriched our view of competence-based education, particularly since our inquiry was grounded in fieldwork by all members of the team, and our diverse beliefs and aims shaped our research method. This method may be unique in its combination of several elements: (1) repeated fieldwork at each site by one member of the team over a three-year period; (2) an agreement among team members to share all field notes from all site visits; (3) team visits to all sites so that every member of the team, while immersed in his or her own site, also did fieldwork relating to a cross-site theme at most of the others; and (4) a broad definition of the domain of research that included the agency funding the research as part of the legitimate field of inquiry.

Of necessity, this recounting of the history of the project must be made from my perspective as director of the project. But it is buttressed by considerable documentation; several thousand pages of field notes and correspondence; records of conversations with officials of the funding agency; three tape recordings of crucial discussions of method (the first, between members of the project team and officers of the agency when the project was under fire in its first year; the second, between the team and the subjects of our investigation midway in the project; and the third, among members of the team during a four-hour discussion at the end of the project); memoranda from all members of the team evaluating the strengths and weaknesses of the project from a methodical point of view; and, finally, a review of a draft of this account by the team members and several of the individuals mentioned in it.

No matter how much documentation is used, however, accounts of method are essentially first-person accounts, sometimes even confessional in tone. At its core, method is autobiographical defects—an account of method reveals how one's scientific beliefs influence one's aims and what one lived through in attempting to realize them. It can also indicate what one believes about the nature of human action and why one has been persuaded to adopt a particular theoretical domain. If this chapter succeeds, the reader will sense both the drama and the confusion of our project, for our choices and decisions were not made under laboratory conditions. Rather, we often acted with a sense of uncertainty, enmeshed in tension and conflict.

Genesis of the Project

In 1973, Thomas Corcoran, then a senior research fellow at the Educational Policy Research Center at Syracuse, obtained a one-year grant from FIPSE to investigate new circular patters in higher education. He and I conferred about nominees for a task force that he planned to assemble as well as about sites they might visit, but I declined Corcoran's invitation to join the task force because I was myself currently pursuing intense fieldwork for a study of reform movements in higher education. By the following spring, Corcoran's task force (including Audrey Cohen of the College for Human Services, Robert Birney of Hampshire College, Morris Keeton of Antioch College, and Zelda Gamson of the University of Michigan) had decided to focus efforts on competence-based education, and FIPSE had decided to earmark a large portion of its grants for competence-based reform. After drafting a proposal for a follow-up grant, Corcoran was offered a position with FIPSE, which he accepted. Shortly thereafter, he approached me to see if I would be interested in assuming leadership of the project.

The project called for a study of innovation processes connected with the spread of competence-based education and giving practitionery program assistance. A task force at each college undertaking a competence-based program would jointly develop a process for monitoring the program and act as resources to one another, with technical assistance provided by Corcoran and two senior-level researchers at the Educational Policy Research Center. I thought that I should refuse Corcoran's offer to lead the project not only because of prior commitments but also because I did not feel qualified to assume Corcoran's technical assistance role. In addition, I lacked the personal relationships with experts in the field that Corcoran had developed in his exploratory grant—relationships important in coordinating a task force of competence-based practitioners.

A short time later, Corcoran reported that the deputy director of FIPSE, Russell Edgerton, wondered whether there were terms on which I might accept leadership of the effort. On further reflection, I decided that the opportunity to examine a major reform movement at an early stage should not be lightly dismissed. The research was congruent with my other interests, and, methodologically, an interesting possibility was beginning to form. I had recently contributed to a volume for the Carnegie Commission in which seventeen authors had been asked to write case studies of institutions that had experienced crises and transformation in the late 1960s and early 1970s (Riesman and Stadtman, 1973). Although some authors had exchanged drafts, the work was done largely in isolation and with no common framework. What if one had called the authors for that book together at the beginning, so that they could have discussed what kind of research ought to be done, developed conceptual frameworks, and remained in communication throughout their field-work? I reconceived Corcoran's proposal along those lines. If the project director's position was made half-time and the two senior research positions eliminated, funds would become available to engage a team selected for their research skills and analytic capabilities. Each member of the team would develop an analysis of some aspect of the competence-based movement in addition to writing a case study. These team members would be external to the institutions being surveyed, thus reducing the tensions possible between practitioners from an institution and the agency funding its programs. The work of the team members would be clearly labeled as research and analysis, with the technical assistance to the institutions largely eliminated.

As revised, the project would be an opportunity to address the problems of educating for competence in American society. This goal was stated as follows in the rewritten proposals: "The intent is not to evaluate programs as successes or failures, not to say in some absolute and definitive sense whether they "worked" or not. Rather, the intent is to investigate the way these programs have been conceptualized and operationalized, to discover how these settings have been created and evolved. The intent is to describe the programs, probe their assumptions, explore the pedagogic issues they raise, and in an open-ended way assess the range of impacts they may have (Educational Policy Research Center, 1974, p. 2).

I told Corcoran that three years of funding would be needed to understand such a complex development, and some days later he called to say that Russell Edgerton was willing to continue discussions about the proposal under those conditions. When I met with Edgerton in Washington, I explained that, in order to study the competence-based movement, a project director would need authority to select a sample of institutions representing different levels of reform and programs preparing students for a wide range of occupations, whether or not such programs were operating under grants from FIPSE, as well as a free hand in choosing the members of the research team. Edgerton expressed some reluctance about the conditions, but did not oppose them outright. When we were joined by several other members of the FIPSE staff, however, and details of the revised proposal became clear to them, the tone of the discussion grew much more skeptical. One asked why a set of case studies and explorations of the issues could not be written on a one-year grant three years hence, thus eliminating two years of funding; he did not seem satisfied with my explanation that one cannot study the "evolution" of a movement on a post hoc basis and achieve the same results as those that accrue from immersion in the movement as it develops. Another scoffed that I proposed nothing other than writing a book: there would be no help to practitioners along the way, and FIPSE was not in the publishing business. While the revised proposal did retain some of the "assistance" function of Corcoran's plan by promising to provide feedback to practitioners and to share interim findings at two conferences, I was candid about the differences. I hoped the quality of research it planned would merit publication at least in part, if not in a book; and I pointed to several recent costly "action-oriented" projects of educational research that had resulted neither in worthy publications nor in much help to practitioners. This did not persuade my chief critic to change his view, and I left the meeting believing the odds were against my somewhat "bookish" project. But Edgerton asked me to spell out the intended outcome of the project more clearly in light of the afternoon's conversation, and on returning to Syracuse I did so, listing five in an addendum to the proposal:

1. A set of case studies of the actual evolution over a three-year period of six to eight competence-based programs selected primarily on the basis of their initial conceptual and programmatic diversity.

2. A synthesis of the ways that competence-based education has been conceptualized and operationalized, and of the critical issues associated with that process.

3. A study of the process of innovation at the institutional level and of the wider diffusion and growth of competence-based education.

4. A refined statement of the applicability, usefulness, and limits of the method of illuminative evaluation.

5. Providing useful feedback, when appropriate and desired, to the institutions participating in the study.

I was as surprised as anyone when two weeks later I received notice that the proposal had been approved and would be funded in its revised form. Although it was obvious that the staff at FIPSE was divided about the worth of the project, an enlightened view (from our perspective, at least) had prevailed. It would be funded for three years, and I was granted the conditions I regarded as essential: to include sites not funded by the agency, to choose the research team myself, and to draw a boundary between our research and FIPSE's monitoring of its own projects. To underscore this last requirement, it was agreed that no case-study materials, even in draft form, would be forwarded to FIPSE until the end of the second year of our project. This would ensure that our accounts would not be used to make decisions about whether projects should be refunded in the next funding cycle.

So-called contract research is in bad odor with many academics. Certainly the conditions under which any research is performed will significantly determine the outcomes. At one extreme the conditions can be such that researchers are virtually part-time employees of the agency and merely carry out quasi-administrative or management tasks. (Thus Horowitz, in his account of the cancellation of the highly controversial Project Camelot, traces much of the difficulty of that project to the failure of the social scientists involved to insist that they were more than hired hands for the Department of Defense: "The Army, however respectful and protective of free expression at the formal level, was 'hiring help' and not openly submitting military problems to the *higher* professional and scientific authority of social science" 1967, p. 36.) But it is also possible—and perhaps more often than traditionally oriented academics assume—to lay the groundwork for high quality work while under contract. Research contracts are open to renegotiations, however, and our agreements came unstuck from time to time as various officers of FIPSE attempted to interpret the proposal in light of what they regarded as more pressing or more useful ends. The boundary defining the researchers' independence had to be vigorously defended more than once.

The work of site selection began immediately. I read scores of proposals submitted to FIPSE in response to its call for experiments in competence-based education. Telephone interviews with a variety of researchers and practitioners led to other suggestions. Wendy Kohli, a member of the project staff, prepared an analysis of institutions developing programs they considered to be competency-based. We tried to identify the universe of institutions that consciously identified with the movement towards competence-based education (whether by the logic of internal developments, because it was required by the state, or in response to a call for proposals by FIPSE or some other agency). A more fundamental approach might have attempted to analyze all forms of higher education in America whether they called themselves competence-based or not. Yet, conceived as a study of a movement, this seemed appropriate though not ideal. And if the competence-based movement could be thought of as a Mississippi flowing through America, our aim was to sample its sources and headwaters, its branches and tributaries, as well as its relationship to other watersheds. However, all this was not thought through with precision. On the contrary, I proceeded in a rush—there was less than sixty days to recruit a staff, select a sample, assemble a team and make arrangements to get them into the field by the opening of most colleges in early September—partly using instinct and intuition and keeping several variables in mind. The sample of colleges selected ought to maximize diversity in the way that they initially conceptualized the problem of developing a competence-based program; a range of institutions by level, type, scope of program, and geographical location was desirable, and the programs ought to be representative of a wide range of career and occupational patterns. Although the proposal promised only eight case studies, twelve institutions were selected in anticipation of some attrition on our team and/or a refusal of some institutions to participate in the study. The twelve were: Alverno College in Milwaukee; Antioch School of Law in Washington, D.C.; College of Community and Public Service, University of Massachusetts at Boston; College for Human Services in New York City; Elgin State Mental Hospital in Illinois (which has pioneered a competence-based program for mental health paraprofessionals in conjunction with Northern Illinois University); Empire State College of the State University of New York; Florida State University in Tallahassee; College IV of the Grand Valley State Colleges in Allendale, Michigan; Justin Morrill College at Michigan State University in East Lansing; Mt. Hood Community College in Gresham, Oregon; Seattle Central Community College in Washington State; and the University of Toledo in Ohio. Nine case studies eventually were completed (Elgin State Mental Hospital, Empire State College, and Justin Morrill were dropped, and Syracuse University was substituted for Toledo), and our fieldwork extended, through short trips or interviews with faculty or administrators, to Bowling Green State University in Ohio; Florida International University in Miami; Mars Hill College in North Carolina; Our Lady of the Lake University in San Antonio, Texas; and Southern Illinois University in Carbondale. The five case studies in this volume illustrate the diversity in the competence-based education movement.

• • •

A Search for Methods

Although a number of important decisions had been reached at the first meeting, some matters were left open quite intentionally. No interview guide had yet been developed, nor even a topical outline for case studies. To a large degree, each researcher was encouraged to interpret the broad aims of the proposal by his or her lights; no formulas or guidelines were presented as to what was meant by "the conceptualization of programs in competence-based education." (I expected to learn a great deal about what was relevant to such a movement by simply sifting the varied interpretations of researchers, who would differ among themselves about what was relevant.) One of the critical differences between qualitatively and quantitatively oriented researchers (if we may use those tired inadequate terms for a moment) is that the latter generally assume that they know the nature of the system they are sampling. They seek to refine understanding of the system and to provide data to correct or improve its functioning—in other words, they seek prediction and control (Habermas, 1971, pp. 309-310). In contrast qualitatively oriented researchers do not assume they know the nature of the system. Their purpose is to discover and to describe it in such a way that the participants recognize it as a portrait of their world—a portrait that, if well done, will contain features the participants themselves may not have fully discerned. They seek not primarily to improve prediction and control of the system but to provide knowledge for more informed and conscious choices.

Members of the team were representative of the humanistic disciplines and the humanistically oriented social sciences, rather than such "hard" or quantitatively oriented disciplines as experimental psychology or economics. Thus the very terms *qualitative* or *quantitative* did not carry much weight with most members, although the more theoretically conscious sociologists among them were likely to refer to themselves as advocates of the qualitative school, more specifically as symbolic interactionists or practitioners of naturalistic sociology. These sociologists were by no means opposed to survey research or quantitative methods and in fact had used such techniques in the past, but they deemed them inappropriate as the primary form of investigation in this instance. All members of the team shared a view of the world that emphasized willful human agency—they saw the world as open and informed by human choice, as continually being remade. The team also agreed to explore topics by means of a free and relatively unstructured set of observational activities. A wide range of data would be sought from interview, analysis of documents and observation of meetings and classes, as well as through team visits. Each researcher would seek to describe the conceptualization and evolution of a particular competence-based program with the consciousness that his or her description would, as one piece of a mosaic, help us to understand and assess the nature of a much broader movement. There was a consensus that one ought to take a very liberal view, particularly in the initial stages of the inquiry, about what might be relevant to such an understanding. Though none of the team members was a professional anthropologist, most would have agreed with Malinowski that it is best to embark on fieldwork guided only by a "foreshadowed notion" of problem areas that may prove interesting.

As the notes began to flow back to Syracuse to be reproduced and distributed by mail to all, the variety of "foreshadowed notions" became evident. Each member of the team was analyzing the evolution of a competence-based program through a unique lens ground out of his or her training and interests. Thomas Ewens, a philosopher with psychoanalytic training, paid especial attention to the hermeneutics of the program at Alverno—when and with what kind of understandings did persons there begin to use the word *competence* and how did those understandings evolve over time? Zelda Gamson, long interested in the processes of innovation in higher education, was particularly sensitive to the ways that an innovation fulfilled institutional needs. John Watt, an historian, paid more careful attention than most other members to early documents and memoranda of competence movements. Virginia Olesen, a sociologist of the symbolic interactionist persuasion, inquired into how meanings were socially constructed by participants. David Riesmann raised questions about the boundaries of the investigation by initially considering the widest possible context for understanding competence-based reforms. Peter Elbow, ever the humanist convinced of the need to honor concrete human experience and skeptical of abstract formulations of any kind, challenged all of us repeatedly, as he did by letter in responding to an earlier version of this chapter: "You talk as though it was interesting because we each had a different method—but some of us had no method at all—didn't know what a method looked like if it hit us in the face—we were scared and had a sense of not knowing which end was up."

Each researcher reading the notes was influenced to some degree by the foreshadowed notions of the others. In some cases, the awareness was expressly reflected in the notes by a comment that so-and-so would have approached an interview quite differently. (Over time, the parenthetical asides in the notes constituted a playful commentary on our various styles as fieldworkers, with all the private jokes and shorthand reference to signal events that one might find in a correspondence among good friends.) Or in team meetings, objections might be made to the use of specialized perspectives, such as psychoanalytic categories, that seemed inappropriate to analyze a particular phenomenon. Intersubjectivity or mutual infiltration of perspectives began to be operative on the consciousness of the group as a whole and to influence the way we established frameworks of analysis. Quite intentionally, there were no restrictions at the beginning as to the range of observations or to the way of generating the categories of observations. But at the end of the first year, some priorities had to be established and some limits set. Zelda Gamson devised a case study guide, and the group adopted it with few changes as a minimal outline of topics that every case study ought to treat. From the beginning, the necessity of some such guide was recognized, although members of the team varied in their eagerness or willingness to establish such categories at earlier stages. From another perspective, of course, this interdisciplinary, inductive approach could be seen as rather aimless mucking around, and such suspicions did play a role in a major crisis the team confronted, an event to be discussed in more detail later.

This guide helped structure the case studies without crushing flexibility of approach or overly restricting any researcher's decisions about salient themes at his or her site, and it undoubtedly reduced anxiety for some of the team members who had never written a case study. It was a straightforward outline of the basis content that the case studies should include: a description of the institution (size, character of faculty and students, significant academic structures, administrative and financial support patterns), an account of who introduced the competence-based program and of how it had developed, a specification of the competencies adopted and their rationale, a description of the ways faculty sought to assess competence in students, and an assessment of the scope and impact of the program. Some kinds of data might never have been collected in a uniform manner without development of the guide, although even at the end some gaps remained.

Fieldwork

The first and last (tenth) meetings of the team were the only two at which the team did not spend at least part of the time in fieldwork at one of the sites in the study. In a typical three-or four-day meeting, a day or a day and a half would be spent in fieldwork by all twelve members of the research team. Prior to the meeting, team members would have been receiving field notes from the worker at that site, along with catalogues and other relevant documents. The researcher responsible for that site, assisted by the project staff, arranged the fieldwork schedule, setting up appointments for interviews, arranging for classroom visits or access to files or records. At institutions such as the College for Human Services or Antioch Law School where students spent time in internships, arrangements were also made for up to half the team to accompany students to their field assignments. The researcher responsible for that site was told to look upon the entire team as research assistants for the portion of the meeting spent in fieldwork. Members of the team varied in the specificity of their directives, but in general schedules were arranged with care and always produced a bountiful harvest of field notes for the case writer. The team was mixed not in its disciplinary affiliation but in background, age, and avocational competence, all of which were taken into account in fieldwork assignments. At Florida State, for example, two research assistants in their twenties talked with students, whereas David Riesman talked with the president and senior administrative officials on the campus. John Watt, an accomplished amateur musician, interviewed faculty in the music program, and Virginia Olesen, who had previously done participant observations in a nursing school, talked to the faculty in nursing. Thus the case writer could see and hear through others what might otherwise be denied him or her because of age or biology or the lack of common interests or expertise with those being interviewed. The teamwork of this kind is not unusual, of course, and consulting firms on contract to the government frequently put such teams in the field. But these are likely to be ad hoc teams thrown together for single visits, unable to develop the kinds of symbiotic relationships that the project team engendered over three years.

Some aspects of our method were invented on the spot and later formalized. For example, at the first team fieldwork visit to my own site, the College for Human Services, colleagues began spontaneously to question me about ambiguities or lacunae in my field notes. How did this event relate to that? Had I interviewed such a person about a particular event? Had I observed any of the sessions at which students were assessed on their performance of "constructive actions," as the performance tests were called at the college? Questions like these were later placed on the formal agenda of our meetings under the heading of "the witness box." They served the purpose of getting all members of the team sensitized to the fieldwork and as a means of constructive criticism of the fieldwork in an atmosphere that enabled the caseworker to think through the case freshly, often providing him or her with new insights into the latent significance of events. Use of the "witness box" was only a heightened form of the mutual adjustment that characterized the project as a whole. Each member's prejudices were open to correction by others, mitigating the dangers of bias that are present in all social research, as well as the impressionism that, given our modes of work, was a particular problem for the team.

The team did not hold its meetings at the college being visited, and usually stayed at a hotel nearby. On the night preceding the fieldwork, the team invited everyone who would be interviewed the next day to a cocktail party at the hotel. This eased entrance of the team into the site, serving to introduce the researchers as persons, not just human tape recorders. At later stages of our research, when we had drafts of papers, representatives of the host institution were invited to join our discussions. In addition, we made an effort to provide feedback to those at the site. This sometimes took the form of presentations by members of the team, followed by questions from faculty and administrators, or of a private report by the case writer, either in person or by letter following the visit. The meetings usually ended with a postmortem analysis of the field experience, although some members of the team urged colleagues to save such analysis for field notes unfiltered by the group discussion. Some members managed to dictate their field notes during breaks between interviews or late in the evening the same day. In other cases retrieval had to be postponed until a day or two later, but long delays between experiences in the field and the recording of notes were not common, and the exceptions were usually quite noticeable in the quality of the notes.

I attempted to respond by letter to field notes as they came in during the first year, giving encouragement, making suggestions for next steps, and occasionally offering interpretations. As time went on, members of the team sometimes responded to each other's notes, and David Riesman in particular was extraordinarily conscientious in this respect. I tried to keep in touch with all members of the team by telephone and through memoranda, and there was a mailing of some kind virtually every week, whether a packet of field notes, a memo, or a journal article or two.

This was not traditional participant-observation in which a researcher might spend months or even years immersed in the local "culture." Most case studies were written on the basis of thirty days of fieldwork (including the team visit as the equivalent of ten to twelve "days"), and perhaps another fifteen to twenty days were spent in analysis of documents and materials from the site. Full-time participant-observation would have been prohibitively expensive, and it is questionable how much more would have been learned for our purposes. A more traditional anthropological style of fieldwork usually comes at a point early in a researcher's career—when the researcher is less rooted to a particular place or position and less expensive to employ. Fieldworkers at that point are also less experienced and knowledgeable. The project team was able to maximize experience and comparative scope through the part-time, in-and-out style we adopted. Such experience is invaluable in order to pierce what House (1974) has called the "ideology inherent in many proposals and regarded as absolutely indispensable in securing . . . funds because it says what the sponsors want to hear." In fact, because so much of the paper flowing between sites and Washington agencies is a semantic screen, an important function of the kind of research the project team engaged in is to get people talking more honestly and less grandiosely about the actual problems in the field, which are often obscured in the elaborate and mandatory "progress" reports. For example, David Riesman pointed out that experimenters at Florida State University felt they had to over-promise in order to meet FIPSE's expectations about expansion of their program, expectations that FIPSE later said it did not have. Experimenters at the site and officials in Washington were each, to some degree, acting with misperceptions of the other. As Virginia Olesen noted, the project team's style of research maximized both continuity, giving each researcher a three-year view of developments at his own and others' sites, and flexibility, enabling each fieldworker to adjust strategies to their site and to periodically reassess the depth and frequency of data gathering. It demanded intensive and exhausting bursts of fieldwork, however, with the need for each researcher to pay attention to maintaining lines of communication with the site between trips. In such a fast-paced style in the field, as Olesen observed in a memorandum, every minute has a "data weight" attached to it: "One must move very quickly very early, which poses keen interactional skills, the possibility of inaccurate judgments, and the risks of failures or mistakes with little leeway to smooth over or patch up."

By the end of the first year, some members of the project were eager to discuss ways of integrating our findings and of achieving greater comparability of data. Based on a reading of the first six months of field notes, I drafted an outline of what seemed to be the emergent issues or critical features of competence-based education. To these I added other questions that I felt ought to be addressed in any intelligent analysis of the movement. Questions to be addressed were arranged under eight categories, or, as they came to be called later, critical issues. These dealt with such issues as images of competence, problems of acquiring and assessing competence, and the limits of the faculty's role in developing competence. This was a rudimentary, first-level attempt to identify some of the major lines of inquiry. For example, the following questions came under the topic of the limits of the faculty's role:

- What is not teachable? Or what can be taught directly, what only indirectly?

- Can affective qualities be taught or stipulated as competencies? Can one speak of a competent lover, a competent mother?

- What are the logical levels of competence? What are differences of degree, what of kind, as one moves from the more specific to the more generic, from being a competent auto mechanic to a competent university president?

- Can one speak only of discrete competencies, or is it possible to specify the configuration, that is, how they are integrated?

I hoped that most members of the team would analyze some critical features of competence-based education or write a paper about it in addition to his or her case study. While retaining responsibility for a particular case, each member would come to have a "specialty" in team fieldwork as we moved across all the sites. One member might pay particular attention to problems of assessment, and another to the processes of change generated by competence-based reforms. Although the outline was only a preliminary draft of what the final report might look like, most team members gave it a cool reception. The outline was interesting, but it was "too early" to begin to sort out the major issues. A few resisted the idea of doing such papers at all. They felt the report ought to have an introduction, a set of case studies, and a concluding summary chapter. Most agreed with the necessity for papers that analyzed the movement at a more general level, but a significant number felt that these should come after the case studies were completed. I agreed with the logic of such a view but argued that to wait until cases were written at the end of the second year of the study would crowd too much into the final year. Since the budget provided for only a fixed number of team meetings each year, I felt the team needed to use these to develop analyses and to criticize drafts. I believed in Rosalie Wax's (1971) realistic rule of thumb: Allow at least as much time for analysis and writing as one does for fieldwork. Hence, at the midpoint of the project (December 1975), writing ought to be underway, even though fieldwork would continue.

With the blessings of hindsight, one can see that such resistance to what were perceive as "laid on" topics (even though largely derived from the members' own field notes) was predictable. A project director should expect professionals to underscore their claims to autonomy and to exhibit the human tendency to be cautious in assuming specific responsibilities. Owing to my inexperience as an administrator, I did not realize this at the time, but my colleagues let me learn on the job. I decided, at any rate, to withdraw the outline because of the dissatisfaction it caused, but I also asked everyone to think more about it and respond by memo. What actually ensued was a negotiation process in which, by letter and phone, I began to sound out members about their preferences. I encouraged some to follow through on their first thoughts and discouraged others, according to my estimates of their strengths and capabilities. By the June 1975 meeting, most had staked out some general topic, and by the fall meeting some had submitted preliminary outlines of topics mutually agreed upon. At the same time fieldwork assignments increasingly reflected these preferences. Peter Elbow, for example, wanted to write about the way the advent of a competence-based program changes a faculty members perception of his or her role, and so he spent much of his time in team fieldwork observing teachers at work and talking to them about such matters.

Renegotiation of the Project

The first year-end meeting developed into a confrontation with FIPSE over issues of who would "guide" the project towards what ends. It proved to be the first round in a crisis that would play itself out over the second year of the project. With the exception of the disgruntlement felt by FIPSE officials at being barred from team meetings, things had gone fairly smoothly for most of the year. Russell Edgerton, deputy director of FIPSE, responded favorably to the first draft of the critical issues (more favorably than the team itself). At a meeting with me midway in the year, he expressed satisfaction that the team had been organized and had begun work in the field with some dispatch, and hinted that although the work might not please everyone, he thought it was not a bad thing to have a group such as ours act as "conservative critics" of the movement. I would have preferred the phrase "unprejudiced critics" or "impartial analysts," but did not object to the word "conservative" if by that he meant the team had not been hired to promote competence-based education.

By late spring, however, somewhat different and mixed signals were emanating from FIPSE. In a discussion of budget proposals for the second-year renewal of the project, Edgerton and others at FIPSE expressed dissatisfaction with the project's approach to the critical issues, and one officer wondered whether the result would not be "just a bunch of essays" that had little connection with fieldwork. There was also criticism that it was unclear what the outcome of the project would be and who would benefit from the research. Edgerton complained that at least some of the persons at the study sites were "confused." Since the members of the project were scheduled to meet in Washington in June in connection with team fieldwork at Antioch School of Law, a meeting with the FIPSE staff was scheduled. A week or two before the meeting, the FIPSE staff received draft copies of a report about the origins and current directions of FIPSE, prepared by two project team research assistants who, as part of the study, had interviewed FIPSE staff members about their role in the competence-based education movement. The report raised the temperature of the ensuing discussions close to the boiling point. Not surprisingly, it showed that experiments in competence-based education had claimed the largest proportion of FIPSE's budget in the preceding year but that the staff held varied opinions as to the nature and purpose of competence-based education—some perceiving it as a means to undermine a course-credit, time-served approach to earning a college degree, others as a means of institutional reform, and still others as a cost-cutting device. The report also indicated what was being fairly widely discussed among insiders in various Washington educational agencies at that time, namely that FIPSE might be absorbed in the new National Institute of Education and that its staff itself was divided about the pro and cons of such a reorganization. Although this was only a passing comment—three lines in a sixteen-page report—it angered at least one top FIPSE official, who told a member of the project team that the report could be used as a damaging document in a bureaucratic fight over FIPSE because it showed that its own staff was divided on one of its major special efforts. From the official's perspective, there were no such differences among staff members, and yet discussions with his staff during lunch prior to the meeting confirmed these differences of opinion. After lunch, the project team and the FIPSE staff were joined by Sister Austin Doherty of Alverno College, one of the sites in the study. She opened the discussion by asking members of the project team what, after nearly a year's study, they had learned. What could they tell her that would be helpful? Such a seemingly plausible question found no ready response. Instead, several of us explained that the team was still trying to sort out many issues and was consciously keeping an open mind about them, rather than trying to draw conclusions. Looking back, it is painfully obvious that this was the first direct encounter in a conflict that we did not comprehend in its full dimensions until much later. We should have anticipated that inductively oriented researchers would not be especially welcome in a movement dedicated to attaining more explicit statements of education outcomes. In a sense, we were violating the central dogma of the movement we were studying. We were the enemy within the gate. (Although this conflict could not have been good, since it centered on our method, it might have been mitigated if I could have given more substantive responses. Researchers in the inductively oriented mode should anticipate that participants being studied will want some hints about the kinds of hypotheses that are beginning to form and ought to give them at least a general account as soon as they can.)

The discussion then turned to an expansion of themes that had been raised earlier by Edgerton in his talks with me, particularly the issue of what audience would benefit from our research. This reopened the question of the degree to which the project was primarily conceived as a form of technical assistance to the institutions under study or as an analysis of the underlying issues of competence-based education and their import for reform of higher education. Although a confrontation is not always the best way to approach an issue, I felt that pressure was building to reorient the project toward the former position, and I drew a hard line, saying the project could not serve those ends in the way some members of FIPSE's staff wished. In order to do so, the team would have to be selected on entirely different criteria (on their expertise in assessment or in particular curriculum areas, for example, rather than on their qualities as observers and analysts), and the project reconceived. The team, as presently constituted, could not succeed in either aim if it tried to do both. Underlying the discussion of this and a number of other issues was the plea that the team "open up" to include both practitioners and members of FIPSE's staff in future meetings.

The discussion revealed that FIPSE itself was divided about the worth and future directions of the project, and it seemed that positions for or against various definitions of the project were implicated in struggles for ascendancy within the agency. At the same time, differences of style and temperament were beginning to appear among members of the research team; under the pressure of fieldwork and the confrontation with FIPSE tempers had flared on several occasions. On the question of "opening up," for example the team was divided; some members felt that to bring others to our meetings might violate confidentiality or too severely limit the scarce time the team had for its own work, while others felt that the practical and moral necessity to be responsive to FIPSE's concerns was overriding. The seams that had begun to show (in an earlier session one team member had heatedly attacked another for failing to properly plan the team's fieldwork at his site) now were beginning to pull apart. In such a situation, one should neither change one's suit too hastily nor pretend that nothing is amiss. One needs to look closely at the points of stress and decide what can be pulled together and what should give way to a new arrangement. Fortunately, the team had a final day to discuss matters privately. Out of that discussion came the agreement that we would hold to our definition of the project—even if this risked renewal of the project—and not attempt to accommodate demands to provide technical assistance, since we could not possibly fulfill them. A compromise was reached on the issue of opening our team meetings to others: it was decided that guests would be invited to every other meeting but that the number would be limited so as not to swamp the team or drain the energies of the central staff in conference planning.

In the weeks following the Washington meeting, FIPSE made two "suggestions." One would have required dismissing a member of the team on the grounds that her site was not really a competence-based experiment. The other, made somewhat later, was that I share an "edited version" of the field notes with the case study institutions as a way of providing feedback at the end of the first year. I declined to do either. In the first instance, I noted that the institution cited was selected largely on the grounds that it had given signs of moving toward a competence-based program. Hence, it provided a unique opportunity to observe an institution in transition. One would be able to learn just as much by discovering why the faculty turned away from competence-based modes as if they eventually embraced them. Arguing from analogy in the second instance, I asked how the FIPSE staff would feel if an edited version of notes taken by the project team during its interview of that staff were furnished to the head of Health, Education, and Welfare? The case study was intended to be the edited version of the field notes. But the agency's officer insisted that, although the proposal had specified a two-year deadline, an interim report was needed because some persons in the institutions were unclear about the purpose and "character" of the investigation. I was not then aware of such confusion, although I would later hear that complaint from the president of Alverno College. I noted that most members of the project had provided feedback during and after field visits but that they would not consider edited field notes as appropriate form of feedback. At the official's request, I did agree to ask members who had not yet made a report to do so in a manner each considered appropriate.

Thomas Ewens, the fieldworker at Alverno College, had also begun to hear complaints that the project had not lived up to its promises to provide feedback, but no one on the team was prepared for the crisis that ensued. Precisely in order to be responsible to requests for information, the meeting at Alverno in September 1975 included guests from four other sites as well as members of Alverno's faculty. An early draft of the chapter on competence in the liberal arts had been prepared by Ewens for the meeting, but President Read declared it was "nondiscussable." She queried us on what we meant by "competence-based eduction." Our response that this was the object of the study—precisely to discover what was signified by numerous initiatives being made under the label of "competence-based education"—was dismissed as unsatisfactory. Furthermore, project members could not respond to a request from a FIPSE official that we attempt on the spot a comparative analysis of the types of programs we were examining, since the logic of the work required that we complete the cases in the spring of 1976 and not begin comparative analysis until the third year.

This meeting was perhaps the low point of the project; members left it feeling frustrated and partially defeated. If anything, it confirmed the wisdom of those who had argued in June that we should resist demands to provide "feed" we didn't have. Alverno College called a moratorium on further field work by Thomas Ewens until it received a report on the team's fieldwork. We sent a forty-three page report several weeks later but never received a reaction to it. In December, Alverno withdrew from the study. President Read politely explained that Alverno did not wish to be included in a study of competence-based education because it feared such inclusion would misrepresent the nature of its "Alverno Learning Process," as the faculty had come to prefer to describe its curriculum. But four other issues seem to have been involved. Although they took their most dramatic form at Alverno, they were not unique to that college, and in one form or another they are likely to arise in all research of this type. They are: (1) the actual or perceived role of the researcher as an agent of change, (2) the threat the researcher poses to the institution's image management, (3) the problem of exchange or reciprocity, and (4) the question of who defines the focus of the investigation. Each of them warrants at least brief attention.

The Researcher as Change Agent. Any researcher coming fresh into an environment has the potential for upsetting the local ecology. The power to ask questions can be used irresponsibly, and even when exercised with care can be perceived as a revolutionary act, as Socrates learned. With the aim of understanding the early conceptualization of the competence program at Alverno, Ewens began his work by conducting a set of extraordinarily perceptive interviews with a wide sampling of informants, including early opponents of the program. He had, of course, gone to the faculty dropouts (some of whom considered themselves "force-outs") who had resigned when the leadership at Alverno decided to put the entire college into the competence-based format. By the end of the first year's research, President Joel Read posed the issue as follows in a letter to Ewens:

> If . . . you take a statement from one of the persons you interviewed here at Alverno and attempt to cross-check it around the institution, it is altogether possible to raise what might have been only one person's question into that of many persons, and thus, to make it an operative dynamic across the institution. Raising questions to levels of consciousness can be a fine art of manipulation or an unconscious politicization or both or neither. But, a person moving freely within an institution, responsible to no one but him or herself, and whose data is said to be held confidentially, can create an institution-wide dynamic which is outside the scope of management unless those responsible know that this is being done. Rumor [and] gossip . . . operate in most institutions and we all survive them like the bacteria we carry within our own organism. But, to deliberately introduce a free agent with the potential to make certain attitudes, approaches, perceptions more sharply focused and thus capable of altering the direction of an institution, can be downright dangerous—perhaps even irresponsible on the part of those answerable for the direction of the institution.

In an earlier letter, President Read had asked for a "clarification" of Ewens' role, saying, "There is a question then as to your position when you seem to be adopting the position of advocate of a particular point of view that exists within the college." In reply, Ewens denied that he was the advocate of any position and was astonished that his interviews would be so interpreted. With regard to her concern that he might be "complicating . . . the management of change," Ewens wrote:

> With regard to your last paragraph, I can only say again that the role of a fieldworker is a difficult one. I am trying to observe a complicated process of change. But of course one cannot merely observe; one's presence, one's questions, one's reactions and interactions inevitably inflect upon and in some minimal way enter into the process itself. I would hope that this does not interfere with the task of those who are trying to manage the change. Indeed I think that the presence of a reasonably discreet outside observer may well facilitate that process in a number of different ways; it can give perspective; it can be therapeutic in allowing hostile or otherwise recalcitrant faculty to express their points of view; it can on occasion lead to new and fruitful questions being pursued. . . . As far as I am concerned, I hope some of these positive, auxiliary outcomes may be brought about, particularly now that I am beginning to know something of your situation at Alverno and of the situations at other institutions which are grappling with some of the same enormously difficult problems. Of course, I cannot guarantee these outcomes any more than I can warrant that unexpected and undesired outcomes will not advene; in neither case do they depend on me only.

Insofar as the research team could determine in its visit to Alverno College during 1975, Ewens had not in any way assumed an advocate's role nor had he been perceived as doing so by faculty. Yet I was told by one of the leaders of the competence-based experiment that she could not understand why Ewens "spent so much time looking into the dark corners" and (to her) so little time interviewing the "central persons." She went on, quite angrily, to say that she was "sick and tired" of hearing "over and over again" how the administration had supposedly "forced the program down everyone's throat." To some degree, an observer who interviews dropouts does stir up old scores and, no doubt, old guilts. But he or she may do this in an entirely unobtrusive way, serving as a neutral conduit of messages that otherwise would not reach the top because only the inflated "good" news that the leadership wants to hear gets passed up through official channels. Participant-observers often do give voice to those whose grievances have been officially silenced.

For example, one of the nurses who was fired in the struggle recounted in Virginia Olesen's account of the competence-based program at Mt. Hood Community College wrote to her: "You and your case history were very important to us—made us feel what we had accomplished was good and what we did was right."

The Threat to Image Management. Suspicions that researchers on the team were grinding special axes arose at other sites, and concern about the political impact of research was always present even when relations between institution and researchers were most cordial. Every institution is concerned about "image management" as well as "management of change." Just as researchers can arouse anxiety by altering or establishing new channels of communication internally, the present the even more potent threat of giving a less-than-flattering profile of the institution to the external world. Even if we set aside the problem of false or distorted representation, selective attention to one aspect of institutional life, no matter how sensitively portrayed, may be resented. In Alverno's case, it did seem odd for the president, after receiving numerous grants for the development of a curriculum publicly announced as competence-based, to cite as a principal reason for her withdrawal from our study that Alverno did not belong in our sample. Yet a president has a legitimate obligation—neglected at peril—to present the most favorable and attractive image of the institution to students, potential donors, and public agencies; and the competence-based label increasingly came to be perceived as a liability at Alverno. The public, however, also has a legitimate right to responsible accounts by qualified observers of educational experiments supported by their tax (and tuition) dollars, no matter what labels they appear under.

The question of the political impact of research goes deeper than issues of labels or cosmetics. The question of manipulation raised by President Read with reference to Ewens' interviewing can also be raised in relation to the institution's attempt to use the researcher for what it considers worthy ends. This dynamic also played itself out at several institutions in the study, most notably at the College of Human Services, where Dean Stephen Sunderland and, to a lesser degree, President Audrey Cohen were highly conscious of the potential impact of my research. A series of discussions with Sunderland came to a head when he made plain that he would not tolerate my presence if he did not think the College for Human Services would eventually benefit from my work. Expanding on this theme in a letter, Sunderland wrote that he viewed the relationship as a potential conversion experience: "I see you as part of a strategy that the college wishes to use to spread the word about the college's good works . . . and as a potential convert to the form of education and assessment that we see as necessary for a different kind of professional, social, and intellectual world." Sunderland was continually on guard whenever I was in the field, questioning "enterprises such as yours in terms of their usefulness in meeting the change goals of the college." At one point, he ushered me out of a tense meeting called by dissatisfied students on the pretext that my personal safety would be endangered, although I had previously established good relations with the students and was in fact invited to the meeting by them. It required several meetings with President Cohen for me to obtain permission to interview sources without "chaperonage" provided by Sunderland and to establish other ground rules I regarded as essential for responsible research, including access to records and random interviews with students and field supervisors.

The sharing of field notes by members of the project team was challenged by President Cohen, who wanted to know what images of the College for Human Services I conveyed to colleagues after my periodic visits to the college. She wanted an opportunity to counter any misleading information at an early stage. When I responded that to share notes with her would compromise confidentiality with sources, she argued that since they were being shared with others (that is, fellow researchers), why not with her? The analogy that I drew—that it was like doctors discussing notes about a patient in confidence—did not carry much weight with her since the College for Human Services sought egalitarian reforms in the professions that would deemphasize such claims of privilege on the part of professionals, whether they were doctors or researchers. In effect, the project team was not treating her as an equal! Realizing my analogy was a weak argument to advance in her court, I thus defended restricted circulation on other grounds namely that field notes had a diarylike quality. They were dictated as "raw" material, often full of contradictions, free associations, conjectures, and highly tentative first interpretations to be checked against other evidence and subsequent observations. As president of the college, her memos to the faculty were public, but when she shared insights in meetings with a "kitchen cabinet" about various aspects of life in the college, such privileged conversations among a few intimates would be analogous to the sharing that went on among our team members through field notes. In such conversations, for example, a close colleague might tell her that one of her ideas was farfetched; team members similarly were able to open themselves to collegial criticism in this way.

Even social scientists do not always share raw field notes, however, and the perception that this practice gave a quasi-public character to interviews was troubling to others. President Joel Read, after a lengthy talk with Ewens about how the struggles within her religious community had affected reforms at Alverno, wrote: "I need some clarification on field notes. First of all, does everything become a part of field notes—that is, substance of conversations and so forth? Secondly, are all field notes of such projects circulated to all other researchers on the other projects? What led to my questions was our lengthy discussion of the relation of my religious community to Alverno. I was willing to discuss that with you because of your background . . . but knowing the general lack of information, much less general lack of understanding of what religious congregations are all about, I did not consider our conversation a source for field notes. But I understand that some 200 pages of field notes already exist on us. I'd appreciate your comment."

Thomas Ewens, like most members of our project, had let it be known in conversations with sources that field notes were being shared in a confidential way among researchers. His reply could stand as a sensitive account of the discretion and self-censorship that members of the team exercised as they attempted to protect individuals even in such privileged communications as field notes:

> What goes into field notes varies widely depending on who is dictating them. Some are brief and laconic; other are quite detailed. Since conversations are a large part of the fieldwork, the substance of conversations is generally noted. Notes are circulated among the immediate members of our group with the understanding that they are strictly confidential. I have made this clear to everybody at Alverno who has asked me and almost everybody has. This is, of course, an extremely delicate matter and places the most stringent requirements of confidentiality and discretion on each one of us. It is, I think, because our group and the institutions which have agreed to cooperate with us share, in principle, the same commitment to the search for truth and understanding that our project, project members and, by implication at least, our *modus operandi* were accepted to begin with.

> With regard to our far-ranging conversation in July and other similar conversations: you and your colleagues have been extremely open with me and I have been told many things, often very intimate and personal, that I consider nobody else's business and would not put in any notes. There is a fine and delicate and supple discretion to be exercised here which would strain anybody's resources of practical wisdom. As a matter of fact I consider the background, history, habits, structures, goals and dynamics of the School Sisters of St. Francis an important factor in the changes that have and are being wrought at Alverno, as does almost everybody I have talked to. Nobody has spoken as insightfully and incisively as you have on certain aspects of that context; it has been very helpful to my own understanding and I would consider it important to share that understanding with others in an appropriate way.

The Problem of Reciprocity. In the end, the refusal of the team to supply field notes to Alverno was seen by its leaders as another indication of the project team's unwillingness to "interact" or provide what they considered adequate feedback. The issue of exchange or reciprocity—of what benefit the host institution receives in turn for its gifts of time, energy, and access to the researcher—has become increasingly salient in all forms of research. It is not unheard of today for researchers to be asked literally to buy their way in, even to pay for interviews or to promise that any royalties or proceeds from the research will be donated to a cause designated by the hosts. Researchers on projects of the type described here are sometimes referred to as "jet-setters," and are occasionally perceived in stereotypical terms as talking only to other researchers, mostly airborne like themselves, and serving no earthly practical purposes. No institution in the study demanded reciprocity in these terms, but the question of the quality and type of feedback provided was an issue in varying degree at most institutions, and most keenly at Alverno. After the Washington meeting in June 1975, Sister Austin Doherty asserted to Ewens that the project was not making good on its promises of feedback, and in September President Read told me that no one in our group seemed interested in giving feedback. "Are we just data?" she asked. "Why don't you want to interact?" In October, she told Ewens, "What I am telling you is that I don't want you to come out here until we have received some information. We have been very open and public; we have denied you nothing. But we do not know what your group is about." She insisted to Ewens that she wanted "more free sharing of information" as the research went on. Ewens indicated that this would be done in the case study the following spring but that he could not make daily reports, as it were, on his interviewing.

In response to concerns expressed at Alverno and from officials at FIPSE, I wrote to all institutions in the study, reemphasizing the provisions for sharing information in the study. I noted that institutions would be invited to criticize its conceptual framework, that special efforts at feedback would be made after each team visit, that each institution would have an opportunity to criticize early drafts of the case study, and that practitioners would be invited to join members of the project for discussion and development of the critical issues. President Read did not regard this letter as resolving differences over the feedback issue: "there is a difference of opinion regarding the methodology and approach of the task force, vis-á-vis the institutions participating in the project. . . . What is the evaluation intended to accomplish? What is its purpose? Who are the audiences? . . . to date, it is not possible to know where the project members are 'coming from.' While a general position on methodology is enunciated in the Case Study Guide, a working statement of your 'collective' philosophy of education and the current state of higher education is left to inference."

Questions about where the researcher is "coming from" often arise in participant observer studies and may reflect the simple human desire to know whether the observer is friend or foe, certainly an open issue in Sunderland's approach to me at the College for Human Services. But that did not seem to be the issue in the same sense at Alverno. In a five-page reply, I indicated that the inductive method used by the team, while loosely modeled on Parlett's illuminative evaluation, allowed for differences of style and approach. I did not regard it as imperative for the group to share a "'collective' philosophy of education." On the contrary, members were selected in part because they represented different views and perspectives and each of them agreed to immerse himself or herself in the work of understanding a variety of attempts to conceptualize and practice competence-based curriculums. I noted that working papers on these issues would be prepared by the spring of 1976 and that "we hope they serve to create some useful dialogue among practitioners and ourselves about these issues." Then I turned to President Read's question about what audiences the project was addressing: "the audiences for this work are several. First, the institutions might benefit from sympathetic criticism and from the kinds of feedback described in my recent letter. Potential studies might make more informed choices as a result of our work. Teachers and administrators in the broader higher education community may benefit by being able to vicariously 'visit' Alverno or the College for Human Services and other institutions where we are developing case studies. Policy makers may be influenced by our analyses. Those who have an interest in the processes of innovation would be another audience, and researchers with an interest in our methodology yet another."

The Problem of Who Defines the Issues. This question of whether practitioners themselves were the primary audience for the project's work was to receive sharp scrutiny within a few weeks.

Institutions in the sample varied enormously, it turned out, in their expectations about the answer. I heard that officials at both Alverno and the College for Human Services were contacting other colleges in the study and raising questions about their continuance in it. At FIPSE, Edgerton warned me of the possibility that other institutions might follow their lead if they pulled out, in which case it would be difficult to justify continued funding of the project. In December, after Alverno did withdraw, Edgerton pressed hard for the point of view that the practitioners were the primary audience for the work and ought to have a major say in determining what issues were analyzed. In his eyes, "the proposal committed the project to a process for determining the issues (coordination of the conceptual framework with the evaluation personnel operating at the program level) which seemed to guarantee that the issues which your team would concentrate on would be recognizable as important by the practitioners trying to put the programs into place."

Since our research was an inquiry into the actual difficulties practitioners encountered in attempting to conceptualize and devise competence-based instructional programs, members of the team felt that both the cases and the critical issues would be regarded as "important" by practitioners, although they would also reflect to some degree the particular interests and competencies of members of the team. Edgerton felt that some of the critical issues we had identified went too far in the latter direction and would result in essays "driven essentially by the interests of the author." But fairminded persons could disagree about the degree to which a given critical issue was related to competence programs. For example, Edgerton cited the essay on the antecedents of competence-based education as an example of too tenuous a connection to the investigations at hand, yet members of the project were unanimous in feeling that it was important to trace the backgrounds of the movement, and practitioners, too, expressed considerable interest in the topic.

The argument seemed to turn on the question of what Edgerton meant by the phrase "determining the issues." Did the "guarantee" that practitioners would regard the issues as important mean in effect that he regarded them as holding a veto power over the researchers' definition of the critical issues? I asked him whether he would have refused to fund Abraham Flexner's investigation of medical schools because some practitioners did not regard Flexner's issues as important? Edgerton responded that it would depend partly on the boundaries of Flexner's research as originally agreed upon. I said that the commitments of the project were to consult and coordinate with practitioners but in no way did that imply any veto power. The boundaries of the project were set by the case study investigations, but the responsibility for identifying the emergent critical issues was primarily in our hands as researchers, and this was not a point that should be left ambiguous.

Yet Alverno's withdrawal, combined with the possibility that other institutions would pull out, generated considerable uncertainty about the continuance of the project. I did not want to take such a hard position without careful reflection and after that conversation sought counsel not only with members of the project but with colleagues at Syracuse, including Lawrence DeWitt, Sheila Huff, Bernard Kaplan, Maureen Webster, and Warren Zeigler. For the most part, these were persons who had had experience directing large-scale research projects in the social sciences. While offering helpful advice about strategy, they generally agreed the position we had taken was right in principle.

Edgerton's questions about the process for identifying the critical issues of the study were not naive ones, however. Edgerton had earned a doctor's degree in political science at Columbia and had taught for five years at the University of Wisconsin; he was not methodologically unsophisticated. Yet he was not particularly sympathetic to our method of avoiding prejudgments of realities, allowing issues to emerge, and reformulating the problems as our research proceeded. To us, the study was open-ended in that it permitted us to revise the explanatory scheme as we learned enough to know which variable deserved more attention and which less, as well as to discover hitherto obscure relationships among them. Edgerton wanted to define the boundaries of the research with more clarity and to get "closure" on the "product." We resisted his effort insofar as we perceived it as predetermining the focal issues of the research. Edgerton's warning had been written as a preface to his meeting with the project team scheduled for January 1976 at Florida State University. Considerable tension had built up prior to the meeting, since FIPSE had explicitly put the project on notice that renewal was not at all assured. The following excerpts of our discussion with Edgerton and Corcoran of the FIPSE staff convey some of the subtleties of a classic problem in a government-sponsored research project:

Grant: A good way to start is to ask you [Edgerton] what you see as the crucial, key issues.

Edgerton: I think that in a complex project in which divergent expectations exist within the Fund, your group, among project directors at the sites and between all those different parties . . . it seems to me that the most important thing . . . is to get as much closure as you can from this point forward on the product you are producing and communicate that to us and the project directors. . . . We need a sense of how the parts come together and what is the balance between the case analysis and the issue analysis.

Grant: You and I have talked about how they come together or connect. This morning's discussion (of the issues) was intended to show how we're grappling with these things. But I wonder whether it's a problem not of connective tissue but that you don't like the issues we've got. Your letter implies that the practitioners in these cases ought to have come veto power.

Edgerton: No, not veto power. . . . One of our expectations is that we expected the issues you would settle upon in your cross-site generalizations would be issues which the practitioners would recognize as important.

Riesman: I wanted to help the practitioners. But I ask myself who are the practitioners. The life of practitioners in this field is very short.

Ewens: Yes, what are we talking about. As Peter Elbows points out, what about all those people who think that CBE [competence-based education] is weird . . . if those practitioners are also part of the audience then that should be made very clear.

Edgerton: I think it is a very good point that the Fund may easily overreact to the constituency of the project and to the project directors (at the sites in the study) in particular. . . . But if you had to state a principle for inclusion or exclusion (of issues), what would you state?

Elbow: What is the point of exclusion? You raised some questions [in your letter] on historical background. But if all the project directors thought it was a waste of time to get background, it doesn't make me think so.

Edgerton: I can't imagine all of you not writing things that are valued. That's not the issue. In our view the [research project] had more boundaries, clear criteria of inclusion and exclusion. In the emergent method there are some points where you diverge outside of the study. . . . It's hard to know [from reading the project's statement of them] what the critical issues are. . . . I had a sense this morning that you yourselves don't know.

Gamson: I think we don't know what the critical answers are, but we know what the critical issues are.

Olesen: There are a lot of emerging themes here. Some of the emerging themes may seem enormously distant, but they are very closely tied to the everyday fieldwork in these sites, and they have emerged out of the definition of what is real for those people in that situation.

Edgerton: I don't know how seriously you want us and the project directors to take your outline [of the critical issues] at this time.

Riesman: Not as seriously as you did.

Edgerton: How seriously should we take what you take seriously? We're talking about a kind of uneasy and turbulent environment and in some cases distrust.

Grant:	We had one institution withdraw. I don't see the distrust that you see. Most people understand what a case study is and what we are doing.
Olesen:	Russ [Edgerton], I want to take serious challenge on that issue. I don't think the rest of us [other than Alverno] have had problems of mistrust. But the fact that I could get in Mt. Hood after a serious rupture last summer indicates there is a modicum of trust. . . . I don't really think there are serious issues of trust in other sites.
Edgerton:	It seems to me that there are. There is a very common feeling across most of the sites that your agenda has not been revealed to them.
Olesen:	I think that is a fundamental problem of all fieldwork. There are always those questions [on the part of people at the site] "What are you people doing here?" Even if you told them two minutes before. I heard such questions nearly every day in three years of my participant observation study of the socialization of student nurses.
Corcoran:	There is another level. The fund [FIPSE] staff itself needs to know what you're up to.
Riesman:	You need ammunition; you need to defend us?
Corcoran:	Well, not necessarily. But we need to persuade colleagues back at the Fund that we know where you're going.
Edgerton:	There's been a hell of a lot of trust [on the part of FIPSE towards the project] for a year and a half.
Watt:	I'd be very surprised if College III (University of Massachusetts, Boston) wasn't one of the places you had to persuade. Last year it was a mine field. . . . I had no idea of the political complexities.
Corcoran:	John [Watt], you have to understand our need to know because if you step on a mine, we get blown up.
Grant:	I want to return to what are the boundaries. What we can write about is limited by the talents that we have and the interests that we have. The critical issues are also bounded by doing case histories at specific institutions. There are boundaries or blinders in ourselves in the sense of our capacities to understand these institutions. Another boundary is indicated by the audience we visualize as composed of the wider kinds of practitioners and faculty at all institutions of higher education who might be interested in these issues—not just project directors at these ten sites.
Corcoran:	We need some idea of the audiences you are trying to reach because we need to ask what is an effective way of reaching them.
Edgerton:	Maybe I'm expecting too much, but it seems to me that you ought to be able to tell the Fund the extent to which you're looking for cost implications.
Olesen:	I don't think we're going to have the time to dig into cost figures. I don't think they would give them to me.
Edgerton:	There is no sort of hard line, rigid architecture. I'm just stating some general concerns and hoping they're accepted as genuine, valid concerns.
Gamson:	There are going to be critical issues [that we'll identify] that however recognizable to the people at the sites will not be top on their list of critical issues and which might seem frivolous to them and not terribly relevant. I think we ought to recognize that.

The meeting was a major turning point for the project, and while no assurances are made about refunding, the tension eased perceptibly. Edgerton volunteered that "your own internal consensus and the research project is a lot further along and better than has been publicly communicated." As a result of participating in discussions of the issues, he was persuaded that "the analysis was really embedded in the cases and [that] that was the structure driving the report." He made a generous concession towards the end of the meeting: "I think we are as sensitive as you are in not wanting to impose process tactics that don't work. It was maybe an unwise attempt to try to get more active relationships between you folks and the project directors." Of course we felt that we have "active relationships" with sources at the sites—relationships that we in fact considered crucial when it came to the question of determining the critical issues. And the meeting had shown that this was the shared view of the project team, including such an experienced investigator as Virginia Olesen, who could tell Edgerton that what he saw as distrust of the team was to some degree to be expected in research of this kind.

Team members also left the meeting with greater appreciation for FIPSE's point of view and the political realities I faced in trying to satisfy multiple constituencies about the worth of the project. This made it easier for me to organize a spring meeting that would include about seventy-five practitioners from various competence-based sites. The project, up to this point, had to some degree been an unwitting victim of its own ethics. Our concern about confidentiality had led to barring the FIPSE staff from meetings, and since field notes were the principal "product" of the research during this first year, little was known about the quality or nature of the work underway. Edgerton was entirely correct in saying there had been a great deal of trust on the agency's side.

After the project team returned from the Florida meeting, a refined version of the critical issues outline was shared with all practitioners in the study and invitations went out for the spring meeting. At the same time—in late January 1976—a survey was made as a follow-up of Edgerton's concerns to see whether this statement of critical issues was "recognized as important" by practitioners. Since the spring conference would be organized around the critical issues as developed by the project team, practitioners were asked whether any topics of concern to them should be added to the conference agenda. Only one was suggested with any frequency—a request to pay more attention to the impact of competence-based education on the way that fees are charged and records are kept in institutions of higher education (subsequently incorporated in Zelda Gamson's analysis of processes of innovation). Within a few weeks it was evident that the distrust Edgerton referred to was apparent at two other sites. However, discussions with persons at those sites led in both cases to decisions to remain in the study. By late spring, nearly every member of the project had met the deadline for submission of first drafts of their case studies, and these received a generally favorable response both at the sites, where they were widely distributed, and at FIPSE. Better than 90 percent of those invited came to the project's June conference at Michigan State University, where in workshops with practitioners we invited criticism of early drafts or outlines of our papers on critical issues. During a panel discussion on the methodology of the project, participants in the case studies asked us about the timing of site visits, our role in offering practical advice to practitioners, the processes by which the research team had decided upon the critical issues, and the comparative validity of the case studies. Indeed, most of the issues discussed in this chapter were raised pointedly from the floor. We attempted to explain why we had proceeded as we had at each of our sites and how this had influenced our understanding of the critical issues.

The FIPSE staff, Edgerton in particular, felt the conference had been quite successful, but one problem remained: What was going to be done about the Alverno case study? Edgerton saw the issue partly in terms of due process. If the team had originally proposed to do three years of field work, was it proper to go ahead and publish the Alverno case after only half that? I responded that the team was unable to carry out the commitment through no fault of its own; hence, the question really turned on whether there was a sufficient data base to complete some part of the intended work. I noted further that the due process provisions included a promise to circulate drafts of the case studies widely at the sites *prior to publication* to give any aggrieved party opportunity for refresh as well as to provide for criticisms of other kinds and contrary interpretations of events. These provisions would be honored in the Alverno case, and it would be Alverno's responsibility to exercise such redress as it deemed appropriate. (As it later turned out, few responses were received from Alverno.) At the end of the Michigan meeting, Edgerton countered that since we differed, the matter should be arbitrated by appointing some panel or third parties to decide the issue. I declined the suggestion on the grounds that collegial peers had the responsibility to decide how and in what manner to make their research public. It would be a denial of academic freedom for some third group to decide what could or could not be published. Edgerton replied that researchers could decide at the end of the project to do or write whatever they wished, however the Fund has a responsibility to decide what it would pay for. This I readily acknowledged, but I did not think members of the project would agree to abort the Alverno case as a condition of third-year funding. Although FIPSE later asked two psychologists for their opinions of Ewens' Alverno draft, one of whom apparently disapproved of its "tone," it refunded the project for the third and final year without placing any conditions on the publication of the Alverno case.

• • •

Lessons

Looking back, one wonders how we could have been so surprised by the conflicts we encountered during the project. Researchers who are bread to "expect" unanticipated consequences should not have been so dense—but we were. Our first surprise resulted from our failure to see how starkly the logic of our research methods contradicted the logic generating the reform we studied. As mentioned earlier, we proceeded by inductive and exploratory methods, discovering, testing, and modifying hypotheses as we enlarged our understanding, whereas most persons at the sites in the study proceeded deductively, deriving curriculums from highly specific sets of desired outcomes. Although such shorthand phrases do not capture the conflict so much as they suggest it, they represent the difference between a person on a hillside who wants to observe what happens when he lets go of a ball and another who wants to have the ball hit a particular target.

In addition to the tension generated by inductive versus deductive logics, we encountered some hostility growing out of differences in "local" versus "cosmopolitan" orientations. At sites where concerns were more local, we were likely to be perceived (to some degree correctly) as jet-setters who would get in the way without offering much practical help and whose research might result in negative publicity for the institution. In contrast, at large, research-oriented institutions, where the outlook was more cosmopolitan, our respondents seemed to place a higher value on research for its own sake apart from any immediate utility it might have. They were more relaxed as to the nature and import of our research and felt less need for formalization of relationships or protection against institutional backlash. Their institutions were more financially secure and less dependent on tuition revenue; they were thus less worried than smaller schools about how the research would affect the institution's image.

The other major conflict—the confrontation with officials of FIPSE—was not so much totally unexpected as it was surprising in its intensity. Somewhat naively, we were not aware of the consequences of including FIPSE itself as a field site in the investigation of the competence-based movement, and we did not realize the degree to which our mode of operating turned the usual understanding of contract research on its head. The funding agency ordinarily sees the researcher as an instrument to accomplish some agency purpose or function, often to help the agency control or manage its field of operations more effectively, and in addition often seeks legitimation of its perceived role from the researchers. The need for great legitimacy was high at FIPSE, a young agency with no developed constituency that was attempting to make its way in Washington at a time when major reorganizations of federal education agencies were being proposed under some of which FIPSE would be absorbed by other agencies. Research that would help ensure the success of its programs and reflect credit on the agency would be most desirable, while research that might reveal confusions about competence-based education outside and within the agency could be very threatening. Our project clearly fell in the latter category, and much of the concern about the need for feedback and clarification of what our research was "really about" should be read in that light. FIPSE had agreed to a set of conditions for our research that placed our project closer to the model of basic rather than contract research. It had agreed in principle to three years of funding (although subject to annual renewal) and to an inductive assessment of the movement. But in practice, as the politically sensitive import of these agreements was discovered, pressures were brought to modify the agreements. Yet, if there are any heroes in this story, they are the officers at FIPSE who, after all, continued to sponsor our research despite great misgivings. They were often forceful proponents of their own view, but they were not ideologues or blind empire builders. They tolerated dissent within the agency; they were willing to look at new evidence; and when we submitted the case studies of the project, they agreed that we had made good on our proposal and continued our funding.

What does one learn from such an experience? It might have been helpful if we had formed an advisory panel made up of a mix of "locals" and "cosmopolitans" who could have helped establish guidelines about feedback and could have reassured FIPSE about the progress of the research at a time when there was little "product" that could be made public. Perhaps even more importantly, we should have expected such conflicts and seen them as an opportunity to better understand the nature of the phenomena under study. In examining my own role, I now realize that I was at times much too defensive and had a tendency to be overprotective of the work of my colleagues. Although there were things to defend—and it is important to note, as Argyris (1971) has in another context, that a researcher who is easily manipulated is not respected—one needs to do so with as little armor and heat as possible. I did not always achieve this, and to the degree that I did, my colleagues deserve thanks for having had the courage to tell me to pull in my horns. But by the conclusion of the project, I feel that I had more of the competence that I needed at the beginning.

To turn finally to the question asked at the outset of this chapter: In what sense has this been a research project rather than a form of social criticism? It has not been research of a form that begins with a hypothesis that can be confirmed or denied. It has been a search into the foundations, understandings, meetings, and imports of the movement toward competence-based education. That search has been disciplined by the work of trying to understand and explicate to practitioners themselves a variety to actual experiments in competence-based education. Of course, as Becker and Geer remind us, "we often do not understand that we do not understand" what we have seen or what has been told to us (1972, p. 104). Our response as colleagues to each other's field notes—and later our direct observation at each site—helped make each of us aware of systematic distortions in our ways of perceiving. It is as though Robert Redfield and Oscar Lewis, the anthropologists who have conflicting accounts of life in the village of Tepotzlan, were asked to reconcile their interpretations before publishing their work. In one or two cases conflict of this kind may have been a factor in a member's decision to leave the team. This element of self-selection means that some systematic bias or outlook may have characterized those of us who remained. But this bias was reduced by sharing drafts of the cases with participants at the sites, who forced awareness of omissions or alternative interpretations of events.

Research is a cooperative enterprise, and it is the disciplined process of cooperation, compelling systematic attention to evidence that does not "fit," that distinguishes it from social criticism, which is the reaction of a single sensibility to an object of perception or field of inquiry. This process of checking inference against "fact" and of compensating for observer bias was much stronger at the level of our case studies than at that of our cross-site analyses. At this thematic level, our research design is much weaker. We worked out the process of determining the critical issues informally, seeking a balance between what in our discussions we felt should be included in our report and what we felt we could do in terms of our talents, competence, and predilections. Thus when no one on the team seemed inclined to write about the issues of assessment, Wendy Kohli and I took on this assignment even though by background and training we did not feel at ease in doing so. Perhaps the team should have been difficult to integrate new members at that point of time even if additional funds had been available. As a result, our critical issue chapters are mixed in form, some using the cases as the data for their analysis, while others merely draw on the cases for illustration. The latter, that is, are closer to the model of informed social criticism than of empircal research although even they are tempered by the process of mutual criticism.

Yet neither cases nor critical issues are replicable. Different persons working from our data might draw different inferences. In that sense, the work of our team is closer to the model of a jury than of a laboratory. It raises many hypotheses and settles few. In assessing such a process, one should ask how the jurors were selected, whether the process exposed hidden interests, whether they considered the relevant evidence, and, finally, whether they were competent to judge this evidence. Readers are not in a better position to assess these matters that I am. Nevertheless, I believe that the special merit in our approach is that our method is uniquely adapted to sorting out the larger implications and potential consequences of nascent educational reforms and thus can help both educators and policy makers better understand the complexities and costs of such movements at an early stage. It is, in other words, a method suited to the observation of a bandwagon while it is still moving slowly enough for careful appraisal.

Afterword: The Passion of Portraiture

Sara Lawrence Lightfoot

Portraiture is a genre whose methods are shaped by empirical and aesthetic dimensions, whose descriptions are often penetrating and personal, whose goals include generous and tough scrutiny. It is a sensitive kind of work that requires the perceptivity and skill of a practiced observer and the empathy and care of a clinician. Throughout this research, I was continually struck by the power of human encounter and its effects on the quality of my work. For generations, anthropologists have written about the struggles of objectivity and the problems of establishing a balance between empathetic regard and over-identification with the subjects of their research. Ethnographers entering a new culture have tried to find the appropriate ratios between being a participant and an observer, fearing that the engrossing and intimate dimensions of the former might distort their role as researcher, and that the distance of the latter might make their subjects untrusting and uncomfortable. Throughout the anthropologist's sojourn in the field, the ratios of participant to observer usually shift over time, reflecting the researcher's adaptation to the setting, the subjects' feelings of trust, and the strategies and tools required for the inquiry. Some of the shifts are conscious, purposely designed to accomplish certain research goals. Others are not under the researcher's control. They often remain unconscious and are defined by contextual and interpersonal forces beyond one's awareness. Often they are only recognized in retrospect, when there is time for contemplation and reflection on one's actions.

In various ways, all researchers who do field work that requires personal contact with subjects in their natural habitat face the challenges, dilemmas, and opportunities of human encounter and struggle with problems of distance and intimacy. Classical anthropologists, who have tended to study foreign, "simple" societies and spend long periods of time in the field, have been most self-conscious and reflective about these issues of adaptation and investigation. Their field notes have recorded their fumbling attempts, their awkwardness, their naiveté as well as their exhilaration at finally making a breakthrough, their excitement at finally understanding the meaning of a ritual. But even those researchers, whose forays into the field are brief, usually become aware of the interventionist quality of their work, the ways in which they have disturbed the environment, and the ways in which personal exchange is a key ingredient of their successful work.

So it was with me as I collected the data for these portraits. From the moment I sought entry into these schools until many months after I crafted the chapters, I was concerned about the personal aspects of this work. It is not only that qualitative research uses "the person" as the research tool, the perceiver, the selector, the interpreter, and that one must always guard against the distortions of bias and prejudice; it is also that one's personal style, temperament, and modes of interaction are central ingredients of successful work. Phenomenologists often refer to the "inter-subjectivity" required in qualitative inquiry—the need to experience and reflect upon one's own feelings in order to successfully identify with another's perspective. Empathetic regard, therefore, is key to good data collection. The researcher must relate to a person before she collects the data and if an impasse develops in the first instance, the empirical work will not be able to proceed. These are old understandings recognized by generations of committed field workers, rituals and rules that are easier to talk about than do well.

In my prior work I have confronted these issues, struggled with them, and found workable but imperfect solutions. What was striking about the portraiture work was my growing awareness of the heightened quality of these dilemmas. The interpersonal aspects of the work were somewhat exaggerated by the relatively short periods of time I spent in the field and by the exploratory methods I was using that allowed little reference to established rules and traditions. Without the elaborate rituals of entry and greeting behavior that characterize long-term field research, much depended on quick, intuitive work, on intense and focused exchanges. Without having the generous, elastic time in which to make contact, build rapport, and develop trust, my interactions with people were more dependent on my ability to seize the moment and take personal risks. Rather than using the patient, receptive approaches that had characterized my earlier work, I was aware of an increased purposefulness and assertiveness on my part. Interestingly, I noticed no evidence of people shrinking back from my more forceful pursuits. In fact, I observed the opposite phenomenon. People seemed to rise to the occasion, responding with intensity and thoughtfulness. They appeared to feel supported and invigorated by the focused attention.

During the interviews, several respondents used words loaded with affect when they described the experience of human encounter. "I feel honored by your interest. You really seem to care," said a senior member of the St. Paul's faculty. "It's like you bring the sunshine," smiled a Puerto Rican girl at Kennedy. "Your attention bathes me in light," said an art teacher with a whimsical style. There was passion in these moments, connections made at deeply personal levels. These respondents were experiencing the glow I had felt when, at eight years old, my seventy year-old friend had drawn me in charcoal. The experience of full and caring attention superseded any concern for how I might be perceived and rendered on paper.

Beyond the emotional content of these encounters, the interviewers' responses to my probing inquiries often referred to the knowledge gained through self-reflection. For the first time, many of them were being asked to reflect upon and think critically about their work, their values, and their goals; and as they talked out loud, they discovered how they felt. Frequently people would say, "I never knew I felt that way," or "That idea just seemed to sneak up on me." Or when I would return the following day, someone would search me out to tell me of thoughts inspired by our conversation of the day before. Sometimes people would refer to the momentary confusions or disorientation that our exchanges had inspired. Claimed a young teacher at Carver High, "You destroyed the balance. I thought I had it all in place." A young English teacher, who was struggling over a decision to leave teaching, wrote me a long, passionate letter after our hour-long conversation.

> Naturally, talking with you managed to stir up the settled silt in mind—about teaching, leaving teaching, and power. I thought I'd take the liberty to restate or enlarge on some of my viewpoints. First the more pressing—these days, I am practically childishly exuberant to be leaving teaching— though the school thinks I may come back and I am prepared to eat those words—you asked me why. On paper, I can see my response much better and see if it's right. I'm tired of being in front of a class. I'm tried of having expectant student eyes upon me, waiting for my kick-off before they return the ball. I'm tried of calling the plays, though this year more than any other I have tried to be a game-player and less the quarterback, if you'll excuse the extended metaphor. I'm tired of having to read everything with teaching it on my mind. Being academic, in that respect, deadens literature for me— ach!—. When I sit down to write myself, I find the immediate need to label what I'm doing—another English teacher offshoot that seems more inhibiting at this time in my life than productive.

Her letter continued with an exploration of her personal and institutional power, her ideological and philosophical views on curriculum and pedagogy, and her notions about success and failure in a professional career. She ended her missive graciously: "Clearly you have inspired me and filled me with energy. I wish you the very, very best."

Whether people are energized, enhanced, disoriented, or made more critical because of the reseacher's presence and inquiry, it is important to be cognizant of the interventionist quality of this work and assume responsibility for establishing the boundaries of interaction and exchange. After spending several days in one school, the principal drove me to the airport. His eyes searched my face as we bid farewell. "I'm not going to make any great speeches," he said haltingly, "but I just want to say that your visit to our school had a tremendous impact on me. It was the high point of my professional career." Such proclamations, generously and openly expressed, were not unusual during my school visits, and they would often shock me into recognizing the power and personal dimensions of this work.

To some extent, my previous research had helped me anticipate the emotionally consuming aspects of portraiture, the struggles to find a balance between investigator and confidante. But never before had I so directly confronted the responses and responsibilities that accompany the research aftermath. Never before had I been brought face to face with the power and pain of portraiture. Certainly, in my past research, I had coped with the ethical and empirical dilemmas of the public exposure of research subjects; worried about the appropriate role for subjects to play in manuscript review; weighed the merits of collaboration with subjects and struggled with reconciling the divergent perspectives of actor and observer. I discovered that portraiture, with its deeply personal imprint invited a heightened concern from research subjects. Their responses to the portraits were vividly reminiscent of my reactions to the painting done of me several years ago when the artist worked "from the inside out." I had been shocked by the artist's portrayal and at first denied its resemblance to me. I complained about the way I had been rendered—the details of my features, the weary stance, and the passivity in my eyes. But even as I denied the portrait's resemblance to my person, I recognized the profound likenesses. The artist had captured my essence, qualities that often remained hidden from view, dimensions that I rarely allowed myself to see. The artist had also captured more than a moment in time. With her piercing gaze she had seen my ancestors and anticipated my future. The scrutiny was threatening. The view of my interior brought denial *and* revelation.

So it was with these high school portraits. The three pieces that originally appeared in *Daedalus* were first read by the school people after their publication. By prior agreement with the schools involved, the editor had not offered the portraits' subjects the chance for pre-publication review. When I negotiated entry with the second wave of schools, I promised the headmasters and principals that they would be given the opportunity to read the pieces immediately after I finished writing them, before I released them to a broader audience. Despite the fact that the leaders of all six schools expressed confidence and pride in their schools and seemed unthreatened by my intrusions or scrutiny, the arrival of the manuscript brought them great trepidation. One headmaster described the "painful" process of reading the "Lightfoot piece": "I received it on Tuesday and couldn't stand to read it immediately and buried it in my briefcase underneath all the trivial paperwork. I waited until Friday night . . . after the family was all in bed. I closed the door to the den, found a comfortable chair, opened up a can of beer and drank it down . . . only then did I turn to the report. I read the first chapter, went and got another beer . . . read the second chapter, another . . . and so on." The beer was the needed lubricant. Another headmaster received the portrait during the middle of the summer. He took it with him to his summer home and read it over several times. "It was the oddest thing, each time it got harder *and* easier to take. All at the same time, I wanted to say 'this is absolutely true . . . and this is wrong.' It was like an emotional seesaw of acceptance and denial." The other school people who spoke about their responses to the pieces were not as reflective or open about the impact of the written word. Yet all of them expressed the trepidation that accompanied their first reading of the manuscript, the "terror" of public scrutiny and criticism, and the combination of denial and recognition. Everyone expressed surprise at the vividly personal character of the pieces. "I didn't expect so many adjectives," said a Milton teacher. "You know, usually research does a good job of masking reality. There is some comfort in that. Your work takes the mask off and that's very hard," claimed a Brookline teacher.

Occasionally, the denial and turmoil lasted a long time and only turned to recognition months later. The portrait of one of the schools published in *Daedalus* caused some furor among the faculty and students when it first appeared in print. I was initially baffled because I felt the piece was laudatory and would have reassured and pleased its readers. According to the reports of some insiders, responses ranged from complete denial (one faculty member put up a public sign denying that I had ever talked to him and claiming that my references to his views were totally false), to expressed differences in perspective, to disputes over details. The headmaster, a wise, confident, and powerful figure, calmed the turbulent seas by commenting on his own responses to the "Lightfoot piece." He admitted to his faculty that parts of the portrait were difficult and painful to read, that he did not share all my views, and that an observer's perspective is potentially useful precisely because it rarely corresponds fully to the views of inhabitants. He also told them that part of the pain they were experiencing reflected the discomforts associated with the uncovering of truths.

At the same time that many of the school's faculty were upset by the portrait, I received several letters from alumni who all commented on the "authenticity" and "candor" of the piece, who expressed pride in their alma mater's openness to scrutiny and criticism. The dissonance between faculty denials and alumni confirmations was striking. More than a year later, when some of the dust had settled, I began to receive missives from a few faculty who thanked me for my "honesty." One commented that my "diagnosis" had begun to challenge some of their most entrenched collective assumptions. "At first we wanted to use your piece to fuel our fires. Now some of us use it to fuel our thoughts," claimed another teacher with surprise in his voice.

The second wave of portraits was read and reviewed by the headmasters and principals before publication. In each case, when I sent them the manuscripts, I said I was eager to hear their reactions and I also asked them to correct any factual errors they found in the piece. I concluded by offering my great thanks for their generosity and helpfulness, saying that I would be glad to discuss the portrait with them or members of their faculty if they thought it would be appropriate and useful. The principals were to decide on the strategies they would use in distributing the document to their colleagues.

In one case, the headmaster interpreted my letter as an invitation for "dialogue." When the two of us met to discuss the portrait, he began by praising the work—its life and perceptivity—and then worried out loud about a few sections that he felt were overly harsh and potentially hurtful to individuals. He also pointed out a few factual errors. I felt no compunction about correcting the errors or softening the sharp edge of several of my words. These charges amounted to minor adjustments in a few paragraphs. Most of our two-hour conversation was spent discussing inter-pretative sections where the headmaster expressed concern about "imbalances" in the manuscript and the "discomfort" and "awkwardness" that might be caused to individuals. These were milder worries that tended to focus on issues about which faculty and administrators felt particularly vulnerable. In a few cases, the headmaster suggested that selected individuals be allowed to review and revise excerpts of the portrait. In no case did he claim that the interpretations were untrue or even unfair. He worried, instead, about the response of his colleagues to portrayals that might reveal them in a way they rarely were seen by the school community. The headmaster admitted that he was expressing his "cautious self" at the same time he recognized that the power of the piece lay in its "sharpness."

This conversation was both difficult and instructive for me. I began to recognize that I had given the headmaster mixed messages when I asked him for his responses to the portrait. I had not been clear whether I was inviting his input and collaboration, or whether I really wanted him to simply comment on a finished document. Certainly neither extreme seemed feasible, but the wide range of possible interactions presented us with a broad and treacherous terrain. In a letter written several days after our meeting, I tried to clear up my ambiguous signals:

> After thinking long and hard about the way we planned to proceed with the review of the manuscript, I began to feel that I needed to clarify my views and correct some misperceptions I might have created. As you know, I was eager to have members of your faculty read and respond to the piece. I value their insights and comments and I would hope that my work might serve as a catalyst for internal conversation and self-criticism at your school. I do distinguish, however, between wanting their response and making changes and revisions on the basis of their suggestions. As you said initially this is my piece, reflecting my perceptions, and it must maintain the coherence and integrity that I have tried to bring to it.
>
> This is very personal work, both for the researcher and the school, and inevitably it creates feelings of exposure and vulnerability on all sides. It is also a kind of work that tends to more fully reveal the interests and preoccupations of the researcher. The work loses its power and honesty, I feel, if it becomes a consensus document. If a collection of people, other than the author, have veto power, it loses the edge of criticism (in its best sense) that makes it useful to you and your colleagues, to researchers, and to other schools that may be coping with many of the same complex issues. As the researcher/author, I have carefully combed through the data, searched my soul on many questions of interpretation, and take full responsibility for my observations. I feel I have substantial evidence (not all of it included in the final document) for most of my views. But given that I bring a "stranger's" external view, I would anticipate contrary opinions from others who necessarily will have different perspectives. I could not, in good conscience, respond to each of these contrasting perceptions.

The response to my letter was immediate and gracious. The headmaster seemed relieved by the clarity of my statement and convinced that "tampering would render the study lifeless and useless."

In another school, the portrait became an opportunity for self-criticism and reflection among the faculty. The headmaster used it as the basis for a staff development day and commented, "It is a live document. . . . You talk about things we see but don't want to notice . . . it will be a valuable vehicle for institutional growth." To the foundation that had funded the study, the headmaster wrote appreciatively:

> It has been several weeks since Sara Lawrence Lightfoot submitted her marvelous portrait of this school to me. It has been read by over 20 staff members here, including the superintendent of schools. It provides a candid picture, a freeze frame of the school. We all agree the portrayal is incredibly perceptive in its ability to capture and highlight the great and deep strength of this institution that are allowing it to respond to the challenges of a changing urban school in the 1980s. The vision many of us have of the school for the year 2000 has become a bit less hazy because of Sara's study. We are grateful for this aid to our ongoing work.
>
> I am aware of the legitimate concern many people in foundations have regarding the impact of their productivity. Let me assure you that in the case "The Lightfoot Report" will be used to energize us. We are currently planning a series of faculty meetings centering upon its content. We plan to use the document to help us continue the stressful task of moving this school and community through changing times and diminished resources.
>
> The report delineates the diversity of our student body. It praises the strengths of our teachers, and it describes the difficult transitional period the school is moving through. But what we like most about the report is that it tried to tell the truth. Some would say that truth-telling is always good teaching, but not always good administration. We would say that we must tell our community the truth about the schools. Otherwise, they will be unable to understand how difficult it is to obtain such elusive objectives as solid achievement and demonstrated competence in the High School of the '80s.

Typically, researchers who have worked "in the field," have stressed the difficulties and challenges of entry, adaptation, and encounter before and during data collection. They have spoken about the need for empathy, sensitivity, and humility in relation to subjects and underscored some of the ethical problems that arise when researchers make decisions solely based on expedience, pragmatics, or "pure" empiricism. Rarely have researchers referred to the aftermath of their work; to the subjects' responses to their efforts as a deliberate part of the research enterprise. Rarely do they see method as extending beyond the crafting of the manuscript.

Through this work I have learned several lessons about the challenges and opportunities that face a researcher engaged in portraiture. One is that the investigator must be conscious of the affective dimensions of this work. By this I am not merely saying that investigators should be aware of the biases that plague their perceptions and try to counter those by the pursuit of contrary evidence. I am also saying that the human encounter, central to the process of data collection, is the opportunity for reflection on and expression of ideas *and* emotion; and researchers must be ready to deal with the empirical *and* clinical dimensions of their work. Portraiture is a highly interactive research form, and the interactions proceed at many levels of human experience.

Because the exchanges between the researcher and subjects can be highly charged, it is important that the researcher not incorporate all the myriad responses as part of his or her self-image. The potent reactions, be they positive or negative, must be listened to attentively, but not taken at face value by the portraitist or used as evidence of his or her goodness or maliciousness. The investigator needs to find a way to hear the responses without feeling devastated by harsh criticism or expanded by high praise. If the portraitist incorporates all of the charged reactions and is vulnerable to all the cycles of emotion, it will inevitably lead to distortions of perception, to the compromising of descriptive powers. Portraiture is essentially a descriptive and interpretive task. It demands generous and benign regard as well as tough criticism. Both require that the researcher not be swayed by responses, but must find an unswerving, confident position that listens and accepts, but is not controlled, enhanced, or diminished by others' perceptions and judgments.

Second, the portraitist should give careful attention to the research aftermath and see it as within the boundaries of the methodological domain. The researcher's "exit," with all of its ritualized, negotiated elements, must be viewed with the same kind of judicious concern as the "entry" into the field. The exit is not only a highly charged, negotiated process, it is also based on dynamics peculiar to the setting. Each negotiation will be shaped by institutional and interpersonal forces that are situationally determined. In this study, each headmaster and his faculty experienced my leaving differently and dealt differently with my request that they review and respond to the manuscript.

Third, there seem to be anticipative stages of reaction that people experience when they read the portraits. The first response reflects the "terror" of exposure and the pain of visibility, no matter whether the words are praising or critical. The second stage seems to combine the elements of denial and recognition. At the same time, people experience the paradoxical sensation of denying that the piece represents them and recognizing that it is profoundly true. The third stage comes after what one teacher called "the healing of time." The subjects have gained some distance and perspective which allows them to embrace the praise and confront the criticism. It is a state in which the portrait can become a tool of institutional diagnosis—the opportunity for self-criticism, reflection, and conscious change.

Finally, the social scientist engaged in portraiture should recognize the potential impact of the work on individuals and institutions. Portraits are not static documents or exclusive texts that are directed towards a small circle of academic colleagues. They directly touch the actors in the portrait and may speak more broadly to a diverse range of people concerned about the issues and ideas expressed in the piece. The personal dimension of the portraits and their literary, aesthetic qualities create symbols and images that people can connect with, offer figures with whom readers can identify, and ground complex ideas in the everyday realities of organizational life. This textured form may serve as a catalyst for change within an institution. It may become an organizational text that invites response and criticism from its inhabitants. The external wide-angle view of the portraitist may contrast sharply with the various perspectives of insiders. But the dissonant strains provide opportunities for examining the power of roles, perspectives, and values in school life. Used in this way, social science portraiture may play a critical role in shaping educational practice and inspiring organizational change.

Beyond "Subjectivity":
The Use of the Self in Social Science

SUSAN KRIEGER

Abstract: Insights about the observer's self can prove useful for understanding others who are the subjects of sociological inquiry. This organizational sociologist studies a midwestern lesbian community using participant observation and in depth interviewing. Subsequent problems with preparing the findings led to development of an analytic technique for dealing with the data. The argument here is that we have much to learn from close examination of the interrelationship between observer and observed.

Recently, in both the social sciences and in related humanistic disciplines, there has been a restimulation of interest in the relationship between observer and observed.[1] Our attention is called to the many ways in which our analyses of others result from highly interactional processes in which we are personally involved.[2] We bring biases and more than biases. We bring idiosyncratic patterns of recognition. We are not, in fact, ever capable of achieving the analytic "distance" we have long been schooled to seek. While recognition of the interactional and contextual nature of social research is not new,[3] how we interpret ourselves during this new period of self-examination may, in fact, add something fresh and significant to the development of sophistication in social science.

I present the following account of my own work with the hope of contributing to a general sharing of personal stories about what we, as social scientists, now do. My account is one of backwards beginnings, wrong ways of doing things, and problems I would rather not have had. Yet precisely because of these things, I think, the story is worth telling. In the following sections, I will tell about some of what went into writing of *The Mirror Dance: Identity in a Women's Community* (1983), a study of a midwestern lesbian social group I conducted during 1977–78. The book focused on problems of likeness and difference, merger and separation, loss and change, and the struggles of individuals for social belonging and personal growth.

I began my research unwittingly. I spent nearly a year participating in the community as a member without the slightest thought of studying it. The community was, for me, as for others, a home away from home, a private social world, a source of intense personal involvements and supportive social activity—a source of parties, dinners, self-help groups, athletic teams, outings, extended-family type ties, a place for finding not only lovers, but also friends. I had moved to a midwestern town to take a job as a visiting assistant professor and had found the community by accident and through need. My participation surprised me. "I did not become a lesbian," I wrote to myself in notes at the time, "to become one of a community." Yet the community won me over in the end, and three months before I was supposed to leave the job and town, I decided to study the community in which I was living, to ask questions of these bold midwestern women.

Data and the Problem of Interpretation

I had, for years, been interested in the subject of privacy and I felt that this private, almost secret sphere of social activity would be a good place to talk to people about it. I wanted to learn about how individuals dealt with how they were known, or not known, to others. I then began two months of intensive interviewing with 78 women who were either members of the community or associated with it. Someone joked that I had solved "the sampling problem" by interviewing the entire community "and then some," which was, by and large, what I did.

My interviews lasted an hour and a half each, were usually conducted in my own home, and focused on personal histories of self-other relationships in the community. I asked each interviewee four basic questions: (1) How would you define privacy (what images come to mind)? (2) How would you define the local lesbian community? (3) Within that community, how have you been concerned about boundaries between public and private, self and other (i.e., what has been your personal and social history)? (4) With respect to the outside world, how have you been concerned about protecting the fact of your lesbianism (who knows, who does not, and why)? Approximately 70% of the time in each interview session was spent on question 3, which concerned internal community relationships. Members of the community and others I approached showed me unusual cooperation. They typically came for interviews within a week of when I called. During the interviews, they spoke to me with great candor.

When I left the community, I took with me, along with my personal memories and accounts, 400 pages of single-spaced typed interview notes, which were, I felt, "rich data" for a study I would soon write up. Then the unexpected happened. For a year I could do nothing with my notes. I picked them up; put them down; moved them around; took notes on the notes; copied them so that one set could sit in loose-leaf binders in my university office while the original set lay in binders on my kitchen table at home. (I had moved the notes to the kitchen table after realizing I kept avoiding them at my desk.) All the while, I kept trying to do simple things; to isolate themes; to find something to say that could be supported by my data. I thought of punching computer cards. I finally culled out the seven interviews with lesbian mothers and attempted to write about their experience, thinking that in some magical way the subject of motherhood would save me. It did not. Then I gave up. I closed the notebooks. I decided to write a novel. Occasionally, I thought about how despite the fact that I was now 1200 miles and many months away from the community, I still did not have a necessary analytic "distance" from the subjects of my study. However, that thought did not help.

Finally, a full year later, done with two drafts of my novel, and haunted still by those volumes of notes—the undefined "promise" of my data, the sense that I should not let the research go to waste—I decided, "I must write about what I can relate to. I must write a personal account." I began writing about what it had been like for me to live in that lesbian community. I wrote many pages, and then I shelved them. What I wrote was interesting, to me. Beyond recalling my experience, it enabled me to see that what I had thought of as a lack of analytic "distance" might more usefully be viewed as lack of personal "separation" from my data, from all those "other women's voices" that rose up each time I took up my notes. But the account I had written was not social science in a conventional sense, and I wanted very much to be conventional.

However, writing the account did give me an insight. The most immediate problem, it seemed to me, was not that I did not have distance from my data, but that I did have, and probably always had, far too much distance. Before dealing with problems of "separation," I had to acknowledge that I was estranged.

I thought about estrangement.[4] I decided that to deal with my data in any "sociologically useful" fashion, I would have to get over my estrangement. I would have to feel that I could "touch" the experience of gathering my data, and in a way that I had not allowed myself before. I would have to begin by expanding my idea of my "data" to include not only my interview notes, but also my entire year of participation in the community. I would have to be willing not only to feel again what the experience of living in the community had been like for me, but also to feel it as fully and deeply as possible and to analyze my feelings. Why did certain things move me? What had unfolded over the year's time? Why had I felt estranged? What did I want? What did I receive? What was I afraid of? How could I bridge the gap between myself and my data?

Because I am not at ease simply "feeling" in an amorphous way, I went about "becoming in touch" with my data very methodically, in a highly disciplined and structured fashion. For the next four to five months, I devoted myself to an exercise which I called a "process of reengagement." The first stage of this exercise was a step-by-step analysis of my experience of involvement in the community, beginning with entry, progressing through entanglements in personal relationships, singling out key events and my emotional responses to them, reviewing the interview period, and ending with my feelings on leaving. The second stage was a step-by-step analysis of my experience in conducting the 78 interviews which were the source of my notes. I later wrote a personal account of this process, called "'Separating Out': A Method for Dealing with Qualitative Data," from which the following is excerpted. This excerpt describes the second stage in my reengagement process and shows how an understanding of the self can help resolve the problem of interpreting one's data.

"Separating Out": A Method for Dealing with Qualitative Data

A Case-Analytic Technique

The strategy in the second part of my reengagement process required that I deal with each of my 78 interview cases. First, I sought to identify and examine my responses to my interviewees as individuals. I reviewed feelings I had with respect to each interviewee, first, in anticipation of our interview session and second, during the interview itself. Finally, I analyzed the data of my interview notes themselves. The analyses in each phase of this process were done by writing down my thoughts and feelings, taking up a separate sheet of paper for each interviewee at each step. When I was through, I had one set of notes reflecting my "preinterview self-assessment," another on my "interview self-assessment," and a third on responses to the interview notes.

Step 1: Preinterview Self-assessment

During this preinterview self-assessment step, I recalled my acquaintance with each interviewee prior to our interview and reviewed how each interview appointment had been made. I remembered social occasions during which the interviewee and I had met and what the biases in introduction had been if the interviewee was known to me primarily through another person. Most important, I noted my personal expectations with respect to each interviewee immediately preceding the session: what I had anticipated with fear, and what with excitement, and what I felt I had wanted for myself in return. In doing this, I sought to identify those prejudices I brought to each interview. It seemed important to separate my personal disappointments and pleasures from my latter interpretations of my data. The following examples are indicative of the preinterview item self-assessment. They are excerpts from longer passages written about each preinterview experience.

> Preinterview #32: B. was one of my neighbors across the street who had been fairly open and friendly with me. I chose her to do one of the first interviews because she had been "public" as a lesbian and I felt she would be knowledgeable about the community and straightforward with me. Yet I was nonetheless concerned that she might not speak personally enough with me.

Preinterview #44: I knew D. mainly through K. and was prejudiced against her, or, more accurately, I felt fear regarding her—that she was judgmental and did not like me because of my relationship with K. and its troubles—that she was primarily K.'s friend.

Preinterview #67: I knew of V. that she was a straight woman in one of the core support groups in the community. Was afraid she would be distant and would withhold. Also, K. had told me V. played "poor me," so I worried I might get impatient with her.

Step 2: Interview Self-assessment

A similar approach informed the next interview self-assessment step. Here, again, I wanted to identify my prejudices and my "hidden" personal agenda I might have had. Yet in this step, even more so than in the preinterview assessment, I was intent on recapturing the force of my emotions at the time, since they seemed to me to surround my waiting notes. For example:

Interview #32: This surprised my expectations, because B. was, it seemed, candid with me and more personal than I'd expected. I did not feel forced to adopt her views or anything of the sort. I really felt for her as a person at the end of the interview, as I had not before.

Interview #44: Interview was very tense for me. I felt D. being defensive. Felt pressure on her part that I join her—see it all her way. Felt she didn't want to be interviewed, felt I was pushing this upon her. I was angry with her because of all these things. When I really wanted to be friends, to win her, to have her like me. In the end, I felt she ran away, wishing she'd not said what she did, angry with me. I wished to run after her, to make it all right—to confront. This is the interview I felt worst about of all of them, it seemed so much a denial and rejection of me. Though I felt its content—what she said— was rich.

Interview #67: Was partly tense because I suspected my own motives about wanting to get to K. through V.—get inside information that would help me settle my troubled feelings. Felt partly pressed by V. to feel as she did. Also that V. was partly confused, yet she felt she had a collar on rationality. The conversation was almost technical, in that she kept much emotion out. Did not like this (angry?—a little, but repressed it) in the end.

Interview #72: M. was the only one to really break down and cry at the time of the interview and want to be held. This scared me—because I did not want to get involved, and did not want her to become dependent on me. I tried to "handle" it by not making a big deal of it, by holding her and then letting her up when I felt she'd be okay. She had brought a tape recorder to record the interview for herself (only one who did this). When she started to cry and ask to be held, I pushed the recorder off. My leftover feelings were fear—that she'd call on me for more holding and that I'd say no. I might do it with someone but somehow I feared her, or she was not the one. I also had feelings that I invited this, with everyone. Then when I got it, drew back from it. This left me uneasy. Feeling angry(?), lonely. What if it were me who wanted to cry and be held?

It became increasingly obvious to me, as I recalled and noted my responses to each case, that I had felt much discomfort and that that had caused me trouble. Yet these were exactly the kinds of things I needed to articulate, since they had been crucial in frustrating my dealings with my data. For instance, the more I noted my responses, the more I became aware of how very often I had been afraid, both prior to the interview sessions and during them. What I had previously identified as anger was really fear. This, I think, was because each interview situation was an intimacy situation for me and an occasion which I felt required proof of myself. I wanted, during the interview sessions, not only to know each of my interviewees, but also for them to know and care about me. I reacted as if it were a denial of myself when an interviewee did not seem to care:

Interview #62: A disappointment. Because M. seemed to me a lot a front—how she wanted to appear, a line, not a real person. I didn't feel the intimacy, the honesty that I wanted. Felt she suspected that I found her false (unconvincing) in this way and that she was angry at this and defensive. When she left, I was let down and angry. Felt she had dealt with me formally, almost as a functionary for herself, rather than as a person. Which I wanted.

The interview self-assessment was difficult. I kept wanting to describe the interviewee and how she appeared to me when she arrived and as she was involved in the session. However, this seemed largely ungrounded, unless I also noted my own reasons for the response—the emotional issue, or issues, each session raised for me. I had to discipline myself to note a reaction of my own for every action of each interviewee that I noted. I had to take time to figure out; the logic of my own reactions, for what they would tell me about barriers to dealing with my data. I had not expected the interview assessment to become highly self-analytic, since I felt that I had already been extremely self-reflective during the earlier stage of reengaging with the entire research experience (Part I of my exercise). Nonetheless, new things were brought to my attention in recalling my specific feelings in each of the interview situations.

My most important recognition occurred after going through approximately one third of the cases. I began to notice that I could distinguish my responses in terms of whether I had felt pressure to become like a particular interviewee, or whether I had felt I could "be myself" during the interview. I then began to look to characteristics of the different interviewees in relation to myself in order to understand why I would feel or not feel pressure. I realized that I would become angry and feel bad in those cases where I felt I had to be like the interviewee. My sense gained from these cases tended to overpower my sense of the actually larger number of cases in which I did not feel this threat. For example:

> Interview #75: Went well. I was impressed with R. as a person—her independence, the carefulness of her thinking, her clarity. I got a good picture of her—because her words were honest?—and so did not feel threatened. Maybe this is mechanism: when the interviewees are confused (due to being defensive or otherwise inauthentic, or confused about themselves), I get threatened and confused about who I am, because the relationship is confused. I don't know what I am relating to: while if the interviewees are more clear about themselves, I can be more clear about myself.

I concluded that I had felt threatened where it seemed to me an interviewee was inauthentic in her presentation of self in ways that set off my own doubts as to who I was. I decided that my feelings concerning this were so strong because of the fact that I shared an intimate identity stake with all the women I interviewed. I looked to them, even in the ostensibly other-oriented interview situation, to help me solve the problem of who I was. Although the interviews were highly controlled and guided by me, my controls did not protect me from threats on the deeper level. The interviews were actually occasions of inner panic, occasions during which I feared that others would not allow me to be myself—to act as the person I truly felt I was. This feeling of threat to my sense of self had not been fully clear to me before I analyzed the individual accounts. But finally it was and I could see in my responses how much I had wanted personal confirmation and acceptance:

> Interview #54: In her office. I was uncomfortable because of her power things—the phone, showing off stuff she'd written, her sensitivity. I felt she was trying to impress me with herself, that I was mostly a pawn to this, a person to be won over, not an independent person to be related to—one who had sensitivity, specialness, etc. And I wanted this other response from her. Perhaps because she was a peer at the university, and an unattached woman, recently out of a relationship. I think I had hopes we might be friends. With sexual possibilities maybe. But even if not, I wanted to be an equal, a real person to her. I left disappointed.

As I analyzed my responses in this way, I felt that my desires for confirmation, while perhaps extreme, might be more widespread in the community. The lesbian community might be functioning as an "identity community" for its members, one in which the most intimate sense of self was frequently on the line, a community in which the power to threaten by lack of confirmation was as strong as the power to confirm.

Reexamining my interview session responses made me aware of something else that was extremely important: the extent to which, even in those special-purpose sessions, I was engaged with the community and acting according to its rules, just as I had been outside the sessions. The interview situations were, in effect, small dramatic reenactments of the social dynamics of the larger community. They were microcosms providing specific examples of expected or acceptable community behaviors. In looking back on my responses, I was shocked for example, to see how often my reactions to interviewees included an element of sexual expectation. In this way, I was clearly a member of the community:

> Interview #2: B. was younger than I had expected and very beautiful, with long straight dark hair. She reminded me of a woman I had been involved with back in California in the winter. I think I felt I would like her to fall in love with me.

> Interview #51: Knew E. casually and occasionally, it seemed to me, she would be showing sexual interest in me. Some part of me, I think, wanted that more and also was repulsed and frightened by it.

The sexual expectation dilemma had been spoken of candidly by one of my interviewees:

> It's like good old sex being such an important part of people's life. And coming to a place with that expectation. Like I am here because other people in this room are here because they have the same sexual orientation I do. It puts a great pressure on you as to what am I up to and what are these people in this room doing? A lot of heterosexual traps I tried to escape, I found here. Because of all those sexual tensions, nobody gets to really know each other or to feeling comfortable with each other.

In this same vein, this interviewee also articulated a predicament referred to in the accounts of others:

> There isn't one woman in the community I haven't considered having a relationship with, just because you're in this community and because of all the pressure to need and want a relationship. Because you're in this community and because you have to relate some intimate details to get along, there is always the question of whether you want to be intimate. In a straight community, you have all these girlfriends who you tell things to. But in this community, you have to worry about whether it means you want to go to bed with them.

It was not easy for me or for my interviewees to acknowledge the pervasive and central sexual tensions of the community, since these were often subtle and personally sensitive. However, by examining my own responses, I was able to arrive at important insights. I concluded that my feelings of sexual expectation had less to do with actual possibilities for sexual relationship than with rules for defining the self in the community. For this was a community in which one's sense of personal identity was closely linked with one's feelings of sexual possibility and in which sexuality often appeared as a route to intimacy, as a means by which an individual might become truly known.

Step 3: Analyzing the Interview Notes

Once having completed both preinterview and interview self-assessments, and interpreting as many of my own responses as I could, I turned to the task of dealing with the content of my interview notes. Initially, I wanted to treat the accounts of my interviewees, as much as possible, as separate and different from my own. I wanted to see my interviewees as sharing my processes and reactions perhaps on occasion, but not as a rule. Yet as I began to review my notes, seeking concepts appropriate for categorizing and "making sense," I found that I was drawing on my understanding of myself with far greater facility than on anything else that came to hand. The task then reformulated itself as one in which I would seek to determine if and how my interviewees shared versions of the problems I had identified in myself.

I would look for words used by my interviewees that were reminiscent of my own, processes that were similar to mine, and assumptions about self in relation to others that were similar. Most centrally, as I read, I would imagine each individual as existing in a problem situation concerning differentiation of self in the community. I would view each individual as seeking, time and again, confirmation for who she was, all the while suspecting she might not belong.

Increasingly, as I examined the notes, I found what seemed to be parallels among the feelings expressed by the interviewees. For example, there was a frequent concern with possibilities for rejection by the community, whether rejection was or was not likely to occur:

> I have a yearning to be part of the community, but I feel, and I know by the grapevine, that I would be rejected.

There was a sense that the community had rules that excluded important aspects of the self, as these excerpts from different interviewees suggest:

> It's hard to capture because all that is implicit—a sense that the community does have these strong rules.

> There are some things you couldn't say. . . .

A sense of the community as unreal or uncertain appeared often in the various accounts:

> The community, for me, became a monster.

> I see several different communities.

> Like the first two years I lived here, I was unaware there was one [a community].

> I think of them as a real tight closed group, that's closed until they know for sure that you're a lesbian, for one thing. And I don't think that you could just go meet them, go hang out with them. I think you have to join them.

In most of the accounts, there was a desire for the community to provide acceptance and self-confirmation:

> The community, to me, is a group of women who I could *know* that I could lean on for support.

> Here is a group of women who can understand me, touch me the way I want to be touched.

> When I had finally found these people, I felt I had finally found people who could accept my whole life.

Along with the need for confirmation were feelings of extreme disillusionment and disappointment when the community seemed to have failed a particular woman:

> You would think it would be easier to assert your differences in a community of women. But it's not. It's real disillusioning.

> I needed reassurance that I was doing all right. I needed some indication that I was appreciated. And they kept spewing forth this ideology of the community, the community, this axial of support when I felt totally abandoned.

During this data analysis step, I used my own insights and developed them further with reference to analyses of the interview notes. This enabled me finally to write a paper about the collective reality of participation in the community (Kreiger, 1980). The reality I described in that paper was, of course, only part of the reality felt by community members, that portion I could be in touch with as a result of my experience. But by now, as a result of clarifying my experience, I was no longer as frightened of my involvement as I had been initially. I could use my own recognitions as a guide, a source not only of personal but of sociological insight.

This is not to suggest that my interpretations of the community were merely interpretations of myself "writ large" and imposed on the testimony of others. I also had to follow additional rules that granted to other members of the community feelings and responses that were different from mine. Throughout the process of analyzing my notes, it was important for me to maintain a sense that there was much in each interview account that fell beyond my own limited experience. My task was to try to uncover what I could with the tool of myself and my personal recognitions. I sought not simply to impose or to apply my newly developed recognitions, but to expand those recognitions by constantly challenging my existing understandings: challenging my perceptions of others with what I now felt I knew about myself and, at the same time, confronting my self-understanding with what my interviewees seemed to be telling me that was different.

I think that often in social research, this is what we really do. We see others as we know ourselves. If the understanding of self is limited and unyielding to change, the understanding of the other is as well. If the understanding of the self is harsh, uncaring and not generous to all the possibilities for being a person, the understanding of the other will show this. The great danger of doing injustice to the reality of the "other" does not come about through use of the self, but through lack of use of a full enough sense of self which, concomitantly, produces a stifled, artificial, limited, and unreal knowledge of others.

Conclusion

The preceding account describes an exercise that helped me to reengage with my data at the same time as "separating out" a sense of myself. The exercise proved immediately useful in generating insights. However, my problem of estrangement was not so easily solved. In 1980 when I returned to California, I again had trouble dealing with my data. I wanted to work with it and, simultaneously, to leave it; to begin new research. At that point, it helped for me to think back on the exercise I had engaged in during the previous year. That exercise had given me some confidence and an initial understanding of the nature of my problem. I knew that I would have to "assert myself," even if my assertion felt uncomfortable, and even if I would continually feel I was illegitimately imposing myself on my data.

Two and a quarter years had passed since the original research for my study was completed. I finally began writing *The Mirror Dance*. I wrote it quickly, relying upon what now seemed deeply imbedded intuitions. The book was published in 1983. Responses from both reviewers and readers suggested that its portrayal was valid, to a surprising and somewhat uncomfortable degree. Yet I knew that what I said in *The Mirror Dance* was dependent on a very personal and idiosyncratic process of data gathering and analysis. Because that process was so personal and because it worked essentially "backwards"—to understand my community, first I had to understand myself—I have presented a partial description here of an analytic exercise that helped me greatly.

The exercise I engaged in was, for me, a way out of a problem. It was a source of insight both about others and about myself. It gave me some confidence when I needed it; it gave me a feeling that "I had a right" to say something that was mine. I had studied a community that I felt I was part of, and, at the same time, that I felt estranged from. I was, at one point, overwhelmed by the voices of all the women in that community. They were all telling me what to do, and they were each telling me something different. It took a long time—longer than I had expected—to find, in myself, a voice by which I could speak back to them.

I found that voice and, as *The Mirror Dance* attests, I hid it. *The Mirror Dance* is written in an unusual ethnographic style, in which the voices of the women of a community interweave with and comment upon one another, analyzing their collective situation. The subjective "I" of the author is hidden in the book, never mentioned, merged finally back in with the community from which it emerged. It is precisely for that reason that the preceding account seems important to me, for it speaks to the origins of the book's inner voice. More crucially, it speaks of a personal process. In social science, I think, we must acknowledge the personal far more than we do. We need to find new ways to explore it. We need to link our statements about; those we study with statements about ourselves, for in reality neither stands alone.

Notes

1. This restimulation has been sparked most dramatically by the development of feminist scholarship across fields. This new scholarship has led to a reexamination not only of the difference that gender makes in determining what we see, and how we see it, but of other perceptual nets as well. In the recent literature, of great interest are the following, although a short list can only be suggestive: Keller (1982; 1983a; 1983b; 1985), dealing with notions of objectivity, subject-object splits, and gender in the work of scientists; Gilligan (1982), concerning women's distinctive developmental experiences and how these can lead to highly contextual ways of seeing; and Chodorow (1978), providing a basic psychoanalytic statement concerning women's self-other relationships. Each of these works, to a significant degree, draws on theories of object-relations, a field in which an important recent contribution is Mahler et al. (1975).

   For the past ten years, feminist anthropologists have been particularly articulate in encouraging the recognition of gender-related observer biases: Atkinson (1982) provides a recent overview; Rosaldo (1980), Reiter (1975), and Rosaldo and Lamphere (1974) frame many of the earlier classic questions. Nonfeminist anthropologists interested in "the new ethnography" have also been concerned specifically with the observer-observed relationship, although in a different vein, e.g., Clifford (1980; 1983); Rabinow (1979; 1983); and the works of Renato Rosaldo and Clifford Geertz. Strathern (1984) provides an astute comparison of differences between the new feminist and nonfeminist anthropologists in their treatment of subject-object. Finally, there is a category of other prominent recent works that either embody or call attention to subject-object and relational issues in a new way: e.g., Meyerhoff (1978); Hochschild (1983); and Bowles and Duelli Klein (1983).

2. Important discussions specific to sociology can be found in Smith (1974; 1979); Millman and Kanter (1975); Reinharz (1979); Gould (1980); Roberts (1981); and Stacey and Thorne (1984).

3. Instructions to field researchers to acknowledge and deal with contextual effects and with personal roles and biases have long been common in sociological texts on qualitative method. Further, many of our classics in sociology have distinctly personal tones and styles. However, I believe there is something new being said today, and it is being said most prominently by feminist scholars. This new statement concerns both what a personal style can be and what we mean by participant-observation. The feminists, in effect, are trying to point out that, traditionally, we have allowed "the personal" only if it was male; we do not even yet fully know what the female social scientist's voice might be. Further, it has never been at all clear exactly what we mean by participant-observation, but certainly the rational balancing of "distance" and "involvement" that is usually implied is something qualitatively different from what Keller, for instance (1983a; 1983b), means when she speaks of "a feeling for the organism," and, indeed, of "love."

4. I read Gearing on studying Fox Indians: "When one is estranged, he is unable to relate because he cannot see enough to relate to . . . [T]he opposite of being estranged is to find a people believable" (Gearing, 1970:5).

References

Atkinson, Jane Mennig
   1982 "Review essay: Anthropology." Signs 8:232–258.
Boeles, Gloria and Renate Duelli Klein (eds.)
   1983 Theories of Women's Studies. London: Routledge & Kegan Paul.
Chodorow, Nancy
   1978 The Reproduction of Mothering: Psychoanalysis and the Sociology of Gender. Berkeley: University of California Press.

Clifford, James
   1980. "Fieldwork, reciprocity and the making of ethnographic texts: The example of Maurice Leenhardt." Man 15:518–32.
   1983 "On ethnographic authority." Representations 1:118–46.
Gearing, Fred
   1970 The Face of the Fox. Chicago: Aldine.
Gilligan, Carol
   1982 In a Different Voice: Psychological Theory and Women's Development. Cambridge: Harvard University Press.
Gould, Meredith
   1980 "Review essay: The new sociology." Signs 5:459–67.
Hochschild, Arlie Russell
   1983 The Managed Heart: Commercialization of Human Feeling. Berkeley: University of California Press.
Keller, Evelyn Fox
   1982 "Feminism and science." Signs 7:589–602.
   1983a, "Feminism as an analytic tool for the study of science." Academe 69, 5:15–21. A Feeling for the Organism: The Life and Work of Barbara McClintock. San Francisco: W.H. Freeman.
   1985 Reflections on Gender and Science. New Haven: Yale University Press.
Krieger, Susan
   1980 "The group as significant other: Strategies for definition of the self." Unpublished paper given at the Annual Meetings of the Pacific Sociological Association.
   1983 The Mirror Dance: Identity in a Women's Community. Philadelphia: Temple University Press.
Mahler, Margaret, Fred Pine and Anni Bergman
   1975 The Psychological Birth of the Human Infant: Symbiosis and Individuation. New York: Basic Books.
Meyerhoff, Barbara
   1978 Number Our Days. New York: Dutton.
Millman, Marcia and Rosabeth Moss Kanter (eds.).
   1975 Another Voice: Feminist Perspectives on Social Life and Social Science. New York: Anchor.
Rabinow, Paul
   1977 Reflections on Fieldwork in Morocco. Berkeley: University of California Press.
   1983 "Facts are a word of God': An essay review of James Clifford's person and myth: Maurice Leenhardt in the Melanesian world." In G.W. Stocking, ed., Observers Observed: History of Anthropology Vol. 1. Madison: University of Wisconsin Press.
Reinharz, Shulamit
   1979 On Becoming a Social Scientist: From Survey Research and Participant Observation to Experiential Analysis. San Francisco: Jossey-Bass.
Reiter, Rayna R. (ed.)
   1975 Toward an Anthropology of Women. New York: Monthly Review Press.
Roberts, Helen (ed.)
   1981 Doing Feminist Research. London: Routledge & Kegan Paul.
Rosaldo, M.Z.
   1980 "The use and abuse of anthropology: reflections on feminism and cross-cultural understanding." Signs 5:389–417.
Rosaldo, Michelle Zimbalist and Louise Lamphere (eds.)
   1974 Woman, Culture, and Society. Stanford: Stanford University Press.

Smith, Dorothy E.

    1974 "Women's perspective as a radical critique of sociology." Sociological Inquiry 44:7–13.

    1979 "A sociology for women." Pp. 135–187 in Julie A. Sherman and Evelyn Torton Beck (eds.), The Prism of Sex: Essays in the Sociology of Knowledge. Madison: University of Wisconsin Press.

Stacey, Judith and Barrie Thorne

    1984 "The missing feminist revolution in sociology." Unpublished paper given at the Annual Meetings of the American Sociological Association.

Strathern, Marilyn

    1984 "Dislodging a world view: Challenge and counter-challenge in the relationship between feminism and anthropology." Unpublished paper. Draft of a lecture given in the series, Changing Paradigms: The Impact of Feminist Theory Upon the World of Scholarship. Adelaide, Australia: Research Centre for Women's Studies.

Ethics: The Failure of Positivist Science

Yvonna S. Lincoln and Egon G. Guba

Despite the widespread proliferation of professional ethical standards such as those of the American Psychological Association (Ad Hoc 1973, 1982), ethical concerns continue to plague social research. The maturing of social science over the past fifty years has not been accompanied by a concomitant maturing of ethical standards. Rather, increasing social complexity has provoked new questions and suggested new issues not covered even by the more recently developed standards. As Bulmer has noted,

> . . . the moral implications for society of natural, medical, and social science research have become sharper. Ethical and related concerns about nuclear physics, genetic engineering, organ transplants, and real-world social experiments have become major public issues. The public scrutiny of scientific work, including social science, is correspondingly keener. . . . Regulation of research is increasing, and social scientists are increasingly likely to find their research activities circumscribed in various ways. Apart from the intrinsic importance of such issues, they are a test of the social relevance, responsibility, usefulness, and moral stature of social science, as well as a challenge to us to explain and justify our activities to the wider society. (1980, 124)

We feel that a major cause of the ethical dilemmas that continue to plague social science inquiry is the set of metaphysical assumptions that undergirds conventional methodologies. These assumptions provide a warrant for near-unethical decisions, raising highly justified concerns on moral grounds. We shall review the present status of ethical guidelines for inquiry and show how the ontological and epistemological belief system on which conventional inquiry rests abets their circumvention. However, these difficulties may be resolved by a shift from a realist ontology and an objectivist epistemology to a relativist ontology and an interactive epistemology, as found, for example, in our earlier work in naturalistic inquiry (Lincoln and Guba 1985) and also shared to a greater or lesser degree by constructivist, hermeneutic, and phenomenological alternatives to postivism (including post-postivism). But of course the shift to another metaphysical system does not remove all ethical dilemmas and, while relieving some, may introduce others of which postivism is relatively free. We shall review the disadvantages as well as the advantages of the proposed shift.

Conventional Responses to Ethical Dilemmas

Social scientists concerned with ethical problems have tried to deal in different ways with the question of what constitutes ethical behavior and how it can be achieved. Some unethical behavior is directed by individual scientists against members of their peer group—for example, concocted data or plagiarism. However, most discussions of ethical behavior focus on the inequities and insults that can be inflicted on hapless research participants, conventionally termed, *subjects*, a word reflecting the concept that research participants have things done to them. We prefer "respondent." Needless to say, participants are relatively powerless compared to the inquirers themselves, especially when the inquirers have the warrant of a university, government, or foundation sponsor. This power disparity led professional groups like the American Psychological Association to devise "rules of the game" since, without the influence of some external controlling mechanism, subjects may be exploited by unprincipled inquirers. Typically, such discussions focus on one of three different concerns: *ethical levels*, the means for taking *moral responsibility*, and *legal definitions*.

Ethical Levels

Edward Diener and Rick Crandall suggest three levels of ethical guidelines: wisdom ethics, which are expressions of "ideal practice" as found, for example, in the *APA Standards* (Ad Hoc 1973, 1980) and which may be thought of as guidelines for anticipating and avoiding ethical problems; *content ethics*, which "state which acts are right and which acts are wrong" (1978, 4). Wisdom and content ethics can at best be markers along a treacherous road, they aver. Ultimately the inquirer must make individual judgments reflecting his or her value structure, the internalized ethical codes of mentors and trainers, and the situation in which the inquiry is conducted. Thus, ethical decisions are basically left to the individual inquirer. Since as Webb et al. (1966) have noted, the "individual moral boiling points" of inquirers differ, so will the ethical decisions they reach, even under similar circumstances.

Moral Responsibility

Moral philosopher Sisella Bok, who has written extensively on the moral dilemmas of lying, concealment, and revelation (1978, 1982), suggests three criteria for judging the ethicality of some inquirer decision or proposed decision. First is the criterion of *publicity*. That is, the dilemma must be "capable of public statement and defense" (1978, 97). Further, this public scrutiny must be carried out with a public of *reasonable persons*, preferably "those who share the perspective of those affected by our choices" (1978, 98). Finally, much depends on the criterion of *discretion*, that is, "the intuitive ability to discern what is and what is not intrusive and injurious" (1982, 41). But the prudent and cautious reserve implied by the criterion of *discretion*, that is, "the intuitive ability to discern what is and what is not intrusive and injurious" (1982, 41). But the prudent and cautious reserve implied by the criterion of discretion is, like Diener and Crandall's concept of ethical decisions, an individual matter. Again, the problem of nonequivalent "boiling points" must be faced.

Legal Responsibilities

It seems apparent from the long, sorry, and well-documented history of ethical abuses that leaving ethical matters to the virtue and/or discretion of individual inquirers is not sufficient. Nothing intrinsic in the conventional processes of inquiry either mandates or rewards ethical behavior. That fact is well recognized in the many legal restraints imposed upon social science inquiry. Here are the most commonly used:

1. *No harm*. Generally accepted principles dictate that respondents not be harmed or placed at risk, including the "lawful" harm that may result when subjects lose, or are cajoled or deceived into giving up, their rights. Of course, harm can also be inflicted if respondents are denied what might have been an auspicious or gainful intervention of "treatment," or when the values of inquirers (or of their sponsors or funders) are served to the detriment of or at the expense of the values of the

subjects themselves. These last tow conditions are frequently overlooked in defining what constitutes physical or psychic harm.

2. *Fully informed consent.* Federal guidelines and regulations now specify what may constitute legitimate informed consent for participating in an inquiry project, including a series of prescriptions that govern inquirer/subject interactions. But the inquirer's definition of "full information" may be far different from the subject's. Inquirers frequently argue that subjects are too unsophisticated about either the content or the process of a given inquiry to make full information possible. We consider this argument mere rationalization, insufficient to override this requirement. Subjects cannot make informed decisions about participation if they are misled about the purposes or procedures of the inquiry.

3. *Protection of privacy and confidentiality.* As in the case of informed consent, federal guidelines and regulations stabilize boundaries around some of the more glaring violations. As a genera rule, individuals are entitled by law to privacy for their persons and confidentiality of information about themselves. Such records as medical claims, school grades, test scores, and financial statements, by law, must be treated as privileged documents, released only with the person's specific permission. Nevertheless, computer access to networked data banks across the country has made this requirement difficult or impossible to enforce. The temptation to access data that are available even though "protected" may be too great to resist.

4. *No deception.* The issue of deception is the most difficult to cope with. Bok (1978) identifies several arguments inquirers use who do feel it necessary to deceive subjects. Sometimes they deceive to "avoid" greater harm, as when physicians lie to a patient with a terminal illness to spare him or her mental anguish and suffering. Others argue that deception is justified in the interest of fairness: to redress a wrong, to right an injustice, or to protect someone's privacy. It is difficult to imagine how a lie might ultimately redress a wrong or right an injustice, but it is easy to see how some lies might protect the privacy of individuals. The minor alteration of names, place descriptions, and the like is virtually *de rigueur* in social science research. Some inquirers urge that deception is justified in the larger end of maintaining or protecting the truth, although once again, it is hard to see how a lie can protect the truth.

But Bok's fourth justification for deception is simultaneously the most perverse and the most frequently cited, implicitly or explicitly, in the interest of defending what might otherwise be deemed morally reprehensible: the lie allows some larger benefit or social good. This argument is often phrased as "serving the interests of science," "the search for truth," or the "public's right to know."

It is precisely in the putative interests of science that deceptions such as those proscribed under the "no harm," "fully informed consent," and "protection of privacy and confidentiality" provisions are so often perpetrated, as eloquently documented by such researchers as Diener and Crandall (1978). Treatments *are* withheld to meet scientific criteria of controlled experimentation. Respondents' values *are* systematically disregarded as mere opinions with no basis in scientific knowledge. Purposes of research *are* systematically withheld from subjects on the ground that were they to know them, the "technical adequacy" of the study would be composed, as for example, through reactivity. Protected personal information *is* accessed when the researcher deems it useful to his or her larger search for truth. Finally, the public's right to know is at best an Occam's Razor, seemingly justifying the abuse of respondents' rights to gain some putative good for the population as a whole.

What can we learn from this brief look at the status of inquiry ethics? First, it seems clear that much depends on the "moral boiling point" of the individual inquirer; different inquirers will make different decisions even when confronted with similar circumstances. Second, it seems clear that nothing inherent in conventional modes of social science research either mandates or rewards ethical behavior. Third, inquirers have managed to find many apparently sound reasons for avoiding "wisdom ethics"—the ideal ethical practices—in conducting their research. How can we account for this state-of-affairs? And is there no way to resolve this problem?

The Tilt of the Conventional Paradigm

The difficulty, as we see it, stems from the metaphysics undergirding conventional (positivist) inquiry, viz., a realist ontology and an objectivist epistemology (Lincoln and Guba 1985). Postivism's fundamental ontological premise is hat there exists an *actual reality*, a "way things really are," that can be discovered (converged on) by the methods of science. This actual reality operates according to a series of natural laws, the "way things really work," which it is also the business of science to determine. If that reality can be discovered and its governing laws determined, then it is possible for science to predict and control future events, to exploit nature for the putative advantage of personkind. Given this ontological position, it follows that scientists, in their work of discovery and determination, must be *objective*, that is, assume a detached stance so that they will not influence the outcome of the inquiry nor allow their values (or those of the client or sponsor) to affect the results. To find out "how things really are" and "how things really work," the inquirer must be in a position to put questions directly to nature and get nature's answers directly back.

With such a metaphysical warrant for the search for truth in hand, the social scientist is free to argue convincingly that his or her research requires and justifies deception. A scientist needs a higher order of "truth"—a "reality" that is described as precisely as possible with its rules and laws plainly understood, so that, ultimately, prediction and control are possible. So long as prediction and control are seen as contributing to some "higher order social good," the warrant becomes complete. Thus, to use the terminology of Diener and Crandall (1978), *wisdom ethics* (ideals) operate to undermine *ethical process decisions* in the conduct of research.

Presumptions about the nature of reality reinforce—and indeed require—treating human research subjects as though they were objects. Objectifying human beings in the process of searching for "truth" has led, as feminist Evelyn Fox Keller (1983) has argued, to the depersonalization and devaluing of human life. The posture on reality assumed by conventional scientific inquirers rest, as Diane Baumrind puts it, on "the logical postivist presupposition that laboratory observations *could* provide unassailable knowledge if only we were able to produce a uniform psychological reality and do away with error variance . . . in the hope that the experimenter can . . . infer unambiguously the existence and direction of causal relations by ruling out alternative causal explanations" (1985, 170). Of course, the flaw in such reasoning lies in assuming the possibility that such "unassailable knowledge" can be obtained or even approximated. Baumrind points out that "the claim that observations can provide value-free, objective knowledge has been challenged by philosophers and scientists at least since Heisenberg's [indeterminacy] principle was enunciated" (1985, 170).

Even if such unassailable knowledge *could* be obtained (an assertion we flatly deny), the costs of obtaining it might be too high. For one thing, conducting research in a way that fully meets the ontological and epistemological requirements of the conventional paradigm may lead to false findings—at least false in the sense of not representing the "way things really are" or the "way things really work." Carefully controlled studies lead to findings generalizable in conventional terms only to other similar carefully controlled settings (e.g., laboratories). Furthermore, even traditional inquirers like Baumrind are now admitting that the price of deceptive research practices is not worth the game. H.W. Reese and W.J. Fremouw posit that "the ethics of *science* deal with the integrity of data; unethical practices undermine science as a body of knowledge. . . . The ethics of *research* deal with the protection of human rights; unethical practices do not undermine science as a body of knowledge, but they undermine society at large through the implications of the research findings or society as embodied in human research participants through the methods used" (1984, 963). Society attempts to bring normal ethics and normative ethics into the conformity by the institution of peer review boards, institutional committees to oversee the protection of human subjects, and federal and state regulation of the human research process; but they challenge "the assumption that ethical conduct has been adequately legislated through peer review or federal regulation" (Reese and Fremouw 1984, 863), since "legislated review boards are more concerned with legalistic due-process compliance than with ethical behavior; they confuse accounting with accountability, etiquette with ethics, responsiveness with responsibility, and religion with faith. They are concerned with form rather than substance, and by legislation they are barely qualified to determine whether proposed research is good science" (p. 871). Thus normative societal ethics rarely get translated into the normal ethics of science.

The implications of this disjunction are serious. When researchers deceive in the name of science, respondents' "rights to autonomy, dignity and privacy are necessarily violated" (Baumrind 1985, 71). In this violation, Baumrind argues, there are three types of costs, each of which is onerous, dangerous, and too high to be borne: costs to the respondents themselves, costs to the profession, and costs to society as a whole.

Costs to the respondents include an undermining of their trust in their own judgment; a loss of trust in fiduciaries; and the psychological stresses of having been duped, including admitting to having been duped and engaging in destructive obedience. Costs to respondents also include the loss of self-determination and the loss of individual locus of control.

Costs to the profession include: "(a) exhausting the pool of naive subjects, (b) jeopardizing community support for the research enterprise, and (c) undermining the commitment to truth of the researchers themselves" (Baumrind 1985, 169).

Costs to society include a loss of "trust in expert authorities . . . , increased self-consciousness in public places, broadening the aura of mistrust and suspicion that pervades daily life, inconveniencing and irritating persons by contrived situations, and desensitizing individuals to the needs of others" (Baumrind 1985, 169–170). Taken together, these costs not only destroy the credibility of social science but also subvert the social principles upon which societies rest and which permit intentional and civil public action.

In sum, the mandate imposed on social scientists to search for a putative truth allows the traditional or conventional scientist to objectify research participants and to deceive respondents in the pursuit of that truth. But social scientists themselves are slowly rejecting the costs of such public deceit as too high and ultimately counterproductive to the research enterprise itself. As a consequence of the criticism, social scientists are asking whether those costs might not be avoided. Such a critique from within the confines of the conventional paradigm itself signals a fundamental reappraisal of how science ought to proceed in the future.

A Possible Solution: The Naturalistic Paradigm

Given legal boundaries, moral principles, and the social costs of engaging in traditional science, how can we avoid unethical behavior and confront or sidestep the problems engendered by postivist social science? The simplest answer to this question is to move to an alternative paradigm, one based on fundamentally different ontological and epistemological assumptions and hence not subject to the critique leveled against postivism. Rather than using a realist ontology and an objective, dualistic epistemology, we propose using a naturalistic paradigm founded on a relativist (constructivist) ontology and a subjective, monistic epistemology. The ontological shift precludes citing a "higher order" or "ultimate" truth as a warrant for unethical behavior, while the latter shift mandates an openness with respondents that precludes deceiving and objectifying them.

Recall the hidden premises of positivism: deception is justified if it leads to greater knowledge, at least so long as it "protects" human subjects, who may, within these parameters, be treated in whole or in part as "objects" of the scientist's investigation. Naturalistic inquiry avoids both of these pitfalls and, in the process, responds to criticism from both the social science community itself and from social scientists who wish to work within another paradigm of inquiry (for example, see Reason and Rowan, 1981, among others).

Naturalistic inquirers respond to the twin problems of positivism in two ways. First, naturalism has no underlying premise that there is a "way things really are" or a "way things really work." Instead, social realities are social constructions, selected, built, and embellished by social actors (individuals) from among the situations, stimuli, and events of their experience. As a result, the naturalist is not interested in pursuing some single "truth," but rather in uncovering the various constructions held by individuals and often shared among members of socially, culturally, familially, or professionally similar groups in some social context. These constructions represent (we would argue, they *are*) the meanings that human beings attach to events, situations, and persons in their effort to impose order on social interaction. In that sense, constructions are intensely personal and idiosyncratic and, consequently, as plentiful and diverse as the people who hold them.

In confronting the proposition that there is not a single, ultimate truth but rather multiple, divergent, and whole-cloth constructions, the naturalist is ill-served by engaging in deception; indeed, deception is absolutely counterproductive to his or her research purpose. Deception merely confuses the participants, who are at a loss to know what kinds of responses the naturalist wants and needs. (Of course it may not be counterproductive for the participant to engage in deception, for example, in the interest of putting his or her best foot forward. But that is not the matter at issue here, and is, in any event, a problem in all paradigms.) Since it is naturalistic inquirer and since deception serves only to obfuscate the naturalist's search, the naturalist is reinforced, even rewarded, for *avoiding* deception. Suddenly, deception ceases to eliminate bias and contribute to validity, as it presumably does in conventional inquiry, but actually frustrates the very search which it was intended to aid. If the inquirer is interested in constructions, then it is pointless to lie to or deceive respondents. A researcher cannot uncover individual and group [emic] constructions by deliberately misleading individuals and groups about the purpose of the research.

The second way in which naturalistic inquiry guards against deception is through the special relationship implied by the interaction between researcher and respondent. Naturalists reject the idea that the researcher-researched relationship ought to be objective and distanced. It is, furthermore, a relationship between equals, built on mutual respect, dignity, and trust. Reinharz (1978) characterizes it as a "lover model" (mutual exchange and respect) rather than a "rape model" (researcher takes what's wanted and leaves).

If scientists have no license to treat others as "objects," then they must build a wholly new relationship on the basis of mutual exchange, the preservation of human dignity, privacy, and confidentiality, and the joint negotiation of research purposes, strategies, and interpretations. This means nothing less than a form of inquiry which is increasingly collaborative or joint (Reason and Rowan 1981), with the researched being equal partners with an equal voice in collecting and interpreting the data and in distributing the "results." The power of agency and the locus of control never leave the province of the respondents, and their decisions regarding information about them—including evaluating the possible harm they may suffer—remain theirs to negotiate in the present and in the future.

Because of the shifts in the metaphysical assumptions—that reality is a multiple entity socially constructed and that respondents cannot be treated as objects but must be accepted as viable partners at every step in the inquiry—naturalistic inquiry demands that *no deception ever be employed in the service of social science research.*

The Ethical Problems of the Naturalistic Paradigm

Of course the naturalistic paradigm, while it may redress certain failings of positivism, has problems of its own. The relativism of naturalism suggests that it is impossible (and always will be) to specify any ultimately true methodology for coming to know. The best we can hope for is for a more sophisticated and informed paradigm than that which guided the giants on whose shoulders we stand. Further, because new paradigms are often constructed, at least initially, to address weaknesses or incompleteness in earlier forms, we need be alert to the strong possibility that the new paradigm has problems. Such is, in fact, the case with naturalistic inquiry, although we prefer its dilemmas to those posed by conventional inquiry.

Among the dilemmas peculiar to naturalistic inquiry (and we do not pretend that our list is complete) are the special nature of intense, face-to-face contacts with participants; the difficulties with maintaining or preserving confidentiality and anonymity; the relationships of trust required which must be constructed in very short periods; the powerful pressure for completely open negotiations in light of the need to honor respondents' emic conditions; and the framing of the resulting case studies (which we believe are the appropriate "product" of any naturalistic inquiry) themselves—what should be included and what excluded, and how should the "self" of the researcher be finally represented? Each of these deserves mention, although our treatment here must necessarily be brief.

Face-to-face Contacts

Since naturalistic inquiry depends of re-creating respondents' realities, gathering and testing those realities necessitates person-to-person data collection with a human being, the inquirer, as instrument (Guba and Lincoln 1981). Dobbert believes that "humans are polyphasic learners who absorb information both coded and uncoded, implicit and explicit, intended and unintended, through simultaneous multiple modalities—the olfactory, auditory, visual, kinesthetic, tactile, positional, cognitive, and emotional ones; and with the ethologist . . . that humans are primates who learn through (if believe) exploration, manipulation, *activity,* and *interaction* (1982, 14–15, italics added). This activity and interaction, however, place both researcher and respondent in jeopardy. That jeopardy revolves about the highly personal relationships which are built as each gives, takes, shares, and teaches the other. Such highly personal interactions create vulnerability as knower and known exchange roles, barter trust, and reconstruct identities.

The inquirer faced with conventional questionnaires never confronts the frightening risk of knowing and being known, nor do his or her research participants need to provide slices of their lives. The instrument buffers the conventional inquirer from research participants, but there is little protection when the instrument *is* the inquirer. The unarmed and inaccessible human in touch with the unarmed and inaccessible participant is an encounter fraught with every possibility that can emerge from human interaction.

Anonymity, Confidentiality, and Privacy

Although the naturalist operates under the same legal rules and regulations as the conventional scientist, he or she may find particular difficulties in maintaining research participants anonymity or privacy. Tom Skrtic, Egon Guba, and Earle Knowlton found this to be exactly the case:

> It is the nature of naturalistic research and the case study reporting method that both are more susceptible to breaches of confidentiality and anonymity than conventional inquiry. Most naturalists are therefore very sensitive to the ethics involved and may go to extraordinary lengths to protect respondents and sites from discovery. . . . It seems to be well established that respondents have a right

to privacy, and if they give up that right in the spirit of cooperation with the researcher, they at least deserve as much protection as the researcher can provide. *As we have seen, such protection may be difficult to extend and impossible to guarantee.* Even if all the names and places and dates are changed "to protect the innocent," it is quite likely that other locals will be able to pinpoint the agencies and parties involved. And *that* breach of confidence may have the most serious consequences of all, for it is these other locals who may be in positions of authority or influence with respect to the research participants, and *thus may have the most powerful sanctions to apply.* (1985, 111; italics added)

As we have made clear earlier (Lincoln and Guba 1985), one of the procedures for establishing trustworthiness is the member check. Research personnel continuously test data and interpretations with members of the groups from which data are solicited. While researchers can be scrupulous in not revealing actual data sources (those data may have been collected from other members of the same audience), nevertheless, expressions or particular views may be recognizable as those of only one or two possible sources. Confidentiality and anonymity obviously cannot be guaranteed. Consequently, the trust relationships which are built must necessarily be negotiated with full disclosure of the risks which respondents are taking.

Trust

Trust between mature adults is built over time, a process complicated by the very human need to present the self at its best. Achieving trust demands forthrightness, clear and fair explication of the purposes of the research, and authentic presentation of the researcher's self—conditions which require time to fulfill. Some projects, however, operate on short time schedules, producing intra- and interpsychic stresses in researcher and researched alike. It is not impossible to establish good rapport in a short time; it is, however, costly (in psychological terms) to both parties. Researchers cannot, in short time frames, afford the repeated casual contacts which permit trust to build; and participants cannot afford to be misled about the intents and purposes of the research. The normal constraints on fieldwork that relies on the human instrument intensify as the time available shortens—hence the need for powerful self-awareness before entering the field.

Negotiation

Negotiation is a characteristic of naturalist inquiry which expresses itself most strongly in the relations between respondents and researchers. The presumption of agency on the part of respondents and the assumption that respondents' constructions are the stuff of which research is made require the researcher to engage in participative modes of inquiry which may seem unfamiliar and initially uncomfortable. The researcher may feel an irresistible desire to "take control," legitimated by the argument that it is necessary to protect the "technical adequacy" of the study. But negotiation—for data, for constructions, for interpretations, for respondents' cooperation—is the best and only way to proceed in an inquiry marked by face-to face contact, by relationships which must be re-formed at every stage of the inquiry process, and by the intense need to have respondents by the ultimate arbiters of credibility and plausibility.

Framing Case Studies

Two ethical problems emerge in framing a case study, particularly in deciding what to include and to exclude. First, how much of the researcher's "self" should be introduced into the case report? To what extent does the researcher be "informed and transformed" in the process? If we abandon the conventional requirement of objectivity, permitting research findings to emerge from the subjective interaction of researcher and researched, must not the self become an intimate part of the process?

The ethical dilemma here is not an unwillingness to give up the objective perspective, but the possibility that the self will be allowed greater weight in determining the outcome than it ought to be. The traditional power relationship between researcher and researched is tipped in favor of the researcher, who has both institutional sanctions and superior substantive background to support his or her personal conclusions. How can we protect the joint participants against disenfranchisement?

The second problem has to do with choices about what material to include and exclude from the case report. These choices are not solely the investigator's. The case report in its final form represents the joint construction to which all concerned parties have come as a result of negotiation. That process sets a context for the report and legitimizes the interpretations made in it. When interpretations are negotiated and settled, then data and incidents supporting those interpretations are chosen. Features of the context which call forth behaviors, activities, and values will need to be presented to ground them in that particular context. Of course, items of information cannot be left out of the report willy-nilly; the negotiation process ought to require confrontation of all data items and to make some reasonable disposition of them. If they are not to be included in the construction that emerges, there ought to be good reasons for their exclusion. The choices, whether of the researcher or the respondents, cannot be arbitrary.

Whose Agenda?

This list of problems by no means exhausts the ethical dilemmas arising from the naturalistic paradigm. The notion of "cooperative" or "participative" inquiry embraces other problems, one of the most acute of which is, "Whose agenda?"
Both Diener and Crandall (1978) and Dobbert (1982) make clear that all social research has some agenda. The former caution, as part of their general guidelines, that "when a study is supported by a funding agency, the scientist must determine whether the research will be used for beneficial purposes. He [or she] should examine the possible applications or social scientific findings and endeavor to make these uses constructive. Before conducting a study the researcher must consider how the information will affect the people being studied" (p. 217).

If the researcher does not undertake the study alone, then he or she has some obligation to discover why the funder wants the study done at all and to what ends the results will (may be) turned. Dobbert is quite clear that this process of sorting out different stakeholders' agendas is part and parcel of the ethical resonsibility of any social scientist (1982, 76-85). She describes two situations but says that there are "just as bad or worse" to be had for the listening at any professional meeting:

> A field worker hired by an agency of any sort to do research and provide recommendations for future policy and actions to the agency has, automatically, two clients—the agency utilizing the research and the study's subjects, for whom the policy or actions are intended. Often the situation is even more complex and five-party situations are not at all rare. A government may, for example, hire a research company to study schools in a certain problem area and make recommendations for their imporvement. The agency in turn hires a fieldworker who goes out to study the local situation, only to discover that there are two very strongly opposed factions attempting to control the schools in question and that each has a different philosophy, which leads to incompatible plans for their schools. Ethically, the fieldworker in this situation is responsible to both hiring agencies . . . ; to himself or herself personally; and to both of the studied groups, who have given time and effort to provide data, with the hopes of having their side of the issue heard. (1982, 82-83)

Our own experience verifies that such a situation is not unusual.

The ethical concern is exacerbated when the agendas to be served are compared to the maze of reality constructions. Whose reality gets presented? The respondents'? Which of the respondent subgroups? The investigators'? The funder's? The contracting agency's? The complexity of the problem can be appreciated from Figure 1.

We raised the issue earlier of the appropriateness of moving toward a more cooperative paradigm of research, one in which both investigators and participants negotiated interpretations of the data gathered (Lincoln and Guba 1985). We are now prepared to state unequivocally that, as an ethical concern, cooperation and negotiation between researcher and respondents/participants are essential both to maintain research authenticity and to fulfill the criterion of safeguarding human dignity. When participants do not "own" the data they have furnished about themselves, they have been robbed of some essential element of dignity, in addition to having been abandoned in harm's way. If they are accorded the dignity of ownership, they have the right to shape that information's use and to assist in formulating the purposes to which they will lend their names and information. To do less is to violate, to intrude, and to condemn to indignity.

Conclusion

We have argued that a central failure of conventional or positivistic inquiry is its inability to acknowledge and correct the socially and morally repugnant fact of deception in research and its violation of such societal ethics as dignity, self-determination, and individual human agency. Deception and the warrant to deceive that investigators inherit in the conventional paradigm have personal, social, and professional costs so high that even conventional inquirers reject them, as do those using a different paradigm (Lincoln and Guba 1985) and those debating the intersection of feminism and science (Keller 1983) or Marxism and science (Reynolds 1980-81).

The ethical concerns embodied in this failure may be seen as moral, legal, or social, although these three dimensions are not exclusive. Moral dimensions include tests for whether reasonable persons would approve the research, whether it would pass the test of publicity, and whether it would afford discretion in restraining intrusiveness and injuriousness. Legal tests revolve about whether the research sufficiently protects individuals from harm, from lapses in informed consent, from deception, and finally, from violations of privacy and confidentiality. Social tests include determining the costs of a cynical public disenchanted with the arrogance of a deceptive social science community.

Conventional inquiry acquires the warrant to engage in deceptive and even injurious research by virtue of its focus on a supposed single "reality." Convergence upon this reality as the single most important focus of research has justified deception as a way of preventing ambiguity of research results. This dubious means, of course, has failed to prevent ambiguity; furthermore, the costs of deception are added to the research, and the research results might not be deemed sufficient compensation.

The costs to research enterprises resulting from real or possible deception can be avoided if the research is conducted with the emergent paradigm of naturalistic inquiry. This paradigm's focus on the multiple realities of divergent social constructions eliminates the search for a single "reality." The emphasis on using rather than compensating for the interactivity of researcher and respondents allows participants to retain their individual loci of control, to make informed decisions about their participation, and to have substantial agency in shaping the processes and results of the inquiry into their lives.

Avoiding the necessity to deceive and the reliance on dominant-subordinate relationships in the research process does not, unfortunately, eliminate all problems associated with ethical social research. The naturalistic paradigm rings a new set of problems—fostering intense, fact-to-face contact with participants, maintaining privacy and confidentiality, building and maintaining trust, negotiating joint responsibility and control, and constructing a case report that controls the intrusiveness of the researcher's self and makes decisions about inclusion and exclusion on the basis of the jointly devised construction.

Nevertheless, although each paradigm resolves one set of problems while raising another, we believe that the warrant to deceive in positivist inquiry raises serious ethical difficulties in social research; the rescinding of that warrant is another powerful reason for seriously considering a paradigm shift.

Bibliography

Ad Hoc Committee on Ethical Standards in Psychological Research. *Ethical Principles in the Conduct of Research with Human Participants.* Washington, D.C.: American Psychological Association, 1982.

_____. *Ethical Principles in the Conduct of Research with Human Participants.* Washington D.C.: American Psychological Association, 1973.

Baumrind, Diane. "Research Using Intentional Deception: Ethical Issues Revisited." *American Psychologist* 40 (1985): 165–74.

_____. "IRBs and Social Science Research: The Costs of Deception." *IRB: A Review of human Subjects Research* 1, no. 6 (1979): 1–4.

Bok, Sisella. *Lying: Moral Choice in Public and Private Life.* New York; Random House, 1978.

_____. *Secrets: On the Ethics of Concealment and Revelation.* New York: Pantheon, 1982.

Bulmer, Martin. "The Impact of Ethical Concerns upon Sociological Research." *Sociology: The Journal of the British Sociological Association* 40 (1980): 125–30.

Diener, Edward, and Rick Crandall. *Ethics in Social and Behavioral Research.* Chicago: University of Chicago Press, 1978.

Dobbert, Marion Lundy. *Ethnographic Research: Theory and Application for Modern Schools and Societies.* New York: Praeger, 1982.

Guba, Egon G., and Yvonna S. Lincoln. *Effective Evaluation.* San Francisco: Jossey-Bass, 1981.

Keller, Evelyn Fox. "Feminism as an Analytic Tool for the Study of Science." *Academe* 69 (1983): 15–22.

Lincoln, Yvonna S., and Egon G. Guba. "Ethics: The Failure of Positivist Science." Paper presented at the annual meeting of the American Educational Research Association, Washington, D.C., April 1987.

_____. *Naturalistic Inquiry.* Beverly Hills, Calif.: Sage Publications, 1985.

Reason, Peter, and John Rowan. *Human Inquiry: A Sourcebook of New Paradigm Research.* San Francisco, Calif.: Jossey-Bass, 1981.

Reese, Hayne Waring, and William J. Fremouw. "Normal and Normative Ethics in Behavioral Sciences." *American Psychologist* 39 (1984): 863–76.

Reinharz, Shulamit. *On Becoming a Social Scientist.* San Francisco: Jossey-Bass, 1978.

Reynolds, David. "The Naturalistic Method of Educational and Social Research." *Interchange* 11 (1980–81): 77–89.

Skrtic, T., E. G. Guba, and H. E. Knowlton. "Interorganizational Special Education Programming in Rural Areas: Technical Report on the Multisite Naturalistic Field Study." Washington, D.C.: National Institute of Education, 1985.

Webb, Eugene J., Donald T. Campbell, Richard D. Schwartz, and Lee Sechrest. *Unobtrusive Measures: Nonreactive Research in the Social Sciences*. Chicago: Rand-McNally, 1966.

Problems of Reliability and Validity in Ethnographic Research

MARGARET C. LECOMPTE AND JUDITH PREISSLE GOETZ

Although problems of reliability and validity have been explored thoroughly by experimenters and other quantitative researchers, their treatment by ethnographers has been sporadic and haphazard. This article analyzes these constructs as defined and addressed by ethnographers. Issues of reliability and validity in ethnographic design are compared to their counterparts in experimental design. Threats to the credibility of ethnographic research are summarized and categorized from field study methodology. Strategies intended to enhance credibility are incorporated throughout the investigative process: study design, data collection, data analysis, and presentation of findings. Common approaches to resolving various categories of contamination are illustrated from the current literature in educational ethnography.

The value of scientific research is partially dependent on the ability of individual researchers to demonstrate the credibility of their findings. Regardless of the discipline or the methods used for data collection and analysis, all scientific ways of knowing strive for authentic results. In all fields that engage in scientific inquiry, reliability and validity of findings are important. A common criticism directed at so-called qualitative investigation (e.g., Magoon, 1977; Reichardt & Cook, 1979) is that it fails to adhere to canons of reliability and validity. This discussion applies the tenets of external and internal validity and reliability as they are used in positivistic research traditions to work done by ethnographers and other researchers using qualitative methods. In so doing, these tenets are translated and made relevant for researchers in the qualitative, ethnographic, or phenomenological traditions.

In this paper ethnographic research is used as a shorthand rubric for investigations described variously as qualitative research, case study research, field research, anthropological research, or ethnography (Smith, 1979). Characteristics of ethnographic research include participant and non-participant observation, focus on natural settings, use of participant constructs to structure the research, and investigator avoidance of purposive manipulation of study variables. Although these approaches are most common in sociology and anthropology, they are used to some extent by all social science disciplines. Wherever they are used, credibility mandates that canons of reliability and validity be addressed, even when ethnographic techniques are adapted within a broader, more positivistic design.

Reliability in ethnographic research is dependent on the resolution of both external and internal design problems (Hansen, 1979). External reliability addresses the issue of whether independent researchers would discover the same phenomena or generate the same constructs in the same or similar settings. Internal reliability refers to the degree to which other researchers, given a set of previously generated constructs, would match them with data in the same way as did the original researcher.

While reliability is concerned with the replicability of scientific findings, validity is concerned with the accuracy of scientific findings. Establishing validity requires determining the extent to which conclusions effectively represent empirical reality and assessing whether constructs devised by researchers represent or measure the categories of human experience that occur (Hansen, 1979; Pelto & Pelto, 1978). Internal validity refers to the extent to which scientific observations and measurements are authentic representations of some reality. External validity addresses the degree to which such representations may be compared legitimately across groups.

Although reliability and validity are problems shared by ethnographers, experimenters, and other researchers, some factors confounding the credibility of findings in experimental designs are inapplicable to ethnographic research; others need to be defined in special ways. In comparing and contrasting threats to validity and reliability recognized by both experimental researchers and ethnographers, we seek to clarify their relevance to other research traditions as well.

The results of ethnographic research often are regarded as unreliable and lacking in validity and generalizability. Some ethnographers ignore such criticisms; others, recognizing potential threats to the credibility of their findings, develop strategies addressing the issues. A few codify their techniques for comprehensibility across research disciplines and traditions (e.g., Cicourel, 1964; Denzin, 1978; Hansen, 1979; Naroll, 1962; Pelto & Pelto, 1978).

Ethnographic research differs from positivistic research, and its contributions to scientific progress lie in such differences. These may involve the data gathering that necessarily precedes hypothesis formulation and revision or may focus on descriptive investigation and analysis. By admitting into the research frame the subjective experiences of both participants and investigator, ethnography may provide a depth of understanding lacking in other approaches to investigation. Ignoring threats to credibility weakens the results of such research, whatever its purpose may be. However, addressing threats to credibility in ethnography requires different techniques from those used in experimental studies. A discussion of reliability and validity problems in ethnographic research properly begins with specification of major differences between the two research traditions.

Differences between Experimentation and Ethnography

Distinctive characteristics of ethnographic research designs (discussed exhaustively elsewhere (e.g., Rist, 1977; Smith, 1979; Wilson, 1977; Wolcott, 1975) result in variations in the ways problems of reliability and validity are approached in ethnographic and experimental research. Three significant areas are the formulation of research problems, the nature of research goals, and the application of research results.

Formulation of Problems

Formulation of an initial research problem involves both the delineation of a content area and the choice of appropriate design and methods for investigation. Positivistic and ethnographic research differ in approach to these issues.

In research focusing on the examination of effects caused by a specific treatment, credibility of the research design and the power of the treatment effect are established by holding constant or eliminating as many of the extraneous and contextual factors as possible. Ethnography, on the other hand, emphasizes the interplay among variables situated in a natural context. It rarely focuses on treatment unless a treatment or experimental manipulation is part of an overall context. Credibility is established by systematically identifying and examining all causal and consequential factors (Goetz & LeCompte, 1981; LeCompte & Goetz, in press; Scriven, 1974). The process involved differs from the post hoc analysis, which provides contextual information in positivistic traditions. The naturalistic setting in which ethnography normally is conducted both facilitates on-the-spot analysis of causes and processes and precludes precise control of so-called extraneous factors. The interrelationship among such factors generally constitutes the focus of ethnographic concern.

Nature of Goals

A second distinction between the two research traditions lies in the nature of their research goals. This issue relates less to initial formulation of a research question than to the stage of the research at which the use of theory becomes salient, the way theoretical considerations are integrated into the study, and the extent to which the goal of the study is to substantiate existing theory or to generate new theories (Goetz & LeCompte, Note 1).

Ethnographers attempt to describe systematically the characteristics of variables and phenomena, to generate and refine conceptual categories, to discover and validate associations among phenomena, or to compare constructs and postulates generated from phenomena in one setting with comparable phenomena in another setting. Hypotheses, or causal propositions fitting the data and constructs generated, then may be developed and confirmed. Ethnographers commonly avoid assuming a priori constructs or relationships. By contrast, experimental research is oriented to the verification or testing of causal propositions developed externally to the specific research site. Having hypothesized specific causal relationships between variables, experimenters test the strength or power of causes on effects. In a sense, experimental researchers hope to find data to match a theory; ethnographers hope to find a theory that explains their data.[1]

Application of Results

Most findings from experiments, survey designs, and quasi-experimental studies are intended to be generalized from the subjects sampled to some wider population. Reichardt and Cook (1979) note that such generalization is warranted only where subjects have been sampled randomly from the entire population to which the findings are applied, and they caution that this statistical condition obtains in few cases. Experimenters and survey analysts more commonly depend on design controls, sample size, and assumptions of equivalence to legitimize their generalizations.

Ethnographers rarely have access even to these nonstatistical conditions for generalization. As a consequence, they aim in application for comparability and translatability of findings rather than for outright transference to groups not investigated. Comparability and translatability are factors that could contribute to effective generalization in experimental studies; they are crucial to the application of ethnographic research.

Comparability requires that the ethnographer delineate the characteristics of the group studied or constructs generated so clearly that they can serve as a basis for comparison with other like and unlike groups (Wolcott, 1973). Translatability assumes that research methods, analytic categories, and characteristics of phenomena and groups are identified so explicitly that comparisions can be conducted confidently. Assuring comparability and translatability provides the foundation upon which comparisons are made. For ethnographers, both function as an analog to the goals of more closely controlled research: generalizability of research findings and production of causal statements.

For comparative purposes, ethnographers may choose phenomena to study because they are similar or because they differ systematically along particular dimensions. In either case, the intention is the clarification, refinement, and validation of constructs. This method can be used to compare phenomena identified in a single research site (Glaser & Strauss, 1967; Goetz & LeCompte,

1981), or it can be used by researchers engaged in ethnographic study of special phenomena in a number of research sites (e.g., Cassell, 1978; Herriott, 1977; Herriott & Gross, 1979; Stake, 1978; Tikunoff, Berliner, & Rist, 1975; Wax, in press; Whiting, 1963; Rist, Note 2).

Triangulating Research Design

Specifications of differences in overall design between experimental and ethnographic research do not preclude legitimate sharing of data collection strategies (Denzin, 1978). Ethnographic techniques may be supplemental, augmenting reliability or validity of an experimental design. Such strategies enhance the replicability of a treatment by providing a procedural and contextual frame for experimental manipulation.

In contrast, an informal experiment occurs when ethnographers use deliberate manipulations to elicit participant sanctions for the violation of social norms or to provoke other reactions from subjects of a study (e.g., King, 1967; Rosenfeld, 1971). In these cases experimental manipulations are supplemental to ethnography, providing special data for a naturalistic study.

This discussion first addresses problems of reliability and their redress in ethnographic studies. An analysis of problems of validity will follow. In certain respects these issues overlap; what threatens reliability in ethnographic research also may threaten the validity of a study. The two are separated here for heuristic purposes, with indications of overlap where necessary. For both issues, the discussion will refer to the three characteristics of ethnographic design delineated above: contextual focus, eclectic approaches to theory, and comparative applications.

Reliability

Reliability refers to the extent to which studies can be replicated. It requires that a researcher using the same methods can obtain the same results as those of a prior study. This poses a herculean problem for researchers concerned with naturalistic behavior or unique phenomena. Establishing the reliability of ethnographic design is complicated by the nature of the data and the research process, by conventions in the presentation of findings, and by traditional modes of training researchers.

Constraints on Ethnography Reliability

When compared to the stringently controlled designs of laboratory experiments or to the regulated procedures of field experiments, ethnographic design may appear to baffle attempts at replication. The type of data and the research process itself may preclude the use of standardized controls so essential in experimental research. Accommodating the strictures of experimental control requires manipulation of phenomena, which distorts their natural occurrence. Attempts at rigorous measurement may impede construction of powerful analytic categories if the phenomena observed are prematurely or inappropriately reduced or standardized.

Ethnographic research occurs in natural settings and often is undertaken to record processes of change. Because unique situations cannot be reconstructed precisely, even the most exact replication of research methods may fail to produce identical results. For example, Fuch's study (1966) of a racial incident at an urban elementary school cannot be replicated exactly because the event cannot be reproduced. Problems of uniqueness and idiosyncrasy can lead to the claim that no ethnographic study can be replicated. However, generation, refinement, and validation of constructs and postulates may not require replication of situations. Moreover, because human behavior is never static, no study can be replicated exactly, regardless of the methods and designs employed.

Among experimental researchers there is substantial familiarity with the analytic and statistical techniques appropriate to particular kinds of data. These are codified in textbooks and are shared across disciplines. Well-established norms also dictate that research reports and proposals include a description of the population studied as well as methods and instruments used, including established measures of reliability and validity and discussion of analytic techniques.[2]

Reliability in ethnography may be affected by traditions and ideologies in anthropology and field sociology regarding the way a report is presented. A consequence of the debate as to whether anthropology is an art (e.g., Evans-Pritchard, 1962) or a science (e.g., Kaplan & Manners, 1972) is the custom of presenting the results of a study artfully and accessibly. While this style is defended as providing effective communication of cultural knowledge, it could lead neophytes to the unwarranted conclusion that the ethnographic process is facile and simplistic.

The tradition of an artful presentation of results, combined with the strictures imposed by journal-length manuscripts, has resulted in the use of shorthand descriptors for research design and analytic techniques meaningful to research peers but deceptive to the uninitiated. Ethnography uses as its primary data collection technique the writing of field notes, either in situ or as immediately following the event observed as is ethically and logistically possible. However, ethnography is also multimodal; ethnographers use a wide range of techniques to supplement and corroborate their field notes, including the manipulations of the field that would be familiar to an experimental researcher (Wilson, 1977). Describing research merely as ethnography may obscure researcher use of on-site observations, structured and unstructured interviews, projective tests, photographs and videotapes, and survey censuses.

Ethnographers share a common intellectual heritage in which knowledge of all these research techniques is acquired in apprenticeships. This knowledge may be assumed on the part of the reader when results are presented. Ethnographic researchers themselves recognize the necessity for probing beyond journal-length articles to the more complete description of design, data collection, and data analysis located in technical reports and monographs. In some cases, replication may require direct communication with the individual who conducted the original research. Researchers untrained in anthropology or sociology may not exercise such care.

The ethnographic process also is personalistic; no ethnographer works just like another. A researcher's failure to specify precisely what was done may create serious problems of reliability.

Failure among ethnographers to provide sufficient design specificity has led to controversy. Pelto and Pelto (1978) and Kaplan and Manners (1972) identify the highly publicized discrepancy between two ethnographers' studies of the same Mexican village (i.e., Lewis, 1951; Redfield, 1930) as a consequence of the differences in their research designs. Redfield and Lewis addressed different issues, used different methods and time periods, and elicited responses from different segments of the population. Their studies were conducted from different, unexplicated world views and scientific assumptions. The problem was aggravated by presenting their results as representative of the belief system and social structure of the village as a whole rather than as derived from the discrete units actually investigated.

Neither external nor internal reliability, as threats to the credibility of inquiry, are problems unique to ethnographers. However, the discussion below examines these two issues in an ethnographic context and identifies ways that ethnographers address them.

External Reliability

Because of factors such as the uniqueness or complexity of phenomena and the individualistic and personalistic nature of the ethnographic process, ethnographic research may approach rather than attain external reliability (Hansen, 1979; Pelto & Pelto, 1978). Ethnographers enhance the external reliability of their data by recognizing and handling five major problems: researcher status position, informant choices, social situations and conditions, analytic constructs and premises, and methods of data collection and analysis.

Researcher status position. This issue can be phrased, "to what extent are researchers members of the studied groups and what positions do they hold?" In some ways, no ethnographer can replicate the findings of another because of the flow of information is dependent on the social role held within the studied group and the knowledge deemed appropriate for incumbents of that role to possess (Wax, 1971). For example, male researchers in tribal societies may find it difficult to obtain information about female rituals and child-rearing practices because these subjects may be unknown to men, known only through an artfully constructed set of myths, or deemed taboo for men even to consider (cf., e.g., Hammond & Jablow, 1976; Paulme, 1963; Reiter, 1975). Similarly, researchers who have friends among student groups and peer cliques (e.g., Cusick, 1973) will obtain different information about student values than those who have little access to students and who must rely on reports from teachers and principals (e.g., Fuchs, 1969).

Ethnographic conclusions are qualified by the investigator's social role within the research site. Other researchers will fail to obtain comparable findings unless they develop corresponding social positions or have research partners who can do so. Although research results generated by ethnographers whose positions were limited in scope may be only narrowly applicable, they are nonetheless legitimate. Such conclusions delineate facets of reality within a group, other aspects of which may be identified by researchers taking other social positions. Glaser and Strauss (1967) refer to these individual facets as slices of data which, taken together, contribute to the total picture of group life. McPherson's analysis (1972) of schooling in a small U.S. town is based on her observations as an elementary schoolteacher. Her description of schoolchildren may represent the relatively narrow perspective of teacher, but can be replicated only by researchers who assume comparable roles. Studies of students in other small U.S. towns, conducted from alternative role positions, must be regarded as supplemental studies rather than replicative studies.

Because ethnographic data depends on the social relationship of researcher with subjects, research reports must clearly identify the researcher's role and status within the group investigated (e.g., Sieber, in press). In addition, some researchers enter settings as nonparticipant observers who develop no personal relationships with members of the groups, while others develop friendships that provide access to some kinds of special knowledge while limiting access to others. Ethnographers customarily label their investigative stance toward participants according to taxonomies such as that developed by Gold (1958) and describe the content and development of the social status and position accorded them by the group participants (e.g., Janes, 1961; Wax, 1971).

Informant choices. Closely related to the role the researcher plays is the problem of identifying the informants who provide data. Different informants represent different groups of constituents; they provide researchers with access to some people, but preclude access to others. For example, in Cusick's ethnographic study (1973) of student culture in a midwestern high school, his initial association with a clique of senior athletes facilitated his entry to groups with whom the athletes associated, but hindered his access to other cliques and to student isolates. In associating with one group, researchers may forfeit information about the life experiences of people in other groups. Berreman's retrospective analysis (1962) of fieldwork in India provides a classic example of the extent to which knowledge gathered is a function of who gives it.

Participants who gravitate toward ethnographers and other field researchers may be atypical of the group under investigation; similarly, those sought by ethnographers as informants and confidants also may be atypical (Dean, Eichhorn, & Dean, 1967). Sometimes this is necessary because people who speak languages comprehensible to researchers, who understand the analytic categories used by ethnographers, and who are introspective and insightful about their own lives are rare in most groups. The qualities that make them valuable as informants and research assistants may mark them as deviant from their own groups.

Threats to reliability posed by informant bias are handled most commonly by careful description of those who provided the data. Such characterization includes personal dimensions relevant to the researcher as well as dimensions significant to the informant and others in the group. External reliability requires both careful delineation of the types of people who served as informants and the decision process invoked in their choice.

Social situations and conditions. A third element influencing the content of ethnographic data is the social context in which they are gathered. What informants feel to be appropriate to reveal in some contexts and circumstances may be inappropriate under other conditions. In Ogbu's study (1974) of education in an ethnic neighborhood of a big city, he distinguishes carefully the information parents reveal when they enter the school context from what they reveal in their home neighborhood. He quotes extensively from his field notes to demonstrate that this discrepancy is recognized and discussed among the parents themselves. Ogbu's experiences highlight the necessity for ethnographers to specify the social settings where data are collected.

Other social circumstances also affect the nature of information revealed. In their analysis of medical school student culture, Becker, Geer, Hughes, and Strauss (1961) differentiate between data gathered from participants alone with the researchers and information acquired from participants in group contexts. Their study indicates that what people say and do varies according to others present at the time.

Delineation of the physical, social, and interpersonal contexts within which data are gathered enhances the replicability of ethnographic studies. To an extent, these factors are subject to change over time. What may be a center for informal gathering among one group of high school seniors, for example, may be anathema to the succeeding class. Consequently, descriptions of contexts should include function and structure as well as specifications of features.

Analytic constructs and premises. Even if a researcher reconstructs the relationships and duplicates the informants and social contexts of a prior study, replication may remain impossible if the constructs, definitions, or units of analysis which informed the original research are idiosyncratic or poorly delineated. Replication requires explicit identification of the assumptions and metatheories that underlie choice of terminology and methods of analysis. For example, the culture concept is defined differently by different researchers. Some use it globally: Linton (1945) identified it as the way of life of a people. Others prefer to define culture more narrowly in terms of observed behavior (e.g., Harris, 1971). Some virtually deny that culture exists independently as an analytic construct, preferring to examine the minute-by-minute interactions by which shared meanings are negotiated among individuals and small groups (e.g., Furlong, 1976; Gearing, 1973, 1975).

If defined idiosyncratically in a study, major organizing constructs such as these can lead to findings that differ widely in their emphasis and interpretation. When underlying assumptions and definitions remain unclarified, the results may be incomprehensible. Researchers may develop their own conceptual schemes in ignorance of disregard of constructs used by other researchers and may fail to provide an analysis of or theory about their implicit structures (Biddle, 1967).

Smith and Brock (1970), for example, note that the work of certain ecological psychologists (i.e., Barker & Wright, 1954) implies the obviation of behavior that appears to have no purpose. In positing both the logical supremacy of the largest unit, the behavioral episode, and a world governed by linear causality, Barker & Wright base their analysis on a simple stimulus-response model of behavior; however, this theoretical underpinning is not made explicit. It may be useful for post hoc analysis of behavior transcripts, but the proposition that behavioral episodes (or any other units of analysis) are natural or intrinsic to the human condition is unverified. Smith and Brock legitimately observe that behavioral episodes may be congruent with common sense, but with common sense as viewed by a given researcher using a specific paradigm. To the extent that invented constructs such as these are mandated by the data, their assumptions, definitions, and limitations should be delineated explicitly, and their relationships to existing concepts should be clarified.

Outlining the theoretical premises and defining constructs that inform and shape the research facilitates replication. However, development of lower level constructs and terms creates problems for internal as well as external reliability. Creating categories for coding is the first step of analysis; it is vital to the process of organizing the naturally occurring stream of behavior into manageable units. Units of analysis should be identified clearly: where they begin and end and, when appropriate, which variables form the framework for data collection and analysis (Goetz & LeCompte, 1981).

Some ethnographers specify clearly their categories of data. They may use standard typologies and checklists (e.g., Henry, 1960; Hilgar, 1966; Whiting, Child, & Lambert, 1966). More problematic are situations in which researchers devise their own schemes. This process may be necessary to provide a valid analytic frame that matches the data collected and the questions posed. However, unless categories are defined carefully and their theoretical antecedents outlined, the dangers of idiosyncrasy and lack of comparability are magnified. Establishing interobserver reliability may be impossible. On the other hand, established classificatory schemes may be used merely because they are well known and easy to administer, even though they may result in premature categorization that misrepresents the data or inadequate standardization and mechanical reduction that trivializes ethnographic findings.

Methods of data collection and analysis. Ideally, ethnographers strive to present their methods so clearly that other researchers can use the original report as an operating manual by which to replicate the study (e.g., Becker, Geer, & Hughes, 1968; Mehan, 1979; Ogbu, 1974; Smith & Geoffrey, 1968; Wolcott, 1973). Failures to specify methods of data collection and analysis may be related to the aforementioned brevity that journals often require in manuscripts. Pelto & Pelto (1978) note the regularity with which journal authors fail to report sufficiently their research designs and methodology. To an extent, this is because of the difficulty of explaining in a few sentences the scope and development of ethnographic research techniques.

Replicability is impossible without precise identification and thorough description of the strategies used to collect data (for compendiums of the range of alternatives, see LeCompte & Goetz, in press; Pelto & Pelto, 1978; Schatzman & Strauss, 1973; Spradley, 1979, 1980; Williams, 1967). Although this admonition may appear elementary to experimental researchers, knowledge of ethnographic techniques is apprehended incompletely and shared unevenly across the disciplines now using them (Burns, 1976; Herriott, 1977; Ianni, 1976; Wolcott, 1971). Until commonly understood descriptors for these complex techniques are developed, shorthand designations will continue to obstruct reliability, and researchers seeking to replicate studies will depend on fugitive monographs, technical reports, and personal communications.

A more serious problem for both external and internal reliability is the identification of general strategies for analyzing ethnographic data. The analytic processes from which ethnographies are constructed often are vague, intuitive, and personalistic. Ethnographers disagree on the extent to which such processes can and should be articulated (cf., e.g., Erickson, 1973; Pelto & Pelto, 1978; Wolcott, 1975; Wolcott, Note 3). Recent efforts to codify techniques for data analysis include Pelto and Pelto's system (1978) of deductive, inductive, and abductive strategies; Smith (1974, 1979) and Smith and Brock's (1970) efforts to generate models of the analytic process, and Goetz and LeCompte's comparative examination (1981) of analytic induction (Mehan, 1979; Robinson, 1951; Znaniecki, 1934), constant comparison (Glazer & Strauss, 1967), typological analyses (e.g., Lofland, 1971), enumerative systems (e.g., McCall, 1969), and standardized protocols (e.g., Flanders, 1970). Because reliability depends on the potential for subsequent researchers to reconstruct original analytic strategies, only those ethnographic accounts that specify these in sufficient detail will be replicable.

Internal Reliability

Problems of internal reliability in ethnographic studies raise the question of whether, within a single study, multiple observers will agree. This issue is especially critical when a researcher or research team plans to use ethnographic techniques to study a problem at several research sites (e.g., Cassell, 1978; Herriott, 1977; Herriott & Gross, 1979; Stake, 1978; Tikunoff, Berliner, & Rist, 1975; Whiting, 1963; Rist, Note 2). Crucial to internal reliability is interrater or interobserver reliability, the extent to which the sets of meanings held by multiple observers are sufficiently congruent so that they describe phenomena in the same way and arrive at the same conclusions about them.

Because ethnographers rarely use the standardized protocols for which some types of interrater reliability are crucial, the more pertinent concern is whether multiple observers agree with each other and with the originator of general constructs on their classifications or on a typology with which to begin categorization. Thus, the agreement ethnographers seek is more appropriately designated interobserver reliability. Agreement is sought on the description or composition of events rather than on the frequency of events.

This is a key concern to most ethnographers. Of necessity, a given research site may admit one or few observers. In the absence of other means of corroboration, such investigations may be idiosyncratic, rather than careful and systematic recordings of phenomena. Ethnographers commonly use any of five strategies to reduce threats to internal reliability: low-inference descriptors, multiple researchers, participant researchers, peer examination, and mechanically recorded data.

Low-inference descriptors. The format, structure, and focus of ethnographic field notes vary with the research problem and design and with the skills and styles of individual ethnographers. However, most guides to the construction of field notes distinguish between two categories of notations. Low-inference descriptors, phrased in terms as concrete and precise as possible, are mandated for all ethnographic research. These include verbatim accounts of what people say as well as narratives of behavior and activity (Lofland, 1971; Pelto & Pelto, 1978; Schatzman & Strauss, 1973). The second category of notation may be any combination of high-inference interpretive comments and will vary according to the analytic scheme chosen.

Low-inference narratives provide ethnographers with their basic observational data. Interpretive comments can be added, deleted, or modified, but the record of who did what under which circumstances should be as accurate as possible (Wax, 1971). This material is analyzed and presented in excerpts to substantiate inferred categories of analysis (Wolcott, 1975). Those ethnographies rich in primary data, which provide the reader with multiple examples from the field notes, generally are considered to be most credible (e.g., Bossert, 1979; Leemon, 1972; Modiano, 1973; Smith & Keith, 1971; Ward, 1971; Wolcott, 1977).

Multiple researchers. The optimum guard against threats to internal reliability in ethnographic studies may be the presence of multiple researchers. In some cases, investigations take place within a team whose members discuss the meaning of what has been observed until agreement is achieved (e.g., Becker et al., 1961, 1968; Peshkin, 1978; Spindler, 1973). Tikunoff, Berliner, and Rist (1975) conducted an intensive, 3-week training period for their 12 observers to prepare them to obtain comparable descriptive protocols from the 40 elementary classrooms examined in a study of effective reading and mathematics instruction.

Ethnographies based on team observation constitute the minority, and most involve only two researchers (e.g., Cicourel & Kitsuse, 1963; Hostetler & Huntington, 1971; Whiting, 1963). The same constraints of time and money that preclude the use of research teams limit the size and scope of teams: ethnographic research often is too time consuming and labor intensive for participation of most lone researchers, let alone multiple investigator teams. Funding is rarely available for more than a single fieldworker. In this case, ethnographers depend on other sources for corroboration and confirmation. Some of the recent, federally funded multiple-site research programs have employed research teams (e.g., Cassell, 1978; Wax, in press); others have used confirmation by short-term observers (e.g., Stake, 1978); more commonly, each field observer is responsible for an independent site (e.g., Herriott, 1977; Herriott & Gross, 1979). Especially under the latter circumstances, problems of establishing internal reliability are much the same as for single-site studies.

Participant researchers. Many researchers enlist the aid of local informants to confirm that what the observer has seen and recorded is being viewed identically and consistently by both subjects and researcher (Magoon, 1977). In some cases, participants serve as arbiters (e.g., Smith & Geoffrey, 1968), reviewing the day's production of field notes to correct researcher misperceptions and misinterpretations. Other researchers (e.g., Carroll, 1977) operate in partnership with particpants, keeping dual accounts of their own observations alongside participant comments. More commonly, ethnographers request reactions to working analyses or processed material from selected informants (e.g., Wolcott, 1973). In this way confirmation may be sought for various levels of the collection and analysis process: description of events and interactions, interpretation of participant meanings, and explanations for overall structures and processes.

Peer examination. Corroboration of findings by researchers operating in similar settings proceeds in three ways. First, ethnographers may integrate descriptions and conclusions from other fieldworkers in their presentations (e.g., Borman, 1978; Clement & Harding, 1978; Sieber, 1979). If discrepancies occur, explanations are proffered (Kaplan & Manners, 1972). Second, findings from studies conducted concurrently at multiple sites, such as those discussed above, may be analyzed and integrated. Independent generation or confirmation of results support the reliability of observation and enhance cross-site validity of conclusions (Campbell, 1979). Finally, the publication of results constitutes an offering of material for peer review. Wolcott's admonition (1975) to fieldworkers to include sufficient primary data in published accounts recognizes the significance of review by colleagues in the evaluation of ethnographic reports. Magoon (1977) cites Scriven's position (1972) that the reliability of various categories of so-called subjective material rests, to an extent, on the observer's established reputation for truthfulness and accuracy. The issue is not, then, to expurgate the subjective experience of the researcher, but to draw on it for insight as well as to provide information regarding its predictions, biases, and possible influences. In this way, ethnographers study themselves within the setting and their influence on it, as well as the setting itself (Wax, 1971).

Mechanically recorded data. Ethnographers use a variety of mechanical devices to record and preserve data. Mehan (1979) argues for the use of observational techniques that record as much as possible and preserve to the greatest extent the raw data, so that the veracity of conclusions may be confirmed by other researchers. Video and audio tape recorders, cameras, and moving-picture cameras are becoming standard equipment in the collection of ethnographic data (e.g., Collier, 1973; Eddy, 2969; Mehan, 1979). Such devices do possess serious limitations. Although cameras and recorders register much that a researcher could forget or ignore, and consequently may increase the reliability of a study, they preserve all data in uncodified and unclassified form and record only that data chosen by the researcher to be preserved. They are an abstraction and yet they may preserve too much data. Thus coding and analysis are imperative to render them usable.

Validity

Validity necessitates demonstration that the propositions generated, refined, or tested match the causal conditions which obtain in human life. There are two questions involved in matching scientific explanations of the world with actual conditions in it.

First, do scientific researchers actually observe or measure what they think they are observing or measuring? This is the problem of internal validity; solving it credibly is considered to be a fundamental requirement for any research design (e.g., Campbell & Stanley, 1963; Cook & Campbell, 1979).

Second, to what extent are the abstract constructs and postulates generated, refined, or tested by scientific researchers applicable across groups? This addresses the issue of external validity; it poses special problems for ethnographers because of the nature of their research designs and methods. Contrasting approaches to these problems are discussed below.

Although the problems of reliability threaten the credibility of much ethnographic work, validity may be its major strength. This becomes evident when ethnography is compared to survey studies, experimentation, and other quantitative research designs for assessment of internal validity (Crain, 1977; Erickson, 1977; Reichardt & Cook, 1979). The claim of ethnography to high internal validity derives from the data collection and analysis techniques used by ethnographers (see Denzin, 1978, for comparison of research designs). First, the ethnographer's common practice of living among participants and collecting data for long periods provides opportunities for continual data analysis and comparison to refine constructs and to ensure the match between scientific categories and participant reality. Second, informant interviewing, a major ethnographic data source, necessarily is phrased more closely to the empirical categories of participants and is formed less abstractly than instruments used in other research designs. Third, participant observation, the ethnographer's second key source of data, is conducted in natural settings that reflect the reality of the life experiences of participants more accurately than do contrived settings. Finally, ethnographic analysis incorporates a process of researcher self-monitoring, termed disciplined subjectivity (Erickson, 1973), that exposes all phases of the research activity to continual questioning and reevaluation.

Although internal and external validity are interrelated issues, they customarily are separated (e.g., Campbell & Stanley, 1963; Cook & Campbell, 1979) to clarify procedures, and this convention is discussed below. Among the measures of scientific credibility—internal and external reliability and internal and external validity—the problems of external validity most frequently are ignored by ethnographers. Reasons for this derive from three common characteristics of the ethnographic process.

First, ethnography focuses on recording in detail aspects of a single phenomenon, whether that phenomenon is a small group of humans or the operation of some social process. Traditionally, ethnographers have concentrated on single research settings. However, studies of a phenomenon, particularly an organizational innovation, over a number of sites have become more common (e.g., Cassell, 1978; Herriott, 1977; Herriott & Gross, 1979; Wax, in press; Rist, Note 2). The task is to reconstruct, in what Lofland (1971) calls loving detail, the characteristics of that phenomenon. Consequently, the ethnographic researcher begins by examining even commonplace groups or processes in a fresh and different way, as if they were exceptional and unique (Erickson, 1973).

In doing this, a second characteristic of ethnographic inquiry emerges. One school of ethnography advocates that researchers enter their fields with an assumption of ignorance or naiveté about the phenomena under investigation; other researchers simply attempt to suspend preconceived notions and even existing knowledge of the field under study. Although they may be familiar with related empirical research and use general theoretical frameworks to initiate studies, fieldworkers assume that detailed description can be constructed more accurately by not taking for granted facets of the social scene (Erickson, 1973).

Third, the problems, goals, and applications of ethnographic research affect how issues of external validity are defined and resolved. As indicated previously the credibility of research, which is contextual, theoretically eclectic, and comparative, is threatened by and grounded in factors different from those pertaining to experimentation and other forms of quantitative research.

Issues pertaining to the validity of ethnographic research, both internal and external, are addressed by fieldworkers operating from the perspective of these characteristics. The following discussion presents the threats to credibility of ethnographic design and their remedies.

Internal Validity

The definition of internal validity presented earlier subsumes the problem of whether conceptual categories understood to have mutual meanings between the participants and the observer actually are shared. For internal validity, the threats that Campbell and Stanley (1963) and Cook and Campbell (1979) describe as posing difficulties for experimental research are equally applicable to ethnographic research although they present somewhat different problems and may be resolved differently. These threats include history and maturation, observer effects, selection and regression, mortality, and spurious conclusions.

History and maturation. The extent to which phenomena observed at entry or at other initial occasions are the same as those observed subsequently becomes salient when process and change are the focus of the research project. Unlike the experimenter who uses various strategies to hold constant the effects of time, the ethnographer conducts research in natural settings where the clock advances. Changes that occur in the overall social scene are what experimenters designate as history; changes that involve progressive development in individuals are considered to be maturation.

Ethnographers assume that history affects the nature of the data collected and that phenomena rarely remain constant. The ethnographic task is to establish which baseline data remain stable over time and which data change (LeCompte & Goetz, in press). Such change may be recurrent, progressive, cyclic, or aberrant; sources of change and their operation also need to be specified (Appelbaum, 1970; Lofland, 1971). This is facilitated by systematic replication and comparison of baseline data, analogous to the pretest data collected by experimenters.

In order to assess the rate and direction of change, ethnographers establish long-term residence in their fields—extending from 6 months to 3 years. This permits time-sampling procedures, the identification of factors intervening in the social scene across some period of time, and the retrospective tracing of phenomena isolated in the terminal phases of a study. In situations where data are required from the preentry period of a field study, ethnographers use informant reconstructions and information located in a variety of documents. They may revisit sites at subsequent intervals in order to verify the time-dependent nature of various phenomena.

The classic instance in educational ethnography of site revisiting is Hollingshead's return (1975) to his Elmtown site and the accompanying analysis of changes that occurred over a 30-year period (cf. Mead, 1956; Wylie, 1974). Wolcott, in his examination of education in a Kwakiutl Indian village in Canada (1967), supplemented his 12-month participant observation with extended visits the following two summers and by retrospective interviews with village informants and educators who had taught in the village school prior to his tenure (cf. Hostetler & Huntington, 1971; King, 1967; Modiano, 1973). Ogbu's study (1974) of the inner-city neighborhood traces the 10-year history and development of the education rehabilitation movement in the community's schools through interviews and the collection and analysis of pertinent documents. These researchers used replication and time-sampling strategies to distinguish phenomena subject to change from phenomena that remained relatively stable.

Many of the techniques used by ethnographers to control for the effects of history are applicable to controlling for maturation. Experimenters manage these variables through such constraints as designing projects of limited duration and assigning subjects randomly to control and experimental groups. When effects of treatments are being measured, maturation may be regarded as a source of contamination. For an experimental study, a biological or quasi-biological model with universal stages of development is posited. Maturation is conceptualized as a universal, normative process, proceedings through well-defined stages. Ethnographers, however, view maturational stages as varying according to cultural norms. Fieldworkers attempt to control for the effects of maturation by identifying explicitly what behaviors and norms are expected in different sociocultural contexts. They are less concerned with what people actually are capable of doing at some developmental stage than with how groups specify appropriate behavior for various developmental stages.

Maturation and development frequently become the focus of ethnographic studies (e.g., Howard, 1970; Moore, 1973). Leemon (1972) and Burnett (1969) used Van Gennep's model (1960) of passage rites to analyze maturation of students in the United States. Other researchers (e.g., Becker et al., 1961) have reconstructed the maturation process through the perceptions of the participants involved. Constant comparison (Glaser & Strauss, 1967), discrepant case analysis (Erickson, 1973; Robinson, 1951; Wolcott, 1975; Znaniecki, 1934), and a variety of logico-deductive strategies (e.g., Scriven's modus operandi, 1974) can be used to distinguish maturation effects from other intervening phenomena in order to identify possible causes, their interactions, and their probable impacts (e.g., Eddy, 1969; Ward, 1971).

Observer effects. The threat to validity posed by observer effects in ethnography is parallel to the threats to experimental and survey studies posed by testing and instrumentation effects. The reactivity of instrumentation (discussed elsewhere, e.g., Campbell & Stanley, 1963; Cook & Campbell, 1979; Phillips, 1971) is as problematic for ethnographers as it is for other social researchers. Participant observation and informant interviewing pose particular problems of their own. The difficulty is amplified by the common practice in ethnography of supplementing these strategies with a variety of standardized instruments.

When data are being gathered through participant observation and informal informant interviewing, reactivity must be assessed. Possible and probable effects of the observer's presence on the nature of the data gathered must be considered (Schwartz & Schwartz, 1955). Such effects operate in a number of ways.

As noted earlier, what observers see and report is a function of the position they occupy within participant groups, the status accorded them, and the role behavior expected of them. Direct observer effects may occur when informants become dependent on the ethnographer for status enhancement or the satisfaction of psychological needs. In such cases, a symbiotic relationship may develop between researcher and informant that precludes obtaining data from other than a single source or that distorts data obtained from other informants who are affected by what they perceive as a special relationship. Ethnographers address this threat by establishing several field relationships (Kahn & Mann, 1952; Miller, 1952; Vidich, 1955), by gradually disengaging themselves from informant relationships (Powdermaker, 1966), and by including in their presentation of results a retrospective analysis of their field positions and relationships (see *Researcher status position* above).

Attempting to avoid problems of entanglement by assuming a position of neutrality can lead the researcher into other distortions. Detachment can destroy rapport and cause informants to infer indifference or even hostility on the part of the researcher. Consequent paranoiac reactions may seriously affect the quality of data (Miller, 1952; Vidich, 1955; Wax, 1971). In settings such as schools, participants may expect, even demand, advocacy from the ethnographer as a condition of rapport (e.g., Cusick, 1973; Goetz, 1976).

Participants may behave abnormally (Argyris, 1952). This may be a consciously planned show in which subjects seek to reveal themselves in the best possible light. Or it may be an unconscious distortion performed to provide what participants believe the researcher wants to see. Interactive situations, in which participants respond spontaneously to the researcher's presence and attention, may result in phenomena comparable to the halo effect documented in experiments and in quasi-experimental field studies (Cook & Campbell, 1979).

Parallel to this problem in observation is the credibility of informant reports in interviewing. Informants may lie, omit relevant data, or misrepresent their claims (Dean & Whyte, 1958). Independent corroboration from multiple informants (e.g., Fuchs, 1969) or other fortuitous observers of the social scene (e.g., Smith & Keith, 1971), sufficient residence in the field to reduce artificial responses (e.g. Wolcott, 1973), and coding participant responses according to situations expected to elicit contrived responses (e.g., Becker et al., 1961; McCall, 1969) are techniques used by ethnographers to control for such distortions in the data.

Unusual observer effects (discussed above as informal social experiments) also may threaten the validity of ethnographic studies. Contrivance effects may distort data gathered: this obtains in situations where the ethnographer plans and executes some exceptional act in order to elicit responses from subjects. Such strategies may violate the research ethics of participant consent (cf., e.g., Denzin, 1978; Jorgensen, 1971; Rynkiewich & Spradley, 1976), although inadvertent faux pas and gaffes are less controversial than deliberate manipulations and do provide valuable information on norms and sanctions. Here the researcher must establish that it is the act itself that elicits the responses rather than the act as performed by the researcher (Webb, Campbell, Schwartz, & Sechrest, 1966).

Two problems are associated with intensive, long-term studies. Research exhaustion, or the saturation of a setting for research purposes (Wolcott, 1975), occurs when the investigation ceases to reveal further new constructs. The ethnographer has become so familiar with the setting that new or discrepant data are no longer observable. Related to this may be the classic problem of going native: ethnographers participate to such a degree in groups that they can no longer maintain sufficient distance from the group role to observe and analyze objectively. Some observers (e.g., Everhart, 1977) interpret these difficulties as an indication that field residence should be terminated; other ethnographers (e.g., Whyte, 1955) advocate periodic temporary withdrawals from the field in order to defamiliarize themselves with the social scene, to reconfirm their primary status as dispassionate researchers, and to provide a respite for participants.

Finally, in cases where presentation of the perspective of participants is important, ethnographers must demonstrate that the categories are meaningful to the participants, reflect the way participants experience reality, and actually are supported by the data. Even where participant-derived constructs are less important, researcher-designated constructs still should be grounded in and congruent with actual data.

In essence, researchers must guard against their own ethnocentrisms and perceptual biases. Disciplined subjectivity (Erickson, 1973) uses the tension arising from the investigator's emotive and affective responses to participant behavior and practice (Wax, 1971) as an indicator of salient phenomena. Through what Wax defines as resocialization, the ethnographer searches for the group's perspectives toward and meanings for significant phenomena (Schatzman & Strauss, 1973), emerging with a dual identity as an outsider-insider which permits authentic presentation of the participant world.

Especially where formal instrumentation is used, ethnographers try to establish the extent to which the measure has the same meaning for both researcher and subject (e.g., Goodman, 1957; Spindler, 1973, 1974). Assumptions underlying instrument items, how they are assessed, and the choice of who scores them, as well as overt meanings of the items and the overall test, should be shared between tester and testee (cf., e.g., Mehan, 1976; Phillips, 1971). Demonstrating equivalence of meaning between researcher and subject is difficult (e.g., Gay & Cole, 1967; Modiano, 1973) and this problem is highlighted in interdisciplinary research where the task is complicated by the necessity for equivalence across different disciplines (Petrie, 1976).

Although sociocultural theories and analytic models provide ethnographers with perspectives for monitoring themselves as members of both participant groups and the scientific community (Schatzman & Strauss, 1973), biases resulting from academic training also may distort data. For example, disciplinary biases may appear, however implicitly, in the categories an investigator chooses as salient for analysis and coding of ethnographic data, regardless of whether participant-derived categories or researcher-designated constructs are used. Researchers with different theoretical backgrounds may choose to focus on quite different aspects of the data. The strategies discussed above for enhancing the reliability of analytic constructs and premises and for ensuring the internal reliability of ethnographic studies also contribute to controlling and managing observer analytic biases. Of these, participant reaction and confirmation—conducted through all levels of the ethnographic process—may be most effective in revealing researcher-induced distortions (Wax, 1971).

Selection and regression. In experimental research, control of selection and regression effects attempts to ensure that measured differences between treatment and control groups are caused by the treatment rather than by differences inherent in the groups. Although ethnographers rarely grapple with the problem of isolating treatment effects, they do cope with distortions in their data and conclusions created by the selection of participants to observe and informants to interview. Wax (1971) emphasizes that the disciplined investigator seeks and maintains contact with a diversity of participants—despite personal preferences and prejudices—as a strategy for correcting bias and distortion. Selectivity becomes a serious problem in situations where the number of participants necessitates gathering data from some sample of the population or where the social scene is sufficiently complex that continual observation of all events, activities, and settings is precluded. Failure to complete an adequate inventory (cf., e.g., LeCompte & Goetz, in press; Schatzman & Strauss, 1973) of subgroups, factions, events, and social scenes in the field site may result in findings representative only of certain participants or of particular circumstances.

Ethnographers commonly initiate investigations by establishing the range of possible informants and participants in a group so as to obtain data from all participant types (e.g., Dean, Eichhorn, & Dean, 1967). In his study of attitudes toward formal education held by American Indian parents and students, Riner (1979) first identified the categories of families sending their children to school and then sampled from that typology. Conclusions reported by Clement and Harding (1978) in their analysis of student relationships in a desegregated elementary school and by Becker et al. (1961) in their study of student culture in a medical school are based on observations sampled from the range of events, activities, and settings identified in the field sites.

Although marginal individuals and other extreme types among a population may serve as liaisons for entry and initial investigation (Kahn & Mann, 1952; Vidich, 1955), ethnographers try to maintain contacts and relationships with as diverse a group of participants as possible. In her analysis of the impact of a state-mandated curriculum on the staff of a school district, Brown (Note 4) verified perceptions of the innovation reported initially by a few teacher informants through subsequent questionnaires administered to all involved teachers.

The tendency for the exotic to be more obvious than the commonplace affects the events and activities the ethnographer notes as well as the selection of informants. Khlief (1974) and Erickson (1973) suggest that this may be remedied by using strategies such as the aforementioned discrepant case analysis, by constantly questioning commonly assumed meanings, and by making comparisons with cross-cultural data and cases.

Because most ethnographers study characteristics and behavior of human groups rather than the effects of specific treatments, ethnographic subjects are chosen for relevance to specific interests. Glaser and Strauss's (1967) use of theoretical sampling—collecting data chosen for relevance to emerging theoretical constructs—is one purposive strategy for implementing this process systematically (for alternative forms of purposive sampling, see Patton, 1980). Following successful access to and entry into particular groups, methodical sampling assures that data adequately represent the population being investigated. Such sampling may take the form of cross-informant interviewing for confirmation and validation of interviews, structured questionnaires, or findings derived from participant observation across the spectrum of subgroups and factions. These strategies are as useful for ensuring external validity as they are for internal validity: if cross-group comparisons are to be credible, they must be grounded in accurate data from individual groups.

Mortality. The ways in which groups change over time as a result of losses and gains in membership pose special difficulties for ethnographers. Although experimenters may replace subjects who are lost from their studies, ethnographers assume that the naturalistic approach precludes the interchangeability of human informants and participants. Loss and replacement as they naturally occur become topics of study in themselves. Growth and attrition are assumed to be normal processes in most group settings, so the ethnographic task becomes the identification of their effects. This requires careful attention to baseline data (discussed above) so that the researcher may compare events and activities occurring across time.

In his study of enculturation, Jocano (1969) examined mobility of young people into and out of a Philippine barrio, as well as the treatment of birth and death, in order to establish cycles of growth and attrition as defined and interpreted by the community. By studying the spring enrollment of a new child into a third-grade classroom, Goetz (1976) was able to validate socialization practices and goals observed among students earlier in the school year. Smith and Keith (1971) approached staff attrition and turnover in a similar manner to illuminate the social dynamics of innovation in an elementary school program. In each of these instances, collection of baseline data enabled researchers to analyze the effects of subsequent loss and replacement.

Spurious conclusions. However thoroughly an ethnographer may have accounted for effects of history and maturation, observer impact, selection and regression, and mortality, relationships posited among observed phenomena nevertheless may be spurious. This problem is comparable to Cook and Campbell's formulation (1979) of statistical conclusion validity. They define this construct as (a) the extent to which a treatment actually caused a predicted effect and (b) the extent to which presumed phenomena actually covary or are causally related. Statistical conclusion validity alerts researchers to search for spurious relationships and to resist assuming relationships where there may be none or assuming nonrelationships where they may be obscured by an artifact of instrumentation or treatment. These issues are paramount to experimental researchers whose designs customarily preclude laborious post hoc examinations of sources of error except where intuition or insight suggest such errors might exist.

In contrast, ethnographic design mandates that Scriven (1974) has designated a modus operandi perspective in which the geneses of observed data are traced retrospectively. All plausible causes are delineated by examination of collected data and through discussion with informants. Postulating associations among phenomena depends on elimination of alternative explanations (Campbell, 1979). Denzin (1978) conceptualizes the adequate support of relational generalizations as requiring establishment of time order, covariance, and elimination of rival hypotheses. He assesses participant observation as excellent, good, and fair, respectively, on these three factors.

Elimination of rival explanations mandates control of factors threatening internal validity. It also requires effective and efficient retrieval systems for ethnographic data and the scrupulous use of corroboratory and alternative sources of data. These serve to support the fieldworker's search for negative instances of tentatively postulated relationships and disconfirming evidence for emergent constructs (Mehan, 1979; Robinson, 1951; Znaniecki, 1934). Although no research design can identify the precise cause of an observed datum, ethnographic data may be quite effective in delineating the most probable causes and in specifying an array of those most plausible.

Participant explanations of events are central among those that ethnographers examine. Factors that many researchers designate as causal may not be so designated by participants. Although Rist (1970) rejected teachers' explanations for student failure in his 3-year study of a group of elementary schoolchildren, he demonstrated that those students who failed were those that the teachers expected to fail. In contrast, Smith and Keith (1971) expanded upon participant accounts and interpretations to explain the failure of innovation in an elementary school.

Longevity in the research site, presupposed in ethnographic research design, facilitates the search for causes and consequences. Ethnographers are likely to have witnessed personally the temporal antecedents of events; where this is impossible, data from informants, documents, and other sources may be substituted. Similarly, long-term field residence permits identification of the covariance of phenomena in natural settings. Nevertheless, Cook and Campbell's counsel (1979) to experimenters is applicable as well to ethnographers:

Estimating the internal validity of a relationship is a deductive process in which the investigator has to systematically think through how each [factor] . . . may have influenced the data. . . . In all of this process, the researcher has to be his or her own best critic, trenchantly examining all of the threats he or she can imagine. (p. 55)

For the ethnographer, the process is an inductive one as well; sources of bias or contamination must be discovered as the study proceeds.

External Validity

In most ethnographic studies, as well as in many quantitative studies, the strictures required for statistical generalization may be difficult to apply. Problems of access may preclude the use of random samples, or random assignments may have to be made from available groups rather than from entire populations. Statistical sampling may even be irrelevant where initial description of a little known or singular phenomenon is desired, where social constructs (to be tested later in more stringently controlled designs) are to be generated, where the goal of the research is explication of meanings or microsocial presses, or where the subject of an investigation is an entire population. To researchers studying special institutions, regions, or populations, selection criteria are different from those required to generate a representative or stratified, random sample. The goal under these circumstances is the development of findings that may be compared and contrasted with many other groups.

Threats to the external validity of ethnographic findings are those effects that obstruct or reduce a study's comparability and translatability. The fieldworker's problem is to demonstrate what Wolcott (1973) conceptualizes as the typicality of a phenomenon, or the extent to which it compares and contrasts along relevant dimensions with other phenomena. Consequently, external validity depends on the identification and description of those characteristics of phenomena salient for comparison with other, similar types. Once the typicality of a phenomenon is established, bases for comparison may be assumed.

This problem is addressed to an extent by multisite ethnographic designs. The classic model for this approach in educational anthropology, Whiting's investigation (1963) of child-rearing practices in six different cultures, incorporated ethnography into a multimethod investigation (Whiting & Whiting, 1975). Although each of the six teams of field researchers produced an independent ethnography, preentry planning and collection of standardized data for other phases of the study resulted in six investigations of comparable phenomena. More recent multisite studies are variations of the Whitings' design (e.g., Cassell, 1978; Herriott, 1977; Herriott & Gross, 1979; Stake, 1978; Tikunoff, Berliner, & Rist, 1975; Wax, in press; Rist, Note 2). Time spent on site, central integration of data collection and analysis processes, number of field researchers per site, and the nature of final products vary across these studies so they cannot be regarded as a homogeneous solution to threats to external validity. All fail to meet the selection requirements for statistical generalization. Nevertheless, the increase in sample size over single-site studies does strengthen the external validity of their findings (Campbell, 1979). Because sample size is an insufficient condition for confident generalization (Reichardt & Cook, 1979), investigators in multisite studies must address threats to external validity as carefully as do single-site ethnographers. Four factors may affect the credibility of a study for cross-group comparisons: selection effects, setting effects, history effects, and construct effects.

Selection effects. Some constructs cannot be compared across groups because they are specific to a single group or because the researcher mistakenly has chosen groups for which the construct does not obtain. This may occur more frequently when researcher-designated categories are used. Here, the researcher's initial task is to determine the degree of match between the categories and the reality of the group, culture, or setting under investigation. When this is neglected, the categories operate on an assumptive level, and invalid comparisons may be drawn. In circumstances in which a researcher is investigating the cross-group occurrence of participant-derived categories, this may be less likely to obtain: awareness of the participant derivation of the constructs may function as a control for threats to validity. Finally, the discovery that data are absent for the support of a construct may be useful information in itself. In some cases, the ethnographer then may reanalyze the data for contrasts across groups.

The ethnographer's virtual obsession with identifying distinct characteristics of investigated populations derives from a recognition of the significance of this information for comparative purposes. Although characterization may be rendered partially in subjective qualities, quantitatively measured attributes of populations are essential. Socioeconomic status, levels of education attained, and racial composition are population characteristics that are readily reported in quantitative terms. In his ethnographic analysis of the role of the principal, Wolcott (1973) typifies the individual studied by describing the individual in comparison with the modal category of a nationwide survey of elementary school principals. Goetz (1981) notes that the cultural broker role assumed by the teachers in her investigation of sex-role enculturation may be dependent on their particular relationship with the community serviced by their school. Cusick (1973) limits his explanations for patterns of student-teacher exchange to schools servicing student populations that are comparable to the groups he examined.

Setting effects. Simply by studying a group, culture, or setting, the investigator affects it in some ways. Constructs generated in one context may not be comparable in others because they are a function of context-under-investigation rather than of context only. The reactive observer effects, discussed above as threats to internal validity, are equally serious when cross-group comparisons are conducted. When the construct is a function of observer-setting interaction, it may be treated as equivalent only for groups being observed in a comparable manner, and the interactive dynamics should be identified clearly. Limitations attributed to school ethnographies conducted by participant observers who functioned as teachers (e.g., King, 1967; McPherson, 1972; Rosenfeld, 1971; Wolcott, 1967) stem from the possibility that findings were distorted by observation-setting interaction effects. Smith and Geoffrey (1968) sought to avoid this problem by collecting observations from two perspectives: teacher and nonparticipant researcher. Wolcott (1974) and King (1974) addressed the issue with retrospective analyses of the dynamics of interactions in their respective settings.

Oversaturation of settings is a second facet of this problem. It relates to group history, a third threat to external validity. Groups and cultures that attract continual or intermittant investigation by social scientists may be assumed to be different from groups and cultures with few or no such experiences. Educational researchers are familiar with this problem as it arises in school districts adjacent to research centers; research activities become so integrated with ongoing teaching and administration that the population is altered permanently. Caudill (1963) cites Appalachia as a subculture that has experienced cyclic attention from scholars. He claims that mountaineers have developed a cautious, cynical response to researchers and practitioners based on repeated experiences of disappointed expectations.

History effects. Cross-group comparisons of constructs may be invalid due to the unique historical experiences of groups and cultures. Researchers are cautioned, for example, in making comparisons between black slavery in the United States and in Latin America. Nevertheless, careful identification of differing historical variables and subsequent comparison of discrepant cases have proved fruitful (e.g., Elkins, 1959).

In his investigation of schooling in a small German village, Spindler (1974) outlined the community's ongoing conversion from rural to urban orientation and the school's introduction of a nationally disseminated curriculum innovation. Cross-site comparison of Spindler's findings with Warren's (1967) earlier study of a school in a similar village would locate urbanizing developments in both places, but would have to take into account variations in school curriculum stemming from the 10-year time differential. Failure to consider differences between groups resulting from histori-cal factors may result in the misapplication of constructs and the assumption that phenomena are equivalent across groups.

The opposite assumption, that all group phenomena are unique, is equally misleading. Studstill (1979) has noted the ethnographic restriction of school studies to complex technological societies. He attributes this to the unquestioned assumption that schools in nonliterate societies have little or nothing in common with the bureaucratic organizations predominant in industrial cultures, despite evidence to the contrary (cf., e.g., Hansen, 1979). Studstill suggests that the failure to identify clearly both common and contrastive features of schools in nonliterate and literate societies has led to the attribution of undeserved uniqueness to schools in complex technological societies.

Construct effects. Construct validity is defined by Cook and Campbell (1979) as the extent to which abstract terms, generalizations, or meanings are shared across times, settings, and popula-tions. This can be interpreted in several ways. Definitions and meanings of terms and constructs can vary (see *Analytic constructs and premises* above).

A second interpretation of construct validity concerns how the effects of observed phenomena are constructed. Explanations regarded as valid among some groups are discounted by others (see *Spurious conclusions* above). Construct validity also may refer to the degree to which instructions for the formats of instruments are mutually intelligible to the instrument designer, to the instrument administrator, and to the subjects to whom the instrument is applied (see *Observer effects* above).

The comparability of ethnographic studies may be reduced or obstructed by idiosyncratic use of initial analytic constructs or by generation of constructs so peculiar to a particular group that they are useless for cross-group examinations. Cook and Campbell (1979) accord sufficient gravity to threats to the construct validity of instruments used in experimental research that they discuss the issue independently of internal and external validity. A number of the effects discussed above affect construct validity. Because a major outcome of ethnographic research is the generation and refinement—through cross-group applications—of constructs, ethnographers must consider issues of construct validity as critical to the credibility of their results.

The elicitation techniques used by ethnographers are designed specifically to intensify equiva-lence in meaning and interpretation between researchers and their subjects. A variety of strategies, including listing, Q-sorting, and constant cross-checking in discussions with informants, support this objective (LeCompte & Goetz, in press). Triangulating many data sources (Denzin, 1978) formalizes the meanings which participants attribute to phenomena. Team research and peer review serve as audits to ensure that interpretation of mundane phenomena are examined rather than assumed.

Where disparities are identified, ethnographers report them as attributes of the groups being examined (e.g., Ogbu, 1974; Smith & Keith, 1971; Wolcott, 1973). This sensitizes other researchers, directing them to examine comparable effects in other populations. In cases where particular group dimensions require the customizing of instruments or initial analytic constructs (e.g., Modiano, 1973; Spindler, 1973, 1974), a common requirement in cross-cultural studies, modifications are included in the presentation of results.

Conclusion

A serious problem in assessing the credibility of ethnographic research, which may be peculiar to this investigative tradition, is that addressing all of the categories of contamination and bias may appear to mandate contradictory measures. Although the term ethnography has been used throughout this discussion as referring to a research process, ethnography also refers to the product of a research effort. It is defined by anthropologists as an analytic description of an intact cultural scene (Spradley & McCurdy, 1972). It delineates the shared beliefs, practices, artifacts, folk knowledge, and behaviors of a group of people. Its objective is the holistic reconstruction of the culture or phenomena investigated.

Given this goal, the ethnographer's primary commitment is to a faithful and accurate rendition of the participant's lifeways. To the extent that these may be eccentric, singular, or idiosyncratic when compared to other groups, they still require reporting. As a consequence, some ethnographers may resist formulation of the constructs and postulates applicable to other groups that are prerequisite for establishing external validity and external reliability. Tailoring these abstractions for cross-group comparisons may appear to distort their derivation. Thus, while confronting the possibility of obtaining noncomparable data and results is a risk undertaken both by experimental and ethnographic researchers, it is perhaps more serious for the latter.

Such dilemmas, which are frequently discussed as dichotomous choices between subjective or objective data and data analysis processes, between replicability or authenticity, between representativeness of samples or purposive sampling, or between generalizability or uniqueness of results (Filstead, 1979; Rist, 1977; Wilson, 1977), are shared across social science research designs. While dichotomous conceptualization of these issues may be useful pedagogically, it may distort and mislead when used to assess and design research activity (Reichardt & Cook, 1979). Educational anthropologists and other educational researchers who use qualitative strategies may be susceptible to viewing these alternatives as mutually exclusive choices because, in their shared commitment to the improvement of curriculum, instruction, and other factors in education, they seek research designs that purport to demonstrate clear-cut causality and that allege to be distortion free. In addition, public and academic concern for direct applicability of educational research overshadows investigation in the field and provokes what are frequently simplistic interpretations of designs and results. The inevitable outcome is that research results rarely are functional in or applicable to real classrooms.

Our position is that the transformation of such issues into dichotomous choices is unnecessary, inaccurate, and ultimately counterproductive. Many research studies include the collection of both objective and subjective data. Similarly, the same investigations may employ data-analysis strategies that range from subjective to objective (Scriven, 1972). Replicability, often viewed as merely a function of standardization of instruments and procedures, is a complex issue that must be addressed by various strategies. If sampling is viewed as a collection of overlapping alternatives to a variety of design problems, then its assessment will depend on how well problems are solved rather than on conformity to a randomness seldom achieved even in quantitative studies. The extent to which results are generalizable or unique depends on such factors as the level of abstraction addressed and will vary by particular construct or relationship posited.

Attaining absolute validity and reliability is an impossible goal for any research model. Nevertheless, investigators may approach these objectives by conscientious balancing of the various factors enhancing credibility within the context of their particular research problems and goals. For decades, reputable ethnographers have used a variety of strategies to reduce threats to reliability and validity. This has been a major source for one of the defining characteristics of present-day ethnography—its multimodality.

Reference Notes

1. Goetz, J.P., & LeCompte, M.D. The role of theory in the design of educational ethnography. Paper presented at the annual meeting of the American Educational Research Association, Los Angeles, April 1981.

2. Rist, R.C. The youthwork national policy study. Paper presented at the annual meeting of the American Educational Research Association, Los Angeles, April 1981.

3. Wolcott, H.F. *How to look like an anthropologist without really being one.* Paper presented at the annual meeting of the American Educational Research Association, Boston, April 1980.

4. Brown, M.J.M. *Triangulation; An approach to the analysis of how one school system implemented a state mandated curriculum innovation.* Paper presented at the annual meeting of the American Educational Research Association, Boston, April 1980.

Notes

This article is based on a paper presented at the annual meeting of the American Anthropological Association, Cincinnati, December 1979. Its revision has benefited from the comments of our colleagues: M. Brightman, M. Ginsburg, J. Levin, M. Melville, L.E. Munjanganja, K. Newman, A.D. Pellegrini, J. Pyper, J. Schreiber, R.T. Sieber, and the *Review of Educational Research's* two anonymous reviewers.

1. A stereotypic distinction labels experimentation as hypothesis verifying and ethnography as hypothesis generating. This simplification has been challenged legitimately by some scholars (e.g., Reichardt & Cook, 1979). Our position is that such dimensions as generation-verification and induction-deduction are continuous rather than discrete processes and that researchers shift along these continua as they proceed through any particular research project and follow some line of investigation. Although ethnographers customarily depend on generative and inductive strategies in the early phases of a research study, they direct later stages of the interactive collection-analysis process to deductive verification of findings. Even where ethnographers begin with an explicit theory to verify (e.g., Erickson, 1943, cited in Campbell, 1979), discrepant data are used first to reject initial explanations and then to generate and verify more adequate explanations. Likewise, experimenters will use unexpected findings as stimuli to generate new theory and will examine its feasibility over a series of studies (Mehan & Griffin, 1980).

2. Claims for the systematic codification across disciplines of experimental, statistical, and other quantitative research techniques are not intended to imply either single-solution approaches to design problems or agreement among scholars on either significance of problems or effectiveness of solutions (see Cook & Campbell, 1979, for delineation of diverse issues in quantitative design). Our treatment of quantitative methods is simplified for contrastive purposes. We do assert, however, that quantitative strategies have been explicated more widely and systematically than qualitative methodology, a factor contributing to the intensity of debates among experimenters, statisticians, and survey analysts.

References

Appelbaum, R.P. *Theories of social change.* Chicago: Markham, 1970.

Argyris, C. Diagnosing defenses against the outsider. *Journal of Social Issues,* 1952, 8(3), 24–34.

Barker, R.G., & Wright, H.F. *Midwest and its children.* Evanston, Ill.: Row, Peterson, 1954.

Becker, H., Geer, B., & Hughes, E. *Making the grade: The academic side of college life.* New York: Wiley, 1968.

Becker, H., Geer, B., & Hughes, E., & Strauss, A. *Boys in white: Student culture in medical school.* Chicago: University of Chicago Press, 1961.

Berreman, G.D. Behind many masks: Ethnography and impression management in a Himalayan village. *Monographs of the Society for Applied Anthropology,* 1962, No. 4.

Biddle, B.J. Methods and concepts in classroom research. *Review of Educational Research,* 1967, 37, 337-357.

Borman, K. Social control and schooling: Power and process in two kindergarten settings. *Anthropology and Education Quarterly,* 1978, 9, 38–53.

Bossert, S.T. *Tasks and social relationships in classrooms: A study of instructional organization and its consequences.* Cambridge: Cambridge University Press, 1979.

Burnett, J.H. Ceremony, rites, and economy in the student system of an American high school. *Human Organization,* 1969, *28,* 1–10.

Burns, A.F. On the ethnographic process in anthropology and education. *Anthropology and Education Quarterly,* 1976, *7*(3), 25–33.

Campbell, D.T. "Degrees of Freedom" and the case study. In T. D. Cook & C. S. Reichardt (Eds.), *Qualitative and quantitative methods in evaluation research.* Beverly Hills, Calif.: Sage, 1979.

Campbell, D.T., & Stanley, J.C. Experimental and quasi-experimental designs for research. Chicago: Rand McNally, 1963.

Carroll, T.G. Work and play: A probe of the formation, use and intersection of adult and child activity domains (Doctoral dissertation, SUNY, Buffalo, 1976). *Dissertation Abstracts International,* 1977, *38,* 5211A–5212A. (University Microfilms No. 77–3520).

Cassell, J. *A fieldwork manual for studying desegregated schools.* Washington, D.C.: The National Institute of Education, 1978.

Caudill, H.M. *Night comes to the Cumberlands: A biography of a depressed area.* Boston: Little, Brown, 1963.

Cicourel, A.V. *Method and measurement in sociology.* New York: Free Press, 1964.

Cicourel, A.V., & Kitsuse, J.I. *The educational decision-makers.* Indianapolis: Bobbs-Merrill, 1963.

Clement, D.C., & Harding, J.R. Social distinctions and emergent student groups in a desegregated school. *Anthropology and Education Quarterly,* 1978, *9.* 272–282.

Collier, J., Jr. *Alaskan Eskimo education: A film analysis of cultural confrontation in the schools.* New York: Holt, Rinehart, & Winston, 1973.

Cook, T.D., & Campbell, D.T. *Quasi-experimentation: Design and analysis issues for field settings.* Chicago: Rand McNally, 1979.

Crain, R.L. Racial tensions in high schools: Pushing the survey method closer to reality. *Anthropology and Education Quarterly,* 1977, *8,* 142–151.

Cusick, P.A. *Inside high school: The student's world.* New York: Holt, Rinehart, & Winston, 1973.

Dean, J.P., Eichhorn, R., & Dean, L.R. Fruitful informants for intensive interviewing. In J.T. Doby (Ed.), *An introduction to social research* (2nd ed.). New York: Meredith, 1967.

Dean, J.P., & Whyte, W.F. How do you know if the informant is telling the truth? *Human Organization,* 1958, *17* (2), 34–38.

Denzin, N.K. *The research act: A theoretical introduction to sociological methods* (2nd ed.). New York: McGraw-Hill, 1978.

Eddy, E.M. *Becoming a teacher: The passage to professional status.* New York: Teachers College Press, 1969.

Elkins, S.M. *Slavery: A problem in American institutional and intellectual life.* New York: Grosset & Dunlap, 1959.

Erikson, E.H. Observations on the Yurok: Childhood and world image. *Publications in American Archaeology and Ethnology,* 1943, *35* (10), I–VII, 257–302.

Erickson, F. What makes school ethnography "ethnographic"? *Anthropology and Education Quarterly,* 1973, *4* (2), 10–19.

Erickson, F. Some approaches to inquiry in school-community ethnography. *Anthropology and Education Quarterly,* 1977, *8,* 58–69.

Evans-Pritchard, E.E. Social anthropology: Past and present. In *Essays in social anthropology.* New York: Free Press, 1962.

Everhart, R.B. Between stranger and friend: Some consequences of "long term" fieldwork in schools. *American Educational Research Journal,* 1977, *14,* 1–15.

Filstead, W.J. Qualitative methods: A needed perspective in evaluation research. In T.D. Cook & C.S. Reichardt (Eds.), *Qualitative and quantitative methods in evaluation research.* Beverly Hills, Calif.: Sage, 1979.

Flanders, N.A. *Analyzing teacher behavior.* Reading, Mass.: Addison-Wesley, 1970.

Fuchs, E. *Pickets at the gate.* New York: Free Press, 1966.

Fuchs, E. *Teachers talk: Views from inside city schools.* New York: Anchor, 1969.

Furlong, V. Interaction sets in the classroom: Towards a study of pupil knowledge. In M. Stubbs & S. Delamont (Eds.), *Explorations in classroom observations.* London: Wiley, 1976.

Gay. J., & Cole, M. *The new mathematics and an old culture: A study of learning among the Kpelle of Liberia.* New York: Holt, Rinehart, & Winston, 1967.

Gearing, F.O. Where we are and where we might go: Steps toward a general theory of cultural transmission. *Anthropology and Education Quarterly,* 1973, *4* (1), 1–10.

Gearing, F.O. Overview: A cultural theory of education. *Anthropology and Education Quarterly,* 1975, *6* (2), 1–9.

Glaser, B.G., & Strauss, A. *The discovery of grounded theory: Strategies for qualitative research.* Chicago: Aldine, 1967.

Goetz, J.P. Configurations in control and autonomy: A microethnography of a rural third-grade classroom (Doctoral dissertation, Indiana University, 1975). *Dissertation Abstracts International,* 1976, *36,* 6175A. (University Microfilms No. 76–6275).

Goetz, J.P. Sex-role systems in Rose Elementary School: Change and tradition in the rural-transitional South. In R.T. Sieber & A.J. Gordon (Eds.), *Children and their organizations: Investigations in American culture.* Boston: G.K. Hall, 1981.

Goetz, J.P., & LeCompte, M.D. Ethnographic research and the problem of data reduction. *Anthropology and Education Quarterly,* 1981, *12,* 51–70.

Gold, R. Roles in sociological field observations. *Social Forces,* 1958, *36,* 217–223.

Goodman, M.E. Values, attitudes, and social concepts of Japanese and American children. *American Anthropologist,* 1957, *59,* 979–999.

Hammond, D., & Jablow, A. *Women in cultures of the world.* Menlo Park, Calif.: Cummings, 1976.

Hansen, J.F. *Sociocultural perspectives on human learning: An introduction to educational anthropology.* Englewood Cliffs, N.J.: Prentice-Hall, 1979.

Harris, M. *Culture, man, and nature.* New York: Crowell, 1971.

Henry, J. A Cross-cultural outlined of education. *Current Anthropology,* 1960, *1* (4), 267–305.

Herriott, R.E. Ethnographic case studies in federally funded multidisciplinary policy research: Some design and implementation issues. *Anthropology and Education Quarterly,* 1977, *8,* 106–115.

Herriott, R.E., & Gross, N. (Eds.). *The dynamics of planned educational change: Case studies and analyses.* Berkeley, Calif.: McCutchan, 1979.

Hilgar, M.I. *Field guide to the ethnological study of child life* (2nd ed.) New Haven, Conn.: Human Relations Area Files Press, 1966.

Hollingshead, A.B. *Elmtown's youth and Elmtown revisited.* New York: Wiley, 1975.

Hostetler, J.A., & Huntington, G.E. *Children in Amish society: Socialization and community education.* New York: Holt, Rinehart, & Winston, 1971.

Howard, A. *Learning to be Rotuman: Enculturation in the South Pacific.* New York: Teachers College Press, 1970.

Ianni, F.A.J. Anthropology and educational research: A report on federal agency programs, policies and issues. *Anthropology and Education Quarterly,* 1976, *7* (3), 3–11.

Janes, R.W. A note on phases of the community role of the participant-observer. *American Sociological Review,* 1961, *26,* 446–450.

Jacano, F.L. *Growing up in a Philippine barrio.* New York: Holt, Rinehart, & Winston, 1969.

Jorgensen, J.G. On ethics and anthropology. *Current Anthropology,* 1971, *12,* 321–334.

Kahn, R., & Mann, F. Developing research partnerships. *Journal of Social Issues,* 1952, *8* (3), 4–10.

Kaplan, D., & Manners, R.A. *Culture theory.* Englewood Cliffs, N.J.: Prentice-Hall, 1972.

Khleif, B.B. Issues in anthropological fieldwork in the schools. In G.D. Spindler (Ed.), *Education and cultural process: Toward an anthropology of education.* New York: Holt, Rinehart, & Winston, 1974.

King. R.A. *The school at Mopass: A problem of identity.* New York: Holt, Rinehart, & Winston, 1967.

King, R.A. The teacher as participant-observer: A case study. In G.D. Spindler (Ed.), *Education and cultural process: Toward an anthropology of education.* New York: Holt, Rinehart, & Winston, 1974.

LeCompte, M.D., & Goetz, J.P. Ethnographic data collection in evaluation research. *Educational Evaluation and Policy Analysis,* in press.

Leemon, T.A. *The rites of passage in a student culture: A study of the dynamics of transition.* New York: Teachers College Press, 1972.

Lewis, O. *Life in a Mexican village: Tepoztlan restudied.* Urbana, Ill.: University of Illinois Press, 1951.

Linton, R. *The cultural background of personality.* New York: Appleton-Century-Crofts, 1945.

Lofland, J. *Analyzing social settings: A guide to qualitative observation and analysis.* Belmont, Calif.: Wadsworth, 1971.

Magoon, A.J. Constructivist approaches in educational research. *Review of Educational Research,* 1977, *47,* 651–693.

McCall, G.J. Data quality control in participant observation. In G.J. McCall & J.L. Simmons (Eds.), *Issues in participant observation: A text and reader.* Reading, Mass.: Addison-Wesley, 1969.

McPherson, G. *Small town teacher.* Cambridge, Mass.: Harvard University Press, 1972.

Mead, M. *New lives for old: Cultural transformations—Manus, 1929–1953*, New York: Morrow, 1956.

Mehan. H. Assessing children's school performance. In M. Hammersley & P. Woods (Eds.). *The process of schooling: A sociological reader*. London: Routledge & Kegan Paul in association with the Open University Press, 1976.

Mehan, H. *Learning lessons: Social organization in the classroom*. Cambridge, Mass.: Harvard University Press, 1979.

Mehan, H., & Griffin, P. Socialization: The view from classroom interactions. *Sociological Inquiry*, 1980, *50* 3–4), 357–398.

Miller, S.M. The participant observer and "over-rapport." *American Sociological Review*, 1952, *17*, 97–99.

Modiano. N. *Indian education in the Chiapus highlands*. New York: Holt, Rinehart, & Winston, 1973.

Moore, A. *Life cycles in Atchálan: The diverse careers of certain Guatemalans*. New York. Teachers College Press, 1973.

Naroll, R. *Data quality control: A new research technique*. New York: Free Press, 1962.

Ogbu, J.U. *The next generation: An ethnography of education in an urban neighborhood*. New York: Academic Press, 1974.

Patton, M.Q. *Qualitative evaluation methods*. Beverly Hills, Calif.: Sage, 1980.

Paulme, D. (Ed.). *Women of tropical Africa*. Berkeley: University of California Press, 1963.

Pelto, P.J., & Pelto, G.H. *Anthropological research: The structure of inquiry* (2nd ed.). Cambridge: Cambridge University Press, 1978.

Peshkin, A. *Growing up American: Schooling and the survival of community*. Chicago: University of Chicago Press, 1978.

Petrie, H.G. Do you see what I see? The epistemology of interdisciplinary research. *Educational Researcher*, 1976, *5* (2), 9–15.

Phillips, D.L. *Knowledge from what? Theories and methods in social research*. Chicago: Rand McNally, 1971.

Powdermaker, H. *Stranger and friend*. New York: Norton, 1966.

Redfield, R. *Tepoztlan—A Mexican village*. Chicago: University of Chicago Press, 1930.

Reichardt, C.S., & Cook, T.D. Beyond qualitative versus quantitative methods. In T.D. Cook & C.S. Reichardt (Eds.), *Qualitative and quantitative methods in evaluation research*. Beverly Hills, Calif.: Sage, 1979.

Reiter, R.R. *Toward an anthropology of women*. New York: Monthly Review Press, 1975.

Riner, R.D. American Indian education: A rite that fails. *Anthropology and Education Quarterly*, 1979, *10*, 236–253.

Rist, R.C. Student social class and teacher expectations: The self-fulfilling prophecy in ghetto education. *Harvard Educational Review*, 1970, *40*, 411–451.

Rist, R.C. On the relations among educational research paradigms: From disdain to detest. *Anthropology and Educational Quarterly*, 1977, *8*, 42–49.

Robinson, W.S. The logical structure of analytic induction. *American Sociological Review*, 1951, *16*, 812–818.

Rosenfeld, G. *"Shut those thick lips!": A study of slum school failure.* New York: Holt, Rinehart, & Winston, 1971.

Rynkiewich, M.A., & Spradley, J.P. (Eds.). *Ethics and anthropology: Dilemmas in fieldwork.* New York: Wiley, 1976.

Schatzman, L., & Strauss, A. *Field research: Strategies for a natural sociology.* Englewood Cliffs, N.J.: Prentice-Hall, 1973.

Schwartz, M.S., & Schwartz, C.G. Problems in participant observations. *American Journal of Sociology*, 1955, *60*, 343–354.

Scriven, M. Objectivity and subjectivity in educational research. In L.G. Thomas (Ed.), *Philosophical redirection of educational research* (71st Yearbook, Part I). Chicago: National Society for the Study of Education, 1972.

Scriven, M. Evaluation perspectives and procedures. In J.W. Popham (Ed.), *Evaluation in education: Current applications.* Berkeley, Calif.: McCutchan, 1974.

Sieber, R.T. Classmates as workmates: Informal peer activity in an elementary school. *Anthropology and Education Quarterly*, 1979, *10*, 207–235.

Sieber, R.T. Many roles, many faces: Researching school-community relations in a heterogeneous American urban community. In D.A. Messerschmidt (Ed.), *Anthropologists at home: Toward an anthropology of issues in America.* New York: Cambridge University Press, in press.

Smith, L.M. Reflections on trying to theorize from ethnographic data. *Anthropology and Education Quarterly*, 1974, *5* (1), 18–24.

Smith, L.M. An evolving logic of participant observation, educational ethnography, and other case studies. *Review of Research in Education*, 1979, *6*, 316–377.

Smith, L.M., & Brock, J.A.M. *"Go, bug, go!": Methodological issues in classroom observational research.* St. Louis: Central Midwestern Regional Educational Laboratory, 1970.

Smith, L.M., & Geoffrey, W. *The complexities of an urban classroom: An analysis toward a general theory of teaching.* New York: Holt, Rinehart, & Winston, 1968.

Smith, L.M., & Keith, P.M. *Anatomy of educational innovation: An organizational analysis of an elementary school.* New York: Wiley, 1971.

Spindler, G.D. *Burgbach: Urbanization and identity in a German village.* New York: Holt, Rinehart, & Winston, 1973.

Spindler, G.D. Schooling in Schönhausen: A study in cultural transmission and instrumental adaptation in an urbanizing German village. In G.D. Spindler (Ed.), *Education and cultural process: Toward an anthropology of education.* New York: Holt, Rinehart, & Winston, 1974.

Spradley, J.P. *The ethnographic interview.* New York: Holt, Rinehart, & Winston, 1979.

Spradley, J.P. *Participant observation.* New York: Holt, Rinehart, & Winston, 1980.

Spradley, J.P., & McCurdy, D.W. *The cultural experience: Ethnography in complex society.* Chicago: Science Research Associates, 1972.

Stake, R.E. *Case studies in science education.* (2 vols.). Washington, D.C.: U.S. Government Printing Office, 1978. (ERIC Document Reproduction Service Nos. ED 166 058 & ED 166 059.)

Stedstill, J.P. Education in a Luba secret society. *Anthropology and Education Quarterly*, 1979, *10*, 67–79.

Taunoff, W.J., Berliner, D., & Rist, R.C. *Special study A: An ethnographc study of 40 classrooms of the BTES known sample*. San Francisco: Far West Laboratory for Educational Development, 1975. (ERIC Document Reproduction Service No. ED 150 110.)

Van Gennep, A. *The rites of passage*. Chicago: University of Chicago Press, 1960.

Valich, A.J. Participant observation and the collection and interpretation of data. *American Journal of Sociology*, 1955, *60*, 354–360.

Ward, M.C. *Them children: A study of language learning*. New York: Holt, Rinehart, & Winston, 1971.

Warren, R.L. *Education in Rebhausen: A German village*. New York: Holt, Rinehart, & Winston, 1967.

Wax, M.L. (Ed.). *When schools are desegregated: Problems and possibilities of students, educators, and the community*. New Brunswich, N.J.: Transaction Books. in press.

Wax, R.H. *Doing fieldwork: Warnings and advice*. Chicago: University of Chicago Press, 1971.

Webb, E.J., Campbell, D.T., Schwartz, R.D., & Sechrest, L. *Unobtrusive measures: Nonreactive research in the social sciences*. Chicago: Rand McNally, 1966.

Whiting, B.B. (Ed.). *Six cultures: Studies of child rearing*. New York: Wiley, 1963.

Whiting, B.B., & Whiting, J.W.M. *Children of six cultures: A psychocultural analysis*. Cambridge, Mass.: Harvard University Press, 1975.

Whiting, J.W.M., Child, I.L., & Lambert, W.W. *Field guide for a study of socialization*. Huntington, N.Y.: Krieger, 1966.

Whyte, W.F. *Street corner society: The social structure of an Italian slum* (2nd ed.). Chicago: University of Chicago Press, 1955.

Williams, T.R. *Field methods in the study of culture*. New York: Holt, Rinehart, & Winston, 1967.

Wilson, S. The use of ethnographic techniques in educational research. *Review of Educational Research;*, 1977, *47*, 245–265.

Wolcott, H.F. *A Kwakiutl village and school*. New York: Holt, Rinehart, & Winston, 1967.

Wolcott, H.F. Handle with care: Necessary precautions in the anthropology of schools. In M.L. Wax, S. Diamond, & F.O. Gearing (Eds.), *Anthropological perspectives on education*. New York: Basic Books, 1971.

Wolcott, H.F. *The man in the principal's office: An ethnography*. New York: Holt, Rinehart, & Winston, 1973.

Wolcott, H.F. The teacher as an enemy. In G.D. Spindler (Ed.), *Education and cultural press: Toward an anthropology of education*. New York: Holt, Rinehart, & Winston, 1974.

Wolcott, H.F. Criteria for an ethnographic approach to research in schools. *Human Organization*, 1975, *34*, 111–127.

Wolcott, H.F. *Teachers versus technocrats: An educational innovation in anthropological perspectives*. Eugene, Ore.: Center for Educational Policy and Management, University or Oregon, 1977.

Wylie, L. *Village in the Vaucluse* (3rd ed.). Cambridge, Mass.: Harvard University Press, 1974.
Znaniecki, F. *The method of sociology*. New York: Farrar & Rinehart, 1934.

Issues of Validity in Openly Ideological Research: Between a Rock and a Soft Place

PATTI LATHER

In this paper, I attempt to reconceptualize validity within the context of openly ideological research.[1] The usefulness of this reconceptualization is tested by applying it to examples from three explicitly value-based research programs: feminist research, neo-Marxist critical ethnography, and Freirian "empowering" research.[2] Finally, validity issues within research committed to a more equitable social order are discussed.

The Context From Which I Speak

The attempt to produce value-neutral social science is increasingly being abandoned as at best unrealizable, and at worst self-deceptive, and is being replaced by social sciences based on explicit ideologies.

Mary Hesse (1980)

To say that positivism remains the orthodox approach to doing empirical research in the human sciences is not to deny that we are in a postpositivist era.[3] Thomas Kuhn wrote that "rather than a single group conversion, what occurs [with a paradigm shift] is an increasing shift in the distribution of professional allegiances" as practitioners of the new paradigm "improve it, explore its possibilities, and show what it would be like to belong to the community guided by it" (1962, pp. 157–158).

The foundation of postpositivism is the cumulative, trenchant, and increasingly definitive critique of the inadequacies of positivist assumptions in the face of the complexities of human experience (Oppenheimer, 1956; Kaplan, 1964; Cronbach, 1975; Bernstein, 1976; Mishler, 1979; Giroux, 1981; Guba & Lincoln, 1981; Feinberg, 1983; Lincoln & Guba, 1985). As the orthodox paradigm for inquiry in the human sciences proves obsolete, new visions are required (Rose, 1979; Schwartz & Ogilvy, 1979; Hesse, 1980; Reason & Rowan, 1981). The result is a rich ferment in contemporary discourse regarding empirical research in the human sciences—a discourse spanning epistemological, theoretical, and to a much lesser degree, methodological issues.[4]

This paper is rooted in that rich ferment and has two basic premises. The first is that "since interest-free knowledge is logically impossible, we should feel free to substitute explicit interests for implicit ones" (Reinharz, 1985, p. 17). As the phrase "openly ideological research" implies, I take issue with the claims of positivism regarding objectivity and neutrality. Feminist research, neo-Marxist critical ethnography, and Freirian "empowering" research all stand in opposition to prevailing scientific norms through their "transformative agendas" and their concern with research as praxis (Rose, 1979). Each argues that scientific "neutrality" and "objectivity" serve to mystify the inherently ideological nature of research in the human sciences and to legitimate privilege based on class, race, and gender.

Within this frame of reference, research which is openly valued based is neither more nor less ideological than is mainstream positivist research. Rather, those committed to the development of research approaches that challenge the status quo and contribute to a more egalitarian social order have made an "epistemological break" from the positivist insistence upon researcher neutrality and objectively (Hesse, 1980, p. 196).

The second premise in this paper is that for those exploring the possibilities of a postpositivist paradigm, the central challenge is to formulate approaches to empirical research which advance emancipatory theory-building through the development of interactive and action-inspiring research designs. There is a pioneering dimension to this task. Since the formation of the Frankfurt School, critical theorists have been calling for such research while spinning obtuse webs of abstract "grand theory" (Mills, 1959; Kellner, 1975, p. 149; Stanley & Wise, 1983, p. 100).

Fifty years ago, the Italian neo-Marxist Antonio Gramsci urged intellectuals to adhere to a "praxis of the present" by aiding developing progressive groups in their effort to become increasingly conscious of their own actions and situations in the world (Salamini, 1981, p. 73). What are the implications of this advice from Gramsci for those seeking empirical approaches which can change, rather than merely describe, the world? The task of this paper is to explore the central questions in the effort to formulate an approach to empirical research which both advances emancipatory theory-building and empowers the researched.

Of the three openly valued-based research programs discussed in this paper, neo-Marxist critical ethnography (Foley, 1979; Ogbu, 1981; Maseman, 1982) is the most advanced in terms of developing empirical approaches for the building of emancipatory social theory. All empirical work within this research program attempts to problematize what goes on in schools in terms of the reproduction of social inequality and the potential for social transformation. Such theoretical emphasis, however, brings to the fore the danger of conceptual overdeterminism: circular reinforcement of theory by experience conditioned by theory.

The recent empirical emphasis in neo-Marxism has been primarily interested in the creation of an empirically informed Marxism to meet the criticisms of those such as Bottomore (1978) and E. P. Thompson (1978) who argue that too much of neo-Marxist social theory is "an immaculate conception which requires no gross empirical impregnation" (Thompson, 1978, p. 13; see also, Kellner, 1975, p. 149; Wright, 1978, p. 10; Krueger, 1981, p. 59; Comstock, 1982, p. 371). Theoretically guided empirical work exploring the mirror-image relationship between schools and the needs of corporate capitalism was the first to be produced (Bowles & Gintis, 1976; Apple, 1979b). More recently, given the extensive critique of an over-socialized conception of human nature as empirically inaccurate and politically suicidal (Apple, 1979a, 1980-81; Wrong, 1961; Giroux, 1981, 1983; 1977), empirical studies of human resistance to hegemonic forces are burgeoning (see, for example, Willis, 1977; McRobbie 1978; Everhart, 1983; Miller, 1983; Anyon, 1983).

Such research is a beginning, but the lack of clear strategies for linking theory and research is pervasive. Although some attention is beginning to be focussed on the need for an approach to research which advances egalitarian transformation (Apple, 1982; Fay, 1977; Comstock, 1982), the methodological implications of critical theory are relatively unexplored (Bredo & Feinberg, 1982, p. 281). There is also a lack of self-reflexivity in the empirical work that exists within critical inquiry. Sabia and Wallulis point out that, too often, critical self-awareness comes to mean "a negative attitude toward competing approaches instead of its own self-critical perspective " (1983, p. 26).

Research within a postpositivist context mandates a self-corrective element to prevent phenomena from being forced into preconceived interpretive schemes. Postpositivism has cleared methodology of prescribed rules and boundaries and has created a constructive turmoil as a result of successful challenges by philosophers of science during the past several decades (Polkinghorne, 1983, pp. 4–5). Because we are not able to assume anything, we must take a self-critical stance regarding the assumptions we incorporate into our empirical approaches. No longer does following the correct method guarantee "true" results: "Method does not give truth; it corrects guesses" (Polkinghorne, 1983, p. 249). If critical theory is to change the way social science is conceived of and practised, it must become genuinely reflexive (Moon, 1983, p. 30).

While the development of empowering approaches to empirical research is at the heart of Freirian research and, increasingly, of feminist research, they, too, by and larger suffer from a lack of self-reflexivity. My central argument is that new paradigm researchers must begin to be more systematic about establishing the trustworthiness of data. Reducing the ambiguity of what we do does not mean we have to deny the essential indeterminancy of human experience, "the irreducible disparity between the being of the world and the knowledge we might have of it" (White, 1973). But if we want illuminating and resonant theory grounded in trustworthy data, we must formulate self-corrective techniques that will check the credibility of our data and minimize the distorting effect of personal bias upon the logic of evidence (Kamarovsky, 1981).

I offer the following reconceptualization of validity in the hope that it will aid those of us who work within openly ideological research programs to focus more of our energies on how best to establish data credibility. Our task is to create a body of research exemplars that will stand as testimony to the vigor that comes, not from positivist retrenchment, but from viewing the move into the postpositivist era with a sense of possibility.

Between a Rock and a Soft Place

Relevance without rigor is no better than rigor without relevance.

Egon Guba (1981)

To recast a familiar metaphor, the "rock" is the unquestionable need for trustworthiness in data generated by alternative paradigms (Guba, 1981) and the "soft place" is the positivist claim to neutrality and objectivity (Campbell, 1981).[5] Within newly emerging patterns of inquiry, approaches to validity must reach beyond the obfuscating claims of objectivity used by positivism to skirt the role placed by researcher values in the human sciences.

Specific techniques of validity are tied to paradigmatic assumptions (Guba & Lincoln, 1981; Morgan, 1983). Positivists formulate tidy, quantifiable procedures based on "the first positivist assumption" that natural science methods are appropriate for the study of human begins (Westkott, 1977). The classic psychometric approach to establishing data trustworthiness focusses on the measurable. In spite of "validity coefficients" and "multitrait-multimethod matrices," however, validity remains elusive. Basic construct validity, so central to theory construction (Cronbach & Meehl, 1955), continues to defy quantification. Error-of-estimate formulae and multiple-regression equations are substituted for the much slipperier process of searching out and establishing independent, external validity criteria.

Within conventional, positivist research, the quantifiable concepts of discriminant and concurrent validity rise to the fore; factor analysis carries the weight of construct validity; and face validity, so inherently impressionistic, is defined as rapport and public relations and relegated to a distinctly second-class concern (Kidder, 1982). Statistical manipulations replace the logical grounding of constructs. Reliability, for example, while held to be necessary but not sufficient in establishing validity, often stands alone in experimental and quasi-experimental research—mute testimony to the lack of attention paid to construct validity. At best, this leads to consistent subjectivity. At worst, it results in the reification of constructs that are the projections of social biases, masculinity-femininity being but one prime example (Constantinople, 1973; Lewin, 1984).

With the present epistemological and methodological ferment in the human sciences, however, paradigmatic uncertainty is leading to the reconceptualization of validity. Efforts to set subjective, tacit knowledge apart from the "context of verification" are seen as "naïve empiricism." The process of inquiry is increasingly viewed as a tapestry in which tacit knowledge is the "warp" and propositional knowledge the "woof" (Heron, 1981, p. 32). With no ready-made formulae to guarantee valid social knowledge, "we must operate simultaneously at epistemological, theoretical and empirical levels with self-awareness" (Sharp & Green, 1975, p. 234). What we are faced with is a lack of workable procedures or specific rules for analyzing and verifying data (Huberman & Miles, 1983, p. 282). Our best shot at present is to construct research designs that push us toward becoming vigorously self-aware.

Going beyond predisposition in our empirical efforts requires techniques that will give confidence in the trustworthiness of data. Reason (1981) wants "objectively subjective" inquiry (p. xiii). Guba and Lincoln (1981) argue, more systematically, for analogues to the major criteria of rigor within the orthodox paradigm. Guba (1981) states that the least we should expect in establishing trustworthy data in new paradigm research is triangulation, reflexivity, and member checks. Reason and Rowan (1981) advise borrowing concepts of validity from traditional research but refining and expanding them in ways appropriate to "an interactive, dialogic logic" (p. 240). Building on all of this, what follows is a reconceptualization of validity appropriate for research openly committed to a more just social order.

Reconceptualizing Validity

The job of validation is not to support an interpretation, but to find out what might be wrong with it. A proposition deserves some degree of trust only when it has survived serious attempts to falsify it.

Lee Cronbach (1980)

Once we recognize that just as there is no neutral education there is no neutral research, we no longer need apologize for unabashedly ideological research and its open commitment to using research to criticize and change the status quo. The development of data credibility checks to protect our research and theory construction from our enthusiasms, however, is essential in our efforts to create a self-reflexive human science. To guard against researcher biases distorting the logic of evidence within openly ideological research, the following guidelines are offered.

Triangulation, expanded beyond the psychometric definition of multiple measures to include multiple *data sources*, *methods*, and *theoretical schemes*, is critical in establishing data trustworthiness. It is essential that the research design seek counterpatterns as well as convergences if data are to be credible.

Construct validity must be dealt with in ways that recognize its roots in theory construction (Cronbach & Meehl, 1955). Emancipatory social theory requires a ceaseless confrontation with the experiences of people in their daily lives in order to stymie the tendency to theoretical imposition which is inherent in theoretically guided empirical work. A *systematized reflexivity*, which gives some indication of how *a priori* theory has been changed by the logic of the data, becomes essential in establishing construct validity in ways that will contribute to the growth of illuminating and change-enhancing social theory.

Face validity needs to be seen as much more integral to the process of establishing data credibility. Guba and Lincoln (1981) refer to "member checks" which they consider to be "the backbone of satisfying the truth-value criterion" (p. 110). Reason and Rowan (1981) argue that such member checks (recycling analysis back through at least a subsample of respondents) need to become a standard part of emancipatory research designs: "Good research at the non-alienating end of the spectrum . . . goes back to the subject with the tentative results, and refines them in the light of the subjects' reactions" (p. 248).

Catalytic validity (Reason & Rowan, 1981, p. 240; Brown & Tandom, 1978) refers to the degree to which the research process re-orients, focusses, and energizes participants in what Freire (1973) terms "conscientization," knowing reality in order to better transform it. Of the guidelines proposed here, this is by far the most unorthodox as it flies directly in the face of the essential positivist tenet of researcher neutrality. My argument is premised not only on a recognition of the reality-altering impact of the research process itself, but also on the need to consciously channel this impact so that respondents gain self-understanding and, ideally, self-determination through research participation.

My concern is that efforts to produce social knowledge that is helpful in the struggle for a more equitable world pursue rigor as well as relevance. Otherwise, just as "pointless precision" (Kaplan, 1964) has proven to be the bane of the conventional paradigm, the rampant subjectivity inherent in the more phenomenologically based paradigms will prove to be the nemesis of new paradigm research.

Feminist Research

The overt ideological goal of feminist research is to correct both the *invisibility* and the *distortion* of female experience in ways relevant to ending women's unequal social position. This entails the substantive task of making gender a fundamental category for our understanding of the social order, "to see the world from women's place in it" (Callaway, 1981, p. 460). The methodological task becomes that of generating and refining interactive, contextualized methods which search for pattern and meaning rather than for prediction and control (Reinharz, 1983). While the first wave of feminist research operated largely within the conventional paradigm (Westkott, 1979), the second wave is more self-consciously methodologically innovative (Eichler, 1980; Reinharz, 1983; Stanley & Wise, 1983; Bowles & Duelli-Klein, 1983).

A few examples will illustrate how such an unabashedly ideological perspective works to frame research approaches and questions. Mies (1984) field-tested seven methodological guidelines for doing feminist research in an action-research project in Cologne, Germany, designed to respond to violence against women in the family. Highly visible street action drew people who were then interviewed regarding their views on wife beating. The resulting publicity led to the creation of Women's House to aid victims of domestic abuse. Principles of action and egalitarian participation, developed through life histories, guided consciousness-raising regarding the sociological and historical roots of male violence in the home. The purpose was to empower the oppressed to come to understand and change their own oppressive realities. Oakley (1981) studied the effects of motherhood on women's lives over an extended period of time through a series of interviews that focussed on "interactive self-disclosure," a collaborative dialogue seeking for greater clarity. Carol Gilligan's work on female moral development (1977, 1982) and the highly contradictory body of work on female achievement motivation (Horner, 1969; Sassen, 1980) serve to counter interpretations that view women as deviants from male-established norms. Such work asks, "How do male-based constructs need to be reformulated from the vantage point of female experience?"[6]

Gilligan's work clarifies the distortion of Kohlberg's androcentric conception of moral development which values autonomy at the expense of interrelatedness. Her research suggests that the female conception of a moral problem may come from conflicting responsibilities rather than from competing rights and that resolution requires contextual thinking rather than formal abstraction.

For women, morality seems defined in terms of interpersonal responsibilities rather than individualistic rights. Gilligan's findings challenge the assumed centrality of male experience in theories of development and expose the all-male samples underlying purportedly "universal theories." Hence, her work is an oft-cited exemplar in feminist research.

Gray (1982) writes that Gilligan's initial concern was the shakiness of construct validity based on hypothetical rather than real-life moral dilemmas. During the Viet Nam War, she intended to interview young men making draft-resistance choices, and she got an all-female sample quite by accident when the war ended (p. 52). Abortion had recently been legalized, and Gilligan soon recognized the moral dilemma of whether to carry a child to full term as a real-life situation with great potential for expanding the methodology of moral development research beyond hypothetical situations.

Twenty-nine women, diverse in age, race, and social class, were referred by abortion and pregnancy counselling services and interviewed. Three of Kohlberg's standardized hypothetical moral dilemmas were administered during the second half of the interview. By allowing categories to arise out of the language of respondents, Gilligan discovered a central tension in women's lives between selfishness and responsibility to self as well as others. In a culture that on the one hand equates feminine goodness with self-sacrifice and on the other hand equates adulthood with separation, individuation, and detachment, women were caught in a classic "double bind."

By structuring the research to focus first on the contextual particularity of a pressing real-life moral dilemma, Gilligan discovered that respondents refused to formulate an ethics abstracted from contextual complications. Their response to the hypothetical dilemmas was, "The wrong questions are being asked," and they insisted on information regarding the lives of the characters. This led Gilligan to surmise that decontextualized hypothetical dilemmas deny the central female experience of contextualized interrelationship and, hence, create Kohlberg's "objective principles of justice" *as a research artifact.*

This is all very interesting as a critique of Kohlberg, but what corrective mechanisms did Gilligan use so that her interview data become scientific research rather than impressionistic journalism?

Triangulation of methods is apparent in the inclusion of both interview data and Kohlberg's standardized hypothetical moral dilemmas, but convergence seems to be sought rather than disconfirmation. Criteria for including/excluding data are not given, and there is no indication of a conscious search for counter-patterns. The triangulation of different data *sources* is not strong; especially at risk is the small (n=29) all-female characteristics of the sample. How can one argue for gender-specific patterns based on a single-sex sample and a gender-specific situation? The triangulation of different *theories* is strong. Gilligan worked with Kohlberg for several years. Her work is, in essence, a critique and revision of his theory-building. The theoretical vitality of what she is doing comes largely out of her strong grounding in Kohlberg's notably different theoretical constructs: the universal, invariant sequence claims, the hierarchical nature of his theory with it relegation of relational concerns to a second-class status, and the assumption that valid data can be evoked on the basis of standardized, hypothetical moral dilemmas.

Construct validity is premised on the convergence of Gilligan's review of psychological and literary sources with the research data and the comparison of Kohlberg's categories with categories arising out of the language of respondents. Some degree of self-reflexivity can be ascertained from the development of theoretical insights, but this is by no means systematized.

Catalytic validity undergoes an interesting development. As respondents began to examine their own thinking, a pattern developed whereby they moved from a conventional feminine construction of the moral problem (equating feminine goodness with self-sacrifice) to a recognition of the conflict between the dependence and self-sacrifice of femininity and the choice and existential responsibility of adulthood. Hence, the research process provided an opportunity for respondents to grow through thoughtful assessment of their experiences. This seems to be an unexpected and relatively unnoted aspect of the research, however, and was in no way consciously invited through the research design. Also, no effort is made to triangulate this growth in self-understanding. This leaves the claims of growth wide open to both the limitations of self-reporting and the projection of the researcher's aspirations for respondents onto the data analysis.

Face validity is perhaps the most seriously lacking. The research design called for two interviews, approximately one year apart. Neither categories nor conclusions were recycled back through respondents. This would have been relatively easy, and the payoff in both construct and catalytic validity would likely have been worth the effort.

The intellectual power of Gilligan's work is such that concern about establishing the trustworthiness of her data is subsumed by the provocativeness of her theorizing. But issues of data trustworthiness concern her—one of her Ph.D. students worked on a coding system that allows reliable data aggregation across interviews in a sample selected to *refuse* a sex differences hypothesis; another worked on self-constructed moral dilemmas that focus on the interaction between justice and caring in an effort to deepen construct validity; Gilligan moved into open-interviewing with adolescent females around self-identity and self-defined moral dilemmas. Additionally, Gilligan and her students work as a team to stress reflexivity.[8] As she and her students move from exploratory, hypothesis-generating work to theory construction and validation within a long-term, ongoing research program, validity issues grow increasingly important. That Gilligan is fully cognizant of this speaks hopefully for the continuing importance of her work.

Neo-Marxist Critical Ethnography

The overt ideological goal of neo-Marxist critical ethnography is to expose the contradictions and delusions of liberal democratic education in order to create less exploitative social and economic relations (Willis, 1977; Apple, 1980–81; Reynolds, 1980–81). The substantive task is the portrayal of the role of schooling in the reproduction of inequality in all of its content and specificity, its contradictions and complexities. The methodological task is the ethnographic revelation of participants' views of reality, where these views come from, and the social consequences of such views, all situated within a context of theory-building. The overriding goal, then, is to produce "an adequate theory of schooling in the context of cultural imperatives" (Ogbu, 1981, p. 9). The theory is to make clear "the order of structural transformation necessary to honor commitments to human rights and justice" (Pinar, 1981, p. 439).

Within this theoretically guided search for data, which is the dominant characteristic of critical ethnography, reality is held to be something more than negotiated accounts. Critical ethnographers hold that by limiting analysis to the actors' perceptions of their situations, nonMarxist ethnographies and phenomenological research reify interpretive procedures and reduce research to a collection of functionalist, subjective accounts that obscure the workings of false consciousness and ideological mystification (Foley, 1979). They argue that Marxism's profound scepticism of both appearances and common sense produces a more valid analysis that does phenomenological research. Such scepticism, however, is tempered by an opposition to reductive forms of determinism as the central theoretical inadequacy of orthodox Marxism: the economistic reduction of humanity to pawns in the great chessgame of capitalism (Apple, 1982; Giroux, 1981; Willis, 1977). Willis writes:

> Capital requires it, therefore schools do it! Humans become dummies, dupes, zombies . . . . This will not do theoretically. It will certainly not do politically. Pessimism reigns supreme in this, the most spectacular of secular relations of predeterminism. (1977, p. 205)

The following examples illustrate how this research program frames its questions. Do progressive, liberal primary schools focus more on liberation than on social control (Sharp & Green, 1975; Apple, 1979b)? How do young working-class males deal with their entrapment in the lower rungs of the hierarchical work world (Willis, 1977)? How do working-class females deal with the school's efforts to prepare them for their primary roles as wife, mother, and reserve labor force (McRobbie, 1978)? Where do teachers' "common-sense" views of student differences come from and how do these views affect kids' life chances (Carlson, 1980)? How do students react to curricular offerings sanitized of any sense of struggle and oppression (McNeil, 1981)?

Paul Willis's *Learning to Labor: How Working Class Kids Get Working Class Jobs* (1977) is the standard work in the critical ethnography of schooling (Apple, 1979a). A three-year participant observation study of 12 "disaffected" male teenages in a working-class British industrial area, it focusses on the transition from school to work in order to shed light on the willing acceptance of restricted work opportunities on the part of working-class youth. Using informal interviewing, regular and recorded group discussion, diaries, and participant observation in and out of school, Willis collected data throughout "the lads'" last two years of schooling and into the first six months of work. Parents, teachers, and work supervisors were included in the interviews. Participant observation included attending classes as a student and working alongside the lads at their jobs. The research design included comparative case studies selected to be similar in sex, patterns of friendship grouping, and likelihood of leaving school at age 16.

Theory guided the search for oppositional, counter-school group members as the main research sample used to substantiate the concept of working-class resistance to official authority. Theory guided the search for contradictions: that between teachers' expressed goal of enabling working-class students to transcend their class-limited lives versus teachers' efforts to stymie the "self-disqualification" of disaffected students from the meritocratic merryground (p. 148); that between the lads' "felt sense of cultural election" as they moved into the adult world of work and money versus the too-late recognition of the determinants that settled a major life decision of their disadvantage (p. 107). Theory guided the "plunge beneath the surface of ethnography in[to] a more interpretive mode" (p. 119) to transcend the limitations of the "ethnography of visible forms" (p. 121) which is as likely to conceal as reveal cultural dynamics. Theory guided the view of humans as active appropriators who reproduce existing structures of inequality only through struggle, contestation, and partial penetration: "Just because there are what we call structural and economic determinants, it does not mean that people will unproblematically obey them" (p. 171). Theory guided the interpretation that while the cultural freedoms of capitalism are essentially used for self-damnation, permanent struggle is the deeper reality.

Within research so theoretically top-heavy, what self-corrective mechanisms did Willis use?

Triangulation of methods is strong, especially the combination of interviewing and participant observation. The triangulation of different data *sources* is also quite strong. The comparative case studies are built into the research design, and the search for counter-patterns as well as convergences is documented. The wide array of subjects observed and interviewed over the course of this extended three-year study is notable. The triangulation of different *theories* is present in that Willis's theoretical advances are premised on reformulations of both the liberal theory of schooling with its espousal of equal opportunity through meritocracy and the over-determinism of orthodox Marxism.

Construct validity is strengthened by collecting data at work and at home as well as at school. Especially powerful in establishing the meaninglessness of working-class jobs is the interview data with fathers and shopfloor supervisors. But there is no systematic self-reflexivity. Given the centrality of theory, it seems of paramount importance to document how researcher perspectives were altered by the logic of the data. With no account of this, one is left viewing the role of theory as nondialectical, unidirectional, an *a priori* imposition that subsumes counter-patterns.

Catalytic validity comes through in the following interview transcript:

> Something should have been done with us, I mean there was so much talent there that it was all fuckin' wasted. . . . We've just been thrust into society too soon, we've been brought up to be too

selfish . . . we couldn't care less, you see on the tele so many people fuckin' affluent, you just want to try and do that, make it, get money, you don't care about others, the working class. (pp. 195–198)

But this was in no way an intended aspect of the research and the lads' continued sense of cultural election in the face of meaningless work comes through clearly, indicating that the catalytic validity was minimal.

Face validity was consciously built into the research design, but only at the end. Willis brought the lads to the university at the conclusion of the research to discuss how they saw his role as researcher and what the "results" of the research meant to them. Marxism has long been infamous for its alienating jargon. The methodological appendix makes clear that the lads had no inkling of what Willis was getting at in his text: "The bits about us were simple enough. . . . It's the bits in between. . . . Well, I started to read it . . . then I just packed it in" (p. 195).

Overall, this is a stellar exemplar of theoretically guided ethnography. The extended time spent in the field using a wide variety of methods and the invitation of disconfirmation through the use of comparative case studies are its methodological strengths. Notable weaknesses are twofold. One is the lack of systematic self-reflexivity; the other is the lack of attention to catalytic validity. Regarding the latter, while Willis acknowledges the general responsibility of the researcher to the researched, he views it in terms of enlightening those with the cultural authority to redirect policy rather than helping respondents gain understanding of and control over their own lives: "The progressive use and mobilization of the research on a wider political and pedagogic place must be the main form of return and repayment [to the researched]" (p. 221). There is a failure to use the research process itself to empower the researched.

Freirian "Empowering" Research

The last of the counter-research programs rooted in the search for a science "derived from the radical needs of the oppressed" (Rose, 1979, p. 280) is modelled after Paulo Freire's *Pedagogy of the Oppressed* (1973). The openly ideological goal is to blur the distinctions between research, learning, and action by providing conditions under which participants' self-determination is enhanced in the struggle toward social justice (Hall, 1975, p. 30; Heron, 1981, p. 35). The substantive task is to delineate collective identification of and solutions to local problems in ways that link this process to larger structural issues (Hall, 1981). The methodological task is to proceed in a reciprocal, dialogic manner, empowering subjects by turning them into co-researchers. Ideally, such research involves participants in the planning, execution, and dissemination of social research (Rowan, 1981, p. 97).

Historically, this research program is a descendent of Lewin's action research. But Lewin's goal was self-management within a society assumed to operate from a consensual value base (Sanford, 1981, p. 178), whereas Freirian research focusses on promoting liberation and growth within a society assumed to be class divided and, hence, inequitable. Two concepts characterize this body of research.

The first is the effort to democratize knowledge and power through the research process (Hall, 1981). Freire's concept of cultural imposition becomes a critique of methods which impose a substantive focus and alienating methods on research subjects. Such a "cult of expertise" is part of the unequal relationships inherent in an oppressive social order. Mainstream researchers "live patronizingly in a delusion of relevance" (Maruyama, 1974). The researcher's role as a privileged possessor of expert knowledge must be reconceptualized as that of a catalyst who works with local participants to understand and solve local problems. The researched become as important as the researcher in formulating the problem, discussing solutions, and interpreting findings (Hall, 1975).

The second concept characterizing Freirian research is designed to have "an arousal effect," to reorient participants' perceptions of issues in ways that influence subsequent attitudes and behaviors (Brown & Tandom, 1978). The "vivification" of "ideas that open beyond themselves" (Torbert,

1981, p. 148) can energize the desire to do things differently *provided the issues are of central importance to the participants.* Self-determination, hence, requires both the demystification of ideologies that distort dominant and oppressive social relationships and the empowerment of the oppressed so that they can take charge of improving their own situations.

Much of the empirical work within this research program is conducted with adult populations in Third World countries. Literacy work is where Freire began to formulate his pedagogical ideas. Others have used local participant-conducted surveys to guide development priorities in Africa (Swantz, 1975); to train inmates to study violence (Maruyama, 1969); to assist Norwegian bank employees to assess the effects of the installation of computer terminals (Elden, 1979); and to help impoverished farmers in India improve local agricultural practices (Tandom, 1981).

While there are no oft-cited exemplars in this research program, Swantz's work (1981) is typical. Working through the University of Norway and the government of Tanzania, Swantz's team conducted a four-year participatory research project to study the process of change in rural villages. Researchers lived in the village and took part in daily activities in order to become familiar with the context of acute problems. The researchers' role was to probe and stimulate the villagers' formulation and to search for solutions to their perceived problems. Theory was used dialectically to problematize the contradictions underlying daily difficulties so that policies and strategies could be formulated that would create long-term solutions (p. 286).

As well as day-to-day informal participant observation, various seminars involving all adult villagers were taped and reports were distributed to all participants (although no mention was made of how literacy rates affected this); villagers were involved in the design of surveys; task groups worked on such projects as collecting local music and storytelling; villagers helped design and conduct training programs for agricultural, veterinary, and health care officers. All phases of the research were characterized by a continuing mutual feedback process.

The self-corrective mechanisms were:

Triangulation of methods is strong: extensive time in the field included participant observation, grounded surveys, and interviews. *Data sources* were extremely varied at both the local and national level. *Theory* triangulation is especially strong. In arriving at a sense of development that reflected villager needs and aspirations, theoretical constructs were triangulated from four sources: (1) concrete case material and the incorporation of the villagers' own thinking on issues; (2) the need for guidelines for national development policies; (3) the commitment to derive theory in ways that would directly benefit the villagers' own micro-level development process; and (4) *a priori,* loosely neo-Marxist theoretical constructs such as sexism and the contradictions inherent in social stratification. What is noteworthy in this process is how concrete situations influenced theory-building and proceeded in a manner that fostered the participants' awareness of their own resources and their right to influence decisions concerning themselves.

Construct validity was grounded in the dialectic between *a priori* theory, the villagers' own ways of thinking, and the researchers' long-term involvement in the productive work of the village.

Catalytic validity was consciously built into the research design and can be detected in the activism of pastoral women over the course of the research, particularly in their growing insistence that they be given literacy skills (p. 286), and the changed behavior of the pastoralists as a group reflected in their insistence on their right to be part of local decision-making (p. 291).

Face validity permeated the research process in both systematic and informal ways. Analytical categories and emerging conclusions were continually recycled back through the respondents. As this was a report of research in progress, it remains to be seen what form the final report will take and whether there will be an effort to assess validity through participant reaction to the results of the research.

A reading of Swantz's earlier work (1975) recommends caution in celebrating the empowering dimensions of participatory research. The gap between intent and practice is noted, but subtle coercion and external imposition permeate her efforts to get villagers to perform a self-study of local resources. Her later work seems more authentically participatory, and one can surmise that important lessons were learned regarding the involvement of participants as co-researchers.

Given this caveat, the strengths of Swantz's research regarding validity are the continuous feedback system and the dialectical development of theory which strengthen construct validity and the changed behavior of villagers which bespeaks the high quality of the study's face and catalytic validity. Its central weakness is the lack of systematized self-reflexivity, but, given the dialectical approach to theory construction, such a lack is by no means as critical in this research program as it is in the theory-laden empirical work of critical ethnography. Additionally, this was a team effort so one can assume a degree of reflexivity, although Reason and Rowan warn against "consensus collusion" (1981, p. 244).

Beyond Predisposition

The structures and procedures of [emancipatory] research are open to many questions and uncertainties; but it seems that social scientists concerned with the analysis of the societally shaped consciousness and subjectivity of various groups should engage in it experimentally, that is, with an open mind. Further exploration of the theoretical and methodological possibilities . . . should be . . . on the agenda.

Marlis Krueger (1981)

These case studies of the treatment of validity in openly ideological research were chosen both for their typicality and in the case of Gilligan and Willis for their exemplary status. By looking at how the best examples of a research program deal with establishing data credibility, potential strengths and troublesome weaknesses become most evident. While by no means exhaustive, the following issues seem of pressing importance for openly ideological researchers.

Is the Method the Message?

The effort to create an emancipatory social science must confront the need for methods that are at least nonalienating, at best empowering. The classic quandry of ends over means can be seen most starkly in comparing the role of the researcher in Freirian and neo-Marxist research. The former works intentionally at thwarting the cult of expertise that has fostered what Reinharz terms the "rape model" of research: career advancement of social scientists built on alienating and exploitative methods (1979, p. 95). Within Freirian research, the inquiry process itself is committed to enhancing the personal power of participants. The neo-Marxist researcher, in contrast, is seen as "interpreter of the world," exposer of false consciousness (Reynolds, 1980-81, p. 87).

This nondialectical perception of the role of the researcher confounds the intent to demystify the world for the dispossessed. Respondents become objects, targets of research, rather than subjects who have been empowered to understand and change their situations. While there is at last some needed revision of the tendency to dismiss resistance to Marxist interpretations as "false consciousness" (Apple, 1980–81, p. 81; Fay, 1977), empirical and theoretical insights continue to be aimed at other intellectuals. Building a more just social order becomes a matter of "getting more people to talk the way they do" (Browning, 1983, p. 55). Only those with advanced education have a shot at piercing through the theory and the jargon and arriving at a greater understanding of social forces.

Neo-Marxist empirical inquiry is too often characterized by an attitude captured in the words of one research team: "We would not expect the teachers interviewed to either agree with or necessarily understand the inferences which were made from their responses" (Bullough, Goldstein & Holt, 1982, p. 133). Given the all-male research team and the largely female teacher subjects, one could make much of the gender politics involved in such a statement. What are at issue here, however, are the implications of such a stance for the purposes of emancipatory theory-building.[9] And what becomes apparent is that the neo-Marxist agenda for equalizing social power is stymied by tendencies to elitism and alienation engendered by its own research methods.

In contrast, participatory research and, increasingly, feminist research stress the use of the research process to empower participants through emphasis on both face and catalytic validity. Yet neo-Marxist theory makes it clear that establishing validity in the eyes of respondents is not enough to make data credible. Neo-Marxist assumptions regarding false consciousness and ideological mystification argue cogently that phenomenological, astructural, ahistorical perspectives stymie the development of emancipatory social theory. Given the reciprocally confirming nature of hegemony, analysis should not be limited to the actors' perceptions of their situation. Our common-sense ways of looking at the world are permeated with meanings that sustain our powerlessness. There are, hence, limits on the degree to which "member checks" (Guba & Lincoln, 1981) can help establish data validity. Perhaps, like reliability within positivism, building catalytic and face validity into our research designs is a necessary but not sufficient technique for establishing data credibility.

Must We Choose Between Conceptual Vigor and Methodological Rigor?

I am not the first to note that leftists are better at criticizing existent research than at creating an empirically informed Marxism (Karabel & Halsey, 1977, p. 55; Dickens, 1983, p. 155). But if the ultimate goal of our work is transformative social praxis, theory is needed which explains lived experience. Such theory can only evolve through empirical grounding. Because of the lack of self-reflexivity in neo-Marxist empirical work, there is no way of assessing the degree to which this happens. On the contrary, one is left with the impression that the research conducted provides empirical specificities for more general, *a priori* theories.

Critical ethnography is an important perspective in the development of a human science that contributes to social change. But praxis is a two-way street produced in the interaction between theory and practice. While there may indeed be not theory-in-dependent facts (Hesse, 1980, p. 172), moving beyond predisposition requires systematizing procedures for minimizing and/or understanding the ways that the investigator's values enter into research. Empirical validation requires a critical stance regarding the inadequacies of our pet theories and an openness to counter-interpretations. In cautioning that conceptual validity precedes empirical accuracy, Michael Apple (1980–81) continues to not see the validity problems inherent in the largely undialectical role that theory plays in critical ethnography. Empirical evidence must begin to be viewed as a mediator for constant self- and theoretical interrogation if neo-Marxist theory is to prove any more useful in the struggle against privilege that has bourgeois liberalism.

Mitroff and Kilman (1978) argue that what makes theory provocative is how *interesting* it is, now how *true* it is. Truth becomes indeterminant at the theoretical level; theory exists precisely because of the need to take credible leaps into the unknown. But the issue is not theoretical vigor versus methodological rigor. The vitality of postpositivist research programs necessitates the development of credibility checks that can be built into the design of openly ideological (and phenomenologically based) research. Both our theory and our empirical work will be the better for the increased attention to the trustworthiness of our data.

I grant that few appropriate mechanisms exist. This is new territory. Though unassailable answers to questions of rigor are the illusion of naïve empiricists, making our data and analyses as public and as credible as possible is essential. The present turmoil in the human sciences creates the freedom to construct new designs based on alternative tenets and epistemological commitments. As Polkinghorne notes:

What is needed most is for practitioners to experiment with the new designs and to submit their attempts and results to examination by other participants in the debate. The new historians of science have made it clear that methodological questions are decided in the practice of research by those committed to developing the best possible answers to their questions, not by armchair philosophers of research. (1983, p. xi)

The task is to get on with it.

What Minimal Standards Might We Begin to Move Toward?

What I have found over and over again in the methodological literature of openly value-based research is a fuzziness on the need for data credibility checks. Reason and Rowan argue for the researcher's self-actualization through engagement in personal and interpersonal development (1981, p. 246). Lacey (1977) and Rose (1979, p. 14) argue that an appeal to the reader's own experiences is at the base of perceptions of truth in research. Sharp and Green (1975, p. 228), Willis (1977), and Mies (1984) argue that the validity of emancipatory empirical work can be judged by its effects on social policy. What rises to the fore in this literature is that researchers recast the issue as the failure of mainstream research in its insistence upon neutrality and scientific objectivity. But to recognize the pervasiveness of ideology in the human sciences and to acknowledge personal bias are not sufficient to foster a body of empirical work suitable for our theory-building. Haphazard considerations of the need for trustworthy data are not enough if openly ideological research is to be accepted as data rather than as metaphor by those who do not share its value premises.

Whether we can do research that appears valid from multiple points of view or whether Heron is correct that truth in research is a function of shared values (1981, p. 33) is presently a moot issue. Given the primitive state of validity issues within openly value-based research (Feinberg, 1983; Reason & Rowan, 1981; White, 1973; Dickens, 1983, p. 151; Moon, 1983, p. 171), we need to recognize that the "spectre of relativism" may be our inevitable companion as we reshape science and move away from its positivist incarnation (White, 1973, p. 170). We also need to recognize Lee Cronbach's point that "to call for value-free standards of validity is a contradiction in terms, a nostalgic longing for a world that never was" (1980, p. 105).

By arguing for a more systematic approach to triangulation and reflexivity, a new emphasis for face validity, and inclusion of the new concern of catalytic validity, I stand opposed to those who hold that empirical accountability is either impossible to achieve or able to be side-stepped in new paradigm research. At minimum, I argue that we must build the following into our research designs:

— triangulation of *methods, data sources,* and *theories*

— reflexive subjectivity (some documentation of how the researcher's assumptions have been affected by the logic of the data)

— face validity (established by recycling categories, emerging analysis, and conclusions back through at least a subsample of respondents)

— catalytic validity (some documentation that the research process has led to insight and, ideally, activism on the part of the respondents)

Conclusion

As the shakiness of validity within the positivist paradigm and the pervasiveness of ideology within the human sciences are increasingly acknowledged (Fay, 1975; Bernstein, 1976; Mishler, 1979; Nowotny & Rose, 1979; Hesse, 1980), we see that what is at first impression the "hard place" of validity coefficients and multitrait-multimethod matrices is, in fact, a soft spot. The "rock" is not the unassailable validity of positivist research findings but rather the need to establish the trustworthiness of data which are "qualitative, fleeting, and, at times, frankly impressionistic" (Reason, 1981, p. 185). For new paradigm researchers, the task becomes the confrontation of issues of empirical accountability in our methodological formulations, the need to offer grounds for accepting a researcher's description and analysis, and the search for novel, *workable* ways of gathering validity data.

Ignoring data credibility within openly value-based research programs will not improve the chances for the increased legitimacy of the knowledge they produce. Agreed-upon procedures are needed to make empirical decision-making public and, hence, subject to criticism. Most importantly, if we fail to develop these procedures, we will fail to protect our work from our own passions, and our theory-building will suffer.

Reason and Rowan's call for "a new rigor of softness" (1981, p. 490), a "validity of knowledge in process" (p. 250), an "objective subjectivity" (p. xiii) may be the best that we can do. But let us begin to move toward that.

Notes

1. I use "ideology" in the expanded neo-Marxist sense of including the need to explore the social genesis, limitations, and transformative possibilities of points of view. This notion is opposed to orthodox Marxist usage which sees ideology as a distortion of reality, protective of existing power arrangements.

   Apple's recent formulation of ideology reflects the revised neo-Marxist usage of the term based on Gramsci and Althusser. Gramsci theorizes that ideology comes in progressive as well as oppressive forms and Althusser distinguishes between practical and theoretical ideologies. The former posits ideology as the material and common-sense aspects of daily life rather than merely ideas. People *inhabit* ideologies which speak to both determinant and creative/autonomous qualities of culture (Apple, 1982, p. 112. See also Wexler, 1982; Giroux, 1983).

   I am aware of the argument that, for analytic usefulness, the term must be bounded. Barrett (1980), for example, argues both against an "unacceptedly expansionist definition of ideology" (p. 253) and for a recognition that the concept is inadequately theorized in both Marxist and feminist theory (p. 84). While thoroughly agreeing with the latter, I would argue against the former if Marxism and feminism themselves are to be viewed as the social constructions that they inherently are. To do otherwise is to become dogmatic, thereby crippling the thrust toward a critical social theory.

2. While it is tempting to use the phrase "openly ideological research paradigms," I agree with Guba and Lincoln that *paradigm* should be reserved for "axiomatic systems characterized essentially by their differing sets of assumptions about the phenomena into which they are designed to inquire" (1981). Neo-Marxism with its theory-generated search for data and its assumptions of a singular material reality of dominance and oppression and the historical inevitability of a more just social order (Ullrich calls this the "doctrine of eventual salvation" [1979, p. 132]) qualifies it as an inquiry paradigm. But Freirian research, although grounded in a dialectical, loose neo-Marxism, shares the assumptions of the naturalistic, interpretive paradigm (Lincoln & Guba, 1985). And feminist research operates out of both the conventional and naturalistic paradigms. Additionally, with the development of Marxist-feminist theory, there is a growing body of feminist empirical work that shares the assumptions of the inquiry paradigm of neo-Marxism (e.g., McRobbie, 1978; Sacks, 1984).

3. In an appendix to his *Methodology for the Human Sciences* (1983), Polkinghorne traces the history of the term "human science." He argues that "behavioral sciences" retain the spectre of behaviorism and the prohibition against consciousness as a part of scientific study. "Social science" carries connotations of natural science in its nomothetic or law-seeking mode of inquiry. "Human science," he argues, is more inclusive, using multiple systems of inquiry, "a science which approaches questions about the human realm with an openness to its special characteristics and a willingness to let the questions inform which methods are appropriate" (p. 289).

4. Exceptions to this lack of attention to the methodological implications of the postpostivist era are: Guba and Lincoln, 1981; Reason and Rowan, 1981; Comstock, 1982; Reinharz, 1983; Polkinghorne, 1983; Lincoln and Guba, 1985.

5. Brofenbrenner originally recast the metaphor in terms of rigor vs. relevance (quoted in Guba, 1980, p.13).

6. An encouraging example of the impact of feminist criticism on more mainstream behavioral researchers is David McClellan's *Power: The Inner Experience* (Irving Press, 1975). Unlike his earlier work on achievement motivation, McClellan looked at both sexes and discovered that power works differently for men and women: "Power motivation apparently helps women develop into higher stages of maturity, just as it hinders men" (p. 96).

   A far less encouraging example is Elizabeth Dodson Gray's discussion of Kohlberg's recent *The Philosophy of Moral Development* (Harper & Row, 1981), with its "Six Universal Stages." Gilligan's work is consigned to one paragraph and dismissed: "The gender implications of her work are never acknowledged, and the limitations they imply for the 'universal stages' are never even raised! . . . How long will male scholars in patriarchy . . . refuse to acknowledge the relativity of their own gender standing point? How long can they ignore the sociology of their own knowledge?" (Gray, 1982, p. 56).

7. For expanded critiques of Gilligan, see *Social Research, 50*(3), 1983, entire issue.

8. Talk delivered by Carol Gilligan at the American Educational Researchers' Association Special Interest Group/Research on Women in Education, mid-year conference, Philadelphia, November, 1982.

9. I explore the methodological implications of critical theory, especially the need to create research designs that empower the researched, in Lather (1986).

References

Anyon, J. (1983). Accommodation, resistance, and female gender. In S. Walker & L. Barton (Eds.), *Gender and education*. Sussex, England: Falmer Press.

Apple, M. (1979a). What Correspondence theories of the hidden curriculum miss. *Review of Education 5*(2), 101–112.

Apple, M. (1979b). *Ideology and curriculum*. London: Routledge & Kegan Paul.

Apple, M. (1980–81). The other side of the hidden curriculum: Correspondence theories and the labor process. *Interchange, 11*(3), 5–22.

Apple, M. (1982). *Education and power*. Boston: Routledge & Kegan Paul.

Barrett, M. (1980). *Women's oppression today: Problems in Marxist–Feminist analysis*. London: Verso.

Bernstein, R. (1976). *The restructuring of social and political theory*. New York: Harcourt, Brace & Jovanovich.

Bernstein, R. (1983). *Beyond objectivism and relativism: Science, hermeneutics, and praxis*. Philadelphia: University of Pennsylvania Press.

Bottomore, T. (1978). Marxism and sociology. In T. Bottomore & R. Nisbet (Eds.), *A history of sociological analysis*. London: Hunemann.

Bowles, S., & Gintis, H. (1976). *Schooling in capitalist American*. NY: Basic Books.

Bowles, G., & Duelli-Klein, R. (1983). *Theories of women's studies*. Boston: Routledge & Kegan Paul.

Bredo, E., & Feinberg, W. (Eds.). (1982). *Knowledge and values in social and educational research*. Philadelphia: Temple University Press.

Brown, D., & Tandom, R. (1978). Interviews as catalysts. *Journal of Applied Psychology, 63*(2), 197–205.

Browning, F. (1983, Jan). Neoradicals rethink marxism. *Mother Jones, 55–56.*

Bullough, R., Goldstein, S., & Holt, L. (1982). Rational curriculum: Teachers and alienation. *Journal of Curriculum Theorizing, 4*(2), 132–143.

Callaway, H. (1981). Women's perspectives: Research as re-vision. In P. Reason & J. Rowan (Eds.), *Human inquiry* (pp. 457–472). NY: John Wiley.

Campbell, P. (1981). *The impact of societal biases on research methods.* Washington, DC: U.S. Department of Education monograph.

Carlson, D. (1980). Making student "types": The links between professional and common-sense knowledge systems and educational practice. *Interchange, 11*(2), 11–29.

Comstock, D. (1982). A method for critical research. In E. Bredo & W. Feinberg (Eds.), *Knowledge and values in social and educational research* (pp. 370–390). Philadelphia: Temple University Press.

Constantinople. A. (1973). Masculinity-feminity: An exception to a famous (cannot read word). *Psychological Bulletin, 80*(5), 389–407.

Cronbach, L., & Meehl, P. (1955). Construct validity in psychological tests. *Psychological Bulletin, 52,* 281–302.

Cronbach, L. (1975, Feb). Beyond the two disciplines of scientific psychology. *American Psychologist,* 116–127.

Cronbach, L. (1980). Validity on parole: Can we go straight? *New Directions for Testing and Measurement, 5,* 99–108.

Dickens, D.R. (1983). The critical project of Jurgen Habermas. In D. Sabia & J. Wallulis (Eds.), *Changing social science* (pp. 131–155). Albany: University of New York Press.

Eichler, M. (1980). *The double standard.* NY: St. Martin's Press.

Elden, M. (1979). Bank employees begin to participate in studying and changing their organization. In M. Nijhoff (Ed.), *Working and the quality of working life: Developments in Europe.* The Hague.

Everhart, R. (1983). *Reading, writing and resistance: Adolescence and labor in a junior high school.* Boston: Routledge & Kegan Paul.

Fay, B. (1975). *Social theory and political practice.* London: George Allen & Unwin.

Fay, B. (1977). How people change themselves: The relationship between critical theory and its audience. In T. Ball (Ed.), *Political theory and praxis* (pp. 200–233). Minneapolis: University of Minnesota Press.

Feinberg, W. (1983). *Understanding education: Toward a reconstruction of educational inquiry.* NY: Cambridge University Press.

Foley, D. (1979). Labor and legitimation in schools: Notes on doing critical ethnography. Unpublished paper.

Freire, P. (1973). *Pedagogy of the oppressed.* NY: Seabury Press.

Gilligan, C. (1977). In a different voice: Women's conceptions of self and morality. *Harvard Education Review, 47*(4), 481–517.

Gilligan, C. (1982). *In a different voice.* Cambridge, MA: Harvard University Press.

Giroux, H. (1981). *Ideology, culture and the process of schooling.* Philadelphia: Temple University Press.

Giroux, H. (1983). *Theory and resistance in education: A pedagogy for the opposition.* MA: Bergin & Garvey.

Glaser, B., & Strauss, A. (1967). *The discovery of grounded theory: Strategies for qualitative research.* Chicago: Aldine.

Gray, E.D. (1982). *Patriarchy as a conceptual trap.* Wellesley, MA: Roundtable Press.

Guba, E. (1980). Naturalistic and conventional inquiry. Paper presented at the American Educational Research Association annual conference.

Guba, E. (1981). Criteria for assessing the trustworthiness of naturalistic inquiries. *Educational Communications and Technology, 29,* 75–81.

Guba, E., & Lincoln, Y. (1981). *Effective evaluation.* San Francisco: Jossey-Bass.

Hall, B. (1975). Participatory research: An approach for change. *Convergence, 8*(2), 24–31.

Hall, B. (1979). Knowledge as a commodity and participatory research. *Prospects, 9*(4), 393–408.

Hall, B. (1981). The democratization of research in adult and non-formal education. In P. Reason & J. Rowan (Eds.), *Human inquiry* (pp. 447–456) New York: John Wiley.

Heron, J. (1981). Experiential research methods. In P. Reason & J. Rowan (Eds.), *Human inquiry* (pp. 153–166). NY: John Wiley.

Hesse, M. (1980). *Revolution and reconstruction in the philosophy of science.* Bloomington, Indiana: Indiana University Press.

Horner, M. (1969). Fail: Bright women. *Psychology Today, 3*(6), 36–38.

Huberman, A. M., & Miles, M. (1983). Drawing valid meaning from qualitative data: Some techniques of data reduction and display. *Quality and Quantity, 17,* 281–339.

Kamarovsky, M. (1981). Women then and now: A journey of detachment and engagement. *Women's Studies Quarterly, 10*(2), 5–9.

Kaplan, A. (1964). *The conduct of inquiry: Methodology for behavioral science.* San Francisco: Chandler.

Karabel, J., & Halsey, A. H. (Eds.). (1977). *Power and ideology in education.* NY: Oxford University Press.

Kellner, D. (1975). The Frankfurt School revisited. *New German Critique, 4,* 131–152.

Kellner, D. (1978). Ideology, Marxism and advanced capitalism. *Socialist Review, 42,* 37–65.

Kidder, L. (1982, June). Face validity from multiple perspectives. In D. Brinberg & L. Kidder (Eds.), *New directions for methodology of social and behavioral science: Forms of validity in research, #12* (pp. 41–57). San Francisco: Jossey-Bass.

Krueger, M. (1981). In search of the "subjects" in social theory and research. *Psychology and Social Theory, 1*(2), 54–61.

Kuhn, T. (1962). *The structure of scientific revolutions.* Chicago: The University of Chicago Press.

Lacey, C. (1977). *The socialization of teachers.* London: Methuen.

Lather, P. (1986). Research as praxis. *Harvard Educational Review, 56*(3), 257-277.

Lewin, M. (Ed.). (1984). *In the Shadow of the Past.* NY: Columbia University Press.

Lincoln, Y., & Guba, E. (1985). *Naturalistic inquiry.* Beverly Hills: Sage.

Malya, S. (1975, spring). Tanzania's literacy experience. *Literacy Discussion,* 45-68.

Maruyama, M. (1969). Epistemology of social science research: Exploration in inculture researchers. *Dialectica, 23,* 229–280.

Maruyama, M. (1974, Oct.). Endogenous research vs "experts" from outside. *Futures,* 389–394.

Maseman, V. (1982). Critical ethnography in the study of comparative education. *Comparative Education Review, 26*(1), 1–15.

McNeil, L. (1981). Negotiating classroom knowledge: Beyond achievement and socialization. *Curriculum Studies, 13*(4), 313–328.

McRobbie, A. (1978). Working class girls and the culture of femininity. In Women's Studies Group, *Women take issue: Aspects of women's subordination* (pp. 96–108). London: Hutchinson.

Mies, M. (1984). Towards a methodology for feminist research. In E. Altbach et al. (Ed.), *German feminism: Readings in politics and literature* (pp. 357–366). Albany: State University of New York Press.

Miller, J. (1983). The resistance of women academics: An autobiographical account. *The Journal of Educational Equity and Leadership, 3*(2), 101–109.

Mills, C. W. (1959). *The sociological imagination.* New York: Oxford University Press.

Mishler, E. (1979). Meaning in context: Is there any other kind? *Harvard Educational Review, 49*(1), 1–19.

Mitroff, I., & Kilman, R. (1978). *Methodological approaches to social science.* San Francisco: Jossey–Bass.

Moon, J. D. (1983). Political ethics and critical theory. In D. Sabia & J. Wallulis (Eds.), *Changing social science* (pp. 171–188). Albany: State University of New York Press.

Morgan, G. (Ed.) (1983). *Beyond method: Strategies for social research.* Beverly Hills, CA: Sage.

Nowotny, H. (1979). Science and its critics: Reflections on anti-science. In Nowotny & Rose (Eds.), *Counter-movements in the sciences: The sociology of the alternatives to big science* (pp. 1–26). Boston: D. Reidel.

Oakley, A. (1981). Interviewing women: A contradiction in terms. In H. Roberts (Ed.), *Doing feminist research* (pp. 30–61). Boston: Routledge & Kegan Paul.

Ogbu, J. (1981). School ethnography: A multilevel approach. *Anthropology and Education Quarterly, 12*(1), 3–29.

Oppenheimer, R. (1956). Analogy in science. *American Psychologist, 11,* 127–135.

Pinar, W. (1981). The abstract and the concrete in curriculum theorizing. In H. Giroux, A. Penna, & W. Pinar (Eds.), *Curriculum and instruction: Alternatives in education* (pp. 431–454): McCutchan.

Polkinghorne, D. (1983). *Methodology for the human sciences: Systems of inquiry.* Albany: State University of New York Press.

Reason, P., & Rowan, J. (1981). Issues of validity in new paradigm research. In P. Reason & J. Rowan (Eds.), *Human inquiry: A sourcebook of new paradigm research* (pp. 239–262). New York: John Wiley.

Reinharz, S. (1979). *On becoming a social scientist.* San Francisco: Jossey-Bass.

Reinharz, S. (1983). Experiential analysis: A contribution to feminist research. In G. Bowles & R. Duelli-Klein (Eds.), *Theories of women's studies.* Boston: Routledge & Kegan Paul.

Reinharz, S. (1985). Feminist distrust: A response to misogyny and gynopia in sociological work. Unpublished paper, 1985. Expanded version. Feminist distrust: Problems of context and content in sociological work. In D. Berg & K. Smith (Eds.), *Clinical demands of social research*. Beverly Hills, CA: Sage.

Reynolds, D. (1980–81). The naturalistic method and education and social research: A marxist critique, *Interchange, 11*(4), 77–89.

Roberts, H. (1981). *Doing feminist research*. London: Routledge & Kegan Paul.

Rose, H. (1979). Hyper-reflexivity—A new danger for the counter-movements. In Nowotny & Rose (Eds.), *Counter-movements in the sciences* (pp. 277–289). Boston: D. Reidel.

Sabia, D., & Wallulis, J. (Eds.). (1983). *Changing social science: Critical theory and other critical perspectives*. Albany: State University of New York Press.

Sacks, K. B. (1984). *My troubles are going to have trouble with me: Everyday trials and triumphs of women workers*. New Brunswick, NJ: Rutgers University Press.

Salamini, L. (1981). *The sociology of political praxis: An introduction to Gramsci's theory*. London: Routledge & Kegan Paul.

Sanford, N. (1981). A model for action research. In P. Reason & J. Rowan (Eds.), *Human inquiry* (pp. 173–182). New York: John Wiley.

Sassen, G. (1980). Success anxiety in women. *Harvard Educational Review, 50*(1), 13–24.

Schwartz, P., & Ogilvy, J. (1979). *The emergent paradigm: Changing patterns of thought and belief. Analytical report: Values and lifestyles program*. Menlo Park, CA: S.R.I. International.

Sharp, R., & Green, A. (1975). *Education and social control: A study in progressive primary education*. Boston: Routledge & Kegan Paul.

Stanley, L., & Wise, S. (1983). *Breaking out: Feminist consciousness and feminist research*. Boston: Routledge & Kegan Paul.

Swantz, M. l. (1975). Research as an educational tool for development. *Convergence: An International Journal of Adult Education, 8*(2), 44–53.

Swantz, M. L. (1981). Culture and development in the bazamoyo district of Tanzania. In P. Reason & J. Rowan (Eds.), *Human inquiry* (pp. 283–291). New York: John Wiley.

Tandom, R. (1981). Dialogue as inquiry and intervention. In P. Reason & J. Rowan (Eds.), *Human Inquiry* (pp. 293–302). New York: John Wiley.

Thompson, E. P. (1978). *The poverty of theory and other essays*. New York: Monthly Review Press.

Torbert, W. (1981). Why educational research has been so uneducational: The case for a new model of social science research based on collaborative inquiry. In P. Reason & J. Rowan (Eds.), *Human inquiry* (pp. 141–152). New York: John Wiley.

Ullrich, O. (1979). Counter-movements in the sciences. In H. Nowotny & Rose (Eds.), *Counter-movements in the sciences* (pp. 127–146) Boston: D. Reidel.

Wexler, P. (1982). Ideology and education: From critique to class action. *Interchange, 13*(1), 53–78.

Westkott, M. (1977). Conservative method. *Philosophy of Social Science, 7*, 67–76.

Westkott, M. (1979). Feminist criticism of the social sciences. *Harvard Educational Review, 49*(4), 422–430.

White, H. (1973). Foucault decoded: Notes from underground. *History and Theory, 12*, 23–54.

Willis, P. (1977). *Learning to labor: How working class kids get working class jobs.* New York: Columbia University Press.

Wright, E. O. (1978), *Class, crisis and the state.* London: National Labor Board.

Wrong, D. (1961). The oversocialized conception of man in modern sociology. *American Sociological Review, 26*(2), 183–193.

PART V
Creating a Text: Writing Up Qualitative Research

Supervising the Text

PAUL ATKINSON

The paper addressed to supervisors of ethnographic research is intended to be a contribution to debates on the training of qualitative researchers. It is argued that research training in the ethnographic tradition should include a critical awareness of the tasks of writing ethnographic accounts. Both the novice and the experienced researcher need to acquaint themselves with the range of available literary and rhetorical conventions. They need to inculcate an understanding of the analytic implications of alternative textual devices.

Introduction

This paper is not specifically about the ethnography of educational settings, relevant though it is to such work, but is concerned primarily with the education of ethnographers themselves. As qualitative research methods are taken up by increasing numbers of researchers, the supervision of ethnographic work becomes a professional responsibility for more academics. In Britain, recent policies and debates concerning the quality and nature of the PhD in social sciences have led to a focus on the processes and outcomes of PhD supervision (see Delamont, 1989; Winfield, 1987). Much of that heart-searching stems from institutional pressures over PhD completion rates and the average length of time taken to finish the doctorate. They have, however, prompted more widespread reflection on the content and conduct of advanced research training. This paper has its origins in reflection of that sort.[1]

The significance of the PhD in the social and educational sciences, however, goes well beyond the specific policy concerns concerning number and completion rates. Most social scientists—ethnographers in particular—learn research skills and orientations of lifelong importance during their doctoral research. The relative autonomy and time available to the postgraduate student are luxuries denied to teaching academics for most of their careers. The PhD thesis may lay the foundations for a subsequent career as a scholar. Many of the important ethnographic monographs in Britain, North America, and elsewhere have their origins in PhD theses. (The relevant literature is extensive. For major monographs in educational ethnography alone that illustrate the British tradition over several decades, see Ball, 1981; Beynon, 1985; Burgess, 1983; Davies, 1984; Hargreaves, 1967; and Lacey, 1970). Over and above the methodological precepts available in textbooks and courses, much of the craft wisdom and the oral tradition of interpretative research is transmitted from generation to generation through the supervisory relationship. It is therefore important that the supervision of postgraduate research should be subject to critical reflection. The direction—as well as the conduct—of qualitative research is multifaceted. It calls for a range of different skills and draws on experience of diverse academic activities. The paper will consider the role of the supervisor and the work of the student in relation to styles of writing. There are, of course, many styles of qualitative research in the social sciences, and there is no attempt here to cover them all. Rather, attention will be restricted to ethnographic fieldwork of a fairly traditional sort.

The student and supervisor of the ethnography together face a potentially daunting task. The classic ethnography is a text of some complexity and considerable scope. Would-be doctoral candidates who pursue ethnographic research may find themselves thrice burdened: time-consuming and often unpredictable fieldwork is followed by complex and labour-intensive analysis, which in turn is followed by major tasks of writing. The construction of "an ethnography" calls for considerable organizational and creative effort, and the ethnographer can rarely fall back on the more ritualized formats that are available for some genres of scientific reporting.

All of those who have supervised ethnographic research, as well as those who have undertaken it, know how important an element the *writing* is. This is so for a number of reasons, both practical and methodological. Not least is the sheer enormity of the task. There is, of course, no inherent or necessary relationship between a style of research method and the absolute length of text which reports that research. Nevertheless, there is a conventional and traditional relationship at work. The discursive nature of qualitative research and its reporting leads readily to the production of long and complex tasks. Even where universities impose word limits on dissertations, we commonly find ethnographic theses stretching and overrunning those limits. Where there is no such external constraint, then the two-volume ethnography is a type as recognizable as the 19th century triple-decker novel. Many of the available role models incline us towards length. The classic ethnographic monograph in social anthropology, sociology, or education is usually a substantial piece of writing. In the case of my own doctoral work (Atkinson, 1976), an obvious model was *Boys in White* (Becker, Geer, Hughes & Strauss, 1961), which runs over 400 pages. Admittedly, that was written by a research team, but tomes of similar length—indeed a series of volumes spanning a lifetime of scholarly output—confront the novice ethnographer. The point here is *not* that *Boys in White* is "too long". There is obviously no ideal or "correct" length for every or any ethnography. Rather, the ethnographic genre inclines novices and their supervisors towards texts of unmanageable proportions. This is but one obvious way in which the discursive reconstruction of social worlds is a major task.

Any commitment to a notion of *holism* is likely to lead the researcher to write lengthy reports. He or she may feel impelled to produce long descriptive accounts of a wide range of actors, settings, and actions. Often in the absence of more summary measures and indices, the author of the ethnography may try to persuade the reader by sheer volume of examples, breadth and depth of coverage, length of exposition, and so on. Whereas for some student authors, the weight of *numbers* provides intellectual and existential security, for the author of a qualitative study the *volume* or text may fulfil a similar function. In any event, the "weight" of evidence, the burden of proof as it were, is frequently carried by the density and complexity, as well as the sheer bulk, of the writing. The burden of proof thus becomes an intellectual burden for the would-be author, as well as a major task. The writing of the ethnography is, for many students and practitioners, the most demanding task of composition they have ever faced.

Length then, is one far from trivial reason why the writing of the thesis (and indeed published monograph) may occupy a disproportionately significant place in the overall enterprise. Certainly the character of qualitative research means that the normal usage and connotations of "writing up" are inappropriate. The conventional of models of the research process which imply clearly demarcated phases (e.g., design, data collection, analysis) and treat writing up not only as separate but a relatively straightforward phase, do not fit. The writing up of qualitative research is a much more extensive and pervasive feature of the research process. The important issues of ethnographic text go far beyond the issue of length *per se*; I use length as an introduction to more far-reaching issues of ethnographic scholarship. As scholars are increasingly led to recognize, the very essence of the ethnographic enterprise requires us to pay close attention to the process of writing.

The Textual Reconstruction of Reality

Data collection itself is often a "literary" activity, especially if it involves the construction of fieldnotes. It is self-evident that fieldnotes are mediated and contrived representations of social events. When the ethnographer produces lengthy "processed" notes, he or she unavoidably uses basic literary or rhetorical devices to produce realistic and vivid accounts of observed settings and actions. An account of every conceivable detail, minute by minute, is practically impossible. It would also violate our normal expectations about the writing and reading of intelligible accounts. The author of fieldnotes therefore constructs narrative accounts of social action and uses metaphorical usage to produce descriptions and characterizations. Many ethnographers have cited extracts from their fieldnotes to give illustration or evidence in their published products. It is clear that many scholars construct fairly polished, "worked-up" accounts that draw on a full range of conventions of "realist" narratives. We glimpse these texts in their fragmentary appearances in papers and monographs. They are rarely available *in toto* for critical inspection. There are some methodological precepts available in the relevant textbooks on how to record one's experiences and impressions in systematic fashion. But we have precious little collective understanding of the literary conventions that are used or of the traditions and genres that may have evolved.

The construction of these "primary" texts remains underexplored. In the absence of standard public availability of fieldnotes and journals, there is no systematic analysis of fieldnotes as text. Equally, therefore, there is a dearth of even conventional wisdom among experienced practitioners about the construction and interpretation of those accounts. There is a very clear parallel between the heroic imagery of the "lone ethnogapher" writing his or her notes, keeping up the daily ration of observation and reporting, and the lone author wrestling with a recalcitrant medium and an elusive inspiration (cf., Brodkey, 1987). But, as Brodkey reminds us, writing is a social act, and when it is also a *sociological* act, then it behoves us to take explicit account of its accomplishment. There is need for more than trial-and-error on the part of the apprentice, or rule-of-thumb advice on the part of the supervisor. If the database of an ethnography is to include the "literary" construction of fieldnotes, then there is need for explicit awareness of what conventional resources are being brought to bear. Collectively, we need secondary analysis of the poetics of fieldnotes. There is a lack of critical vocabulary with which the oral tradition and its craft knowledge can be brought under critical scrutiny. A framework for critical understanding is required if elementary aspects of the ethnographic task are to be transmitted and supervised in a disciplined fashion. Much of the necessary groundwork remains to be done. It calls for an acquaintance with contemporary scholarship in cultural and critical theory. The same is true when it comes to the work of constructing and interpreting the final "products" of ethnography—dissertations, monographs, and papers.

The "analysis" of the data is dependent on their arrangement and discussion in extended discursive presentations. Quite apart from niceties of theory and epistemology, it is a practical task of some magnitude. It is intellectually demanding and time-consuming. The successful construction of an ethnographic account may involve repeated drafting and redrafting of working papers and chapters before the ordering and presentation of the material starts to "work". There is, moreover, a strong element of unpredictability in these tasks. As author or as supervisor, one is often unsure how the analysis will work out, what connections are to be found and elaborated on, until preliminary drafting has been done. The analytic induction of categories, themes, and relationships; the explication of meaning; and the understanding of action may all proceed via the writing itself. Neither the novice nor the experienced practitioner can assume that "the findings" will be formulated as a set of propositions, simply to be reported and filled in through a more-or-less mechanical set of compositional steps. The role of the supervisor may need to be more actively focused on the writing than is the case in other styles of research. The supervisor will need to be concerned not simply with the "progress" of the writing and keeping the student on schedule; the interest will go beyond the factual accuracy of the reportage; rather, the supervisor may need to consider the *form* of the writing. A systematic understanding of the work, to be shared between supervisor and apprentice, will encompass as appreciation of the textual possibilities and choices that are available, the characteristics of exemplary texts, the use of narrative, metaphor, and other tropes.

There is, therefore, a profound sense in which the writing is an integral feature of the research enterprise. It is not always appreciated by colleagues unversed in qualitative research, but the anthropological or sociological "findings" are inscribed in the ways we write about things; they are not detached from the presentation of observations, reflections, and interpretations. We all know how difficult we can find it, on our own or our students' behalf, to answer "What are your conclusions?" or "What have you proved?" It *is* possible to derive propositional theory and summary findings from ethnographic research and equivalent writing. But it is normally a very pale reflection of the "thick" descriptive work of the thesis or monograph and in no way substitutes for it. The desired response to the naive question is "Well, read the ethnography."

A pertinent case in point, although perhaps an extreme version of the "literary" style, is the published work of Erving Goffman. Lofland (1980) demonstrates the point with reference to several of Goffman's texts. From *Asylums*—the nearest Goffman got to a standard ethnographic monograph in style—one can derive propositions of the order of:

> *If* persons are placed in total institutions, *then* their selves will be mortified. *If* persons are placed in total institutions, *then* they will develop secondary adjustments to protect themselves from the identity implications of the organization's theory of human nature.

But propositions of this sort seem exceptionally jejune in comparison with the dense complexity of Goffman's own texts. Indeed, Goffman's sociological analysis is substantially conveyed through the rhetorical devices and formats of his published
works (Atkinson, 1989).

The "writing up" of the qualitative study is not merely a major and lengthy task; it is *intrinsic* to the "analysis," the "theory," and the "findings." The success or failure of the entire project can depend on the felicity of the writing. To a considerable extent, therefore, the craft of qualitative research implies craft skill in organizing the products of that research into satisfying and plausible products.

On the whole, however, students and their advisers have little methodological advice to guide them in the construction of ethnographic texts. The majority of methods textbooks are reticent, if not totally silent, on the topic of writing. That is understandable, given the paucity of shared knowledge about the processes and products involved. We have devoted a great deal of methodological imagination to fieldwork practitioners, ethics, social relationships, data storage and retrieval, even theory building, but, until very recently, much less to writing. To a considerable extent, methods texts in qualitative traditions, despite authors' intentions to the contrary, have reflected the implicit logic of more positivistic styles. The collection of valid and reliable data is treated as paramount. Their literary transformation into texts is relegated to the extra-curricular. Some general methods texts do include advice in writing, but they tend to lack grounding in a technical appreciation of critical theory.

I suppose that we have all been aware, if only at a preconscious level, that successful ethnographies have certain kinds of stylistic, aesthetic qualities. We ourselves have often assimilated the stylistic characteristics of admired exemplars. Lacking clear guidelines, even of a typological sort, we have perhaps advised a student to take an admired monograph from the bookshelf and emulate it. It is noteworthy that this strategy would no longer pass for sound methodological advice for any other phase or feature of the research.

The collective amnesia concerning literary modes of representation reflects a number of historical contrasts and appositions. Modern scientific discourse has diverged from its erstwhile companion of rhetoric. Until very recent years, rhetoric has been neglected (except for a very enfeebled existence in the teaching of composition to American undergraduates). Rhetoric has been relegated to "mere" presentation and "rhetoric" contrasts with matters of substance. In a broader vein, the crudest images that have governed our conceptions of positive science have been dismissive of the aesthetic elements of scholarly endeavour. More specifically, the search for academic respectability and the supposed claims for well-founded "factual" status have easily led qualitative scholarship to distance itself from more overtly literary activities. The indication of close affinities and stylistic similarities between ethnography and journalism or fictional writing is sometimes treated as a threat to our scholarly standards and the veracity of our accounts.

In recent years, however, a small but growing number of anthropologists, sociologists, and others in the "human sciences" have turned their attention to the textual character of our productions (Atkinson, 1982, 1990; Bazerman, 1981, 1987; Brown, 1977, 1983; Clifford, 1978, 1981, 1983; Crapanzano, 1977; Geertz, 1983, 1988; Marcus, 1980; Marcus & Cushman, 1982; Van Maanen, 1988). The specific analytic approaches vary and include the range of perspectives current in literary-critical theory. The various authors also espouse different epistemological and political positions. Analyses have included attempts to explicate ideological inscriptions in textual practices, the uses of literary tropes to convey sociological or anthropological insight, textual devices to establish the authority of the author, and varieties of narrative genre to be found among ethnographic texts. While approaches differ in their emphases, they are in broad agreement in suspending the conventional distinction between "fact" and "fiction," in the recognition that *all* texts are constructed in accordance with socially shared conventions. The authors and the readers of "factual" accounts draw on conventions actively to "make sense," just as to the readers and writers of "fiction". This perspective does *not* result in a promiscuous or nihilistic approach. The methodological suspension of taken-for-granted distinctions allows for the recognition and exploration of the textuality of "factual" accounts; it does not lead to a disregard for the circumstances of their production.

Irrespective of the epistemological or methodological claims for a piece of research, the text in which it is reported must be *persuasive*. This is the guiding rationale for Edmondson's (1984) application of rhetorical analyses to a sample of sociological texts. Edmondson's analytic scope is modest, and the emphasis on classical rhetoric means that a much broader tradition of critical theory is glossed over. Nevertheless, Edmondson's treatment is useful; it provides a clear exposition of various textual devices whereby sociological authors persuade (or attempt to persuade) their readers of the cogency and strength of their argument and of their evidence. The examples chosen to illustrate qualitative methods are Rex and Moore's (1967) *Race, Community and Conflict* and Willis's (1977) *Learning to Labour*.

Edmondson (1984) addresses a number of related issues. First, attention is drawn to the achievement of *ordering and relative emphasis* in the chosen texts. Of Willis (1977), for instance, it is noted that his book has a rather unusual structure. The book is explicitly divided into two sections. The first section presents a graphic, descriptive "ethnography"; the second contains a detailed and heavily theorized "analysis." Edmondson suggests that this particular arrangement

> enables the reader to evolve a certain personal response to its subjects *before* the author advances a detailed sociological account of their situation. The response which the first part of the book is clearly intended to evoke is one of sympathy; sympathy not just in the sense of particular feelings towards Willis's subjects, but also in the sense of a preparedness to consider their points of view and to refrain from the dismissive evaluations of their conduct which are usual (the book makes clear) from people outside their own class and group. (p. 42)

It is noteworthy that Willis presents the more engaging aspects of "the lads" in the earlier passages, while the discussions of their "sexism" and "racism"are kept back: "they are arranged, that is, in order of least likelihood to alienate the reader" (p. 44). (See also Hammersley & Atkinson, 1983, p. 222.)

Second, Edmondson (1984) draws attention to the use of "examples" and deals especially with the chosen texts' use of atypical and unrepresentative examples of illustrations. In that context Edmondson emphasizes that the *reader* is often required to draw conclusions and see contrasts. The analysis of Willis (1977) and Rex and Moore (1967) underlines the fact that the ethnography communicates by way of a persuasive relationship with the reader, rather than through formal models. Writing, for instance, about the use of quotations in *Learning to Labour*, Edmondson suggests

> we should not regard quotations such as those from .Joey and Councillor Collett in the light of evidence as it is used in the natural sciences, and that the question whether they are literally typical in the statistical sense does not arise. . . . If instead we regard such citations as rhetorical devices for enabling and encouraging readers to perceive the force of general remarks, we can expect examples to exhibit particularly concentrated cases of what happens generally but, perhaps, less remarkably. (p. 50)

Edmondson goes on to suggest that "forceful examples compensate the reader for his or her narrower experience of the field than the author's" (p. 50).

As Edmondson (1984) demonstrates, the use of example is important, functioning as they do as "actual types": "These examples, I believe, function rhetorically as signs: signs as symptoms of states in some way which enables the reader to interpret future situations, and only very rarely necessary signs of state affairs" (p. 52). Edmondson's analysis alerts us to the pervasive feature of ethnographic texts: the interweaving of extracts, episodes, and narratives on the one hand; and interpretation, observation, commentary, and generalization on the other.

Edmondson's (1984) rhetorical analysis does not tell us anything we do not practise already, and it is a disappointingly sparse treatment of the potential range of topics. Nevertheless, we are usefully alerted to the fact that our, and our students', written products very largely stand or fall on the successful manipulation of rhetorical or literary conventions. The ethnographic thesis and monograph are members of a genre and are expected to correspond to the canons of that genre. Or, more precisely, we should recognize that there have been and are several sub-types of ethnographic genre, each with its own set of transformations on the basic conventional requirements.

John Lofland's (1974) work is one of the few discussions by an experienced reader and writer of ethnographic work in sociology of how such conventions inform the reception of such texts. His observations come from editorial work on journal submissions. Many of the general points are, however, common to article-length and thesis- or monograph-length texts. Lofland's contribution is based on an analysis of referees' comments on papers reporting qualitative research and his general expertise in the area. While it is clear that his remarks bear on more than just this issue, it also is clear that content and style are inextricably intertwined in readers' receptions and reports. The reader of qualitative research cannot proceed "as if" there were a neutral textual format independent of the scientific message to be conveyed. Lofland (1974) comments on this, noting that there is a division within sociology when it comes to styles of reporting:

> At one extreme, practitioners of laboratory and experimental work share a highly routinized set of working procedures and schemes for reporting research. Drawing from physical science models of inquiry perhaps facilitates their achieving such consensus. The stylistic and organizational features of their publications reproduce the stylistic and organizational features of physical science journals in particularly striking fashion. While not nearly as shared and codified, demographic and survey practitioners still draw upon a rather consensual pool of research strategies, technical steps, and standardized conceptions of the structure and content of their research reports. Moreover, one even

senses a high degree of working agreement among library researchers who employ bodies of historical and substantive materials. (p. 101)

In contrast, Lofland (1974) suggests a *relative* lack of consensus among those who report qualitative research findings: "Qualitative field research seems distinct in the degree to which its practitioners lack a public, shared, and codified conception of how what they do is done, and how what they report should be formulated" (p. 101). Of course, as Lofland himself acknowledges, the uniformity of the more clearly "positivist" styles is itself a textual achievement, a matter of organization and style. Indeed, one strand of contemporary sociology of science pays particular attention to the literary representation of scientific findings and discoveries. On the other hand, though Lofland is correct in suggesting a lack of consensual models for the reporting of qualitative research, that does not imply a total lack of available models and devices. On the contrary, there are many generic conventions that inform the production of the text and its reading. Lofland goes on to discuss several evaluative criteria that are applied to qualitative research reports, each of which implies some textual element or arrangement.

First, there is the criterion invoked by readers which reflects the extent to which "the report was organized by means of a *generic* conceptual framework" (Lofland, 1974, p. 102). This refers to the extent to which a particular topic or setting is "framed" according to more general themes. Such themes are used not simply as explicit sociological theory, but as more general articulatory themes, images, and devices. The successful text weaves together the local and the generic—often by means of metaphorical allusions—in achieving a satisfactory mixture of data and discussion, example and generalization. Interestingly, Lofland suggests that readers can predict the presence of a generic frame of reference from the opening sentences of a report. He cites the opening of Bigus (1972) as an instance of the successful deployment of such an introductory framing passage:

> America is a service society—so much so that essentially non-service institutions, such as stores, take
> on service-like characteristics. . . . This emphasis on service has given rise to a preponderance of a
> particular kind of social activity, which I shall refer to as "cultivating," and to an associated kind of
> social relationship which I will refer to as a "cultivated relationship." (Bigus, 1972, p. 131)

This passage is used to frame an ethnographic account of the daily relationship between milkmen and their customers. The sort of "framework" is detected by the reader at the outset and provides him or her with an initial attitude from which the significance of the paper is foreshadowed and projected. While openings like the Bigus passage state their theme, they have the rhetorical function of persuading the sympathetic reader that the report addresses "real" or "important" themes *and* that the specific case to be explored is a relevant one.

Lofland (1974) goes on to suggest that readers who positively evaluate a "generic" frame will find unsatisfactory reports that do not use organizational motifs of that sort. He refers, among others, to the "Then They Do This" style, in which a report is organized so that it "makes evident that participants do many kinds of things over and over, hour to hour, day to day, week to week" (Lofland, 1974, p. 104). Interestingly, Lofland notes that a text can, as it were, "get away with" such an organizational format provided that the setting is sufficiently "exotic": otherwise readers will allege that the text is merely based on "cute," "interesting," or "startling" descriptive content.

Lofland goes on to detail other types of evaluative criteria invoked by readers of research reports. Readers may seek a "novel frame," or, when absolute freshness is impossible, then at least a "slightly late" frame may be employed—that is, somebody else's recent novelty. As Lofland (1974) says,

> In recent years, the frames of Erving Goffman have been applied with particular assiduousness.
> Researchers report: yes, mental hospitals are total institutions; yes, this or that category of deviant
> experiences stigma; yes, inmates do use making out" devices. Slightly more novel, look over here,
> public housing has characteristic's of total institutions. (pp. 105–106)

Readers, Lofland reports, find such second-hand novelties acceptable up to a point, but beyond that point the frame starts to lose its novelty value, and the readers are likely to condemn the text as mere dreary repetition. The achievement of adequate novelty and freshness is not simply a function of which authors and examples are selected in order to illuminate the findings. To a considerable extent, "freshness of the presentation will depend upon the literary skills with which those allusions, connotations, examples, and citations are deployed. The reader will be swayed by criteria which are partly aesthetic: the "lightness of touch" whereby other authors, studies, and empirical parallels are filled in and elaborated on; the appositeness of those comparisons and contrasts; the extent to which they reveal "imagination" and depart from the obvious and hackneyed.

The extreme example of the latter failing is contained in Lofland's (1974) type of the "intro text style":

> Notions that are "common knowledge" in American society or that sociologists can find in elementary textbooks will likely be defined as "obvious." Few qualitative field reports discover such introductory textbook frames as socialization, norms, deviance, social control, culture or informal organization. (P. 106)

The successful text, it would appear, is neither so "novel" as to be *outré* or bizarre, nor so familiar as to be stale. Moreover, as Lofland (1974) indicates, a successful textual arrangement should be adequately elaborated and enriched. First, the analytic "frame" should be "elaborated"—it should be couched in a text which "specifies constituent elements of the frame, draws out implications, shows major variations, and uses all these as the means by which the qualitative data are organized and presented" (p. 106). Further, for many readers, it should be "eventful"—richly endowed with "concrete interactional events, incidents, occurrences, episodes, anecdotes, scenes, and happenings someplace in the real world" (p. 107). On the other hand, it should not be overburdened with the repetitious rehearsal of incidents and illustrations. Otherwise, it may topple over into the failing of being "hyper-eventful." These delicate balances are achieved in the textures of the writing itself.

A final evaluative criterion is closely related. The analytic frame and the qualitative data it comments on should be "interpenetrated" if the text is to be judged satisfactory:

> Taken separately, each is likely to be viewed as having little sociological interest or merit. . . . The frame taken separately is dull because the reader has little conception of the concrete empirical reality to which the frame might refer. The "data" alone are dull because the reader has no notion of what sort of social structure or process might be involved. But interpenetrated through the minute and continual alteration between data and frame-elements the whole is more than the parts. (Lofland, 1974, pp. 108-109)

These by no means exhaust Lofland's (1974) observations, and his are not exhaustive of the textual arrangements of qualitative sociology. They are not alluded to in order to produce a prescriptive model for ethnographic texts, but to illustrate the sort of thing that sociological readers (including, presumably, supervisors and external examiners) seem to bring to such texts in evaluating their success or failure. The most important general issue to emerge from Lofland's analysis, as from Edmondson's (1984), is the importance of textual arrangement itself. The text has a certain force or effect which is not based simply on some evaluation of whether or not it is "correct." Indeed, it is difficult to think how any written or spoken text convey "facts" or "findings," let alone analyses, hypotheses, conjectures, criticisms, and refutations, without recourse to conventionally appropriate textual formats. In the reader's evaluative readings, then, form and content are inextricably linked. The text need not simply transcribe or report; it must also persuade. The reader must be drawn into its own frame of reference and come to share the perspectives of the text; it must be found plausible and engaging, arresting, or novel; it must establish relations of similarity and difference with the social world it reports—it needs to reproduce a recognizable world of concrete detail, but not appear to be an unremarkable recapitulation of it.

Lofland's (1974) analysis is important in that it highlights—from actual experience—the bases of readers' judgements. It does little, however, to illuminate the fine detail of how "literary" and "rhetorical" conventions are used to construct plausible texts. Among recent sociological commentators, Van Maanen (1988) is notable for his contribution on ethnographic writing. He combines advice and a degree of prescription with a delineation of genre within the ethnographic cannon. Van Maanen does not enter into detailed discussion of textual conventions, but outlines types of "story" that ethnographers typically recount. He distinguishes between "realist," "confessional," and "impressionist" tales. The first type capitalizes on the traditions of realist reportage and fiction, inscribing the difference between the observer and the observed, and the relative disengagement of the researcher. It draws on a tradition of literary conventions that implicitly deny their conventionality. The tendency is to treat the text as an unproblematic representation of reality.

The confessional is not really an alternative genre, since it is in a relation of complementarity rather than contrast. Ethnographers who have produced their realist accounts are frequently given to publishing autobiographical accounts in which the personal, the problematic, and the narrative elements are in the foreground. For most authors, the confessional is contained within a separate account, and collections of such first-hand narrative of fieldwork experience have become a major sector in the published literature. (For general examples of the type, see Bell & Encel, 1978; Bell & Newby, 1978; Bell & Roberts, 1984; McKeganey & Cunningham-Burley, 1987; Messerschmidt, 1982; and Whyte, 1985. For recent examples that refer specifically to educational research, see Burgess, 1984, 1985a, 1985b, 1985c; Fetterman, 1984; Spindler, 1982; and Walford, 1988.) To some extent, therefore, the separation of the "realist" and the "confessional" accounts leaves the former relatively uncontaminated by the contingencies reflected in the latter.

In Van Maanen's (1988) third type, the "impressionist" tale, the entire account is permeated with a self-conscious deployment of the more "literary" resources. The detachment of the realist genre is not sustained. The ethnography constructs a more explicitly vivid and metaphorical account. Van Maanen explores the characteristics of these alternatives and commends a more explicit adoption of "impressionist" approaches. He advocates—and is not alone in this—a more wholehearted recognition and celebration of the more "literary" and metaphoric elements of ethnographic writing. Van Maanen's is a valuable contribution to the methodological literature. He may be faulted for overstating the distinctions between the genres he identifies; all three may be found within the work of a single author, or indeed within the same monograph. Nevertheless, his provision of an accessible and systematic review will be a common reference point for students and their supervisors.

For further illumination one must also look to some recent texts that have been based on anthropological rather than sociological discourse. In recent years, cultural anthropologists in North America have become especially sensitive to the textual representation of anthropological work. They have drawn on semiotic and structuralist or poststructuralist theory to identify such issues as the devices establishing the "authority" of the text and the "narrative contract" between writer and reader, the writing of cultural "difference" and the representation of the cultural "other," and the self-representation of the ethnographer in the text. The range of analytic issues (by no means restricted to anthropological writing) is summarized by Clifford in the introduction to Clifford and Marcus (1986);

> Ethnographic writing is determined in at least six ways; (1) contextually (it draws from and creates meaningful social milieux); (2) rhetorically (it uses and is used by expressive conventions); (3) institutionally (one writes within, and against, specific traditions, disciplines, audiences); (4) generically (an ethnography is usually distinguishable from a novel or a travel account); (5) politically (the authority to represent cultural realities is unequally shared and at times contested); (6) historically (all the above conventions and constraints are changing). These determinations govern the inscription of coherent ethnographic fictions. (p. 6)

The deliberately challenging use of "fictions" by authors in this vein is used to alert us to the *constructed* character of texts, whether they report, in the conventional sense, fact or fiction. As Clifford says in the same context, "The making of ethnography is artisanal, tied to the worldly work of writing" (p. 6).

Anthropologists, far more than sociologists, have explored the textual nature of ethnographic writing as part of an epistemological and ideological crisis in the discipline. The agenda is in part political; the authority of the narrator is implicitly (but powerfully) claimed in the conventional style of "ethnographic realism" or "ethnographic naturalism" (cf., Spencer, 1989). That authority, rests on the textual construction of the *object* of description as "the other" (cf., Fabian, 1983). Anthropological texts, it is claimed, present an unacceptably objectified account of a "strange" culture; they transform the dialogues of fieldwork into a monologic, privileged account. Arguably, anthropologists of this persuasion have become too thoroughly seduced by their own rhetoric of postmodernism. There is a danger of taking the literary-critical perspective too literally. As Spencer (1989) argues, by focusing too narrowly on the texts of anthropology, the contemporary critics themselves decontextualize the work of writing from the other tasks of scholarship, including the tasks of fieldwork itself. Ironically for the discipline of anthropology, there is the parallel danger that the cultural and historical context of anthropological work is too readily reduced merely to phenomena of "intertextuality." Relations with other texts and genre are important but do not exhaust the intellectual and social context of their production or reception.

All genres, including the genres of scholarly, authoritative accounts, are rhetorically produced. The varieties of qualitative research—ethnographic, life-history, ethnomethodological—all deploy characteristic conventions. It is part of their paradigm-like coherence that different styles of research are embodied in different styles of reportage. Now, it is not the task of this paper to review all the rapidly growing literature on these and related topics. Nor is it to reflect that for all the current work in this area, there remains scope for much more good work on the "textual construction of reality" in the social sciences. Rather, we need to reflect on some of the practical and methodological issues that face us as practitioners, supervisors, and examiners. It is easy to make the deceptively simple point that apprenticeship in the craft skills of writing is an essential element in research training. It is undeniable in principle that our students need to develop, and be helped to appreciate, the necessary disciplines for adequate writing. Equally valuable, from a slightly different perspective, will be Wolcott's (1990) synthesis of personal reflection and practical advice on the writing of ethnographic accounts. It is vital to treat seriously the "artisan" skills of textual construction. Many colleagues and students report finding Howard Becker's (1986) recent book an invaluable source of inspiration, sound advice, and "insider" wrinkles. Students frequently need help to realize that writing is not easy for anybody; that their own shortcomings and blocks are not profound moral failings; that writing tasks can be approached as interesting intellectual puzzles, and so on. There are practical steps that can be taken to help with these and related matters. We can encourage groups of students to participate in writing workshops, in which mutual aid and sympathetic criticism are encouraged; where published texts are dissected and subjected to "practical criticism"; where the organization of texts and draft passages are tried out with peers before being subjected to the scrutiny of a supervisor, an examiner, or a journal's referees. These activities alone are difficult enough to achieve. They demand a social context of trust and mutual support, for even the most hardened can find the critical evaluation of their writing deeply threatening. Students have to be prepared to give time for each other rather than working in isolation. Through such activities, students (and teachers) may also come to appreciate some of the more far-reaching intellectual implications.

As already indicated, the textual construction of qualitative research goes far beyond the problems of producing serviceable thesis drafts. The purpose of reflection is not just to encourage the production of more "polished" writing (welcome though that is). Rather, it should encourage the student group to understand their writing as encompassing methodological and analytic strategies. If we take seriously the thrust of recent work on the rhetoric and semiotics of ethnographic texts, then it is apparent that we cannot regard those texts as "innocent." It must become part of our reflexive self-awareness that we recognize the rhetorical and stylistic conventions with which we deal, not in order that textual analysis should substitute for fieldwork, but in order to bring it within our explicit methodological and epistemological understanding. Gone are the days when *writing* could be regarded as neutral. We have not yet reached the stage at which we can expect a shared understanding of our shared textual conventions.

The achievement of such reflexive awareness is not easy, and in advocating it one no doubt is preaching an unattainable ideal (if ideal it be). For it requires an acquaintance with recent and contemporary literary theory and with parallel work on the poetics of economics, history, law, and so on. It suggests the development of collaborative relationships between social scientists and practitioners of "literary" analysis. Nonetheless, I believe that it is worth cultivating at least some degree of critical reflection on the *form* of ethnographic writings as well as its content. The more that practitioners of qualitative research can cultivate such an informed understanding, the better students can be helped explicitly and self-consciously to deploy the literary conventions within which and against which they may formulate their work.

Furthermore, if we encourage our students to take explicit account of their textual practices, then we must recognize that this places on them a further burden. The more explicit and reflexive we render the methodology, the harder things get. It is easier to copy a taken-for-granted model than it is to understand the possibilities, to manipulate the conventions, and to experiment with them. The last thing is important. If we recognize that the conventional formats of "realistic" reportage are essentially as arbitrary as any other, then we can open up the possibility of alternatives. Indeed, we may come to the view that the normal canons of written scientific discourse are inappropriate for the representation of complex and multiple social realities. Of course, we do not want to encourage a spate of modernist ethnographic texts (or whatever) just in order to promote novelty. But there is surely no harm in exploring alternative modes of representation in the light of an informed understanding of literary theory.

Some authors have made tentative steps in the direction of more self-conscious texts. Krieger (1979, 1983, 1984), for instance, claims quite explicitly to have written her ethnography taking "stream of consciousness" novels as inspiration. Likewise, Bluebond-Langner (1980) employs dramatic conventions in presenting narrative and scenes. Both texts are noteworthy for trying to innovate rather than for any startling success. But the point is that some authors have tried. In recent years Michael Mulkay's (1985) uses of unusual textual genre (including the "dialogue" form, parody, short story, and one-act play) make up the most sustained attempt to exploit the relationship between literary conventions and sociological arguments. Indeed, in recent British sociology of science, the use of "new literary forms" has come to occupy a particular niche, equivalent to a theoretical or methodological sub-paradigm in the field. (For recent examples, see Ashmore, Mulkay & Pinch, 1989; Woolgar, 1988). Finally, there are two corollaries. First, if students are encouraged and able to explore such possibilities, then examiners must be willing to treat them seriously and sympathetically. (There are no extra marks for being gratuitously avant-garde, of course.) Second, the academy may need to be more open to masters and doctoral theses in which textual experimentation is a major *raison d'étre*; we cannot treat them as less important than any other methodological concerns.

Note

1. This paper was originally prepared for an Economic and Social Research Council-sponsored conference for supervisors of qualitative research in sociology and education, held at the University of Warwick, December 17-18, 1987. It is grounded in British experience. The British system, though subject to modification, places primary emphasis on the lone apprentice-scholar. Coursework has not been a part of the PhD

until the recent introduction of doctoral programmes in some disciplines, departments, and universities. Specific references to supervision and examination thus presuppose a single supervisor and an examiner external to the university, rather than, say, the North American committee system. The thrust of the argument is intended to apply more generally.

References

Ashmore, M., Mulkay, M., & Pinch, T. (1989) *Health and efficiency: a sociology of health economics*. Milton Keynes: Open University Press.

Atkinson, P. (1976) *The clinical experience: an ethnography of medical education*. Unpublished doctoral dissertation. University of Edinburgh.

Atkinson, P. (1982) *Writing ethnography* In H. J. Helle (Ed.), *Kultur und Institution* (Culture and institution) (pp. 77-105). Berlin: Duncker und Humblot.

Atkinson. P. (1989) Goffman's poetics. *Human Studies, 12,* 59-76.

Atkinson, P. (1990) *The ethnographic imagination: textual constructions of reality*. London: Routledge.

Ball, S. (1981) *Beachside comprehensive*. Cambridge: Cambridge University Press.

Bazerman, C. (1981) What written knowledge does: three examples of academic discourse. *Philosophy of Social Sciences, 11,* 361-387.

Bazerman, C. (1987) Codifying the social scientific style: the APA Publication Manual as a behaviorist rhetoric. In J. S. Nelson, A. Megill & D. N. McCloskey (Eds.), *The rhetoric of the human sciences* (pp. 125-144). Madison: University of Wisconsin Press.

Becker. H. S. (1986) *Writing for social scientists*. Chicago: University of Chicago Press.

Becker, H. S., Geer, B., Hughes, E. C. & Strauss, A. L. (1961) *Boys in white*. Chicago: University of Chicago Press.

Bell, C. & Encel, S. (Eds.) (1978) *Inside the whale*. Oxford: Pergamon.

Bell, C. & Newby, H. (Eds.) (1978) *Doing sociological research*. London: Allen and Unwin.

Bell, C. & Roberts, H. (Eds.) (1984) *Social researching*. London: Allen and Unwin.

Beynon, J. (1985) *Initial encounters in the secondary school*. London: Falmer.

Bigus, O. E. (1972) The milkman and his customer: a cultivated relationship. *Urban Life and Culture, 1,* 131-165.

Bluebond-Langner, M. (1980) *The private worlds of dying children*. Princeton, NJ: Princeton University Press.

Brodkey, L. (1987) *Academic writing as social practice*. Philadelphia: Temple University Press.

Brown, R. H. (1977) *A poetic for sociology*. Cambridge: Cambridge University Press.

Brown, R. H. (1983) Dialectical irony, literary form and sociological theory. *Poetics Today, 4,* 543-564.

Burgess, R. G. (1983) *Experiencing comprehensive education*. London: Bethuen.

Burgess, R. G. (Ed.) (1984) *The research process in educational settings: ten case studies*. London: Falmer.

Burgess, R. G. (Ed.) (1985a) *Field methods in the study of education*. London: Falmer.

Burgess, R. G. (Ed.) (1985b) *Issues in educational research*. London: Falmer.

Burgess, R. G. (Ed.) (1985c) *Strategies of educational research*. London: Falmer.

Clifford, J. (1978) Hanging up looking glasses at odd corners: ethnobiolographical perspectives. *Harvard English Studies, 8,* 41-56.

Clifford, J. (1981) On ethnographic surrealism. *Comparative Studies in Society and History, 23,* 539-564.

Clifford, J. (1983) On ethnography authority. *Representations, 1,* 118-146.

Clifford, J. & Marcus, G. E. (Eds.) (1986) *Writing culture*. Berkeley: University of California Press.

Crapanzano, V. (1977) The writing of ethnography. *Dialectical Anthropology, 2,* 69-73.

Davies, L. (1984) *Pupil power: deviance and gender in school*. London: Falmer.

Delamont, S. (1989) Gender and British postgraduate funding policy: a critique of the Winfield Report. *Gender and Education, 1,* 53-59.

Edmondson, R. (1984) *Rhetoric in sociology*. London: Macmillan.

Fabian, J. (1983) *Time and the other: how anthropology makes its object*. New York: Columbia University Press.

Fetterman, D. (Ed.) (1984) *Ethnography in educational evaluation*. Beverly Hills, CA: Sage.

Geertz, C. (1983) Slide show: Evans-Pritchard's African transparencies. *Raritan, 3,* 62-80.

Geertz, C. (1988) *Works and lives: the anthropologist as author*. Cambridge: Polity.

Hammersley, M. & Atkinson, P. (1983) *Ethnography: principles in practice*. London: Tavistock.

Hargreaves, D. H. (1967) *Social relations in a secondary school*. London: Routledge and Kegan Paul.

Krieger, S. (1979) Research and the construction of a text. In. N. Denzin (Ed.), *Studies in symbolic interaction* (Vol. 2, pp. 167-187). Greenwich, CT: JAI Press.

Krieger, S. (1983) *The mirror dance: identity in a women's community*. Philadelphia: Temple University Press.

Krieger, S. (1984) Fiction and social science. In N. Denzin (Ed.), *Studies in symbolic interaction* (Vol. 5, pp. 269-286). Greenwich, CT: JAI Press.

Lacey, C. (1970) *Hightown grammar*. Manchester: Manchester University Press.

Lofland, J. (1974) Styles of reporting qualitative field research. *American Sociologist, 9,* 101-111.

Lofland, J. (1980) Early Goffmam: style, structure, substance, soul. In J. Ditton (Ed.), *The view from Goffman* (pp. 24-51). London: Macmillan.

McKeganey, N. & Cunningham-Burley, S. (Eds.) (1987) *Enter the sociologist*. Aldershot, UK: Gower.

Marcus, G. E. (1980) Rhetoric and the ethnographic genre in anthropological research. *Current Anthropology, 21,* 507-510.

Marcus, G. E. & Cushman, D. (1982) Ethnographies as texts. *Annual Review of Anthropology, 11,* 25-69.

Messerschmidt, D. S. (Ed.) (1982) *Anthropologists at home in North America*. New York: Cambridge University Press.

Mulkay, M. (1985) *The word and the world*. London: Allen and Unwin.

Rex, J. & Moore, R. (1967) *Race, community and conflict*. London: Oxford University Press.

Spencer, J. (1989) Anthropology as a kind of writing. *Man, 2*, 145-164.

Spindler. G. (Ed.) (1982) *Doing the ethnography of schooling*. New York: Holt, Rinehart and Winston.

Van Maanen, J. (1988) *Tales of the field: on writing ethnography*. Chicago: University of Chicago Press.

Walford, G. (Ed.) (1988) *Doing the sociology of education*. London; Falmer.

Whyte, W. F. (1985) *Learning from the field*. Beverly Hills, CA: Sage.

Willis, P. (1977) *Learning to labour: how working class kids get working class jobs*. Farnborough: Saxon House.

Winfield, G. (1987) *The social science PhD: the ESRC inquiry on submission rates*. London: Economic and Social Research Council.

Wolcott, H. F. (1990) *Writing up qualitative research*. Beverly Hills, CA: Sage.

Woolgar, S. (Ed.) (1988) *Knowledge and reflexivity: new frontiers in the sociology of knowledge*. Beverly Hills, CA: Sage.

Recording the Miracle: Writing

David M. Fetterman

The difference between the right word and the nearly right word is the same as that between lightning and the lightning bug.

—*Mark Twain*

Writing is hard work. Writing well is even harder. Ethnography requires good writing skills at every stage of the enterprise. Research proposals, field notes, memoranda, interim reports, final reports, articles, and books are the tangible products of ethnographic work. The ethnographer can share these written works with participants to verify their accuracy and with colleagues for review and consideration. Ethnography offers many intangibles, through the media of participation and verbal communication. However, written products, unlike transitory conversations and interactions, withstand the test of time.

Ethnographic writing is as difficult and as satisfying as descriptions of nature. From simple notes about small events, special landmarks, or even the temperature to efforts to describe an experience or explain a sudden insight, ethnographic writing requires an eye for detail, an ability to express that detail in its proper context, and the language skills to weave small details and bits of meaning into a textured social fabric. The ethnographic writer must recreate the varied forms of social organization and interaction that months of observation and study have revealed. The manifold symbolism every culture displays and the adaptiveness of people to their environment must somehow come to life on this page.

Ethnographic writing comes in a variety of styles, from clear and simple to byzantine. Many ethnographers model their efforts after those of an author they admire. They adapt their model to suit various subjective and objective considerations: tone, context, message, time constraints, purpose, and so on. As a result, each writer develops a literary voice that becomes clearer and more individual with experience. However, all ethnographers—regardless of how well developed their style—need to adapt their writing to suit their particular and varying audiences. As is the case with every writer, the ethnographer's ability to write to different audiences will determine the effectiveness of the work.

Writing good field notes is very different from writing a solid and illuminating ethnography or ethnographically informed report. Note taking is the rawest kind of writing. The note taker typically has an audience of one. Thus, although clarity, concision, and completeness are vital in note taking, style is not a primary consideration.

Writing for an audience, however, means writing to that audience. Reports for academics, government bureaucrats, private and public industry officials, medical professionals, and various educational program sponsors require different formats, languages, and levels of abstraction. The brevity and emphasis on findings in a report written for a program-level audience might raise some academics' eyebrows and cause them to question the project's intellectual effort. Similarly, a refereed scholarly publication would frustrate program personnel, who would likely feel that the researcher is wasting their time with irrelevant concerns, time that they need to take care of business. In essence, both parties feel that the researcher is simply not in touch with their reality. These two audiences are both interested in the fieldwork and the researcher's conclusions, but have different needs and concerns. Good ethnographic work can usually produce information that is relevant to both parties. The skillful ethnographer will communicate effectively with all audiences—using the right smoke signals for the right tribe. (See Fetterman, 1987b, for a discussion about the ethnographer as rhetorician. See also Yin, 1984, for a discussion about differing audiences in the presentation of a case study.)

Writing is part of the analysis process as well as a means of communication (see also Hammersley & Atkinson, 1983). Writing clarifies thinking. In sitting down to put thoughts on paper, an individual must organize those thoughts and sort out the specific ideas and relationships. Writing often reveals gaps in knowledge. If the researcher is still in the filed when those gaps are discovered, additional interviews and observations of specific settings are necessary. If the researcher has left the field, field notes and telephone calls must suffice. Embryonic ideas often come to maturity during writing, as the ethnographer crystallizes months of thought on a particular topic.

From conception—as a twinkle in the ethnographer's eye—to delivery in the final report, an ethnographic study progresses through written stages. A brief review of some of the milestones in the ethnographic life cycle highlights the significance of writing in ethnography.

Research Proposals

The ethnographer's ideas have their first expression in the research proposal. Sponsors judge the quality of the design, the significance of the problem, the methodology, including analysis, and the budget—all through this written exercise. The enormity of a specific problem and the sophistication of research tools can be described in myriad ways. However, only a few approaches will compete favorably with other deserving proposals. Sponsors are a very special, pivotal audience. Each sponsor has idiosyncratic standards, requirements, criteria, topics or interest, and funding capabilities. The ethnographer's ability to communicate with sponsors will directly affect the success, shape, and tone of the research endeavor.

Careful and deliberate writing can ensure an appropriate match between sponsor and researcher. Like an employment interview, the proposal is the first communication between individuals who must decide quickly whether they can work together and then must learn to do so. A meticulously drafted proposal can chart the way for both the researcher and the sponsor. Clear, direct statements—free of circumlocutions, jargon, qualifying clauses, and vague, passive phrasing—can assure both parties about what the ideas are, how the study will carry them out, who will conduct the work, and for how much and how long. Shared understandings and values minimize misunderstandings, miscommunications, and consequent tensions. Ambiguity invites misunderstanding and turmoil. Lack of clarity may also indicate to the sponsor that the ethnographer's thinking is fuzzy. Writing is thus both an exercise in clarifying thoughts and plans and a form of self-presentation.

Planning and foresight are essential in ethnographic research. The more organized the effort, the smoother its progress. The proposal's language and structure reflect the writer's organization. In addition, proper planning during the proposal stage can ensure that enough time and money are available for important aspects of the research effort. Improper planning can result in terminating a project before it has addressed all the salient issues. It can also result in research that follows an aimless pattern, like a ship adrift, wasting time and effort. When the proposal is accepted and the work funded, after the carefully crafted letters necessary to gain entry to the community, the next significant writing challenge lies in taking good field notes.

Field Notes

Field notes are the brick and mortar of an ethnographic structure. These notes consist primarily of data from interviews and daily observation. They form an early stage of analysis during data collection and contain the raw data necessary for later, more elaborate analyses. Many field note guidelines and techniques are available to assist ethnographers. The most important rule, however, is to write the information down.

Fieldwork inundates the ethnographer with information, ideas, and events. Ethnographic work is exhausting, and the fieldworker will be tempted to stop taking notes or to postpone typing the day's hieroglyphics each night. However, memory fades quickly, and unrecorded information will soon be overshadowed by subsequent events. Too long a delay sacrifices the rich immediacy of concurrent notes.

Shorthand, Symbols, and Mnemonics

Ethnographers use numerous techniques to improve their accuracy in recording events in the field. For example, they learn a highly personalized shorthand for recording interviews. Short phrases or key words represent an event, an image, or parts of a conversation. Standard abbreviations and symbols are common aids in note taking: ♀, ♂, +, $, and so on. Question marks and exclamation points are useful notations, reminding the ethnographer of a finding or another unanswered question. These devices enable the ethnographer to take extensive notes during the day, capturing both depth and breadth. Ideally, the translation of these notes takes place immediately after the interview or observation, when the memory is sharpest. However, routine end-of-day translation is more usual and more practical in many cases. These abbreviations and symbols are written snapshots or mnemonic devices. They trigger the memory, carrying a rush of images to the brain and enabling the ethnographer to reconstruct entire episodes.

Reconstruction

Note taking is inappropriate in some situations—for example, funerals, fights, and certain religious festivals. Field notes are still important, but taking them is more difficult. In this case, a complete reconstruction is necessary. In his study of tramps, Spradley ran to the lavatory after almost every interview with drunks to transcribe events. Many of his interviewees thought that he had a bladder problem. Powdermaker (1966) sat in her car for hours, writing up sensitive conversations. Recalling long passages of conversation accurately requires practice. However, like bards who memorize thousands of lines of song, ethnographers can accurately remember vast amounts of data with training and experience. Unlike the bards, however, the ethnographer must write down this information as quickly as possible before absorbing new material.

Field Note Organization

Keeping field notes organized and cross-referenced can facilitate formal stages of analysis, from preliminary hypothesis testing in the field to the final writing stage. Notes can be organized by topic in a loose-leaf folder as easily as in a database on a 20- or 40-megabyte hard disk. The database approach greatly facilitates analysis, as Chapter 4 discussed, and minimizes the time necessary for most ethnographers to write an ethnography. (See Wolcott, 1975, concerning the amount of time typically required to write an ethnograghy. Also see Levine, 1985, for a discussion about organizational strategies, specifically the principles of data storage and retrieval.)

Speculations, cues, lists, and personal diary-type comments should remain in a separate category from observation notes. Such notes are working documents that help guide the ethnographer's work. They serve as a reminder to follow up on a long list of topics and tasks. Written on the back of an envelope or on a mainframe computer with an automatic reminder program, these notes also document part of the ethnographic process. Using them, the ethnographer can retrace steps to identify the strategy that helped to uncover a specific layer of meaning during the research. A personal diary can be both an effective coping strategy during particularly difficult and dangerous fieldwork and a quality-control mechanism. Notes about the researcher's mood, attitude, and prejudice during a specific stage of the research endeavor can provide a context from which to view primary field notes at that stage. Maintaining these separate files thus becomes a quality control on data collection and analysis. (See Schwandt & Halpern, 1988, concerning auditing field notes. See also Bogdan & Biklen, 1982, for an additional discussion about writing field notes.)

Organization of Field Notes

A variety of useful ways of organizing field notes are available. I have found that one approach in particular ensures an efficient and effective fieldwork experience and, in the process, greatly facilitates the process of writing.

Field notes can be organized in a looseleaf folder, with tabs to identify each section. The first section consists of a running index, which can be used to help find specific topic areas or passages. The second section consists of the proposal/contract. The third section holds the time and budget records necessary to administer the effort properly. The fourth section holds all correspondence, and the fifth section contains preliminary notes used during the early survey phase of the research effort. (Field notes in this section of the notebook are used to develop the proposal and the delimit further the ethnographer's scope during the early stages of fieldwork.) The remaining sections are all subsets of the proposal. The proposal identifies the major categories for study, each section containing a research topic.

The first page of each section is a cover sheet containing purpose, methods, findings, conclusions, and recommendations. This system compels the ethnographer to clarify the purpose of the task, accurately record the specific methods in use to explore the topic, and summarize findings and conclusions. In addition, this organizational aid provides a convenient reference throughout the study for recommended future courses of action. The cover sheet also enables the ethnographer to generate memoranda or other summary communications to share with colleagues, sponsors, and people in the field. The memoranda in turn—together with participant responses—generate the report or ethnography.

The findings section of the cover sheet is cross-referenced to the specific field notes, photographs, and tape recordings or transcripts that document each finding. For example, the field notes of an interview represent the raw data. The interview notes might be accompanied by observational records, matrices, and pictures used to triangulate the information. These documents or raw data refer back to the summary sheet for convenience . (The same set of observational notes or interview data can be used to support a number of findings in other sections of the folder or work papers.)

The ethnographer can develop new topics or subsets of existing ones. A computer can maintain and organize many of these records, as discussed in Chapter 4. In many cases, however, hard copy, as well as photographic records, is essential. This approach to field note organization reminds the ethnographer of the study's purpose and direction; allows the fieldworker easy access to preliminary findings, conclusions, and recommendations; and enables others to review the research efforts.

Memoranda

Ethnographers produce summaries of the research effort during various stages of their work. This synthesizing tool helps ethnographers gauge their progress. In my work in higher education, I find brief memoranda useful in consolidating my understanding of a situation. I share them with the people I am working with and ask for feedback. This interactive mode places a check on my perceptions before I use them as a base for understanding the next stage or development. In addition, memoranda provide participants with an opportunity to share in the research process.

Writing memoranda throughout a study also makes report writing much easier. The ethnographer can draw introductory and background sections from the proposal, modified after field experience. The core of the report then comes directly from the memoranda and feedback generated throughout the study. Thus the ethnographer needs only to finish the final synthesis, which explains how all the memoranda and the responses fit together. Participants should have no significant surprises at the end of the process.

Interim Reports

In contract research work, interim reports are more common than memoranda. These reports are preliminary summaries of the ethnographer's knowledge at prespecified intervals during the study. These reports go to sponsors, participants, and colleagues for review. In testing an ethnographer's understanding of the program or culture and allowing specific feedback for each aspect of the report, interim reports are an invaluable contribution to the quality of the research effort.

Final Reports, Articles, and Books

The last stage in ethnographic research is writing the final report, article, or book. These final products often represent the ethnographer's last opportunities to present a refined, analyzed picture of the culture under study. These three forms of highly crystallized expression require the same foundation of data, hard work, and insight, but differ in tone, style, format, distribution, and economic value in the marketplace.

The variety of reports, articles, and books is so great that in one chapter I can do little more than discuss a few generic characteristics and guidelines for each type. A brief review of the most common forms of ethnographic publishing is essential, however, because sharing knowledge, which usually involves publishing findings, is a critical part of an ethnographer's work. Publishing is an ethnographer's way of sharing observations and conclusions and then learning from the feedback generated by the published material.

A government report is typically more pragmatic than an article or book. It is likely to have an immediate impact on the program or group under study. Typically, the ethnographer focuses on a specific policy issue in the report. The language is likely to be bureaucratese, full of abstract jargon (words like *prioritization* and *implementation*)—a must for communicating effectively with government agencies. The report may contain a technical and a non technical compilation of the findings. It will typically have an executive summary for policymakers who do not have the time or inclination to read the entire report. Advisory panels—composed of academics, practitioners, and government commissioners—maintain quality control on the effort and the product. In many cases, the panels play a direct role in negotiating the wording of key passages.

An article is a cross section or a highly condensed version of the ethnographer's overall effort. It often discusses a specific issue in depth. The author typically will indicate briefly how the work contributes to knowledge development, theory, or methodology. The audience usually consists of academic colleagues, who have direct impact on the shape of the author's work in refereed journals because they recommend publication or rejection. They also recommend specific revisions. The author must respond to such suggestions before the article is accepted for publication. Collegial influence can have a dramatic effect on the final product—refining and improving it or forcing the author to make an inappropriate detour. (For more about writing journal articles, see Bogdan & Biklen, 1982, pp. 183–190; Van Til, 1987.)

A book's greater length provides the ethnographer with more latitude than an article. The audience, once again, is composed primarily of academic colleagues. The structure of ethnographic manuscripts varies, but an ethnography typically discusses fundamental elements about the culture, such as its structure and organization, history, politics, religion, economy, and worldview. A specific theme that emerged during the ethnography might become the focal point of discussion throughout the text. This theme might be a critical feature of the culture, its ethos, or the manner in which members adapt or fail to adapt to their environment. On receipt of a manuscript, the publisher requests reviews from appropriate colleagues in the field to help make a go/no-go decision. The reviews can determine the fate of the manuscript as well as its tone or emphasis. Authors can seek out other publishers or journals if their work is rejected or if they disagree with the recommended changes. However, some publishers and journals are so prized in the field that the author has no realistic alternative. (See Powell, 1985, for a discussion about the decision-making process in scholarly publishing.)

In addition to disciplinary and status differences among reports, articles, and books, differences exist in subtopic focus and in whether the orientation is basic or applied. Whatever the work, the ethnographer must select the most appropriate audience to write to—the readers upon whom the work will have an impact and who will judge it appropriately. Once the ethnographer has determined the appropriate audience, he or she then must gear the writing style to that audience.

Reports usually have limited circulation, targeting sponsors, various government agencies, program personnel, and some academic colleagues. Reports may or may not be copyrighted and generally do not generate royalties; they are products that are delivered and paid for as part of a research project. Report deadlines are a double-edged sword. They ensure a timely response to specific policy questions, but preclude much stylistic refinement.

The circulation of articles depends on the journal in which they appear. An ethnographer interested in reaching the largest possible audience within the general boundaries of the topic will attempt to publish in a scholarly journal with a large circulation. If the aim is simply to share knowledge with a very small, specialized group of scholars, highly specific journals are the best choice. In both instances, the ethnographer makes trade-offs in terms of exposure and impact or influence. Refereed journals are more highly respected and prestigious than nonrefereed journals because they have built-in quality control and publishing in them is more difficult. Journal articles are usually copyrighted. The journal holds the copyright, and the author generally has the right to use the article in any book or collection he or she authors or edits. Journal articles do not produce any royalties unless they are reprinted in a book. Such articles are less timely than reports, but more timely than books. Manuscript review for a journal article may take two to eight months. Revisions, galley proofing, and general production time may delay publication another two to six months. (For this reason, many high-energy physicists prefer on-line electronic articles to traditionally published articles—they need to keep up with rapid changes in their field.)

Scholarly books are more difficult to write than articles—a result in part of their greater length and in part of the larger scope of intellectual effort they require. Stamina and concentration are essential: An article requires tremendous effort to reduce mountains of data and pools of analysis into concise expression. A book requires the same effort multiplied many times. In addition, a book is the ultimate scholarly format and will be judged by generation after generation of readers.

Books—unlike most articles—are reviewed publicly (for illustrations, see Feterman, 1986c, 1986d). Although most reviewers try to give an honest critique of the work (see Janesick, 1986), a poor match between reviewer and text can be disastrous. Almost all reviewers look for errors, sins of omission, and conceptual flaws in a text. Some have the wisdom to judge a book on its own merits; others judge it against an ideal but unrelated model. (For additional discussion on this topic, as well as a case example, see Bank, 1986; Fetterman, 1986a.) In some cases, the publisher selects a reviewer precisely because his or her view of the topic is completely different from that of the author. Colleagues familiar with the players learn how to interpret reviewer comments and can learn a great deal from this exercise. Although review comments must sometimes be taken with a grain of salt, the review process—with all its faults—appears to be the best system available.

How widely books circulate depends on the publisher. Some publishers have highly integrated dissemination systems, including databases of professional association membership lists, classified according to interest and topic area. Such systems enable publishers to identify their market and target their advertising resources. The author has a direct interest in this process because the author of a book typically receives royalties. The publisher owns the copyright—to prevent competition from that same author—and the author retains limited publication rights.

A book is usually an ethnographer's least timely published effort. Some ethnographies are written many years after the fieldwork. Once a publisher accepts a manuscript, actual publication may take an additional year or two. Exceptions do exist. Some publishers now request camera-ready copy of the author's manuscript to expedite the process. Given the typical lag between acceptance and publication, however, authors are fortunate that most scholarly ethnographic books are timeless and have a long shelf life. (See Whyte's *Street Corner Society*, 1955, for a classic example. See also Lareau, 1987, for discussion about the delay in publication of this text.)

All written ethnographic expressions share some common features. Most important are thick description and verbatim quotations. Use of the ethnographic present and an explicit statement of the role of the ethnographer are also characteristic.

Thick Description and Verbatim Quotations

Thick description and verbatim quotations are the most identifiable features of ethnographic field notes, reports, articles, and books. Ethnographers take great pains to describe a cultural scene or event in tremendous detail. The aim is to convey the feel as well as the facts of an observed event. Ideally, the ethnographer shares the participant's understanding of the situation with the reader. Thick description is a written record of cultural interpretation. Chapter 2 discusses the difference between a wink and a blink in the section on cultural interpretation. A thin description would simply describe a rapid closing of the eyelid. A thick description gives context, telling the reader whether the movement was a blink caused by a piece of dust in someone's eye or a romantic signal transmitted across a crowded room. Thus the description would incorporate the cultural meaning and the ethnographer's analysis.

Thick description can portray a variety of cultural scenes and episodes. The example below comes from a discussion about ethical dilemmas during fieldwork in the inner city.

> On what was to have been the last day of the site visit a student befriended me. After a few hours of conversation about his life and the neighborhood, he decided to show me around. He introduced me to a number of the leaders running life in the streets. It was getting hot and he knew I was from California, so he brought me to a health food store for a cold drink and a snack. We went in and my new friend winked at the owner of the store and told him to give me a granola bar with some natural soda. I said thanks and reached out my hand for the granola bar and felt something else under the bar. It was a nickel bag of marijuana. I looked at the owner, then I looked at my friend. I did not want to show any form of disapproval or ingratitude, but this was not exactly what I had in mind when I agreed to play the role of guest, visitor, and friend.
>
> A moment later, I heard steps in perfect stride. I looked over to the front window and saw two policemen walking by, looking right in the window. My hand was still in the air with the mixed

contents for all to see. My heart dropped to the floor. My first thought was, "I'm going to get busted. How am I going to explain this to my colleagues at the research corporation?"

Fortunately, the police disappeared as quickly as they had appeared. I asked my friend what had just transpired. He explained to me that the police were paid off regularly and would bother you only if they needed money or if an owner had not made a contribution. (Fetterman, 1986e, pp. 27–28)

Thick descriptions start out as long, unwieldy, redundant entities in note form during field-work. The author must carefully select and prune these notes to illustrate a point or present an interpretation in a report or book. Ethnographic writing is a process of reduction, as the ethnographer moves from field notes to written text. The goal is to represent reality in a concise but complete fashion, not to reproduce every detail and word. A complete reproduction is not possible or desirable: It is not science, and no one will take the time to read it all.

Verbatim quotations are also a sine qua non of ethnography. They are a permanent record of a person's thoughts and feelings. Verbatim quotations convey fear, anger, frustration, exhilaration, and joy of a human being, and contain surface and deep, embedded meanings about the person's life. They can present a host of ideas to the reader: basic "factual" data, social and economic indicators, and internal consistency or patterned inconsistencies. The reader can extrapolate the values and worldview of the speaker from these passages.

Long verbatim quotations help convey a sense of immediacy to the reader. In addition, judicious use of such raw data in reports and ethnographies can provide the reader with sufficient data to determine whether the ethnographer's interpretations and conclusions are warranted.

During the study of the dropout program, I learned about the practice of arson for hire in the community from a young mother who lived in the neighborhood. Her words conveyed a vivid picture of this crime. Corina said that she

woke up to a phone call at two in the morning. The man over the phone said to be out of the house in 15 minutes because it was going to burn. That's what they do when it's arson, they call you just like that at two in the morning. I had my rollers on and I was in my bathrobe, that's all I had. I was on the second floor and my grandma she was on the third. I can still remember seein' the flames all around her wheelchair. I tried to get her out but I couldn't. I had rheumatic fever you know, so I'm weak. She was so heavy I just couldn't. I got my babies out but she was so heavy. I just watched her die. I still go to the county [psychiatrist] even now. I dream about it. It still frightens me. I couldn't save her. (Fetterman, 1983, p. 218)

The dimensions of Corina's personal tragedy and the personal nature of this crime would have been lost in a third-person description. Her verbatim quotation provides a concise, accurate, and personal description of the effects of arson for hire in the community. Thick description and verbatim quotations have tremendous face validity in ethnography. (See Ryles as credited and represented in Geertz, 1973.)

Ethnographic Present

Ethnographers are usually written in ethnographic present. The ethnographic present is a slice of life—a motionless image. This literary illusion suggests that the culture stands still through time—even after the time the ethnography describes. Ethnographers are keenly aware of change in sociocultural systems. They often focus on change in a program, a culture, or any group. Fieldwork may have taken years, but the ethnographer writes about the events as if they were occurring today. This convention is partly a matter of linguistic convenience. However, it is also a way to maintain consistency in description and to keep the story alive. Fundamentally, the ethnographer uses the present tense because fieldwork—which could continue indefinitely—must end at some arbitrary point. Time and other resources are not inexhaustible, and natives tire of being observed.

The ethnographer realizes that no matter how long the study, the culture will change the moment the fieldwork ends. The best the ethnographer can do is to describe the culture as accurately as possible up to the point of departure. Ideally, the ethnographic present is true to the ethnographer's image of the culture at the time of the study.

Ethnographic Presence

Ethnographers attempt to be unobtrusive, to minimize their influence on the natural situation. Their purpose is to describe another culture as it operates naturally. However, ethnographers are honest. They recognize that their presence is a factor in this human equation. Thus, rather than present an artificial and antiseptic picture, ethnographers openly describe their roles in events during fieldwork. The ethnographic presence tells the reader how close the ethnographer is to the people and to the data. The technique can contribute additional credibility to the researcher's findings. These embedded self-portraits simultaneously serve as quality control, documenting the degree of contamination or influence the ethnographer has on the people under study.

At the same time, the ethnographer should not dominate the setting, nor should the ethnographer's signature be in every word or every page. The researcher need not include every parenthetical thought to demonstrate intellectual prowess. In describing a culture, the focus of the writing should be on the topic. Alfred Hitchcock's signature—appearing on screen for a few seconds in each of his movies—is an example of an explicit presence. His style, particularly his use of cameral angles, is an example of implicit presence. Ethnographers leave both explicit and implicit signatures on their work. Some are subtle, others are as bold as van Gogh's brush strokes in his *Cornfield with Crows*. An artfully crafted ethnographic presence can convey the depth and breadth of the ethnographer's experience in the field.

Ethnographically Informed Reports

Ethnographers do not always have the luxury of completing a full-blown ethnography. Instead, they must write ethnographically informed reports or other publication efforts. An ethnographically informed report may require the same effort as an ethnography, or it may approximate the effort by applying some ethnographic concepts and techniques to research. In either case, the report has the flavor of an ethnography, but its structure and format resemble those of publications funded by the public- or private-sector sponsor. An ethnographically informed report is as useful as a full-blown ethnography to the right audience. However, ethnographically informed reports that only approximate the effort a traditional ethnography requires will not be as credible because the writer loses many built-in quality controls when ethnographic concepts and methods are not used in an integrated fashion.

Literature

Literary artists are keen observers of the human drama. They have created classic stories and characters who represent fundamental values and social relationships. Literary works can be useful to the ethnographer at various stages in the work. During fieldwork, the events of everyday life often parallel the plots of masterpieces. These parallels can help to unravel the complex performances that the ethnographer attends.

Literature is probably most useful, however, as a tool to help ethnographers communicate their insights. A number of literary conventions and writing techniques are available for the ethnographer to use. The author may assume the voice of different speakers, may appear omniscient or transparent. The author can expand or contract through narrative pace. Use of concrete metaphors, rich similes, parallelism, irony and may other devices on a larger plane convey the true feel, taste, and smell of a moment.

Ethnographers use this wordcraft to make their science meaningful and effective. I used Shakespeare's resonant phrase "a comedy of errors" in my "Blaming the Victim" article about the dropout program. The phrase aptly characterized in a concise and instantly comprehensible fashion the misuse of the treatment-control design and the federal bureaucratic intervention in the study. The phrase—as a description of the behavior of educational agencies and researchers in a national research effort—conveys the absurdity of the experience as well as its tragedy (misevaluation) (see Fetterman, 1981b).

Henrik Ibsen's story "An Enemy of the People" provided a powerful image that accurately reflected my experience in attempting to publish my research findings about the misapplication of the treatment-control design in the dropout study. In this story, Dr. Stockmann, the play's protagonist and a medical official, attempts to publish his discovery of contaminants in the town's famous baths. He encounters significant resistance from the townspeople, who derive their income from tourist frequenting the baths. I used this poignant story to convey my own frustration; it captured the emotional tension and outrage I experienced in the face of harsh resistance to a public discussion of the misuse of a paradigm fundamental to educational research (see Fetterman, 1982b). Writing about art can also be an effective way to communicate. In the same article, I used art to illustrate a conceptual point, to abstract the situation from the reader and the observer—like Dali's painting of Dali painting Dali painting, ad infinitum.

Revising and Editing

The last stages of writing always include revising and editing. Writing is both mechanical and artistic. Paragraphs must be shifted to fit in the right organizational or conceptual sequence. Sentences should be grammatical. Participles shouldn't dangle, and citations should correspond to references. Phrases must be carefully crafted to capture the imagination of the reader and yet remain scientific. Examples must be compelling and precise. Titles must catch the reader's eyes and remain honest. The author must polish all these facets of the work in addition to making sure the work it cogent, conceptually coherent, and comprehensive, yet concise. All these tasks take time. (For useful writing guides, see Bernstein, 1965, 1977; Strunk & White, 1959.)

Proper organization can reduce the time necessary to write drafts of ethnographic products, but revising and polishing take additional time and a tremendous amount of effort. The amount of time depends on the quality of the first draft, the writer's talent, and the amount of time available. Attention to detail, including proofing galleys, is important. The absence of a single word or letter can inadvertently change meanings. Passages supporting a complex argument can be lost between copyediting and galley stages. Without sufficient attention to the role of editing manuscripts, opportunities for last-minute updates can be lost. Time devoted to these tasks is always time well spent.

PART VI
Reading Text: Examples of Qualitative Research

Double Vision:
The Experience of Institutional Stability

Anna Neumann

Stability as Stress

Studies of resource stress in higher education focus primarily on economic change (especially downturns), on strategic responses to such change, and on approaches and techniques for cutting back (Zammuto 1987). A second strand of research studies how leaders and other campus participants respond within their colleges during tough times (Cameron, Kim, and Whetten 1987; Cyert 1978; Peterson 1984a, 1984b; Rubin 1977; Whetten 1984). However, with only a few exceptions (e.g., Chaffee 1984; Chaffee and Tierney 1988; Neumann, in press), we have paid little attention to the cognitive and affective dimensions of leadership during hard financial times: how leaders and faculty members learn about troublesome resource conditions, how they experience such news, and how this affects their well-being. Although several studies examine how leaders and others around them think, know, and learn (Bensimon 1990, 1991; Neumann 1990a, 1991b), few explore the link between cognition and context—for example, asking how people construct and experience the phenomenon of hard times.

While we know a fair amount about how administrative leaders and others act during times of financial strain, including how they respond instrumentally (Pfeffer 1981)—for example, by launching a new marketing strategy or by cutting costs—we know very little about how they learn that they are faced with financial difficulties in the first place or how they feel about that situation. This enlarged perspective on financial stress requires us to assume a double vision of sorts— viewing a college's financial condition simultaneously as a material object to be changed and as a socially constructed (Berger and Luckmann 1973) and socially shared understanding to be planted and shaped within our own and others' minds. The latter perspective defines financial stress as a cultural artifact of organization.

The ambiguity that accompanies resource loss makes it particularly important to study how we construct our resource realities and how we experience those constructions. But the focus on resource difficulty suggests that stable organizations are less interesting. That is, we assume that colleges with strong or growing resource feel little of the strain typically associated with economic decline. For the most part, researchers have not examined the dynamics of financial stability and financial growth as closely as they have examined the dynamics of financial hardship, despite the fact that a significant number of higher education institutions are, in fact, stable (see Cameron, Kim, and Wheaton 1987). In sum, while we have given little attention to how administrators and faculty construct and experience the phenomenon of troubled financial times, we have given virtually no attention to how they construct and experience the absence of financial trouble.

This tendency to overlook resource stability as a contextual organizational feature in its own right is both puzzling and worrisome. For example, in attending purely to questions of how faculty and administrators experience financial downturn, we may neglect to consider how they experience stasis and growth, including what it is like to live during a period of "no change" or "restrained change," and also what it is like to live in a time of "positive change." Interestingly, organizational scholars have recently reoriented their views of change—including negative change—to consider, not only its physical, observable, and behavioral form (e.g., Bennis, Benne, and Chin 1969; Downs and Mohr 1976; Lewin 1947; Munson and Pelz 1981; Zaltman and Duncan 1977), but also its cognitive and affective manifestation (e.g., Bartunek 1984, 1988; Ford and Baucus 1987; Isabella 1990). It may be just as important to supplement our current understanding of stasis, as the antithesis of change, by considering its subjective aspects, particularly in an era of decline when the only alternative to negative change for many institutions of higher education may, in fact, be stasis. While the prospect of living in a stable institutional environment may be preferable to negative financial change, we know little about the internal conditions that administrators create as they pursue or maintain stability; we know even less about how faculty members experience those conditions.

In a related study I show that when the faculty experience the ambiguity that often attends financial hardship—usually because their leaders have neglected to mediate that ambiguity—the faculty may question their own and their leader's professional competence (Neumann, in press). Other researchers have pointed out that when professionals question their own competence, they are likely to falter also in the sense of personal efficacy (Rosenhltz 1980) that drives professional performance—for example, their teaching and their continuous scholarly learning. While we know something about the dynamics of financial stress, including its likely effects on the faculty's sense of efficacy, we know very little about how stasis and the administrative actions that produce it affect faculty members' conceptions of themselves, their work, and their leaders.

This study considers the inverse of what we have typically been concerned with in higher education. Rather than looking at an institution in financial trouble, it presents the case of Continental College, an institution that has achieved enviable financial comfort and organizational stability. Rather than focusing on how campus members deal instrumentally with their financial condition, it focuses on how they learn about it and how they feel about the resource strategy that frames their world. Rather than considering only the views and feelings of administrative leaders, it emphasizes the perceptions of persons outside the top administrative circle, especially the faculty, thereby assessing how the work of leaders is mirrored in the minds of "followers." Moreover, this is not a study of what Continental College, a financially and structurally stable institution, is or how it works; rather, it is a study of what it looks and feels like to live and work within it.

The major assumption that frames this study is the belief that the material objects comprising an organization's reality reflect both surface-level and deep-level meanings in the minds of those who strive to apprehend them (Dandridge, Mitroff, and Joyce 1980). Because deep-level interpretations of organizational occurrences are often intensely personal, even inarticulable (Schutz 1970), the meaning of any object or event may vary drastically from person to person, from place to place, and from time to time (Daft 1983; Morgan, Frost, and Pondy 1983; Pfefer 1981; Tierney 1989). Leadership involves the ability to work simultaneously at surface- and deep-level meaning, both for oneself and for others, as one strives to apprehend that which others know and feel, while reflecting simultaneously on the messages that one emits as one speaks, gestures, or simply stands before another, even as one assumes the attitude of listening or otherwise striving to know (Schutz 1970). The conceptual focus of this study is on how faculty and administrators signify meaning and how they apprehend or misconstrue each other's meaning.

The college budget and the general state of a college's financial affairs are primary examples of organizational objects and circumstances whose surface-level and deep-level meanings often carry equal force for the faculty, requiring a leadership that is capable of attending simultaneously to both. This sort of leadership double vision is particularly important during tough financial times when the need to cut back may lead to deep-level ascriptions of value to the contributions that people make to the life of their academic community and, by association, to those people themselves (Neumann, in press). Thus, the leadership of hard times requires equal attention to the decisions that must be made for substantive, instrumental reasons (surface) and to the symbolic messages (deep) simultaneously inscribed within them (Pfeffer 1981).

However, the double vision may be equally important during times of stability. Faculty and administrators are likely to experience even the most stable of environments in different ways, and they are likely to interpret administrative strategies for achieving stability differently as well. While administrators may view their actions as rational and beneficial at a surface level, the deep-level meaning of their actions, for example, as construed by the faculty, may be quite different. In the case of Continental College, I show that administratively induced stability can, in fact, be quite stressful at a deep level to the faculty, even as the faculty voice gratitude for a leadership that helps their college avert the devastation of hard times.

I present the case of Continental College in three parts. First, I describe how stability manifests itself at Continental College—financially, structurally, and operationally—and how administrators make the stability happen, namely by institutionalizing a leadership philosophy centered on rationality, delegation, and minimized conflict. In this section, I also describe how administrators perpetuate the stability that they have created, for example, by maintaining preestablished routines whereby organizational members learn and interact, and whereby they generate, acquire, decipher, and interpret information. In the second section of the case I consider how the faculty experience their stable institutional world—including how they make sense of and how they feel about the rationality, delegation, peace, and patterned learning inscribed within their daily lives and institutional careers. I conclude, in the third section, with faculty leaders' reflections on their experiences of their organization, including emerging hopes for change. To foreshadow the results, I find that Continental's stability—as evidenced by its steady resources and administrative structure—leads to an undercurrent of malaise among the faculty. This suggests that, in at least some cases, administratively induced stability may be as much a source of stress for the faculty as financial hardship.

Method

Continental College[1] is one of eight colleges and universities participating in a study of organizational and leadership dynamics under diverse degrees of resource stress. The eight institutions share a prominent (but not necessarily exclusive) commitment to the teaching function, especially at the undergraduate level. Four of the institutions (two private and two public) were financially stressed in 1986–87, the first year of the study; the remaining four (two private and two public) were financially stable. At the time of the study, Continental College fell in the latter set. While Continental College was growing steadily and securely in its resources, it was hardly changing in substance or structure; as I show later, it seemed to purposefully avert change, whether positive or negative. Viewed in terms of this structural and resource stability,[2] Continental College differs dramatically from the other seven institutions in the sample—for example, from the institutions under clear and immediate financial stress (reported in Neumann, in press; 1990b), from those struggling for direction and meaning in the aftermath of financial disaster, and from those experiencing new-found growth and change after a sustained time of stasis (reported in Neumann 1991a).

For the purpose of this analysis and other related reports, I define resource stress in both normative and interpretive terms. First, I define resource stress as resource loss or instability exceeding the limits deemed acceptable by normative standards (e.g., as defined formally through standard economic indexes) and also by criteria established by formal institutional leaders. Viewed this way, Continental College was exceedingly stable, a pattern I established primarily through analyses of documentary data acquired through public and institutional sources such as HEGIS-IPEDS financial and enrollment data, and also through accreditation reports, institutional planning documents, administrators' assessments, and so forth. Second, I consider resource stress in a more subjective and interpretive light—that is, positing it as a social construction (Berger and Luckmann 1973) that exists in people's minds. Viewed this way, resource stress reflects the beliefs and feelings of "non-experts," particularly faculty, about their financial condition, regardless of whether their definitions are consistent with the normative criteria for measuring stress. Viewed through an interpretive lens, individuals within an institution may be convinced that the institution is financially stressed, while in normative terms that institution may look quite stable; the reverse may also be true.

The eight institutions participating in this study, including Continental College, were selected from a larger sample of thirty-two institutions of diverse type, size, structure, curriculum, and leadership orientation, participating in the Institutional Leadership Project, a national, longitudinal study of administrative, trustee, and faculty leadership in higher education; the eight institutions participating in the study reflected this diversity as well. During the 1986–87 academic year, and again in 1988–89, a researcher spent three days on each campus interviewing up to fifteen persons in sittings that ranged between one and three hours per person. In 1988–89 these interviewees typically included the president, a trustee, four cabinet-level administrators, and between five and seven faculty leaders (i.e., the head of the faculty senate, informal leaders among the faculty, knowledgeable department chairs, and other mid-level academic administrators viewed as faculty leaders). With the aid of a structured interview protocol comprised, for the most part of open-ended questions.[3] I typically aksed interviewees to portray their institutional conditions and their leadership; I also asked the faculty leaders to describe the views and experiences of their faculty colleagues as best they could.

The larger analysis of the eight institutions has moved comparatively from case to case (Yin 1984). In constructing an interpretive image or images for each campus, I have purposefully "revisited" each campus conceptually with every review of or reimmersion in the data. With each conceptual revisit, I have re-recorded my "field notes," tightening or enlarging the narrative description—the process philosopher Paul Ricoeur calls "textualization" (in Van Maanen 1988, 95)—of what I had heard on site, especially as patterns of similarity and difference became apparent. For Continental College, this has involved seven rewritings of the case. In this way, I have moved iteratively from thorough but non-systematic recording of what I originally heard and saw, to more ordered and systematic description based on emerging categories, and finally to analysis across categories. This process resembles methods of qualitative analysis originally described by Leonard Schatzman and Anselm Strauss (1973). While this study is limited in the small proportion of faculty leaders included in the study, particularly in comparison to the proportion of top administrators, it manages nonetheless to identify points of convergence and difference in how these two sets of leaders construe their realities, including how they conceive of themselves and each other. However, I also search for differences within each leadership set, noting patterns of repetition and diversity among the faculty leaders, and to the extent possible, among the administrators.

Rather than laying claim to one particular vision of collegiate reality (whether verbalized by a key leader or signified by economic indicators), this study purposefully searches for multiple interpretations and, thereby, for multiple realities. It also probes the means whereby institutional actors construct their diverse realities and the consequences of the coexistence of these multiple constructions within a single locale and at a particular time.[4] While it makes no effort to generalize beyond the locale of Continental College, it attempts to show, in particularistic detail (Erickson

1986), how diverse, complex, and confusing any "cultural place" is likely to be, regardless of its espoused stability and singularity (see Frost, et al. 1991).

In portraying the multiple voices of leaders at Continental College, I provide numerous quotations from personal interviews, selecting those that capture most clearly the patterns emerging from my retrospective reconstruction of the site that I visited. To preserve confidentiality, I designate each voice with a code (e.g., F1, F2, A1, A2, P, T), in which F = faculty/academic leader, A = administrator, P = president, T = trustee, and the numbers represent different individuals in those roles. The codes reflect only the order of appearance of a particular voice within this text, and the numbering scheme starts over for each section and subsection of the case. For the case as a whole, I quote seven faculty/academic leaders who describe their own and the faculty's perceptions generally, five cabinet-level administrators (including the president), and one trustee.

For example, in the subsection on "Different Learning Roles," I refer to six faculty/academic leader voices (F1, F2, F3, F4, F5, F6) and four administrative voices (A1, A2, A3, P), while in the subsection called, "Opportunities for Interaction," I refer to three faculty/academic leader voices (F1, F2, F3) and three administrative voices (A1, A2, P). This scheme tells the reader how many faculty and administrative interviewees contributed to the framing of each section; however, each section's numbering scheme is self-contained. Voice "F1" in one section is not necessarily the same person as voice "F1" in another section. When the speaker is clearly designated within the text, I usually omit the designation by code, unless further clarification is desirable.

The Stability of Continental College

Continental College leaves a visitor with the feeling that it is extremely stable, particularly in its operation. Classes meet, faculty teach, research, and write, department heads pore over program plans and class schedules, administrative processes run with only a few hitches, and students of predictable type matriculate and graduate in relatively predictable numbers. Except for sporadic, short-run outbursts about a certain campus routine or tradition, the student newspaper features a smooth stream of official campus events. A college trustee sums up the tone and meter of college life by saying that the campus runs "like a fine-tuned Swiss watch." And a vice president describes governance as "very stable" with "normal turnover among deans and chairs" while "the faculty has remained the same size, the student body has remained the same size . . . [with] no new significant programs . . . added."

From the visitor's perspective, the college's operational stability is matched by its resource stability. In its public documents, the institution displays a steady and healthy enrollment, a sound inflow of grants and contracts, an extremely successful fund-raising program, a long history of balanced budgets, and minimal debt accumulation. The findings of a coarse but objective financial assessment are consistent with the message that Continental projects to its publics. Over a recent six-year period, Continental's rate of inflation-adjusted revenue increases have matched or exceeded the average growth rate for all American colleges and universities.[5] It is noteworthy that while the college's inflation-adjusted revenues have grown substantially, its enrollment level has remained relatively unchanged. In sum, Continental College runs like clockwork, with small deviations quickly caught and just as quickly corrected. The college is financially solid. Its leadership knows it and says so publicly.

Organizing for Stability

In describing how the college has achieved its smooth operation and its current level of resource sufficiency, the administrators and trustees of Continental College evoke three principles of operation: rational leadership, delegated responsibility, and minimized conflict.

The president explains that it is his job, as Continental's chief leader, to envision what the college is to become and to direct its members toward that end—first, by impressing his goals on them, and second, by providing them with what they need to achieve those goals, namely "the peace to do it, and the resources." At Continental College, the concept of "peace" refers to the absence of conflict and disruption. In the words of a vice president, "We don't have confrontations here, and we avoid it at all costs. . . . There is no room for argument" [A1]. The president explains that after providing the "resources" and the "environment," he "delegates the rest," because he "can't get involved in detail" and "faculty do the work" of achieving goals.

Below the president, administrators explain that they are expected to work autonomously or, as one vice president described it, the president "gives to and expects his VPs to deal with issues in their areas" [A2]. At Continental it is assumed that the vice presidents and other administrators will bring only a minimal number of distracting circumstances to the attention of those in superordinate positions. In the words of a top-level administrator: "If a subordinate is not screwing things up, don't get in his or her way. If you have to substitute for [the person] often, get a new one. I don't want to work with [the people reporting to my subordinate] in any direct sense—it means that other people aren't doing their job" [A3]. To balance the autonomy that comes with delegation, the president claims final authority: "My level is decisive. I'm not a rubber stamp."

While feeling responsible for their own divisional tasks, the vice presidents also feel the weight and scope of the president's authority. They describe him as "an aloof delegator" [A4] and as "a very, very effective leader" whose "initiative" has helped to "bring strength here—financially, organizationally, operationally" [A2]. One vice president describes him as exerting effects "on every thing there is" because "he is implicitly in all. . . . You can't divorce him from anything" [A3]. These administrators also reflect the belief that, with few exceptions, the president's ethos of rationality dominates their organization. In the words of one, "What we don't have here that you see at other places is this—the fiefdoms. . . . There is no political environment here. . . . We have highly centralized authority" [A1].

In sum, from the perspective of its top administrative cadre, Continental College runs like a classic bureaucracy with the president clearly at its helm. "He has transformed the college," praises one vice president, "and now it is pointed to become a great institution. . . . He has done this by skillfully using subordinates, listening to their counsel, and by giving out resources to carry out the plans that people have made together" [A4]. But how does the cognitive side of the functionally smooth bureaucracy work? How do people in a bureaucratic structure learn about the outcomes of their college's resource strategy? How do they come to know the state of their resources in the first place?

Learning Roles, Opportunities, and Information

Learning, as defined here, refers to the process whereby individuals assume the common understanding of an organization's resource reality, regardless of whether they actively define it on their own or in the company of others, or whether they adopt, critically or without question, the definitions that others create. This section identifies the roles that the administrators, trustees, and faculty of Continental College typically play as they "learn" about their shared resource reality. It also assesses the opportunities that these actors have for sharing, enlarging, or refining their learning through interaction with others. Finally, it examines the nature of the information that is available for learning.

Different Learning Roles

Years ago, an important, top-level administrator at Continental assumed, virtually single-handedly, the responsibility of setting out in handbook form the types of data that college members rely on to evaluate the institution's financial condition. Today the data handbook continues to serve as the institution's central reference guide, in that it contains various statistics and indicators of the college's financial health, updated regularly. It also serves as a dictionary of sorts that registers the type of data that campus members typically use to assess officially the state of the campus' financial health. In the words of the handbook originator:

> We've had it since 19__ . . . when I inaugurated it. . . . It is a summary paper. . . . Each operating VP gives me his or her best assessment of the most important developments in their areas . . . pithy statements . . . on academic programs, accreditation reviews, admissions. . . . It is up-to-date information. We do this so that if there are problems we will be able to handle them. [A1]

The administrator who originally developed the handbook still plays a prominent leadership role at Continental, and he is known, throughout the campus, as the conceptual force behind the college's very effective budgeting system. In addition to his original, prominent defining role, he assumes today two additional roles: He regulates the campus' budgeting process by setting out its calendar, by initiating and directing the activities of individuals and groups invovled in the process, and by bringing the process to closure when its final product (the budget) is complete. In his words, "I established the categories that [the college] is using. I am expected to provide the synthesis for all the on-going operations of Continental." This administrator also gives voice to the budget, proclaiming its "reality" to the faculty who, in turn, view him as "influential in terms of how money is distributed" [F1], compared to to the president, whom they see as the college's more externally directed "money man" [F2]. In the words of one faculty leader, when it comes to learning about resource matters," [The long-term administrator] is who we hear from" [F2].

While the handbook-originator has played a prominent defining role, other institutional leaders (e.g., the trustees, president, vice presidents, and others) have, over the years, adopted and internalized the conceptual core that the handbook represents. While these other leaders share a combined receiving and using role, that role takes on two distinctly different forms. Some, including several cabinet-level officers and academic administrators, use the handbook actively as the material of their thinking—for example, using the statistical information to make decisions about how to staff, schedule, or develop their programs and classes. According to one vice president, the fact that "we rely on the handbook data" helps assure that "we are conscious of how many staff people there are to students" and that "we will not proliferate administrators around here" [A2].

Other campus leaders (e.g., the president, trustees) use the data handbook, along with other selected information, to oversee college activities, according to the perceptions of the handbook-originator. In his view, the data keep the hands of the president and trustees on internal college activities while simultaneously releasing them to attend to their external responsibilities (e.g, fund-raising, building outside support, etc.). As a result, he says, the president and trustees have only "a passive involvement" in internal campus affairs; but because of their access to key financial and operational data, they are "able to intervene . . . at any time" [A1]. This administrator refers to the data as a "surrogate for their [the president's and the trustees'] involvement" in activities that would otherwise distract them from the external duties to which they give their primary energy. "The president is truly knowledgeable of everything," said the college's prominent administrator and creator of the handbook. "He is in a position to exercise control, and he needs to be. . . . The trustees don't want to run the university, but they have to balance that with their needing to be knowledgeable . . . [needing to be prepared] for involvement at any time . . . able to intervene" [A1]. The president confirms his colleague's observation: "I know how to read a balance sheet. This is how you monitor programs." The chair of Continental's board of trustees concurs: "The university does a grand job of keeping details like this. . . . You can go into the most infinite detail."

The faculty of Continental College are also in an information-receiving position; but as their leaders describe it, the faculty's version of the role precludes information use in both the active and the passive senses that apply to Continental's administrators and trustees. In the words of campus participants, the faculty are merely "kept apprised" [F3], "information is given out" to them [F1], and they are "handed decisions" [A3] but "without . . . consultation" [F4]. The faculty may receive reports describing the state of institutional resources; but as targets of an institutional dissemination effort (rather than as potential users of information), they rarely respond to the administrators who deliver these messages. "They [faculty] get it [budgetary information], and they glance at it," said one faculty leader, but he notes that they rarely respond [F5]. "The budget seems to be . . . not a secret," said another faculty leader, but the faculty "never read it. . . . They don't have time . . . They have always had the budget in the administrator's hands" [F6].

Opportunities for Interaction

The extent to which the faculty engage among themselves differs dramatically from how administrators and trustees interact. An analysis of the interviews shows that, in comparison to administrators and trustees, the faculty gather far less frequently as a group to exchange information and opinions, to voice their understandings of what is happening in the college, and to learn how others interpret and feel about what they see. From the perspective of at least some of the faculty leaders, institutional logistics simply do not support the opportunity for faculty colleagues to meet and learn what is on each other's minds. "There is no place here to bring faculty together. No psychological space—no physical space," said one interviewee [F1]. And another commented that, except for the assistant professors who "have their own network, . . . most of us in the departments are remarkably isolated" [F2]. In the absence of a forum that would provide a campus-wide faculty voice or a horizontal linking structure that would create a real group, they turn inward. In the words of one faculty leader: "Many people have retreated into their own bailiwicks. Department chairs . . . take care of their departments, but they are not campus leaders. . . . Some people have pulled their horns in out of frustration. . . . We don't have any strong leaders here. . . . There's no power base because of focus on departments." [F3]

The trustees and administrators interact among themselves in ways that differ sharply from those of the faculty. Within the administration, the cabinet meets as a whole irregularly and infrequently as needed; but despite the formal distance, cabinet members remain in contact with each other as a "group" through formal memoranda and reports. One administrator explains that in their roles as cabinet officers, administrators rarely mix with each other for informal or personal purposes. The "ideal relationship" between cabinet-level officers involves "merely greeting each other cordially" and avoiding "talk" that would be equated with "gassing" and "vapor" [A1]. Thus, although the administrators as members of the cabinet do not exercise their opportunity to meet often, they have a formal, albeit restricted, structure to do so when necessary.

However, the top administrative group has carved out for itself another type of opportunity to interact as colleagues with selected "others"—one that is exercised more than it is talked about. At an informal level, the cabinet breaks into two subgroups; and in their roles as members of these subgroups, individuals interact more among themselves than they do in their roles as members of the larger, formal cabinet. For example, when a person thinks up a bright idea that needs testing or elaboration, she does not hesitate to call her subgroup together or to walk over to a colleague's office to chat informally about it. Also within their protective inner subgroups, administrators feel free to vent doubts, concerns, anxieties, and frustrations that they do not show on the outside. "We use each other as sounding boards," said one vice president, "I use the other VPs . . . . I am able to lay out issues on the table and discuss them in an open and forthright manner" [A2].

In sum, within their subgroups, administrators exhibit qualitatively different brands of member interaction than they do in the larger, formal structure of the cabinet. Within each subgroup, there is less restriction on what is exchanged among members because there are relatively few formal restrictions on how the exchange may occur.

While faculty leaders portray themselves and their colleagues as alienated and while the top administrative leaders portray their cabinet as fractured, the trustees present an image of comfortable and meaningful cohesion. According to the chair of the board and the president, the trustees meet frequently among themselves and with the administration, but they have very little contact with the faculty. Although the board meets occasionally with various cabinet officers, their primary institutional contact is the president, whom they see frequently at regular board meetings and, more importantly, talk to in one-to-one informal visits or telephone calls.

Although the frequency with which the president and trustees speak with one another appears important, what they say to each other, how they say it, and how they come to see and feel about each other as they say it may be much more important. As part of his larger, self-defined fund-raising duties, the president spends extensive time "spelling out" to trustees and other external supporters exactly what Continental College stands for, how it works, and how it relates to their own lives. The president's fund-raising philosophy reflects his belief that the cultivation of external financial support really means the cultivation of the human sources that provide it. What this means to the president, who defines himself as the institution's chief fund-raiser, is that he must dedicate himself to shaping how supporters and potential supporters understand and feel about the institution. That is, he works persistently at keeping the institution foremost in their minds: "[The] public has to understand what Continental College is. . . . [They] *must* continue to reflect on this" [P].

In this way, the president builds a close cognitive and emotional bond between himself, as representative of the college, and external supporters. This relationship differs dramatically from the relationship that he shapes with the faculty, which he defines in more instrumental terms and which be believes could distract him from what he views as his primary external obligations.

The Nature of Information Flows

Although the information contained in Continental's budgetary data handbook is distributed routinely, administrators, trustees, and faculty differ in what and how much they get, and also in when and how they get it. As a result, these three sets of campus actors differ in what, when, and how they learn.

Within the college, faculty are at the narrowest end of the information funnel, while top administrators, as they have access to the total handbook, are at the widest. According to one interviewee, "As you go up the chain of command, you get more and more reports and summaries" [A1]. The trustees receive selected—but regular and frequent—reports based on the handbook.

The information that administrators, faculty, and trustees get also differs in its specificity and in the amount of interpretation that accompanies it. The faculty get a "short form" [F1, P] and "rough categories" [F2]. Like the faculty, the trustees get a picture of "the large and rough distribution" [P]. The difference between what trustees and faculty get is the amount of interpretation that accompanies statistics, the personal or impersonal style through which the interpretation is delivered, and the extent to which the data are custom fit, in a sense, to meet the needs of one group as opposed to another—or at least, the extent to which receivers perceive senders as genuinely concerned with their unique interests.

What do the numbers mean? The president explains that along with the data, "we give [the trustees] the principles [that underlie them] and we guide them" [P]. The guidance that administrators provide to the trustees is delivered to them personally, for example, in the president's interactions with them, one to one or in small groups. In return, the chair of the board of trustees, speaking from the perspective of his board colleagues, praises "the grand job" that administrators do of keeping "beautiful records . . . like a business"—how easy it is for the average trustee to see how revenues balance with expenses and how "the capital infrastructure" is being maintained [T].

The faculty, on the other hand, receive only brief information, which some say "is presented in such a way that all you need to do is to glance at it to know that things are better" [F1]. Some faculty accept this message with few comments or questions, claiming that "they are not interested" [F2] or that "they don't have time" [F3]. Others explain their silence in the face of the budgetary "mysteries" [F4] by complaining that the faculty can learn little if all they see is "the budget broken into rough categories" or if all that they get are data that "come through in small pieces" with "no benchmarks" of meaning [F2].

According to these faculty leaders, then, some of their colleagues prefer to ignore budgetary matters, resting in the assurance that their college is doing well, but others feel the frustration of not being able to understand the little information they do get—even if it indicates (albeit in a general way) the good news that Continental College is in solid financial shape. Moreover, they explain that the faculty receive financial data through the institution's official dissemination process, that is, by way of the "normal vehicles" [A2] such as "annual reports [F1, F3, F4], . . . admissions reports [F3, F5], . . . faculty senate minutes [F5, F6]." Given the more personalized information that is directed to trustees, in comparison to the more impersonal information that the faculty get, a faculty leader points out that it is easy to conclude that "the information is really prepared for the trustees" with the faculty getting only the "copy" [F2]. It is easy to see how trustees may become engaged with meaningful data, delivered to them personally by college administrators, while the faculty, who derive little meaning from the "rough" information that they receive through impersonal channels, are likely to remain unengaged.

Experience: The Faculty Perspective

From the perspective of most administrators, Continental College functions like the classic bureaucracy. But individuals outside the top administrative circle, especially the faculty, have different views. That which seems smooth, rational, and functional to some people (i.e., top administrators) looks and feels quite different to others (i.e., faculty leaders). What most administrators (particularly the president) and trustees (particularly the chair of the board) view as a singular, objective reality, the faculty experience in a subjectively different way. The differences are especially apparent when we listen to faculty leaders describe their organization and the process of how they learn about its health and status.

The Faculty Experience of Rationality

In contrast to the administrators' descriptions of their reality as rational, structural, orderly, and predictable, the faculty describe their experience, under this cover of formal organization, as more fluid and malleable: "There is a lot of centralized decision making, but there is flexibility down below. . . . The ultimate decisions are strategic. But then we implement these—but we also do different things with them [i.e., in the process of implementation]" [F1]. For example, while top administrators describe what they experience as an efficient budgeting process that always leads to a balanced bottom line and to a surplus that is allocated on the basis of articulated need, some faculty leaders describe how the system, as it is set up, forces academic and faculty leaders to "learn to scheme. . . . [and] compete" [F2], and how it forces mid-level academic leaders to "put more into those [budget requests] than any chapter [they] have ever written" [F2]. And while top-level administrators list a string of official memoranda and reports as the primary "vehicles" [A1] for shaping the faculty's understanding of the college's status (with faculty leaders acknowledging that these documents are, in fact, "thrust on" them [F3]), the faculty leaders explain that they and their colleagues learn what is happening from the "scuttlebutt" around the college [F4] or simply from "informal" talks [F2] with trusted administrators willing to speak with them.

The theme of rationality as a harbor for political and emotional events not subject to purely rational justification is echoed in other ways throughout the organization. For example, while top administrators (i.e., looking downward) subscribe, in a rather direct and simple way, to their own final authority over institutional events and resources (in the president's words, "I am responsible for everything"), persons in hierarchically subordinate positions explain how they carefully fashion their words and actions to induce their superiors to act in one way or another. For example, an academic administrator also acting as a faculty leader explains how he crafts "a carefully written report about what we have accomplished and [what] we need" on the assumption that "if it [the report] is readable, it will stick" in the minds of those who have the power to allocate resources [F2]. And an administrator trying to stave off a potentially harmful program change explains how she lobbies the top administrators to whom she reports because she feels that they may act purely on the basis of a detached analysis of program costs and productivity without acknowledging the feelings of the faculty and students:

> My fear is that [the administrator] will lose patience before I do and tell me to [make the program change] before I am ready. I am keeping him *fully* informed. . . . I am trying to plead with him, . . . lobby him for time. . . . I am not sure that I will talk him into it. . . . We don't want to make this [program change] widely known among the faculty. It would lead to a descending spiral—faculty, students, quality of teaching, and so on. . . . I am not sure that I have the president's attention on this. . . . We need him [the president] for . . . clout [i.e., with other decision makers]. [A2]

And there are other inconsistencies in how those "down below" (both faculty and administrators) view their institutional reality, compared to those in top administrative roles. As suggested in previous sections, while top administrators assert a theme of impersonality, rational analysis, and individual responsibility—often to the exclusion of human and political considerations—those who are subordinate on the collegiate hierarchy speak of forming "networks" [F3] and using each other as "sounding boards" [A3] in informal and friendship-based advice giving sessions. While top administrators speak with unwavering certainty about a sense of institutional direction that they believe is just as much alive today as it has always been ("spelling out our intentions . . . continuing to reexamine what we're about" [P]), some faculty express feelings of directionlessness. "I get the feeling," said one faculty leader, "that there is not a general plan for the next ten to fifteen years here—what it is that we *can* be. . . . I have yet to hear this articulated" [F5].

In sum, while the upper echelon of administrators at Continental College espouse a fairly rational and straightforward perspective on college life, faculty and academic leaders present it in more complex ways, considering, for example, the rationally based administrative view alongside alternative politically based perspectives.

The Faculty Experience of Delegation

The principle of delegation reserves for the president the job of acquiring resources. Simultaneously it releases him from involvement in the work he delegates to others (e.g., curriculum and instruction) and from the campus life that others create through their work together. Although administrators see the president's self-release from campus events as a necessity, some faculty interpret it as distancing, and others still conceive of it as exclusion: The administrators "sit on the periphery. . . . They are distant. All deliberations occur physically and metaphysically at a distance from us. They don't try to encourage faculty involvement" [F1].

Faculty leaders justify their own and their colleagues noninvolvement—or simply their lack of awareness—concerning resource matters, in various ways. Some, for example, explain that the faculty are uninvolved because "they are not interested" [F2], because "they don't have time" [F3], because they "are so preoccupied with their own bailiwicks" [F1], because financial information "is boring" [F4], and because "we don't need to know each others' salaries and efficiency ratings" [F5]. Some also see themselves as unable to make sense of budgets, either because budgetary data are presented in categories that are too "rough" to interpret meaningfully [F2] or because they lack the skill to think in budgetary terms: "I don't have the expertise to read it" [F4]. Some look beyond themselves and beyond the data as potential causes of their non-involvement, explaining that at Continental this is simply how the system works: "The administrative style here is not to consult with faculty. . . . Faculty have the sense that [the budget] is out of their control" [F5].

In sum, while the college's delegation system effectively releases the president from what would otherwise be an overwhelming responsibility, at least as he describes it, faculty leaders construe the system of delegation as creating distance between themselves and administrators. With the increasing distance, top administrators and faculty appear to disengage from each other's concerns. While the administrators say little about this growing separation—suggesting that perhaps they do not see it— the faculty are acutely aware of it.

The Faculty Experience of "Peace"

Life at Continental College is conducive to the view of peace defined as absence of conflict. There is a feeling here of "continuity" and minimized change, or, as one interviewee describes it, "only as a river changes flowing on" [A1]. The image of stasis suggests that the urge to question, evaluate, challenge, and disagree over the appearance of something new or different—over "disjunctures" [A1] in the flow of institutional continuity—is minimized.

In addition, the structural quality of the college, reflecting the institutionalization of its philosophy of delegation and division of labor, shields the faculty from the noise, bustle, and news generated by administrative activity. For example, the faculty here have little contact with administrators other than those immediately above them on the official hierarchy. And conversely, administrators rarely reach beyond their immediate subordinates. A faculty leader described one of the institution's top administrators in this way: "He believes in the hierarchy and is more concerned with the views of people one notch below him and not five below him. This [mode of interaction] pervades the university and people don't like it' [F1]. The implication of this approach for administrative-faculty relations is that administrators remain within their official niche, keeping the faculty distant physically and cognitively: "[Administration] seems like an alien territory—unfathomable. It becomes an easy target because no one [i.e., faculty] knows who is in the administration building or what they are doing. There is less a sense of community. The initiative must come from them [administrators] to involve us [faculty]" [F2]. Because the college's structural design emphasizes separation and distance, it minimizes the opportunity for differences in views to arise. In minimizing the potential for conflict, it assures a form of "peace."

Some faculty leaders describe themselves as grateful not be caught up in conflict and are careful to prevent any upset. In the words of one, "I don't want to be overly critical" [F3]. Although several faculty interviewees [F2, F4, F5] and at least one administrator [A2] acknowledged, at least briefly, that "too much is done by administrators without faculty consultation" [F5], many also point out that their colleagues are comfortable with things as they are. "They [faculty] may complain," said one, "and the next day they will be happy as a clam to be left alone" [F2].

However, faculty interviewees also make the point that they are not worried about administrative dominance or faculty noninvolvement as such but rather the "mindless system" [F2] and passivity ("we just listened . . ." [F5]) that result. Interviewees explained that as long as the faculty get the resources they want, "people don't complain" [F1]. In the words of one faculty leaders, "We get lulled" [F4].

The flip side of administratively imposed "peace" is the implication that in minimizing the opportunity for conflict, the college simultaneously minimizes the faculty's need to engage in skepticism.

The Faculty Experience of Learning

In the absence of a larger, clearer, and more engaging picture of the college's resource condition, and in light of norms discouraging cross-departmental interaction, what do faculty count on for information at Continental, and what do they see through it?

For some faculty, financial knowledge derives from interpretations offered by colleagues who profess to understand institutional data that they themselves find vague: "[The administrator] puts out a statement [excerpts from the data handbook]—I don't have the expertise to read it or the desire to. I think that people get a distilled version of it from each other. I don't read it, but I have a sense of it because of the distillation" [F1].

Some interviewees also rely on intuition ("I will go with what I can sense" [F2]) or inferences from observations: "We have just finished [putting up a new] building, [and] . . . have finances [for refurbishing] this building. . . . There are good faculty salary raises, . . . the place is clean, . . . painting and repairs [occur promptly]. . . . Nothing looks [like we're in financial trouble]" [F2].

In referring to the condition of the college, several refer to their own departments—the "bailiwicks" [F3] within which they spend their time and to which their attention is riveted by virtue of a college organization that emphasizes "the quality of the delivery of departments" [T]. At Continental, trustees and others assess college progress by examining "line items for various departments" [T], by poring through year-end "departmental reports" [P], and by regularly analyzing student enrollment levels by department [F1]. A faculty leader elaborates: Every unit has the flexibility to run its own shop and it is held accountable for it—by that I mean each department. . . . It means that leadership here is distributed and that multiple people are encouraged to take the ball and to run with it" [F4].

While Continental's budgetary process focuses on academic departments, the college's official governance process underscores that focus: "We don't have a lot of structures or faculty involvement except at the . . . departmental level" [P]. According to a faculty leader, as a result of the college's departmental emphasis, the faculty learn to "retreat into their own bailiwicks." And their knowledge of the institution is filtered through their daily life in their individual departments. In the absence of a larger, shared definition of at least some aspects of institutional reality, the college becomes a conglomerate of multiple, particularistic views and definitions of what is happening, at least as the faculty collectively see that reality.

How does the faculty's view compare to that of trustees and administrators? As noted earlier, through their data handbook, the trustees and administrators have rich access to global (institutional) information, and administrators have access as well to particularistic (departmental) data. Their understanding, however, is limited to statistical and economic interpretation—to the language of the data handbook—and thus, both trustees and administrators miss the human and political dynamics occurring beneath their purely economic interpretations of organization. While giving direction and consistency to their thinking, the data handbook serves to solidify (and restrict) the span of their attention; their interpretation misses the intricacies and richness of the human and political life of their organization.

The realities that the people of Continental College perceive around them are bounded (Dearborn and Simon 1958, Simon 1961) in diverse ways. Faculty members' understandings are bounded largely by their immediate and diverse surroundings, especially by the departmental settings in which they spend most of their time. Administrators' understandings are largely bounded by the data handbook that acts simultaneously as a conceptual frame and as a conceptual blinder. Trustees' understandings are bounded by their reliance on administrative interpretation. Thus, what faculty, administrators, and trustees see and what they believe to be the singular reality of Continental College differs according to their institutional roles. Viewed interpretively, Continental College is not one place, but many."[6]

Evaluation: Reflections on Experience

Continental College has been extremely successful in meeting its financial goals. Admittedly, its administrative and academic processes run like clockwork. From the standpoint of objective measures, this is a financially solid college; and following the conventional wisdom, we might expect to find a relatively satisfied community that may be primarily concerned about maintaining its current level of security. This is, in fact, the view of the president and trustees who assert that the kind of organization and leadership that the college needs now is "exactly what we've got" [T] and that the current "game plan is exactly as it was before . . . to keep the place humming along" [P].

Most faculty leaders agree with administrators that "we need to continue to have fiscal strength" [F1], and they praise the administration's strategy of "letting you feel comfortable . . . confident . . . financially," adding that the institution "has flourished under this president" [F2]. "We have done that so well," said one faculty leader [F3] in reference to the college's financial solidity. And another faculty leader commented on the important contributions of the long-term administrator who brought about the data handbook: "He has been a great force . . . especially fiscally" [F4].

But below this surface of expressed comfort and gratitude, there are signs of searches for something different. Faculty leaders say that, with its financial security, the college can now afford to be "a little more risky" [F3], and that it may be time to "wake the sleeping giant" [F5] and to become a "social actor" [F5] rather than being just "a good neighbor" [F5]. In describing what they need now, some call for leadership that "can articulate what Continental College is about" to its faculty and to a larger external audience [F1], and for leadership that is "more visible, charismatic, dynamic" [F5]. One individual points out that while "it is better to be cautious than reckless, . . . you can be so cautious that you don't act" and that what the college needs now is leadership that is more "aggressive" [F4].

Looking internally, a faculty leader also notes the need for a change—that while "people here like what the leadership has done" for them, they are concerned about "how it has done it." He adds, moreover, that what the faculty need now is "more time spent collegially" [F3]. In focusing on what they and their colleagues need, some briefly paint a picture of a very different institution: "We need . . . a greater sense of collegiality. There is the sense that [the administration] is a big box from which decisions emanate. . . . We have to have people talk to each other and trust that good will come—that things will be more unruly" [F2]. For this interviewee, the goodness of stability has come into question. In invoking "unruliness," he probably calls less for disorder than for a loosening of the constraints of Continental's stability.

These comments suggest that while faculty may appreciate the comfort and security of their stability, several are simultaneously imagining the possibility of a different reality.

Comparing Realities

Several qualities stand out about Continental College as different campus actors experience it. First, in contrast to the assertions of its board chair and its top administrators (particularly the president and the budget administrator), the college, like most institutions of higher education, is a bundle of self-contained contradictions. While the college's top administrators describe it as rational, linear, absolute in form, and uninterrupted by emotive distraction, faculty and academic leaders portray it as political and malleable. While the president and other top administrators believe that the college's rational structure, particularly its system of delegation, is good because it contributes to its efficiency of operation and its task-centeredness, faculty and academic leaders see the division of institutional labor into tasks that are carried out by people working separately rather than jointly as distancing and depersonalizing. While administrators see their rational structuring as providing faculty with the peace that they need to work productively, faculty and academic leaders suggest that the nature of peace at Continental College reflects a noiselessness which, while assuring tranquility, results in a seeming mindlessness that stands counter to the academic ideals of skeptical inquiry and creative productivity.

Second, the persons who seem most attuned to the differences in the realities of administrators and faculty are not the college's formal administrative leaders. Rather, the people who are most aware of contradictory realities for different people in the college are the faculty and academic leaders who have learned to play on the plane of administrative rationality (for example, so that they can make effective budget requests), and who have also mastered the politics and ambiguity that reign below this surface, usually in the faculty's departmental homes. In this institution, unlike many others that I have examined through previous studies (Neumann, in press; 1990b; 1991a), the college's faculty and academic leaders appear more complex (Bensimon, Neumann, and Birnbaum 1989; Birnbaum 1988), behaviorally and cognitively, than their top-level formal leaders. In brief, the faculty leaders of Continental College appear more skilled in exercising double vision than most top administrators.

Third, if we view leadership as the process of defining a reality that others, as followers, come to adopt and use (Smircich and Morgan 1982), then we may think of Continental's leadership as having occurred in the past when the defining originally occurred—for example, when the long-term administrator first created and defined the elements of the budgetary data handbook that people throughout the college eventually adopted as a dictionary for thinking about and responding to financial issues. In contrast, the task of Continental College, at the time of the visits, seemed to be one of maintenance—assuring the continuance of college life within the bounds of those basic handbook definitions established long ago.

Moreover, the task of defining a reality, as opposed to identifying and elaborating issues within a predefined reality, implies two very different forms of learning for college members: First, as I have indicated (Neumann 1990a), the task of defining evokes an image of interpretive or reinterpretive learning, whereby persons question and rethink the base of what they know, often transforming it (see, for example, Argyris 1982, Argyris and Schon 1978, Freire 1984). Second, the task of using predefined concepts or frames to better understand that which yet needs to be addressed (for example, as indicated by previously established definitions) is more consistent with acquisitive than interpretive learning. Through acquisitive learning, people add incrementally to a knowledge base that remains conceptually unchanged (Neumann 1990a). At the time of the research visits, college members' learning appeared to be almost totally acquisitive as they strove to understand their world mostly through the lens of the previously defined data handbook. There were few (if any) attempts at new interpretation or at reinterpretation, except that most of the interviewees in faculty and academic leadership positions voiced a growing need to take a new and different look at the reality around them—for example, urging the college to become more of a "social actor" rather than just "a good neighbor" [F1].

Fourth, Continental College displays diverse forms of "followership." The vice presidents and academic administrators, for example, adopt the definitions that others give to them, actively using those definitions in fulfilling concrete tasks. The president and trustees adopt definitions for more passive purposes—to monitor and control from a distance, interceding only for corrective purposes in a cybernetic (Birnbaum 1988) fashion—while they devote their primary attention to such external responsibilities as garnering institutional support. In this way, the president and trustees act more like followers than leaders in that they relinquish the leader's prerogative to define reality

(Smircich and Morgan 1982) to the handbook originator, whose definitions they then accept. Another group of followers, the faculty, are merely informed or apprised of what is happening, usually in a general way, and serve as targets of dissemination rather than as users of data in a meaningful way. And finally, there are followers (e.g., the long-term administrator who created the handbook) who were definers in the past, and who, in the present, follow only in the lines of their former thinking.

Fifth, the delegation system that administrators count on heavily as the basis of their organizing strategy serves, on the other hand, to relieve top administrators, especially the president, from the interruptions of internal college affairs, particularly with regard to instructional and curricular matters. At the same time, however, this system distances administrators from internal college life as they devote their attention and energies outwardly rather than inwardly. Moreover, this "delegation as distancing" phenomenon manifests itself behaviorally and cognitively. As administrators and faculty build different realities for themselves through work that, by virtue of the delegation scheme, they do apart from each other, their thinking and their knowing of their common campus also separates. While existing in the same locale, they come to know it in very different ways.

Sixth, while the underlying principle of peace, defined as a form of noiselessness, serves to minimize disagreement and destructive conflict, it also appears to mute criticism, questioning, critical thought, and even voice by discouraging the airing of opposing views. Rather than providing opportunities for productive thought and action, peace at Continental College becomes, for some, a lulling.

Seventh, while this camping displays an elaborate information system, the communication that occurs between the administrators and the faculty, who are bureaucratically separated from each other, is very limited. While administrators communicate freely and informally within their own administrative subgroups and with the board, their communication with faculty generally flows in only one direction—from them to the professorial ranks. The means that administrators use to communicate with the faculty resembles a dissemination model whereby administrators send out information with the expectation that faculty will return little or nothing for them to build upon, and which they might then return to the faculty for additional comment. Moreover, the communication that occurs between administrators and faculty is significantly less engaging, cognitively and emotionally, than the communication that occurs within the administrative subgroups and between the president and the trustees. This is probably because the information that the faculty get is less consistent with the faculty's sense of what a college is all about compared to how the trustees and administrators construe a college. The faculty, in fact, get the message that the financial information that they do receive is really intended for another audience.

Where there is engagement, cohesion seems to follow, and thus the trustees and president (and some of the other administrators) form a close and interactive group. Where there is little engagement, cohesion falters and fragmentation often sets in, as it does among the faculty who separate, willing or not, from the administration, and who separate also among themselves as they "retreat into their [departmental] bailiwicks" [F2]. The president of Continental College appears to build a stronger following among his external public, who bind themselves closely to him, than among his faculty, with whom he has fewer emotive ties.

Eighth, while administrators and trustees see their college and their leadership as complete and at its peak, a number of faculty evoke images of incompleteness and unfulfilled possibility. They point especially to the need to think beyond fundamental issues of financial security, even if this means opening the door to conflict and ambiguity, or in the words of one—to a life that is more "unruly" [F3] than their current, highly controlled design. What is striking about the faculty view is its double perspective on financial security as assuring, on the one hand, and confining, on the other. In describing the college's financial status, administrators focus only on the protective aspects of leadership (assuring financial reserves in the event of financial difficulty) but saying little about the constraints on creativity that this approach implies.

Ninth, while administrators present campus life as financially, administratively, and academically balanced and serene, faculty, and academic leaders present an image of internal stress and difficulty as they straddle the demands of administratively defined rationality, on the one hand, and the more human and political aspects of day-to-day departmental life, on the other. They also express a sense of incompleteness and unfulfilled possibility in their institution.

Tenth, administrators' and trustees' learning is more active, concrete, direct, meaningful, and personal than that of faculty. As a result they are more engaged with their context than are the faculty who are relatively disengaged, to the point, as one described it, of feeling "lulled" [F1].

Summary

This study raises an important conceptual issue for scholars of higher education organizations. While the general organizational literature portrays managers and leaders as primarily concerned with acquiring, controlling, and coordinating resources and with buffering the organization's productive or technical core (in this case, the faculty) from environmental intrusions (Kast and Rosenzweig 1985; Katz and Kahn 1978; Pfeffer and Salancik 1978; Scott 1981), proving the disparate realities of Continental College brings into question the degree to which this view can be applied wholesale to higher education settings. What is the price, to an educational institution, of having a leadership that is oriented almost exclusively to the job of resource-hunting and resource-caretaking? What is the educational price of buffering conducted in the name of peace? Although this study cannot address these questions directly because it did not set out to do so, they merit close attention in future research. Three concerns follow.

First, the case of Continental College indicates that stability—of finances, structure, and leadership—is not clearly associated with faculty vitality and improved morale. Rather, the study shows that a leadership and organizational approach that leads to solid finances and clear structures—with little concern for how the faculty experience what it takes to get there—may result in feelings of disengagement or frustration for the faculty.

Second, the case also points out that administrative images of rational control and stability, whether for structures or finances, may shield disordered, political, and stressful internal realities. In doing so, it questions the concept of stress as we commonly think of it. It is possible that there may be as much stress and hardship associated with conditions of balance or equilibrium (i.e., a financially and operationally stable institution) as with unstable conditions (i.e., an institution experiencing resource loss, leadership change, etc.) In the disturbed state, stress is at least acknowledged and, most often, is also addressed. In the balanced state, stress is contained, and little attention is paid to its pervasive presence or the damage it may be wreaking bit by bit. If this conception of stress is accurate, then perhaps we should be as concerned about stable institutions as about those openly experiencing hardship—whether in the form of financial downturn, structural change, conflicts over governance, or leadership turnover.

Third, as scholars of higher education, we all too frequently separate concerns about learning from concerns about leadership, thinking that the job-related or professional learning that leaders and faculty do (for example, about their resource condition or their institutional context generally) is something quite different from the "real academic learning" that students do. This study raises the question of whether we can and should continue to make this distinction. Helping students become critically engaged within their personal, social, and professional contexts has been defined as a primary aim of undergraduate education (Gamson and Associates 1984). It is hard to imagine how faculty who are not critically engaged within their own everyday, professional contexts can deliver effectively on this aim. As administrators and as scholars, we have often wondered how much conflict and upheaval education can tolerate and still remains as good education. This study raises a parallel question: How much stability can it take?

Notes

1. To maintain the confidentiality promised during the research, I have masked numerous features of institutional and personal identity. Continental College is a pseudonym; and although I refer to it as a "college," I use this term in the most generic sense and without reference to any Carnegie (institutional) type. The gender that I ascribe to individuals does not necessarily reflect a person's true gender. All position titles (e.g., president, trustee, department chair, etc.) and all names of official groups (e.g., cabinet, faculty senate, etc.), events, and institutional artifacts are generic, reflecting their general use in the field rather than their specific name in this institution.

2. The case of Continental College shows that institutional stability is anything but a simple construct. People in different roles vary in how they define it and in how they experience it. Moreover, the concept of stability intertwines with many institutional factors including resources, routines, and leadership. At Continental, the overarching aura of stability is reflected in stable resources and stable routines for resource acquisition, allocation, and use; it is further coupled with stable leadership that is oriented toward maintaining routine and secure resource levels. While I emphasize the college's resource condition as my point of entry to this research, I acknowledge also that resources are but one of a host of organizational artifacts that contribute to the construction—and continuous reconstruction—of the reality of stability at Continental College.

3. Interviewees were selected through telephone conversations with an institutional contact person designated by the president. During 1986–87, I relied heavily on the contact person's advice in selecting interviewees; in 1988–89, with a base of experience in the institution, I requested interviews with specific persons. In 1988–89 I typically reinterviewed one-third of the people originally interviewed in 1986–87; the remaining interviewees included individuals whose names were mentioned in the course of the earlier interviews or who had assumed positions previously occupied by others.

   The three-day campus visits consisted of one-to-one interviews usually in the administrator's or faculty member's office or, when this was not possible, in a room reserved specifically for my use. In 1988–89 the interview protocol asked individuals to provide their perceptions of: (1) changes in the college's financial status, college-wide morale, campus governance, and quality, (2) leadership activities and interactions with others on campus, especially about financial matters, (3) the nature of the college's resource base (including the interviewee's approach to assessing its viability), (4) critical campus incidents and how they were addressed, and (5) perceptions of campus leadership and what individuals learned from occupying leadership roles or from observing others who held them.

4. The time span of the study is 1986–87 through 1988–89. While base-line data collected during 1986–87 were critical to the research project, this analysis draws more heavily on the data collected during the follow-up visit in 1988–89.

5. Comparisons were based on the "Higher Education Prices and Price Indexes" (Research Associates 1988).

6. After rereading the field notes for the 1986 research visit to Continental College, I wrote: "I am left with the following impressions—that the faculty live in one world, the administration in another, and that the primary home of the faculty is the departmental structure."

   After the 1988–89 visit, I added another note of my overridding impression: "This institution is bureaucratic and hierarchical—this is how [the president and other administrators] characterize it. They see rational principles . . . tying levels together. . . . However, once you get inside this organization and past the [words that the administrators use to frame their worlds], it is not that clean or clear-cut. . . . There is jousting, scheming, and lobbying. . . . There are complaints and unhappiness. There are concerns about the . . . character of this institution. There are concerns about . . . who's really in charge. There is a voiced desire for change. . . . This institution appears very fragmented, and faculty are so very clearly tuned into their departments as their universes."

Bibliography

Argyris, Chris. "The Executive Mind and Double-Loop Learning." *Organizational Dynamics* 11 (1982): 5–22.

Argyris, Chris, and Donald Schön. *Organizational Learning*. Reading, Mass.: Addison-Wesley, 1978.

Bartunek, Jean M. "Changing Interpretive Schemes and Organizational Restructuring: The Example of a Religious Order." *Administrative Science Quarterly* 29 (September 1984): 355–72.

Bartunek, Jean M. "The Dynamics of Personal and Organizational Reframing." In *Paradox and Transformation, Toward a Theory of Change in Organization and Management*, edited by Robert E. Quinn and Kim S. Cameron, 137–62. Cambridge, Mass.: Ballinger Publishing Company, 1988.

Bennis, Warren G., Kenneth D. Benne, and Robert Chin. *The Planning of Change*. 2nd ed. New York: Holt, Rinehart, and Winston, 1969.

Bensimon, Estela M. "Viewing the Presidency: Perceptual Congruence Between Presidents and Leaders on Their Campuses." *Leadership Quarterly* 1, no. 2 (1990): 71–90.

_____. "The Social Processes through Which Faculty Shape the Image of New President." *Journal of Higher Education* 62, no. 6 (November/December 1991): 637–60.

Bensimon, Estela M., Anna Nuemann, and Robert Birnbaum. *Making Sense of Administrative Leadership: The 'L' Word in Higher Education*. ASHE-ERIC Higher Education Report No. 1. Washington, D.C.: School of Education and Human Development, George Washington University, 1989.

Berger, Peter L., and Thomas Luckmann. *The Social Construction of Reality*. London: Penguin, 1973.

Birnbaum, Robert. *How Colleges Work, The Cybernetics of Academic Organization and Leadership*. San Francisco, Calif.: Jossey-Bass Publishers, 1988.

Cameron, Kim S., Myung U. Kim, and David A. Whetten 1987. "Organizational Effects of Decline and Turbulence." *Administrative Science Quarterly* 32, no. 2 (June 1987): 222–40.

Chaffee, Ellen E. "Successful Strategic Management in Small Private Colleges." *Journal of Higher Education* 55, no. 2 (1984): 212–41.

Chaffee, Ellen E., and William G. Tierney. *Collegiate Culture and Leadership Strategies*. New York: American Council on Eduction and Macmillan Publishing Company, 1988.

Cyert, Richard M. "The Management of Universities of Constant or Decreasing Size." *Public Administration Review* 4 (July/August 1978): 344–49. Reprint No. 20, *University Administration*, Carnegie-Mellon University.

Daft, Richard L. "Symbols in Organizations: A Dual-Content Framework for Analysis." In *Organizational Symbolism*, edited by Louis R. Pondy, Gareth Morgan, Peter J. Frost, and Thomas C. Dandridge, 199–206. Greenwich, Conn.: JAI Press, 1983.

Dandridge, Thomas C., Ian Mitroff, and William F. Joyce. "Organizational Symbolism: A Topic to Expand Organizational Analysis." *Academy of Management Review* 5, no. 1 (1980): 77–82.

Dearborn, DeWitt C., and Herbert A. Simon. *Sociometry* 21 (1958): 140–44.

Downs, George W., and Lawrence B. Mohr. "Conceptual Issues in the Study of Innovation." *Administrative Sciences Quarterly* 21 (December 1976): 700–14.

Erickson, Frederick. "Qualitative Methods in Research on Teaching." In *Handbook of Research on Teaching*, edited by Merlin C. Wittrock, 119–61, 3rd ed. New York: Macmillan, 1986.

Ford, Jeffrey D., and David A. Baucus. "Organizational Adaptation to Performance Downturns: An Interpretation-Based Perspective." *Academy of Management Review* 12, no. 2 (1987): 366–80.

Freire, Paulo. *Pedagogy of the Oppressed.* New York: Continuum, 1984.

Frost, Peter J., Larry F. Moore, Meryl Reis Louis, Craig C. Lundberg, and Joanne Martin, eds. *Reframing Organizational Culture.* Newbury Park, Calif.: Sage, 1991.

Gamson, Zelda F., and Associates. *Liberating Education.* San Francisco, Calif.: Jossey-Bass Publishers, 1984.

Isabella, Lynn A. "Evolving Interpretations as a Change Unfolds: How Managers Construe Key Organizational Events." *Academy of Management Journal* 33, no. 1 (March 1990): 7–41.

Kast, Fremont E., and James E. Rosenzweig. *Organization and Management, A Systems and Contingency Approach,* 4th ed. New York: McGraw-Hill Book Company, 1985.

Katz, Daniel, and Robert L. Kahn. *The Social Psychology of Organizations,* 2nd ed. New York: John Wiley and Sons, 1978.

Lewin, Kurt. "Frontiers in Group Dynamics." *Human Relations* 1 (1947): 5–41.

Morgan, Gareth; Peter J. Frost, and Louis R. Pondy. "Organizational Symbolism." In *Organizational Symbolism,* edited by Louis R. Pondy, Gareth Morgan, Peter J. Frost, and Thomas C. Dandridge, 3–35. Greenwich, Connecticut: JAI Press, 1983.

Munson, Fred C., and Donald C. Pelz. *Innovating in Organizations: A Conceptual Framework.* Ann Arbor: The University of Michigan, Institute for Social Research, 1981.

Neumann, Anna. "Making Mistakes: Error and Learning in the College Presidency." *Journal of Higher Education* 61, no. 4: (July/August 1990a): 386–407.

_____. "On the Making of 'Good Times' and 'Hard Times': The Social Construction of Resource Stress." Paper presented at the annual meeting of the Association for the Study of Higher Education, Portland, Oregon, November 1990b.

_____. "A Case Analysis of Collegiate Leadership and Cultural Change." Paper presented at the annual meeting of the American Education Research Association, Chicago, Illinois, April 1991a.

_____. "The Thinking Team: Toward a Cognitive Model of Administrative Teamwork in Higher Education." *Journal of Higher Education* 62, no. 5 (September/October 1991b): 485–513.

_____ "College Under Pressure: Budgeting, Presidential Competence, and Faculty Uncertainty," *The Leadership Quarterly,* in press.

Peterson, Marvin W. "Decline, New Demands, and Quality: The Context for Renewal." *The Review of Higher Education* 7, no. 3 (Spring 1984a): 187–203.

_____. "In a Decade of Decline, the Seven R's of Planning." *Change* 16, no. 4 (May/June 1984b): 43–46.

Pfeffer, Jeffrey. "Management as Symbolic Action: The Creation and Maintenance of Organizational Paradigms." *Research in Organizational Behavior* 3 (1981): 1–52.

Pfeffer, Jeffrey, and Gerald G. Salancik. *The External Control of Organizations: A Resource Dependency Perspective.* New York: Harper and Row, 1978.

Research Associates of Washington. "Higher Education Prices and Price Indexes: 1988 Update," Washington, D.C., September 1988.

Rosenholtz, Susan J. *Teachers' Workplace: The Social Organization of Schools*. New York: Longman Press, 1989.

Rubin, Irene. "Universities in Stress: Decision Making Under Conditions of Reduced Resources." *Social Science Quarterly* 58, no. 2 (September 1977): 242–54.

Schatzman, Leonard, and Anselm L. Strauss. *Field Research, Strategies for a Natural Sociology*. Englewood Cliffs, NJ.: Prentice-Hall, Inc., 1973.

Schutz, Alfred. *On Phenomenology and Social Relations*. Chicago: University of Chicago Press, 1970.

Scott, W. Richard. *Organizations: Rational, Natural, and Open Systems*. Englewood Cliffs, N.J.: Prentice-Hall, 1981.

Simon, Herbert A. *Administrative Behavior*. New York: Macmillan, 1961.

Smircich, Linda, and Gareth Morgan. "Leadership: The Management of Meaning." *Journal of Applied Behavioral Science* 18, no. 3 (1982): 257–73.

Tierney, William G. "Symbolism and Presidential Perceptions of Leadership." *The Review of Higher Education* 12, no. 2 (Winter 1989): 153–66.

Van Maanen, John. *Tales of the Field, On Writing Ethnography*. Chicago: University of Chicago Press, 1988.

Whetten, David A. "Effective Administrators: Good Management on the College Campus." *Change* 16, no. 8 (November/December 1984): 38–43.

Yin, Robert K. *Case Study Research: Design and Methods*. Beverly Hills, Calif.: Sage, 1984.

Zaltman, Gerald, and Robert Duncan. *Strategies for Planned Change*. New York: John Wiley and Sons, 1977.

Zammuto, Raymond F. "Managing Declining Enrollments and Revenues." In *Key Resources on Higher Education Governance, Management, and Leadership* edited by Marvin W. Peterson and Lisa A. Mets, 347–65. San Francisco, Calif.: Jossey-Bass Publishers, 1987.

Re-Visioning Leadership in Community Colleges

Marilyn J. Amey and Susan B. Twombly

From its modest beginnings as small junior colleges has emerged a system of community colleges that enrolls millions of credit/non-credit, non-traditional/traditional students from all racial, ethnic, gender, and social class groups. This system has been labeled the success story of twentieth-century U.S. education (Breneman and Nelson, 1981). However, the generation of leaders who oversaw two decades of tremendous growth during the 1960s and 1970s is approaching retirement, and the system faces an inevitable transition in leadership.

This transition has not gone unheralded. Jess Parrish, president of Midland Community College in Midland, Texas, summarized: "The alarm has been sounded in speeches, articles, reports, and conversations among colleagues: the first generation of great community college leadership is passing from the scene, and its replacement is uncertain" (1988, [1]). The changing of the guard is understandably a concern for community colleges because, as Dale Tillery and William Deegan observed, "No other educational institution has been so shaped and promoted by so few leaders as has the community college" (1985, 14). The importance of leadership is heightened because most community colleges are entering stages in their organizational life cycles at which they are on the verge of renewal or decline. Appropriate leadership may be the key variable in determining whether the community college movement as a whole and individual colleges are able to engage in effective renewal or whether they will enter a period of decline.

The type of leadership behavior and qualities sought in new leaders in community colleges, as in all organizations, is influenced by context and the particular demands of a social situation (Selznick 1984). We argue, drawing on insights from discourse analysis and organizational life cycle theory, that ideas about leadership are also shaped and constrained by beliefs and images about the kind of leadership called for and the characteristics required in those who assume leadership positions. The language in which these images are communicated serves both symbolic and political purposes—defining legitimate leadership regardless of contextual demands for leadership. Obviously, the consequences of images that no longer fit can hamper the effectiveness of an institution.

A striking element about the language of community college leadership literature is the vivid descriptors and images that have been used over time. Although critical, conceptual, or theoretical discussions of institutional leadership may be rare, the scholarship is so replete with heroic images of leaders, triumphantly constructing this unique sector of higher education, that the literature on four-year college leaders seems pale by comparison. The reader may question the "what" of community college leadership but the "who" of leadership is never in doubt. The certainty, perpetuated through vivid imagery, about the desired and even necessary style of community college leaders invited a more critical analysis of that language from the early 1900s to the present. We feel certain that those images will, in the absence of purposeful intervention, shape future community college leadership.

Our purposes in this study were to (1) identify the images and rhetoric of leadership in junior / community colleges; (2) observe the sociohistorical and organizational context of these images; and (3) examine the effect of images and rhetoric on leadership behavior—specifically on the types of individuals who could be considered leaders and on the future of leadership in community colleges. Jess Parrish noted, "A generation of community college lore is available to current and up-and-coming leaders, and the smart ones are using it" (1988, [1]). It is that lore, as evidenced in published materials, which we are going to critically examine. In short, we are going to engage in what author Adrienne Rich calls re-visioning: "The act of looking back, of seeing with fresh eyes, of entering an old text from a new critical direction" (Kolodny 1985, 59). By engaging in the process of re-visioning, we hope to provide the basis for developing new models of effective leadership that reflect not only changes in the organizational life cycle but changes in the rhetoric and images of leadership.

Discourse Analysis

Our purpose is to analyze and question the dominant ideology that has permeated the community college leadership literature from two perspectives: (1) to question the relevance of the images of leadership for the different stages in the organizational life cycle through which community colleges have developed, and more importantly, (2) to question how the ideologies behind these images of leadership have maintained a particular type of leader and have excluded or severely limited access to leadership positions by those who do not fit that specific image. This critical perspective allows us to move away from assumptions so fundamental that they have been taken as objective truths and instead focus on the literature as social constructions of leadership, where social and historical contexts are important considerations.

Our approach to the research tasks was grounded generally in critical theory and more specifically in discourse analysis. F. Michal Connelly and D. Jean Clandinin (1990) argue that narrative inquiry—the study of texts—is both a phenomenon and method. And so, we argue, is discourse analysis both a framework for looking at the community college literature and a way of analyzing what we found. Richard Terdiman defines discourse as "the complexes of signs and practices which organize social existence and social reproduction" (Giroux 1988, 219). Discourse encompasses such "signs and practices" as language and narrative or stories.

Critical theorists whose work is based in an analysis of discourse believe that discourse serves very important social functions, giving "differential substance to membership of a social group or class or formation, which mediate[s] an internal sense of belonging, and outward sense of other-ness" (Terdiman in Giroux 1988, 219). Sociologists and social psychologists point out how discourse becomes an instrument for consolidating and manipulating concepts and relationships in areas of power and control as well as other areas of ideological / social structure (e.g., Gergen 1988; Potter and Wetherell 1987; Shotter and Logan 1988). Language is used to enforce existing positions of authority, exploit privilege, give a sense of belonging, or communicate a sense of otherness in both obvious and subtle ways. The intentional use of language reinforces the status and roles on which people base their claims to exercise power and, in turn, those which perpetuate subservience (Fowler 1985).

Because the dominant class has the power to make and perpetuate meaning through its control of language and its dissemination through such outlets as scholarly journals, we can see that language is not only a reflection of inequality but that it, in effect, fosters inequality and operates as censorship, exclusion, blockage, and repression (Michel Foucault in Cherryholmes 1988, 34–36). In the United States, the dominant class consists largely of white, middle- or upper-class men. By constructing and reiterating certain selected images, phrases, and stories the dominant class can insist that a selected set of concepts make up social reality. In our case, we found that a relatively few writers have created, used, and perpetuated persuasive images of leadership in community colleges.

For those who match these images, it obviously benefits them to maintain, reinforce, and legitimate that particular understanding of the world, "regardless of how incomplete it may be" (Nielson 1990, 11). But obviously some groups are excluded. Dale Spender (1980) argues that as white men have constituted the dominant class, women (and by implication, blacks and other nondominant groups) have largely been excluded from formulations of cultural meanings, including their production of forms of thought, images, and symbols. She points out that women are forced to use language which they had no role in creating but which has become so ingrained in organizational culture that changing the language or accepting new images is very difficult.

Discourse often refers to spoken language, but Emile Benveniste emphasizes that the written word (texts)—for our purposes, scholarly books and articles—are also legitimate discourse and part of the social world (Cherryholmes 1988). As an active shaper of administrative culture and practice, scholarly discourse should be open to critical scrutiny from all sectors. Cleo Cherryholmes (1988) asserts that constructs and discourses, particularly of professional life, are often accepted with little analysis or criticism. In not being critical in our analysis of the language used in scholarship, we continue to replicate text, talk, and images as though they were natural, required, or predestined descriptions of reality; the present social order is legitimated.

Our analysis of community college leadership literature builds from these perspectives. We use discourse analysis as a means of focusing "reflexively" on "the rhetorical structure" of knowledge (Warren 1988, 48). To determine what a word means, one looks to the discourse and not just to the word. To determine what a discourse means, we need to examine its history, culture, politics, economics, conventions, and institutions to account for how it operates to produce "truth" and what is said. Rules of inclusion and exclusion are sometimes explicit, sometimes implicit; they govern what is said, what remains unsaid, who can speak with authority, and who must listen. The rules of discourse are based on ideas, concepts, values, and power arrangements that both transcend and ground what is said and done (Cherryholmes 1988, 33; Lather 1991, 86–92).

Through the use of discourse analysis, we begin to grasp how such features of the social context as gender, status, power, and roles impact on the style, thematic structure, or cognitive interpretation of text and talk (van Dijk 1985, 4–5). Using this analytic approach allows the researcher to do more than just say that there are differences; it illuminates how the participants in a given social interaction enact social roles, show power, and exert control through language. Discourse analysis also reminds the researcher of the part that literature and research (discourse) play in reproducing larger societal problems, "in social and political decision procedures, and in institutional management and representation of such issues" (van Dijk 1885, 7).

In short, an approach to a body of literature rooted in discourse analysis brings to the fore a different set of conceptual questions about knowledge and meaning than those typically asked. Whose knowledge is represented in the literature? What is the context of this knowledge? Whose meaning is perpetuated by word and action? In looking at leadership issues, whose issues do we focus on? Whose definitions of leadership are perpetuated as real? The focus of our discourse analysis moves to the different meanings that images and expectations of leadership can have, according to the ideological position of those images' creators. We can also determine the effects of the sociohistorical conditions in which these symbols have been produced.

Organizational Life Cycle Theory

The organizational life cycle of the junior/community college provides an appropriate sociohistoric context within which to analyze leadership. Kim Cameron (1984) suggests that organizations progress through at least four sequential, though recyclable, stages with recognizable characteristics and general problems to overcome. He emphasizes the important role managers play in facilitating or impeding progress through the organizational adaptations. More specifically, an organizational structure or leadership style effective at one stage of development may be inappropriate or even dysfunctional at another (Greiner 1972; Cameron and Zammuto 1983). Therefore we would expect to observe different leadership images, expectations, and styles associated with organizational structure and mission at various stages in community college development.

Although there are many life cycle schema from which to choose, we have selected John Gardner's (1986) four-stage organizational life cycle, in conjunction with Deegan and Tillery's (1985) description of generations of community college development to provide a sociohistoric context for our analysis. Gardner's stages are (1) birth, corresponding roughly to Deegan and Tillery's first generation, (2) growth, corresponding to Deegan and Tillery's second and third generations, (3) maturity, corresponding to Deegan and Tillery's fourth generation, and (4) renewal or decline, corresponding to Deegan and Tillery's fifth generation. The community college movement and most individual community colleges have experienced the first three of these stages and now face the challenges of renewing mature colleges (Hudgins 1990). If Larry Greiner's (1972) description of stage-style match is correct, then we would expect analysts and scholars to advocate different leadership expectations and styles for this new period in organizational development. In the discourse on leadership in each new organizational life stage and context, we would also expect to find different images of leadership with different meanings ascribed to those images as stages change.

Data Analysis

We undertook a comprehensive examination of the community college leadership literature from the early 1900s to the present. This literature base included published articles and books as well as unpublished materials found in *Resources in Education*, conference and workshop materials provided by the American Association of Community and Junior Colleges, and *Leadership Abstracts* published by the League of Innovation in the Community College. We conducted this review of the literature, or scholarly discourse, according to the stages of the community college life cycle identified by Gardner (1986) and Tillery and Deegan (1985), following existing guidelines for engaging in discourse analysis. Within this broad framework, we were interested in identifying the organizational context and structure, expectations of leadership, and most importantly, the images and language used to describe and reinforce leadership.

Tillery and Deegan segment the evolution of two-year colleges into five generations based on institutional characteristics. We discuss each of these periods according to tasks of leadership associated with organizational growth and development:

1. Tillery and Deegan's High School Extension, 1900–30. We call this period Birth and Youth.

2. Tillery and Deegan's period of the Junior College, approximately 1930–50. We discuss this period under the heading, "Changing Expectations."

3. Tillery and Deegan's generation of the Community College 1950–70. We discuss this metamorphosis of junior colleges into larger, more comprehensive schools under the heading "Growth and Maturation" along with their fourth category.

4. Tillery and Deegan's generation of the Comprehensive Community College, mid-1970s to mid-1980s. We discuss this development under "Growth and Maturation."

5. Tillery and Deegan did not have an appropriate label in 1985 for contemporary times. We discuss what seems to be an emerging fifth generation under the heading, "Alternative Images."

Clearly, the years associated with each period are somewhat arbitrary; and while many junior colleges may have become comprehensive by the mid-1970s, surely not all had. The years associated with the Tillery and Deegan schemata should be used as guidelines rather than as definitive "watershed" dates. Likewise, many others wrote both retrospectively and about the present, making it inaccurate to associate particular authors and sources with specific periods. Many of the most telling images of leadership emerged out of attempts to characterize the past in a way that made sense to contemporary scholars. Indeed, it is partially the point of this paper that Jesse Bogue, for example, writing in 1950, or Steven Brint and Jerome Karabel in 1989, chose to characterize early leaders as they did.

As with other forms of meta-analysis, there are several viable approaches to discourse analysis. We relied on Cherryholmes's approach to post-structural criticism; it involves a five-step, interdependent process of reading, interpretation, criticism, communication, and evaluation and judgment (1988, 153–77). As we read, we looked for stories within the texts, stories which are connected to and by "codes in language, culture, and society." These stories are subject to multiple readings and submit to different tellings. The overlapping meanings which result connect reading with the next step in the process—interpretation—as a means of "getting from the said and read, to the unsaid" (Robert Scholes in Cherryholmes 1988, 155–56). In this way, we, the researchers, engage in interpretation, which will eventually become a new story or text.

It is important to emphasize at this point the role of the reader and the complex of perspectives and biases she or he brings to the task of reading and interpreting the text. This phenomenon has been emphasized by feminist literary critics. (See, for example, Annette Kolodny, 1985.) Readers of this article, for example, may not agree with our interpretation of the literature; however, we assume that multiple interpretations of any text are possible. Interpretation of texts allows for the identification of binary distinction/oppositions, metaphors, models, modes of argumentation, inferences, and repetitions within a larger context. We move from noting the cultural codes to understanding the attitudes taken toward the codes by the makers of the text.

During the third step, criticism, variant readings of the literature emerge, some of them different from the traditional and dominant interpretations of the text. These variant interpretations are especially important when texts present themselves as "objective" descriptions of the way things really are. In this step of the process, the reader evaluates, discusses, examines, and questions the categories, orientations, and metaphors distinguished during the identification step of the process. "Reading produces stories," says Cherryholmes. ". . . Interpretation provides context. Criticism brings to light and evaluates that which narrative and interpretation has omitted, suppressed, devalued, silenced, and opposed as well as what has been claimed, asserted, and argued" (1988, 159).

Criticism, like interpretation, depends on the perspectives and background of the critiquing individual. The results of moving through these first three stages of discourse analysis do not necessarily lead to some "new truth." But the process has brought us to a place where we may enter the fourth stage—communicating to others the criticisms of the literature which we discovered during our reading and interpretation. Those who use or respond to our work will continue the discourse on community college leadership.

Our analysis of the community college leadership literature produced two major findings. First, the discourse used to recount the organizational development of the community college sector continuously reinforces the ideology of both a particular institution—the community college—and a specific dominant class—a relatively small group of white male scholars and practitioners. The discourse has crystallized into relevancy a set of concepts about community colleges such as constant change, democratic ideals concerning their role in society, and powerful autocratic leaders. By continually speaking and writing in heavily value-laden images, community college scholars and practitioners (and even their critics) have been able to maintain a strong sense of cohesion, organizational definition, and professional boundaries over time. From an organizational development perspective, this pattern may have been critical in the early stages of birth and growth; however, it may be ineffective as a means of addressing organizational renewal if ideas about effective leadership are inappropriate to critical organizational tasks.

Second, the effect of such writing has been the systematic exclusion of, or failure to include, those who do not use the same language, exhibit the characteristic behaviors, or fit the symbolic image of leadership perpetuated by "mainstream" authors who have been almost exclusively white men. The community college literature rings with pervasive and persuasive nouns, verbs, and phrases which create and reinforce a particular image of leadership—the "great man" (both literally and figuratively). This image, we argue, precludes others from being seen as legitimate leaders and shapers of the community college future.

Birth and Youth: Images of the 1900–1930s

Jesse Bogue, former president of the American Association of Junior Colleges (AAJC) said, "The community college is not an institution. It is a movement" (1950, 239). A strong case can be made that, during the first half-century of junior college existence, the "movement" had leaders and individual institutions had administrators. Prominent university leaders like Alexis Lange of the University of California, William Rainey Harper of the University of Chicago, Henry Tappan of the University of Michigan, and David Starr Jordan of Stanford, and successive generations of national junior/community college leaders generally are credited with conceptualizing the idea of the junior college and solidifying the junior college's position in the structure of the U.S. educational system by developing, rationalizing, and communicating a mission and organizational form. In short, these few men are widely credited with creating and molding the paradigm for the contemporary comprehensive community college. Although it is doubtful that university leaders like Harper were actually involved in the development of individual junior colleges (Ratcliff 1987), the junior college literature almost universally cites their instrumental role in developing the junior/community college movement.

The paradigm offered by these "great men" was often at odds with the views of faculty, students, and parents, further reinforcing their influence (Brint and Karabel 1989). The "great man" theory of leadership dominated during this early period (Ratcliff 1987). These few early leaders actually wrote very little about leadership *per se*; however, they modeled a style of leadership about which others wrote admiringly; and as models, they continue to define normative leadership even in the 1990s. Consequently, it is from those who wrote about these "great men" and their role in the junior college movement that we get our ideas about leadership during the birth and youth periods.

The founding of the American Association of Junior Colleges in 1920 and the rising influence of Leonard Koos, Walter Eells, and Doak Campbell had more long-term impact on the identity and mission of these fledgling institutions than did their university benefactors. Koos, Eells, and Campbell are universally regarded as the movement's first real leaders—leaders it could call its own, leaders committed totally to the development of the junior college for its own sake. Koos and Eells were both university professors; and Campbell, a former college president, was the first president of AAJC. These men have been described as missionaries of middle-class, small-town, religious backgrounds who were educated in small colleges (Brint and Karabel 1989; Goodwin 1971). The motives ascribed to these men, like those of their Progressive contemporaries, were those of searching for a means of uplifting society; junior colleges, they believed, would help channel students to their proper station in an orderly and efficient society (Brint and Karabel 1989; Goodwin 1971).

Even more interesting for this study is how authors have described junior colleges and their leaders in frontier, pioneer, and military images. George Zook, a higher education specialist for the U.S. Department of Education and a contributing author of the influential President's Commission on Higher Education Report (1947), described the junior college movement in 1940 "as an army of 'struggling frontiersmen' put together by 'General Koos and Colonel Eells and Campbell,' who then led them into all parts of the country, even storm(ing) the New England citadel" (Brint and Karabel 1989, 35). Steven Brint and Jerome Karabel then comment: "The analogy is apt in may ways. These intellectual commanders did undertake a massive job of organization. They did lead their recruits to fight many battles before their institutions were accepted, and many more before their vision of the junior colleges became widely adopted" (1989, 35).

Brint and Karabel further reinforce the vivid images portrayed by Zook, as other contemporary community college writers repeatedly do, by describing Koos, Eells, and Campbell as the "vanguard" (also a military term) of the community college movement. They not only created and established a paradigm for two-year postsecondary education, which they helped to institutionalize, but also, according to Brint and Karabel's thesis, they and their successors successfully refocused the junior/community college's focus from transfer to vocational mission, despite the wishes of students, faculty, and parents. Although one may disagree with the motives Brint and Karabel attribute to these men, Koos, Eells, and Campbell were transformational leaders in the truest meaning of the term. Furthermore, Koos, Eells, and Campbell groomed a generation of junior/community college men to take their places—including Jesse Bogue, Joseph Cosand, Leland Medsker, S.V. Martorana, Raymond Schultz, and Edmund Gleazer, to name but a few. More recently still, Arthur Cohen, John Roueche, George Vaughan, and Dale Parnell, among others, have assumed prominence on the national level while a group of college presidents has also gained attention, among them, William Priest, Judith Eaton, Robert McCabe, and Larry Tyree.

In this early period, presidents of AAJC were identified as important leaders of the movement. Through its annual meeting and journal, the AAJC served as a forum for the discussion and spread of ideas. Early AAJC presidents like Doak Campbell and Jesse Bogue are portrayed as having particular influence on the institutionalization and rationalization of a paradigm for the modern comprehensive community college. We argue that as the movement itself and individual institutions have matured, the influence of campus leaders has increased, while the direct influence of the AACJC (formerly AAJC) presidents have decreased—although they each made an attempt at transforming the overall mission of the community college in some way. For example, Edmund Gleazer (1980) advocated that community colleges become the "nexus" of community activity— perhaps even dropping the designation "college." More recently, Dale Parnell pressed for a reemphasis on the vocational mission through a 2 (high school) + 2 (community college) plan for the "neglected majority" (1985, 14). Although his book sold thousands of copies, the concept of tracking students into a community college vocational program in the tenth grade has not been widely embraced.

Several factors affected expectations and actions of early *institutional* leaders, notably the newness of the two-year college as an educational form and its relationship to the public school. Heads of private junior colleges, of which there were many in this early period, held the title of president, while early public junior college leaders held the title of dean and typically reported to district school superintendents or principals, reflecting organizational relationships with public school districts (Brothers, 1928; and Green in Eells 1931; Lee and Rosenstengel 1938). Interestingly, the second most important administrative position in these early colleges was the dean of women (Eells 1931; Foster 1933; Hill 1927). Unfortunately, little is written about this position or the women who held it after the early treatises on the junior college.

Early authors were not satisfied with the status, duties, or roles of these early college deans. A post-structuralist classification of objects would find a binary opposition in leadership discourse between the active images of "pioneer," "commander," and "builder" and the passive image of the "errand boy," who has few significant responsibilities and little power. Proctor (1927) noted that the dean of the junior college should be a general advisor to students. Fifteen years later, J.R. Johnson, president of the Nebraska Association of Junior Colleges, and W.W. Carpenter, professor of education at the University of Missouri doubted that "deans actually have the position of educational leader." Do they not "merely carry out the instructions of the board of education and superintendent of schools?", they asked, and quoted an unnamed dean as asking, "I wonder if the dean of public junior college isn't after all, primarily an errand boy?" (1942, 381). They concluded, based on a survey, that deans were not over-burdened with responsibilities and were not given much latitude in critical areas of policy making.

Eells, looking toward the future, said: "It is plainly evident that many of the deans were denied, in whole or in part, important administrative functions" and quoted Green, who agreed but also argued that the rapidly developing junior college presented unlimited opportunities for leadership ability and that deans must be prepared and willing to assume such functions (1931, 372).

Changing Expectations: Images of the 1930s–50s

In the 1940s and 1950s, a change in the imagery describing desirable and actual leadership practices began to emerge in the writings about junior colleges. Tillery and Deegan (1985) describe these two decades as the period during which leaders began to seek college identity and to gain independence from the secondary schools.

In 1951, Pierce described a line-staff relationship between presidents and deans of junior colleges. He saw the president as the leader in policy making, the liaison between the board of control and the college, and the chief public relations and chief business officer. Pierce concluded, "It appears, then, that junior colleges are coming more and more to have two general administrative officers, a chief administrator most often called 'president' and a second in command called 'dean'; and with the line-and-staff administrative organization, the other administrative officers are usually co-ordinates of equal rank serving under the leadership of the president and the dean" (1951, 366).

Recognizing the importance of the board of control to leadership of the college, Bogue insisted that "standards and practices should be revised to include definite provisions for preparation, functions and limitations of the *supreme* elected officers" (1950, 282; italics ours). Use of *supreme* leaves little doubt of his feeling that junior colleges should be governed by their own boards and that these boards should take charge. The chief executive officer, he stated, must be directly responsible to the board of control. Furthermore, this chief executive officer was expected to delegate authority as well as assume it. "Be in command, if that is your assignment," he approvingly quoted James C. Miller, president of Christian College. "Never by autocratic, but always be in command. No one feels secure with an administrator who is vacillating and weak. Always be fair, but be positive and constructive in performing your administrative duties" (1950, 287). Bogue then describes the ideal junior/community college leader:

> Especially for the community college, one needs an element of inspiration, the spirit of the pioneer and a sense of thrilling adventure. The quality referred to is sometimes called inspiring leadership ability. While it must have a foundation in character that creates confidence, sound judgement that enlists respect, intellectual honesty and scholarship that men trust, it nevertheless reaches beyond these characteristics. It is almost indefinable: one applauds the star when he appears on stage; the colorful gamey athlete when he runs onto the playing field; the rugged, courageous sea captain when he takes command of his ship. Just as one knows the difference between a day of sunshine and one of shadows so one knows the difference between a leader and a follower. It might be represented by the

sharp line between the batter who "steps into it" when the balls come over the plate and the other who hesitates. (1950, 299)

On the same page, he adds yet another image: "The kingpin is the chief executive. His acumen in financial affairs, his ability to recognize and select the right kind of associates and delegate authority to them, his character, attitudes, and personality that create confidence in all the publics of the college naturally give him the leading role. If he plays his part well, he will have the wholehearted support of his entire cast and the applause of the audience" (1950, 299). There was no question in Bogue's mind or images about the centrality of the president in the junior college.

Bartky spoke directly about the preferred leadership style of presidents in the post-war period. Drawing on his experience in the U.S. Navy, Bartky likened the junior college to a battleship. Because society's objectives for the junior college

> . . . are value judgements approaching absolutes when applied to junior colleges . . . a junior college should approach its objectives in the manner of a well-trained battleship. Society has set its objectives and expects them to be attained. There is no place for debate that frustrates society's designated purposes. It is undemocratic to act in ways that hamper society's designated leadership. The junior college organization has a job to perform and must not dissipate its efforts with too much consideration of the whims of the faculty and with tolerance toward those who would dilly dally with its socially defined purposes. In this way only it can become a truly democratic organization. (1957, 7)

It says much about the character of the times that such openly advocated disregard for faculty opinion can be held up as a "truly democratic" ideal. And commanding this "well-trained battleship," naturally, is the president.

The studies reported here seem to represent the sum total of the published material on leaders and leadership before 1950. Thus, an unanswered historical question is when and how the "errand boy" image disappeared from the consciousness of junior/community college leadership to be replaced by the "commander." Nevertheless, it seems clear that World War II reinforced some of the changes in leadership rhetoric. Lee and Rosenstengel, writing as the conflict in Europe began, observed: "War emphasizes the responsibility of the administrative officer usually called the dean. To him is delegated the grave responsibility of keeping the machinery of the college rolling and in good order and contributing to the total defense of America" (1938, 21). Thus, not only did junior colleges contribute to the orderly assignment of people to their places in life but they also played a part in defending America (Brint and Karabel 1989; Bartky 1957).

The change in title from dean to president occurred between 1930 and 1950, coinciding with the separation of junior colleges from the public schools. Oddly enough, the reasons and conditions surrounding the separation are not discussed in the literature. The imagery of commanders and kingpins coincides with the stage in the history and organizational life cycle of community colleges when the struggle for independence dominated other considerations. Junior college authors seem to have seen this extremely active, even domineering, "great man" leadership style as necessary before the junior college could break away from the public schools and fulfill its "manifest destiny," a phrase George Vaughan applies to the development of community colleges.

By 1972, Richardson, Blocker, and Bender described community colleges as having "autocratic leaders making all the major decisions in the context of rigid bureaucracy, secrecy and attitude, 'if you don't like it, you can leave'" (p. v). The once-positive image of the "commander" leading the ship had given way to the image of the autocrat, which under specific organizational conditions, was not viewed as acceptable by at least some writers. The idea of shared decision-making that Richardson et al. advocated provided a brief interlude in the pursuit of the "great man" ideal of leadership. The contrasts between the "errand boy" of the junior college under control of the public school, and the supreme elected officer, kingpin, gamey athlete, and the commander of the post-war years, and the autocratic leader of the 1960s suggests that the attribution of autocratic leadership styles to community college leaders is, more appropriately, a function of history and organizational life cycle—partially a result of the community college struggle for independence from the public schools, rather than a result of its origins there.

Growth and Maturation: Imagery of the 1960s to mid-1980s

As community colleges continued to develop and more clearly define their educational roles during the 1960s, they entered a period of growth and maturation. Leadership images are still predominantly those of the "commander" and "great man," probably because the explosive growth in the number of community colleges meant that many institutions were individually replicating the earlier historical patterns of the 1940s and 1950s. Many of the characteristics—particularly "inspiration" and a "pioneering" spirit—once attributed to the national leaders in the community college movement became part of the rhetoric used to describe institutional leaders as well. Many new college presidents approached their office in the tradition of those prominent national figures.

John Roueche, George Baker, and Robert Rose, describing the 1960s, characterized them as "times [that] demanded builders, political persuaders, organizers and master plan developers" (1989, 40). The "builders" were great pioneers with great visions who translated their ideas and dreams into programs and buildings. Presidents were (and, as importantly, were expected to be) competitive, innovative, fast-moving, flexible, calculated risk takers, tough, dominating, and ones who played to win (Brint and Karabel 1989; Deegan and Tillery 1985). Even as the administrative infrastructure of the developing community college became more differentiated, most community college presidents continued to adopt the strong authoritarian and power figure role of the early national leaders (Alfred and Smydra 1985, 204).

Institutional growth, increased organizational complexity, and expanded involvement by a wide range of constituents characterized community colleges during the late 1960s and early 1970s. It had been critical that the founding presidents be visionaries, able to engage the community in the concept of community colleges as a viable educational sector, and that they have the quality of inspiring leadership (Bogue 1950). During the period of organizational growth and maturation, community colleges needed presidents who were efficient managers, rather that visionaries. The emphasis of the manager-leader president was on efficiency and increased productivity during the late 1960s and 1970s, coupled with the internal and external environmental changes related to organizational maturity. This inward focus belies a subtle shift in the presidential role from provider of a global community college vision to individual institutional vision, although not all presidents effectively communicated local visions. In many cases, college presidents were unwilling, unable, or at least very hesitant to clearly interpret and articulate their institutional missions to relevant constituency groups (Hall and Alfred 1985; Vaughan 1988). Sometimes this silence resulted in constituent confusion and disenchantment; but, in fact, during this period when community colleges truly attempted to be "all things to all people," there may have been benefits in not attempting to clarify mission.

Community colleges as educational organizations approaching maturity during the late 1970s no longer faced rapid expansion or abundant funding. Roueche et al. suggest that this slowed growth "resulted in myopic vision" (1989, 116) in community college leaders which, in turn, eventually led to constituent demands for reinforcing a broader, comprehensive sense of institutional identity. In looking to the 1990s and beyond, James Hudgins, president of Midlands Technical College, captures the growth of community college organizations in these life cycle images: "Most [community colleges] experienced the excitement of birth in the 1960s, the headiness of growth in the 1970s, and the trials and difficulties of adolescence and young adulthood in the 1980s" (1990, [1]). Maturity is characterized by stabilization of growth (Lorenzo 1989), after which the organization faces the inevitable choice of renewal or decline. Both Hudgins and Lorenzo agree that the primary leadership task for community college presidents during the maturity phase is to establish a basis upon which organizational renewal can occur. Inevitably, this foundation involves the reclarification and/or reinterpretation of the institutional mission.

One of the conflicts in resolving the organizational positioning of community colleges for the future seems to stem, in part, from the sense that this reclarified mission should be a dramatic and sweeping vision, something radically new that fundamentally alters the nature of the community college. For example, Roueche et al. urge leaders "to create something new out of something old"— a major change, not just "incremental adjustments of transactional leadership" (1989, 32). The traditional perspective on transformational leadership, as described by J. MacGregor Burns (1978), is an emphasis on change, usually an all-consuming overhauling of mission, goals, and values concerned with ideals such as liberty, justice and equality. This definition, however, also implies that leadership originates from a "single, highly visible individual" who then communicates it persuasively and powerfully, down to the faculty and out to the community (Bensimon, Neumann, and Birnbaum 1989, 74). The logical candidate for this position is the dynamic community college "commander."

Transformational leadership, in its traditional form, has usually been associated with national or social movements, which makes it natural to see great-man leadership in the community college movement as well. At an institutional level, however, transformational leadership is most relevant for an institution in crisis where an autocratic, charismatic leader is not only needed but welcomed. Although they certainly face important choices at this stage of organizational maturity, most community colleges are no longer in crisis nor are they likely to accept willingly a dominating "great man" president again.

On the one hand, this emphasis on transforming leadership, the "great man," and dynamic change should come as no surprise. These images have been consistent in community college literature over time and are currently popular in trade publications. Given the stage in the organizational life cycle of most community college literature over time and are currently popular in trade publications. Given the stage in the organizational life cycle of most community colleges, we question the appropriateness of this popularity, however. A closer examination of the research which provided the substance of the Roueche et al. (1989) book, *Shared Vision: Transformational Leadership in American Community Colleges*, emphasizes elements of effective leadership (for example, cultural awareness and continuity with change) that resemble those Estela Bensimon (1989) describes as "trans-vigorational" and that John Gardner (1986) describes as renewal. Yet, as "mainstream" community college authors, Roueche et al. chose to call their leadership behaviors "transformational" and their leaders, "blue chippers," both terms continuing the traditional, elite imagery. There is an apparent recognition of the kind of leadership required for community colleges in the maturity life cycle stage, yet there is an equally strong reluctance to relinquish the heroic images ingrained in the literature and in the minds of scholars and critics. It is as though choosing to use alternative language somehow makes the leadership images less real, less valid.

Roueche et al. (1989) are not alone in their inability to re-vision leadership for the future of community colleges by finding persuasive images of participative or renewing leaders. Several authors describe the activities community college leaders must undertake to move their institutions into renewal and away from decline, indicating a certain understanding about this stage of the organizational life cycle. In some cases, these activities are outlined in "image neutral" phrases. For instance, George Vaughan (1986), a scholar of the community college in addition to being a former community college president, defines the four primary roles of community college presidents for the 1990s as interpreting and communicating the institutional mission, managing the institution, creating the campus climate, and serving as educational leader. John Keyser (1988), president of Clackamas Community College, advocates collaborative decision making for the future, as does the report *Building Communities: A Vision for a New Century* (Commission 1988).

In other cases, some authors reinforce the imagery of command when describing appropriate leadership behaviors for renewal, which continues to legitimate "great man" leadership. John Jacob (1989), president and chief executive officer of the National Urban League, invokes military images when he talks of leaders who need to "marshall" community support and "join forces" with community organizations. An editor's note in *Leadership Abstracts* quotes certain leadership traits that *U.S. News & World Report* advocated for the executive of the twenty-first century as applicable to community college leaders of the future. Among them were "Master of Technology" and the "Leader/Motivator" who would be "less a commander than a coach" (Doucette 1988 [1–2]). Again, while the leadership behaviors (for example, technological innovation and motivation) seem appropriate for an institution moving toward renewal, the repeated use of male pronouns, male nouns (Doucette uses only male examples), and military and athletic metaphors project into the twenty-first century a community college executive image that continues to be exclusionary.

Jess Parrish (1988) also uses athletic imagery in discussing future leaders of community colleges: "Leaders, like athletes, are bigger, stronger, quicker, and better coaches than ever. A generation of community college lore is available to current and up-coming leaders, and the smart ones are using it. . . . Somewhere out there is another Priest, another Cosand, and another Fordyce" (1988, [1]). Parrish's new leader is simply a new version of the old hero who should be relying on the lore (stories, myths, legends, etc.) to understand his or her role. We would argue that the use of such language has become so ingrained in the community college literature and the leadership images created by this language so normative that the authors may not realize the limitations of the message they are reinforcing.

Alternative Voices

There have been and continue to be alternative voices and images of leadership. Writing in 1972, Richard Richardson, Clyde Blocker, and Louis Bender provided the earliest, most obvious alternative when they disapprovingly described the "autocratic" style of community college leaders (p. v). They proposed instead a model of shared governance, with ideals of participation. Although some scholars picked up the concept, our review suggests that major community college authors have only recently adopted it.

Alternative voices and images of leadership, while not exclusively those of women, have most frequently emerged from the feminist movement. Alternative images have allowed women to be included where traditional images exclude them. At least two widely read books on the community college presidency have attempted, more or less successfully, to address past inattention to women presidents often by devoting a chapter specifically to women presidents. For example, Roueche, Baker, and Rose include such a chapter, written by a woman graduate student who was listed as chapter author but was not accorded a place as one of the book's authors (1989, 235–63). Only four of the fifty elite "blue chippers," who are the focus of the entire volume, are women.

George Vaughan (1989) also reserves a chapter for women presidents, but much of its attention goes to the problems women have in becoming and being presidents rather than the opportunities for creative leadership that they offer. The overall message is thus a discouraging one for women, even though Vaughan reports that the presidency is described as "asexual" by those women who make it, which in itself may not be an encouraging note. Former community college president Judith Eaton makes a serious contribution toward a new image by asking whether leadership, as traditionally defined, is important to enhancing individual capacity, whether educational institutions can make a difference in individuals, and even whether presidents, by themselves, can make a difference in modern society (Eaton 1988). She seems to be calling for a more involving form of leadership, a sharing of leadership roles.

The most significant of the current alternative voices emanates from the National Institute for Leadership Development. Supported by the American Association of Women in Community and

Junior Colleges, the Maricopa Community College District, and now also by the League for Innovation in the Community College, the National Institute seeks to promote "leadership in a different voice": leadership based on connectedness and collaboration rather than hierarchy, authority, and power. Rooted in the work of Carol Gilligan (1982), the National Institute assumes that women's leadership styles and preferences are different from men's, and thus provides a new model of leadership based on the many threads in the web of campus life rather than on the all-powerful leader. Carol Cross and John Ravekes praise Mildred Bulpit and Carolyn Desjardins as

> . . . leaders for their work in running the National Institute for Leadership Development. These women have been a major influence on the way that a significant number (over 1,100) of the women in community colleges view themselves and their jobs. They are also central to the growing national women's network among community college personnel. Few presidents have such direct impact on the people they direct as these women do on the colleagues they nurture. (1990, 12)

The fact that Bulpit and Desjardins are praised for nurturing rather than commanding is significant. At least in the work of the National Institute, nurturing is an alternative image to be encouraged.

The *AAWCJC Journal* is another example of an alternative voice, where the image of leadership reflected in various articles printed in 1988, 1989, and 1990 issues conveys connectedness, cooperation, and "webs and nets" rather than pyramids and hierarchical ladders. These alternative voices, however, are frequently marginalized. The *AAWCJC Journal* is received only by members, is indexed on ERIC only by entire issue, not by author or title, and is not received by most libraries. In work that is more widely disseminated, alternative models and voices are relegated to a chapter typically toward the end of the book, if they are included at all (for example, Vaughan 1989). On the occasion of the National Institute for Leadership Development's tenth anniversary, it was formally honored for its work by the League for Innovation at the league's Summer Institute. Once recognized by the "mainstream," perhaps this group will acquire more legitimacy.

Conclusion

In this paper we have attempted to show, through an examination of the literature, that the leadership behaviors exemplified by "General Koos and Colonels Eells and Campbell" have become immortalized in the community college lore about leadership. These strong, often militaristic, descriptors have perpetuated the "great man" style of leadership, even when the writers sometimes recognize a need for a different type of leadership (e.g., Roueche et al. 1989). Contemporary writers (e.g., Deegan and Tillery 1985; Parrish 1988; Brint and Karabel 1989), like those of the past (e.g. Bogue 1950), reinforce the "great man" view of leadership by repeatedly referring to the few great leaders who have shaped the movement. They tell us that community colleges, more so than any other segment of postsecondary education, have been shaped and promoted by a handful of influential leaders. Furthermore, we are reminded of the critical need of replacing these specific leaders when they retire from active duty. (For example, Parrish referred to Priest, Cosand, Fordyce, Colvert, Martorana, and others [1988, (1)]). Perhaps we should expect no less from institutions that are considered part of a larger movement. The very use of this term implies some great force at work that demands great leadership from a select few.

One consequence of this approach to leadership is its unspoken but effective removal of leader candidates who do not fit the images and the marginalization of writers who do not use the same language in their writing.

Two aspects of this finding merit discussion. The first relates to the creation and control of knowledge itself. A relatively few scholars or writers have been stamped as the spokespersons for the community college movement and have retained control of knowledge and the discourse by which it is disseminated. The scholars, with a few exceptions, have been relatively closed to research done by individuals outside of the circle and defensive in the face of criticism or change. The research of the core writers on community college leadership, such as that of Vaughan, Roueche et al., has been criticized for sacrificing objectivity for message.[1] Gaining access to the inner circle of accepted writers in the field is also difficult, especially for those promoting alternative images. Consequently one of the concerns for leadership in community colleges, particularly since they are so reliant on the "lore," is who is writing and will write on the topic in the future.

This concern is directly related to the second point: Can women and minorities possibly fit the images of leadership portrayed in the literature? As Rosemary Gillett-Karam (1989) concluded, effective leadership is "a concept relating attributes of community college presidents without reference to their sex" (1989, 255). In other words, she found few differences between women and men on major dimensions of leadership behavior. This is consistent with Cynthia Epstein's (1988) review of much of the gender research of the last two decades. Epstein concludes that gender differences are not empirically "real." Rather, because of how gender and gender relations are socially constructed, we persist in believing that there are differences. We perpetuate these differences in our language, writing, symbols, and images. For instance, it is not easy to imagine women or minorities as pioneers[2], commanders, builders, athletes, and even blue-chippers.

Even as women slowly gain access to community college presidencies, their accomplishments are marginalized or discussed in terms of "problems" rather that potential. For example, Vaughan observes: "Although women encounter certain difficulties that men do not when seeking the presidency, to assume that being female caused failure to be selected for a given presidency is to greatly oversimplify the presidential selection process. . . . Trustees are obligated to determine the right fit, or chemistry for a college at a particular time and location. There are some cases when the right fit requires a white male president and other cases when it requires a female president" (1989, 76). Such a statement dramatically reinforces our point: Images of leadership, in this, case, gender images, whether appropriate or not, determine who gains access to positions of power.

Yet can community colleges, serving such diverse constituencies, afford to maintain images of leadership that are narrow and exclusionary? Organizationally, can they afford to perpetuate the great-man model of leadership when many writers agree that different behaviors are called for?

Linda Alcoff (1988) commented that post-structuralism deconstructs but offers no alternative construction in its wake. The challenge facing community college scholars and practitioners is to create alternative construction(s) of leadership that reflect and convey the rich tradition, history, and spirit of the community college movement, that meet the demands of leadership for organizational renewal, and do not recreate the binary oppositions (commander/subordinate) which have permeated the discourse in the past. Using terms like *great man, pioneer, builder, commander, visionary* (and their opposites) in effect excludes groups of people who do not fit the image and perpetuates the view that the success or failure of any community college rests in the hands of one or a few "great leaders."

More promising images of leaders are also found in John Gardner's pathfinder (1990, 128) and Harland Cleveland's (1985) knowledge executive. Although more inclusive than military or sports images and more reflective of behaviors necessary for organizational renewal in the twenty-first century, these images still focus on *the* leader in positions of influence. However, if leadership is viewed as a process rather than a position one might adopt verbs such as *empower, facilitate, collaborate,* and *educate,* and metaphors such as *weaver, cultivator, networker,* and *connector* to capture the essences of effective leadership.

Attempting to conceptualize alternative images of leadership has demonstrated the difficult challenge confronting community colleges, as well as other organizations. Our study underscores how strongly Western conceptions of leadership are grounded in the ideology of the philosopher-king and military hero even when behaviors associated with such leadership are viewed as inappropriate. It might be fruitful to search other cultures for alternative images. The Chinese philosopher Lao Tzu instructs leaders: "Imagine that you are a midwife. . . . You are assisting at someone else's birth. . . . The leader is helping others to find their own success. There is plenty to go around. Sharing success with others is very successful" (in Heider 1989, 162–63). How different might community colleges (and the world) be if these were the images of leadership to which we ascribe and to which we aspired? And where are these more appropriate than for institutions called *community* colleges?

Notes

1. We do not intend to imply this situation is different from or worse than writing on leadership in four-year colleges and universities. We argue that bias in that sector is thinly veiled as science and results from theoretical and methodological choices.

2. Much has recently been written about women pioneers in western history. These accounts tell of the activities of the women who went west, rather than ignoring women based on an a priori definition of *pioneer* that would exclude the activities of women.

Bibliography

Alcoff, Linda. "Cultural Feminism Versus Post-structuralism: The Identity Crisis in Feminist Theory." In *Reconstructing the Academy*, edited by Elizabeth Minnich, Jean O'Barr, and Rachel Rosenfeld, 257–88. Chicago: University of Chicago Press, 1988.

Alfred, Richard L., and David F. Smydra. "Reforming Governance: Resolving Challenges to Institutional Authority." In *Renewing the American Community College*, edited by William L. Deegan, Dale Tillery, and Associates, 199–228. San Francisco: Jossey-Bass, Inc., 1985.

Bartky, John. "The Nature of Junior College Administration." *Junior College Journal* 28 (1957): 3–7.

Bensimon, Estela M. "Transactional, Transformational and 'Trans-vigorational' Leaders." *Leadership Abstracts* 2, no. 6 (April 1989), not paginated. Newsletter of the League for Innovation in the Community College.

Bensimon, Estela M., Anna Neumann, and Robert Birnbaum. *Making Sense of Administrative Leadership: The 'L' Word in Higher Education*. ASHE-ERIC Higher Education Report No. 1. Washington, D.C.: School of Education and Human Development, George Washington University, 1989.

Bogue, Jesse. P. *The Community College*. New York: McGraw-Hill, 1950.

Brint, Steven, and Jerome Karabel. *The Diverted Dream: Community Colleges and the Promise of Educational Opportunity in America, 1900–1985*. New York: Oxford University Press, 1989.

Brothers, E.Q. "Present Day Practices and Tendencies in the Administration and Organization of Public Junior Colleges." *School Review* 36 (1928): 665–74.

Burns, J. MacGregor. *Leadership*. New York: Harper and Row, 1978.

Cameron, Kim. "Organizational Adaptation and Higher Education." *The Journal of Higher Education* 55 (April/May 1984): 122–44.

Cameron, Kim, and Ray Zammuto. "Matching Managerial Strategies to Conditions of Decline." *Human Resource Management* 22, no. 4 (Winter 1983): 359–75.

Carpenter, W.W., and J. R. Johnson. "The Junior College Dean." *Junior College Journal* 13 (1942): 19–21.

Cherryholmes, Cleo. *Power and Criticism: Poststructural Investigations in Education.* New York: Teachers College Press, 1988.

Cleveland, Harlan. *The Knowledge Executive: Leadership in an Information Society.* New York: E.P. Dutton, 1985.

Commission on the Future of Community Colleges. "Building Communities: A Vision for a New Century." *Leadership Abstracts* 1, no. 12 (July 1988), not paginated. Newsletter of the League for Innovation in the Community College.

Connelly, F. Michal, and D. Jean Clandinin. "Stories of Experience and Narrative Inquiry." *Educational Research* 19 (June/July 1990): 2–14.

Cross, Carol, and John E. Ravekes. "Leadership in a Different Voice." *AAWCJC Journal* 1990, 7–14.

Doucette, Don, ed. "The 21st Century Executive." *Leadership Abstracts* 1, no. 8 (April 1988), not paginated. Newsletter of the League for Innovation in the Community College.

Eaton, Judith S. "Love Me, Lead Me, and Leave Me Alone." In *Leaders on Leadership: The College Presidency,* edited by James L. Fisher and Martha W. Tack, 75–80. New Directions for Higher Education No. 61. San Francisco: Jossey-Bass, Inc., 1988.

Eells, William C. *The Junior College.* Boston: Houghton Mifflin Co., 1931.

Epstein, Cynthia. *Deceptive Distinctions: Sex, Gender, and the Social Structure.* New Haven: Yale University Press and New York: Russell Sage Foundation, 1988.

Foster, F.M. "Uniformity in Administrative Nomenclature. *Junior College Journal.* 3 (1933): 362–64.

Fowler, Roger. "Power." In *Handbook of Discourse Analysis, Volume 4,* edited by Teun A. van Dijk, 61–82. London: Academic Press, 1985.

Gardner, John W. *On Leadership* New York: Free Press, 1990.

———. *Tasks of Leadership.* Leadership Papers No. 2. Washington, D.C.: Independent Sector, 1986.

Gergen, Mary McCanney. "Feminist Critique of Science and the Challenge of Social Epistemology." In *Feminist Thought and the Structure of Knowledge,* edited by Mary McCanney Gergen, 87–104. New York: New York University Press, 1988.

Gillett-Karam, Rosemary. "Women in Leadership Roles." In *Shared Vision: Transformational Leadership in American Community Colleges,* edited by John E. Roueche, George A. Baker III, and Robert R. Rose, 235–63. Washington D.C.: The Community College Press and the American Association of Community and Junior Colleges, 1989.

Gilligan, Carol. *In a Different Voice: Psychological Theory and Women's Development.* Cambridge, Mass.: Harvard University Press, 1982.

Giroux, Henry A. *Schooling and the Struggle for Public Life: Critical Pedagogy in the Modern Age.* Minneapolis: University of Minnesota Press, 1988.

Greiner, Larry. "Evolution and Revolution as Organizations Grow." *Harvard Business Review* 50 (July-August 1972): 37–46.

Hall, Robert A., and Richard L. Alfred. "Applied Research on Leadership in Community Colleges." *Community College Review* 12 (1985): 36–41.

Heider, John. "The Leader Who Knows How Things Happen." In *Contemporary Issues in Leadership,* edited by William E. Rosenbach and Robert L. Taylor, 161–67. Boulder, Colo.: Westview Press, 1989.

Hill, Morton. "Steps in the Organization of the Junior College." In *The Junior College: Its Organization and Administration*, edited by W.M. Proctor, 26–40. Palo Alto, Calif.: Stanford University Press, 1927.

Hudgins, J.L. "Renewing a Mature Community College." *Leadership Abstracts 3*, no. 4 (February 1990), not paginated. Newsletter of the League for Innovation in the Community College.

Jacob, John E. "Education and the Revitalization of Urban America." *Leadership Abstracts* 2, no. 19 (1989), not paginated. Newsletter of the League for Innovation in the Community College.

Johnson, J.R., and W.W. Carpenter. "Dean or Errand Boy?" *Junior College Journal* 13 (1943): 381–83.

Keyser, John S. "Collaborative Decision-making." *Leadership Abstracts* 1, no. 17 (October 1988), not paginated. Newsletter of the League for Innovation in the Community College.

Kolodny, Annette. "A Map for Rereading: Gender and the Interpretation of Literary Texts." In *Feminist Criticism: Essays on Women, Literature and Theory* edited by E. Showalter, 46–62. New York: Pantheon Books, 1985.

Lather, Patti, *Getting Smart: Feminist Research and Pedagogy with/in the Postmodern*. New York: Routledge, 1991.

Lee, Charles, and W.E. Rosenstengel. "Philosophy of Junior College Administration." *Junior College Journal* 8 (1938): 227–30.

Lorenzo, Albert L. "A Foundation for Renewal." *Leadership Abstracts* 2, no. 12 (July 1989), not paginated. Newsletter of the League for Innovation in the Community College.

Nielsen, Joyce McCarl. Introduction. In *Feminist Research Methods: Exemplary Readings in the Social Sciences*, edited by Joyce McCarl Nielsen, 1–37. Boulder: Westview Press, 1990.

Parrish, Jess H. "Individual and Group Responsibility for Leadership Development." *Leadership Abstracts* 1, no. 7 (April 1988), not paginated. Newsletter of the League for Innovation in the Community College.

Pierce, A.C. "Deans in the Organization and Administration of Junior Colleges." *Junior College Journal* 21 (1951): 364–66.

Potter, Jonathan, and Margaret Wetherell. *Discourse and Social Psychology: Beyond Attitudes and Behavior*. London: Sage Publications, 1987.

President's Commission on Higher Education. *Higher Education for American Democracy*. Washington, D.C.: U.S. Government Printing Office, 1947.

Proctor, W.M. *The Junior College: Its Organization and Administration*. Palo Alto, Calif.: Stanford University Press, 1927.

Ratcliff, James L. "'First' Public Junior Colleges in an Age of Reform." *Journal of Higher Education* 58 (1987): 151–80.

Richardson, Richard C., Clyde E. Blocker, and Louis W. Bender, *Governance for the Two-Year College*. Englewood Cliffs, N.J.: Prentice-Hall, 1972.

Roueche, John E., George A. Baker III, and Robert R. Rose. *Shared Vision: Transformational Leadership in American Community Colleges*. Washington, D.C.: The Community College Press and the American Association of Community and Junior Colleges, 1989.

Selznick, Philip. *Leadership in Administration*. 1957; reprint ed., Berkeley and Los Angeles: University of California Press, 1984.

Shotter, John, and Josephine Logan. "The Pervasiveness of Patriarchy: On Finding a Different Voice." In *Feminist Thought and the Structure of Knowledge,* edited by Mary McCanney Gergen, 69–86. New York: New York University Press, 1988.

Spender, Dale. *Man Made Language.* London: Routledge & Kegan Publishers, 1980.

Tillery, Dale, and William L. Deegan. "The Evolution of Two-Year Colleges through Four Generations." In *Renewing the American Community College: Priorities and Strategies for Effective Leadership*, edited by William L. Deegan and Dale Tillery, 3–33. San Francisco: Jossey-Bass, Inc., 1985.

van Dijk, Teun A. "Introduction: The Role of Discourse Analysis in Society." In *Handbook of Discourse Analysis, Volume 4*, edited by Teun A. van Dijk, 1–8. London: Academic Press, 1985.

Vaughan, George B. *The Community College Presidency.* New York: ACE/Macmillan, 1986.

_____. Bringing Focus to the Presidency. *Leadership Abstracts* 1, no. 6 (March 1988), not paginated. Newsletter of the League for Innovation in the Community College.

_____. *Leadership in Transition: The Community College Presidency.* New York: ACE/Macmillan, 1989.

Warren Carol A.B. *Gender Issues in Field Research.* Newbury Park Calif.: Sage Publications, 1988.

E Pluribus Unum?
Academic Structure, Culture, and
the Case of Feminist Scholarship

Patricia J. Gumport

E pluribus unum—out of many, one. Higher education scholars have used this phrase both descriptively and prescriptively. Both as metaphor and motto, the phrase suggests that, despite a plurality of interests and specialities in academic life, there is a cohesion within the organization of academic work and that this cohesion corresponds to lines of formal structure based on one's disciplinary and institutional affiliation. In this article, I call into question the utility of this idealized image as a conceptual frame for understanding complex variations in academics culture. Drawing on recent empirical data about the formation of intentional intellectual communities, I analyze feminist scholarship as a contemporary current in academic life.

Two significant findings are: (1) Faculty seek and find intellectual communities beyond lines of formal structure (e.g., department, institutional); and (2) The departmental organization of academic work does not necessarily function as an integrating framework for resolving conflicting interests and advancing common ones. This analysis concludes with an invitation to rethink the premise about culture and structure that are implicit in prevailing conceptual frameworks for studying change in higher education organizations.

Frameworks for Understanding Academic Change

The current configuration of departments and disciplines across campuses evolved in an evolutionary process of intellectual and social differentiation, according to functionalist accounts of academic change in American higher education (e.g., Blau 1973; Clark 1983; Rudolf 1981; Trow 1984). From this perspective, disputes over curricula and new academic programs have been handled by additive solutions—that is, expanding to cover a plurality of interests rather than replacing what counts as worthwhile academic pursuits. Regardless of whether this explanation is the definitive historical explanation, it is apparent that differentiation has its limits. Fewer resources and more capital-intensive academic endeavors render infinite expansion an untenable solution for solving conflicting academic visions.

With varying degrees of urgency over the past decade, some scholars have challenged higher education to "pull itself together" against the current proliferation of new fields and the "blurring of genres" (Geertz 1983; Clark 1983, 1987). Other scholars have warned that "faculty are even more sharply divided than in previous years, . . . and the end of this . . . fragmentation is not in sight"

(Bowen and Schuster 1986, 152). One assessment of this state of academic affairs is to assure us of *e pluribus unum*, that is an enduring, harmonious system where faculty are held together by a devotion to knowledge, dual commitments to one's discipline and institution, a unified system albeit constituted by a pluralistic landscape of interests, as Clark (1987, 145) has proposed. An alternative assessment is to view the contemporary scene as a site of oppositional discourses, imbued with fundamental conflicts of vision and resistance to new ideas, such that the revision of the current departmental organization may be imminent (Lincoln 1986).

Such divergent assessments of how things are and how they may be in the future compel us to reconsider some assumptions about academia. In the broadest sense, when we speak of the organization of academic work or of the academic profession, we usually presuppose some degree of integration, whether it be cohesion among people around a knowledge base by discipline or by department, or whether it be cohesion around a professional ideal of purpose or service.

Yet, both within and across disciplines as well as within and across departments on any given campus, such cohesion appears to be waning or, if present, is buried under an array of dramatically different visions of the nature and content of academic knowledge. Debates over the value of Euro-centric scholarship and Western culture undergraduate requirements in the curricula, to name two recent examples, illustrate not only different but conflicting interests. Although the metaphor of organizational culture has been implicitly used in higher education for over two decades (e.g., Clark, 1970, 1972), the increased popularity and refinement of cultural perspectives among higher education researchers and managers attest to the pervasive interest in understanding the glue that holds academia together. The theoretical and empirical work on organizational culture in higher education is, at least in part, a response to this functionalist concern.

Whether positing structural dimensions of organizations as a foil or merely as an analytical complement, deliberate cultural analysis in higher education settings has provided an alternative set of concepts and methods for studying cultural artifacts (e.g., myths, symbols, and rituals) in higher education organizations. The purpose of such research is to uncover beliefs and values among organizational participants, with the promise of more accurately portraying organizational life (Clark 1983; Dill 1982; Gumport 1988; Harman 1988; Masland 1985; Tierney 1988).

Most of such higher education research has been constructed and disseminated within a functionalist paradigm that implicitly seeks to uncover layers of academic order and mechanisms of integration. For example, Andrew T. Masland proposes that culture be seen as "a force that provides stability and a sense of continuity" (1985, 165). Along similar lines, William G. Tierney suggests that the study of cultural dynamics can help us "to decrease conflict" and "to understand and, hopefully, to reduce adversarial relationships" (1988, 18, 5).

Grounded in an *e pluribus unum* premise of organic solidarity (Durkheim 1933), such frameworks for understanding academic organization may be appealing for their currency as a motto, if not as a metaphor, for the hoped-for, ensuing coordination. However, as a conceptual frame for analyzing academic culture, the approach limits inquiry by assuming equilibrium rather than investigating it as an open empirical question. Conflict among organizational participants is seen as either a transient condition that erupts in an otherwise smoothly running system or as a more substantial difference of interest that nonetheless can and should be remedied or resolved. The solution may be structural (by creating a new organizational unit) or cultural (by accepting a divergence of beliefs). Conflict in academic culture is conceptually rendered part of a trend toward differentiation and pluralism.

An alternative starting point for the analysis of academic culture is to ask a different question than what glue is holding everything together, for it may be that things will fall apart or fall out along different lines. Rather than beginning with integration as an *a priori* analytical strait-jacket, we can examine what faculty do—"not what others think they do or should be doing," as George Kuh and Elizabeth Whitt have proposed (1988, 109). What becomes centrally problematic is to examine the nature of individuals' interests and commitments. In other words, the researcher should try not only to find out whether faculty really have dual commitments to their disciplines and institutions, but also to describe faculty perceptions of how their commitments are constructed in different academic settings. This approach leaves open the possibility for ambiguity, conflict, and disintegration. Moreover, this line of inquiry dovetails with an enduring interest in the sociology of knowledge and of science to determine the interplay between social structures and the development of ideas.

Accordingly, my analysis is framed by two questions: First, how do faculty seek and find intellectual community? And second, how do patterns of association differ in different campus organizational settings? I have found that the emergence of feminist scholarship and its associated academic networks call into question the accuracy of the *e pluribus unum* framework. The analysis is based on interview data from twenty-seven full-time faculty located on two campuses and case study data analyzing how different organizations frame the possibilities for forming intentional communities. These data are drawn from a larger two-year study in which I conducted seventy-five semi-structured, in-depth interviews with administrators and a stratified, random sample of women faculty across ten campuses and three disciplines (Gumport 1987). By supplementing the interviews with case study research and by conceptually anchoring faculty at the center of the analysis, I examined how faculty are constrained by, yet contribute to, their academic settings.

A major substantive line of inquiry int he interviews was examining whether and how these faculty became involved with feminist scholarship and its teaching arm, women's studies. Some of the faculty were located in conventional departments (sociology, history, and philosophy); others were in autonomous women's studies programs. Since they were all women who were in academia at a time of heightened gender consciousness, the contemporary emergence of academic feminism provided a set of intellectual, social, and political interests that they could ignore or embrace. Voluntary association was the major mechanism whereby faculty became participants in this newly emerging, not-yet-legitimate academic specialty. Feminist scholarship is interdisciplinary, potentially of interest to faculty in a wide range of disciplines, and controversial. Some scholars interpret it as having an explicitly political and oppositional agenda. These factors make it a suitable empirical opportunity to examine contemporary lines of academic culture on different campuses.

Analysis

Through an iterative, grounded theory analysis of the interview data (Glaser and Strauss 1967), I discerned patterns that reflected a complex process of finding intellectual affinity and forming intentional networks that cross-cut structural lines of departments. Faculty described individual and group processes as characterized by ambiguity of purpose and conflict of vision as well as by an absence of forethought, conscious planning, or likelihood of academic rewards. In fact, more often than not, the reference group and source of authority were identified as outside the departments and sometimes outside academia entirely. Visible communities of feminist scholars emerged across departments as well as across campuses.

Faculty career histories and intellectual biographies enable us to examine what compelled them to associate and what subsequent senses of intellectual and organizational community emerged. First, I address the individual level of how faculty conceive of their intellectual community. Second, I analyze the campus levels for the distinctive informal networks that emerged.

Although individual variations may be interesting in and of themselves, different patterns among individuals provide greater insight for the analysis of social action. The faculty in this sample may be grouped into the following four patterns: (1) scholars whose interests matched their conventional departments and who had no interest or participation in feminist thinking; (2) feminist scholars working primarily in their department and discipline of training but who had some dual or mixed loyalties; (3) feminist scholars in departments yet whose primary loyalty was to women's studies as an autonomous unit separate from the conventional department; and (4) feminist scholar-activists located in women's studies programs who saw themselves as change agents to develop women's studies as an autonomous unit, and whose primary affinity was to the broader national feminist movement.

In this sample, those in the first group were fewer in number, especially among those who entered graduate school in the 1960s. The other three groups reflected some involvement with feminist scholarship and conveyed varying experiences of fragmentation and conflict in academia, both internally and interpersonally. They expressed a sense of conflicting membership within their departments and even internally within an emerging women's studies subculture. I examine each group in turn.

Faculty Identifying with Departments

The scholars who were oriented to their department and discipline agendas did not see their work as intersecting with feminist scholarship in a meaningful way. They did not become involved with feminist research or teach women's studies, deeming them either irrelevant or inappropriate due to the perceived political nature of feminist scholarship.

Four quotations illustrate this sense of detachment. A philosopher commented, "I was conscious of there being a feminist movement; but since there weren't any differences for me as a women at the time, I more or less ignored all of it."

"I could see it as an area of interest but not something that can stand alone," said a sociologist. "It could get into trouble if it becomes a matter of taking sides rather than material that can be analyzed and looked at critically. It's fine to see women as victims, but that should be separate from the academic milieu. I feel uncomfortable with that."

"I just don't understand it," admitted a second sociologist, and added, "I don't think I agree with it. It worries me a little . . . because I can see people saying we need a Catholic or Jewish sociology; we need a sociology of white supremacy or anti-white supremacy. It gets off into directions I feel real uncomfortable with. . . . I'm not very comfortable with a larger political role. I don't have any problem with people trying to shift the agenda of the discipline as an intellectual activity, but I have problems with combining the roles—using their academic credentials to legitimate a particular political position. . . . I prefer to keep them separate."

"The label is a disservice," a historian charged. "I've had enough ideologies and dogmas. I have not found [feminist scholars] a natural audience. . . . I'm mistrustful. . . . They want something more doctrinaire, much more ideological."

These four scholars conceived of themselves and their sense of community as clearly anchored in their departments and disciplines. Their networks and associations were not problematic, since they followed the formal structure; but they were only a few voices in my sample.

Faculty with Mixed Loyalties

The second group tried to balance the dual loyalties of their department/discipline and their emerging interests in feminist scholarship.

For some, the balancing act worked. These were usually historians who found a niche in the emerging subfield of women's history. For example, one historian explained she "fell into" feminist scholarship "by accident." Initially she was worried about possible consequences and

> . . . toyed briefly with not telling anyone here that I was working on it, because I was afraid of how it might be perceived, especially as I was coming up for tenure at the time. But I decided not to. There was the practical reason that people would wonder what I was working on. . . . Then it also just didn't seem right. Then I presented some of it in the form of a paper to colleagues in my department. It went

very well. I was amazed. Some of the issues that I dealt with are at the intersection of sex and power. They are interested in that. . . . They were very supportive and made good suggestions, and I was much releived.

Recalling her relations with departmental colleagues prior to her feminist research, she realized in retrospect that there was no need to worry: "I had established such a moderate or really a conservative facade in my department that . . . I felt it would not be detrimental." This scholar thus conceived of herself and her community as centered in history, yet able to accommodate a feminist research project.

Others found no convergence between interests in historical and feminist scholarship. They either felt pulled in two different directions or tried to enact a new kind of scholarly identity.

Another historian described herself as "balancing on women's history and French history. Each of them takes me in a direction away from the other. I do pursue women's history outside of France and French history outside of women's history. But in different periods of my life, I'm concentrating on either on one or the other."

Her primary professional involvement was the American Historical Association, although she characterized that group as "not exciting." In contrast, she was "attached to" the Berkshire Conference of women's historians and feminist scholars with related interests: "It's special and it's happening. To go to a place where you know your going to be indulging your professional interests with other women . . . perks you up in a sense because it takes away a burden you don't even know is there when you're working in a male-dominated place like this." In spite of her identification with those who attend the Berkshire Conference, her sense of her work and community was still problematic. She felt pulled apart, unable to find a home entirely in either location.

In trying to reconcile this kind of tension, some scholars in history, sociology, and philosophy generated a research agenda and tried to establish a new intellectual and organizational identity created from the intersection of disciplinary and feminist interests. Historians were most likely to succeed in making this a viable option, although others made concerted efforts.

One historian, who described herself as a pioneer, characterized her efforts:

> I was pulling together the politics and the scholarship and feeling like it had to be done. . . . I still do it that way. You can see all my articles start out with the contemporary political issue and end up with it, too. And I do the history in between. . . . Now I define myself as someone in women's history and a feminist. I have a network of women's historians around the country. It's an intellectual community: we read each others' work and comment on it . . . and go to conferences. We also socialize at those gatherings and other times. It's also active as a political network.

She had a clear sense of belonging in a feminist scholarly community. Rather than feeling pulled in two separate directions or working in two separate worlds, she had constructed a new primary identity as a "feminist historian." Simultaneously she retained a strong disciplinary orientation, which reflected a comfortable congruence with her being located in the history department at a leading research university: "I'm very wedded to history," she described herself. "I read other fields, but I really believe in history and in having strong disciplinary training, that without it people can float too much. So my primary identity is as a feminist historian."

It is noteworthy that both this historian and the one who described herself as "balancing" between feminism and history were in the same department at the same institution. Yet their experiences differed, one ending up with the dual loyalties while the second ended up constructing a new sense of self and community.

Two philosophers also spoke of finding a new scholarly path which united their divergent scholarly interests. However, they characterized this orientation as more problematic, both in the process and in the outcome, than for the historians. Both philosophers described the difficulty of, first, establishing an intellectual and organizational niche and, second, finding an audience for their research.

The first philosopher observed, "In college I was definitely not a feminist," but over the past two decades, she became a self-described "feminist and a philosopher." She described the process: "The challenge for me as my own person and independent thinker was to get the blend that is desirable. I felt that it was too difficult . . . to meet the narrow constraints of the discipline, so I shifted into a women's studies program for a while. That context was invaluable for me [in being] able to develop my thinking freely." Then she took a position in a philosophy department. Her sense of her work was that "it is not straight philosophy." Her most recent paper probably will not be accepted for the American Philosophical Association annual conference because "it's too bizarre in its multidisciplinary approach." In sum, this scholar did not see herself fitting comfortably into her discipline.

A second philosopher also sought to "have something to say to both feminist and philosophical audiences," a task she conceived of as doing something new for her field.

> I take the current [feminist] agenda and ask myself is there something useful a philosopher can do here. . . . When I'm speaking to a feminist audience . . . , I have to make my work relevent in ways that I don't have to when I'm speaking to a philosophical audience. . . . After the initial encounter between the disciplinary work and feminist concerns, then the work develops its own momentum and generates its own sorts of questions, so that it no longer seems appropriate to talk about my work as bridging some gap between my subfield in philosophy and separate [feminist] concerns.

This philosopher still saw negative consequences for not "doing straight philosophy," so she spent time developing a feminist scholarly network and trying to publish in both feminist and philosophy journals.

In sum, the pattern characteristic of this group was mixed loyalties that they tried, with different degrees of success, to balance or blend through different strategies. Historians tended to find more resolution in carving out an intellectual and organizational niche for themselves and their community.

Faculty Identifying Primarily with Women's Studies

A third pattern in this sample was scholars who, although located in conventional departments, found their intellectual and social center outside the department. For the most part, they were extensively involved with a campus women's studies program and read, attended, and published primarily in women's studies forums. They consistently reported feeling "more and more distance" from their departments. (Not surprisingly, these scholars were employed at a comprehensive state university, not a research university, which is a point I will address later in the analysis.)

As an example of this pattern, a historian described how she has struggled with this dimension of academic life since graduate school in the late 1960s. She stayed in history, even though her identity and interests gradually moved into women's studies. As a graduate student, she recalled, the discipline was more a heavy hand than an intellectual home. "Where there was a question of my values being in direct conflict with the trajectory of the disciplinary career, I got slapped down and I was very well aware of that. I could see that happening. I cried. I wept. I said it was unfair. And I changed."

Years later, her intellectual affinities turned toward women's studies, even though she had a full-time position in a history department. she did not find it feasible to be in both worlds, so she, in effect, "dropped out of the history department." She remembered: "I wouldn't serve on any committees and I wouldn't socialize with anyone. I had nothing to do with the department. . . . All of my orientation was with the women's studies program. Because that was a confrontational program at the time, the separation was absolute. I could be here, or I could be there. But I couldn't be in both places."

In retrospect, she characterized herself as having been "professionally dumb" to make a primary commitment to women's studies without thinking about the consequences. Still, her identification with women's studies was so strong that "if someone had said don't risk it, it would have had to have been the leader of our feminist movement. If the chair of the [history] department had said to me, `Look, I'm with you and I love what you're doing for women's studies but I'm not going to be able to get you through the department,' I would have said `screw you.'" She gained tenure in her department, probably because of her outstanding teaching record; her courses, which were cross-listed with women's studies, were popular and consistently well-enrolled.

Naturally faculty located in women's studies programs most frequently expressed the feeling of having an intellectual and organizational home in women's studiers. Since they were not located in conventional departments, they would have greater opportunity to find congruence between their interests, expertise, and organizational niche. However, such positions lacked the security of appointments in more traditional departments. Only some women's studies faculty had "retreat rights" to another department in the event of program dissolution. However, the perceived marginality of women's studies coupled with a lack of common intellectual interests made those future scenarios unsatisfactory. One women's studies program director, who was simultaneously a full professor in a sociology department, explained her own situation: "The loss of collegiality with my `home' department is something I hadn't anticipated would happen. I no longer go to their meetings—on campus or nationally in the association. I can't do both." The center of her academic life was clearly in women's studies, locally, regionally, and nationally—an orientation shared by some other women's studies scholars who had departmental appointments.

Faculty identifying with Feminism

Some faculty with positions in women's studies differed from their departmental colleagues in having a distinctive nonacademic orientation, where the faculty member conceived of her work and her community as lying outside the academy. In those cases, the primary loyalty and reference group became more the political movement than academy.

For example, one faculty member reported having had a series of terminal appointments over the last seven years, part-time on and off, later full-time in a women's studies program. "Basically I've been a gypsy scholar and to me it [politics and academics] is not an internal conflict. If it's a choice between my political convictions and a job, the job can go to hell. . . . I will never make those kinds of compromises. It's not an internal conflict, but it's a conflict with the system." She identifies herself as a feminist scholar and black scholar who believes in women's studies programs as "an essential institutional power base . . . not . . . in it being a safe harbor, but in it being a real space for women . . . scholars and women students." She describes having a primary political agenda.

She is located in a women's studies program on a campus where the program functions much like a department; a handful of other full-time faculty in women's studies ostensibly share her feminist scholarly interests. However, this setting has not become a complete home. As a women of color, she felt that she was hired to boost enrollments; and other women's studies faculty felt threatened when she wanted to change things, "threatened enough to complain to the administration." She felt betrayed:

> Most of the tension has come in women's studies because they didn't realize what it'd mean to have a woman of color who is not a clone of traditional feminist theory. . . . They put on file with the administration a criticism saying that I was not collegial because I did not validate the work of the women who went before me, that I moved too fast. And they refused to talk with me about it. . . . So that's saying to me we don't want you here, and if we want you here we want you under our control.

Although this particular case may seem extreme, it is a useful reminder that the basic organizing units of academic life do not necessarily convey cohesion of purpose and loyalty. Both on the individual level and the interpersonal level, fragmentation and conflict may be pervasive. Even in a case where women's studies functions like a department, there may be less cohesion than we presume. In fact, faculty involved with women's studies and feminist scholarship admit to internal lack of consensus on program content , visions for change, and even who qualifies as members in their enterprise (Gumport 1990). As one director of a women's studies program observed: "People differ in what they mean by feminist and feminist scholarship, and some programs have been torn apart over it."

Campus Networks

These four patterns of faculty orientations also coincide with different higher education organizational settings. Individuals oriented toward conventional departments without interest or involvement in feminist work as well as individuals who felt pulled in two directions from conflicting departmental and feminist scholarly associations were located at a leading research university. Those whose primary affinities were in autonomous women's studies programs or who were highly politicized and oriented outside academia entirely were located at a comprehensive state university.

At the common-sense level and in a functionalist framework, this pattern is no surprise. One obvious hypothesis is that either the individual women self-selected organizational settings that matched their interests or the research-oriented and teaching-oriented institutions each selected faculty with orientations that fit their particular campus culture. However, rather than assuming conscious choice on either part, and examining disaggregated individual behaviors, it is more illuminating to examine the kinds of informal networks that developed in each campus setting.

The reward system within research universities for departmental and disciplinary research and the emphasis in comprehensive state universities on teaching suggest that the different organizational settings provide different possibilities for cross-departmental networks among feminist scholars. The case study data from the two campuses point to a distinctive pattern: the comprehensive university had a thriving cross-departmental feminist, scholarly network; the leading research university had a floundering one.

At the comprehensive university, the faculty in general were described as "progressive" and "having a radical bent." The core of the feminist scholarly community revolved around the women's studies program, which was established in early 1970s and, at the time of this research, boasted fifty undergraduate majors, eighteen courses a semester, and a dozen faculty (including part-timers) with women's studies appointments. The faculty network also included over a dozen more active feminist located in departments.

The faculty network originated in and has been sustained by students' grass-roots efforts to establish a women's studies program. In the early years, there was a student alliance, where students either ran the courses or taught them informally. Since the courses were well-enrolled and highly politicized, the administration took notice. As an administrator remembered: "It scared the administration. The mere size of the thing, the numbers of people involved, the energy generated around it! I think all that was significant enough to carry us ultimately into the women's studies program itself." Years later, the alliance became an ad hoc committee which has been the intellectual, social, and political center for feminist faculty and students ever since. Many departmental faculty became connected formally by cross-listing courses or serving on committees, or informally by socializing. Their focus shifted to formulating a master's program in women's studies and whether to make women's studies a general education requirement, thereby changing small, personal classes into large required ones.

As faculty described the campus milieu, they often referred to "the administration." "The administration," they said, "does not penalize us for being involved in women's studies." What seemed to count most was generating and sustain high enrollment programs. Since departmental involvement and women's studies involvement were not differentially valued, participating in a feminist network on campus had a pay-off.

In contrast to the thriving feminist scholarly network at the comprehensive university, the research university has had a small though growing faculty group, whose members tended to keep an intellectual and organizational anchor in their departments. The women's studies program at the research university was small and had no permanent autonomous faculty lines; except for an occasional visitor, the program relied on cross-listed departmental courses. Established relatively late vis-a-vis the national scene, the program did not grant degrees; students petitioned individually to an interdisciplinary majors committee for a bachelor's degree in women's studies.

At the time of this research, the dozen or so most visible feminist faculty in the departments wanted the teaching program to flourish but recognized the constraints in faculty recruitment and hiring practices in the departments. A historian explained: "The reality of the university is so discipline-based that you do a disservice to create something outside the disciplines. . . . Strategically, people need to be based in the disciplines. . . . And it's not just strategically but intellectually as well." However, the women's studies program director acknowledges that the institution was willing to support women's studies, provided that it demonstrated "strong scholarship" and an "assurance or respectability." The willingness came from the competitive drive for excellence—the fact that "entrepreneurs get their way here. . . . It's survival of the fittest. . . . You survive if you get a high level of visibility, if you are judged by your peers as at the top."

Participating in an emerging informal feminist scholarly network on this campus would have little pay-off for faculty, given the strong disciplinary orientations and time constraints from pressure to publish. In addition, according to one observer in the humanities:

> It's a little risky that no matter how committed you are, you have to draw the line somewhere because there is so much to be done. There are considerations of practicality, of what you need to do and can do if you want to stay here. . . . Most people are much more cautious about getting involved in anything besides writing their books. . . . It's getting labeled—not as a feminist or a women's studies person per se. It's getting labeled as a person who will do non-scholarly, collaborative, student-oriented things. . . . It's the kiss of death.

In spite of the risk, participating in a feminist network on a small scale provides intellectual, social, or political support for faculty who are trying to balance or blend feminist with disciplinary interests. Although informal feminist networks connect people who would otherwise be dispersed and isolated in conventional departments, they may also do disservice. A philosopher explained: "In general there isn't a location for feminist work in the field. . . . The status of feminist work is still fairly fragile. . . . It's mostly women doing it. And so, of course, [since] women are all engaged in this funny kind of work just really confirms people's initial prejudice that women can't do real philosophy . . . [but] are doing this other thing which isn't really philosophy." In any case, despite the scrutiny and stigma, a scholar with this orientation may still seek a feminist scholarly network as an intellectual and organizational home. Another philosopher explained her own decision to do so and remarked on the same inclination of her colleagues:

> If you are working on feminist stuff, you are likely to feel embattled. . . . The women in philosophy who see themselves as feminist scholars will generally be the only person doing feminist work in a department and may sometimes be the only woman period. [They] may feel cut off or deprived of collegial relationships among departmental colleagues and may develop closer relationships with colleagues in women's studies [located] in other departments. . . . Those are the only places where you get both philosophical colleagueship and feminist colleagueship. You get both of them at the same time, in the same place, in the same sentence. And for most women philosophers that is extremely rare.

Thus, both the advantages and disadvantages of associating with a feminist scholarly network are heightened in the constraints of the research university than in the comprehensive university.

The contrast between these two campuses raises questions about the organizational factors that might account for these differences. The inability of the research university to generate—let alone sustain—a thriving feminist scholarly network reflects a distinctive structure and culture which stand in dramatic contrast to that of the comprehensive university.

At the research university, faculty were oriented primarily to their disciplinary colleagues; and departments did the essential work of research and graduate education. In a sense, this peer culture became coercive, guiding faculty behavior and time management as a means of social coordination. In effect, it kept people on their assigned academic tasks, not only junior faculty who faced the "publish or perish" criteria for tenure but senior faculty who earned merit increases in promotion. Since departmental senior faculty held the power, other faculty were not inclined to spend too much time and energy on voluntary associations. Those who chose to do so essentially ran against the grain at their own risk by leaping across discrete departmental building blocks on which the university organization rests. When it comes to peer review, they ran an even greater risk of not fitting in (Gumport 1990). A feminist scholar who had been denied tenure at a leading research university explained it this way: "It's harder to work when it's not fitting into your discipline in a particular way. You can't expect to get clear judgements and rewards, although you'll get different opinions about it. . . . The problem is the people who could judge it are out there and not in here in my department and my discipline."

In contrast, the locus of power at the comprehensive university lay with administrators, not with a departmental/disciplinary peer culture. Administrators' power was linked to their discretion over academic programs and teaching loads. Enrollment-driven data carried clout. Consequently, there was a greater organizational distance between the faculty and the central administration. Faculty and administrators ended up antagonists, no matter what voluntary associations faculty formed. Since course enrollments were the currency for leverage, it was less important whether a feminist faculty member was participating in women's studies centrally, marginally, or in a conventional department. The issue simply lacked the salience it assumed in the disciplinary peer culture of the research university.

In light of these fundamental differences in organizational settings, it becomes clear that overarching academic beliefs like academic freedom and devotion to knowledge are mediated by local settings. Moreover, each setting coordinates academic work with a different emphasis so that faculty are encouraged to attend different concerns. Thus, each setting is more likely to raise different possibilities for the formation of a cross-departmental feminist scholarly network. Although these patterns appear to warrant an *e pluribus unum* conclusion, such a conclusion would be overly simplistic and premature. As the first part of this analysis shows, participants interpret and reenact beliefs according to their subjective perceptions and have the potential to reconstitute the settings in which they work.

Conclusion

In an analysis of recent empirical data, I reexamine the functionalist premise of *e pluribus unum*—out of many, one. Rather than beginning with the assumption of past, present, or future cohesion among organizational participants, as other higher education scholars have, I bring the analysis down to the level of individuals to examine how they enter, negotiate, and play out structural and cultural dimensions of their particular organizational settings. The interview data reveal that faculty conceive of their commitments and their sense of community in ways that do not always correspond with idealized conceptions of academic organization in which departmental and institutional affinities reign supreme.

Setting aside the sub-group in this small sample whose orientations did correspond to their departments, the three other groups of women scholars exemplify a kind of intellectual and social incongruence with their organizational locations. There are plenty of academics whose work does not fit neatly into their so-called home departments and disciplines. In fact, many of the quotations cited in the preceding analysis could have been spoken by faculty in such fields as area studies, urban studies, environmental studies, science policy studies, and ethnic studies—to name a few. These are contemporary fields whose scholarly content and practice do not match the current departmental organization. These are fields where, effort to reconstitute academic knowledge, people seek and find intentional communities that are cross-departmental and sometimes even nonacademic.

In a fundamentalist sense, the emergence of faculty with orientations that diverge significantly from their departments/disciplines of training remains a puzzle. Are they self-chosen outliers, deviants, or examples of inadequate disciplinary socialization? Do they reflect the particular dynamics of those with distinctive special interests? Or are their experiences characteristic of academics who are engaged in the formation of new specialities or interdisciplinary fields?

While I am not proposing generalizability from this small sample of women faculty, I am suggesting that the data may illuminate some persistent dynamics of conflict and ambiguity in academic life that are overlooked when one begins in the aggregate by attributing cohesion of purpose to departments and institutions. Whether it be for academics who engage in not-yet-legitimate academic pursuits or even for those who apparently have conventional disciplinary and departmental affiliations, the process of forming a scholarly identity, the nature of interpersonal communication, and positioning oneself within the academic reward system may be central features of academic organizational life that have been understudied and undertheorized.

The nature of academic organization needs to be reconceptualized because departmental units do not necessarily or inevitably determine behavior, interests, and, more profoundly, the pace and direction of knowledge change. That is, the formation of intentional communities may be integral to the process of negotiating the tension between constraints and academic reward structure and personal ambitions, between the designation of what is cutting edge versus trivial, and between determining what is legitimately innovative versus what is off the map. The consequences for innovation in higher education are significant, as there is a perennial need to consider which administrative frameworks foster scholarly creativity. As Dean MacHenry has noted: "In scholarship, as in farming, the most fertile soil may be under the fences, rather than at the center of long-established fields" (1977, ix). Similarly, Angela Simeone has proposed that "there are some who would argue that these networks constitute the most vital development within the recent history of American higher education" (1987, 99).

Functionalist conceptions do not make problematic how, where and why faculty seek and find intellectual community, since a premise of overlapping memberships assures that affinities will converge along two primary lines of disciplinary and campus affiliations. Such an orientation assumes that beliefs lead to commitments (Clark 1987, 106–7) and commitments lead to community. Beliefs and increasingly specialized orientations more or less correspond to, or at least complement, one's departmental affiliation; otherwise, a new unit will be differentiated. A further functionalist presupposition is one of coordination, where the organization of academic work and knowledge acts as a "framework for both resolving conflicting interests and advancing common ones" (Clark 1987, 109). In spite of "narrow groups that in turn generate their own separate subcultures," cultural overlap emerges from a common commitment to shared, overarching principles and beliefs (Clark 1987, 109, 140–42).

While my analysis challenges Clark's rationalistic premises, one functionalist proposition finds support in this analysis: beliefs get played out differently in organizational settings (Clark 1987, Chapt. 5). At research universities, disciplinary and cutting edge scholarship are valued; whereas in the comprehensive college sector, both faculty and administration, the "they" to whom faculty often refer, turn their attention to teaching and undergraduate enrollments. Using this analytical distinction, I examined how these different organizational settings may inhibit or foster informal, cross-departmental faculty networks.

As the analysis revealed, location was linked with distinctive patterns of association among faculty. Feminist scholarly activity at the comprehensive university most closely approximates a subculture, although this particular subculture seems more likely to subvert that status quo enterprise than enhance it. The research university could not generate and sustain a viable cross-departmental network; instead faculty behavior tended to either correspond to, or complement, lines of differentiation in the formal structure. Both patterns illustrate that structural and cultural features of organizational life may be a coercive force. Yet faculty are active agents who may try to reshape their immediate academic settings; further, faculty's innovative interests may be tied to wider external culture. Thus, when supposedly shared beliefs are viewed in their respective organizational embodiments, far more variation, fragmentation, conflict and ambiguity exist than the *e pluribus unum* framework presumes.

For those who study higher education, a theoretical and methodological directive is clear. The kinds of questions we need to ask about academic life need to reflect complexity, not only of structures but of processes; not of distinct levels but of mechanisms that cross-cut and potentially undermine the levels; not of daily life inside an organization but of how daily life is necessarily situated in wider socio-cultural circumstances. The questions locate both the realities or organizational life and the potentials for change in people's subjective experiences, not solely in *a priori* notions of formal structure, dominant norms, and beliefs as determinative.

Indeed, an even further diversity of perspectives is necessary to understand something as complex as the nature of academic change. As illustrative of one emerging approach, a critical culture perspective signifies a marked departure from functionalist premises in order to take seriously the interplay between prevailing social structures and individuals' perceptions and agency (Tierney 1991). The intention is to yield a more accurate portrayal, not only of the variation in academic life in its myriad settings but also of the ways in which research from a functionalist perspective advances a myth of unity in pluralism. The aim is to examine how interests may conflict and come to be differently valued, "not to celebrate organization as a value, but to question the ends it serves" (Smircich 1983, 355). Nor is it the intention to remain silent on the unresolved and unacknowledged controversies underlying established departmental categories, but rather "to think about them and to recognize they [themselves are] the product of theoretical choices" (Graff 1987, 8).

Although some proponents of this line of inquiry approach their data with an etic standpoint from the top down, other proponents of a critical cultural analysis advocate inductive inquiry that begins at the local level from the inside out. From either perspective, a cultural analysis makes problematic conventional functionalist analyses of such essential academic processes as curricular change, faculty hiring and promotion, and academic program planning. It forces us to rethink concepts such as hierarchy—an all-important context of academic life. For instance, rather than seeing hierarchy as an ordered arrangement that promotes coordination and excellence, hierarchy may also be examined as a means of social control which is contested between the Weberian bureaucratic interests for self-regulation and autonomy.

From this line of inquiry, empirical study on the problem of social integration generates a wider range of questions worth pursuing, ultimately for revising theoretical explanations of the nature of academic organization. For example, how and under what conditions do academic organizations reflect enduring systemic disequilibria, either in the contemporary era or historically? Are there new types of social and intellectual integration that have emerged beyond the administratively decentralized, rational organizational order; if so, how has the formation of intentional communities played a role in academic change? Are current faculty commitments pointing to a disintegration of the modern academic role, or possibly to a postmodern legitimacy for explicit expression of political and economic commitments, or perhaps to an institutionally mediated academic role in which certain commitments and behaviors—such as political protest or economic entrepreneurship—are deemed acceptable lines of partnership in certain kinds of campus settings but not in others?

As researchers of higher education define directions for further organizational studies, they will determine whether the various structural and cultural analyses of higher education may be used in a complementary manner or may be judged incompatible on the basis of divergent directives for what to study, how to study it, and to what end. It remains to be seen whether this uncertainty should be interpreted as a sign of knowledge growth and differentiation in a maturing field of study or as a sign of impending fragmentation and cultural ambiguity in a field of study that is itself inescapably embedded in multiple nested contexts.

Bibliography

Blau, Peter. *The Organization of Academic Work.* New York: John Wiley & Sons, 1973.

Bowen, Howard, and Jack Schuster. *American Professors: A National Resource Imperiled.* New York: Oxford University Press,1986.

Clark, Burton R. *The Distinctive College.* Chicago: Aldine, 1970.

_____. "The Organizational Saga in Higher Education." *Administrative Science Quarterly* 17 (June 1972): 178–84.

_____. *The Higher Education System: Academic Organization in Cross National Perspective.* Berkeley: University of California Press, 1983.

_____, ed. *The Academic Life: Small Worlds, Different Worlds.* Princeton: The Carnegie Foundation for the Advancement of Teaching, 1987.

Dill, David D. "The Management of Academic Culture: Notes on the Management of Meaning and Social Integration." *Higher Education* 11 (May 1982): 303–20.

Durkheim, Emile. *The Division of Labor in Society.* 1933; reprint ed., New York: The Free Press,1984.

Geertz, Clifford. "The Way We Think Now: Toward an Ethnography of Modern Thought." In his *Local Knowledge: Further Essays in Interpretive Anthropology.* 147-66. New York: Basic Books, 1983.

Glaser, Barney, and Anselm Strauss. *The Discovery of Grounded Theory: Strategies for Qualitive Research.* New York: Aldine, 1967.

Graff, Gerald. *Professing Literature: An Institutional History.* Chicago: The University of Chicago Press, 1987.

Gumport, Patricia J. "The Social Construction of Knowledge: Individual and Institutional Commitments to Feminist Scholarship." Ph.D.diss., Stanford University, 1987.

_____. "Curricula as Signposts of Cultural Change." *Review of Higher Education* 12 (Autumn 1988): 49–61.

_____. "Feminist Scholarship as a Vocation." *Higher Education* 20 (October 1990): 231–43.

Harman, Kay. "The Symbolic Dimension of Academic Organization: Academic Culture at the University of Melbourne." Ph.D. diss., La Trobe University, 1988.

Kuh, George, and Elizabeth Whitt. *The Invisible Tapestry: Culture in American Colleges and Universities.* ASHE-ERIC Higher Education Reports, Washington, D.C.: Association for the Study of Higher Education, 1988.

Lincoln, Yvonna S. "Toward a future-Oriented Comment on the State of the Profession." *Review of Higher Education 10* (Winter 1986): 135–42.

MacHenry, Dean. "Preface." In *Academic Departments,* edited by Dean MacHenry and Associates, ix-xvi. San Francisco: Jossey-Bass, 1977.

Masland, Andrew T. "Organization Culture in the Study of Higher Education." *Review of Higher Education* 8 (Winter 1985): 157–68.

Rudolph, Frederick. *Curriculum: A History of the American Undergraduate Curriculum Since 1936.* San Francisco: Jossey-Bass, 1981.

Simeone, Angela. *Academic Women: Working Toward Equality.* South Hadley, Mass.: Bergin and Garvey; 1987.

Smircich, Linda. "Concepts of Cultural and Organizational Analysis." *Administrative Science Quarterly* 28 (1983): 339–58.

Tierney, William G. "Organizational Culture in Higher Education: Defining the Essentials." *Journal of Higher Education 59* (January/February 1988): 2–21.

_____, ed. *Culture and Ideology in Higher Education: Advancing a Critical Agenda.* New York: Praeger, 1991.

Trow, Martin. "The Analysis of Status." In *Perspectives on Higher Education,* edited by Burton Clark, Chap. 5. Berkeley: University of California Press, 1984.

A Feminist Reinterpretation of Presidents' Definitions of Leadership*

ESTELA MARA BENSIMON

Asked what the word leadership means, College President Wittman responded by saying;

> . . . it means being first among equals. It is not hierarchical. It means persuading, educating, consulting, pulling, shoving, biting in directions you want people to move. It includes the elements of democracy. It means leading by example, goal-setting. You must have vision. Without it the people and the institution perish.

President Franz answered the same question in the following manner:

> Leadership is the totality of the person. Leadership is understanding that the university existed before you came and it will continue after you leave. The leader must assimilate and articulate the goals, massage and reorient them some, and by doing this, by nudging, the leader can move the organization in the direction of the goals. It is a cheerleader role-making the institution feel good about itself by symbolic things that the leader does.

Using four organizational frames—bureaucratic, collegial, political, and symbolic—I analyzed the content of these two college presidents' definitions of leadership and found that their conceptions of it were similar (Bensimon, 1989). Both definitions had elements associated with the collegial, political, and symbolic organizational frames.

President Franz and President Wittman also look remarkably similar on the basis of other coding schemes used to analyze interviews in which they participated in 1986-87 as part of a study of institutional leadership. For example, Neumann and Bensimon (1990) found both presidents to be internally connected to their institutions; Neumann (1989) found that both presidents made use of interpretive strategy and Birnbaum (1989) found that both considered leadership a two-way process of mutual influence.

What none of these studies reveal is that President Wittman is a man and President Franz a woman. They are part of a cohort of 32 presidents participating in a 5-year study of institutional leadership.[1] In addition to President Franz, this cohort includes seven other women presidents. Yet, none of the studies that have emerged from this body of research look at the women in the group separately from the men. This is not unusual, as most works on management and leadership assume that women experience leadership in the same way as their male counterparts. However, feminist analysis and scholarship maintain that the submergence of women in an all-encompassing male or genderless category distorts their unique experiences. Moreover, the failure to look at women separately imposes severe limitations on the understanding of leadership if we assume that gender plays a critical role in issues of power and decision making.

My intent in this paper is twofold. First, I will provide a brief feminist critique of the prevailing conceptual frameworks and methods upon which we rely to examine leadership in colleges and universities. I shall do this by returning to the "frames study" in which I originally portrayed presidents Wittman and Franz and suggesting that the conceptual orientations and analytic methods of analysis used in that study contributed to the suppression of women's particular experiences and, therefore, to the exclusion of their distinct voice from our examination of leadership. I chose to focus on the frames study because its conceptual base reflects conventional views of organizations as bureaucracies, collegiums, political systems, or organized anarchies (see Bensimon, Neumann, & Birnbaum 1989, for a general description and review; also Birnbaum, 1988; Bolman & Deal, 1984).

In the second part of the paper, I will follow up the critique with a feminist reinterpretation of the definitions of leadership provided above by presidents Wittman and Franz. This time, I will not filter their replies through the frames but permit them to speak more naturally, in their own voices and, thereby retain their individual identity. My intent is to set up a more free-flowing analysis that permits a fuller examination of the the apparent similarity of their concepts of leadership. The analysis I am about to undertake is based on only two individuals; therefore, I wish to stress that I am neither attempting to generalize nor to portray one as being good and the other as bad.

Part I: Critique

In the spirit that "knowledge is the result of constant assault on conventionally understood boundaries" (Ring, 1987, p. 763) I propose to confront my own work and test it by means of the "woman question." Posing the woman question means determining to what extent conceptual frameworks, research designs, methodologies, and the interpretation of findings fail "to take into account the experiences and values that seem more typical of women than of men" (Bartlett, 1990, p. 837). The woman question pushes us to consider how the epistemological and ontological bases of conceptual frameworks may misrepresent the experiences of women as leaders, thereby distorting our specific knowledge of such experiences and our general knowledge of the phenomenon of leadership as gender-encompassing. According to Bartlett (1990), the woman question assumes that how we know what we know "may be not only nonneutral in a general sense, but also 'male' in a specific sense. The purpose of the woman question is how to expose those features and how they operate, and to suggest how they might be corrected" (p. 837).

The "Frames Study"

In the "frames study" I used standard methods of content analysis to code references[2] in the presidents' discussions of leadership by their correspondence to four organizational frames: bureaucratic, collegial, political, and symbolic:

- In the *bureaucratic frame* the institution is seen as a mechanistic hierarchy with clearly established lines of authority. Presidents using a bureaucratic frame are likely to emphasize their role in making decisions, getting results, and establishing systems of management.

- In the *collegial frame* the institution is seen as a collegium, a community of equals, or a community of scholars (Goodman, 1962; Millett, 1962). Presidents who use a collegial frame are consensus-oriented and seek participative and democratic decision making.

- In the *political frame* the institution is seen as a composite of formal and informal groups vying for power to control institutional processes and outcomes. In the political frame the president is a mediator or negotiator between shifting power blocs, a statesman presiding over a cabinet form of administration.

- In the *symbolic frame* the institution is seen as a cultural system of shared meanings and beliefs in which organizational structures and processes are invented. Presidents who adhere to the symbolic frame are primarily catalysts or facilitators in a continual process of organization. They do not so much lead the institution as channel its activities in subtle ways. They do not plan rationally but try to apply preexisting solutions to current problems. (Baldridge, Curtis, Ecker, & Riley, 1978)

The frames' androcentric roots. Even though androcentrism in the frames varies in intensity (i.e., more in the bureaucratic; less in the collegial and symbolic), all four derive from theories developed through studies of men. The schools of thought associated with the bureaucratic and collegial models, despite being philosophically different (e.g., scientific management *vs.* human relations), share a common concern—how to increase the productivity of men usually engaged in physical or mechanical work. The political and symbolic frames, though more contemporary, are inspired by models in organizational sociology and organization theory which also neglect gender issues (Blackmore, 1989; Hearn & Parkin, 1983).

Androcentrism lies not only in the epistemological origins of the frames, but also in the manner in which they have been adapted to the study of academic organizations and their administration. The key features of the bureaucratic, collegial, and political conceptualizations of leadership in colleges and universities were delineated and refined through studies of academic decision making that did not take gender into consideration. Thus they are a more accurate representation of men's experiences in academic organizations. For example, the central concepts in the collegial model, despite their resonance to the feminist concept of connectedness (Gilligan, 1982), refer to the experiences, values, and beliefs of a collectivity or community of scholars that was (and still is) dominated by males.

The political model derives from a case study of male administrators in a research university (Baldridge, 1971). It is a distinctly masculinist model in that it subscribes to a form of decision-making—the balancing of opposing claims—which is more typical of men than women. Furthermore, it promulgates a conception of power that is based on the idea of control and domination. Carroll (1984) critiques this view of power and leadership by citing Nancy Harstock's (1981) observation that:

> Most social scientists have based their discussions of power on definitions of power as the ability to compel obedience, or as control and domination. They link this definition with Bertrand Russell's statement that power is the production of intended effects, and add that power must be power over someone—something possessed, a property of an actor such that he can alter the will or actions of others in a way that produces results in conformity with his own will. (pp. 3–4)

The symbolic model differs somewhat in its gender orientation from the collegial and political models in that the sample of 42 presidents upon which it is based included several women presidents, although the exact number is not specified. Yet *Leadership and Ambiguity* (Cohen & March, 1974), which introduced us to the idea of leadership in the "organized anarchy" and is to date one of the best analyses of the academic presidency from a symbolic perspective, gives no indication that the study design took into account differences between the men and women presidents. Cohen and March suggest ways in which administrators can overcome organizational constraints and make changes supporting their own desired outcomes. A feminist critique takes issue with these tactics because, first of all, they are purely instrumental. But a second and much more serious point of contention would have to be the tactics' reliance on deception. For example, Cohen and March's recommendation to leaders to "interpret history" suggests that administrators should put off preparing records of meetings, decisions made, and significant campus activities until enough time has elapsed so that the accounts can be written in a manner that is consistent with actions seen as desirable in the present. A feminist critique argues that such a tactic is abhorrent as it implies deceit. Moreover, it is the kind of tactic frequently used by powerful elites to silence minority voices and deflate their positions.

Overlooking gender in the frame analysis. The most conspicuous omission in the "frames" study was my failure to report the findings on the basis of gender. Even though the study cohort included eight women presidents, analysis proceeded on the basis of institutional type and presidents' length of tenure, thus foregoing the opportunity to bring women's definitions of leadership into the discourse.

By treating institutional (e.g., Carnegie type) and career (president's length of tenure) characteristics, rather than gender, as the major determinants of a president's conception of leadership, I reinforced the idea of leadership as a phenomenon that is shaped by objective and independent variables. This understanding of leadership is more consistent with the functionalist/positivist perspective (e.g., see Lincoln & Guba, 1985; Tierney, 1988) which feminists have criticized as reflecting a predominantly male interpretation of organizations and their management (Blackmore, 1989).

A basic premise of feminist theory is that women experience the social world differently than men do and that this translates into a particular epistemology and a particular ethic (Donovan, 1990). We might also say that it translates into a different experience and exercise of leadership. Sandra Harding (1986) maintains that "gender is a fundamental category within which meaning and value are assigned to everything in the world, a way of organizing human social relations" (p. 57). Therefore, if the study of leadership starts with the premise that it is a socially constructed phenomenon, gender must be taken into consideration.

Part II: Reinterpretation

Because the organizational frames are based on the experience of men, they reflect the dominant discourse on leadership: a discourse in which the leader is apart from the rest of the organization in a position that provides a more global perspective, and is therefore responsible for ensuring the survival of the organization.

A feminist perspective on leadership focuses on the influence of gender (rather than the abstract conceptions of organizational frames) on interpretations of leadership. Feminist analysis assumes that the characteristic experiences of men, as more privileged beings, and of women, as the "second sex," result in different conceptions of good leadership, and seeks to understand leadership from the point of view of women.

Obviously women are not bound by a single world view. However, recent scholarship on moral development reveals important differences between women and men which can serve as a point of departure, for a feminist analysis of leadership. These differences can be summarized as follows:

- Women, as a group, tend to define their identity in the terms of relationships, as opposed to men, who define their identity in terms of separation (Gilligan, 1982; Gilligan, Lyons, & Hammer, 1990).

- Women view themselves as interdependent and judge themselves by standards of responsibility and care toward others. Men view themselves primarily as independent and judge themselves by standards of individual achievement and competency (Ferguson, 1984).

- Women perceive a world made up of physically and socially embodied "things," which are concrete, particularistic, and continuous with one another, governed by wants and needs rather than rational control. Men perceive a world made up of physically and socially *dis*embodied "things," governed by uniform laws or rules that can be rationally understood and controlled by individuals (Ferguson, 1984).

I propose to return to Wittman's and Franz's definitions of leadership, provided at the beginning of the article, and to reinterpret their discourse from a feminist perspective. Within the parameters of the frames study, Allison Franz and Douglas Wittman were found to interpret "good presidential leadership" similarly. Their definitions included elements of the collegial, political, and symbolic frames. But what happens if the frames are put aside and the presidents' definitions of leadership are allowed to stand on their own? How alike do their definitions then seem? Is it possible that the organizational frames, when applied to their discourse, mask differences reflecting the way women and men experience leadership?

Before turning to these questions, I offer a brief description of the two presidents. Douglas Wittman and Allison Franz are presidents of public comprehensive colleges of approximately the same size, located in communities that are predominantly blue-collar. The students who attend their colleges tend to be the first in their families to go beyond high school. Their educational aspirations are fueled by the desire for professional careers. Both presidents are highly aware of the educational needs of their students and concerned with improving educational opportunities for minority students. Both also enjoy strong support from administrators and faculty. They have excellent relationships with faculty leaders on their campuses, are generally described in very positive terms, and are considered successful presidents.

The one major difference between them as presidents, in addition to that of gender, is that Allison Franz is a relative newcomer, while Douglas Wittman has been in office longer and therefore has greater experience.

Collegiality Reinterpreted as Differentiation and Holism

Wittman: Leadership . . . it means being first among equals. It is not hierarchical.

Franz: Leadership is the totality of the person . . . understanding that the university existed before you came and it will continue after you leave.

When these statements were analyzed through the use of the frames, they seemed to reflect a collegial perspective. The collegial element appears in the presidents' conceptions of their role within the context of an academic community. President Wittman's definition of the leader's role as "first among equals" brings to mind the classic image of the university as a community of scholars. President Franz exhibits a collegial orientation by specifically recognizing the perpetuity of the university.

However, when these statements are viewed from a feminist perspective a different interpretation emerges. Douglas Wittman's definition calls attention to the differentiation between the leader and members of the academic community by emphasizing positional ("first among equals") and structural ("it is not hierarchical") considerations that disembody leadership from the person.

In Allison Franz' definition a sense of holism is conveyed through the notion that leadership is indistinguishable from one's being, " . . . the totality of the person." Leadership, she implies, is based on the beliefs and values to which the individual subscribes. The themes of differentiation and holism are also discernable in the role these presidents accord the university within their definitions of leadership. In Wittman's definition the university is not mentioned, making it appear, by its absence, an amorphous entity, existing only as an extension of the president. In the definition given by Franz, the university emerges as a human organization that constructs its own reality. This theme—university-as-human-organization—is even more apparent in her elaboration of the process of leadership provided below.

The aspects of differentiation and holism are particularly apparent in the language of the presidents. Wittman's language gives prominence to the leader; in Franz's, the leader is imperceptible. Despite his explicit denial, Wittman implies the existence of hierarchy by his use of the phrase "first among equals." To be first is to stand out from the others, in importance and privilege. Franz's allusions to totality, existence, and continuity reflect less of a concern with the act of leadership and more with the context in which it takes place.

Political Skill Reinterpreted as the Accrual of Power Through Separation and Connection

> Wittman: Leadership means persuading, educating, consulting, pulling, shoving, biting in directions you want people to move.... It means leading by example, goal setting.

> Franz: The leader must assimilate and articulate the goals, massage, and re-orient them some, and by doing this, by nudging, the leader can move the organization in the direction of the goals.

In the frames study, the series of verbs in Wittman's statement ("persuading, educating, consulting, pulling, shoving, biting") was understood as a reference to the political processes involved in the exercise of leadership. Consistent with the political model, Wittman construes power as the ability to move people in the direction which he, as the leader, sets for the institution. In Franz' definition the term "nudging" was also construed as an indication of involvement in political processes such as persuading and negotiating.

However, the frames perspective does not show that, even though Wittman and Franz conceive of the process of leadership in terms of *moving people* in a predetermined direction, they have a different understanding of how this is accomplished. Wittman explains the process of leadership by means of a string of action verbs that denote increasing coerciveness. The focus is on accomplishing the leader's desired ends—collegially or forcefully—which are presumed to be synonymous with the needs of the institution. His explanation conveys an image of the leader, separate from the institution, gathering all his energy and skills to move it in the right direction.

Allison Franz, while also concerned with moving people, sees the source of movement as a force of *attraction* emanating from the mission (or goals) of the institution, rather than from the leader. She situates leadership within the context of the university. The university, not the leader, is the focus of attention in her definition. Her identify as leader depends on becoming part of the university. The image of the leader assimilating the university's goals, rather than imposing them, infuses her definition with a relational quality. It suggests that before she can exercise leadership, she has to become part of the existing culture. Thus she creates a sense of continuity and connection with the institution.

Symbolic Management Reinterpreted as Instrumentalism and Responsiveness

> Wittman: You [the president] must have vision. Without it the people and the institution perish.

> Franz: If [the president's role] is a cheerleader role—making the institution feel good about itself by symbolic things that the leader does.

In the frames study Wittman's image of the president as a visionary and Franz' as a cheerleader were interpreted to indicate that leadership is essentially the symbolic management of meaning. But a feminist analysis suggests an alternative interpretation. Wittman has a view of leadership that is strongly individualistic and instrumental. In portraying the leader as the creator of a vision that becomes a motivating force for others, the leader assumes a central place, while everyone else recedes to the edges. This suggests that the leader has a broader view of the institution and its environment and therefore a more complete picture than others inside the institution. Such a leader assumes the almost heroic proportions of a protector, a role typically associated with men.

Franz has a less grandiose image of the leader, mainly because she construes the role in responsive terms—being aware of the needs of the organization and celebrating its accomplishments so that it will continue to flourish. The leader as cheerleader suggests someone who is content to be on the sidelines, helping others attain their goals. Rather than fixing her attention on the outcome (e.g., survival of the institution), she provides the encouragement for others to fulfill their aspirations.

Allison Franz' definition of leadership is more difficult to fix with precision than Wittman's. His is more tangible because it describes leadership in terms of a quest for some specific end. Hers is more elusive because it is shaped by a concern to be responsive to human needs, reflecting her belief that "leadership is the totality of the person." It is exactly this quality—leadership as a process that is attached to, and continuous with, the person of the leader—that eludes a reductive explanation.

In sum, from a feminist perspective these two presidents' definitions are substantively different. Franz's originates in a conception of the university as a human organization and implies that the basis of academic leadership is the union between the leader and the university. The main point of divergence between the leader and the university. The main point of divergence between the two definitions is what Wittman's rests completely on the potential of the leader—on his visionary capacity, his ability to set goals that will seal the fate of the organization. Her definition achieves an integrative quality, while his reinforces the idea of leadership as differentiation and separation between the leader and the led. His view of leadership is more instrumental; he is an agent of organizational transformation. Hers is more expressive: She cares about the reality of the institution and is therefore open to the possibility of being transformed by it.

When these two presidents' narratives are juxtaposed and the organizational frames not applied to them, there is no question that their theories of leadership are dramatically different. The contrast between them suggests that the axioms of the collegial, political, and symbolic frames reflect Wittman's definition of leadership more accurately than Allison Franz's.

Part III: Conclusion

Because the four frames seem more representative of male constructions of organizational life, I am compelled to consider the gender implications of having used them as the interpretive tools for women's definitions of leadership. In making a blanket application of the frames to the definitions of leadership provided by women, I acted on the assumption that it is valid to interpret their experience through male-derived categories. In submitting the frames study to the "woman question" it becomes clear that to rigidly superimpose these particular organizational models (or any other leadership constructs) on the experience of women is to deprive them of their own story (Heilbrun, 1988). It also serves to perpetuate an incomplete understanding of administrative leadership in higher education.

In the case of Allison Franz, feminist theories of moral development (Gilligan, 1982; Noddings, 1984) can provide a more complete and sensible explanation for her definition of leadership, the enactment of leadership, and her self-perceptions as a leader. Such theories reveal important differences between men and women in how they see and know themselves, as well as in the standards they apply to moral decision making. The theories ascribe to women an identity of connection and an ethic of responsibility, and to men, an identity of separation and an ethic of rights.

Allison Franz's discourse is about connectedness. It is a prevailing characteristic of her talk. Her identity as president—as the leader of the institution—inheres in her ability to achieve a union with the campus community. When the language of connectedness is examined from the frames perspective, it can easily be misread as a manifestation of collegial, political, and symbolic awareness.

But when we examine it through feminist lenses we see that connectedness is much more fundamental: It shapes the very identity of the leader.

Allison Franz considers it important for the leader to accept the institution on its own terms. Feminist epistemology interprets such a stance positively, as an expression of acceptance of different realities. Josephine Donovan (1990) approves this posture as an unwillingness:

> . . . to wrench that context apart or to impose upon it alien abstractions or to use implements that subdue it intellectually or physically. Such an epistemology provides the basis for an ethic that is non-imperialistic, that is life-affirming, and that reverences the concrete details of life. (p. 173)

On the other hand, Ferguson (1984) points out that such a stance can be problematic if it is a reflection of women's experience as accommodation to the power of man.

The woman question revealed how conventional organizational constructs "silently and without justification submerge the perspectives of women and other excluded groups" (Bartlett, 1990, p. 836). Feminist critique has likewise exposed the exclusion of women's experiences in the conceptual models and methodologies that guide scholarship in the disciplines (Ferguson, 1984; Harding, 1986; Millman & Kanter, 1987) and practice in the professions (Bartlett, 1990; Blackmore, 1989; Noddings, 1984); it has also exposed the androcentric tendencies of these models.

This raises a question that I shall try to answer in conclusion: "Why is it that feminist thinking has not had demonstrable consequences, either critically or conceptually, in the study of the organization and administration of colleges and universities?" One possible reason is that, with a few noteworthy exceptions, women are largely invisible as interpreters of organizational life and leadership in the academy.

A more plausible reason is the fear of marginalization, both for the women we write about and for ourselves as women writing on a topic that is predominantly male. In bringing Allison Franz into the mainstream discourse on leadership there is the risk that because she does not speak the normative language of leadership, she will be dismissed. As I studied her definition of leadership I asked myself, "Why is it so disturbing to explain her stance of responsiveness? Why is her approach so much harder to describe than Douglas Wittman's?" The answer is obvious. The language used to express her stance of responsiveness is associated with women's role as nurturer. I feared that because she speaks a language that reflecting values associated with women, she would be trivialized. And that in placing her side by side with Douglas Wittman and revealing how differently she defines leadership, she would be misunderstood.

By focusing on the experiences of women, gender theory has provided a new perspective for viewing moral development (Gilligan, 1982), ways of knowing (Belenky, Clinchy, Goldberger, & Tarule, 1986), and the construction of social reality (Harding, 1986, 1987). Gender theory offers a means of access to Allison Franz's experience and thought that normative models of leadership cannot provide. Through such insights we can gain a better understanding of leadership, not only that of Allison Franz, but also Douglas Wittman's as well.

Notes

The author would like to express her gratitude to Anne Ard, Robert Birnbaum, Judith Glazer, Anna Neumann, William G. Tierney, and Kelly Ward, all of whom provided comments on an earlier draft of this article.

*This document was prepared pursuant to a grant from the Office of Educational Research and Improvement/Department of Education (OERI/ED). However, the opinions expressed herein do not necessarily reflect the position or policy of the OERI/ED and no official endorsement of the OERI/ED should be inferred. Support for this work was also provided by the Lilly Endowment, Inc. and TIAA-CREF.

1. The Institutional Leadership Project is a 5-year longitudinal study of presidents, vice-presidents, trustees, and faculty leaders in 32 colleges and universities, conducted as part of the National Center for Postsecondary

Governance and Finance. The purpose of the ILP is to study how individuals in formal leadership positions set goals, conduct agendas, communicate and interact, transmit values, and evaluate their effectiveness.

2. In the frames study I constructed the presidents' theories of leadership by abstracting data from the total interview transcript and their responses to the following question: "How does President X [the respondent] define good presidential leadership?" To identify presidents' frames, I analyzed espoused theories of leadership as if they were made up of two distinct components: leadership as the process of providing direction to a group or an institution and the ways in which presidents prefer to provide direction. I used content analysis to code references to elements of the four frames in a sustained interview passage. The excerpts reflecting President Wittman's and President Franz's definitions of leadership provided in the opening paper represent only a portion of the actual passage used to determine their espoused theories of leadership. I considered that presidents used a frame if their responses contained at least two references to it (Bensimon, 1989, pp. 111–112).

References

Baldridge, J.V. (1971). *Power and conflict in the university*. New York: John Wiley & Sons.

Baldridge, V.J., Curtis, D.V., Ecker, G., & Riley, G. (1978). *Policy making and effective leadership: A national study of academic management*. San Francisco: Jossey-Bass.

Bartlett, K.T. (1990). Feminist legal methods. *Harvard Law Review. 103* (4), 829–888.

Belenky, M.F., Clinchy, B.M., Goldberger, N.G., & Tarule, J.M. (1986). *Women's ways of knowing: The development of self, voice, and mind*. New York: Basic Books.

Bensimon, E.M. (1989). The meaning of "good presidential leadership": A frame analysis. *The Review of Higher Education, 12*, 107–123.

Bensimon, E.M., Neumann, A., & Birnbaum, R. (1989. *Making sense of administrative leadership: The "L" word in higher education*. Washington, DC: ASHE-ERIC Higher Education Reports.

Birnbaum, R. (1988). *How colleges work: The cybernetics of academic organization and leadership*. San Francisco: Jossey-Bass.

Birnbaum, R. (1989). The implicit leadership theories of college and university presidents. *Review of Higher Education, 12*, 125–136.

Blackmore, J. (1989). Educational leadership: A feminist critique and reconstruction. In J. Smyth (Ed.), *Critical perspectives on educational leadership* (pp. 93–129). London: Falmer Press.

Bolman, L.G., & Deal, T.E. (1984). *Modern approaches to understanding and managing organizations*. San Francisco: Jossey-Bass.

Carroll, S.J. (1984). Feminist scholarship on political leadership. In B. Kellerman (Ed.), *Leadership: Multidisciplinary perspectives* (pp. 139–156). Englewood Cliffs, NJ: Prentice-Hall.

Cohen, M.D., & March, J.G. (1974). *Leadership and ambiguity: The American college presidency*. New York: McGraw-Hill.

Donovan, J. (1990). *Feminist theory: The intellectual traditions of American feminism*. New York: Continuum.

Ferguson, K.E. (1984). *The feminist case against bureaucracy*. Philadelphia: Temple University Press.

Gilligan, C. (1982). *In a different voice: Psychological theory and women's development*. Cambridge, MA: Harvard University Press.

Gilligan, C., Lyons, C.P., & Hammer, T.J. (Eds.). (1990). *Making connections; The relational worlds of adolescent girls at Emma Willard's school.* Cambridge, MA: Harvard University Press.

Goodman, P. (1962). *The community of scholars.* New York: Random House.

Harding, S. (1986). *The science question in feminism.* Ithaca, NY: Cornell University Press.

Harding, S. (Ed.) (1987). *Feminism and methodology.* Bloomington, IN: Indiana University Press.

Harstock, N. (1981). Political change: Two perspectives on power. In C. Bunch (Ed.), *Building Feminist Theory.* New York: Longman.

Hearn, J.P., & Parkin, W. (1983). Gender and organizations: A selective review and a critique of a neglected area. *Organizational Studies, 4,* 219–242.

Heilbrun, C.G. (1988). *Writing a woman's life.* New York: Ballantine Books.

Lincoln, Y.S., & Guba, E.G. (1985). *Naturalistic inquiry.* Beverly Hills, CA: Sage.

Millett, J.D. (1962). *The academic community: An essay on organization.* New York: McGraw-Hill.

Millman, M., & Kanter, R. (1987). Introduction to another voice: Feminist perspectives on social life and social science. In S. Harding (Ed.), *Feminism and methodology* (pp. 29–36). Bloomington, IN: Indiana University Press.

Neumann, A. (1989). Strategic leadership: The changing orientations of college presidents. *The Review of Higher Education, 12,* 137–151.

Neumann, A., & Bensimon, E.M. (1990). Constructing the presidency: College presidents' images of their leadership roles, a comparative study. *Journal of Higher Education, 61* (6), 676–701.

Noddings, N. (1984). *Caring: A feminine approach to ethics and moral education.* Berkeley, CA: University of California Press.

Ring, J. (1987). Toward a feminist epistemology. *American Journal of Political Science, 31* (4), 753–772.

Tierney, W.G. (1988). Organizational culture in higher education. *Journal of Higher Education, 59,* 2–21.

New Faculty as Colleagues

Robert Boice

This study, based on repeated interviews, tracked four successive cohorts of new faculty at a large state university over each of their semesters on campus. It documents trends for these new hires, notably in how they coped with social and intellectual isolation, with conflicts between their own and senior faculty's values, and with finding social support. New faculty evidenced differences as a function of the degree of their experience and of return from non-academic careers. Older and more experienced new faculty found fewer friends and social supports on campus. New faculty needed at least three years to feel a real part of campus.

This paper describes a longitudinal study of new faculty adjusting to a large state university over four successive cohorts and four successive years. It addresses an unmet need in the study of higher education; as yet we know little about how faculty fare through transitional phases in their careers (Menges & Mathis, 1988) or about what contributes to recruiting and retaining them. What we do know, all too well, is that ever fewer talented individuals opt for careers as professors (Bowen & Schuster, 1986).

Three of the best studies in this area show the promises and limitations of existing studies of new faculty. One, by Braskamp, Fowler, and Ory (1984), shows that assistant professors often are narrowly oriented to scholarly productivity, not to teaching excellence. Another, by Fink (1984), confirms the impression that new faculty experience heavy work loads and want more support and feedback. The third study, by Sorcinelli (1985), documents the satisfactions and concerns of faculty, including new hires. But these studies do not inquire beyond a single year or gather histories of new faculty's broad experiences as colleagues, scholars, and teachers.

The present study is the first of three longitudinal studies of new faculty, divided into the domains of collegiality, scholarly productivity, and teaching success. This paper depicts new faculty as colleagues who deal, over semesters, with problems of collegiality, including social and intellectual isolation, cultural conflicts with senior faculty, and finding social support. It follows the tradition of researchers who have studied the careers of academics via life history accounts (for example, Evetts, 1989) and it attempts, in the style of other qualitative studies (for example, Beynon, 1985), to use descriptive data as a basis for understanding the new faculty experience.

Interviewing Cohorts of New Faculty

All the new faculty interviewed for this study came from one campus, a "comprehensive university" with some 35,000 students and about 1,000 full-time faculty. All but one to three new tenure-track faculty in each of the four successive cohorts volunteered for participation in this program of repeated interviews and visits. While participants technically were volunteers, they often had to be coaxed into agreement; initial contacts were marred by faculty failing to be in their offices for appointments, carrying out other business during interviews, and questioning the credentials of the two interviewers. Eventually, though, all the participants came to welcome these visits, often commenting that we were their only outlets for complaining and perhaps the only people on campus who took a sustained interest in them.

Cohorts

The four successively hired cohorts of new faculty began with 29, 40, 48, and 68 participants. Although no participants dropped out of the study as long as they remained on campus, numbers dropped to 20, 24, 40 and 62 by the last set of interviews. Some new faculty had left campus in each cohort. All four cohorts cut across the university's colleges and disciplines (applied arts & sciences, business, education, engineering, fine arts, humanities, natural sciences, and social & behavioral sciences). These cohorts represented the first major hiring activity in 15 years for most academic departments. The burst of hiring signalled a formal change; new faculty were hired with a clear expectation of publishing.

As the study progressed, a critical distinction emerged; new faculty were differentiated as inexperienced (with less than three years beyond the terminal degree), returning (from careers outside academe), and experienced (at full-time teaching on another campus). Beginning numbers for inexperienced new faculty were 18, 13, 14, and 21 over the four cohorts. Beginning numbers for returning faculty were 3, 6, 5, and 2 over the four cohorts. Beginning numbers for experienced new faculty were 8, 21, 29, and 47 over the four cohorts.

Interviews and Other Visits

The interview formats have been published elsewhere (Turner & Boice, 1987). Interviews continued over semesters, for as long as four years. Briefly, the interview forms directed new faculty to speak about and rate their recent experiences, collegial interactions, scholarly productivity, academic philosophy, teaching concerns and successes, and career plans. (Only material pertaining to collegiality is reported here.) During the first three years, until budget cuts set in, Jimmie L. Turner shared the interviewing responsibilities with me. By the end of the fourth year, further budget cuts on campus ended my presence there.

The visits to new faculty, however, consisted of much more than structured interviewing. Interactions lasted at least an hour, almost always with success in getting new faculty to add open-ended responses to structured answers. Thus, beyond the set questions, individuals chose what to emphasize and develop.

The First Semester on Campus

Loneliness

Except for two or three individuals per cohort, new faculty uniformly emphasized feelings of loneliness and intellectual understimulation. This was their most salient complaint and took clear precedence over workload and busyness. One assistant professor from the first cohort typified her colleagues' comments;

> In graduate school, I always had people around me to talk with, people who were doing similar things, people who worried about me and me about them. What worries me most about being here is not so much the lack of social contact—I can understand, I suppose, why most of my colleagues are rarely here on campus—as it is the lack of ideas and of caring about my teaching and research. I

worry that I may never have ideas of my own for research. I guess that I'm a lot more dependent on the people around me for ideas and motivation than I realized.

But feelings of isolation and understimulation were not exclusive to inexperienced new faculty. Returning new faculty felt just as isolated although they already had learned that the supportiveness of graduate school may evaporate in real-life jobs. A returning faculty member observed in quiet, bemused fashion,

> Now that I'm here I realize that they hired me only because they couldn't find anyone else qualified in my speciality area and with a Ph. D. Now that I'm here no one pays much attention to me. That's disappointing, I suppose, but I should have known that this would happen. The other people in the department have their own business to take care of. I wish this were a happier place, one where we took more interest in what each other teaches.

Experienced faculty were the most surprised at their isolation. Almost without exception, these faculty had been hired because they already were productive as researchers on other campuses. As a rule, the recruitment process had set up the false expectations expressed by an associate professor who brought a substantial grant to campus:

> When they recruited me they couldn't be complimentary enough. They courted me. Now that I'm on campus, I feel ignored. They not only don't care about my lab and my research, they've actually undermined my efforts to set it up. If I had known what things would be like here, I would never have come. It puzzles me. Does this sort of thing happen to other new faculty?

Changes in Collegiality Over Time

Isolation and understimulation relate to collegiality. In every interview administered in first semesters on campus, new faculty were asked to rate their departmental colleagues for collegiality. Table l shows simple, descriptive data over cohorts. The data are not broken down according to backgrounds because the responses of the three groups were closely identical. The striking result shown in Table l is one repeated throughout this study; that is, across cohorts, the collegial climate seems to have improved over time. Whereas newcomers in 1985 and 1986 routinely reported hostile comments from colleagues with more seniority, new faculty who began in 1987 and 1988 rarely commented on such matters.

The most commonly reported categories of cultural conflict (irrespective of their decline in frequency over the four cohorts) are these rank-ordered complaints about more senior faculty: (a) Senior faculty routinely excluded them from departmental decisions, (b) senior faculty complained about new faculty's greater interest in gaining national visibility rather than local visibility as professionals, (c) senior faculty were disinterested in accounts of new faculty's research, (d) senior faculty complained of new faculty's narrow interests in teaching speciality courses, and (e) senior faculty loudly designated teaching and research as mutually incompatible activities.

Table 1
New faculty reporting different levels of collegial support/help, first semester

Level of support/help	Year cohort began			
	1985	1986	1987	1988
High	28%	38%	46%	49%
Medium	31%	35%	46%	41%
Low	41%	27%	8%	10%

Perhaps because these indices of cultural conflict declined strikingly over the four cohorts, the ratings of collegial support shown in Table 1 improved accordingly. As we will see presently, new faculty may have been responding to more than the lessening of hostilities in rating the collegial climate as friendlier. In subsequent years on campus, they reported finding increased collegial support and help. New faculty who began in years 3 and 4 of this study reported hearing, from both recent hires and old hands, that acceptance of new faculty had improved noticeably. A comment from an assistant professor in cohort 3 illustrates the point:

> I gather that things have gotten better for new people here . . ., who started here two years ago, told me some horror stories about how the old timers treated him. They seemed threatened by the presence of someone new, someone who is doing research, someone whom the students seemed to like a lot. But, according to him, that tension or resentment seems to have lessened. As far as I can tell, the same people who had trouble adjusting to new comers have quieted down. They generally leave me alone; they're friendly in a superficial way . . . when I see them. Sometimes I wish they would show more interest, but then I'm not sure they would understand what I'm doing.

The Substance of Collegial Help

As new faculty's colleagues were perceived as friendlier, the substance of help improved slightly. The number of new faculty reporting advice specific to professional activities went up from 17% to 30% over successive first semesters for each cohort. Still, two other aspects of advice from senior colleagues disappointed new faculty across all cohorts. First, the level of gossip and political intrigue always was far higher than new faculty would have preferred (it comprised about 50% of all advice given over first semesters). Second, of all work-related advice, useful hints about teaching were the rarest (never exceeding 3% of the total content). Excerpts from the notes on inexperienced assistant professors in cohorts 1 and 3 illustrate the point;

> Most of my colleagues like to complain about each other. They warn me about the people to avoid because they are deadwood or because they are explosive. They tell me stories about assistant professors who have failed—I could do without that, especially considering that these stories don't really tell me much about how I can survive.

> [In response to my question about whether colleagues give much advice about teaching]: No, almost none, except to complain about the poor quality of students here. As a matter of fact, when I've mentioned teaching in terms of wanting to do well, I've been looked at askance. Some of my colleagues seem to be more comfortable talking about almost anything else.

> There are few people, like . . . and . . ., who talk to me but I wish I could tell you that the conversations were worthwhile. It is mostly gossip, so much so that I wonder what they will say about me. Some of it is good-natured, though. The problem is that very little of it is about what must be done to get tenure . . . except for some vague comments like "you'll have to publish."

Another surprising result from this interview question was that the three kinds of new faculty (inexperienced, experienced, and returning) reported no differences among themselves in terms of help and support received. In later years on campus, though, inexperienced faculty indicated greater levels of help received. The seeming paradox was this: senior faculty often reported (in a more informal series of interviews) feeling that they should leave new faculty alone awhile, until they were settled. New faculty, as we have seen, felt very differently. Still, new faculty were notably passive about seeking collegial support; they generally expected others to come to them, much as had happened during the recruitment process.

A separate question was asked about specific plans to collaborate (as researchers or as teachers) with colleagues on campus. The percentages went up over cohorts (from around 20% to nearly 40% for research, and from 7% to 21% for coteaching), but not as much as anticipated. Clearly, new faculty were not feeling very optimistic, especially in terms of their own, much higher ratings of hoped-for collaboration. Data from other campuses may help to put this result in perspective. Sorcinelli and Near (1989), for instance, found that faculty at a campus with a strong research tradition cherished the supports and the milieu that greeted them.

When asked to describe their departmental colleagues in terms of most and least positive qualities, new faculty produced rank-orderings. Senior faculty were seen as *positive* in the following respects:

1. Liking both teaching and their students;

2. Appreciating their job security;

3. Appreciating their geographic location;

4. Envisioning a brighter future for their campus.

Senior faculty were seen as *negative* in these respects:

1. Burnout;

2. Overconcern with campus politics;

3. Paranoia;

4. Complaints about campus resources;

5. Complaints about poor quality students.

Perceptions of senior faculty as generally tired, unproductive, cynical, and even embarrassing persisted throughout the four years of this study.

Indeed, senior faculty presented a problem that is conspicuously absent in the literature about new faculty (see Seldin, 1987). They often were unable or unwilling to provide the kinds of effective supports and models that newcomers said they wanted in the midst of stressful transitions (and, possibly, in the midst of establishing lasting habits as professors). A sampling of typical comments of new faculty in their first year on campus helps to substantiate the point:

> [Assistant professor, inexperienced, cohort 1]: The older people here amaze me, They don't even look or act like professors. I don't think they're too comfortable having someone like me here. For sure, they haven't made me feel welcome. Let me tell you about what one guy said to me. He said, "Listen, what you want to do is get settled in your courses and then enjoy life. You'll see me out sailing when I can. You think you want to do research but you'll learn. I did."

> [Associate professor, experienced, cohort 3]: The old timers in my department do things that interfere, including saying negative things to students. Students come to me and actually tell me that . . . or . . . told them not to work with me. Fortunately, the students think it's a joke. I don't.

> [Associate professor, returning, cohort 2]: My problem here is the chairman and his friends. They have their own clique and they're not interested in helping me. They stick me with courses that they don't want to teach. They act like they don't have information on how to teach my courses.

A final trend in semester 1 proved to be of particular interest. Over cohorts, the campus seemed to hire new faculty with decreasing needs for collegiality. The percentage of interviewees who rated collegial support as important for job satisfaction and professional success generally decreased over cohorts (72%, 82%, 58% and 34%). But another explanation could account for the same data. Perhaps because they came to a campus growing more congenial to newcomers, succeeding cohorts felt less concerned about collegiality and, thus, rated their need for it lower.

Additional support for the first interpretation came from responses to another question. With each succeeding cohort, the percentage of new faculty who placed themselves toward the "independent" end of an imaginary continuum of preferred collegial style grew from 28%, to 25%, to 46% and then 53%. Over cohorts, then, new faculty described themselves as relatively noncollegial individuals of long-standing nature. For example,

> [Assistant professor, inexperienced, cohort 4]: I've always been able to do my best work alone. I like to have people to talk to, but I really don't need them as collaborators. Even in graduate school, I didn't need much help with things like my dissertation.

Without realizing it, the campus may have increasingly selected for new hires who would not barrage them with complaints about neglect once on campus. This same prejudice, if it existed, may have been evidenced in a growing preference vocalized by departmental hiring committees for more experienced faculty as new hires. At a campus-wide meeting for recruitment committees in 1987, senior faculty talked repeatedly about what they saw as a shortcoming of inexperienced new faculty already on campus: The new hires, presumably, were overly eager to leave campus for better jobs. The consensus was that the campus would fare better by hiring faculty who would show more "loyalty."

Experienced new faculty did rate themselves, incidentally, as more independent on the continuum of collegiality than did inexperienced new faculty. They rarely talked to me about planning to leave campus soon. And, over cohorts, proportionately more experienced new faculty were hired.

Second Semester on Campus

Collegial Support

Ratings of collegiality across all cohorts went down by the second semester on campus. Nonetheless, each successive cohort reported slightly higher levels of support from colleagues. Spontaneous comments provided an idea of what caused this drop in morale during the second semester. By the time they had been on campus for a semester, realities had set in. In particular, new faculty reported feeling depressed about the competence of senior faculty; familiarity was breeding contempt. This meant that plans for collaboration, especially where new faculty had no junior colleagues with similar interests, remained pessimistic.

Still, of newcomers from the three kinds of backgrounds, inexperienced faculty were more generous in rating their senior as being, on the average, competent (13%, 17%, 28% and 20% of inexperienced new faculty gave such ratings for senior colleagues) than were experienced and returning new faculty (their ratings ranged from 0% to 15% over the four cohorts).

Intellectual Stimulation

Not only did satisfaction with collegiality reach bottom in semester 2, but complaints also peaked about intellectual understimulation. Table 2 shows the result; the great majority of inexperienced new faculty rated intellectual stimulation as poor across all four cohorts.

In contrast, only about a third of experienced new faculty (who earlier had tended to rate themselves as needing little collegial support) complained about a serious lack of intellectual stimulation. Returning new faculty fell midway between the others in complaints about feeling berefit of ideas and prods in their departments.

Accordingly, inexperienced new faculty expressed the most concerns about this situation; they typically worried about how productive they could be as researchers if they were not stimulated to think beyond themselves. They wondered aloud how motivated they would remain in a context where almost no one else seemed excited about research and teaching. Experienced and returning new faculty, on the other hand, commented about the need to accept the situation as it was and, at best, to look for ideas from reading journals and attending conferences.

Table 2
New faculty, distinguished by background and cohort,
who rated intellectual stimulation as poor during semester 2

Year cohort began	Background of new faculty		
	Inexperienced	Returning	Experienced
1985	87%	50%	33%
1986	88%	50%	42%
1987	61%	60%	19%
1988	70%	60%	28%

Third Semester on Campus

Collegial Support

By the midpoint of their third semester on campus, new faculty reported a rebound from the low point of the second semester; the result of ratings of collegiality was about the same as for semester 1. That is, successive cohorts continued to rate collegiality somewhat higher, more so for inexperienced new faculty. But, nonetheless, ratings were only a little higher than for semester 1.

Descriptive accounts provided reasons for this inertia. First, almost everyone still reported feeling very much like newcomers. New faculty, in the best scenarios, might have found a mentor and a friend or two, but they rarely knew most of their colleagues (who continued to seem invisible and frugal with help). Second, new faculty felt even more pressure than in semester 1 to get on with research and publishing. During the summer between years 1 and 2 they had not, as a rule, fulfilled their plans of doing much research and writing. New faculty in year 2 supposed that one reason for their lack of professional progress was a dearth of support, including physical facilities (for example, equipped laboratories) and personnel (for example, secretaries and assistants) essential to productivity. In other words, new faculty held their colleagues responsible, not only for the lack of a friendly environment, but also for the absence of a research culture.

> [Assistant professor, inexperienced, cohort 3]: No, I don't feel that things are any more conducive to feeling good about the campus than last year. People seem no more interested than they were before; that's how things will probably stay. What I should be doing, what I planned to be doing, is to get some collaborations set up here. That's a big disappointment, not having anyone to share things with. And I can't see it changing soon; nobody else around here seems to be doing much. I didn't know how reliant I could be on other people to help get things done.

Experienced and returning faculty offered few spontaneous comments about collegiality by semester 3. When asked, they typically responded with resignation; they saw the campus as a commuter culture where senior faculty spent little time in their offices or interacting with colleagues.

Fourth semester on campus

Collegiality

With the exception of a handful of inexperienced newcomers, new faculty persisted in reports of social isolation and intellectual understimulation.

> [Assistant professor, inexperienced, cohort 3]: When will it end? Or maybe I should say when will I end? I just don't see how I'm going to make it here. I feel like Admiral Byrd in his book *Alone*. I'm as

alone as if I were in the Antarctic in his stead. What's going to happen, if I don't go crazy first, is that I'll get to be just like my colleagues who spend very little time on campus. Some of them have businesses elsewhere, you know. But I don't want to be like that. I still like students and teaching. And I still want to do research, something worthwhile. I don't like what this place is doing to me.

[Associate professor, experienced, cohort 4]: What are we in, my fourth semester on campus, right? I'll have to admit that I'm surprised how hard it is to get to know people here. I end up spending all my time preparing for classes and, more than that, spending lots of time with students in my office. They're not hard to get to know. I fret over the things I'm missing in not having colleagues in the department to interact with, especially on my research. I notice that I'm not getting much done of what I told you I had planned to do.

So, by the end of their second year on campus, new faculty could be categorized according to whether or not they had found substantial social support. In the 14 cases where new faculty had found systematic mentoring, they reported a feeling of acceptance on campus.

Fifth Semester on Campus

Transition Point

For most new faculty, year 3 on campus brought a sense of relief. Regardless of how collegially assimilated they felt, they returned to campus with a certainty that things at last were going to be easier. Curiously, the near majority of new faculty who already felt a part of campus attributed this feeling to finding social support. New faculty who still felt estranged, on the other hand, explained their newfound comfort in terms of having mastered the time-consuming aspects of the job (for example, course preparations). In either case, some new faculty seemed to have completed the stage that developmental theorists call the entry period (Braskamp, Fowler, & Ory, 1984), but not until well after the "compressed" period usually predicated—perhaps two years. Two reasons for the lengthy entry period seem to be (a) the social upheaval of bringing new faculty to a campus that had done little hiring for over a decade, and (b) a new set of professional values for incoming cohorts.

Socialization Rates

Inexperienced new faculty expressed delight in having, as a rule, by their third year on campus at least one friend (someone with whom they socialized off campus) and one potential collaborator (someone with whom they discussed academic matters at least weekly and in ways that might lead to coauthored projects). Experienced and returning new faculty, again, reported less success in establishing these kinds of social networks. Table 3 distributes four kinds of collegial activity cross the three types of experience levels of new faculty.

Without a doubt, the somewhat older, more experienced newcomers were not finding social support at levels shown by inexperienced new faculty. And by their own admission, experienced and returning new faculty were not adjusting happily to campus life, even by their third year. The four exceptions to this rule were experienced faculty who themselves became mentors for new faculty (n = 2), or whose departments had agreed to hire their friends from other campuses as even newer faculty (n = 2).

Table 3 shows another result worth mentioning. For new faculty in their third year on campus, rates of socialization seemed rather low. When asked why they thought this happened, new faculty offered remarkably uniform answers.

Table 3
New faculty reporting various social contacts in year 3

| Year cohort began (and type) | Type of regular weekly contact | | | |
	Visits to Colleagues	Visits from Colleagues	Visits with Chairs	Discuss Plans
1985 I	75%	50%	42%	58%
R	0%	251%	0%	0%
E	40%	30%	20%	30%
1986 I	86%	71%	36%	71%
R	20%	20%	10%	10%
E	58%	43%	29%	29%

Notes: I, inexperienced; R, returning; E, experienced

[Assistant professor, inexperienced, cohort 2]: The answer couldn't be more obvious. I have been too busy to try to do much socializing. I meant to. I wanted to (and I still want to). But I just haven't had the time.

[Associate professor, experienced, cohort 1]: I think I know why. I expected the people here, especially the chair, to come to me, to display more interest in me. It's part of the responsibility of the senior people to help make people like me feel at home.

[Associate professor, returning, cohort 2]: One good reason is that I haven't done as much as I could have. I really haven't made the effort to go around and talk to people. Part of it is due to shyness. Part of it is due to busyness; I've put other things first. Besides, I should have expected this. I sort of knew that a campus wasn't going to be like industry where they pay so much attention to you when you first arrive. Part of what attracted me here was being left alone to operate autonomously. But now I'm not sure I relish the result.

Collegiality as Evaluation

Year 3 also marked the real emergence of another dimension of collegiality, experiencing one's colleagues as judges. Some peer evaluations by more senior faculty already had occurred in earlier semesters, but the fifth semester was when preoccupation with colleagues in this role reached threshold. New faculty's treatment in the Retention/Tenure/Promotion (R/T/P) process became the number one source of complaints.

R/T/P committees consisted almost entirely of senior faculty who evaluated new hires in written formats (typically with added evaluations from departmental chairpersons). Fifty-eight percent of new faculty found these evaluations unfair and disheartening. Complaint levels were nearly equal across experience types.

Spontaneous complaints about the R/T/P process also remained similar across cohorts in a rank-order.

1. Feedback emphasized criticisms and rarely included praise.

2. Standards were enforced that most enforcers (senior faculty) could not themselves meet.

3. Single failings of new faculty, especially relating to poor student evaluations of teaching, were overemphasized and then reemphasized in subsequent evaluations.

Even new faculty who had not complained about the fairness of evaluations joined their peers in complaining about the generally unspecified criteria by which new faculty were judged.

> [Assistant professor, inexperienced, cohort 2]: I can't find out how much is enough. And no one else seems to know either. It would help to know how many publications are enough, and to know what level of student evaluations I should aim for. But I guess that all this gets decided on an individual basis; it makes the whole thing seem political, capricious.

> [Assistant professor, inexperienced, cohort 4]: Let me tell you what the effect of the R/T/P process is on me. Because I really don't know how the system works and because most of what I hear about is rumor (most of it horror stories), I end up feeling like avoiding the whole issue. I end up not working on the things I know I should because the system makes me feel helpless.

The commonality of concerns about an ill-defined process of evaluation may be seen in the fact that of the 50 new faculty participating in semester 2, only 5 reported receiving specific, sufficient information on what they probably needed to do for approval in the R/T/P process. What new faculty apparently wanted most was what their kin on other campuses reportedly wanted—more support and useful feedback (Fink, 1984).

Sixth Semester on Campus

Collegiality Evolving as Collaborating Versus Distancing

Once again this midpoint of a spring semester brought many reports of dysphoria; new faculty ruminated about the hopelessness of working on their adopted campus. But amidst all that, collegiality was a bright spot for slightly less than half of all new faculty by year 4 (most so, as usual, for inexperienced new faculty). While their opinions of departments remained low, new faculty showed less emotion in disparaging their home bases. They were, in effect, showing some "distancing," a presumably healthy event in adjusting to some aspects of a new job. Distancing also took on a discriminatory character where new faculty actively decided which colleagues to ignore and which to pursue as resources and friends.

In a way, though, distancing was proceeding with remarkable slowness. Two-thirds of new faculty reported that they still carried strong resentment about unpleasant experiences with campus administrators in semester 1. Invariably these reports included descriptions of rude managers/bureaucrats who treated new faculty in patronizing fashion, usually when trying to obtain resources that had been promised during the recruitment phase. New faculty reported that the memory of these events still rankled and sometimes motivated them to try to move to another campus. The durability of these critical incidents suggests that campuses should pay more attention to the delivery of promised resources.

Seventh Semester on Campus

Collegial Support

How much had this critical aspect of campus life changed over the four years? In their first year on campus, cohort 1 reported a surprisingly low level of collegial support and help: only 28% of them rated it as high, while 41% rated it as low (Table 1). Each succeeding cohort, as we have seen, rated collegiality somewhat higher, suggesting that the climate became more congenial to newcomers. Consistent with that trend, cohort 1 reported more help and support in each of their four years under study; by the fourth year 40% of them rated collegiality highly (most so for inexperienced new faculty).

By the fourth year another trend was confirmed further; new faculty reported less need for collegiality over years and over cohorts. Cohort 1 began with one of the highest expressed levels of need for collegiality, with 72% rating their needs at the maximum level. By year 4 only 36% rated their need for collegiality as highly as they once had.

Intellectual Stimulation

The low estimates of intellectual stimulation from colleagues also showed improvement over years, from the 87% of new faculty who rated it as poor in year 1 to just under 50% in year 4. Here again, those who elicited this sort of social support reported having taken a discriminatory stance; clearly, only a few colleagues could be counted on to provide intellectual stimulation. New faculty who did not find this stimulation generally reported finding or maintaining sources off campus (or, nearly as often for experienced and returning new faculty, learning to cope without the ideas and prods they had hoped for).

Usefulness of Collegial Advice

A form of social support that did not show improvement over the four years was the quality of collegial advice. By year 4 new faculty reported, with some surprise, that they still were getting advice on academic survival from more senior colleagues. But they did not report an improvement over the gossip/politics-laden information that had dominated such exchanges in year 1. With a prod to consider their own role in encouraging this sort of advice, only about one-third of new faculty admitted to such a possibility.

Mentors

New faculty in cohorts 1 and 2 found the fewest mentors over the study period, at rates below 15% and 34% respectively. Despite their continuing uninvolvement as mentees, 12 faculty in these cohorts became mentors for more junior new hires. While tradition might have dictated an expectation that these mentors would come from the ranks of experienced faculty, two-thirds of the faculty who met the criteria for participation came from the junior ranks. New faculty who acted as formal mentors were, not surprisingly, unusually well-connected to social networks and were satisfied with their jobs.

Eighth Semester on Campus

In general, few observable changes occurred between semesters 7 and 8; new faculty were settled into seemingly stable social patterns by this time. The most notable development during the fourth year involved an aspect of sociality heretofore neglected, social life off campus, including family life.

Negative Spillover

New faculty invariably listed a desire to balance their professional and personal lives during year l. In reminders of this priority during subsequent semesters, responses were comical. Balance, if it ever would come, was not an immediately foreseeable reality; new faculty felt too busy, too overscheduled, too far behind on writing projects, too insecure about gaining tenure to even try to give social life off campus as high a priority as academic activities.

What new faculty exhibited in this regard through their first three years on campus can be called negative spillover. In their study of faculty, Sorcinelli and Near (1989) found that new faculty especially were likely to allow their jobs to overwhelm (that is, negatively spill over into) their home lives. In the present study, new faculty in years 1 and 2 routinely admitted that they were neglecting their social life off campus.

> [Assistant professor, inexperienced, cohort 2, year 1]: I really don't have any social life at all. I always have work that I take home in the evenings and weekends. If I'm not preparing lectures, I'm grading papers. I'm waiting for Christmas vacation to get at some writing. Plus, when I do get some free time, I'm tired.

By year 4, most new faculty had taken concrete steps to reduce negative spillover. Fourteen of the 20 members of cohort 1 detailed specific plans for community and/or family-based activities (for example, membership in a choir, weekend camping trips), compared to a previous high of four such reports. Curiously, this move generally came in conjunction with a decision that could have undermined it. During this year, nearly a third of the new faculty had found part-time employment off campus.

Their roles off campus, typically as consultants, had two reported impacts beyond financial considerations. First, consulting provided them with reminders of their competence as professionals; outside jobs clearly were more likely to produce compliments than was work on campus. Second, having to fit the part-time job into an already crowded schedule helped teach new faculty that they could manage more than the lecture-related activities that had dominated their lives.

Taking outside employment, a step that usually preceded the move to develop a more substantial social life off campus, assumed the special appearance of a signal activity. It seemed to coincide with the realization that new faculty could get on with their lives. In a way, this may have been the most telling end point of the entry period.

General Discussion

One of the most important findings of this study concerned its practicality. Despite concerns of campus administrators that new faculty might be noncompliant, all but five of the substantial number of potential interviewees cooperated. Although new faculty usually showed reluctance initially to be interviewed, they came to welcome these twice-annual contacts. And even while displaying some understandable initial rudeness, new faculty were eager to share their experiences on campus. Later reflections of new faculty suggested that the initial interview appearances demanded a kind of self-scrutiny that only would remind them of how little they were getting done.

Some findings in this longitudinal study were anticipated. I expected that new faculty would complain of busyness and of some social isolation. Still, the extent of complaining, especially about the slow rate of change from the busyness and isolation of the first semester, proved surprising. Even urgently needed corrections, including areas related to health (for example, family and social life, exercising), came slowly and incompletely over the four years.

A related surprise was the length of the entry period, the phase during which new faculty still felt that they were not a part of campus. This period lasted for three and sometimes four years. The length of this socialization stage could have been elongated by the commuter culture of the study campus; presumably, campuses with senior faculty more in attendance might effect quicker socialization by more frequent contracts with new hires.

The biggest surprise was the ostensible neglect and mistreatment of new faculty at a campus well-known for its interest in faculty development. Was this campus calloused in its treatment of new hires? My own consulting efforts on a variety of other campuses suggest that this reaction of new faculty is typical. As a rule, new faculty seem to feel neglected, isolated, overworked, and deprived of vital supports and feedback. In fact, few American campuses do more than provide their new faculty with a brief orientation and a packet of information about insurance options. If campuses vary in the kinds of problems expressed in this study, it probably is in terms of duration. For example, because the study campus had not hired many new faculty in over a decade, it may have been slower than the norm to adjust to them.

Given the apparent commonality of socially isolating new faculty, at least on large, commuter-oriented campuses, we might wonder if this practice has adaptive value. When I asked new faculty this question, they typically supposed that academe still operates on Social Darwinist principles. "Just as graduate schools let many students sink or swim in the dissertation stage," one inexperienced new assistant professor commented, "we also seem to willingly let people, even good people, fail here if they don't figure things out on their own." Not one of the new faculty in this sample thought that social isolation served a useful purpose.

Other longitudinal studies of new faculty might well pay special attention to the rates of change in perceived collegiality over cohorts and over years of study. In this study, a gradual warming of the collegial climate occurred in both dimensions. Attention to new faculty's backgrounds also paid dividends. In the new faculty scrutinized here, inexperienced new faculty were the quickest to find support and to feel a part of campus. Their counterparts, experienced and returning new faculty, showed slower, often incomplete, assimilation to campus. Reasons for the poorer adjustment of these two groups seem to include (a) assumptions of senior faculty that only inexperienced new faculty needed significant help and support, (b) defensiveness of senior faculty about the publication records of experienced and returning new faculty that translated into not wanting to assist these newcomers, and (c) more passivity in seeking collegial help on the part of experienced and returning new faculty who saw themselves as less in need of guidance. Returning new faculty added a special problem that they often mentioned. They had been away from academic culture for a long time and, thus, had to adjust to what now seemed a peculiarly political and competitive situation that showed little respect for their years of accumulated knowledge in real-world contexts.

The two sequels to follow this report tie the rates of collegial adjustments to new faculty's successes at mastering teaching and at research/writing/publication. Briefly, when taken together the data suggest that the three domains of collegiality, teaching, and research work in concert. As a rule, the new faculty who adjusted most easily and effectively to, say, the demands of teaching also evidenced above average skills in coping in the other two domains (see Boice, 1984).

A final point brings us back to the first. Not only was this interview procedure practical and informative, but its results showed promising parallels to findings about career development in other organizational settings. The most thorough-going and well-known of these, by Howard and Bray (1988), suggested that employees become more autonomous and less affiliative with age. A similar process apparently distinguished the new faculty studied here. Related work in the same American Telephone & Telegraph project (London & Stumpf, 1986) posited three critical predictors of how new employees will adjust and thrive: (a) resilience (how effectively they persist in the face of frustrations), (b) insight (how realistically they see their problems and potentials), and (c) identification (how much a part of their organization they felt). Each of these factors played a critical role in the collegial adjustment of new faculty studied here.

Resilience represented new faculty's persistence in looking for collegial support, eventually by discriminating the few senior faculty who could be helpful. It meant not taking the feeling of isolation and understimulation personally. And it meant taking some initiative in finding and accepting collegiality.

The presence of insight was tantamount to new faculty expressing realistic concerns about problems they faced, while avoiding the temptation to see everything as catastrophe and to take all gossip seriously. Identification, finally, was reflected in the rapidity with which new faculty ended their entry periods (and, at last, felt a part of campus).

Considered together, these indices can provide a set of predictors to assess the probability of new faculty's success and the areas in which they (and their campus culture) need remediation. Such an attempt is an ultimate goal of this project, to be pursued in the two subsequent studies of success at teaching (Boice, in press) and productivity at writing/publishing. In these reports, two other indices will be extended, information about the most difficult tasks facing new faculty and how the most successful newcomers cope with those problems.

References

Benyon, J. (1985). Institutional change and career histories in a comprehensive school. In S. J. Ball and I. F. Goodson (Eds.), *Teachers' lives and careers* (pp. 158–179). Lewes: Falmer.

Boice, R. (1984). Reexamination of traditional emphases in faculty development. *Research in Higher Education, 21,* 195–209.

Boice, R. (1987). Is released–time an effective device for faculty development? *Research in Higher Education, 26,* 311–326.

Boice, R. (in press). New faculty as teachers. *Journal of Higher Education.*

Braskamp, L. A., Fowler, D. L., & Ory, J. C. (1984). Faculty development and achievement: a faculty's view. *The Review of Higher Education, 7,* 205–222.

Bowen, J. R., & Schuster, J. H. (1986). *American professors: a national resource imperiled.* New York: Oxford University Press.

Evetts, J. (1989). Married women and career: career history accounts of primary head teachers. *International Journal of Qualitative Studies in Education, 2(2),* 89–105.

Fink, L. D. (1984). *The first year of college teaching.* San Francisco: Jossey-Bass.

Howard, A., & Bray, D. W. (1988). *Managerial lives in transition.* New York: Guilford.

London, M. & Strumpf, S. A. (1986). Individual and organizational career development in changing times. In D. T. Hall (Ed.). *Frontier series in individual and organizational psychology.* San Francisco: Jossey-Bass.

Menges, R. J., & Mathis, B. C. (1988). *Key resources on teaching, learning, curriculum, and faculty development.* San Francisco: Jossey-Bass.

Seldin, P. (Ed.). (1987). *Coping with faculty stress.* San Francisco: Jossey-Bass.

Sorcinelli, M. D. (1985). Faculty careers: satisfactions and discontents. *To Improve the Academy, 4,* 44–62.

Sorcinelli, M. D., & Near, J. P. (1989). Relations between work and life away from work among university faculty. *Journal of Higher Education, 60,* 59–81.

Turner, J. L., & Boice, R. (1987). Starting at the beginning: concerns and needs of new faculty. *To Improve the Academy, 6,* 41–55.

Faculty Perspectives and Practice in an Urban Community College

Lois Weis

*"When you're up to your ass in alligators
It's hard to remember that your initial goal was to drain the swamp."*

(Placard in a faculty office)

This article explores faculty perspectives and practice at one Urban Community College in the United States. Data were gathered as part of a larger ethnography on the culture which lower class black students produce in an urban institution. My goal here is to describe elements of faculty culture, explore reasons why faculty culture takes the shape and form that it does, and discuss the ways in which this culture may be linked to institutional outcomes. In so doing, I offer a framework through which the structural genesis of faculty-student conflict and the relationship between faculty culture and institutional outcomes may be viewed.

This article explores faculty perspectives and practice at one urban community college (which I call "Urban College") located in a large northeastern city in the United States. Data presented here were gathered as part of a larger ethnography on the culture which lower class black students produce in an urban institution. The participant-observation was carried out during the academic year 1979-80, during which time I attended classes, conducted in-depth interviews with faculty and students and, in general, immersed myself in the institution for a full academic year. While my identity was not hidden, I essentially assumed the role of "student."

I have argued elsewhere that the culture students produce at Urban College acts primarily to ensure that the vast majority of students will return to the ghetto streets (Weis, 1983, 1985). Students drop in and out of school, exert little effort, arrive late to class, and engage in extensive drug use in spite of the fact that they value education highly and attend Urban College with every intention of escaping the urban underclass.

What role, if any, do faculty play in the creation of this culture—a culture which contributes to an exceedingly low "success" rate in traditional academic terms? [1]. My intent here is to discuss the nature of faculty culture in an urban institution and the reasons why this culture takes the shape and form that it does. I will also speculate as to the ways in which faculty culture might be linked in an often unanticipated fashion to institutional outcomes. Data are discussed with an eye toward providing a framework through which the relationship between faculty culture and institutional outcomes may be viewed. The structural genesis of student-faculty conflict will no doubt differ by type of institution and nature of clientele served. It is my intent here to focus on the dynamic itself through presenting data collected in the urban community college setting. The way in which these processes play themselves out in other institutions can profitably be addressed in future research efforts.

Faculty Views Toward the College

Howard London (1978) and others have argued that community college faculty look upon themselves as "second class"—that they actively desire to obtain positions in four-year colleges and universities. Many of the faculty in London's "City Community College," which serves a white working class clientele, see themselves as too intellectual, too abstract, for their present position. A majority of them resent the fact that they are teaching on a community college level.

Within this context, it is noteworthy that, for the most part, faculty at Urban College are not disappointed with their responsibilities at Urban College and would not prefer to teach in a four-year institution. They may not have initially envisioned themselves at a community college, but most have come to terms with their position and actively embrace their career. *It is this very coming to terms with their position in the particular site in which they work that constitutes a major component of their own culture.* Elements of faculty culture did not emerge full-blown. Faculty culture, like student culture, is dynamic and best understood as the product of collective human activity.

As the interviews below suggest, faculty were initially struck by the exceedingly low level of student academic skills. The lack of basic skills, coupled with the fact that faculty could view their predominantly ghetto student population as "other" than themselves, contributed to a rising antagonism on the part of faculty and students. This antagonism took on a distinctively race form in this setting, recreating and reinforcing a fundamental antagonism in American society. While this antagonism is not necessarily vicious or even overt within the college itself, the very fact that faculty (close to 70 percent of whom are white) increasingly see students as fundamentally "different" from themselves serves to reproduce racial antagonisms which lie at the very heart of society. Where faculty feel comfortable with those "other" than themselves, it is generally due to the fact that they lived in the ghetto at one time (as college students, for example) or had other previous contact with ghettoized minorities. The tendency to see students as "other" does not diminish under these circumstances.

It can be argued that faculty in any institution view students as "other." In the graduate school setting, for example, it is not uncommon to hear faculty discuss the fact that students at their current institution are "not as good as"—not as motivated or bright as—"we" were when we were students at Harvard, University of Michigan and so forth. The tendency to see students as "other" probably exists in all institutions, except perhaps in the highly elite sector (this, however, is an empirical question). My point here is that seeing students as "other" takes a different shape and form and has varying consequences depending upon the faculty-student mix. At Urban College, the fact that a largely white faculty increasingly see their predominantly black ghetto student population as fundamentally different from themselves sets into motion a dynamic that differs from that in institutions which serve a predominantly white middle class population. Faculty everywhere perhaps see students as "other." The consequences of this, however, are likely to be very different depending on the context in which this dynamic is played out. In Urban College, this very "normal" dynamic serves to reinforce a fundamental antagonism in American society. Once again, however, this is not vicious nor even overt within the college itself. I have chosen to quote at length here in order to allow faculty to speak for themselves [2]. The discussions below are with white faculty: the views of black faculty will be considered separately.

> Phil: I'd like to talk about Urban College and my various stages of growth or whatever in dealing with the urban student. I went through several shocks in dealing with the students. First of all, the general lifestyle and then what they didn't know so far as the basic simple ideas of mathematics.

> LW: Such as?

Phil: Well, not being able to deal with decimals or fractions and them my wondering how they are able to purchase a television set on credit or how they are able to deal with consumer-type problems, and I've since found out that they don't. They just let "the man," so to speak, decide those things for them and make those decisions. So that if a new car costs $150.00 a month that's what it is and there's no real feel for how much interest they're paying or anything else.

LW: When you say people don't have basic concepts in mathematics, what about addition, subtraction, multiplication, and division?

Phil: It's really a conceptual problem in fractions and decimals. In adding and subtracting there's no real problem. In multiplication there's a problem because they don't know the times table, and of course I'm talking about the majority, there's some who can. But when it comes to division, that is a terrible problem. I don't think they *ever* learned division—*ever*.

(. . .) So they can add and subtract, some can multiply and very few can divide a two digit number into a three digit number. And then it gets worse from there because no one really knows what a half means or what is a third. There's no light that flashes in their mind.

(a Mathematics instructor)

• • •

LW: When you first came here did you have any problems orienting yourself?

Hugh: That's right. As bad as I thought it would be, student intelligence-wise, it was worse. I just couldn't believe some of the things students couldn't understand. But I'm very patient. I didn't get angry or mad. But I wondered if it was possible for these students to learn (. . .) For example, not knowing that two-dash-three [2/3] means two divided by three. I tried to understand this and finally came to the realization that what the students didn't know was that the word *increase* means get bigger. Without exaggeration! *So the problem is that you're teaching in English and they don't understand English* (my emphasis). So all of a sudden that hits you. I was very disillusioned when I first came. Even though I imagined that the students were not that good, they were absolutely non-students for a long time.

(. . .) I have found a level that I'm quite satisfied with. Students are not always so satisfied with it. I think it's the right thing to do. I'm satisfied in *my* mind. What happens is that I suffer a lot of attrition in my courses. I also have decided that I don't mind attrition at this level.

(. . .) I certainly expect these problems now [lack of basic skills] whereas I didn't expect them at first. So when I want to do a certain thing that requires knowledge of mathematics, I now forget that certain thing and teach mathematics.

Having decided to do this now, I'm not going to accept *less than*, you know what I mean?

(. . .) The material is covered. For example, I might take a topic that I cover in one week and delay it by covering it in two or three weeks. That's the difference between ten years ago [when I first began teaching here] and today.

(. . .) I think it's ok to take twenty people and graduate five.

(a Science instructor)

• • •

LW: When you first came here did you have any difficulties orienting yourself to this school?

Dennis: Yes, academically. I was very surprised how poor the students were. Reading comprehension and especially writing—I couldn't believe how bad it was (. . .) Even now when I give exams I give almost totally objective exams. Almost totally objective (. . .) The English teachers are going to have to handle the comprehension and the writing.

(. . .) I've got students who are graduating in May and I look at their exams and it takes me twenty minutes to figure out what they're trying to say (. . .) I'll have fill-ins. Every once in a while I'll slip one in. Even when I'll need five words it'll be unbelievable.

(a Criminal Justice instructor)

• • •

LW: When you first came to Urban College did you have any difficulty orienting yourself?

Jim: No, I had lived in [a large Eastern city] for three years. I lived in what was then, well it was called the "the gut" (. . .) My neighbors and the people I worked with while I was going to school were the economically disadvantaged, were the minorities, were the poor, so I had a great deal of experience dealing with the people that are very familiar to students here.

Jim: (. . .) [But] occasionally the students would go to the department and say [I am] a racist and they said that about most of the white faculty at one time or another, and periodically over the last ten years I've been accused of that (. . .) That's part of working here, especially if you're going to demand a great deal from the students. There's always going to be a certain group that are not making it and have to find some excuse for not making it and being a racist is a good way.

(. . .) I have been keeping track in my records over the years because I'm concerned. I don't want to somehow without knowing it have become a racist and so I look at grades from one semester to the next and so far I've seen no grade indication that it has anything to do with race, sex, age or anything else. It has to do with their performance in the course. I've also learned to set up course requirements, exams and so forth, so that the accusation can't be made (. . .) I structure my tests so that they are more or less objective. Wherever possible I ask objective kinds of things and (. . .) in the essays I ask for a very specific kind of response (. . .) [Also] by curving exams it allows the students to really compete against each other using my exam, and that way it's done much more objectively and it eliminates any accusation of favoritism, etc.

LW: (. . .) How do you define success in your teaching?

Jim: [Laughter] Depending on my frame of mind in the semester it can be one student in a class who all of a sudden really has it together. Like I've got one student that I can think of offhand this semester that throughout the semester thus far has been doing passing work but not really outstanding work but now he's shown me the beginning of this last paper and it's such an *incredible* improvement. So well organized and thought out. Well researched. That kind of thing is thrilling very honestly here and I think you've got to take your successes where you find them. You don't have a lot of success (. . .) I feel good when I see progress and sometimes it's only one student in a semester.

(an English instructor)

Faculty were initially disappointed with the quality of their students, particularly the low level of academic skills. Most admit that they respond by teaching concepts that they had expected students to know already, and by relying increasingly on objective examinations which require little or no writing [3]. Hugh, for example, suggests that "when I want to do a certain thing that requires knowledge of mathematics, I now forget that certain thing and teach mathematics," and Dennis points out that he gives almost "totally objective exams (. . .) The English teachers are going to have to handle the comprehension and the writing." Thus curricular form and content at Urban College developed over time and in relation to a dynamic student culture [4]. It is not a question, then, of community college faculty *imposing* a particular curricular form on their largely black student clientele, thereby reproducing inequalities in the larger society. The form and content of the curriculum is in large part the result of ongoing interaction between faculty and students at the level of their own culture. I am not attempting to suggest here that faculty consciousness develops *only* in relation to students, nor that curricular form and content develop *only* in relation to faculty consciousness. Both faculty consciousness and curricular form are arguably the product of more than the interaction between students and faculty. My point here is that students exert a powerful effect on the development of both. The form and content of curriculum cannot be understood as the *simple* imposition of a form of control applied to particular groups. This is especially true at the tertiary level where faculty exert substantial control over the curriculum [5]. The way in which faculty "choice" over curricular matters may serve to reproduce existing social inequalities despite the good intentions of faculty becomes quite important here.

The data also suggest that faculty, over time, begin to define success as reaching one or two students per term, and many admit that they except attrition and no longer mind it. Hugh states that he "doesn't mind attrition at this level" and Bill, an English instructor, argues similarly below.

> Bill: Sometimes we have an attrition rate problem (. . .); that is the nature of the beast. We do have a high attrition rate and we do come to accept that. Since we are a full opportunity program college, we cannot by law turn anyone away, but as is obvious, everyone is not qualified to go on to higher education but at least we have to give them the opportunity (. . .) I have a lot of high attrition, there's no doubt about that (. . .) I consider it a weeding out area. The weeding out comes in the classroom.

Faculty thus focus increasingly on the one or two who "make it" and devote less energy to the vast numbers who do not. They define high attrition as "normal" at the same time that they define success in terms of one or two. This collectively held set of attitudes must be seen in relation to students. It emerged in its present form (and appears structural) only through years of collective interaction within this site.

It is also important that faculty, despite initial disappointment in the quality of students, have, overall, a very positive attitude toward the school. Unlike faculty in London's study, Urban College faculty enjoy the institution and do not, for the most part, wish they were elsewhere. At the same time, they do not generally pinpoint students as a reason for enjoying their jobs. Given that the *raison d'être* of the community college is teaching, what then, accounts for their positive outlook? The discussions with Alex, Jim, and Hugh below shed light on these issues.

> Alex: I never thought of myself as a community college teacher. I was caught up in the notion of teaching at a prestigious university, with graduate students and majors, but at a period of time when I had a physical injury—I smashed my pelvis in an automobile accident—I was being removed from the job for political reasons and blacklisted as I have evidence to show, documentary evidence, I had a difficult time getting a job so for me, teaching at a community college meant putting bread on the table (. . .) I saw a newspaper story saying that this campus was opening up so then I applied and got the job. That was ten years ago. It was not ideological, just the need to have a job.

> LW: (. . .) Do you see yourself staying here, or would you like to move on?

> Alex: Well, I don't think I have any job mobility (. . .) but on the other hand this is a good place to end up, so I have accepted my final placement at this institution and don't see it as a stepping stone to anything but as a world unto itself. So I think that I lack the desire but I also lack the means to move in the current climate (. . .) On the other hand, I am very well positioned here so it isn't like we [sic] want to leave a bad situation. I have very good personal relationships with people here. There is no alienation from this institution. I don't have to hide in my classroom. I can relate to the affairs of the school. I have a lot of informal input and a lot of informal influence through persuasion in my position. So it is a good position; it is enviable from many points of view.

> (an English instructor)

● ● ●

> Jim: I don't think I'm going to enjoy teaching any place as much as here. Part of the problem here is that I work with a group of people that I think are phenomenal. They are just beautiful people and they're great to work with, and I don't think there are very many places in the world where you can get that sense of community camaraderie and I appreciate that much more than I do necessarily the title or the prestige of the institution.

(. . .) There is a good interaction between faculty and administration which again, doesn't happen in a lot of places (. . .) I like to be in a place where you've got to fight—One of the things I really like about this campus is that it is the poor cousin out of the three [in the county system]—I enjoy a good fight!

(an English instructor)

• • •

LW: What is it that you like about being here?

Hugh: Well, I like teaching. From the day I started teaching as a teaching assistant in graduate school, I liked it. It's a great way to make a living and I would sacrifice money if it came to that. What I like about teaching is that it is so diversified. Every day is different, every year is different (. . .) In addition to that, here I'm into so many things. Heading a whole department which is perfect for me (. . .) And I have here the head coaching job for the baseball team. One of the reasons I came here to begin with is that they told me that I could have the baseball team at this campus (. . .) So the baseball aspect here takes up many, many more hours than the other part. It's just like I'm two different people. Six out of seven days a week I'm involved in baseball, either playing or coaching in the summer.

(. . .) That is why I really feel unique and why I like this place so much. Also I find the administrators here to be absolutely super. They're either very poor and don't know what to do, or they have enough sense to let certain people run their own show. I've always been able to do pretty much what I wanted. Not that I've ever wanted to do anything improper, but the kind of teaching that I've wanted to do, the courses I've wanted to run, the kind of courses I've wanted to teach. I've pretty much had my way, which contributes to the good feeling I've had here.

(a Science instructor)

It is apparent that faculty not only alter curricula in response to students, but they define other aspects of their job as more intrinsically satisfying. This is particularly interesting since students are the *raison d'être* of the community college and faculty are paid to teach, not to produce knowledge as is arguably the case at the university. It is, therefore, noteworthy that, in the absence of an alternative mission such as universities have, faculty locate the primary source of their satisfaction in relations with colleagues, "community camaraderie," positive experiences with administrators, sports, and, as one faculty member put it, "a good fight" (referring to the political position of Urban College vis-à-vis the county). This is not to suggest that these factors are unrelated to one's classroom teaching. Indeed at least some of them are related in some rather powerful ways. It is nevertheless telling that faculty discuss these factors without *ever* mentioning their student clientele. It is only after I asked faculty what constitutes success in their teaching that students were mentioned at all.

Despite the ability of faculty to define their experience in the college positively in terms other than students, faculty must continually clarify, if only to themselves, why it is that student behavior is as it is. Why, in particular, do students exhibit so little success in traditional academic terms? Why is the graduation rate persistently so low? This is exceptionally important since faculty, despite their apparent ability to create a positive climate for themselves, must nevertheless confront students daily in five courses per week. Significantly, this must be done on an individual rather than a collective level.

Faculty Views of the Student Culture

Despite their generally positive feelings about the school, faculty are forced to grapple with why the student culture takes the form it does. Faculty must confront on a daily basis increasingly empty classes and low "success" rates in traditional academic terms [6]. Faculty, therefore, at the level of their own culture, attempt to explain student behavior, which in turn has an impact on their own classroom practice. Basically these attempts take one of two forms: (1) students are just there for the grant money and never *were* serious about education, or (2) while students may be serious about education and genuinely desire upward mobility, problems associated with lower class ghetto life make the pursuit of education exceedingly difficult.

I have argued elsewhere that student culture at Urban College is inherently contradictory (Weis, 1983, 1985). Students engage in extensive drug use, drop in and out of school semester after semester (even after obtaining grant money to attend school), and arrive late to class. At the same time they affirm rather that contradict legitimate knowledge. It is, therefore, significant that faculty, in an attempt to explain and respond to student culture, focus almost exclusively on the pattern of dropping in and out. The other elements of culture (including of course, its contradictory nature), are, by and large, not acknowledged.

It must be pointed out here that since the college is a Full Opportunity Program (FOP) branch of State University, all applicants who have high school or general equivalency diplomas are admitted. More than 90 percent of the students receive some form of financial aid. The issue of grant money is thus an important one at Urban College.

The first set of interviews below reflects faculty perception that students attend the college simply for grant money. The second set reflects an attempt to situate the pattern of dropping in and out within a broader class cultural context.

Tim: Dislikes? I get ticked off sometimes at the immaturity of the students. "Written homework—who me, are you crazy?"

LW: Why do people [students] come here?

Tim: Well there's no doubt in my mind that some people are here for the money. My classes have gone down about 25 percent. But see, it's not just the quick-buck artists that hit us once. People come here because they have nothing else to do in a shitty, pardon my expression, economy. People will say, "Well, I'll try it." They get paid a little bit for it and they're not getting paid that much. It's not worth their time, but people say "heck, I get paid for it and I might as well do something." (. . .) Some come here for Paralegal or Radiologic Technology—they come here with definite career goals in minds. It's a small percentage though.

(a Business Administration instructor)

• • •

Dave: Well, I think there's a lot of abuse here in most of the financial aid programs. I've been here two terms and I see students come—stay for two or three weeks—get their money and leave, and they come back again [the following semester]. I have one student—a good student, capable of getting probably straight A's in all her courses—she was in about halfway last term, she was in about halfway this term, and now she's gone, and I'm sure she's going to be there next Fall. Hey, what the hell, you can continue doing that probably forever.

LW: Why do you think these students are here?

Dave: Well, again, I have to suspect there's money motivation here. I used every penny I have coming to me under VA [Veterans] benefits and I encouraged my brother to do likewise, not to mention other friends I've talked with. I think a person is foolish if they don't take advantage of federal programs where they can get government help in getting an education. The point is, if we're going to take the government's money to get ourselves an education, they by God we ought to apply ourselves and get that education, not just take the money and disappear.

LW: You see that as a real problem?

Dave: I see abuse. I've seen more abuse here (. . .) than I've seen any place else. (. . .) This term

(. . .) I've seen several repeat students who were here last year come and do the same thing this year. (. . .) I have a feeling from advisement that some of these students have been around here for quite some time. Not just one or two years, not just one or two semesters, but *several* years. Again, you can get that kind of information from teachers who have been here the past 6-8 years.

Dave and Tim emphasize the idea that students are *simply* there for the money. The pattern of dropping in and out is seen as a case of "ripping off" the system for monetary gain. Faculty below tend to emphasize the constraints imposed by lower class life. Faculty of both categories, however, focus on a single element of student culture—the pattern of dropping in and out—and neither consider the effects that the school itself might have (including faculty) on the production of student culture. With the exception of Phil (the first faculty member below), faculty by and large focus on only this one element of culture and define it as a "student problem." This categorization not only loses the contradictory nature of the culture but its relational quality as well.

LW: The attrition rate is high in your classes [mathematics]. Why do you think that is?

Phil: Well I would say that the attrition rate is high, one, because we have no support services to really speak of, that is no active support services, and then we're probably not starting at the place where we should be starting in our math sequence. In other words, we say that arithmetic is the lowest you can go, and then we try to do a lot in one semester. We try to go through arithmetic and include a bit of algebra. We stick to that schedule so that when the attrition rate begins to climb we don't let up; we just continue to do it.

LW: Do you think it's just the frustration of failure?

Phil: I think there's a lot that goes on in their outside life that causes them to miss. For example, I saw the name of two of my students last semester in the paper as being picked up for being prostitutes. Another student in my class—we were talking about budget a few weeks ago—told me that she made $100.00 a night, you know [as a prostitute], and that she was amazed that it added up the way it did because she didn't get all that money, her boyfriend did.

So there's really a variety of factors that cause attrition, and I'm not sure how many of them are school related and how many are related to their outside work,

(a Mathematics instructor)

• • •

LW: What prevents you from being as successful [in teaching] as you would like?

Bill: That's a tough question. Maybe something that I have no control over, and that is outside influences on the student. Pressures on them, not scholastic pressures, but economic pressures, community pressures, social pressures.

LW: Can you give an example of what you mean?

Bill: Someone who has to walk to school and can't make it all the time. I've had people like that. Someone who has trouble heating their home during the winter, feeding their kids the way they should be fed, feeding themselves properly. I think we have a higher incidence of sickness at Urban College during the winter because I think that some of our people have problems heating, feeding, and clothing themselves properly. Fro a number of reasons—economics is one of them. Background—not having been taught how to keep themselves properly.

(an English instructor)

The point here is not only that faculty are unaware of the contradictory nature of student culture, but that they see this culture as a simple extension of lower class black culture. Student culture is seen simply as "hustling" or, less negatively, a response to problems associated with lower class life. Faculty miss the way in which their own located culture in part *creates* the very culture they are attempting to understand. Student culture is at least partially a response to collectively-held faculty perspectives and subsequent behavior, whether rooted in a "liberal" or "conservative" model [7].

Perceptions of Black Faculty

Black faculty, by virtue of their lived experiences, warrant distinct analysis. It is indeed important, for example, that of the three faculty members interviewed below, two have a firmer grasp on the contradictory nature of student culture than white faculty. Significantly, the third black faculty member grew up in West Africa and is not rooted in the Afro-American experience. It is also noteworthy that of all the faculty interviewed, it is only black faculty who specifically cite students as a reason for enjoying the institution. Vivian, for example, exemplifies this position.

> Vivian: Right now I'm into teaching. I enjoy it. I get a lot of satisfaction out of the interaction with the students (. . .) I think a good part of my being here and enjoying it a lot is because I'm black and the vast majority of students I'm associated with are black students and I get a lot of pleasure and intense enjoyment out of thinking, not knowing, that I provide a little bit more pleasure and enjoyment to someone who is also black and striving to get somewhere.

> (a Social Science instructor)

In many ways, however, the views of black and white faculty with respect to student culture are similar. The difference between black and white faculty lies more in their *understanding* of the roots of student cultural form than in their valuation of this form. It is also the case that black faculty are often put in positions vis-à-vis students what white faculty are not, making the relationship between black faculty and the institution a somewhat more difficult one. This is articulated most clearly by Percy, whose comments are reproduced at some length.

> Percy: [On first teaching at Urban College] People kind of assume that because you're black or minority that you can relate instantly to minority people. I *could* relate on different levels, but educationally it was very difficult. They [students] didn't have the skills I thought they should have (. . .) I just assumed certain things even though I was teaching some remedial type of courses in composition here.

> LW: What did you assume?

> Percy: I assumed that they could at least write sentences, that students had some idea of grammar. I assumed [that they knew something about their own history]. I would say, you know, Martin Luther King or Malcolm X. They would look at you like who's that?

> (. . .) The matter of being scholars too. I guess I'm somewhat of a scholar and I guess I try to project that onto my students—to be excellent in what they do. In fact that is what I always say the first day of class—that you will be excellent and you will do very good in this class. I didn't realize that some of these students had no orientation in studying or in being a scholar or being intellectually curious. That's sort of disheartening.

> LW: Do you still find that people assume that because you're black you have some kind of understanding?

> Percy; Yes [and] obviously I do have a link. Having been born in the south and grew up on the east side of ——,of course I have, But I also have other kinds of training and background.

> (. . .) Students get the impression that you are not *supposed* to know or do that [appreciate Mozart, enjoy caviar]. You know, "you're like us and why can't you give us a break?" (. . .) They look for the break in terms of "don't be so hard on us because you understand that we come from this poor background and we are so destitute" and so on.

I tell them "bull." Don't tell me about poor backgrounds; don't tell me about walking the streets; don't tell me about drugs and all that kind of stuff. I've seen it and I've been there. You don't *know* prejudice. I knew prejudice in the 40's and the 50's—I'll tell you about prejudice. You have to make it on your own. You are really responsible for yourself and you *can* learn."

LW: What is the response to that?

Percy: "Yeah, but you made it." Yeah, and I'll tell you *how* I made it. My mother scrubbed other people's floors while I took care of the other three kids and she went out to the suburbs and scrubbed floors. I washed dishes in the city's restaurants for about two years; every summer I worked in a drug store, paid my tuition to [State College] myself, so don't talk about that. I don't want to hear about that.

LW: (. . .) When you were talking about—"hey you're just like us, give us a break"—is that a reaction of men or women or both?

Percy: The men more than the women and I find black men unfortunately have an attitude of give it to me (. . .) "Man, I'm trying to make it and this world is terrible, especially on black men." I've worked it out somewhat. The kinds of societal pressures on black men as we know in America, in their wanting to *make* it, but more than that, their (. . .) feeling of wanting gratification *now*. They don't think in terms of deferred gratification because we have been taught as black men that tomorrow is not promised; you gotta do this *now*. The men are more apt to want to do it now, try to get it now, therefore they're more inclined to want me to give them a break now, slide them through now because they had a jail record or that sort of thing, and that's not stereotypic because a lot of black men do have jail records. They come from the ghetto.

(an English instructor)

Percy argues that black students, particularly males, expect him, as a black faculty member, to "understand" their background and "give them a break"—to slide them through because they have jail records, for example. Percy's response to this is "'bull'—don't tell me about poor backgrounds; don't tell me about walking the streets; don't tell me about drugs and all that kind of stuff. I've seen it and I've been there (. . .) You have to make it on your own. You are really responsible for yourself and you *can* learn!" Percy's remarks embody a spirit of individualism in that he argues that the individual can always "make it" if only he or she is willing to try hard enough. This is not to say that Percy is unaware of structural barriers for blacks. Any black American knows full well the extent of racial prejudice in the United States. The individual, nevertheless, *can* escape the urban underclass, and this is what Percy stresses. Percy resents the fact that he is "hustled" by black students and responds by being even more rigorous than many white faculty. He responds negatively to the expression that he should "understand" students, and therefore pass them, whether they meet course requirements or not. Students do not, in contrast, expect this same "understanding" from white faculty.

Although Percy responds negatively to what he perceives as a "hustle," he does understand the contradictory nature of student culture. This is clear from the discussion below.

Percy: Academia is very scary. It's foreign and a lot of black students see it as a white world. A lot of them feel that it is completely foreign to them.

LW: Why?

Percy: How it was presented to them before (. . .) attitude on the part of other teachers, administrators, people for whom they have worked. The kind of orientation that America gives us. You get a feeling (. . .) from seeing the companies or advertisements white oriented and so on [and the fact] that larger universities have white students, and (. . .) the kinds of things they learned in school are white oriented.

(. . .) When I say [to students] "you're going to be excellent," that's (. . .) hard to take, because I'm imposing on them another value that is foreign in many ways, that I don't think should be foreign. I think excellence should be across the board, but to them often times excellence means being kind of white.

LW: Is that negative?

Percy: Yeah, it's negative sometimes. That kind of excellence is negative here.

LW: But yet, what are people doing here?

Percy: They don't know often times. They can get money to come here—some—so it's a ticket to getting a new stereo. They can get some extra money that perhaps their husband, boyfriend, or father or their child isn't giving them. That's one of the reasons.

(. . .) It's also style. [Like a guy] I see around here all the time whom I know is not in class, but he dresses to a "t." He wears a suit—you probably have seen him—very tall person, wears glasses, in his own way fashionable, and I don't think he is [ever in] a class. He was in my class for a while, but he was kind of a pretty boy who'd come in and I flattened his conceit one day and I never saw him again (. . .) He would come in so the girls could see him walk in, a mirror of fashion.

LW: So in part you think it's prestige?

Percy: Oh, definitely so. To say "I'm a college student." (. . .) I got a "D" average but I go to [State College].

Percy is quite critical of many aspects of student culture, and, while he links student behavior to the position of blacks in the American class structure, he is nevertheless highly critical of the way in which response to this class structure is played out in educational institutions. At the same time, he acknowledges the contradictory nature of the culture, which is not true for white faculty. Percy articulates clearly the contradictions with respect to education embedded within the black American experience that Eugene Genovese (1976) discusses so eloquently. Percy notes, for example, that "excellence means being kind of white" and therefore, excellence is perceived negatively by many black students. He also suggests that "academia is very scary. It's foreign and a lot of black students see it as a white world. A lot of them feel that it is completely foreign to them."

At least on one level, then, Percy argues that college knowledge is perceived as "not ours"—it is white, not black. At the same time, he pinpoints the contradictory attitude toward education by suggesting that many students at Urban College attend the school for reasons of "style." Being a college student also carries some prestige in the culture. He admits that some students are there for "a new stereo, (. . .) some extra money perhaps their husband, boyfriend or father of their child isn't giving them," but at the same time stresses the contradictory nature of these impulses. On the one hand, education *is* valued (even by those who are there for a new stereo); on the other hand, education is not part of *our* culture—it is white and therefore must be contradicted. This could explain why so many students adopt the *form* of college attendance without engaging in its substance. Again, however, this does not mean that college knowledge is totally rejected either consciously or unconsciously. The point here is that it is both embraced *and* rejected at one and the same time.

The position of Eboe, a Social Sciences instructor who grew up in West Africa, contrasts sharply with both that of Percy and Vivian and more closely resembles that of white faculty. This suggests that those rooted in the African-American experience have a clearer understanding of student culture (whether they approve of it or not) than those outside the experience, whether black or white.

Eboe: One of the biggest problems at Urban College is that there is a lot of con people—slick people—those who would use their disadvantage that they have as an excuse not to do their work. It took me a long time to learn that.

(. . .) I ask them "Don't you know that things are rougher out there now than ever before? You have to work harder."

"Yes, yes brother, we see that." "Then why don't you work harder?" [The student] laughs. That is strange and it is disheartening.

LW: (. . .) Where does that come from?

Eboe: It might come from the fact that some of the guys have had to take money or make things the illegal way, the only way he knows. Therefore he thinks that if I don't get it I can cheat, I can do this, he always thinks everything is going to come easy or the illegal way.

LW: But why are the men here?

Eboe: For the money. It's like a job to certain people. To a big degree [it characterizes] most of the men [here], especially those that you don't find in class after the checks are given out. Some people stay because they know that if they don't stay they might get F's and next semester they will not be able to come back to pick up those checks. So they stay and do mediocre work until the semester is over.

Most faculty are unaware of the contradictions embedded within student culture. Even if they recognize these contradictions (for example, Percy), faculty, on a day to day basis, must interact with student culture, and the pattern of dropping in and out assumes primary importance. This *is* the aspect of culture that faculty truly live—that they come into contact with day after day, year after year.

Students, on the other hand, interact on a day to day basis with faculty who see student culture largely in terms of chronic absence. It is the interaction between student and faculty cultures that produce and reinforce aspects of the lived culture of each, drawing out and emphasizing particular elements of respective cultural form. It is these very interactions on a day to day basis that in part produce and reinforce aspects of dominant ideology and structure. This is not to deny the impact of dominant ideology on these emerging forms. Certainly aspects of faculty and student culture (or at least a tendency toward certain forms) existed prior to their shared community college experience. At the same time, both faculty and students are actively involved in shaping their own reality and, by extension, their own futures.

Student and Faculty Cultures

I have argued that faculty, in response to both the low level of student academic skills and what they see as the non-serious nature of the student body, turn their attention away from students and begin to define enjoyment in their work more and more as lying *outside* of students. In addition, they define success increasingly in terms of the one or two who will "make it," while at the same time minimizing their labor in the classroom. Many faculty admit, for example, to the fact that they rely more on tapes, filmstrips, and other pre-packaged material than ever before. Many also use worksheets in class and have students exchange papers and correct them before class is over. Actual *teaching* and preparation time is thus lessened. An increased reliance on multiple-choice tests, rather than essay questions, reflects this same tendency. Not only do objective tests take less time to correct, but such tests can easily be corrected by others. Several faculty mentioned that their children correct examinations by using a "key." These practices all serve to lessen teacher labor. Significantly, most faculty did not start out using these materials and practices—they began using them only over time in this particular site. Faculty perspectives and important aspects of practice are therefore shaped, at least in part, by the student culture itself. In particular, they are shaped by faculty perceptions of this culture. In the final analysis, faculty adopt a set of classroom practices that are increasingly routinized and simplified. It is here that faculty culture embodies its own contradictions. In response to student culture, faculty focus increasingly on one or two students who will succeed and define their own success in terms of such students. At the same time, they provide these one or two students with a less demanding curriculum (more objective tests, relatively simple concepts that students "ought to know") due to a second, contradictory response to the group logic. Thus, while faculty see themselves as teaching to only a few, they are, in fact, working from a curriculum that they designed in response to the group.

It is here that dominant ideology plays a critical role. Racial antagonisms are deeply rooted in American culture. When faculty and student cultures polarize as they do in this particular site, faculty can draw upon already existing antagonisms to support their own perceptions and subsequent practice. Thus faculty are able to withdraw more and more from students and gain support for such action by an ideology which emphasizes "equality of opportunity." They are thus able to minimize their labor to some extent within the classroom and distance themselves from students and the educational process. This enables them to place their efforts elsewhere (for example, "a good fight") [8]. For the faculty, then, the *raison d'être* of the college is defined more and more in terms other than direct involvement with students. It must be stressed that this is a largely *unconscious* process. Interestingly enough, dominant ideology plays two roles here: it sustains the urban community college (and faculty jobs) in that the college offers "equal educational opportunity" at one and the same time that it enables faculty to distance themselves from students. Its effects, then, are inherently contradictory.

Faculty consciousness, in turn, affects student cultural form. While students affirm both the idea of teachers and the content of school knowledge, they are critical of faculty insofar as they do not, according to students, encourage a *fair* transaction. In return for respect/obedience, faculty are expected to share their knowledge. Where students express negativity, it is in terms of faculty not caring enough, or not working hard enough, to ensure that students learn [9].

> James: There may be some [faculty] who don't have what I consider a dedication, they are just there to get the money. They are not unlike the students themselves. They are there to get paid and they are going to do as less as they can. This works to the detriment of the student because what it does is lower standards and makes the person think that they are getting an education when they are not. Then they leave this facility and go someplace else, they get a job, go to another school, then they cannot pass the entrance test, or they get in class then they can't maintain because the proper groundwork hasn't been laid over there (. . .) I feel that the ones who are not dedicated should be held to performance within the scope of their employment. If they cannot perform, then it's about standing aside and allowing someone to assume the position who can (. . .) I want my teachers to be dedicated in teaching me, not just there to get the dollar.
>
> (a Paralegal student)

• • •

> Johnnie: As far as professors, I'd attempt to keep their attendance in line (. . .) because the professors at Urban College tend to just take for granted the students in this school.
>
> (. . .) They take the attitude that the student at this school doesn't really want to learn. He's here for some other reason or another other than to learn. So I'm going to miss this day and I'm going to miss that day.
>
> (. . .) This is my first semester. I started off with five classes and now I'm presently at four. Out of four classes I have two good instructors that are there when they are supposed to be and the way they go about instructing is compatible, you know, you can really get into it. But I have two other instructors that are hardly ever there; what they teach they don't test on, and they use attendance as their chain on you or something. He says if you don't attend, you don't get a good grade, but if you attend and he's not there, your motivation about getting to this class tends to drop somewhat.
>
> (. . .) There's a lot of good instructors there but *they don't apply themselves* [emphasis mine]. I know the students don't either and that has the instructor's motivation drop somewhat (. . .) I can understand that, but that is their job.

• • •

Jerome: At Urban College the instructors tend to make that assumption that everybody is on the same footing when they're not. Certain people can't even understand whiteys, so there's a communications breakdown. Then you have a personality clash between some teachers and students (. . .) You know, I take the attitude, you're white, you don't care, you get paid anyway. I know you don't care if I learn. That don't caring attitude—it's transmitted over a period of time. Students are off into that, so that there's no communication between students and teachers (. . .)

LW: Could you be a bit more specific?

Jerome: In a sense like, you have various wealth of people, most of them are people you can categorize as being unemployed, underemployed, social service recipients, you know, uh, poorly educated in the sense that the reading level and the math skills are below par of most high school kids now. So you know that with that knowledge that most instructors up there have, they are still around there with that Harvard School attitude and that's not Harvard. "I'm going to do my job and fail three-quarters of them and the two/three good ones can just slip through," you know.

                                                                    (a Business Administration student)

Students, then correctly perceive that faculty minimize their labor in the classroom to some extent, ant they have seen through a widely held acceptance of high attrition rates and a definition of success that rests on two or three students. They understand that faculty do not, for the most part, define success in terms of the group.

At the same time, students take some responsibility for faculty practice. As Johnnie states, "I know the students don't [apply themselves] either and that has the instructor's motivation drop somewhat, "and James argues that "they [faculty] are just there to get the money (. . .) not unlike the students themselves." Faculty, on the other hand, do not perceive their own likely role in the creation of student culture. Faculty see it solely as "a student problem." In response to collective faculty consciousness (which they partially see through), it can be speculated that students, in turn, emphasize particular aspects of their already contradictory culture. They drop out, arrive late, exert little effort, and engage in drugs. It is the case, however, that there is a genuine affirmation of learning within the culture as well. Given that this affirmation is in itself contradictory (although knowledge is respected, it is nevertheless white), faculty consciousness and practice encourage students to act on *certain* aspects of a highly contradictory set of cultural elements. The school is not neutral here. I am suggesting that faculty culture plays an important role in the form that student culture ultimately takes within the institution. As noted earlier, it is this very student culture that, in part, gives rise to faculty culture to begin with.

That faculty tend not to see their role in this process is linked, once again, to a dominant ideology which stresses the usefulness of education and the fact that "if you fail, it is your fault." Thus dominant ideology plays a role here, but it is truly recreated at the lived cultural level; it is not simply imposed. It is also noteworthy that while students may blame faculty, in the final analysis, they also blame themselves. Thus students not only reassert their "otherness" in an institution designed to break down such "otherness," but they also take some responsibility for their own position in a highly stratified class structure.

In so arguing, I do not mean to imply that if only faculty culture would change, student culture and ultimately institutional outcomes would change. It is probably not this simple and faculty respond "sensibly" in many ways to their own lived conditions. It is therefore not my intent to blame them for the compromises they make (compromises which I believe that I myself would have made), nor institutional outcomes generally. As I have argued elsewhere (Weis, 1985) student culture arises in relation to a number of internal institutional factors as well as factors external to the institution. Faculty, nevertheless, appear to contribute to institutional outcomes in unanticipated ways by virtue of the form their culture takes—a form that represents a set of accommodations to their own lived realities.

The data presented here were gathered in an urban community college and the analysis is geared toward that setting. The issues raised are, nonetheless, potentially relevant to institutions of higher education generally. On any campus students and faculty construct their own cultures. It is my contention that such cultures are linked in critical ways to institutional outcomes. It is, after all, students who achieve or who do not achieve, thereby turning institutional goals into realities. Faculty, by virtue of their perspectives and practice, possess the power to thwart, whether consciously or not, institutional goals. The cultures faculty and students construct for themselves in educational settings potentially determine, at least partially, educational outcomes.

It is therefore important to understand the genesis of faculty and student cultures and the way in which each creates aspects of the other. In the case of the urban community college I have suggested that faculty and student cultures take shape and polarize in such a way as to help produce widespread educational failure. Neither faculty nor students wish this to be the case. It is certainly not an intended outcome of the institution or the community college movement generally.

Studies of cultural creation such as that presented here can be pursued fruitfully in a variety of institutional settings. This should be done with an eye toward understanding the shape and form such cultures take, the reasons for this form, and the way in which cultures are linked in possibly unanticipated ways to institutional outcomes such as in the Urban College example. Institutional outcomes are, after all, created by both faculty and students as they go about living and working within colleges and universities. Outcomes are not and cannot be decreed from above. They are at least partially the result of ongoing interaction within institutional settings. It is this ongoing interaction that deserves our full attention. It is only in this way that we will be able to understand the way in which practices emerge within institutions and the way in which such practices may be related to institutional outcomes.

Notes

This article will appear in a somewhat different form in Lois Weis, *Between Two Worlds: Black Students in an Urban Community College* (Boston: Routledge and Kegan Paul, 1985). My thanks to Lionel Lewis for his comments on an earlier version of this paper.

1. It has been estimated that of the 827 students admitted into degree programs in the Fall of 1977, only 93, or 11 percent, graduated in May 1979. The figure is somewhat higher for the following year: of 527 students admitted in Fall of 1978, it has been estimated that 131, or 25 percent, graduated in May 1980. Even assuming a three-year cycle, only 131 of the 827 (16 percent) admitted in the Fall of 1977 graduated three years later. Urban College Task Force *Student Enrollment: Retention and Placement 1976–1981 Data Bank*.

2. Information reported here was obtained through formal interviews as well as informal interaction with faculty. All formal interviews were taped with permission of the respondents.

3. An objective test here refers to one with a forced choice format.

4. This is not an inconsequential point. There has been far too little attention paid to the way in which curricular form emerges in educational institutions. It is not *simply* a form of control applied to specific groups. Although Linda McNeil (1981, 1983) does not focus on student race or class, I am in agreement with her basic argument regarding the shaping of curriculum.

5. Faculty at Urban College, like faculty on the university level, are basically in control of their own curriculum. Clearly such "choice" is dependent upon what is available in the marketplace. See Michael Apple (1982, Chapters 2 and 5).

6. In-class observations indicate absenteeism as follows: A class in Fashion Merchandising began with close to 35 students in early September; by December 14, 1979, between 7 and 12 students were attending the course. Twelve of an original 32 students were attending a Salesmanship class by November 17. Twenty-four students were attending Business Seminar (a remedial course) on February 8; attendance had dropped to between 4 and 11 by May 5. Additional data on absenteeism are reported in Weis (1983, 1985).

7. London (1978) has categorized faculty in the community college as having conservative, liberal or radical perspectives. While this may be true, subsequent practice in the classroom may not follow from such perspectives.

8. This in not to deny the very real politics surrounding Urban College that may necessitate "a good fight." It is significant, however, that faculty enjoy action outside the classroom to a greater extent than they do action within the classroom.

9. I have discussed this point at length in Weis, (1985, Chapter 2).

References

Apple, Michael (1982). *Education and Power*. Boston: Routledge and Kegan Paul.

Apple, Michael and Weis, Lois (eds.) (1983). *Ideology and Practice in Schooling*. Philadelphia: Temple University Press.

Carnegie Commission for Higher Education (1970). *The Open Door Colleges*. New York: McGraw-Hill.

Clark, Burton (1960). "The 'cooling-out' function in higher education," *The American Journal of Sociology* 65: 569–76.

Fields, R. R. 1962). *The Community College Movement*. New York: McGraw-Hill.

Genovese, Eugene (1976). *Roll Jordan Roll: The World the Slaves Made*. New York: Vintage Books.

Gleazer, E. J. (1968). *This is the Community College*. Boston: Houghton Mifflin.

Karabel, Jerome (1972). "Community colleges and social stratification," *Harvard Educational Review* 42 (4): 521–562.

London, Howard (1978). *The Culture of a Community College*. New York: Praeger.

McNeil, Linda (1981). "Negotiating classroom knowledge: beyond achievement and socialization," *Journal of Curriculum Studies* 13 (4): 313–328.

McNeil, Linda (1983). "Defensive teaching and classroom control," in M. Apple and L. Weis (eds.), *Ideology and Practice in Schooling*. Philadelphia: Temple University Press, pp. 114–142.

Olivas, Michael (1979). *The Dilemma of Access: Minorities in Two-Year Colleges*. Washington, DC: Howard University Press.

Pincus, Fred (1980). "The false promises of community colleges: class conflict and vocational education," *Harvard Educational Review* 50 (3): 33–360.

Weis, Lois (1985): *Between Two Worlds: Black Students in an Urban Community College*. Boston: Routledge and Kegan Paul.

Weis, Lois (1983). "Schooling and cultural production: a comparison of black and white lived culture," in M. Apple and L. Weis (eds.), *Ideology and Practice in Schooling*. Philadelphia: Temple University Press, pp. 235–261.

"Hit the Ground Running": Experiences of New Faculty in a School of Education

Elizabeth J. Whitt

The greatest investment an institution of higher education makes during the coming decades may well be the hiring of new faculty members (Mathis 1979). Aside from salary, a new faculty member requires a significant investment in search committee time and activities, reduced course and advising loads, and special evaluations. Most faculties think that these efforts are worthwhile because they assume (or hope) that new faculty will be long-term productive members of the institutional community.

In the early years of an academic appointment, new faculty members must learn what their colleagues and students expect of them, acquire facility in dealing with organizational structures and processes, and grasp the history and traditions of their new institutional setting (Baldwin 1979; Mathis 1979). At the same time, new faculty members must also explore and become comfortable with their roles as members of the academic profession, including teaching, research, and service (Bess 1978).

New faculty members are likely to make faster and more satisfactory adjustments to their academic roles and their new institution if there is a good match between their expectations, values, and skills, those of their individual department, and those of the institution as a whole (Mathis 1979; Van Maanen 1976). For example, a faculty member who prefers close relationships with colleagues and involvement in collaborative research will thrive best in a setting in which collegial interaction is frequent and supportive. If her new colleagues are distant—even absent—the new faculty member's satisfaction and productivity may fall far short of what she hoped and also what the institution expected (Corcoran and Clark 1984; Schein 1968).

Studies of new faculty experiences describe high levels of stress and low levels of occupational satisfaction (i.e., Baldwin 1979; Baldwin and Blackburn 1981; Mager and Myers 1982; Reynolds 1988; Sorcinelli 1985; Sorcinelli 1988). Mary Deane Sorcinelli (1988) concluded that department chairs play a crucial role in facilitating or hindering the adjustment of new faculty. If that is the case, to what extent are department chairs aware of and responsive to the feelings of new faculty about their experiences? Also, how much congruence is there between the expectations and perceptions of those new faculty and their chairs? If a department chair incorrectly assumes that a new faculty member already knows everything she needs to know to be effective, the chair may unintentionally play a very negative role in the new faculty member's adjustment.

My purposes in this study were (1) to examine and describe the experiences of new faculty in the School of Education (SOE) at a large midwestern research university and (2) to compare new faculty experiences with SOE administrators' expectations and perceptions of those new faculty experiences.

Experiences of New Faculty

Socialization is cultural learning which takes place in a social context. From the perspective of individuals within an organization, organizational socialization is the process by which the newcomer learns what is important in the organization, including its norms and values, and the behaviors expected of members of the organization (Schein 1968). From the perspective of the organization, socialization is the "mechanism through which the existing consensus structure and communication practices are transferred to new generations and participants" (Etzioni 1975, 254). The outcomes of socialization processes largely depend on the organization's ability to select and use methods that communicate clearly which behaviors elicit valued rewards (Van Maanen 1976).

The period of organizational entry is the point at which an individual is most susceptible to organizational socialization efforts; John Van Maanen observes: "The importance of this set of initial experiences in determining how both the individual and the organization will view one's career cannot be overstated" (1976, 77). Indeed, David Berlow and Douglas Hall, in their study of AT&T managers, asserted that "what he [or she] learns at the beginning will become the core of his [or her] organizational identity" (1966, 210). However, "that portion of his [or her] life space corresponding to the organization is blank" (1966, 210). Newcomers, during organizational entry, are anxious to fill in the blank—to define expectations of others and relate themselves to those expectations.

Newcomers are also likely to experience "reality shock," or conflicts between what they anticipated and what they believe they have found. To reduce the anxiety inherent in reality shock, they try to learn the social and functional requirements of their new roles as quickly as possible (Orth 1963; Van Maanen 1975). "The newcomer's most pressing task is to build a set of guidelines and interpretations to explain and make meaningful the myriad of activities observed as going on in the organization" (Van Maanen 1978, 21).

Accomplishing this task may be particularly difficult for new faculty members as much of what is expected of them is unstated and unwritten (Corcoran and Clark 1984). Van Maanen (1984) asserted that unstated expectations are typical of organizations whose socialization processes are based on the assumption that newcomers bring with them the skills and knowledge they need to be successful. Thus, it may not be surprising that newcomers to institutions of higher education are, for the most part, left alone to figure out what they are supposed to do and rely on experiences and interpretations from previous settings to make sense of events and activities in the new setting. Because the new setting typically lacks persons and processes that provide newcomers with socialization assistance, newcomers must look backward for lessons from old roles to create understandings of their new roles. In this type of organization, then, prior socialization settings represent "the main conceptual resource and skill repository to be drawn on when adjusting to changes in . . . life situations" (Van Maanen 1984, 238).

The first faculty position continues the educational process begun in graduate school; new faculty members become more fully socialized into the academic profession while they simultaneously learn and adapt to the norms and values of the new employing organization (Bess 1982). The anxiety produced by these demands may be exacerbated by the shift from graduate student to the new "adult status" of faculty member (Lortie 1968, 259). This new role demands "adult" behavior, including performing the roles of a faculty member without assistance from others in the new setting. Roger Baldwin (1979), in his study of the careers of faculty members at twelve liberal arts colleges, found that many of them remembered their first years in a faculty position as a particularly difficult career stage, characterized by high levels of stress and low levels of occupational satisfaction. New faculty members confessed to feeling very worried about succeeding, being unfamiliar with the governance and informal operational structures in their new setting, and being very open to receiving help from more experienced colleagues (Baldwin and Blackburn

1981). Many senior faculty members interviewed confirmed that their first college teaching position had a significant effect on their later career. "In other words, the problems and performance of novice faculty members influence their later occupational progress," Baldwin summarized (1979, 17). These research results support the view that newcomers enter new settings with much role- and setting-related anxiety, that they are particularly susceptible to organizational socialization processes, whatever their nature, and that their early experiences have a critical impact on their future careers.

Other studies of faculty experiences and attitudes reveal similar characterizations of the lives of new faculty members (Mager and Myers 1982; Reynolds 1988; Sorcinelli 1985; Sorcinelli 1988). Specific concerns of new faculty include ambiguous measures of success, feelings of isolation, difficult interactions with and among other faculty members including competition and departmental politics (Mager and Myers 1982); extreme time pressures, difficulty finding time for research, and fear of not getting tenure (Sorcinelli 1985).

Anne Reynolds (1988) identified six concerns of beginning faculty: advice—mostly contradictory; finances, including salaries lower than the cost of living; ill health (a problem for over half of her respondents); identity, including feelings of being an imposter "pretending" to be a faculty member; friendship deprivation, including an absence of junior colleagues, lack of time to find friends, and barriers of time, age, and and interest separating new faculty from senior colleagues; and tenure, a major source of worry, confusion, and conversation, resulting in marital problems, intimidation by senior faculty, and feelings of competition among junior faculty.

Sorcinelli's (1988) longitudinal study of faculty members at a research university captured both the positive and negative experiences of new faculty. New faculty identified their sources of satisfaction as the nature of academic work, their autonomy as faculty members, and securing a tenure track position at a research university when the academic job market was tight. Stressors for new faculty included lack of time to do their work (especially research), the need to balance many professional and personal demands, coping with the contradiction between teaching requirements and institutional rewards for research, lack of collegial relationships ("the most surprising and disappointing aspect of their first year" 1988, 3), tenure, and administration. New faculty members who had come directly from graduate school or postdoctoral study felt particularly overwhelmed by the stress and contradictory demands (Sorcinelli 1988).

Research Methods

Qualitative research methods are particularly useful in understanding the nature of culture and cultural process (Goetz and LeCompte 1984; Morgan 1986; Whitt and Kuh, in press); thus, they constitute excellent tools for probing institutional values, expectations and socialization.

I selected six key respondents, three men and three women who were newly employed in full-time faculty positions in the School of Education at a large, midwestern research university. Two had come directly from doctoral programs, two had held full-time faculty positions at other institutions, one had held a non-university research position, and one had been a full-time administrator at a research university. Four of the key respondents had responsibility for program development and/or administration in addition to teaching, research, and service activities. I also interviewed six School of Education department chairs and four administrators who served on the dean's staff to obtain information about the context in which faculty worked, as well as to examine Sorcinelli's (1988) findings that the behavior and attitudes of department chairs toward new faculty were crucial in new faculty adjustment.

The limitations that a small number of respondents from a single setting place on generalization of findings are obvious; however, such an investigation allows for deep, rather than broad, examination and, it is hoped, correspondingly deep understanding. My purpose was to generate a clear, accurate, and trustworthy picture of the perceptions and experiences of one group of individuals in a particular context, not generalizable conclusions.

Secondary data sources were academic handbooks, the tenure and promotion handbook, and the School of Education's policy manual. They helped generate questions for the respondents and provided information about the setting of the study. I also attended a SOE faculty retreat and a tenure workshop conducted by the university's office of women's programs as an observer.

Data collection and analysis were conducted concurrently, so that the early stages of interviewing informed my later interviews and interpretations (Lincoln and Guba 1985; Miles and Huberman 1984). These interviews were semi-structured, becoming more structured as the investigation proceeded; respondents generated additional questions for the study and, as data analysis progressed, gaps in information became evident. I conducted twenty-one interviews with the six new faculty members over the course of a semester and interviewed each administrator once.

Data analysis was inductive; that is, I developed categories of information from the interviews themselves using the processes of unitization and categorization (Lincoln and Guba 1985; Miles and Huberman 1984). The reliability of these two processes was tested according to the effective percentage agreement formula described by Myrtle Scott and J.G. Hatfield (1985).

Results of the Study

Analysis of the data revealed five recurring themes in the experiences of these new faculty: (1) collegiality, (2) the school's attitudes and expectations regarding new faculty members, (3) the role of department chairs, (4) workload, and (5) the feelings of new faculty about their experiences.

Collegiality

Collegiality was a high priority for new faculty, and they brought with them from past settings high expectations for collegial relationships in the SOE. The new faculty looked forward to a work environment characterized by shared values and commitments and collaborative research. For one newcomer, the question, "Could I see these people as colleagues?" was the factor that "probably weighed heaviest for me" in deciding where to work. Another reported with satisfaction, "I've been able to find people who share my interests here."

However, although they all hoped for the ideal, they found a less satisfactory reality, one that required negotiating the omni-present tensions between the autonomous and communal aspects of faculty life. The six key respondents perceived the SOE faculty community as fragmented— divided by work-space, time commitments, interests, and age. In most cases, they were disappointed by what one of the new faculty called "a lack of collegiality." For example, "I [have gotten] sort of a consensus that 'we all work to capacity in a quality way and each of us is working toward some kind of ideal, but we interconnect very rarely'." Also, "my picture of the culture here is one of fragmentation, probably due to the fact that everyone must do research and research happens to be a very lonely type of thing unless people team together. When I say fragmentation, I could mean isolation." Another key respondent had similar feelings: "There is a terrific sense of isolation. That's one of my biggest frustrations, not being able to find a sounding board that will enable me to sort things out." Some expressed concerns about sounding naive, unprofessional, or disorganized by asking for help from senior faculty: "If I say anything, they might wonder if I'm really doing my job," a big risk to take with those who make decisions about tenure.

The new faculty members were surprised to find out that they had to take the initiative in interacting with colleagues, a difficult task in a setting of new people and unknown norms. "Senior faculty talk about collegiality, but they never take the initiative," described one, "and that's hard." "My experience is not what I expected," admitted one new faculty member. "I expected others to come to me because I'm new here. I also expected more linkages with departments, I expected a sharing of ideas, I expected like-minded people to call me to work with them."

Department chairs emphasized that senior faculty were an important source of socialization for new faculty; but two acknowledged barriers to relationships between the most senior faculty members and junior faculty: "Full professors provide little contact and little support for new faculty," admitted one. "New faculty have very few interactions with full professors," the other agreed. "They just aren't around, aren't usually interested."

New faculty also identified the "cohort issue" as a major barrier to collegiality. Generational differences between junior and senior faculty seemed to create different subcultures. As one newcomer put it: "There was a cohort of people that came up in the late '50s and '60s. I don't want to say they had it easy, but there certainly was a different set of expectations. I've heard some of the senior faculty say that tenure was more informal and the economic situation of professors was a lot better." These differences create "a large gap between those people who've been here and are in stable positions and those of us just starting out." Another new faculty member stated, "I learned early not to complain, that it's not expected—it's almost like 'we did it, you can do it.' There's just a total lack of understanding of what it means to be a junior faculty member now and a general lack of sympathy."

Relationships within departments reflected both positive and negative elements of the SOE community. Department chairs asserted that they and other faculty encouraged new members to have equal input into departmental decisions and discussions. New faculty said that they had trusted and respected their immediate colleagues. One observed, in a statement that was typical of others, "They seem like reasonable people and I'm assuming that if there were something I was doing wrong, someone would tell me." Another commented that he "enjoyed . . . faculty meetings with those people." However, the long histories some departments had shared frustrated the new faculty members who wanted to effect change: "I'm the only person in the department who has worked anywhere else within the last ten years," pointed out one. "That gives me a real different feel for what's possible. They say, 'Well, we used to . . .', 'We always . . .'—there's always a deference to history.' New faculty also reported difficulty in figuring out the dynamics of relationships and alignments in the department: "I think that leaves me as a faculty member at some distance away from them in not totally understanding what the positions are and so being leery of getting involved in something they don't want me involved in." As a consequence, new faculty felt, to some extent, like outsiders.

Administrators' Attitudes and Expectations

Comments from the department chairs and dean's staff revealed concern for the adjustment of new faculty and expressions of commitment to helping them succeed. For example, one administrator told me, "The School of Education philosophy toward new faculty has been that they are valued because they are so rare—like precious jewels." Another put it this way: "Our attitude is that they should be given a lot of support. We want to keep them and we want them to succeed and we want them to be quality faculty members." A third called them "an investment. It's an issue of departmental survival to do whatever is possible to help them." This chair added, "It's absolutely critical that they get off to a good start, to feel good about their situation . . . and we have to help them grow into the role of a faculty member."

At the same time, the administrators described clear expectations of new faculty members, expectations that, in some cases, communicated more rigor than support. None said anything to indicate that they expected new faculty members to need a year or two to settle in, learn their way around, and focus on their goals. On the contrary, both department chairs and dean's staff agreed that they expected new faculty to already know a great deal about being a faculty member, to be experienced researchers and teachers, to have values and goals consistent with their new institution, and to possess appropriate work habits. As one department chair said, "We look at research. Have they done any? Do they know what it takes? Have they been introduced to norms?" If they haven't, he said, "there [are] a limited number of ways you can help. . . . It's difficult to give someone a research orientation to the world."

One phrase occurred spontaneously so many times that it was tantamount to a slogan in this School of Education: "hit the ground running." According to a member of the dean's staff, "We want to remove obstacles for them, but they couldn't wait for us to anticipate their needs. We're not here to coddle them. . . . If they've had research opportunities, we hope that [those] attitudes and habits have rubbed off and they can hit the ground running." A department chair echoed the same phrase: "We want new faculty who've already demonstrated that they can do what we want them to do, who can come in and set their course and hit the ground running." A second chair agreed: "They need to be assertive and self-motivating. . . . This is a publish or perish institution. If they're going to survive, they have to get out there and do thing . . . to be productive they have to hit the ground running."

Fortunately, new faculty knew about this expectation and also shared it, even though it was intimidating for some. One new faculty member reported, "A senior faculty member told me that he's heard positive things about my coming here and being able to hit the ground running. . . . I do think that I came in with an understanding of what a faculty member does, but the specific information I needed to carry that out was a little nebulous."

Another used the identical terminology in his comments, "I think graduate school shaped me. . . . I moved quickly, applying for grants—really hit the ground running, so to speak. . . . I think that's a fair expectation coming into a major research university. But" he added ruefully, "the image that comes to mind is,'they hit the ground running, so let's drop a load of bricks on them and see what they do.' If they'd just allowed me to hit the ground running . . . but the resources—time and information and money—just aren't there."

Like this newcomer, none of the other five resisted the expectation that they "hit the ground running." None of them asked for a longer or more leisurely adjustment period. But most of them expressed the same frustration at being expected to already know everything an effective faculty member needed to know. As one put it, "Coming in and knowing what it is to be a faculty member here—how am I supposed to know that?" "There's a lot of time spent spinning your wheels before you find out what you need to know," agreed another. A third one said, "I was just told I had to learn it somehow as I carried my load. . . . It's like I was thrown into a swimming pool without knowing how to swim."

Another pinpointed contradictions in the attitudes of administrators toward new faculty: "To expect us to hit the ground running and say they need to support faculty to help them succeed—those are mutually exclusive. . . . It doesn't make sense for [this university] to produce doctoral students who haven't been intentionally trained to be faculty, but then think that our sister institutions are producing students who *are* trained to do that."

The Role of Department Chairs

Both dean's staff and department chairs asserted that department chairs are "critical" to the adjustment of new faculty, although the staff members believed that some department chairs were more effective than others: "How do new faculty learn to become faculty members? First, from their department chairs, although some anticipate new faculty needs better than others." Also, "the departments chair's attitude is key—an attitude that it is part of the job of the chair to provide unusual support for the new faculty to make sure that they become good teachers, establish a meaningful program of research, and receive honest feedback and praise." But, "department chair performance is variable. A good chair will provide a meaningful annual review, serve as a mentor to new faculty or make sure that mentoring is taking place—good chairs assign mentors—and can tell you who is being mentored by whom."

Not all department chairs were so specific or saw their roles in the same way, though all four perceived themselves as a source of aid: "We want to make sure they make it here. I constantly ask, 'How's your research coming along? What do you need?'" Another department chair, who admittedly focused on "their progress toward tenure," explained how he saw his responsibilities: "I think we ought to work extra hard to help new faculty adjust quickly and learn quickly what they need to know. I give them assignments that are intended to help them develop and succeed, because if we lose someone, we may not be able to replace them." He also added, "My role is to make sure that no faculty member is isolated. . . . It's also my role to be positive and enthusiastic, and encourage development of new ideas by finding ways to make things happen." Two chairs said that they assigned each new faculty member in their departments to a senior mentor, someone to provide guidance, support, and opportunities for collaboration.

When new faculty described the roles department chairs played in their socialization and adjustment, they communicated the variable performance the dean's staff had noted rather than the chairs' own view that they were consistently supportive. A few of the new faculty praised their chairs and expressed appreciation for their concern and assistance: "I think I have a sponsor in the department chair. I've appreciated that—rather than saying, 'Well, you're here. We'll check in with you in six months.' It's real important to help someone get integrated into a new organization." Another key respondent appreciatively noted that her chair "has been extremely helpful. He comes in from time to time, asking me how I am, have I seen such and such."

But most felt that their chairs were not adequately involved with them nor as helpful as they could, or should, have been: "The role of the department chair should be socialization," mused one. "[The] department chair and dean can take the place of a mentor. Maybe it's me, but I haven't felt touched by that." Another noted wryly, "I've had contact with him about twice a semester. I saw him at merit review time—when something comes up." A third seemed wary of her chair: "About some things he's given me very sketchy information, like 'it's in the catalogue,' but it's not that easy! And a couple of times he gave me wrong information. . . . A lot [with him] is unspoken cues." It is interesting to note that neither of the two faculty members whose chairs said that they assigned mentors to new faculty thought they had a mentor in the SOE, although all wished they did.

Workload

Most new faculty members said that they had expected very heavy workloads and also felt that it was what others expected of them: "I knew that I was getting myself into a pressure cooker, but that didn't bother me," as one put it, while another said, "I expected to be busy . . . that there was an expectation that I'd get a research program underway and that I'd been given a light [course] load to support that."

Nevertheless, they also identified some negative consequences in very demanding workloads and conflicting demands: "I work all the time. I keep thinking its going to get better, that eventually I'll get caught up, but there's always something new. I never go home and do nothing. I always work." A second worried, "It really is like having to catch six things coming at you at once [but] I tend not to say 'no' very often for fear of violating the norm." Another metaphor was "plate spinning—you run and spin the plate just as it's about to fall down, then you run back and spin another. That really . . . can burn you out." Still another painted a sober picture of the long-term consequences of these demands: "When you're spending that much time on the job, there really isn't time to answer those broad 'why am I here?' questions without driving yourself crazy. . . . I have an image of a faculty member as gray. I guess gray hair is a metaphor for what I see as worried. . . . The harried and haggard professor has replaced the absent-minded professor."

Feelings of New Faculty About Their Experiences

I wanted to know to what extent the administrators had thought about the feelings of new faculty or tried to put themselves in the place of new faculty members.

Interestingly enough, dean's staff members, for the most part, emphasized difficulties: "Being a new faculty member here is scary, unless you're unusual," said one. "I think they're terrorized by the threat of the tenure process." Another added, "They get mixed messages from what they're asked to do and what is expected for tenure—incongruity between responsibilities and rewards." Another administrator stated that assuming "the faculty role is probably the "most difficult" part of the new faculty member's job. "In their prior socialization as graduate students . . . arrogance and assertive behavior aren't rewarded—deference is. The faculty role is that of an authority, and it's a shock to cope with. They also have a problem being taken seriously because most of the [other] faculty members are so senior."

The department chairs, in contrast, painted a brighter picture, occasionally acknowledging its threatening aspects but stressing its excitement and challenges. "Being a new faculty member is more a matter of survival than of being effective. They're in a vulnerable position, torn in different directions by very heavy demands for teaching, advising, research, and service. I think they also have financial worries. . . . I would hope that the new faculty feel loved and warmly regarded." Another expressed the opinion that "new faculty probably feel a lot of ambiguity: 'Can I make it? What do they expect?' There's an awful lot of support, so it's not threatening for a new faculty member, but there's some stress, especially about money." Another confidentially stated, "A new faculty member in this department feels real satisfaction that 'I can develop here', 'I'm supported'. . . . There is also probably some tension—but without threat. . . . Being a new faculty member here is challenging . . . but it's hard to avoid a level of paranoia in a place like this." On the other hand, another chair asserted that "a new faculty member is probably impressed with the expectations of a place like this and is likely to find them threatening."

When asked, "What is it like to be a new faculty member?" new faculty described their feelings and experiences as predominantly negative. Typically, they expressed confusion: "I have no idea what's going on,' "I get no messages from this place," "I feel I've been thrown into a big pool without knowing how to swim." Also, "the word that comes to mind is stressful. . . . I'd say threatening. I wish there was a way of being clear to people how hard it's going to be. . . . If only someone had told me I would be twice as poor as an assistant professor as I was in graduate school and that it's probably five times more frustrating."

Despite administrators' assertions that support for new faculty was a priority, new faculty keenly felt a lack of emotional and financial support. One new faculty member lamented, "There are virtually no resources provided for gearing up one's own research program. What I hear is 'we're not going to give you the resources to do what we're asking you to do . . . [and] the salary is probably the hardest thing about the job.'" Another asserted, "This is a very unhelpful place—not an evil or un-nice place, but it's not a very warm way to take care of people. . . . Some days, particularly days you're asked to do a lot, there's nobody to take care of you and that makes me angry." Another reflected, "I didn't think to ask in interviews, 'How do you support people?' . . . It was more different from what I was doing before than I'd expected."

In addition to having a lot to do, some of the new faculty felt a great deal of pressure to perform—to be effective faculty members and to keep up with the standards set by senior faculty: "I feel as though I have to earn the respect of others through evidence of the work I'm doing. This is difficult because these are people with major names. . . . You're involved with people with national reputations and you try to stay up with them." For another new faculty member, "There's almost a constant pressure to perform—to get grants in competition with other researchers, to get articles published in highly competitive journals . . . you can't ever get out of the competition because you have to achieve at a certain level [to get tenure]."

The three newcomers who had never been faculty members before and who were new to this particular university I termed "very new" faculty. In particular, they struggled with issues of professional identity, concerns about tenure, and feeling of intense isolation.

In addition to normal adjustment problems, the very new faculty were uneasy with their new identity as professors and with titles that accompanied that identity: "At a departmental picnic, a graduate student and [I] were talking and she said, 'Oh, you're a professor,' and I said, 'No, not really' and sort of shuffled my feet and so on. Suddenly I saw this barrier go up. . . . The funny part about this job is that you don't suddenly have this metamorphosis where you know exactly what to do." Another very new faculty member said "the first couple of weeks it was 'what am I doing here?' . . . I mostly felt I should keep busy so I'd look like I was doing something even though I didn't know what I was doing."

Concerns about tenure were not unique to this group, but their level of anxiety about it was intense. One said in great frustration, "I don't know how I'm going to get tenure. They want me to put out a significant amount of research, yet I have to battle every step of the way to get myself time to do that." Another had decided that "there is a difference between doing your best and doing the right things. Every once in a while I think I'll just say "big deal' to tenure."

The sense of isolation expressed by all six newcomers was intensified for the three very new faculty because they believed that they were alone in feeling isolated, overwhelmed, and inadequate. During the debriefings when I described the feelings of other new faculty, these very new faculty said: "It's good to hear I'm not alone. . . . I spend a lot of time wondering, 'Is it just me?'. 'Am I being particularly negative?'" Another stated, "It's helpful to feel that I'm not alone. Sometimes I wonder if I'm just sitting here being a malcontent."

Summary of the Results

What then, can be said about the experiences of these new faculty members in this School of Education?

1. New faculty were expected to "hit the ground running"—to establish themselves quickly as teachers and researchers, to get acquainted with practitioners, to apply for grants, and to adjust to their new work setting. Administrators expected them to bring with them much of what they needed to know about being faculty members. They were expected to have prior socialization to research and teaching; appropriate values, expectations, and work habits; a research orientation; and a program of research already in progress. Although department chairs and the dean's staff expressed strong commitments to helping new faculty succeed, they also had no intention of "coddling" new faculty.

    While new faculty believed that hitting the ground running was an appropriate expectation at a major research university, they thought their path was blocked with an unexpected and bewildering number of obstacles. They believed that inadequate orientation to the institution and the absence of adequate financial and emotional resources hampered their ability to quickly adjust to and perform their new roles.

2. Being a new faculty member can be s stressful and negative experience. New faculty struggled with conflicting demands on their time while trying to figure out, with little assistance, what they should be doing and how they ought to be allocating their time. New faculty perceived themselves as striving to meet high expectations in an environment that provided less research funding, salary, and emotional support than they expected and felt they needed.

3. The experiences of "very new" faculty and "old new" faculty are somewhat different. Faculty members new to the institution and to teaching were more uncertain about their

roles and felt more isolated from other faculty. At the same time, all of the new faculty were concerned about how little assistance they were given in adjusting to their new setting.

4.   New faculty and department chairs perceive the experiences of new faculty very differently. Chairs characterized the experiences as primarily positive while the new faculty were mostly negative. Also, the department chairs perceived themselves as more helpful (e.g., answering questions, anticipating concerns) than the new faculty did.

Discussion

New faculty in this study used a variety of metaphors to describe their expectations in their first year in the School of Education at a research university: spinning plates, being thrown into the middle of the pool without knowing how to swim, spinning their wheels, living in a pressure cooker, hitting the ground running, hitting the ground running while carrying a load of bricks, and turning gray. All of these metaphors communicate pressure, uncertainty, little time to think—only to act, and feelings of isolation—carrying that heavy load alone. Particularly hard hit by concerns about identity, isolation, and uncertainty were the very new faculty. At the same time, all of the key respondents spoke in positive terms of the opportunities they found in the SOE to fulfill their commitment to research, teaching, and educational practice.

These findings reinforce the portrayals in existing research of new faculty members at research universities as harried by competing professional and personal demands, pressured to perform in a competitive environment, disappointed at the lack of collegiality in their departments, yet challenged in a positive way by their teaching and research (Reynolds 1988; Sorcinelli 1985, 1988). Sorcinelli (1988) also found that faculty right out of graduate school—very new faculty—were especially overwhelmed by the stresses of being new faculty members.

The contrast between how new faculty viewed their experiences and the perceptions of department chairs is noteworthy. Both the chairs and the dean's staff emphasized the key role chairs played in the adjustment of new faculty. The chairs perceived themselves as caring and supportive, and described a number of actions—for example, "constantly checking" on new faculty and assigning mentors—as evidence of their concern. In contrast, the new faculty felt that their chairs were not as helpful as they could or should have been. In fact, several of the new faculty seemed to be unaware of the supportive behaviors the chairs described: the chair who "constantly" checked with the new faculty member was characterized as largely absent, and the new faculty did not think that they had mentors.

Perhaps some new faculty had such high expectations of their chairs that they were bound to be disappointed. Or perhaps the experience of being new faculty members was so overwhelming that the chairs' supportive actions did not come close to meeting their needs or went unnoticed. Perhaps some of the chairs portrayed themselves as they wished they could be. It is also possible that the chairs and the new faculty had different perceptions about what actions were helpful. For example, a chair might see providing grant information to a new faculty member as evidence of support, while the new faculty member might see it as additional pressure.

Also striking is the discrepancy between the department chairs' impressions of how new faculty members felt about their experiences and the feelings new faculty reported. Chairs perceived new faculty experiences as "exciting," "challenging," and "non-threatening," and thought new faculty felt "loved" and "warmly regarded." New faculty, however, described confusion, anxiety, isolation, and lack of support. The dean's office staff, who used words like "terrorized" and "threatened," seemed more in touch with the feelings of new faculty.

It may be the case that new faculty were reluctant to discuss their true feelings with their chairs because they did not want to appear incompetent or weak. The message that new faculty must "hit the ground running" may also imply that they must do so without ever stumbling, getting tired, or asking for help. If contact between new faculty members and their department chairs was limited to a quick "how's it going?" or an annual merit review meeting, the new faculty members would probably not feel comfortable revealing their confusion, self-doubts, and disappointments. Perhaps department chairs, too, took the "hit the ground running" message to heart and assumed that these well-prepared and talented individuals would have no trouble adjusting to their new roles or might even be insulted by questions about their progress or offers of assistance.

A question that must be raised is to what extent the "sink or swim," (Weick 1984, 25) nature of the socialization of new faculty is reflected in reported feelings of stress, pressure, uncertainty, and isolation, as well as positive challenges, freedom, and flexibility? The experiences of this particular group of new faculty would lead me to speculate that having to be responsible for their own socialization may have added to the already heavy workload of new faculty. Having to spend time "spinning their wheels" finding out answers to questions—or finding out questions—exacerbated the sense of carrying "a load of bricks."

In addition, the perceived lack of collegiality seems to have grown logically from the absence of formal orientation processes and the concomitant perceptions that new faculty must take the initiative for obtaining information and establishing connections with other faculty. That belief may have been enhanced by the new faculty members' fears about taking the initiative. Their senior colleagues were not only responsible for tenure and promotion decisions, but also "major names" to whom new faculty would not want to communicate vulnerability or lack of total competence. All of these concerns may have enhanced feelings of isolation and set the tone for a perceived lack of emotional support.

If the adjustment processes for new faculty do contribute to the negative challenges and stresses they feel, then we must ask whether those stresses are desirable. Research universities value faculty autonomy (Clark 1984; Kuh and Whitt 1988; Weick 1984); thus, the experiences of the new SOE faculty may have been exactly what they needed. In other words, the socialization process itself teaches faculty the independence that will be required for success. The fact that new faculty were left alone to "hit the ground running" may be the most effective way to communicate that faculty members at a research university must work autonomously, discovering their own answers to problems of everyday academic life as well as complex research questions. The message that senior faculty are extremely busy and have more important things to do than help new faculty may also be a lesson essential to their future survival or success.

In this study, administrators clearly stated that new faculty were the future of the School of Education, and as such, were to be given as much support as possible without being coddled. The administrators also expressed the hope that new faculty felt "warmly regarded" and "loved." At the same time, the administrators expected that new faculty would already have all they needed to be effective faculty members. New faculty were aware of that expectation but felt that fulfilling it was undermined by a *lack* of support from department chairs and other faculty. Perhaps, as one of the new faculty members noted, high and rigorous expectations for new faculty are incompatible with hopes that new faculty will feel that they are being cared for.

Even if senior colleagues and administrators view the negative challenges presented to new faculty as undesirable, the question remains whether efforts to provide more support and direction for new faculty are worthwhile. Are the potential benefits of more formal orientation processes and more help from senior faculty and department chairs worth their cost? The answer to that question probably varies from institution to institution, or college to college. Issues to consider in addressing the question of costs and benefits include available resources (both human and financial), expectations for and attitudes about how new and senior faculty should spend their time, and needs of new faculty. The administrators and faculty of the SOE in which this study took place have decided that, at least for the time being, the results justify the cost and have implemented an on-going orientation program for new faculty.

If new faculty are, in fact, "precious jewels" whose ability to survive and thrive is critical to the future of institutions of higher education, the nature of their experiences as new faculty should concern their administrator and faculty colleagues. The first-year experiences of six new faculty offered here may increase understanding about that experience and encourage discussions about whether, and how, their experiences can, or should, be different. New faculty want to "hit the ground running" and even expect to have to clear some hurdles, but they need clearer directions about the track, more consistent information about the events in which they are running, and a much louder cheering section.

Bibliography

Baldwin, Roger G. "Adult and Career Development: What Are the Implications for Faculty?" *Current Issues in Higher Education, No. 2.* Washington, D.C.: American Association for Higher Education, 1979.

Baldwin, Roger G., and Robert T. Blackburn. "The Academic Career as a Developmental Process: Implications for Higher Education." *Journal of Higher Education* 52 (1981): 598–614.

Berlew, David, and Douglas T. Hall. "The Socialization of Managers: Effects of Expectations on Performance." *Administrative Science Quarterly* 11 (1966): 207–223.

Bess, James L. "Anticipatory Socialization of Graduate Students." *Research in Higher Education* 8 (1978): 289–317.

_____. *University Organization: A Matrix Analysis of the Academic Professions.* New York: Human Sciences Press, 1982.

Corcoran, Mary, and Shirley M. Clark. "Professional Socialization and Contemporary Career Attitudes of Three Faculty Generations." *Research in Higher Education* 20 (1984): 131–53.

Etzioni, Amatai. *A Comparative Analysis of Complex Organizations: On Power, Involvement, and Their Correlates.* Revised. New York: The Free Press, 1975.

Goetz, Judith P., and Margaret D. LeCompte. *Ethnography and Qualitative Design in Educational Research.* Orlando, Fla.: Academic Press, 1984.

Kuh, George D., and Elizabeth J. Whitt. *The Invisible Tapestry: Culture in American Colleges and Universities.* ASHE-ERIC Higher Education Report Series, No. 1. Washington, D.C.: Association for the Study of Higher Education, 1988.

Lincoln, Yvonna S., and Egon G. Guba. *Naturalistic Inquiry.* Beverly Hills, Calif.: Sage, 1985.

Mager, Gerald, and Betty Myers. "If First Impressions Count: New Professors' Insights and Problems." *Peabody Journal of Education* 50 (1982): 100–106.

Mathis, B. Claude. "Academic Careers and Adult Development: A Nexus for Research." *Current Issues in Higher Education, No. 2.* Washington, D.C.: American Association for Higher Education, 1979.

Miles, Matthew B., and A. Michael Huberman. *Qualitative Data Analysis: A Sourcebook of New Methods.* Beverly Hills, Calif.: Sage, 1984.

Morgan, Gareth. *Images of Organization.* Beverly Hills, Calif.: Sage, 1986.

Orth, Charles D. *Social Structure and Learning Climate: The First Year at the Harvard Business School.* Boston: Graduate School of Business, Harvard University, 1963.

Reynolds, Anne. "Making and Giving the Grade: Experiences of Beginning Professors at a Research University." Paper presented at the annual meeting of the American Educational Research Association, New Orleans, 1988.

Schein, Edgar H. "Organizational Socialization and the Profession of Management." *Industrial Management Review* 9 (1968): 1–16.

Scott, Myrtle M., and James G. Hatfield. "Problems of Analyst and Observer Agreement in Naturalistic Narrative Data." *Journal of Educational Measurement* 22 (1985): 207–18.

Sorcinelli, Mary Deane. *Summary of Interview Data: The School of Education.* Faculty Career Development Project, Dean of the Faculties Office. Mimeographed. Bloomington: Indiana University, 1985.

_____. "Satisfaction, Stress High for New Faculty." *Campus Report: Indiana University-Bloomington* 11 (1988): 1–4.

Van Maanen, John. "Police Socialization: A Longitudinal Examination of Job Attitudes in an Urban Police Department." *Administrative Science Quarterly* 20 (1975): 207–28.

_____. "Breaking In: Socialization to Work." In *Handbook of Work, Organization, and Society*, edited by R. Dubin, 67–130. Chicago: Rand McNally, 1976.

_____. "People Processing: Strategies of Organizational Socialization." *Organizational Dynamics* (1978): 19–36.

_____. "Doing New Things in Old Ways: The Chains of Socialization." In *College and University Organization: Insights from the Behavioral Sciences*, edited by James L. Bess, 211–47. New York: New York University Press, 1984.

Weick, Karl. "Contradictions in a Community of Scholars: The Cohesion-Accuracy Tradeoff." In *College and University Organization: Insights from the Behavioral Sciences*, edited by James L. Bess, 15–30. New York: New York University Press, 1984.

Whitt, Elizabeth J., and George D. Kuh. "The Use of Qualitative Methods in a Team Approach to Multiple Institution Studies." *Review of Higher Education*, in press.

Rethinking the Study of the Outcomes of College Attendance

LOUIS C. ATTINASI, JR.

The author critiques the way in which researchers typically study the outcomes of college attendance, provides a rationale for an alternative approach, and demonstrates the potential of the alternative approach for providing insight into how and why particular outcomes occur.

The outcomes for individuals of enrolling in institutions of higher education have long been of interest to researchers (Feldman & Newcomb, 1969; Pace, 1979; Pascarella & Terenzini, 1991) and policymakers. Aside from purely academic interest, the need to justify the expenditure of public and individual funds on higher education has primarily motivated this line of inquiry. Thus, outcomes research has the potential to answer the following question: In consideration of the benefits that individual college-goers, and by extension members of the general public, receive through college enrollment, is the investment of resources in higher education merited?

The focus of outcomes research has been (a) short-term outcomes, for example, whether or not, and why or why not, currently enrolled students make the decision to maintain their enrollment for another year; and (b) outcomes that occur much later in the life of the individual. Typical of the latter is the cultural, civic, or work force participation of individuals in the years following their graduation (Pace, 1979); the interest here is whether or not and, if so, how going to college influences the nature and level of such participation.

In studying the immediate or long-term outcomes of college attendance, researchers have chiefly used quantitative research approaches. These involve the collection of data through the administration of surveys with precoded response alternatives and the analysis of these data by means of multivariate statistical techniques of varying sophistication. Through such procedures the researcher is able to test the hypothesized relationships of various independent and mediating variables to one another and to the dependent variable—some measure of the outcome of interest (Pascarella, 1982). To a large extent, the success of this approach in illuminating the factors the influence student outcomes depends on the prior conceptualization that informs the selection of the survey questions or, in other words, the variables and their indicators, and the particular statistical technique(s) employed (Attinasi & Nora, 1987; Pascarella, 1982). But even the most well-done studies in this genre of outcomes research are limited in their ability to help one understand why and how particular outcomes occur because of their inability to capture more than superficially the perspectives of the individuals whose outcomes are of concern.

In this article, I argue that college student outcomes cannot be truly understood in the absence of an understanding of how students construe the persons (including themselves) with whom, the places in which, and the events in the course of which the outcomes occur. Second, I describe a research method—phenomenological interviewing—that can be used to capture the student's perspective of aspects of his or her own life-world. Finally, I illustrate usage of phenomenological interviewing in the study of one college outcome: freshman-year persistence.

Limitations of Current Approaches to the Study of College Student Outcomes

Underlying current approaches to the study of college student outcomes is the (tacit) assumption that why and how such outcomes occur can be understood in the absence of an understanding of the point of view of those individuals whose outcomes are being investigated. This is evident in the use of a research strategy that largely imposes the researcher's frame of reference on the data collection and analysis procedures and that essentially forecloses any opportunity to obtain the student's perspective of his or her own life-world (that is, the reliance on questionnaires calling for fixed-choice responses to a fixed number of preselected items that are analyzed with aggregative multivariate statistical techniques).

Researchers who use these methods of data collection and analysis either assume they already understand the meanings that things have for the individuals they are studying or they ignore such meanings under the assumption that they are not important for understanding outcomes. "Meaning is either taken for granted and thus pushed aside as unimportant or it is regarded as a mere neutral link between the factors responsible for human behavior and this behavior as the product of such factors" (Blumer, 1969, p. 2). Thus, meaning is swallowed up in sociological factors (e.g., social position, social roles, or norms and values), psychological factors (e.g., attitudes, motives, or stimuli), or both, which are used to account for the behavior under study.

To the contrary position, however, that human behavior is understandable only to the extent that the actor's definitions, and the processes by which he or she constructs them, are understood, there is increasing subscription. Many researchers have come to recognize what seems to be an inescapable fact—namely, that "people act, not on the basis of predetermined responses to predefined objects, but rather as interpreting, defining, symbolic animals whose behavior can only be understood by having the researcher enter into the defining process" (Bogdan & Biklen, 1982, p. 33). Following this line of reasoning, it is argued here that further significant advances in our understanding of student outcomes are unlikely except as research is designed to take account of the 'subjects' (i.e., students') meanings. Weber's injunction (cited in Runciman, 1978) is operative: "Without adequacy at the level of meaning, our generalizations remain mere statements of statistical probability, either not intelligible at all or only imperfectly intelligible; this is no matter how high the probability of outcome . . . and no matter how precisely calculable in numerical terms it may be" (p. 10).

Limits of Variable Analysis

In his classic critique of the traditional analysis of variables in sociological research, Blumer (1956) observed that one of the primary problems with this approach is that it does not accommodate the process of interpretation or definition that goes on in human groups, which is "the core of human action" (p. 685).

> The conventional procedure is to identify something which is presumed to operate in a group life and treat it as an independent variable, and then to select some form of group activity as the dependent variable. The independent variable is put at the beginning of the process of interpretation and the dependent variable at the terminal part of the process. The intervening process is ignored or, what amounts to the same thing, taken for granted as something that need not be considered. (p. 686)

But in areas of group life the independent variable does not automatically exercise its influence on the dependent variable. Rather, there is a process of definition intervening between the events of experience presupposed by the independent variable and the formed behavior represented by the dependent variable. To use Blumer's example, the relationship between the presentation of political programs on the radio and the (resulting) expression of the intention to vote cannot be understood in the absence of a consideration of the interpretation by the listeners of the political programs.

Arguing that the process of interpretation lacks "the qualitative constancy that is logically required in a variable" (p. 688), Blumer (1956) called for an alternative to traditional variable analysis when investigating areas where the process is important. What was needed, in Blumer's view, was research that sought to trace the lines of defining experience through which ways of living, patterns of relations, and social forms are developed, rather than to relate these formations to a set of selected items. This necessitates "the study of group activity through the eyes and experience of the people who have developed the activity" (p. 689).

If one accepts the view that the complexes of experiences that lead to various college student outcomes are areas of human life in which the process of interpretation is central, then one must acknowledge the need for inquiries into these outcomes that are designed to accomplish what Blumer (1956) proposed. Lacking such research, one cannot expect the processes leading to the outcomes, and hence the outcomes themselves, to be more than poorly understood. The focus of this article is an approach—there are others—that will permit the researcher to approach human activity "through the eyes and experience" of the actors. What immediately follows is a description of that approach, which is called *phenomenological interviewing*. Subsequently, the potential of phenomenological interviewing for illuminating college student outcomes is demonstrated through a recent investigation of the freshman-year persistence of Mexican American university students.

An Alternative Approach to the Study of College Student Outcomes

Phenomenological Interviewing

The purpose of phenomenological interviewing is to gain access to the meaning an individual makes of his or her own experience (Tesch, 1988). A basic premise of the approach is that such meaning is accessible when the individual reflects on the constitutive factors of personal experience (Schutz, 1932/1967). The task of the phenomenological interviewer, then, is to encourage interviewees to "reconstruct their experience and reflect on the meaning they make of that experience" (Seidman, 1985, p. 15).

To accomplish this, the phenomenological interviewer uses a qualitative research interview of the type described by Kvale (1983). Such an interview seeks detailed "description and understanding of the meaning of themes in the life-world of the interviewee" (Kvale, 1983, p. 174). Technically, it is semistructured (Gorden, 1987), being neither a free conversation nor a highly structured questionnaire. It is carried through according to an interview guide, which rather than containing exact questions focuses on certain themes. The interview is taped and transcribed verbatim. The typed transcription together with the tape constitute the material for subsequent interpretation of meaning.

With phenomenological interviewing, data collection and data analysis take place more or less simultaneously. The process has several phases that can be thought of as occurring at different points along a continuum between description and interpretation. There are six possible phases (Kvale, 1983), described as follows:

1. The interviewee describes his or her life-world with respect to the phenomenon of interest. This is a spontaneous description, without any special interpretation of the description from either the interviewee or the interviewer.

2. The interviewee discovers new relations, sees new meaning in his or her life-world on the basis of the spontaneous descriptions. Again, this occurs without any direct influence from interpretations by the interviewer.

3. The interviewer during the interview condenses and interprets the meaning of what the interviewee describes and, perhaps, "sends" the interpreted meaning back for confirmation or clarification.

4. The interviewer or another person alone interprets the completed and transcribed interview on three different levels: (a) the self-understanding of the interviewee; (b) a commonsense interpretation that involves extending the meaning of what the interviewee said by reading between the lines and by drawing in broader contexts than the interviewee did; and (c) more theoretical interpretations, based on, for example, an existing social or sociopsychological theory.

5. The interviewer gives the interpretations, based on his or her analysis of the completed interview, back to the interviewee in a second interview. This provides an opportunity for the interviewer to correct and elaborate the interpretations.

6. There may be an extension of the description-interpretation continuum to action. Perhaps the interviewee begins to act from new insights gained during the interview, or the researcher and the interviewee together, in a program of action research, act on the basis of experiences and insights about social situations developed through the interviews.

These phases are not to be thought of as presupposing each other logically or chronologically in any strict sense, nor will every study include all six phases. Furthermore, "the offerings of each phase have their own worth and can stand and be utilized independently of the others" (Wertz, 1985, p. 161).

Phenomenological Interviewing in the Study of Student Outcomes: An Illustration

A Phenomenological Study of Persistence in the University

A study of Mexican American university students that I recently conducted (Attinasi, 1989a) serves to illustrate the use of phenomenological interviewing to investigate college student outcomes. The purpose of the inquiry was to obtain detailed descriptions of what going to college meant for these students at various points in their lives, how they came to have those meanings, and how they used them in deciding, in the first place, to enter college and, in the second place, to sustain their enrollment through the freshman year. I wanted to understand the entire sociopsychological context in which they made these decisions. Toward that end, I interviewed phenomenologically and in-depth 18 individuals, from a single entering class of a large public university in the Southwest, who were either sophomores (13 informants) or freshman-year leavers (5 informants) at the time of the interview.

An interview guide with general, open-ended questions was used in obtaining from each interviewee a detailed description of the meaning of college-going for him or her, both prior to and during the freshman year, and of the processes through which he or she obtained and used those meanings. These interviews took place at locations of the interviewees' choosing, including the university library and dormitories, the interviewees' homes and the library of a local community college. Each interview lasted between 1-1/2 and 2 hours and was audiotaped. The tapes were transcribed verbatim.

Analysis was by means of qualitative induction (Erickson, 1986). That is, concepts and hypotheses emerged from an examination of the concrete details of the informants' lives reported in the interviews. The induction process was constrained only by the research perspective (see description that follows).

The analysis began with open coding of the interview transcriptions; that is, the coding of their contents in as many ways as possible. The coding categories related to context and setting, informants' definitions of situations, informants' ways of thinking about people and objects, process (sequence of events, changes over time), activities, events, strategies, relationships, and social structure (Bogdan & Biklen, 1982). A total of 119 coding categories were initially assigned to the contents of the interviews. This was followed by a data reduction step in which the number of coding categories was reduced and the analysis began to take shape conceptually. Saliency of the categories, as judged by rate of occurrence, uniqueness, and apparent connectedness to other categories, was the criterion for initial decisions to retain, merge, or discard coding categories.

Subsequently, clustering was used to further reduce the coding categories. That is, it became possible to link categories to one another through higher order categories. A higher order category, or concept, was one under which another category could be fitted without sacrificing the latter's integrity. In this way initial coding categories became subcategories or properties of higher level categories. Eventually, connections between higher level categories were established. The writing of research memos (Glaser & Strauss, 1967), notes to myself of varying lengths in which I speculated on relationships between categories beyond what may have been literally justified by the evidence at hand, assisted in the process of moving from lower level to higher level categories.

The collection and analysis of the data were guided by a broad research perspective—the sociology of everyday life (Douglas, 1980). This is actually a collection of research perspectives in sociology, all of which focus on everyday social interaction in natural situations and have as their starting points (a) the experiences and observation of people interacting in concrete, face-to-face situations, and (b) an analysis of the actors' meanings. In particular, two of the sociologies of everyday life—symbolic interactionism and ethnomethodology—were used in conducting the inquiry.

Symbolic interactionism emphasizes social interaction as a process that forms human conduct: It is from the interaction of the individual with others that the meaning of things arise, and it is on the basis of their meaning that the individual acts toward things. Shared emergent meanings are the concern of symbolic interactionists. *Ethnomethodology* seeks to understand how actors go about the task of seeing, describing, and explaining the world in which they live; that is, the process of creating shared emergent meanings and using them to account for things in one's everyday world. The research perspective led to two critical assumptions of the study: (a) Persistence behavior is the consequence of a process in which the student is an active participant: He or she takes account of various things in the everyday world and acts on the basis of how he or she interprets them; and (b) persistence behavior is related to the manner in which the university becomes and remains, through everyday social interaction, a reality for the student.

The Researcher's Commonsense Interpretation of Meanings

The data collection and analysis is this study involved the first four phases of Kvale's (1983) interviewing process, discussed previously. The result of the fourth phase—the researcher's interpretation of the completed and transcribed interviews—was at the commonsense level of bithematic scheme for understanding the meaning of college-going for the interviewees. The first theme—*getting ready*—had to do with the interviewees' perceptions of various activities that intentionally or unintentionally got them ready for college. The second scheme—*getting in*—centered on the interviewees' perceptions, upon matriculation, of the university as a tripartite geography (physical, social, and academic) too large and complex to be easily negotiated, and on their use of certain strategies that assisted them in the negotiation of the geography (that is, in "getting in" the university).

Getting Ready

Many of the informants described an early expectation that they would go to college, which was primarily a consequence of parental exhortation (*initial expectation engendering*). Subsequent "getting ready" experiences provided substance, in the form of descriptions, prescriptions, and predictions about college-going, for this early generalized expectation of college-going. For example, experiences labeled *familial modeling* referred to an informant's observations of the college-going of an older relative, particularly an older sibling. This had two potential consequences for the informant: first, a belief that he or she, too, would go to college one day; and second, a belief that his or her eventual college-going was likely to be of the kind that was described by the sibling.

Another source of descriptions of college-going was provided by high school teachers who related their own experiences of and attitudes toward college. This kind of modeling or defining of college-going made its strongest impression on an informant when he or she perceived the teacher to be a mentor. Hence, it has been labeled *mentor modeling*. A teacher could also influence an informant's perceptions of college-going by simulating for the informant what being a college student was like. He or she did this by making prescriptive or predictive statements about college-going. As with familial and mentor modeling, knowledge acquisition through *indirect simulation* was strictly vicarious.

In the case of *direct simulation*, however, the informants engaged in a whole range of on-campus activities that provided them with firsthand experience of college life. In some cases, the activities (e.g., using the gymnasium) were very short in duration, involved little interaction with campus personnel, and were unrelated to college-going per se. In others, such as accompanying an official enrollee to classes or actually being a class enrollee, the activities closely resembled those of a matriculated student. Between these cases was a wide range of experiences that varied in the extent to which they (a) were related to college-going per se, (b) involved the informants in interaction with campus personnel, and (c) kept the informants on campus, and in terms of the roles occupied by the informants while having them.

Getting In

In describing their early impressions of the university, the informants were virtually unanimous in emphasizing a perception of bigness. The descriptor *big* turned out to be a gloss for articulating the perceived dimensions, mass, distance, and complexity, of three campus geographies: (a) a physical geography, (b) a social geography, and (c) an academic-cognitive geography. Many of the postmatriculation experiences reported by the informants were the working out of strategies for fixing themselves in one or more of these geographies (that is, for "getting in"). Two primary strategies for "getting in" were identified as follows: *getting to know* and *scaling down*.

"Getting to know" refers to strategies used by the informants to rapidly increase their familiarity with the geographies. There were at least two ways in which they accomplished this: (a) through mentoring relationships with veteran students who showed them the ropes (*mentoring*), or (b) through information-sharing relationships with fellow neophytes (*peer information sharing*), which resulted in cooperative exploring of the geographies. Through "scaling down" the informants perceptually and physically bounded the geographies, effectively reducing the amount of each with which they had to be familiar in order to locate themselves.

One focus of both the "getting to know" and "scaling down" kinds of experiences was the process of *majoring in*. In addition to its manifest function—initiating a focused study of that part of the curriculum that is most closely related to one's life and career goals—selecting an academic major had another, more latent function. It provided a vehicle for locating oneself in the physical, social, and academic-cognitive geographies; it promoted "getting in."

The Researcher's Theoretical Interpretations

I interpreted the contents of the interview on a more theoretical level by drawing upon elements of existing social and sociopsychological theories. For example, the concepts of significant others and anticipatory socialization illuminated certain aspects of "getting ready," whereas the notions of social integration and cognitive mapping were useful for understanding "getting in."

Getting Ready

Significant Other. The construct significant other, particularly as worked out by Haller and Woelfel (1972), turned out to be useful in considering the significance of "getting ready." In their study of the occupational and educational goals of high school students, Haller and Woelfel came to define a significant other as "a person, known to the focal individual, who either through direct interaction (a definer) or by example (a model) provides information which influences the focal individual's conception of himself in relation to educational or occupational roles or influences his conception of such roles (a conception of an object)" (pp. 594—595).

In my study, parents, high school teachers, and, less frequently, siblings were definers with respect to college-going. These individuals communicated to the informant the fact that he or she belonged to the category of future college-goers and defined for him or her what it meant to be a college-goer. In addition, high school teachers and siblings created expectations with respect to going to college by modeling college-going behavior. The mere departure of an older sibling for college might have signaled to the informant his or her membership in the category of (future) college-goers. Subsequently, the informant's observations of college-going behavior by siblings and teachers provided insight into the nature of the college-going role.

Anticipatory Socialization. A second construct that was useful for drawing out the theoretical significance of "getting ready" was anticipatory socialization. Anticipatory socialization refers to a premature taking on or identification with the behavior and attitudes of an aspired to group that "may serve the two functions of aiding [an individual's] rise into [the aspired to] group and of easing his adjustment after he has become part of it" (Merton & Kitt, 1950, p. 87). The concept has been primarily worked out in relation to occupational preparation (Pavalko, 1971) and the formation of political views (Sheinkopf, 1973), but there has been some consideration of it with respect to the role of college student.

Parsons (1959), for example, argued that because, as early as elementary school, high achievers are culled from their classmates so they can be directed toward a college preparatory curriculum, the decision of a high achiever to attend college may be the result of a long period of anticipatory socialization. Silber et al. (1961) have reported that some high school students prepare themselves for college by rehearsing forms of behavior they associate with college students. This role rehearsing may include taking special courses that are viewed as trial college experiences and carrying out assignments the teacher identifies as what one does in college.

Role rehearsing was clearly an element of "getting ready." It may have been very indirect, such as the simulation of certain aspects of college-going in college preparatory classes. A more direct kind of rehearsing occurred when the individual participated in on-campus activities: living in dormitories, going to parties, and attending classroom lectures. Another component of anticipatory socialization, the forecasting of future situations, was a feature of "getting ready"; such as, for example, when the informant, upon observing an older sibling depart for college, predicted his or her own matriculation, or when a high school teacher predicted that college professors would treat the informant and his or her high school classmates much differently than he or she (the high school teacher) did.

Getting In

Social Integration. In drawing out the theoretical significance of the concept "getting in," I again found two existing concepts helpful. My consideration of *social integration* as a theoretical datum for comparison with the concept of "getting in" was initially prompted by my reading of other conceptually oriented investigations of the behavior of undergraduate students. Spady (1970) and later Tinto (1975) borrowed this concept from the French sociologist Durkheim (1871/1951) as he had elaborated it in his treatise on the causes of suicide, in order to conceptualize student withdrawal from college. Durkheim argued that suicide was likely in populations for which rates of interaction (collective affiliation) were too low because this led to a lack of common sentiments and values (moral consensus) and the precedence of individual interests over social ones. As the individual increasingly frees himself or herself from the social control of the group, he or she removes himself or herself from its prophylactic influence and finds little meaning in life, which then comes to appear as an intolerable burden.

Spady (1970) (and Tinto, 1975, after him), in adapting these concepts to an explanation of student withdrawal from college, specified a lack of collective affiliation (friendship) and a lack of moral consensus (cognitive congruence) as having separate effects on dropping-out behavior; that is, independently influencing the level of one's social integration. The results of my study suggest that moral consensus is neither the (principal) outcome of collective affiliation (as postulated by Durkheim) nor an independent cause of one's persisting in life or college (as postulated by Spady and Tinto). A student's interaction with others is important for persistence in college not simply or primarily because it leads to the sharing of general values and orientations, but because it assists the student in developing specific strategies for negotiating the physical, social, and cognitive geographies. The "getting to know" category of "getting in" defines *collective affiliations* with specific individuals—mentors and peers—who integrate the student into the physical and academic-cognitive geographies as well as the social geography by providing him or her with knowledge of these geographies and the skills to negotiate them. According to this interpretation, then, students become integrated for distinctly more cognitive, and less moral, reasons.

Cognitive Mapping. In theorizing about exactly how students, with the assistance of mentors and peer, come to locate themselves in the perceived geographies, the concept of cognitive mapping proved helpful. It has been hypothesized (Stea, 1969) that when significant environments are too large to be apprehended at once (e.g., a large university campus encountered by a student for the first time), people form conceptions of them. These conceptions, or cognitive maps, are a complex of things learned about the environment, including expectations, stereotypes, and value judgments. In developing cognitive maps of large and complex spaces, individuals make certain simplifications and adjustments in accordance with their own needs and experience. This means, of course, that cognitive maps and map-making exhibit considerable interpersonal variation.

The basis of cognitive map formation is the identification of significant objects in the environment, the establishment of the connectedness of the objects to one another and to the observer, and the assignment of meaning, whether emotional or practical, to the objects and their relationships. As the word *map* implies, the origin and major implication of the cognitive map lie in the spatial domain. But people are thought to organize other phenomena, for example, social interrelations, affective bonds, and temporal relationships, in the same way (Kaplan & Kaplan, 1978).

The student's initial perceptions of the campus geographies may be understood to reflect the absence of cognitive maps. Thus, the geographies were perceived to be large-scale environments in which objects stood separated from one another and seemed incapable of being resolved into meaningful components. The student's strategies for "getting in" are conceptualized to be mechanisms for assisting the acquisition of these maps. For example, "getting to know" behaviors—knowledge sharing with other neophytes and mentoring relationships with veteran students—are shortcuts to acquiring representations of specific objects within the various geographies and the associations between these representations. "Scaling down" behaviors result in more detailed maps of smaller portions of the geographies—areas of particular concern to the individual.

My commonsense and theoretical interpretations of the meaning of college-going to the interviewees, both prior to and following matriculation at the university, suggest possible interventions by family, high school, and university to enhance the likelihood of Mexican American students entering and remaining in the university (Attinasi, 1989a). Had I chosen to do so, I could have given these interpretations immediately back to the interviewees not only to obtain clarification and elaboration of them but also, and more important, to provide the informants themselves with the option of acting on the basis of the interpretations (fifth and sixth steps of Kvale's, 1983, interviewing process).

Summary and Conclusion

Progress in understanding college student outcomes such as persistence has been retarded by our failure to adequately take into consideration the meanings the phenomenon of going to college holds for students. It is on the basis of meanings that human beings act. Yet those who study outcomes tend to ignore student meanings either because they assume they already know them or because they consider them irrelevant. As with social researchers generally, their focus is on the relationship between static independent and dependent variables with little concern for the intervening process of interpretation.

This article describes one method—phenomenological interviewing—for obtaining the actor's meanings. Data collection and analysis in phenomenological interviewing occur in a series of phases, involving at first primarily spontaneous, uninterpreted description by the interviewee but, as the study proceeds increasing interpretation and greater participation by the researcher. The researcher's interpretation of the completed interviews include the following: (a) the interviewee's self-understanding, (b) a commonsense understanding of the phenomenon that extends the meaning of the interviewee, and (c) more theoretical interpretations that are based on concepts that are drawn from existing disciplinary or interdisciplinary theory.

To illustrate the use of phenomenological interviewing to illuminate student outcomes, I described my own recent study (Attinasi, 1989a) of the meaning of college going for Mexican American university students, which was conducted in anticipation of illuminating the context within which they make decisions to persist or withdraw during the freshman year. Eighteen persisting and nonpersisting students were interviewed in-depth during their sophomore year (or, for leavers, what would have been their sophomore year) to obtain their understanding of college-going during and prior to their freshman year.

At the commonsense level, the meaning of college-going for the students could be understood in terms of a bi-thematic scheme. The first theme is preparing for college attendance; the second, negotiating the university environment. Existing social and psychological concepts such as significant others, anticipatory socialization social integration, and cognitive mapping were drawn upon to illuminate various aspects of the scheme. Both the commonsense and theoretical interpretations of the interviews suggested possible interventions by family, high school, and university to enhance the likelihood of Mexican American students succeeding during their first year of university attendance and of persisting into the second.

The line of research begun with that study had been continued (Attinasi, 1989b) with a subsequent investigation in which I interviewed in depth both Mexican American and non-Hispanic White students from a single entering class on a continuous basis (about every ? weeks) over the course of their freshman year. My purpose was to verify, refine, and elaborate the understanding—both commonsense and theoretical—emanating from the initial study. Preliminary results of this follow-up study (Attinasi, 1989b) are consistent with, but extend the findings of, the first investigation and provide additional support for the usefulness of the in-depth interviewing approach for inquiry into the outcomes of college.

It should be pointed out that the literature of higher education is not otherwise devoid of reports of inquiries based on in-depth, phenomenological interviewing. Seidman (1985) and Seidman, Sullivan, and Schatzkamer (1983), for example, interviewed faculty phenomenologically in an attempt to develop new perspectives on improving the quality of instruction in community colleges. Seidman et al. operated under the premise that the faculty's "description of their own experiences and reflection on the meaning of that experience provide valuable insights into the problems within community colleges" (Seidman, 1985, p. xi). Earlier, Schuman (1982) interviewed college graduates phenomenologically to ascertain the impact of college education on everyday life. Involving extended conversations (with a small number of informants) that focused on the meaning college now held for them and its perceived contribution(s) to their postcollegiate lives, the latter research was intended as a novel approach to policy analysis in higher education.

In-depth, phenomenological interviewing is but one of an arsenal of qualitative research approaches (see Crowson, 1987, for a survey of these) that can help us to "get beyond a superficial understanding of central phenomena in the life-world of people" (Kvale, 1983, p. 194) who populate our institutions of higher education. If this article, which offers an apologia for the use of phenomenological interviewing in the study of college student outcomes and illustrates how the method can be so employed, encourages others to adopt such approaches for inquiry into this important subject, its purpose will be well-served and, it may be anticipated, understanding of what college does to and for our students thereby advanced.

References

Attinasi, L., & Nora, A. (1987, November). *The next step in the study of student persistence in college.* Paper presented at the meeting of the Association for the Study of Higher Education, Baltimore.

Attinasi, L. (1989a). Getting in: Chicano students' perceptions of university attendance and the implications for freshman year persistence. *Journal of Higher Education, 60,* 247–277.

Attinasi, L. (1989b, November). *Negotiating the first year of college: Case studies of Mexican American and non-Hispanic White university students.* Paper presented at the meeting of the Association for the Study of Higher Education, Atlanta.

Blumer, H. (1956). Sociological analysis and the "variable." *American Sociological Review, 21,* 683–690.

Blumer, H. (1969). *Symbolic interactionism: Perspective and method.* Englewood Cliffs, NJ: Prentice-Hall.

Bogdan, R.C., & Biklen, S.K. (1982). *Qualitative research for education: An introduction to theory and methods.* Boston: Allyn & Bacon.

Crowson, R.L. (1987). Qualitative research methods in higher education. In J.C. Smart (Ed.), *Higher education: Handbook of theory and research* (Vol. 3, pp. 1–56). New York: Agathon Press.

Douglas, J.D. (1980). Introduction to the sociologies of everyday life. In J.D. Douglas (Ed.), *Introduction to the sociologies of everyday life* (pp. 1–19). Boston: Allyn & Bacon.

Durkheim, E. (1951). *Suicide: A study in sociology* (J.A. Spaulding & G. Simpson, Trans.). Glencoe, IL: Free Press. (Original work published 1897.)

Erickson, F. (1986). Qualitative methods in research on teaching. In M.C. Wittrock (Ed.), *Handbook of research on teaching* (3rd ed., pp. 119–161). New York: Macmillan.

Feldman, K.A., & Newcomb, T.M. (1969). *The impact of college on students: An analysis of four decades of research.* San Francisco: Jossey-Bass.

Glaser, B.G., & Strauss, A. (1967). *The discovery of grounded theory: Strategies for qualitative research.* New York: Aldine.

Gorden, R.L. (1987). *Interviewing: Strategy, techniques, and tactics* (4th ed.). Homewood, IL: Dorsey.

Haller, A.O., & Woelfel, J. (1972). Significant others and their expectations: Concepts and instruments to measure interpersonal influence on status aspirations. *Rural Sociology, 37,* 591–622.

Kvale, S. (1983). The qualitative research interview: A phenomenological and hermeneutical mode of understanding. *Journal of Phenomenological Psychology, 14,* 171–196.

Kaplan, S., & Kaplan, R. (1978). Introduction to Chapter 3. In S. Kaplan & R. Kaplan (Eds.), Humanscope: Environments for people (pp. 42–43). North Scituate, MA: Duxbury Press.

Merton, R.K., & Kitt, A.S. (1950). Contributions to the theory of reference group behavior. In R.K. Merton & P.F. Lazarsfeld (Eds.), *Continuities in social research: Studies in the scope and method of "The American Soldier"* (pp. 40–105). Glencoe, IL: Free Press.

Pace, C.R. (1979). *Measuring outcomes of college: Fifty years of findings and recommendations for the future.* San Francisco: Jossey-Bass.

Parsons, T. (1959). The school class as a social system: Some of its functions in American society. *Harvard Educational Review, 29,* 297–318.

Pascarella, E.T. (Ed.). (1982). *Studying student attrition* (New Directions for Institutional Research No. 36). San Francisco: Jossey-Bass.

Pascarella, E.T., & Terenzini, P. (1991). *How college affects students: Findings and insights from twenty years of research.* San Francisco: Jossey-Bass.

Pavalko, R.M. (1971). *Sociology of occupations and professions.* Itasca, IL: Peacock.

Runciman. W.G. (Ed.). (1978). *Max Weber: Selections in translation* (E. Matthews, Trans.), Cambridge: Cambridge University Press.

Schuman, D. (1982). *Policy analysis, education, and everyday life: An empirical reevaluation of higher education in America.* Lexington, MA: Heath.

Schutz, A. (1967). *The phenomenology of the social world* (G. Walsh & F. Lehnert, Trans.). Evanston, IL: Northwestern University Press. (Original work published 1932.)

Seidman, E. (1985). *In the words of the faculty: Perspectives on improving teaching and educational quality in community colleges.* San Francisco: Jossey-Bass.

Seidman, E., Sullivan, P.J., & Schatzkamer, M.B. (1983). *The work of community college faculty: A study through in-depth interviews. Final report to the National Institute of Education.* Amherst, MA: University of Massachusetts, School of Education, (ERIC Document Reproduction Service No. ED 243 499.)

Sheinkopf, K.G. (1973). Family communication patterns and anticipatory socialization. *Journalism Quarterly, 50,* 24–30, 133.

Silber, E.D., Hamburg, D.A., Coelho, G.V., Murphey, E.B., Rosenberg, M., & Pearlin, L.I. (1961). Adaptive behavior in competent adolescents: Coping with the anticipation of college. *Archives of General Psychiatry, 5,* 354–365.

Spady, W.G. (1970). Dropouts from higher education: An interdisciplinary review and synthesis. *Interchange, 1,* 64–85.

Stea, D. (1969). The measurement of mental maps: An experimental model for studying conceptual spaces. In K.R. Cox & R.G. Golledge (Eds.), *Behavioral problems in geography: A symposium* (pp. 228–253). Evanston, IL: Northwestern University Department of Geography.

Tesch, R. (1988, April). *The contribution of a qualitative method: Phenomenological research.* Paper presented at the meeting of the American Educational Research Association, New Orleans.

Tinto, V. (1975). Dropout from higher education: A theoretical synthesis of recent research. *Review of Educational Research, 45,* 89–125.

Wertz, F.J. (1985). Method and findings in a phenomenological psychological study of a complex life-event: Being criminally victimized. In A. Giorgi (Ed.), *Phenomenology and psychological research* (pp. 155–216). Pittsburgh: Duquesne University Press.

The Politics of Race: Through the Eyes of African-American Teachers

Michèle Foster

Research on teachers, though extensive, has generally failed to include the experiences of African-American teachers.[1] Studies of teacher thinking do not consider the influence of the racial identity of teachers on their belief systems and teaching practice; likewise, they ignore the influence of particular classroom contexts, including the social identity of the students, in shaping teachers' pedagogy. The more recent literature on teaching has sought to capture the "wisdom of practice" of experienced teachers, but these studies have also ignored the experiences of teachers of color, particularly those who teach African-American students (Shulman, 1987). Though the sociological, anthropological, and first-person literature on teachers is substantial, in large measure it has also failed to capture the experiences of African-American teachers. Sympathetic and balanced portrayals of African-American teachers such as those by Sara Lightfoot (1978), Philip Sterling (1972), and Gerda Lerner (1972) are rare. All too often African-American teachers are depicted as uncaring, unsympathetic, rigid individuals who, regardless of their class origins, neither identify with nor relate well to their working-class African-American pupils (Conroy, 1972; Rist, 1970, 1973; Spencer, 1986). A number of the first-person teacher accounts deal specifically with the instruction of African-American pupils, but most of these accounts have been written by socially conscious white teacher activists and reformers (Decker, 1969; Herndon, 1968; Kohl, 1967; Kozol, 1967).

Though the first-person literature does not include many accounts by African-American teachers, perhaps characteristic of the genre, when African-American teachers do write about their own practice, many of them include information about their political views and how these views influence their teaching practice. Narratives by Fannie Jackson-Coppin (1913), Septima Clark (1962), James Haskins (1971), Dorothy Robinson (1974), and Mamie Fields (1985), all works by African-American teachers written in this century, exemplifying this orientation.

If one believes that the views of majority and minority teachers will be similar, then the omission noted earlier will be inconsequential. If, on the other hand, researchers assume as Ivor Goodson (1988) does that teachers' backgrounds, identities, and culture help shape their views of teaching, as well as essential elements of their practice, then this omission will severely restrict our knowledge of teaching. Though sparse, research comparing African-American and majority teachers has concluded that the groups differ in how they perceive the profession, the school environment, and the changes needed to help students overcome their educational deficiencies (Metropolitan Life, 1988; Provenzo, 1988).

Historically paid less than their white counterparts, rarely employed except to teach African-American pupils, opposed by unions seeking to preserve seniority rights for their largely white constituencies, dismissed in large numbers following the *Brown v. Board of Education* decision, and denied access to teaching positions through increased testing at all levels, the lives and careers of African-American teachers have been seriously affected by racism (Anderson, 1989; Curry, 1981, Dilworth, 1984; Ethridge, 1979; Franklin, 1979; Tyack, 1974). This paper, with its focus on the politics of race, emerges from a larger ongoing study of African-American teachers. It examines the attitudes and views of 16 African-American teachers on issues related to race. It considers the racism they encountered in their own schooling, their experiences in both segregated and desegregated school systems, and their understanding of the structural constraints imposed by race. Finally, it examines how these experiences have shaped and influenced their teaching practice and pedagogy. The paper contends that these teachers have been exploited, victimized, and marginalized by the larger society as well as by the educational institutions in which they work. As a result, as I have argued elsewhere (Foster, in press), they understand the structural constraints of race in their own lives and on their teaching practice better than they do those imposed by gender and class.

Listening to African-American Teachers Tell Their Own Stories

I have interviewed 16 exemplary teachers, 12 female and 4 male, who were chosen by community nomination.[2] Using open-ended life history methods, I asked them about their childhood, their family and community life, their schooling experiences at the elementary, secondary, and post-secondary levels, their current and previous teaching positions, and their personal philosophies and pedagogies of education. These teachers ranged in age from 45 to 84, the majority in their forties and fifties, and their years of teaching experience from 20 to 66. Seven have been employed as elementary teachers for most of their careers, 8 as high school teachers, and 1 as a junior high teacher. All of these teachers began their careers in predominantly Black schools; 13 teachers still teach in predominantly low-income Black schools in urban or rural communities.

All of these teachers grew up—and most began their professional lives—during the time that separate but equal was the law of the United States. Eleven of them spent their entire childhoods in officially segregated communities where laws dictated separate schools for Blacks and whites. Four grew up in communities not segregated by law and one woman spent half of her childhood in a legally segregated community but by early adolescence had moved north where she completed school.

Experiences in Communities of Orientation

Raised in different environments, each group experienced the brand of racism peculiar to their region. Many of those who grew up in segregated communities recalled walking to school while white children passed them by on buses. They recalled attending school in buildings in disrepair, and studying from books handed down from white schoolchildren. Despite these negative aspects of their schooling experiences, the teachers also remembered African-American teachers who lived or boarded in their communities, often acting as surrogate parents who were involved with the students outside of school in church and community life. In contrast, though most of the teachers from northern communities began their schooling in racially isolated schools by secondary school all were students in majority-white schools which employed few, if any African-American teachers and in which they were one of a handful of African-American pupils enrolled. In fact, not one of the teachers raised in northern communities was taught by an African-American teacher prior to attending college. Thus, while the teachers growing up in segregated communities were firmly anchored in their African-American communities, with their community life reinforced by their schooling experiences, northern informants were forced to leave their communities of origin to secure favorable schooling.

The differences in the northern and southern schooling experiences of these teachers is captured best by the account of one woman who attended school in Austin, Texas through grade six before relocating with her family to Boston.[3]

> I don't really feel that I had the closeness of the teachers there [in Boston] that I had of those in the other school, because they were Black teachers in Austin. I don't remember a Black teacher until . . . I'm trying to think. One does not stick out in my mind. Yeah, in Roxbury. I think when I was in the South, I felt closer to my teachers. I also knew some of them as human beings, and where they lived, and some of them were even part of the churches. I don't think I knew the teachers there [in Boston] as well. I kind of feel, too, that as I look back with the teachers that I had in Austin, they were even involved in after school activities and some other kinds of things with kids. That was not the case [in Boston]. I'm not saying they weren't good teachers, but I remember so many kinds of things that in elementary school . . . as I told you the PE teacher who taught us to dance, the programs. I remember the little drill team that she had and I remember the soccer games we had in elementary school and the PE teacher even had some little cheerleaders, although in her own way even with what she had to work with. I didn't have that [in Boston].

At issue is that regardless of the setting in which they were raised, all of these teachers were aware of the marginal position that they and other African-Americans held in the larger society.

Experiences Before Desegregation

At the time these teachers entered the profession, between 1928 and 1968, teaching was one of the few jobs available to college-educated African-Americans. Though the period during which these 16 teachers began their careers spans 40 years, all except 2 of the participants in this study began their careers in all-Black or majority-Black schools. This fact reflects the laws of de jure segregated school systems and the practices of de facto segregated school systems of the times. For those who began their careers in legally segregated communities, the place of African-American teachers was unambiguous; though all African-American teachers were concentrated in separate schools, within these confines they had access to the full range of teaching and administrative opportunities. Northern communities, on the other hand, used unofficial and more subtle practices to concentrate African-American teachers in certain schools and to keep them out of certain grade levels.

Three teachers who began their careers in the Boston and Hartford public school systems in the 1950s remembered the unofficial policies of the central office that placed African-American teachers in certain schools and at specific grade levels. One said:

> Because at the time I started teaching, Black teachers were assigned to just that strip going from the South End into Roxbury, between, let me see, Tremont Street and Washington. You didn't get any choice. That's where you were sent and most of the Black teachers had a very hard time out of town [the area where Black teachers were assigned].

Another said:

> Then I came to Hartford. Did not get a job immediately. I applied. This was in 53. I applied each year that I went back to West Virginia, but they didn't have any openings, or they never called me. . . . I subbed at the Noah Webster School which was in the Northwest section of the city which was predominantly white—it was white. I was a long-term sub for two months because the teacher there was on maternity leave. At the end of June the principal asked me what was I gonna do next year. I said I didn't know. She said, "Well, why don't you put your application in." I told her it had been in, so she called downtown and she said, "I want Bobbie here." They say, "We don't have an application." Course, I know where the application went. When I applied, it went in the waste basket. Because of the color of my skin. This was in 1953. I don't know how many Black teachers it might

have been, maybe six or seven in the city. I'm not sure of how many at the time, but there weren't that many Black teachers.

Finally, a certified high school English teacher with several years of experience in Florida recalled how she was denied a position in Hartford because she was not licensed for elementary school, where the majority of African-American teachers were placed. Not until she acquired an elementary certificate was she able to secure permanent employment in the Hartford public schools.

Though there are some documented exceptions (Jones, 1981; Sowell, 1974; 1976), the inferiority of segregated Black schools is a widely accepted fact. Detailed descriptions of Black schools in segregated southern school systems make this point (Kluger, 1975). There is no doubt that segregated schools were severely underfunded and lacking supplies and equipment. Still, it cannot unilaterally be assumed that the students enrolled in segregated schools were automatically deprived of a challenging academic curriculum.[4] A retired teacher who taught in a rural North Carolina school district for 41 years, 27 in segregated and 14 in desegregated schools, Everett Dawkins, agreed that segregation had a deleterious effect on the amount and quality of materials available to his country's Black public schools. Nonetheless, it was Dawkins who introduced the first advanced math class in the Country, which he taught to his students in the all-Black segregated school. Learning of the course the county school board forced him to stop teaching advanced math until the white schools in the county could implement a similar course. Though forced to comply, Dawkins recognized the cancellation of the course as a political struggle over who was to control the content of Black education.

The theme of controlling the education of African-American children surfaced repeatedly in the life histories of teachers who began teaching in legally segregated schools. Another instance is evident in the incident told by Miss Ruthie, an 80-year-old South Carolina teacher. Remembering the fight waged by the teachers and parents when Georgetown County tried to force the closing of a local Episcopal parochial school known for its excellent academic curriculum, she describes how African-American parents and teachers actively resisted the county's efforts to control their children's education:

> The county had just built a new school and they wanted all of us to go together to the new school. So we told them no. So they said that they were gonna see that this school closed down. My husband told them, "We'll see that it stays open." So that was the argument between the superintendent and us. So they stirred the people up telling them how they felt. They said if the children came here to school that when they finished here they couldn't go into public school for a higher education. And that's when the parents started to roll and we started keeping Columbia hopping. We got the Department of Education hopping. To answer the questions that they were putting out. We kept on going, but some of the parents, you know how they can frighten some off. The next year, the Diocese said they couldn't support the school, but if we wanted to keep it open we could do it. They did everything they could to make us close the school. And we didn't. So then the Diocese said if we wanted to keep it and the community wanted it we could do it without support and that's what we've been doing ever since.

Experiences in Desegregated Schools

The civil rights movement, most notably the struggle for desegregated schools, had a profound impact on the professional lives of African-American teachers. A number of the teachers in this study were involved in the early desegregation efforts undertaken in their school districts. This fact notwithstanding, 12 of the teachers are currently employed, 10 as teachers, in schools where students of color make up the majority; only 1 teacher works in a school system where pupils of color are not the majority.[5]

African-American teachers who have been transferred to desegregated schools have experienced conflicts with colleagues, administrators, and white parents, the latter often challenging their competence as teachers solely on the basis of race. A teacher in the Boston public schools since the 1950s described white parents' hostility when, during the first year of desegregation in 1974, they found out that she would be teaching their children. Their animosity increased even further when she tried to add diversity to her curricular offerings by teaching her pupils the Langston Hughes poem "I am the Darker Brother" to recite at a school assembly.

Other teachers reiterated this theme, noting similar conflicts with white parents. A veteran teacher with 35 years of experience, one of only four teachers transferred from the segregated school in an East Texas town and currently the only African-American teacher in the town's elementary school, described the confrontation she had with a white parent who tried to remove her daughter from this teacher's class:

> One morning I came up three years ago. I didn't realize it was people still that prejudiced. I knew they were prejudiced. And she came up. And Mr. Wooten [the principal] had come up here and gotten me and he said he wanted me to come and go to my room and have a parent conference. And I said, "This morning? You mean I got a parent in my room this early?" So he said, "You can handle it." Well, I came in here and she has her hands on her hip and they had opened my room, and that had made me mad, too. And, she said, "I want my kid out of your room." I said, "Is there a problem?" "Yes, I want my daughter to have a college education. And I don't want her in your room." And I said, "Don't we all want our daughters to have a college education?" I said, "Oh, it's a racial issue, is it?" And she said, "Yes." I said, "In that case, lady," and she had her husband with her, "I think we ought to go to the office." And we went to the office and I slammed that door. And I said, "Mr. Wooten, this lady wants her kid out of my room." And he said, "What's the problem?" And I said, "This, my color."

In the end, in accord with this teacher's wishes, the principal refused to transfer the child to another class. Though frustrated by conflicts with white parents, some of the teachers recognize that their presence and ultimately their success forces white parents and students to confront their own feelings of superiority.

In a few cities, voluntary interdistrict programs have been used to achieve desegregation. Boston and St. Louis are two such cities. Believing that such programs benefit suburban districts at the expense of city districts, two teachers, who work in cities which participate in urban-suburban desegregation, commented that the programs in their communities subtly discriminate against African-American teachers. A high school teacher, the 1974 Missouri Biology Teacher of the Year, recalled how she and another African-American science teacher were recruited to work in two suburbs participating in desegregation. After learning she was being hired to teach only Black students from the city, and white students in the lowest tracks, she declined. Unaware of her teaching assignment, the other teacher transferred to the suburbs only to find that all of the Black students were placed in one of her five classes. These school districts are continuing but slightly altering a practice set during desegregation: they are siphoning off the most competent Black teachers from all-Black schools to desegregate the faculty, and in this case enlisting them to teach "undesirable" students.[6]

Earlier, I argued that irrespective of region, African-American teachers have been victimized by racist hiring practices. In Boston, for example, prior to the 1974 desegregation order, African-American teachers were severely underrepresented among the teaching force; the Boston Teachers' Union, in order to maintain the privileged status of its largely white membership, attempted to restrict further the number of Blacks entering their ranks by shrouding the issue in the cloak of seniority. Though they support improved pay and working conditions for teachers, many of the northern Black teachers in this study avoid the combative actions of unions which in their estimation do not give equal emphasis to strengthening relationships with parents and community and insuring accountability for students' academic achievement. Though she thought that the union's concerns for better working conditions were valid, a retired teacher with 32 years in the Hartford public schools recalled that she always refused to go on strike:

> A lot of teachers felt that is for their own good that they would be in those kinds of organizations, because they were the ones who got the ball rolling as far as salaries and things like that are concerned. I was a member of both [organizations]. I joined both. I never struck though. They had three strikes while I was there, but I never went out on strike. But I would never cross their picket lines. What I would do was go to school before the picket lines started and wait until after school then when they left, then I would leave. Well, that was respect for them. I just didn't feel that as a teacher I should strike. The school had to stay open as far as I was concerned. The kids had to be taught. It never caused me any trouble because I just told them in the very beginning that I was not going to strike.

In the southern and border states, because of laws mandating dual school systems prior to desegregation, African-American teachers were employed in far greater numbers than in cities with unitary school systems such as Boston (Franklin, 1979; Tyack, 1974). One result of desegregation, however, was that in the southern and border states the ranks of African-American teachers were decimated (Ethridge, 1979). In many southern school systems, African-American teachers were simply dismissed. Negative and unfair evaluations resulted in the firings of many others, an in other cases the most competent African-American teachers were reassigned to white schools. Obscured by these grim statistics are the untold stories of large numbers of African-American teachers. Examining the experiences of two of these teachers, both of whom began teaching in segregated schools in small southern towns and were later transferred to desegregated schools, tells the partial story. More importantly, it exposes the racism that eliminated large numbers of African-American teachers and thwarted the careers of many others.

A retired male teacher from a rural North Carolina community explained how in the newly integrated high school, he and another African-American teacher were forced into stereotyped roles: they were assigned to coach the football, basketball, and baseball teams, even though neither had participated in any kind of college athletics. The continuing racism experienced by African-American teachers in small southern towns is expressed in the account of another teacher.

Ella Jane, raised in an East Texas community, attended the consolidated K-12 for Black pupils, studied to be a teacher at Prairie View A & M, and returned to teach for nine years in the same school she had once attended. Summoned from her classroom to the superintendent's office in the spring of 1964, she was informed that she was one of four Black teachers to be sent to the newly desegregated school:

> I got in the car, left the school which was about eight miles out and came over to the administration building. I was sandwiched between two high school principals and a secretary and the superintendent. And they carried me through the wringer. That 's how I got here. The questions they asked were ridiculous. They said, "Ella Jane, did you know that we have to have some Black teachers?" And I said, "Yes." And he said, "Did you know that you are going to be very fortunate because you are going to be one of the Black teachers that we're going to hire?" And he said, "You're the best teacher I have in the system, Black or white. I did not have to tell you that and if you tell anyone I said that, I'm gonna tell'em you lied." He says, "Do you get my meaning?" And he said, "It should make you feel very proud whether you do or not that you're going to be one of the ones who are retained." That's how that happened.

Ella Jane went on to say that though she and her cousin, each of whom possessed master's degrees, reported to school each day, neither of them was given a class. Instead, because the townspeople were unwilling to accept them as teachers for their children, they sat in a classroom for half of the school year without teaching a single student. Finally, after the white teachers complained, the school board created classes of remedial reading students, composed of 9 to 12 students all of whom were Black or poor white, for them to teach. For three years, they continued teaching remedial reading classes. During this entire period, the other teachers showed their contempt for them and the Black students. Ella Jane speaks about how they were treated:

> We were just glorified students. Incidentally, I couldn't use the bathroom with the teachers and everything. I would use the bathroom with the students. I didn't eat with them [the other teachers]. You know, they just kind of treated me like dirt. We brought our Black students. The teachers, the white teachers, would put the Black kids, this is the truth, on one side and white ones on the other so they wouldn't touch, and so they wouldn't mingle and that's the truth. This was starting in 64. This went on for a long time.

For 26 years, Ella Jane has found herself caught between the institutional racism of the school system and her belief that she is both qualified and entitled to teacher there. Long ago, realizing that "everywhere Blacks were getting flak and that it was hard after integration for us to get jobs," she has resisted the school system's effort to push her and chosen instead to confront the individual racism of white colleagues who resent and challenge her position as grade leader, by remaining in her job.

In their own ways, all of these teachers have resisted the institutional racism they confronted in their lives and in their professional careers. Though each story represents a personal triumph, the value lies not in the individual stories. Rather the lesson is in what they reveal about the institutional racism and structural conditions that continue to limit the professional lives of African-American teachers and strangle educational possibilities for African-American pupils.

Seeing Black Students Through the Eyes of Black Teachers

Though desegregation was supposed to provide equal educational opportunity for African-American students, these interviews cast doubt on the educational benefits that have actually accrued to these students. Several teachers described the tracking, lowered expectations, and unprincipled support of athletically inclined Black students in desegregated schools. Though he did not pinpoint specific examples, one high school teacher spoke about the negative expectations that white teachers had for African-American students:

> I saw a lot of my little Black brothers get into classes that were taught by white instructors who went into the class saying, not very loudly, but very clearly, the Black kids can't make it. And I think that bothered me to no end.

Describing the treatment of Black students in her school system an elementary teacher in the South expanded on this theme:

> The Black kids are really pushed back. The only thing that they can excel in here is athletics. And, if you're a good athlete, they'll try and keep your GPA up enough for you to participate in the athletic program, but if you're academically inclined and Black you'll only get a C. We have a gifted and talented program here. There's only one Black kid in the entire gifted and talented program. He's good. I don't know how he got in there.

Another teacher described what happened to two of her students who transferred from the parochial school to the local public school in South Carolina. Though they had earned the highest average coming out of eighth grade, these African-American students were almost denied the honor of being valedictorians. According to this teacher, this incident crystallizes the discrimination in desegregated schools, whose faculty rarely expect or promote academic achievement among African-American students:

> The teachers won't give you one point. I remember because I had two that finished valedictorian over at the public school there. Some of the teachers would not vote for her to get valedictorian. But, she got it. She got it. And she came to me and said, Miss Ruthie, some of the teachers wouldn't vote for

me. The same thing happened with her sister. The commencement was on Thursday, but they waited until Tuesday to tell her to get something to say.

An African-American Teaching Philosophy

These teachers share the perspective that the effective teaching of African-American students involves more than merely imparting subject matter. They reason that desegregation has sharply curtailed African-American teachers' ability to talk with African-American students, in terms they understand, about the personal value, the collective power, and the political consequences of choosing academic achievement. As a result, they contend not only that desegregation has weakened their solidarity with Black students, but that desegregation has also limited their ability to engage in critical dialogue with African-American students, dialogue necessary to engage students in their own learning. A male high school teacher comments on the difficulties of achieving this goal with African-American students in mixed classrooms:

> The big difference was that I can see we were able to do more with the Black students. In other words, if I wanted to come in this morning, have my kids put their books under the desk or on top of the desk and I'd get up on top of my desk and sit down and just talk to them. "Why are you here? Are you here just to make out another day? Or are you here because the law says you must go to school? Are you here to try to better yourself?" This kind of thing I could talk to them about. "Well, now I'm here to better myself. Well what must you do? What are the requirements? Do you know where your competition is?" And I could talk to them about things like that. "Your competition is not your little cousin that's sittin' over there. Your competition is that white person over there in that other school. He's your competition. He's the one you've got to compete with for a job. And the only way that you're going to be able to get that job is that you can't be as good as he is, you got to be better." And I could drill that into their heads. But once you integrated, I mean you didn't feel, I didn't—I don't feel comfortable really in a mixed setting to really get into the things that the whites did to us as Black people. I don't really feel too comfortable doing that in a mixed group because I think I know how I felt when they talked about me. And surely they have feelings even though sometimes I didn't think they had any, but that kind of thing we, I mean I, couldn't do. I didn't want to pull them aside because then they would feel that they had been moved out of the mainstream because then you were just talking to just Blacks. But, this is the big difference that I saw, that you couldn't do. Well, I guess another thing, I got disillusioned with integration because of that type thing, because I could not get to my people and tell them all the things that they needed to know. I could not beat into their minds that they had to be better—that to compete with that white kid on an equal basis was not enough. I couldn't tell them that. I couldn't stop my class and tell him that so that he would understand. I think this is one of the things that they miss, Black kids, in general.

Another teacher repeats this theme, noting that desegregation has hindered the ability of African-American teachers to adopt the multifaceted and protean roles of admonisher, urger, and meddler:

> I think that integration, when I'm talking I could talk about it two ways. It's like integration is great and we need to know each other, but they miss the big picture. I know that in one way integration is worthwhile because you're going into the workforce. But, on the other hand, it's been so detrimental to kids. I mean maybe it's great for white people. Because I don't think the kids even know where they're supposed to be themselves. The kids say, "Well, I've got a C, so hey, that's wonderful." But, see nobody Black would let him get away with that. They would say, "You know you're supposed to do better than that." In the olden days. What integration as a whole has done to the Black teacher. In the olden days where you could just stand there in front of your class and tell'em, you can't do that. I mean, I can't do that when I got Blacks and whites, you know what I mean? I mean you could do it in your own little way, but you can't just stand there and say, "You're being hurt by this, wake up and smell the coffee," kind of thing. They really don't understand what's happening to them. That's the sad part.

These teachers understand clearly the contradictions inherent in the equal educational opportunity ideology of desegregated schools, especially as it has affected the motivation and consequent achievement of African-American students. A North Carolina high school teacher with experience in both segregated and desegregated schools commented on African-American students' reactions after the schools were desegregated:

> Black kids are not hungry now. There are some few of them that want to be on top, but they're not really hungry. They want to be there because they heard somebody say that it's nice to be on top, but they do not hunger and thirst after righteousness, if I can use that expression from the Bible. They don't hunger and thirst for it and the reason they don't is because nobody tells them that they need to hunger and thirst for these things. And I'm talking about that kid out there whose parents maybe get up in the morning and maybe go to work and they don't see them any more until six or seven o'clock at night. There's nothing that's pushing them when they went into an integrated situation, they looked back they look at Martin Luther King's address and he said, "I have seen the promised land." They say, "I have reached the promised land. Now that I"m here I don"t need to be concerned anymore."

These interviews are suffused with the theme that teaching African-American learners effectively demands more than knowing subject matter and the accompanying pedagogical skills. It is evident from what these teachers say that undergirding their practice with African-American students is a "hidden curriculum" which they believe has been severely compromised in desegregated schools, with negative consequences for many African-American students. This research corroborates findings from my earlier ethnographic study of an African-American teacher (Foster, 1987). The comments in these interviews as well as the behavior and speech events of the teacher in the previous study illustrate a pattern of interest and concern demonstrated by African-American teachers that both urges students to invest in learning and explains the political reasons for doing so. In both studies, the teachers assert their connectedness to and identification with Black students and the larger Black community.

Communicating and teaching across ethnic and cultural lines is complicated by the sociopolitical relationship between dominant and subordinate groups. Ray McDermott (1974, 1977) maintains that teachers and students from different cultural and ethnic backgrounds often collude in maintaining the status quo. Using their shared racial consciousness and their experiences with racism illustrated earlier, these teachers work to undo the status quo. In the following excerpt, Pam Owens, a high school teacher, explains why lack of trust often results in counterproductive relationships between white teachers, Black students, and their parents.

> The Black kids have just been hurt. They've bought into a lot of the things that white people have told them. You know if you're Black you can't do this, you can't do that. I mean, we talk about high expectations and this, I think for the most part they [white teachers] don't have 'em. I mean for God's sake, they're victims of their own society and their own upbringing. Like I was saying, why should they want some Black child to achieve? What is in it for him? But then, on the other hand, there are only so many things Black parents are gonna let white teachers do to their children, as well. Just because they don't have that kind of faith. They might put their lives into a Black teacher's hand. We have some kind of community in terms of knowing what's going on in this person's head.

Combined, the comments above suggest that though unfamiliar with McDermott's argument, these teachers understand its essence.

So far, because desegregation has merely rearranged and not changed the power arrangements in American schools, it has failed to stop the socialization of racism through the school system which both Black teachers and students experience. In fact, in desegregated schools, it has often been assumed that African-American students rather than institutional racism or unequal power relations are the problem. One teacher recalls an inservice workshop that reinforced that view:

In 1970 we had a workshop, a three-day workshop. They paid us to go to this workshop—Black and white teachers; we were integrating the school. So the first day, they came in and they had these experts who knew everything. They told these white teachers: "Now this is what you can expect from Black kids. Whatever it was don't expect them to come in and say, "yes mam" and "no mam" to you. They're gonna say "'yes" and "no" and so you're going to have to accept that even though you're not used to it. I mean this is basic. "They're not going to bring all their homework in everyday, even though that's what you're kind of accustomed to from these white kids," which was a lie by the way. But the first day we spent a whole six hours and they were telling that white teacher how to get along with that Black kid. Came in the second day, we spent six hours telling that white teacher how to get along with that Black kid. Another six hours. We came in that third day and the first three hours we spent with these so-called experts telling these white teachers how to get along with Black kids. So when we came back in after lunch break on the third day, they started the same stuff again. And I stood up: "Now wait a minute, we have spent two and half days here, and you have told these white teachers how to get along with these Black kids. You have not told me yet how to get along with that white kid." I said, "You got some of them out there just as nasty as any Black kid you ever seen, so far as conduct is concerned; this is what I'm talking about. They're not coming in that classroom and sit down and be little angels. And I see it as something wrong if they did; they are children they are children just like the Black child is. But you have not said anything to me as to how to get along with the white kid? Why was that white teacher told how to deal with the problems that he was going to face with the Black kid? Why wasn't I told how to deal with problems that I'm going to face in dealing with that white kid. When I was a youngster, fortunately or unfortunately, my parents drilled into me when you go to Miss Ann's house you go to the back door and knock. Now, I got this little stinker in my class who is gonna try and run me out and I am not going anywhere. Now, I got to go and visit that parent—you haven't told me whether or not I should go to the front door, the back door, the side door, or anything. I mean this kind of thing that I thought was very important and that white kids is going to give you problems too. But the basic premise that they were dwelling on is that you going to have trouble with Black kids. I know he was a problem. I had problems with Black children, and I'm Black, but I did. But don't tell me that because he's Black that he's automatically going to be a problem and that white child because he's white he's not going to be a problem. You going to have some problems with them."

What teachers working in integrated schools complained about most was not the loss of personal autonomy, nor the individual or institutional acts of discrimination aimed at them, but their diminishing ability to influence positively the educational futures of African-American students.

Structural Conditions in Society

When I asked these teachers to discuss the changes that have occurred during their careers regarding teaching African-American pupils, most often they commented on the changing societal conditions that limit students' futures by robbing them of meaningful participation in the economic system.

Miss Ruthie, who has been teaching since 1938 on a South Carolina sea island that has fallen victim to the "recreation explosion."[7] A version of gentrification, commented on the systematic and deliberate land taking schemes by which African-Americans have lost their lands:

There were Blacks all over there back in times before. [The land] not owned by all whites. But now, it's all white understand. All this over here—we call it Palmetto Beach. Blacks owned it. All right, the whites wanted it. So they put the taxes up so high that their heirs couldn't pay it. So after they wouldn't sell it to them, they put it on auction. Blacks got together—a group of men and women who were in business—got the money together and were determined they were going to save it. The Blacks had brought $75,000.00 and they were willing to go. So all right, they bid, and they bid, and they bid and they bid. Every time the Blacks would outbid them. Finally they quit at $50,000.00 and the Negroes got the beach. But you know they wouldn't give 'em a fair deed so they can develop that beach.

Continuing this theme, Jean Vander, a Boston elementary schoolteacher with 35 years experience, discusses displacement along with other problems facing many of the first graders who attend her school:

> They [the city] have ideas of moving those people right out of Orchard Park [the housing project where many of her children reside]. They will move poor people into areas where they will not be able to survive—just survive the situation, but they'll be out there someplace. Orchard Park is full of drugs. That is a given. It is full of drugs. One mother met me in the supermarket. She said "Mrs. Vander, I have my children with me all the time because of the drugs." They haven't got the money. They see no way out, and this is true, Michéle. Things cost. Do you know what that's going to mean? Total loss for Black kids. Because some of those kids are dealing with so much. They'll say, "I didn't come in yesterday because my cousin got shot or my father went to jail," or you know, they have some pretty serious situations. Really. Because the kids have so many more health problems. A lot of kids come in hungry. Because I think that the sixties encouraged the use of drugs too along with building up of Black self-image. I think the business of drugs has a strong, definite stronghold in poor neighborhoods. Because that's the only way of subsisting for some of these people. They are selling the shit. They are selling drugs. And they are selling to whomever will buy. Because they have to live, too. People weren't outside of the law as much before. People are more and more outside the law. Women are hustling, Michéle, to make money 'cause they can't make it out here with collard greens a dollar a pound.

While all of these teachers believe they are competent and have influenced the lives of most of the students who have been in their classrooms, they agree that changes in schools without the corresponding societal changes will not change the prospects for the majority of African-American pupils. When asked what happens to the children from her school once they leave her, an elementary teacher with 30 years in the same Philadelphia school describes the life changes of students in her community.

> Yeah, they [the students] come back all the time. Or they send word or whatever. But there's nothing in the middle. They either do very well, or poorly. There's nothing in the middle. I don't mean just college. I mean they graduate from high school, and they get responsible jobs, and they're fine people, and they read. That's important. And then you know, so many of them graduate from college, lawyers, doctors, all that. I haven't had a doctor, but I had two lawyers. And some in jail. No middle. That's the way of the neighborhood. They have to get out of it. They have to get out to do better. Then if they want to come back, well, that's okay. But they have to go away to school or go away to the army, or just go away, because it'll just eat you alive.

An English teacher who for 31 years has worked at Phillips High School, a school whose students come from Chicago's Robert Taylor Homes, echoes this theme. He concludes that the obstacles facing African-American students growing up in the large cities are so intractable that, based on his experiences, "only three out of ten students are likely to escape."

What is significant about all of these comments is that they do not blame parents or students for societal conditions that are not of their making.

Conclusion

A number of conclusions can be drawn from these interviews. An obvious one is that not only has desegregation had little effect on the schooling of large numbers of African-American students, but the process has created significant problems for African-American teachers. It has weakened these teachers' voice in the education of African-American pupils. There are other conclusions that may be less obvious. Although this article has documented teachers' beliefs and does not include observation of their practice, it is clear that teachers are unlikely to teach students effectively if they blame them instead of society for their condition. What characterizes these expert teachers is that they understand the structural conditions but are not totally overwhelmed by them. In spite of the limitations imposed by the schools and larger society, they have fashioned a teaching philosophy and pedagogy that enables them to act as social agents in ways that both change and construct their own and their pupils' realities. As noted earlier, these teachers share the belief that teaching African-American students successfully requires more than merely mastering subject matter and the accompanying pedagogical skills, but consists of engaging them in dialogue that continually questions and seeks to change the status quo. Consequently, they are neither overly optimistic nor pessimistic.

In too many instances, however, teachers of Black pupils blame the victim, her family, or the larger society for whatever problems they encounter. In fact, a recent survey of the Great City Council of Schools, made up of 44 of the nation's largest cities, has concluded that these districts are more likely to blame parents' and students' attitudes and external conditions than to blame the internal schooling conditions over which they have the most control (Lytle, 1990). Likewise, a recent study by Joyce King and Gloria Ladson-Billings (1990) showed that (largely white) pre-teaching majors in an elite Jesuit university tended to blame African-Americans' problems on supposed cultural deficits rather than on institutional racism and structural inequities. That being said, it is important to underscore the fact that not all African-American teachers are as politically aware and as sensitive to the life circumstances of their pupils as are the teachers in this study. By no means should my analysis be construed to suggest as much. It is my contention, in fact, that certain societal changes, in particular the dismantling of the "separate but equal" laws, have created an illusion and convinced many Americans, including a substantial number of younger Blacks, that institutional racism is a thing of the past. But, as noted earlier, the power arrangements have merely been rearranged, not changed. Studies that have analyzed Black teachers have often found them lacking in the kind of political perspective required to successfully teach students who have historically been oppressed by society. Nonetheless, as this study has demonstrated, not all African-American teachers are guilty of holding the perspectives suggested by earlier studies.

In conclusion, the failure to include the voices and perspectives of experienced, exemplary African-American teachers means that researchers may be cutting off an important source of understanding about how to improve the education of poor African-American children. Because teachers of color are more likely to work in school districts with greater proportions of low-income pupils of color, this omission could have serious consequences for educating students currently least well served by schools (Metropolitan Life, 1988).

Notes

I acknowledge funding from the University of Pennsylvania Research Foundation and The Spender Small Grant Program. A Spencer Postdoctoral Fellowship from The National Academy of Education, a University of North Carolina Minority Postdoctoral Fellowship, and a Faculty Fellowship from the Smithsonian Institution provided me with the funds that enabled me to work full-time on this research. I would also like to thank Joyce King for her comments on an earlier draft of this article and Jeanne Newman for her careful transcription of the interviews.

1. In this paper, both the terms *Black* and *African-American* are used. I use *Black* only to refer to students' or teachers' physical characteristics without regard to historical or cultural background. *African-American* refers to Black students and teachers who are Americans of African heritage.

2. *Community nomination,* a term coined by this author specifically for this study, means that teachers were chosen by direct contact with African-American communities. Periodicals, community organizations, and individuals provided the names of the teachers.

3. All informants' names are pseudonyms. The place names remain unchanged.

4. From the beginning, many have assumed that schools staffed by Black teachers would be inferior. However, this was not necessarily the case. James Anderson (1989, pp. 21–22), refers to an 1867 report by Frank R.

Chase, the Freedmen's Bureau superintendent of education for Louisiana, which notes that "many of the most prosperous schools in the State are taught by competent colored teachers."

5. Two teachers were retired when interviewed. Since the first interview, one teacher has taken a position as a district-level multicultural curriculum coordinator.

6. For an excellent discussion of how suburban districts have benefited by interdistrict plans at the expense of urban districts and students, see Daniel Monti (1985).

7. For a discussion of the term "recreation explosion" with respect to the development of coastal South Carolina, see Russell & Silvernail (1966).

References

Anderson, J. (1989). *The education of Blacks in the South, 1860–1935*. Chapel Hill: University of North Carolina Press.

Clark, S. (1962). *Echo in my soul*. New York: E.P. Dutton.

Conroy, P. (1972). *The water is wide*. Boston: Houghton-Mifflin.

Curry, L.P. (1981). *The free Black in America, 1800–1850*. Chicago: University of Chicago Press.

Decker, S. (1969). *An empty spoon*. New York: Harper and Row.

Dilworth, M. (1984). *Teachers' totter: A report on certification issues*. Washington, DC: Institute for the Study of Educational Policy, Howard University.

Ethridge, S. (1979). Impact of the 1954 *Brown v. Topeka Board of Education* decision on Black educators. *Negro Educational Review, 30* (3–4), 217–232.

Fields, M. with Fields, K. (1985). *Lemon Swamp: A Carolina memoir*. New York: The Free Press.

Foster, M. (1987). *"It's cookin' now": An ethnographic study of a successful Black teacher in an urban community college*. Unpublished EdD dissertation, Harvard University.

Foster, M. (1989). "It's cookin' now": A performance analysis of the speech events of a Black teacher in an urban community college. *Language in Society, 18* (1), 1–29.

Foster, M. (in press). Constancy, change and constraints in the lives of Black women teachers: Some things change, most stay the same. *NWSA Journal*.

Franklin, V.P. (1979). *The education of Black Philadelphia: The social and educational history of a minority community 1900–1950*. Philadelphia: University of Pennsylvania Press.

Goodson, I. (1988). Teachers' lives. In *Qualitative research in education: Teaching and learning qualitative traditions* (pp. 150–159). Proceedings of the second annual conference of the Qualitative Interest Group, Athens, GA.

Haskins, J. (1971). *Diary of a Harlem schoolteacher*. New York: Grove Press.

Herndon, J. (1968). *The way it spozed to be*. New York: Simon & Schuster.

Jackson-Coppin, F. (1913). *Reminiscences of school life and hints on teaching*. Philadelphia: AME Book Concern.

Jones, F. (1981). *A traditional model of excellence: Dunbar High School of Little Rock, Arkansas*. Washington: Howard University Press.

King, J., & Ladson-Billings, G. (1990, April). *Dysconscious racism and multicultural illiteracy: The distorting of the American mind.* Paper presented at the meeting of the American Educational Research Association, Boston.

Kluger, R. (1975). *Simple justice.* New York: Vintage.

Kohl, H. (1967). *36 children.* New York: Signet.

Kozol, J. (1967). *Death at an early age. The destruction of the hearts and minds of Negro children in the Boston public schools.* Boston: Houghton-Mifflin.

Lerner, G. (1972). *Black women in white America: A documentary history.* New York: Vintage.

Lightfoot, S. (1978). *Worlds apart: Relationships between families and schools.* New York: Basic Books.

Lytle, J. (1990, April). *Minority student access to and preparation for higher education.* Paper presented at the annual meeting of the American Educational Research Association, Boston.

McDermott, R. (1974). Achieving school failure. In G.D. Spindler (Ed.), *Education and cultural process* (pp. 82–118). New York: Holt, Rinehart & Winston.

McDermott, R. (1977). Social relations as contexts for learning in school. *Harvard Educational Review, 47,* 198–213.

Metropolitan Life (1988). *Strengthening the relationship between teachers and students.* New York: Metropolitan Life Insurance Company.

Monti. D. (1985). *A semblance of justice: St. Louis school desegregation and order in urban America.* Columbia: University of Missouri Press.

Provenzo, E. (1988, April). *Black and white teachers: Patterns of similarity and difference over twenty years.* Paper presented at the annual meeting of the American Educational Research Association, New Orleans.

Rist, R. (1970). Student social class and teacher expectations: The self-fulfilling prophecy in ghetto education. *Harvard Educational Review, 40,* 411–451.

Rist, R. (1973). *The urban school: A factory for failure.* Cambridge: MIT Press.

Robinson, D.R. (1974). *The bell rings at four: A Black teacher's chronicle of change.* Austin: Madrona Press.

Russell, J., & Silvernail, R.G. (1966). The impact of recreation on coastal South Carolina. *Business and Economic Review, 13,* 3–8.

Shulman, L. (1987). *The wisdom of practice: Managing complexity in medicine and teaching.* In. D. Berliner & B. Rosenshine (Eds.), *Talks to teachers: A festschrift for N.L. Gage* (pp. 369–386). New York: Random House.

Sowell, T. (1974). Black excellence—The case of Dunbar High School. *Public Interest.* No. 35, pp. 3–21.

Sowell, T. (1976). *Patterns of Black excellence. Public Interest,* No. 43. pp. 26–58.

The Thinking Team:
Toward a Cognitive Model of Administrative Teamwork in Higher Education

ANNA NEUMANN

Most college presidents have a circle of top-level administrators who report directly to them and with whom they work closely. Presidents may refer to this group, which often includes all or part of the presidential cabinet, as their "administrative team" or "inner circle." In this study I refer to this group as *the team*, and to the individuals who comprise it (for example, president, vice presidents, others designated by the president) as team members.[1]

In assessing how the individual members of the administrative team contribute to collegiate leadership, we usually consider their functional roles, including their institutional, divisional, and specialized professional responsibilities. For example, a vice president for business affairs, commonly a team member, may represent the college at community or state-level functions (institutional responsibility). She or he is also likely to oversee the activities and personnel of the college's division of finance and administration (divisional responsibility) and to be personally responsible for generating financial analyses or forecasts (specialized professional responsibilities). What this breakdown fails to consider is the time and energy that this vice president, like other team members, gives to the collective work of the administrative team. This omission is surprising given continuing calls for teamwork, collaborative leadership, and joint effort at top administrative team. This omission is surprising given continuing calls for teamwork, collaborative leadership, and joint effort at top administrative levels [16, 28, 35, 39, 74], especially during stressful times when the capacities of a single leader may be stretched to the limit, regardless of her or his personal abilities, talents, and expertise [55].

Furthermore, in examining collegiate leadership, we have focused more on how leaders position themselves to *act* effectively rather than to *think* effectively [56, 57]. We have numerous descriptions of how leaders organize themselves to achieve goals and to respond to hardship and opportunity [17, 24, 48, 49, 59, 78]. However, except for analyses of formal strategic planning processes for addressing resource stress [46, 52] we know very little about how college leaders organize themselves to improve or extend the thinking behind their goal-setting, problem-solving, and opportunity-seeking activities.

This research takes a step toward addressing such gaps by viewing top-level administrative leadership as a joint, interactive process of defining and learning about college reality [70]. Moreover, it follows up on recent assertions that effective leadership is less likely to come from a single heroic figure than from a "density of administrative competence" [51, p. 29], or from a combined team intelligence [32, 54, 76]. My objective was to consider whether team members construct their own and each others' roles on the team in terms of their collective *knowing and thinking* (as opposed to their collective *doing*), and how they may do so.

Theoretical Perspective

In this study I view the administrative team as a mini-organization, and I assume that like an organization, a team may be viewed as a system [27, 33, 47]. Given his perspective, it becomes possible to apply to the administrative team three systems metaphors [15] more commonly applied to the larger organization [19]. Accordingly, we can think of a team as a machine system focused on production [17], or as a living biological system concerned with subsistence and self-maintenance [21, 64]. However, we can also think of a team as a cognitive and sensemaking system patterned after the human mind and capable of perceiving, thinking, learning, and learning to learn [3, 15, 50, 53, 65, 67]. Viewed cognitively, teams engage in collective knowing [22, 66, 68, 69].

These three metaphors—machine, biological organism, and human mind—suggest three different conceptual frames for viewing individual members' roles on the team. For example, in teams with machine-like characteristics, members may think of their roles in terms of goal or task accomplishment. In biological team systems, members may define their roles in terms of collective knowing, thinking, and learning. A single influential member's preconceptions about which metaphor should prevail for the team as a whole (for example, as espoused by the president as team architect [10]) may frame and delimit the roles [26, 67]. However, the reverse may also be true: How team members act and think as individuals and how they negotiate among themselves the team "part" that each will play [30] may contribute additively to an emerging metaphor.

This study assumes that a team, like an organization, constructs its own reality [12, 60, 75], regardless of whether that reality is cast in the image of the machine, the living organism, or the human mind, and regardless of whether the image arises from any one person's preconceived notion of what a team is meant to do or from the team's negotiated culture [4, 5, 30, 34]. In this study I do not consider team roles in light of the machine or biological metaphor may arise. I have limited this study to the following questions: To what extent do team members think of their roles and their teammates' roles in view of a *cognitive team model*? And in particular, how do they see and think of these roles?

In sum, the purpose of this study is to generate hypotheses about the extent to which team members may organize themselves, prospectively or retrospectively, around a model of the cognitive team. Team members engaged in this kind of introspective "organizing" may be viewed as grafting a particular type of "sense" onto what would otherwise appear as a senseless maze of "team" activity [75]. The focus of this study, then, is how individual team members make sense of their own and each other's activities on the team (for example, by constructing certain types of roles) and not with the nature or effects of the activities themselves. As a result, I am concerned with capturing the *images* that team members have of the roles that they and their teammates play, and not with an image that I, as an outside observer, might construct of their actions directly. In sum, I am concerned with how *they* make sense of their own behaviors and those of their teammates, rather than with how *I* might do so.

Tradition and Change in the Study of Groups

Early studies of groups examined the traits and behaviors of individual groups and tasks [23, 41]. Many of these early studies asked whether group members should be alike or different on certain attributes, often concluding that a mixture of diversity and commonality is preferable to extreme homogeneity or heterogeneity [41, 42, 43, 44] yet revealing little about the specific components of an effective group "mix" [36, 37].

There are other obvious shortcomings to this clinical tradition in small-group research. Generally, experimental studies involved only decontextualized groups, thus neglecting groups' relationships to their larger social or organizational contexts. These early studies tended to focus excessively on temporary groups, formed specifically for experimentation and disbanded immediately afterward, thereby excluding consideration of a group's "history." They typically viewed group members' characteristics as static, often failing to consider the possibility that individuals may behave differently in diverse situations or that group members may learn from experience, thereby changing in some of their characteristics over time. They also focused heavily on group members' observable behaviors, often missing cognitive and affective dimensions. Finally, the majority of these studies strived for objective, researcher-constructed presentations of team members' roles, thereby omitting members' personal experiences within the team.

Despite the popularity of the clinical approach, a small number of scholars have, over the years, employed alternative perspectives useful for studying groups. Examples include Alderfer's [1, 2], Friedlander's [27], and Golembiewski's [33] analyses of how groups relate to their larger organizational and social contexts; Bales and Slater's [5] and Goffman's [30, 31] insights into the relationship between role-negotiation and culture creation; Hambrick's [38] attention to groups' cognitive profiles; Hare's [40] assessments of how group members perceive themselves and their teammates; and Belbin's [7] long-term observations of how professional management teams work. By considering the larger natural contexts within which groups are embedded, by focusing on cognition and emotion alongside behavior, and by examining groups' internal cultures over time, studies such as these have addressed and raised questions that clinical research, while providing other useful insights, often left untouched: What kinds of cognitive (as opposed to behavioral) contributions do group members make, for example, in non-laboratory settings where members work together for extended periods of time and on diverse, multiple tasks? How do groups interrelate with their larger social contexts? How do team members come to know the issues and tasks that confront them—not merely taking action in response to them—and how do individual members participate in constructing the group's agenda? What exactly are "roles" and how are they assumed? Why do groups arise, what makes them persist, and why do they dissolve? What is it like to be on a team—and to be outside one?

Questions such as these call for perspectives, research designs, and methodologies that differ from the conventional approach. They call for a social science that is concerned with how groups exist naturally in the field and over time, rather than striving to contrive them in the laboratory. They require researchers who are intent on understanding a group's subjectively constructed experience, rather than observing its short-term responses to controlled test environments. In sum, they require a social science concerned with interpretation of subjective meaning rather than detached objectivity. [62].

While limited to an exploration of cognition as an organizing rubric for the team, my approach in this study centers on group members' interpretations of their own and each other's roles on the team. Rather than asking, "Do the members of this team act like a cognitive team?" I asked, "To what extent do team members construct their roles on the team in cognitive terms, and with what results?"

Methodology

During 1988–89 two researchers visited fifteen campuses (nationally distributed) participating in the Institutional Leadership Project (I.L.P.) of the National Center for Post secondary Governance and Finance and conducted individual interviews with the president and up to four members of her or his administrative team (identified by the president[2]) about the nature of the team's organization, functions, and internal dynamics. A total of seventy individuals were interviewed. The institutions involved in this study are diverse in type, control, size, program emphasis, geographic location, presidential tenure, gender, and team composition.

In this study, I relied on methods of case comparison [77] and qualitative analysis [29, 63, 72] to identify and examine team members' views of how they and their teammates contribute to the cognitive aspects of their teamwork. Initially, I reviewed all interview transcripts (70) with the following analytic questions in mind:

> How does the interviewee describe her or his own contributions to the team's deliberations?

> How does the interviewee describe the contributions of other members to the team's deliberations?

This initial review revealed two sets of teams within the sample of fifteen: (a) eight teams where interviewees spoke extensively and clearly about individual members' cognitive contributions, and (b) seven teams where members volunteered less about members' cognitive contributions.

In this study I concentrated on the first set of teams (interviewees focused on cognitive contributions), reviewing the transcribed interviews in multiple iterations, assembling subcatagories of similar team member contributions and behaviors (which I eventually clustered into "roles"), and comparing the subcategories across cases. In a later review of the second set of teams (interviewees gave less attention to cognitive contributions), I identified instances of "realized absence" whereby interviewees articulated the absence of one or more cognitive roles or the teams need for such roles. I matched these expressions to the "clearly present" roles emerging from the first set of teams.

A study of this type reflects several limitations. First, the sample is small, and therefore these results should be viewed as propositions and hypotheses in need of further verification and elaboration. Second, this study only considers how team members make sense of role enactment, but it does not check whether their sensemaking aligns with role behavior, for example, as viewed by other team members or external observers. This kind of assessment was beyond the scope of this study. Third, while I considered the extent to which members where consistent in their views of each other's contributions, the data did not permit me to measure specifically for degrees of agreement. Finally, although this study acknowledges that role differences may be related to larger contextual differences (for example, institutional type, control, size, financial status, and so on), the sample's small size, coupled with its internal diversity, limited such analysis.

Results

In describing their own and their colleagues' participation in team deliberations, interviewees appeared to be thinking in terms of up to eight prototypical roles which I labeled: the Definer, the Analyst, the Interpreter, the Critic, the Synthesizer, the Disparity Monitor, the Task Monitor, and the Emotional Monitor. In this section, I present examples of these and other differences, and I discuss how the teams with clearly articulated cognitive roles differ from the teams where cognitive roles are less clear.

The Definer: Creating the Team's Reality

> [The Definer] will push, put a lot of things on the agenda and push us to resolve them. . . .

The Definer identifies and proposes the problems and topics to which the team attends—in short, formulates the team's agenda. Some teams have only one Definer (usually the president) whereas others have several, and in some cases all team members share in the Definer role. The difference between the solo Definer versus the shared Definer is exemplified in the orientations of two sample presidents:

> President 1: I set things going and let them [team members] worry about it. . . . I set up the structure.

> President 2: One important thing for me to make certain is that all members have been involved in developing the agenda.

Team members frequently describe the Definer as "knowledgeable" and "well read," and they are likely to see this individual as providing "tons of information" and, in some instances, as having the final word (within the boundaries of the team) on the state of the topic under discussion:

> [The Definer] brings a lot, including an understanding of [the topic] and the direction to go in, and the problems we will encounter in pursuing that. [The Definer] keeps us informed and aware of what other institutions are doing nationally.

In sum, the Definer's contribution to the team is a formulation of the reality to which the team attends.

The Analyst: Exploring and Mapping the Team's Reality

Given the agenda, the team's Analyst tackles it item by item. The Analyst elaborates on the topic of concern, considering its parts and interrelationships and the overall dynamics. One interviewee described the Analyst on her team as knowing "how the pieces fit together . . . communicating that well to the group . . . knowing when things are out of balance."

Persons in this role also consider the likely impacts and ramifications of team issues, especially if these are likely to grow or change. More simply, they focus on "where we will be if we continue to do what we are doing." Thus, one of their functions is to project effects. One interviewee said that, compared to other team members, those who typically assume the Analyst role "are the most hard-nosed in making hard choices, considering the ramifications for people . . . giving implications for years down the line."

Analysts often try out different angles in examining a problem or issue in order to map its multiple faces and likely effects. At one sample institution, while most team members argued for a certain major capital expenditure on the grounds that it would be symbolically important to the internal college community, the Analyst took an opposite stand. She explained, in detail, how departmental budgets would be affected by the proposed expenditure, how special faculty and staff requests would have to be denied due to the exhaustion of slack resources, and how the community's mood might falter as a result of the increased budgetary restrictiveness.

Some Analysts are generalists, drawing their analytic frames from diverse fields of knowledge. Others are specialists, bringing more focused professional frames (for example, legal, financial) to bear on team issues. The Analyst's contribution to a team is depth of understanding of those issues previously defined as being at hand.

The Interpreter: Predicting What Others Are Likely to See

The Interpreter, like the Analyst, takes the Definer's agenda as a point of departure. This suggests that although the persons in these first three roles perform different tasks, they are conceptually "in tune" with each other.

The team's Interpreter is especially sensitive to the fact that persons outside the team may not see, experience, or understands issues in the same way as the team sees and understands them. Given her or his familiarity with a certain organizational constituency, the Interpreter's task is to predict how that constituency will see the team's actions. One interviewee, for example, described the Interpreter on his team as having "good instincts for how things will look to others" and as knowing "what kinds of things will be irritating to others."

The Interpreter provides the team with conceptual translations of actions and events that, to the team itself, would appear to hold just one meaning. For example, one type of Interpreter, the institutional "historian" or keeper of the "institutional memory," might consider how the team's efforts to institute a new management process would be viewed by the faculty in light of similar prior attempts. The historian is a long-time observer of (or participant in) the faculty-administrative relationship and can make experience-based guesses about how the academic community would view and respond to this kind of leadership initiative. Another type of Interpreter with different expertise or experience might consider how critical external groups (for example, legislators and alumni) would view such an initiative. Some teams consist of several persons in the Interpreter role, with each providing unique translations of these issues at hand, for example: "bringing the faculty perspective . . . seeing things from a students standpoint . . . bringing insights from how budgeting works . . . representing the parents' point of view. . . ."

Like the Analyst, Interpreters process issues that they receive from Definers, but rather than looking intensively within any one issue (as the Analyst would do), the Interpreter recasts the issue, explaining how important institutional actors, outside the team, would likely see it. Collectively, a team's Interpreters contribute an appreciation of the multiple awareness alive in any organization. On many teams, they are acknowledged and praised for pointing out to the team the unrealized "messages that we are sending with whatever [we are] doing." They add breadth to a team's understanding of any issue and help sensitize other teams members to the multiple meanings embedded in their organization.

The Critic: Redefining, and Re-interpreting the Team's Reality

The Critic takes the work of the Definers, Analysts, and Interpreters and proposes revision. The result may be viewed as an "expression of contrary views," as a "challenge" to established understanding, or as a "confrontation," with the Critic "saying things [to persons in authority] that others would not say."

The Critic may propose minor or major alterations to prevailing team views. As an example of minor change, the Critic may reformulate a problem in a more or less urgent light:

> [We must] make sure that we don't become complacent and satisfied [or] that we would stop pushing back the edges of where we are. . . . You can become mature, entrenched, satisfied, routinized. . . . I don't think that we are there, but there is the danger of us becoming that, and we have to be on the alert that may be happening . . . that we should become stodgy . . . not challenging one another.

The Critic often questions or counters the work of the Definer, the Analyst, or the interpreter. For example, a Definer may present an agenda, and a Critic may propose modifications to its content. An Analyst may disaggregate a complex problem and the Critic may propose an alternative frame of analysis. An Interpreter may recast a problem in terms of the academic community's perceptions, and the Critic may point out the costs of catering to established views. Because by definition, the Definer, Analyst, and the Interpreter are likely to be working in concert, in challenging one, the Critic is likely to disrupt the other two as well.

Some Critics are long-term members of the team, but many are just entering the team from other lines of work or other institutions where they viewed similar issues in different ways. Their tendency to "come at things differently" may elicit either positive or negative reactions from other team members.

> Team 1: [The Critic] brings freshness . . . like a breath of fresh air.

Team 2: [The Critic] keeps things stirred up. He may go too far and irritate the others too much. . . . He exerts political influence almost bordering on divisiveness.

Critics may be depicted by their teammates as creative, non-traditional, iconoclastic, or argumentative. Regardless, the contribution of the Critic is alternate understanding derived from a revised definition, analysis, or interpretation of the team's agenda.

The Synthesizer: Orchestrating What the Team Knows

The Synthesizer receives the substantive contributions of Definers, Analysts, Interpreters, and Critics and builds from them a summative explanation of the reality the team is facing. One type of Synthesizer is a cognitive arbitrator or compromiser among diverse intellects:

> I [Synthesizer] am able to work with a wide range of people, to pull a group together. I tend to listen to all points of view and propose solutions that are satisfying to all. I tend to be the peace maker. . . .

> [The Synthesizer] . . . will be quiet and then bring together several ideas. When there is polarization on issues, he, through his own viewpoint, will try to bring the parts together.

A second type of Synthesizer "frames issues," melding what she or he learns from individual team members into a larger, multifaceted picture of the team's reality.

> As for myself[Synthesizer], I have to see more than what each of them sees individually. . . . I have to be a catalyst, bring divergent views together. . . . I have to understand the tension of being the head for all of them but being open to learning from them.

> [The Synthesizer] can touch all the bases. So she is the balance or the center point for what we [team] do.

Under conditions of ambiguity when the team's cognitive efforts are strained, the Synthesizer helps team members "face reality" of human limitations, and "move on."

The Synthesizer encourages team members to play their roles, for example, "by asking the right questions . . . [to] stimulate our thinking" and by "providing an atmosphere for candid interchange." In short, the Synthesizer elicits members' role contributions and uses them to revise the team's initial views of problems or issues. The Synthesizer also acknowledges the team's human limitations in deliberating over complex problems.

The Disparity Monitor: Gauging What Outsiders Think

The role of the Disparity Monitor is to bring to the team information on what organizational members outside the team are currently talking and thinking about, especially their views on administrative actions. Persons in this role:

> keep an ear to the ground . . . [listening for the things that] you would hear over coffee . . . emotional gripes or comments that would never surface in formal reporting lines. . . .

Presidents who are intent on "finding out peoples concerns about the institution" rely heavily on the Disparity Monitor role, requesting that their administrative team members, "talk . . . about what [they] are hearing and seeing."

The Disparity Monitor appears similar to the Interpreter in that both sensitize the team to the views of the outsiders. However, there is an important difference. The Interpreter uses her or his well-developed understanding to predict how others will view and respond to administrative initiatives, whereas the Disparity Monitor collects and relays what outsiders are in fact saying, doing, and feeling. The Interpreter helps the team be preventative; the Disparity Monitor helps it be corrective.

The Disparity Monitor provides a check on how the team views the institution's reality, helping team members gauge disparities between what they see and attend to, and what the faculty and others have on their minds.

The Task Monitor: Keeping the Team on Course

Like the Definer (and often, the Critic), the Task Monitor is concerned with the shape of the team's agenda. However, there are important differences: The Definer formulates the agenda and the Critic often revises it, but the Task Monitor expedites and supports its progress and completion, for example, by "keeping the group focused on [the pertinent] issues."

Some individuals in the Task Monitoring role make it their business to assess regularly whether the team is progressing on its "critical path . . . [or] getting bogged down." In this function, the Task Monitor:

> gets decisions ordered in terms of long-range goals [and asks if what we are doing is] . . . getting us where we want to go, or [if it] is ancillary. . . . Is what we are trying to achieve what we set out to do, and are we being economic and efficient.

The Task Monitor may also refer team members faced with new or unusual problems to other individuals with special expertise on the topic. She or he may consider whether the problems that the team is addressing would be better handled by others in the institution. Or acting like "a utility infielder," the Task Monitor may provide other team members with whatever backup is needed to get a job done. Some Task Monitors are particularly attuned to the team's readiness for action, looking for the appropriate moment to draw closure to the team's thinking.

> It may well be that my [Task Monitor's] role in our meetings is to bring closure to discussion. My colleagues say that if I am not there that the discussions never end. . . . I like things to come to some kind of closure. I will call the question.

As a tactician, the Task Monitor focuses on task accomplishment and on the means of task accomplishment. Her or his primary contribution to the team is practical help in staying on course and getting task accomplished.

The Emotional Monitor: Remembering Emotions

The Emotional Monitor is attuned to the human side of teamwork—the emotions that brew as diverse intellects mix and as the intensity of the team's business rises and subsides. One type of Emotional Monitor enacts her or his role by forcing the team to confront a comical or more relaxed interpretation of their situation—by making room for a "loud gusty laugh" as a respite from intense deliberations. One team member in the sample described his Emotional Monitoring role in this way:

> There should be a court jester. . . . One thing I try to do is set a climate that is fun. I make more of the jokes to lighten it up when there is tension. . . . Things ought to be fun. Or I will say, "You are pushing too hard. We have difficult decisions to make and I don't think you can drag people there."

Another type of Emotional Monitor offers "psychological support" to her or his colleagues on the team, "encouraging" them when they "get to feeling down." Some individuals in the Emotional Monitoring role push substantive issues aside long enough to "emphasize" with the personal feelings that may underlie emotionally strained discussions. The Emotional Monitor is also concerned with mediating and firming up "relationships" among team members. When one of the sample presidents was asked how he handled a conflict among team members, he responded in the Emotional Monitoring role:

[I handle conflict] very directly by meeting with the people involved. . . . . I become mindful of what is going on. I clarified [the vice presidents'] positions and relations . . . [described changing a reporting relationship]. I will also make comments to them [like],"I thought you were more sensitive."

Other individuals in the Emotional Monitoring role try to create team experiences that are meaningful to all team participants. One president, functioning as an Emotional Monitor, made it a point to ask frequently, "Is everyone on the team having fun or just [me]?" Emotional Monitors are particularly sensitive to new members who have not yet become a part of the team and who risk "being isolated" by others who take the routine of team interaction for granted.

To summarize, the Emotional Monitor contributes what several interviewees referred to as an emotional "glue" that binds the group as it proceeds in its work.

Different Roles on Different Teams: Patterns of Variation

I separated teams where members were fairly clear in describing roles in cognitive terms from teams where members did this less clearly, although even in this second group, interviewees occasionally commented on the nature or quality of group deliberations. In this section, I will use the cognitive role typology to guide a comparison of these two groups which, for shorthand purposes, I will refer to here as the MORE teams (cognitive roles articulated more clearly) and the LESS teams (cognitive roles articulated less clearly). I designated eight of the fifteen sample teams as MORE teams, but in this analysis, I will consider only seven of them.[3] I designated the remaining seven as LESS teams.

Role Content and the Quality of Role Performance

The most prominent difference between the MORE and LESS teams was, of course, in how members spoke of their own and each others' team participation. MORE team members emphasize cognitive contributions to the team, although they also referred to functional responsibilities (for example, representing the college, formulating the budget, coordinating faculty). In contrast, the members of LESS teams occasionally referred to cognitive roles but tended to emphasize functional responsibilities, for example, describing themselves and their teammates as "[having] budgeting skills . . . raising money . . . tapping the community purse . . . [and] focusing on traditional academic skills."

In contrast to the MORE teams whose members saw the cognitive roles as attributes of their team reality, the members of LESS teams often spoke of cognitive roles relative to what they saw the team as missing. In fact, what was particularly distinctive about the LESS teams was the tendency of several interviewees to express longing for one or more *missing* (but desirable) cognitive roles— for example, saying that the team needs someone to lay out an agenda (a Definer), or to "pin down" the president on the likely effects of certain actions (Analyst), or to "provide a different point of view" (Critic).

Despite these fundamental differences, the members of MORE teams and LESS teams were equally diverse in how they judged the quality of the cognitive role performance that they saw. Members of both MORE and LESS teams ranged widely in their evaluations of their teammates' role performance, from very positive to very negative. For example, a Definer could be praised for picking out issues in need of attention, or criticized for overloading the team's agenda. An Interpreter might be seen as providing valuable insights on how the college community typically responds to certain issues, or as taking an archconservative stand. A Critic might be viewed as providing novel insights, or as generating "hare-brained ideas."

Stage of Team Development and Team Integration

Both MORE teams and LESS teams were experiencing changes in their membership (including the entrance or departure of a president).[4] However, the LESS teams articulated a greater sense of discomfort with the changes than the MORE teams. The discomfort in LESS teams was expressed in different ways: Some members described their teams as avoiding important institutional issues or (as noted earlier) missing important cognitive roles. Others said that their own and their team-mates' functional responsibilities were not clearly delineated. Others said that the team had not yet formed a whole.

One of the difficulties experienced by LESS teams, as described by their members, was the presence of one or more persons who had been "inherited" from the previous administration. Inherited members on LESS teams usually described themselves as having been deeply engaged in the previous president's team, but as being "on the outs" with the new team. Their teammates tended to concur in this view, often describing their unassimilated, inherited colleagues as trouble-some or inactive, or as lacking desirable competence. The MORE teams also included several inherited team members, but they appeared to be as well integrated into the team as those members who were brought in by the president.

Role Prevalence

Three of the seven MORE teams considered here reflected the presence of all eight cognitive roles, with the remaining four deleting up to three roles. The roles most likely to be *present* included the Definer, Analyst, Interpreter, Critic, and Synthesizer. The roles most likely to be *absent* were the Disparity Monitor, Task Monitor, and Emotional Monitor.

The LESS teams reflected no more than four cognitive roles and some reflected as few as two. It was not possible to identify patterns of role prevalence and absence for the LESS teams, with these two exceptions: The Definer role was present in half the LESS teams and absent in the other half; the Synthesizer role was absent from all LESS teams.

Role Configuration

In the MORE group, any one team member might reflect two or more team roles, but no role clustering patterns were evident. For example, a member designated as a Definer was as likely to be an Emotional Monitor as a Task Monitor or a Critic, and the ascription of these four roles (plus others) to one person would not be unusual. An Interpreter was as likely to be a Critic as an Analyst and could, in fact, be all three.

Another characteristic of the MORE group was that any one role could be shared by two or more team members. For example, a team might have two or more Analysts, two or more Synthesizers, and so on. The Definer role was the clearest case in point. In all but one of these teams, the Definer role was ascribed to two or more team members, and in some cases team activities were structured so as to encourage and even require all team members to try out the Definer role. In one institution this was done by developing the team's meeting agenda around very broad categorical topics (for example, advisory issues) with team members being free to bring in questions and concerns that other team members could help them think over. In another institution the president held regular meetings of the team as a whole, but she also scheduled regular, frequent, one-to-one meetings with teams members, requiring them to take full charge of those meeting agendas while she took the more responsive position. In a MORE team, the president always reflected the Definer role, and nearly always played the Synthesizer and Task Monitor roles, but other members would assume those roles as well.

These patterns of role sharing and role distribution within a team were not as clear for the LESS teams. Some teams appeared to work on a "one role per member" basis with some members reflecting no roles. Other LESS teams seemed to have one member playing multiple roles while the remaining members played few or none. A frequent complaint on LESS teams was that, in the absence of a "traffic cop" to introduce important but frequently uncomfortable issues (that is, a Definer), the team's overall agenda tended to be haphazard, "jumping from topic to topic." Moreover, the members of LESS teams presented the Definer role in one of two ways: as minimally active to the point of being absent, or as highly active and prominent but restricted to the president. This, of course, contrasts sharply with how the members of MORE teams saw the Definer role, namely, as shared by two or more team members.

Cognitive Differentiation and Cognitive Complexity

MORE teams present themselves as more cognitively differentiated—that is, as having a more diverse array of cognitive roles—than LESS teams. Not only are there more roles on MORE teams, but the roles are played by more members. In sum, the MORE team, as a whole, projects an image of complex cognitive activity in comparison to LESS teams where fewer roles are generally played by fewer members. Although cognitive complexity has been defined as an attribute of an individual mind [6], it may also be viewed as a property of a social unit (in this case, the team).

Managing Cognitive Differentiation

Despite its obvious allure, a team that is cognitively differentiated presents difficulties: Cognitive differentiation may be hard to elicit, hard to coordinate and control, hard to bring to closure, hard to understand and be patient with, and hard to hold to standards of efficiency, especially during stressful times when the ability to respond rapidly may be essential. The data suggest three ways to manage cognitive differentiation: through the Synthesizer role, team norms, and team meetings.

The Synthesizer role appears to mediate the difficulties associated with cognitive differentiation by creating a context in which members feel free to enact their thinking roles. In addition, the Synthesizer recasts issues introduced by a Definer as others (Analysts, Interpreters, Critics) rework these issues in their minds, and then moves the team to action on the enlarged understanding. Thus, the Synthesizer elicits the different cognitive roles, blending their contributions into a sensible product. The Synthesizer, then, must comprehend, tolerate, and appreciate the variety of team roles, seeking them out and "playing them" as needed. In short, the Synthesizer must be able to tolerate and work with the cognitive complexity of a MORE team. What does this say about the cognitive complexity of the *individual* in the Synthesizer role? Because most of the MORE presidents were Synthesizers, whereas the LESS presidents were not, it is instructive to pursue this question by comparing MORE and LESS presidents in terms of their cognitive complexity.

A follow-up analysis of the I.L.P.'s presidential data, previously coded according to the presidents' cognitive complexity [9, 56] and updated to reflect data collected in subsequent rounds, shows that six out of the seven MORE presidents were "cognitively complex," in comparison to one out of seven LESS presidents. What this suggests is that a cognitively differentiated team (MORE) is likely include a cognitively complex president playing a complex Synthesizing team role. (The data also suggest that a LESS team is not likely to include a cognitively complex president, and that the Synthesizer is likely to be absent.)

Prior studies of higher education leadership have associated a leader's cognitive complexity with her or his effectiveness in relating to the external environment and the *larger* organization (that is, the college) [9, 11, 13, 56]. This study suggests an association between a cognitively complex presidential leader and her or his *smaller* organization (that is, the team). This finding gives credence to Bartunek, Gordon, and Weathersby's [6] assertion that the relationship between an individual's cognitive team may represent a critical link in a complex chain: Leadership effectiveness may not be the result of a single leader's capabilities. Rather, it may result, at least in part, from a team's more complex capabilities. However, the ability of the team to be a "cognitive team" may well depend on that one leader.

Team norms aimed at preserving cognitive differences may also aid in team management. Several interviews conducted during the course of this research suggest that conflicts of "rough spots" among team members might be explained in terms of how an individual's ability or willingness to tolerate cognitive differences varies from the team norm. For example, several members of a MORE team described their experience with a new team member whose strong, singular view of how a team should run negated the team's traditional, preferred mode of operation. The team member, who became increasingly uncomfortable with a group that insisted on continuing to think and talk informally among themselves rather than acting as "an august body," eventually left her post, and the cognitive team was preserved.

However, team norms, as promulgated by a prominent team member, can have an opposite effect: In other sample institutions, a president whose view of the team was more singularly utility-oriented would overlook the contributions of a cognitively oriented team member (many times, inherited) or describe the member as ineffectual. That team member would often speak at length about the cognitive roles that she or he saw the team as missing. These patterns suggest that for a team to function as a cognitive unit, all of its members, and probably the president in particular, should be able to tolerate, respect, and appreciate each other's cognitive differences—even if, at times, they appear confusing and disruptive.

Team meetings represent a third means of eliciting and supporting cognitive differentiation. The members of MORE teams spoke of frequent meetings, formal and informal, among the whole team and among subgroups, with or without the president. In contrast, the members of LESS teams usually said that the team rarely met as a whole, and they portrayed individual team members (including themselves) as being more closely related to the president than to other members of the team. Meetings—formal or not—represent the "settings" in which roles may be enacted. Without "settings," there is no time and place for "enactment," and by extension, there are no "roles." Further, if meetings stimulate the thinking team," their absence may suppress it.

Observations and Discussion

This study yields several considerations for researchers and practitioners wanting to learn about teams and how they work: (1) that teams may be analyzed as systems; (2) that teams, viewed as cognitive systems, reflect internal tension and balance; (3) that teams may stimulate personal and organizational learning; (4) that teams can be both organizational assets and liabilities; and (5) that teams may represent an important "missing link" in the study of organizational and leadership effectiveness.

Teams as Systems

Five of the eight cognitive roles presented in this study focus on the *substance* of team deliberation, including the Definer who introduces the content of team deliberations; the Analyst and Interpreter who, in a sense, process it; the Critic who sharpens, refashions, and often redirects the work of Definers, Analysts, and Interpreters; and the Synthesizer who recognizes and articulates the final result of the overall deliberative process. The remaining three roles focus on maintaining and supporting the deliberative *process*, for example, by providing feedback on external perceptions and effects (Disparity Monitor), by expediting internal tasks (Task Monitor), and by looking after individual members' emotional well-being (Emotional Monitor).

These roles may be translated into "systems" language [47] as follows: The Definer infuses issues (the agenda) as inputs to the cognitive team system. Together, the Analyst and Interpreter perform a *transforming* function as they process issues one by one. The Synthesizer packages and sends out the final *product* or *output—that* is, the issue enlarged and recast. To extend the systems analogy further, the Analyst and Interpreter represent the *productive subsystem* or *technical core* because they carry out the system's central purpose (in this case, enlarging what the team knows). The Definer and Synthesizer represent the *production-supportive subsystem* in that they acquire inputs and dispose of the system's outputs. The Emotional Monitor and Task Monitor represent the *maintenance subsystem* in caring for the functional and emotional well-being of system participants. The Critic represents the *adaptive subsystem* in identifying alternative ways of thinking about and performing system functions.[5] Viewed this way, the individual roles, in interaction, could represent the parts of a complex thinking system capable of superseding the cognitive efforts of any individual team member.

Other systems concepts, previously reserved for the study of organizations, might serve as points of departure in analyzing teams. For example, it may be possible to adapt, at least roughly, Bolman and Deal's [14] multi-frame perspective on organizations by considering the bureaucratic, human, political, and symbolic dimensions of team dynamics. Smircich's [69] analysis of an insurance company's executive staff as a small organization within the larger company is an example of how a team might be studied from a cultural or symbolic perspective. Or, extending Pfeffer and Salancik's [61] resource dependency model, it is possible to conceive of a team as one of many potentially interactive team systems "nested" within a larger context [22] which, in this case, is the larger organization itself [1, 2, 27, 33].

Internal Tension and Balance

A review of the eight roles suggested opportunities for tension and balance within the team. For example, the views of the Definer, Analyst, and Interpreter are likely to differ considerably from those of the Critic. The Task Monitor who wants to move the team along in its work may clash with the Analyst and Interpreter, who require time to complete their processing tasks, or with the Emotional Monitor, who is typically more concerned with emotional well-being than task completion. A Task Monitor intent on "calling the question" may overlap with the Synthesizer role. An Interpreter who is overly focused on past organizational events or patterns of operation may not be receptive to a Disparity Monitor bringing more current information.

These differences suggest that a president may want to focus on unique institutional needs in selecting and orchestrating the administrative team. Several considerations are apparent: New presidents intent on making a difference in their institutions may become overly attentive to Critics who see creative, new approaches, while giving insufficient attention to Interpreters who could foretell the reactions of a particular constituency to administrative initiatives. This might be an especially important consideration for new presidents still in the process of "getting to know . . . and getting known in" their new settings [8]. Similarly, new presidents who try to please critical college players may take action in light of what they learn from Disparity Monitors (namely what outsiders see and think) without attending to Analysts' warnings about potential side-effects. In contrast, presidents who have been in office for many years and who have worked comfortably with a stable and loyal administrative team may downplay the Critic and Disparity Monitor roles, attending instead to Interpreters. The resulting rule-of-thumb may be that new presidents (and new teams) may want to moderate the influence of Critics and Disparity Monitors while giving weight to Interpreters' voices. Experienced presidents (and their teams) may want to moderate the influence of Interpreters and encourage the contributions of Critic and Disparity Monitors.

The ability of a college to put together a good administrative team may be superseded in importance only by the ability of a college to find a president who can put together and support the work of a good team. The findings of this study, in relation to the work of the larger Institutional Leadership Project, show that while college presidents, in and of themselves, can claim no superhuman qualities [11,13], they may possess the ability to compose and orchestrate a team that, together, can see or do more than any one member alone could see or do. What the professional field of higher education administration lacks at this times is a clarification of the specific synthesizing skills and abilities that presidents need in order to be able to do this, as well as an understanding of how such skills might be fostered and how they might be identified by members of presidential search committees. Initial studies of cognitive complexity [9,13], leadership strategy [18,19,56], and organizational cultures [20,55,73] represent a step in this direction.

Learning in Teams, Learning by Teams

One of the tasks of a new president is to create a team setting that elicits the best capabilities as well. It would seem possible that by watching and listening to each other, members could learn how to play new roles. In one incident reported through this study, the president and vice president (a close team colleague) instigated this kind of role-learning when the VP assumed the Definer and Critic roles while the president took on the Analyst role. From this and similar incidents, the other team members, previously unaccustomed to such role reversals, learned that they to could assume the Definer and Critic roles—in short, "that it is okay to argue with the president" and to take a hand in directing the team's thinking. There may be several benefits to this type of role-learning: expanding the scope of individual members' understanding of how to use the contributions that others make, and personal learning and growth for those who acquire new roles.

Furthermore, it seems likely that a key role to be learned and shared could be the Definer role. From the perspective of the cognitive model, the person who is the Definer holds the primary initiating role. Other persons, with no Defining responsibilities, are likely to assume more receptive or supportive team roles in that they process and remold (or sustain the processing and remolding of) that which the Definer has already created. If the Definer role is held by just one person, then initiative—namely the prerogative and power to create—is centered in just that individual. If the Definer role is shared with other team members, then initiative is also shared and the whole team may become more active and *creating* in its orientation. Thus in constructing a shared Definer role, the entire character of a team could be affected. Although the team, its individual members, and the institution may benefit from a shared Definer role, the president may also gain from the increased flexibility that comes with playing—or learning to play—other team roles, and from the decreased pressure to appear "leader like" [13] at all times.

Another key role, occasionally absent and frequently controversial, is the Critic. If the team is viewed as an open system emphasizing an input-processing-output cycle [47] along the lines of simple biological systems [15], then the Critic role is superfluous. In questioning and rethinking the nature of the issues, ideas, problems, considerations, and "facts" that Definers introduce to the team system, and by finding and offering alternative analyses and interpretations, the Critic converts the purpose of the team system—from a focus on continuance to a focus on learning. The Critic represents the team's self-reflecting, searching, and experimenting eye.

The Cognitive Team as an Organizational Asset and Liability

To view the team as a means for enlarging what the organization knows, and how it thinks and learns, is appealing in its implications for enhancing organizational performance: If we have a larger and sharper picture of our organizational world and how it works, then we should be better able to devise action that will work to improve that world, than we would be if our understanding of it were more limited.

The other side of the coin is the risk that the cognitive team will become too much of a team, in effect turning into a "cognitive clique." This could happen in several ways. For example, in spending extended time together (that is, in formal and informal meetings), team members may grow to like and appreciate each other [45], and in making choices of whom to talk to, they may choose the team over other institutional members. Over time, team members may come to attend to the needs of the administrative division (for example, academic affairs, student affairs, business affairs, external affairs). They may also come to rely less on Disparity Monitors (who would bring the views of outsiders to the team) as they become more established and confident in their knowledge of how the institution works and what their constituents expect of them (thereby becoming Interpreters in their own right). What occurrences such as these suggest is that a team that works together particularly well may, over time, cut itself off from other aspects of institutional life. This kind of administrative teamwork, with or without a cognitive orientation, may be more harmful than the absence of any teamwork at all.

Cognitive Teams and Effectiveness

This study suggests that administrative teams vary in the roles that their members play and that are more thinking-and-learning-oriented than others. Moreover, some teams appear to organize themselves according to a model of complex cognitive activity (for example, the MORE teams) while others seem to overlook or simplify the cognitive aspects of team organization (for example, the LESS teams). In this study the cognitive teams (MORE) exhibited both cognitive and behavioral complexitivity in four ways: (1) in the composition of the group as a whole with persons in various roles articulating diverse perspectives; (2) in the person of the Synthesizer (most commonly, the president), who elicits and orchestrates these views; (3) in team norms that promote tolerance for and encouragement of cognitive diversity; and (4) in formal and informal team meetings permitting complex interactions. In sum, this study provides evidence for associating "cognitive teams" with "cognitive complexity," a quality identified by others [6,11,13,75] as contributing to effective leadership, albeit at the individual level.

But does cognitive complexity, at the level of the team, matter as much as it may at the level of the individual? And particularly, does a cognitive complex team make an organization and its leadership more effective? While additional research is needed to assess the relationship between cognitive teams and organizational effectiveness, studies of leaders facing conceptually difficult problems—over time and at points of crisis—reveal that those who compose cognitively diverse teams are likely to achieve greater levels of success than those who prefer to work alone, who ignore issues of cognition in building their team, or who develop teams with members who think very much alike [7,37,38]. a similar finding resulted from this study; The teams that were less cognitively oriented and less complex (LESS) were also less comfortable with the quality of their deliberative efforts than the teams with stronger cognitive orientations (MORE). For example, the members of LESS teams often said that their group would be more effective if one or more cognitive roles were present and if the team would act as a thinking whole.

While studies of possible linkages between complexity and effectiveness among the individual leader, the team, and the organization are rare, one recent study [58], also conducted through the Institutional Leadership Project, showed that presidents concerned with enhancing their team's complexity (that is, using the team to increase what team members do individually or together) were more likely to govern in financially stable and high-morale colleges than presidents with more reductive aims (that is, using the team to delimit or simplify the roles of individual team members). Moreover, the presidents who created complex teams were typically more cognitively complex than those who sought to simplify their team's structure. Although the cross-sectional design of this earlier study prevented assessment of casualty (for example, do complex presidents and teams create favorable conditions, or do favorable conditions permit presidents and teams to be complex?), its findings are consistent with the proposition that the "thinking team" is an important link in evolving conceptions of effective institutional leadership.

Finally, while this study provokes questions about how a team's cognitive complexity relates to leadership and organizational effectiveness, it also raises questions about difficulties commonly associated with complexity: What can team members do to enhance their abilities to tolerate and make use of their colleagues' unique (but different) cognitive skills? How can an individual come to know and appreciate those cognitive differences in others that are beyond the realm of her or his own scheme of knowing? How can broad-ranging cognitive diversity be managed? How can people with diverse mindsets find enough common ground within the range of their combined knowing and thinking to be a "team"? Although the potential benefits of the cognitive team need exploring, so do its limitations and its challenges.

Notes

This research was funded by a grant from the Lilly Endowment, Inc., with support from TIAA-CREF, and prepared pursuant to a grant from the Office of Educational Research and Improvement/Department of Education (OERI/ED). However, the opinions expressed herein do not necessarily reflect the position or policy of the OERI/ED and no official endorsement by the OERI/ED should be inferred.

I am grateful to Estela M. Bensimon, Robert Birnbaum, Aaron M. Pallas, Robert J. Silverman, and the *Journal*'s anonymous reviewers for helpful criticism, advice, and encouragement. My special thanks to Jill Glickman who assisted in organizing the data and conducting library research and to Eleanor Fujita for assistance througout the life of the Institutional Leadership Project. An earlier version of this article was presented at the annual meeting of Association for the Study of Higher Education, November 1989.

1. To comply with pledges of confidentiality, I refer to all sample institutions as "colleges" or "institutions." In addition, I have disguised the gender of interviewees, attributing feminine and masculine pronouns randomly; the gender used in this article does not necessarily reflect the true gender of an interviewee. I also changed specific position titles to reflect generic roles. Thus a person with the title, "chancellor," would be referred to here as "the president," a person with the title, "vice president for administration and finance," would be called "the vice president for business affairs," and so on.

2. Presidents described their teams as consisting of as few as two or as many as ten persons, with an average team size of seven (these figures include the president as a team member). Although the composition of the team varied by campus, the typical team consisted of members of the president's cabinet and occasionally members of her or his office staff (executive assistant, secretary, public relations specialist, and so on). For the purpose of this study, interviews were limited to the president and four other team members identified by the president as her or his closest working associates, Given this design, the typical slate of interviewees per campus included: the president, the chief academic officer, the chief business officer, the chief student affairs officer, and the chief external affairs or development officer.

3. The membership of one of the MORE teams was very small, and although its members appeared to be very sensitive to their own and each other's cognitive contributions to the team, the small number of team participants limited the kind of self-analysis that seemed possible in larger teams.

4. An analysis by presidential tenure was difficult because out of the fifteen presidents in the study, only three were senior (in office for over five years). Therefore, the majority of the sample (12) consisted of junior presidents who had been in office for less than two years. The MORE group included the three senior presidents and five junior presidents, one of whom was brand new. The LESS group consisted of seven junior presidents, two of whom were brand new. There were no senior presidents in the LESS group.

5. It may be significant that no role fits as neatly with what Katz and Kahn [47] call "the managerial subsystem" in charge of coordinating the other roles (or subsystems). The Synthesizer may represent this subsystem to some degree, for example, by creating an environment whereby team members can enact their roles or try out new ones, and by orchestrating the team's final product. In a sense, the Task Monitor, who is concerned with the system's efficiency and productivity, may also be seen as representing the managerial subsystem

to some degree. I would speculate, however, that the managerial subsystem in the team is better represented by team norms, established early in the life of the team system, than by any of the cognitive roles. Viewed this way, inner team management (or inner team leadership) might be defined as the establishing and maintaining of those norms.

References

1. Alderfer, C.P. "Group and Intergroup Relations." In *Improving Life at Work: Behavioral Sciences Approaches to Organizational Change,* edited by J.R. Hackman and J.L. Suttle, pp. 227-96. Santa Monica, Calif.: Goodyear Publishing Co., 1977.

2. _____."An Intergroup Perspective on Group Dynamics." In *Handbook of Organizational Behavior,* edited by J.W. Lorsch, pp. 190-219. Englewood Cliffs, N.J.: Prentice-Hall, 1987.

3. Argyris, C., and D.A. Schön. *Organizational Learning.* Reading, Mass.: Addison-Wesley, 1978.

4. Bales R. F. "A Set of Categories for the Analysis of Small Group Interaction." *American Sociological Review,* 15 (April 1950), 257–63.

5. Bales, R. F., and P. E. Slater. "Role Differentiation in Small Decision-Making Groups." In *The Family, Socialization, and Interaction Process,* edited by T. Parsons, R. F. Bales, and others, pp. 259–306. Glencoe, Ill.: Free Press, 1955.

6. Bartunek, J. M., J R. Gordon, and R. P. Weathersby. "Developing 'Complicated' Understanding in Administrators." *Academy of Management Review,* 8 (1983), 273–84.

7. Belbin, R. M. *Management Teams, Why They Succeed or Fail.* New York: John Wiley and Sons, 1981.

8. Bensimon, E. M. "The Discovery Stage of Presidential Succession." Paper presented at the national meeting of the Association for the Study of Higher Education, Baltimore, Md., 1987.

9. _____. "The Meaning of 'Good Presidential Leadership': A Frame Analysis." *Review of Higher Education,* 12 (19849), 107–23.

10. _____."How College Presidents Use Their Administrative Groups: 'Real' and 'Illusory' Teams." *Journal for Higher Education Management,* in press.

11. Bensimon, E. M., A. Neumann, and R. Birnbaum. *Making Sense of Administrative Leadership: The "L" Word in Higher Education.* ASHE-ERIC Higher Education Report, No. 1. Washington, D.C.: School of Education and Human Development, The George Washington University, 1989.

12. Berger, P., and T. Luckmann. *The Social Construction of Reality.* New York: Doubleday, 1966.

13. Birnbaum, R. *How Colleges Work: The Cybernetics of Academic Organization and Leadership.* San Francisco: Jossey-Bass, 1988.

14. Bolman, L. G., and T. E. Deal. Modern Approaches to Understanding and Managing Organizations. San Francisco: Jossey-Bass, 1984.

15. Bouling, K. E. "General Systems Theory—the Skeleton of Science," *Management Science,* 2 (1956), 197–208.

16. Bowen, W. G. "The Role of the Business Officer in Managing Educational Resources." *NACUBO Professional File,* 2 (December 1971), 1–8.

17. Brown, D. G. *Leadership Roles of Chief Academic Officers.* New Directions for Higher Education, no. 47. San Francisco: Jossey-Bass, 1984.

18. Chaffee, E. E. "Successful Strategic Management in Small Private Colleges." Journal of Higher Education, 55 (March/April 1984), 212–41.

19. _____. "The Concept of Strategy: From Business to Higher Education." In *Higher Education: Handbook of Theory and Research*, Vol. 1, edited by J. C. Smart, pp. 133–71. New York: Agathon Press, 1985.

20. Chaffee, E. E., and W. G. Tierney. *Collegiate Culture and Leadership Strategies*. New York: American Council on Education/Macmillan, 1988.

21. Collins, B. E., and H. Guetzkow. *A Social Psychology of Group Processes for Decision-Making*. New York: John Wiley and Sons, 1964.

22. Daft, R. L., and K. E. Weick, "Toward a Model of Organizations as Interpretation Systems." *Academy of Management Review*, 9 (1984), 284–95.

23. Davis, J. H., P. R. Laughlin, and S. D. Komorita. "The Social Psychology of Small Groups: Cooperative and Mixed-Motive Interaction." In *Annual Review of Psychology*, Vol. 27, edited by M. R. Rosenzweig and L. W. Porter, pp. 501–41. Palo Alto, Calif. Annual Reviews, 1976.

24. Dill, D. D. "The Nature of Administrative Behavior in Higher Education." *Educational Administration Quarterly*, 20 (1984), 69–99.

25. Eble, K. E. *The Art of Administration: A Guide for Academic Administrators*. San Francisco: Jossey-Bass, 1978.

26. Fiske, S. T., and S. E. Taylor. *Social Cognition*. New York: Random House, 1984.

27. Friedlander, F. "The Ecology of Work Groups." In *Handbook of Organizational Behavior*, edited by J. W. Lorsch, pp. 301–14. Englewood Cliffs, N. J.: Prentice-Hall, 1987.

28. Gardiner, J. "Building Leadership Teams," In *Leaders for a New Era*, edited by M. Green, pp. 137–53. New York: American Council on Education and Macmillan Publishing Co., 1988.

29. Glaser, B. G. and A. L. Strauss. *The Discovery of Grounded Theory*. New York: Aldine, 1967.

30. Goffman, E. *The Presentation of Self in Everyday Life*. Garden City. N.Y.: Doubleday Anchor Books, 1959.

31. _____. Interaction Ritual, Essays on Face-to-Face Behavior. New York: Pantheon Books, 1967.

32. Goleman, D. "Recent Studies Explain Why Some Meetings Fail." *The New York Times*, June 7, 1988.

33. Golembiewski, R. T. "Small Groups and Large Organizations." In *Handbook of Organizations*, edited by J. G. March, pp. 87–141. Chicago: Rand McNally and Co., 1965.

34. Graen, G. "Role-Making Processes within Complex Organizations." In *Handbook of Industrial and Organizational Psychology*, edited by M. D. Dunnette, pp. 1201–45. Chicago: Rand McNally College Publishing Co., 1976.

35. Guskin, A. E., and M. A. Bassis. "Leadership Styles and Institutional Renewal, In *Leadership and Institutional Renewal, New Directions for Higher Education*, no. 49, edited by R. M. Davis, pp. 13–22. San Francisco: Jossey-Bass, 1985.

36. Hackman, J. R. "The Design of Work Teams." In *Managerial Control and Organizational Democracy*, edited by S. S. Streufert and F. E. Fiedler, pp. 61–91. Washington D. C.: Winston and Sons, 1977.

37. _____. "The Design of Work Teams." In *Handbook of Organizational Behavior*, edited by J. W. Lorsch, pp. 315–42. Englewood Cliffs, J. J.: Prentice-Hall, 1987.

38. Hambrick, D. C. "The Top Management Team: Key to Strategic Success." *California Management Review*, 30 (Fall 1987), 112–19.

39. Hardaker, M., and B. K. Ward. "Getting Things Done: How to Make a Team Work." *Harvard Business Review*. No. 6 (November–December 1987), 112–19.

40. Hare, A. P. *Handbook of Small Group Research*. 2nd ed. New York: Free Press, 1976.

41. Helmrich, R., R. Bakeman, and L. Scherwitz. "The Study of Small Groups." In *Annual Review of Psychology*, Vol. 24, edited by P. H. Mussen and M. R. Rosenzweig, pp. 337–54. Palo Alto, Calif.: Annual Reviews, Inc., 1973.

42. Hill, G. W. "Group Versus Individual Performance: Are $N + 1$ Heads Better Than One?" *Psychological Bulletin*, 91 (1982), 517–39.

43. Hoffman, L. R., and N. R. F. Maier. "Quality and Acceptance of Problem Solutions by Members of Homogeneous and Heterogeneous Groups." *Journal of Abnormal and Social Psychology*, 62 (1961), 401–07.

44. Hoffman, L. R., E. Harburg, and N. R. F. Maier. "Differences and Disagreement as Factors in Creative Group Problem Solving." *Journal of Abnormal and Social Psychology*, 64 (1962), 206–14.

45. Homans, G. C. *The Human Group*. New York: Harcourt, Brace, and World, 1950.

46. Jedamus, P., M. W. Peterson, and associates. *Improving Academic Management: A Handbook of Planning and Institutional Research*. San Francisco: Jossey-Bass, 1980.

47. Katz, D., and R. L. Kahn. *The Social Psychology of Organizations*, 2nd ed. New York: John Wiley and Sons, 1978.

48. Kerr, C. *Presidents Make a Difference: Strengthening Leadership in Colleges and Universities*. Washington, D. C.: Association of Governing Boards of Universities and Colleges, 1984.

49. Kerr, C., and M. L. Gade. *The Many Lives of Academic Presidents: Time, Place, and Character*. Washington, D. C.: Association of Governing Boards of Universities and Colleges, 1986.

50. Levitt, B., and J. G. March. "Organizational Learning." In *Annual Review of Sociology*, Vol. 14, edited by W. R. Scott and J. Blake, pp. 319–40. Palto Alto, Calif.: Annual Reviews, Inc., 1988.

51. March, J. G. "How We Talk and How We Act: Administrative Theory and Administrative Life." In *Leadership and Organizational Culture*, edited by T. J. Sergiovanni and J. E. Corbally, pp. 18–35. Urbana, University of Illinois Press, 1984.

52. Mingel, J. R., and associates. *Challenges of Retrenchment: Strategies for Consolidating Programs, Cutting Costs, Reallocating Resources*. San Francisco: Jossey-Bass, 1981.

53. Morgan, G. *Images of Organization*. Beverly Hills, Calif.: Sage, 1986.

54. Nadler, D. A. "What Every New Chief Executive Should Know: The Fine Art of Managing Change." *The New York Times*, November 29, 1987.

55. Neumann, A. "Colleges Under Pressure: Budgeting, Presidential Competence, and Faculty Uncertainty." Paper presented at the annual meeting of the American Educational Research Association, San Francisco, 1989.

56. _____. "Strategic Leadership: The Changing Orientations of College Presidents." Review of Higher Education, 12 (1989), pp. 137–51.

57. _____. "Making Mistakes: Error and Learning in the College Presidency." *Journal of Higher Education*, 61 (July/August 1990), 386–407.

58. Neumann, A., and E. M. Bensimon. "Constructing the Presidency: College Presidents' Images of Their Leadership Roles, A Comparative Study." *Journal of Higher Education*, 61 (November/December 1990), 386–407.

59. Peck, R. D. "The Entrepreneurial College Presidency." *Educational Record*, 64 (1983), 18–25.

60. Pettigrew, A. M. "On Studying Organizational Cultures." *Administrative Science Quarterly*, 24 (1979), 570–81.

61. Pfeffer, J., and G. R. Salancik. *The External Control of Organizations, A Resource Dependence Perspective*, New York: Harper and Row, 1978.

62. Rabinow, P., and W. M. Sullivan (eds.) *Interpretive Social Science, A Second Look*. Berkeley, Calif.: University of California Press, 1987.

63. Schatzman, I., and A. L. Strauss. *Field Research Strategies for a Natural Sociology*. Englewood Cliffs, N. J.: Prentice-Hall, 1973.

64. Schein, E. H. *Process Consultation*. Volume 1: *Its Role in Organization Development*. Reading, Mass.: Addison-Wesley Publishing Co., 1988.

65. Schön, D. A. *The Reflective Practitioner: How Professionals Think in Action*. New York: Basic Books, 1983.

66. Shulman, L. S., and N. B. Carey. "Psychology and the Limitations of Individual Rationality: Implications for the Study of Reasoning and Civility." *Review of Educational Research*, 54 (1984), 501–24.

67. Sims, H. P., D. A. Gioia, and associates. *The Thinking Organization: Dynamics of Organizational Social Cognition*. San Francisco: Jossey-Bass, 1986.

68. Smircich, L. "Concepts of Culture and Organizational Analysis." *Administrative Science Quarterly*, 28 (1983), 339–58.

69. _____. "Organizations as Shared Meaning." In *Organizational Symbolism*, edited by L. R. Pondy, G. Morgan, P. J. Frost, T. C. Dandridge, pp. 55–65. Greenwich, Conn.: JAI Press, 1983.

70. Smircich, L., and G. Morgan. "Leadership: The Management of Meaning." *Journal of Applied Behavioral Science*, 18 (1982), 257–73.

71. Steiner, I. D. *Group Process and Productivity*. New York: Academic Press, 1972.

72. Strauss, A. L. *Qualitative Analysis for Social Scientists*, Cambridge, Mass.: Cambridge University Press, 1987.

73. Tierney, W. G. "Organizational Culture in Higher Education." *Journal of Higher Education*, 59 (January/February 1988), 2–21.

74. Walker, D. E. *The Effective Administrator*. San Francisco: Jossey-Bass, 1979.

75. Weick, K. E. *The Social Psychology of Organizing*. New York: Random House, 1979.

76. Williams, W. M., and R. J. Sternberg. "Group Intelligence: Why Some Groups Are Better Than Others," *Intelligence*, 12 (1988), 351–77.

77. Yin, R. K. *Case Study Research: Design and Methods*. Beverly Hills, Calif.: Sage, 1984.

78. Zammuto, R. F. "Managing Declining Enrollments and Revenues." In *Key Resources in Higher Education Governance, Management, and Leadership*, edited by M. W. Peterson and L. A. Mets, pp. 347–65. San Francisco: Jossey-Bass, 1987.

Bibliography

REBECCA ROPERS-HUILMAN AND CLIFTON F. CONRAD

I. Explicating Frames of Reference: The Multiple Faces of Qualitative Research

Anderson, Gary L. "Critical Ethnography in Education: Origins, Current Status, and New Directions." *Review of Educational Research* 59 (Fall, 1989), pp. 249–270.

Anderson, Gary L. "Toward a Critical Constructivist Approach to School Administration: Invisibility, Legitimation, and the Study of Non–Events." *Educational Administration Quarterly* 26 (August, 1990), pp. 38–59.

Bahm, Archie J. "Science is Not Value–Free." *Policy Sciences* 2 (December, 1971), pp. 391–396.

Bartky, Sandra Lee. *Femininity and Domination: Studies in the Phenomenology of Oppression.* New York: Routledge, 1990.

Bates, Richard J. "Educational Administration, the Sociology of Science, and the Management of Knowledge." *Educational Administration Quarterly* 16 (Spring, 1980), pp. 1–20.

Berger, Peter L. and Luckmann, Thomas. *The Social Construction of Reality: A Treatise in the Sociology of Knowledge.* New York: Doubleday, 1967.

Bernstein, Richard J. *Beyond Objectivism and Relativism: Science, Hermeneutics, and Praxis.* Philadelphia: University of Pennsylvania Press, 1983.

Bernstein, Richard J. *The New Constellation: The Ethical-Political Horizons of Modernity/Post-modernity.* Cambridge, Massachusetts: MIT Press, 1992.

Bloland, Harland G. "Higher Education and High Anxiety: Objectivism, Relativism, and Irony." *Journal of Higher Education* 60 (September/October, 1989), pp. 519–543.

Bloland, Harland G. "Interpretive Sociologies and the Study of Higher Education Organizations." *Review of Higher Education* 3 (Fall, 1979), pp. 1–14.

Bourdieu, Pierre. *Homo Academicus.* (Peter Collier, Trans.) Stanford, California: Stanford University Press, 1988.

Bourdieu, Pierre and Wacquant, Loic J.D. *An Invitation to Reflexive Sociology.* Chicago: University of Chicago Press, 1992.

Bruner, Jerome. *Acts of Meaning*. Cambridge, Massachusetts: Harvard University Press, 1990.

Bruner, Jerome. *Actual Minds, Possible Worlds*. Cambridge, Massachusetts: Harvard University Press, 1986.

Buchman, Margaret and Floden, Robert E. "Research Traditions, Diversity, and Progress." *Review of Educational Research* 59 (Summer, 1989), pp. 241–248.

Bulmer, Martin. *The Chicago School of Sociology: Institutionalization, Diversity, and the Rise of Sociological Research*. Chicago: University of Chicago Press, 1984.

Burbules, Nicholas C. and Rice, Suzanne. "Dialogue Across Differences: Continuing the Conversation." *Harvard Educational Review* 61 (November, 1991), pp. 393–416.

Burrell, Gibson. "Modernism, Postmodernism, and Organizational Analysis 2: The Contribution of Michel Foucault." *Organization Studies* 9 (1988), pp. 221–235.

Calinescu, Matei. *Five Faces of Modernity: Modernism, Avant-Garde, Decadence, Kitsch, and Postmodernism*. Durham, North Carolina: Duke University Press, 1987.

Capper, Colleen A. "Educational Administration in a Pluralistic Society: A Multiple Paradigm Approach." In *Educational Administration in a Pluralistic Society*, edited by Colleen A. Capper. Albany, New York: State University of New York Press, 1993.

Capper, Colleen A. "A Feminist Poststructural Analysis of Nontraditional Approaches in Educational Administration." *Educational Administration Quarterly* 28 (February, 1992), pp. 103–124.

Carr, Wilfred and Kemmis, Stephan. *Becoming Critical: Education, Knowledge, and Action Research*. London: Falmer Press, 1986.

Carspecken, Phil Francis and Apple, Michael. "Critical Qualitative Research: Theory, Methodology, and Practice." In *The Handbook of Qualitative Research in Education*, edited by Margaret D. LeCompte, Wendy L. Millroy, and Judith Preissle. San Diego: Academic Press, 1992, pp. 507–553.

Cherryholmes, Cleo H. *Power and Criticism: Poststructural Investigations in Education*. New York: Teachers College Press, 1988.

Collins, Patricia Hill. *Black Feminist Thought: Knowledge, Consciousness, and the Politics of Empowerment*. New York: Routledge, 1991.

Collins, Patricia Hill. "Learning from the Outsider Within: The Sociological Significance of Black Feminist Thought." *Social Problems* 33 (December, 1986), pp. S14–S32.

Conrad, Clifton F. "Meditations on the Ideology of Inquiry in Higher Education: Exposition, Critique, and Conjecture." Review of Higher *Education* 12 (Spring, 1989), pp. 199–220.

Cooper, Robert and Burrell, Gibson. "Modernism, Postmodernism, and Organizational Analysis: An Introduction." *Organization Studies* 9 (1988), pp. 91–112.

Corder, Jim W. and Baumlin, James S. "Opinion Is, Of Course, Bad; Research, On the Other Hand, Is Quite Good: The Tyranny (Or is it Myth?) of Methodology." *Journal of Higher Education* 58 (July/August, 1987), pp. 463–469.

Cott, Nancy F. *The Grounding of Modern Feminism*. New Haven, Connecticut: Yale University Press, 1987.

Denzin, Norman K. "Postmodern Social Theory." *Sociological Theory* 4 (Fall, 1986), pp. 194–204.

Denzin, Norman K. *Interpretive Interactionism*. Newbury Park, California: Sage, 1989.

Derrida, Jacques. *Positions*. (Alan Bass, Trans.) Chicago: University of Chicago Press, 1981.

DiMaggio, Paul J. and Powell, Walter W. "The Iron Cage Revisited: Institutional Isomophism and Collective Rationality in Organizational Fields." *American Sociological Review* 48 (April, 1983), pp. 147–160.

Donmoyer, Robert. "The Rescue from Relativism: Two Failed Attempts and an Alternative Strategy." *Educational Researcher* 14 (December, 1985), pp. 13–20.

Douglas, Jack D. (Ed.). *Understanding Everyday Life: Toward the Reconstruction of Sociological Knowledge*. Chicago: Aldine, 1970.

Douglas, Jack D. *Introduction to the Sociologies of Everyday Life*. Boston: Allyn and Bacon, 1980.

Eisner, Elliot W. and Peshkin, Alan (Eds.). *Qualitative Inquiry in Education: The Continuing Debate*. New York: Teachers College Press, 1990.

Ellsworth, Elizabeth. "Why Doesn't This Feel Empowering?: Working Through the Repressive Myths of Critical Pedagogy." *Harvard Educational Review* 59 (August, 1989), pp. 297–324.

Fay, Brian. *Critical Social Science: Liberation and Its Limits*. Ithaca, New York: Cornell University Press, 1987.

Feinberg, Walter. *Understanding Education: Toward a Reconstruction of Educational Inquiry*. New York: Cambridge University Press, 1983.

Feyerabend, Paul K. *Against Method: Outline of an Anarchistic Theory of Knowledge*. London: Verso, 1978.

Firestone, William A. "Meaning in Method: The Rhetoric of Quantitative and Qualitative Research." *Educational Researcher* 16 (October, 1987), pp. 16–21.

Flax, Jane. "Postmodernism and Gender Relations in Feminist Theory." *Signs* 12 (Summer, 1987), pp. 621–643.

Fonow, Mary Margaret and Cook, Judith A. (Eds.). *Beyond Methodology: Feminist Scholarship as Lived Research*. Bloomington, Indiana: Indiana University Press, 1991.

Foster, William P. "Administration and the Crisis of Legitimacy: A Review of Habermasian Thought." *Harvard Educational Review* 50 (November, 1980), pp. 496–505.

Foster, William P. "Toward a Critical Theory of Educational Administration." In *Leadership and Organizational Culture*, edited by Thomas J. Sergiovanni and John E. Corbally. Urbana, Illinois: University of Illinois Press, 1984, pp. 240–259.

Foucault, Michel. *Power/Knowledge: Selected Interviews and Other Writings*. (Colin Gordon, et al., Trans.). New York: Pantheon, 1980.

Fraser, Nancy and Nicholson, Linda. "Social Criticism Without Philosophy: An Encounter Between Feminism and Postmodernism." In *Universal Abandon?: The Politics of Postmodernism*, edited by Andrew Ross. Minneapolis: University of Minnesota Press, 1988, pp. 83–104.

Franzosa, Susan Douglas. "The Texture of Educational Inquiry: An Exploration of George Herbert Mead's Concept of the Scientific." *Journal of Education* 166 (Fall, 1984), pp. 254–272.

Gergen, Kenneth J. *The Saturated Self: Dilemmas of Identity in Contemporary Life*. New York: Basic Books, 1991.

Gilligan, Carol. *In a Different Voice: Psychological Theory and Women's Development*. Cambridge, Massachusetts: Harvard University Press, 1982.

Gilligan, Carol. "Remapping Development: The Power of Divergent Data." In *The Impact of Feminist Research in the Academy*, edited by Christie Farnham. Bloomington, Indiana: Indiana University Press, 1987, pp. 77–94.

Giola, Dennis A. and Pitre, Evelyn. "Multiparadigm Perspectives on Theory Building." *Academy of Management Review* 15 (October, 1990), pp. 584–602.

Giroux, Henry A. *Authority, Ethics, and the Politics of Schooling.* Minneapolis: University of Minnesota Press, 1988.

Giroux, Henry A. *Border Crossings: Cultural Workers and the Politics of Education.* New York: Routledge, 1992.

Giroux, Henry A. "Border Pedagogy in the Age of Postmodernism." *Journal of Education* 170 (Fall, 1988), pp. 162–181.

Giroux, Henry A. "The Politics of Postmodernism." *Journal of Urban and Cultural Studies* 1 (1990), pp. 5–37.

Giroux, Henry A. *Theory and Resistance in Education: A Pedagogy for the Opposition.* South Hadley, Massachusetts: Bergin and Garvey, 1983.

Gitlin, Andrew, Siegel, Marjorie, and Boru, Kevin. "The Politics of Method: From Leftist Ethnography to Educative Research." *International Journal for Qualitative Studies in Education* 2 (July/September, 1989), pp. 237–253.

Goffman, Erving. *Interaction Ritual: Essays on Face-to-Face Behavior.* New York: Pantheon Books, 1967.

Goffman, Erving. *The Presentation of Self in Everyday Life.* Garden City, New York: Doubleday, 1959.

Gordon, Beverly M. "The Necessity of African-American Epistemology for Educational Theory and Practice." *Journal of Education* 172 (Fall, 1990), pp. 88–105.

Gordon, Edmund W., Miller, Fayneese, and Rollock, David. "Coping with Communicentric Bias in Knowledge Production in the Social Sciences." *Educational Researcher* 19 (April, 1990), pp. 14–19.

Greenfield, T.B. "Theories of Educational Organization: A Critical Perspective." In *The International Encyclopedia of Education: Research and Studies* (Vol. 9), edited by Torsten Husen and T. Neville Postlethwaite. New York: Pergamon, 1985, pp. 5240–5251.

Guba, Egon G. "The Context of Emergent Paradigm Research." In *Organizational Theory and Inquiry: The Paradigm Revolution*, edited by Yvonna S. Lincoln. Beverly Hills, California: Sage, 1985, pp. 79–104.

Guba, Egon G. *The Paradigm Dialog.* Newbury Park, California: Sage, 1990.

Gumport, Patricia J. "Feminist Scholarship as a Vocation." *Higher Education* 20 (October, 1990), pp. 231–243.

Habermas, Jurgen. *The Theory of Communicative Action.* (Thomas McCarty, Trans.) Boston: Beacon, 1983.

Habermas, Jurgen. *Knowledge and Human Interests.* (Jeremy J. Shapiro, Trans.) Boston: Beacon Press, 1971.

Haraway, Donna. "Situated Knowledges: The Science Question in Feminism and the Privilege of Partial Perspective." *Feminist Studies* 14 (Fall, 1988), pp. 575–599.

Harding, Sandra. "After the Neutrality Ideal: Science, Politics, and 'Strong Objectivity'." *Social Research* 59 (Fall, 1992), pp. 567–587.

Harding, Sandra (Ed.). *Feminism and Methodology.* Bloomington, Indiana: Indiana University Press, 1987.

Harding, Sandra. *The Science Question in Feminism.* Ithaca, New York: Cornell University Press, 1986.

Harding, Sandra. *Whose Science? Whose Knowledge? Thinking from Women's Lives.* Ithaca, New York: Cornell University Press, 1991.

Hartsock, Nancy. "Rethinking Modernism: Minority vs. Majority Theories." *Cultural Critique 7* (Fall, 1987), pp. 187–206.

Harvey, David. *The Condition of Postmodernity: An Enquiry into the Origins of Cultural Change.* New York: Blackwell, 1989.

Hassard, John. "Multiple Paradigms and Organizational Analysis: A Case Study." *Organization Studies* 12 (1991), pp. 275–299.

Hawkesworth, Mary E. "Knowers, Knowing, Known: Feminist Theory and Claims of Truth." *Signs* 14 (Spring, 1989), pp. 533–557.

hooks, bell. "Culture to Culture: Ethnography and Cultural Studies as Critical Intervention." In *Yearning: Race, Gender, and Cultural Politics.* Boston, Massachusetts: South End Press, 1990, pp. 123–134.

hooks, bell. "Postmodern Blackness." In *Yearning: Race, Gender, and Cultural Politics.* Boston: South End Press, 1990, pp. 23–32.

hooks, bell. "Representations of Whiteness." In *Black Looks: Race and Representation.* Boston: South End Press, 1992, pp. 165–178.

hooks, bell. "Saving Black Folk Culture: Zora Neale Hurston as Anthropologist and Writer." In *Yearning: Race, Gender, and Cultural Politics.* Boston: South End Press, 1990, pp. 135–144.

Horkheimer, Max. *Critical Theory.* (Matthew J. O'Connell, Trans.) New York: Herder and Herder, 1972.

House, Ernest R. "Realism in Research." *Educational Researcher* 20 (August/September, 1991), pp. 2–9, 25.

Howe, Kenneth R. "Against the Qualitative-Quantitative Incompatibility Thesis or Dogmas Die Hard." *Educational Researcher* 17 (1988), pp. 10–16.

Howe, Kenneth and Eisenhart, Margaret. "Standards for Qualitative (and Quantitative) Research: A Prolegomenon." *Educational Researcher* 19 (May, 1990), pp. 2–9.

Howe, Kenneth R. "Two Dogmas in Educational Research." *Educational Researcher* 14 (October, 1985), pp. 10–18.

Jackson, Norman and Carter, Pippa. "In Defence of Paradigm Incommensurability." *Organization Studies* 12 (1991), pp. 109–127.

Jacob, Evelyn. "Qualitative Research Traditions: A Review." *Review of Educational Research 57* (Spring, 1987), pp. 1–50.

Jacob, Evelyn. "Clarifying Qualitative Research: A Focus on Traditions." *Educational Researcher* 17 (January/February, 1988), pp. 16–19, 22–24.

Jameson, Fredric. "Postmodernism or the Cultural Logic of Late Capitalism." *New Left Review* 146 (July/August, 1984), pp. 53–92.

Jayaratne, T.E. and Stewart, A. "Quantitative and Qualitative Methods in the Social Sciences: Current Feminist Issues and Practical Strategies." In *Beyond Methodology: Feminist Scholarship as Lived Research*, edited by Mary Margaret Fonow and Judith A. Cook. Bloomington, Indiana: Indiana University Press, 1991, pp. 85–106.

Keller, Evelyn Fox. *Reflections on Gender and Science*. New Haven, Connecticut: Yale University Press, 1985.

Keller, George. "Trees Without Fruit." *Change* 17 (January/February, 1985), pp. 7–10.

Kellner, Douglas. *Critical Theory, Marxism, and Modernity*. Baltimore, Maryland: Johns Hopkins University Press, 1989.

Lacan, Jacques. *Ecrits*. Paris: Editions du Sevil, 1966.

Lakoff, George and Johnson, Mark. *Metaphors We Live By*. Chicago: University of Chicago Press, 1980.

Lamphere, Louise. "Feminism and Anthropology: The Struggle to Reshape Our Thinking About Gender." In *The Impact of Feminist Research in the Academy*, edited by Christie Farnham. Bloomington, Indiana: Indiana University Press, 1987, pp. 11–33.

Lather, Patti. "Feminist Perspectives on Empowering Research Methodologies." *Women's Studies International Forum* 11 (November/December, 1988), pp. 569–581.

Lather, Patti. *Feminist Research in Education: Within/Against*. Victoria, Australia: Deakin University Press, 1991.

Lather, Patti. *Getting Smart: Feminist Research and Pedagogy With/In the Postmodern*. New York: Routledge, 1991.

Lather, Patti. "Research as Praxis." *Harvard Educational Review* 56 (August, 1986), pp. 257–277.

Lincoln, Yvonna S. "A Future-Oriented Comment on the State of the Profession." *Review of Higher Education* 10 (Winter, 1986), pp. 135–142.

Lincoln, Yvonna S. "The Substance of the Emergent Paradigm: Implications for Researchers." In *Organizational Theory and Inquiry: The Paradigm Revolution*, edited by Yvonna S. Lincoln. Beverly Hills, California: Sage, 1985, pp. 137–157.

Lincoln, Yvonna S. "Trouble in the Land: The Paradigm Revolution in the Academic Disciplines." In *Higher Education: Handbook of Theory and Research* (Vol. 5), edited by John C. Smart. New York: Agathon Press, 1989, pp. 57–133.

Liston, Daniel P. "Examining Marxist Explanations of Schools." *American Journal of Education* 96 (May, 1988), pp. 323–350.

Livingstone, David W. and Others. *Critical Pedagogy and Cultural Power*. South Hadley, Massachusetts: Bergin and Garvey, 1987.

Lyotard, Jean-Francois. *The Postmodern Condition: A Report on Knowledge*. Manchester, England: Manchester University Press, 1984.

MacKinnon, Catherine A. "Feminism, Marxism, Method, and the State: Toward Feminist Jurisprudence." *Signs* 8 (Summer, 1983), pp. 635–658.

Mascia-Lees, Frances E., Sharpe, Patricia, and Cohen, Colleen Ballerina. "The Postmodernist Turn in Anthropology: Cautions from a Feminist Perspective." *Signs* 15 (Autumn, 1989), pp. 7–33.

Manicas, Peter T. and Secord, Paul F. "Implications for Psychology of the New Philosophy of Science." *American Psychologist* 38 (April, 1983), pp. 399–413.

Marcus, George E. and Fisher, Michael M. J. *Anthropology as Cultural Critique: An Experimental Moment in the Human Sciences*. Chicago: University of Chicago Press, 1986.

Marshall, Margaret and Barritt, Loren. "Choices Made, Worlds Created: The Rhetoric of AERJ." *American Educational Research Journal* 27 (Winter, 1990), pp. 589–609.

Martin, Joanne. "Deconstructing Organizational Taboos: The Suppression of Gender Conflicts in Organization." *Organization Science* 1 (November, 1990), pp. 339–359.

Mead, George Herbert. *Mind, Self, and Society*, edited by Charles W. Morris. Chicago: University of Chicago Press, 1962.

Meisenhelder, Thomas. "Habermas and Feminism: The Future of Critical Theory." In *Feminism and Sociological Theory*, edited by Ruth A. Wallace. Newbury Park, California: Sage, 1989, pp. 119–132.

Merton, Robert K. "Insiders and Outsiders: A Chapter in the Sociology of Knowledge." *American Journal of Sociology* 78 (July, 1972), pp. 9–47.

Meyer, John W. and Rowan, Brian. "Institutionalized Organizations: Formal Structure as Myth and Ceremony." *American Journal of Sociology* 83 (September, 1977), pp. 340–363.

Milam, John H., Jr. "The Presence of Paradigms in the Core Higher Education Journal Literature." *Research in Higher Education* 32 (August, 1991), pp. 651–668.

Milam, John H., Jr. "Using Alternative Paradigms: Four Case Studies." In *Higher Education: Handbook of Theory and Research* (Vol. 8), edited by John C. Smart. New York: Agathon Press, 1992, pp. 305–344.

Miller, Steven I. and Fredericks, Marcel. "Postpositivistic Assumptions and Educational Research: Another View." *Educational Researcher* 20 (May, 1991), pp. 2–8.

Mills, C. Wright. *The Sociological Imagination*. New York: Oxford University Press, 1959.

Minnich, Elizabeth K. *Transforming Knowledge*. Philadelphia: Temple University Press, 1990.

Nicholson, Linda J. (Ed.). *Feminism/Postmodernism*. New York: Routledge, 1990.

Nielsen, Joyce McCarl (Ed.). *Feminist Research Methods*. Boulder, Colorado: Westview Press, 1990.

Peshkin, Alan. "From Title to Title: The Evolution of Perspective in Naturalistic Inquiry." *Anthropology and Education Quarterly* 16 (1985), pp. 214–224.

Phillips, D.C. "After the Wake: Postpositivistic Educational Thought." *Educational Researcher* 12 (May, 1983), pp. 4–12.

Phillips, Denis Charles. *Philosophy, Science, and Social Inquiry: Contemporary Methodological Controversies in Social Science and Related Applied Fields of Research*. New York: Pergamon, 1987.

Popkewitz, Thomas S. *Paradigm and Ideology in Educational Research: The Social Functions of the Intellectual*. New York: Falmer Press, 1984.

Poster, Mark. *Critical Theory and Poststructuralism: In Search of a Context*. Ithaca, New York: Cornell University Press, 1989.

Rabinow, Paul and Sullivan, William M. (Eds.). *Interpretive Social Science: A Reader*. Berkeley, California: University of California Press, 1979.

Reason, Peter (Ed.). *Human Inquiry in Action: Developments in New Paradigm Research*. London: Sage, 1988.

Reason, Peter and Rowan, John (Eds.). *Human Inquiry: A Sourcebook of New Paradigm Research*. New York: John Wiley, 1981.

Reiter, Rayna R. *Toward an Anthropology of Women*. New York: Monthly Review Press, 1975.

Roberts, Helen (Ed.). *Doing Feminist Research*. Boston: Routledge and Kegan Paul, 1981.

Rosaldo, Renato. *Culture and Truth: The Remaking of Social Analysis*. Boston: Beacon Press, 1989.

Rosenau, Pauline Marie. *Post-Modernism and the Social Sciences: Insights, Inroads, and Intrusions*. Princeton, New Jersey: Princeton University Press, 1992.

Ross, Andrew. "Introduction." In *Universal Abandon?: The Politics of Postmodernism*, edited by Andrew Ross. Minneapolis: University of Minnesota Press, 1988, pp. vii–xviii.

Sandoval, Chela. "U.S. Third World Feminism: The Theory and Method of Oppositional Consciousness in the Postmodern World." *Genders* 10 (Spring, 1991), pp. 1–24.

Schrag, Francis. "In Defense of Positivist Research Paradigms." *Educational Researcher* 21 (June/July, 1992), pp. 5–8.

Schutz, Alfred. *The Phenomenology of the Social World*. Evanston, Illinois: Northwestern University Press, 1967.

Schwandt, Thomas A. "Solutions to the Paradigm Conflict: Coping with Uncertainty." *Journal of Contemporary Ethnography* 17 (January, 1989), pp. 379–407.

Scott, Joan W. "Deconstructing Equality-Versus-Difference or the Uses of Poststructuralist Theory for Feminism." *Feminist Studies* 14 (Spring, 1988), pp. 33–50.

Sirotnik, Kenneth A. and Oakes, Jeannie (Eds.). *Critical Perspectives on the Organization and Improvement of Schooling*. Boston: Kluwer-Nijhoff, 1986.

Smart, Barry. *Foucault, Marxism, and Critique*. London: Routledge and Kegan Paul, 1983.

Smith, Dorothy E. "The Everyday World as Problematic: A Feminist Methodology." In *The Everyday World as Problematic: A Feminist Sociology*. Boston: Northeastern University Press, 1987, pp. 105–145.

Smith, Dorothy E. "Institutional Ethnography: A Feminist Research Strategy." In *The Everyday World as Problematic: A Feminist Sociology*. Boston: Northeastern University Press, 1987, pp. 151–179.

Smith, Dorothy E. "Women's Perspective as a Radical Critique of Sociology." *Sociological Inquiry* 44 (1974), pp. 7–13.

Smith, David. "The Limits of Positivism in Social Work Research." *British Journal of Social Work* 17 (August, 1987), pp. 401–416.

Smith, John K. and Heshusius, Lous. "Closing Down the Conversation: The End of the Quantitative-Qualitative Debate Among Educational Inquirers." *Educational Researcher* 15 (January, 1986), pp. 4–12.

Smith, John K. "Quantitative versus Qualitative: An Attempt to Clarify the Issue." *Educational Researcher* 12 (March, 1983), pp. 6–13.

Smyth, John (Ed.). *Critical Perspectives on Educational Leadership*. London: Falmer, 1989.

Stacey, Judith. "Can there be a Feminist Ethnography?" *Women's Studies International* 11 (January/February, 1988), pp. 21–27.

Tetrault, Mary Kay. "Feminist Phase Theory." *Journal of Higher Education* 56 (July/August, 1985), pp. 363–384.

Thelin, John R. "The Search for Good Research: Looking for 'Science' in All the Wrong Places." *Review of Higher Education* 10 (Winter, 1986), pp. 151–158.

Tierney, William C. (Ed.). *Culture and Ideology in Higher Education: Advancing a Critical Agenda.* New York: Praeger, 1991.

Tierney, William G. "Facts and Constructs: Defining Reality in Higher Education Organizations." *Review of Higher Education* 11 (Autumn, 1987), pp. 61–73.

Tierney, William G. and Rhoads, Robert A. "Postmodernism and Critical Theory in Higher Education: Implications for Research and Practice." In *Higher Education: Handbook of Theory and Research* (Vol. 9), edited by John C. Smart. New York: Agathon Press, 1993.

Townsend, Barbara. "Feminist Scholarship in Core Higher Education Journals: Where Art Thou? *Review of Higher Education,* in press.

Twombley, Susan. "New Directions for Studying Women in Higher Education: Lessons from Feminist Phase Theory." *Initiatives* 54 (Spring, 1991), pp. 9–17.

Tyler, Stephen A. *The Unspeakable: Discourse, Dialogue, and Rhetoric in the Postmodern World.* Madison, Wisconsin: University of Wisconsin Press, 1987.

Warren, Carol A.B. *Gender Issues in Field Research.* Beverly Hills, California: Sage, 1988.

Weber, Max. "Science as a Vocation." In *From Max Weber: Essays in Sociology,* translated and edited by Hans Heinrich Gerth and C. Wright Mills. New York: Oxford University Press, 1946, pp. 129–156.

Weedon, Chris. *Feminist Practice and Poststructuralist Theory.* New York: Basil Blackwell, 1987.

Wertsch, James V. *Voices of the Mind: A Sociocultural Approach to Mediated Action.* Cambridge, Massachusetts: Harvard University Press, 1991.

West, Cornel. "Philosophy and the Afro-American Experience." *Philosophical Forum,* 9 (Winter/Spring, 1977–78), pp. 117–148.

Witherell, Carol and Noddings, Nel (Eds.). *Stories Lives Tell: Narrative and Dialogue in Education.* New York: Teachers College Press, 1991.

Yeakey, Carol Camp, Johnston, Gladys Styles, and Atkinson, Judith A. "In Pursuit of Equity: A Review of the Literature on Minorities and Women in Education." *Educational Administration Quarterly* 22 (Summer, 1986), pp. 110–149.

II.   Approaching Inquiry: Methods and Techniques

A. Methods and Techniques

Agar, Michael H. *The Professional Stranger: An Informal Introduction to Ethnography.* New York: Academic Press, 1980.

Agar, Michael H. *Speaking of Ethnography.* Beverly Hills, California: Sage, 1986.

Atkinson, Paul. *The Ethnographic Imagination: Textual Constructs of Reality.* London: Routledge, 1990.

Baldwin, Roger G. and Thelin, John R. "Thanks for the Memories: The Fusion of Quantitative and "Qualitative Research on College Students and the College Experience." In *Higher Education: Handbook of Theory and Research* (Vol. 6), edited by John C. Smart. New York: Agathon Press, 1990, pp. 337–360.

Becker, Howard S. "Problems of Inference and Proof in Participant Observation." In *Sociological Work: Method and Substance*, edited by Howard S. Becker. Chicago: Aldine, 1970, pp. 25–38.

Beekman, Ton. "Stepping Inside: On Participant Experience and Bodily Presence in the Field." *Journal of Education* 168 (Fall, 1986), pp. 39–45.

Bernard, H. Russell. *Research Methods in Cultural Anthropology*. Beverly Hills, California: Sage, 1988.

Bogdan, Robert C. and Biklen, Sari Knopp. *Qualitative Research for Education: An Introduction to Theory and Methods*. Boston: Allyn and Bacon, 1992.

Campbell, Donald T. "'Degrees of Freedom' and the Case Study." In Qualitative *and Quantitative Methods in Evaluation Research*, edited by Thomas D. Cook and Charles S. Reichardt. Beverly Hills, California: Sage, 1979, pp. 49–67.

Chambers, Erve. *Applied Anthropology: A Practical Guide*. Prospect Heights, Illinois: Waveland Press, 1989.

Charmaz, Kathy. "The Grounded Theory Method: An Explication and Interpretation." In *Contemporary Field Research*, edited by Robert M. Emerson. Boston: Little, Brown, 1983, pp. 109–126.

Coe, David E. "Levels of Knowing in Ethnographic Inquiry." *International Journal of Qualitative Studies in Education* 14 (October/ December, 1991), pp. 313–331.

Connelly, F. Michael and Clandinin, D. Jean. "Stories of Experience and Narrative Inquiry." *Educational Researcher* 19 (June/July, 1990), pp. 2–14.

Connidis, Ingrid. "Integrating Qualitative and Quantitative Methods in Survey Research on Aging: An Assessment." *Qualitative Sociology* 6 (Winter, 1983), pp. 334–352.

Cooper, Joanne E. "Telling Our Own Stories: The Reading and Writing of Journals or Diaries." In *Stories Lives Tell: Narrative and Dialogue in Education*, edited by Carol Witherell and Nell Noddings. New York: Teachers College Press, 1991, pp. 96–112.

Conrad, Clifton F. "Grounded Theory: An Alternative Approach to Research in Higher Education." *Review of Higher Education* 5 (Fall, 1982), pp. 239–249.

Corbin, Juliet and Strauss, Anselm. "Grounded Theory Research: Procedures, Canons, and Evaluative Criteria." *Qualitative Sociology* 13 (Spring, 1990), pp. 3–21.

Crowson, Robert L. "Qualitative Research Methods in Higher Education." In *Higher Education: Handbook of Theory and Research* (Vol. 3), edited by John C. Smart. New York: Agathon Press, 1987, pp. 1–56.

Denzin, Norman K. *The Research Act: A Theoretical Introduction to Sociological Methods*. Chicago: Aldine, 1970.

Dobbert, Marion Lundy. *Ethnographic Research: Theory and Application for Modern Schools and Societies*. New York: Praeger, 1984.

Eisner, Elliot W. *The Educational Imagination: On the Design and Evaluation of School Programs*. New York: Macmillan, 1985.

Eisner, Elliot W. *The Enlightened Eye: Qualitative Inquiry and the Enhancement of Educational Practice.* New York: Macmillan, 1991.

Eisner, Elliot W. "On the Differences between Scientific and Artistic Approaches to Qualitative Research." *Educational Researcher* 10 (April, 1981), pp. 5–9.

Ely, Margot, Anzul, Margaret, Friedman, Teri, Garner, Diane, and Steinmetz, Ann McCormack. *Doing Qualitative Research: Circles Within Circles.* New York: Falmer, 1991.

Emerson, Robert M. (Ed.). *Contemporary Field Research.* Boston: Little, Brown, 1983.

Erickson, Frederick. "Qualitative Methods in Research on Teaching." In *Handbook of Research on Teaching* (3rd Ed.), edited by Merlin C. Wittrock. New York: Macmillan, 1985, pp. 119–161.

Erickson, Frederick. "Some Approaches to Inquiry in School-Community Ethnography." *Anthropology and Education Quarterly* 8 (May, 1977), pp. 58–69.

Erickson, Frederick. "What Makes School Ethnography 'Ethnographic?'" *Anthropology and Education Quarterly* 15 (Spring, 1984), pp. 51–66.

Faraday, Annabel and Plummer, Kenneth. "Doing Life Histories." *Sociological Review* 27 (November, 1979), pp. 773–798.

Fetterman, David M. *Ethnography: Step by Step.* Newbury Park, California: Sage, 1989.

Fetterman, David M. "Ethnography in Educational Research: The Dynamics of Diffusion." *Educational Researcher* 11 (March, 1982), pp. 17–22, 29.

Fetterman, David M. *Using Qualitative Methods in Institutional Research.* San Francisco: Jossey-Bass, 1991.

Fielding, Nigel G. and Lee, Raymond M. (Eds.). *Using Computers in Qualitative Research.* Newbury Park, California: Sage, 1991.

Fox, Mary Frank and Faver, Catherine A. "Independence and Cooperation in Research: The Motivations and Costs of Collaboration." *Journal of Higher Education* 55 (May/June, 1984), pp. 347–359.

Garfinkel, Harold. *Studies in Ethnomethodology.* Englewood Cliffs, New Jersey: Prentice-Hall, 1967.

Geertz, Clifford. "Thick Description: Toward an Interpretive Theory of Culture." In *The Interpretation of Cultures*, edited by Clifford Geertz. New York: Basic Books, 1973, pp. 3–30.

Geiger, Susan. "Women's Life Histories: Method and Content." *Signs* 11 (Winter, 1986), pp. 344–351.

Gitlin, Andrew David. "Educative Research, Voice, and School Change." *Harvard Educational Review* 60 (November, 1990), pp. 443–466.

Glaser, Barney G. and Strauss, Anselm L. *The Discovery of Grounded Theory: Strategies for Qualitative Research.* Chicago: Aldine, 1967.

Glesne, Corrine and Peshkin, Alan. *Becoming Qualitative Researchers: An Introduction.* White Plains, New York: Longman, 1992.

Goetz, Judith P. and LeCompte, Margaret D. *Ethnography and Qualitative Design in Educational Research.* Orlando, Florida: Academic Press, 1984.

Goodchild, Lester F. and Huk, Irene Pancner. "The American College History: A Survey of Its Historiographic Schools and Analytic Approaches from the Mid-Nineteenth Century to the

Present." In *Higher Education: Handbook of Theory and Research* (Vol. 6), edited by John C. Smart. New York: Agathon Press, 1987, pp. 201–290.

Hammersley, Martyn and Atkinson, Paul. *Ethnography: Principles in Practice*. London: Tavistock Publications, 1983.

Herriott, Robert E. and Firestone, William A. "Multisite Qualitative Policy Research: Optimizing Description and Generalizability." *Educational Researcher* 12 (February, 1983), pp. 14–19.

Jaeger, Richard M. (Ed.). *Complementary Methods for Research in Education*. Washington, D.C.: American Educational Research Association, 1988.

Kaestle, Carl F. "Recent Methodological Developments in the History of American Education." In *Complementary Methods for Research in Education*, edited by Richard M. Jaeger. Washington, D.C.: American Educational Research Association, 1988, pp. 61–73.

Kincheloe, Joe L. "Educational Historiographical Meta-Analysis: Rethinking Methodology in the 1990s." *International Journal of Qualitative Studies in Education* 4 (July/September, 1991), pp. 231–245.

Kuh, George D. "Assessing Student Cultures." In *Assessing Academic Climates and Cultures: New Directions for Institutional Research*, edited by William G. Tierney. San Francisco: Jossey-Bass, 1990, pp. 47–60.

Kuh, George D. and Andreas, Rosalind E. "It's About Time: Using Qualitative Methods in Student Life Studies." *Journal of College Student Development* 32 (September, 1991), pp. 397–405.

Lancy, David F. *Qualitative Research in Education: An Introduction to the Major Traditions*. New York: Longman, 1993.

Light, Richard J., Singer, Judith D., and Willet, John H. *By Design: Planning Research on Higher Education*. Cambridge, Massachusetts: Harvard University Press, 1990.

Lincoln, Yvonna S. and Guba, Egon G. *Naturalistic Inquiry*. Beverly Hills, California: Sage, 1985.

Lofland, John. *Analyzing Social Settings: A Guide to Qualitative Observation and Analysis*. Belmont, California: Wadsworth, 1971.

MacKay, Kathleen A. and Schuh, John H. "Practical Issues Associated with Qualitative Research Methods." *Journal of College Student Development* 32 (September, 1991), pp. 424–432.

Majchrzak, Ann. *Methods for Policy Research*. Beverly Hills, California: Sage, 1984.

Marshall, Catherine and Rossman, Gretchen B. *Designing Qualitative Research*. Newbury Park, California: Sage, 1989.

McCall, George J. and Simmons, J. L. (Eds.). *Issues in Participant Observation*. Reading, Massachusetts: Addison-Wesley, 1969.

McPhee, Robert D. "Alternative Approaches to Integrating Longitudinal Case Studies." *Organization Science* 1 (November, 1990), pp. 393–405.

Merriam, Sharan B. *Case Study Research in Education: A Qualitative Approach*. San Francisco: Jossey-Bass, 1988.

Merton, Robert King, Fiske, Marjorie, and Kendal, Patricia L. *The Focused Interview: A Manual of Problems and Procedures*. New York: Free Press, 1990.

Miles, Matthew B. "New Methods for Qualitative Data Collection and Analysis: Vignettes and Pre-structured Cases." *International Journal of Qualitative Studies in Education* 3 (January/March, 1990), pp. 37–51.

Mitchell, Jack N. "An Exchange of Communication: Permanence and Change in the Ethnomethodology of Harold Garfinkel." In *Social Exchange, Dramaturgy, and Ethnomethodology: Toward a Paradigmatic Synthesis*. New York: Elsevier, 1978, pp. 130–159.

Morgan, Gareth. *Beyond Method: Strategies for Social Research*. Beverly Hills, California: Sage, 1983.

Nelson, Linda Williamson. "Code-Switching in the Oral Life Narratives of African-American Women: Challenges to Linguistic Hegemony." *Journal of Education* 172 (Fall, 1990), pp. 142-155.

Ogbu, John. "School Ethnography: A Multilevel Approach." *Anthropology and Education Quarterly* 12 (Spring, 1981), pp. 3-29.

Patton, Michael Quinn. *Qualitative Evaluation and Research Methods*. Newbury Park, California: Sage, 1990.

Patton, Michael J. "Qualitative Research on College Students: Philosophical and Methodological Comparisons with the Quantitative Approach." *Journal of College Student Development* 32 (September, 1991), pp. 389-396.

Pettigrew, Andrew M. "On Studying Organizational Cultures." *Administrative Science Quarterly* 24 (December, 1979), 570-581.

Polkinghorne, D. *Methodology for the Human Sciences: Systems of Inquiry*. Albany, New York: State University of New York Press, 1983.

Reinharz, Shulamit. *Feminist Methods in Social Science Research*. New York: Oxford University Press, 1992.

Reinharz, Shulamit. *On Becoming a Social Scientist: From Survey Research and Participant Observation to Experiential Analysis*. New Brunswick, New Jersey: Transaction Publishers, 1991.

Rist, Ray C. "Blitzkrieg Ethnography: On the Transformation of a Method into a Movement." *Educational Researcher* 9 (February, 1980), pp. 8-10.

Salomon, Gavriel. "Transcending the Qualitative-Quantitative Debate: Analytic and Systemic Approaches to Educational Research." *Educational Researcher* 20 (August/September, 1991), pp. 10–18.

Sanday, Peggy Reeves. "The Ethnographic Paradigm(s)." *Administrative Science Quarterly* 24 (December, 1979), pp. 527–538.

Schatzman, Leonard and Strauss, Anselm L. *Field Research: Strategies for a Natural Sociology*. Englewood Cliffs, New Jersey: Prentice-Hall, 1973.

Schulman, Judith H. "Now You See Them, Now You Don't: Anonymity Versus Visibility in Case Studies of Teachers." *Educational Researcher* 19 (August/September, 1990), pp. 11–15.

Schwartz, Gary and Merten, Don. "Participant Observation and the Discovery of Meaning." *Philosophy of the Social Sciences* 1 (1971), pp. 279–298.

Schwartz, Howard and Jacobs, Jerry. *Qualitative Sociology: A Method to the Madness*. New York: Free Press, 1979.

Scott, M.M. "Naturalistic Research: Applications for Research and Professional Practice with College Students." *Journal of College Student Development* 32 (September, 1991), pp. 416–423.

Shaffir, William B. and Stebbins, Robert A. (Eds.). *Experiencing Fieldwork: An Inside View of Qualitative Research*. Newbury Park, California: Sage, 1991.

Sharp, Rachel. "Self-Contained Ethnography or a Science of Phenomenal Forms and Inner Relations." *Journal of Education* 164 (Winter, 1982), pp. 48–63.

Skrtic, Thomas M. "Doing Naturalistic Research into Educational Organizations." In *Organizational Theory and Inquiry: The Paradigm Revolution*, edited by Yvonna S. Lincoln. Beverly Hills, California: Sage, 1985, pp. 185–220.

Smith, Allen G. and Robbins, Albert E. "Structured Ethnography." *American Behavioral Scientist* 26 (September/October, 1982), pp. 45–61.

Smith, Carolyn D. and Kornblum, William (Eds.). *In the Field: Readings on the Field Research Experience*. New York: Praeger, 1989.

Spindler, George (Ed.). *Doing the Ethnography of Schooling: Educational Anthropology in Action*. New York: Holt, Rinehart, and Winston, 1982.

Spindler, George and Spindler, Louise. *Interpretive Ethnography of Education: At Home and Abroad*. Hillsdale, New Jersey: Erlbaum, 1987.

Spradley, James P. and McCurdy, David W. *The Cultural Experience: Ethnography in a Complex Society*. Chicago: Science Research Associates, 1972.

Spradley, James P. *Participant Observation*. New York: Holt, Rinehart, and Winston, 1980.

Stage, Frances (Ed.). *Flexibility in Assessing and Conducting Research on College Students*. Alexandria, Virginia: ACPA Media, 1992.

Stake, Robert E. "Case Study Methods in Educational Research: Seeking Sweet Water." In *Complementary Methods for Research in Education*, edited by Richard M. Jaeger. Washington, D.C.: American Educational Research Association, 1988, pp. 253–269.

Stewart, David W. and Shamdasani, Prem N. *Focus Groups: Theory and Practice*. Newbury Park, California: Sage, 1990.

Taylor, Steven J. and Bogdan, Robert. *Introduction to Qualitative Research and Methods: The Search for Meaning*. New York: Wiley, 1984.

Thompson, Paul R. *The Voice of the Past: Oral History*. Oxford: Oxford University Press, 1988.

Tierney, William G. (Ed.). *Assessing Academic Climates and Cultures*. San Francisco: Jossey-Bass, 1990.

Tierney, William G. "Ethnography: An Alternative Evaluation Methodology." *Review of Higher Education* 8 (Winter, 1985), pp. 93–105.

Van Maanen, John. *Qualitative Methodology*. Beverly Hills, California: Sage, 1983.

Van Maanen, John, Dabbs, James M., Jr., and Faulkner, Robert R. *Varieties of Qualitative Research*. Beverly Hills, California: Sage, 1982.

Wax, Rosalie H. *Doing Fieldwork: Warnings and Advice*. Chicago: University of Chicago Press, 1971.

Werner, Oswald and Fenton, Joann. "Method and Theory in Ethnoscience or Ethnoepistemology." In *A Handbook of Method in Cultural Anthropology*, edited by Raoul Naroll and Ronald Cohen. New York: Columbia University Press, 1970, pp. 537–578.

Whitt, Elizabeth J. "Artful Science: A Primer on Qualitative Research." *Journal of College Student Development* 32 (September, 1991), pp. 406–415.

Whitt, Elizabeth J. and Kuh, George D. "Qualitative Methods in a Team Approach to Multiple-Institution Studies." *Review of Higher Education* 14 (Spring, 1991), pp. 317–338.

Whyte, William Foote (Ed.). *Participatory Action Research.* Newbury Park, California: Sage, 1991.

Wilson, Stephen. "The Use of Ethnographic Techniques in Educational Research." *Review of Educational Research* 47 (Winter, 1977), pp. 245–265.

Wolcott, Harry F. "Ethnographic Research in Education." In *Complementary Methods for Research in Education,* edited by Richard M. Jaeger. Washington, D.C.: American Educational Research Association, 1988, pp. 187–210.

Yin, Robert K. *Case Study Research: Design and Methods.* Newbury Park, California: Sage, 1988.

B.   Interviewing

Bradburn, Norman M., Sudman, Seymour, and Others. *Improving Interview Method and Questionnaire Design.* San Francisco: Jossey-Bass, 1979.

Briggs, Charles L. *Learning How to Ask: A Sociolinguistic Appraisal of the Role of the Interview in Social Science Research.* Cambridge, England: Cambridge University Press, 1986.

DeVault, Marjorie L. "Talking and Listening from Women's Standpoint: Feminist Strategies for Interviewing and Analysis." *Social Problems* 37 (February, 1990), pp. 96–116.

Dexter, Lewis Anthony. *Elite and Specialized Interviewing.* Evanston, Illinois: Northwestern University Press, 1970.

Fitchen, Janet M. "How Do You Know What To Ask If You Haven't Listened First?: Using Anthropological Methods to Prepare for Survey Research." *Rural Sociologist* 10 (Spring, 1990), pp. 15–22.

Gordon, Raymond L. *Interviewing: Strategy, Techniques, and Tactics.* Homewood, Illinois: Dorsey Press, 1975.

Krueger, Richard A. *Focus Groups: A Practical Guide for Applied Research.* Newbury Park, California: Sage, 1988.

Kvale, S. "The Qualitative Research Interview: A Phenomenological and Hermenuetical Mode of Understanding." *Journal of Phenomenological Psychology* 14 (1983), pp. 171–196.

McCracken, Grant. *The Long Interview.* Beverly Hills, California: Sage, 1988.

Measnor, Lynda. "Interviewing: A Strategy in Qualitative Research." In *Strategies of Educational Research: Qualitative Methods,* edited by Robert G. Burgess. New York: Falmer Press, 1985, pp. 55–78.

Mishler, Elliot G. *Research Interviewing: Context and Narrative.* Cambridge, Massachusetts: Harvard University Press, 1986.

Morgan, David L. *Focus Groups as Qualitative Research.* Newbury Park, California: Sage, 1988.

Oakley, Ann. "Interviewing Women: A Contradiction in Terms." In *Doing Feminist Research,* edited by Helen Roberts. London: Routledge and Kegan Paul, 1981, pp. 30–61.

Patton, Michael Quinn. "Qualitative Interviewing." In *Qualitative Evaluation and Research Methods.* Newbury Park, California: Sage, 1990, pp. 277–359.

Pope, Maureen and Denicolo, Pam. "Intuitive Theories—a Researcher's Dilemma: Some Practical Methodological Implications." *British Education Research Journal* 12 (1986), pp. 153–166.

Seidman, I.E. *Interviewing as Qualitative Research: A Guide for Researchers in Education and the Social Sciences.* New York: Teachers College Press, 1991.

Snow, David A., Zurcher, Louis A., and Sjoberg, Gideon. "Interviewing by Comment: An Adjunct to the Direct Question." *Qualitative Sociology* 5 (Winter, 1982), pp. 285–311.

Spradley, James P. *The Ethnographic Interview.* New York: Holt, Rinehart and Winston, 1979.

Whyte, William Foote. "Interviewing in Field Research." In *Human Organization Research: Field Relations and Techniques,* edited by Richard Adams and Jack J. Preiss. Homewood, Illinois: Dorsey Press, 1960, pp. 352–373.

C.   Documents, Photographs, Statistics, and Other Quantitative Data

Altheide, David L. "Ethnographic Content Analysis." *Qualitative Sociology* 10 (Spring, 1987), pp. 65–77.

Andrew, Alison. "In Pursuit of the Past: Some Problems in the Collection, Analysis, and Use of Historical Documentary Data." In *Strategies of Educational Research: Qualitative Methods,* edited by Robert Burgess. New York: Falmer Press, 1985, pp. 153–178.

Ball, Michael S. and Smith, Gregory W. H. *Analyzing Visual Data.* Newbury Park, California: Sage, 1992.

Hughes, Everett C. "The 'Gleichschaltung' of the German Statistical Yearbook: A Case in Professional Neutrality." In *Men and Their Work.* Glencoe, Illinois: Free Press, 1958, pp. 145–156.

Purvis, Jane. "Reflections Upon Doing Historical Documentary Research from a Feminist Perspective." In *Strategies of Educational Research: Qualitative Methods,* edited by Robert Burgess. New York: Falmer Press, 1985, pp. 179–206.

Schwartz, Dona. "Visual Ethnography: Using Photography in Qualitative Research." *Qualitative Sociology* 12 (Summer, 1989), pp. 119–154. Thelin, John R. and Townsend, Barbara K. "Fiction to Fact: College Novels and the Study of Higher Education." In *Higher Education: Handbook of Theory and Research* (Vol. 4), edited by John C. Smart. New York: Agathon Press, 1988, pp. 183–211.

Webb, Eugene J., Campbell, Donald T., Schwartz, Richard D., and Sechrest, Lee. *Unobtrusive Measures: Nonreactive Research in the Social Sciences.* Chicago: Rand McNally, 1966.

Whitt, Elizabeth J. "Document Analysis." In *Flexibility in Assessing and Conducting Research on College Students,* edited by Frances Stage. Alexandria, Virginia: ACPA Media, 1992.

III.   Doing Fieldwork: Data Collection and Analysis

Ball, Michael S. and Smith, Gregory W. *Analyzing Visual Data.* Newbury Park, California: Sage, 1992.

Bogdan, Robert C. and Biklen, Sari Knopp. "Data Analysis." In *Qualitative Research for Education: An Introduction to Theory and Methods.* Boston: Allyn and Bacon, 1992, pp. 153–183.

Clark, Christopher M. "Computer Storage and Manipulations of Field Notes and Verbal Protocols: Three Cautions. *Anthropology and Education Quarterly* 18 (1987), pp. 56–58.

Conrad, Peter and Reinharz, Shulamit (Eds.). "Special Issue: Computers and Qualitative Data." *Qualitative Sociology* 7 (Spring/Summer, 1984).

Constas, Mark A. "Qualitative Analysis as a Public Event: The Documentation of Category Development Procedures." *American Educational Research Journal* 29 (Summer, 1992), pp. 253–266.

Fetterman, David M. "A Wilderness Guide: Methods and Techniques." In *Ethnography: Step by Step.* Newbury Park, California: Sage, 1989, pp. 41–72.

Fetterman, David M. "Finding Your Way Through the Forest: Analysis." In *Ethnography: Step by Step.* Newbury Park, California: Sage, 1989, pp. 88–103.

Fielding, Nigel G. and Lee, Raymond M. (Eds.). *Using Computers in Qualitative Research.* Newbury Park, California: Sage, 1991.

Glesne, Corrine and Peshkin, Alan. "Finding Your Story: Data Analysis." In *Becoming Qualitative Researchers: An Introduction.* White Plains, New York: Longman, 1992, pp. 127–149.

Goetz, Judith P. and LeCompte, Margaret D. "Ethnographic Research and the Problem of Data Reduction." *Anthropology and Education Quarterly* 12 (Spring, 1981), pp. 51–70.

Guba, Egon G. and Lincoln, Yvonna S. *Effective Evaluation.* San Francisco: Jossey-Bass, 1981.

Hammersley, Martyn, and Atkinson, Paul. "Recording and Organizing Data." In *Ethnography: Principles and Practice.* London: Tavistock Publications, 1983, pp. 144–173.

Holsti, Ole R. *Content Analysis for the Social Sciences and Humanities.* Reading, Massachusetts: Addison-Wesley, 1969.

Huberman, Michael and Matthew, Miles. "Some Procedures for Causal Analysis of Multiple-Case Data." *International Journal of Qualitative Studies in Education* 2 (January/March, 1989), pp. 55–68.

Lareau, Annette. "Common Problems in Field Work: A Personal Essay." In *Home Advantage: Social Class and Parental Intervention in Elementary Education.* New York: Falmer Press, 1989, pp. 187–223.

McCutcheon, Gail. "On the Interpretation of Classroom Observations." *Educational Researcher* 10 (May, 1981), pp. 5–10.

Miles, Matthew B. "Qualitative Data as an Attractive Nuisance: The Problem of Analysis." In *Qualitative Methodology,* edited by John Van Maanen. Beverly Hills, California: Sage, 1983, pp. 117–134.

Miles, Matthew B. and Huberman, A. Michael. *Qualitative Data Analysis: A Sourcebook of New Methods.* Beverly Hills, California: Sage, 1984.

Mishler, Elliot G. "Validation in Inquiry-Guided Research: The Role of Exemplars in Narrative Studies." *Harvard Educational Review* 60 (November, 1990), pp. 415–442.

Padilla, Raymond V. "Using Computers to Develop Concept Models of Social Situations." *Qualitative Sociology* 14 (Fall, 1991), pp. 263–274.

Patton, Michael Quinn. *How to Use Qualitative Methods in Evaluation.* Newbury Park, California: Sage, 1987.

Russell, Ruth V. and Stage, Frances K. "Triangulation: Intersection Assessment and Research Methods." In *Diverse Methods for Research and Assessment of College Students,* edited by Frances K. Stage. Washington, D.C.: American College Student Personnel Association 1992, pp. 123–128.

Seidel, John V. and Clark, Jack A. "The Ethnograph: A Computer Program for the Analysis of Qualitative Data." *Qualitative Sociology* 7 (Spring/Summer, 1984), pp. 110–125.

Strauss, Anselm L. *Qualitative Analysis for Social Scientists.* New York: Cambridge University Press, 1987.

Strauss, Anselm L. and Corbin, Juliet. *Basics of Qualitative Research: Grounded Theory Procedures and Techniques*. Newbury Park, California: Sage, 1990.

Tesch, Renata. *Qualitative Research: Analysis Types and Software Tools*. New York: Falmer Press, 1990.

Werner, Oswald and Schoepfle, G. Mark *Systematic Fieldwork: Volume 1, Foundations of Ethnography and Interviewing*. Newbury Park, California: Sage, 1987.

Werner, Oswald and Schoepfle, G. Mark *Systematic Fieldwork: Volume 2, Ethnography Analysis and Data Management*. Newbury Park, California: Sage, 1987.

Whyte, William Foote. *Learning from the Field*. Beverly Hills, California: Sage, 1984.

IV. Interacting With Self and Others: Reflections In/On Qualitative Inquiry

A. Self and Others

Anzul, Margaret and Ely, Margot. "Halls of Mirrors: The Introduction of the Reflective Mode." *Language Arts* 65 (November, 1988), pp. 675–687.

Cassell, Joan. "Risks and Benefits to Subjects of Fieldwork." *The American Sociologist* 13 (August, 1978), pp. 134–143.

Daniels, Arlene Kaplan. "Self-Deception and Self-Discovery in Fieldwork." *Qualitative Sociology* 6 (Fall, 1983), pp. 195–214.

Everhart, Robert B. "Between Stranger and Friend: Some Consequences of 'Long Term' Fieldwork in Schools." *American Educational Research Journal* 14 (Winter, 1977), pp. 1–15.

Glesne, Corrine. "Rapport and Friendship in Ethnographic Research." *International Journal of Qualitative Studies in Education* 2 (January/March, 1989), pp. 45–54.

Grant, Gerald. "New Methods for the Study of a Reform Movement." In *On Competence: A Critical Analysis of Competency-Based Reforms in Higher Education*. Chicago: University of Chicago Press, 1979, pp. 439–490.

Gurney, Joan Neff. "Not One of the Guys: The Female Researcher in a Male Dominated Setting." *Qualitative Sociology* 8 (Spring, 1985), pp. 42–62.

Holland, Dorothy C. and Eisenhart, Margaret A. "The Odyssey behind the Case." In *Educated in Romance: Women, Achievement, and College Culture*.

Krieger, Susan. "Beyond 'Subjectivity': The Use of the Self in Social Science." *Qualitative Sociology* 8 (Winter, 1985), pp. 309–324.

Krieger, Susan. *Social Science and the Self: Personal Essays on an Art Form*. New Brunswick, New Jersey: Rutgers University Press, 1991.

Lather, Patti. "Staying Dumb? Student Resistance to Liberatory Curriculum." In *Getting Smart: Feminist Research and Pedagogy With/In the Postmodern*. New York: Routledge, 1991, pp. 123–152.

Lightfoot, Sara Lawrence. "Afterword: The Passion of Portraiture." In *The Good High School: Portraits of Character and Culture*. New York: Basic Books, 1983, pp. 369–378.

MacLeon, Jay. "Social Immobility in the Land of Opportunity." In *Ain't No Makin' It: Leveled Aspirations in Low-Income Neighborhoods*. Boulder, Colorado: Westview Press, 1987, pp. 1–8.

Martin, Joanne. "A Personal Journey: From Integration to Differentiation to Fragmentation to Feminism." In *Reframing Organizational Culture*, edited by Peter J. Frost, Larry F. Moore, Meryl Reis Louis, Craig C. Lundberg, and Joanne Martin. Newbury Park, California: Sage, 1991, pp. 352–355.

Reinharz, Shulamit. "Reclaiming Self-Awareness as a Source of Insight." In *Becoming a Social Scientist*. New Brunswick, New Jersey: Transaction Publishers, 1991, pp. 240–263.

Rosaldo, Renato. "Subjectivity in Social Analysis." In *Culture and Truth: The Remaking of Social Analysis*. Boston: Beacon Press, 1989, pp. 168–195.

Savage, Mary C. "Can Ethnographic Narrative Be a Neighborly Act?" *Anthropology and Education Quarterly* 19 (March, 1988), pp. 3–19.

B. Ethics

Bulmer, Martin. *Social Research Ethics*. New York: Holmes and Meier, 1982.

Cronbach, Lee. "Validity on Parole: Can We Go Straight?" *New Directions for Testing and Measurement* 5 (1980), pp. 99–108.

Diener, Edward and Crandall, Rick. *Ethics in Social and Behavioral Research*. Chicago: University of Chicago Press, 1978.

Jorgensen, Joseph G. "On Ethics and Anthropology." *Current Anthropology* 12 (June, 1971), pp. 321–334.

Kimmel, Allan J. *Ethics and Values in Applied Social Research*. Beverly Hills, California: Sage, 1988.

Lincoln, Yvonna S. and Guba, Egon G. "Ethics: The Failure of Postivist Science." *Review of Higher Education* 12 (Spring, 1989), pp. 221–240.

Punch, Maurice. *The Politics and Ethics of Fieldwork*. Beverly Hills, California: Sage, 1986.

Rhoades, Gary. "Is Love the Answer? A Commentary on Naturalistic Ethics." *Review of Higher Education* 14 (Winter, 1991), pp. 239–250.

Rynkiewich, Michael A. and Spradley, James P. *Ethics and Anthropology: Dilemmas in Fieldwork*. New York: John Wiley, 1976.

Soltis, Jonas F. "The Ethics of Qualitative Research." *International Journal of Qualitative Studies in Education* 2 (April/June, 1989), pp. 123–130.

Van Maanen, John. "The Moral Fix: On the Ethics of Fieldwork." In *Contemporary Field Research*, editedy Robert M. Emerson. Boston: Little, Brown, 1983, pp. 225–268.

C. Trustworthiness

Acker, Joan, Barry, Kate, and Esseveld, Johanna. "Objectivity and Truth: Problems in Doing Feminist Research." In *Beyond Methodology: Feminist Scholarship as Lived Research*, edited by Mary Margaret Fonow and Judith A. Cook. Bloomington, Indiana: Indiana University Press, 1991.

Cannon, Lynn Weber, Higginbotham, Elizabeth, and Leung, Marianne L. A. "Race and Class: Bias in Qualitative Research on Women." *Gender and Society* 2 (December, 1988), pp. 449–462.

Dean, John P. and Whyte, William Foote. "How Do You Know If the Informant is Telling the Truth." *Human Organization* 17 (Summer, 1958), pp. 34–38.

Guba, Egon G. and Lincoln, Yvonna S. *Fourth Generation Evaluation*. Newbury Park, California: Sage, 1989.

Heider, Karl G. "The Rashomon Effect: When Ethnographers Disagree." *American Anthropologist* 90 (March, 1988), pp. 73–81.

Jick, Todd D. "Mixing Qualitative and Quantitative Methods: Triangulation in Action." In *Qualitative Methodology*, edited by John Van Maanen. Beverly Hills, California: Sage, 1983, pp. 135–148.

Kirk, Jerome and Miller, Marc L. *Reliability and Validity in Qualitative Research*. Beverly Hills, California: Sage, 1986.

Lakotas, Imre. "Falsification and the Methodology of Scientific Research Programmes." In *Criticism and the Growth of Knowledge*, edited by Imre Lakotas and Alan Musgrave. Cambridge, England: Cambridge University Press, 1970, pp. 91–195.

Lather, Patti. "Issues of Validity in Openly Ideological Research: Between a Rock and a Soft Place." *Interchange* 17 (Winter, 1986), pp. 63–84.

LeCompte, Margaret D. and Goetz, Judith Preissle. "Problems of Reliability and Validity in Ethnographic Research." *Review of Educational Research* 52 (Spring, 1982), pp. 31–60.

Lincoln, Yvonna S. and Guba, Egon G. "Judging the Quality of Case Study Reports." *International Journal of Qualitative Studies in Education* 3 (Fall, 1990), pp. 53–59.

Lincoln, Yvonna S. and Guba, Egon G. "Case Reporting, Member Checking, and Auditing." In *Naturalistic Inquiry*. Newbury Park, California: Sage, 1985, pp. 357–381.

Mathison, Sandra. "Why Triangulate?" *Educational Researcher* 17 (March, 1988), pp. 13–17.

Maxwell, Joseph A. "Understanding and Validity in Qualitative Research." *Harvard Educational Review* 62 (Fall, 1992), pp. 279–300.

Miles, Matthew and Huberman, A. Michael. "Drawing Valid Meaning from Qualitative Data: Toward a Shared Craft." *Educational Researcher* 13 (May, 1984), pp. 20–30.

Mishler, Elliot G. "Validation in Inquiry-Guided Research: The Role of Exemplars in Narrative Studies." *Harvard Educational Review* 60 (November, 1990), pp. 415–442.

Page, Helen E. "Dialogic Principles of Interactive Learning in the Ethnographic Relationship." *Journal of Anthropological Research* 44 (Summer, 1988), pp. 163–181.

Reason, Peter and Rowan, John. "Issues of Validity in New Paradigm Research." In *Human Inquiry*, edited by Peter Reason and John Rowan. New York: John Wiley, 1981, pp. 239–250.

Russell, Ruth V. and Stage, Frances K. "Triangulation: Intersecting Assessment and Research Methods." In *Diverse Methods for Research and Assessment of College Students*, edited by Frances K. Stage. Washington, D.C.: National College Personnel Association, 1992, pp. 123–138.

Wax, Rosalie H. "The Ambiguities of Fieldwork." In *Contemporary Field Research*, edited by Robert M. Emerson. Boston: Little, Brown, 1983, pp. 191–202.

V.   Creating a Text: Writing Up Qualitative Research

Atkinson, Paul. *Understanding Ethnographic Texts*. Newbury Park, California: Sage, 1992.

Atkinson, Paul. "Supervising the Text." *International Journal of Qualitative Studies in Education* 4 (April/June , 1991), pp. 161–174.

Becker, Howard S. *Writing for Social Scientists: How to Start and Finish Your Thesis, Book, or Article.* Chicago: University of Chicago Press, 1986.

Clifford, James and Marcus, George E. (Eds.). *Writing Culture: The Poetics and Politics of Ethnography.* Berkeley, California: University of California Press, 1986.

Fetterman, David M. "Recording the Miracle: Writing." In *Ethnography: Step by Step.* Newbury Park, California: Sage, 1989, pp. 104–119.

Frank, Francine Wattman and Treichler, Paula A. *Language, Gender, and Professional Writing: Theoretical Approaches and Guidelines for Nonsexist Usage.* New York: The Modern Language Association of America, 1989.

Geertz, Clifford. *Works and Lives: The Anthropologist as Author.* Stanford, California: Stanford University Press, 1988.

Glesne, Corrine and Peshkin, Alan. "Writing Your Story: What Your Data Say." *Becoming Qualitative Researchers: An Introduction.* White Plains, New York: Longman, 1992, pp. 151–172.

Krieger, Susan. "Fiction and Social Science." In *The Mirror Dance: Identity in a Women's Community.* Philadelphia: Temple University Press, 1983, pp. 173–199.

Lofland, John. "Styles of Reporting Qualitative Field Research." *The American Sociologist* 9 (August, 1974), pp. 101–111.

Roth, Paul A. "Narrative Explanations: The Case of History." *Studies in the Philosophy of History* 27 (1988), pp. 1–13.

Smith, Mary Lee. "Publishing Qualitative Research." *American Educational Research Journal* 24 (Summer, 1987), pp. 173–183.

Van Maanen, John. "The Fact of Fiction in Organizational Ethnography." In *Qualitative Methodology,* edited by John Van Maanen. Beverly Hills, California: Sage, 1983, pp. 37–55.

Van Maanen, John (Ed.). "Special Issue: The Presentation of Ethnographic Research." *Journal of Contemporary Ethnography* 19 (April, 1990).

Van Maanen, John. *Tales of the Field: On Writing Ethnography.* Chicago: University of Chicago Press, 1988.

Wolcott, Harry F. *Writing Up Qualitative Research.* Newbury Park, California: Sage, 1990.

VI. Examples of Qualitative Research

A. Higher and Postsecondary Education

Abel, Emily K. *Terminal Degrees: The Job Crisis in Higher Education.* New York: Praeger, 1984.

Amey, Marilyn J. and Twombly, Susan B. "Re-Visioning Leadership in Community Colleges." *Review of Higher Education* 15 (Winter, 1992), pp. 125–150.

Aper, Jeffery P. and Hinkle, Dennis E. "State Policies for Assessing Student Outcomes: A Case Study with Implications for State and Institutional Authorities." *Journal of Higher Education* 62 (September/October, 1991), pp. 539–555.

Attinasi, Louis C., Jr. "Getting In: Mexican Americans' Perceptions of University Attendance and the Implications for Freshman Year Persistence." *Journal of Higher Education* 60 (May/June, 1989), pp. 247–277.

Attinasi, Louis C., Jr. "Rethinking the Study of the Outcomes of College Attendance." *Journal of College Student Development* 33 (January, 1992), pp. 61–70.

Becker, Howard S., Geer, Blanche, Hughes, Everett, and Strauss, Anselm. *Boys in White: Student Culture in a Medical School*. Chicago: University of Chicago Press, 1961.

Becker, Howard, Geer, Blanche, and Hughes, Everett C. *Making the Grade: The Academic Side of College Life*. New York: Wiley, 1968.

Bensimon, Estela M. "A Feminist Reinterpretation of Presidents' Definitions of Leadership." *Peabody Journal of Education* 66 (1991), pp. 143–155.

Bensimon, Estela M. "The Meaning of 'Good Presidential Leadership': A Frame Analysis." *Review of Higher Education* 12 (Winter, 1989), pp. 107–123.

Bensimon, Estela M. "The Social Processes Through Which Faculty Shape the Image of a New President." *Journal of Higher Education* 62 (November/December, 1991), pp. 637–660.

Bensimon, Estela M., Neumann, Anna, and Birnbaum, Robert. *Making Sense of Administrative Leadership: The "L" Word in Higher Education*. ASHE-ERIC Report No. 1. Washington, D.C.: Association for the Study of Higher Education, 1989.

Bensimon, Estela M. and Neumann, Anna. *Redesigning Collegiate Leadership: Teams and Teamwork in Higher Education*. Baltimore, Maryland: Johns Hopkins University Press, 1993.

Birnbaum, Robert. "The Implicit Leadership Theories of College and University Presidents." *Review of Higher Education* 12 (Winter, 1989), pp. 125–136.

Birnbaum, Robert. "Will You Love Me in December as You Do in May?: Why Experienced College Presidents Lose Faculty Support." *Journal of Higher Education* 63 (January/February, 1992), pp. 1–25.

Boice, Robert. "New Faculty as Colleagues." *International Journal of Qualitative Studies in Education* 4 (January/March, 1991), pp. 29–44.

Chaffee, Ellen E., Tierney, William G., Ewell, Peter T., and Krakower, Jack Y. *Collegiate Culture and Leadership Strategies*. New York: American Council on Education and Macmillan, 1988.

Christie, Nancy G. and Dinham, Sarah M. "Institutional and External Influences on Social Integration in the Freshman Year." *Journal of Higher Education* 62 (July/August, 1991), pp. 412–436.

Clark, Burton R. *The Academic Life: Small Worlds, Different Worlds*. Princeton, New Jersey: Carnegie Foundation for the Advancement of Teaching, Princeton University Press, 1987.

Clark, Burton R. "The 'Cooling Out' Function in Higher Education." *American Journal of Sociology* 65 (May, 1960), pp. 569–576.

Clark, Burton R. *The Distinctive College: Antioch, Reed, & Swarthmore*. Chicago: Aldine, 1970.

Clark, Shirley M. and Corcoran, Mary. "Perspectives on the Professional Socialization of Women Faculty: A Case of Accumulative Disadvantage?" *Journal of Higher Education* 57 (January/February, 1986), pp. 20–43.

Conrad, Clifton F. "A Grounded Theory of Academic Change." *Sociology of Education* 51 (April, 1978), pp. 101–112.

Conrad, Clifton F., Haworth, Jennifer Grant, and Millar, Susan Bolyard. *A Silent Success: Master's Education in the United States.* Baltimore, Maryland: Johns Hopkins University Press, 1993.

Cottle, Thomas J. "A Family Prepares for College." *Journal of Higher Education* 62 (January/February, 1991), pp. 79–86.

Cyphert, Frederick R. and Boggs, David L. "The Transition from Administrator to Professor: Expectations and Experiences." *Review of Higher Education* 9 (1986), pp. 325–333.

Darling, Ann L. and Staton, Ann Q. "Socialization of Graduate Teaching Assistants: A Case Study in an American University." *International Journal of Qualitative Studies in Education* 2 (July/September, 1989), pp. 221–235.

Dill, David D. "The Management of Academic Culture: Notes on the Management of Meaning and Social Integration." *Higher Education* 11 (May, 1982), pp. 303–320.

Eisenhart, Margaret A. "Learning to Romance: Cultural Acquisition in College." *Anthropology and Education Quarterly* 21 (March, 1990), pp. 19–40.

Eisenhart, Margaret A. "Women Choose Their Careers: A Study of Natural Decision Making." *Review of Higher Education* 8 (Spring, 1985), pp. 247–270.

Finkelstein, Martin J., Farrar, David, and Pfinster, Allan O. "The Adaptation of Liberal Arts Colleges to the 1970s." *Journal of Higher Education* 55 (March/April, 1984), pp. 242–268.

Gamson, Zelda F. *Higher Education and the Real World: The Story of CAEL.* Wolfeboro, New Hampshire: Longwood, 1989.

Gamson, Zelda F. and Others. *Liberating Education.* San Francisco: Jossey-Bass, 1984.

Grant, Gerald and Others. *On Competence: A Critical Analysis of Competency-Based Reforms in Higher Education.* San Francisco: Josey-Bass, 1979.

Grant, Gerald and Riesman, David. *The Perpetual Dream: Reform and Experiment in the American College.* Chicago: University of Chicago Press, 1977.

Gumport, Patricia J. "The Contested Terrain of Academic Program Reduction." *Journal of Higher Education*, in press.

Gumport, Patricia J. "E Pluribus Unum? Academic Structure, Culture, and the Case of Feminist Scholarship." *Review of Higher Education* 15 (Fall, 1991), pp. 9–29.

Gumport, Patricia J. "Fired Faculty: Reflections on Marginalization and Academic Identity." In *Naming Silenced Lives: Personal Narratives and the Process of Educational Change,* edited by Daniel McLaughlin and William Tierney. New York: Routledge, 1993.

Hammond, Martine F. "Survival of Small Private Colleges: Three Case Studies." *Journal of Higher Education* 55 (May/June, 1984), pp. 360–388.

Hancock, Elise. "Zoos, Tunes, and Gweeps—A Dictionary of Campus Slang." *Journal of Higher Education* 61 (January/February, 1990), pp. 98–106.

Heinrich, Kathleen T. "Loving Partnerships: Dealing with Sexual Attraction and Power in Doctoral Advisement Relationships." *Journal of Higher Education* 62 (September/October, 1991), pp. 514–538.

Holland, Dorothy C. and Eisenhart, Margaret A. *Educated in Romance: Women, Achievement, and College Culture.* Chicago: University of Chicago Press, 1990.

Horowitz, Helen L. *Campus Life: Undergraduate Cultures from the End of the Eighteenth Century to the Present.* Chicago: University of Chicago Press, 1987.

Jencks, Christopher and Riesman, David. *The Academic Revolution.* Garden City, New York: Doubleday, 1968.

Keller, Evelyn Fox. "The Anomaly of a Woman in Physics." In *Working it Out,* edited by Sara Ruddick and Pamela Daniels. New York: Pantheon, 1977, pp. 78–91.

Kempner, Ken. "Faculty Culture in the Community College: Facilitating or Hindering Learning?" *Review of Higher Education* 13 (Winter, 1990), pp. 215–235.

Kerr, Clark and Gade, Marian L. *The Many Lives of Academic Presidents: Time, Place, and Character.* Washington, D.C.: Association of Governing Boards, 1986.

Kirk, Deborah and Todd-Mancillas, William R. "Turning Points in Graduate Student Socialization: Implications for Recruiting Future Faculty." *Review of Higher Education* 14 (Spring, 1991), pp. 407–422.

Kolmen, Eileen and Hossler, Don. "The Influence of Institutional Culture on Presidential Selection." *Review of Higher Education* 10 (Summer, 1987), pp. 319–332.

Kuh, George D., Schuh, John H., Whitt, Elizabeth J., and Associates. *Involving Colleges: Successful Approaches to Fostering Student Learning and Development Outside the Classroom.* San Francisco: Jossey-Bass, 1991.

London, Howard B. *The Culture of a Community College.* New York: Praeger, 1978.

McEwen, Marylu K., Williams, Terry E., and Engstrom, Cathy McHugh. "Feminization in Student Affairs: A Qualitative Investigation." *Journal of College Student Development* 32 (September 1991), pp. 440–446.

McLaughlin, Judith Block and Riesman, David. *Choosing a College President: Opportunities and Constraints.* Princeton, New Jersey: Carnegie Foundation for the Advancement of Teaching, Princeton University Press, 1990.

Mitchell, Mary B. "The Process of Department Leadership." *Review of Higher Education* 11 (Winter, 1987), pp. 161–176.

Moffatt, Michael. *Coming of Age in New Jersey: College and American Culture.* New Brunswick, New Jersey: Rutgers University Press, 1989.

Moffatt, Michael. "College Life: Undergraduate Culture and Higher Education." *Journal of Higher Education* 62 (January/February, 1991), pp. 44–61.

Murguia, Edward, Padilla, Raymond V., and Pavel, Michael. "Ethnicity and the Concept of Social Integration in Tinto's Model of Institutional Departure." *Journal of College Student Development* 32 (September, 1991), pp. 433–439.

Neumann, Anna. "Colleges Under Pressures: Budgeting, Presidential Competence, and Faculty Uncertainty." *Leadership Quarterly* 3 (Autumn, 1992), pp. 191–215.

Neumann, Anna. "Double Vision: The Experience of Institutional Stability." *The Review of Higher Education* 15 (Summer, 1992), pp. 341–371.

Neumann, Anna. "Making Mistakes: Error and Learning in the College Presidency." *Journal of Higher Education* 61 (July/August, 1990), pp. 386–407.

Neumann, Anna. "The Thinking Team: Toward a Cognitive Model of Administrative Teamwork in Higher Education." *Journal of Higher Education* 62 (September/October, 1991), pp. 485–513.

Neumann, Anna. "Strategic Leadership: The Changing Orientations of College Presidents." *Review of Higher Education* 12 (Winter, 1989), pp. 137–151.

Neumann, Anna and Bensimon, Estela M. "Constructing the Presidency: College Presidents' Image of Their Leadership Roles, A Comparative Study." *Journal of Higher Education* 61 (November/December, 1990), pp. 678–701.

Newcombe, Judith P. and Conrad, Clifton F. "A Theory of Mandated Academic Change." *Journal of Higher Education* 52 (November/December, 1981), pp. 555–577.

Padilla, Raymond V. "Using Dialogical Research Methods to Study Chicano College Students." *Urban Review* 24 (September, 1992), pp. 175–183.

Perry, William G. *Forms of Intellectual and Ethical Development in the College Years: A Scheme.* New York: Holt, Rinehart and Winston, 1970.

Peterson, Marvin W. and Others. *Black Students on White Campuses: The Impact of Increased Black Enrollments.* Ann Arbor, Michigan: Survey Research Center, Institute for Social Research, University of Michigan, 1978.

Ragland-Sullivan, Ellie and Barglow, Peter. "Job Loss: Psychological Response of University Faculty." *Journal of Higher Education* 52 (January/February, 1981), pp. 45–66.

Rhoades, Gary. "Calling on the Past: The Quest for the Collegiate Ideal." *Journal of Higher Education* 61 (September/October, 1990), pp. 512–534.

Rhoades, Gary and Slaughter, Sheila. "The Public Interest and Professional Labor: Research Universities." In *Culture and Ideology in Higher Education: Advancing a Critical Agenda,* edited by William Tierney. New York: Praeger, 1991, pp. 187–211.

Riesman, David, Gusfield, Joseph, and Gamson, Zelda. *Academic Values and Mass Education.* Garden City, New York: Doubleday, 1970.

Ruscio, Kenneth P. "Bridging Specializations: Reflections from Biology and Political Science." *Review of Higher Education* 10 (Fall, 1986), pp. 29–46.

Schwartz, Harriet L. "An Interview Study of Former Student Leaders' Perceptions of an Ethical Conflict Involving the College or University President." *Journal of College Student Development* 32 (September, 1991), pp. 447–454.

Slaughter, Sheila. "From Serving Students to Serving the Economy: Changing Expectations of Faculty Role Performance." *Higher Education* 14 (February, 1985), pp. 41–56.

Thelin, John R. "Beyond Background Music: Historical Research on Admissions and Access in Higher Education." In *Higher Education: Handbook of Theory and Research* (Vol. 1), edited by John C. Smart. New York: Agathon, 1985, pp. 349–380.

Tierney, William G. "Academic Work and Institutional Culture: Constructing Knowledge." *Review of Higher Education* 14 (Winter, 1991), pp. 199–216.

Tierney, William G. "Cultural Politics and the Curriculum in Postsecondary Education." *Journal of Education* 171 (Fall, 1989), pp. 72–88.

Tierney, William G. *Curricular Landscapes. Democratic Vistas: Transformative Leadership in Higher Education*. New York: Praeger, 1989.

Tierney, William G. *Official Encouragement, Institutional Discouragement: Minorities in Academe*. Norwood, New Jersey: Ablex, 1992.

Tierney, William G. "Symbolism and Presidential Perceptions of Leadership." *Review of Higher Education* 12 (Winter, 1989), pp. 153–166.

Weis, Lois. *Between Two Worlds: Black Students in an Urban Community College*. Boston: Routledge and Kegan Paul, 1985.

Weis, Lois. "Faculty Perspectives and Practice in an Urban Community College." *Higher Education* 14 (October, 1985), pp. 553–574.

Whitt, Elizabeth J. "'Hit the Ground Running': Experiences of New Faculty in a School of Education." *Review of Higher Education* 14 (Winter, 1991), pp. 177–197.

Williams, Joyce E. and Johansen, Elinor. "Career Disruption in Higher Education." *Journal of Higher Education* 56 (March/April, 1985), pp. 144–160.

B.   Education, Social Sciences, and the Professions

Anderson, Elijah. *Streetwise: Race, Class, and Change in an Urban Community*. Chicago: University of Chicago Press, 1990.

Astin, Helen S. and Leland, Carole. *Women of Influence, Women of Vision*. San Francisco: Jossey-Bass, 1991.

Belenky, Mary F., Clinchy, Blythe M., Goldberger, Nancy R., and Tarule, Jill M. *Women's Ways of Knowing: The Development of Self, Voice, and Mind*. New York: Basic Books, 1986.

Berger, Bennett M. (Ed.). *Authors of Their Own Lives: Intellectual Autobiographies by Twenty American Sociologists*. Berkeley: University of California Press, 1990.

Biklen, Sari Knopp. *School Work: The Cultural Construction of Gender and Teaching*. New York: Teachers College Press, 1992.

Brown, Lyn Mikel and Gilligan, Carol. *Meeting at the Crossroads: Women's Psychology and Girls' Development*. Cambridge, Massachusetts: Harvard University Press, 1992.

Bullough, Robert V. *First-Year Teacher: A Case Study*. New York: Teachers College Press, 1989.

Burnett, Jacquetta Hill. "Ceremony, Rites, and Economy in the Student System of an American High School." *Human Organization* 28 (Spring, 1969), pp. 1–10.

Carnoy, Martin and Levin, Henry M. "Reproduction and the Practices of Schooling." In *Schooling and Work in the Democratic State*. Stanford, California: Stanford University Press, 1985, pp. 110–143.

Connell, R.W., Ashenden, D.J., Kessler, S., and Dowsett, G.W. *Making the Difference: Schools, Families and Social Division*. Boston: Allen and Unwin, 1982.

Cookson, Peter W. and Persell, Caroline Hodges. *Preparing for Power: America's Elite Boarding Schools*. New York: Basic Books, 1985.

Cusick, Philip A. *Inside High School: The Student's World*. New York: Holt, Rinehart, and Winston, 1973.

Dantley, Michael E. "The Ineffectiveness of Effective Schools Leadership: An Analysis of the Effective Schools Movement from a Critical Perspective." *Journal of Negro Education* 59 (Fall, 1990), pp. 585–598.

Eckert, Penelope. *Jocks and Burnouts: Social Categories and Identities in the High School.* New York: Teachers College Press, 1989.

Erickson, Frederick. "Gatekeeping and the Melting Pot: Interaction in Counseling Encounters." *Harvard Educational Review* 45 (February, 1975), pp. 44–70.

Everhart, Robert B. *Reading, Writing and Resistance: Adolescence and Labor in a Junior High School.* Boston: Routledge and Kegan Paul, 1983.

Evetts, Julia. "Married Women and Career: Career History Accounts of Primary Headteachers." *International Journal of Qualitative Studies in Education* 2 (April/June, 1989), pp. 89–105.

Fine, Michelle. *Framing Dropouts: Notes on the Politics of an Urban High School.* Albany, New York: State University of New York Press, 1991.

Fink, Deborah. *Open Country, Iowa: Rural Women, Tradition, and Change.* Albany, New York: State University of New York Press, 1986.

Foley, Douglas E. *Learning Capitalist Culture: Deep in the Heart of Texas.* Philadelphia: University of Pennsylvania Press, 1990.

Foster, Michele. "The Politics of Race: Through the Eyes of African-American Teachers." *Journal of Education* 172 (Fall, 1990), pp. 123–141.

Fraatz, J.M.B. "Political Principals: Efficiency, Effectiveness, and the Political Dynamics of School Administration." *International Journal of Qualitative Studies in Education* 2 (January/March, 1989), pp. 3–24.

Fuchs, Estelle. *Pickets at the Gate.* New York: Free Press, 1966.

Fuchs, Estelle. *Teachers Talk: Views from Inside City Schools.* Garden City, New York: Anchor, 1969.

Gerson, Kathleen. *Hard Choices: How Women Decide About Work, Career, and Motherhood.* Berkeley, California: University of California Press, 1985.

Gilligan, Carol, Lyons, Nona P., and Hanmer, Trudy J. (Eds.). *Making Connections: The Relational Worlds of Adolescent Girls at Emma Willard School.* Cambridge, Massachusetts: Harvard University Press, 1990.

Giroux, Henry A. *Schooling and the Struggle for Public Life: Critical Pedagogy in the Modern Age.* Minneapolis: University of Minnesota Press, 1988.

Glasman, N.S. "Student Achievement and the School Principal." *International Journal of Qualitative Studies in Education* 2 (1988), pp. 283–296.

Goffman, Erving. *Asylums: Essays on the Social Situation of Mental Patients and Other Inmates.* Garden City, New York: Anchor, 1961.

Griffin, Pat. "Identity Management Strategies Among Lesbian and Gay Educators." *International Journal of Qualitative Studies in Education* 4 (July/September, 1991), pp. 189–202.

Grumet, Madeleine R. *Bitter Milk: Women and Teaching.* Amherst, Massachusetts: University of Massachusetts Press, 1988.

Harper, Douglas A. *Working Knowledge: Skill and Community in a Small Shop.* Chicago: University of Chicago Press, 1987.

Krieger, Susan. *The Mirror Dance: Identity in a Women's Community.* Philadephia: Temple University Press, 1983.

Ladson-Billings, Gloria. "Like Lightening in a Bottle: Attempting to Capture the Pedagogical Excellence of Successful Teachers of Black Students." *International Journal of Qualitative Studies in Education* 3 (October/December, 1990), pp. 335–344.

Lareau, Annette. *Home Advantage: Social Class and Parental Intervention in Elementary Education.* New York: Falmer Press, 1989.

LeCompte, Margaret. "Learning to Work." *Anthropology and Education Quarterly* 1 (Spring, 1978), pp. 22–37.

Leithwood, K.A. and Montgomery, D.J. "The Role of the Elementary School Principal in Program Improvement." *Review of Educational Research* 52 (1982), pp. 309–339.

Lesko, Nancy. *Symbolizing Society: Stories, Rites, and Structure in a Catholic High School.* New York: Falmer Press, 1988.

Lightfoot, Sara Lawrence. *The Good High School: Portraits of Character and Culture.* New York: Basic Books, 1983.

Louis, Karen S. and Miles, Matthew B. *Improving the Urban High School: What Works and Why.* New York: Teachers College Press, 1990.

Lynd, Robert Staughton. *Middletown: A Study in Modern American Culture.* New York: Harcourt, Brace, 1956.

MacLeod, Arlene Elowe. "Hegemonic Relations and Gender Resistance: The New Veiling as Accommodating Protest in Cairo." *Signs* 17 (Spring, 1992), pp. 533–557.

MacLeod, Jay. *Ain't No Makin' It: Leveled Aspirations in Low-Income Neighborhoods.* Boulder, Colorado: Westview Press, 1987.

McLaren, Peter. *Life in School: An Introduction to Critical Pedagogy in the Foundations of Education.* New York: Longman, 1988 or 1989.

McNeil, Linda M. *Contradictions of Control: School Structure and School Knowledge.* New York: Routledge and Kegan Paul, 1986.

Metz, Mary H. *Classrooms and Corridors: The Crisis of Authority in Desegregated Secondary Schools.* Berkeley, California: University of California Press, 1978.

Oakes, Jeannie. *Keeping Track: How Schools Structure Inequality.* New Haven, Connecticut: Yale University Press, 1985.

Ogbu, John U. *The Next Generation: An Ethnography of Education in an Urban Neighborhood.* New York: Academic Press, 1974.

Page, Reba Neukom. *Lower-Track Classrooms: A Curricular and Cultural Perspective.* New York: Teachers College Press, 1991.

Peshkin, Alan. *The Color of Strangers, The Color of Friends: The Play of Ethnicity in School and Community.* Chicago: University of Chicago Press, 1991.

Peshkin, Alan. *Growing Up American: Schooling and the Survival of Community.* Chicago: University of Chicago Press, 1978.

Peshkin, Alan. *God's Choice, The Total World of a Fundamentalist Christian School.* Chicago: University of Chicago Press, 1986.

Reyes, Pedro and Capper, Colleen A. "Urban Principals: A Critical Perspective on the Context of Minority Student Dropout." *Educational Administration Quarterly* 27 (November, 1991), pp. 530–557.

Schofield, Janet Ward. *Black and White in School: Trust, Tension, or Tolerance?* New York: Praeger, 1982.

Schubert, William H., and Ayers, William (Eds.). *Teacher Lore: Learning from Our Own Experience.* White Plains, New York: Longman, 1992.

Spindler, George and Spindler, Louise (Eds.). *Interpretive Ethnography of Education: At Home and Abroad.* Hillsdale, New Jersey: Erlbaum, 1987.

Spindler, George (Ed.). *Doing the Ethnography of Schooling: Educational Anthropology in Action.* New York: Holt, Rinehart and Winston, 1982.

Stelling, Joan and Bucher, Rue. "Vocabularies of Realism in Professional Socialization." *Social Science and Medicine* 7 (September, 1973), pp. 661–675.

Swidler, Ann. *Organization Without Authority: Dilemmas of Social Control in Free Schools.* Cambridge, Massachusetts: Harvard University Press, 1979.

Tetreault, Mary Kay Thompson. "It's So Opinioney." *Journal of Education* 168 (Spring, 1986), pp. 78–95.

Tobin, Joseph J., Wu, David Y. H., and Davidson, Dana H. *Preschool in Three Cultures.* New Haven, Connecticut: Yale University Press, 1989.

Trueba, Henry T., Spindler, George, and Spindler, Louise (Eds.). *What Do Anthropologists Have to Say About Dropouts?* New York: Falmer Press, 1989.

Trueba, Henry T. *Raising Silent Voices: Educating the Linguistic Minorities for the 21st Century.* New York: Newbury House, 1989.

Van Maanen, John. "The Smile Factory: Work at Disneyland." In *Reframing Organizational Culture,* edited by Peter J. Frost, Larry F. Moore, Meryl Reis Louis, Craig C. Lundberg, and Joanne Martin. Newbury Park, California: Sage, 1991, pp. 58–76.

Whyte, William Foote. *Street Corner Society: The Social Structure of an Italian Slum.* Chicago: University of Chicago Press, 1955.

Williams, Terry M. *The Cocaine Kids: The Inside Story of a Teenage Drug Ring.* Reading, Massachusetts: Addison-Wesley, 1989.

Willis, Paul E. *Learning to Labour.* New York: Columbia University Press, 1977.

Wolcott, Harry F. *The Man in the Principal's Office: An Ethnography.* Prospect, Illinois: Waveland Press, 1984.